A complete list of Self-Assessme̶ ^{W9-BEF-334} available in the text and online:

In-text

Active Listening Skills Inventory
Assessing Your Personal Need for Structure
Connor-Davidson Resilience Scale (CD-RISC)
Corporate Culture Preference Scale
Identifying Your Preferred Organizational Structure
Identifying Your Self-Monitoring Personality
It All Makes Sense?
Measuring Your Creative Personality
Measuring Your Equity Sensitivity

Leadership Dimensions Instrument
School Commitment Scale
Team Roles Preferences Scale
The Dutch Test for Conflict Handling
The Team Player Inventory
Tolerance of Change Scale
Upward Influence Scale
What is Your Attitude Toward Money?

Online

Self-Assessments

Active Listening Skills Inventory
Appreciating and Valuing Diversity
Assessing How Personality Type Impacts
  Your Goal-Setting Skills
Assessing Your Creativity Quotient
Assessing Your Emotional Empathy
Assessing Your Emotional Intelligence
Assessing Your Empathy Skills
Assessing Your Ethical Decision-Making Skills
Assessing Your Flexibility
Assessing Your Leader-Member Exchange
Assessing Your Perspective Taking
Assessing Your Self-Leadership
Career Planning Based on Brain Dominance
  & Thinking Styles Inventory
Corporate Culture Preferences Scale
Decision Making Style Inventory
Dispositional Mood Scale
Do You Have What It Takes to Be a Leader?
Guanxi Orientation Scale
Identifying Your Dominant Values
Identifying Your Locus of Control
Identify Your Preferred Organizational Structure
Individualism-Collectivism Scale
Machiavellianism Scale
Matching Holland's Career Types
Measuring Your Growth Need Strength
Perceived Stress Scale
Perceptions of Politics Scale (POPS)
Propensity to Trust Scale

Stress Coping Preference Scale
Student Empowerment Scale
Team Roles Preferences Scale
Telework Disposition Assessment
Testing Your Creative Bench Strength
Type "A" Scale
What is Your Communication Style Under Stress?
What is Your Level of Self-Esteem?
What is Your Primary Conflict-Handling Style?
Work Addiction Risk Test
Your Preferred Decision-Making Style

Test Your Knowledge

Appraisal Methods
Barriers to Effective Communications
Characteristics of Successful Entrepreneurs
Choosing the Best Communications Medium
Comparing Affirmative Action, Valuing Diversity,
  and Managing Diversity
Elements of the Planning Process
Ethics
Facilities Layout
Managerial Functions
Maslow's Hierarchy of Needs
Mentoring
Project Planning
Styles of Handling Conflict
SWOT Analysis
Technological Change
Training Methods

Organizational Behavior

Emerging Realities for the Workplace Revolution

Organizational Behavior

Steven L. McShane
The University of Western Australia

Mary Ann Von Glinow
Florida International University

4th Edition

McGraw-Hill
Irwin

Boston   Burr Ridge, IL   Dubuque, IA   Madison, WI   New York   San Francisco   St. Louis
Bangkok   Bogotá   Caracas   Kuala Lumpur   Lisbon   London   Madrid   Mexico City
Milan   Montreal   New Delhi   Santiago   Seoul   Singapore   Sydney   Taipei   Toronto

McGraw-Hill Irwin

ORGANIZATIONAL BEHAVIOR:
EMERGING REALITIES FOR THE WORKPLACE REVOLUTION
Published by McGraw-Hill/Irwin, a business unit of The McGraw-Hill Companies, Inc., 1221
Avenue of the Americas, New York, NY, 10020. Copyright © 2008 by The McGraw-Hill
Companies, Inc. All rights reserved. No part of this publication may be reproduced or
distributed in any form or by any means, or stored in a database or retrieval system, without
the prior written consent of The McGraw-Hill Companies, Inc., including, but not limited to, in
any network or other electronic storage or transmission, or broadcast for distance learning.
Some ancillaries, including electronic and print components, may not be available to customers
outside the United States.

This book is printed on acid-free paper.

1 2 3 4 5 6 7 8 9 0 WCK/WCK 0 9 8 7 6

ISBN   978-0-07-304977-9
MHID   0-07-304977-8

Editorial director: *John E. Biernat*
Senior sponsoring editor: *Ryan Blankenship*
Senior developmental editor: *Christine Scheid*
Editorial coordinator: *Allison J. Belda*
Associate marketing manager: *Margaret A. Beamer*
Media producer: *Greg Bates*
Lead project manager: *Mary Conzachi*
Lead production supervisor: *Michael R. McCormick*
Senior designer: *Kami Carter*
Photo research coordinator: *Lori Kramer*
Photo researcher: *Jennifer Blankenship*
Media project manager: *Joyce J. Chappetto*
Cover and interior design: *Pam Verros, pv design*
Typeface: *10/12 Times New Roman*
Compositor: *GTS – York, PA Campus*
Printer: *Quebecor World Versailles Inc.*

Library of Congress Cataloging-in-Publication Data
McShane, Steven Lattimore.
    Organizational behavior: emerging realities for the workplace revolution / Steven L.
McShane, Mary Ann Von Glinow. –4th ed.
        p. cm.
    Includes index.
    ISBN-13: 978-0-07-304977-9 (alk. paper)
    ISBN-10: 0-07-304977-8 (alk. paper)
    1. Organizational behavior. I. Von Glinow, Mary Ann Young, 1949- II. Title.
HD58.7.M42 2008
658–dc22

                                                                                2006028304

about the authors

Steven L. McShane

Steven L. McShane is Professor of Management in the Graduate School of Management at the University of Western Australia, where he receives high teaching ratings from students in Perth, Singapore, and other cities in Asia where UWA offers its programs. He is also an Honorary Professor at Universiti Tunku Abdul Rahman (UTAR) in Malaysia and previously taught in the business faculties at Simon Fraser University and Queen's University in Canada. Steve has conducted executive seminars with Nokia, Wesfarmers Group, ALCOA World Alumina Australia, and many other organizations. He is also a popular visiting speaker, having given four-dozen talks to faculty and students in almost a dozen countries over the past three years.

Steve earned his Ph.D. from Michigan State University in organizational behavior, human resource management, and labor relations. He also holds a Master of Industrial Relations from the University of Toronto, and an undergraduate degree from Queen's University in Canada. Steve has served as President of the Administrative Sciences Association of Canada (the Canadian equivalent of the Academy of Management) and Director of Graduate Programs in the business faculty at Simon Fraser University.

Along with co-authoring *Organizational Behavior*, 4e, Steve is the author of *Canadian Organizational Behaviour* 6th ed. (2006) and co-author (with Tony Travaglione) of *Organisational Behaviour on the Pacific Rim*, 2e (2007) and co-author (with Mary Ann von Glinow) of *Organizational Behavior: Essentials* (2007). He has also published several dozen articles, book chapters, and conference papers on diverse topics, including managerial decision making, organizational learning, socialization of new employees, gender bias in job evaluation, wrongful dismissal, media bias in business magazines, and labor union participation.

Steve enjoys spending his leisure time swimming, body board surfing, canoeing, skiing, and traveling with his wife and two daughters.

Mary Ann Von Glinow

Dr. Von Glinow is Director of the Center for International Business Education and Research (CIBER) and is Research Professor of Management and International Business at Florida International University. She also is the 2006 Vice President of the Academy of International Business (AIB) and an editor of JIBS. Previously on the Marshall School faculty of the University of Southern California, she has an MBA and Ph. D in Management Science from The Ohio State University. Dr. Von Glinow was the 1994-95 President of the Academy of Management, the world's largest association of academicians in management and is a Fellow of the Academy, and the Pan Pacific Business Association. She sits on eleven editorial review boards and numerous international panels. She teaches in executive programs in Latin America, Central America, the Caribbean region, Asia and the U.S.

Dr. Von Glinow has authored over 100 journal articles and eleven books. Her most recent include *Managing Multinational Teams*, by Elsevier 2005; *Organizational Learning Capability* by Oxford University Press, 1999 (in Chinese and Spanish translation) which won a Gold Book Award from the Ministry of Economic Affairs in Taiwan in 2002. She also has a popular textbook: *Organizational Behavior*, 2007, McGraw-Hill/Irwin and a recently published *OB Essentials* (2007). She heads an international consortium of researchers delving into "Best International Human Resource Management Practices," and her research in this arena won an award from the American Society for Competitiveness' Board of Trustees. She also received an NSF grant to study globally-distributed work. Dr. Von Glinow is the 2005 Academy of Management recipient of the Distinguished Service Award, one of the Academy's 3 highest honors bestowed.

Mary Ann consults to a number of domestic and multinational enterprises, and serves as a mayoral appointee to the Shanghai Institute of Human Resources in China. Since 1989, she has been a consultant in General Electric's "Workout" and "Change Acceleration Program" including "Coaching to Management." Her clients have included Asia Development Bank, American Express, Diageo, Knight-Ridder, Burger King, Pillsbury, Westinghouse, Southern California Edison, The Aetna, State of Florida, Kaiser Permanente, TRW, Rockwell Int'l, Motorola, N.Y. Life, Amoco, Lucent, and Joe's Stone Crabs, to name a few. She is on the Board of Friends of WLRN, Fielding University, Friends of Bay Oaks, Pan-Pacific Business Association and Animal Alliance in Los Angeles. She is actively involved in several animal welfare organizations and received the 1996 Humanitarian Award of the Year from Miami's Adopt-a-Pet.

Dedicated with love and devotion to Donna, and to our wonderful daughters, Bryton and Madison
—S.L.M.

To my family and my virtual, globally-distributed family!
—M.A.V.G.

brief contents

PART 1 Introduction   1

Chapter 1   Introduction to the Field of Organizational Behavior   2

PART 2 Individual Behavior and Processes   31

Chapter 2   Individual Behavior, Values, and Personality   32
Chapter 3   Perception and Learning in Organizations   66
Chapter 4   Workplace Emotions and Attitudes   102
Chapter 5   Motivation in the Workplace   132
Chapter 6   Applied Performance Practices   166
Chapter 7   Work-Related Stress and Stress Management   196

PART 3 Team Processes   223

Chapter 8   Decision Making and Creativity   224
Chapter 9   Foundations of Team Dynamics   256
Chapter 10   Developing High-Performance Teams   284
Chapter 11   Communicating in Teams and Organizations   312
Chapter 12   Power and Influence in the Workplace   340
Chapter 13   Conflict and Negotiation in the Workplace   368
Chapter 14   Leadership in Organizational Settings   400

PART 4 Organizational Processes   427

Chapter 15   Organizational Structure   428
Chapter 16   Organizational Culture   458
Chapter 17   Organizational Change   486

Additional Cases   513

Case 1: Arctic Mining Consultants   513
Case 2: Big Screen's Big Failure   515
Case 3: High Noon at Alpha Mills   520
Case 4: Keeping Suzanne Chalmers   522
Case 5: Magic Cable   523
Case 6: MexFabrics   527
Case 7: Nirvana Art Gallery   529
Case 8: Woodland Community Center Corporation   531
Video Summaries   533

Appendix A
Theory Building and Systematic Research Methods   538

Appendix B
Scoring Keys for Self-Assessment Activities   545

Glossary 556
References 562
Photo Credits 615
Organization Index 617
Name Index 620
Subject Index 637
URL Index 653

contents

Preface   xvii

Part 1   Introduction   1

Chapter 1   Introduction to the Field of Organizational Behavior   2

The Field of Organizational Behavior   4
What Are Organizations?   4
Why Study Organizational Behavior?   5
Organizational Behavior Trends   7
Globalization   7
Workforce Diversity   8
Connections 1.1 Attracting Talent through Work–Life Balance   11
Evolving Employment Relationships   11
Virtual Work   13
Workplace Values and Ethics   14
The Five Anchors of Organizational Behavior   16
The Multidisciplinary Anchor   17
The Systematic Research Anchor   18
The Contingency Anchor   18
The Multiple Levels of Analysis Anchor   19
The Open Systems Anchor   19
Knowledge Management   21
Knowledge Management Processes   21
Organizational Memory   22
The Journey Begins   23
Chapter Summary   24
Key Terms   24
Critical Thinking Questions   24
Case Study 1.1: Introducing Work–Life Balance at Oxford Manufacturing   25

BusinessWeek *Case Study 1.2:   27*
Team Exercise 1.3: Human Checkers   28
Web Exercise 1.4: Diagnosing Organizational Stakeholders   28
Self-Assessment 1.5: It All Makes Sense?   29
Self-Assessment 1.6: Telework Disposition Assessment   30

PART 2   Individual Behavior and Processes   31

Chapter 2   Individual Behavior, Values, and Personality   32

MARS Model of Individual Behavior and Results   32
Employee Motivation   35
Ability   36
Role Perceptions   37
Situational Factors   37
Types of Individual Behavior in Organizations   38
Task Performance   38
Exhibiting Organizational Citizenship   38
Counterproductive Work Behaviors   39
Joining and Staying with the Organization   39
Connections 2.1 Google Goes Guerrilla in the War for Talent   40
Maintaining Work Attendance   40
Values in the Workplace   41
Types of Values   42
Values and Individual Behavior   43
Values Congruence   44

Values across Cultures 45

Individualism and Collectivism 45

Power Distance 46

Other Cross-Cultural Values 47

Ethical Values and Behavior 48

Three Ethical Principles 48

Moral Intensity, Ethical Sensitivity, and Situational Influences 49

Supporting Ethical Behavior 50

Personality in Organizations 51

Personality and Organizational Behavior 51

The Big Five Personality Dimensions 52

Myers-Briggs Type Indicator 53

Other Personality Traits 54

Personality and Vocational Choice 55

Chapter Summary 57

Key Terms 57

Critical Thinking Questions 58

Case Study 2.1: Cox-2 Inhibitor Drugs 58

Case Study 2.2: Pushing Paper Can Be Fun 60

BusinessWeek *Case Study 2.3: 61*

Team Exercise 2.4: Comparing Cultural Values 62

Team Exercise 2.5: Ethics Dilemma Vignettes 62

Self-Assessment 2.6: Identifying Your Self-Monitoring Personality 63

Self-Assessment 2.7. Identifying Your Dominant Values 65

Self-Assessment 2.8: Individualism–Collectivism Scale 65

Self-Assessment 2.9: Identifying Your Locus of Control 65

Self-Assessment 2.10: Matching Holland's Career Types 65

Chapter 3 Perception and Learning in Organizations 66

The Perceptual Process 68

Selective Attention 69

Perceptual Organization and Interpretation 69

Social Identity Theory 71

Perceiving Others through Social Identity 72

Stereotyping in Organizational Settings 73

Why Stereotyping Occurs 73

Connections 3.1 Stereotyping and Social Identity Discourage Women from Entering Engineering 74

Problems with Stereotyping 74

Minimizing Stereotyping Bias 76

Attribution Theory 77

Attribution Errors 79

Self-Fulfilling Prophecy 79

Contingencies of Self-Fulfilling Prophecy 80

Other Perceptual Errors 81

Primacy Effect 82

Recency Effect 82

Halo Effect 82

Projection Bias 82

Improving Perceptions 83

Improving Perceptions through Empathy 83

Know Yourself: Applying the Johari Window 83

Learning in Organizations 85

Learning Explicit and Tacit Knowledge 85

Behavior Modification: Learning through Reinforcement 86

A–B–Cs of Behavior Modification 86

Contingencies of Reinforcement 86

Schedules of Reinforcement 87

Behavior Modification in Practice 88

Social Learning Theory: Learning by Observing 89

Behavior Modeling 89

Learning Behavior Consequences 89

Self-Reinforcement 89

Learning through Experience 90

Experiential Learning in Practice 90

Chapter Summary 92

Key Terms 93

Critical Thinking Questions 93

Case Study 3.1: From Lippert-Johanson Incorporated to Fenway Waste Management 94

BusinessWeek *Case Study 3.2: 96*

Class Exercise 3.3: The Learning Exercise 97

Team Exercise 3.4: Who Am I? 97

Web Exercise 3.5: Analyzing Corporate Annual Reports 98

Self-Assessment 3.6: Assessing Your Personal Need for Structure 98

Self-Assessment 3.7: Assessing Your Perspective Taking (Cognitive Empathy)　100

Self-Assessment 3.8: Assessing Your Emotional Empathy　100

Chapter 4　Workplace Emotions and Attitudes　102

Emotions in the Workplace　104

Types of Emotions　105

Emotions, Attitudes, and Behavior　106

Connections 4.1: Serious Fun　109

Managing Emotions at Work　110

Conditions Requiring Emotional Labor　111

Emotional Dissonance　111

Emotional Intelligence　113

Improving Emotional Intelligence　114

Job Satisfaction　115

Job Satisfaction and Work Behavior　116

Job Satisfaction and Performance　117

Job Satisfaction and Customer Satisfaction　118

Organizational Commitment　119

Consequences of Organizational Commitment　119

Building Organizational Commitment　120

Psychological Contracts　121

Types of Psychological Contracts　121

Psychological Contracts across Cultures and Generations　122

Chapter Summary　123

Key Terms　124

Critical Thinking Questions　124

Case Study 4.1: Diana's Disappointment: The Promotion Stumbling Block　125

BusinessWeek　*Case Study 4.2:　126*

Class Exercise 4.3: Stem-and-Probe Interview Activity　127

Team Exercise 4.4: Ranking Jobs by Their Emotional Labor　128

Self-Assessment 4.5: School Commitment Scale　129

Self-Assessment 4.6: Dispositional Mood Scale　129

Chapter 5　Motivation in the Workplace　132

Motivating Employees　134

Needs, Drives, and Employee Motivation　135

Maslow's Needs Hierarchy Theory　135

What's Wrong with Needs Hierarchy Models?　138

Four-Drive Theory　138

Theory of Learned Needs　140

Practical Implications of Needs/Drive-Based Theories　142

Expectancy Theory of Motivation　143

Expectancy Theory Model　143

Expectancy Theory in Practice　144

Does Expectancy Theory Fit Reality?　146

Goal Setting and Feedback　146

Characteristics of Effective Goals　147

Characteristics of Effective Feedback　148

Sources of Feedback　149

Evaluating Goal Setting and Feedback　151

Organizational Justice　152

Distributive Justice and Equity Theory　152

Procedural Justice　156

Organizational Justice in Practice　157

Chapter Summary　158

Key Terms　159

Critical Thinking Questions　159

Case Study 5.1: Buddy's Snack Company　160

BusinessWeek　*Case Study 5.2:　161*

Class Exercise 5.3: Needs Priority Exercise　162

Team Exercise 5.4: A Question of Feedback　163

Self-Assessment 5.5: Measuring Your Equity Sensitivity　163

Self-Assessment 5.6: Measuring Your Growth Need Strength　165

Chapter 6　Applied Performance Practices　166

Financial Reward Practices　168

Membership- and Seniority-Based Rewards　168

Job Status–Based Rewards　170

Competency-Based Rewards　171

Performance-Based Rewards   171

Improving Reward Effectiveness   174

Connections 6.1 When Rewards Go Wrong   175

Job Design Practices   176

Job Design and Work Efficiency   176

Job Design and Work Motivation   178

Job Design Practices That Motivate   180

Empowerment Practices   182

Supporting Empowerment   183

Self-Leadership Practices   184

Personal Goal Setting   185

Constructive Thought Patterns   185

Designing Natural Rewards   186

Self-Monitoring   186

Self-Reinforcement   186

Self-Leadership in Practice   186

Chapter Summary   188

Key Terms   188

Critical Thinking Questions   189

Case Study 6.1: The Regency Grand Hotel   189

BusinessWeek *Case Study 6.2:   191*

Team Exercise 6.3: Is Student Work Enriched?   191

Self-Assessment 6.4: What Is Your Attitude Toward Money?   193

Self-Assessment 6.5: Assessing Your Self-Leadership   194

Self-Assessment 6.6: Student Empowerment Scale   195

Chapter 7   Work-Related Stress and Stress Management   196

What Is Stress?   198

General Adaptation Syndrome   199

Stressors: The Causes of Stress   200

Interpersonal Stressors   200

Role-Related Stressors   202

Task Control Stressors   204

Organizational and Physical Environment Stressors   204

Work–Nonwork Stressors   204

Stress and Occupations   206

Individual Differences in Stress   206

Resilience and Stress   207

Workaholism and Stress   208

Consequences of Distress   208

Physiological Consequences   209

Psychological Consequences   209

Behavioral Consequences   210

Managing Work-Related Stress   210

Remove the Stressor   211

Withdraw from the Stressor   213

Change Stress Perceptions   215

Control the Consequences of Stress   215

Receive Social Support   215

Chapter Summary   216

Key Terms   217

Critical Thinking Questions   217

Case Study 7.1: How Did I Get Here?   217

BusinessWeek *Case Study 7.2:   219*

Team Exercise 7.3: Stage Fright!   220

Self-Assessment 7.4: Connor-Davidson Resilience Scale   220

Self-Assessment 7.5: Work Addiction Risk Test   222

Self-Assessment 7.6: Perceived Stress Scale   222

Self-Assessment 7.7: Stress Coping Preference Scale   222

PART 3   Team Processes   223

Chapter 8   Decision Making and Creativity   224

Rational Choice Paradigm of Decision Making   226

Problems with the Rational Choice Paradigm   227

Identifying Problems and Opportunities   227

Problems with Problem Identification   228

Connections 8.1 Famous Missed Opportunities   229

Identifying Problems and Opportunities More Effectively   230

Evaluating and Choosing Alternatives   230

Problems with Goals   231

Problems with Information Processing   231

Problems with Maximization   232

Evaluating Opportunities   232

Emotions and Making Choices   232

Intuition and Making Choices   233

Making Choices More Effectively   234

Evaluating Decision Outcomes   235

Escalation of Commitment   235

Evaluating Decision Outcomes More Effectively   237

Employee Involvement in Decision Making   237

Benefits of Employee Involvement   238

Contingencies of Employee Involvement   239

Creativity   240

The Creative Process Model   240

Creative People and Work Environments   241

Activities That Encourage Creativity   243

Chapter Summary   244

Key Terms   245

Critical Thinking Questions   245

Case Study 8.1: Employee Involvement Cases   246

BusinessWeek *Case Study 8.2:   247*

Class Exercise 8.3: For What It's Worth   248

Team Exercise 8.4: Where in the World Are We?   249

Team Exercise 8.5: Winter Survival Exercise   251

Class Exercise 8.6: The Hopping Orange   252

Class Exercise 8.7: Creativity Brainbusters   252

Self-Assessment 8.8: Measuring Your Creative Personality   253

Self-Assessment 8.9: Testing Your Creative Bench Strength   254

Self-Assessment 8.10: Decision Making Style Inventory   254

Chapter 9   Foundations of Team Dynamics   256

Teams and Groups   258

Why Rely on Teams?   259

Why People Belong to Informal Groups   260

A Model of Team Effectiveness   261

Organizational and Team Environment   262

Team Design Features   263

Task Characteristics   264

Team Size   265

Team Composition   265

Connections 9.1 Team Diversity Challenges Students in Shell's Gourami Business Challenge   266

Team Processes   268

Team Development   268

Team Norms   270

Team Roles   272

Team Cohesiveness   272

The Trouble with Teams   276

Process Losses and Brooks's Law   276

Social Loafing   277

Chapter Summary   278

Key Terms   279

Critical Thinking Questions   279

Case Study 9.1: Treetop Forest Products   280

BusinessWeek *Case Study 9.2:   281*

Team Exercise 9.3: Team Tower Power   282

Self-Assessment 9.4: Team Roles Preferences Scale   282

Chapter 10   Developing High-Performance Teams   284

Self-Directed Work Teams   286

Sociotechnical Systems Theory and SDWTs   287

Applying STS Theory and Self-Directed Work Teams   288

Challenges to Self-Directed Work Teams   288

Connections 10.1 Chrysler's Lean Self-Directed Work Teams   289

Virtual Teams   291

Designing High-Performance Virtual Teams   292

Team Trust   294

Individual Differences in Trust   296

Dynamics of Trust in Teams   296

Team Decision Making   297

Constraints on Team Decision Making   297

Team Structures to Improve Creativity and Decision Making   299

Team Building 303

Types of Team Building 304

Is Team Building Effective? 305

Chapter Summary 305

Key Terms 306

Critical Thinking Questions 306

Case Study 10.1: The Shipping Industry Accounting Team 307

BusinessWeek *Case Study 10.2: 308*

Team Exercise 10.3: Egg Drop Exercise 309

Self-Assessment 10.4: The Team Player Inventory 309

Self-Assessment 10.5: Propensity to Trust Scale 311

Chapter 11 Communicating in Teams and Organizations 312

A Model of Communication 314

Communication Channels 315

Verbal Communication 315

Electronic Communication 316

Nonverbal Communication 318

Connections 11.1 Nonverbal Gestures Help Crowd Control during Iraq War 319

Choosing the Best Communication Channels 319

Media Richness 319

Symbolic Meaning of the Medium 321

Communication Barriers (Noise) 322

Perceptions 322

Filtering 322

Language Barriers 322

Information Overload 323

Cross-Cultural and Cross-Gender Communication 324

Nonverbal Differences 325

Gender Differences in Communication 326

Improving Interpersonal Communication 327

Getting Your Message Across 327

Active Listening 327

Communicating in Organizational Hierarchies 329

Workspace Design 329

E-Zines, Blogs, and Wikis 330

Employee Surveys 330

Direct Communication with Top Management 331

Communicating through the Grapevine 331

Grapevine Characteristics 332

Grapevine Benefits and Limitations 332

Chapter Summary 333

Key Terms 333

Critical Thinking Questions 333

Case Study 11.1: Bridging the Two Worlds—The Organizational Dilemma 334

BusinessWeek *Case Study 11.2 335*

Team Exercise 11.3: Analyzing the Blogosphere 335

Team Exercise 11.4: Active Listening Exercise 336

Team Exercise 11.5: Cross-Cultural Communication Game 337

Self-Assessment 11.6: Active Listening Skills Inventory 338

Chapter 12 Power and Influence in the Workplace 340

The Meaning of Power 342

A Model of Power in Organizations 343

Sources of Power in Organizations 343

Legitimate Power 344

Reward Power 345

Coercive Power 345

Expert Power 345

Referent Power 345

Information and Power 346

Contingencies of Power 347

Substitutability 347

Centrality 348

Discretion 348

Visibility 348

Connections 12.1 New York Transit Strike Reveals Its Centrality, But Also Its Substitutability 349

Networking and Power 350

Influencing Others 351

Types of Influence Tactics 351

Consequences and Contingencies of Influence Tactics 355

Gender Differences in Influence Tactics 357

Influence Tactics and Organizational Politics 357

Conditions Supporting Organizational Politics   358

Connections 12.2 Politics at WorldCom Leads to Record-Breaking Accounting Fraud   359

Chapter Summary   360

Key Terms   361

Critical Thinking Questions   361

Case Study 12.1: Rhonda Clark: Taking Charge at the Smith Foundation   362

BusinessWeek *Case Study 12.2:   364*

Team Exercise 12.3: Budget Deliberations   364

Self-Assessment 12.4: Upward Influence Scale   365

Self-Assessment 12.5: Guanxi Orientation Scale   367

Self-Assessment 12.6: Machiavellianism Scale   367

Self-Assessment 12.7: Perceptions of Politics Scale (POPS)   367

Chapter 13   Conflict and Negotiation in the Workplace   368

The Conflict Process   370

Conflict Perceptions and Emotions   371

Manifest Conflict   371

Conflict Outcomes   371

Sources of Conflict in Organizations   373

Incompatible Goals   373

Differentiation   374

Task Interdependence   375

Scarce Resources   375

Ambiguous Rules   375

Connections 13.1 Ambiguous Fee Structure Creates Fractious Divisions at Arthur Andersen   376

Communication Problems   377

Interpersonal Conflict Management Styles   377

Choosing the Best Conflict Management Style   379

Cultural and Gender Differences in Conflict Management Styles   380

Structural Approaches to Conflict Management   380

Emphasizing Superordinate Goals   380

Reducing Differentiation   381

Improving Communication and Understanding   382

Reducing Task Interdependence   383

Increasing Resources   383

Clarifying Rules and Procedures   384

Resolving Conflict through Negotiation   384

Bargaining Zone Model of Negotiations   385

Situational Influences on Negotiations   386

Negotiator Behaviors   387

Third-Party Conflict Resolution   387

Choosing the Best Third-Party Intervention Strategy   388

Chapter Summary   390

Key Terms   391

Critical Thinking Questions   391

Case Study 13.1: Conflict in Close Quarters   392

BusinessWeek *Case Study 13.2:   393*

Class Exercise 13.3: The Contingencies of Conflict Handling   394

Team Exercise 13.4: Ugli Orange Role-Play   398

Self-Assessment 13.5: The Dutch Test for Conflict Handling   398

Chapter 14   Leadership in Organizational Settings   400

What Is Leadership?   402

Shared Leadership   402

Perspectives of Leadership   403

Competency Perspective of Leadership   404

Competency (Trait) Perspective Limitations and Practical Implications   406

Behavioral Perspective of Leadership   407

Choosing Task-Oriented versus People-Oriented Leadership   407

Contingency Perspective of Leadership   408

Path–Goal Theory of Leadership   408

Path–Goal Leadership Styles   408

Contingencies of Path–Goal Theory   410

Practical Implications and Limitations of Path–Goal Theory   411

Other Contingency Theories   412

Situational Leadership Theory   412

Fiedler's Contingency Model   412

Leadership Substitutes   413

Transformational Perspective of Leadership   414

Transformational versus Transactional Leadership   414

Transformational versus Charismatic Leadership   415

Elements of Transformational Leadership   415

Connections 14.1 Procter & Gamble Trades Charisma for Transformational Substance   416

Evaluating the Transformational Leadership Perspective   418

Implicit Leadership Perspective   418

Stereotyping Leadership   419

Attributing Leadership   419

Need for Situational Control   419

Cross-Cultural and Gender Issues in Leadership   420

Gender Differences in Leadership   421

Chapter Summary   421

Key Terms   422

Critical Thinking Questions   422

Case Study 14.1: A Window on Life   423

BusinessWeek *Case Study 14.2   424*

Team Exercise 14.3: Leadership Diagnostic Analysis   425

Self-Assessment 14.4: Leadership Dimensions Instrument   425

PART 4   Organizational Processes   427

Chapter 15   Organizational Structure   428

Division of Labor and Coordination   430

Division of Labor   430

Coordinating Work Activities   431

Elements of Organizational Structure   433

Span of Control   433

Centralization and Decentralization   434

Formalization   435

Mechanistic versus Organic Structures   436

Forms of Departmentalization   438

Simple Structure   438

Functional Structure   439

Divisional Structure   439

Matrix Structure   441

Team-Based Structure   444

Connections 15.1 The Extreme Team Structure of W. L. Gore & Associates Inc.   445

Network Structure   446

Contingencies of Organizational Design   448

External Environment   448

Organization Size   449

Technology   449

Organizational Strategy   450

Chapter Summary   451

Key Terms   452

Critical Thinking Questions   452

Case Study 15.1: FTCA—Regional and Headquarters Relations   452

BusinessWeek *Case Study 15.2:   454*

Team Exercise 15.3: The Club Ed Exercise   455

Self-Assessment 15.4: Identifying Your Preferred Organizational Structure   455

Chapter 16   Organizational Culture   458

Elements of Organizational Culture   460

Content of Organizational Culture   461

Organizational Subcultures   463

Deciphering Organizational Culture through Artifacts   463

Organizational Stories and Legends   464

Rituals and Ceremonies   464

Organizational Language   465

Physical Structures and Symbols   465

Is Organizational Culture Important?   466

Contingencies of Organizational Culture and Performance   466

Adaptive Cultures   467

Organizational Culture and Business Ethics   468

Merging Organizational Cultures   469

Bicultural Audit   469

Strategies to Merge Different Organizational Cultures   470

Changing and Strengthening Organizational Culture   472

Connections 16.1 Defeated by the HP Way   473

Actions of Founders and Leaders   473

Introducing Culturally Consistent Rewards   473

Aligning Artifacts   474

Selecting and Socializing Employees   474

Organizational Socialization   476

Stages of Socialization   476

Improving the Socialization Process   478

Chapter Summary   479

Key Terms   480

Critical Thinking Questions   480

Case Study 16.1: Hillton's Transformation   480

BusinessWeek   Case Study 16.2:   482

Web Exercise 16.3: Diagnosing Corporate Culture Proclamations   482

Team Exercise 16.4: Truth in Advertising   483

Self-Assessment 16.5: Corporate Culture Preference Scale   483

Chapter 17   Organizational Change   486

Lewin's Force Field Analysis Model   488

Restraining Forces   489

Unfreezing, Changing, and Refreezing   491

Creating an Urgency for Change   492

Reducing the Restraining Forces   493

Connections 17.1 Carlos Ghosn Relies on High Involvement to Transform Nissan   496

Refreezing the Desired Conditions   498

Strategic Visions, Change Agents, and Diffusing Change   498

Change Agents   499

Diffusion of Change   499

Three Approaches to Organizational Change   500

Action Research Approach   500

Appreciative Inquiry Approach   502

Parallel Learning Structure Approach   503

Cross-Cultural and Ethical Issues in Organizational Change   504

Personal Change for the Road Ahead   505

Understand Your Needs and Values   505

Understand Your Competencies   505

Set Career Goals   506

Maintain Networks   506

Get a Mentor   506

Organizational Behavior: The Journey Continues   506

Chapter Summary   507

Key Terms   507

Critical Thinking Questions   507

Case Study 17.1: The Excellent Employee   508

BusinessWeek   Case Study 17.2:   509

Team Exercise 17.3: Strategic Change Incidents   510

Self-Assessment 17.4: Tolerance of Change Scale   511

Additional Cases   513

Case 1: Arctic Mining Consultants   513

Case 2: Big Screen's Big Failure   515

Case 3: High Noon at Alpha Mills   520

Case 4: Keeping Suzanne Chalmers   522

Case 5: Magic Cable   523

Case 6: MexFabrics   527

Case 7: Nirvana Art Gallery   529

Case 8: Woodland Community Center Corporation   531

Video Cases   533

Appendix A

Theory Building and Systematic Research Methods   538

Appendix B

Scoring Keys for Self-Assessment Activities   545

preface

Welcome to a new era of organizational behavior! Virtual teams are replacing committees. Values and self-leadership are replacing command-and-control supervision. Knowledge is replacing infrastructure. Companies are looking for employees with emotional intelligence, not just technical smarts. Globalization has become the mantra of corporate survival. Co-workers aren't down the hall; they're at the other end of an Internet connection located somewhere else on the planet.

Organizational Behavior, Fourth Edition, is written in the context of these emerging workplace realities. This edition explains how emotions guide employee motivation, attitudes, and decisions; how values have become the new resource to shape workplace behavior; how companies rely on creativity and a learning orientation as their source of competitive advantage in the knowledge economy; and how appreciative inquiry has become one of the emerging strategies for organizational change. This book also presents the new reality that organizational behavior is not just for managers; it is relevant and useful to anyone who works in and around organizations.

Linking Theory with Reality

Every chapter of *Organizational Behavior*, Fourth Edition, is filled with real-life examples to make OB concepts more meaningful and reflect the relevance and excitement of this field. For example, you will read how Whole Foods Market applies a "yoghurt culture" model to maintain and strengthen its organizational culture as it expands; how W. L. Gore & Associates remains nimble through an organizational structure that has no bosses; how Dubai's Department of Economic Development is becoming a values-based organization; how DaimlerChysler is racing to improve productivity and quality through self-directed work teams in Mexico and the United States; and how Sun Microsystems and IBM are improving internal and external communication through blogs and wikis.

These real-life stories appear in many forms. Every chapter of *Organizational Behavior,* Fourth Edition, offers several detailed photo captions and many more in-text anecdotes. Lengthier stories are distinguished in a feature we call *Connections,* because it "connects" OB concepts with real organizational incidents. Case studies in each chapter and video case studies in each part also connect OB concepts to the emerging workplace realities. These stories provide representation across the United States and around the planet. They also cover a wide range of industries—from software to government, and from small businesses to the Fortune 500.

Global Orientation

One of the first things you might notice about this book is its strong global orientation. This goes beyond the traditional practice of describing how U.S. companies operate in other parts of the world. Instead, this book takes a truly global approach by continually illustrating how organizational behavior concepts and practices are relevant to companies in every part of the world. For example, you will read how Nitro, the Shanghai-based boutique advertising agency, is taking the world by storm with its organic structure; how Panafric Hotel in Nairobi, Kenya, motivates its employees with good old-fashioned recognition; how John Fletcher, CEO of Australian retailer Coles Myer Group, is maintaining the momentum for change after the company's significant improvements to date; and how Infosys, one of India's leading information technology services companies, is developing a better understanding of organizational leadership.

This global orientation is also apparent in our discussion of many organizational behavior topics. The first chapter of *Organizational Behavior,* Fourth Edition, introduces the concept of globalization. Global issues are then highlighted throughout this book, such as cross-cultural values and ethics, job satisfaction and displaying emotions in different societies, employee stress from overwork in China and Japan, cross-cultural issues in the success of self-directed work teams, problems with cross-cultural communication, cultural values and expectations as a factor in the preferred influence tactics, cross-cultural conflict, and preferred leadership styles across cultures.

Active Learning and Critical Thinking Support

We teach organizational behavior, so we understand how important it is to use a textbook that offers deep support for active learning and critical thinking. The fact that business school accreditation associations also emphasize the importance of the learning experience further reinforces our attention on classroom activities. *Organizational Behavior,* Fourth Edition, includes more than two-dozen case studies, many written by instructors from the United States, Mexico, Canada, Malaysia, and Australia. It offers three-dozen self-assessments, including scales that measure emerging concepts such as Guanxi orientation and resilience. This book is also a rich resource for in-class activities, some of which are not available in other organizational behavior textbooks, such as Where in the World are We? and the Cross-Cultural Communication Game.

Contemporary Theory Foundation

Organizational Behavior, Fourth Edition, has a solid foundation of contemporary and classic scholarship. You can see this in the references. Each chapter is based on dozens of articles, books, and other sources. The most recent literature receives thorough coverage, resulting in what we believe is the most up-to-date organizational behavior textbook available. These references also reveal that we reach out to information systems, marketing, and other disciplines for new ideas. At the same time, this textbook is written for students, not the scholars whose work is cited. So, while this book provides new knowledge and its practical implications, you won't find detailed summaries of specific research studies. Also, this textbook rarely names specific researchers and their university affiliations; it focuses on organizational behavior knowledge rather than "who's-who" in the field.

Organizational Behavior was the first textbook in this field to discuss workplace emotions, affective events theory (but without the jargon), somatic marker theory (also without the jargon), social identity theory, appreciative inquiry, bicultural audits, future search events, Schwartz's values model, the effects of job satisfaction on customer service, learning orientation, workaholism, and several other groundbreaking topics. Along with documenting numerous ongoing developments in OB knowledge, this edition continues to lead the way with the latest knowledge on four-drive theory, resilience, employee engagement, communication blogs and wikis, separating socioemotional conflict from constructive conflict, exceptions to media richness theory, employer branding, problems in identifying opportunities, Goleman's emotional intelligence model, and the automaticity and emotionality of the perceptual process.

Organizational Behavior Knowledge for Everyone

Another distinctive feature of *Organizational Behavior,* Fourth Edition, is that it is written for everyone in organizations, not just "managers". The new reality is that people throughout the organization–systems analysts, production employees, accounting professionals–are assuming more responsibilities as companies remove layers of bureaucracy and give non-management staff more autonomy over their work. Consequently, the philosophy of this book is that everyone who works in and around organizations needs to understand and make use of organizational behavior knowledge.

Changes to the Fourth Edition

Organizational Behavior, Fourth Edition, is the result of reviews over the past three years by more than 100 organizational behavior scholars and teachers in several countries. Chapter structure changes in the previous (3rd) edition proved very popular with instructors, so this 4th edition largely keeps the previous organization of chapters. In addition to substantially updated examples throughout the book, most of the improvements to this edition are in the new and updated topics summarized below:

- *Chapter 1: Introduction to the Field of Organizational Behavior.* This chapter offers more details about work-life balance and reorganizes the organizational behavior trends to include virtual work as a theme. This chapter also updates discussion of globalization effects, such as offshoring and work intensity, and introduces surface and deep level diversity concepts in the section on workforce diversity.

- *Chapter 2: Individual Behavior, Values, and Personality.* This chapter introduces students to the emerging concept of employee engagement, and links this concept to the MARS model of individual behaviour and performance. It also introduces employer branding and guerrilla recruitment to attract job applicants. The section on personal values is also updated with more details about different forms of values congruence.

- *Chapter 3: Perception and Learning in Organizations.* This chapter reflects current thinking about selective attention, organization, and interpretation as automatic unconscious emotional (rather than logical/mechanical) processes. It also writes about categorical thinking as part of the perceptual process, introduces "thin slices" research on perceptions, updates the highly popular concept of social identity theory, provides new details about when self-fulfilling prophecy is more (or less) likely to occur, adds new cross-cultural information about fundamental attribution error, introduces the concept of positive organizational behavior, and further highlights the importance of the learning orientation concept in experiential learning.

- *Chapter 4: Workplace Emotions and Attitudes.* This edition describes the emotions attitudes-behavior model more clearly in two parts (cognitive vs emotional) and includes discussion of situations where cognitions and emotions conflict with each other. It also describes the important marketing concept about how people "listen in" on their emotions when forming attitudes. This chapter also updates discussion of emotional display norms across cultures, and includes shared values as a predictor of organizational commitment.

- *Chapter 5: Motivation in the Workplace.* Recognizing that needs hierarchy models lack research support, *Organizational Behavior* was the first OB textbook to introduce four-drive theory as an alternative model to understand the dynamics of needs and drives in organizational settings. This edition further explains how that model works, and identifies its implications for practice in the workplace. This chapter also explains the ongoing relevance of Maslow's ideas, and further emphasizes the role of procedural justice in organizational justice.

- *Chapter 6: Applied Performance Practices.* This chapter has relatively minor changes. The chapter is somewhat shorter in this edition by condensing the section on the meaning of money and types of rewards. The chapter also refines some of the details about scientific management and updates details about how self-leadership is applied in the workplace.

- *Chapter 7: Work-Related Stress and Stress Management.* This edition introduces the important emerging concept of resilience as an individual difference in the reaction to stress. Psychological harassment has been added to this edition, integrating previous edition writing on workplace bullying. The chapter also cites three explanations for the increasing incidence of work overload, and offers a little more detail on how companies monitor or audit stress in the workplace.

- *Chapter 8: Decision Making and Creativity.* The chapter offers a brief history of the origins of the rational choice paradigm. It provides a clearer overview of the reasons why decision makers have difficulty identifying problems, and identifies three ways that emotions affect the evaluation of alternatives. This edition also introduces new evidence about escalation of commitment, intuition in decision making, and how people evaluate opportunities.

- *Chapter 9: Foundations of Team Dynamics.* This edition more explicitly explains why organizations rely on teams. It also lists several types of formal teams in organizations, adds new information about faultlines in team diversity, and provides more details about Brooks's law (mythical man-month).

- *Chapter 10: Developing High Performance Teams.* This chapter further refines our knowledge of self-directed work teams and sociotechnical systems theory. It also updates the section on team trust, including propensity to trust as an individual difference. This chapter also incorporates new research on team decision making, including new knowledge about constructive conflict, groupthink, and brainstorming

- *Chapter 11: Communicating in Teams and Organizations.* Along with updating information about e-mail and instant messaging, this edition discusses the role of blogs and wikis in corporate communication. This chapter also provides new information about the exceptions to media richness, as well as employee attitudes toward the organizational grapevine.

- *Chapter 12: Power and Influence in the Workplace.* This chapter updates our knowledge of power and influence derived from social networks. It organizes influence tactics more clearly around hard and soft tactics, and introduces three contingencies to consider when applying various influence tactics.

- *Chapter 13: Conflict and Negotiation in the Workplace.* This edition offers new information about the relationship between constructive (task-related) conflict and socioemotional conflict, and identifies ways to minimize the latter while engaging in the former. It also summarizes current thinking about how to minimize conflict through communication and understanding. including the role of talking circles.

- *Chapter 14: Leadership in Organizational Settings.* This chapter further elaborates the concept of shared leadership. It also updates information about leadership substitutes, the implicit leadership perspective, and gender differences in leadership. In addition, it provides further evidence separating charismatic from transformational leadership.

- *Chapter 15: Organizational Structure.* This edition updates information about coordination mechanisms, the optimal level of decentralization, and problems with matrix structures. It revises and updates writing on the divisionalized structure, including challenges in choosing the preferred divisionalized structure. The section on contingencies of organizational design has been re-organized to emphasize the external environment as a central contingency.

- *Chapter 16: Organizational Culture.* This chapter revises the organizational culture model to reflect emerging views on its elements. It sharpens the focus on the advantages and limitations of strong organizational cultures. The section on changing and strengthening organizational culture has been revised to reflect key issues and more detailed discussion of these practices.

- *Chapter 17: Organizational Change.* This chapter provides additional information about creating an urgency to change and diffusing change from a pilot project. It also updates information on contingencies of appreciative inquiry.

Supporting the Learning Process

The changes described above refer only to the text material. *Organizational Behavior,* Fourth Edition, also has improved technology supplements, cases, videos, team exercises, and self-assessments. The detailed Walkthrough on the following pages highlights the many learning features available to students and instructors who adopt *Organizational Behavior,* Fourth Edition.

Student-Focused Learning Features

With its core philosophy being "OB is for everyone," every chapter of **Organizational Behavior** is filled with innovative features and exercises to help students learn and apply the knowledge they've gained from chapter material.

What does a swarm of robot bees sound like? Cory Hawthorne tried to figure that out by listening to dozens of sounds and loops. Suddenly the sound effects specialist at Radical Entertainment found the right combination when he mixed his humming through a kazoo with the noise of operating an electric beard trimmer across the surface of his bathtub. The robot bees now had a menacing audio effect in the electronic game that Hawthorne was working on: *The Simpsons: Hit and Run.*

Radical depends on Cory Hawthorne and its other 230 employees to have plenty of such discovery moments to succeed in the competitive video game marketplace. "Hit games are made by people who have the freedom and support to put unconventional ideas in motion," explains Ian Wilkinson, founder and CEO of the Vancouver, Canada, company (now a division of Los Angeles–based Vivendi Universal Games). "So we give our employees the autonomy to drive real change, whatever their role in the company. No other game developer offers this level of creative freedom."

Radical Entertainment founder Ian Wilkinson (third from right) meets with employees every week to reinforce the Vancouver-based games developer's emphasis on creative decision making and employee involvement.

Danielle Michael, Radical's vice president of business development, echoes Wilkinson's view that the best decisions in this fast-paced industry come from employee involvement and autonomy: "People are hugely empowered to be creative, to go beyond the call of duty to come up with great ideas and to actually implement them," says Michael.

To help guide employee decision making, posters hung throughout Radical's headquarters state the company's succinct values, including this one: "Take risks, always learn." Wilkinson takes these values seriously. He lunches with a half dozen employees each week (as shown in this photo—Wilkinson is third from the right), encouraging them to apply the company's values in their everyday decisions.

Creative ideas are also cross-pollinated through Radical's monthly "game fair" day, in which teams show off their products and make presentations to other teams in the organization. "I don't want to be hearing what other companies are doing," Wilkinson advises staff. "I want to do innovative stuff and have some people say we're crazy."[1]

A half-dozen years ago, district and store managers at Home Depot made their own decisions, routinely ignored directives from the head office, and opposed anything that looked like bureaucracy or hierarchy. "Whether it was an aisle, department, or store, you were truly in charge of it," recalls a former store operations manager. This decentralized, freewheeling culture likely fueled Home Depot's phenomenal growth, but it turned into a liability when Lowe's and Wal-Mart brought more intense competition to the marketplace. Home Depot needed more structure and efficiency, so the board of directors plucked Robert Nardelli from General Electric (GE) to become the new CEO and chief architect for change. His objective, not surprisingly, was to "GE-ize" Home Depot, turning it into a much more regimented, centralized, and measurement-focused organization.

Home Depot CEO Robert Nardelli has dramatically changed the big box retailer's culture by introducing systems that reinforce the new values.

Nardelli took a structural approach to change by introducing precise measures of corporate performance and drilling managers with weekly performance objectives around those metrics. The previous hodge-podge of subjective performance reviews was replaced with one centralized fact-based system to evaluate store managers and weed out poor performers. Nardelli instituted quarterly business review meetings in which objective measures of revenue, margins, inventory turns, cash flow, and other key indicators were analyzed across stores and regions. A two-hour weekly conference call became a ritual in which Home Depot's top executives were held accountable for the previous week's goals.

These changes occurred with lightning speed. "The rate of change internally has to be greater than the rate of change externally or else you're pedaling backward," advises Nardelli. For example, Dennis Donovan, one of several GE alumni Nardelli hired into key management posts, was given 90 days to develop a centralized purchasing system that would leverage more buying power than the existing decentralized process. "In the game of change, velocity is your friend," says Donovan, adding that Nardelli works by a stopwatch, not a time clock.

These rapid structural change interventions have helped Home Depot increase operating efficiency and double sales and profits over Nardelli's first five years. Employee engagement scores initially suffered, but they have now risen above the industry average. However, critics point out that these changes resulted in the departure of almost all of Home Depot's top management as well as ongoing turnover rates well above those at Lowe's. "[Nardelli's] lost so much good talent out of that place," observes one former executive. "The guys I still talk to there say they're waiting for the next shoe to drop."

Equally troubling is that Home Depot's customer service levels have sunk to new lows (one survey ranks Home Depot dead last among major U.S. retailers). "[Nardelli's] made Home Depot much more profitable and more streamlined, but messed up everything that has to do with serving the customer," complains one retail consultant. Wall Street isn't impressed, either; Home Depot's share price hasn't budged since Nardelli arrived.[1]

OPENING VIGNETTE

Each chapter begins with an engaging **opening vignette** that sets the stage for the chapter. These brief but interesting case studies introduce students to critical issues, challenge their preconceptions, and highlight some of today's hottest companies.

Foundations of Team Dynamics

LEARNING OBJECTIVES

After reading this chapter you should be able to

1. Define *teams* and distinguish them from informal groups.
2. Discuss the potential benefits of teams in organizations.
3. Outline the model of team effectiveness.
4. Identify six organizational and team environmental elements that influence team effectiveness.
5. Explain how a team's task, size, and composition influence its effectiveness.

6. Summarize the team development process.
7. Discuss how team norms develop and are maintained and how they may be altered.
8. List six factors that influence team cohesiveness.
9. Discuss the limitations of teams.
10. Explain how companies minimize social loafing.

LEARNING OBJECTIVES

A topical guide for the student, a list of Learning Objectives not only can be found at the beginning of each chapter, but correspondingly throughout chapter.

---

any special circumstances or ulterior motives. A second explanation is provided by social identity theory, which states that individuals define themselves by their group affiliations. Thus we join informal groups—particularly groups viewed favorably by others and that are similar to our existing values—because they shape and reinforce our self-images.[9]

A third reason why people join informal groups is to accomplish tasks that cannot be achieved by individuals working alone. For example, employees will sometimes form a group to oppose organizational changes because the group collectively has more power than individuals complaining alone. A fourth explanation for informal groups is that in stressful situations we are comforted by the mere presence of other people and are therefore motivated to be near them. When in danger, people congregate near each other even though it serves no apparent purpose. Similarly, employees tend to mingle more often when hearing rumors that the company might be sold.[10]

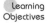
Learning Objectives

> **After reading the next three sections you should be able to**
> 3. **Outline the model of team effectiveness.**
> 4. **Identify six organizational and team environmental elements that influence team effectiveness.**
> 5. **Explain how a team's task, size, and composition influence its effectiveness.**

CAPTIONS BEYOND CURSORY

Going beyond the simple caption, richly detailed photos are accompanied by more in-depth narrative.

Chapter 5 *Motivation in the Workplace*   137

Belongingness Needs Top the Hierarchy for Some Employees These UBS Warburg employees in Chicago seem to be enjoying each other's company, suggesting that they are experiencing some fulfillment of their belongingness needs. But do they all have the same needs hierarchy? Not according to emerging research and writing on this subject. Contrary to Maslow's well-known theory, needs are not hardwired into a universal hierarchy. Instead a person's needs hierarchy seems to be strongly influenced by his or her value system, so needs hierarchies vary from one person to the next and possibly from one culture to the next. The UBS Warburg staff in this photo probably have somewhat different value systems, so their needs hierarchies would be different.

motivation experts had splintered needs and drives into dozens of categories, each studied in isolation using nontypical subjects (usually animals or people with severe

Connections 4.1

CONNECTIONS

Connections boxes connect OB concepts with real organizational incidents.

Serious Fun

Walk into the offices of CXtec in Syracuse, New York, and you might think employees are in the middle of a birthday party. Around the cubicles are colorful clusters of helium-filled balloons, each representing a small token of the company's appreciation for performing their work effectively. Employees at the computer networking equipment company also enjoy a break room with billiards, foosball, and air hockey. And if staff want a little more enjoyment, the company also sponsors miniature golf tournaments in the office, tricycle races around the building, and "CXtec Idol" competitions. Of course all of this fits in with what the company stands for: "Part of our core values is that work is fun," explains Paula Miller, CXtec's director of employee and community relations.

Fun at work? It sounds like an oxymoron. But to attract and motivate valuable talent, companies are finding creative ways to generate positive emotions in the workplace. About six times each year, credit department staff at Zebra Technologies in Vernon Hills, Illinois, head off to the Whirlyball center, a large rink where employees grab and toss a ball using handheld scoops and electric bumper cars. The Malaysian operations of Scope International, a division of British bank Standard Chartered, won an award for bringing fun into the workplace—such as color coordination days, in which employees wear the same color clothing on a particular day. Along with enjoying office nerf gun fights, robot combat tournaments, movie nights, and wine tours, employees at Nuvation in San Jose, California, showcase a life-size fiberglass blue and orange moose. "We like to take the moose out to our parties," says Nuvation cofounder Geoff White.

These fun and games may seem silly, but some corporate leaders are serious about their value. "It's pretty

CXtec employees in Syracuse, New York, like to live up to their company values, which include having fun at work.

simple," explains an executive at Quebecor. "If you want to make the most money, you must attract the best people. To get the best people, you must be the most fun."

Sources: J. Elliott, "All Work and No Play Can Chase Workers Away," *Edmonton Journal*, 28 February 2000; M.A. Tan, "Management: Having Fun at Work," *The Edge Malaysia*, 10 February 2003; R. Deruyter, "Firm's Goals Are Business Success and Having Fun," *Kitchener-Waterloo Record*, 30 October 2004, p. F1; S.K. Wong, "How Do Some Big companies Spell Teamwork? Whirlyball," *The Columbian* (Vancouver, WA), 19 March 2006, p. E1; T. Knauss, "Small Company Is a Happy Place to Work," *Post Standard/Herald-Journal* (Syracuse, New York), 21 March 2006, p. A1.

End-of-Chapter Material Geared Toward Application

SELF-ASSESSMENTS

Experiential exercises and **self-assessments** represent an important part of the active learning process. *Organizational Behavior*, Fourth Edition, offers one or two **team exercises** in every chapter. Many of these learning activities are not available in other organizational behavior textbooks, such as "Where in the World are We?" (Chapter 8) and "A Cross-Cultural Communication Game" (Chapter 11). This edition has **three-dozen self-assessments** in the book or part of the premium content offered with the Online Learning Center or Enhanced Cartridges for course management systems. The self-assessments feature personalize the meaning of several organizational behavior concepts, such as workaholism, corporate culture preferences, self-leadership, empathy, stress, creative disposition, and tolerance of change.

Self-Assessment 12.5
GUANXI ORIENTATION SCALE (STUDENT OLC)

Guanxi, which is translated as interpersonal connections, is an important element of doing business in China and some other Asian countries with strong Confucian cultural values. Guanxi is based on traditional Confucian values of helping others without expecting future repayment. This instrument estimates your guanxi orientation–that is, the extent to which you accept and apply guanxi values. This self-assessment is completed alone so you can rate yourself honestly without concerns of social comparison. However, class discussion will focus on the meaning of guanxi and its relevance for organizational power and influence.

Self-Assessment 12.6
MACHIAVELLIANISM SCALE (STUDENT OLC)

Machiavellianism is named after Niccolò Machiavelli, the 16th-century Italian philosopher who wrote *The Prince*, a famous treatise about political behavior. Out of Machiavelli's work emerged this instrument that estimates the degree to which you have a Machiavellian personality. Indicate the extent to which you agree or disagree that each statement in this instrument describes you. Complete each item honestly to get the best estimate of your level of Machiavellianism.

Self-Assessment 12.7
PERCEPTIONS OF POLITICS SCALE (POPS) (STUDENT OLC)

Organizations have been called "political arenas" environments where political tactics are common because decisions are ambiguous and resources are scarce. This instrument estimates the degree to which you believe the school where you attend classes has a politicized culture. This scale consists of several statements that might or might not describe the school where you are attending classes. These statements refer to the administration of the school, not the classroom. Please indicate the extent to which you agree or disagree with each statement.

 After reading this chapter, if you need additional information, see www.mhhe.com/mcshane4e for more in-depth interactivities that correspond with this material.

TEAM EXERCISES

Team Exercise 8.4 WHERE IN THE WORLD ARE WE?

PURPOSE This exercise is designed to help you understand the potential advantages of involving others in decisions rather than making decisions alone.

MATERIALS Students require an unmarked copy of the map of the United States with grid marks (Exhibit 2). Students are not allowed to look at any other maps or use any other materials. The instructor will provide a list of communities located somewhere on Exhibit 2. The instructor will also provide copies of Exhibit 2. The instructor will also provide copies of the answer sheet after students have individually and in teams estimated the locations of communities.

INSTRUCTIONS

1. Write in Exhibit 1 the list of communities identified by your instructor. Then, working alone, estimate the location in Exhibit 2 of these communities, all of which are in the United States. For example, mark a small "1" in Exhibit 2 on the spot where you believe the first community is located. Mark a small "2" where you think the second community is located, and so on. Please be sure to number each location clearly and with numbers small enough to fit within one grid space.

2. The instructor will organize students into roughly equal teams (typically five or six people per team). Working with your team members, reach a consensus on the location of each community listed in Exhibit 1. The instructor might provide teams with a separate copy of the map, or members can identify the team's numbers using a different color pen on the individual maps. The team's decision for each location should occur by consensus, not voting or averaging.

3. The instructor will provide an answer sheet showing the correct location of the communities. Using this answer sheet, count the minimum number of grid squares between the location you individually marked and the true location of each community. Write the number of grid squares in the third column of Exhibit 1, then add up the total. Next, count the minimum number of grid squares between the location the team marked and the true location of each community. Write the number of grid squares in the fourth column of Exhibit 1, then add up the total.

4. The instructor will ask for information about the totals, and the class will discuss the implications of these results for employee involvement and decision making.

Exhibit 1
List of Selected Communities in the United States

Number	Communities	Individual distance in grid units from the true location	Team distance in grid units from the true location
1			
2			
3			
4			
5			
6			
7			
8			
		Total:	Total:

© 2002 Steven L. McShane.

249

CRITICAL THINKING QUESTIONS

Critical Thinking Questions

1. This chapter begins by suggesting that motivating employees has become more challenging in recent years, partly because younger employees (Generation-X and Generation Y) have different expectations than baby boomers. How do you think these younger and older generation groups differ in their expectations? Generally speaking, what would motivate a typical Generation-Y worker (under 25 years old) more than a typical baby boomer worker (over 45 years old)?

2. Four-drive theory is conceptually different from Maslow's needs hierarchy (as well as ERG theory) in several ways. Describe these differences. At the same time, needs are typically based on drives, so the four drives should parallel the seven needs that Maslow identified (five in the hierarchy and two additional needs). Map Maslow's needs to the four drives in four-drive theory.

3. Use all three components of expectancy theory to explain why some employees are motivated to show up for work during a severe storm whereas others make no effort to leave their homes.

4. What are the limitations of expectancy theory in predicting an individual's work effort and behavior?

5. Using your knowledge of the characteristics of effective goals, establish two meaningful goals related to your performance in this class.

6. When do employees prefer feedback from nonsocial rather than social sources? Explain why nonsocial sources are preferred under these conditions.

7. Several service representatives are upset that a newly hired representative with no previous experience will be paid $3,000 a year above the usual starting salary in the pay range. The department manager explained that the new hire would not accept the entry-level rate, so the company raised the offer by $3,000. All five reps currently earn salaries near the top of the scale ($15,000 higher than the new recruit), although they all started at the minimum starting salary a few years earlier. Use equity theory to explain why the five service representatives feel inequity in this situation.

8. Organizational injustice can occur in the classroom as well as in the workplace. Identify classroom situations in which you experienced feelings of injustice. What can instructors do to maintain an environment that fosters both distributive and procedural justice?

BUSINESS WEEK CASE STUDIES

Found at the end of each chapter, ***BusinessWeek* case studies** introduce the online full-text article and provide critical thinking questions for class discussion or assignments. These cases encourage students to understand and diagnose real-world issues using organizational behavior knowledge. For example, one case study challenges students to analyze how team dynamics supported development of Motorola's highly successful cell phone, the Razr. Another case study asks students to explain who Boeing experienced several serious incidents of ethical misconduct, and to evaluate the likely success of Boeing's actions to improve ethical conduct at the aerospace company.

Case Study 9.2 MOSH PITS OF CREATIVITY

BusinessWeek The Razr, Motorola's highly successful ultralight cell phone, was designed through a process that differed from the electronics company's traditional research and development center. Much of the critical work on the phone was done in an innovation lab where cross-functional teams of engineers, marketers, and others work together in funky open-space offices that foster information sharing. Mattel, Steelcase, Boeing, Wrigley, Procter & Gamble, and many other firms are also turning to cross-functional teams to creatively and efficiently design new products or solve perplexing problems. Some companies have also designed their workplace to improve informal group dynamics that support the creative process.

This *BusinessWeek* case study examines this trend toward collaborative cross-functional teamwork in product development. It describes the characteristics of these "mosh pits," including their separation from the normal corporate bureaucracy and how employees are rotated through these special centers for inspiration. Read the full text of this *BusinessWeek* article at www.mhhe.com/mcshane4e and prepare for the discussion questions below.

Discussion Questions

1. What elements of the team dynamics model are Motorola, Procter & Gamble, and other companies applying to make these product development teams successful?

2. Identify the potential team dynamics challenges these product development teams might face in the situations described in this case study.

3. How are these companies supporting informal groups, and how might these groups aid the creative process?

Source: J. Weber, "'Mosh Pits' of Creativity," *BusinessWeek*, 7 November 2005, 98.

281

Case Study 5.1 BUDDY'S SNACK COMPANY

Russell Casey, Clayton State University, and Gloria Thompson, University of Phoenix

Buddy's Snack Company is a family-owned company located in the Rocky Mountains. Buddy Forest started the business in 1951 by selling homemade potato chips out of the back of his pickup truck. Nowadays Buddy's is a $36 million snack food company that is struggling to regain market share lost to Frito-Lay and other fierce competitors. In the early eighties Buddy passed the business to his son, Buddy Jr., who is currently grooming his son, Mark, to succeed himself as head of the company.

Six months ago Mark joined Buddy's Snacks as a salesperson, and after four months he was quickly promoted to sales manager. Mark recently graduated from a local university with an MBA in marketing, and Buddy Jr. was hoping that Mark would be able to implement strategies that could help turn the company around. One of Mark's initial strategies was to introduce a new sales performance management system. As part of this approach, any salesperson who receives a below-average performance rating would be required to attend a mandatory coaching session with his or her supervisor. Mark Forest is hoping that these coaching sessions will motivate employees to increase their sales. This case describes the reaction of three salespeople who have been required to attend a coaching session because of their low performance over the previous quarter.

Lynda Lewis

Lynda is a hard worker who takes pride in her work ethic. She has spent a lot of time reading the training material and learning selling techniques, viewing training videos on her own time, and accompanying top salespeople on their calls. Lynda has no problem asking for advice and doing whatever needs to be done to learn the business. Everyone agrees that Lynda has a cheery attitude and is a real "team player," giving the company 150 percent at all times. It has been a tough quarter for Lynda due to the downturn in the economy, but she is doing her best to make sales for the company. Lynda feels that failure to make quota during this past quarter is due not to lack of effort, but just bad luck in the economy. She is hopeful that things will turn around in the next quarter.

160

Lynda is upset with Mark about having to attend the coaching session because this is the first time in three years that her sales quota has not been met. Although Lynda is willing to do whatever it takes to be successful, she is concerned that the coaching sessions will be held on a Saturday. Doesn't Mark realize that Lynda has to raise three boys by herself and that weekends are an important time for her family? Because Lynda is a dedicated employee, she will somehow manage to rearrange the family's schedule.

Lynda is now very concerned about how her efforts are being perceived by Mark. After all, she exceeded the sales quota for the previous quarter, yet she did not receive thanks or congratulations for those efforts. The entire experience has left Lynda unmotivated and questioning her future with the company.

Michael Benjamin

Michael is happy to have his job at Buddy's Snack Company, although he really doesn't like sales work that much. Michael accepted this position because he felt that he wouldn't have to work hard and would have a lot of free time during the day. Michael was sent to coaching mainly because his customer satisfaction reports were low; in fact, they were the lowest in the company. Michael tends to give canned presentations and does not listen closely to the customer's needs. Consequently, Michael makes numerous errors in new sales orders, which delay shipments and lose business and goodwill for Buddy's Snack Company. Michael doesn't really care because most of his customers do not spend much money, and he doesn't think it is worth his while.

There has been a recent change in the company commission structure. Instead of selling to the warehouse stores and possibly earning a high commission, Michael is now forced to sell to lower-volume convenience stores. In other words, he will have to sell twice

CHAPTER CASES AND ADDITIONAL END-OF-TEXT CASES

Every chapter includes at least one short **case study** that challenges students to diagnose issues and apply ideas from that chapter. Additional comprehensive cases appear at the end of the book. Several cases are new to this book and are written by instructors around the United States and from other countries. Other cases, such as Arctic Mining Consultants, are classics that have withstood the test of time.

Chapter Summary

Motivation refers to the forces within a person that affect his or her direction, intensity, and persistence of voluntary behavior in the workplace. Motivation has become more challenging because of an increasingly turbulent work environment, the removal of direct supervision as a motivational instrument, and the lack of understanding about what motivates the new generations of people entering the workforce.

Maslow's needs hierarchy groups needs into a hierarchy of five levels and states that the lowest needs are initially most important, but higher needs become more important as the lower ones are satisfied. Although very popular, the theory lacks research support—as does ERG theory, which attempted to overcome some of the limitations in Maslow's needs hierarchy. Both models assume that everyone has the same hierarchy, whereas emerging evidence suggests that needs hierarchies vary from one person to the next based on their personal values.

Four-drive theory states that everyone has four innate drives—the drives to acquire, bond, learn, and defend. These drives create competing emotions, however, so we consciously reconcile these competing impulses through a skill set that considers social norms, past experience, and personal values. Four-drive theory offers considerable potential for understanding employee motivation, but it still requires clarification and research to understand how people translate competing emotions into motivated behavior.

McClelland's learned needs theory argues that needs can be strengthened through learning. The three needs studied in this respect have been need for achievement, need for power, and need for affiliation.

The practical implication of needs/drives-based motivation theories is that corporate leaders must provide opportunities for everyone in the workplace to regularly

fulfill all four drives; that organizations should avoid too much or too little opportunity to fulfill each drive; and that employees should be offered a choice of rewards rather than given the same reward as everyone else.

Expectancy theory states that work effort is determined by the perception that effort will result in a particular level of performance (E-to-P expectancy); the perception that a specific behavior or performance level will lead to specific outcomes (P-to-O expectancy); and the valences the person feels for those outcomes. The E-to-P expectancy increases by improving the employee's ability and confidence to perform the job. The P-to-O expectancy increases by measuring performance accurately, distributing higher rewards to better performers, and showing employees that rewards are performance-based. Outcome valences increase by finding out what employees want and using these resources as rewards.

Goal setting is the process of motivating employees and clarifying their role perceptions by establishing performance objectives. Goals are more effective when they are specific, relevant, and challenging; have employee commitment; and are accompanied by meaningful feedback. Participative goal setting is important in some situations. Effective feedback is specific, relevant, timely, credible, and sufficiently frequent (which depends on the length of the task cycle and the employee's knowledge and experience with the task). Two increasingly popular forms of feedback are multisource (360-degree) assessment and executive coaching. Feedback from nonsocial sources is also beneficial.

Organizational (perceived fairness our contribution others) and pro used to decide ory, which cons

Key Terms

distributive justice, p. 152	four-drive theory, p. 138	need for power (nPow), p. 141
drives, p. 135	goal setting, p. 146	needs, p. 135
equity sensitivity, p. 154	Maslow's needs hierarchy, p. 135	positive organizational
equity theory, p. 152	motivation, p. 134	behavior, p. 137
ERG theory, p. 138	multisource (360-degree)	procedural justice, p. 162
executive coaching, p. 150	feedback, p. 149	self-actualization, p. 135
expectancy theory, p. 143	need for achievement (nAch), p. 141	valence, p. 144
feedback, p. 148	need for affiliation (nAff), p. 141	

Supplementary Choices

Organizational Behavior, Fourth Edition, includes a variety of **supplemental materials** to help instructors prepare and present the material in this textbook more effectively.

INSTRUCTOR'S CD-ROM

The **Instructor's CD-Rom** contains the **Instructor's Manual,** the **Computerized Test Bank, PowerPoint presentation,** and additional downloads of **art from the text.** Written by Steve McShane, the IM includes the learning objectives, glossary of key terms, a chapter synopsis, and complete lecture outline with thumbnail images of corresponding PowerPoint slides, suggested solutions to the end-of-chapter discussion questions. It also includes teaching notes for the chapter case(s), team exercises, and self-assessments and transparency masters. The Test Bank, written with assistance from Amit Shah, Frostburg State University, includes more than 2,400 multiple-choice, true/false, and essay questions, the majority of which have been tested in class examinations. We've also aligned our Testbank with new AACSB guidelines, tagging each question according to its knowledge and skills areas. Categories include Global, Ethics and Social Responsibility, Legal and other External Environment, Communication, Diversity, Group Dynamics, Individual Dynamics, Production, and IT. Previous designations aligning questions with Learning Objectives and features still exist as well.

POWERPOINT

Organizational Behavior includes a complete set of **PowerPoint Presentation** files, with at least 18 slides relating to each chapter. These slides have received high praise for their clean design, use of graphics, and inclusion of some photos from the textbook.

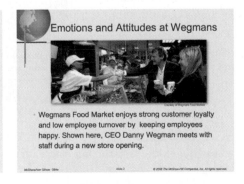

GROUP AND VIDEO RESOURCE MANUAL: An Instructor's Guide to an Active Classroom (in print 0073044342 or online at www.mhhe.com/mobmanual)

This manual created for instructors contains everything needed to successfully integrate activities into the classroom. It includes a menu of items to use as teaching tools in class. All of our self-assessment exercises, Test Your Knowledge quizzes, group exercises, and Manager's HotSeat exercises are located in this one manual along with teaching notes and PowerPoint slides to use in class. Group exercises include everything you would need to use the exercise in class — handouts, figures, etc.

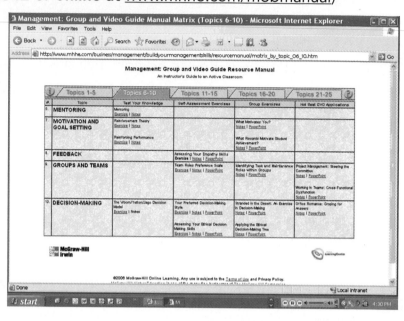

This manual is organized into 25 topics like ethics, decision-making, change and leadership for easy inclusion in your lecture. A matrix is included at the front of the manual that references each resource by topic. Students access all of the exercises and self-assessments on their textbook's website. The Manager's Hot Seat exercises are located online at www.mhhe.com/MHS

MANAGER'S HOTSEAT ONLINE: www.mhhe.com/MHS

In today's workplace, managers are confronted daily with issues such as **ethics**, **diversity**, **working in teams**, and the **virtual workplace**. The Manager's HotSeat is interactive software that allows students to watch video of 15 real managers as they apply their years of experience to confront these issues.

Students assume the role of the manager as they watch the video and answer multiple choice questions that pop up forcing them to make decisions on the spot. They learn from the manager's mistakes and successes, and then do a report critiquing the manager's approach by defending their reasoning.

Reports can be e-mailed or printed out for credit. These video segments are a powerful tool for your course that truly immerses your students in the learning experience.

VIDEO DVD

The new video collection features PBS, NBC, and *BusinessWeek* footage, and original business documentaries that relate to examples and cases in the text. With segments like:

Troubles at General Motors

Good Business Deeds

Workplace Bias

America: An Overworked Nation (Working Smart)

ONLINE LEARNING CENTER

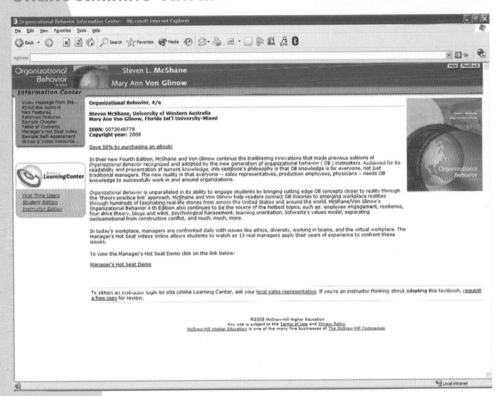

www.mhhe.com/mcshane4e

The Online Learning Center (OLC) is a one-stop shopping Web site with additional course materials, supplements, links, and exercises found chapter by chapter. As students read the book, they can go online to take self-grading quizzes, review material, or work through interactive exercises. OLCs can be delivered in multiple ways—professors and students can access them directly through the textbook Web site, or within a course management system (e.g., WebCT, Blackboard, or eCollege).

acknowledgments

Have you ever worked on a high-performance team where everything just seems to "click"? We have—on this edition! Sure, we spend plenty of time alone writing and researching for this book, and of course there are challenges along the way. But is amazing how teamwork *really does* make a difference. Several people provided valued expertise to smooth out the rough spots of writing, search out the most challenging photos, create a fantastic design, develop the various forms of student and instructor support, and pull together these many pieces into a comprehensive textbook. This teamwork is even more amazing when you consider that the team members live throughout the United States and around the world.

Sponsoring editor Ryan Blankenship led the way with enthusiasm and foresight, while clearing the way of any challenges. Christine Scheid (Senior Development Editor) demonstrated amazingly cool coordination skills as we pushed deadline limits so students have the latest OB knowledge. The keen copy editing skills of Meg McDonald made Organizational Behavior, Fourth Edition, incredibly error-free. Mary Conzachi, our Lead Project Manager, was a true professional as she guided the project through a tight production schedule. Kami Carter delivered an elegant design that captures the global and future-focus themes of this textbook. Jen Blankenship, our photo researcher, makes Sherlock Holmes look like an amateur—she can track down photos from the most obscure sources. Jodi Dowling and the Techbooks team composited the book to high standards. Meg Beamer, our marketing manager, kept everyone focused on customer needs. Thanks to you all. This has been an exceptional team effort!

As was mentioned earlier, more than 100 instructors around the world reviewed parts or all of *Organizational Behavior*, Fourth Edition, or its regional editions over the past three years. Thank you for sharing your thoughts and ideas about what an organizational behavior textbook should look like. Your compliments were energizing, and your suggestions significantly improved the final product. We also want to thank reviewers of previous editions for helping us develop this textbook. The following people from American colleges and universities provided feedback specifically for *Organizational Behavior,* Fourth Edition:

Dr. Gibb Dyer
Brigham Young University

Eleanor H. (Holly) Buttner
UNC-Greensboro

Sandra Deacon Carr
Boston University

Floyd Ormsbee
Clarkson University

George Redmond
Franklin University

B. Kay Snavely
Miami University

Carole Barnett
University of New Hampshire

Joy Benson
University of Illinois–Springfield

Greg Bier
Stephens College

Weldon Blake
Bethune Cookman College

Antonia Bos
Tusculum College

James Breaugh
University of Missouri–St. Louis

Holly Buttner
University of North Carolina–Greensboro

Michael Camarata
Marywood University

Sandra Deacon Carr
Boston University

Beth Chung
San Diego State University

Roger Dean
Washington & Lee University

George Dodge
Clearwater Christian College

Sally Dresdow
University of Wisconsin–Green Bay

Richard Feltman
San Diego State University

Marilyn Fox
Minnesota State University–Mankato

Janice Gates
Western Illinois University

Ronald Humphrey
Virginia Commonwealth University

Rusty Juban
Dallas Baptist University

Dong Jung
San Diego State University

Tom Kolenko
Kennesaw State University

Susan Manring
Elon College

Jennifer Martin
York College of Pennsylvania

Linda Morable
Richland College

Emile Pilafidis
University of La Verne

Liz Ravlin
University of South Carolina

Pete Richardson
Southwest Missouri State University

Jill Roberts
Campbellsville University

Lena Rodriguez
San Diego State University

Michael Shaner
St. Louis University

Jason Shaw
University of Kentucky–Lexington

Tracy Sigler
Northern Kentucky University

Vikki Sitter
Milligan College

Randall Sleeth
Virginia Commonwealth University

Maryalice Smith
Tarrant County College–NE

Gary Stark
University of Minnesota–Duluth

Pat Stubblebine
Miami University–Oxford

Bill Turnley
Kansas State University

Matthew Valle
Elon College

Andrew Ward
Emory University

The authors also extend their sincerest thanks to Amit Shah for assisting Steve with the test Bank. They are also very grateful to the many instructors in the United States and other countries who contributed cases and exercises to this edition of *Organizational Behavior.*

- Marc Bacon, Fabgroups Technologies Inc
- Alicia Boisnier, SUNY at Buffalo
- Martha Burkle, Monterrey Institute of Technology
- Gerard A. Callanan, West Chester University Of Pennsylvania
- Sharon Card, (formerly at) Saskatchewan Institute of Applied Science & Technology
- Russell Casey, Clayton State University
- Jeewon Cho, SUNY at Buffalo
- Mary Gander, Winona State University
- Swee C. Goh, University of Ottawa
- Cheryl Harvey, Wilfrid Laurier University
- Arif Hassan, International Islamic University Malaysia

- Christine Ho, University of Adelaide
- Lisa Ho, Prada, Singapore
- Joseph Kavanaugh, Sam Houston State University
- Theresa Kline, University of Calgary
- Henry S. Maddux III, Sam Houston State University
- Rosemary Maellaro, University of Dallas
- Fiona McQuarrie, University College of the Fraser Valley
- Kim Morouney, Wilfrid Laurier University
- David F. Perri, West Chester University Of Pennsylvania
- Harry Gene Redden, Sam Houston State University
- Joseph C. Santora, Essex County College & TST, Inc.
- Christina Stamper, Western Michigan University
- Gloria Thompson, University of Phoenix
- William Todorovic, Purdue University
- Lisa V. Williams, SUNY at Buffalo
- Thivagar Velayutham, International Islamic University Malaysia

The authors would also like to extend our sincerest thanks to the many instructors in the United States and other countries who contributed cases and exercises to previous editions of *Organizational Behavior:*

- Jeffrey Bagraim, *University of Cape Town, South Africa*
- Hazel Bothma, *University of Cape Town, South Africa*
- Sharon Card, *Saskatchewan Institute of Applied Science & Technology*
- Cynthia Larson-Daugherty, *National University*
- Carolynn Larson-Garcia, *Assesso*
- Aneil Mishra, *Wake Forest University*
- Karen Mishra, *Wake Forest University*
- Joseph C. Santora, *Essex County College and TSTDCG, Inc.*
- James C. Sarros, *Monash University*

Steve would also like to extend special thanks to his students in Perth, Singapore, and Manila for sharing their learning experiences and assisting with the development of the three organizational behavior textbooks in the United States, Canada, and the Pacific Rim, as well as their adaptations in Asia, India, and elsewhere. Steve is also very grateful to his colleagues at the Graduate School of Management, The University of Western Australia, for patiently listening to his ideas, diplomatically redirecting his wayward thoughts, and sharing their experiences using the American and Pacific Rim editions of this book in several locations around Asia and Oceania. But more than anything else, Steve is forever indebted to his wife Donna McClement and to their wonderful daughters, Bryton and Madison. Their love and support give special meaning to Steve's life.

Mary Ann would like to thank the many, many students who have used and hopefully enjoyed this book. I've been stopped on my campus and at occasional meetings by students who tell me that they recognize my picture and wanted to thank me! There are a few that have actually asked for my autograph! (Note, that didn't happen when I was President of the Academy of Management!) Thus it is to the students that I acknowledge many thanks, particularly for making this learning venture fun and exciting. Also, I would like to thank the faculty and staff at Florida International University, who have been very supportive of this effort. By far and away, my coauthor Steve McShane is the penultimate scholar. He has boundless energy and a mind that doesn't seem to quit, particularly with those late night or early morning e-mails! Steve is also the techno-wizard behind this edition. Finally I would like to thank my family—John, Rhoda, Lauren, Lindsay, and Christy—as well as some very special people in my life—Janet, Peter, Bill, Karen, Jerry, Barbara, Kate, Joanne, Mary, Linda, and Steve. I know I never get a chance to thank them enough, so thank you my friends! I also thank Emma, Zack, Molly, and Googun, my babies! A final note of thanks goes to my CIBER family: Tita, Sonia, Juan, Elsa, and KK—you are simply the best! Thank you all, for being there for me!

Steven L. McShane
Mary Ann Von Glinow

Organizational Behavior

Part One
Introduction

Chapter 1   Introduction to the Field of Organizational Behavior

Friends were puzzled when Rob Pike decided a few years ago to leave his 20-year career at the prestigious Bell Labs in New Jersey to join a Web search start-up in California with a name that sounded like baby talk. The respected computer scientist's move had nothing to do with money. "I took a huge pay cut to come here," says Pike about his decision to join Google. "The reason is, it's an exciting place to work."

Google, the company behind the ubiquitous search engine, has a freewheeling, geeky culture that attracts Rob Pike and other creative thinkers who want to make a difference in the Internet world. Employees are expected to devote a quarter of their time to new ideas of their choosing and to get those ideas into practice as quickly as possible. "Here, you can have an idea on Monday and have it on the Web site by the end of the week," says Pike, citing Google Maps and Gmail as examples of the company's rapid innovation.

Google has leveraged the power of organizational behavior to attract talented employees who want to make a difference in the Internet world.

Google's culture has clashed to some extent with its meteoric global growth to more than 6,000 employees over the past eight years. In response, the company's chaotic style has been reined in with a more stable structure around teams assigned to projects and functions. "It has scaled [up] pretty well," says Google CEO Eric Schmidt. Google's unofficial ethical philosophy—Don't be evil—is the guideline by which it refuses to favor paid advertisers in its search results (unlike some other search engines) or to allow Web sites that speak against anyone. However, Google has also faced global ethical challenges, such as when it agreed to support China's censorship of democracy and opposition against government policy.

Along with its culture and ethics, Google attracts talent with the Googleplex, the company's campuslike headquarters where high-density team clusters, playful décor, and a legendary cafeteria make everyone feel as though they haven't yet left school. Meetings even start a few minutes after the hour, just like class schedules in a lot of colleges. "That (campus) model is familiar to our programmers," explains Schmidt. "We know it's a very productive environment."

Google chief financial officer George Reyes sums up the main reason for the company's phenomenal success. "We want Google to be the very place to work for the very best computer scientists in the world," says Reyes. "Google is truly a learning organization."[1]

Introduction to the Field of Organizational Behavior

LEARNING OBJECTIVES

After reading this chapter, you should be able to

1. Define organizational behavior and give three reasons for studying this field of inquiry.

2. Describe five organizational behavior trends and discuss their effects on the workplace.

3. Debate the advantages and disadvantages of workforce diversity.

4. Summarize the benefits and challenges of telecommuting.

5. Define values and explain why they have become more important in recent years.

6. Define corporate social responsibility and argue for or against its practice in organizations.

7. Identify the five anchors on which organizational behavior is based.

8. Diagram an organization from an open systems view.

9. Define knowledge management and intellectual capital.

10. Identify specific ways in which organizations acquire, share, and preserve knowledge.

Google has become a powerhouse on the Internet, but its real power comes from applying organizational behavior theories and practices. More than ever, organizations are relying on organizational behavior knowledge to remain competitive. For example, Google has an engaged workforce because of its exciting work opportunities, supportive team dynamics, and "cool" workplace. It attracts talented people through its strong culture and ethical values and an environment that supports creativity and a learning organization. These and many other organizational behavior concepts and practices make a difference in the organization's success and employee well-being.

This book is about people working in organizations. Its main objective is to help you understand behavior in organizations and to work more effectively in organizational settings. Although organizational behavior knowledge is often presented for "managers," this book takes a broader and more realistic view that organizational behavior ideas are relevant and useful to anyone who works in and around organizations. In this chapter we introduce you to the field of organizational behavior, outline the main reasons why you should know more about it, highlight some of the trends influencing the study of organizational behavior, describe the anchors supporting the study of organizations, and introduce the concept that organizations are knowledge and learning systems.

Learning Objectives

After reading this section you should be able to

1. **Define organizational behavior and organizations and give three reasons for studying this field of inquiry.**

The Field of Organizational Behavior

organizational behavior (OB)
The study of what people think, feel, and do in and around organizations.

Organizational behavior (OB) is the study of what people think, feel, and do in and around organizations. OB researchers systematically study individual, team, and organizational-level characteristics that influence behavior within work settings. By saying that organizational behavior is a field of study, we mean that OB experts have been accumulating a distinct knowledge about behavior within organizations—a knowledge base that is the foundation of this book.

By most estimates, OB emerged as a distinct field around the 1940s.[2] However, its origins can be traced much further back in time. The Greek philosopher Plato wrote about the essence of leadership. The writings of Chinese philosopher Confucius in 500 BC are beginning to influence contemporary thinking about ethics and leadership. In 1776 Adam Smith advocated a new form of organizational structure based on the division of labor. One hundred years later German sociologist Max Weber wrote about rational organizations and initiated discussion of charismatic leadership. Soon after, Frederick Winslow Taylor introduced the systematic use of goal setting and rewards to motivate employees. In the 1920s Elton Mayo and his colleagues discovered the importance of formal and informal group dynamics in the workplace, resulting in a dramatic shift towards the "human relations" school of thought. As you can see, OB has been around for a long time; it just wasn't organized into a unified discipline until after World War II.

What Are Organizations?

Organizations have existed for as long as people have worked together. Massive temples dating back to 3500 BC were constructed through the organized actions of many people. Craftspeople and merchants in ancient Rome formed guilds, complete with elected managers. And more than 1,000 years ago, Chinese factories were producing 125,000 tons of iron a year.[3] We have equally impressive examples of contemporary organizations, ranging from Wal-Mart, the world's largest and most successful retailer, to Google, the world's leading search engine. "A company is one of humanity's most amazing inventions," says Steven Jobs, CEO of Apple Computer and Pixar Animation Studios. "It's totally abstract. Sure, you have to build something with bricks and mortar to put the people in, but basically a company is this abstract construct we've invented, and it's incredibly powerful."[4]

organizations
Groups of people who work interdependently toward some purpose.

So what are **organizations?** They are groups of people who work interdependently toward some purpose.[5] Organizations are not buildings or government-registered entities. Rather, they consist of people who interact with each other to achieve a common purpose. "A business is just a registered name on a piece of paper," explains Grahame Maher, who leads Vodafone's operations in the Czech Republic. "It's nothing more than that unless there's a group of people who care about a common purpose for why they are, where they are going, how they are going to be when they are there."[6]

Some OB experts are skeptical about the relevance of goals in a definition of organizations.[7] They argue that an organization's mission statement may be different from its true goals. Also, they question the assumption that all organizational members believe in the same goals. These points may be true, but imagine an organization without goals: It would consist of a mass of people wandering around aimlessly without any sense of direction. Overall, as Vodafone's Grahame Maher stated, organizations consist of people with a collective sense of purpose. This purpose might not be fully understood or agreed upon, but it helps employees to engage in structured patterns of interaction. In other words, they expect each other to complete various tasks in a coordinated way—in an *organized* way.

Why Study Organizational Behavior?

Organizational behavior seems to get more respect from people who have been in the workforce a while than from students who are just beginning their careers. Many of us specialize in accounting, marketing, information systems, and other fields with corresponding job titles, so it's understandable that students focus on these career paths. After all, who ever heard of a career path leading to a "vice president of OB" or a "chief OB officer"? Even if organizational behavior doesn't have its own job title, most people eventually come to realize that this field is a potential gold mine of valuable knowledge. The fact is, everyone in the workforce needs to understand, predict, and influence behavior (both our own and that of others) in organizational settings (see Exhibit 1.1). Marketing students learn marketing concepts, and computer science students learn about circuitry and software code. But everyone benefits from organizational behavior knowledge to address the people issues when trying to apply marketing, computer science, and other fields of knowledge.

Understanding, Predicting, and Influencing   Each of us has an inherent need to understand and predict the world in which we live.[8] Because much of our time is spent working in or around organizations, OB theories are particularly helpful in satisfying this innate drive to make sense of the workplace. OB theories also give you the opportunity to question and rebuild your personal mental models that have developed through observation and experience.

Exhibit 1.1
Reasons for Studying Organizational Behavior

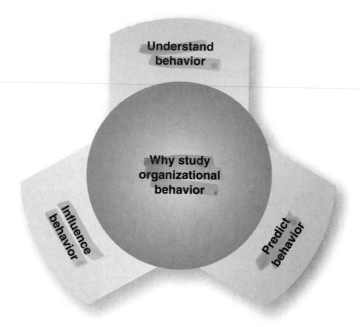

Understand behavior

Why study organizational behavior

Influence behavior

Predict behavior

Understanding and predicting are important, but most of us also need to influence the organization in various ways. Whether you are trying to introduce a new marketing strategy, encourage staff to adopt new information technology, or negotiate more flexible work arrangements with your boss, you'll find that OB concepts play an important role in performing your job and working more effectively within organizations. This practical side of organizational behavior is, according to some experts, a critical feature of the best OB theories.[9]

Organizational Behavior Is for Everyone This book takes the view that organizational behavior knowledge is for everyone—not just managers. We all need to understand organizational behavior and to master the practices that influence organizational events. That's why you won't find very much emphasis in this book on "management." Yes, organizations will continue to have managers, but their roles have changed. More important, the rest of us are now expected to manage ourselves, particularly as companies remove layers of management and delegate more responsibilities. In the words of one forward-thinking organizational behavior writer many years ago: Everyone is a manager.[10]

OB and the Bottom Line So far our answer to the question "Why study OB?" has focused on how OB knowledge benefits you as an individual. But organizational behavior knowledge is just as important for the organization's financial health. According to one estimate, firms that apply performance-based rewards, employee communication, work–life balance, and other OB practices have three times the level of financial success as companies where these practices are absent. Another study concluded that companies that earn "the best place to work" awards have significantly higher financial and long-term stock market performance. Essentially these firms leverage the power of OB practices, which translate into more favorable employee attitudes, decisions, and performance. The benefits of OB are well known to Warren Buffett and other financial gurus; they consider the organization's leadership and quality of employees as two of the best predictors of the firm's financial potential.[11]

Learning Objectives

After reading this section you should be able to

2. **Describe five organizational behavior trends and discuss their effects on the workplace.**
3. **Debate the advantages and disadvantages of workforce diversity.**
4. **Summarize the benefits and challenges of telecommuting.**
5. **Define values and explain why they have become more important in recent years.**
6. **Define corporate social responsibility and argue for or against its practice in organizations.**

Organizational Behavior Trends

There has never been a better time to learn about organizational behavior. The pace of change is accelerating, and most of the transformation is occurring in the workplace. Let's take a brief tour through five trends in the workplace: globalization, workforce diversity, evolving employment relationships, virtual work, and workplace values and ethics.

Globalization

Google didn't exist a decade ago, yet today it is one of the best-known names on the Internet around the planet. The Mountain View, California, company offers Web search services in over 100 languages, and over half of its search engine queries come from outside the United States. One-third of Google's revenue is from other countries, and it is already facing sensitive issues in China, France, and other countries that want o censor search results. So far Google has not outsourced work to contractors in low-wage countries, but it has opened its own research centers in India and Japan.[12]

Google is a rich example of the globalization of business over the past few decades. **Globalization** refers to economic, social, and cultural connectivity with people in other parts of the world. Google and other organizations globalize when they actively participate in other countries and cultures. Although businesses have traded goods

globalization
Economic, social, and cultural connectivity (and interdependence) with people in other parts of the world.

Whirlpool's Journey to Globalization In the late 1980s 95 percent of Whirlpool's revenue and most of its manufacturing occurred in the United States. Yet executives at the Benton Harbor, Michigan, company knew from excursions to other countries that globalization would soon transform the industry. "We came to the conclusion that the industry would become a global one and that someone had to shape it," recalls David Whitwam, Whirlpool's recently retired CEO. Today Whirlpool is the global leader in the appliance industry, with microwave ovens engineered in Sweden and assembled in China, refrigerators made in Brazil for European consumers, top-loading washers made in Ohio, and front-loading washers made in Germany (shown in photo). This journey toward globalization has required tremendous organizational change. "We need a diverse workforce with diverse leadership," says Whitwam, as well as "strong regional leadership that lives in the culture." Whitwam also believes a global company requires broad-based involvement and an organizational structure that encourages the flow of knowledge.[13]

across borders for centuries, the degree of globalization today is unprecedented because information technology and transportation systems allow a much more intense level of connectivity and interdependence around the planet.[14]

Globalization has given Google and other firms new markets and resources as well as a broader net to attract valuable knowledge and skills. Some experts also argue that globalization potentially improves the financial and social development of poorer nations, although other experts dispute that claim.[15] Against its potential benefits, globalization is criticized for increasing competitive pressures and market volatility. It is also linked to "offshoring"–outsourcing work to lower-wage countries. Collectively these events potentially reduce job security, increase work intensification, and demand more work flexibility from employees. Thus globalization might partly explain why many of us now work longer hours, have heavier workloads, and experience more work–family conflict than at any time in recent decades.[16]

Globalization is now well entrenched, so rather than debate its advantages and disadvantages, the real issue is how corporate leaders and employees alike can lead and work effectively in this emerging reality.[17] OB researchers are turning their attention to this topic, such as determining how well OB theories and practices work across cultures. In the Best Practices Project, for instance, over three dozen scholars are discovering human resource management practices based on companies around the globe. Another consortium, called Project GLOBE, is studying leadership and organizational practices across dozens of countries.[18] Globalization also has important implications for how we learn about organizational behavior. The best-performing companies may be in Helsinki, Singapore, or São Paulo, not just in New York or Miami. That's why this book presents numerous examples from around the planet. We want you to learn from the best, no matter where their headquarters are located.

Workforce Diversity

Walk into the offices of Verizon Communications around the United States and you can quickly see that the communications service giant reflects the communities it serves. Minorities make up 30 percent of Verizon's workforce of 200,000 and 18 percent of top management positions. Women represent 43 percent of its workforce and 32 percent of top management. Verizon's inclusive culture has won awards from numerous organizations representing Hispanics, African Americans, gays and lesbians, people with disabilities, and other groups. You can also see this diversity at Google. Its California headquarters employs people from most countries, which creates a challenge for the company's restaurant staff. "It's a global community here, and you can't just go with one kind of cuisine," says Charlie Ayers, the chef who created Google's kitchens. Even Google's smaller European operations in Dublin, Ireland, employ people from more than 40 nationalities.[19]

Verizon Communications and Google are model employers that reflect the increasing diversity of people living in the United States and in many other countries. Workforce diversity takes many forms. The primary categories in Exhibit 1.2 represent **surface-level diversity,** which include observable demographic or physiological differences in people, such as their race, ethnicity, gender, age, and physical disabilities. This most obvious form of diversity has changed considerably in the United States over the past few decades.

People with nonwhite or Hispanic origin represent one-third of the American population, and this fraction is projected to increase substantially over the next few decades. The Hispanic population recently replaced African Americans as the second largest ethnic group. Within the next 50 years one in four Americans will be

surface-level diversity Observable demographic or physiological differences in people, such as their race, ethnicity, gender, age, and physical disabilities.

Exhibit 1.2
**Primary and
Secondary
Dimensions of
Workforce Diversity**

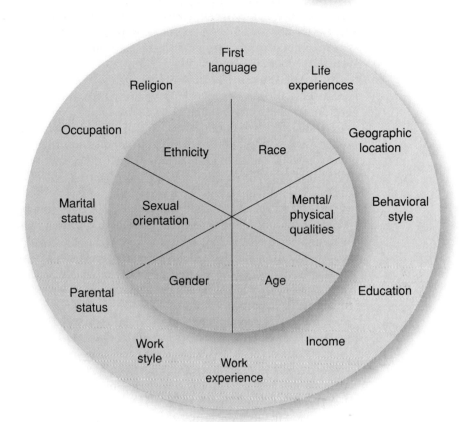

Sources: Adapted from M. Loden, *Implementing Diversity* (Chicago: Irwin, 1996); S. Bradford, "Fourteen Dimensions of Diversity: Understanding and Appreciating Differences in the Workplace," in J. W. Pfeiffer (Ed.), *1996 Annual: Volume 2 Consulting* (San Diego: Pfeiffer and Associates, 1996), pp. 9–17.

Hispanic, 14 percent will be African American, and 8 percent will be of Asian descent. By 2060 non-Hispanic whites will be a minority.[20] Many other countries are also experiencing increasing levels of racial and ethnic diversification. Meanwhile women now account for nearly half of the paid workforce in the United States—more than double the participation rate a few decades ago. Gender-based shifts continue to occur within many occupations. For example, women represent 59 percent of accountants in the United States, compared to just 17 percent in 1960. Similarly, the percentage of women enrolled in medical schools has jumped from 9 percent in 1970 to almost 50 percent today.[21]

Deep-Level Diversity   Surface-level diversity is the most obvious and easiest-to-measure form of diversity. In contrast, **deep-level diversity** represents differences in the psychological characteristics of employees, including personalities, beliefs, values, and attitudes.[22] We can't directly see deep-level diversity, but it is evident in a person's decisions, statements, and actions. The secondary dimensions of diversity shown in Exhibit 1.2 don't represent psychological differences, but they and the primary dimensions influence deep-level diversity. Religion and geographic location, for example, influence a person's personal values. Education and work

deep-level diversity
The differences in
the psychological
characteristics of
employees, including
personalities, beliefs,
values, and attitudes.

experience shape a person's beliefs and attitudes on a variety of issues. An individual's personal wealth (income), parental status, and other factors influence personal needs and preferences.

One illustration of deep-level diversity is the different attitudes and expectations held by employees across generational cohorts.[23] *Baby boomers*—people born between 1946 and 1964—seem to expect and desire more job security and are more intent on improving their economic and social status. In contrast, *Generation-X* employees—those born between 1965 and 1979—expect less job security and are motivated more by workplace flexibility, the opportunity to learn (particularly new technology), and working in an egalitarian and "fun" organization. Meanwhile, some observers suggest that *Generation-Y* employees (those born after 1979) are noticeably self-confident, optimistic, multitasking, and more independent than even Gen-X coworkers. These statements certainly don't apply to everyone in each cohort, but they reflect the fact that different generations have different values and expectations.

Consequences of Diversity   Diversity presents both opportunities and challenges in organizations.[24] In some circumstances and to some degree, diversity can become a competitive advantage by improving decision making and team performance on complex tasks. For many businesses a diverse workforce also provides better customer service in a diverse society. For example, many Vietnamese customers insisted that Southern California Gas Co. field staff remove their steel-toed work boots when entering their homes, yet doing so would violate safety regulations. Some of the gas company's Vietnamese employees found a solution: Customers would be satisfied if employees wore paper booties over the boots. PepsiCo offers a more precise calculation of the diversity advantage. It recently estimated that one-eighth of revenue growth is directly attributable to new products inspired by diversity efforts, such as guacamole-flavored Doritos chips that appeal to Hispanic customers and a wasabi-flavored snack for Asian Americans.[25]

Against the evidence that workforce diversity is a sound business proposition, several experts suggest that the benefits are more subtle and contingent on a number of factors. In fact, the general conclusion is that most forms of diversity offer both advantages and disadvantages.[26] As we will discuss more fully in Chapter 9, diverse employees usually take longer to become a high-performing team. Chapter 11 looks into communication problems that exist between people from different backgrounds. Chapter 13 will explain how diversity is a source of conflict, which can lead to lack of information sharing and, in extreme cases, morale problems and higher turnover.

Whether or not workforce diversity is a business advantage, companies need to make it a priority because surface-level diversity is a moral and legal imperative. Ethically, companies that offer an inclusive workplace are, in essence, making fair and just decisions regarding employment, promotions, rewards, and so on. Fairness is a well-established influence on employee loyalty and satisfaction. "Diversity is about fairness; we use the term *inclusive meritocracy*," says Ann M. Limberg, president of Bank of America New Jersey. "What it does for our workforce is build trust and ensures that individual differences are valued."[27] In contrast, firms that fail to represent the diversity of people in the relevant labor force are unfairly discriminating against those who are significantly underrepresented. Altogether, diversity can make a difference to the organization's reputation and bottom line, but we still need to untangle what types of diversity make a difference and under what circumstances the benefits overtake the problems.

Attracting Talent through Work–Life Balance

Five years ago partners at Gray Plant Mooty made the tough decision to reduce the minimum number of billable hours (time paid through client fees) rather than raise the salaries of associates at the Minneapolis law firm. The partners might have expected a backlash when they announced that pay would not increase. Instead the law firm's associates gave the partners a standing ovation. By reducing billable hours, staff could now work fewer hours and have better work–life balance.

Work–life balance has become an important issue for staff at Gray Plant Mooty in Minneapolis as well as in most other companies. In its recent survey of more than 9,000 American university students, Universum Communications reported that more flexible work hours had become the top-ranked attribute that students are looking for in a prospective employer. When 1,000 Canadians were asked to identify the "top indicators of success in your own career," work–life balance ranked first, far ahead of salary level, challenging job, level of responsibility, and other alternatives. Another recent study reporting that work–life balance is the top priority for Canadians considering a new job offer. When 10,000 members of the New Zealand Institute of Chartered Accountants were asked to identify the prime motivation for them to choose and stay in their current jobs, one-third indicated work–life balance, beating out career advancement and money.

Work–life balance isn't always the top priority in employment. American university students placed it lower a few years ago when job prospects were limited. And university students in Europe and Asia place this factor below career advancement and challenging work or international assignments.

But even in these countries where it isn't the top priority, work–life balance is now well established as a business issue. Fuji Xerox's business in Singapore is an example. Not long ago the local managing director would arrive at work around 7:30 in the morning and stay until 10 at night. He would then continue working at home for a few more hours, sending employees e-mail messages with tasks he wanted completed "first thing in the morning." Fuji Xerox staff dutifully followed their boss's schedule, arriving at work much earlier in time to complete the assignments that had been e-mailed overnight. Eventually the managing director realized this unrelenting pace was wearing out both the staff and himself. Now he is out of the office by 6:30 p.m. and shoos his staff out at the same time. Fuji Xerox also gives employees the opportunity to work from home as well as flexibility regarding when they want to begin and end their workdays.[28]

Sources: Ipsos-Reid, "What Are Canadians' Top Indicators of Career Success?" Ipsos-Reid News release (Toronto: 7 May 2003); S.-A. Chia and E. Toh, "Give Employees a Break," *Straits Times* (Singapore), 23 July 2005; S. Shellenbarger, "Forget Vacation Time, New Grads Want Stability and a Good Retirement Plan," *The Wall Street Journal,* 16 February 2006, p. D1; D. Healey, "Families Come First," *Hamilton Spectator* (Canada), 16 March 2006, p. A16; S. Hsieh, "Minneapolis Law Firm Promotes Core Values," *Minnesota Lawyer,* 10 April 2006; M. Perry, "Stable Companions?" *Accountancy Age,* 13 April 2006, p. 18; "Money Comes Distant Third on Accountants' Wish List," *Scoop.co.nz,* 6 April 2006.

Evolving Employment Relationships

Globalization and increasing workforce diversity have produced two contrasting changes in relationships between employers and employees: (1) aligning the workplace with emerging workforce expectations and (2) increasing workforce flexibility to increase organizational competitiveness.

work–life balance
Minimizing conflict between work and nonwork demands.

Aligning the Workplace with Emerging Workforce Expectations   **Work–life balance**—minimizing conflict between work and nonwork demands—was seldom mentioned a couple of decades ago. Most employees assumed that they would put in long hours to rise up through the corporate ladder. Asking the boss to accommodate nonwork responsibilities and interests was almost a sign of betrayal.[29] But as Connections 1.1 describes, work–life balance has become one of the most important factors in the employment relationship. Probably the main reason is that technology has turned many former 9-to-5 jobs into 24/7 employment, so people are pushing back with demands for more work–life balance. A second reason is that two-income families put more demands on both partners to provide time for household duties. Gen-X/Gen-Y expectations represent a third factor. Young people today are less willing to completely wrap themselves in their jobs, possibly because they witnessed the problems with this workaholic style in their baby boomer parents.

Along with providing more work–life balance, companies are adjusting to emerging workforce expectations of a more egalitarian workplace by reducing hierarchy and replacing command-and-control management with facilitating and teaching-oriented leaders. Gen-X/Gen-Y employees also want to work in companies that make a difference, which may explain why employers are paying more attention to serving the community rather than just shareholders—a trend we'll discuss in more detail later in this chapter.

Younger employees tend to view the workplace as a community where they spend a large part of their lives (even with work–life balance), so many expect opportunities for more social fulfillment and fun. Again, several companies are making this shift in the employment relationship. Google is a sparkling example. The company's Googleplex (headquarters) in Mountain View, California, "resembles a glimmering playground for 20-somethings," says one observer. The building is outfitted with lava lamps, exercise balls, casual sofas, foosballs, pool tables, workout rooms, video games, a restaurant with free gourmet meals, and a small pool where swimmers exercise against an artificial current. Beach volleyball matches are held in the courtyard, and roller hockey games are in the parking lot. Google executives had to remind some employees that making the Googleplex their permanent residence was against building code regulations.[30]

Increasing Workforce Flexibility

As some companies are aligning employment practices with emerging workforce expectations, they are also demanding more flexibility from employees to remain responsive to globalization and other sources of turbulence. This increased flexibility occurs partly through **employability,** in which employees are expected to manage their own careers by anticipating future organizational needs and developing new competencies that match those needs.[31] From this perspective, organizations are customers, and employees keep their jobs by continuously developing new competencies for the future and performing a variety of work activities over time. Furthermore, employability shifts the burden of this adaptability to employees rather than employers, although the latter are expected to offer the resources and opportunities to assist in the process. "I think people are starting to understand the concept of lifetime employability rather than lifetime employment," says Rich Hartnett, global staffing director at aerospace manufacturer Boeing. "It's a good idea to stay current with what's out there and take personal responsibility for our own employability."[32]

Contingent Work

Along with employability, companies are making more use of **contingent work** to increase workforce flexibility. Contingent work includes any job in which the individual does not have an explicit or implicit contract for long-term employment, or one in which the minimum hours of work can vary in a nonsystematic way. This employment relationship includes anyone with temporary or seasonal employment, freelance contractors (sometimes called "free agents"), and temporary staffing agency workers.[33] By some estimates more than 15 percent of the U.S. workforce is employed in some sort of contingent work arrangement. Some experts predict that this trend will continue.

Why has contingent work increased? One reason is that it allows companies to reduce costs by more closely matching employment levels and competencies with product or service demands. This is particularly apparent in service industries, where

employability

An employment relationship in which people perform a variety of work activities rather than hold specific jobs, and are expected to continuously learn skills that will keep them employed.

contingent work

Any job in which the individual does not have an explicit or implicit contract for long-term employment, or one in which the minimum hours of work can vary in a nonsystematic way.

casual work is most common. It is also the preferred employment relationship for "free agents" with high-demand skills who enjoy a variety of interesting assignments. At the same time, research suggests that contingent workers potentially have higher accident rates as well as lower performance and loyalty. However, these outcomes depend on the type of contingent workers (for example, "free agent" contractors versus new hires on temporary status) as well as whether contingent workers are separated from, or interact regularly with, permanent staff. Another concern is that permanent employees may feel injustice against their employers if contingent workers are treated as second-class citizens.[34]

Virtual Work

virtual work
Work practices whereby employees use information technology to perform their jobs away from the traditional physical workplace.

Rush hour isn't much of a rush for Tan Swee Hoong. She enjoys breakfast with her three children, heads them off to school, then walks from the kitchen to her study. There the relocation manager at Hewlett-Packard's offices in Singapore checks e-mail and uses the telephone to connect with teammates on her work projects.[35] Tan Swee Hoong's daily routine is an example of **virtual work,** whereby employees use information technology to perform their jobs away from the traditional physical workplace. Tan's variation of virtual work, called *telecommuting* or *teleworking,* involves working at home rather than commuting to the office. Virtual work also includes employees connected to the office while on the road or at clients' offices.

Telecommuting is still rare in most Asian countries, making Tan Swee Hoong more of a pioneer than a typical employee in that region. It is somewhat more common in Japan, where 6 percent of employees telecommute. To ease traffic congestion and air pollution, the Japanese government wants to increase that figure to 20 percent by 2010. Various surveys estimate that around 20 percent of Americans work at home at least one day each month. In some firms telecommuting and other forms of virtual work are the norm rather than the exception. For instance, nearly 50 percent of employees at Sun Microsystems complete some of their work from home, cafés, drop-in centers, or clients' offices. More than two-thirds of the employees at Agilent Technologies engage in virtual work some or all of the time.[36]

Some research suggests that virtual work, particularly telecommuting, potentially reduces employee stress by offering better work–life balance and dramatically reducing time lost through commuting to the office. AT&T estimates that by avoiding daily travel, telecommuters reduce pollution and are about 10 percent more productive than before they started working from home. Nortel Networks reports that 71 percent of its U.K. staff feels more empowered through virtual work arrangements. Others point out that virtual work reduces the cost of office space and reduces traffic congestion.[37]

Against these potential benefits, virtual workers face a number of real or potential challenges.[38] Although telecommuting is usually introduced to improve work–life balance, family relations may suffer rather than improve if employees lack sufficient space and resources for a home office. Some virtual workers complain of lack of recognition, although virtual work does not seem to undermine career progression or performance ratings. Social isolation is another common complaint, particularly among virtual workers who rarely visit the office. Virtual work is clearly better suited to people who are self-motivated, organized, can work effectively with broadband and other technology, and have sufficient fulfillment of social needs elsewhere in their life. Virtual work also functions better in organizations that evaluate employees by their performance outcomes rather than by "face time."

Virtual Teams

virtual teams
Teams whose members operate across space, time, and organizational boundaries, and who are linked through information technologies to achieve organizational goals.

Virtual Teams   Another variation of virtual work occurs in **virtual teams:** cross-functional groups that operate across space, time, and organizational boundaries with members who communicate mainly through information technology.[39] Virtual teams exist when some members telecommute, but also when team members are located on company premises at different sites around the country or world. Teams have varying degrees of virtualness, depending on how often and how many team members interact face-to-face or at a distance. Currently a flurry of research activity is studying the types of work best suited to virtual teams and the conditions that facilitate and hinder their effectiveness. As with telecommuting, some people are also better suited than others to virtual team dynamics. Chapter 10 will examine these virtual team issues in detail.

Workplace Values and Ethics

Search through most annual reports and you'll soon discover that corporate leaders view values as the sine qua non of organizational excellence. For example, as described in the opening story to this chapter, Google places paramount importance on the motto "Don't be evil." Vodafone, Xerox, Dell Computer, and a host of other organizations around the world have also reexamined the values that direct employee decisions and behavior. Xerox chief executive Anne Mulcahy claims that reaffirming the company's values "helped save Xerox during the worst crisis in our history."[40]

values
Stable, long-lasting beliefs about what is important in a variety of situations, that guide our decisions and actions.

Values represent stable, long-lasting beliefs about what is important in a variety of situations that guide our decisions and actions. They are evaluative standards that help define what is right or wrong, or good or bad, in the world. Values dictate our priorities, our preferences, and our desires. They influence our motivation and decisions.[41] Although leaders refer to the core values of their companies, values really exist only within individuals as *personal values.* However, groups of people might hold the same or similar values, so we tend to ascribe these *shared values* to the team, department, organization, profession, or entire society.

Importance of Values in the Workplace   Values are not new to organizational behavior, but they have become the subject of several popular books, the mantra of corporate leaders, and the foundation of many corporate transformations in recent years.[42] One reason for this attention is that as today's workforce rejects command-and-control supervision, leaders are turning to values as a more satisfactory approach to aligning employees' decisions and actions with corporate goals. Values represent the unseen magnet that pulls employees in the same direction.[43] A second reason is

Values-Based Leadership at Dubai's Department of Economic Development The senior management team at the Department of Economic Development (DED) in the Emirate of Dubai recently devoted several months to identifying the agency's core values: accountability, teamwork, and continuous improvement. Each of these three values is anchored with specific behavior descriptions to ensure that employees and other stakeholders understand their meaning. DED also organized a series of workshops (shown in photo) in which employees participated in a "Values Mystery" exercise to help them recognize values-consistent behaviors. To develop a values-based organization, DED will also use these three values to evaluate employee performance, assess employee competencies, and identify management potential.[44]

that globalization has raised our awareness of and sensitivity to cultural differences in values and beliefs. Increasing cultural diversity also presents new challenges as organizations try to discover shared values acceptable to all employees.

The third reason why values have gained prominence is that organizations are under increasing pressure to engage in ethical practices and corporate social responsibility. **Ethics** refers to the study of moral principles or values that determine whether actions are right or wrong and outcomes are good or bad. We rely on our ethical values to determine "the right thing to do." Ethical behavior is driven by the moral principles we use to make decisions. These moral principles represent fundamental values. Unfortunately executives are receiving low grades on their ethics report cards these days, so ethics and values will continue to be an important topic in OB teaching.

ethics
The study of moral principles or values that determine whether actions are right or wrong and outcomes are good or bad.

Corporate Social Responsibility
Over 30 years ago economist Milton Friedman pronounced that "there is one and only one social responsibility of business—to use its resources and engage in activities designed to increase its profits." Friedman is a respected scholar, but this argument was not one of his more popular—or accurate—statements. Today any business that follows Friedman's advice will face considerable trouble in the marketplace. Four out of five Americans say that a company's commitment to a social issue is an important factor in deciding whether to work there and whether to buy the company's products or services. Another poll reported that 97 percent of American and European MBA students would relinquish significant financial benefits to work for an organization with a better reputation for ethics and corporate social responsibility. Almost 80 percent of Canadians say a company's record of corporate social responsibility has either a moderate or a great deal of influence on their decision where to work.[45]

corporate social responsibility (CSR)
An organization's moral obligation toward its stakeholders.

stakeholders
Shareholders, customers, suppliers, governments, and any other groups with a vested interest in the organization.

Corporate social responsibility (CSR) refers to an organization's moral obligation toward all of its **stakeholders.** Stakeholders are the shareholders, customers, suppliers, governments, and any other groups with a vested interest in the organization.[46] As part of corporate social responsibility, many companies have adopted the *triple bottom line* philosophy. This means that they try to support or "earn positive returns" in the economic, social, and environmental spheres of sustainability. Firms that adopt the triple bottom line aim to survive and be profitable in the marketplace (economic), but they also intend to maintain or improve conditions for society as well as the physical environment. For instance, Stratham, New Hampshire–based Timberland Co. pays employees to work on community projects and engage in more environmentally friendly behaviors. At The Warehouse, New Zealand's largest retailer, stores are evaluated monthly not just on their sales and profits, but also on how little landfill waste they produced to generate those financial returns.[47]

Corporate leaders seem to agree that corporate social responsibility is an important part of the organization's obligations, yet many have difficulty translating their good intentions into corresponding behavior. Wal-Mart, the world's largest retailer, claims that it monitors suppliers with one of the toughest codes of conduct in the industry; yet an undercover camera crew recently revealed child labor openly practiced in some overseas factories that manufacture Wal-Mart products. For more than a decade Interface, the world's largest floor covering company, has tried to transform itself into an ecologically friendly manufacturer. The LaGrange, Georgia, firm has made better progress than others in the industry; but critics point out that Interface has fallen short of its original well-publicized goals for sustainability and may have exaggerated a few of its achievements.[48] The point here is that CSR is receiving a lot of attention, but in many organizations the rhetoric runs well ahead of actions.

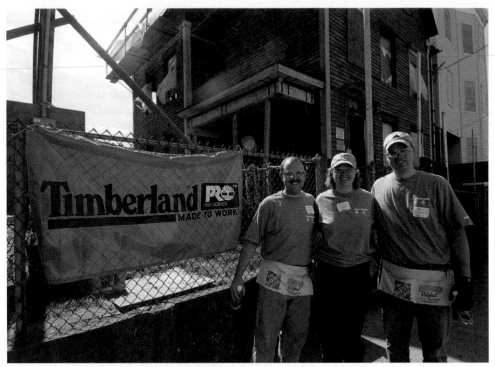

Selling Outdoor Gear and CSR at Timberland Anyone who thinks companies must choose between profits and corporate social responsibility (CSR) should have a conversation with Jeffrey Swartz. The CEO of Timberland Co. doesn't see the dilemma and, in fact, will enthusiastically point out how they can potentially complement each other. The U.S. designer and retailer of outdoor-themed clothing, shoes, and accessories seems to be a good example. Timberland has both growth and profitability, yet it stands out further than most firms in supporting the community and environment. Employees get 40 hours of paid leave every year to work on community projects. The company also closes operations for one day each year so staff can work together to help the community, such as cleaning up or rebuilding playgrounds and homeless shelters. To help the environment, Timberland pays employees $3,000 rebates and gives them preferred parking spots if they buy environmentally friendly hybrid cars. The company is also switching to solar energy in some of its operations.[49]

Learning Objectives

After reading this section you should be able to

7.   **Identify the five anchors on which organizational behavior is based.**
8.   **Diagram an organization from an open systems view.**

The Five Anchors of Organizational Behavior

Globalization, workforce diversity, evolving employment relationships, virtual work, and workplace values and ethics are just a few of the trends that we will explore in this textbook. To understand these and other topics, the field of organizational behavior relies on a set of basic beliefs or knowledge structures (see Exhibit 1.3). These conceptual anchors represent the way that OB researchers think about organizations and how they should be studied. Let's look at each of these five beliefs that anchor the study of organizational behavior.

Exhibit 1.3
Five Philosophical Anchors of Organizational Behavior

Multidisciplinary anchor	OB should import knowledge from many disciplines.
Systematic research anchor	OB should study organizations using systematic research methods.
Contingency anchor	OB theory should recognize that the effects of actions often vary with the situation.
Multiple levels of analysis anchor	OB knowledge should include three levels of analysis: individual, team, and organization.
Open systems anchor	OB should view organizations as open systems that interact with their environment.

The Multidisciplinary Anchor

Organizational behavior is anchored around the idea that the field should develop from knowledge in other disciplines, not just from its own isolated research base. Some OB experts have recently argued that the field suffers from a "trade deficit"—importing far more knowledge from other disciplines than is exported to other disciplines. Although this is a possible concern, organizational behavior has thrived through its diversity of knowledge from other fields of study.[50]

The upper part of Exhibit 1.4 identifies the traditional disciplines from which organizational behavior knowledge has developed. For instance, sociologists have

Exhibit 1.4
Multidisciplinary Anchor of Organizational Behavior

Discipline	Relevant OB topics
Traditional disciplines	
Psychology	Drives, perception, attitudes, personality, job stress, emotions, leadership
Sociology	Team dynamics, roles, socialization, communication patterns, organizational power, organizational structure
Anthropology	Corporate culture, organizational rituals, cross-cultural dynamics, organizational adaptation
Political science	Intergroup conflict, coalition formation, organizational power and politics, decision making, organizational environments
Economics	Decision making, negotiation, organizational power
Industrial engineering	Job design, productivity, work measurement
Emerging disciplines	
Communications	Knowledge management, electronic mail, corporate culture, employee socialization
Information systems	Team dynamics, decision making, knowledge management
Marketing	Knowledge management, creativity, decision making
Women's studies	Organizational power, perceptions

contributed to our knowledge of team dynamics, organizational socialization, organizational power, and other aspects of the social system. The field of psychology has aided our understanding of most issues relating to individual and interpersonal behavior. Recently even the field of neuroscience has contributed new ideas about human drives and behavior.[51]

The bottom part of Exhibit 1.4 identifies some of the emerging fields from which organizational behavior knowledge is acquired. The communications field helps us understand the dynamics of knowledge management, electronic mail, corporate culture, and employee socialization. Information systems scholars are exploring the effects of information technology on team dynamics, decision making, and knowledge management. Marketing scholars have enhanced our understanding of job satisfaction and customer service, knowledge management, and creativity. Women's studies scholars are studying perceptual biases and power relations between men and women in organizations.

The Systematic Research Anchor

scientific method
A set principles and procedures that help researchers to systematically understand previously unexplained events and conditions.

A second anchor for organizational behavior researchers is their belief in the value of studying organizations through systematic research methods. Traditionally scholars have relied on the **scientific method** by forming research questions, systematically collecting data, and testing hypotheses against those data. This approach relies mainly on quantitative data (numeric information) and statistical procedures to test hypotheses. The idea behind the scientific method is to minimize personal biases and distortions about organizational events.

grounded theory
A process of developing theory through the constant interplay between data gathering and the development of theoretical concepts.

More recently OB scholars have also adopted qualitative methods and, in particular, **grounded theory** to understand the workplace. Grounded theory is a process of developing a theory through the constant interplay between data gathering and the development of theoretical concepts. Through observation, interviews, and other forms of data collection, researchers form concepts and theories. But as they return to gather more information each time, they also test the concepts and theory created up to that point in the research study.[52] Appendix A at the end of this book provides an overview of research design and methods commonly found in organizational behavior studies.

The Contingency Anchor

contingency approach
The idea that a particular action may have different consequences in different situations.

"It depends" is a phrase that OB scholars often use to answer a question about the best solution to an organizational problem. The statement may seem evasive, yet it reflects an important way of understanding and predicting organizational events, called the **contingency approach.** This anchor states that a particular action may have different consequences in different situations. In other words, no single solution is best in all circumstances.[53]

The contingency anchor explains why OB experts tend to be skeptical about surefire recommendations that are so common in the media and consulting literature. Although the ideal situation might be to identify universal theories—where the concepts and practices have equal success in every situation—in reality there are usually too many exceptions to make these "one best way" theories useful. Even when a theory seems to work everywhere, OB scholars remain doubtful: An exception is somewhere around the corner. For example, in Chapter 14 we will learn that leaders should use one style (such as participation) in some situations and another style (perhaps direction) in other situations. Thus when faced with a particular problem or opportunity, we need to understand and diagnose the situation and select the strategy most appropriate *under those conditions.*[54]

Although contingency-oriented theories are necessary in most areas of organizational behavior, we should also be wary about carrying this anchor to an extreme. Some contingency models add more confusion than value over universal ones. Consequently, we need to balance the sensitivity of contingency factors with the simplicity of universal theories.

The Multiple Levels of Analysis Anchor

This textbook divides organizational behavior topics into three levels of analysis: individual, team, and organization. The individual level includes the characteristics and behaviors of employees as well as the thought processes that are attributed to them, such as motivation, perceptions, personalities, attitudes, and values. The team level of analysis looks at how people interact. This includes team dynamics, decisions, power, organizational politics, conflict, and leadership. At the organizational level we focus on how people structure their working relationships and on how organizations interact with their environments.

Although an OB topic is typically pegged into one level of analysis, it usually relates to multiple levels.[55] For instance, communication is located in this book as a team (interpersonal) process, but we also recognize that it includes individual and organizational processes. Therefore, you should try to think about each OB topic at the individual, team, and organizational levels—not just at one of these levels.

The Open Systems Anchor

Northwestern Mutual may have several buildings and financial investments, but CEO Ed Zore says that the insurance company is a living system with several interconnected subsystems. "Together, we're a living organism," suggests Zore in a recent annual meeting. "Every part is integrated, every part is interdependent, and every part is important."[56]

Ed Zore is depicting Northwestern Mutual in terms of the fifth anchor of organizational behavior—the view that organizations are **open systems**. The open systems anchor of organizational behavior refers to the notion that organizations are organic systems that need to interact effectively with the external environment. Organizations take their sustenance from the environment and, in turn, affect that environment through their output. Thus a company's survival and success depend on how well employees sense environmental changes and alter their patterns of behavior to fit those emerging conditions.[57] In contrast, a closed system has all the resources needed to survive without dependence on the external environment. Organizations are never completely closed systems, but monopolies come close because they operate in very stable environments and can ignore stakeholders for a fairly long time without adverse consequences.

As Exhibit 1.5 illustrates, organizations acquire resources from the external environment, including raw materials, employees, financial resources, information, and equipment. Inside the organization are numerous subsystems, such as processes (communication and reward systems), task activities (production, marketing), and social dynamics (informal groups, power dynamics). With the aid of technology (such as equipment, work methods, and information), these subsystems transform inputs into various outputs. Some outputs (products and services) may be valued by the external environment, whereas other outputs (employee layoffs, pollution) have adverse effects. The organization receives feedback from the external environment regarding the value of its outputs and the availability of future inputs. This process is cyclical and, ideally, self-sustaining so that the organization may continue to survive and prosper.

---

open systems

Organizations that take their sustenance from the environment and, in turn, affect that environment through their output.

Exhibit 1.5
**Open Systems View
of Organizations**

External Environment and Stakeholders   As open systems, successful organizations monitor their environments and are able to maintain a close fit with those changing conditions.[58] They do so by reconfiguring their outputs (new products and services, reducing waste) and transforming their processes. At the same time this dynamic capability must not be accelerated to the point where it depletes the organization's resources or gets too far ahead of market demand. The point here is that organizations need to adapt to changing environments—but not so much that they overspend their resources or overshoot stakeholder needs.

Stakeholders represent a central part of the internal and external environment. As mentioned earlier, these include any person or entity with a vested interest in the organization. Stakeholders influence the firm's access to inputs and ability to discharge outputs. And unless they pay attention to the needs of all stakeholders, organizational leaders may find their business in trouble. For instance, leaders may put their organization at risk if they pay attention only to shareholders and ignore the broader corporate social responsibility.[59] We see this stakeholder misalignment when job applicants avoid companies that ignore corporate social responsibility and when organizations fail to treat their employees and suppliers with respect.

Systems as Interdependent Parts   The open systems anchor states that organizations consist of many internal subsystems that need to be continuously aligned with each other. As companies grow, they develop more and more complex subsystems that must coordinate with each other in the process of transforming inputs to outputs.[60] These interdependencies can easily become so complex that a minor event in one subsystem may amplify into serious unintended consequences elsewhere in the organization.

The open systems anchor is an important way of viewing organizations. However, it has traditionally focused on physical resources that enter the organization and are processed into physical goods (outputs). This was representative of the industrial economy but not of the "new economy," where the most valued input is knowledge.

Learning
Objectives

After reading this section you should be able to

9. **Define knowledge management and intellectual capital.**
10. **Identify specific ways in which organizations acquire, share, and preserve knowledge.**

Knowledge Management

In the opening story to this chapter, Google's chief financial officer George Reyes said that his company "is truly a learning organization." This perspective of organizations, called **knowledge management,** includes any structured activity that improves an organization's capacity to acquire, share, and use knowledge in ways that improve its survival and success.[61] Knowledge management is an offshoot of the open systems view because it presumes that organizations need to interact with their environment.

For instance, Google is a learning organization—it actively applies knowledge management—because it actively seeks out knowledgeable people (such as Rob Pike), supports knowledge sharing and creativity, and encourages employees to quickly transform that knowledge into valuable services such as Google's search engine, Google Desktop, Gmail, Google News, and Google Translate. Even after services have been created, the organization learns from feedback about how the public uses those services.

The stock of knowledge that resides in an organization is called its **intellectual capital,** which is the sum of everything known in an organization that gives it competitive advantage—including its human capital, structural capital, and relationship capital:[62]

- *Human capital.* This is the knowledge that employees possess and generate, including their skills, experience, and creativity.

- *Structural capital.* This is the knowledge captured and retained in an organization's systems and structures. It is the knowledge that remains after all the human capital has gone home.

- *Relationship capital.* This is the value derived from an organization's relationships with customers, suppliers, and other external stakeholders who provide added mutual value for the organization. For example, this includes customer loyalty as well as trust between the organization and its suppliers.

Knowledge Management Processes

To maintain a valuable *stock* of knowledge (intellectual capital), organizations depend on their capacity to acquire, share, and use knowledge more effectively. This *process* is often called *organizational learning* because companies must continuously learn about their various environments to survive and succeed through adaptation.[63] The "capacity" to acquire, share, and use knowledge means that companies have established systems, structures, and organizational values that support the knowledge management process. Let's look more closely at some of the strategies companies use to acquire, share, and use knowledge.

Knowledge Acquisition   Knowledge acquisition includes the process of extracting information and ideas from the external environment as well as through insight. One of the fastest and most powerful ways to acquire knowledge is by hiring individuals or acquiring entire companies. Knowledge also enters the organization when employees learn from external sources, such as discovering new resources from suppliers or becoming aware of new trends from clients. For instance, a team of

knowledge management
Any structured activity that improves an organization's capacity to acquire, share, and use knowledge in ways that improve its survival and success.

intellectual capital
The sum of an organization's human capital, and relationship capital.

employees at Amcor, one of the world's largest packaging companies, continuously searches around the world for intellectual property and patent licensing opportunities. This knowledge acquisition process recently helped the company develop plastic packaging that prevented table grapes from falling off their stems. A third knowledge acquisition strategy is through experimentation. Companies receive knowledge through insight as a result of research and other creative processes.[64]

An important contingency with knowledge acquisition is that organizations must have enough absorptive capacity to acquire the knowledge. **Absorptive capacity** refers to the ability to recognize the value of new information, assimilate it, and apply it to commercial ends. The absorptive capacity to acquire new knowledge depends on the company's existing store of knowledge. Without basic knowledge of plastics and package manufacturing processes, Amcor engineers could not have effectively applied outside knowledge to improve packaging for table grapes. Thus acquiring new knowledge from the environment requires absorptive capacity, which depends on the organization's existing foundation of knowledge. This absorptive capacity also applies to the ability of entire societies to develop.[65]

absorptive capacity
The ability to recognize the value of new information, assimilate it, and apply it to commercial ends.

Knowledge Sharing   Many organizations are reasonably good at acquiring knowledge, but they waste this resource by not effectively spreading it around. As several executives have lamented, "I wish we knew what we know."[66] Valuable ideas sit idly—rather like unused inventory—or remain hidden as "silos of knowledge" throughout the organization. Many organizations improve knowledge sharing by creating digital repositories of knowledge: computer intranets in which employees document and store new knowledge as it becomes available. Although somewhat useful, these electronic storage systems can be expensive to maintain; they also overlook the fact that a lot of knowledge is difficult to document.[67]

An alternative strategy for knowledge sharing is to give employees more opportunities for informal online or face-to-face communication. One such approach is through **communities of practice:** groups bound together by shared expertise and passion for a particular activity or interest.[68] One pioneer in communities of practice is Clarica Life Insurance Company. Realizing that its agents possess valuable knowledge that is often isolated from other agents, the company created an online forum where knowledge among sales agents can be actively shared with others.[69]

communities of practice
Informal groups bound together by shared expertise and passion for a particular activity or interest.

Knowledge Use   Acquiring and sharing knowledge are wasted exercises unless knowledge is effectively put to use. To do this, employees must realize that the knowledge is available and that they have enough freedom to apply it. This requires a culture that supports experiential learning, which we will describe in Chapter 3.

Organizational Memory

The Olympic Games are mammoth projects requiring deep knowledge about managing sports events; yet until recently little knowledge was documented and passed on to the next Olympic organizing committee. "You had a situation where every two years, a $2–4 billion Olympic event would be staged somewhere, and every time the organizers would start all over again—no historical data, no corporate knowledge," explains Craig McLatchey, former secretary general of the Australian Olympic Committee and board member of the Sydney Organizing Committee for the Olympic Games (SOCOG). "You would see SOCOG staff literally sitting in front of a blank sheet of paper, trying to work things out."[70]

SOCOG's experience is a reminder that corporate leaders are the keepers of an organizational memory.[71] This unusual metaphor refers to the storage and preservation of intellectual capital. It includes information that employees possess as well as

Evercare's Hard Lesson in Organizational Memory A few years ago Evercare (formerly Helmac) decided to move its headquarters and manufacturing from Flint, Michigan, to Georgia. The move nearly killed the manufacturer of Lint Pic-up products because none of Evercare's production employees wanted to leave Flint. So when the company's executives arrived in Georgia to set up production, they struggled to rebuild the company's manufacturing and distribution systems from scratch. "Nothing was documented," recalls manufacturing vice president John Moore, shown here with vice president of distribution Barbara Tomaszewski. "All of the knowledge, all of the practices were built in people's heads." The good news was that the rebuilt company seems stronger because employees did not learn some of the past practices that didn't work.[72]

knowledge embedded in the organization's systems and structures. It includes documents, objects, and anything else that provides meaningful information about how the organization should operate. One way to maintain an organizational memory is to keep good employees. Progressive companies attract and retain high-quality staff by adopting employment practices compatible with emerging workforce expectations, including work–life balance, egalitarian hierarchy, and a workplace that generates more fun.

A second organizational memory strategy is to systematically transfer knowledge before employees leave. This occurs when new recruits apprentice with skilled employees, thereby acquiring knowledge that is not documented. A third approach is to transfer knowledge into structural capital. This includes bringing out hidden knowledge, organizing it, and putting it in a form that can be available to others. SOCOG applied this strategy by asking every division and functional area to complete an extensive "how to" template based on their experiences in the Sydney Olympics. After the event, SOCOG had produced 90 manuals documenting each area's mission and objectives, key risks, key stakeholders, key interactions, operations plans, budget, organizational charts, multiyear staffing, key considerations, and key lessons and recommendations. This documented memory of the Sydney Olympics became a major resource for Athens and other Olympics.

Before leaving the topic of organizational memory and knowledge management, you should know that successful companies also unlearn. Sometimes it is appropriate for organizations to selectively forget certain knowledge.[73] This means that they should cast off routines and patterns of behavior that are no longer appropriate. Employees need to rethink their perceptions, such as how they should interact with customers and which is the "best way" to perform a task. As we will discover in Chapter 17, unlearning is essential for organizational change.

The Journey Begins

This chapter has given you some background about the field of organizational behavior. But it's only the beginning of our journey. Throughout this book we will challenge you to learn new ways of thinking about how people work in and around organizations. We begin this process in Chapter 2 by presenting a basic model of individual behavior, then introducing over the next six chapters various stable and mercurial characteristics of individuals that relate to elements of the individual behavior model. Next this book moves to the team level of analysis. We examine a model of team effectiveness and specific features of high-performance teams. We also look at decision making and creativity, communication, power and influence, conflict and negotiation, and leadership. Finally we shift our focus to the organizational level of analysis, where the topics of organizational structure, organizational culture, and organizational change are examined in detail.

Chapter Summary

Organizational behavior is the study of what people think, feel, and do in and around organizations. Organizations are groups of people who work interdependently toward some purpose. OB concepts help us to predict and understand organizational events, adopt more accurate theories of reality, and influence organizational events. This field of knowledge also improves the organization's financial health.

There are several trends in organizational behavior. Globalization requires corporate decision makers to be sensitive to cultural differences. Another trend is increasing workforce diversity. Employment relations are also evolving as companies adapt workplace practices to support emerging workforce expectations while also demanding more flexibility through employability and contingent work.

Virtual work, a fourth trend, occurs when employees use information technology to perform their jobs away from the traditional physical workplace. Virtual work includes telecommuting as well as virtual teams—cross-functional groups that operate across space, time, and organizational boundaries with members who communicate mainly through information technology. Values and ethics represent the fifth trend. In particular, companies are learning to apply values in a global environment, and they are under pressure to abide by ethical values and higher standards of corporate social responsibility.

Organizational behavior scholars rely on a set of basic beliefs to study organizations. These anchors include

beliefs that OB knowledge should be multidisciplinary and based on systematic research; that organizational events usually have contingencies; that organizational behavior can be viewed from three levels of analysis (individual, team, and organization); and that organizations are open systems.

The open systems anchor suggests that organizations have interdependent parts that work together to continually monitor and transact with the external environment. They acquire resources from the environment, transform them through technology, and return outputs to the environment. The external environment consists of the natural and social conditions outside the organization. External environments are generally highly turbulent today, so organizations must become adaptable and responsive.

Knowledge management develops an organization's capacity to acquire, share, and use knowledge in ways that improve its survival and success. Intellectual capital is knowledge that resides in an organization, including its human capital, structural capital, and relationship capital. Organizations acquire knowledge through various practices, including individual learning and experimentation. Knowledge sharing occurs mainly through various forms of communication, including communities of practice. Knowledge use occurs when employees realize that the knowledge is available and that they have enough freedom to apply it. Organizational memory refers to the storage and preservation of intellectual capital.

Key Terms

absorptive capacity, p. 22

communities of practice, p. 22

contingency approach, p. 18

contingent work, p. 12

corporate social
responsibility (CSR), p. 15

deep-level diversity, p. 9

employability, p. 12

ethics, p. 15

globalization, p. 7

grounded theory, p. 18

intellectual capital, p. 21

knowledge management, p. 21

open systems, p. 19

organizational behavior (OB), p. 4

organizations, p. 5

scientific method, p. 18

stakeholders, p. 15

surface-level diversity, p. 8

values, p. 14

virtual teams, p. 14

virtual work, p. 13

work–life balance, p. 11

Critical Thinking Questions

1. A friend suggests that organizational behavior courses are useful only to people who will enter management careers. Discuss the accuracy of your friend's statement.

2. Look through the list of chapters in this textbook and discuss how globalization could influence each organizational behavior topic.

3. Corporate social responsibility is one of the hottest issues in corporate boardrooms these days, partly because it is becoming increasingly important to employees and other stakeholders. In your opinion, why have stakeholders given CSR more attention recently? Does abiding by CSR standards potentially cause companies to have conflicting objectives with some stakeholders in some situations?

4. "Organizational theories should follow the contingency approach." Comment on the accuracy of this statement.

5. A number of years ago, employees in a city water distribution department were put into teams and encouraged to find ways to improve efficiency. The teams boldly crossed departmental boundaries and areas of management discretion in search of problems. Employees working in other parts of the city began to complain about these intrusions. Moreover, when some team ideas were implemented, the city managers discovered that a dollar saved in the water distribution unit may have cost the organization two dollars in higher costs elsewhere. Use the open systems anchor to explain what happened here.

6. After hearing a seminar on knowledge management, a mining company executive argues that this perspective ignores the fact that mining companies could not rely on knowledge alone to stay in business. They also need physical capital (such as digging and ore processing equipment) and land (where the minerals are located). In fact, these two may be more important than what employees carry around in their heads. Discuss the merits of the mining executive's comments.

7. At a recent seminar on information technology, you heard a consultant say that over 30 percent of U.S. companies use software to manage documents and exchange information, whereas firms in Europe are just beginning to adopt this technology. Based on this, the consultant concluded that "knowledge management in Europe is at its beginning stages." In other words, few firms in Europe practice knowledge management. Comment on this consultant's statement.

8. BusNews Corp. is the leading stock market and business news service. Over the past two years BusNews has experienced increased competition from other news providers. These competitors have brought in Internet and other emerging computer technologies to link customers with information more quickly. There is little knowledge within BusNews about how to use these computer technologies. Based on the knowledge acquisition processes for knowledge management, explain how BusNews might gain the intellectual capital necessary to become more competitive in this respect.

Case Study 1.1 INTRODUCING WORK–LIFE BALANCE AT OXFORD MANUFACTURING

Fiona McQuarrie, University College of the Fraser Valley

Oxford Manufacturing is a company with 350 employees in a large Midwestern city. It specializes in producing custom plastic products, although it also manufactures a range of small plastic items (such as storage boxes and water bottles) that it sells to wholesale distributors. Because of the variety of products the firm produces, its workers have a wide range of skill levels and qualifications: engineers with university degrees work on design and production specifications for customized products, and assembly line workers, some of whom did not finish high school, operate machines in the production facility. The company's plant operates 12 hours a day, seven days a week—although if a large order cannot be produced during regular hours, operating hours may be added to meet that demand.

Over the last few years, where Oxford is located, the demand for workers has begun to exceed the supply. Oxford's owners have realized that the company can no longer afford to sit back and let potential employees find them, as was the case in the past. They also realize that the company is now increasingly competing for employees, especially skilled ones, with other manufacturing firms in the same area. These realities have led Oxford's owners to decide that Oxford needs to be seen as a "preferred employer" if it is going to attract and retain the best employees. They have decided to make Oxford a preferred employer by emphasizing how much the company cares about employees' work–life balance. The message communicated to potential and current employees is that Oxford wants to help them achieve a lifestyle in which work and nonwork commitments are equally important. The company has adopted a policy giving each employee five "free days" off per year to use for whatever purpose the employee desires, in addition to generous vacation and sick leave benefits. The company also has encouraged department managers to schedule workers' shifts to accommodate the workers' outside commitments as much as possible. The company managers feel that offering such benefits will not only attract good workers to Oxford but also help retain the ones already working there.

Peter MacNee is a manager of one of the production areas. He has received requests from two of his employees to accommodate their work schedules to their nonwork commitments.

- John Mason is an engineer whose marriage has recently ended. He is now a single parent to a daughter, age 9, and a son, age 6. His parents are helping him with child care, but they are not always available to take care of the children during the day when John is at work. In addition, John's daughter was badly affected by her parents' divorce; occasionally she has temper tantrums and refuses to go to school or stay with her grandparents, insisting that only her father can take care of her. These situations have occasionally resulted in John having to miss work on short notice. Peter has allowed John to use three of his five annual free days to cover these situations, even though company policy states that employees wishing to take free days must notify their supervisor two weeks before the date of the absence. John is asking to work only in the evenings because his parents are regularly available to supervise his children then. He is also offering to work unpaid overtime in exchange for formally being allowed to take his two remaining free days as needed without the required period of notification. He is willing to continue to be available for unpaid overtime if the company gives him a yearly allocation of five additional free days.

- Jane Collier is a supervisor on the production line. She also participates in curling at the local recreation center. When a friend encouraged her to take up curling for fun a few years ago, she was having problems with her health and was also somewhat shy. Because she has been curling regularly, her fitness level has increased, and her health problems are no longer affecting her attendance at work. In addition, because success in curling requires working effectively as part of a team, her social and supervisory skills at work have noticeably improved. Jane's curling team has an opportunity to join a new curling league that is more competitive than the one they currently belong to, but this will allow them to compete at regional, national, and possibly even international levels. Jane's team has decided not only to join this league but also to start working with a coach to improve their technique. Jane is asking to be scheduled for day shifts only because of the time demands of this new level of participation and because most of her curling-related activities will take place in the evenings. She is also asking for two weeklong unpaid leaves per year to attend curling bonspiels (competitions) out of town.

Peter is not sure what to do with these requests. He knows that the company encourages employee work–life balance and expects its managers to support employees trying to manage both work and nonwork activities. He realizes that John and Jane would not have made their requests unless they felt the requested accommodations were the only way they could successfully balance their work lives with their nonwork commitments. However, there is no way he can grant both requests: The products John helps design are manufactured by the production line Jane supervises, and both of them need to be at work at the same time at least twice a week to share information about the products they are working on. He is also aware that John and Jane are talented and experienced employees, and if he turns down these requests, they will have no trouble finding comparable jobs with any of Oxford's competitors.

As Peter is considering this dilemma, he shuffles through the pile of mail that arrived on his desk that morning. An interoffice memo catches his eye, and he pulls it out of the pile and opens it. The memo is from the three office administrators in his area. The administrators complain that they are becoming increasingly upset with their co-workers, most of whom are married and have families, "dumping" work on them because of family crises. The memo describes several recent incidents in which co-workers received phone calls about family problems and then left for the rest of the day, asking the office administrators to cover for them and complete their work. After dealing with their co-workers' unfinished tasks, the administrators often had to stay beyond the end of their scheduled shifts to finish their own work. The last paragraph of the memo states, "We don't mind helping out once in a while, but not having kids or elderly parents to take care of doesn't mean we don't have anything to do besides work. If we have to stay late on short notice, we often have to cancel activities that are important to us. This is unfair; and if other people can't manage their family responsibilities, they should be the ones making the adjustments, not us. We want you to address this problem immediately because it is occurring more and more frequently."

Discussion Questions

1. How should Peter deal with John's and Jane's requests and the complaint from the administrators?

2. What can the organization as a whole do to address problems like these?

3. What organizational behavior issues can you identify in this case?

Case Study 1.2 WAL-MART REACHES FOR THE WHITE HAT

BusinessWeek Wal-Mart Stores, Inc., has weathered unpaid hours and sex discrimination lawsuits, claims of supporting sweat-shop factories in Asia, union busting, and other public relations nightmares over the past few years. Now, the world's largest retailer is trying to fight back by more actively embracing corporate social responsibility, and by hiring some of the top guns in the public relations industry to get that message out to the public. Wal-Mart responded quickly with help to victims of Hurricane Katrina. It is working with anit-sweatshop groups to improve monitoring of factories where it purchases products. The retailer is even working with environmental groups to open eco-friendly stores and generally find ways to reduce the amount of packaging.

This *BusinessWeek* case study describes Wal-Mart's responses to criticism that it has failed the corporate social responsibility test. Read the full text of this *BusinessWeek* article at www.mhhc.com/mcshane4e and prepare for the discussion questions below.

Discussion Questions

1. Evaluate Wal-Mart's corporate social responsibility initiatives in the context of the triple bottom line. What else could it do to fulfil the triple bottom line mandate?

2. In addition to introducing new corporate social responsibility initiatives, Wal-Mart is actively communicating its practices through public relations experts. Is this action necessary and appropriate, in your opinion? What are the risks of Wal-Mart's public relations activities?

Source: R. Berner, "Can Wal-Mart Fit Into a White Hat?" *BusinessWeek*, 3 October, 2005, p. 94.

Team Exercise 1.3 HUMAN CHECKERS

PURPOSE This exercise is designed to help you understand the importance and application of organizational behavior concepts.

MATERIALS None, but the instructor has more information about the team's task.

INSTRUCTIONS

1. Form teams with six students. If possible, each team should have a private location where team members can plan and practice the required task without being observed or heard by other teams.

2. All teams will receive special instructions in class about the team's assigned task. All teams have the same task and will have the same amount of time to plan and practice the task. At the end of this planning and practice, each team will be timed while completing the task in class. The team that completes the task in the least time wins.

3. No special materials are required or allowed (see the following rules) for this exercise. Although the task is not described here, you should learn the following rules for planning and implementing the task:

   a. You cannot use any written form of communication or any props to assist in the planning or implementation of this task.

   b. You may speak to other students in your team at any time during the planning and implementation of this task.

   c. When performing the task, you must move only in the direction of your assigned destination. In other words, you can move only forward, not backward.

   d. When performing the task, you can move forward to the next space, but only if it is vacant (see Exhibit 1).

   e. When performing the task, you can move forward two spaces if that space is vacant. In other words, you can move around a student who is one space in front of you to the next space if that space is vacant (see Exhibit 2).

Exhibit 1   Exhibit 2

4. When all teams have completed their task, the class will discuss the implications of this exercise for organizational behavior.

DISCUSSION QUESTIONS

1. Identify the organizational behavior concepts that the teams applied to complete this task.

2. What personal theories of people and work teams were applied to complete this task?

3. What organizational behavior problems occurred? What actions were (or should have been) taken to solve them?

Web Exercise 1.4 DIAGNOSING ORGANIZATIONAL STAKEHOLDERS

PURPOSE This exercise is designed to help you understand how stakeholders influence organizations as part of the open systems anchor.

MATERIALS You need to select a company and, prior to class, retrieve and analyze information publicly available over the past year or two about that company. This may include annual reports, which are usually found on the Web sites of publicly traded companies. Where possible, you should also scan full-text newspaper and magazine databases for articles published over the previous year about the company.

INSTRUCTIONS The instructor may have you work alone or in groups for this activity. Select a company and investigate the relevance and influence of various stakeholder groups on the organization. Stakeholders can be identified from annual reports, newspaper articles, Web site statements, and other available sources. Stakeholders should be rank ordered in terms of their perceived importance to the organization.

Be prepared to present or discuss your rank ordering of the organization's stakeholders, including the evidence you used.

DISCUSSION QUESTIONS

1. What are the main reasons why certain stakeholders are more important than others for this organization?

2. Based on your knowledge of the organization's environmental situation, is this rank ordering of stakeholders in the organization's best interest, or should specific other stakeholders be given higher priority?

3. What societal groups, if any, are not mentioned as stakeholders by the organization? Does this lack of reference to these unmentioned groups make sense?

Self-Assessment 1.5

IT ALL MAKES SENSE?

PURPOSE This exercise is designed to help you understand how organizational behavior knowledge can help you understand life in organizations.

INSTRUCTIONS (*Note:* This activity may be done as a self-assessment or as a team activity.) Read each of the following statements and circle whether each statement is true or false, in your opinion. The class will consider the answers to each question and discuss the implications for studying organizational behavior.

Due to the nature of this activity, the instructor will provide the answers to these questions. There is no scoring key in Appendix B.

1. True   False   A happy worker is a productive worker.
2. True   False   Decision makers tend to continue supporting a course of action even though information suggests that the decision is ineffective.
3. True   False   Organizations are more effective when they prevent conflict among employees.
4. True   False   It is better to negotiate alone than as a team.

5. True   False   Companies are more effective when they have a strong corporate culture.
6. True   False   Employees perform better without stress.
7. True   False   Effective organizational change always begins by pinpointing the source of current organizational problems.
8. True   False   Female leaders involve employees in decisions to a greater degree than do male leaders.
9. True   False   People in Japan value group harmony and duty to the group (high collectivism) more than Americans do (low collectivism).
10. True   False   The best decisions are made without emotion.
11. True   False   If employees feel they are paid unfairly, then nothing other than changing their pay will reduce their feelings of injustice.

Self-Assessment 1.6

TELEWORK DISPOSITION ASSESSMENT (STUDENT OLC)

Some employees adapt better than others do to telework (also called telecommuting) and other forms of virtual work. This self-assessment measures personal characteristics that seem to relate to telecommuting, and therefore provides a rough indication of how well you might adapt to telework. The instrument asks you to indicate how much you agree or disagree with each of the statements provided. You need to be honest with yourself to get a reasonable estimate of your telework disposition. Please keep in mind that this scale considers only your personal characteristics. Other factors, such as organizational, family, and technological systems support, must also be taken into account.

After reading this chapter, if you need additional information, see www.mhhe.com/mcshane4e for more in-depth interactivities that correspond with this material.

Part Two

Individual Behavior
and Processes

Chapter 2   Individual Behavior, Values, and Personality

Chapter 3   Perception and Learning in Organizations

Chapter 4   Workplace Emotions and Attitudes

Chapter 5   Motivation in the Workplace

Chapter 6   Applied Performance Practices

Chapter 7   Work-Related Stress and Stress Management

Shutting down two production furnaces for major repairs effectively idled half of the production employees at Owens Corning's plant in Jackson, Tennessee. But rather than invoke a massive layoff, the company rotated everyone through a one-week quality management training program at full pay. This decision had an immediate and powerful effect. "As our employees returned from training, they were more engaged and more aware of waste," says Owen Corning's plant operations leader. This observation was supported a few months later when the plant's employee engagement scores jumped by 12 points from the previous survey.

Owens Corning is making employee engagement a cornerstone of its business strategy to become a world-class organization.

Employee engagement has become the watchword at Owens Corning and many other organizations. It refers to how much employees identify with and are emotionally committed to their work, are cognitively focused on that work, and possess the ability and resources to do the work. Royal Bank of Scotland calculated that when their employee engagement scores increase, productivity rises and staff turnover falls.

Two separate consultant reports estimate that only about a quarter of American employees are highly engaged, fewer than 60 percent are somewhat engaged, and approximately one-fifth have low engagement or are actively disengaged. Actively disengaged employees tend to be disruptive at work, not just dissatisfied. One recent report estimated that employees in Mexico and Brazil have the highest levels of engagement, whereas several Asian countries (notably Japan, China, and South Korea) and a few European countries (notably Italy, Netherlands, and France) have the lowest levels. Surveys by other consulting firms reveal similar employee engagement scores across countries.

ASB Bank scored well above average in its first employee engagement survey, but that wasn't good enough for the New Zealand financial institution. "We were absolutely shattered," recalls an ASB Bank executive, expecting to be in the top quartile. To boost its employee engagement levels, ASB Bank produced videos showing how managers with the most engaged subordinates perform their jobs. Managers also meet with staff each month, and the bank's chief executive personally teaches new employees about the company's customer service vision. The company also provides opportunities for employees to socialize after work. Today, ASB Bank's employee engagement scores are in the top 10 percent globally, and the company receives some of the highest ratings in New Zealand for customer service.[1]

Individual Behavior, Values, and Personality

After reading this chapter you should be able to

1. Identify the four drivers of individual behavior and results.
2. Describe three ways to match individual competencies to job requirements.
3. Identify five types of individual behavior in organizations.
4. Define *values* and explain why values congruence is important.
5. Define five values commonly studied across cultures.
6. List three ethical principles.
7. Explain how moral intensity, ethical sensitivity, and the situation influence ethical behavior.
8. Identify the "Big Five" personality dimensions.
9. Summarize the personality concepts behind the Myers-Briggs Type Indicator.
10. Explain how personality relates to Holland's model of vocational choice.

employee engagement
Employees' emotional and cognitive (rational) motivation, their ability to perform their jobs, their possessing a clear understanding of the organization's vision and their specific roles in that vision, and a belief that they have been given the resources to get their jobs done.

The groundswell of interest in **employee engagement** makes a great deal of sense because this concept includes most of the drivers of individual behavior and performance results. It refers to employees' emotional and cognitive (rational) motivation, their ability to perform their jobs, their possessing a clear understanding of the organization's vision and their specific roles in that vision, and a belief that they have been given the resources to get their jobs done. This chapter begins by presenting the MARS model, which outlines the four drivers of individual behavior and results. Next this chapter briefly describes the five main types of individual behavior in the workplace.

The latter half of this chapter looks at values and personality—two deeply held characteristics of people that influence their attitudes, motivation, and behavior in the workplace. The section about values describes Schwartz's model of personal values, issues relating to values congruence, the dynamics of cross-cultural values, and key features of ethical values in the workplace. The section about personality introduces the five-factor model of personality, the Myers-Briggs Type Indicator, and other personality characteristics that are often discussed in organizational behavior research.

Learning Objectives

After reading the next two sections you should be able to

1. **Identify the four drivers of individual behavior and results.**
2. **Describe three ways to match individual competencies to job requirements.**
3. **Identify five types of individual behavior in organizations.**

MARS Model of Individual Behavior and Results

Why do individuals behave the way they do and perform well or poorly in the workplace? This question has been the center of much research in organizational behavior, and it is the focus of this chapter and the next five chapters in this book. We begin to answer this question by presenting a basic model of individual behavior and results (called the MARS model) and outlining the main types of behavior in organizational settings. Then we set out to examine the main individual difference topics underlying the MARS model, beginning with two of the most stable influences: values and personality.

The MARS model, illustrated in Exhibit 2.1, is a useful starting point to understanding the drivers of individual behavior and results. The model highlights the four factors that directly influence an employee's voluntary behavior and resulting performance—motivation, ability, role perceptions, and situational factors. These four factors are represented by the acronym "MARS" in the model's name.[2] The MARS model shows that these four factors have a combined effect on individual performance. If any factor weakens, employee performance will decrease. For example, enthusiastic salespeople (motivation) who understand their job duties (role perceptions) and have sufficient resources (situational factors) will not perform their jobs as well if they lack sufficient knowledge and sales skill (ability). Look back at the opening story, and you will see that employee engagement captures all four MARS drivers of individual behavior and results. No wonder employee engagement has become such a popular concept among executives and consultants!

Exhibit 2.1 also shows that the four factors in the MARS model are influenced by several other individual variables that we will discuss over the next few chapters. Personality and values are the most stable characteristics,[3] so we look at them later in this chapter. Emotions, attitudes, and stress are much more fluid characteristics,

Exhibit 2.1   MARS Model of Individual Behavior and Results

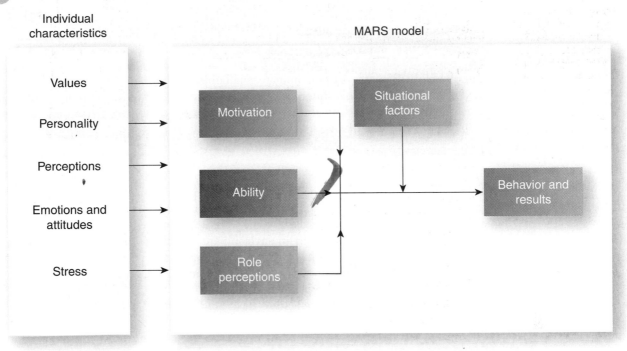

whereas individual perceptions and learning usually lie somewhere between. Each of these factors relates to the MARS model in various ways. For example, personal values affect an employee's motivation through emotions and tend to shape role perceptions through the perceptual process. Learning influences ability, role perceptions, and motivation, as we will learn in Chapter 3. Before examining these individual characteristics, let's briefly introduce the four elements of the MARS model, followed by an overview of the different types of individual behavior in the workplace.

Employee Motivation

motivation
The forces within a person that affect his or her direction, intensity, and persistence of voluntary behavior.

Motivation represents the forces within a person that affect his or her direction, intensity, and persistence of voluntary behavior.[4] *Direction* refers to the path along which people engage their effort. This sense of direction of effort reflects the fact that people have choices about where they put their effort. In other words, motivation is goal-directed, not random. People are motivated to arrive at work on time, finish a project a few hours early, or aim for many other targets. The second element of motivation, called *intensity,* is the amount of effort allocated to the goal. For example, two employees might be motivated to finish their projects a few hours early (direction), but only one of them puts forth enough effort (intensity) to achieve this goal. In other words, intensity is how much you push yourself to complete a task.

Finally, motivation involves varying levels of *persistence*—that is, continuing the effort for a certain amount of time. Employees sustain their efforts until they reach their goals or give up beforehand. To help remember these three elements of motivation, consider the metaphor of driving a car in which the thrust of the engine is your effort. Direction refers to where you steer the car; intensity is how strongly you put your foot down on the gas pedal; and persistence is how long you drive toward that destination.

Ability

Employee abilities also make a difference in behavior and task performance. **Ability** includes both the natural aptitudes and learned capabilities required to successfully complete a task. *Aptitudes* are the natural talents that help employees learn specific tasks more quickly and perform them better. For example, some people have more natural ability than others to manipulate small objects with their fingers (called finger dexterity). There are many different physical and mental aptitudes, and our ability to acquire skills is affected by these aptitudes. *Learned capabilities* are the skills and knowledge you have actually acquired. These include the physical and mental skills you possess as well as the knowledge you acquire and store for later use.

Employee Competencies   Skills, knowledge, aptitudes, values, drives, and other underlying personal characteristics that lead to superior performance are typically bunched together into the concept of **competencies.** Competencies are relevant to an entire job group rather than just to specific jobs. For instance, American Express recently determined that to thrive in an environment of rapid change and globalization, it would require leaders who have strong competencies in commercial excellence, driving innovation and change, focus on customer and client, and demonstrating personal excellence.[5] Most large organizations spend a lot of money identifying key competencies, but some competencies are described so broadly that they offer little guidance for hiring and training people. Also, companies wrongly assume that everyone should have the same set of competencies, whereas the truth seems to be that people with another combination of competencies may be equally effective.[6]

Person–Job Matching   There are three approaches to matching individual competencies with job requirements. One strategy is to select applicants whose existing competencies best fit the required tasks. This includes comparing each applicant's competencies with the requirements of the job or work unit. A second approach is to provide training so employees develop required skills and knowledge.

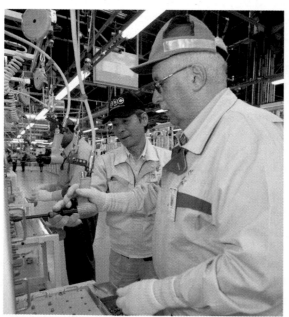

Training the Toyota Way Poised to become the world's largest automaker, Toyota Motor Company is ramping up its training programs around the world to maintain the company's quality standards. Toyota's training methods make extensive use of visual and cognitive aptitudes that require considerable practice and coaching. For example, trainees learn how to spot defects on metal sheet panels where most of us would see none. They also develop visual gap measuring, such as determining how well the edge of the engine hood lines up with the adjacent part of the front grill. This photo shows Toyota production employee Ray Howley (right) from South Africa learning from master trainer Kazuo Hyodo how to tighten bolts so they are snug without being too tight.[7]

The third way to match people with job requirements is to redesign jobs so employees are given only tasks within their capabilities. AT&T's customer service operations in Dallas took this approach when they realized that many employees were overwhelmed by the increasing variety of products (cable, Internet, HDTV, home theater, and so on). "Our employees just said, 'Help! This is way too complex, we're trained on three things and we need help!'" recalls an executive at the American telecommunications giant. AT&T's solution was to redesign jobs so employees could begin with one area of product knowledge, such as video cable, and then progress to a second knowledge area when the first product was mastered.[8]

Role Perceptions

Florida Power & Light (FPL) crew members scrambled to restore power after Hurricane Wilma, the most intense hurricane ever recorded in the Atlantic basin, devastated parts of South Florida. In Boynton Beach alone, 750 FPL staff and electrical workers from other states worked tirelessly from dawn to past dusk to put the area's power grid back together. Dave Bromley, FPL's logistics site manager for the Boynton Beach staging location, admits that it was a challenge to provide accommodation, food, transportation, supplies, laundry services, and other resources to so many people so quickly under such harsh conditions. Yet FPL employees and staff at other organizations that provided logistics support were so dedicated and focused on their tasks that the process soon worked smoothly. "After two or three days, it's a well-oiled machine," says Bromley proudly.[9]

Employees at Florida Power & Light and its service organizations acted like a "well-oiled machine" not just because they knew how to perform their jobs; they had also developed accurate *role perceptions*. Employees have clear role perceptions in three ways. First, they understand the specific tasks assigned to them: They know the specific duties or consequences for which they are accountable. Second, they understand the relative importance of those tasks; in other words, they know the priorities of their various responsibilities, such as the relative importance of quality versus quantity. Third, they understand the preferred behaviors to accomplish those tasks. This refers to situations where more than one method could be applied to a task. Employees know which of these methods is preferred by the organization.

Employees with clear role perceptions feel more engaged in their work because they know where to direct their effort. The most basic way to improve role perceptions is for staff to receive clear job descriptions and ongoing coaching. For instance, the opening vignette to this chapter described how ASB Bank clarified perceptions about the importance of customer service, while managers watched video programs of colleagues to discover the best way to engage employees. Employees also clarify their role perceptions as they work together over time and receive frequent and meaningful performance feedback.

Situational Factors

Even with clear role perceptions and high levels of motivation and ability, employees won't perform their jobs well unless situational factors also support their task goals. Situational factors include conditions beyond the employees' immediate control that constrain or facilitate their behavior and performance.[10] Some situational characteristics—such as consumer preferences and economic conditions—originate from the external environment and, consequently, are beyond the employees' and organization's control. However, other situational factors—such as time, people, budget, and physical work facilities—are controlled by people in the organization. Corporate leaders need to carefully arrange these conditions so employees can achieve their performance potential.

Motivation, ability, role perceptions, and situational factors affect all conscious workplace behaviors and their performance outcomes. The next section outlines the five categories of behavior in organizational settings.

Types of Individual Behavior in Organizations

People engage in many different types of behavior in organizational settings. Exhibit 2.2 highlights the five types of behavior discussed most often in the organizational behavior literature: task performance, organizational citizenship, counterproductive work behaviors, joining and staying with the organization, and work attendance.

Task Performance

Task performance refers to goal-directed behaviors under the individual's control that support organizational objectives. Task performance behaviors transform raw materials into goods and services or support and maintain technical activities.[11] For example, foreign exchange traders at Wachovia make decisions and take actions to exchange currencies. Employees in most jobs have more than one performance dimension. Foreign exchange traders must be able to identify profitable trades, work cooperatively with clients and co-workers in a stressful environment, assist in training new staff, and work on special telecommunications equipment without error. Some of these performance dimensions are more important than others, but only by considering all of them can we fully evaluate an employee's contribution to the organization.

Exhibiting Organizational Citizenship

One of the defining characteristics of engaged employees is that they perform beyond task performance standards or expectations. "When employees become engaged, they develop a stronger conscientiousness about what they can do," explains Bill Erikson, vice chairman of consulting firm Kenexa. "They will go the extra step, or maybe even the extra mile, to support the interest of the organization." In short,

Exhibit 2.2

Types of Work-Related Behavior

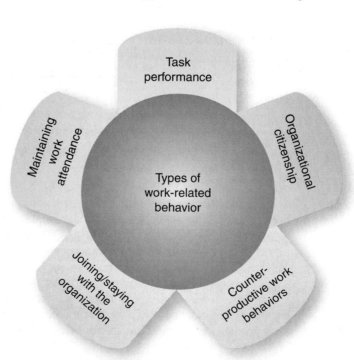

engaged employees practice **organizational citizenship.** They help others without selfish intent, are actively involved in organizational activities, avoid unnecessary conflicts, perform tasks beyond normal role requirements, and gracefully tolerate impositions. Several factors described throughout this book explain why some employees are good organizational citizens and others are not. Later in this chapter, for example, we learn that people with a conscientiousness personality trait have higher organizational citizenship.[12]

Counterproductive Work Behaviors

Although organizations benefit from task performance and organizational citizenship, we also need to recognize that employees sometimes succumb to **counterproductive work behaviors (CWBs)**—voluntary behaviors that have the potential to directly or indirectly harm the organization. Organizational behavior experts have organized CWBs into five categories: abuse of others (insults and nasty comments), threats (threatening harm), work avoidance (tardiness), work sabotage (doing work incorrectly), and overt acts (theft). CWBs are not minor concerns. One recent study found that units of a fast-food restaurant chain with higher CWBs had a significantly worse performance, whereas organizational citizenship had a relatively minor benefit. Throughout this book we'll identify several ways to minimize counterproductive work behaviors, including better organizational justice (Chapter 5) and less workplace stress (Chapter 7), as well as the propensity of people with a political personality trait known as Machiavellianism to engage in CWBs (Chapter 12).[13]

Joining and Staying with the Organization

Task performance, organizational citizenship, and the lack of counterproductive work behaviors are obviously important; but if qualified people don't join and stay with the organization, none of these performance related behaviors will occur. Attracting and retaining talented people is particularly important as worries about skills shortages heat up. For instance, a shortage of qualified truck drivers is the main factor restricting growth at Contract Freighters in Joplin, Missouri. "We have plenty of freight; we have plenty of trucks," says company president Herb Schmidt, but the "severe shortage" of qualified drivers is making it impossible to satisfy the growing customer base. Hotels in many parts of the United States are also struggling to find enough staff to keep up with demand. "We're woefully understaffed," says the owner of a St. Petersburg, Florida, resort that employs 265 people and still has 40 unfilled vacancies. "It's horrible."[14] Even Google, which is one of the most widely recognized employer "brands," is feeling the challenge in the war for talent. However, as Connections 2.1 describes, the California-based Internet search engine company has reduced some of its skills shortage through various guerilla recruiting tactics.

A reputable employer brand may attract qualified applicants, but the war for talent also includes ensuring that they stay with the company. Chapter 1 described how much of an organization's intellectual capital is the knowledge carried around in employees' heads. Organizations may try to document information about work processes, corporate values, and customer needs; but much of it remains in employees' heads. Consequently, retaining valued employees is a critical knowledge management strategy. The problem is that many employees don't plan on staying with their current employer very long. A few surveys report that between one-third and one-half of employees say they would change companies if offered a comparable job.[15]

Why do people quit their jobs? Traditionally, OB experts have identified low job satisfaction as the main cause of turnover. **Job satisfaction** is a person's evaluation of his or her job and work context (see Chapter 4). Employees become dissatisfied with

Google Goes Guerrilla in the War for Talent

To keep up with its blistering growth, Google needs to hire thousands of people in the United States each year. The California-based company that created the world's most popular Internet search engine is also expanding rapidly in India and many other countries. The problem is that Google can't find enough talent to keep up with its growth plans. "Can we hire the quality and quantity of people we want to? No," cofounder Sergey Brin admitted to several hundred investment analysts. "We're under-investing in our business because of the limitations of hiring."

Fortunately Google has also become a master of guerrilla recruiting. Rather than passively waiting for applicants to reply to recruitment ads, Google actively and creatively seeks out talent. One successful tactic has been to host competitions such as "Code Jam," in which contestants around the world are challenged to write code to solve specific problems, then find ways to "break" the code that others have written. Winners in the final round of 100 contestants (out of thousands in the first round) receive up to $10,000, a trip to the Google-plex (Google headquarters), and a job offer.

A related form of guerrilla recruiting is to host internships. Google recently funded a "Summer of Code" event in which 410 college-level students (out of thousands who submitted proposals) received mentoring support from several partner organizations while writing open-source software code. Google paid a small stipend to mentors at the other organizations and $4,500 to students who completed their projects. Summer of Code gave Google (and the other mentoring firms) an inside track on high-quality applicants. "It was a way to start a dialogue with people around the world who might not necessarily be looking for a job—but might become a future employee," says Judy Gilbert, Google's staffing program director.

Even Google's recruitment ads take on a creative guerrilla twist. One example is the billboard (shown in the accompanying

Google relies on guerrilla recruiting, including this innovative ad, to win the war for talent.

photo) and subway banners Google has created, luring curious commuters to follow a series of Web sites with math problems. Only those with top-notch math skills could decipher each puzzle, which eventually led to Google's Web site with an invitation to submit a résumé. "One thing we learned while building Google is that it's easier to find what you're looking for if it comes looking for you," said the Google Web page. "What we're looking for are the best engineers in the world. And here you are!"

Sources: "Google Entices Job Searchers with Math Puzzle," *NPR*, 14 September 2004; S. Olsen, "Google Recruits Eggheads with Mystery Billboard," *CNET News.com*, 9 July 2004; "Google Expansion Is Being Held Back by Hiring Process," *The Wall Street Journal*, 10 February 2005, p. B5; C. Hymowitz, "Busy Executives Fail to Give Recruiting Attention It Deserves," *The Wall Street Journal*, 21 November 2005, p. B1; V. Kopytoff, "How Google Woos the Best and Brightest," *San Francisco Chronicle*, 18 December 2005, p. A1; J. Puliyenthuruthel, "How Google Searches—for Talent," *BusinessWeek*, 11 April 2005; P.-W. Tam and K.J. Delaney, "Talent Search: Google's Growth Helps Ignite Silicon Valley Hiring Frenzy," *The Wall Street Journal*, 23 November 2005, p. A1; "Google Code Jam 2005" (Mountain View, California, 2005), http://www.google.com/codejam/ (accessed 1 March 2006).

their employment relationship, which motivates them to search for and join another organization with better conditions. Although job dissatisfaction builds over time and eventually affects turnover, the most recent opinion is that specific "shock events" need to be considered.[16] These shock events, such as a boss's unfair decision or a conflict episode with a co-worker, create strong emotions that trigger employees to think about and search for alternative employment.

Maintaining Work Attendance

Along with attracting and retaining employees, organizations need everyone to show up for work at scheduled times. Absenteeism occurs for a variety of reasons. One factor is conditions largely beyond employees' control, such as a major storm, car breakdowns, or sick kids with no one else to care for them. Motivation is another factor. Employees who experience job dissatisfaction or work-related stress are more likely to be absent or late for work because taking time off is a way to temporarily withdraw from stressful or dissatisfying conditions. Absenteeism is also higher in organizations with generous sick leave because this benefit limits the negative financial impact of taking time away from work. Yet another factor is team norms. Studies have found that absenteeism is higher in teams with strong absence norms, meaning that team members tolerate and even expect co-workers to take time off.[17]

The MARS model and the five types of individual behavior and results provide a foundation for the ideas presented over the next few chapters. For the remainder of this chapter we will look at two of the most stable individual differences: values and personality.

Learning Objectives

After reading the next two sections you should be able to

4. **Define values and explain why values congruence is important.**
5. **Define five values commonly studied across cultures.**

Values in the Workplace

Tom's of Maine encourages its employees to pay attention to their values, not just corporate goals. "It's management by values and objectives, not just management by objectives," says Tom Chappell, who cofounded the personal care products with his wife, Kate Chappell. Chappell explains that objectives are the domain of the mind, whereas values are the domain of the heart. "Values bring the whole person to work," he explains. "We employ the whole person, the mind and the soul." Values are so important that Tom Chappell contributed to the establishment of The Saltwater Institute, a foundation that helps CEOs and entrepreneurs integrate their personal values with their workplace decisions.[18]

values
Stable, long-lasting beliefs about what is important in a variety of situations, that guide our decisions and actions.

Several best-selling management books conclude that Tom's of Maine and other successful companies have a deeply entrenched and long-lasting set of core values.[19] To emulate this success, executives have been keen to identify, communicate, and align a set of core values in their own firms. Values are stable, evaluative beliefs that guide our preferences for outcomes or courses of action in a variety of situations.[20] They are perceptions about what is good or bad, right or wrong. Values tell us what we "ought" to do. They serve as a moral compass that directs our motivation and, potentially, our decisions and actions. Values partly define who we are as individuals and as members of groups with similar values.

People arrange values into a hierarchy of preferences, called a *value system*. Some individuals value new challenges more than they value conformity. Others value generosity more than frugality. Each person's unique value system is developed and reinforced through socialization from parents, religious institutions, friends, personal experiences, and the society in which he or she lives. As such, a person's hierarchy of values is stable and long-lasting. For example, one study found that value systems of a sample of adolescents were remarkably similar 20 years later as adults.[21]

Notice that our description of values has focused on individuals, whereas executives often describe values as though they belong to the organization. In reality, values exist only within individuals, which we call *personal values*. However, groups of people might hold the same or similar values, so we tend to ascribe these *shared values* to the team, department, organization, profession, or entire society. The values shared by people throughout an organization (*organizational values*) will receive fuller discussion in Chapter 16 because they are a key part of corporate culture. The values shared across a society (*cultural values*) will receive attention later in this chapter.

Before discussing workplace values in more detail, we need to distinguish between espoused and enacted values.[22] *Espoused values* represent the values that we say we use and, in many cases, think we use. Corporate leaders might say they value environmentalism, creativity, and politeness, whether or not they really do value these things in practice. Values are socially desirable, so people create a positive public image by claiming to believe in values that others expect them to embrace. Also, corporate values are usually considered espoused values because, although leaders might abide by them, we don't know whether lower-level employees share this commitment. *Enacted values,* on the other hand, represent the values we actually rely on to guide our decisions and actions. These values-in-use are apparent by watching people in action. Just as we judge an individual's personality by behavioral tendencies, so too do we judge enacted values by behavioral tendencies.

Types of Values

Values come in many forms, and experts on this topic have devoted considerable attention to organizing them into coherent groups. The model in Exhibit 2.3, developed and tested by social psychologist Shalom Schwartz, has become the most widely

Exhibit 2.3   **Schwartz's Values Circumplex**

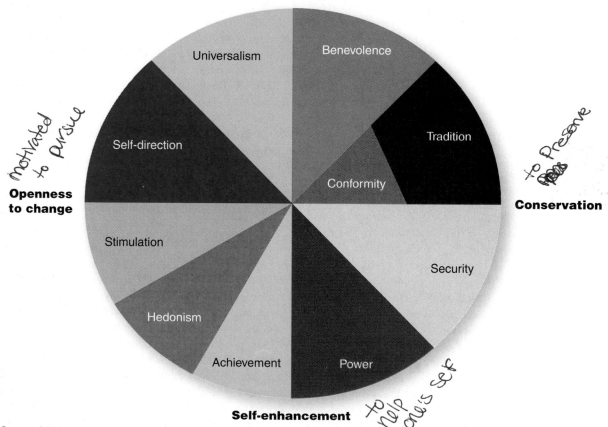

Sources: S.H. Schwartz, "Universals in the Content and Structure of Values: Theoretical Advances and Empirical Tests in 20 Countries," *Advances in Experimental Social Psychology* 25 (1992), pp. 1–65; S.H. Schwartz and G. Sagie, "Value Consensus and Importance: A Cross-National Study," *Journal of Cross-Cultural Psychology* 31 (July 2000), pp. 465–97.

studied and generally accepted model today.[23] Schwartz reduced dozens of personal values into these 10 broader domains of values and further organized these domains around two bipolar dimensions.

Along the left side of the horizontal dimension in Schwartz's model is *openness to change,* which represents the extent to which a person is motivated to pursue innovative ways. Openness to change includes the value domains of self-direction (independent thought and action) and stimulation (excitement and challenge). *Conservation,* the opposite end of Schwartz's horizontal dimension, is the extent to which a person is motivated to preserve the status quo. Conservation includes the value clusters of conformity (adherence to social norms and expectations), security (safety and stability), and tradition (moderation and preservation of the status quo).

The vertical dimension in Schwartz's model ranges from self-enhancement to self-transcendence. *Self-enhancement*–how much a person is motivated by self-interest–includes the values of achievement (pursuit of personal success) and power (dominance over others). The opposite of self-enhancement is *self-transcendence,* which refers to the motivation to promote the welfare of others and nature. Self-transcendence includes the values of benevolence (concern for others in one's life) and universalism (concern for the welfare of all people and nature).

Values and Individual Behavior

Values have gained a lot of respect in recent years because they are viewed as anchors that stabilize behavior and keep employees moving collectively in the same direction. They are also considered beacons that keep managers on course under turbulent conditions. "I've always thought that values are a core part of leadership," says Richard Brajer, CEO of LipoScience, a diagnostic testing and analytical company headquartered in Raleigh, North Carolina. "Why? . . . Because, quite frankly, the stresses of a leadership role are very strong. You need to have a solid foundation."[24]

Personal values guide our decisions and actions to some extent, but this connection isn't always as strong as some would like to believe. Habitual behavior tends to be consistent with our values, but our everyday conscious decisions and actions apply our values much less consistently. The main reason for the "disconnect" between personal values and individual behavior is that values are abstract concepts that sound good in theory but are less easily followed in practice. A lot of people say that benevolence is an important value to them, yet they don't think about being benevolent in a lot of situations. Benevolence becomes a truism that gets lost in translation in everyday life.

Benevolence and other values do influence decisions and behavior if three conditions are met.[25] First, a specific value affects our behavior when something makes us mindful (consciously aware) of that value. Co-workers tend to treat each other with much more respect and consideration immediately after a senior executive gives a speech on the virtues of benevolence in the workplace. The speech makes employees temporarily mindful of this value, so they think about it in their behavior toward others. Second, even if a particular value is important and we are mindful of it, we still need to have logical reasons in our head for applying that value. In other words, we tend to apply our values only when we can think of specific reasons for doing so. For example, you will be more motivated to switch your vacation time with a co-worker who needs that time off if you are mindful of your value of benevolence *and* you can think of reasons why it's good to be benevolent.

The third condition that improves the linkage between our values and behavior is the situation. Work environments shape our behavior, at least in the short term—so they necessarily encourage or discourage values-consistent behavior. The fact is that our jobs sometimes require us to act in ways that are inconsistent with our personal values. This incongruence between our personal values and work requirements can also have a powerful effect on employee attitudes and other behaviors, as we'll see next.

Values Congruence

Earlier in this section we noted that Tom's of Maine asks its employees to pay attention to their values. Bill Hetzel is one such employee. As head of purchasing and supply chain management, Hetzel applies Tom's environmental values every day. "Every decision I make is laced with business, technological, environmental, and social factors," explains the MIT chemical engineer and MBA graduate. Equally important, Hetzel is comfortable working within this values framework because it is congruent with his own environmentally conscious values. "It makes a huge difference every day at work that I share the values of my colleagues and my company," he says.[26]

values congruence
A situation wherein two or more entities have similar value systems.

Bill Hetzel experiences a high degree of **values congruence** in his job at Tom's of Maine because his personal values are very similar to the organization's value system. This particular form of values congruence, called *person–organization values congruence,* seems to be elusive in many organizations. Three out of four managers surveyed in one study said their company's values conflict to some extent with their own personal values. Another study reported that managers saw significant differences between their personal values and organizational practices.[27]

Person–organization values incongruence has a number of undesirable consequences, including higher stress and turnover as well as lower organizational citizenship, loyalty, and job satisfaction. Values are guideposts, so incongruence also reduces the chance that employees will make decisions compatible with the organization's values.[28] Does this mean that the most successful organizations perfectly align employee values with the organization's values? Not at all! Although a comfortable degree of values congruence is necessary for the reasons just noted, organizations also benefit from some level of values incongruence. Employees with diverse values offer different perspectives, which often leads to better decision making (see Chapter 8). Furthermore, too much congruence can create a "corporate cult" that potentially undermines creativity, organizational flexibility, and business ethics (see Chapter 16).[29]

Creating Congruent Values at Coles Myer Coles Myer staff indicated through employee surveys that they wanted a coherent set of values to help bind the company together. Chief executive John Fletcher and his executive team felt that these values should come from the employees themselves so that personal and organizational values would be highly congruent. To accomplish this, more than 2,300 employees across all levels at Australia's second largest retailer participated in 203 focus groups around the country. Several dozen employees later met for two days to condense 153 pages of focus group feedback into four values: integrity, respect and recognition, a passion for excellence, and working together. Next, thousands of Coles Myer managers attended one-day workshops where they developed a better understanding of the four values and what behaviors are associated with those values. The company also revised its performance appraisal system to tie 20 percent of managers' bonuses to how well they perform against those values.[30]

Other Types of Values Congruence A second type of values congruence refers to how closely the values apparent in our actions (enacted values) are consistent with what we say we believe in (espoused values). This *espoused–enacted values congruence* is especially important for people in leadership positions because any obvious gap between espoused and enacted values undermines their perceived integrity, a critical feature of effective leaders (see Chapter 14). For instance, Albuquerque, New Mexico, accounting firm Meyners & Co. surveys each manager's subordinates and peers each year to determine how consistent their decisions and actions are with the company's espoused values. Even for nonmanagement staff, espoused–enacted values congruence affects how much co-workers can trust them, which has implications for team dynamics.[31]

A third type of values congruence refers to the compatibility of an organization's dominant values with the prevailing values of the community or society in which it conducts business.[32] For example, an organization headquartered in one country that tries to impose its value system on stakeholders located in another culture may experience higher employee turnover and have more difficult relations with the communities in which the company operates. This creates a delicate balancing act: Companies depend on shared values to maintain consistent standards and behaviors. Airbus, which employs 55,000 people from 80 nationalities, recognizes cross-cultural differences, but it also believes that a few of its values must be applied everywhere. "There are some values that must be retained wherever Airbus components are manufactured," explains Gustav Humbert, CEO of the world's largest commercial aircraft manufacturer. "So as we spread our industrial network [to other countries], the values of quality, safety, and customer care will remain key to making a successful integrated industrial network."[33] Let's look more closely at how values vary across cultures.

Values across Cultures

Anyone who has worked long enough in other countries will know that values differ across cultures. Some cultures value group decisions, whereas others think that the leader should take charge. Meetings in Germany usually start on time, whereas they might be half an hour late in Brazil without much concern. We need to be sensitive to the fact that cultural differences exist and, although often subtle, can influence decisions, behavior, and relations among employees.

Individualism and Collectivism

individualism
The extent to which a person values independence and personal uniqueness.

collectivism
The extent to which people value duty to groups to which they belong, and to group harmony.

Let's start by looking at the two most commonly mentioned cross-cultural values: individualism and collectivism. **Individualism** is the extent to which we value independence and personal uniqueness. Highly individualist people value personal freedom, self-sufficiency, control over their own lives, and appreciation of the unique qualities that distinguish them from others. This value relates most closely to the self-direction dimension shown earlier in Exhibit 2.3. **Collectivism** is the extent to which we value our duty to groups to which we belong, as well as group harmony. Highly collectivist people define themselves by their group membership and value harmonious relationships within those groups.[34] Collectivism is located within the conservation range of values (security, tradition, conformity) in Exhibit 2.3.

You might think from these definitions that high individualism is the same as low collectivism and vice versa. Until recently many scholars thought so, too. However, research indicates that the two concepts are actually unrelated.[35] Some people and cultures might have both high individualism and high collectivism, for example. Someone who highly values duty to his or her group does not necessarily give a low priority to personal freedom and self-sufficiency.

Exhibit 2.4

Individualism and Collectivism in Selected Countries

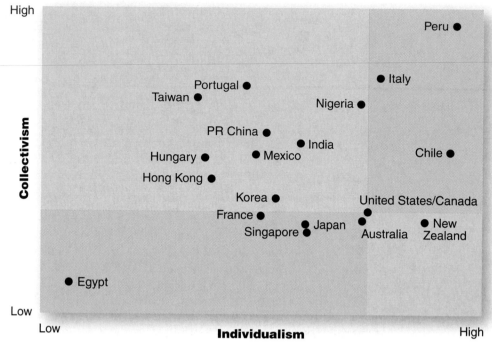

Source: Based on information in D. Oyserman, H.M. Coon, and M. Kemmelmeier, "Rethinking Individualism and Collectivism: Evaluation of Theoretical Assumptions and Meta-Analyses," *Psychological Bulletin* 128 (2002), pp. 3–72. The countries shown here represent only a sample of those in Oyserman's meta-analysis.
Note: The United States/Canada data refer only to people with European heritage in those countries.

How individualistic and collectivistic are people in various countries? Exhibit 2.4 provides the best available answer because it is based on dozens of previous studies combined into a massive single analysis. These findings indicate that Americans with European heritage are more individualistic than people in many other countries. Only people in some South American countries (such as Chile and Peru) apparently score higher on individualism. In contrast, people from Taiwan, Hong Kong, Hungary, and Portugal are among those with much lower individualism. Exhibit 2.4 also shows that Americans, Canadians, and Australians have relatively low collectivism, whereas people in Italy, Taiwan, Peru, Nigeria, and most other countries have higher collectivism.

One notable observation in Exhibit 2.4 is that people in Japan have lower levels of collectivism than people in most other cultures. This is a stark contrast to statements in many cross-cultural books that Japan is one of the most collectivist countries on the planet! The problem was that a major study more than 20 years ago identified Japan as collectivist, but it measured collectivism in a way that bears little resemblance to how the concept is usually defined.[36] Subsequent studies have reported that Japan is relatively low on the collectivist scale (as Exhibit 2.4 reveals), but these persistent results have been slow to replace the old views on this matter.

Power Distance

Stephen Roberts was born in Australia, but experienced a cultural shock after returning to that country following nearly a decade as a manager in Asia. "Managing in Asia was a relatively easy process because no one pushed back," says Roberts,

Anticipating Cross-Cultural Differences at Lenovo A few years ago several Chinese-born managers living in Silicon Valley were recruited to work in Beijing for Lenovo Group, China's giant computer manufacturer. Many of them quit a year later because after living in the United States for several years, they had difficulty with China's high power distance culture. Every morning Lenovo employees had to sing the company song. Their whereabouts in and out of the office was closely monitored throughout the day. Those late for meetings had to stand behind their chairs for a minute in humiliation to discourage future tardiness. "It's very militaristic," recalls one former Lenovo employee recruited from the United States. "You just have to do what you're told." Now, as Lenovo takes control of IBM's personal computer business, cross-cultural differences will likely be apparent again for IBM staff in the United States. "We regard cultural integration as the key factor of our eventual success," says Lenovo CEO Yang Yuanqing. Although Yang points out the good product fit, he acknowledges that there "will be big cultural conflicts and challenges" in bringing together employees from two diverse cultures.[37]

who is currently chief executive of Citigroup Australia/New Zealand. "I remember arriving in Australia and I was asked to present to an executive committee of our equities team, and it felt like a medical examination. I walked out battered and bruised."[38]

Stephen Roberts experienced the difference between Australia and every Asian country on the value called **power distance:** the extent to which people accept unequal distribution of power in a society.[39] People in Asian countries (with Malaysia and Philippines among the highest) tend to have high power distance scores. They accept and value unequal power, value obedience to authority, and are comfortable receiving commands from their superiors without consultation or debate. High power distance individuals also prefer resolving differences or contradicting their boss indirectly through formal procedures rather than directly.

In contrast, people in Israel, Austria, Denmark, Australia, and other countries with low power distance expect relatively equal power sharing. They view the relationship with their boss as one of interdependence, not dependence; that is, they believe their boss is also dependent on them, so they expect power sharing and consultation before decisions affecting them are made. As Stephen Roberts discovered soon after returning to Australia, employees with low power distance are very comfortable approaching and contradicting their boss.

power distance
The extent to which people accept unequal distribution of power in a society.

Other Cross-Cultural Values

Cross-cultural researchers have investigated many other values, but the only two that we will mention here are uncertainty avoidance and achievement–nurturing orientation. **Uncertainty avoidance** is the degree to which people tolerate ambiguity (low uncertainty avoidance) or feel threatened by ambiguity and uncertainty (high uncertainty avoidance). Employees with high uncertainty avoidance value structured situations where rules of conduct and decision making are clearly documented. They usually prefer direct rather than indirect or ambiguous communications. Uncertainty avoidance scores tend to be high among people living in Greece, Portugal, Japan, and South Korea. Studies report low uncertainty avoidance scores in Singapore and Jamaica, and moderately low scores in Malaysia, Hong Kong, and China. Americans score around the middle of the range.

uncertainty avoidance
The degree to which people tolerate ambiguity or feel threatened by ambiguity and uncertainty.

achievement–nurturing orientation
A competitive versus cooperative view of relations with other people.

Achievement–nurturing orientation reflects a competitive versus cooperative view of relations with other people.[40] People with a high achievement orientation value assertiveness, competitiveness, and materialism. They appreciate people who are tough and favor the acquisition of money and material goods. In contrast, people in nurturing-oriented cultures emphasize relationships and the well-being of others. They focus on human interaction and caring rather than competition and personal success. People in Sweden, Norway, and Denmark score very low on achievement orientation (that is, they have a high nurturing orientation). In contrast, high achievement orientation scores have been reported in Japan and Hungary. The United States and United Kingdom score near the middle, slightly toward the achievement orientation.

Before leaving this topic, we need to point out two concerns about the cross-cultural values information provided here.[41] First, the statements about how high or low people in various countries score on power distance, uncertainty avoidance, and achievement–nurturing orientation are based on a survey of IBM employees worldwide more than a quarter century ago. Over 100,000 IBM staff in dozens of countries completed that survey, but it is possible that these IBM employees do not represent the general population. There is also evidence that values have changed quite a bit in some countries since then. A second concern is the assumption that everyone in a society has similar cultural values. This may be true in a few countries, but multiculturalism—where several microcultures coexist in the same country—is becoming more common. On this point, one study reported significantly different values among Javanese, Batik, and Chinese Indonesians. By attributing specific values to an entire society, we are engaging in a form of stereotyping that limits our ability to understand the more complex reality of that society.

Learning Objectives

After reading this section you should be able to

6. **List three ethical principles.**
7. **Explain how moral intensity, ethical sensitivity, and the situation influence ethical behavior.**

Ethical Values and Behavior

When employees are asked to list the most important characteristic they look for in a leader, the top factor isn't intelligence, courage, or even being inspirational. Although these characteristics are important, the most important factor in most surveys is honesty/ethics.[42] **Ethics** refers to the study of moral principles or values that determine whether actions are right or wrong and outcomes are good or bad. People rely on their ethical values to determine "the right thing to do."

ethics
The study of moral principles or values that determine whether actions are right or wrong and outcomes are good or bad.

Unfortunately an ongoing stream of incidents involving corporate wrongdoing continues to raise serious questions about the ethical values of many corporate leaders. Scandals at Enron, Worldcom, Tyco, and other companies led to the Sarbanes-Oxley Act in 2002, which put more controls on U.S. companies and auditing firms to minimize conflict of interest and disclose companies' financial pictures more fully. This legislation might reduce some unethical conduct, but wrongdoing is unlikely to disappear completely. For instance, the founder and former CEO of Gemstar-TV Guide International Inc. was fined for significantly overstating the company's revenue. Ethical problems also continue outside the United States. Several Hong Kong–listed companies have recently suffered heavy losses due to embezzlement by their own executives. And a United Nations report accused the Australian Wheat Board (AWB) of transferring more than $300 million to former Iraq president Saddam Hussein through an intricate system of kickbacks.[43]

Three Ethical Principles

To better understand the ethical dilemmas facing organizations, we need to consider three distinct types of ethical principles: utilitarianism, individual rights, and distributive justice.[44] Although you might prefer one principle more than the others based on your personal values, all three should be actively considered to put important ethical issues to the test.

end justifies the means

- *Utilitarianism.* This principle advises us to seek the greatest good for the greatest number of people. In other words, we should choose the option providing the highest degree of satisfaction to those affected. This is sometimes known as a consequential principle because it focuses on the consequences of our actions, not on how we achieve those consequences. One problem with utilitarianism is that it is almost impossible to evaluate the benefits or costs of many decisions, particularly when many stakeholders have wide-ranging needs and values. Another problem is that most of us are uncomfortable engaging in behaviors that seem, well, unethical, to attain results that are ethical.

- *Individual rights.* This principle reflects the belief that everyone has entitlements that let them act in a certain way. Some of the most widely cited rights are freedom of movement, physical security, freedom of speech, fair trial, and freedom from torture. The individual rights principle includes more than legal rights; it also includes human rights that everyone is granted as a moral norm of society. For example, access to education and knowledge isn't a legal requirement everywhere, but most of us believe that it is a human right. One problem with individual rights is that certain individual rights may conflict with others. The shareholders' right to be informed about corporate activities may ultimately conflict with an executive's right to privacy, for example.

- *Distributive justice.* This principle suggests that people who are similar in relevant ways should receive similar benefits and burdens; those who are dissimilar should receive different benefits and burdens in proportion to their dissimilarity. For example, we expect that two employees who contribute equally in their work should receive similar rewards, whereas those who make a lesser contribution should receive less. A variation of the distributive justice principle says that inequalities are acceptable where they benefit the least well off in society. Thus employees in risky jobs should be paid more if this benefits others who are less well off. One problem with the distributive justice principle is that it is difficult to agree on who is "similar" and what factors are "relevant." Most of us agree that race and gender should not be relevant when paychecks are distributed. But should rewards be determined purely by an employee's performance? Or should effort, seniority, and other factors also be taken into account?

Moral Intensity, Ethical Sensitivity, and Situational Influences

Along with ethical principles and their underlying values, we need to consider three other factors that influence ethical conduct in the workplace: the moral intensity of the issue, the individual's ethical sensitivity, and situational factors.

moral intensity
The degree to which an issue demands the application of ethical principles.

Moral intensity is the degree to which an issue demands the application of ethical principles. Decisions with high moral intensity are more important, so the decision maker needs to more carefully apply ethical principles to resolve it. Stealing from your employer is usually considered high on moral intensity, whereas borrowing a company pen for personal use is much lower on the scale. Several factors influence the moral intensity of an issue, such as the extent to which

- The issue clearly produces good or bad consequences.
- Others in the society think it is good or evil.
- The issue quickly affects people.
- The decision maker feels close to the issue.
- How much control the person has over the issue.[45]

ethical sensitivity
A personal characteristic that enables people to recognize the presence and determine the relative importance of an ethical issue.

Even if an issue has high moral intensity, some employees might not recognize its ethical importance because they have low ethical sensitivity. **Ethical sensitivity** is a personal characteristic that enables people to recognize the presence and determine the relative importance of an ethical issue.[46] Ethically sensitive people are not necessarily more ethical. Rather, they are more likely to recognize whether an issue requires ethical consideration; that is, they can more accurately estimate the moral intensity of the issue. Ethically sensitive people tend to have higher empathy. They also have more information about the specific situation. For example, accountants would be more ethically sensitive regarding the appropriateness of specific accounting procedures than would someone who has not received training in this profession.

The third important factor explaining why good people do bad things is the situation in which the unethical conduct occurs. A few recent surveys have reported that employees regularly experience corporate pressure that leads to selling beyond customers' needs, lying to clients, or making unrealistic promises. In one academic study nearly two-thirds of the managers stated that pressure from top management causes people further down in the hierarchy to compromise their beliefs, whereas 90 percent of top management disagreed with this statement.[47] The point here is not to justify unethical conduct. Rather, we need to recognize the situational factors that influence wrongdoing so that organizations can correct these problems in the future.

Supporting Ethical Behavior

Most large and medium-sized organizations in the United States, United Kingdom, and several other countries apply one or more strategies to improve ethical conduct. Ethical codes of conduct are the most common. Ninety-five percent of the *Fortune* 500 companies in the United States and 57 percent of the 500 largest United Kingdom

Long before the scandals at Enron, Worldcom, and Tyco, Adolph Coors Co. put together a variety of ethical practices that today makes it one of the best workplaces in the United States. A cross-functional team rewrote the Golden, Colorado, brewer's ethics code so it would be clearer and user-friendly. Performance evaluations explicitly consider how well employees model this ethics code. An online training program guides employees through real-world scenarios where they see how the company's ethics principles apply to everyday work situations. The activity is set up as an expedition in which employees progress down a mountain to several "camps," where they must resolve ethics violations. The problems begin with clear violations of the company's ethics code, but later camps have much fuzzier dilemmas requiring more careful thought about underlying values. "The goal of the program is to step beyond rules and guidelines and teach employees how to think, clarify, and analyze situations," says Warren Malmquist, shown here with another Coors ethics leader, Caroline McMichen.[48]

companies now have codes of ethics.[49] Critics point out that ethics codes alone do little to reduce unethical conduct. After all, Enron had a well-developed code of ethical conduct, but that document didn't prevent senior executives from engaging in wholesale accounting fraud, resulting in the energy company's bankruptcy. Still, ethics codes lay the foundation for other strategies to support ethical behavior.

Many firms bolster the effectiveness of their ethics codes through training. For instance, Sun Microsystems puts each of its 35,000 employees worldwide through a basic online ethics training program, while its top 1,200 executives participate in a two-day ethics boot camp. Food manufacturer H. J. Heinz Co. is one of many companies that rely on an ethics hotline that employees can use to raise ethical issues or concerns about ethical conduct. At Heinz the hotline operates around the clock and in 150 languages for its global workforce. "They know how to use the hot line in China," comments Jack W. Radke, Heinz's director of ethics. Radke adds that the hotline "has provided an early warning signal of problems we were not aware of."[50]

These programs seem to have some influence on ethical conduct, but the most powerful foundation is a set of shared values—in other words, a strong organizational culture—that supports ethical decisions and behavior. "If you don't have a culture of ethical decision making to begin with, all the controls and compliance regulations you care to deploy won't necessarily prevent ethical misconduct," warns Devin Brougham, director of Vodafone, the British communications giant. This culture is supported by the ethical conduct and vigilance of corporate leaders. By acting with the highest standards of moral conduct, leaders not only gain support and trust from followers; they role-model the ethical standards that employees are more likely to follow.[51]

Learning Objectives

After reading this section you should be able to

8. **Identify the "Big Five" personality dimensions.**
9. **Summarize the personality concepts behind the Myers-Briggs Type Indicator.**
10. **Explain how personality relates to Holland's model of vocational choice.**

Personality in Organizations

Ethical, cultural, and personal values are relatively stable characteristics, so they are an important influence on individual behavior. Another individual characteristic that has long-term stability is personality. In fact, there is considerable evidence that values and personality traits are interrelated and reinforce each other.[52] **Personality** refers to the relatively stable pattern of behaviors and consistent internal states that explain a person's behavioral tendencies. Personality has both internal and external elements. External traits are the observable behaviors that we rely on to identify someone's personality. For example, we can see that a person is extroverted by the way he or she interacts with other people. The internal states represent the thoughts, values, and genetic characteristics that we infer from the observable behaviors. Experts continue to debate the extent to which personality is genetically coded through evolution or shaped from childhood and other early life experiences.[53]

We say that personality explains behavioral tendencies because individuals' actions are not perfectly consistent with their personality profiles in every situation. Personality traits are less evident in situations where social norms, reward systems, and other conditions constrain our behavior.[54] For example, talkative people remain relatively quiet in a library where "no talking" rules are explicit and strictly enforced.

personality
The relatively stable pattern of behaviors and consistent internal states that explain a person's behavioral tendencies.

Personality and Organizational Behavior

Brigitte Catellier's final hurdle to become vice president of legal affairs at Astral Media Inc. wasn't quite what she might have anticipated. For seven hours Catellier sat through eight aptitude, preferences, and personality tests, some of which asked unusual questions such as whether she would prefer to be an astronaut or an acrobat. "I was told very directly there are two candidates and you are both doing the same tests," says Catellier, who was later offered the job at the Montreal-based media giant. Astral decided a few years ago to include psychological tests in the hiring process, including instruments that measure personality traits such as dominance and tolerance. "This helps us to avoid mistakes, and we have made mistakes from time to time in the past," says Astral's vice president of human resources, referring to people hired in the past whose personality didn't fit the company or job requirements.[55]

Astral Media is among the growing number of firms around North America that have introduced psychological testing in the hiring process. Although aptitude tests have been used regularly for decades, personality tests have had a rocky experience in choosing job applicants. At one time scholars commonly explained employee behavior in terms of personality traits, and companies regularly administered personality tests to job applicants. This changed in the 1960s when researchers reported that the relationship between personality and job performance is very weak.[56] They cited problems with measuring personality traits and explained that the connection between personality and performance exists only under narrowly defined conditions. Companies stopped using personality tests due to concerns that these tests might unfairly discriminate against visible minorities and other identifiable groups.

Over the past decade personality has regained some of its credibility in organizational settings.[57] Recent studies have reported that specific personality traits predict specific work-related behaviors, stress reactions, and emotions fairly well under specific conditions. Research indicates that effective leaders have identifiable traits and that personality explains some of a person's positive attitudes and life happiness. Personality traits also seem to help people find the jobs that best suit their needs.[58] Personality is a remote concept, so it isn't the best predictor of most jobs; but it is increasingly clear that some personality traits are relevant. Some of the most relevant personality traits for job performance and well-being are found in the Big Five personality dimensions.

The Big Five Personality Dimensions

Since the days of Plato scholars have been trying to develop lists of personality traits. About 100 years ago a few personality experts tried to catalog and condense the many personality traits that had been described over the years. They found thousands of words in Roget's thesaurus and Webster's dictionary that represented personality traits. They aggregated these words into 171 clusters, then further shrank them down to five abstract personality dimensions. Using more sophisticated techniques, recent investigations identified the same five dimensions—known as the **Big Five personality dimensions**.[59] These five dimensions, represented by the handy acronym CANOE, are outlined in Exhibit 2.5 and described here:

"Big Five" personality dimensions
The five abstract dimensions representing most personality traits: conscientiousness, agreeableness, neuroticism, openness to experience, and extroversion (CANOE).

- *Conscientiousness.* Conscientiousness refers to people who are careful, dependable, and self-disciplined. Some scholars argue that this dimension also includes the will to achieve. People with low conscientiousness tend to be careless, less thorough, more disorganized, and irresponsible.

- *Agreeableness.* This includes the traits of being courteous, good-natured, empathic, and caring. Some scholars prefer the label of "friendly compliance" for

Exhibit 2.5

Big Five Personality Dimensions

'Big Five' Dimension	People with a high score on this dimension tend to be more
Conscientiousness	Careful, dependable, self-disciplined
Agreeableness	Courteous, good-natured, empathic, caring
Neuroticism	Anxious, hostile, depressed
Openness to experience	Sensitive, flexible, creative, curious
Extroversion	Outgoing, talkative, sociable, assertive

this dimension, with its opposite being "hostile noncompliance." People with low agreeableness tend to be uncooperative, short-tempered, and irritable.

- *Neuroticism.* Neuroticism characterizes people with high levels of anxiety, hostility, depression, and self-consciousness. In contrast, people with low neuroticism (high emotional stability) are poised, secure, and calm.

- *Openness to experience.* This dimension is the most complex and has the least agreement among scholars. It generally refers to the extent to which people are sensitive, flexible, creative, and curious. Those who score low on this dimension tend to be more resistant to change, less open to new ideas, and more fixed in their ways.

- *Extroversion.* **Extroversion** characterizes people who are outgoing, talkative, sociable, and assertive. The opposite is **introversion,** which refers to those who are quiet, shy, and cautious. Introverts do not necessarily lack social skills. Rather, they are more inclined to direct their interests to ideas than to social events. Introverts feel quite comfortable being alone, whereas extroverts do not.

extroversion
A "Big Five" personality dimension that characterizes people who are outgoing, talkative, sociable, and assertive.

introversion
A "Big Five" personality dimension that characterizes people who are quiet, shy, and cautious.

These five personality dimensions affect work-related behavior and job performance to varying degrees.[60] People with high emotional stability tend to work better than others in high-stress situations. Those with high agreeableness tend to handle customer relations and conflict-based situations more effectively. However, conscientiousness has taken center stage as the most valuable personality trait for predicting job performance in almost every job group. Conscientious employees set higher personal goals for themselves, are more motivated, and have higher performance expectations than do employees with low levels of conscientiousness. High-conscientiousness employees tend to have higher levels of organizational citizenship and work better in workplaces that give employees more freedom than in traditional command-and-control workplaces. Employees with high conscientiousness, as well as agreeableness and emotional stability, also tend to provide better customer service.

Myers-Briggs Type Indicator

More than half a century ago the mother-and-daughter team of Katherine Briggs and Isabel Briggs-Myers developed the **Myers-Briggs Type Indicator (MBTI),** a personality inventory designed to identify individuals' basic preferences for perceiving and processing information. The MBTI builds on the personality theory proposed in the 1920s by Swiss psychiatrist Carl Jung that identifies the way people prefer to perceive their environment as well as obtain and process information. Jung suggested that everyone is either extroverted or introverted in orientation and has particular preferences for perceiving (sensing or intuition) and judging or deciding on action (thinking or feeling). The MBTI is designed to measure these as well as a fourth dimension relating to how people orient themselves to the outer world (judging versus perceiving).[61] Extroversion and introversion were discussed earlier, so let's examine the other dimensions:

- *Sensing/intuition.* Some people like collecting information through their five senses. Sensing types use an organized structure to acquire factual and preferably quantitative details. In contrast, intuitive people collect information nonsystematically. They rely more on subjective evidence as well as their intuition and sheer inspiration. Sensers are capable of synthesizing large amounts of seemingly random information to form quick conclusions.

- *Thinking/feeling.* Thinking types rely on rational cause–effect logic and systematic data collection to make decisions. They weigh the evidence objectively and unemotionally. Feeling types, on the other hand, consider how their choices affect others. They weigh the options against their personal values more than rational logic.

- *Judging/perceiving*—Some people prefer order and structure in their relationship with the outer world. These judging types enjoy the control of decision making and want to resolve problems quickly. In contrast, perceiving types are more flexible. They like to spontaneously adapt to events as they unfold and want to keep their options open.

The MBTI questionnaire combines the four pairs of traits into 16 distinct types. For example, ESTJ is one of the most common types for managers, meaning that they are extroverted, sensing, thinking, and judging types. Each of the 16 types has its strengths and weaknesses. ENTJs are considered natural leaders, ISFJs have a high sense of duty, and so on. These types indicate people's preferences, not the way they necessarily behave all of the time.

Effectiveness of the MBTI
Is the MBTI useful in organizations? The city council in Portsmouth, Virginia, thinks so; every council member completed the MBTI prior to recent budget deliberations so they could better understand each other's preferences. Dell founder Michael Dell and company president Kevin Rollins also completed the MBTI to figure out their similarities and differences. In fact, the MBTI is one of the most widely used personality tests in work settings and is equally popular for career counseling and executive coaching.[62] Still, evidence regarding the effectiveness of the MBTI and Jung's psychological types is mixed.[63] The MBTI does a reasonably good job of measuring Jung's psychological types. The MBTI predicts preferences for information processing in decision making and preferences for particular occupations. However, other evidence is less supportive regarding the MBTI's ability to predict job performance. Overall, the MBTI seems to improve self-awareness for career development and mutual understanding, but it probably should not be used in selecting job applicants.

Finding a Career That Fits the Personality While working as a navy diver, Dan Porzio prepared for his next career in financial planning. But he was far from happy in his new field, so he took a job selling cellular telephones. Still unhappy, Porzio moved into the investment industry, where he worked for three years. During that time he visited a career counselor and discovered why he lacked interest in his work. "I thought those other jobs were ones that I wanted to do, but I found out I was doing things that didn't jive with my character," Porzio explains. With that knowledge in hand, Porzio found a job that fit his personality as captain of the Annabelle Lee Riverboat in Richmond, Virginia (where Porzio is shown in photo).[64]

Other Personality Traits

The Big Five personality dimensions represent a broad categorization of personality traits, but organizational behavior also considers traits that are more specific or fall outside the five clusters. Two other personality traits that help to explain individual behavior in the workplace are locus of control and self-monitoring.

locus of control
A personality trait referring to the extent to which people believe events are within their control.

Locus of Control   **Locus of control** refers to a generalized belief about the amount of control people have over their own lives. Individuals who feel that they are very much in charge of their own destiny have an internal locus of control; those who think that events in their life are due mainly to fate, luck, or powerful others have an external locus of control. Locus of control is a generalized belief, so people with an external locus can feel in control in familiar situations (such as opening a door or serving a customer). However, their underlying locus of control would be apparent in new situations in which control over events is uncertain. Compared to people with an external locus of control, people with a moderately strong internal locus of control tend to perform better in most employment situations, are more successful in their careers, earn more money, and are better suited for leadership positions. Internals are also more satisfied with their jobs, cope better in stressful situations, and are more motivated by performance-based reward systems.[65]

self-monitoring
A personality trait referring to an individual's level of sensitivity to the expressive behavior of others and the ability to adapt appropriately to these situational cues.

Self-Monitoring   **Self-monitoring** refers to an individual's level of sensitivity to the expressive behavior of others and the ability to adapt appropriately to these situational cues. High self-monitors can adjust their behavior quite easily, whereas low self-monitors are more likely to reveal their emotions, so predicting their behavior from one situation to the next is relatively easy.[66] The self-monitoring personality trait has been identified as a significant factor in many organizational activities. Employees who are high self-monitors tend to be better at social networking, interpersonal conversations, and leading people. They are also more likely than low self-monitors to be promoted within the organization and to receive better jobs elsewhere.[67]

Personality and Vocational Choice

Self-monitoring, locus of control, conscientiousness, and the many other personality traits help to explain individual behavior in organizations. One fairly successful application of personality is in the area of vocational choice. Vocational choice is not just about matching your skills with job requirements. It is a complex alignment of personality, values, and competencies with the requirements of work and characteristics of the work environment. You might be very talented at a particular job, but your personality and values must also be aligned with what the job offers.

John Holland, a career development scholar, was an early proponent of this notion that career success depends on the degree of congruence between the person and his or her work environment.[68] Holland argued that people can be classified into different types relating to their personality and that they seek out and are more satisfied in work environments that are congruent with their particular profiles. Thus *congruence* refers to the extent that someone has the same or similar personality type as the environment in which he or she is working. Some research has found that high congruence leads to better performance, satisfaction, and length of time in that career; but other studies are less supportive of the model.[69]

Holland's Six Types   Holland's theory classifies both individual personalities and work environments into six categories: realistic, investigative, artistic, social, enterprising, and conventional. Exhibit 2.6 defines these types of people and work environments and suggests sample occupations representing those environments. Few people fall squarely into only one of Holland's classifications. Instead Holland refers to a person's degree of *differentiation*–that is, the extent to which the individual fits into one or several types. A highly differentiated person is aligned with a single category, whereas most people fit into two or more categories.

Because most individuals fit into more than one personality type, Holland developed a model shaped like a hexagon with each personality type around the points of the model. Consistency refers to the extent that a person is aligned with similar types,

Exhibit 2.6
Holland's Six Types of Personalities and Work Environments

Holland type	Personality traits	Work environment characteristics	Sample occupations
Realistic	Practical, shy, materialistic, stable.	Work with hands, machines, or tools; focus on tangible results.	Assembly worker; dry cleaner, mechanical engineer.
Investigative	Analytic, introverted, reserved, curious, precise, independent.	Work involves discovering, collecting, and analyzing; solving problems.	Biologist, dentist, systems analyst.
Artistic	Creative, impulsive, idealistic, intuitive, emotional.	Work involves creation of new products or ideas, typically in an unstructured setting.	Journalist, architect, advertising executive.
Social	Sociable, outgoing, conscientious, need for affiliation.	Work involves serving or helping others; working in teams.	Social worker, nurse, teacher, counselor.
Enterprising	Confident, assertive, energetic, need for power.	Work involves leading others; achieving goals through others in a results-oriented setting.	Salesperson, stockbroker, politician.
Conventional	Dependable, disciplined, orderly, practical, efficient.	Work involves systematic manipulation of data or information.	Accountant, banker, administrator.

Sources: Based on information in D.H. Montross, Z.B. Leibowitz, and C.J. Shinkman, *Real People, Real Jobs* (Palo Alto, CA: Davies-Black, 1995); and J.H. Greenhaus, *Career Management* (Chicago: Dryden, 1987).

which are next to each other in the hexagon, whereas dissimilar types are opposite. For instance, the enterprising and social types are next to each other in Holland's model, so individuals with both enterprising and social personalities have high consistency.

Practical Implications of Holland's Theory Holland's vocational fit model is the basis of much career counseling today. Still, some aspects of the model don't seem to work. Holland's personality types represent only some of the Big Five personality dimensions, even though other dimensions should be relevant to vocational fit.[70] Also, research has found that some "opposing" categories in Holland's hexagon are not really opposite to each other. There are also doubts about whether Holland's model can be generalized to other cultures. Aside from these concerns, Holland's model seems to explain individual attitudes and behavior to some extent, and it is the dominant model of career testing today.[71]

Personality and values lay some of the foundation for our understanding of individual behavior in organizations. However, people are, of course, also influenced by the environments in which they live and work. These environments are perceived and learned, the two topics presented in the next chapter.

Chapter Summary

Employee engagement refers to how much employees identify with and are emotionally committed to their work, are cognitively focused on that work, and possess the ability and resources to do the work. This concept refers to the four elements of the MARS model—motivation, ability, role perceptions, and situational factors—which identify the four direct predictors of all voluntary behavior and performance. Motivation consists of internal forces that affect the direction, intensity, and persistence of a person's voluntary choice of behavior. Ability includes both the natural aptitudes and learned capabilities required to successfully complete a task. Role perceptions are a person's beliefs about what behaviors are appropriate or necessary in a particular situation. Situational factors are environmental conditions that constrain or facilitate employee behavior and performance. Collectively, these four factors are included in the concept of employee engagement.

The five main types of workplace behavior are task performance, organizational citizenship, counterproductive work behaviors, joining and staying with the organization, and work attendance.

Values are stable, evaluative beliefs that guide our preferences for outcomes or courses of action in a variety of situations. They influence our decisions and interpretation of what is ethical. People arrange values into a hierarchy of preferences called a value system. Espoused values—what we say and think we use as values—are different from enacted values, which are values evident from our actions. Shalom Schwartz grouped the dozens of individual values described by scholars over the years into 10 broader domains, which are further reduced to four quadrants of a circle.

Values are abstract concepts that are not easily followed in practice. A personal value influences our decisions and actions when (1) something makes us mindful of that value, (2) we can think of specific reasons for applying the value in that situation, and (3) the work environment supports behaviors consistent with the value. Values congruence refers to the similarity of value systems between two entities. Person–organization values incongruence has a number of undesirable consequences, but some incongruence is also desirable. Espoused–enacted values congruence is contrary to effective leadership and undermines trust.

Five values that differ across cultures are individualism, collectivism, power distance, uncertainty avoidance, and achievement–nurturing orientation. Three values that guide ethical conduct are utilitarianism, individual rights, and distributive justice. Three factors that influence ethical conduct are the extent that an issue demands ethical principles (moral intensity), the person's ethical sensitivity to the presence and importance of an ethical dilemma, and situational factors that cause people to deviate from their moral values. Companies can improve ethical conduct through a code of ethics, ethics training, ethics hot lines, and the conduct of corporate leaders.

Personality refers to the relatively stable pattern of behaviors and consistent internal states that explain a person's behavioral tendencies. Personality is shaped by both heredity and environmental factors. Most personality traits are represented within the Big Five personality dimensions (CANOE): conscientiousness, agreeableness, neuroticism, openness to experience, and extroversion. Conscientiousness is a relatively strong predictor of job performance.

The Myers-Briggs Type Indicator measures how people prefer to focus their attention, collect information, process and evaluate information, and orient themselves to the outer world. Another popular personality trait in organizational behavior is locus of control, which is a generalized belief about the amount of control people have over their own lives. Another trait, called self-monitoring, refers to an individual's level of sensitivity and ability to adapt to situational cues. Holland's model of vocational choice defines six personalities and their corresponding work environments.

Key Terms

ability, p. 36

achievement–nurturing orientation, p. 47

Big Five personality dimensions, p. 52

collectivism, p. 45

competencies, p. 36

counterproductive work behaviors (CWBs), p. 39

employee engagement, p. 34

ethical sensitivity, p. 50

ethics, p. 48

extroversion, p. 53

individualism, p. 45

introversion, p. 53

job satisfaction, p. 39

locus of control, p. 55

moral intensity, p. 49

motivation, p. 35

Myers-Briggs Type Indicator (MBTI), p. 54

organizational citizenship, p. 38

personality, p. 51

power distance, p. 47

self-monitoring, p. 55

uncertainty avoidance, p. 47

values, p. 41

values congruence, p. 44

Critical Thinking Questions

1. This chapter begins by identifying employee engagement as a combination of the four factors in the MARS model. In your opinion, why would all four factors be important? Also, is it possible for employees to have high levels of engagement and be unethical or unproductive?

2. An insurance company has high levels of absenteeism among the office staff. The head of office administration argues that employees are misusing the company's sick leave benefits. However, some of the mostly female staff members have explained that family responsibilities interfere with work. Using the MARS model, as well as your knowledge of absenteeism behavior, discuss some of the possible reasons for absenteeism here and how it might be reduced.

3. Most large organizations spend a lot of money identifying the key competencies for superior work performance. What are the potential benefits and pitfalls associated with identifying competencies? Are there other useful ways to select employees?

4. Executives at a major consumer products company devoted several days to a values identification seminar in which they developed a list of six core values to drive the company forward. All employees attended sessions in which they learned about these values. In spite of this effort and ongoing communication regarding the six values, the executive team concluded two years later that employees were often making decisions and engaging in behaviors that were inconsistent with these values. Provide three possible explanations why employees have not enacted the values espoused by top management at this company.

5. This chapter discussed the concept of values congruence in the context of an employee's personal values with the organization's values. But values congruence also relates to the juxtaposition of other pairs of value systems. Explain how values congruence is relevant to organizational versus professional values.

6. People in a particular South American country have high power distance and high collectivism. What does this mean, and what are the implications of this information when you (a senior executive) visit employees working for your company in that country?

7. "All decisions are ethical decisions." Comment on this statement, particularly by referring to the concepts of moral intensity and ethical sensitivity.

8. Look over the four pairs of psychological types in the Myers-Briggs Type Indicator and identify the personality type (the four letters) that would be best for a student in this course. Would this type be appropriate for students in other fields of study (such as biology or fine arts)?

Case Study 2.1 COX-2 INHIBITOR DRUGS

Christine Stamper, University of Western Michigan

Treating chronic pain conditions associated with growing older, such as arthritis, has become more important (and more profitable) with the aging of the baby boomers, the largest generation in U.S. society. Pain medications produced by pharmaceutical companies take many forms, including both over-the-counter (aspirin, Tylenol, Motrin, Aleve, and the like) and prescription types of medicine. Investment in the research and development of new drugs costs pharmaceutical companies billions of dollars each year, with approximately 4–6 percent of all researched drugs actually receiving the approval of the Food and Drug Administration (FDA), the watchdog government agency tasked with maintaining public safety pertaining to medicines. Given this low "to-market" rate, top managers in pharmaceutical companies try to protect the drugs that are on the market at all costs.

The last few years have witnessed much concern over a class of drugs called Cox-2 inhibitors, such as Vioxx (manufactured by Merck) and Celebrex and Bextra (both produced by Pfizer). Despite the fact that all of these drugs were approved by the FDA (Celebrex in 1998, Vioxx in 1999, and Bextra in 2001), recent independently conducted research has shown significant negative health effects in people who have taken these medicines long term (for more than three months). Specifically, all three drugs have been found to increase the risk of heart attack and stroke in patients, and Bextra also may cause fatal skin reactions. Subsequently, Vioxx was taken off the market by Merck in September 2004, and Pfizer stopped selling Bextra in April 2005 at the request of the FDA. However, Celebrex remains on the market.

When first introduced, Cox-2 inhibitors were hailed as a type of "super-aspirin," alleviating the suffering of the patient while causing little risk. They were also viewed as a preferred alternative to existing NSAIDs, which are nonsteroidal anti-inflammatory drugs like aspirin, naproxen (sold as Aleve and Naprosyn), and ibuprofen (sold as Advil and Motrin). When taken for three months or longer, these NSAIDs pose a risk of internal bleeding in the stomach and small intestine areas (approximately 16,000 people die from these effects each year). Vioxx, Celebrex, and Bextra were produced to provide pain relief while protecting the lining of the gastrointestinal tract.

Even knowing that Cox-2 inhibitors carry a potentially large cardiovascular health risk, there are chronic pain sufferers who would voluntarily (and happily) continue to take these drugs. For example, it was reported that one man who suffers from chronic knee, hip, and shoulder pain thought, ". . . whom do I know who has some but isn't taking it? How can I get as much of it as possible before it disappears from the shelves?" He, and many others, would willingly tolerate the health risks of these medicines instead of living with chronic pain. The acting director of the FDA's Center for Drug Evaluation and Research has recognized, in light of the new information about health risks, that it is important to balance these risks with the potential benefits of the medicines before deciding whether to remove them from the market. However, the associate director for science and medicine at the FDA's Office of Drug Safety has argued strongly that the health risks associated with Cox-2 drugs vastly outweigh any potential benefits.

In December 2004 (prior to its request to pull Bextra off the market) the FDA recommended that doctors limit their prescriptions of all Cox-2 inhibitors, including Celebrex, to only those patients at risk for gastrointestinal bleeding. Researchers at Stanford and the University of Chicago argued that millions of patients who did not face this risk were prescribed either Vioxx or Celebrex by their doctors. Each of these drugs can cost 10–15 times as much as the NSAIDs available to treat the same pain symptoms, and critics of big pharmaceutical companies argue that the Cox-2 inhibitors were marketed too aggressively and deceptively to potential patients. It is not clear whether the increase in prescriptions for the Cox-2 inhibitors in lieu of NSAIDs was due to patients asking their doctors specifically for either Vioxx or Celebrex, or to recommendations by physicians that the patients change their medications.

Both Pfizer and Merck still assert the relative safeness of the Cox-2 inhibitors. In February 2005 an FDA advisory panel recommended that Vioxx, Celebrex, and Bextra should continue to be sold despite their health risks because the potential benefits of the drugs outweigh the risks for some patients. The doctors on the panel stated that they felt Vioxx posed the greatest risk to consumers and that Celebrex had the fewest side effects. Research estimates show that

Celebrex increases the risk for heart problems by 1 percent, but only for individuals who routinely take double the normal dosage of 200 milligrams. Also, another recent study indicated that Celebrex may suppress the typical immune function of the body, which may benefit some arthritis sufferers.

The FDA does not always follow the recommendations of its advisory groups, and it subsequently decided to request that Pfizer pull Bextra from the market. A statement released by Pfizer said the company ". . . respectfully disagreed with the FDA's decision on Bextra and that it would work with the agency on Celebrex's label." The FDA has requested that a "black box" warning label be placed on Celebrex, which is the strongest warning procedure available in product labeling. However, the FDA also requested "black box" warnings on NSAIDs like Motrin, Advil, and Aleve. Pfizer has also stopped public advertising of Celebrex, but still argues that it should be available to patients who need it, according to a doctor's recommendation. Two additional Cox-2 drugs are now waiting for the FDA's approval, one of which (Arcoxia) is produced by Merck. Arcoxia has been approved for use in 51 countries worldwide.

As this case was written, Pfizer had just finished a widely publicized strategic planning meeting addressing the future of the company. In the press releases from this meeting, and prior to the FDA asking Pfizer to remove Bextra from the market, corporate representatives expressed their desire to revitalize the sales of both Celebrex and Bextra in the coming months. With the removal of Bextra from the market, financial analysts predicted that Pfizer's earnings would continue to decline for 2005, and the recent predictions for double-digit earnings growth for 2006 and 2007 would have to be revised. In 2004 sales associated with Bextra were $1.3 billion, and Celebrex's sales were estimated at $3.3 billion. Together Bextra, Celebrex, and Vioxx totaled more than 50 million prescriptions in the United States in 2004 (Bextra = 13 million, Vioxx = 14 million, and Celebrex = 24 million).

Discussion Questions

1. Should Pfizer voluntarily pull Celebrex off the market, given that the other two drugs in its class have been withdrawn? What factors are the most important in making this decision? What should the FDA do about Arcoxia?

2. What are the responsibilities (if any) of Merck, Pfizer, and the FDA for the deaths of individuals who took the Cox-2 inhibitors? Who holds primary responsibility?

3. How many deaths per 100,000 people pose an acceptable risk for a drug to be viewed as marketable? Should individual patients have the right to determine if the risk is too great for them? What roles do organizations and consumers play in maintaining consumer safety?

Sources: T. Agovino, "Pfizer's Outlook Darkens with Bextra Ban," Associated Press, as printed in the *Kalamazoo Gazette,* 10 April 2005; Associated Press, "All Drugs Like Vioxx May Cause Problems, Says Merck Official," MSNBC.com, 16 February 2005; Associated Press, "Painkiller Bextra Pulled from Market," MSNBC.com, 7 April 2005; B.J. Feder, "More Lawsuits over Pfizer's Bextra Expected," *The New York Times,* as printed in the *Kalamazoo Gazette,* 10 April 2005; A. Goodnough, "Consumers Weigh Risks of Painkillers, Life without Them," *The New York Times,* as printed in the *Kalamazoo Gazette,* 10 April 2005; Reuters, "Cox-2 Drugs May Suppress Immune Function," MSNBC.com, 7 April 2005; Reuters, "FDA Rules in Favor of Painkillers," MSNBC.com, 19 February 2005; Reuters, "FDA Should Pull Pain Drugs, Says Group," MSNBC.com, 24 January 2005; Reuters, "FDA Tells Doctors to Limit Painkiller Use," MSNBC.com, 31 December 2004; Reuters, "Painkillers May Damage Small Intestines," MSNBC.com, 3 January 2005; Reuters, "Researcher Says 139,000 Harmed by Vioxx," MSNBC.com, 3 January 2005; Reuters, "Scientist: No Need for Arthritis Drugs," MSNBC.com, 17 February 2005; Reuters, "U.S. May Pull Painkillers, Researchers Say," MSNBC.com, 15 February 2005; Reuters, "Vioxx, Celebrex May Be Overprescribed," MSNBC.com, 24 January 2005.

Case Study 2.2 PUSHING PAPER CAN BE FUN

A large city government was putting on a number of seminars for managers of various departments throughout the city. At one of these sessions the topic discussed was motivation—how to motivate public servants to do a good job. The plight of a police captain became the central focus of the discussion:

I've got a real problem with my officers. They come on the force as young, inexperienced rookies, and we send them out on the street, either in cars or on a beat. They seem to like the contact they have with the public, the action involved in crime prevention, and the apprehension of criminals. They also like helping people out at fires, accidents, and other emergencies.

The problem occurs when they get back to the station. They hate to do the paperwork, and because they dislike it, the job is frequently put off or done inadequately. This lack of attention hurts us later on when we get to court. We need clear, factual reports. They must be highly detailed and unambiguous. As soon as one part of a report is shown to be inadequate or incorrect, the rest of the report is suspect. Poor reporting probably causes us to lose more cases than any other factor.

I just don't know how to motivate them to do a better job. We're in a budget crunch, and I have absolutely no financial rewards at my disposal. In fact, we'll probably have to lay some people off in the near future. It's hard for me to make the job interesting and challenging because it isn't—it's boring, routine paperwork, and there isn't much you can do about it.

Finally, I can't say to them that their promotions will hinge on the excellence of their paperwork. First of all, they know it's not true. If their performance is adequate, most are more likely to get promoted just by staying on the force a certain number of years than for some specific outstanding act. Second, they were trained to do the job they do out in the streets, not to fill out forms. All through their careers the arrests and interventions are what get noticed.

Some people have suggested a number of things, like using conviction records as a performance criterion. However, we know that's not fair—too many other things are involved. Bad paperwork increases the chance that you lose in court, but good paperwork doesn't necessarily mean you'll win. We tried setting up team competitions based on the excellence of the reports, but the officers caught on to that pretty quickly. No one was getting any type of reward for winning the competition, and they figured why should they bust a gut when there was no payoff.

I just don't know what to do.

Discussion Questions

1. What performance problems is the captain trying to correct?
2. Use the MARS model of individual behavior and performance to diagnose the possible causes of the unacceptable behavior.
3. Has the captain considered all possible solutions to the problem? If not, what else might be done?

Source: T.R. Mitchell and J.R. Larson Jr., *People in Organizations,* 3r ed. (New York: McGraw-Hill, 1987), p. 184. Used with permission.

Case Study 2.3 CLEANING UP BOEING

BusinessWeek W. James McNerney Jr. didn't mince words when he took the helm of troubled Boeing. At the giant aerospace company's annual meeting held after his arrival, McNerney bluntly warned attendees that "management had gotten carried away with itself," that too many executives had become used to "hiding in the bureaucracy," that the company had failed to "develop the best leadership." McNerney wasn't exaggerating. Boeing had been battered by several ethical scandals ranging from embarrassing to costly. Boeing's former chief financial officer was jailed for holding illegal job negotiations with a senior Pentagon official. A Boeing manager allegedly stole some 25,000 pages of proprietary documents from his former employer, Lockheed Martin Corp. Boeing was accused to pay discrimination against women, and one judicial review concluded that the company helped cover up internal studies supporting those sex discrimination complaints.

This *BusinessWeek* case study looks at the actions that McNerney and his executive team are invoking to improve Boeing's ethical conduct. Read the full text of this *BusinessWeek* article at www.mhhe.com/mcshane4e and prepare for the discussion questions below.

Discussion Questions

1. List the reasons that McNerney and the author of this article identify why Boeing experienced these and possibly other unethical behaviors. Are these explanations reasonably accurate, in your opinion? Are there any other causes that come to mind?
2. What steps is McNerney taking to improve Boeing's ethical conduct? In your opinion, will these actions be effective? What other steps would you take, if in McNerney's situation, to improve the company's ethical conduct?

Source: S. Holmes, "Cleaning Up Boeing," *BusinessWeek,* 13 March 2006, 62.

Team Exercise 2.4 COMPARING CULTURAL VALUES

PURPOSE This exercise is designed to help you determine the extent to which you hold similar assumptions about the values that dominate in other countries.

INSTRUCTIONS The names in the left column represent labels that a major consulting project identified with businesspeople in a particular country, based on its national culture and values. These names appear in alphabetical order. In the right column are the names of countries, also in alphabetical order, corresponding to the labels in the left column.

1. Working alone, connect the labels with the countries by relying on your perceptions of these countries. Each label is associated with only one country, so each label will be connected to only one country, and vice versa. Draw a line to connect the pairs, or put the label number beside the country name.

2. The instructor will form teams of four or five students. Members of each team will compare their results and try to reach consensus on a common set of connecting pairs.

3. Teams or the instructor will post the results for all to see the extent that students hold common opinions about businesspeople in other cultures.

Class discussion can then consider the reasons why the results are so similar or different, as well as the implications of these results for working in a global work environment.

Values Labels and Country Names

Country label (alphabetical)	Country name (alphabetical)
1. Affable humanists	Australia
2. Ancient modernizers	Brazil
3. Commercial catalysts	Canada
4. Conceptual strategists	China
5. Efficient manufacturers	France
6. Ethical statesmen	Germany
7. Informal Egalitarians	India
8. Modernizing traditionalists	Netherlands
9. Optimistic entrepreneurs	New Zealand
10. Quality perfectionists	Singapore
11. Rugged individualists	Taiwan
12. Serving merchants	United Kingdom
13. Tolerant traders	United States

Source: Based on R. Rosen, P. Digh, M. Singer, and C. Phillips, *Global Literacies* (New York: Simon & Schuster, 2000).

Team Exercise 2.5 ETHICS DILEMMA VIGNETTES

PURPOSE This exercise is designed to make you aware of the ethical dilemmas people face in various business situations, as well as the competing principles and values that operate in these situations.

INSTRUCTIONS The instructor will form teams of four or five students. Team members will read each of the following cases and discuss the extent to which the company's action in each case was ethical. Be prepared to justify your evaluation using ethics principles and the perceived moral intensity of each incident.

CASE ONE An employee at a major food retailer wrote a Weblog (blog) and, in one of his writings, complained that his boss wouldn't let him go home when he felt sick and that his district manager refused to promote him because of his dreadlocks. His blog named the employer, but the employee didn't use his real name. Although all blogs are on the Internet, the employee claims that his was low-profile and that it didn't show up when doing a Google search of his name or the company. Still, the employer somehow discovered the blog, figured out the employee's real name, and fired him for "speaking ill of the company in a public domain."

CASE TWO Computer printer manufacturers usually sell printers at a low margin over cost and generate much more income from subsequent sales of the high-margin ink cartridges required for each printer. One global printer manufacturer now designs its printers so they work only with ink cartridges made in the same region. Ink cartridges purchased in the United States will not work for the same printer model sold in Europe, for example. This "region coding" of ink cartridges does not improve performance. Rather, this action prevents consumers and gray marketers from buying the product at a lower price in another region. The company says this action allows it to maintain stable prices within a region rather than continually changing prices due to currency fluctuations.

CASE THREE For the past few years the design department of a small (40-employee) company has been using a particular software program, but the three employees who use the software have been complaining for more than a year that the software is out of date and is slowing down their performance. The department agreed to switch to a competing software program costing several thousand dollars. However, the next version won't be released for six months, and buying the current version will not allow much discount toward the next version. The company has put in advance orders for the next version. Meanwhile, one employee was able to get a copy of the current version of the software from a friend in the industry. The company has allowed the three employees to use this current version of the software even though they did not pay for it.

Self-Assessment 2.6

IDENTIFYING YOUR SELF-MONITORING PERSONALITY

PURPOSE This self-assessment is designed to help you to estimate your level of self-monitoring personality.

INSTRUCTIONS The statements in this scale refer to personal characteristics that might or might not be characteristic of you. Mark the box indicating the extent to which the statement describes you. This exercise should be completed alone so you assess yourself honestly without concerns of social comparison. However, class discussion will focus on the relevance of self-monitoring personality in organizations.

64

Self-Monitoring Scale

Indicate the degree to which you think the following statements are true or false:	Very false	Somewhat false	Slightly more false than true	Slightly more true than false	Somewhat true	Very true
1. In social situations, I have the ability to alter my behavior if I feel that something else is called for.	☐	☐	☐	☐	☒	☐
2. I am often able to read people's true emotions correctly through their eyes.	☐	☐	☐	☐	☒	☐
3. I have the ability to control the way I come across to people, depending on the impression I wish to give them.	☐	☐	☐	☐	☐	☒
4. In conversations, I am sensitive to even the slightest change in the facial expression of the person I'm conversing with.	☐	☐	☐	☐	☐	☒
5. My powers of intuition are quite good when it comes to understanding others' emotions and motives.	☐	☐	☐	☐	☒	☐
6. I can usually tell when others consider a joke in bad taste, even though they may laugh convincingly.	☐	☐	☐	☐	☒	☐
7. When I feel that the image I am portraying isn't working, I can readily change it to something that does.	☐	☐	☐	☐	☒	☐
8. I can usually tell when I've said something inappropriate by reading the listener's eyes.	☐	☐	☐	☐	☒	☐
9. I have trouble changing my behavior to suit different people and different situations.	☐	☒	☐	☐	☐	☐
10. I have found that I can adjust my behavior to meet the requirements of any situation I find myself in.	☐	☐	☐	☐	☐	☒
11. If someone is lying to me, I usually know it at once from that person's manner of expression.	☐	☐	☐	☐	☒	☐
12. Even when it might be to my advantage, I have difficulty putting up a good front.	☐	☒	☐	☐	☐	☐
13. Once I know what the situation calls for, it's easy for me to regulate my actions accordingly.	☐	☐	☐	☐	☐	☒

Source: R.D. Lennox and R.N. Wolfe, "Revision of the Self-Monitoring Scale," *Journal of Personality and Social Psychology* 46 (June 1984), pp. 1348–64. The response categories in this scale have been altered slightly due to limitations with the original scale responses.

Self-Assessment 2.7

IDENTIFYING YOUR DOMINANT VALUES (STUDENT OLC)

Values have taken center stage in organizational behavior. Increasingly, OB experts are realizing that our personal values influence our motivation, decisions, and attitudes. This self-assessment is designed to help you estimate your personal values and value system. The instrument consists of several words and phrases, and you are asked to indicate whether each word or phrase is highly opposed or highly similar to your personal values, or some point in between these two extremes. As with all self-assessments, you need to be honest with yourself when completing this activity to get the most accurate results.

Self-Assessment 2.8

INDIVIDUALISM–COLLECTIVISM SCALE (STUDENT OLC)

Two of the most important concepts in cross-cultural organizational behavior are individualism and collectivism. This self-assessment measures your levels of individualism and collectivism with one of the most widely adopted measures. This scale consists of several statements, and you are asked to indicate how well each statement describes you. You need to be honest with yourself to receive a reasonable estimate of your levels of individualism and collectivism.

Self-Assessment 2.9

IDENTIFYING YOUR LOCUS OF CONTROL (STUDENT OLC)

This self-assessment is designed to help you estimate the extent to which you have an internal or external locus of control personality. The instrument asks you to indicate the degree to which you agree or disagree with each of the statements provided. As with all self-assessments, you need to be honest with yourself when completing this activity to get the most accurate results. The results show your relative position in the internal–external locus continuum and the general meaning of this score.

Self-Assessment 2.10

MATCHING HOLLAND'S CAREER TYPES (STUDENT OLC)

This self-assessment is designed to help you understand Holland's career types. Holland's theory identifies six different types of work environments and occupations in which people work. Few jobs fit purely in one category, but all have a dominant type. Your task is to identify the Holland type that you believe best fits each of the occupations presented in the instrument. While completing this self-assessment, you can open your book to the exhibit describing Holland's six types.

 After reading this chapter, if you feel that you need additional information, see **www.mhhe.com/ mcshane4e** for more in-depth interactivities that correspond to this material.

Don't try looking for Grahame Maher in his office; he doesn't have one. Instead the Vodafone executive (currently head of the British telecommunication's company's Czech operations) uses temporary workspace near employees in various departments. Every few months he packs up his cell phone, laptop, personal organizer, and a few files and moves to another department to sharpen his perceptions about the organization. "I haven't had an office for years," says Maher. "[Working among employees] is where I learn most about the business."

Few executives follow Maher's lead by permanently working near frontline staff, but an increasing number improve their understanding of their businesses by occasionally working in or around frontline jobs. David Neeleman, the founder of New York–based discount airline JetBlue, works in the trenches each month with his baggage handlers and ticket takers. Ikea executives work on the shop floor or tend the cash registers during the Swedish retailer's annual Anti-bureaucracy Week. Indianapolis Power & Light (IPL) CEO Ann Murtlow regularly visits line crews in the field, sits in on line crew safety schools, and finds other opportunities to interact with employees throughout the organization. "The plant guys [are] not surprised to see her in a manhole," says Murtlow's executive assistant. "She wants to know what everybody is doing and how it works."

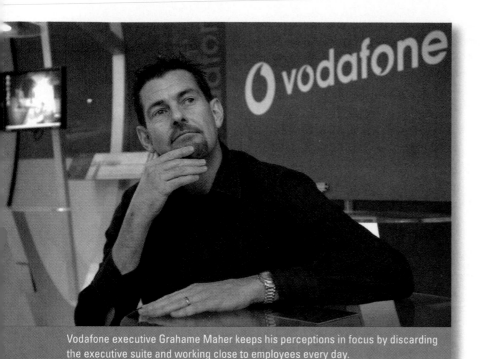

Vodafone executive Grahame Maher keeps his perceptions in focus by discarding the executive suite and working close to employees every day.

Some companies have extended this practice so nonmanagement staff also understand each other better. Everyone at the head office of British department store Debenhams adopts a store for a year and works on the floor of that store once or twice each month. Newly hired information technology staff at Marriott International spend a week working in one of the company's hotels, shadowing people in sales, front desk, engineering, food services, housekeeping, and other business functions. Every new hire at 1-800-GOT-JUNK?, North America's largest rubbish removal company, spends an entire week on a junk removal truck to better understand how the business works. "How can you possibly empathize with someone out in the field unless you've been on the truck yourself?" asks CEO and founder Brian Scudamore.[1]

Perception and Learning in Organizations

After reading this chapter you should be able to

1. Outline the perceptual process.
2. Explain how we perceive ourselves and others through social identity.
3. Outline the reasons why stereotyping occurs and describe ways to minimize its adverse effects.
4. Describe the attribution process and two attribution errors.
5. Summarize the self-fulfilling prophecy process.
6. Explain how empathy and the Johari Window can improve a person's perceptions.

7. Define *learning* and explain how it affects individual behavior.
8. Describe the A-B-C model of behavior modification and the four contingencies of reinforcement.
9. Describe the three features of social learning theory.
10. Describe Kolb's experiential learning model and the action learning process.

perception
The process of receiving information about and making sense of the world around us.

Grahame Maher, David Neeleman, Ann Murtlow, and other executives work in frontline jobs or otherwise keep in close contact with staff and customers in order to improve their perceptions of the world around them and to learn about the consequences of their actions. **Perception** is the process of receiving information about and making sense of the world around us. It entails deciding which information to notice, how to categorize this information, and how to interpret it within the framework of our existing knowledge. This chapter begins by describing the perceptual process: the dynamics of selecting, organizing, and interpreting external stimuli. Social identity theory, which has become a leading perceptual theory in organizational behavior, is then introduced, followed by a description of stereotyping, including ways of minimizing stereotype biases in the workplace. Next we look at attribution, self-fulfilling prophecies, and other perceptual issues, followed by an overview of empathy and Johari Window as general strategies to minimize perceptual problems.

The opening vignette also refers to the topic of learning because executives working on the front lines learn about what employees and customers experience every day. Indeed, it is difficult to discuss perceptions without also referring to the knowledge and skills learned from those perceptions. That's why perceptions and learning are combined in this chapter. The latter part of this chapter introduces the concept of learning as well as the related concepts of tacit and explicit knowledge. We then look at three perspectives of learning: behavior modification, social learning theory, and experiential learning.

Learning Objectives

After reading the next two sections you should be able to

1. **Outline the perceptual process.**
2. **Explain how we perceive ourselves and others through social identity.**

The Perceptual Process

The Greek philosopher Plato wrote long ago that we see reality only as shadows reflected on the rough wall of a cave.[2] In other words, reality is filtered through an imperfect perceptual process. This imperfect process, which is illustrated in Exhibit 3.1,

Exhibit 3.1
Model of the Perceptual Process

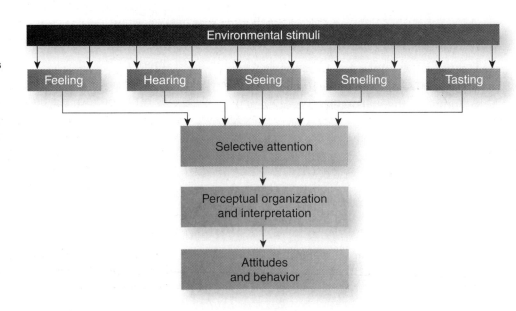

begins when environmental stimuli are received through our senses. Most stimuli are screened out; the rest are organized and interpreted. The resulting perceptions influence our conscious emotions and behavior toward those objects, people, and events.[3]

Selective Attention

Our five senses are constantly bombarded with stimuli. Some things are noticed, but most are screened out. A nurse working in postoperative care might ignore the smell of recently disinfected instruments or the sound of co-workers talking nearby. Yet a small flashing red light on the nurse station console is immediately noticed because it signals that a patient's vital signs are failing. This process of attending to some information received by our senses and ignoring other information is called **selective attention.** Selective attention is influenced by two sets of factors: (1) characteristics of the person or object being perceived and (2) characteristics of the individual doing the perceiving.[4]

selective attention
The process of filtering information received by our senses.

Characteristics of the Object   Some things stand out more than others because of their size, intensity, motion, repetition, and novelty. The red light on the nurse station console receives attention because it is bright (intensity), flashing (motion), and a rare event (novelty). As for people, we would notice two employees having a heated debate if co-workers normally don't raise their voices (novelty and intensity). Notice that selective attention is also influenced by the context in which the target is perceived. You might be aware that a client had a German accent if the meeting took place in Houston, but not if the conversation took place in Germany—particularly if you had been living there for some time. On the contrary, your accent would be noticed!

Characteristics of the Perceiver   Characteristics of the perceiver play an important role in selection attention, much of it without our awareness.[5] When information is received through the senses, our brain quickly and unconsciously assesses whether it is relevant or irrelevant to us. Emotional markers (worry, happiness, anger) are attached to the relevant information based on this rapid evaluation, and these emotionally tagged bits of stimuli compete for our conscious attention. In extreme cases our emotions almost completely take over. For example, a number of armed off-duty police officers or plainclothes detectives have been killed by "friendly fire" when colleagues thought they were suspects. Strong emotions cause officers to instinctively react to the sight of the handgun, screening out other information suggesting the victim is also an officer.[6]

Although largely unconscious, selective attention is also consciously influenced through our anticipation of future events.[7] If you expect a co-worker to send you some important information by e-mail today, then that e-mail is more likely to get noticed despite the daily bombardment of messages. Unfortunately, expectations also delay our awareness of unexpected information. If we form a theory too early regarding a particular customer trend, we might not notice information indicating a different trend. In other words, our expectations and cognitive attention toward one issue tend to reduce our sensitivity to information about other issues. The solution here is to keep an open mind and take in as much information as possible without forming theories too early.

categorical thinking
The mostly unconscious process of organizing people and objects into preconceived categories that are stored in our long-term memory.

Perceptual Organization and Interpretation

People make sense of information even before they become aware of it. This sense making partly includes **categorical thinking**—the mostly unconscious process of organizing people and objects into preconceived categories that are stored in our

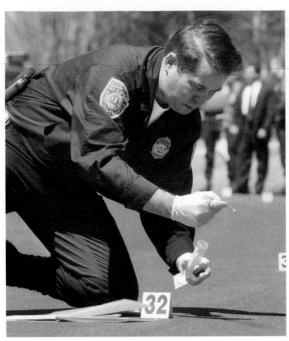

Detectives Avoid Tunnel Vision with Art Appreciation Good detective work involves more than forming a good theory about the crime. It also involves *not* forming a theory too early in the investigation. Keith Findley, codirector of the Wisconsin Innocence Project, warns that becoming preoccupied with a single theory causes police to "focus on a suspect, select and filter the evidence that will build a case for conviction, while ignoring or suppressing evidence that points away from guilt." To minimize this selective attention problem, officers in the New York Police Department are attending art classes, where they learn observation skills and how to develop multiple perspectives. "[The class] reminded me to stop and take in the whole scene and not just have tunnel vision," says NYPD captain David Grossi, who credits the class for helping him to discover evidence outside the area he otherwise would have investigated.[8]

long-term memory.[9] Categorical thinking relies on a variety of automatic perceptual grouping principles. Things are often grouped together based on their similarity or proximity to others. If you notice that a group of similar-looking people includes several professors, for instance, you will likely assume that the others in that group are also professors. Another form of perceptual grouping is based on the need for cognitive closure, such as filling in missing information about what happened at a meeting that you didn't attend (who was there, where it was held). A third form of grouping occurs when we think we see trends in otherwise ambiguous information. Several research studies have found that people have a natural tendency to see patterns in what really are random events, such as presumed winning streaks among sports stars or in gambling.[10]

Making sense also involves interpreting incoming information, and this happens just as quickly as the brain selects and organizes that information. The brain attaches emotional markers to incoming stimuli, which are essentially quick judgments about whether those stimuli are good or bad for us. To give you an idea about how quickly and systematically this unconscious perceptual process occurs, consider the following study:[11] Eight observers were shown video clips of university instructors teaching an undergraduate class, then rated the instructors on several personal characteristics (optimistic, likable, anxious, active, and the like). The observers did not know the instructors and completed their ratings independently, yet they agreed with each other on many characteristics. Equally important, these ratings matched the ratings completed by students who actually attended the entire classes.

These results may be interesting, but the extraordinary discovery is that the observers formed their perceptions based on as little as *six seconds* of video—three segments of two seconds each selected randomly across the one-hour class! Furthermore, the video didn't have any sound. In spite of these very thin slices of information, the observers developed similar perceptions of the instructors, and those perceptions were comparable to the perceptions formed by students attending the entire classes. Other studies have reported parallel results using two 15-second video segments of high school teachers, courtroom judges, and physicians. Collectively these "thin slice" studies reveal that selective attention as well as perceptual organization and interpretation operate very quickly and to a large extent without our awareness.

Mental Models   To achieve our goals with some degree of predictability and sanity, we need road maps of the environments in which we live. These road maps, called **mental models,** are internal representations of the external world.[12] They consist of broad worldviews or templates of the mind that provide enough stability and predictability to guide our preferences and behaviors. For example, most of us have a mental model about attending a class lecture or seminar. We have a set of assumptions and expectations about how people arrive, arrange themselves in the room, ask and answer questions, and so forth. We can create a mental image of what a class would look like in progress.

We rely on mental models to make sense of our environment through perceptual grouping; they fill in the missing pieces, including the causal connection among events. Yet mental models may also blind us from seeing that world in different ways. For example, accounting professionals tend to see corporate problems in terms of accounting solutions, whereas marketing professionals see the same problems from a marketing perspective. Mental models also block our recognition of new opportunities. How do we change mental models? It's a tough challenge. After all, we developed models from years of experience and reinforcement. The most important way to minimize the perceptual problems with mental models is to constantly question them. We need to ask ourselves about the assumptions we make. Working with people from diverse backgrounds is another way to break out of existing mental models. Colleagues from different cultures and areas of expertise tend to have different mental models, so working with them makes our own assumptions more obvious.

Social Identity Theory

The perceptual process is an interesting combination of our self-perceptions and perceptions of others. Increasingly, experts around the world are discovering that how we perceive the world depends on how we define ourselves. This connection between self-perception and perception of others is explained through **social identity theory.**[13] According to social identity theory, people maintain a *social identity* by defining themselves in terms of the groups to which they belong and have an emotional attachment. For instance, someone might have a social identity as an American, a graduate of the University of Massachusetts, and an employee at Oracle Corporation (see Exhibit 3.2). Everyone engages in this social categorization process because it helps to make sense of where we fit within the social world.

Along with a social identity, people have a *personal identity*–characteristics that make them unique and distinct from people in any particular group. For instance, an unusual achievement that distinguishes you from other people typically becomes a personal identity characteristic. Personal identity refers to something about you as an individual without reference to a larger group. Social identity, on the other hand, defines you in terms of characteristics of the group. By perceiving yourself as an employee at Oracle Corporation, you are assigning characteristics to yourself that you believe are also characteristics of Oracle employees in general.

Social identity is a complex combination of many memberships arranged in a hierarchy of importance. One factor determining this importance is how obvious our membership is in the group. We define ourselves by our gender, race, age, and other observable characteristics because other people can easily identify our membership

mental models
The broad worldviews or "theories in-use" that people rely on to guide their perceptions and behaviors.

social identity theory
A conceptual framework based on the idea that how we perceive the world depends on how we define ourselves in terms of our membership in various social groups.

Exhibit 3.2

Self-Perception and Social Perception through Social Identity

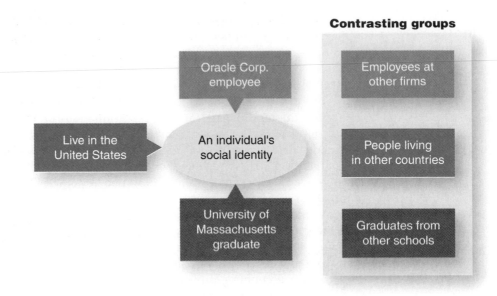

in those groups. It is difficult to ignore your gender in a class where most other students are the opposite gender, for example. In that context gender tends to become a stronger defining feature of your social identity than in social settings where there are many people of the same gender.

Along with our demographic characteristics, group status is typically an important influence on our social identity. Most of us want to have a positive self-image, so we identify with groups that have higher status or respect. Medical doctors usually define themselves in terms of their profession because of its high status, whereas people in low-status jobs tend to define themselves in terms of nonjob groups. Some people define themselves in terms of where they work because their employer has a favorable reputation in the community; other people never mention where they work if the firm has a poor reputation in the community.[14]

Perceiving Others through Social Identity

Social identity theory explains more than just how we develop self-perceptions. It also explains the dynamics of *social perception*—how we perceive others.[15] This social perception is influenced by three activities in the process of forming and maintaining our social identity: categorization, homogenization, and differentiation.

- *Categorization.* Social identity is a comparative process, and that comparison begins by categorizing people into distinct groups. By viewing someone (including yourself) as a Texan, for example, you remove that person's individuality and instead see him or her as a prototypical representative of the group called Texans. This categorization allows you to distinguish Texans from people who live in, say, California or elsewhere.

- *Homogenization.* To simplify the comparison process, we tend to think that people within each group are very similar to each other. For instance, we think Texans collectively have similar attitudes and characteristics, whereas Californians collectively have their own set of characteristics. Of course every individual is unique, but we tend to lose sight of this fact when thinking about our social identity and how we compare to people in other social groups.

- *Differentiation.* Social identity fulfills our inherent need to have a distinct and positive identity—in other words, to feel unique and good about ourselves. To achieve this, we do more than categorize people and homogenize them; we also differentiate groups by assigning more favorable characteristics to people in our groups than to people in other groups. This differentiation is often subtle. Even by constructing favorable images of our own social identity groups, we implicitly form less favorable images of people belonging to other social categories. However, when other groups compete or conflict with our groups, the "good guy–bad guy" contrast becomes much stronger. Under these conditions, the negative image of opponents preserves our self-image against the threatening outsiders.[16]

To summarize, the social identity process explains how we perceive ourselves and other people. We identify ourselves partly in terms of our membership in social groups. This comparison process includes categorizing people into groups, forming a homogeneous image of people within those groups, and differentiating groups by assigning more favorable features to our own groups than to other groups. This perceptual process makes our social world easier to understand and fulfills an innate need to feel unique and positive about ourselves. This social identity process is also the basis for stereotyping people in organizational settings, which we discuss next.

Learning Objectives

After reading the next three sections you should be able to

3. **Outline the reasons why stereotyping occurs and describe ways to minimize its adverse effects.**
4. **Describe the attribution process and two attribution errors.**
5. **Summarize the self-fulfilling prophecy process.**

Stereotyping in Organizational Settings

stereotyping
The process of assigning traits to people based on their membership in a social category.

Stereotyping is an extension of social identity theory and a product of our natural process of organizing information.[17] The first step in stereotyping occurs when we develop social categories and assign traits that are difficult to observe. For instance, students might form a stereotype that professors are both intelligent and absent-minded. Personal experiences shape stereotypes to some extent, but stereotypes are provided to us mainly through cultural upbringing and media images (such as movie characters).

The second step in stereotyping involves assigning people to one or more social categories based on easily observable information about them, such as their gender, appearance, or physical location. Observable features allow us to assign people to a social group quickly and without much investigation. The third step consists of assigning the stereotyped group's cluster of traits to people identified as members of that group. For example, we tend to think that professors are absentminded because people often include this trait in their stereotype of professors.

Why Stereotyping Occurs

Stereotyping occurs for three reasons.[18] First, stereotyping relies on categorical thinking which, as we learned earlier, is a natural process to simplify our understanding of the world. We depend on categorical thinking and stereotyping because it is impossible to recall all the unique characteristics of every person we meet. Second, we have an innate need to understand and anticipate how others will behave. We don't have much information when first meeting someone, so we rely heavily on stereotypes to fill in the missing pieces. As you might expect, people with a stronger need for this cognitive closure have a higher tendency to stereotype others.

The third reason why stereotyping occurs is that it enhances our self-perception and social identity. Recall from social identity theory that we tend to emphasize the positive aspects of the groups to which we belong, which implicitly or explicitly generates less favorable views of people in contrasting groups. This explains why we are particularly motivated to use negative stereotypes toward people who hurt our self-esteem.[19] Stereotypes of aloof, greedy executives often fill employees' minds during layoffs, for instance.

Problems with Stereotyping

Stereotypes tend to have some inaccuracies, some overestimation or underestimation of real differences, and some degree of accuracy.[20] Still, they cause numerous problems in the workplace that need to be minimized. One concern is that stereotypes do not accurately describe every person in a social category. For instance, the widespread "bean counter" stereotype of accountants collectively views people in this profession as "single-mindedly preoccupied with precision and form, methodical and conservative, and a boring joyless character."[21] Although this may be true of some accountants, it is certainly not characteristic of all—or even most—people in this profession.

One unfortunate consequence of these negative stereotypes is that they discourage some social groups from entering various professions. As Connections 3.1 describes, the "geek" or "nerd" stereotype of people in engineering and computer science is partly responsible for the low percentage of women in these occupations. Notice how the individual's social identity also plays an important role in deciding whether to enter these professions.

Another problem with stereotyping is that it lays the foundation for discriminatory behavior. Most people experience *unintentional (systemic) discrimination* (also called *disparate impact*), which sometimes occurs when decision makers rely on stereotypes to establish notions of the "ideal" person in specific roles. A person who doesn't fit the ideal is likely to receive a less favorable evaluation. This subtle discrimination often shows up in age discrimination claims, where employers say they are looking for "new blood" or "young dynamic" individuals. Ryanair recently lost an age discrimination case after the Irish discount airline used the latter phrase in its recruitment advertising. The tribunal learned that none of the 28 applicants who applied for Ryanair's job opening was over 40 years old.[22] Recruiters say they aren't biased against older job applicants; yet older workers have a much more difficult time gaining employment even though research indicates they are well qualified.

A more overt form of discrimination is **prejudice,** which refers to unfounded negative emotions and attitudes toward people belonging to a particular stereotyped group.[23] Overt prejudice is less apparent today than a few decades ago, but it still exists. In one recent incident a hotel clerk told two Wisconsin investigators of Hispanic and southeast Asian descent, respectively, that there were no vacancies; yet a female colleague who telephoned soon afterward was told the hotel had plenty of rooms available. The Australian army has taken a hammering recently for several examples of overt racism, including one incident where soldiers dressed as Ku Klux Klan members to taunt nonwhite soldiers in the unit. A tribunal in Quebec was recently shocked to discover that one of Canada's largest vegetable farms prevented black employees from eating in the regular cafeteria. Instead they were relegated to a "blacks only" eating area that lacked heat, running water, proper toilets, and refrigeration. Claude

prejudice
The unfounded negative emotions and attitudes toward people belonging to a particular stereotyped group.

Stereotyping and Social Identity Discourage Women from Entering Engineering

Women represent 57 percent of university graduates in the United States but only 19 percent of engineering graduates. One reason for this gap is that the stereotype of engineers and computer scientists doesn't fit the social identities that most women want for themselves. "If you ask a woman to characterize a typical IT professional, she is likely to describe a young man with excess facial hair, sitting behind a computer all day munching pizza and guzzling Coke," quips Ann Swain, chief executive of the Association of Technology Staffing Companies in the United Kingdom. Jo-Ann Cohen, associate dean at North Carolina State University, says the same image problem exists for engineering and science. "I think women have a hard time envisioning themselves as scientists," she says. "There's a lack of role models."

Even if women are not put off by social identity problems, family and friends offer them stereotypical advice. Edna Lee grew up with aspirations of becoming a chemical engineer, but her parents had other ideas. "My parents said that a woman would not be able to get very far as an engineer," recalls Edna, who has since become an accountant. "They thought that engineering was more a 'male' job." Kirsty Last, a third-year mechanical engineering student at the University of Wollongong in Australia, says that this stereotyping exists in subtle ways. "People still gasp when I tell them I'm doing engineering," says Last.

To correct these perceptions, many universities have established summer camps where high school girls meet successful female engineers and discover through hands-on activities that science and math can be fun and fit their self-image. CalTech went one step further five years ago by

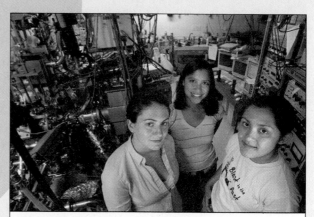

CalTech and other universities are trying to attract more women to engineering and computer science by altering stereotypes and revising programs.

revising its chemical engineering curriculum to include topics that seem more relevant and appealing, particularly for women (biochemistry, environmental engineering). Today nearly half of the Pasadena college's chemical engineering class consists of women, including (from left in this photo) Shannon Lewis, Michelle Giron, and Haluna Gunterman.[24]

Sources: A. Swain, "Easing a Skills' Shortage—Women in IT," *Guardian (London),* 13 March 2003, p. 6; P. Shih, "Breaking Down Barriers," *Jasmine Magazine,* Premiere Issue (2003); L. Giovanelli, "Gender Divide," *Winston-Salem Journal,* 3 July 2005, p. 1; V. Reitman, "Caltech to Harvard: Redo the Math," *Los Angeles Times,* 20 June 2005; C. Trenwith, "Engineering a Gender Balance," *Illawarra Mercury (Australia),* 13 September 2005, p. 22.

Bebear, CEO of French insurance giant AXA, has called for anonymous résumés because he believes that many employers in France routinely "throw away the résumés of people who are from bad parts of town which are supposed to have Arabs or blacks."[25]

Minimizing Stereotyping Bias

If stereotyping is such a problem, shouldn't we try to avoid this process altogether? Unfortunately it's not that simple. Most experts agree that categorical thinking (including stereotyping) is an automatic and unconscious process. Intensive training can minimize stereotype activation to some extent, but for the most part the process is hardwired in our brain cells.[26] Also remember that stereotyping helps us in several valuable (although fallible) ways described earlier: minimizing mental effort, filling in missing information, and supporting our social identity. The good news is that although it is very difficult to prevent the *activation* of stereotypes, we can minimize the *application* of stereotypical information. In other words, we can avoid using our stereotypes in our decisions and actions toward other people. Three strategies for minimizing the application of stereotyping are diversity awareness training, meaningful interaction, and decision-making accountability.

Diversity Awareness Training and Assessment

Diversity awareness training tries to minimize discrimination by dispelling myths about people from various cultural and demographic groups and by identifying the organizational benefits of diversity and the problems with stereotyping. Some sessions rely on role-playing and other exercises to help employees discover the subtle yet pervasive effects of stereotyping in their decision making and behavior. Another approach is to complete self-assessments, such as the Implicit Association Test (IAT), which detect subtle race, age, and gender bias in people.[27]

Diversity training and assessment do not correct deep-rooted prejudice; they probably don't even change stereotypes in tolerant people. What they can potentially do, however, is to increase our sensitivity to equality and motivate us to block inaccurate perceptions arising from ingrained stereotypes. Consider Jennifer Smith-Holladay, who recently completed the IAT. Smith-Holladay was surprised to learn that she is biased in favor of white people, a group to which she belongs, and in favor of heterosexuals, a group to which she does not belong. "I discovered that I not only have some ingroup favoritism lurking in my subconscious, but also possess some internalized oppression in terms of my sexuality." Smith-Holladay suggests that this revelation will make her more aware of personal biases and help her minimize their application in decision making. "In the case of my own subconscious ingroup favoritism for white people, for example, my charge is to be color-conscious, not color-blind, and to always explicitly consider how race may affect behaviors and decisions," she says.[28]

Meaningful Interaction

The more meaningful interaction we have with someone, the less we rely on stereotypes to understand that person.[29] This statement, which describes the **contact hypothesis,** sounds simple enough; but in reality it works only under specific conditions. Participants must have close and frequent interaction working toward a shared goal where they need to rely on each other (that is, cooperate rather than compete with each other). Everyone should have equal status in that context and should be engaged in a meaningful task. An hour-long social gathering between executives and frontline employees does not satisfy these conditions. On the other hand, having executives work in frontline jobs, which we described at the beginning of this chapter, does seem to represent meaningful interaction. By working in frontline jobs these executives reduce their status differences with other staff, cooperate toward a common goal, and have close and frequent interaction with frontline employees.

contact hypothesis
A theory stating that the more we interact with someone, the less we rely on stereotypes to understand that person.

Decision-Making Accountability

A third way to minimize the biasing effects of stereotyping is to hold employees accountable for their decisions.[30] This accountability encourages more active information processing and, consequently, motivates decision makers to suppress stereotypical perceptions in favor of more precise and logical information. In contrast, less concern about accountability allows decision makers to engage in more passive information processing, which includes more reliance on discriminatory stereotypes.

Overall, social identity theory and stereotyping are central activities in the perceptual process, most of which occurs automatically and unconsciously. Without our awareness, our brain identifies and organizes the incoming information around preconceived categories and assigns emotional markers representing an initial reaction

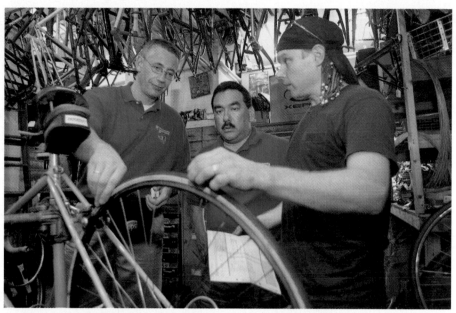

UPS Managers Gain Meaningful Interaction   Every year since 1968, the UPS Community Internship Program (CIP) has transported up to 50 UPS managers out of their busy world of package delivery for four weeks and into communities that need their help and are far removed from their own lives. CIP interns help in drug abuse centers, homeless shelters, job training programs, and other community services in Texas, Tennessee, and New York. For example, this photo shows UPS managers (from left) Dirk Fricke and Dan Sotello assisting bike repairer Ed Matthiack at a bicycle recycling shop and job training center in Brooklyn. UPS senior vice president Cal Darden explains that CIP is an important part of leadership development at UPS because it creates meaningful interaction that "develops sensitivity to issues that our employees and communities face every day." "CIP brings you back down to earth," says Michael Michelak, who recently completed the program by assisting the needy in Chattanooga, Tennessee. The UPS manager from Indiana explains further, "When an issue arises, I am more empathetic in dealing with employees."[31]

to whether the information is good, bad, or irrelevant. It may be difficult to prevent this categorization and activation of stereotypes, but we can consciously control the application of stereotypes in decision making and behavior. Now let's look at another perceptual activity: attribution.

Attribution Theory

attribution process
The perceptual process of deciding whether an observed behavior or event is caused largely by internal or by external factors.

The **attribution process** is the process of deciding whether an observed behavior or event is caused largely by the person (internal factors) or the environment (external factors).[32] Internal factors include the individual's ability or motivation, such as believing that an employee performs a job poorly because he or she lacks the necessary competencies or motivation. External factors include lack of resources, other people, or just luck. An external attribution would occur if we believe that the employee performs a job poorly because he or she doesn't receive sufficient resources to do the task.

People rely on the three attribution rules shown in Exhibit 3.3 to determine whether someone's behavior has mainly an internal or external attribution. Internal attributions are made when the observed individual behaved this way in the past (high consistency) and behaves like this toward other people or in different situations

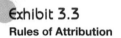

Exhibit 3.3

Rules of Attribution

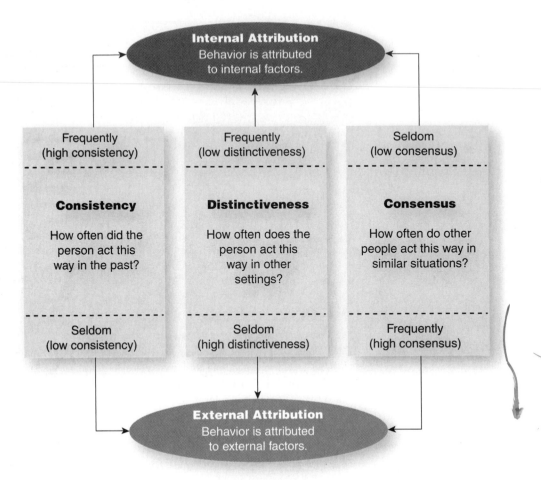

(low distinctiveness), and other people do not behave this way in similar situations (low consensus). On the other hand, an external attribution is made when there is low consistency, high distinctiveness, and high consensus.

Here's an example that will help to clarify the three attribution rules. Suppose an employee is making poor-quality products one day on a particular machine. We would probably conclude that there is something wrong with the machine (an external attribution) if the employee has made good-quality products on this machine in the past (low consistency), the employee makes good-quality products on other machines (high distinctiveness), and other employees have recently had quality problems on this machine (high consensus). We would make an internal attribution, on the other hand, if the employee usually makes poor-quality products on this machine (high consistency), other employees produce good-quality products on this machine (low consensus), and the employee also makes poor-quality products on other machines (low distinctiveness).[33]

Attributions are an essential part of our perceptual world because they link together the various pieces of that world in cause–effect relationships. As a result, our decisions and actions are influenced by our prior attributions.[34] Students who make internal attributions about their poor performance are more likely to drop out of their programs. Our satisfaction with work accomplishments is influenced to a large degree by whether we take credit for those accomplishments or attribute the success to external causes. Whether employees support or resist organizational change initiatives depends on whether they believe management introduced those changes due to external pressures or their personal motives.

Attribution Errors

fundamental attribution errors
The tendency to attribute the behavior of other people more to internal than to external factors.

People are far from perfect when making attributions. One bias, called **fundamental attribution error,** refers to our tendency to see the person rather than the situation as the main cause of that person's behavior.[35] If an employee is late for work, observers are more likely to conclude that the person is lazy than to realize that external factors may have caused this behavior. One reason why fundamental attribution error occurs is that observers can't easily see the external factors that constrain the person's behavior. We didn't see the traffic jam that caused the person to be late, for instance. Another reason is that we tend to believe in the power of the person; we assume that individuals can overcome situational constraints more than they really can.

Although it is fairly common in the United States and other Western countries, fundamental attribution error is less common in Asian cultures.[36] The reason for this East–West difference is that Asians are taught from an early age to pay attention to the context in interpersonal relations and to see everything connected in a holistic way. Westerners, on the other hand, learn about the importance and independence of the individual; the person and situation are separate from each other, not seamlessly connected.

self-serving bias
A perceptual error whereby people tend to attribute their favorable outcomes to internal factors and their failures to external factors.

Another attribution error, known as **self-serving bias,** is the tendency to attribute our favorable outcomes to internal factors and our failures to external factors. Simply put, we take credit for our successes and blame others or the situation for our mistakes. Self-serving bias protects our self-esteem, but it can have the opposite effect for people in leadership positions. We expect leaders to take ownership of their failures, so we have less respect for executives who blame the situation rather than take personal responsibility. Still, self-serving bias is consistently found in annual reports; executives mainly refer to their personal qualities as reasons for the company's gains and to external factors as reasons for the company's losses.[37]

Self-Fulfilling Prophecy

self-fulfilling prophecy
Occurs when our expectations about another person cause that person to act in a way that is consistent with those expectations.

Another important perception—and perceptual error—in organizations is **self-fulfilling prophecy.** Self-fulfilling prophecy occurs when our expectations about another person cause that person to act in a way that is consistent with those expectations. In other words, our perceptions can influence reality. Exhibit 3.4 illustrates the four

Exhibit 3.4
The Self-Fulfilling Prophecy Cycle

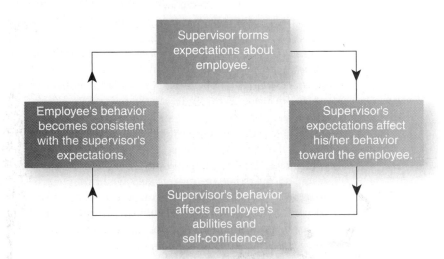

Supervisor forms expectations about employee.

Supervisor's expectations affect his/her behavior toward the employee.

Supervisor's behavior affects employee's abilities and self-confidence.

Employee's behavior becomes consistent with the supervisor's expectations.

steps in the self-fulfilling prophecy process using the example of a supervisor and subordinate:[38]

1. *Expectations formed.* The supervisor forms expectations about the employee's future behavior and performance. These expectations are sometimes inaccurate because first impressions are usually formed from limited information.
2. *Behavior toward the employee.* The supervisor's expectations influence his or her treatment of employees. Specifically, high-expectancy employees (those expected to do well) receive more emotional support through nonverbal cues (such as more smiling and eye contact), more frequent and valuable feedback and reinforcement, more challenging goals, better training, and more opportunities to demonstrate their performance.
3. *Effects on the employee.* The supervisor's behaviors have two effects on the employee. First, through better training and more practice opportunities, a high-expectancy employee learns more skills and knowledge than a low-expectancy employee. Second, the employee becomes more self-confident, which results in higher motivation and willingness to set more challenging goals.[39]
4. *Employee behavior and performance.* With higher motivation and better skills, high-expectancy employees are more likely to demonstrate desired behaviors and better performance. The supervisor notices this, which supports his or her original perception.

There are plenty of examples of self-fulfilling prophecies in work and school settings.[40] Research has found that women score lower on math tests when people around them convey a negative stereotype of women regarding their perceived ability to do math. Women perform better on these tests when they are not exposed to this negative self-fulfilling prophecy. Another study reported that the performance of Israeli Defense Force trainees was influenced by their instructor's expectations regarding the trainee's potential in the program. Self-fulfilling prophecy was at work here because the instructors' expectations were based on a list provided by researchers showing which recruits had high and low potential, even though the researchers had actually listed these trainees randomly.

Contingencies of Self-Fulfilling Prophecy

Self-fulfilling prophecies are more powerful under some conditions than others.[41] Manager expectations have a stronger effect on employee behavior at the beginning of the relationship (when employees are first hired) than after they have known each other for some time. Self-fulfilling prophecy is also more powerful when several people have these expectations toward an individual than when the expectations are perceived by just one person. In other words, we might be able to ignore one person's doubts about our potential, but not the collective doubts of several people.

A third factor is the individual's past achievements. Both positive and negative self-fulfilling prophecies have a stronger effect on people with a history of low achievement than of those with high achievement. High achievers are less affected by negative expectations because they can draw on the strength of their successful past experiences. Low achievers don't have these past successes to support their self-esteem, so they give up more easily when they sense their boss's low expectations. Fortunately, the opposite is also true: Low achievers respond more favorably than high achievers to positive self-fulfilling prophecy. Low achievers don't receive this positive encouragement very often, so it probably has a strong effect on their motivation to excel.[42]

Positive Self-Fulfilling Prophecies Strengthen Cocoplans After only a dozen years in business, Cocoplans is recognized throughout the Philippines as a top-performing pre-needs (pension and education) insurance company with excellent customer service. This success is partly due to the way Cocoplans executives perceive their sales staff. "At Cocoplans, we treat salespeople as our internal customers, while plan holders are our external customers," explains Cocoplans president Caesar T. Michelena. Michelena believes that by treating employees as customers, Cocoplans managers have positive expectations of those employees, which then results in higher performance results. "It's a self-fulfilling prophecy. If you believe that [employees] will not last, your behavior toward them will show it. . . . You get what you expect."[43]

positive organizational behavior

An emerging philosophy that focuses on building positive qualities and traits within individuals or institutions as opposed to focusing on just trying to fix what might be wrong with them.

The main lesson from the self-fulfilling prophecy literature is that leaders need to develop and maintain a positive, yet realistic, expectation toward all employees.[44] This recommendation is consistent with the emerging philosophy of **positive organizational behavior** (a variation of *positive psychology*), which focuses on building positive qualities and traits within individuals or institutions as opposed to focusing on just trying to fix what might be wrong with them. Perceiving and communicating hope are so important that they are identified as critical successful factors for physicians and surgeons. Unfortunately, training programs that make leaders aware of the power of positive expectations seem to have minimal effect. Instead, generating positive expectations and hope depends on a corporate culture of support and learning. Hiring supervisors who are inherently optimistic toward their staff is another way of increasing the incidence of positive self-fulfilling prophecies.

Other Perceptual Errors

Self-fulfilling prophecy, attribution, and stereotyping are processes that both assist and interfere with the perceptual process. Four other well-known perceptual biases in organizational settings are primacy effect, recency effect, halo effect, and projection bias.

Primacy Effect

First impressions are lasting impressions. This well-known saying isn't a cliché; it's a well-researched observation known as the **primacy effect.** The primacy effect refers to our tendency to quickly form an opinion of people based on the first information we receive about them.[45] This rapid perceptual organization and interpretation occurs because we need to make sense of the world around us. The problem is that first impressions—particularly negative first impressions—are difficult to change. After categorizing someone, we tend to select subsequent information that supports our first impression and screen out information that opposes that impression. Negative impressions tend to "stick" more than positive impressions because negative characteristics are more easily attributed to the person, whereas positive characteristics are often attributed to the situation.

Recency Effect

The **recency effect** occurs when the most recent information dominates our perceptions.[46] This effect is most common when people (especially those with limited experience) make an evaluation involving complex information. For instance, auditors must digest large volumes of information in their judgments about financial documents, and the most recent information received prior to the decision tends to get weighted more heavily than information received at the beginning of the audit. Similarly, when supervisors evaluate the performance of employees over the previous year, the most recent performance information dominates the evaluation because it is the most easily recalled. Some employees, aware of the recency effect, use it to their advantage by getting their best work on the manager's desk just before the performance appraisal is conducted.

Halo Effect

Halo effect occurs when our general impression of a person, usually based on one prominent characteristic, colors our perception of other characteristics of that person.[47] If a supervisor who values punctuality notices that an employee is sometimes late for work, the supervisor might form a negative image of the employee and evaluate that person's other traits unfavorably as well. Generally one trait important to the perceiver forms a general impression, and this impression becomes the basis for judgments about other traits. Halo effect is most likely to occur when concrete information about the perceived target is missing or we are not sufficiently motivated to search for it. Instead we use our general impression of the person to fill in the missing information.

Projection Bias

Projection bias occurs when we believe other people have the same beliefs and behaviors that we do.[48] If you are eager for a promotion, you might think that others in your position are similarly motivated. If you are thinking of quitting your job, you start to believe that other people are also thinking of quitting. Projection bias is also a defense mechanism to protect our self-esteem. If we break a work rule, projection bias justifies this infraction by claiming "everyone does it." We feel more comfortable with the thought that our negative traits exist in others, so we believe that others also have these traits.

Learning Objectives

After reading this section you should be able to

6. **Explain how empathy and the Johari Window can improve a person's perceptions.**

Improving Perceptions

We can't bypass the perceptual process, but we should make every attempt to minimize perceptual biases and distortions. Earlier we learned about diversity awareness, meaningful interaction, and accountability practices to minimize the adverse effects of biased stereotypes. Two other broad practices to improve perceptions are developing empathy and improving self-awareness.

Improving Perceptions through Empathy

empathy
A person's understanding and sensitivity to the feelings, thoughts, and situation of others.

Empathy refers to a person's understanding of and sensitivity to the feelings, thoughts, and situations of others. Empathy has both a cognitive (thinking) and emotional component.[49] The cognitive component, which is sometimes called *perspective taking*, represents a cognitive awareness of another person's situational and individual circumstances. The emotional component of empathy refers to experiencing the feelings of the other person. You have empathy when actively visualizing the other person's situation (perspective taking) and feeling that person's emotions in that situation. Empathizing with others improves a person's sensitivity to external causes of another person's performance and behavior, thereby reducing fundamental attribution error. A supervisor who imagines what it's like to be a single mother, for example, would become more sensitive to the external causes of lateness and other events among these employees.

Our empathy toward others improves through feedback, such as from a supervisor, co-worker, or coach. Executive coaches—consultants who help executives develop their competencies—also provide empathy-related feedback by attending meetings and later debriefing executives regarding how well they demonstrated empathy toward others in the meeting.[50] Another way to improve empathy is to literally walk in the other person's shoes. The opening story to this chapter described how several executives are following this practice by working in frontline jobs once in a while. The more you personally experience the environment in which other people live and work, the better you will understand and be sensitive to their needs and expectations.

Know Yourself: Applying the Johari Window

Johari Window
The model of personal and interpersonal understanding that encourages disclosure and feedback to increase the open area and reduce the blind, hidden, and unknown areas of oneself.

Knowing yourself—becoming more aware of your values, beliefs, and prejudices—is a powerful way to improve your perceptions.[51] Let's say that you had an unpleasant experience with lawyers and developed negative emotions toward people in this profession. Being sensitive to these emotions should enable you to regulate your behavior more effectively when working with legal professionals. Furthermore, if co-workers are aware of your antipathy to lawyers, they are more likely to understand your actions and help you to be objective in the future.

The **Johari Window** is a popular model for understanding how co-workers can increase their mutual understanding.[52] Developed by Joseph Luft and Harry Ingram (hence the name *Johari*), this model divides information about you into four

Exhibit 3.5
Johari Window

Source: Based on J. Luft, *Group Processes* (Palo Alto, CA: Mayfield, 1984).

"windows"—open, blind, hidden, and unknown—based on whether your own values, beliefs, and experiences are known to you and to others (see Exhibit 3.5). The *open area* includes information about you that is known both to you and to others. For example, both you and your co-workers may be aware that you don't like to be near people who smoke cigarettes. The *blind area* refers to information that is known to others but not to you. For example, your colleagues might notice that you are self-conscious and awkward when meeting the company chief executive, but you are unaware of this fact. Information known to you but unknown to others is found in the *hidden area.* We all have personal secrets about our likes, dislikes, and personal experiences. Finally, the *unknown area* includes your values, beliefs, and experiences that aren't known to you or others.

The main objective of the Johari Window is to increase the size of the open area so that both you and colleagues are aware of your perceptual limitations. This is partly accomplished by reducing the hidden area through *disclosure*—informing others of your beliefs, feelings, and experiences that may influence the work relationship.[53] The open area also increases through *feedback* from others about your behaviors. This information helps you to reduce your blind area because co-workers often see things in you that you do not see. Finally, the combination of disclosure and feedback occasionally produces revelations about information in the unknown area.

The Johari Window applies to some diversity awareness and meaningful contact activities that we described earlier. By learning about cultural differences and communicating more with people from different backgrounds, we gain a better understanding of their behavior. Engaging in open dialogue with co-workers also applies the Johari Window. As we communicate with others, we naturally tend to disclose more information about ourselves and eventually feel comfortable providing candid feedback to them.

The perceptual process represents the filter through which information passes from the external environment to our brain. As such, it is really the beginning of the learning process, which we discuss next.

Learning Objectives

After reading the next four sections you should be able to

7. Define *learning* and explain how it affects individual behavior.
8. Describe the A-B-C model of behavior modification and the four contingencies of reinforcement.
9. Describe the three features of social learning theory.
10. Describe Kolb's experiential learning model and the action learning process.

Learning in Organizations

What do employees at Wipro Technologies appreciate most about working at the Indian software giant? Financial rewards and challenging work are certainly on the list, but one of the top benefits is learning. "Wipro provides great learning opportunities," says CEO Vivek Paul. "The core of how employees think about us and value us revolves around training. It simply isn't something we can back off from."[54]

learning

A relatively permanent change in behavior (or behavior tendency) that occurs as a result of a person's interaction with the environment.

Learning is a relatively permanent change in behavior (or behavior tendency) that occurs as a result of a person's interaction with the environment. Learning occurs when the learner behaves differently. For example, we can see that you have "learned" computer skills when you operate the keyboard and software more quickly than before. Learning occurs when interaction with the environment leads to behavior change. This means that we learn through our senses, such as through study, observation, and experience.

Learning influences individual behavior and performance through three elements of the MARS model (see Chapter 2). First, people acquire skills and knowledge through learning opportunities, which gives them the competencies to perform tasks more effectively. Second, learning clarifies role perceptions. Employees develop a better understanding of their tasks and relative importance of work activities. Third, learning occurs through feedback, which motivates employees when they see that they are accomplishing their tasks.

Learning Explicit and Tacit Knowledge

When employees learn, they acquire both explicit and tacit knowledge. Explicit knowledge is organized and can be communicated from one person to another. The information you receive in a lecture is mainly explicit knowledge because the instructor packages and consciously transfers it to you. Explicit knowledge can be written down and given to others.

tacit knowledge

Knowledge embedded in our actions and ways of thinking, and transmitted only through observation and experience.

However, explicit knowledge is really only the tip of the knowledge iceberg. Most of what we know is **tacit knowledge.**[55] You have probably said to someone, "I can't tell you how to do this, but I can show you." Tacit knowledge is not documented; rather, it is action-oriented and known below the level of consciousness. Some writers suggest that tacit knowledge also includes the organization's culture and a team's implicit norms. People know these values and rules exist, but they are difficult to describe and document. Tacit knowledge is acquired through observation and direct experience. For example, airline pilots learn to operate commercial jets more by watching experts and practicing on flight simulators than through lectures. They acquire tacit knowledge by directly experiencing the complex interaction of behavior with the machine's response.

The rest of this chapter introduces three perspectives on learning tacit and explicit knowledge: reinforcement, social learning, and direct experience. Each perspective offers a different angle for understanding the dynamics of learning.

Behavior Modification: Learning through Reinforcement

behavior modification
A theory that explains learning in terms of the antecedents and consequences of behavior.

One of the oldest perspectives on learning, called **behavior modification** (also known as *operant conditioning* and *reinforcement theory*), takes the rather extreme view that learning is completely dependent on the environment. Behavior modification does not question the notion that thinking is part of the learning process, but it views human thoughts as unimportant intermediate stages between behavior and the environment. The environment teaches us to alter our behaviors so that we maximize positive consequences and minimize adverse consequences.[56]

A–B–Cs of Behavior Modification

The central objective of behavior modification is to change behavior (B) by managing its antecedents (A) and consequences (C). This process is nicely illustrated in the A–B–C model of behavior modification, shown in Exhibit 3.6.[57]

Antecedents are events preceding the behavior, informing employees that certain behaviors will have particular consequences. An antecedent may be a sound from your computer signaling that an e-mail message has arrived or a request from your supervisor to complete a specific task by tomorrow. These antecedents let employees know that a particular action will produce specific consequences. Notice that antecedents do not cause behaviors. The computer sound doesn't cause us to read our e-mail. Rather, the sound is a cue telling us that particular consequences are likely to occur if we engage in particular behaviors.

Although antecedents are important, behavior modification focuses mainly on the *consequences* of behavior. Consequences are events following a particular behavior that influence its future occurrence. Generally speaking, people tend to repeat behaviors that are followed by pleasant consequences and are less likely to repeat behaviors that are followed by unpleasant consequences or no consequences at all.

Contingencies of Reinforcement

Behavior modification identifies four types of consequences that strengthen, maintain, or weaken behavior. These consequences, collectively known as the *contingencies*

Exhibit 3.6   A–B–Cs of Behavior Modification

| **Antecedents**
What happens before behavior. | **Behavior**
What person says or does. | **Consequences**
What happens after behavior. |

Examples

| Warning light flashes on operator's console. | Operator switches off the machine's power supply. | Co-workers thank operator for stopping the machine. |

Sources: Adapted from T.K. Connellan, *How to Improve Human Performance* (New York: Harper & Row, 1978), p. 50; F. Luthans and R. Kreitner, *Organizational Behavior Modification and Beyond* (Glenview, IL: Scott, Foresman, 1985), pp. 85–88.

of reinforcement, include positive reinforcement, punishment, negative reinforcement, and extinction:[58]

positive reinforcement
Occurs when the introduction of a consequence increases or maintains the frequency or future probability of a behavior.

- *Positive reinforcement.* **Positive reinforcement** occurs when the *introduction* of a consequence *increases or maintains* the frequency or future probability of a specific behavior. Receiving a bonus after successfully completing an important project is considered positive reinforcement because it typically increases the probability that you will use those behaviors in the future.

punishment
Occurs when a consequence decreases the frequency or future probability of a behavior.

- *Punishment.* **Punishment** occurs when a consequence decreases the frequency or future probability of a behavior. This consequence typically involves introducing something that employees try to avoid. For instance, most of us would consider a demotion or being ostracized by our co-workers as forms of punishment.[59]

negative reinforcement
Occurs when the removal or avoidance of a consequence increases or maintains the frequency or future probability of a behavior.

- *Negative reinforcement.* **Negative reinforcement** occurs when the removal or avoidance of a consequence increases or maintains the frequency or future probability of a specific behavior. Supervisors apply negative reinforcement when they *stop* criticizing employees whose substandard performance has improved. When the criticism is withheld, employees are more likely to repeat behaviors that improved their performance. Notice that negative reinforcement is not punishment. It actually reinforces behavior by removing punishment.

extinction
Occurs when the target behavior decreases because no consequence follows it.

- *Extinction.* **Extinction** occurs when the target behavior decreases because no consequence follows it. In this respect, extinction is a do-nothing strategy. Generally, behavior that is no longer reinforced tends to disappear; it becomes extinct. For instance, research suggests that when managers stop congratulating employees for their good performance, that performance tends to decline.[60]

Which contingency of reinforcement should we use in the learning process? In most situations positive reinforcement should follow desired behaviors, and extinction (do nothing) should follow undesirable behaviors. This approach is preferred because punishment and negative reinforcement generate negative emotions and attitudes toward the punisher (supervisor) and organization. However, some form of punishment (dismissal, suspension, demotion) may be necessary for extreme behaviors, such as deliberately hurting a co-worker or stealing inventory. Indeed, research suggests that, under certain conditions, punishment maintains a sense of equity among co-workers.[61]

Schedules of Reinforcement

Along with the types of reinforcement, the frequency and timing of those reinforcers also influence employee behaviors.[62] These reinforcement schedules can be continuous or intermittent. The most effective reinforcement schedule for learning new tasks is *continuous reinforcement*–providing positive reinforcement after every occurrence of the desired behavior. Employees learn desired behaviors quickly and, when the reinforcer is removed, extinction also occurs very quickly.

The other schedules of reinforcement are intermittent and are distinguished by whether they are based on a period of time (interval) or number of behavioral events (ratio), and whether that interval or ratio is fixed or variable. Most people get paid with a *fixed interval schedule* because they receive their reinforcement (paycheck) after a fixed period. A *variable interval schedule* is common for promotions: Employees are promoted after a variable amount of time. If you are given the rest of the day off after completing a fixed amount of work (for example, serving a specific number of customers), then you have experienced a *fixed ratio schedule*–reinforcement after a fixed number of behaviors or accomplishments.

Finally, companies often use a *variable ratio schedule* in which employee behavior is reinforced after a variable number of times. Salespeople experience variable ratio reinforcement because they make a successful sale (the reinforcer) after a varying number of client calls. They might make four unsuccessful calls before receiving an order on the fifth one, then make 10 more calls before receiving the next order, and so on. The variable ratio schedule is a low-cost way to reinforce behavior because employees are rewarded infrequently. It is also highly resistant to extinction. Suppose your boss walks into your office at varying times of the day. Chances are that you would work consistently better throughout the day than if your boss visits at exactly 11 a.m. every day. If your boss doesn't walk into your office at all on a particular day, you might still expect a visit right up to the end of the day if previous visits were random.

Behavior Modification in Practice

Everyone practices behavior modification in one form or another. We thank people for a job well done, are silent when displeased, and sometimes try to punish those who go against our wishes. Behavior modification also occurs in various formal programs to reduce absenteeism, encourage safe work behaviors, and improve task performance. In Arkansas, for example, the North Little Rock School Board introduced an absenteeism reduction plan in which teachers can earn $300 after every six months with perfect attendance. Those with no more than one day of absence receive $100. The Dallas Area Rapid Transit (DART) introduced a behavior modification program in which employees earn points for wellness activities, including getting an annual physical examination, engaging in fitness workouts, and attending wellness lectures. Every point is equivalent to one dollar, which can be used to buy gifts at DART's wellness store and, at the end of each year, a cash payout.[63]

Although behavior modification can be effective, it has several limitations.[64] One problem is "reward inflation," in which the reinforcer is eventually considered an entitlement. For this reason most behavior modification programs must run infrequently and for short durations. A second problem is that some people revolt against the lottery-style variable ratio schedule because they consider gambling unethical. Third, behavior modification's radical "behaviorist" philosophy (that human thinking processes are unimportant) has lost favor because it is now evident that people can learn through mental processes, such as observing others and thinking logically about possible consequences.[65] Thus without throwing away the principles of behavior modification, most learning experts today also embrace the concepts of social learning theory.

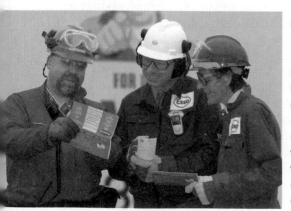

ExxonMobil Reinforces Safety with Leading Indicators

ExxonMobil seems to win as many safety awards as it produces barrels of oil. The Houston-based energy company relies on extensive safety training and leadership, but it also uses classic behavior modification practices to reinforce safe work behaviors. To some extent ExxonMobil rewards employees and work units for accident-free milestones and similar "lagging indicators." In Malaysia, for instance, the company distributes awards to worksites and contractors with zero lost time injuries. However, ExxonMobil mainly reinforces "leading indicators"—work behaviors that prevent accidents. ExxonMobil's U.K. Fawley refinery (shown in the photo) introduced a "Behave Safely Challenge" program in which supervisors rewarded employees and contractors on the spot when they exhibited good safety behavior or intervened to improve the safe behavior of co-workers. The company also introduced a system in which co-workers observe each other's safety behaviors.[66]

Social Learning Theory: Learning by Observing

Social learning theory states that much learning occurs as we observe others and then model the behaviors that lead to favorable outcomes and avoid behaviors that lead to punishing consequences.[67] Three related features of social learning theory are behavior modeling, learning behavior consequences, and self-reinforcement.

Behavior Modeling

People learn by observing the behaviors of a role model on a critical task, remembering the important elements of the observed behaviors, and then practicing those behaviors.[68] Behavior modeling works best when the model is respected and the model's actions are followed by favorable consequences. For instance, recently hired college graduates learn better by watching a previously hired college graduate who successfully performs a task.

Behavior modeling is a valuable form of learning for two reasons. First, tacit knowledge and skills are acquired from others mainly through observation. The adage that a picture is worth a thousand words applies here. It is difficult to document or verbally explain every detail of how a master baker kneads dough. Instead this information is more effectively learned by observing the baker's actions and the consequences of those actions. Second, employees have a stronger belief that they can perform work after seeing someone else perform the task. This effect is particularly strong when observers identify with the model, such as someone who is similar with respect to age, experience, and gender. For instance, students are more confident about taking a challenging course when they are mentored by students similar to them who have just completed that course.

Learning Behavior Consequences

A second element of social learning theory says that we learn the consequences of behavior through logic and observation, not just through direct experience. People logically anticipate desirable consequences after completing a task well and undesirable consequences (punishment or extinction) after performing the job poorly. It just makes sense to expect these outcomes until we learn otherwise. We also learn behavioral consequences by observing the experiences of other people. This process, known as *vicarious learning*, occurs all the time in organizational settings. You might notice how co-workers mock another employee who dresses formally at work. By observing this incident, you learn about the group's preference for wearing casual attire. You might see how another worker serves customers better by keeping a list of their names, which teaches you to do the same. In each case you have learned vicariously, not through your own experience.[69]

Self-Reinforcement

Self-reinforcement, the third element of social learning theory, occurs whenever an employee has control over a reinforcer but doesn't "take" it until completing a self-set goal.[70] For example, you might be thinking about having a snack after you finish reading the rest of this chapter. You could take a break right now, but you don't use this privilege until you have achieved your goal of reading the chapter. Raiding the refrigerator is a form of self-induced positive reinforcement. Self-reinforcement can take many forms, such as taking a short walk, watching a movie, or simply congratulating yourself for completing the task. Self-reinforcement has become increasingly important because employees are given more control over their working lives and are less dependent on supervisors to dole out positive reinforcement and punishment.

social learning theory
A theory stating that much learning occurs by observing others and then modeling the behaviors that lead to favorable outcomes and avoiding the behaviors that lead to punishing consequences.

self-reinforcement
Occurs whenever someone has control over a reinforcer but delays it until a self-set goal has been completed.

Learning through Experience

Mandy Chooi is about to attend a meeting with a lower-level manager who has botched a new assignment. She is also supposed to make a strategy presentation to her boss in three hours, but the telephone won't stop ringing and she is deluged with e-mail. It's a stressful situation. Fortunately the challenges facing the Motorola human resources executive from Beijing on this particular day are not real. Chooi is sitting in a simulation to develop and test her leadership skills. "It was hard. A lot harder than I had expected," she says. "It's surprising how realistic and demanding it is."[71]

Many organizations are shifting their learning strategy away from the classroom and toward a more experiential approach. Classrooms transfer explicit knowledge that has been documented; but most tacit knowledge and skills are acquired through experience as well as observation. Experiential learning has been conceptualized in many ways, but one of the most enduring perspectives is Kolb's experiential learning model, shown in Exhibit 3.7. This model illustrates experiential learning as a cyclical four-stage process.[72]

Concrete experience involves sensory and emotional engagement in some activity. It is followed by *reflective observation,* which involves listening, watching, recording, and elaborating on the experience. The next stage in the learning cycle is *abstract conceptualization.* This is the stage in which we develop concepts and integrate our observations into logically sound theories. The fourth stage, *active experimentation,* occurs when we test our previous experience, reflection, and conceptualization in a particular context. People tend to prefer and operate better in some stages than in others due to their unique competencies and personality. Still, experiential learning requires all four stages in proper balance.

Experiential Learning in Practice

Learning through experience works best in organizations with a strong **learning orientation**—they value learning opportunities and, in particular, the generation of new knowledge while employees perform their jobs. If an employee initially fails to perform a task, then the experience might still be a valuable learning opportunity. In other words, such organizations encourage employees to appreciate the process of individual and team learning, not just the performance results.

learning orientation
The extent that an organization or individual supports knowledge management, particularly opportunities to acquire knowledge through experience and experimentation.

Exhibit 3.7
Kolb's Experiential Learning Model

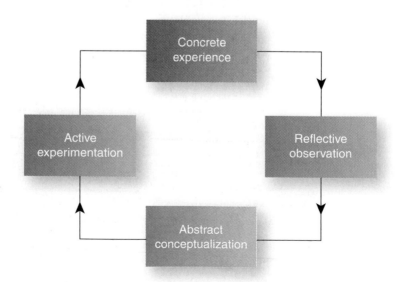

Organizations achieve a learning orientation culture by rewarding experimentation and recognizing mistakes as a natural part of the learning process. They encourage employees to take reasonable risks to ultimately discover new and better ways of doing things. Without a learning orientation, mistakes are hidden and problems are more likely to escalate or reemerge later. It's not surprising, then, that one of the most frequently mentioned lessons from the best-performing manufacturers is to expect mistakes. "[Mistakes] are a source of learning and will improve operations in the long run," explains an executive at Lockheed Martin in Bethesda, Maryland. "[They] foster the concept that no question is dumb, no idea is too wild, and no task or activity is irrelevant."[73]

Action Learning   One application of workplace experiential learning that has received considerable interest, particularly in Europe, is **action learning.** Action learning occurs when employees, usually in teams, investigate and apply solutions to a situation that is both real and complex, with immediate relevance to the company.[74] In other words, the task becomes the source of learning. Kolb's experiential learning

action learning
A variety of experiential learning activities in which employees are involved in a "real, complex, and stressful problem," usually in teams, with immediate relevance to the company.

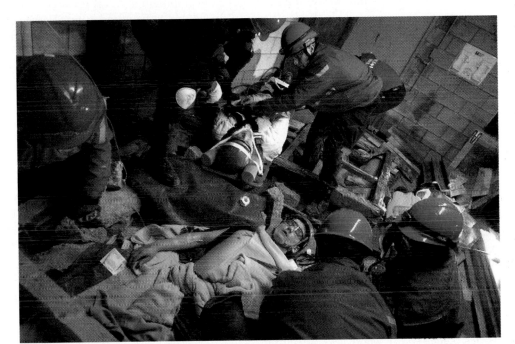

Emergency Response Teams Learn through Simulations Physicians Jonathan Sherbino and Ivy Chong (far right) prepare to amputate the leg of Wesley Bagshaw, who is pinned by a fallen beam in this collapsed building. "If we don't do this, you're going to die," says Sherbino in response to Bagshaw's anguished protests. Fortunately for Bagshaw, the bone saw cuts through a pig's leg rather than his own. The entire incident was a mock disaster to help train the Heavy Urban Search and Rescue (HUSAR) team in Toronto, Canada. For four hours HUSAR crews located the victims with dogs and search equipment at this special operations training center site, secured the structure, treated Bagshaw and 15 other "victims," and extricated them to a mock hospital at a nearby community college. In all over 300 HUSAR and medical professionals were involved. "People from the hospitals love these exercises because they get to try out all the ideas they have and no one is (adversely) affected," explains one of the event's organizers. "It was definitely a lot more realistic than anything we've done in the past."[75]

model presented earlier is usually identified as the main template for action learning. Action learning requires concrete experience with a real organizational problem or opportunity, followed by "learning meetings" in which participants reflect on their observations about that problem or opportunity. Then they develop and test a strategy to solve the problem or realize the opportunity. The process also encourages plenty of reflection so the experience becomes a learning process.

Action learning is considered one of the best ways to develop leadership competencies because it combines conceptual knowledge with real-world issues and reflective learning. Although slowly gaining popularity in North American firms (such as GE and Boeing), action learning is well established in Europe, where companies such as Heineken appreciate how this learning process can add value to the organization. "Action learning has become the primary vehicle for generating creative ideas and building business success at Heineken," says the chairman of the executive board at Europe's largest brewer. MTR Corporation, which operates Hong Kong's commuter train system, recently introduced action learning projects as part of its executive development program. One action learning team discovered a cost savings measure that would fund executive development at MTR for several years.[76]

This chapter has introduced you to two fundamental activities in human behavior in the workplace: perceptions and learning. These activities involve receiving information from the environment, organizing it, and acting on it as a learning process. Our knowledge about perceptions and learning in the workplace lays the foundation for the next chapter, which looks at workplace emotions and attitudes.

Chapter Summary

Perception involves selecting, organizing, and interpreting information to make sense of the world around us. Selective attention is influenced by characteristics of the person or object being perceived (size, intensity, motion, repetition, and novelty) and characteristics of the person doing the perceiving. Perceptual organization engages categorical thinking—the mostly unconscious process of organizing people and objects into preconceived categories that are stored in our long-term memory. To a large extent, our perceptual interpretation of incoming information occurs before we are consciously aware of it. Mental models—broad worldviews or templates of the mind—also help us make sense of incoming stimuli.

The social identity process explains how we perceive ourselves and other people. We identify ourselves partly in terms of our membership in social groups. This comparison process includes categorizing people into groups, forming a homogeneous image of people within those groups, and differentiating groups by assigning more favorable features to our own groups than to other groups.

Stereotyping is a derivative of social identity theory, in which people assign traits to others based on their membership in a social category. Stereotyping economizes mental effort, fills in missing information, and enhances our self-perception and social identity. However, it also lays the foundation for prejudice and systemic

discrimination. It is very difficult to prevent the activation of stereotyping, but we can minimize the application of stereotypical information in our decisions and actions. Three strategies to minimize the influence of stereotypes are diversity awareness training, meaningful interaction, and decision-making accountability.

The attribution process involves deciding whether a behavior or event is due largely to the situation (external attributions) or personal characteristics (internal attributions). Attributions are decided by perceptions of the consistency, distinctiveness, and consensus of the behavior. This process links together the various pieces of our world in cause–effect relationships, but it is also subject to attribution errors, including fundamental attribution error and self-serving bias.

Self-fulfilling prophecy occurs when our expectations about another person cause that person to act in a way that is consistent with those expectations. Essentially, our expectations affect our behavior toward the target person, which then affects the target person's opportunities and attitudes, which then influences his or her behavior. Self-fulfilling prophecies tend to be stronger at the beginning of relationships (such as when employees first join a department), when several people hold similar expectations of the employee, and when the employee has a history of low achievement.

Four other perceptual errors commonly noted in organizations are primacy effect, recency effect, halo effect, and projection bias. We can minimize these and other perceptual problems through empathy and becoming more aware of our values, beliefs, and prejudices (the Johari Window).

Learning is a relatively permanent change in behavior (or behavior tendency) that occurs as a result of a person's interaction with the environment. Learning influences individual behavior and performance through ability, role perceptions, and motivation. Some learning results in explicit knowledge, which can be verbally transferred between people. But much of what we learn is tacit knowledge, which is embedded in our actions without conscious awareness.

The behavior modification perspective of learning states that behavior change occurs by altering its antecedents and consequences. Antecedents are environmental stimuli that provoke (not necessarily cause) behavior. Consequences are events following behavior that influence its future occurrence. Consequences include positive reinforcement, punishment, negative reinforcement, and extinction. The schedules of reinforcement also influence behavior.

Social learning theory states that much learning occurs as we observe others and then model behaviors that seem to lead to favorable outcomes and avoid behaviors that lead to punishing consequences. It also recognizes that we often engage in self-reinforcement. Behavior modeling is effective because it transfers tacit knowledge and enhances the observer's confidence in performing the task.

Many companies now use experiential learning because employees do not acquire tacit knowledge through formal classroom instruction. Kolb's experiential learning model is a cyclical four-stage process that includes concrete experience, reflective observation, abstract conceptualization, and active experimentation. Action learning is experiential learning in which employees investigate and act on significant organizational issues.

Key Terms

action learning, p. 91

attribution process, p. 77

behavior modification, p. 86

categorical thinking, p. 69

contact hypothesis, p. 76

empathy, p. 83

extinction, p. 87

fundamental attribution error, p. 79

halo effect, p. 82

Johari Window, p. 83

learning, p. 85

learning orientation, p. 90

mental models, p. 70

negative reinforcement, p. 87

perception, p. 68

positive organizational behavior, p. 81

positive reinforcement, p. 87

prejudice, p. 75

primacy effect, p. 82

projection bias, p. 82

punishment, p. 87

recency effect, p. 82

selective attention, p. 69

self-fulfilling prophecy, p. 79

self-reinforcement, p. 89

self-serving bias, p. 79

social identity theory, p. 71

social learning theory, p. 89

stereotyping, p. 73

tacit knowledge, p. 85

Critical Thinking Questions

1. You are part of a task force to increase worker responsiveness to emergencies on the production floor. Identify four factors that should be considered when installing a device that will get every employee's attention when there is an emergency.

2. What mental models do you have about attending a college or university lecture? Are these mental models helpful? Could any of these mental models hold you back from achieving the full benefit of the lecture?

3. Contrast "personal" and "social" identity. Do you define yourself in terms of the university or college you attend? Why or why not? What are the implications of your answer for your university of college?

4. During a diversity management session, a manager suggests that stereotypes are a necessary part of working with others. "I have to make assumptions about what's in the other person's head, and stereotypes help me do that," she explains. "It's better to rely on stereotypes than to enter a working relationship with someone from another culture without any idea of what they believe in!" Discuss the merits of and problems with the manager's statement.

5. Several studies have reported that self-serving bias occurs in corporate annual reports. What does this mean, and how would it be apparent in these reports? Provide hypothetical examples of self-serving bias in these documents.
6. Describe how a manager or coach could use the process of self-fulfilling prophecy to enhance an individual's performance.

7. Describe a situation in which you used behavior modification to influence someone's behavior. What specifically did you do? What was the result?
8. Why are organizations moving toward the use of experiential approaches to learning? What conditions are required for success?

Case Study 3.1 FROM LIPPERT-JOHANSON INCORPORATED TO FENWAY WASTE MANAGEMENT

Lisa V. Williams, Jeewon Cho, and Alicia Boisnier, SUNY at Buffalo

Part One

Catherine O'Neill was very excited to finally be graduating from Flagship University at the end of the semester. She had always been interested in accounting, following from her father's lifelong occupation, and she very much enjoyed the challenging major. She was involved in many highly regarded student clubs in the business school and worked diligently to earn good grades. Now her commitment to the profession would pay off, she hoped, as she turned her attention to her job search. In late fall she had on-campus interviews with several firms, but her interview with the prestigious Lippert-Johanson Incorporated (LJI) stood out in her mind as the most attractive opportunity. That's why Catherine was thrilled to learn she made it to the next level of interviews, to be held at the firm's main office later that month.

When Catherine entered the elegant lobby of LJI's New York City offices, she was immediately impressed by all there was to take in. Catherine had always been one to pay attention to detail, and her acute observations of her environment had always been an asset. She was able to see how social and environmental cues told her what was expected of her, and she always set out to meet and exceed those expectations. On a tour of the office, she had already begun to size up her prospective workplace. She appreciated the quiet, focused work atmosphere. She liked how everyone was

dressed: Most people wore suits, and their conservative apparel supported the professional attitudes that seemed to be omnipresent. People spoke to her in a formal but friendly manner and seemed enthusiastic. Some of them even took the time to greet her as she was guided to the conference room for her individual interviews. "I like the way this place feels, and I would love to come to work here every day," Catherine thought. "I hope I do well in my interview!"

Before she knew it, Catherine was sitting in a nicely appointed office with one of the eight managers in the firm. Sandra Jacobs was the picture of a professional woman, and Catherine naturally took her cue from her about how to conduct herself in the interview. It seemed to go very quickly, although the interview lasted an hour. As soon as Catherine left the office, she could not wait to phone her father about the interview. "I loved it there, and I just know I'm a good fit!" she told her proud father. "Like them, I believe it is important to have the highest ethical standards and quality of work. Ms. Jacobs really emphasized the mission of the firm, as well as its policies. She did say that all the candidates have an excellent skill set and are well qualified for the job, so mostly they are going to base their hiring decision on how well they think each of us will fit into the firm. Reputation is everything to an accounting firm. I learned that from you, Dad!"

After six weeks of apprehensive waiting, Catherine's efforts were rewarded when LJI and another firm contacted her with job offers. Catherine knew she would accept the offer from LJI. She saw the firm as very ethical, with the highest standards for work quality and an excellent reputation. Catherine was grateful to have been selected from such a competitive hiring process. "There couldn't be a better choice for me! I'm so proud to become a member of this company!"

Catherine's first few days at LJI were a whirlwind of a newcomer's experiences. She had meetings with her supervisor to discuss the firm's mission statement, her role in the firm, and what was expected of her. She was also told to spend some time looking at the employee handbook, which covered many important policies of the firm, such as dress code, sick time, grievances, the chain of command and job descriptions, and professional ethics. Everyone relied on the handbook to provide clear guidance about what was expected of each employee. Also, Catherine was informed that she would soon begin participating in continuing professional education, which would allow her to update her skills and knowledge in her field. "This is great," thought Catherine, "I'm so glad to know the firm doesn't just talk about its high standards—it actually follows through with action."

What Catherine enjoyed most about her new job were her warm and welcoming colleagues, who invited her to their group lunches beginning with her first day. They talked about work and home; they seemed close, both professionally and personally. She could see that everyone had a similar attitude about work: They cared about their work and the firm; they took responsibility for their own tasks, and they helped one another out. Catherine also got involved in LJI activities outside work—like baseball and soccer teams, happy hours, picnics, and parties—and she enjoyed the chance to mingle with her co-workers. In what seemed like no time at all, Catherine started to see herself as a fully integrated member of LJI.

Before tax season started, Catherine attended some meetings of the AICPA and other professional accounting societies. There she met many accountants from other firms who all seemed impressed when she told them where she worked. Catherine's pride and appreciation of being a member of LJI grew as she realized how highly regarded the firm was among others in the accounting industry.

Part Two

Over the past seven years Catherine's career in New York had flourished. Her reputation as one of the top tax accountants in her company was well established and was recognized by colleagues outside the firm as well. However, Catherine entered a new chapter of her life when she married Ted Lewis, an oncology intern, who could not turn down an offer of residency at a top cancer center in upstate New York. Wanting to support Ted's once-in-a-lifetime career opportunity, Catherine decided it was time to follow the path of many of her colleagues and leave public accounting for a position that would be more conducive to starting a family. Still, her heart was in the profession, so she took an available position as a controller of a small recycling company located a few miles from Catherine and Ted's new upstate home. She knew that with this position she could both have children and maintain her career.

Fenway Waste Management was small—about 35 employees. There were about 25 people who worked in the warehouse, three administrative assistants, two supervisors, and five people in management. Catherine found that she had to adjust to her new position and surroundings. Often she found herself doing work that formally belonged to someone else; because it was a smaller company managers seemed to "wear many hats." This was quite different from what she had experienced at LJI. In addition, the warehouse workers often had to handle greasy materials, and sometimes they tracked the grease into the offices. Catherine both laughed and worried when she saw a piece of paper pinned to the wall that said, "Clean Up After Yourself!" She supposed that the nature of the business was why the offices were functional but furnished with old pieces. She couldn't imagine having a business meeting there. Also, for most of the employees, the casual dress matched the casual attitudes. But Catherine continued to wear a dressed-down version of her formal LJI attire, even though her new co-workers considered her overdressed.

With all the changes Catherine had experienced, she maintained one familiar piece of her past. Although it was not required for her new position, Catherine still attended AICPA meetings and made a point of continually updating her knowledge of current tax laws. At this year's conference, she told a former colleague, "Being here, I feel so much more like myself—I am so much more connected to these people and this environment than to those at my new job. It's too bad I don't feel this way at Fenway. I guess I'm just more comfortable with professionals who are similar to me."

Discussion Questions

1. Discuss the social identity issues present in this case.

2. What indicated Catherine's positive evaluation of the groups described in Part 1? How did her evaluations foster her social identity?

3. What theory helps us understand how Catherine learned about appropriate behaviors at LJI?

4. Compare and contrast LJI and Fenway.

5. What was Catherine's reaction after joining Fenway Waste Management, and why was her level of social identification different from that at LJI?

6. Is there evidence that Catherine experienced the categorization–homogenization–differentiation process? What details support your conclusion?

Case Study 3.2 HOW FAILURE BREEDS SUCCESS

BusinessWeek Coca-Cola Chairman and CEO E. Neville Isdell knows that the best companies embrace their mistakes and learn from them. That's why Isdell doesn't mind rhyming off the list of Coke's failures over the years. In fact, he is keen to convince employees and shareholders that he will tolerate the failures that will inevitably result from the bigger risks that he wants Coke to take. At the same time, say analysts, balancing a learning culture with a performance culture is a perennial challenge. Intuit, the tax software company, thinks it has a solution. When one of its marketing strategies recently flopped, the company celebrated the failure and spent a lot of time dissecting it.

This *BusinessWeek* case study describes several ways that companies learn from their mistakes while still maintaining a strong focus on performance and the bottom line. Read the full text of this *BusinessWeek* article at www.mhhe.com/mcshane4e and prepare for the discussion questions below.

Discussion Questions

1. Use Kolb's experiential learning model to describe the process that Intuit and other companies follow to learn from their mistakes and failures.

2. What perceptual problems do managers need to overcome with failures? How can these perceptual problems be minimized?

Source: J. McGregor, "How Failure Breeds Success," *BusinessWeek*, 10 July 2006, 42.

Class Exercise 3.3 THE LEARNING EXERCISE

PURPOSE This exercise is designed to help you understand how the contingencies of reinforcement in behavior modification affect learning.

MATERIALS Any objects normally available in a classroom will be acceptable for this activity.

INSTRUCTIONS The instructor will ask for three volunteers, who will be briefed outside the classroom. The instructor will spend a few minutes telling the remaining students in the class about their duties. Then one of the three volunteers will enter the room to participate in the exercise. When the first volunteer has finished, the second volunteer will enter the room and participate in the exercise. Finally the third volunteer will enter the class and participate in the exercise.

For you to gain the full benefit of this exercise, no other information will be provided here. However, your instructor will have more details at the beginning of this fun activity.

Team Exercise 3.4   WHO AM I?

PURPOSE   This exercise is designed to help you understand the elements and implications of social identity theory.

MATERIALS   None.

INSTRUCTIONS

1. Working alone (no discussion with other students), use the space provided here or a piece of paper to write down 12 words or phrases that answer the question "Who am I?" Write your words or phrases describing you as they come to mind; don't worry about their logical order. Please be sure to fill in all 12 spaces.

Phrases that describe you	Circle S or P	
1. I am _Independent_	S	(P)
2. I am _Confident_	S	P
3. I am _Complicated_	S	(P)
4. I am _Social_	S	(P)
5. I am _Smart_	S	(P)
6. I am _Witty_	S	(P)
7. I am _Indian_	(S)	P
8. I am _American_	(S)	P
9. I am _Floridian_	(S)	P
10. I am _business savy_	S	(P)
11. I am _intuitive_	S	(P)
12. I am _spontaneous_	S	(P)

2. Circle the "S" beside the items that define you in terms of your social identity, such as your demographics and formal or informal membership in a social group or institution (school, company, religious group). Circle the "P" beside the items that define you in terms of your personal identity—that is, unique personality traits, values, or experiences that are not connected to any particular social group. Next underline one or more items that you believe will still be a strong characteristic of you 10 years from now.

3. Form small groups. If you have a team project for this course, your project team would work well for this exercise. Compare your list with those that others in your group wrote about themselves. Discuss the following questions in your group, and prepare notes for class discussion and possible presentation of these questions:

   a. Among members of this team, what was the typical percentage of items representing social versus personal identity? Did some team members have many more or fewer social identity items compared to other team members? Why do you think these large or small differences in emphasis on social or personal identity occurred?

   b. What characteristics did people in your group underline as being the most stable (remaining the same 10 years from now)? Were these underlined items mostly social or personal identity features? How similar or different were the underlined items among team members?

   c. What do these lists say about the dynamics of your group as a team (whether or not your group for this activity is actually involved in a class project for this course)?

Sources: M.H. Kuhn and T.S. McPartland, "An Empirical Investigation of Self-Attitudes," *American Sociological Review* 19 (February 1954), pp. 68–76; C. Lay and M. Verkuyten, "Ethnic Identity and Its Relation to Personal Self-Esteem: A Comparison of Canadian-Born and Foreign-Born Chinese Adolescents," *Journal of Social Psychology* 139 (1999), pp. 288–99; S.L. Grace and K.L. Cramer, "The Elusive Nature of Self-Measurement: The Self-Construal scale versus the Twenty Statements Test," *Journal of Social Psychology* 143 (2003), pp. 649–68.

Web Exercise 3.5 ANALYZING CORPORATE ANNUAL REPORTS

PURPOSE This exercise is designed to help you diagnose evidence of stereotyping and corporate role models that minimize stereotyping in corporate annual reports.

MATERIALS You need to complete your research for this activity prior to class, including selecting a publicly traded company and downloading the past four or more years of its fully illustrated annual reports.

INSTRUCTIONS The instructor may have you work alone or in groups for this activity. Select a company that is publicly traded and makes its annual reports available on the company Web site. Ideally annual reports for at least the past four years should be available, and these reports should be presented in the final illustrated format (typically PDF replicas of the original hard copy report).

Examine closely the images in your selected company's recent annual reports in terms of how women, visible minorities, and older employees and clients are presented. Specifically, be prepared to discuss and provide details in class regarding the following:

1. The percentage of images showing women, visible minorities, and older workers and clients. Be sensitive to the size and placement of these images on the page and throughout the annual report.

2. The roles in which women, visible minorities, and older workers and clients are depicted. For example, are women shown more in traditional or nontraditional occupations and nonwork roles in these annual reports?

3. If several years of annual reports are available, pick one that is at least a decade old and compare its visual representation of and role depictions of women, visible minorities, and older employees and clients.

If possible, pick one of the most blatantly stereotypical illustrations you can find in these annual report to show in class, either as a printout or as a computer projection.

Self-Assessment 3.6

ASSESSING YOUR PERSONAL NEED FOR STRUCTURE

PURPOSE This self-assessment is designed to help you estimate your personal need for perceptual structure.

INSTRUCTIONS Read each of the following statements and decide how much you agree with each according to your attitudes, beliefs, and experiences. Then use the scoring key in Appendix B of this book to calculate your results. There are no right or wrong answers to these questions. This self-assessment should be completed alone so that you can rate yourself honestly without concerns of social comparison. However, class discussion will focus on the meaning of need for structure in terms of how we engage differently in the perceptual process at work and in other settings.

Personal Need for Structure Scale

To what extent do you agree or disagree with each of these statements about yourself?	Strongly agree	Moderately agree	Slightly agree	Slightly disagree	Moderately disagree	Strongly disagree	
1. It upsets me to go into a situation without knowing what I can expect from it.	☒	☐	☐	☐	☐	☐	6
2. I'm not bothered by things that interrupt my daily routine.	☐	☒	☐	☐	☐	☐	2
3. I enjoy being spontaneous.	☒	☐	☐	☐	☐	☐	1
4. I find that a well-ordered life with regular hours makes my life tedious.	☐	☒	☐	☐	☐	☐	2
5. I find that a consistent routine enables me to enjoy life more.	☐	☐	☐	☒	☐	☐	3
6. I enjoy having a clear and structured mode of life.	☐	☐	☒	☐	☐	☐	4
7. I like to have a place for everything and everything in its place.	☒	☐	☐	☐	☐	☐	6
8. I don't like situations that are uncertain.	☐	☒	☐	☐	☐	☐	5
9. I hate to change my plans at the last minute.	☐	☐	☒	☐	☐	☐	4
10. I hate to be with people who are unpredictable.	☐	☐	☒	☐	☐	☐	4
11. I enjoy the exhilaration of being in unpredictable situations.	☐	☐	☐	☒	☐	☐	4
12. I become uncomfortable when the rules in a situation are not clear.	☐	☒	☐	☐	☐	☐	5

Source: M.M. Thompson, M.E. Naccarato, and K.E. Parker, "Assessing Cognitive Need: The Development of the Personal Need for Structure and the Personal Fear of Invalidity Scales." Paper presented at the annual meeting of the Canadian Psychological Association, Halifax, Nova Scotia (1989).

Self-Assessment 3.7

ASSESSING YOUR PERSPECTIVE TAKING (COGNITIVE EMPATHY) (STUDENT OLC)

Empathy is an important perceptual ability in social relations, but the degree to which people empathize varies considerably. This self-assessment provides an estimate of one form of empathy, known as *cognitive empathy* or *perspective taking*. This means that it measures the level of cognitive awareness of another person's situational and individual circumstances. To complete this scale, indicate the degree to which each of the statements presented does or does not describe you well. You need to be honest with yourself to get a reasonable estimate of your level of perspective taking. The results show your relative position along the perspective-taking continuum and the general meaning of this score.

Self-Assessment 3.8

ASSESSING YOUR EMOTIONAL EMPATHY (STUDENT OLC)

Empathy is an important perceptual ability in social relations, but the degree to which people empathize varies considerably. This self-assessment provides an estimate of one form of empathy, known as *emotional empathy*. This refers to the extent to which you are able to experience the emotions or feelings of another person. To complete this scale, indicate the degree to which each of the statements presented does or does not describe you well. You need to be honest with yourself to get a reasonable estimate of your level of emotional empathy. The results show your relative position along the emotional empathy continuum and the general meaning of this score.

After reading this chapter, if you feel that you need additional information, see **www.mhhe.com/ mcshane4e** for more in-depth interactivities that correspond to this material.

Employees seem to be as genuinely happy as the customers at Wegmans Food Market. That's probably because the company, which is consistently rated as one of the best places to work in America (and number one in two recent years), bends over backward to make sure its employees get plenty of positive emotions at work. In fact, Wegmans motto is "Employees first, customers second." The Wegmans family believes that happy employees provide the best customer service.

Wegmans Food Market enjoys strong customer loyalty and low employee turnover by keeping employees happy.

Wegmans' 33,000 staff members in New York and four nearby states enjoy above-average pay, health benefits, and other perks, resulting in labor costs of about 16 percent of sales compared to 12 percent at most supermarkets. But it's the everyday "family" feeling that seems to make the biggest difference. "The best way to describe it is a family atmosphere," says Mark Fursman, a bakery manager in Buffalo who has worked at Wegmans for 17 years.

Katie Southard echoes this view. "It's more you're not part of a company, you're part of a family," says Southard, who works in customer service at a Wegmans' store in Rochester, New York. "You're treated as an individual, not just one of the 350 persons in the store."

Wegmans also invests in its employees, then gives them the freedom to do their jobs. The company sent cheese manager Terri Zodarecky on a 10-day trip to cheesemakers in London, Paris, and Italy. Steve O'Malley has also received "a lot of education," including sojourns to California and advanced training at the Culinary Institute of America. Armed with this knowledge, employees are given the freedom to serve customers as best they see fit. "They let me do whatever comes into my head, which is kind of scary sometimes," says part-time meat department worker Bill Gamer. Wegmans operations chief Jack DePeters agrees, half-jokingly suggesting that "We're a $3 billion company run by 16-year-old cashiers."

The financial rewards, family culture, investment in employees, and employee autonomy seem to have the desired effect. While many grocery chains are shrinking or pulling out, Wegmans continues to expand. With happy employees, Wegmans enjoys one of the highest levels of customer loyalty and lowest levels of employee turnover in the industry. Brenda Hidalgo, who works at Wegmans in Buffalo, sums up the positive experience: "I've worked at other places where you wake up and you say 'Ech, I have to go to work,'" she recalls. "Now I love to go to work."[1]

4

Workplace Emotions and Attitudes

After reading this chapter, you should be able to

1. Define *emotions* and identify the two dimensions around which emotions are organized.

2. Explain how cognitions and emotions influence attitudes and behavior.

3. Identify the conditions that require and the problems associated with emotional labor.

4. Describe the four dimensions of emotional intelligence.

5. Summarize the effects of job dissatisfaction in terms of the exit–voice–loyalty–neglect model.

6. Discuss the relationships between job satisfaction and performance as well as between job satisfaction and customer satisfaction.

7. Distinguish affective and continuance commitment, and discuss their influences on employee behavior.

8. Describe five strategies to increase organizational commitment.

9. Contrast transactional and relational psychological contracts, and explain how they vary across cultures and generational cohorts.

Wegmans is a role model for giving employees positive emotional experiences at work. That's because emotions and attitudes can make a huge difference in individual behavior and well-being, as well as in the organization's performance and customer satisfaction. Over the past decade the field of organizational behavior has experienced a dramatic change in thinking about workplace emotions, so this chapter begins by introducing the concept and explaining why researchers are so eager to discover how emotions influence attitudes and behavior.

Next we consider the dynamics of emotional labor, including the conditions requiring emotional labor. This is followed by the popular topic of emotional intelligence, in which we examine the components of emotional intelligence and ways of improving this ability. The specific work attitudes of job satisfaction and organizational commitment are then discussed, including their association with various employee behaviors and work performance. Organizational commitment is strongly influenced by the psychological contract, so the final section of this chapter looks briefly at this topic.

Learning Objectives

After reading this section you should be able to

1. Define *emotions* and identify the two dimensions around which emotions are organized.

2. Explain how cognitions and emotions influence attitudes and behavior.

Emotions in the Workplace

emotions
Psychological, behavioral, and physiological episodes experienced toward an object, person, or event that create a state of readiness.

Emotions have a profound effect on almost everything we do in the workplace. This is a strong statement—and one that you would rarely find a decade ago in organizational behavior research or textbooks. For most of its history the field of OB assumed that a person's thoughts and actions are governed primarily by conscious reasoning (called *cognitions*). Yet groundbreaking neuroscience discoveries have revealed that our perceptions, attitudes, decisions, and behavior are influenced by both cognition and emotion, and that the latter often has the greater influence. By ignoring emotionality, many theories have overlooked a large piece of the puzzle about human behavior in the workplace. Today OB researchers and their colleagues in marketing, economics, and many other social sciences are catching up by making emotions a key part of their research and theories.[2]

So what are emotions? **Emotions** are physiological, behavioral, and psychological episodes experienced toward an object, person, or event that create a state of readiness.[3] There are four key elements of this definition. First, emotions are brief events or *episodes*. Your irritation with a customer, for instance, would typically subside within a few minutes. Second, emotions are directed toward someone or something. We experience joy, fear, anger, and other emotional episodes toward tasks, customers, public speeches we present, a software program we are using, and so on. This contrasts with *moods,* which are less intense emotional states that are not directed toward anything in particular.[4]

Third, emotions are experiences. They represent changes in a person's physiological conditions, such

© 1999 Ted Goff

"Biosensors. The whole company knows instantly when I'm displeased."

as blood pressure, heart rate, and perspiration, as well as changes in behavior, such as facial expression, voice tone, and eye movement. These emotional reactions are involuntary and often occur without our awareness. When aware of these responses, we also develop feelings (worry, fear, boredom) that further mark the emotional experience. The experience of emotion also relates to the fourth element—namely, that emotions put people in a state of readiness. When we get worried, for example, our heart rate and blood pressure increase to better prepare our body to engage in fight or flight. Emotions are also communications to our conscious selves. Some emotions (such as anger, surprise, and fear) are particularly strong "triggers" that interrupt our train of thought, demand our attention, and generate the motivation to take action. They make us aware of events that may affect our survival and well-being.[5]

Types of Emotions

Emotions come in many forms, and experts have generally organized them around two or three dimensions. The most widely recognized arrangement is the circumplex model of emotions shown in Exhibit 4.1, which organizes emotions on the basis of their pleasantness and activation (the extent that the emotion produces alertness and motivation to act).[6] Fear, for example, is an unpleasant experience (we try to avoid conditions that generate fear) and has high activation (it motivates us to act).

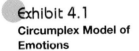

Exhibit 4.1

Circumplex Model of Emotions

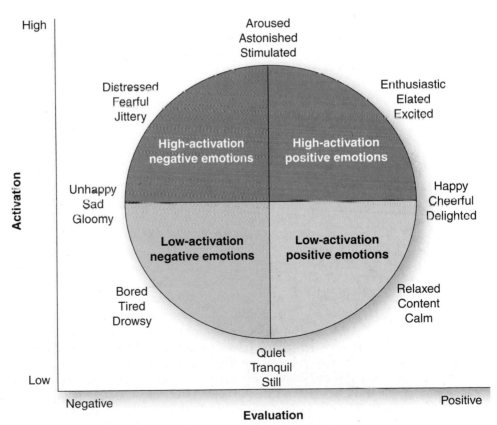

Source: Adapted from J. Larson, E. Diener, and R.E. Lucas, "Emotion: Models, Measures, and Differences," in *Emotions in the Workplace*, ed. R.G. Lord, R.J. Klimoski, and R. Kanfer (San Francisco: Jossey-Bass, 2002), pp. 64–113; J.A. Russell, "Core Affect and the Psychological Construction of Emotion," *Psychological Review* 110, no. 1 (2003), pp. 145–72.

Emotions on the opposite side of the circle have the opposite effect. As we see in Exhibit 4.1, calm is the opposite of fear; it is a pleasant experience that produces little activation in us.

Emotions, Attitudes, and Behavior

attitudes

The cluster of beliefs, assessed feelings, and behavioral intentions toward an object.

Emotions influence our thoughts and behavior, but to explain this effect we first need to know about attitudes. **Attitudes** represent the cluster of beliefs, assessed feelings, and behavioral intentions toward a person, object, or event (called an *attitude object*).[7] Attitudes are *judgments,* whereas emotions are *experiences.* In other words, attitudes involve conscious logical reasoning, whereas emotions operate as events, often without our awareness. We also experience most emotions briefly, whereas our attitude toward someone or something is more stable over time.

Attitudes include three components—beliefs, feelings, and behavioral intentions—and we'll look at each of them using attitude toward mergers as an illustration:

- *Beliefs.* These are your established perceptions about the attitude object—what you believe to be true. For example, you might believe that mergers reduce job security for employees in the merged firms. Or you might believe that mergers increase a company's competitiveness in this era of globalization. These beliefs are perceived facts that you acquire from past experience and other forms of learning.

- *Feelings.* Feelings represent your positive or negative evaluations of the attitude object. Some people think mergers are good; others think they are bad. Your like or dislike of mergers represents your assessed feelings toward the attitude object.

- *Behavioral intentions.* These represent your motivation to engage in a particular behavior with respect to the attitude object. You might plan to quit rather than stay with the company during a merger. Alternatively, you might intend to e-mail the company CEO to say that this merger was a good decision.

Traditional Cognitive Model of Attitudes   Until recently, attitude experts assumed that these three attitude components are connected to each other and to behavior only through the cognitive (logical reasoning) process shown on the left side of Exhibit 4.2. Let's look at the left side of the model more closely. First, our beliefs about mergers are formed from various learning experiences, such as reading about the effects of mergers in other organizations or personally experiencing them in the past.

Next, beliefs about mergers shape our feelings toward them. Suppose you are certain that mergers improve the organization's competitiveness (positive outcome with high probability) and sometimes reduce job security (negative outcome with medium probability) for employees in the merged organization. Overall you might have a somewhat positive attitude toward mergers if your feelings about corporate competitiveness are stronger than your feelings about reduced job security. The probabilities of those outcomes also weight their effect on your feelings.

In the third step of the model, feelings directly influence behavioral intentions.[8] However, two people with the same feelings might have different behavioral intentions based on their past experience and personality. Some employees with negative feelings toward mergers may intend to quit, whereas others might want to complain about the decision. People choose the behavioral intention that they think will work best or make them feel most comfortable.

Exhibit 4.2

Model of Emotions, Attitudes, and Behavior

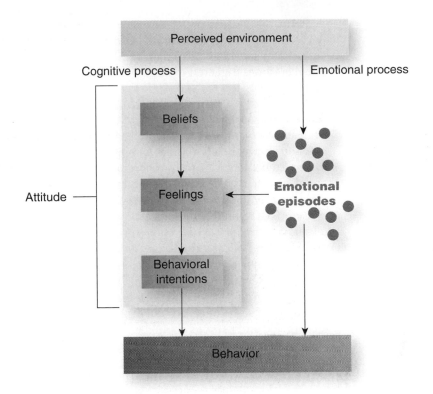

In the final step, behavioral intentions are better than feelings or beliefs at predicting a person's behavior because they are specific to that behavior. Even so, behavioral intentions might not predict behavior very well because intentions represent only the motivation to act, whereas behavior is also caused by the other three factors in the MARS model—ability, role perceptions, and situational factors. You might plan to send an e-mail to management complaining about the announced merger, but perhaps you never get around to this task due to a heavy workload and family obligations.

How Emotions Influence Attitudes and Behavior   The cognitive model has dominated attitude research for decades, yet we now know that it describes only partially what really happens.[9] According to neuroscience research, incoming information from our senses is routed to the emotional center as well as the cognitive (logical reasoning) center of our brain.[10] We have already described the logical reasoning process, depicted on the left side of Exhibit 4.2. The right side of Exhibit 4.2 offers a simple depiction of how emotions influence our attitudes and behavior.

The emotional side of attitude formation begins with the dynamics of the perceptual process, particularly perceptual interpretation, described in Chapter 3. When receiving incoming sensory information, we automatically form emotions regarding that information before consciously thinking about it.[11] More specifically, the emotional center quickly and imprecisely evaluates whether the incoming sensory information supports or threatens our innate drives, then attaches emotional markers to the information. These are not calculated feelings; they are automatic and unconscious emotional responses based on very thin slices of sensory information.

Returning to our previous example, you might experience excitement, worry, nervousness, or happiness upon learning that your company intends to merge with a competitor. The large dots on the right side of Exhibit 4.2 illustrate these multiple emotional episodes triggered by the merger announcement, subsequent thinking about the merger, discussion with co-workers about the merger, and so on. These emotions are transmitted to the logical reasoning process, where they swirl around and ultimately shape our conscious feelings toward the attitude object.[12] Thus while you consciously evaluate the merger—that is, logically figure out whether it is a good or bad thing—your emotions have already formed an opinion that then sways your thoughts. If you experience excitement, delight, comfort, and other positive emotions whenever you think about or discuss the merger, then these positive emotional episodes will lean your logical reasoning toward positive feelings regarding the merger.[13]

Emotions operate automatically and unconsciously most of the time, but research tells us that the logical reasoning process actually "listens in" on the person's emotions and uses this information when translating beliefs into feelings.[14] When thinking about whether the announced merger is good or bad, we try to understand our emotional reactions to the event, then use this emotional awareness as factual information in our logical evaluation. In some cases the perceived emotions change the values of some beliefs or the probabilities that they are true. If you sense that you are worried and nervous about the merger, then your logical analysis might pay more attention to your belief about job insecurity and put less weight on your belief that mergers increase the organization's competitiveness.

You can see how emotions affect workplace attitudes. When performing our jobs or interacting with co-workers, we experience a variety of emotions that shape our longer-term feelings toward the company, our boss, the job itself, and so on. The more we experience positive emotions, the more we form positive attitudes toward the targets of those emotions.

The opening story to this chapter described how Wegmans strategically tries to ensure that employees experience plenty of positive emotional episodes each day. Many firms specifically teach employees four principles developed at Pike Place Fish Market in Seattle, Washington. These Fish! principles—play, make their day, be there, and choose your attitude—help staff to be more upbeat at work and contribute to positive emotions in others. The Fish! principles emerged when Pike Place fishmongers turned a money-losing, morale-draining business into a world-famous attraction by deciding to have fun at work. Connections 4.1 looks at other means by which organizations have created positive emotions.

When Cognitions and Emotions Conflict   The influence of both logical reasoning and emotions on attitudes is most apparent when they disagree with each other. Everyone occasionally experiences this mental tug-of-war, sensing that something isn't right even though they can't think of any logical reason to be concerned. This conflicting experience indicates that our logical analysis of the situation (left side of Exhibit 4.2) can't identify reasons to support the automatic emotional reaction (right side of Exhibit 4.2).[15] Should we pay attention to our emotional response or our logical analysis? This question is not easy to answer because, as we just learned, the emotional and rational processes interact with each other so closely. However, some studies indicate that while executives tend to make quick decisions based on their gut feelings (emotional response), the best decisions tend to occur when executives spend time logically evaluating the situation.[16] Thus we should pay attention to both the cognitive and emotional sides of the attitude model, and hope they agree with each other most of the time!

Serious Fun

Walk into the offices of CXtec in Syracuse, New York, and you might think employees are in the middle of a birthday party. Around the cubicles are colorful clusters of helium-filled balloons, each representing a small token of the company's appreciation for performing their work effectively. Employees at the computer networking equipment company also enjoy a break room with billiards, foosball, and air hockey. And if staff want a little more enjoyment, the company also sponsors miniature golf tournaments in the office, tricycle races around the building, and "CXtec Idol" competitions. Of course all of this fits in with what the company stands for: "Part of our core values is that work is fun," explains Paula Miller, CXtec's director of employee and community relations.

Fun at work? It sounds like an oxymoron. But to attract and motivate valuable talent, companies are finding creative ways to generate positive emotions in the workplace. About six times each year, credit department staff at Zebra Technologies in Vernon Hills, Illinois, head off to the Whirlyball center, a large rink where employees grab and toss a ball using handheld scoops and electric bumper cars. The Malaysian operations of Scope International, a division of British bank Standard Chartered, won an award for bringing fun into the workplace—such as color coordination days, in which employees wear the same color clothing on a particular day. Along with enjoying office nerf gun fights, robot combat tournaments, movie nights, and wine tours, employees at Nuvation in San Jose, California, showcase a life-size fiberglass blue and orange moose. "We like to take the moose out to our parties," says Nuvation cofounder Geoff White.

These fun and games may seem silly, but some corporate leaders are serious about their value. "It's pretty

CXtec employees in Syracuse, New York, like to live up to their company values, which include having fun at work.

simple," explains an executive at Quebecor. "If you want to make the most money, you must attract the best people. To get the best people, you must be the most fun."

Sources: J. Elliott, "All Work and No Play Can Chase Workers Away," *Edmonton Journal,* 28 February 2000; M.A. Tan, "Management: Having Fun at Work," *The Edge Malaysia,* 10 February 2003; R. Deruyter, "Firm's Goals Are Business Success and Having Fun," *Kitchener Waterloo Record,* 30 October 2004, p. F1; S.K. Wong, "How Do Some Big companies Spell Teamwork? Whirlyball," *The Columbian* (Vancouver, WA), 19 March 2006, p. E1; T. Knauss, "Small Company Is a Happy Place to Work," *Post Standard/Herald-Journal* (Syracuse, New York), 21 March 2006, p. A1.

One last observation about the attitude model in Exhibit 4.2 relates to the arrow directly from the emotional episodes to behavior. This indicates that people have direct behavioral reactions to their emotions. Even low-intensity emotions automatically change your facial expressions. High-intensity emotions can have a more powerful effect, which is apparent when an upset employee bangs a fist on a desk or an overjoyed colleague embraces someone nearby. These actions are not carefully thought out. They are fairly automatic emotional responses that serve as coping mechanisms in that situation.[17]

Cognitive Dissonance   Emotions and attitudes usually lead to behavior, but the opposite sometimes occurs.[18] Suppose you volunteered to take a foreign assignment. You weren't particularly interested in the posting, but thought that it might be necessary for promotion into senior management. However, you later learn that most people become senior managers in this firm without spending any time in foreign

cognitive dissonance

A psychological tension that occurs when people perceive an inconsistency between their beliefs, feelings, and behavior.

assignment. This inconsistency between a person's beliefs, feelings, and behavior situation creates an uncomfortable tension called **cognitive dissonance.** In this example your behavior (taking a foreign assignment) is inconsistent with your beliefs and feelings toward foreign postings.

Behavior is usually the most difficult element to change, particularly when that behavior has been observed by others (it can't be denied), was done voluntarily, and can't be undone. Thus people usually change their beliefs and feelings to reduce the inconsistency. In our example you might convince yourself that the foreign posting is not so bad after all because it will develop your management skills. Alternatively, you might downplay the features that previously made the foreign posting less desirable. Suddenly a somewhat negative attitude toward foreign assignments has changed to a more favorable one.

Emotions and Personality   Coverage of the dynamics of workplace emotions wouldn't be complete unless the role of personality was also mentioned. The extent to which people experience positive or negative emotions at work is partly determined by their personalities, not just workplace experiences.[19] Some people experience positive emotions as a natural trait. These people are generally extroverted—outgoing, talkative, sociable, and assertive (see Chapter 2). In contrast, some people have a tendency to experience more negative emotions. Positive and negative emotional traits affect a person's attendance, turnover, and long-term work attitudes. For example, several studies have found that people with a negative emotional trait have lower levels of job satisfaction. Also, employees with a natural tendency to experience negative emotions tend to have higher levels of job burnout.[20] Although these positive and negative personality traits have some effect, other research concludes that the actual situation in which people work has a noticeably stronger influence on their attitudes and behavior.[21]

Learning Objectives

After reading the next two sections you should be able to

3.   **Identify the conditions that require and the problems associated with emotional labor.**

4.   **Describe the four dimensions of emotional intelligence.**

Managing Emotions at Work

The Elbow Room Café is packed and noisy on this Saturday morning. A customer at the restaurant in Vancouver, Canada, half-shouts across the room for more coffee. A passing waiter scoffs, "You want more coffee, get it yourself!" The customer only laughs. Another diner complains loudly that he and his party are running late and need their food. This time restaurant manager Patrick Savoie speaks up: "If you're in a hurry, you should have gone to McDonald's." The diner and his companions chuckle.

To the uninitiated, the Elbow Room Café is an emotional basket case, full of irate guests and the rudest staff on Canada's West Coast. But it's all a performance—a place where guests can enjoy good food and play out their emotions about dreadful customer service. "It's almost like coming to a theater," says Savoie, who spends much of his time inventing new ways to insult the clientele.[22]

Whether it's the most insulting service at Elbow Room Café in Vancouver or the friendliest service at Wegmans in Rochester or Albany, New York, employees are usually expected to manage their emotions in the workplace. **Emotional labor** refers to the effort, planning, and control needed to express organizationally desired emotions during interpersonal transactions.[23] When interacting with co-workers,

emotional labor

The effort, planning, and control needed to express organizationally desired emotions during interpersonal transactions.

suppliers, and others, employees are expected to abide by *display rules*. These rules are norms requiring employees to display certain emotions and withhold others.

Conditions Requiring Emotional Labor

Don't be surprised if you hear a cheerful voice when calling the Golden Inn. The Atlantic City hotel sent 175 of its employees to a special customer service training program sponsored by New Jersey's Casino Reinvestment Development Authority (CRDA). CRDA arranged the training program for area businesses to correct one of the biggest complaints mentioned by tourists to the Jersey Shore—rude staff. Guest ratings of employee friendliness and courtesy shot up 5 percent after employees completed the program, prompting general manager John Ellison to award staff a 50-cent-per-hour bonus. "We look for smiles," says Ellison, who now carefully considers a person's positive attitude during job interviews. "You can never have too many smiles at the Shore."[24]

Golden Inn and just about every other organization expect employees to engage in some level of emotional labor, and many provide training so staff know exactly what emotions to display and when to display them. For instance, the Ritz-Carlton Hotel Company's motto is "Smile—we are on stage." To ensure that this standard is maintained at the 60 properties it manages around the world, the Ritz developed a detailed training program that teaches staff how to look pleasant in front of guests. Its orientation manual even includes two pages on phrases to use and to avoid saying, such as "My pleasure" rather than "OK, sure." Emotional labor is higher in jobs requiring a variety of emotions (such as anger as well as joy) and more intense emotions (showing delight rather than smiling weakly), as well as where interaction with clients is frequent and for longer durations. Emotional labor also increases when employees must precisely rather than casually abide by the display rules.[25]

Emotional Display Norms across Cultures   How much we are expected to hide or reveal our true emotions in public depends to some extent on the culture in which we live. Cultural values in some countries—particularly Ethiopia, Korea, Japan, and Austria—expect people to display a neutral emotional demeanor. In the workplace and other public settings, employees try to subdue their emotional expression and minimize physical contact with others. Even voice intonation tends to be monotonic. In other countries—notably Kuwait, Egypt, Spain, and Russia—cultural values allow or encourage open display of one's true emotions. People are expected to be transparent in revealing their thoughts and feelings, dramatic in their conversational tones, and animated in their use of nonverbal behaviors to get their messages across. These cultural variations in emotional display can be quite noticeable. One survey reported that 83 percent of Japanese believe it is inappropriate to get emotional in a business context, compared with 40 percent of Americans, 34 percent of French, and only 29 percent of Italians. In other words, Italians are more likely to accept or tolerate people who display their true emotions at work, whereas this would be considered rude or embarrassing in Japan.[26]

Emotional Dissonance

Emotional labor can be challenging for most of us because it is difficult to conceal true emotions and to display the emotions required by the job. The main problem is that joy, sadness, worry, and other emotions automatically activate a complex set of facial muscles that are difficult to restrain and equally difficult to fake. Our true emotions tend to reveal themselves as subtle gestures, usually without our awareness. Meanwhile,

Localizing Emotional Display Rules at Four Seasons Hotels As one of the world's leading operators of luxury hotels, Four Seasons Hotels and Resorts trains employees and audits hotel performance to ensure that guests consistently experience the highest standards of service quality. Yet Four Seasons also adapts its legendary service to the local culture. "McDonald's is the same all over. We do not want to be that way; we are not a cookie-cutter company," says Four Seasons executive David Crowl. One of the most obvious forms of localization is in the way Four Seasons staff are allowed to display emotions that reflect their own culture. "What changes [from one country to the next] is that people do it with their own style, grace, and personality," explains Antoine Corinthios, president of Four Seasons' operations in Europe, Middle East, and Africa. "In some cultures you add the strong local temperament. For example, an Italian concierge has his own style and flair. In Turkey or Egypt you experience different hospitality."[27]

pretending to be cheerful or concerned is difficult because several specific facial muscles and body positions must be coordinated. More often than not, observers see when we are faking and sense that we feel a different emotion.[28]

emotional dissonance
A conflict between a person's required and true emotions.

Emotional labor also tends to create a conflict between required and true emotions, called **emotional dissonance.** The larger the gap between the required and true emotions, the more employees tend to experience stress, job burnout, and psychological separation from self.[29] One way to minimize emotional dissonance is by hiring people with a natural tendency to display the emotions required for the job. For example, when CiCi's Pizza opens new stores, it looks for job applicants with a "happy, cheery" attitude. The restaurant franchise believes that it is easier to teach new skills than attitudes. "We hire for attitude and train for skill," says one of CiCi's franchisees.[30]

But even with a good fit between the person's natural disposition and the required emotions for the job, some acting is required to perform the job. The problem is that most of us engage in *surface acting;* we modify our behavior to be consistent with required emotions but continue to hold different internal feelings. For instance, we force a smile while greeting a customer whom we consider rude. The solution is to follow the practice of great actors—namely, engage in *deep acting*. Deep acting involves changing true emotions to match the required emotions. Rather than feeling irritated by a rude customer, you might view your next interaction with that person as an opportunity to test your sales skills. This change in perspective can potentially generate more positive emotions next time you meet that difficult customer, which produces friendlier displays of emotion.[31] However, it also requires considerable emotional intelligence, which we discuss next.

Emotional Intelligence

GM Holden's new production facility at Port Melbourne was General Motors' largest investment in Australia in decades, so executives carefully selected the plant's design team, managers, and production staff. Still, it wasn't long before the project unraveled due to infighting and interpersonal tensions. Consultants called in to analyze the problems offered the following solution: Employees need to improve their emotional intelligence. With this advice, the 30 plant design team members and over 300 other employees from production through management completed an emotional intelligence assessment and attended training modules on effective self-expression, understanding others, controlling emotions, and related topics.

To overcome skepticism about its touchy-feely nature, the emotional intelligence and leadership development program was evaluated to see whether employee scores improved and behavior changed. The results found an average 50 percent increase on EI scores, while behavior became much more cooperative and diplomatic. "It has greatly improved communication within the team and with other teams outside the plant," says GM Holden quality systems engineer Vesselka Vassileva. Some employees also note that it has improved their interpersonal behavior outside the workplace. "I'm not so aggressive or assertive," says manufacturing engineer Alf Moore. "I feel better, and it's helped me at home."[32]

GM Holden's new production facility started up more smoothly than might have occurred because the company paid attention to **emotional intelligence (EI)**. EI is the ability to perceive and express emotion, assimilate emotion in thought, understand and reason with emotion, and regulate emotion in oneself and others.[33] In other words, EI represents a set of *competencies* that allow us to perceive, understand, and regulate emotions in ourselves and in others. Exhibit 4.3 illustrates the most recent EI model. According to this model, EI can be organized into four dimensions representing the recognition of emotions in ourselves and in others, as well as the regulation of emotions in ourselves and in others. Each dimension consists of a set of emotional competencies that people must possess to fulfill that dimension of emotional intelligence.[34]

emotional intelligence (EI)
The ability to perceive and express emotion, assimilate emotion in thought, understand and reason with emotion, and regulate emotion in oneself and others.

Exhibit 4.3
Dimensions of Emotional Intelligence

	Self (personal competence)	Other (social competence)
Recognition of emotions	**Self-Awareness** • Emotional self-awareness • Accurate self-assessment • Self-confidence	**Social Awareness** • Empathy • Organizational awareness • Service
Regulation of emotions	**Self-Management** • Emotional self-control • Transparency • Adaptability • Achievement • Initiative • Optimism	**Relationship Management** • Inspirational leadership • Influence • Developing others • Change catalyst • Conflict management • Building bonds • Teamwork and collaboration

Sources: D. Goleman, R. Boyatzis, and A. McKee, *Primal Leadership* (Boston: Harvard Business School Press, 2002), Chapter 3; D. Goleman, "An EI-Based Theory of Performance," in *The Emotionally Intelligent Workplace, ed.* C. Cherniss and D. Goleman (San Francisco: Jossey-Bass, 2001), p. 28.

- *Self-awareness.* Self-awareness refers to having a deep understanding of one's own emotions as well as strengths, weaknesses, values, and motives. Self-aware people are better able to listen to their emotional responses to specific situations and to use this awareness as conscious information.[35]

- *Self-management.* This represents how well we control or redirect our internal states, impulses, and resources. It includes keeping disruptive impulses in check, displaying honesty and integrity, being flexible in times of change, maintaining the drive to perform well and seize opportunities, and remaining optimistic even after failure. Self-management involves an inner conversation that guides our behavior.

- *Social awareness.* Social awareness is mainly about *empathy*–having understanding and sensitivity to the feelings, thoughts, and situations of others (see Chapter 3). This includes understanding another person's situation, experiencing the other person's emotions, and knowing their needs even though unstated. Social awareness extends beyond empathy to include being organizationally aware, such as sensing office politics and understanding social networks.

- *Relationship management.* This dimension of EI refers to managing other people's emotions. It is linked to a wide variety of practices, such as inspiring others,- influencing people's beliefs and feelings, developing others' capabilities, managing change, resolving conflict, cultivating relationships, and supporting teamwork and collaboration. These activities also require effective emotional expression–intentionally communicating emotions to others, usually to influence their emotions and behavior.

These four dimensions of emotional intelligence form a hierarchy.[36] Self-awareness is the lowest level of EI because it does not require the other dimensions; instead it is a prerequisite for the other three dimensions. Self-management and social awareness are necessarily above self-awareness in the EI hierarchy. You can't manage your own emotions (self-management) if you aren't good at knowing your own emotions (self-awareness). Relationship management is the highest level of EI because it requires all three other dimensions. In other words, we require a high degree of emotional intelligence to master relationship management because this set of competencies requires sufficiently high levels of self-awareness, self-management, and social awareness.

EI has its roots in the social intelligence literature introduced more than 80 years ago, but scholars since then focused mainly on cognitive intelligence (IQ). Now leaders at GM Holden and other companies are realizing that EI is an important set of competencies in the performance of most jobs. Recall from Chapter 2 that people perform better when their aptitudes–including general intelligence–match the job requirements. But most jobs also involve social interaction, so employees also need emotional intelligence to work effectively in social settings. The evidence so far indicates that people with high EI are better at interpersonal relations, perform better in jobs requiring emotional labor, and are more successful in many aspects of job interviews. Teams whose members have high emotional intelligence initially perform better than teams with low EI.[37]

Improving Emotional Intelligence

Emotional intelligence is associated with conscientiousness and other personality traits. However, EI can also be learned to some extent, so GM Holden and other companies put employees through EI training programs. "We've developed a seven-hour training program on emotional intelligence," says an executive at BB&T Corp., a large financial services company based in Winston-Salem, North Carolina. "We believe it really helps people grow as employees." In support of the training approach, a recent study reported that business students scored higher on emotional intelligence after taking an undergraduate interpersonal skills course.[38] Although training helps, a more effective way to improve EI is through personal coaching, plenty of practice, and frequent feedback. EI also increases with age; it is part of the process called maturity. Overall, emotional intelligence offers considerable potential, but we also have a lot to learn about its measurement and effects on people in the workplace.

So far this chapter has laid out the model of emotions and attitudes, but we also need to understand specific workplace attitudes. The next two sections of this chapter look at two of the most widely studied attitudes: job satisfaction and organizational commitment.

Learning Objectives

After reading this section you should be able to

5. **Summarize the effects of job dissatisfaction in terms of the exit–voice–loyalty–neglect model.**
6. **Discuss the relationships between job satisfaction and performance as well as job satisfaction and customer satisfaction.**

Job Satisfaction

job satisfaction
A person's evaluation of his or her job and work context.

Job satisfaction, a person's evaluation of his or her job and work context, is probably the most studied attitude in organizational behavior.[39] It is an *appraisal* of the perceived job characteristics, work environment, and emotional experiences at work. Satisfied employees have a favorable evaluation of their jobs, based on their observations and emotional experiences. Job satisfaction is really a collection of attitudes about different aspects of the job and work context. You might like your co-workers but be less satisfied with the workload, for instance.

How satisfied are employees at work? In the most recent surveys, more than 85 percent of Americans are somewhat or very satisfied with their jobs—a level that has been consistent for more than a decade. Exhibit 4 4 shows that Americans also have high levels of job satisfaction compared with people in most other countries. Only employees in Denmark, India, and Norway say they are happier at work. Another survey found that Americans had the third highest job satisfaction, after Brazilians and Canadians, among the 10 largest economies in the world. In contrast, employees in most Asian countries report lower job satisfaction. One study of 115,000 Asian employees reported that 63 percent are satisfied overall with their jobs.[40]

It's probably fair to conclude that employees in India and the United States are more satisfied than in some other parts of the world, but we also need to be somewhat cautious about these and other job satisfaction surveys. One problem is that surveys often use a single direct question, such as "How satisfied are you with your job?" Many dissatisfied employees are reluctant to reveal their feelings in a direct question because this is tantamount to admitting that they made a poor job choice and are not enjoying life. For instance, three recent surveys in the United States, Canada, and Malaysia found that although most employees in those countries say they are satisfied with their job and work environment, more than half would abandon their employers if offered comparable jobs elsewhere![41]

A second problem is that cultural values make it difficult to compare job satisfaction across countries. People in China, South Korea, and Japan tend to subdue their emotions in public, so they probably avoid extreme survey ratings such as "very satisfied." A third problem is that job satisfaction changes with economic conditions.

Exhibit 4.4   **Job Satisfaction across Cultures**

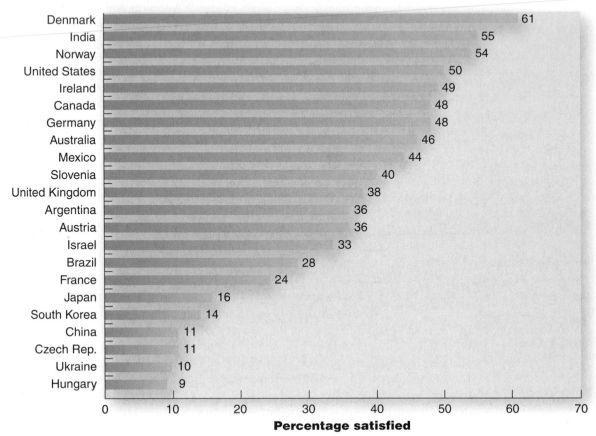

Source: Based on Ipsos-Reid survey of 9,300 employees in 39 countries in mid-2000. See "Ipsos-Reid Global Poll Finds Major Differences in Employee Satisfaction around the World," Ipsos-Reid News Release, 8 January 2001. A sample of 22 countries across the range is shown here, including all of the top-scoring countries.

Employees with the highest job satisfaction tend to be in countries where the economies are booming at the time of the survey.[42]

Job Satisfaction and Work Behavior

Job satisfaction affects many of the individual behaviors mentioned in Chapter 2. A useful template to organize and understand the consequences of job dissatisfaction is the **exit–voice–loyalty–neglect (EVLN) model.** As the name suggests, the EVLN model identifies four ways in which employees respond to dissatisfaction:[43]

exit-voice-loyalty-neglect (EVLN) model
The four ways, as indicated in the name, employees respond to job dissatisfaction.

- *Exit.* Exit refers to leaving the organization, transferring to another work unit, or at least trying to make these exits. Employee turnover is a well-established outcome of job dissatisfaction, particularly for employees with better job opportunities elsewhere. Exit usually follows specific "shock events," such as when your boss treats you unfairly.[44] These shock events generate strong emotions that energize employees to think about and search for alternative employment.

- *Voice.* Voice refers to any attempt to change, rather than escape from, a dissatisfying situation. Voice can be a constructive response, such as recommending ways for management to improve the situation; or it can be more confrontational, such as filing formal grievances.[45] In the extreme, some employees might engage in counterproductive behaviors to get attention and force changes in the organization.

- *Loyalty.* Loyalty has been described in different ways, but the most widely held view is that "loyalists" are employees who respond to dissatisfaction by patiently waiting–some say they "suffer in silence"–for a problem to work itself out or get resolved by others.[46]

- *Neglect.* Neglect includes reducing work effort, paying less attention to quality, and increasing absenteeism and lateness. It is generally considered a passive activity that has negative consequences for the organization.

Which of the four EVLN alternatives do employees use? It depends on the person and situation. One determining factor is the availability of alternative employment. With poor job prospects, employees are less likely to use the exit option. Those who identify with the organization are also more likely to use voice rather than exit. Highly conscientious people are less likely to engage in neglect and more likely to engage in voice. Some experts suggest that employees differ in their EVLN behavior depending on whether they have high or low collectivism. Finally, past experience influences our choice of action. Employees who were unsuccessful with voice in the past are more likely to engage in exit or neglect when experiencing job dissatisfaction in the future.[47]

Job Satisfaction and Performance

One of the oldest beliefs in the business world is that "a happy worker is a productive worker." Is this statement true? Over several decades, organizational behavior scholars have flip-flopped on their answers on this question. Long ago they were reasonably confident that the statement was true. Later, doubts emerged as studies found a weak or negligible association between job satisfaction and task performance.[48] Now the evidence suggests that the popular saying may be correct after all. Citing problems with the earlier studies, a recent meta-analysis (which combines results from the previous studies) concluded that there is a *moderate* relationship between job satisfaction and job performance. In other words, happy workers really are more productive workers *to some extent*.[49]

Even with a moderate association between job satisfaction and performance, there are a few underlying reasons why the relationship isn't even stronger.[50] One argument is that general attitudes (such as job satisfaction) don't predict specific behaviors very well. As we learned with the EVLN model, job dissatisfaction can lead to a variety of outcomes rather than lower job performance (neglect). Some employees continue to work productively while they complain (voice), look for another job (exit), or patiently wait for the problem to be fixed (loyalty).

A second explanation is that job performance leads to job satisfaction (rather than vice versa), but only when performance is linked to valued rewards. Higher performers receive more rewards and, consequently, are more satisfied than low-performing employees who receive fewer rewards. The connection between job satisfaction and performance isn't stronger because many organizations do not reward good performance. The third explanation is that job satisfaction might influence employee motivation, but this has little influence on performance in jobs where employees have little control over their job output (such as assembly line work). This point explains why the job satisfaction–performance relationship is strongest in complex jobs, where employees have more freedom to perform their work or to slack off.

Job Satisfaction and Customer Satisfaction

The opening story to this chapter revealed that Wegmans Food Markets has an unusual motto: Employees first, customers second. The grocery chain definitely puts employees on top of the stakeholder list, but why not customers first? Wegmans' rationale is that customer satisfaction follows from employee satisfaction. In other words, it is difficult to keep customers happy if employee morale is low. Virgin Group founder Sir Richard Branson agrees with that theory. "It just seems common sense to me that if you start with a happy, well-motivated workforce, you're much more likely to have happy customers," says Branson.[51]

Fortunately, research generally agrees that job satisfaction has a positive effect on customer satisfaction.[52] There are two main reasons for this relationship. First, employees are usually in a more positive mood when they feel satisfied with their jobs and working conditions. Employees in a good mood display friendliness and positive emotions more naturally and frequently, and this creates positive emotions for customers. Second, satisfied employees are less likely to quit their jobs, so they have better knowledge and skills to serve clients. Lower turnover also gives customers the same employees to serve them, so there is more consistent service. There is some evidence that customers build their loyalty to specific employees, not to the organization, so keeping employee turnover low tends to build customer loyalty.[53]

Before leaving this topic, it's worth mentioning that job satisfaction does more than improve work behaviors and customer satisfaction. Job satisfaction is also an ethical issue that influences the organization's reputation in the community. People spend a large portion of their time working in organizations, and many societies now expect companies to provide work environments that are safe and enjoyable. Indeed, employees in several countries closely monitor ratings of the best companies to work for—an indication that employee satisfaction is a virtue worth considerable goodwill to employers. This virtue is apparent when an organization has low job satisfaction. The company tries to hide this fact, and when morale problems become public, corporate leaders are usually quick to improve the situation.

Happy Staff Means Happy Guests at Outback Restaurants Outback Steakhouse, Inc., has become a phenomenal success story in America's competitive restaurant industry. In 1988 Outback's four partners each opened a restaurant in Tampa, Florida, based on popular images of casual lifestyle and tucker in the land Down Under. Today Outback's 65,000 employees work in 1,100 restaurants around the United States and Canada. Although the Australian theme launched the company's success, Outback founder and CEO says staff quality deserves as much credit. Long before scholars pointed out that satisfied employees provide better customer service, Outback was applying this principle. "Outback's theory of success is that you hire the right people and take care of them," explained founder Chris Sullivan and three colleagues in a recent journal article. The company hires and creates a culture that supports energized employees who stay with the company and provide excellent service. This service makes customers happy, which brings them back and encourages them to recommend Outback to friends. The result of such customer satisfaction is higher sales, which improve company profits.[54]

Learning Objectives

After reading the next two sections you should be able to

7. **Distinguish affective and continuance commitment, and discuss their influences on employee behavior.**
8. **Describe five strategies to increase organizational commitment.**
9. **Contrast transactional and relational psychological contracts, and explain how they vary across cultures and generational cohorts.**

Organizational Commitment

Along with job satisfaction, OB researchers have been intently interested in an attitude called organizational commitment. **Organizational commitment** refers to the employee's emotional attachment to, identification with, and involvement in a particular organization.[55] This definition refers specifically to *affective commitment* because it is an emotional attachment—our feelings of loyalty—to the organization.

Another form of commitment, called **continuance commitment,** occurs when employees believe it is in their own personal interest to remain with the organization. It is a calculated rather than emotional attachment to the organization.[56] Employees have high continuance commitment when they do not particularly identify with the organization where they work but feel bound to remain there because it would be too costly to quit. This reluctance to quit may be due to the risk of losing a large bonus by leaving early or because they are well established in the community where they work.[57]

Consequences of Organizational Commitment

Corporate leaders have good reason to pay close attention to employee loyalty because it can be a significant competitive advantage. Employees with high levels of affective commitment are less likely to quit their jobs and be absent from work. Organizational commitment also improves customer satisfaction because long-tenure employees have better knowledge of work practices, and clients like to do business with the same employees. Employees with high affective commitment also have higher work motivation and organizational citizenship, as well as somewhat higher job performance.[58]

Employees can also have too much affective commitment. One concern is that organizational loyalty reduces turnover, which may limit the organization's opportunity to hire new employees with different knowledge and fresh perspectives. Another concern is that loyalty results in conformity, which can undermine creativity and ethical conduct. For instance, a former executive at Arthur Andersen claims that one reason for the accounting firm's downfall was that it created a cultlike level of employee loyalty where no one questioned or second-guessed top management's decisions.[59]

Consequences of Continuance Commitment Creating too much affective commitment is probably much less of a problem compared with concerns about company practices that increase continuance commitment. Many firms tie employees financially to the organization through low-cost loans, stock options, deferred bonuses, and other "golden handcuffs." Brokerage firms on Wall Street apparently suppress employee turnover through a deferred compensation scheme in which brokers agree to receive up to 25 percent of their pay (often in the form of discounted company stock) two years later, but only if they stay until then.[60]

organizational commitment
The employee's emotional attachment to, identification with, and involvement in a particular organization.

continuance commitment
A calculative decision to remain with an organization because quitting would be costly.

These financial incentives (or penalties) to remain with the organization tend to reduce turnover, but they also increase continuance commitment, not affective commitment. Research suggests that employees with high levels of continuance commitment have *lower* performance ratings and are *less* likely to engage in organizational citizenship behaviors! Furthermore, unionized employees with high continuance commitment are more likely to use formal grievances, whereas employees with high affective commitment engage in more constructive problem solving when employee–employer relations sour.[61] Although some level of financial connection may be necessary, employers should not confuse continuance commitment with employee loyalty. Employers still need to win employees' hearts (affective commitment) beyond tying them financially to the organization (continuance commitment).

Building Organizational Commitment

There are almost as many ways to build organizational loyalty as topics in this textbook, but the following list is most prominent in the literature:

- *Justice and support.* Affective commitment is higher in organizations that fulfill their obligations to employees and abide by humanitarian values, such as fairness, courtesy, forgiveness, and moral integrity. These values relate to the concept of organizational justice that we discuss in the next chapter. Similarly, organizations that support employee well-being tend to cultivate higher levels of loyalty in return.[62]

- *Shared values.* The definition of affective commitment refers to a person's identification with the organization, and that identification is highest when employees believe their values are congruent with the organization's dominant values. Also, employees experience more comfort and predictability when they agree with the values underlying corporate decisions. This comfort increases their motivation to stay with the organization.[63]

- *Trust.* **Trust** refers to positive expectations one person has toward another person in situations involving risk.[64] Trust means putting faith in the other person or group. It is also a reciprocal activity: To receive trust, you must demonstrate trust. Employees identify with and feel obliged to work for an organization only when they trust its leaders. This explains why layoffs are one of the greatest blows to employee loyalty—by reducing job security, companies reduce the trust employees have in their employers and the employment relationship.[65]

- *Organizational comprehension.* Affective commitment is a person's identification with the company, so it makes sense that this attitude is strengthened when employees understand the company, including its past, present, and future. Thus loyalty tends to increase with open and rapid communication to and from corporate leaders, as well as with opportunities to interact with co-workers across the organization.[66]

- *Employee involvement.* Employee involvement increases affective commitment by strengthening the employees' social identity with the organization. Employees feel that they are part of the organization when they take part in decisions that guide the organization's future. Employee involvement also builds loyalty because giving this power is a demonstration of a company's trust in its employees.

Look closely at some of these recommendations: You will see that one of the key influences on organizational commitment is the employment relationship. In particular, affective commitment is sensitive to how well the organization fulfills the psychological contract, which we look at in the last section of this chapter.

trust
A person's positive expectations toward another person in situations involving risk.

Psychological Contracts

When Katherine Certain joined an ad agency not long ago, her expectations included a wide range of job duties, such as calling potential clients and evaluating marketing plans. The recent college graduate did get those responsibilities, along with a few that weren't on her list—such as watering the plants and walking the owner's dogs each day. After the initial shock that she had been given these tasks, Certain began to feel degraded and confused. Less than a year later Certain jumped to a larger ad agency, where so far she hasn't experienced any surprises.[67]

Katherine Certain experienced the shock of having her psychological contract violated. This isn't unusual. According to one university study, 24 percent of employees are "chronically" angry at work, mostly because they feel their employer violated basic promises and didn't fulfill the psychological contract.[68] The **psychological contract** refers to the individual's beliefs about the terms and conditions of a reciprocal exchange agreement between that person and another party. This is inherently perceptual, so one person's understanding of the psychological contract may differ from the other party's understanding. In employment relationships, psychological contracts consist of beliefs about what the employee is entitled to receive and is obliged to offer the employer in return.[69] For example, Katherine Certain believed that her employer would give her responsibilities related to her career interests. Being assigned the duties of watering plants and walking the boss's dogs clearly violated her expectations.

psychological contract
The individual's beliefs about the terms and conditions of a reciprocal exchange agreement between that person and another party.

Types of Psychological Contracts

Psychological contracts vary in many ways.[70] One of the most fundamental differences is the extent to which they are transactional or relational. As Exhibit 4.5 indicates, *transactional contracts* are primarily short-term economic exchanges. Responsibilities are well defined around a fairly narrow set of obligations that do not change over the life of the contract. People hired in temporary positions and as consultants tend to have transactional contracts. To some extent, new employees also form transactional contracts until they develop a sense of continuity with the organization.

Exhibit 4.5

Types of Psychological Contracts in Employment

Contract Characteristics	Transactional	Balanced	Relational
Focus	Economic		Economic and socioemotional
Time frame	Closed-ended and short-term		Open-ended and indefinite
Stability	Static		Dynamic
Scope	Narrow		Pervasive
Tangibility	Well-defined		More subjective

Source: Based on information in D.M. Rousseau and J.M. Parks, "The Contracts of Individuals and Organizations," *Research in Organizational Behavior* 15 (1993), pp. 1–43; D.M. Rousseau, *Psychological Contracts in Organizations* (Thousand Oaks, CA: Sage, 1995).

Japan's Freeters Turn the Psychological Contract Upside Down More than 2 million young Japanese have become "freeters": casual workers with an equally casual psychological contract that emphasizes personal freedom over loyalty. Generally they want employment that is short-term, transactional, and flexible—just the opposite of what their parents expected in an employment relationship. "Living as a freeter, I get more freedom and I like that," says Mika Onodera, a 28-year-old bakery employee in Tokyo (shown in this photo). Japan's struggling economy partially explains why an increasing number of young people are willing to accept temporary work; but recent surveys also suggest that freeters simply don't worry at all about long-term careers, and they think job-hopping is a badge of honor. The Japanese government is so concerned about the freeter trend that it provides financial aid to companies who hire freeters so they can "test-drive" a permanent job. It has also introduced a program in high schools to teach students the value of holding a full-time job.[71]

Relational contracts, on the other hand, are rather like marriages; they are long-term attachments that encompass a broad array of subjective mutual obligations. Employees with a relational psychological contract are more willing to contribute their time and effort without expecting the organization to pay back this debt in the short term. Relational contracts are also dynamic, meaning that the parties are more flexible regarding when they expect a payback for their contributions to the relationship. Not surprisingly, organizational citizenship behaviors are more likely to prevail under relational than transactional contracts. Permanent employees are more likely to believe they have a relational contract.

Psychological Contracts across Cultures and Generations

Psychological contracts are influenced by the social contexts in which the contracting process occurs.[72] In other words, they vary across cultures and groups of employees based on their unique cultures and cohort experiences. For instance, employees in the United States, United Kingdom, and several other countries expect some involvement in company decisions (that is, they have low power distance), whereas employees in Taiwan and Mexico are more willing to accept arbitrary orders from their supervisors (they have high power distance).

In Japan, employees traditionally expected lifetime employment in return for loyalty and hard work. However, this relational psychological contract shifted as a result of the country's extended recession in the 1990s. The emerging psychological contract among many young Japanese is a startling contrast to their parents. Specifically, Japan is experiencing a rising tide of "freeters" – young people who hop from one job to the next, usually with a distinctly transactional psychological contract. The psychological contract expectations of freeters has motivated the Japanese government to introduce various schemes intended to change their views on the employment relationship.

Psychological contracts also seem to vary across generations of employees. Older employees grew up with "organization man" expectations in which dedicated employees worked in secure jobs with steady promotions through the hierarchy. They often devoted their entire lives to the same company, put in regular hours, and rarely thought about changing employers.[73] The implicit contract was that if you are loyal to the company and perform your job reasonably well, the company will be loyal to you by providing job security and managing your career development. When the "new deal" of employability arrived, these older employees felt betrayed—their psychological contracts had been violated (see Chapter 1).[74]

However, some scholars suggest that job security has less value to Generation-X and Generation-Y employees than to baby boomers. Workforce newcomers have mainly experienced a psychological contract based on employability and are comfortable with weaker job security. "Employees are developing the view that their only job security in the future must be based on their ability and their competence," says Gary L. Howard, a Motorola vice president, "and not on keeping a job at some particular company."[75]

Psychological contracts are changing, as is the entire field of organizational behavior as it embraces new knowledge about emotions in the workplace. Emotional brain centers, emotional labor, emotional intelligence, and other topics in this chapter were unheard of 10 or 15 years ago. Now they are essential reading to improve our grasp of the complex dynamics of employee attitudes and behavior. You will see several references to emotions-related concepts throughout this book, including the next chapter about employee motivation.

Chapter Summary

Emotions are physiological, behavioral, and psychological episodes experienced toward an object, person, or event that create a state of readiness. Emotions are typically organized into a bipolar circle (circumplex) based on their pleasantness and activation. Emotions differ from attitudes, which represent the cluster of beliefs, feelings, and behavioral intentions toward a person, object, or event. Beliefs are a person's established perceptions about the attitude object. Feelings are positive or negative evaluations of the attitude object. Behavioral intentions represent a motivation to engage in a particular behavior with respect to the target.

Attitudes have traditionally been described as a process in which we logically calculate our feelings toward the attitude object based on an analysis of our beliefs. Thus beliefs predict feelings, which predict behavioral intentions, which predict behavior. But this traditional perspective overlooks the role of emotions, which have an important influence on attitudes and behavior. Emotions typically form before we think through situations, so they influence this rational attitude formation process. This dual process is apparent when we internally experience a conflict between what logically seems good or bad and what we emotionally feel is good or bad in a situation. Emotions also affect behavior directly.

Behavior sometimes influences our subsequent attitudes through cognitive dissonance. People also have personality traits that affect their emotions and attitudes.

Emotional labor is the effort, planning, and control needed to express organizationally desired emotions during interpersonal transactions. This is more common in jobs requiring a variety of emotions and more intense emotions, as well as where interaction with clients is frequent and for longer durations. The extent to which we are expected to hide or reveal our true emotions in public depends to some extent on the culture in which we live.

Emotional labor can be challenging for most of us because it is difficult to conceal true emotions and to display the emotions required by the job. It also creates emotional dissonance when required and true emotions are incompatible with each other. Deep acting can minimize this dissonance, as can the practice of hiring people with a natural tendency to display desired emotions.

Emotional intelligence is the ability to perceive and express emotion, assimilate emotion in thought, understand and reason with emotion, and regulate emotion in oneself and others. This concept includes four components arranged in a hierarchy: self-awareness, self-management, social awareness, and relationship management. Emotional intelligence can be learned to some extent, particularly through personal coaching.

Job satisfaction represents a person's evaluation of his or her job and work context. Although surveys indicate Americans are moderately or very satisfied with their jobs, these results may be somewhat inflated by the use of single-item questions and distorted by cultural differences. The exit–voice–loyalty–neglect model outlines four possible consequences of job dissatisfaction. Job satisfaction has a moderate relationship with job performance and with customer satisfaction. Job satisfaction is also a moral obligation in many societies.

Affective organizational commitment (loyalty) refers to the employee's emotional attachment to, identification with, and involvement in a particular organization. This contrasts with continuance commitment, which is a calculated bond with the organization. Affective commitment improves motivation and organizational citizenship and produces somewhat higher job performance, whereas continuance commitment is associated with lower performance and organizational citizenship. Companies build loyalty through justice and support, shared values, trust, organizational comprehension, and employee involvement.

The psychological contract refers to the individual's beliefs about the terms and conditions of a reciprocal exchange agreement between that person and another party. Transactional psychological contracts are primarily short-term economic exchanges, whereas relational contracts are long-term attachments that encompass a broad array of subjective mutual obligations. Psychological contracts seem to vary across cultures as well as across generations of employees.

Key Terms

attitudes, p. 106

cognitive dissonance, p. 110

continuance commitment, p. 119

emotional dissonance, p. 112

emotional intelligence (EI), p. 113

emotional labor, p. 110

emotions, p. 104

exit–voice–loyalty–neglect (EVLN) model, p. 116

job satisfaction, p. 115

organizational (affective) commitment, p. 119

psychological contract, p. 121

trust, p. 120

Critical Thinking Questions

1. After a few months on the job, Susan has experienced several emotional episodes ranging from frustration to joy about the work she has been assigned. Explain how these emotions affect Susan's level of job satisfaction with the work itself.

2. A recent study reported that college instructors are frequently required to engage in emotional labor. Identify the situations in which emotional labor is required for this job. In your opinion, is emotional labor more troublesome for college instructors or for telephone operators working at an emergency service?

3. "Emotional intelligence is more important than cognitive intelligence in influencing an individual's success." Do you agree or disagree with this statement? Support your perspective.

4. Describe a time when you effectively managed someone's emotions. What happened? What was the result?

5. The latest employee satisfaction survey in your organization indicates that employees are unhappy with some aspects of the organization. However, management tends to pay attention to the single-item question asking employees to indicate their overall satisfaction with the job. The results of this item indicate that 86 percent of staff members are very or somewhat satisfied, so management concludes that the other results refer to issues that are probably not important to employees. Explain why management's interpretation of these results may be inaccurate.

6. "Happy employees create happy customers." Explain why this statement might be true, and identify conditions in which it might not be true.

7. What factors influence an employee's organizational loyalty?

8. This chapter argues that psychological contracts vary across cultures and generations. Identify some of the psychological contract expectations around which younger and older employees differ in the country where you live.

Case Study 4.1 DIANA'S DISAPPOINTMENT: THE PROMOTION STUMBLING BLOCK

Rosemary Maellaro, University of Dallas

Diana Gillen had an uneasy feeling of apprehension as she arrived at the Cobb Street Grille corporate offices. Today she was meeting with her supervisor, Julie Spencer, and regional director, Tom Miner, to learn the outcome of her promotion interview for the district manager position. Diana had been employed by this casual dining restaurant chain for 12 years and had worked her way up from waitress to general manager. Based on her track record, she was the obvious choice for the promotion; and her friends assured her that the interview process was merely a formality. Diana was still anxious, though, and feared that the news might not be positive. She knew she was more than qualified for the job, but that didn't guarantee anything these days.

Nine months ago, when Diana interviewed for the last district manager opening, she thought her selection for the job was inevitable. She was shocked when that didn't happen. Diana was so upset about not getting promoted then that she initially decided not to apply for the current opening. She eventually changed her mind—after all, the company had just named her "restaurant manager of the year" and trusted her with managing their flagship location. Diana thought her chances had to be really good this time.

A multi-unit management position was a desirable move up for any general manager and was a goal to which Diana had aspired since she began working in the industry. When she had not been promoted the last time, Julie, her supervisor, explained that her people skills needed to improve. But Diana knew that explanation had little to do with why she hadn't gotten the job—the real reason was corporate politics. She heard that the person they hired was some superstar from the outside—a district manager from another restaurant company who supposedly had strong multi-unit management experience and a proven track record of developing restaurant managers. Despite what she was told, she was convinced that Tom, her regional manager, had been unduly pressured to hire this person, who had been referred by the CEO.

The decision to hire the outsider may have impressed the CEO, but it enraged Diana. With her successful track record as a store manager for the Cobb Street Grille, she was much more capable, in her opinion, of overseeing multiple units than someone who was new to the operation. Besides, district managers had always been promoted internally from among the store managers, and she was unofficially designated as the next one to move up to a district position. Tom had hired the outside candidate as a political maneuver to put himself in a good light with management, even though it meant overlooking a loyal employee like her in the process. Diana had no patience with people who made business decisions for the wrong reasons. She worked very hard to avoid politics—and it especially irritated her when the political actions of others negatively impacted her.

Diana was ready to be a district manager nine months ago, and she thought she was even more qualified today—provided the decision was based on performance. She ran a tight ship, managing her restaurant completely by the book. She meticulously adhered to policies and procedures and rigorously controlled expenses. Her sales were growing, in spite of new competition in the market, and she received relatively few customer complaints. The only number that was a little out of line was the higher turnover among her staff.

Diana was not too concerned about the increasing number of terminations, however; there was a perfectly logical explanation for this. It was because she had high standards for both herself and her employees. Any employee who delivered less than 110 percent at all times would be better off finding a job somewhere else. Diana didn't think she should bend the rules for anyone, for whatever reason. A few months ago, for example, she had to fire three otherwise good employees who decided to try a new customer service tactic—a so-called innovation they dreamed up—rather than complying with the established process. As the general manager, it was her responsibility to make sure that the restaurant was managed strictly in accordance with the operations manual, and she could not allow deviations. This by-the-book approach to managing had served her well for many years. It got her promoted in the past, and she was not about to jinx that now. Losing a few employees now and then—particularly those who had difficulty following the rules—was simply the cost of doing business.

During a recent store visit Julie suggested that Diana might try creating a friendlier work environment because she seemed aloof and interacted with employees somewhat mechanically. Julie even told her that she overheard employees refer to Diana as the "ice maiden" behind her back. Diana was surprised that Julie brought this up because her boss rarely criticized her. They had an unspoken agreement: Because Diana was so technically competent and always met her financial targets, Julie didn't need to give her much input. Diana was happy to be left alone to run her restaurant without needless advice.

At any rate, Diana rarely paid attention to what employees said about her. She wasn't about to let something as childish as a silly name cause her to modify a successful management strategy. What's more, even though she had recently lost more than the average number of employees due to "personality differences" or "miscommunications" over her directives, her superiors did not seem to mind when she consistently delivered strong bottom-line results every month.

As she waited in the conference room for the others, Diana worried that she was not going to get this promotion. Julie had sounded different in the voicemail message she left to inform her about this meeting, but Diana couldn't put her finger on exactly what it was. She would be very angry if she was passed over again and wondered what excuse they would have this time. Then her mind wandered to how her employees would respond to her if she did not get the promotion. They all knew how much she wanted the job, and she cringed at how embarrassed she would be if she didn't get it. Her eyes began to mist over at the sheer thought of having to face them if she was not promoted today.

Julie and Tom entered the room then, and the meeting started. They told Diana, as kindly as they could, that she would not be promoted at this time; one of her colleagues would become the new district manager. She was incredulous. The individual who got promoted had been with the company only three years—and Diana had trained her! She tried to comprehend how this happened, but it did not make sense. Before any further explanation could be offered, she burst into tears and left the room. As she tried in vain to regain her composure, Diana was overcome with crushing disappointment.

Discussion Questions

1. Within the framework of the emotional intelligence domains of self-awareness, self-management, social awareness, and relationship management, discuss the various factors that might have led to Diana's failure to be promoted.

2. What competencies does Diana need to develop to be promotable in the future? What can the company do to support her developmental efforts?

Case Study 4.2 TROUBLING EXITS AT MICROSOFT

BusinessWeek For most of its three decades, Microsoft has faced intense criticism, mostly from the outside world regarding its heavy-handed tactics. Now, the Redmond, Washington-based company is receiving its sharpest criticism from its own current and former employees. When superstar computer scientist Kai-Fu Lee bolted for Google, he called his former employer "incompetent." Around the same time, two current employees sent Microsoft chairman Bill Gates a memo saying that "everyone sees that a crisis is imminent." The 12-page document outlined "10 crazy ideas" to help Microsoft get out of its crisis.

This *BusinessWeek* case study describes several criticisms that Microsoft employees have complained about to their employer, and what some of them have done about the situation. The article examines some of the perks that Microsoft employees appreciate, as well as some of the current concerns they have working at the world's largest software company. Read the full text of this *BusinessWeek* article at <u>www.mhhe.com/mcshane4e</u> and prepare for the discussion questions below.

Discussion Questions

1. Use the exit-voice-loyalty-neglect model to describe some of the behaviors of Microsoft employees who seem dissatisfied with the software company.

2. What factors seem to dampen employee loyalty at Microsoft? Do you think continuance commitment is weak or strong here?

Source: J. Greene, "Troubling Exits at Microsoft," *BusinessWeek*, 26 September 2005, 98.

Class Exercise 4.3 STEM-AND-PROBE INTERVIEW ACTIVITY

PURPOSE To help you develop better awareness of others as well as to observe the effects of positive organizational behavior.

MATERIALS None.

INSTRUCTIONS This simple yet powerful exercise consists of students conducting and receiving a detailed stem-and-probe interview with other students in the class. Each student will have an opportunity to interview and be interviewed. However, to increase the variation and novelty of this experience, the student conducting the first interview should *not* be interviewed by the student who was just interviewed. Instead the instructor will either form groups of four students (two pairs) at the beginning of this exercise, or have two pairs of students swap after the first round. Each of the two sets of interviews should take 10 to 15 minutes and use a stem-and-probe interview method. The stem-and-probe method, as well as the topic of the interview, are described next.

STEM-AND-PROBE INTERVIEWING This interview method attempts to receive more detail from the interviewee than typically occurs in semistructured or structured interviews. The main interview question, called the "stem," is followed by a series of probing questions that encourages the interviewee to provide more details relating to a particular incident or situation. The stem question for this exercise is provided next. The interviewee can use several "probes" to elicit more detail; the best probe depends on the circumstances, such as what information has already been provided. Some common probe questions include these:

- "Tell me more about that."
- "What did you do next?"
- "Could you explain that further, please?"
- "What else can you remember about that event?"

Notice that these probes are open-ended questions, not closed-ended questions such as "Is there anything else you want to tell me?" in which a simple yes or no is possible. Stem-and-probe interviewing also improves when the interviewer engages in active listening and isn't afraid of silence—giving the interviewee time to think and motivating him or her to fill in the silence with new information.

INTERVIEW TOPIC In both sets of interviews, the "stem" question is this: "Describe two or three things you did this past week that made someone else feel better."

Throughout this interview process, the interviewer's task is to receive as much information as possible (that the interviewee is willing to divulge) about the details of these two or three things that the interviewee did over the past week.

Following the two sets of interviews (when each student has interviewed and been interviewed once), the class will discuss the emotional and attitudinal dynamics of this activity.

Team Exercise 4.4 RANKING JOBS BY THEIR EMOTIONAL LABOR

PURPOSE This exercise is designed to help you understand the jobs in which people tend to experience higher or lower degrees of emotional labor.

INSTRUCTIONS

1. Individually rank order the extent to which the jobs listed here require emotional labor. Assign a "1" to the job you believe requires the most effort, planning, and control to express organizationally desired emotions during interpersonal transactions. Assign a "10" to the job you believe requires the least amount of emotional labor. Mark your rankings in column 1.

2. The instructor will form teams of four or five members, and each team will rank order the items based on consensus (not simply averaging the individual rankings). These results should be placed in column 2.

3. The instructor will provide expert ranking information. This information should be written in column 3. Then you can calculate the differences in columns 4 and 5.

4. The class will compare the results and discuss the features of jobs with high emotional labor.

Occupational Emotional Labor Scoring Sheet

Occupation	(1) Individual Ranking	(2) Team Ranking	(3) Expert Ranking	(4) Absolute Difference of 1 and 3	(5) Absolute Difference of 2 and 3
Bartender	5		4	1	
Cashier	8		8	✓	
Dental hygienist	6		7	1	
Insurance adjuster	4		6	2	
Lawyer	3		5	2	
Librarian	7		9	2	
Postal clerk	10		10	✓	
Registered nurse	2		2	✓	
Social worker	1		1	✓	
Television announcer	9		3	6	
			TOTAL		

(The lower the score, the better)   Your score   Team score

Self-Assessment 4.5

SCHOOL COMMITMENT SCALE

PURPOSE This self-assessment on page 130 is designed to help you understand the concept of organizational commitment and to assess your commitment to the college or university you are currently attending.

OVERVIEW The concept of commitment is as relevant to students enrolled in college or university courses as it is to employees working in various organizations. This self-assessment adapts a popular organizational commitment instrument, so it refers to your commitment as a student to the school you are attending.

INSTRUCTIONS Read each of the following statements and circle the response that best fits your personal belief. Then use the scoring key in Appendix B of this book to calculate your results. This self-assessment is completed alone so that you can rate yourself honestly without concerns of social comparison. However, class discussion will focus on the meaning of the different types of organizational commitment and how well this scale applies to the commitment of students toward the college or university they are attending.

Self-Assessment 4.6

DISPOSITIONAL MOOD SCALE (STUDENT OLC)

This self-assessment is designed to help you understand mood states or personality traits of emotions and to assess your own mood or emotion personality. This self-assessment consists of several words representing various emotions that you might have experienced. For each word presented, indicate the extent to which you have felt this way generally across all situations *over the past six months*. You need to be honest with yourself to receive a reasonable estimate of your mood state or personality trait on these scales. The results provide an estimate of your level on two emotional personality scales. This instrument is widely used in research, but it is only an estimate. You should not assume that the results are accurate without a more complete assessment by a trained professional.

School Commitment Scale

To what extent does each statement describe you? indicate your level of agreement by marking the appropriate response on the right	Strongly agree	Moderately agree	Slightly agree	Neutral	Slightly disagree	Moderately disagree	Strongly disagree
1. I would be very happy to complete the rest of my education at this school.	☒	☐	☐	☐	☐	☐	☐
2. One of the difficulties of leaving this school is that there are few alternatives.	☐	☐	☐	☐	☐	☐	☐
3. I really feel as if this school's problems are my own.	☐	☒	☐	☐	☐	☐	☐
4. Right now, staying enrolled at this school is a matter of necessity as much as desire.	☐	☐	☐	☐	☐	☐	☐
5. I do not feel a strong sense of belonging to this school.	☐	☐	☐	☐	☐	☐	☐
6. It would be very hard for me to leave this school right now even if I wanted to.	☐	☐	☐	☐	☐	☐	☐
7. I do not feel emotionally attached to this school.	☐	☐	☐	☐	☒	☐	☐
8. Too much of my life would be disrupted if I decided to move to a different school now.	☒	☐	☐	☐	☐	☐	☐
9. I do not feel like part of the "family" at this school.	☐	☐	☒	☐	☐	☐	☐
10. I feel that I have too few options to consider leaving this school.	☐	☐	☐	☐	☐	☐	☐
11. This school has a great deal of personal meaning for me.	☒	☐	☐	☐	☐	☐	☐
12. If I had not already put so much of myself into this school, I might consider completing my education elsewhere.	☐	☐	☐	☐	☐	☐	☐

Source: Adapted from: J.P. Meyer, N.J. Allen, and C.A. Smith, "Commitment to Organizations and Occupations: Extension and Test of a Three-Component Model," *Journal of Applied Psychology* 78 (1993), pp. 538–51.

After reading this chapter, if you need additional information, see www.mhhe.com/mcshane4e for more in-depth interactivities that correspond with this material.

David Gachuru lives by a motto that motivates employees more than money can buy: "If an employee's work calls for a thumbs-up, I will appreciate him or her as many times as possible." Translating this advice into practice is a daily event for the general manager of Panafric Hotel in Nairobi, Kenya. In addition to thanking staff personally and through e-mail messages, Gachuru holds bimonthly meetings where top-performing employees are congratulated and receive paid holidays with their family. Employee achievements are also celebrated in the hotel's newsletter, which is distributed to guests as well as employees.

Panafric Hotel in Nairobi, Kenya, motivates its employees through plenty of praise and recognition. "If an employee's work calls for a thumbs-up, I will appreciate him or her as many times as possible," says Panafric general manager David Gachuru, shown in this photo (left) presenting an award to employee of the month Matayo Moyale.

Panafric Hotel and other firms are returning to good old-fashioned praise and recognition to motivate staff. Share options can evaporate and incentive plans might backfire, but a few words of appreciation almost always create a warm glow of satisfaction and renewed energy. The challenge of recognition is to "catch" employees doing extraordinary things. Keyspan Corporation chairman Bob Catell resolves this by regularly asking managers for lists of "unsung heroes" at the New England gas utility. He calls an employee every week, often spending the first few minutes convincing the listener that the CEO really is calling. "They start by saying, 'Hey, you can't fool me, this isn't Catell!' But once they realize it is me, they are pleased that I would take the time to do this."

Along with recognition from managers, approximately one-third of large American firms rely on peer recognition as one way to motivate employees. Among them is Yum Brands Inc., the parent company of KFC, Taco Bell, and Pizza Hut. Yum's restaurants around the world use a recognition program in which employees reward colleagues with "Champs" cards, an acronym for KFC's values (cleanliness, hospitality, and so on). The Ritz Carlton Hotel in Kuala Lumpur, which is rated as one of the best places to work in Asia, applies a similar peer recognition process using First Class cards. Nancy Teoh, Ritz Carlton Kuala Lumpur's human resources manager, explains that "congratulatory messages or words of appreciation are written down by any member of the team to another and even as far as from the hotel and corporate senior leaders." Teoh adds, "This serves as a motivational aspect of the work environment."[1]

Motivation in the Workplace

After reading this chapter you should be able to

1. Explain why motivating employees has become more challenging in recent years.

2. Summarize Maslow's needs hierarchy and discuss Its contribution and limitations to employee motivation.

3. Describe four-drive theory and explain how these drives influence motivation.

4. Summarize McClelland's learned needs theory, including the three needs he studied.

5. Discuss the practical implications of motivation theories relating to needs and drives.

6. Diagram the expectancy theory model and discuss its practical implications for motivating employees.

7. Describe the characteristics of effective goal setting and feedback.

8. Summarize the equity theory model, including how people try to reduce feelings of inequity.

9. Identify the factors that influence procedural justice, as well as the consequences of procedural justice.

After reading this section you should be able to

1. **Explain why motivating employees has become more challenging in recent years.**

Motivating Employees

motivation
The forces within a person that affect his or her direction, intensity, and persistence of voluntary behavior.

First Class cards at Ritz Carlton Hotel, Champs cards at Yum Brands, telephone calls from the CEO of Keyspan, and various celebrations for good performance at Panafric Hotel are designed to maintain and improve employee motivation. **Motivation** refers to the forces within a person that affect the direction, intensity, and persistence of voluntary behavior.[2] Motivated employees are willing to exert a particular level of effort (intensity) for a certain amount of time (persistence) toward a particular goal (direction). Motivation is one of the four essential drivers of individual behavior and performance (see the MARS model in Chapter 2) and, consequently, is an integral component of employee engagement. An engaged workforce is an important predictor of an organization's competitiveness, so it's easy to see why employee motivation is continuously on the minds of corporate leaders.

The quest for a motivated and engaged workforce has not been easy, however. Most employers—92 percent of them, according to one major survey—say that motivating employees has become more challenging. Three factors seem to be responsible for this increasing challenge. First, globalization, information technology, corporate restructuring, and other changes have dramatically altered the employment relationship. These changes potentially undermine the levels of trust and commitment necessary to energize employees beyond minimum standards.[3]

Second, in decades past, companies typically relied on armies of supervisors to closely monitor employee behavior and performance. Even if commitment and trust were low, employees performed their jobs with the boss watching them closely. But most companies thinned their supervisory ranks when they flattened organizational structure to reduce costs. Supervisors now have many more employees, so they can't possibly keep a watchful eye out for laggards. This is just as well because today's educated workforce resents the old command-and-control approach to performance management. Most people enjoy the feeling of being motivated, but this requires the right conditions; so employers need to search for more contemporary ways to motivate staff.

The third challenge is that a new generation of employees has brought different expectations to the workplace. A few years ago various writers disparaged Generation-X and Generation-Y employees as slackers, cynics, whiners, and malcontents. Now we know that the problem wasn't their lack of motivational potential; it was that employers didn't know how to motivate them! It seems that many companies still haven't figured this out: According to one report more than 40 percent of employees aged 25 to 34 sometimes or frequently feel demotivated, compared to 30 percent of 35- to 44-year-olds and just 18 percent of 45- to 54-year-olds.[4]

We begin the process of understanding and facilitating employee motivation by looking at the core theories of motivation in organizational settings. The chapter begins by describing Maslow's needs hierarchy theory and explaining the shortfalls of this incredibly popular theory as well as other needs hierarchy models. We then turn to four-drive theory and McClelland's learned needs theory, both of which offer more promise. Next this chapter introduces expectancy theory, which is a rational decision approach to employee motivation. The fourth section of this chapter covers the key elements of goal setting and feedback, including the topics of multisource feedback and executive coaching. In the final section we look at organizational justice, including the dimensions and dynamics of equity theory and procedural justice.

After reading this section you should be able to

2. **Summarize Maslow's needs hierarchy and discuss its contribution and limitations to employee motivation.**

3. **Describe four-drive theory and explain how these drives influence motivation.**

4. **Summarize McClelland's learned needs theory, including the three needs he studied.**

5. **Discuss the practical implications of motivation theories relating to needs and drives.**

Needs, Drives, and Employee Motivation

needs
Deficiencies that energize or trigger behaviors to satisfy those needs.

Motivation begins with individual needs and their underlying drives. In spite of some confusion in the literature regarding these terms, we will define **needs** as deficiencies that energize or trigger behaviors to satisfy those needs. Unfulfilled needs create a tension that makes us want to find ways to reduce or satisfy those needs. The stronger your needs, the more motivated you are to satisfy them. Conversely, a satisfied need does not motivate. **Drives** are instinctive or innate tendencies to seek certain goals or maintain internal stability. Drives are hardwired in the brain—everyone has the same drives—and they most likely exist to help the species survive.[5] Needs are typically produced by drives, but they may also be strengthened through learning (reinforcement) and social forces such as culture and childhood upbringing. We'll discuss needs and drives later in this section after describing Maslow and other needs hierarchy theories.

drives
Instinctive or innate tendencies to seek certain goals or maintain internal stability.

Maslow's Needs Hierarchy Theory

Maslow's needs hierarchy theory
Maslow's motivation theory of five instinctive needs arranged in a hierarchy, whereby people are motivated to fulfill a higher need as a lower one becomes gratified.

More people have probably heard about **Maslow's needs hierarchy theory** than any other concept in organizational behavior. Developed by psychologist Abraham Maslow in the 1940s, the model has been applied in almost every human pursuit, from marketing products to rehabilitating prison inmates. This incredible popularity is rather odd considering that most research has reported little or no support for the theory. According to his later journal entries, even Maslow was amazed that people had accepted his theory wholeheartedly with any critique. Normally a theory that fails to live up to its predictions is laid to rest. However, Maslow's model is described here because it significantly altered the way experts now think about and study motivation and behavior in the workplace.

Maslow's needs hierarchy theory condenses and integrates the long list of needs that had been studied previously into a hierarchy of five basic categories.[6] As Exhibit 5.1 illustrates, physiological needs (food, air, water, shelter, and the like) are at the bottom of the hierarchy. Next are safety needs—the need for a secure and stable environment and the absence of pain, threat, or illness. Belongingness includes the need for love, affection, and interaction with other people. Esteem includes self-esteem through personal achievement as well as social esteem through recognition and respect from others. At the top of the hierarchy is **self-actualization**, which represents

self-actualization
The need for self-fulfillment—a sense that a person's potential has been realized.

Exhibit 5.1

Maslow's Needs Hierarchy

Source: Based on information in: A.H. Maslow, "A Theory of Human Motivation," *Psychological Review* 50 (1943), pp. 370–96.

the need for self-fulfillment—a sense that a person's potential has been realized. In addition to these five, Maslow describes the need to know and need for aesthetic beauty as two needs that do not fit within the hierarchy.

Maslow says that we are motivated simultaneously by several needs, but the strongest source is the lowest unsatisfied need at the time. As a person satisfies a lower-level need, the next higher need in the hierarchy becomes the primary motivator and remains so even if never satisfied. Physiological needs are initially the most important, and people are motivated to satisfy them first. As they become gratified, safety needs emerge as the strongest motivator. As safety needs are satisfied, belongingness needs become most important, and so forth. The exception to this need fulfillment process is self-actualization; as people experience self-actualization, they desire more rather than less of this need. Thus while the bottom four groups are *deficiency needs* because they become activated when unfulfilled, self-actualization is known as a *growth need* because it continues to develop even when fulfilled.

As was mentioned earlier, Maslow's needs hierarchy theory has not received much scientific support.[7] Researchers have found that needs do not cluster neatly around the hierarchy's five categories. Also, gratification of one need level does not necessarily lead to increased motivation to satisfy the next higher need level. Some people can be very hungry and yet strive to fulfill their social needs; others can self-actualize while working in a risky environment. The theory also assumes that need priorities shift over months or years, whereas the importance of a particular need likely changes more quickly with the situation.

Maslow's Contribution to Motivation Theories   In spite of the flaws of needs hierarchy theory, Maslow's writing dramatically shifted the study of human motivation to one that is more holistic, humanistic, and positive. First, Maslow brought a more holistic perspective by introducing the notion that needs are related to each other and, consequently, should be studied together. Prior to his needs hierarchy model,

Belongingness Needs Top the Hierarchy for Some Employees These UBS Warburg employees in Chicago seem to be enjoying each other's company, suggesting that they are experiencing some fulfillment of their belongingness needs. But do they all have the same needs hierarchy? Not according to emerging research and writing on this subject. Contrary to Maslow's well-known theory, needs are not hardwired into a universal hierarchy. Instead a person's needs hierarchy seems to be strongly influenced by his or her value system, so needs hierarchies vary from one person to the next and possibly from one culture to the next. The UBS Warburg staff in this photo probably have somewhat different value systems, so their needs hierarchies would be different.

motivation experts had splintered needs and drives into dozens of categories, each studied in isolation using nontypical subjects (usually animals or people with severe psychological dysfunctions).[8] He argued that isolating narrowly defined needs and drives was inappropriate because human behavior is typically initiated by more than one of these needs or drives with varying degrees of influence on that behavior. Second, when most researchers focused on human instincts as direct drivers of employee motivation and behavior, Maslow argued that higher-order needs are influenced by social dynamics and culture, not just instincts. In other words, he explained how human thoughts play a role in motivation.

Maslow's third contribution was to introduce a more positive perspective of employee motivation. Previously scholars focused on drive "deprivation" (particularly hunger), whereas Maslow suggested that need "gratification" is just as important in motivating people. Indeed Maslow's most important contribution is his work on self-actualization, which he considered far more important than the needs hierarchy model.[9] Throughout his career Maslow emphasized that people are naturally motivated to reach their potential (once lower needs are fulfilled) and that organizations and societies need to be structured to help people continue and develop this motivation. Maslow called for more "enlightened management" to provide meaningful work and freedom, rather than tedious work with oppressive bureaucratic controls, so employees can experience self-actualization and fulfill their other needs.[10] This view of employee motivation, which was novel at the time, has become the foundation of **positive organizational behavior** (a variation of *positive psychology*), which focuses on building positive qualities and traits within individuals or institutions as

positive organizational behavior

Building positive qualities and traits within individuals or institutions as opposed to focusing on just trying to fix what might be wrong with them.

opposed to focusing on just trying to fix what might be wrong with them. In other words, this approach emphasizes building on strengths rather than trying to correct weaknesses.[11]

What's Wrong with Needs Hierarchy Models?

Maslow's theory is not the only attempt to map employee needs onto a single hierarchy. The most comprehensive of the alternative models is **ERG theory**, which reorganizes Maslow's five groups into three—existence, relatedness, and growth.[12] Unlike Maslow's theory, which only explained how people progress up the hierarchy, ERG theory also describes how people regress down the hierarchy when they fail to fulfill higher needs. ERG theory seems to explain human motivation somewhat better than Maslow's needs hierarchy, but that's mainly because it is easier to cluster human needs around ERG's three categories than Maslow's five categories. Otherwise, the research findings are fairly clear that ERG theory only marginally improves our understanding of human needs.[13]

Why have Maslow's needs hierarchy, ERG theory, and other needs hierarchies largely failed to explain the dynamics of employee needs? The most glaring explanation is that people don't fit into a single universal needs hierarchy. Some people seem preoccupied with social status even though they haven't fulfilled their lower needs; others consider personal development and growth an ongoing priority over social relations or status. There is increasing evidence that needs hierarchies are unique, not universal, because needs are strongly influenced by each individual's personal values. If your most important values lean toward stimulation and self-direction, you probably pay more attention to self-actualization needs. If power and achievement are at the top of your value system, then status needs might be stronger most of the time. This connection between values and needs suggests that a needs hierarchy is unique to each person and can change over time, just as values change over a lifetime.[14]

ERG theory
A needs hierarchy theory consisting of three instinctive needs—existence, relatedness, and growth.

Four-Drive Theory

Motivation experts have mostly abandoned needs hierarchy theories, but not the notion that needs and drives are relevant. On the contrary, recent discoveries about how the brain functions have prompted experts to consider a more coherent and integrated approach to innate drives. Building on recent research on neuroscience, emotions, anthropology, and emotional intelligence, Harvard Business School professors Paul Lawrence and Nitin Nohria have proposed **four-drive theory** to explain human motivation.[15] This model is both holistic (it pulls together the many drives and needs) and humanistic (it considers human thought and social influences rather than just instinct). These were two conditions that Maslow felt were essential for a solid theory of human motivation.

four-drive theory
A motivation theory based on the innate drives to acquire, bond, learn, and defend that incorporates both emotions and rationality.

Four Fundamental Drives   Four-drive theory organizes drives into four categories: the drives to acquire, bond, learn, and defend. These drives are innate and universal, meaning that they are hardwired in our brains through evolution and are found in everyone. They are also independent of each other, so one drive is neither dependent on nor inherently inferior or superior to another drive. Four-drive theory also states that these four drives are a complete set—no other fundamental drives are excluded from the model. Another key feature is that three of the four drives are "proactive," meaning that we regularly try to fulfill them. Thus any notion of fulfilling drives is temporary at best.

- **Drive to acquire.** This is the drive to seek, take, control, and retain objects and personal experiences. The drive to acquire extends beyond basic food and water; it includes the need for relative status and recognition in society. Thus it is the foundation of competition and the basis of our need for esteem. Four-drive theory states that the drive to acquire is insatiable because the purpose of human motivation is to achieve a higher position than others, not just to fulfill our physiological needs.

- **Drive to bond.** This is the drive to form social relationships and develop mutual caring commitments with others. It also explains why people form social identities by aligning their self-image with various social groups (see Chapter 3). Research indicates that people invest considerable time and effort forming and maintaining relationships without any special circumstances or ulterior motives. Indeed, recent evidence shows that people who lack social contact are more prone to serious health problems.[16] The drive to bond motivates people to cooperate and, consequently, is a fundamental ingredient in the success of organizations and the development of societies.

- **Drive to learn.** This is the drive to satisfy our curiosity, to know and understand ourselves and the environment around us. When observing something that is inconsistent with or beyond our current knowledge, we experience a tension that motivates us to close that information gap. In fact, studies in the 1950s revealed that people who are removed from any novel information will crave even boring information (outdated stock reports) to satisfy their drive to learn![17] The drive to learn is related to the higher-order needs of growth and self-actualization described earlier.

- **Drive to defend.** This is the drive to protect ourselves physically and socially. Probably the first drive to develop, it creates a "fight or flight" response in the face of personal danger. The drive to defend goes beyond protecting our physical selves. It includes defending our relationships, our acquisitions, and our belief systems. The drive to defend is always reactive—it is triggered by threat. In contrast, the other three drives are always proactive—we actively seek to improve our acquisitions, relationships, and knowledge.

How Drives Influence Employee Motivation To understand how these four drives translate into employee motivation, recall from previous chapters that our perceptions of the external world are influenced by our emotions. Every meaningful bit of information we receive is quickly and unconsciously tagged with emotional markers that subsequently shape our logical analysis of the situation. Our motivation to act is a result of rational thinking influenced by these emotional markers.[18]

The four drives fit into this tango of emotionality and rationality because they determine which emotional markers, if any, are attached to the perceived information. For example, suppose your department has just received a new computer program that you are curious to try out (triggered by your drive to learn). However, your boss says that you are not experienced enough to use the new system yet, which makes you somewhat angry (triggered by your drive to defend against the "inexperience" insult). Both the curiosity about the software program and your anger from the boss's beliefs about your experience demand your attention and energize you to act. The key point here is that the four innate drives determine which emotions are generated in each situation.

Four-drive theory further explains that this process is conscious (humanistic) rather than instinctive because these drives produce independent and often competing

Exhibit 5.2   **Four-Drive Theory of Motivation**

Source: Based on information in P.R. Lawrence and N. Nohria, *Driven: How Human Nature Shapes Our Choices* (San Francisco: Jossey-Bass, 2002).

signals that often require our attention.[19] As Exhibit 5.2 illustrates, we resolve these dilemmas through a built-in skill set that takes into account social norms, past experience, and personal values. The result is goal-directed decision making and effort that fit within the constraints of cultural and moral expectations. In other words, our conscious analysis of competing demands from the four drives generates needs that energize us to act in ways acceptable to society and our own moral compass.

Evaluating Four-Drive Theory   Four-drive theory potentially offers a rich explanation for employee motivation. It avoids the assumption found in needs hierarchy theories that everyone has the same needs hierarchy. Instead it explains how our needs are based on innate drives, how emotions are generated from those drives in the context of a specific situation, and how personal experience and cultural values influence the intensity, persistence, and direction of effort. Four-drive theory also provides a much clearer understanding about the role of emotional intelligence in employee motivation and behavior. Employees with high emotional intelligence are more sensitive to competing demands from the four drives, are better able to avoid impulsive behavior from those drives, and can judge the best way to act to fulfill those drive demands in a social context.

Four-drive theory is based on some fairly solid evidence regarding (1) the existence and dynamics of the four innate drives and (2) the interaction of emotions and cognitions (logical thinking) in employee behavior. However, the overall model is quite new and requires much more work to clarify the role of skill sets in forming goal-directed choice and effort. The theory also ignores the fact that needs can be strengthened through learning. Four-drive theory likely accommodates the notion of learned needs, but it does not explain them. Fortunately other motivational researchers, notably David McClelland, have provided some clarification about learned needs, which we examine next.

Theory of Learned Needs

At the beginning of this chapter we learned that needs typically originate from drives. For instance, your need for belongingness is created out of the innate drive to bond. But needs can also be strengthened through reinforcement, including through childhood learning, parental styles, and social norms. Psychologist David McClelland popularized the idea of learned needs years ago through his research on three learned needs: achievement, power, and affiliation.

need for achievement (nAch)
A learned need in which people want to accomplish reasonably challenging goals, and desire unambiguous feedback and recognition for their success.

- *Need for achievement (nAch).* People with a strong **need for achievement (nAch)** want to accomplish reasonably challenging goals through their own effort. They prefer working alone rather than in teams, and they choose tasks with a moderate degree of risk (neither too easy nor impossible to complete). High nAch people also desire unambiguous feedback and recognition for their success. Money is a weak motivator, except when it provides feedback and recognition.[20] In contrast, employees with a low nAch perform their work better when money is used as an incentive. Successful entrepreneurs tend to have a high nAch, possibly because they establish challenging goals for themselves and thrive on competition.[21]

need for affiliation (nAff)
A learned need in which people seek approval from others, conform to their wishes and expectations, and avoid conflict and confrontation.

- *Need for affiliation (nAff).* **Need for affiliation (nAff)** refers to a desire to seek approval from others, conform to their wishes and expectations, and avoid conflict and confrontation. People with a strong nAff try to project a favorable image of themselves. They tend to actively support others and try to smooth out workplace conflicts. High nAff employees general work well in coordinating roles to mediate conflicts, and in sales positions where the main task is cultivating long-term relations. However, they tend to be less effective at allocating scarce resources and making other decisions that potentially generate conflict. People in decision-making positions must have a relatively low need for affiliation so that their choices and actions are not biased by a personal need for approval.[22]

need for power (nPow)
A learned need in which people want to control their environment, including people and material resources, to benefit either themselves (personalized power) or others (socialized power).

- *Need for power (nPow).* People with a high **need for power (nPow)** want to exercise control over others and are concerned about maintaining their leadership positions. They frequently rely on persuasive communication, make more suggestions in meetings, and tend to publicly evaluate situations more frequently. McClelland pointed out that there are two types of nPow. Those who enjoy their power for its own sake use it to advance personal interests, and wear their power as a status symbol have *personalized power*. Others mainly have a high need for *socialized power* because they desire power as a means to help others.[23] McClelland asserted that leaders are more effective when they have a high need for socialized rather than personalized power. They should have a high degree of altruism and social responsibility and must be concerned about the consequences of their own actions on others.

Learning Needs   McClelland argued that achievement, affiliation, and power needs can be strengthened through learning, so he developed training programs for this purpose. In his achievement motivation program, trainees write achievement-oriented stories and practice achievement-oriented behaviors in business games. They also complete a detailed achievement plan for the next two years and form a reference group with other trainees to maintain their newfound achievement motive style.[24] These programs seem to work. Participants attending a need for achievement course in India subsequently started more new businesses, had greater community involvement, invested more in expanding their businesses, and employed twice as many people as nonparticipants. Research on similar achievement motive courses for American small business owners reported dramatic increases in the profitability of the participants' businesses.

Practical Implications of Needs/Drive-Based Theories

Needs- and drive-based theories, and particularly four-drive theory, offer some practical advice for motivating employees. The main recommendation that Lawrence and Nohria provide from four-drive theory is to ensure that individual jobs and workplaces provide balanced opportunities to fulfill the drives to acquire, bond, learn, and defend.[25] There are really two key recommendations here. The first one is that everyone in the workplace needs to regularly fulfill all four drives. This contrasts sharply with the ill-fated needs hierarchy theories, which suggested that employees are motivated mainly by one need at a time. Four-drive theory says that each of us continuously seeks fulfillment of our innate drives. Thus the best workplaces for motivation and morale provide sufficient rewards, learning opportunities, social interaction, and so forth for all employees.

The second recommendation from four-drive theory is that these four drives must be kept in "balance"; that is, organizations should avoid too much or too little opportunity to fulfill each drive. The reason for this advice is that the four drives counterbalance each other. Companies that help employees fulfill one drive but not the others will face long-term problems. An organization that energizes the drive to acquire without the drive to bond may eventually suffer from organizational politics and dysfunctional conflict. Change and novelty in the workplace will aid the drive to learn, but too much of it will trigger the drive to defend so that employees become territorial and resistant to change. Creating a workplace that supports the drive to bond can, at extreme levels, undermine the diversity and constructive debate required for effective decision making.

Another recommendation from the needs/drives-based theories is to offer employees a choice of rewards rather than giving everyone the same specific reward. Although we possess the same drives and require their ongoing fulfillment, people differ in their needs at any given time. Due to their unique value systems and experiences, some employees generally have a strong need to achieve, whereas others are motivated more by social factors. A narrow application of this recommendation is to let employees choose their own rewards. Farm Fresh Supermarkets accomplishes this by awarding points to employees for good customer service. These points are later redeemed for reward gifts from a catalog. "There are several hundred items in [the catalog], and they can get everything from a T-shirt to a toaster oven, coffee maker, and a vacuum

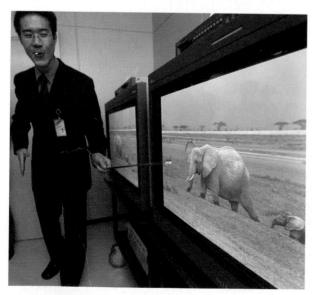

Sony Suffers from Lack of Four-Drive Balance According to four-drive theory, companies that help employees fulfill one drive much more than the others will face long-term problems. This seems to explain the current challenges facing Sony. The Japanese company, which led the electronics world a decade ago with its Walkman and Playstation innovations, is now struggling to keep up with competitors. One reason for the current difficulties is that Sony executives allowed a hypercompetitive culture to develop, where engineers were encouraged to outdo each other rather than work together. This competitive culture fed employees' drive to acquire, but the lack of balance with the drive to bond led to infighting and information hoarding. For instance, competitive rivalries within Sony delayed the company's launch of a digital music player and online music service to compete against Apple's iPod and iTunes music Web site.[26]

cleaner," explains Ron Dennis, president of the Virginia Beach, Virginia–based grocery chain.[27] At a broader level, employees need to have career choices and diverse opportunities to discover and experience their potential. One of the enduring recommendations from Maslow's work on self-actualization is that employees must have sufficient freedom to discover their potential. It cannot be assumed or dictated by management.

Learning Objectives

After reading this section you should be able to

6. Diagram the expectancy theory model and discuss its practical implications for motivating employees.

Expectancy Theory of Motivation

expectancy theory
The motivation theory based on the idea that work effort is directed toward behaviors that people believe will lead to desired outcomes.

The theories described so far mainly explain what motivates employees. But how do these drives and needs translate into specific effort and behavior? One of the best theories to answer this question is expectancy theory of motivation. **Expectancy theory is based on the idea that work effort is directed toward behaviors that people believe will lead to desired outcomes.**[28] Through experience, we develop expectations about whether we can achieve various levels of job performance. We also develop expectations about whether job performance and work behaviors lead to particular outcomes. Finally, we naturally direct our effort toward outcomes that help us fulfill our needs.

Expectancy Theory Model

The expectancy theory model is presented in Exhibit 5.3. The key variable of interest in expectancy theory is *effort*—the individual's actual exertion of energy. An individual's effort level depends on three factors: effort-to-performance (E-to-P) expectancy, performance-to-outcome (P-to-O) expectancy, and outcome valences (V). Employee motivation is influenced by all three components of the expectancy theory model. If any component weakens, motivation weakens.

E-to-P Expectancy The *effort-to-performance (E-to-P) expectancy* is the individual's perception that his or her effort will result in a particular level of performance. Expectancy is defined as a probability and therefore ranges from 0.0 to 1.0. In some

Exhibit 5.3
Expectancy Theory of Motivation

situations employees may believe that they can unquestionably accomplish the task (a probability of 1.0). In other situations they expect that even their highest level of effort will not result in the desired performance level (a probability of 0.0). For instance, unless you are an expert skier, you probably aren't motivated to try some of the black diamond ski runs at Vale. The reason is a very low E-to-P expectancy. Even your best effort won't get you down the hill on your feet! In most cases the E-to-P expectancy falls somewhere between these two extremes.

P-to-O Expectancy   The *performance-to-outcome (P-to-O) expectancy* is the perceived probability that a specific behavior or performance level will lead to specific outcomes. This probability is developed from previous learning. For example, students learn from experience that skipping class either ruins their chance of a good grade or has no effect at all. In extreme cases employees may believe that accomplishing a particular task (performance) will definitely result in a particular outcome (a probability of 1.0), or they may believe that this outcome will have no effect on successful performance (a probability of 0.0). More often the P-to-O expectancy falls somewhere between 0.0 and 1.0.

One important issue in P-to-O expectancies is which outcomes we think about. We certainly don't evaluate the P-to-O expectancy for every possible outcome; there are too many of them. Instead we think only about outcomes of interest to us at the time. Sometimes your motivation to complete a task may be fueled mainly by the likelihood of getting off work early to meet friends. At other times your motivation to complete the same task may be based more on the P-to-O expectancy of a promotion or pay increase. The main point is that your motivation depends on the probability that a behavior or job performance level will result in outcomes that you think about.

valence
The anticipated satisfaction or dissatisfaction that an individual feels toward an outcome.

Outcome Valences   The third element in expectancy theory is the **valence** of each outcome that you consider. Valence refers to the anticipated satisfaction or dissatisfaction that an individual feels toward an outcome. It ranges from negative to positive. (The actual range doesn't matter; it may be from −1 to +1 or from −100 to +100.) An outcome valence represents a person's anticipated satisfaction with the outcome.[29] Outcomes have a positive valence when they are consistent with our values and satisfy our needs; they have a negative valence when they oppose our values and inhibit need fulfillment. If you have a strong need for social interaction, for example, you would value group activities and other events that help to fulfill that need. Outcomes that move you further away from fulfilling your social need—such as working alone from home—will have a strong negative valence.

Expectancy Theory in Practice

One of the appealing characteristics of expectancy theory is that it provides clear guidelines for increasing employee motivation by altering the person's E-to-P expectancies, P-to-O expectancies, and/or outcome valences.[30] Several practical implications of expectancy theory are listed in Exhibit 5.4 and described next.

Increasing E-to-P Expectancies   E-to-P expectancies are influenced by the individual's belief that he or she can successfully complete the task. Some companies increase this can-do attitude by assuring employees that they have the necessary competencies, clear role perceptions, and necessary resources to reach the desired levels of performance. Matching employees to jobs based on their abilities and clearly communicating the tasks required for the job is an important part of this process. Similarly, E-to-P expectancies are learned, so behavioral modeling and supportive

Exhibit 5.4   Practical Applications of Expectancy Theory

Expectancy theory component	Objective	Applications
E→P expectancies	To increase the belief that employees are capable of performing the job successfully.	• Select people with the required skills and knowledge. • Provide required training and clarify job requirements. • Provide sufficient time and resources. • Assign simpler or fewer tasks until employees can master them. • Provide examples of similar employees who have successfully performed the task. • Provide coaching to employees who lack self-confidence.
P→O expectancies	To increase the belief that good performance will result in particular (valued) outcomes.	• Measure job performance accurately. • Clearly describe the outcomes that will result from successful performance. • Describe how the employee's rewards were based on past performance. • Provide examples of other employees whose good performance has resulted in higher rewards.
Valences of outcomes	To increase the expected value of outcomes resulting from desired performance.	• Distribute rewards that employees value. • Individualize rewards. • Minimize the presence of countervalent outcomes.

feedback (positive reinforcement) typically strengthen the individual's belief that he or she is able to perform the task.[31]

Increasing P-to-O Expectancies

The most obvious ways to improve P-to-O expectancies are to measure employee performance accurately and distribute more valued rewards to those with higher job performance. Unfortunately many organizations have difficulty putting this straightforward idea into practice. Some executives are reluctant to withhold rewards for poor performance because they don't want to experience conflict with employees. Others don't measure employee performance very well. For instance, fewer than half of the 6,000 employees surveyed in one study said they know how to increase their base pay or cash bonuses. In other words, most employees and managers have a generally low P-to-O expectancy regarding their paychecks.[32] Chapter 6 looks at reasons why rewards aren't connected to job performance.

P-to-O expectancies are perceptions, so employees should believe that higher performance will result in higher rewards. Having a performance-based reward system is important, but this fact must be communicated. When rewards are distributed, employees should understand how their rewards have been based on past performance. More generally, companies need to regularly communicate the existence of a performance-based reward system through examples, anecdotes, and public ceremonies.

Increasing Outcome Valences

Performance outcomes influence work effort only when those outcomes are valued by employees. This brings us back to what we learned from the needs/drives-based theories of motivation—namely, that companies should develop more individualized reward systems so that employees who perform well are offered a choice of rewards. Expectancy theory also emphasizes the need to discover and neutralize countervalent outcomes. These are performance outcomes that have negative valences, thereby reducing the effectiveness of existing reward systems. For example, peer pressure may cause some employees to perform their jobs at the minimum standard even though formal rewards and the job itself would otherwise motivate them to perform at higher levels.

Does Expectancy Theory Fit Reality?

Expectancy theory remains one of the better theories for predicting work effort and motivation. In particular, it plays a valuable role by detailing a person's thinking process when translating the competing demands of the four drives into specific effort. Expectancy theory has been applied to a wide variety of studies, such as predicting student motivation to participate in teaching evaluations, using a decision support system, leaving the organization, and engaging in organizational citizenship behaviors.[33] Research also indicates that expectancy theory predicts employee motivation in different cultures.[34]

One limitation is that expectancy theory seems to ignore the central role of emotion in employee effort and behavior. As we learned earlier in this and previous chapters, emotions serve an adaptive function that demands our attention and energizes us to take action. The valence element of expectancy theory captures some of this emotional process, but only peripherally. Thus theorists probably need to redesign the expectancy theory model in light of new information about the importance of emotions in motivation and behavior.

After reading this section you should be able to

7. **Describe the characteristics of effective goal setting and feedback.**

Goal Setting and Feedback

Walk into almost any call center and you will notice that performance is judged on several metrics such as average pickup time (time to answer the call), length of time per call, and abandon rates (customers who hang up before the call is handled by a customer service representative). For example, one recent survey reported that the average pickup time for call centers in the United States is 35 seconds, the average talk time is 11 minutes for government and 6.5 minutes for private call centers, and the average time on hold is 33 seconds. Some call centers have large electronic boards showing how many customers are waiting and the average time they have been waiting. Employees sometimes receive feedback on their computers, such as the average length of time for each call at their workstation.[35] Associated with these numbers are specific goals, and supervisors conduct goal-setting sessions with each employee to help them understand and achieve those objectives.

goal setting
The process of motivating employees and clarifying their role perceptions by establishing performance objectives.

Call centers rely on goal setting and feedback to motivate employees and achieve superior performance.[36] **Goal setting** is the process of motivating employees and clarifying their role perceptions by establishing performance objectives. It potentially improves employee performance in two ways: (1) by stretching the intensity and persistence of effort and (2) by giving employees clearer role perceptions so that their effort is channeled toward behaviors that will improve work performance.

Stretch Goals Send Speedera Staff to the Beach Near the end of a recent financial quarter, Speedera Network's 120 employees in Bangalore, India, and Santa Clara, California, received an enticing challenge from founder and CEO Ajit Gupta: "If we pull together to achieve our business targets [for the next quarter], then we'll all be on a beach in May." Employees at the Internet applications company (now merged with Akamai) even voted on the preferred destination (a Hawaiian resort). Speedera would cover employee expenses as well as 50 percent of a spouse's or family member's expenses for four days. Everyone worked feverishly toward the company's goals, which included a hefty increase in revenue. Their motivation was further fueled with constant reminders of the Hawaiian trip. "The offices were transformed to look like tropical islands," says Gupta. Staff also received postcards and brochures with tempting images of the resort and its attractions. Much to everyone's delight, the company achieved its goals and Speedera staff from both countries had a memorable bonding experience on Hawaiian beaches.[37]

Characteristics of Effective Goals

Goal setting is more complex than simply telling someone to "do your best." Instead it requires six conditions to maximize task effort and performance: specific goals, relevant goals, challenging goals, goal commitment, participation in goal formation (sometimes), and goal feedback.[38]

- *Specific goals.* Employees put more effort into a task when they work toward specific goals rather than "do your best" targets.[39] Specific goals have measurable levels of change over a specific and relatively short time frame, such as "reduce scrap rate by 7 percent over the next six months." Specific goals communicate precise performance expectations so employees can direct their effort more efficiently and reliably.

- *Relevant goals.* Goals must also be relevant to the individual's job and within his or her control. For example, a goal to reduce waste materials would have little value if employees don't have much control over waste in the production process.

- *Challenging goals.* Challenging goals (rather than easy ones) cause people to raise the intensity and persistence of their work effort and to think through information more actively. They also fulfill a person's need for achievement or self-actualization needs when the goal is achieved. General Electric, Goldman Sachs, and many other organizations emphasize *stretch goals*. These goals don't just stretch your abilities and motivation; they are goals that you don't know how to reach, so you need to be creative to achieve them.[40]

- *Goal commitment.* Although goals should be challenging, employees also need to be committed to accomplishing goals. Thus we need to find an optimal level of goal difficulty where the goals are challenging, yet employees are still motivated to achieve them.[41] This is the same as the E-to-P expectancy that we learned about in the section about expectancy theory. The lower the E-to-P expectancy that the goal can been accomplished, the less committed (motivated) the employee is to the goal.

- *Goal participation* (sometimes). Goal setting is usually (but not always) more effective when employees participate in setting goals.[42] Employees identify more with goals they are involved in setting than goals assigned by a supervisor. In fact, today's workforce increasingly expects to be involved in goal setting and other decisions that affect them. Participation may also improve goal quality because employees have valuable information and knowledge that may not be known to managers who develop these goals alone. Thus participation ensures that employees buy into the goals and have the competencies and resources necessary to accomplish them.

- *Goal feedback.* Feedback is another necessary condition for effective goal setting.[43] **Feedback** is any information that people receive about the consequences of their behavior. Feedback lets us know whether we have achieved a goal or are properly directing our effort toward it. Feedback is also an essential ingredient in motivation because our growth needs can't be satisfied unless we receive information about goal accomplishment. Feedback is so central to goal setting that we will look more closely at it next.

feedback
Any information that people receive about the consequences of their behavior.

Characteristics of Effective Feedback

Feedback is a key ingredient in goal setting and employee performance. It communicates what behaviors are appropriate or necessary in a particular situation (that is, it clarifies role perceptions) and improves ability by frequently providing information to correct performance problems. Information that identifies a gap between actual and ideal performance is known as *corrective feedback* because it raises awareness of performance errors and identifies ways to correct those errors.

Under some circumstances, feedback also motivates employees. This is particularly true when feedback is positive, such as the peer-to-peer recognition activities described in the opening vignette to this chapter. These recognition programs communicate feedback as rewards, so they have the double benefit of informing employees about their performance and fulfilling their needs. Constructive feedback can also be motivating when employees have a strong "can-do" attitude toward the task and a learning orientation. For these people, less-than-ideal performance feedback triggers the drive to learn (improve their performance), not their drive to defend.[44]

Many of the characteristics of effective goal setting also apply to effective feedback (see Exhibit 5.5). First, feedback should be *specific*. The information provided should be connected to the details of the goal, rather than subjective and general phrases such as "your sales are going well." Second, feedback must be *relevant*; it must relate to the individual's behavior rather than to conditions beyond the individual's control. This ensures that the feedback is not distorted by situational factors. Third, feedback should be *timely*; it should be available as soon as possible after the behavior or results. Timeliness helps employees see a clear association between their behavior and its consequences. The fourth characteristic of effective feedback is that it should be *credible*. Employees are more likely to accept feedback (particularly corrective feedback) from trustworthy and credible sources.

Finally, feedback should be *sufficiently frequent*. How frequent is "sufficiently"? The answer depends on at least two things. One consideration is the employee's knowledge and experience with the task. Feedback is a form of reinforcement, so employees working on new tasks should receive more frequent corrective feedback because they require more behavior guidance and reinforcement (see Chapter 3). Employees who are repeating familiar tasks can receive less frequent feedback. The second factor is how long it takes to complete the task. Feedback is necessarily less frequent in jobs with a long cycle time (executives and scientists) than in jobs with a short cycle time (grocery store cashiers).

Exhibit 5.5
Characteristics of Effective Feedback

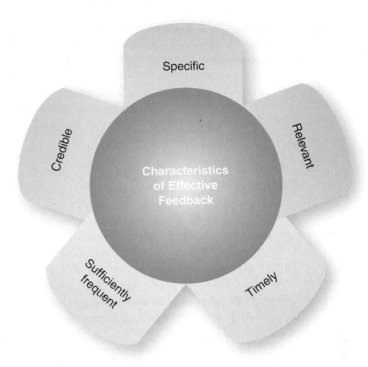

Sources of Feedback

Feedback can originate from nonsocial or social sources. Nonsocial sources provide feedback without someone communicating that information. The opening paragraph to this section mentioned that call centers have various forms of nonsocial feedback, such as electronic displays showing how many callers are waiting and the average time they have been waiting.[45] Some professionals have "executive dashboards" on their computer screens that display the latest measures of sales, inventory, and other indicators of corporate success. The job itself can be a nonsocial source of feedback. Many employees see the results of their work effort while making a product or providing a service where good and poor performance is fairly obvious.

Social sources of feedback include supervisors, clients, co-workers, and anyone else who communicates information about the employee's behavior or results. Supervisors in some call centers meet with each employee a few times each month to review monitored calls and discuss ways to improve those events. In most other organizations employees receive formal feedback maybe once or twice each year, but informal feedback occurs more often. Customer surveys have become a popular form of feedback for teams of employees, such as everyone who works at a bank branch.

multisource (360-degree) feedback
Performance feedback received from a full circle of people around an employee.

Multisource (360-Degree) Feedback According to some estimates, managers at almost all *Fortune* 500 firms receive feedback about their job performance from a full circle of people, including direct reports, peers, bosses, vendors, customers, and partners.[46] Most plans (87 percent) also give employees complete freedom to choose who will rate them. This **multisource or 360-degree feedback** tends to provide more complete and accurate information than feedback from a supervisor alone. It is particularly useful when the supervisor is unable to observe the employee's behavior or performance throughout the year. Lower-level employees also feel a greater sense of fairness and open communication when they are able to provide upward feedback about their boss's performance.[47]

However, multisource feedback also creates challenges. Having several people review so many co-workers can be expensive and time-consuming. With multiple opinions, the 360-degree process can also produce ambiguous and conflicting feedback, so employees may require guidance to interpret the results. A third concern is that peers may provide inflated rather than accurate feedback to avoid conflicts over the forthcoming year. A final concern is that critical feedback from many people can create stronger emotional reactions than if the critical judgment originates from just one person (your boss).[48]

Executive Coaching

Soon after his promotion to a senior management position at P&O Nedlloyd (now Maersk Line), Bob Kemp hired an executive coach to help him discover and repair his vulnerabilities. He was particularly keen to shore up his self-awareness skills because, as the top executive, there was no one above him at the shipping and logistics firm to regularly monitor his interpersonal style as a leader. Over several sessions, the executive coach teased out Kemp's weak spots, such as listening skills and being approachable. Before long Kemp's colleagues and wife noticed a positive change. "Very early in the process, people started telling me I was changing and I started to feel more at ease in the new role," Kemp recalls. He also noticed that people were "walking out of my office with a slightly more positive attitude."[49]

executive coaching
A helping relationship using behavioral methods to assist clients in identifying and achieving goals for their professional performance and personal satisfaction.

Bob Kemp and numerous other executives have turned to **executive coaching**, which uses a variety of behavioral methods to help clients identify and achieve goals for their performance and well-being. Executive coaching is usually conducted by an external consultant and is essentially one-on-one "just-in-time" personal development using feedback and other techniques. Coaches do not provide answers to the employee's problems. Rather they are "thought partners" who offer more accurate feedback, open dialogue, and constructive encouragement to improve the client's performance and personal well-being.

The evidence so far is that executives who work with an executive coach perform better than those who do not. Coaching comes in many forms, so this positive result should be treated cautiously. Still, executive coaching has become a popular form of feedback and development for executives in many countries. For instance, a few years ago Alison Clark was burning out from overwork, and her business, Tickles Child Care Center in Te Puke, New Zealand, was suffering from high staff turnover. With the guidance of an executive coach, Clark discovered the leadership issues she needed to address and thereby improve the business and her personal life. The ongoing coaching had a demonstrable effect: Clark recently earned awards for her entrepreneurship and team development among businesses in New Zealand.[50]

Choosing Feedback Sources

With so many sources of feedback—executive coaching, multisource feedback, executive dashboards, customer surveys, equipment gauges, nonverbal communication from your boss, and so on—which one works best under which conditions? The preferred feedback source depends on the purpose of the information. To learn about their progress toward goal accomplishment, employees usually prefer nonsocial feedback sources, such as computer printouts or feedback directly from the job. This is because information from nonsocial sources is considered more accurate than information from social sources. Corrective feedback from nonsocial sources is also less damaging to self-esteem. This is probably just as well because social sources tend to delay negative information, leave some of it out, and distort the bad news in a positive way.[51] When employees want to improve their

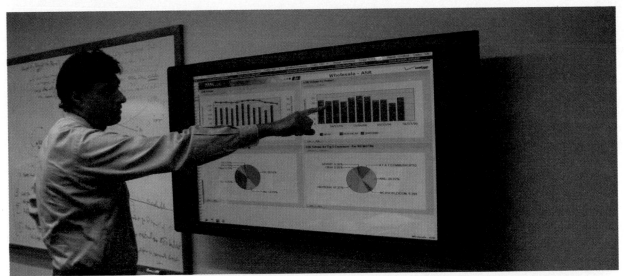

Executive Feedback Drives through the Dashboard Corporate intranets now allow many executives to receive feedback instantaneously on their computer, usually in the form of graphic output on an executive dashboard. Almost half of Microsoft employees use a dashboard to monitor project deadlines, sales, and other metrics. Microsoft CEO Steve Ballmer regularly reviews dashboard results in one-on-one meetings with his seven business leaders. "Every time I go to see Ballmer, it's an expectation that I bring my dashboard with me," says Jeff Raikes, who heads the Microsoft Office division. Verizon CIO Shaygan Kheradpir (shown in this photo) also appreciates the instant feedback provided by his dashboard, which is a huge plasma screen on the wall of his office. Called the "Wall of Shaygan," the screen displays the status of more than 100 network systems around the country in green, yellow, or red lights. Another part of the screen also shows sales, voice portal volumes, call center results, and other business metrics.[52]

self-image, they seek out positive feedback from social sources. It feels better to have co-workers say that you are performing the job well than to discover this from a computer printout.

Evaluating Goal Setting and Feedback

A recent survey of organizational behavior researchers recently identified goal setting as one of the top OB theories in terms of validity and usefulness.[53] This high score is not surprising given the impressive research support and wide application of this concept in a variety of settings. In partnership with goal setting, feedback also has an excellent reputation for improving employee motivation and performance.

Nevertheless, both goal setting and feedback have a few limitations.[54] One problem is that combining goals with monetary incentives motivates many employees to set up easy rather than difficult goals. In some cases employees have negotiated goals with their supervisor that have already been completed! Another limitation is that goal setting potentially focuses employees on a narrow subset of measurable performance indicators while ignoring aspects of job performance that are difficult to measure. The saying "What gets measured, gets done" applies here. A third problem is that setting performance goals is effective in established jobs, but it seems to interfere with the learning process in new, complex jobs. Thus we need to be careful not to apply goal setting where an intense learning process is occurring.

After reading this section you should be able to

8. **Summarize the equity theory model, including how people try to reduce feelings of inequity.**

9. **Identify the factors that influence procedural justice, as well as the consequences of procedural justice.**

Organizational Justice

Patti Anderson came from a family of Boeing engineers, so she was proud to also work as a manufacturing engineer at the aerospace company's commercial airplane division in Renton, Washington. But that pride evaporated when Anderson discovered that the men in her family earned more than her at Boeing for performing the same work. "My husband, brother, and dad also performed the same job as me, and each was paid more than me and consistently received higher raises than I did," said Anderson in a legal statement. "I know this because I saw their pay stubs."[55]

Most corporate leaders know that treating employees fairly is both morally correct and good for employee motivation, loyalty, and well-being. Yet the feelings of injustice that Patti Anderson describes are regular occurrences in a variety of situations. To minimize these incidents, we need to first understand that there are two forms of organizational justice: distributive justice and procedural justice.[56] **Distributive justice** refers to perceived fairness in the outcomes we receive relative to our contributions and the outcomes and contributions of others. **Procedural justice,** on the other hand, refers to fairness of the procedures used to decide the distribution of resources. Patti Anderson felt distributive injustice because male colleagues were paid significantly more than she was, even though their contribution to the organization was comparable. Andersen also experienced procedural injustice because of the way Boeing initially responded to her concerns.

distributive justice
The perceived fairness in outcomes we receive relative to our contributions and the outcomes and contributions of others.

procedural justice
The fairness of the procedures used to decide the distribution of resources.

Distributive Justice and Equity Theory

The first thing we usually think about and experience in situations of injustice is distributive injustice—the belief (and its emotional response) that the distribution of pay and other outcomes is unfair. What is considered "fair" varies with each person and situation. We apply an *equality principle* when we believe that everyone in the group should receive the same outcomes. Companies apply this principle when allocating some employee benefits and parking spaces, for example. The *need principle* is applied when we believe that those with the greatest need should receive more outcomes than others with less need. Patti Anderson applied the *equity principle* by inferring that people should be paid in proportion to their contribution. The equity principle is the most common distributive justice rule in organizational settings, so let's look at it in more detail.

equity theory
A theory that explains how people develop perceptions of fairness in the distribution and exchange of resources.

Elements of Equity Theory   To explain how the equity principle operates in our heads, OB scholars developed **equity theory,** which says that employees determine feelings of equity by comparing their own outcome/input ratio to the outcome/input ratio of some other person.[57] The outcome/input ratio is the value of the outcomes you receive divided by the value of inputs you provide in the exchange relationship. Anderson probably included her skills and level of responsibility as inputs. Other inputs might include experience, status, performance, personal reputation, and amount of time worked. Outcomes are the things employees receive from the organization in exchange for the inputs. For Anderson, the main outcomes are the paycheck and pay raises. Some other outcomes might be promotions, recognition, or an office with a window.

Equity theory states that we compare our outcome/input ratio with a comparison other.[58] In our earlier example, Anderson compared herself with her male family members and likely other men who worked in the same jobs at Boeing. However, the comparison other may be another person, group of people, or even yourself in the past. It may be someone in the same job, another job, or another organization. Chief executives have no direct comparison within the firm, so they tend to compare themselves with their counterparts in other organizations. Some research suggests that employees frequently collect information about several referents to form a "generalized" comparison other.[59] For the most part, however, the comparison other varies from one person to the next and is not easily identifiable.

Equity Evaluation   We form an equity evaluation after determining our own outcome/input ratio and comparing this with the comparison other's ratio. Let's consider the experience of Patti Anderson again. Anderson feels *underreward* inequity because her male counterparts receive higher outcomes (pay) for inputs that are, at best, comparable to what she contributes at Boeing. This condition is illustrated in Exhibit 5.6(a).

In the equity condition Anderson would believe that her outcome/input ratio is similar to the ratio of male colleagues. Specifically, if she believes that she provides the same inputs as male family members and other men who work in the same jobs at Boeing, then she would feel equity if both men and women received the same pay and other outcomes (see Exhibit 5.6(b)). It is also possible that Anderson's male family members experience *overreward* inequity (Exhibit 5.6(c)). They would feel that their performance is similar to Anderson's performance, yet they earn more money. However, overreward inequity isn't as common as underreward inequity because people quickly change their perceptions to justify the higher outcomes.

Correcting Inequity Feelings   We experience an emotional tension with perceived inequities; and when sufficiently strong, the tension motivates us to reduce the inequities. But what are we motivated to do to reduce this tension? Research has identified several reactions that people have to inequity. Some actions are reasonable, whereas others are dysfunctional; some are illegal, such as theft and sabotage. Here are the main ways that people correct inequity feelings when they are underrewarded compared to a co-worker (comparison other):[60]

Exhibit 5.6
Equity Theory Model

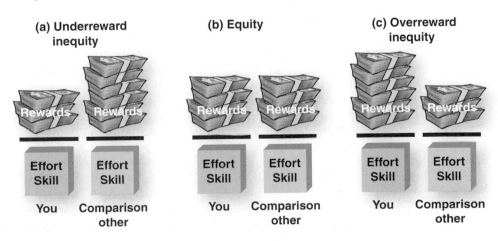

| (a) Underreward inequity | (b) Equity | (c) Overreward inequity |

"O.K., if you can't see your way to giving me a pay raise, how about giving Parkerson a pay cut?"

- *Reduce our inputs.* Perform at a lower level, give fewer helpful suggestions, engage in less organizational citizenship behavior.

- *Increase our outcomes.* Ask for a pay increase, make unauthorized use of company resources.

- *Increase the comparison other's inputs.* Subtly ask the better-off co-worker to do a larger share of the work to justify his or her higher pay or other outcomes.

- *Reduce comparison other's outcomes.* Ask the boss to stop giving favorable treatment to the co-worker.

- *Change our perceptions.* Believe the co-worker really is doing more (such as working longer hours) or that the higher outcomes (perhaps a better office) he or she receives really aren't so much better than what we get.

- *Change the comparison other.* Compare ourselves to someone else closer to our situation (job duties, pay scale).

- *Leave the field.* Avoid thinking about the inequity by keeping away from the office where the co-worker is located, taking more sick leave, moving to another department, or quitting the job.

Although the categories remain the same, people who feel overreward inequity would, of course, act differently. For example, overrewarded employees don't usually correct this tension by working harder. Instead they might encourage the referent to work at a more leisurely pace or, more likely, change their perceptions to justify why they are given more favorable outcomes. As the author Pierre Burton once said, "I was underpaid for the first half of my life. I don't mind being overpaid for the second half."[61]

Individual Differences: Equity Sensitivity   Thus far we have described equity theory as though everyone has the same feelings of inequity in a particular situation. The reality, however, is that people vary in their **equity sensitivity**—that is, their outcome/input preferences and reactions to various outcome/input ratios.[62] At one end of

equity sensitivity
A person's outcome/ input preferences and reaction to various outcome/input ratios.

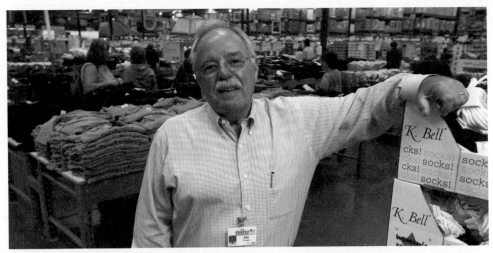

Costco Wholesale CEO Keeps Executive Pay Equitable John Pierpont Morgan, who in the 1800s founded the financial giant now called J.P. Morgan Chase, warned that no CEO should earn more than 20 times an average worker's pay. That advice didn't stop William B. Harrison Jr., the current CEO of J.P. Morgan Chase, from receiving $15–20 million in pay, bonuses, and stock options for each of the past few years. That's more than 700 times the pay of the average employee in the United States. Costco Wholesale chief executive Jim Sinegal (shown in this photo) thinks such a large wage gap is blatantly unfair and can lead to long-term employee motivation problems. "Having an individual who is making 100 or 200 or 300 times more than the average person working on the floor is wrong," says Sinegal, who cofounded the Issaquah, Washington, company. With annual salary and bonus of $550,000, Sinegal ranks as one of the lowest-paid executives even though Costco is one of the country's largest retailers and its employees among the highest paid in the industry.[63]

the equity sensitivity continuum are the "benevolents"—people who are tolerant of situations where they are underrewarded. They might still prefer equal outcome/input ratios, but they don't mind if others receive more than they do for the same inputs. In the middle are people who fit the standard equity theory model. These "equity sensitives" want their outcome/input ratio to be equal to the outcome/input ratio of the comparison other. Equity sensitives feel increasing inequity as the ratios become different. At the other end are the "entitleds." These people feel more comfortable in situations where they receive proportionately more than others. They might accept having the same outcome/input ratio as others, but they would prefer receiving more than others performing the same work.[64]

Evaluating Equity Theory

Equity theory is widely studied and quite successful at predicting various situations involving feelings of workplace injustice, such as major baseball league salary disputes and remuneration of British CEOs.[65] Feelings of inequity are regular occurrences in every workplace. Some tensions are minor and temporary misunderstandings of the situation; others produce unpleasant emotions or worse, major theft and sabotage of company resources. Feelings of inequity are based on the moral principle of distributive justice (see Chapter 2), so companies that act unfairly toward their employees also face the charge of unethical conduct.

In spite of its research support, equity theory has a few limitations. One concern is that the theory isn't sufficiently specific to predict employee motivation and behavior. It doesn't indicate which inputs or outcomes are most valuable, and it doesn't identify the comparison other against which the outcome/input ratio is evaluated. These vague and highly flexible elements may explain why OB experts think equity theory is highly valid but only moderately useful.[66] A second problem is that equity theory incorrectly assumes people are individualistic, rational, and selfish. In reality, people are social creatures who define themselves as members of various groups (see the discussion of social identity theory in Chapter 3). They share goals with other members of these groups and commit themselves to the norms of their groups. A third limitation is that recent studies have found that equity theory accounts for only some of our feelings of fairness or justice in the workplace. Experts now say that procedural justice, which we look at next, is at least as important as distributive justice.

Procedural Justice

For many years OB scholars believed that distributive justice was more important than procedural justice in explaining employee motivation, attitudes, and behavior. This belief was based on the assumption that people are driven mainly by self-interest, so they try to maximize their personal outcomes. Today we know that people seek justice for its own sake, not just as a means to improve their paychecks. Thus procedural justice seems to be as important as (and some experts say more important than) distributive justice in explaining employee attitudes, motivation, and behavior.[67]

Structural Rules of Justice   Procedural justice is influenced by both structural rules and social rules (see Exhibit 5.7).[68] Structural rules represent the policies and practices that decision makers should follow. The most frequently identified structural rule in procedural justice research is people's belief that they should have a "voice" in the decision process.[69] Voice allows employees to convey what they believe are relevant facts and views to the decision maker. Voice also provides a "value-expressive" function;

Exhibit 5.7   **Components of Organizational Justice**

employees tend to feel better after having an opportunity to speak their minds. Other structural rules are that the decision maker is unbiased, relies on complete and accurate information, applies existing policies consistently, has listened to all sides of the dispute, and allows the decision to be appealed to a higher authority.[70]

Social Rules of Justice   Along with structural rules, procedural justice is influenced by social rules—that is, how well the decision maker treats employees during the process. The two key social rules are respect and accountability. Employees feel greater procedural justice when they are treated with respect. For instance, one study found that nonwhite nurses who experienced racism tended to file grievances only after experiencing disrespectful treatment in their attempt to resolve the racist situation. Another study found that employees with repetitive strain injuries were more likely to file workers' compensation claims after experiencing disrespectful behavior from management. A third recent study noted that employees have stronger feelings of injustice when the manager has a reputation of treating people unfairly most of the time.[71]

The other social rule that has attracted attention is accountability. People believe that they are entitled to explanations about decisions, particularly when the results have potentially negative consequences for them. For instance, suppose a co-worker receives a better office than you do (distributive injustice). Chances are that you will feel less injustice after hearing the decision maker's explanation for that decision.

Consequences of Procedural Injustice   Procedural justice strongly influences a person's emotions and motivation. Employees tend to experience anger toward the source of the injustice, which generates various response behaviors that scholars categorize as either withdrawal or aggression.[72] Notice how these response behaviors are similar to the fight-or-flight responses described earlier in the chapter regarding situations that activate our drive to defend. Withdrawal behaviors might include avoiding those who acted unjustly or being less willing to comply with their future requests. For instance, employees who believe their boss relies on an unfair decision process may be less likely to "walk the extra mile" in the future and might complete any assigned work only at a minimal standard.

Aggressive responses to procedural injustice include several counterproductive work behaviors, such as sabotage, theft, conflict, and acts of violence.[73] However, most employees who experience injustice respond with milder forms of retaliation, such as showing indignation and denouncing the decision maker's competence. Research suggests that being treated unfairly undermines our self-esteem and social status, particularly when others see that we have been unjustly treated. Consequently employees retaliate to restore their self-esteem and reinstate their status and power in the relationship with the perpetrator of the injustice. Employees also engage in these counterproductive behaviors to educate the decision maker, thereby minimizing the chance of future injustices.[74]

Organizational Justice in Practice

One of the clearest lessons from equity theory is that we need to continually treat people fairly in the distribution of organizational rewards. Unfortunately this is perhaps one of life's greatest challenges because most of us seem to have unique opinions about the value of inputs and outcomes. Decision makers need to carefully understand these dynamics along with the distribution rules—equity, equality, or need—that the organization wants to apply. From the procedural justice literature, we can see that justice also depends on whether employees believe the decision-making process follows a fair set of rules and whether they are personally treated fairly in that process.

In spite of the many challenges of creating justice in the workplace, managers can improve their procedural fairness through training programs. In one study, supervisors participated in role-play exercises to develop several procedural justice practices in the disciplinary process, such as maintaining the employee's privacy, giving employees some control over the process, avoiding arbitrariness, and exhibiting a supportive demeanor. Judges subsequently rated supervisors who received the procedural justice training as behaving more fairly than supervisors who did not receive the training. In another study, managers received procedural justice training through lectures, case studies, role-playing, and discussion. Three months later subordinates of the trained managers had significantly higher organizational citizenship behaviors than the subordinates of managers who did not receive procedural justice training.[75] Overall it seems that justice can be improved in the workplace.

Chapter Summary

Motivation refers to the forces within a person that affect his or her direction, intensity, and persistence of voluntary behavior in the workplace. Motivation has become more challenging because of an increasingly turbulent work environment, the removal of direct supervision as a motivational instrument, and the lack of understanding about what motivates the new generations of people entering the workforce.

Maslow's needs hierarchy groups needs into a hierarchy of five levels and states that the lowest needs are initially most important, but higher needs become more important as the lower ones are satisfied. Although very popular, the theory lacks research support—as does ERG theory, which attempted to overcome some of the limitations in Maslow's needs hierarchy. Both models assume that everyone has the same hierarchy, whereas emerging evidence suggests that needs hierarchies vary from one person to the next based on their personal values.

Four-drive theory states that everyone has four innate drives—the drives to acquire, bond, learn, and defend. These drives create emotional markers that motivate us. The drives generate competing emotions, however, so we consciously reconcile these competing impulses through a skill set that considers social norms, past experience, and personal values. Four-drive theory offers considerable potential for understanding employee motivation, but it still requires clarification and research to understand how people translate competing emotions into motivated behavior.

McClelland's learned needs theory argues that needs can be strengthened through learning. The three needs studied in this respect have been need for achievement, need for power, and need for affiliation.

The practical implication of needs/drives-based motivation theories is that corporate leaders must provide opportunities for everyone in the workplace to regularly fulfill all four drives; that organizations should avoid too much or too little opportunity to fulfill each drive; and that employees should be offered a choice of rewards rather than given the same reward as everyone else.

Expectancy theory states that work effort is determined by the perception that effort will result in a particular level of performance (E-to-P expectancy); the perception that a specific behavior or performance level will lead to specific outcomes (P-to-O expectancy); and the valences that the person feels for those outcomes. The E-to-P expectancy increases by improving the employee's ability and confidence to perform the job. The P-to-O expectancy increases by measuring performance accurately, distributing higher rewards to better performers, and showing employees that rewards are performance-based. Outcome valences increase by finding out what employees want and using these resources as rewards.

Goal setting is the process of motivating employees and clarifying their role perceptions by establishing performance objectives. Goals are more effective when they are specific, relevant, and challenging; have employee commitment; and are accompanied by meaningful feedback. Participative goal setting is important in some situations. Effective feedback is specific, relevant, timely, credible, and sufficiently frequent (which depends on the length of the task cycle and the employee's knowledge and experience with the task). Two increasingly popular forms of feedback are multisource (360-degree) assessment and executive coaching. Feedback from nonsocial sources is also beneficial.

Organizational justice consists of distributive justice (perceived fairness in the outcomes we receive relative to our contributions and the outcomes and contributions of others) and procedural justice (fairness of the procedures used to decide the distribution of resources). Equity theory, which considers the most common principle applied in distributive justice, has four elements: outcome/input ratio, comparison other, equity evaluation, and consequences of inequity. The theory also explains what people are motivated to do when they feel inequitably treated. Equity sensitivity is a personal characteristic that explains why people react differently to varying degrees of inequity.

Procedural justice is influenced by both structural rules and social rules. Structural rules represent the policies and practices that decision makers should follow; the most frequently identified is giving employees a voice in the decision process. Social rules refer to standards of interpersonal conduct between employees and decision makers; they are best observed by showing respect and providing accountability for decisions. Procedural justice is as important as distributive justice, and it influences organizational commitment, trust, and various withdrawal and aggression behaviors.

Key Terms

distributive justice, p. 152
drives, p. 135
equity sensitivity, p. 154
equity theory, p. 152
ERG theory, p. 138
executive coaching, p. 150
expectancy theory, p. 143
feedback, p. 148

four-drive theory, p. 138
goal setting, p. 146
Maslow's needs hierarchy, p. 135
motivation, p. 134
multisource (360-degree) feedback, p. 149
need for achievement (nAch), p. 141
need for affiliation (nAff), p. 141

need for power (nPow), p. 141
needs, p. 135
positive organizational behavior, p. 137
procedural justice, p. 152
self-actualization, p. 135
valence, p. 144

Critical Thinking Questions

1. This chapter begins by suggesting that motivating employees has become more challenging in recent years, partly because younger employees (Generation-X and Generation-Y) have different expectations than baby boomers. How do you think these younger and older generation groups differ in their expectations? Generally speaking, what would motivate a typical Generation-Y worker (under 25 years old) more than a typical baby boomer worker (over 45 years old)?

2. Four-drive theory is conceptually different from Maslow's needs hierarchy (as well as ERG theory) in several ways. Describe these differences. At the same time, needs are typically based on drives, so the four drives should parallel the seven needs that Maslow identified (five in the hierarchy and two additional needs). Map Maslow's needs to the four drives in four-drive theory.

3. Use all three components of expectancy theory to explain why some employees are motivated to show up for work during a severe storm whereas others make no effort to leave their homes.

4. What are the limitations of expectancy theory in predicting an individual's work effort and behavior?

5. Using your knowledge of the characteristics of effective goals, establish two meaningful goals related to your performance in this class.

6. When do employees prefer feedback from nonsocial rather than social sources? Explain why nonsocial sources are preferred under these conditions.

7. Several service representatives are upset that a newly hired representative with no previous experience will be paid $3,000 a year above the usual starting salary in the pay range. The department manager explained that the new hire would not accept the entry-level rate, so the company raised the offer by $3,000. All five reps currently earn salaries near the top of the scale ($15,000 higher than the new recruit), although they all started at the minimum starting salary a few years earlier. Use equity theory to explain why the five service representatives feel inequity in this situation.

8. Organizational injustice can occur in the classroom as well as in the workplace. Identify classroom situations in which you experienced feelings of injustice. What can instructors do to maintain an environment that fosters both distributive and procedural justice?

Case Study 5.1 BUDDY'S SNACK COMPANY

Russell Casey, Clayton State University, and Gloria Thompson, University of Phoenix

Buddy's Snack Company is a family-owned company located in the Rocky Mountains. Buddy Forest started the business in 1951 by selling homemade potato chips out of the back of his pickup truck. Nowadays Buddy's is a $36 million snack food company that is struggling to regain market share lost to Frito-Lay and other fierce competitors. In the early eighties Buddy passed the business to his son, Buddy Jr., who is currently grooming his son, Mark, to succeed himself as head of the company.

Six months ago Mark joined Buddy's Snacks as a salesperson, and after four months he was quickly promoted to sales manager. Mark recently graduated from a local university with an MBA in marketing, and Buddy Jr. was hoping that Mark would be able to implement strategies that could help turn the company around. One of Mark's initial strategies was to introduce a new sales performance management system. As part of this approach, any salesperson who receives a below-average performance rating would be required to attend a mandatory coaching session with his or her supervisor. Mark Forest is hoping that these coaching sessions will motivate employees to increase their sales. This case describes the reaction of three salespeople who have been required to attend a coaching session because of their low performance over the previous quarter.

Lynda Lewis

Lynda is a hard worker who takes pride in her work ethic. She has spent a lot of time reading the training material and learning selling techniques, viewing training videos on her own time, and accompanying top salespeople on their calls. Lynda has no problem asking for advice and doing whatever needs to be done to learn the business. Everyone agrees that Lynda has a cheery attitude and is a real "team player," giving the company 150 percent at all times. It has been a tough quarter for Lynda due to the downturn in the economy, but she is doing her best to make sales for the company. Lynda feels that failure to make quota during this past quarter is due not to lack of effort, but just bad luck in the economy. She is hopeful that things will turn around in the next quarter.

Lynda is upset with Mark about having to attend the coaching session because this is the first time in three years that her sales quota has not been met. Although Lynda is willing to do whatever it takes to be successful, she is concerned that the coaching sessions will be held on a Saturday. Doesn't Mark realize that Lynda has to raise three boys by herself and that weekends are an important time for her family? Because Lynda is a dedicated employee, she will somehow manage to rearrange the family's schedule.

Lynda is now very concerned about how her efforts are being perceived by Mark. After all, she exceeded the sales quota for the previous quarter, yet she did not receive thanks or congratulations for those efforts. The entire experience has left Lynda unmotivated and questioning her future with the company.

Michael Benjamin

Michael is happy to have his job at Buddy's Snack Company, although he really doesn't like sales work that much. Michael accepted this position because he felt that he wouldn't have to work hard and would have a lot of free time during the day. Michael was sent to coaching mainly because his customer satisfaction reports were low; in fact, they were the lowest in the company. Michael tends to give canned presentations and does not listen closely to the customer's needs. Consequently, Michael makes numerous errors in new sales orders, which delay shipments and lose business and goodwill for Buddy's Snack Company. Michael doesn't really care because most of his customers do not spend much money, and he doesn't think it is worth his while.

There has been a recent change in the company commission structure. Instead of selling to the warehouse stores and possibly earning a high commission, Michael is now forced to sell to lower-volume convenience stores. In other words, he will have to sell twice as much product to earn the same amount of money. Michael does not think this change in commission is fair, and he feels that the coaching session will be a waste of time. He believes that the other members of the sales team are getting all of the good leads, and that is why they are so successful. Michael doesn't socialize with others in the office and attributes others' success and promotions to "whom they know" in the company rather than the fact that they are hard workers. He thinks that no matter how much effort is put into the job, he will never be adequately rewarded.

Kyle Sherbo

For three of the last five years Kyle was the number one salesperson in the division and had hopes of being promoted to sales manager. When Mark joined the company, Kyle worked closely with Buddy Jr. to help Mark learn all facets of the business. Kyle thought this close relationship with Buddy Jr. would assure his upcoming promotion to the coveted position of sales manager, and he was devastated to learn that Mark received the promotion that he thought was his.

During the past quarter there was a noticeable change in Kyle's work habits. It has become commonplace for Kyle to be late for appointments or miss them entirely, not return phone calls, and not follow up on leads. His sales performance declined dramatically, which resulted in a drastic loss of income. Although Kyle had been dedicated and fiercely loyal to Buddy Jr. and the company for many years, he is now looking for other employment. Buddy's Snacks is located in a rural community, which leaves Kyle with limited job opportunities. He was, however, offered a position as a sales manager with a competing company in a larger town, but Kyle's wife refuses to leave the area because of her strong family ties. Kyle is bitter and resentful of his current situation and now faces a mandatory coaching session that will be conducted by Mark.

Discussion Questions

1. You have met three employees of Buddy's Snacks. Explain how each employee's situation relates to equity theory.

2. Explain the motivation of these three employees in terms of the expectancy theory of motivation.

Case Study 5.2 FAT MERGER PAYOUTS OF CEOs

 Mergers have roared back in corporate America, and with them have come highly lucrative payouts for the executives who triggered or accepted the acquisitions. One example is Gillette CEO James M. Kilts, who received a whopping $165 million, including stock options and severance, for selling the razor maker to Procter & Gamble. Bruce L. Hammonds, CEO of MBNA Corp., was apparently promised $102 million in connection with the credit-card company's acquisition by Bank of America Corp. Further behind but still well ahead of the average employee's lifetime income is Toys 'R' Us Inc. CEO John H. Eyler, who will receive cash and benefits worth about $63 million when the struggling toy retailer is purchased by an investment group. But several observers say these special perks are blatantly unfair. Others point out that the bonuses perversely reward the people who made the company vulnerable to takeover.

This *BusinessWeek* case study examines the new "Gilded Age" of executive payouts from mergers and acquisitions. It considers the complaints hurled at these generous rewards and justifications that the beneficiaries give in response. Read the full text of this *BusinessWeek* article at www.mhhe.com/mcshane4e and prepare for the discussion questions below.

Discussion Questions

1. Use equity theory to explain some of the criticisms that are leveled against these large merger payouts.

2. The article states that some CEOs are quite persistent about negotiating their payouts. Use four-drive theory to explain why this is so.

3. What are these golden payouts supposed to motivate in these executives? What unintended behaviors might they also (or alternatively) motivate?

Source: E. Thornton, "Fat Merger Payouts of CEOs," *Business Week*, 12 Decmeber 2005, 34.

Class Exercise 5.3 NEEDS PRIORITY EXERCISE

PURPOSE This class exercise is designed to help you understand the characteristics and contingencies of employee needs in the workplace.

INSTRUCTIONS

1. The accompanying table lists in alphabetical order 14 characteristics of the job or work environment. Working alone, use the far left column to rank order these characteristics in terms of how important they are to you personally. Write "1" beside the most important characteristic, "2" for the second most important, and so on through to "14" for the least important characteristic on this list.

2. In the second column, rank order these characteristics in the order that you think human resource managers believe they are important for their employees.

3. Your instructor will provide results of a recent large-scale survey of employees. When these results are presented, identify the reasons for any noticeable differences. Relate these differences to your understanding of the emerging view of employee needs and drives in work settings.

Importance to you	What HR managers believe are important to employees	
6		Autonomy and independence
7	1	Benefits (health care, dental, and so on)
12		Career development opportunities
4		Communication between employees and senior managers
2	2	Compensation/pay
8	3	Feeling safe in the work environment
9		Flexibility to balance work/life issues
5	4	Job security
13		Job specific training
14		Management recognition of employee job performance
11		Opportunities to use skills and abilities
10		Organization's commitment to professional development
3		Relationship with immediate supervisor
1		The work itself

Team Exercise 5.4 A QUESTION OF FEEDBACK

PURPOSE   This exercise is designed to help you understand the importance of feedback, including problems that occur with imperfect communication in the feedback process.

MATERIALS   The instructor will distribute a few pages of exhibits to one person on each team. The other students will need a pencil with an eraser and some blank paper. Movable chairs and tables in a large area are helpful.

INSTRUCTIONS

1. The class will be divided into pairs of students. Each pair is ideally located in a private area, away from other students and where one person can write. One student is given the pages of exhibits from the instructor. The other student in each pair is not allowed to see these exhibits.

2. The student holding the materials will describe each of the exhibits; the other student's task is to accurately replicate each exhibit. The pair of students can compare the replication with the original at the end of each drawing. They may also switch roles for each exhibit if they wish. If roles are switched, the instructor must distribute exhibits separately to each student so that they are not seen by the other person. Each exhibit has a different set of limitations, as described here:

    *   *Exhibit 1.* The student describing the exhibit cannot look at the other student or at the student's drawing. The student drawing the exhibit cannot speak or otherwise communicate with the person describing the exhibit.

    *   *Exhibit 2.* The student describing the exhibit may look at the other student's diagram. However, he or she may say only "yes" or "no" when the student drawing the diagram asks a specific question. In other words, the person presenting the information can use only these words for feedback and only when asked a question by the writer.

    *   *Exhibit 3* (optional, if time permits). The student describing the exhibit may look at the other student's diagram and may provide any feedback at any time to the person replicating the exhibit.

3. The class will gather to discuss this exercise. This may include conversation about the importance of feedback and the characteristics of effective feedback for individual motivation and learning.

Self-Assessment 5.5

MEASURING YOUR EQUITY SENSITIVITY

PURPOSE   This self-assessment is designed to help you estimate your level of equity sensitivity.

INSTRUCTIONS   Read each of the following statements and circle the response that you believe best reflects your position regarding each statement. Then use the scoring key in Appendix B to calculate your results. You will complete this exercise alone so you can assess yourself honestly without concerns of social comparison. However, class discussion will focus on equity theory and the effect of equity sensitivity on perceptions of fairness in the workplace.

Equity Preference Questionnaire

To what extent do you agree or disagree that...	Strongly agree	Agree	Neutral	Disagree	Strongly disagree
1. I prefer to do as little as possible at work while getting as much as I can from my employer.	☐	☐	☐	☐	☐
2. I am most satisfied at work when I have to do as little as possible.	☐	☐	☐	☐	☐
3. When I am at my job, I think of ways to get out of work.	☐	☐	☐	☐	☐
4. If I could get away with it, I would try to work just a little bit more slowly than the boss expects.	☐	☐	☐	☐	☐
5. It is really satisfying to me when I can get something for nothing at work.	☐	☐	☐	☐	☐
6. It is the smart employee who gets as much as he or she can while giving as little as possible in return.	☐	☐	☐	☐	☐
7. Employees who are more concerned about what they can get from their employer rather than what they can give to their employer are the wisest.	☐	☐	☐	☐	☐
8. When I have completed my tasks for the day, I help out other employees who have yet to complete their tasks.	☐	☐	☐	☐	☐
9. Even if I receive low wages and poor benefits from my employer, I would still try to do my best at my job.	☐	☐	☐	☐	☐
10. If I had to work hard all day at my job, I would probably quit.	☐	☐	☐	☐	☐
11. I feel obligated to do more than I am paid to do at work.	☐	☐	☐	☐	☐
12. At work, my greatest concern is whether I am doing the best job I can.	☐	☐	☐	☐	☐
13. A job that requires me to be busy during the day is better than a job that allows me a lot of loafing.	☐	☐	☐	☐	☐
14. At work, I feel uneasy when there is little work for me to do.	☐	☐	☐	☐	☐
15. I would become very dissatisfied with my job if I had little or no work to do.	☐	☐	☐	☐	☐
16. All other things being equal, it is better to have a job with a lot of duties and responsibilities than one with few duties and responsibilities.	☐	☐	☐	☐	☐

Source: K.S. Sauleya and A.G. Bedeian, "Equity Sensitivity: Construction of a Measure and Examination of Its Psychometric Properties," *Journal of Management* 26 (September 2000), pp. 885–910.

Self-Assessment 5.6

MEASURING YOUR GROWTH NEED STRENGTH (STUDENT OLC)

Abraham Maslow's needs hierarchy theory distinguished between deficiency needs and growth needs. Deficiency needs become activated when unfulfilled, such as the need for food or belongingness. Growth needs, on the other hand, continue to develop even when temporarily fulfilled. Maslow identified self-actualization as the only category of growth needs. Research has found that Maslow's needs hierarchy theory overall doesn't fit reality, but specific elements such as the concept of growth needs have not been rejected. This self-assessment is designed to estimate your level of growth need strength. This instrument asks you to consider what about a job is most important to you. Please indicate which of the two jobs you personally would prefer if you had to make a choice between them. In answering each question, assume that everything else about the jobs is the same. Pay attention only to the characteristics actually listed.

After reading this chapter, if you need additional information, see www.mhhe.com/mcshane4e for more in-depth interactivities that correspond with this material.

Fifteen years ago Nucor was an upstart in an industry dominated by Bethlehem Steel, National Steel, and other megafirms. Today, battered by global competition, two-thirds of American steel companies have disappeared or are under bankruptcy protection. Nucor, on the other hand, has become the largest steel company in America and 10th largest in the world. And although it now employs 11,000 people, Nucor remains nimble, highly competitive, and profitable, handily beating most other companies in the Standard & Poor's 500 index in shareholder returns over the past five years.

Nucor has survived and thrived in the turbulent steel industry through the benefits of performance-based rewards, job design, and empowerment.

What's Nucor's secret to success? Aside from technological innovations and avoiding "legacy" payroll costs, the company relies on applied performance practices that create phenomenal levels of employee engagement. To begin with, it has an extreme performance reward system. The average Nucor steelworker earns more than $70,000 in a typical year, but only one-third of that is guaranteed. "We pay a real low base wage, but high bonuses on a weekly basis," explains Nucor human resources vice president Jim Coblin. "The bonuses are based on the quality and tons produced and shipped through a team. The average base pay is about $9 to $10 an hour, but they could get an additional $15 to $20 an hour for bonuses."

Nucor's team-based bonus system also includes penalties. If employees catch a bad batch of steel before it leaves the minimill, they lose their bonus for that shipment. But if a bad batch makes its way to the customer, the team loses three times its usual bonus. A profit-sharing bonus (recently more than $15,000) on top of the fixed and bonus pay further motivates Nucor employees to keep mills running and to discover ways to improve steel quality and output.

Along with rewarding performance, Nucor gives employees the freedom and job flexibility to make key decisions and adjust their work to fit demands. Most decisions are made at the plant level—in fact, the head office in North Carolina has only 65 people—and employees take the initiative without waiting for management approval.

Consider the recent incident in which the electrical grid failed at Nucor's minimill in Hickman, Arkansas, potentially shutting down the operation for an entire week. When three Nucor electricians in North Carolina and Alabama heard the news, they drove or flew to Hickman and within three days had the minimill back in business. Nucor management didn't tell them to go, and their heroism didn't come with any extra pay. Yet these three Nucor employees gave up their weekend because they knew their effort could make a huge difference to Nucor's success. While remarkable in most companies, this is just a routine example at Nucor. "It happens daily," says a Nucor executive.[1]

6

Applied Performance Practices

After reading this chapter you should be able to

1. Discuss the advantages and disadvantages of the four reward objectives.

2. Identify several team- and organization-level performance-based rewards.

3. Describe five ways to improve reward effectiveness.

4. Discuss the advantages and disadvantages of job specialization.

5. Diagram the job characteristics model of job design.

6. Identify three strategies to improve employee motivation through job design.

7. Define *empowerment* and identify strategies to support empowerment.

8. Describe the five elements of self-leadership.

Nucor's success is a testament to the potential value of rewards, job design, and empowerment. This chapter looks at each of these applied performance practices as well as a fourth practice, self-leadership, which is also evident in Nucor employees. The chapter begins with an overview of financial reward practices, including the different types of rewards and how to implement rewards effectively. Next we look at the dynamics of job design, including specific job design strategies to motivate employees. We then consider the elements of empowerment as well as conditions that support empowerment. The final part of this chapter explains how employees manage their own performance through self-leadership.

Learning Objectives

After reading this section you should be able to

1. **Discuss the advantages and disadvantages of the four reward objectives.**
2. **Identify several team- and organization-level performance-based rewards.**
3. **Describe five ways to improve reward effectiveness.**

Financial Reward Practices

Financial rewards is probably the oldest—and certainly the most fundamental—applied performance practice in organizational settings. At the most basic level, financial rewards represent a form of exchange; employees provide their labor, skill, and knowledge in return for money and benefits from the organization. From this perspective, money and related rewards align employee goals with organizational goals.

However, financial rewards do much more than pay employees back for their contributions to organizational objectives. They are a symbol of success, a reinforcer and motivator, a reflection of employees' performance, and a source of reduced anxiety. With so many different purposes, it is little wonder that people rank pay and benefits as two of the most important features in the employment relationship.[2]

The value and meaning of money also vary considerably from one person to the next. One large-scale survey revealed that men in almost all of the 43 countries studied attach more importance or value to money than do women. This result is consistent with public opinion polls reporting that money has a higher priority for men than for women, particularly as a symbol of power and status.[3] Cultural values also seem to influence the meaning and value of money. People in countries with high power distance (such as China and Japan) tend to have a high respect and priority for money, whereas people in countries with a strong egalitarian culture (such as Denmark, Austria, and Israel) are discouraged from openly talking about money or displaying their personal wealth.[4]

Financial rewards come in many forms, which can be organized into the four specific objectives identified in Exhibit 6.1: membership and seniority, job status, competencies, and performance.

Membership- and Seniority-Based Rewards

Membership- and seniority-based rewards (sometimes called "pay for pulse") represent the largest part of most paychecks. Some employee benefits, such as free or discounted meals in the company cafeteria, remain the same for everyone, whereas

Exhibit 6.1   **Reward Objectives, Advantages, and Disadvantages**

Reward objective	Sample rewards	Advantages	Disadvantages
Membership/seniority	• Fixed pay. • Most employee benefits. • Paid time off.	• May attract applicants. • Minimizes stress of insecurity. • Reduces turnover.	• Doesn't directly motivate performance. • May discourage poor performers from leaving. • Golden handcuffs may undermine performance.
Job status	• Promotion-based pay increase. • Status-based benefits.	• Tries to maintain internal equity. • Minimizes pay discrimination. • Motivates employees to compete for promotions.	• Encourages hierarchy, which may increase costs and reduce responsiveness. • Reinforces status differences. • Motivates job competition and exaggerated job worth.
Competencies	• Pay increase based on competency. • Skill-based pay.	• Improves workforce flexibility. • Tends to improve quality. • Consistent with employability.	• Subjective measurement of competencies. • Skill-based pay plans are expensive.
Task performance	• Commissions. • Merit pay. • Gainsharing. • Profit sharing. • Stock options.	• Motivates task performance. • Attracts performance-oriented applicants. • Organizational rewards create an ownership culture. • Pay variability may avoid layoffs during downturns.	• May weaken job content motivation. • May distance reward giver from receiver. • May discourage creativity. • Tends to address symptoms, not underlying causes of behavior.

others increase with seniority. For example, employees at the City of Pawtucket, Rhode Island, receive longevity bonuses of approximately $2,000 or more after completion of four years of service. Police officers in Petaluma, California, were recently awarded a 30 percent increase over three years to catch up to pay rates of officers in other Bay Area communities.[5] In many companies employees with greater seniority receive longer vacation time. Many Asian companies distribute a "13th month" bonus, which every employee expects to receive each year no matter how well the company performed over the previous year.

These membership- and seniority-based rewards potentially attract job applicants (particularly those who desire predictable income) and reduce turnover. However, they do not directly motivate job performance; on the contrary, they discourage poor performers from seeking work better suited to their abilities. Instead the good

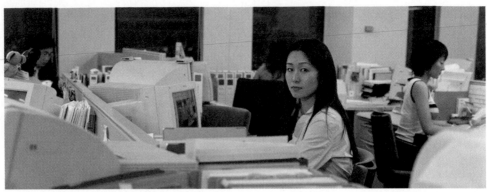

Japanese Firms Reward Age, Seniority, and Babies Since World War II employees in most large Japanese companies have received pay rates and increases determined entirely by their age or seniority, usually topping out around age 45. Not even the value of the specific jobs performed affected how much employees earned. Tough times in the 1990s forced many Japanese firms to introduce performance-based pay systems in which annual pay increases varied with employees' contributions. The shift toward pay for performance continues today, but labor groups still oppose such programs, and a few companies have not been happy with the results. Concerned that employees were becoming too stressed over their variable pay rates each year, Tokai Rubber Industries Ltd. recently reintroduced an age-based bonus pay system. "Even during that period [when they can't perform as well as expected], we raise salaries according to their age," says Tokai Rubber president Akira Fujii. Meanwhile Japanese firms are replacing monthly family allowances (where employees receive higher pay for the number of children they support) with a one-time lump sum childbirth bonus. For example, employees at Daiwa House Industry Co. in Osaka previously received an extra $45 per month for each child. Now the company pays a one-time lump sum of $9,000 for each childbirth.[6]

performers are lured to better-paying jobs. Some of these rewards are also golden handcuffs, which, as we learned in Chapter 4, can potentially weaken job performance by creating continuance commitment.

Job Status–Based Rewards

job evaluation
Systematically evaluating the worth of jobs within an organization by measuring their required skill, effort, responsibility, and working conditions.

Almost every organization rewards employees to some extent based on the status or worth of the jobs they occupy. **Job evaluation** is commonly used to rate the worth or status of each job, with higher pay rates going to jobs that require more skill and effort, have more responsibility, and have more difficult working conditions.[7] Aside from receiving higher pay, employees with more valued jobs sometimes receive larger offices, company-paid vehicles, and other perks.

Job status–based rewards maintain feelings of equity (people in higher-valued jobs should get higher pay) and motivate employees to compete for promotions. However, when companies are trying to be more cost efficient and responsive to the external environment, job status–based rewards potentially do the opposite by encouraging bureaucratic hierarchy. These rewards also reinforce a status mentality, whereas Generation-X and Generation-Y employees expect a more egalitarian workplace. Furthermore, status-based pay potentially motivates employees to compete with each other for higher-status jobs and to raise the value of their own jobs by exaggerating job duties and hoarding resources.[8]

Competency-Based Rewards

Many firms have shifted from job status to competency-based rewards. For instance, Syracuse University in upstate New York replaced its 20 pay-grade hierarchy with just 7 wider pay bands. Employees now receive pay increases within each pay band partly based on how well they have acquired new knowledge and skills.[9] *Skill-based pay* is a variation of competency-based rewards in which employees are rewarded for the number of skill modules mastered and consequently the number of jobs they can perform.

Competency-based rewards improve workforce flexibility by motivating employees to learn a variety of skills and thereby perform a variety of jobs. Product or service quality tends to improve because employees with multiple skills are more likely to understand the work process and know how to improve it. Competency-based rewards are also consistent with employability because they reward employees who continuously learn skills that will keep them employed. One potential problem is that measuring competencies can be subjective, particularly when described as personality traits or personal values. Skill-based pay systems measure specific skills, so they are usually more objective. However, they are expensive because employees spend more time learning new tasks.[10]

Performance-Based Rewards

Performance-based rewards have existed since Babylonian days in the 20th century BC, but their popularity has increased dramatically over the past couple of decades.[11] Here is an overview of some of the most popular individual, team, and organizational performance-based rewards.

Individual Rewards   Many employees receive individual bonuses or awards for accomplishing a specific task or exceeding annual performance goals. Real estate agents and other salespeople typically earn *commissions*, in which their pay increases with sales volume. Piece rate systems reward employees based on the number of units produced. For example, lawn care staff at The Lawn Mowgul in Dallas, Texas, earn a form of piece rate (called "piecemeal") based on the number of yards cut; housekeeping staff in some British hotels earn a piece rate for each room they clean (about $3 per room).[12] At Pretoria Portland Cement in South Africa, employees individually receive financial rewards for suggestions that improve productivity. Hong Kong communications company PCCW rewards employees with up to one month's pay if they exceed their performance goals.[13]

Team Rewards   Most brokerage firms on Wall Street, as well as other financial institutions, are shifting their focus from individuals to teams. Consequently, employees in these companies are finding a larger part of their total paycheck determined by team performance. One example is National City Bank in Cleveland, where brokers now earn bonuses based on the collective sales performance of their team. As was described at the beginning of this chapter, most of the paycheck that Nucor employees receive is determined by team performance. Specifically, employees at each minimill are organized into teams, and individuals earn bonuses based on the volume and quality of the team's output. A few years ago Home Depot introduced team-based rewards whereby employees earn a bonus based on how well their store meets or exceeds specific financial goals.[14]

Gainsharing plans are a form of team-based compensation that calculates bonuses from the work unit's cost savings and productivity improvement. At Whole Foods Market, for example, each department within a store is run by a team with a

gainsharing plan
A reward system in which team members earn bonuses for reducing costs and increasing labor efficiency in their work process.

monthly payroll budget. If payroll money is unspent at the end of the month, the surplus is divided among members of that Whole Foods' team. Most gainsharing plans distribute some of the gains and return the rest to the company's coffers. The majority of mining companies in North America have a gainsharing bonus system, typically where mining teams share the cost savings of extracting more ore at lower cost. With considerable caution, American hospitals have introduced gainsharing programs in which surgeons and other medical staff are rewarded for cost reductions in surgery and patient care.[15] Gainsharing plans tend to improve team dynamics, knowledge sharing, and pay satisfaction. They also create a reasonably strong link between effort and performance because much of the cost reduction and labor efficiency is within the team's control.

Organizational Rewards   Along with individual-and team-based rewards, many firms rely on organization-level rewards to motivate employees. **Employee stock ownership plans** (**ESOPs**) encourage employees to buy shares of company stock, usually at a discounted price or with a no-interest loan. Employees are subsequently rewarded through dividends and market appreciation of those shares. Approximately 10 percent of the private sector U.S. workforce participates in an ESOP. Sears Roebuck and UPS were two of the earliest companies to distribute stocks to their employees. ESOPs are also gaining popularity in other countries. For example, Dairibord Zimbabwe employees own more than one-fifth of the outstanding shares of the Zimbabwe dairy products company. Most Dairibord workers who bought a few thousand shares a decade ago are now millionaires from the share appreciation and receive a sizable bonus from the annual dividend.[16]

Whereas ESOPs involve actually purchasing company shares, **stock options** give employees the right to purchase shares from the company at a future date at a predetermined price up to a fixed expiration date. For example, an employer might offer employees the right to purchase 100 shares at $50 anywhere between two and six years from now. If the stock price is, say, $60 two years later, employees could earn $10 from these options or wait for up to six years for the stock price to rise further. If the stock never rises above $50 during that time, then employees are "out of the money" and would just let the options expire. The intention of stock options is to motivate employees to make the company more profitable, which should raise the company's stock price and thereby allow them to reap the value above the exercise price of the stock options.

Profit-sharing plans, a third organization-level reward system, calculate bonuses from the previous year's level of corporate profits. As was noted in the opening vignette to this chapter, Nucor employees earn a profit-sharing bonus on top of their fixed pay and team bonuses. Specifically, the steelmaker distributes 10 percent of its earnings before taxes to employees each year, which recently amounted to more than $17,000 per employee.[17]

A fourth organization-level reward strategy, called **balanced scorecard** (**BSC**), is a goal-oriented performance measurement system that rewards people (typically executives) for improving performance on a composite of financial, customer, and internal processes, as well as employee factors. The better the measurement improvements across these dimensions, the larger the bonus awarded. Best Buy, Ingersoll-Rand, Crown Castle, and, according to some sources, almost 60 percent of major companies use some variation of BSC, usually to reward and direct the performance of management staff, although the system is also used to reward nonmanagement employees. For instance, KT (formerly Korea

employee stock ownership plans (ESOPs)
A reward system that encourages employees to buy stock in the company.

stock options
A reward system that gives employees the right to purchase company stock at a future date at a predetermined price.

profit sharing plans
A reward system that pays bonuses to employees based on the previous year's level of corporate profits.

balanced scorecard (BSC)
A reward system that pays bonuses for improved results on a composite of financial, customer, internal process, and employee factors.

Telecom) relied on BSC to transform the former government-owned telephone company into a more competitive business after privatization. "It guided our employees with clear direction and balanced perspectives," says Song Young-han, KT's executive senior vice president. "By gathering all the employees around BSC, we were able to concentrate our foundation for the performance-oriented organization culture."[18]

Evaluating Organization-Level Rewards

How effective are organization-level rewards? ESOPs, stock options, and balanced scorecards tend to create an "ownership culture" in which employees feel aligned with the organization's success. Balanced scorecards have the added benefit of aligning rewards to several specific measures of organizational performance. However, BSC is potentially more subjective and requires a particular corporate culture for effective implementation. Profit sharing tends to create less ownership culture, but it has the advantage of automatically adjusting employee compensation with the firm's prosperity, thereby reducing the need for layoffs or negotiated pay reductions during recessions.[19]

The main problem with ESOPs, stock options, and profit sharing (less so with balanced scorecards) is that employees often perceive a weak connection between individual effort and corporate profits or the value of company shares. Even in small firms, the company's stock price or profitability is influenced by economic conditions, competition, and other factors beyond the employees' immediate control. This low individual performance-to-outcome expectancy weakens employee motivation. Another

Hugo Stays Boss with Balanced Scorecard In the highly competitive fashion industry, Hugo Boss Industries commands an impressive brand image and market share (30 percent for business suits in some markets). This success is due in part to a balanced scorecard that captures diverse performance measures across the Swiss company's various product groups. "You can't expect miracles, and no tool is going to do the job," concedes Werner Lackas, HBI's head of operations. "But the scorecard serves a very important purpose in focussing attention on the things that are being measured and where we are trying to go." Lackas explains that the scorecard gives HBI managers and employees "a pretty rigid skeleton" within which to be flexible and creative. The scorecard, which includes a range of hard (e.g., return on capital) and soft (e.g., staff development and satisfaction) objectives, is the foundation of performance bonuses received by all of HBI's 350 employees and managers.[20]

concern is that some companies in a few countries (including the United States) use ESOPs as a replacement for employee retirement plans. This is a risky strategy because company stock pension funds lack diversification. If the company goes bankrupt, employees lose both their jobs and a large portion of their retirement savings.[21]

Improving Reward Effectiveness

Performance-based rewards have come under attack over the years for discouraging creativity, distancing management from employees, distracting employees from the meaningfulness of the work itself, and being quick fixes that ignore the true causes of poor performance. Although these issues have kernels of truth under specific circumstances, they do not necessarily mean that we should abandon performance-based pay. On the contrary, the top-performing companies around the world are more likely to have performance-based rewards.[22] Reward systems do motivate most employees, but only under the right conditions. Here are some of the more important strategies to improve reward effectiveness.

Link Rewards to Performance
Behavior modification theory (Chapter 3) and expectancy theory (Chapter 5) both recommend that employees with better performance should be rewarded more than those with poorer performance. Unfortunately this simple principle seems to be unusually difficult to apply. In one recent large-scale survey, fewer than half of Malaysian employees said they believe their company rewards high performance or deals appropriately with poor performers. A Gallup survey at an American telecommunications company revealed an equally devastating observation: Management's evaluation of 5,000 customer service employees was uncorrelated with the performance ratings that customers gave those employees. "Whatever behavior the managers were evaluating were irrelevant to the customers," concluded Gallup executives. "The managers might as well have been rating the employees' shoe sizes, for all the customers cared."[23]

How can companies improve the pay–performance linkage? Inconsistencies and bias can be minimized by introducing gainsharing, ESOPs, and other plans that use objective performance measures. Where subjective measures of performance are necessary, companies should rely on multiple sources of information, such as 360-degree feedback. Companies also need to apply rewards soon after the performance occurs, and in a large enough dose (such as a bonus rather than pay increase) so employees experience positive emotions when they receive the rewards.[24]

Ensure That Rewards Are Relevant
Companies need to align rewards with performance within the employee's control. The more employees see a "line of sight" between their daily actions and a reward, the more they are motivated to improve performance. Wal-Mart applies this principle by rewarding bonuses to top executives based on the company's overall performance, whereas frontline employees earn bonuses based on the sales volume of the stores where they work. Reward systems also need to correct for situational factors. Salespeople in one region may have higher sales because the economy is stronger there than elsewhere, so sales bonuses need to be adjusted for these economic factors.

Use Team Rewards for Interdependent Jobs
Team rewards should be used rather than individual rewards when employees work in highly interdependent jobs because it is difficult to measure individual performance in these situations. Nucor relies on team-based bonuses for this reason; steelmaking is a team effort, so employees earn bonuses based on team performance. Team rewards also encourage cooperation,

When Rewards Go Wrong

There is an old saying that "what gets rewarded, gets done." But what companies reward isn't always what they had intended for employees to do. Here are a few dramatic examples:

- Stock options are supposed to motivate executives to improve corporate performance. Instead they seem to motivate some leaders to inflate share values through dodgy accounting practices. Recent research estimates that for every 25 percent increase in stock options awarded to executives, the risk of fraud rises by 68 percent. The companies with the largest corporate fraud in recent years have, on average, eight times as many options as similar companies that did not experience fraud.
- Integrated steel companies often rewarded managers for increased labor efficiency. The fewer labor hours required to produce a ton of steel, the larger the manager's bonus. Unfortunately steel firms usually didn't count the work of outside contractors in the formula, so the reward system motivated managers to hire expensive contractors in the production process. By employing more contractors, managers actually increased the cost of production.
- Toyota rewards its dealerships based on customer satisfaction surveys, not just car sales. What Toyota discovered, however, is that this motivates dealers to increase satisfaction scores, not customer satisfaction. One Toyota dealership received high ratings because it offered free detailing to every customer who returned a "Very Satisfied" survey. The dealership even had a special copy of the survey showing clients which boxes to check. This increased customer ratings but not customer satisfaction.
- Donnelly Mirrors (now part of the Magna International empire) introduced a gainsharing plan that motivated employees to reduce labor but not material costs. Employees at the automobile parts manufacturer knew they worked faster with sharp grinding wheels, so they replaced the expensive diamond wheels more often. This action reduced labor costs, thereby giving employees the gainsharing bonus. However, the labor savings were offset by much higher costs for diamond grinding wheels.

Sources: F.F. Reichheld, *The Loyalty Effect* (Boston, MA: Harvard University Press, 1996), p. 236; D.R. Spitzer, "Power Rewards: Rewards That Really Motivate," *Management Review*, May 1996, pp. 45–50; J.A. Byrne, "How To Fix Corporate Governance," *Business Week*, 6 May 2002, p. 68; A. Holeck, "Griffith, Ind., Native Takes Over as Steel Plant Manager," *Northwest Indiana Times*, 25 May 2003; H. Connon, "Overhyped, Overpaid, and Overextended," *The Observer* (London), 20 March 2005, p. 5.

which is more important when work is highly interdependent. A third benefit of team rewards is that they tend to support employee preferences for team-based work. One concern, however, is that employees (particularly the most productive employees) in the United States and many other low-collectivism cultures prefer rewards based on their individual performance rather than team performance.[25]

Ensure That Rewards Are Valued   It seems obvious that rewards work best when they are valued. Yet companies sometimes make false assumptions about what employees want—with unfortunate consequences. The solution, of course, is to ask employees what they value. Campbell Soup did this a few years ago at its distribution centers in Canada. Executives thought the employees would ask for more money in a special team reward program. Instead, distribution staff said the most valued reward was a leather jacket with the Campbell Soup logo on the back. These leather jackets cost much less yet were worth much more than the financial bonus the company had otherwise intended to distribute.[26]

Watch Out for Unintended Consequences   Performance-based reward systems sometimes have an unexpected—and undesirable—effect on employee behavior. Consider the pizza company that decided to reward its drivers for on-time delivery. The plan got more hot pizzas to customers on time, but it also increased the accident rates of its drivers because the incentive motivated them to drive recklessly.[27] Connections 6.1 describes a few other examples where reward systems had unintended consequences. The solution here is to carefully think through the consequences of rewards and, where possible, test incentives in a pilot project before applying them across the organization.

Financial rewards come in many forms and, as was mentioned at the outset of this section, influence employees in complex ways. But money isn't the only thing that motivates people to join an organization and perform effectively. "High performers don't go for the money," warns William Monahan, CEO of Oakdale, Minnesota-based Imation Corp. "Good people want to be in challenging jobs and see a future where they can get even more responsibilities and challenges." Rafik O. Loutfy, a Xerox research center director, agrees with this assessment. "Our top stars say they want to make an impact—that's the most important thing," he says. "Feeling they are contributing and making a difference is highly motivational for them."[28] In other words, Imation, Xerox, and other companies motivate employees mainly by designing interesting and challenging jobs, which we discuss next.

Learning Objectives

After reading this section you should be able to

4. **Discuss the advantages and disadvantages of job specialization.**
5. **Diagram the job characteristics model of job design.**
6. **Identify three strategies to improve employee motivation through job design.**

Job Design Practices

How do you build a better job? That question has challenged organizational behavior experts as well as psychologists, engineers, and economists for centuries. Some jobs have few tasks and usually require little skill. Other jobs are immensely complex and require years of experience and learning for mastery. From one extreme to the other, jobs have different effects on work efficiency and employee motivation. The challenge, at least from the organization's perspective, is to find the right combination so work is performed efficiently but employees are motivated and engaged.[29] This challenge requires careful **job design**—the process of assigning tasks to a job, including the interdependency of those tasks with other jobs. A job is a set of tasks performed by one person. To understand this issue more fully, let's begin by describing early job design efforts aimed at increasing work efficiency through job specialization.

job design
The process of assigning tasks to a job, including the interdependency of those tasks with other jobs.

Job Design and Work Efficiency

One production line at the Magna Steyr manufacturing plant in Graz, Austria, is responsible for assembling Chrysler's European minivan. On average, assembly workers on this line take three minutes to attach their assigned pieces to the chassis before repeating their work on the next vehicle. In North America, Chrysler employees assembling the same vehicle have an average job cycle time of 64.5 seconds. The difference isn't that Austrian employees are slower. Rather, Chrysler's North American employees are assigned fewer tasks in their work cycles. In other words they have somewhat more **job specialization**.[30]

Job specialization occurs when the work required to build an automobile—or any other product or service—is subdivided into separate jobs assigned to different people. Each resulting job includes a narrow subset of tasks, usually completed in a short cycle time. *Cycle time* is the time required to complete the task before starting over with a new work unit. Chrysler's minivan assemblers have an average cycle time of 64.5 seconds, which means they repeat the same set of tasks about 58 times each hour and probably about 230 times before they take a meal break.

job specialization
The result of division of labor in which each job includes a subset of the tasks required to complete the product or service.

Why would companies divide work into such tiny bits? The simple answer is that job specialization improves work efficiency. In fact, the economic benefits of dividing work into specialized jobs have been described and applied for at least two millennia. More than 2,300 years ago the Chinese philosopher Mencius and Greek philosopher Plato noted that division of labor improves work efficiency. In AD 1436 the waterways of Venice became an assembly line loading 10 galleons in just six hours. More than 200 years ago economist Adam Smith described a small factory where 10 pin makers collectively produced as many as 48,000 pins per day because they performed specialized tasks, such as straightening, cutting, sharpening, grinding, and whitening the pins. In contrast, Smith explained that if these 10 people worked alone producing complete pins, they would collectively manufacture no more than 200 pins per day.[31]

One reason why job specialization potentially increases work efficiency is that employees have fewer tasks to juggle and therefore spend less time changing activities. They also require fewer physical and mental skills to accomplish the assigned work, so less time and resources are needed for training. A third reason is that employees practice their tasks more frequently with shorter work cycles, so jobs are mastered quickly. A fourth reason why work efficiency increases is that employees with specific aptitudes or skills can be matched more precisely to the jobs for which they are best suited.[32]

Scientific Management

One of the strongest advocates of job specialization was Frederick Winslow Taylor, an American industrial engineer who introduced the principles of **scientific management** in the early 1900s.[33] Scientific management consists of a toolkit of activities. Some of these interventions—training, goal setting, and work incentives—are common today but were rare until Taylor popularized them. However, scientific management is mainly associated with high levels of job specialization and standardization of tasks to achieve maximum efficiency.

scientific management
Involves systematically partitioning work into its smallest elements and standardizing tasks to achieve maximum efficiency.

According to Taylor, the most effective companies have detailed procedures and work practices developed by engineers, enforced by supervisors, and executed by employees. Even the supervisor's tasks should be divided: One person manages operational efficiency, another manages inspection, and another is the disciplinarian. Taylor and other industrial engineers demonstrated that scientific management significantly improves work efficiency. No doubt some of the increased productivity can be credited to the training, goal setting, and work incentives; but job specialization quickly became popular in its own right.

Frederick Taylor and his contemporaries focused on how job specialization reduces labor "waste" by improving the mechanical efficiency of work (matching skills, faster learning, less switchover time). Yet they didn't seem to notice how this extreme job specialization has an adverse effect on employee attitudes and motivation. Some jobs—such as assembling Chrysler minivans—are so specialized that they quickly become tedious, trivial, and socially isolating. Employee turnover and absenteeism tend to be higher in specialized jobs with very short time cycles. Companies sometimes have to pay higher wages to attract job applicants to this dissatisfying, narrowly defined work.[34]

Job specialization often reduces work quality because employees see only a small part of the process. As one observer of an automobile assembly line work reports, "Often [employees] did not know how their jobs related to the total picture. Not knowing, there was no incentive to strive for quality—what did quality even mean as it related to a bracket whose function you did not understand?"[35]

Equally important, Taylor's reliance on job specialization to improve employee performance ignores the motivational potential of jobs. As jobs become specialized, the work tends to become easier to perform but less motivating. As jobs become more complex, work motivation increases but the ability to master the job decreases. Maximum job performance occurs somewhere between these two extremes, where most people can eventually perform the job tasks efficiently, yet the work is interesting.

Job Design and Work Motivation

motivator–hygiene theory
Herzberg's theory stating that employees are primarily motivated by growth and esteem needs, not by lower-level needs.

Industrial engineers may have overlooked the motivational effect of job characteristics, but it is now the central focus of many job design changes. Organizational behavior scholar Frederick Herzberg is credited with shifting the spotlight when he introduced **motivator–hygiene theory** in the 1950s.[36] Motivator–hygiene theory proposes that employees experience job satisfaction when they fulfill growth and esteem needs (called *motivators*), and they experience dissatisfaction when they have poor working conditions, job security, and other factors categorized as lower-order needs (called *hygienes*). Herzberg argued that only characteristics of the job itself motivate employees, whereas the hygiene factors merely prevent dissatisfaction. It might seem obvious to us today that the job itself is a source of motivation, but it was radical thinking when Herzberg proposed the idea.

job characteristics model
A job design model that relates the motivational properties of jobs to specific personal and organizational consequences of those properties.

Motivator–hygiene theory didn't find much research support, but Herzberg's ideas generated new thinking about the motivational potential of the job itself.[37] Out of subsequent research emerged the **job characteristics model** shown in Exhibit 6.2.

Exhibit 6.2
The Job Characteristics Model

Source: J.R. Hackman and G. Oldham, *Work Redesign* (Reading, MA: Addison-Wesley, 1980), p. 90. Used with permission.

The job characteristics model identifies five core job dimensions that produce three psychological states. Employees who experience these psychological states tend to have higher levels of internal work motivation (motivation from the work itself), job satisfaction (particularly satisfaction with the work itself), and work effectiveness.[38]

Core Job Characteristics

The job characteristics model identifies five core job characteristics. Under the right conditions, employees are more motivated and satisfied when jobs have higher levels of these characteristics:

- *Skill variety.* **Skill variety** refers to the use of different skills and talents to complete a variety of work activities. For example, sales clerks who normally only serve customers might be assigned the additional duties of stocking inventory and changing storefront displays.

- *Task identity.* **Task identity** is the degree to which a job requires completion of a whole or identifiable piece of work, such as assembling an entire broadband modem rather than just soldering in the circuitry.

- *Task significance.* **Task significance** is the degree to which the job affects the organization or society. For instance, many employees at Medtronic, the Minneapolis-based maker of pacemakers and other medical equipment, have high job specialization, yet 86 percent say their work has special meaning and 94 percent feel pride in what they accomplish. The reason for their high task significance is that they attend seminars that show how the products they manufacture save lives. "We have patients who come in who would be dead if it wasn't for us," says a Medtronic production supervisor.[39]

- *Autonomy.* Jobs with high levels of **autonomy** provide freedom, independence, and discretion in scheduling the work and determining the procedures to be used to complete the work. In autonomous jobs, employees make their own decisions rather than relying on detailed instructions from supervisors or procedure manuals.

- *Job feedback.* Job feedback is the degree to which employees can tell how well they are doing based on direct sensory information from the job itself. Airline pilots can tell how well they land their aircraft, and road crews can see how well they have prepared the roadbed and laid the asphalt.

Critical Psychological States

The five core job characteristics affect employee motivation and satisfaction through three critical psychological states shown in Exhibit 6.2. One of these psychological states is *experienced meaningfulness*—the belief that one's work is worthwhile or important. Skill variety, task identity, and task significance directly contribute to the job's meaningfulness. If the job has high levels of all three characteristics, employees are likely to feel that their jobs are highly meaningful. Meaningfulness drops as a job loses one or more of these characteristics.

Work motivation and performance increase when employees feel personally accountable for the outcomes of their efforts. Autonomy directly contributes to this feeling of *experienced responsibility*. Employees must be assigned control of their work environment to feel responsible for their successes and failures. The third critical psychological state is *knowledge of results*. Employees want information about the consequences of their work effort. Knowledge of results can originate from co-workers, supervisors, or clients. However, job design focuses on knowledge of results from the work itself.

---

skill variety
The extent to which employees must use different skills and talents to perform tasks within their job.

task identity
The degree to which a job requires completion of a whole or an identifiable piece of work.

task significance
The degree to which the job has a substantial impact on the organization and/or larger society.

autonomy
The degree to which a job gives employees the freedom, independence, and discretion to schedule their work and determine the procedures used in completing it.

Individual Differences   Job design doesn't increase work motivation for everyone in every situation. Employees must have the required skills and knowledge to master the more challenging work. Otherwise job design tends to increase stress and reduce job performance. The original model also suggests that increasing the motivational potential of jobs will not motivate employees who are dissatisfied with their work context (such as working conditions or job security) or who have a low growth need strength. However, research findings have been mixed, suggesting that employees might be motivated by job design no matter how they feel about their job context or how high or low they score on growth needs.[40]

Job Design Practices That Motivate

Three main strategies can increase the motivational potential of jobs: job rotation, job enlargement, and job enrichment. This section also identifies several ways to implement job enrichment.

Job Rotation   At the beginning of this topic on job design, we mentioned that assembly line employees at Chrysler have a high degree of specialization. Chrysler executives are aware of the motivational and physiological problems that this repetitive work can create, so they have introduced a policy where employees work in teams and rotate to a different workstation within that team every few hours. **Job rotation** is the practice of moving employees from one job to another. "The whole idea of job rotation makes a big difference," says Chrysler executive vice president of manufacturing Frank Ewasyshyn. "The job naturally gets better, quality improves, throughput improves." The Jeep assembly plant in Toledo, Ohio, was Chrysler's first U.S. facility to switch to team assembly, and significant improvements in productivity and morale became apparent within the first year. Job rotation offers "important ergonomic benefits to workers, improvements in product quality, and higher employee satisfaction," says Tom Maxon, a senior Chrysler manager in Toledo.[41]

From the experience at Chrysler and many other companies, we can identify three potential benefits of job rotation. First, it minimizes health risks from repetitive strain and heavy lifting because employees use different muscles and physical positions in the various jobs. Second, it supports multiskilling (employees learn several jobs), which increases workforce flexibility in the production process and in finding replacements for those on vacation. A third benefit of job rotation is that it potentially reduces the boredom of highly repetitive jobs. However, organizational behavior experts continue to debate whether job rotation really is job redesign because each job is still highly specialized. Critics argue that job redesign requires changes within the job, such as job enlargement.

Job Enlargement   **Job enlargement** adds tasks to an existing job. This might involve combining two or more complete jobs into one, or just adding one or two more tasks to an existing job. Either way, skill variety increases because there are more tasks to perform. Video journalists represent a clear example of an enlarged job. As Exhibit 6.3 illustrates, a traditional news team consists of a camera operator, a sound and lighting specialist, and the journalist who writes and presents or narrates the story. One video journalist performs all of these tasks.

Job enlargement significantly improves work efficiency and flexibility. However, research suggests that simply giving employees more tasks won't affect motivation, performance, or job satisfaction. Instead these benefits result only when skill variety is combined with more autonomy and job knowledge.[42] In other words, employees

job rotation
The practice of moving employees from one job to another.

job enlargement
Increasing the number of tasks employees perform within their job.

Exhibit 6.3

Job Enlargement of Video Journalists

Traditional news team

Employee 1
Operates camera

Employee 2
Operates sound

Employee 3
Reports story

Video journalist

• Operates camera
• Operates sound
• Reports story

are motivated when they perform a variety of tasks *and* have the freedom and knowledge to structure their work to achieve the highest satisfaction and performance. These job characteristics are at the heart of job enrichment.

job enrichment

Giving employees more responsibility for scheduling, coordinating, and planning their own work.

Job Enrichment   **Job enrichment** occurs when employees are given more responsibility for scheduling, coordinating, and planning their own work.[43] People in enriched jobs usually experience higher job satisfaction and work motivation, along with lower absenteeism and turnover. Productivity is also higher when task identity and job feedback are improved. Product and service quality tend to improve because job enrichment increases the jobholder's felt responsibility and sense of ownership over the product or service.[44]

One way to increase job enrichment is by combining highly interdependent tasks into one job. This *natural grouping* approach is reflected in the video journalist job. Video journalist was earlier described as an enlarged job, but it is also an example of job enrichment because it naturally groups tasks together to complete an entire product (a news clip). By forming natural work units, jobholders have stronger feelings of responsibility for an identifiable body of work. They feel a sense of ownership and therefore tend to increase job quality. Forming natural work units increases task identity and task significance because employees perform a complete product or service and can more readily see how their work affects others.

A second job enrichment strategy, called *establishing client relationships*, involves putting employees in direct contact with their clients rather than using the supervisor as a go-between. By being directly responsible for specific clients, employees have more information and can make decisions affecting those clients.[45] Establishing client relationships also increases task significance because employees see a line-of-sight connection between their work and consequences for customers. This was apparent among medical secretaries at a large regional hospital in Sweden after the hospital reduced its workforce by 10 percent and gave the secretaries expanded job duties. Although these employees experienced more stress from the higher workloads, some of them also felt more motivated and satisfied because they now had direct interaction with patients. "Before, I never saw a patient; now they have a face," says one medical secretary. "I feel satisfied and pleased with myself; you feel someone needs you."[46]

Video Journalists Get Enriched on the Job Traditionally up to four people have been required to shoot a video news clip: a reporter, camera operator, sound operator, and production editor. Now, thanks to technology and innovative thinking about job design in the newsroom, many TV networks are turning staff into video journalists (VJs) who perform all of these tasks in one job. Michael Rosenblum, who became one of the world's first VJs two decades ago, has transformed BBC, NYT-TV, Oxygen, and many other television companies into VJ shops. He also recently trained staff at KRON-TV in San Francisco, which is now making the transition. This photo shows one of KRON's VJs at work. "The VJ model will empower a new breed of broadcast journalist who will take a story from concept to finished segment," says Mark Antonitis, president and general manager of KRON-TV. "This sort of complete ownership will provide the station with stories that have a singular and unique voice."[47]

Forming natural task groups and establishing client relationships are common ways to enrich jobs, but the heart of the job enrichment philosophy is to give employees more autonomy over their work. This basic idea is at the core of one of the most widely mentioned—and often misunderstood—practices, known as empowerment.

Learning Objectives

After reading the next two sections you should be able to

7. Define empowerment and identify strategies to support empowerment.
8. Describe the five elements of self-leadership.

Empowerment Practices

A large American hotel had a policy that if a guest questioned a bill, front-desk staff were supposed to defend the bill no matter what. If the guest asked to speak with the manager, the manager would override the charge. The hotel manager thought that this "good cop, bad cop" approach was useful; but Rick Garlick, a consultant hired by the hotel, suggested that they immediately change the policy. Instead front-desk staff should have the autonomy to decide alone whether the complaint was justified. The result? Within a few months the hotel's guest satisfaction scores soared from near the bottom to near the top among hotels in the company's chain. "Empowering employees was one of a number of key improvements in manager–staff relations that ultimately resulted in much higher guest satisfaction," says Garlick.[48]

Empowerment is a term that has been loosely tossed around in corporate circles and has been the subject of considerable debate among academics. However, the most widely accepted definition is that empowerment is a psychological concept represented by four dimensions: self-determination, meaning, competence, and impact of the individual's role in the organization. Empowerment consists of all four dimensions. If any dimension weakens, the employee's sense of empowerment will weaken.[49]

- *Self-determination.* Empowered employees feel that they have freedom, independence, and discretion over their work activities.

- *Meaning.* Employees who feel empowered care about their work and believe that what they do is important.

- *Competence.* Empowered people are confident about their ability to perform the work well and have a capacity to grow with new challenges.

- *Impact.* Empowered employees view themselves as active participants in the organization; that is, their decisions and actions have an influence on the company's success.

Supporting Empowerment

Chances are that you have heard corporate leaders say they are "empowering" the workforce. What these executives really mean is that they are changing the work environment to support empowerment.[50] Numerous individual, job design, and organizational or work context factors support empowerment. At the individual level, employees must possess the necessary competencies to be able to perform the work as well as handle the additional decision-making requirements. Although other individual factors have been proposed (such as locus of control), they do not seem to have any real effect on whether employees feel empowered.[51]

Job characteristics clearly influence the dynamics of empowerment.[52] To generate beliefs about self-determination, employees must work in jobs with a high degree of autonomy with minimal bureaucratic control. To maintain a sense of meaningfulness, jobs must have high levels of task identity and task significance. And to maintain a sense of self-confidence, jobs must provide sufficient feedback.

Several organizational and work context factors also influence empowerment. Employees experience more empowerment in organizations where information and other resources are easily accessible. Empowerment also requires a learning orientation culture. In other words, empowerment flourishes in organizations that appreciate the value of the employee learning and that accept reasonable mistakes as a natural part of the learning process. Furthermore, empowerment requires corporate leaders who trust employees and are willing to take the risks that empowerment creates. "Executives must give up control and trust the power of talent," advises Ricardo Semler, head of Semco Corporation in São Paulo, Brazil.[53]

With the right individuals, job characteristics, and organizational environment, empowerment can have a noticeable effect on motivation and performance. For instance, a study of bank employees concluded that empowerment improved customer service and tended to reduce conflict between employees and their supervisors. Other research links empowerment with higher trust in management, which ultimately influences job satisfaction, belief and acceptance of organizational goals

empowerment

A psychological concept in which people experience more self-determination, meaning, competence, and impact regarding their role in the organization.

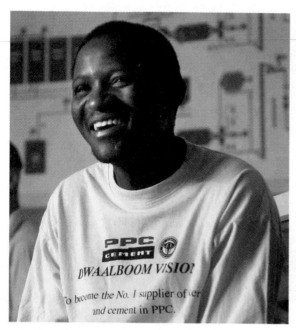

Kambuku Empowerment   Kambuku is the name of one of the largest tusked elephants in Africa. It is also the symbolic title for a "people focused, value added" initiative that has transformed Pretoria Portland Cement (PPC) into a performance-oriented company and one of South Africa's best employers. The company had a long way to go to reach its goal. A few years ago PPC was a top-down, autocratic organization where managers gave "oodles of supervision and checking that people do the right things," recalls PPC chief executive John Gomersall. Now he says, "We have passed the ownership to the people." Departments and teams are given much more autonomy. Company leaders seek out employee ideas, offer continuous training, and reward teams and individuals for their performance. "We attribute our ongoing success and strength to the fact that every employee in the company has the opportunity to make a contribution and be recognized for their input to achieving success," says chief operating officer Orrie Fenn. "Empowered employees ensure a committed workforce, which eventually translates into sustainable business performance."[54]

and values, and organizational commitment. Empowerment also tends to increase personal initiative because employees identify with and assume more psychological ownership of their work.[55]

Self-Leadership Practices

What is the most important characteristic that companies look for in their employees? Leadership potential, ability to work in a team, and good communication skills are important, but a survey of 800 British employers concludes that they don't top the list. Instead the most important employee characteristic is self-motivation. The staff at Universal Insurance Services, Inc., can identify with those results. The Grand Rapids insurance company is one of Michigan's "cool places to work" because, according to its own Web site, "Our culture encourages self-management and total accountability." This isn't a blank statement. Universal's employees are expected to score their own performance and provide evidence of that score![56]

Most of the concepts introduced in this chapter and Chapter 5 have assumed that corporate leaders do things to motivate employees. Certainly these theories and practices are valuable; but they overlook the fact that the most successful employees ultimately motivate and manage themselves. In other words, they engage in self-leadership.

Self-leadership refers to the process of influencing oneself to establish the self-direction and self-motivation needed to perform a task.[57] This concept includes a toolkit of behavioral activities borrowed from social learning theory and goal setting. It also includes constructive thought processes that have been extensively studied in sports psychology. Overall, self-leadership takes the view that individuals mostly regulate their own actions through these behavioral and cognitive (thought) activities.

self-leadership
The process of influencing oneself to establish the self-direction and self-motivation needed to perform a task.

Exhibit 6.4   **Elements of Self-Leadership**

| Personal goal setting | → | Constructive thought patterns | → | Designing natural rewards | → | Self-monitoring | → | Self-reinforcement |

Although we are in the early stages of understanding the dynamics of self-leadership, Exhibit 6.4 identifies the five main elements of this process. These elements, which generally follow each other in a sequence, are personal goal setting, constructive thought patterns, designing natural rewards, self-monitoring, and self-reinforcement.[58]

Personal Goal Setting

The first step in self-leadership is to set goals for your own work effort. This applies the ideas learned in Chapter 5 about goal setting, such as identifying goals that are specific, relevant, and challenging. The main difference is that self-leadership involves setting goals alone rather than having them assigned by or jointly decided with a supervisor. Research suggests that employees are more focused and perform better when they set their own goals, particularly in combination with other self-leadership practices.[59]

Constructive Thought Patterns

Before beginning a task and while performing it, employees should engage in positive (constructive) thoughts about that work and its accomplishment. In particular, employees are more motivated and better prepared to accomplish a task after they have engaged in positive self-talk and mental imagery.

Positive Self-Talk   Do you ever talk to yourself? Most of us do, according to a major study of university students.[60] **Self-talk** refers to any situation in which we talk to ourselves about our own thoughts or actions. Some of this internal communication assists the decision-making process, such as weighing the advantages of a particular choice. Self-leadership is mostly interested in evaluative self-talk, in which you evaluate your capabilities and accomplishments.

The problem is that most evaluative self-talk is negative; we criticize much more than encourage or congratulate ourselves. Negative self-talk undermines our confidence and potential to perform a particular task. In contrast, positive self-talk creates a "can-do" belief and thereby increases motivation by raising our effort-to-performance expectancy. We often hear that professional athletes "psych" themselves up before an important event. They tell themselves that they can achieve their goal and that they have practiced enough to reach that goal. They are motivating themselves through positive self-talk.

Mental Imagery   You've probably heard the phrase "I'll cross that bridge when I come to it!" Self-leadership takes the opposite view. It suggests that we need to mentally practice a task and imagine successfully performing it beforehand. This process, known as **mental imagery** has two parts. One part involves mentally practicing the task, anticipating obstacles to goal accomplishment, and working out solutions to those obstacles before they occur. By mentally walking through the activities required to accomplish the task, we begin to see problems that may occur. We can then imagine what responses would be best for each contingency.[61]

self-talk
Talking to ourselves about our own thoughts or actions for the purpose of increasing our self-confidence and navigating through decisions in a future event.

mental imagery
Mentally practicing a task and visualizing its successful completion.

While one part of mental imagery helps us to anticipate things that could go wrong, the other part involves visualizing successful completion of the task. We imagine the experience of completing the task and the positive results that follow. Everyone daydreams and fantasizes about being in a successful situation. You might imagine yourself being promoted to your boss's job, receiving a prestigious award, or taking time off work. This visualization increases goal commitment and motivates us to complete the task effectively. This is the strategy that Tony Wang applies to motivate himself. "Since I am in sales, I think about the reward I get for closing new business—the commission check—and the things it will allow me to do that I really enjoy," explains Wang. "Or I think about the feeling I get when I am successful at something and how it makes me feel good, and use that to get me going."[62]

Designing Natural Rewards

Self-leadership recognizes that employees actively craft their jobs. To varying degrees, they can alter tasks and work relationships to make the work more motivating.[63] One way to build natural rewards into a job is to alter how a task is accomplished. People often have enough discretion in their jobs to make slight changes to suit their needs and preferences. For instance, you might try out a new software program to design an idea rather than sketching the image with pencil. By using the new software, you are adding challenge to a task that may have otherwise been mundane.

Self-Monitoring

Self-monitoring is the process of keeping track at regular intervals of one's progress toward a goal using naturally occurring feedback. Some people can receive feedback from the job itself, such as a road crew that can see how well they are laying the roadbed and asphalt. But many of us are unable to observe our work output so readily. Instead many people need to design feedback systems. Salespeople might arrange to receive monthly reports on sales levels in their territory. Production staff might have gauges or computer feedback systems installed so they can see how many errors are made on the production line. Research suggests that people who have control over the timing of performance feedback perform their tasks better than those with feedback assigned by others.[64]

Self-Reinforcement

Self-leadership includes the social learning theory concept of self-reinforcement. Self-reinforcement occurs whenever an employee has control over a reinforcer but doesn't "take" the reinforcer until completing a self-set goal.[65] A common example is taking a break after reaching a predetermined stage of your work. The work break is a self-induced form of positive reinforcement. Self-reinforcement also occurs when you decide to do a more enjoyable task after completing a task that you dislike. For example, after slogging through a difficult report, you might decide to spend time doing a more pleasant task, such as catching up on industry news by scanning Web sites.

Self-Leadership in Practice

Self-leadership is shaping up to be a valuable applied performance practice in organizational settings. A respectable body of research shows consistent support for most elements of self-leadership. Self-set goals and self-monitoring increased the frequency

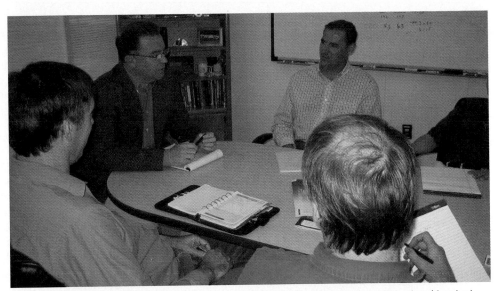

eSilicon Corp. Flies with Employees Who Lead Themselves   Jack Harding (top left in photo) has had his share of ups and downs over his career as an entrepreneur in Silicon Valley. Fortunately the company he founded in 2000, eSilicon Corp., has become the fastest-growing private company in Silicon Valley and is winning accolades throughout the industry for its design and manufacturing of custom chips for electronics companies. Looking back, Harding says that employee self-leadership played a key role in the company's growth. "You look for character and experience" when hiring new employees, Harding suggests. "They need to be smart, team players and self-motivated—and you can't instill that."[66]

of wearing safety equipment among employees in a mining operation. Airline employees who received constructive thought training experienced better mental performance, enthusiasm, and job satisfaction than co-workers who did not receive this training. Mental imagery helped supervisors and process engineers in a pulp and paper mill to transfer what they learned in an interpersonal communication skills class back to the job.[67] Studies also indicate that self-set goals and constructive thought processes improve individual performance in swimming, tennis, ice skating, soccer, and other sports. Indeed, studies show that almost all Olympic athletes rely on mental rehearsal and positive self-talk to achieve their performance goals.[68]

Self-leadership behaviors are more frequently found in people with specific personality characteristics, notably conscientiousness and extroversion.[69] However, one of the benefits of self-leadership is that it can be learned. Training programs have helped employees to improve their self-leadership skills. Organizations can also encourage self-leadership by providing sufficient autonomy and establishing rewards that reinforce self-leadership behaviors. Employees are also more likely to engage in self-monitoring in companies that emphasize continuous measurement of performance. Overall, self-leadership promises to be an important concept and practice for improving employee motivation and performance.

Self-leadership, job design, empowerment, and rewards are valuable approaches to improving employee performance. However, performance is also affected by work-related stress. As we learn in the next chapter, too much stress is causing numerous problems with employee performance and well-being, but there are also ways to combat this epidemic.

Chapter Summary

Money and other financial rewards are a fundamental part of the employment relationship, but their value and meaning vary from one person to the next. Organizations reward employees for their membership and seniority, job status, competencies, and performance. Membership-based rewards may attract job applicants and seniority-based rewards reduce turnover, but these reward objectives tend to discourage turnover among those with the lowest performance. Rewards based on job status try to maintain internal equity and motivate employees to compete for promotions. However, they tend to encourage bureaucratic hierarchy, support status differences, and motivate employees to compete and hoard resources. Competency-based rewards are becoming increasingly popular because they improve workforce flexibility and are consistent with the emerging idea of employability. However, they tend to be subjectively measured and can result in higher costs as employees spend more time learning new skills.

Awards and bonuses, commissions, and other individual performance–based rewards have existed for centuries and are widely used. Many companies are shifting to team-based rewards such as gainsharing plans and to organizational rewards such as employee stock ownership plans (ESOPs), stock options, profit sharing, and balanced scorecards. ESOPs and stock options create an ownership culture, but employees often perceive a weak connection between individual performance and organizational rewards.

Financial rewards have a number of limitations, but reward effectiveness can be improved in several ways. Organizational leaders should ensure that rewards are linked to work performance, rewards are aligned with performance within the employees' control, team rewards are used where jobs are interdependent, rewards are valued by employees, and rewards have no unintended consequences.

Job design refers to the process of assigning tasks to a job, including the interdependency of those tasks with other jobs. Job specialization subdivides work into separate jobs for different people. This increases work efficiency because employees master the tasks quickly, spend less time changing tasks, require less training, and can be matched more closely with the jobs best suited to their skills. However, job specialization may reduce work motivation, create mental and physical health problems, lower product or service quality, and increase costs through discontentment, absenteeism, and turnover.

Contemporary job design strategies reverse job specialization through job rotation, job enlargement, and job enrichment. The job characteristics model is a template for job redesign that specifies core job dimensions, psychological states, and individual differences. Organizations introduce job rotation to reduce job boredom, develop a more flexible workforce, and reduce the incidence of repetitive strain injuries. Two ways to enrich jobs are clustering tasks into natural groups and establishing client relationships.

Empowerment is a psychological concept represented by four dimensions: self-determination, meaning, competence, and impact regarding the individual's role in the organization. Individual characteristics seem to have a minor influence on empowerment. Job design is a major influence—particularly autonomy, task identity, task significance, and job feedback. Empowerment is also supported at the organizational level through a learning orientation culture, sufficient information and resources, and corporate leaders who trust employees.

Self-leadership is the process of influencing oneself to establish the self-direction and self-motivation needed to perform a task. This includes personal goal setting, constructive thought patterns, designing natural rewards, self-monitoring, and self-reinforcement. Constructive thought patterns include self-talk and mental imagery. Self-talk refers to any situation in which a person talks to himself or herself about his or her own thoughts or actions. Mental imagery involves mentally practicing a task and imagining successfully performing it beforehand.

Key Terms

autonomy, p. 179

balanced scorecard (BSC), p. 172

employee stock ownership plans (ESOP), p. 172

empowerment, p. 183

gainsharing plans, p. 171

job characteristics model, p. 178

job design, p. 176

job enlargement, p. 180

job enrichment, p. 181

job evaluation, p. 170

job rotation, p. 180

job specialization, p. 176

mental imagery, p. 185

motivator–hygiene theory, p. 178

profit-sharing plans, p. 172

scientific management, p. 177

self-leadership, p. 184

self-talk, p. 185

skill variety, p. 179

stock options, p. 172

task identity, p. 179

task significance, p. 179

Critical Thinking Questions

1. As a consultant, you have been asked to recommend either a gainsharing plan or a profit-sharing plan for employees who work in the four regional distribution and warehousing facilities of a large retail organization. Which reward system would you recommend? Explain your answer.

2. You are a member of a team responsible for developing performance measures for your college or university department or faculty unit based on the balanced scorecard approach. Identify one performance measurement for each of the following factors: financial, customer satisfaction, internal processes, and employee performance.

3. Numbat Tire Corp. redesigned its production facilities around a team-based system. However, the company president believes that employees will not be motivated unless they receive incentives based on their individual performance. Give three explanations why Numbat Tire should introduce team-based rather than individual rewards in this setting.

4. What can organizations do to increase the effectiveness of financial rewards?

5. Most of us have watched pizzas being made while waiting in a pizzeria. What level of job specialization do you usually notice in these operations? Why does this high or low level of specialization exist? If some pizzerias have different levels of specialization than others, identify the contingencies that might explain these differences.

6. Can a manager or supervisor "empower" an employee? Discuss this fully.

7. Describe a time when you practiced self-leadership to successfully perform a task. With reference to each step in the self-leadership process, describe what you did to achieve this success.

8. Can self-leadership replace formal leadership in an organizational setting?

Case Study 6.1 THE REGENCY GRAND HOTEL

Lisa Ho, Prada Singapore under the supervision of Steven L. McShane

The Regency Grand Hotel is a five-star hotel in Bangkok, Thailand. The hotel was established 15 years ago by a local consortium of investors and has been operated by a Thai general manager throughout this time. The hotel is one of Bangkok's most prestigious hotels, and its 700 employees enjoy the prestige of being associated with the hotel. The hotel provides good welfare benefits, above–market rate salary, and job security. In addition, a good year-end bonus amounting to four months' salary is rewarded to employees regardless of the hotel's overall performance during the year.

Recently the Regency was sold to a large American hotel chain that was very keen to expand its operations into Thailand. When the acquisition was announced, the general manager decided to take early retirement when the hotel changed ownership. The American hotel chain kept all of the Regency employees, although a few were transferred to other positions. John Becker, an American with 10 years of management experience with the hotel chain, was appointed as the new general manager of Regency Grand Hotel. Becker, was selected as the new general manager because of his previous successes in integrating newly acquired hotels in the United States. In most of the previous acquisitions Becker, took over operations with poor profitability and low morale.

Becker is a strong believer in empowerment. He expects employees to go beyond guidelines and standards to consider guest needs case by case. That is, employees must be guest-oriented at all times to provide excellent customer service. From his U.S. experience Becker has found that empowerment increases employee motivation, performance, and job satisfaction, all of which contribute to a hotel's profitability and customer service ratings. Soon after becoming general manager in Regency Grand, Becker introduced the practice of empowerment to replicate the successes that he had achieved back home.

189

The Regency Grand hotel has been very profitable since it opened 15 years ago. The employees have always worked according to management's instructions. Their responsibility was to ensure that the instructions from their managers were carried out diligently and conscientiously. Innovation and creativity were discouraged under the previous management. Indeed, employees were punished for their mistakes and discouraged from trying out ideas that had not been approved by management. As a result, employees were afraid to be innovative and to take risks.

Becker met with Regency's managers and department heads to explain that empowerment would be introduced in the hotel. He told them that employees must be empowered with decision-making authority so that they could begin to use their initiative, creativity, and judgment to satisfy guest needs or handle problems effectively and efficiently. However, he stressed that the more complex issues and decisions were to be referred to superiors, who were to coach and assist rather than provide direct orders. Furthermore, Becker stressed that although mistakes were allowed, the same mistakes could not be tolerated more than twice. He advised his managers and department heads not to discuss with him minor issues and problems and not to consult with him about minor decisions. Nevertheless, he told them that they were to discuss important and major issues and decisions with him. He concluded the meeting by asking for feedback. Several managers and department heads told him that they liked the idea and would support it, while others simply nodded their heads. Becker, pleased with the response, was eager to implement his plan.

In the past the Regency had emphasized administrative control, resulting in many bureaucratic procedures throughout the organization. For example, the front counter employees needed to seek approval from their manager before they could upgrade guests to another category of room. The front counter manager would then have to write and submit a report to the general manager justifying the upgrade. Soon after his meeting with managers, Becker reduced the number of bureaucratic rules at the Regency and allocated more decision-making authority to frontline employees. This action upset those who previously had decision-making power over these issues. As a result, several of these employees left the hotel.

Becker also began spending a large portion of his time observing and interacting with the employees at the front desk, lobby, restaurants, and various departments. This direct interaction with Becker helped many employees to understand what he wanted and expected of them. However, the employees had much difficulty trying to distinguish between major and minor issues and decisions. More often than not, supervisors would reverse employee decisions by stating that they were major issues requiring management approval. Employees who displayed initiative and made good decisions in satisfying the needs of the guests rarely received any positive feedback from their supervisors. Eventually most of these employees lost confidence in making decisions, reverting back to relying on their superiors for decision making.

Not long after the implementation of the practice of empowerment, Becker realized that his subordinates were consulting him more frequently than before. Most of them came to him with minor issues and decisions. He had to spend most of his time attending to his subordinates. Soon he began to feel frustrated and exhausted, and often he would tell his secretary that "unless the hotel is on fire, don't let anyone disturb me."

Becker thought that the practice of empowerment would benefit the overall performance of the hotel. However, contrary to his expectations, the business and overall performance of the hotel began to deteriorate. There had been an increasing number of guest complaints. In the past the hotel had minimal guest complaints. Now there were a significant number of formal written complaints every month. Many other guests voiced their dissatisfaction verbally to hotel employees. The number of mistakes made by employees had increased. Becker was very upset when he realized that two local newspapers and an overseas newspaper had published negative feedback about the hotel's service. He was most distressed when an international travel magazine voted the hotel as "one of Asia's nightmare hotels."

The stress levels of the employees were continuously mounting since the introduction of the practice of empowerment. Absenteeism due to illness was increasing at an alarming rate. In addition, the employee turnover rate had reached an all-time high. The good working relationships that were established under the old management had been severely strained. The employees were no longer united and supportive of each other. They were quick to point fingers at or to backstab one another when mistakes were made and when problems occurred.

Discussion Questions

1. Identify the symptoms indicating that problems exist in this case.

2. Diagnose the problems in this case using organizational behavior concepts.

3. Recommend solutions to overcome or minimize the problems and symptoms in this case.

Note: This case is based on true events, but the industry and names have been changed.

Case Study 6.2 THE BOTTOM LINE ON OPTIONS

BusinessWeek Stock options became popular in the 1990s as a tool that was supposed to "align the interests" of shareholders and management—in other words, reward CEOs for concentrating on raising their stock price. The popularity of these options—more than 10 million employees received them at the height of the options boom in 2002—was partly due to accounting rules in which stock options cost nothing when handed out. Not any more. The new rules require U.S. companies to count stock options as an expense. The result is that companies are turning to other forms of financial rewards for top executives and, in many cases, curtailing financial rewards altogether for professional and lower management staff.

This *BusinessWeek* case study describes how several companies have responded to new accounting rules regarding stock options. It also looks at the motivational effect of stock options. Read the full text of this *BusinessWeek* article at www.mhhe.com/mcshane4e and prepare for the discussion questions below.

Discussion Questions

1. When are stock options effective for motivating and rewarding employees?

2. How have financial rewards for senior executives shifted since the new stock option accounting rules were introduced? In your opinion, will the new financial rewards motivate executives differently than did stock options?

Source: M. Gimein, "The Bottom Line on Options," *BusinessWeek*, 3 April 2006, 32.

Team Exercise 6.3 IS STUDENT WORK ENRICHED?

PURPOSE This exercise is designed to help you learn how to measure the motivational potential of jobs and to evaluate the extent to which jobs should be further enriched.

INSTRUCTIONS Being a student is like a job in several ways. You have tasks to perform, and someone (such as your instructor) oversees your work. Although few people want to be students most of their lives (the pay rate is too low!), it may be interesting to determine how enriched your job is as a student.

1. Students are placed into teams (preferably four or five people).

2. Working alone, students complete both measures in this exercise. Then, using the guidelines here, they individually calculate the score for the five core job characteristics as well as the overall motivating potential score for the job.

3. Members of each team compare their individual results. The group should identify differences of opinion about each core job characteristic. They should also note which core job characteristics

191

have the lowest scores and recommend how these scores could be increased.

present their comparisons and recommendations for a particular core job characteristic.

4. The entire class meets to discuss the results of the exercise. The instructor may ask some teams to

Job Diagnostic Survey

Circle the number on the right that best describes student work.	Very little ▼		Moderately ▼			Very much ▼	
1. To what extent does student work permit you to decide on your own how to go about doing the work?	1	2	3	4	5	6	7
2. To what extent does student work involve doing a whole or identifiable piece of work, rather than a small portion of the overall work process?	1	2	3	4	5	6	7
3. To what extent does student work require you to do many different things, using a variety of your skills and talents?	1	2	3	4	5	6	7
4. To what extent are the results of your work as a student likely to significantly affect the lives and well-being of other people (within your school, your family, or society)?	1	2	3	4	5	6	7
5. To what extent does working on student activities provide information about your performance?	1	2	3	4	5	6	7

Circle the number on the right that best describes student work.	Very inaccurate ▼		Uncertain ▼		Very accurate ▼		
6. Being a student requires me to use a number of complex and high-level skills.	1	2	3	4	5	6	7
7. Student work is arranged so that I do NOT have the chance to do an entire piece of work from beginning to end.	7	6	5	4	3	2	1
8. Doing the work required of students provides many chances for me to figure out how well I am doing.	1	2	3	4	5	6	7
9. The work students must do is quite simple and repetitive.	7	6	5	4	3	2	1
10. The work of a student is one where a lot of other people can be affected by how well the work gets done.	1	2	3	4	5	6	7
11. Student work denies me any chance to use my personal initiative or judgment in carrying out the work.	7	6	5	4	3	2	1
12. Student work provides me the chance to completely finish the pieces of work I begin.	1	2	3	4	5	6	7
13. Doing student work by itself provides few clues about whether I am performing well.	7	6	5	4	3	2	1
14. As a student, I have considerable opportunity for independence and freedom in how I do the work.	1	2	3	4	5	6	7
15. The work I perform as a student is NOT very significant or important in the broader scheme of things.	7	6	5	4	3	2	1

Adapted from the Job Diagnostic Survey, developed by J.R. Hackman and G.R. Oldham. The authors have released any copyright ownership of this scale. See J.R. Hackman and G.R. Oldham, *Work Redesign* (Reading, MA: Addison-Wesley, 1980), p. 275.

CALCULATING THE MOTIVATING POTENTIAL SCORE

SCORING CORE JOB CHARACTERISTICS Use the following calculations to estimate the motivating potential score for the job of being a student. Use your answers from the Job Diagnostic Survey that you just completed.

Skill variety (SV) $\dfrac{\text{Questions } 3 + 6 + 9}{3} = \underline{\quad}$

Task identity (TI) $\dfrac{\text{Questions } 2 + 7 + 12}{3} = \underline{\quad}$

Task significance (TS) $\dfrac{\text{Questions } 4 + 10 + 15}{3} = \underline{\quad}$

Autonomy $\dfrac{\text{Questions } 1 + 11 + 14}{3} = \underline{\quad}$

Job feedback $\dfrac{\text{Questions } 5 + 8 + 13}{3} = \underline{\quad}$

CALCULATING MOTIVATING POTENTIAL SCORE (MPS) Use the following formula and the previous results to calculate the motivating potential score. Notice that skill variety, task identity, and task significance are averaged before being multiplied by the score for autonomy and job feedback.

$$\left(\frac{SV + TI + TS}{3}\right) \times \text{Autonomy} \times \text{Job feedback}$$

$$\left(\frac{\underline{\quad} + \underline{\quad} + \underline{\quad}}{3}\right) + \underline{\quad} + \underline{\quad} = \underline{\quad}$$

Self-Assessment 6.4

WHAT IS YOUR ATTITUDE TOWARD MONEY?

PURPOSE This exercise is designed to help you understand the types of attitudes toward money and to assess your own attitude toward money.

INSTRUCTIONS Read each of the following statements and circle the response that you believe best reflects your position regarding each statement. Then use the scoring key in Appendix B to calculate your results. This exercise is completed alone so you can assess yourself honestly without concerns of social comparison. However, class discussion will focus on the meaning of money, including the dimensions measured here and other aspects of money that may influence behavior in the workplace.

Money Attitude Scale

To what extent do you agree or disagree that...	Strongly agree ▼	Agree ▼	Neutral ▼	Disagree ▼	Strongly disagree ▼
1. I sometimes purchase things because I know they will impress other people.	(5)	4	3	2	1
2. I regularly put money aside for the future.	5	4	(3)	2	1
3. I tend to get worried about decisions involving money.	5	(4)	3	2	1
4. I believe that financial wealth is one of the most important signs of a person's success.	5	(4)	3	2	1
5. I keep a close watch on how much money I have.	5	4	3	(2)	1
6. I feel nervous when I don't have enough money.	5	(4)	3	2	1
7. I tend to show more respect to people who are wealthier than I am.	(5)	4	3	2	1
8. I follow a careful financial budget.	5	4	3	(2)	1
9. I worry about being financially secure.	5	4	(3)	2	1
10. I sometimes boast about my financial wealth or how much money I make.	5	4	3	2	(1)
11. I keep track of my investments and financial wealth.	5	4	(3)	2	1
12. I usually say "I can't afford it" even when I can afford something.	5	4	(3)	2	1

Sources: Adapted from J.A. Roberts and C.J. Sepulveda, "Demographics and Money Attitudes: A Test of Yamauchi and Templer's (1982) Money Attitude Scale in Mexico," *Personality and Individual Differences* 27 (July 1999), pp. 19–35; K. Yamauchi and D. Templer, "The Development of a Money Attitudes Scale," *Journal of Personality Assessment* 46 (1982), pp. 522–28.

Self-Assessment 6.5

ASSESSING YOUR SELF-LEADERSHIP (STUDENT OLC)

This exercise is designed to help you understand self-leadership concepts and to assess your self-leadership tendencies. Self-leadership is the process of influencing yourself to establish the self-direction and self-motivation needed to perform a task. Please indicate the extent to which each statement in this instrument describes you very well or does not describe you at all. Complete each item honestly to get the best estimate of your score on each self-leadership dimension.

Self-Assessment 6.6

STUDENT EMPOWERMENT SCALE (STUDENT OLC)

Empowerment is a concept that applies to people in a variety of situations. This instrument is specifically adapted to your position as a student at this college or university. Indicate the extent to which you agree or disagree with each statement in this instrument. Then request the results, which provide an overall score as well as scores on each of the four dimensions of empowerment. Complete each item honestly to get the best estimate of your level of empowerment.

After reading this chapter, if you need additional information, see www.mhhe.com/mcshane4e for more in-depth interactivities that correspond with this material.

547-548

Joe Straitiff realized that his leisure life was in trouble when his boss hung a huge neon sign in the workplace with the words "Open 24 Hours." The former Electronic Arts (EA) software developer also received frequent e-mail messages from the boss to the team, saying that he would see them on the weekend. "You can't work that many hours and remain sane," says Straitiff, who no longer works at the Redwood City, California, electronic games company. "It's just too harsh."

Straitiff's complaints were not exaggerations. Two days after joining EA's Los Angeles operations, video programmer Leander Hasty was sucked into a "crunch" period of intense work on *Lord of the Rings: the Battle for Middle Earth*. Soon the entire team was working 13-hour days, seven days per week. Exasperated, Hasty's fiancée, Erin Hoffman, wrote a lengthy diatribe on the Internet describing the dire situation. "The love of my life comes home late at night complaining of a headache that will not go away and a chronically upset stomach," she wrote. Within two days she received more than 1,000 sympathetic messages from people at EA and other video game companies. This flashpoint sparked several lawsuits against EA for unpaid overtime.

Josh Holmes has fond memories of working at EA, but he admits that the long hours were stressful. "From the minute I joined the company (EA), I put every waking hour of my day into my work....It definitely took its toll," says Holmes. After 10 years at EA, Holmes was burned out, so he quit. "We had done a lot of really long grueling hours. I know I was thinking that there's got to be a way to do things a little differently."

So in their quest for a less stressful electronic games company, Holmes and three other senior EA staff formed Propaganda Games (now part of Disney's video game division, Buena Vista Games) with the unique values of creativity, risk taking, and work–life balance. "Senior management knows what it's like to burn out on the job. They've been there," says Propaganda's Web site. "That's why they've set up the studio right from the start to reflect work–life balance. Normal working hours. Proper planning. And, above all, keeping things in perspective."[1]

Electronic Arts (EA) faced a barrage of criticism for creating a stressful workplace. Former EA employee Josh Holmes (shown above) co-founded a video games development company that offers more work-life balance.

Work-Related Stress and Stress Management

After reading this chapter you should be able to

1. Define *stress* and describe the stress experience.

2. Outline the stress process from stressors to consequences.

3. Identify the different types of stressors in the workplace.

4. Explain why a stressor might produce different stress levels in two people.

5. Discuss the physiological, psychological, and behavioral effects of stress.

6. Identify five work–life balance initiatives.

7. Describe the five strategies to manage workplace stress.

Working longer hours has been a serious concern among staff at EA and in many other video game development companies. But they are not alone in the rising tide of work-related stress. One survey reported that almost one-third of college-educated male adults in the United States regularly log 50 hours or more per week at work, up from 22 percent in 1980. A recent poll conducted by the New York–based Families and Work Institute revealed that 44 percent of Americans say they are often or very often overworked, with 26 percent of them experiencing this in the previous month. Another survey stated that 80 percent of Americans feel too much stress on the job; nearly half indicate that they need help coping with it.

Chronic work-related stress is not just an American affliction. Approximately one in every four employees in the United Kingdom feels "very or extremely stressed," and this condition has become the top cause of absenteeism there. A survey of 4,700 people across Asia reported that one-third were feeling more stress than in the recent past. People in Taiwan reported the highest stress; those in Thailand reported the lowest stress. More than half of Australian employees across all occupations feel under pressure a significant amount of the time; one in five say they feel exhausted on the job. The Japanese government, which tracks work-related stress every five years, has found that the percentage of Japanese employees who feel "strong worry, anxiety, or stress at work or in daily working life" has increased from 51 percent in 1982 to almost two-thirds of the population today.[2]

In this chapter we look at the dynamics of work-related stress and how to manage it. The chapter begins by describing the stress experience. Next the causes and consequences of stress are examined, along with the factors that cause some people to experience stress when others do not. The final section of this chapter looks at ways to manage work-related stress from either an organizational or individual perspective.

Learning Objectives

After reading the next two sections you should be able to

1. Define *stress* and describe the stress experience.
2. Outline the stress process from stressors to consequences.
3. Identify the different types of stressors in the workplace.

What Is Stress?

stress

An individual's adaptive response to a situation that is perceived as challenging or threatening to the person's well-being.

Stress is an adaptive response to a situation that is perceived as challenging or threatening to a person's well-being.[3] The stress response is a complex emotion that produces physiological changes to prepare us for "fight or flight"–to defend ourselves from the threat or flee from it. Specifically, our heart rates increase, muscles tighten, breathing speeds up, and perspiration increases. Our bodies also moves more blood to the brain, release adrenaline and other hormones, fuel the system by releasing more glucose and fatty acids, activate systems that sharpen our senses, and conserve resources by shutting down our immune systems.

We often hear about stress as a negative consequence of modern living. People are stressed from overwork, job insecurity, information overload, and the increasing pace of life. These events produce *distress*–the degree of physiological, psychological, and behavioral deviation from healthy functioning. There is also a positive side of stress, called *eustress*, which refers to the healthy, positive, constructive outcome of stressful events and the stress response. Eustress is the stress experience in moderation, enough to activate and motivate people so that they can achieve goals, change

Exhibit 7.1
Selye's General Adaptation Syndrome

Source: Adapted from H. Selye, *The Stress of Life* (New York: McGraw-Hill, 1956).

their environments, and succeed in life's challenges. In other words, we need some stress to survive.[4] However, most research focuses on distress because it is a significant concern in organizational settings. Employees frequently experience enough stress to hurt their job performance and increase their risk of mental and physical health problems. Consequently our discussion will focus more on distress than on eustress.

General Adaptation Syndrome

general adaptation syndrome
A model of the stress experience, consisting of three stages: alarm, resistance, and exhaustion.

The stress experience was first documented 50 years ago by stress research pioneer Hans Selye.[5] Selye determined that people have a fairly consistent physiological response to stressful situations. This response, called the **general adaptation syndrome**, provides an automatic defense system to help us cope with environmental demands. Exhibit 7.1 illustrates the three stages of the general adaptation syndrome: alarm, resistance, and exhaustion. The line in this exhibit shows the individual's energy and ability to cope with the stressful situation.

Alarm Reaction The alarm reaction stage occurs when a threat or challenge activates the physiological stress responses that we noted earlier, such as increased respiration rate, blood pressure, heartbeat, and muscle tension. The individual's energy level and coping effectiveness decrease in response to the initial shock. In extreme situations this shock can result in incapacity or death because the body is unable to generate enough energy quickly enough. Most of the time the alarm reaction alerts the person to the environmental condition and prepares the body for the resistance stage.

Resistance The person's ability to cope with the environmental demand rises above the normal state during the resistance stage because the body activates various biochemical, psychological, and behavioral mechanisms. For example, we have higher-than-normal levels of adrenaline and glucose during this stage, which give us more energy to overcome or remove the source of stress. At the same time, the body shuts down the immune system to focus energy on the source of the stress. This explains why people are more likely to catch a cold or other illness when they experience prolonged stress.

Exhaustion People have a limited resistance capacity, and if the source of stress persists, they will eventually move into the exhaustion stage. In most work situations the general adaptation syndrome process ends long before total exhaustion. Employees resolve tense situations before the destructive consequences of stress become manifest, or they withdraw from the stressful situation, rebuild their survival capabilities, and return later to the stressful environment with renewed energy. However, people who frequently experience the general adaptation syndrome have increased risk of long-term physiological and psychological damage.[6]

The general adaptation syndrome describes the stress experience, but this is only part of the picture. To effectively manage work-related stress, we must understand its causes and consequences as well as individual differences in the stress experience.

Stressors: The Causes of Stress

stressors

The causes of stress, including any environmental conditions that place a physical or emotional demand on the person.

Stressors, the causes of stress, include any environmental conditions that place a physical or emotional demand on a person.[7] There are numerous stressors in organizational settings and other life activities. Exhibit 7.2 lists the four main types of work-related stressors: interpersonal, role-related, task control, and organizational and physical environment stressors.

Interpersonal Stressors

Among the four types of stressors, interpersonal stressors seem to be the most pervasive in the workplace. The trend toward teamwork generates interpersonal stressors because employees must interact more with co-workers. Organizational politics, which we'll discuss in Chapter 12, are another interpersonal stressor. Bad

Exhibit 7.2
Causes and Consequences of Stress

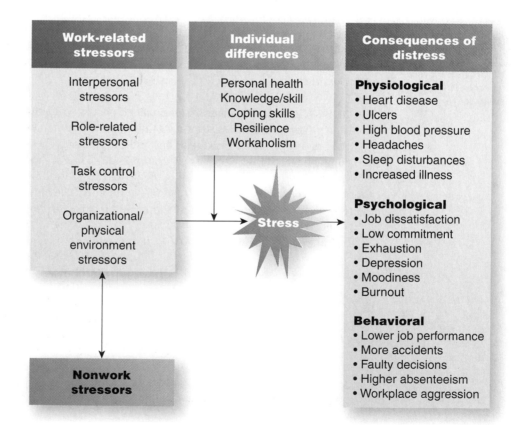

bosses can also be quite stressful. For instance, one study discovered that female health care assistants experienced much higher blood pressure when working with an ineffective rather than an effective supervisor. Over a sustained period this higher blood pressure would increase the risk of stroke by 38 percent![8] Two other interpersonal stressors are workplace violence and harassment, which are discussed next.

Workplace Violence   Workplace violence is a serious interpersonal stressor. In the United States more than 600 employees are murdered on the job each year, and 2 million others experience lesser forms of physical violence. An International Labor Organization study reported that more than 60 percent of health care staff in Bulgaria, Australia, South Africa, and Portugal experienced at least one incident of physical or psychological violence in the previous year. A recent survey reported that more than a quarter of the 3,000 British nurses questioned had been physically attacked at work, half of those within the previous 12 months.[9]

Victims of workplace violence experience severe stress symptoms. Those who observe the violence also tend to experience stress. After a serious workplace incident, counselors assist many employees, not just the direct victims. Even employees who have not directly experienced or observed violence may show signs of stress if they work in jobs that expose them to a higher incidence of violence.

Psychological and Sexual Harassment   One of the fastest-growing sources of workplace stress is **psychological harassment**. Psychological harassment includes repeated and hostile or unwanted conduct, verbal comments, actions, or gestures that affect an employee's dignity or psychological or physical integrity and that result in a harmful work environment for the employee. This covers a broad landscape of behaviors, from threats and bullying to subtle yet persistent forms of incivility.[10] Three large surveys reported strikingly similar results—namely that 70 percent or more Americans think people are less civil today than 20 years ago. In another U.S. poll 10 percent of respondents said they witness incivility daily in their workplaces and are targets of that abuse at least once each week.[11]

Psychological harassment also permeates workplaces in other countries. One global survey reported that almost 40 percent of German and Dutch finance and human resource professionals have experienced workplace bullying, compared with 33 percent in New Zealand, 25 percent in Australia and the United Kingdom, and only 9 percent in Italy. Other polls suggest that these figures might underestimate the actual levels of psychological harassment. A recent survey suggests that more than half of U.K. human resource managers have been bullied at work, mostly by their immediate supervisors. More than half of the 1,800 lawyers polled in the Australian state of New South Wales say they have been bullied or intimidated. When the province of Quebec, Canada, recently passed the first workplace antiharassment legislation in North America (modeled after similar laws in Sweden, France, and Belgium), nearly 5,000 complaints were received during the first two years![12]

Sexual harassment is a variation of harassment in which a person's employment or job appraisal is conditional on unwanted sexual relations (called *quid pro quo*) and/or the person experiences sexual conduct from others (such as posting pornographic material) that unreasonably interferes with work performance or creates an intimidating, hostile, or offensive working environment (called a *hostile work environment*). One study points out that men tend to have a narrower interpretation than do women over what constitutes a hostile work environment, so they sometimes engage in this

psychological harassment
Repeated and hostile or unwanted conduct, verbal comments, actions, or gestures that affect an employee's dignity or psychological or physical integrity and that result in a harmful work environment for the employee.

sexual harassment
Unwelcome conduct of a sexual nature that detrimentally affects the work environment or leads to adverse job-related consequences for its victims.

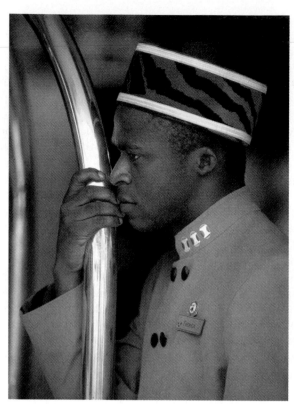

Five-Star Bullying in Posh London Hotels Working at a London five-star hotel has not been pleasant for Ahmet (not his real name). For the past six long months the Moroccan migrant worker has experienced racial harassment, as well as shouting and screaming from managers and customers who pointed their fingers at his head. At one point the harassment became so severe that Ahmet burst into tears, had to go on medication, and received counseling. Another five-star hotel, which welcomes migrant workers in its induction as a "home away from home," is apparently just as abusive. Workers there complain about the daily verbal attacks from managers, who hurl profanities and ridicule one ethnic group against another. "These are the top luxury hotels. Just imagine the rest of them," says Julio Haro, race equality officer of Britain's General Union, adding that these incidents are the norm, not the exception, in the hotel industry.[13]

form of sexual harassment without being aware of their transgressions.[14] Another issue is that sexual harassment sometimes escalates into psychological harassment after the alleged victim complains about the sexual wrongdoing. The good news, however, is that the number of charges alleging sexual harassment in the United States has declined steadily from 16,000 in 2000 to less than 13,000 in 2005. The Equal Employment Opportunity Commission attributes the improvement to better supervisor training and concerted management action to address harassment issues before they reach litigation.

Psychological and sexual harassment are stressful experiences that undermine employee well-being and performance. Past behavior is the best predictor of future behavior, so companies should carefully screen applicants for past incidents. Multisource feedback is another valuable tool to let employees know that co-workers and direct reports find their behavior intimidating or sexually inappropriate. Along with these practices, companies need to develop a grievance, mediation, or other conflict resolution process that employees trust when they become victims of workplace harassment.

Role-Related Stressors

Role-related stressors include conditions in which employees have difficulty understanding, reconciling, or performing the various roles in their lives. Three types of role-related stressors are role conflict, role ambiguity, and work overload. **Role conflict** refers to the degree of incongruity or incompatibility of expectations associated with a person's role. Some people experience stress when they have two roles that conflict with each other. For example, various studies have recently reported this

role conflict
Incongruity or incompatibility of expectations associated with a person's role.

inter-role conflict among human service workers and health care providers, where workloads and bureaucratic procedures interfered with their ability to serve clients or patients.[15] Role conflict also occurs when an employee's personal values are incompatible with organizational values, a topic that was detailed in Chapter 2.

role ambiguity
A lack of clarity and predictability of the outcomes of a person's behavior.

Role ambiguity refers to the lack of clarity and predictability of the outcomes of a person's behavior. Role ambiguity produces unclear role perceptions, which directly affect job performance. It is also a source of stress in a variety of situations, such as joining an organization or working in a new joint venture, because people are uncertain about task and social expectations.[16]

Work Overload   A half-century ago social scientists predicted that technology would allow employees to enjoy a 15-hour workweek at full pay by 2030.[17] So far it hasn't turned out that way. As the opening vignette to this chapter described, employees at Electronic Arts and many other companies in the video games industry are experiencing stress due to *work overload*—working more hours and more intensely during those hours than they can reasonably handle.

Why do employees work such long hours? One explanation is the combined effects of technology and globalization. "Everyone in this industry is working harder now because of e-mail, wireless access, and globalization," says Christopher Lochhead, chief marketing officer of Mercury Interactive, a California-based consultancy with offices in 35 countries. "You can't even get a rest on the weekend," he says. A second cause, according to a recent study, is that many people are caught up in consumerism; they want to buy more goods and services, which require more income

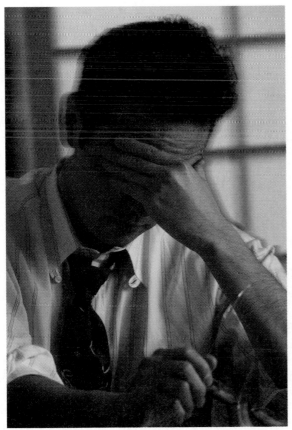

Asian Professionals Are Dying to Get Ahead Throughout Asia professionals are working long hours as a badge of honor. For some this is a short-lived honor. According to the Japanese government, employees who work more than 80 hours of overtime per month have a significantly higher risk of *karoshi*—death from overwork. Currently more than 20 percent of male Japanese employees exceed that level of overtime. Governments in South Korea—which has among the world's highest average work hours—and Taiwan are also paying closer attention to workplace casualties linked to long work hours. In China, the media are now using the term *guolaosi* (overwork death) to describe this disturbing trend. In one recent incident two young faculty members at China's top engineering school died suddenly, apparently from exhaustion and overwork. The Chinese media themselves seem to suffer from *guolaosi*. A study of journalists in China's major news outlets revealed that the average age of death was 46 years. Long hours and corresponding poor lifestyle were identified as factors in this shorter life expectancy.[18]

through longer work hours. A third reason, called the "ideal worker norm," is that professionals expect themselves and others to work longer work hours. For many people, toiling away far beyond the normal workweek is a badge of honor, a symbol of their superhuman capacity to perform above others.[19] This badge of honor is particularly pronounced in Japan, South Korea, Taiwan, China, and several other Asian countries, to the point where "death from overwork" is now part of the common language (*karoshi* in Japanese and *guolaosi* in Chinese).

Task Control Stressors

As a private driver for an executive in Jakarta, Eddy knows that traffic jams are a way of life in Indonesia's largest city. "Jakarta is traffic congestion," he complains. "All of the streets in the city are crowded with vehicles. It is impossible to avoid this distressing fact every day." Eddy's boss complains when traffic jams make him late for appointments, which makes matters even more stressful. "Even watching soccer on TV or talking to my wife doesn't get rid of my stress. It's driving me mad."[20] Eddy and many other people experience stress due to a lack of task control. Along with driving through congested traffic, low task control occurs where the employee's work is paced by a machine, the job involves monitoring equipment, or the work schedule is controlled by someone else. Computers, cell phones, and other technology also increase stress by limiting a person's control of time and privacy.[21]

The degree to which low task control is a stressor increases with the burden of responsibility the employee must carry. Assembly line workers have low task control, but their stress can be fairly low if their level of responsibility is also low. In contrast, sports coaches are under immense pressure to win games (high responsibility) yet have little control over what happens on the playing field (low task control). Similarly, Eddy (the Jakarta driver) is under pressure to get his employer to a particular destination on time (high responsibility), yet he has little control over traffic congestion (low task control).

Organizational and Physical Environment Stressors

Organizational and physical environment stressors come in many forms. Downsizing is stressful for those who lose their jobs. Even those who keep their jobs (called layoff survivors) experience stress because of the reduced job security, chaos of change, additional workloads, and guilt of having a job as others lose theirs. For example, one study reported that long-term sick leave doubled among surviving government employees in Finland after a major downsizing.[22] Physical work environment stressors include excessive noise and poor lighting. People working in dangerous environments also tend to experience higher stress levels.

Work–Nonwork Stressors

The stress model shown earlier in Exhibit 7.2 has a two-way arrow, indicating that stressors from work spill over into nonwork and vice versa.[23] There are three types of work–nonwork stressors: time-based, strain-based, and role-based conflict.

Time-Based Conflict   *Time-based conflict* refers to the challenge of balancing the time demanded by work with family and other nonwork activities. Time-based conflict relates back to the work overload stressor described earlier. The problem of longer work hours that we discussed earlier (as well as more intensely during those hours) is

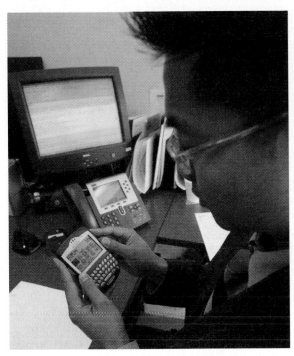

Blackberry Divorce Nick Salaysay (shown in this photo) admits that his work routinely gets mixed in with his personal time. "I have a BlackBerry, so I check my e-mail a lot when I'm supposed to be on vacation," says the corporate lawyer at Gowling Lafleur Henderson in Calgary, Canada. Salaysay also acknowledges that having work spill over into his time off "really annoys my girlfriend." Amy Schulman is another dedicated BlackBerry user. The New York–based partner with law firm DLA Piper Rudnick Gray Cary recalls that "the BlackBerry was at first a significant intrusion on family life," but she believes family members now understand that the device makes it easier for her to process several hundred e-mail messages each day. As a consolation, Schulman adds that "I don't generally look at my e-mail during mealtimes, and I try not to look at it in movie theaters." Nick Salaysay and Amy Schulman are comfortable using their BlackBerries during family time. But research indicates that when electronic devices spill work into home life, they increase the risk of strain-based stress and possibly result in the additional stress of relationship and marital problems.[24]

compounded by the fact that employees have little time or energy left for themselves and their family. Inflexible work schedules, business travel, and rotating shift schedules also take a heavy toll because they reduce the ability to effectively juggle work and nonwork.[25] Time-based conflict is usually more acute for women than for men because housework and child care continue to fall more on their shoulders as a "second shift" in most dual-career families.

Strain-Based Conflict   *Strain-based conflict* occurs when stress from one domain spills over to the other. Relationship problems, financial difficulties, and loss of a loved one usually top the list of nonwork stressors. New responsibilities, such as marriage, birth of a child, and a mortgage, are also stressful to most of us. Stress at work spills over to an employee's personal life and often becomes the foundation of stressful relations with family and friends. Strain-based conflict may be increasing as technology allows work and nonwork activities to spread from one domain to the other. For instance, many professionals now routinely use their cell phones, pagers, and BlackBerry wireless devices for work-related tasks while at home and even on vacation. Similarly, many employees use technology at work to complete household obligations, such as online banking or purchases.[26]

Role Behavior Conflict   A third work–nonwork stressor, called *role behavior conflict,* occurs when people are expected to act quite differently at work than in nonwork roles. For instance, people who act logically and impersonally at work have difficulty switching to a more compassionate behavioral style in their personal lives. Thus stress occurs in this adjustment from one role to the other.[27]

Exhibit 7.3   Stressors in Occupations

Low-stress occupations	Medium-stress occupations	High-stress occupations
Accountant	Hospital manager	U.S. president
Artist	Physician (GP)	Prison officer
Auto mechanic	Psychologist	Teacher
Forester	School principal	Nurse

Stress and Occupations

Several studies have attempted to identify which jobs have more stressors than others.[28] These lists are not in complete agreement, but Exhibit 7.3 identifies a representative sample of jobs and their relative level of stressors. We need to view this information with some caution, however. One problem with rating occupations in terms of their stress levels is that a particular occupation may have considerably different tasks and job environments across organizations and societies. A nurse's job may be less stressful in a small-town medical clinic, for instance, than in the emergency room of a large city hospital.

Another important point to remember when looking at Exhibit 7.3 is that a major stressor to one person may be less significant to another. Thus not everyone in so-called high-stress occupations actually experiences more stress than people in other occupations. High-stress jobs have more stressors, but people don't experience more stress if they are carefully selected and trained for this type of work. The next section discusses individual differences in stress.

Learning Objectives

After reading the next two sections you should be able to

4. **Explain why a stressor might produce different stress levels in two people.**

5. **Discuss the physiological, psychological, and behavioral effects of stress.**

Individual Differences in Stress

Due to unique personal characteristics, people have different stress experiences when exposed to the same stressor. One reason is that they have different threshold levels of resistance to the stressor. Younger employees generally experience fewer and less severe stress symptoms than older employees because they have a larger store of energy to cope with high stress levels. Exercise and healthful lifestyles (including work-free holidays) are discussed later in this chapter as ways to manage stress because these activities rebuild this store of energy. A second reason for different stress outcomes is

Stress-Free at Finster Honey Farms Working around honeybees is a heart-thumping experience for most of us. But Hakija Pehlic (shown here) doesn't worry when he pushes his nose through a layer of European honeybees to determine the type of honey produced on a honeycomb frame. Pehlic, a beekeeper at Finster Honey Farms in Schuyler, New York, doesn't experience much stress in this situation because he is trained to know when it's safe to smell the honey and how to avoid getting stung. Most of the time, says Pehlic, honeybees are gentle insects that won't bother you. Maybe so, but you probably shouldn't try this at home.[29]

that people use different coping strategies, some of which are more effective than others. Research suggests that employees who try to ignore or deny the existence of a stressor suffer more in the long run than those who try to find ways to weaken the stressor and seek social support.[30]

The third reason why some people experience less stress than others in the same situation is that they have different beliefs about the threat and their ability to withstand it. This explanation really has two parts. The first part refers to the notion that people with more knowledge and skill usually feel more confident about successfully managing or overcoming the threat. Someone who flies a plane for the first time tends to experience much more stress than an experienced pilot, for instance. The second part refers to the idea that people who are optimistic, confident, and often experience positive emotions tend to feel less stress.[31] This characteristic extends beyond the person's knowledge and skill; it refers to an important emerging concept known as *resilience*.

Resilience and Stress

resilience
The capability of individuals to cope successfully in the face of significant change, adversity, or risk.

Resilience is the capability of individuals to cope successfully in the face of significant change, adversity, or risk. Everyone has some resilience; it occurs every time we pull through stressful experiences. Although the word literally means to "leap back," resilience in this context refers mainly to withstanding adversity rather than recovering from it. Although everyone needs to recuperate to some extent following a stressful experience, people with high resilience are better able to maintain an equilibrium and consequently have lost little ground in the first place. In fact, some writers believe that resilience moves people to a higher plateau after the adversity.[32]

Experts have looked at the characteristics of resilience from different perspectives. One perspective is that resilient people have personality traits that generate more optimism, confidence, and positive emotions. These traits include high extroversion, low neuroticism, internal locus of control, high tolerance of change, and high self-esteem.[33]

A second perspective is that resilience involves specific competencies and behaviors to respond and adapt more effectively to stressors. Research indicates that resilient people have higher emotional intelligence and good problem-solving skills. They also apply productive coping strategies, such as analyzing the sources of stress and finding ways to neutralize these problems. In contrast, people with low resilience tend to avoid or deny the existence of stressors.[34]

The third perspective is that resilience is an inner force that motivates us to move forward. This emerging view is connected to the concept of self-actualization that psychologist Abraham Maslow popularized and made his life's work a half-century ago (see Chapter 5). It is also connected to recent OB writing on *workplace spirituality*, which investigates a person's inner strength and how it nurtures and is nurtured by the workplace. Resilience as an inner force has some empirical support. Research has found that resilience is stronger when people have a sense of purpose and are in touch with their personal values.[35]

Workaholism and Stress

workaholic
A person who is highly involved in work, feels compelled to work, and has a low enjoyment of work.

While resilience helps people to withstand stress, another personal characteristic—workaholism—attracts more stressors and weakens the capacity to cope with them. The classic **workaholic** (also called *work addict*) is highly involved in work, feels compelled or driven to work because of inner pressures, and has a low enjoyment of work. He or she is compulsive and preoccupied with work, often to the exclusion and detriment of personal health, intimate relationships, and family. Work addicts are typically hard-driving, competitive individuals who tend to be impatient, lose their tempers, and interrupt others during conversations.[36] These latter characteristics are collectively known as the **Type A behavior pattern**.

Type A behavior pattern
A behavior pattern associated with people having premature coronary heart disease; type As tend to be impatient, lose their temper, talk rapidly, and interrupt others.

According to a large-scale study at Israel's University of Haifa, 12.7 of Americans are traditional workaholics, followed by 9.3 percent of Japanese workers and 8.1 percent of Israeli workers. Further down the workaholism scale are employees in Belgium (6.8 percent) and the Netherlands (6.5 percent). Along with classic workaholics, the academic literature identifies two other workaholic types: *enthusiastic workaholics* and *work enthusiasts*. Enthusiastic workaholics have high levels of all three components—high work involvement, drive to succeed, and work enjoyment. Work enthusiasts have high work involvement and work enjoyment, but low drive to succeed.

Workaholism is relevant to this discussion of stress because classic work addicts are more prone to job stress and burnout. They also have significantly higher scores on depression, anxiety, and anger than do nonworkaholics, as well as lower job and career satisfaction. Furthermore, work addicts of both sexes report more health complaints.[37]

Consequences of Distress

The previous sections on workplace stressors and individual differences in stress have made some reference to the various outcomes of the stress experience. These stress consequences are typically grouped into physiological, psychological, and behavioral categories.

Physiological Consequences

Stress takes its toll on the human body.[38] The stress response shuts down the immune system, which makes us more vulnerable to viral and bacterial infection. Many people experience tension headaches due to stress. Others get muscle pain and related back problems. These physiological ailments are attributed to muscle contractions that occur when people are exposed to stressors.

Cardiovascular disease is one of the most disturbing effects of stress in modern society. Strokes and heart attacks were rare a century ago but are now among the leading causes of death among adults in the United States and other countries. Stress also influences hypertension (high blood pressure). In spite of better lifestyle and medical treatment, recent evidence suggests that hypertension continues to increase, particularly among older people and non-Hispanic blacks in the United States. Along with these health problems, a recent study of 60,000 people in Norway found that those with high scores on an anxiety test were 25 percent more likely to have premalignant tumors seven years later.[39]

Psychological Consequences

Stress produces various psychological consequences, including job dissatisfaction, moodiness, depression, and lower organizational commitment.[40] Emotional fatigue is another psychological consequence of stress and is related to job burnout.

job burnout
The process of emotional exhaustion, cynicism, and reduced efficacy (lower feelings of personal accomplishment) resulting from prolonged exposure to stress.

Job Burnout **Job burnout** refers to the process of emotional exhaustion, cynicism, and reduced feelings of personal accomplishment resulting from prolonged exposure to stress.[41] It is a complex process that includes the dynamics of stress, coping strategies, and stress consequences. Burnout is caused by excessive demands made on people who serve or frequently interact with others. In other words, burnout is due mainly to interpersonal and role-related stressors, and is most common in helping occupations (nurses, teachers, police officers).

Exhibit 7.4 diagrams the relationship among the three components of job burnout. *Emotional exhaustion*, the first stage, is characterized by a lack of energy, tiredness, and a feeling that one's emotional resources are depleted. Emotional exhaustion is sometimes called *compassion fatigue* because the employee no longer feels able to give as much support and care to clients.

Exhibit 7.4
The Job Burnout Process

Cynicism (also called *depersonalization*) follows emotional exhaustion. It is identified by an indifferent attitude toward work and the treatment of others as objects rather than people. At this stage employees become emotionally detached from clients and cynical about the organization. This detachment is to the point of callousness—far beyond the normal level in helping occupations. Cynicism is also apparent when employees strictly follow rules and regulations rather than trying to understand the client's needs and searching for a mutually acceptable solution.

Reduced professional efficacy (also called *reduced personal accomplishment*), the final component of job burnout, refers to feelings of diminished confidence in one's ability to perform the job well. In these situations employees develop a sense of learned helplessness as they no longer believe that their efforts make a difference.

Behavioral Consequences

Moderate levels of stress focus our attention and concentrate resources where they are most needed. But when stress becomes distress, job performance falls, memory becomes impaired, workplace accidents are more frequent, and decisions are less effective.[42] You have probably experienced this in an exam or emergency work situation. You forget important information, make mistakes, and otherwise "draw a blank" under intense pressure.

Overstressed employees also tend to have higher levels of absenteeism. One reason is that stress makes people susceptible to viral and bacterial infections. The other reason is that absenteeism is a coping mechanism. At a basic level, we react to stress through "fight or flight." Absenteeism is a form of flight—temporarily withdrawing from the stressful situation so that we can reenergize. Companies may try to minimize absenteeism, but it sometimes helps employees avoid the exhaustion stage of the stress experience.[43]

Workplace Aggression   Workplace aggression is more than the serious interpersonal stressor described earlier. It is also an increasingly worrisome behavioral consequence of stress. Aggression represents the fight (instead of flight) reaction to stress. In its mildest form, employees engage in verbal harassment. They "fly off the handle" and are less likely to empathize with co-workers. Like most forms of workplace behavior, co-worker aggression is caused by both the person and the situation. Although certain individuals are more likely to be aggressive, their behavior is also usually a consequence of extreme stress to some extent.[44] In particular, employees are more likely to engage in aggressive behavior if they believe they have been treated unfairly, experience other forms of frustration beyond their personal control, and work in physical environments that are stressful (such as being hot or noisy).

Learning
Objectives

After reading this section you should be able to

6.   **Identify five work–life balance initiatives.**

7.   **Describe the five strategies to manage workplace stress.**

Managing Work-Related Stress

Tony Bates had a high-flying career as head of private banking at Macquarie Bank, but he preferred a shorter workweek with proportionately lower pay. When Bates tried to discuss his need for work–life balance with the three executives above him—all

Exhibit 7.5
Stress Management
Strategies

baby boomers with no children—one replied, "If you work your guts out for 30 years, you'll retire at 55 and get [work–life] balance in the last 30 years."

That was enough for Bates, a Generation-Xer and father of three children. He started his own boutique financial planning business, spacing his work across four days per week. "I'm on about 60 percent of the money I used to make, and working fewer hours," says Bates. "Just knowing I can pick up the kids after school takes out the stress, so I'm happier at home and happier at work."

Tony Bates was fortunate. He was able to change his work habits before matters got worse. Unfortunately many of us deny the existence of our stress until it is too late. This avoidance strategy creates a vicious cycle because the failure to cope with stress becomes another stressor on top of the one that created the stress in the first place. The solution is for both employers and employees to discover the toolkit of effective stress management strategies identified in Exhibit 7.5 and to determine which ones are best for the situation.[45]

Remove the Stressor

From the categories in Exhibit 7.5, some writers argue that the only way companies can effectively manage stress is by removing the stressors that cause unnecessary strain and job burnout. Other stress management strategies may keep employees "stress-fit," but they don't solve the fundamental causes of stress.

Removing the stressor usually begins by identifying areas of high stress and determining its main causes. Ericsson conducts this diagnosis in its North American operations through an annual survey that includes a stress index. Executives at the telecommunications company use the index to identify departments where stress problems may be developing. "We look at those scores, and if there appears to be a problem in a particular group, we put in action plans to try and remedy and improve the work situation that may be causing the stress," explains an Ericsson executive.[46]

Monitoring stress is one of the first steps in a more comprehensive stress management strategy—changing the corporate culture to support a work–life balance rather than dysfunctional workaholism. Another strategy is to give employees more control over their work and work environment. Role-related stressors can be minimized by selecting and assigning employees to positions that match their competencies. Noise and safety risks are stressful, so improving these conditions would also go a long way to minimize stress in the workplace. Workplace harassment can be minimized by carefully selecting employees and having clear guidelines of behavior and feedback to people who violate those standards.[47]

Employees can also take an active role in removing stressors. If stress is caused by ambiguous role expectations, for example, employees might seek more information from others to clarify these expectations. If a particular piece of work is too challenging, they might break it into smaller sets of tasks so that the overall project is less threatening or wearing. To some extent employees can also minimize workplace harassment by learning to identify early warning signs of aggression in customers and co-workers and by developing interpersonal skills that dissipate aggression.

Work–Life Balance Initiatives   In a variety of ways companies can help employees experience a better balance between their work and personal lives. Five of the most common work–life balance initiatives are flexible work time, job sharing, telecommuting, personal leave, and child care support.

- *Flexible work time.* Some firms are flexible on the hours, days, and amounts of time employees work. For instance, accounting firm Deloitte & Touche allows employees to work part-time as well as to take up to five years off for personal leave. Flexible and part-time work schedules have become so popular at PricewaterhouseCoopers that the accounting firm now has an online program for employees to schedule them.

- *Job sharing.* Job sharing splits a career position between two people so they experience less time-based stress between work and family. They typically work different parts of the week with some overlapping work time in the weekly schedule to coordinate activities. Although traditionally aimed at nonmanagement positions, job sharing is also starting to occur in executive jobs.[48]

Flexible Accounting   Several years ago, Deloitte & Touche partners discovered that many promising female accountants were leaving because they wanted more flexibility in their work schedule. Today, the accounting giant is a leader in flexible work arrangements and other forms of work-life balance. Tricia Schetz, a senior manager for Deloitte's audit group in Grand Rapids, Michigan, is a case in point. Schetz works 16 to 20 hours a week so she can spend more time raising her two children. Cathy Levatino (shown in this photo with her two children), also works a reduced schedule at Deloitte & Touche to satisfy her work-balance needs. Even on this flexible schedule, Levatino was recently admitted to the partnership.[49]

- *Telecommuting.* Chapter 1 described how an increasing number of employees are telecommuting. This reduces the time and stress of commuting to work and makes it easier to fulfill family obligations, such as temporarily leaving the home office to pick the kids up from school. Research suggests that telecommuters experience a healthier work–life balance.[50] However, telecommuting may increase stress for those who crave social interaction and who lack the space and privacy necessary to work at home.

- *Personal leave.* Employers with strong work–life values offer extended maternity, paternity, and personal leave to care for a new family or take advantage of a personal experience. The U.S. Family and Medical Leave Act gives expecting mothers (and anyone considered to have an "illness") 12 weeks of unpaid, job-protected leave. However, almost every other developed nation requires employers to provide paid maternity leave. In Austria, for instance, both parents are entitled to paid parental leave of two years.[51]

- *Child care support.* According to one estimate, almost one-quarter of large American employers provide on-site or subsidized child care facilities. Child care support reduces stress because employees are less rushed to drop off children and less worried during the day about how well they are doing.[52]

Given the high levels of work–life conflict that we have read about, you would think that organizations are encouraging employees to apply these initiatives. The reality, according to some critics, is that while these practices are available, employees either feel guilty about using them or are discouraged from using them. To ensure that employees actually develop a work–life balance, the top 500 managers at accounting firm RSM McGladrey, Inc., receive annual 360-degree reviews in which peers, subordinates, and managers rate how well the executives respect and encourage "balance of work and personal life priorities" among employees.[53]

Withdraw from the Stressor

Removing the stressor may be the ideal solution, but it is often not feasible. An alternative strategy is to permanently or temporarily remove employees from the stressor. Permanent withdrawal occurs when employees are transferred to jobs that better fit their competencies and values.

Temporary Withdrawal Strategies   Temporarily withdrawing from stressors is the most frequent way that employees manage stress. SAS Institute employees in Cary, North Carolina, enjoy live piano recitals at lunch. Consulting firms Segal Co. in New York and Vielife in London have nap rooms where staff can recover with a few winks of sleep. Admiral Insurance doesn't have sleep facilities yet, but the Welsh insurance company offers other ways for employees to take temporary breaks from work. "We have an Indian head-masseur who visits monthly, we have a number of chill-out rooms with sofas, TVs, and games consoles for all staff to use, and we are currently trialing a 'relaxation chair,' which reclines and massages the user while playing chilled-out music through headphones," says an Admiral Insurance spokesperson.[54]

Personal days off and vacations represent somewhat longer temporary withdrawals from stressful conditions. Oxygen Business solutions in Auckland, New Zealand, offers employees two "wellness" days per year "so people can call in and say they're too well to come to work today," says Oxygen chief executive Mike Smith. Sabbaticals represent an extended version of vacations, whereby employees take up to several months of paid leave after several years of service. Approximately 5 percent of U.S. companies offer paid sabbaticals to some employees. McDonald's Corp. has had paid sabbaticals for the past 40 years, offering employees eight weeks of paid time off after every 10 years of service.[55]

Change Stress Perceptions

Earlier we learned that employees often experience different levels of stress in the same situation because they have different levels of self-confidence and optimism. Consequently corporate leaders need to look at ways for employees to strengthen their confidence and self-esteem so that job challenges are not perceived as threatening. Self-leadership practices seem to help here. For example, positive self-talk can boost self-confidence. A study of newly hired accountants reported that personal goal setting and self-reinforcement can also reduce the stress that people experience when they enter new work settings.[56] Humor can also improve optimism and create positive emotions by taking some psychological weight off the situation.

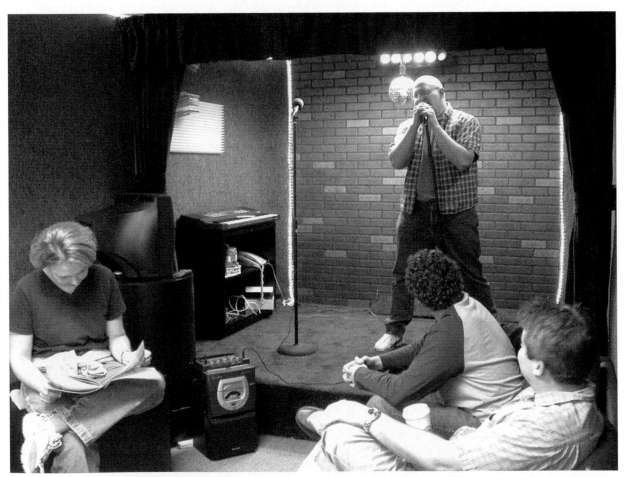

Singing the Stress Away When employees at Liggett-Stashower Inc. need a short break from the daily stresses of work, they retreat to one of three theme rooms specially designed for creativity and respite. Staff at the Cleveland advertising firm can enter the bowling room and knock down a few pins. Or they might try out the Zen room, which serves as a quiet, relaxing place to think. The third room features karaoke in which frustrated employees can belt out tunes. "The higher the stress level, the more singing there is going on," says Kristen Flynn, a Liggett art director.[57]

Control the Consequences of Stress

Coping with workplace stress also involves controlling its consequences. For this reason many companies have fitness centers where employees can keep in shape. Research indicates that physical exercise reduces the physiological consequences of stress by helping employees moderate their breathing and heart rates, muscle tension, and stomach acidity.[58] Another way to control the physiological consequences of stress is through relaxation and meditation. For instance, employees at Wilmington, Delaware–based pharmaceutical company AstraZeneca practice a form of meditation called Qi Gong during department meetings and coffee breaks. Research has found that Qi and other forms of meditation reduce anxiety, reduce blood pressure and muscle tension, and moderate breathing and heart rate.[59]

Along with fitness and relaxation/meditation, 81 percent of U.S. employers with at least 50 employees have wellness programs. These programs educate and support employees in better nutrition and fitness, regular sleep, and other good health habits. For example, employees at Pitney-Bowes receive up to $200 for completing online wellness surveys three times each year. More than 80 percent of Minitab Inc. employees in State College, Pennsylvania, participate in the software developer's wellness program, which includes annual on-site checkups and meditation classes.[60]

Many large employers offer **employee assistance programs** (**EAPs**)—counseling services that help employees overcome personal or organizational stressors and adopt more effective coping mechanisms. Most EAPs are "broadbrush" programs that assist employees with any work or personal problems. Family problems often represent the largest percentage of EAP referrals, although this varies with industry and location. For instance, major banks provide posttrauma stress counseling for employees after a robbery. EAPs can be one of the most effective stress management interventions when the counseling helps employees to understand the stressors, acquire stress management skills, and practice those stress management skills.[61]

employee assistance programs (EAPs)
Counseling services that help employees overcome personal or organizational stressors and adopt more effective coping mechanisms.

Receive Social Support

Social support from co-workers, supervisors, family members, friends, and others is generally regarded as one of the more effective stress management practices. However, this benefit occurs when the stressed individual reaches out for support, not when the support is imposed by others. *Social support* refers to the person's interpersonal transactions with others and involves providing either emotional or informational support to buffer the stress experience. Seeking social support is called a "tend and befriend" response to stress, and research suggests that women often follow this route rather than the "fight-or-flight" alternative that was mentioned earlier in this chapter.[62]

Social support reduces stress in at least three ways.[63] First, employees improve their perceptions that they are valued and worthy. This, in turn, increases resilience because they have higher self-esteem and confidence to cope with stressors. Second, social support provides information to help employees interpret, comprehend, and possibly remove stressors. For instance, social support might reduce a new employee's stress if co-workers describe ways to handle difficult customers. Finally, emotional support from others can directly help to buffer the stress experience. This last point reflects the idea that "misery loves company." People seek out and benefit from the emotional support of others when they face threatening situations.[64]

Social support is an important way to cope with stress that everyone can practice by maintaining friendships. This includes helping others when they need a little support from the stressors of life. Organizations can facilitate social support by providing opportunities for social interaction among employees as well as their families. People in leadership roles also need to practice a supportive leadership style when employees work under stressful conditions and need this social support. Mentoring relationships with more senior employees may help junior employees cope with organizational stressors.

Chapter Summary

Stress is an adaptive response to a situation that is perceived as challenging or threatening to a person's well-being. Distress represents high stress levels that have negative consequences, whereas eustress represents the moderately low stress levels needed to activate people. The stress experience, called the general adaptation syndrome, involves moving through three stages: alarm, resistance, and exhaustion. The stress model shows that stress is caused by stressors, but the effect of these stressors on stress is moderated by individual characteristics.

Stressors are the causes of stress and include any environmental conditions that place a physical or emotional demand on a person. Stressors are found in the physical work environment, employees' various life roles, interpersonal relations, and organizational activities and conditions. Conflicts between work and nonwork obligations are a frequent source of employee stress.

Two people exposed to the same stressor may experience different stress levels because they have different threshold levels of resistance to the stressor, use different coping strategies, or have different beliefs about the threat and their ability to withstand it. People experience less stress when they have high resilience—the capability of individuals to cope successfully in the face of significant change, adversity, or risk. Classic workaholics (work

addicts)—those who are highly involved in work, feel compelled or driven to work because of inner pressures, and have a low enjoyment of work—tend to experience more stress.

Intense or prolonged stress can cause physiological symptoms such as cardiovascular disease, headaches, and muscle pain. Psychologically, stress reduces job satisfaction and organizational commitment and increases moodiness, depression, and job burnout. Job burnout refers to the process of emotional exhaustion, cynicism, and reduced efficacy resulting from prolonged exposure to stress. It is mainly due to interpersonal and role-related stressors and is most common in helping occupations. Behavioral symptoms of stress include lower job performance, poorer decisions, more workplace accidents, higher absenteeism, and more workplace aggression.

Many interventions are available to manage work-related stress. Some directly remove unnecessary stressors or remove employees from the stressful environment. Others help employees alter their interpretation of the environment so that it is not viewed as a serious stressor. Wellness programs encourage employees to build better physical defenses against stress experiences. Social support provides emotional, informational, and material resource support to buffer the stress experience.

Key Terms

employee assistance programs (EAPs), p. 215
general adaptation syndrome, p. 199
job burnout, p. 209
psychological harassment, p. 201

resilience, p. 207
role ambiguity, p. 203
role conflict, p. 202
sexual harassment, p. 201

stress, p. 198
stressors, p. 200
Type A behavior pattern, p. 208
workaholic, p. 208

Critical Thinking Questions

1. Several Web sites—including www.unitedmedia.com/comics/dilbert/ and www.cartoonbank.com—use humor to describe problems that people experience at work. Scan through these and other Web sites and determine what types of work-related stressors are depicted.

2. Is being a full-time college or university student a stressful role? Why or why not? Contrast your response with other students' perspectives.

3. Two recent college graduates join the same major newspaper as journalists. Both work long hours and have tight deadlines to complete their stories. They are under constant pressure to scout out new leads and be the first to report new controversies. One journalist is increasingly fatigued and despondent and has taken several days of sick leave. The other is getting the work done and seems to enjoy the challenges. Use your knowledge of stress to explain why these two journalists are reacting differently to their jobs.

4. Resilience is an individual characteristic that plays an important role in moderating the effect of stressors. Suppose you have been put in charge of a task force in a large government department to ensure that employees are highly resilient. What would you and your task force do to accomplish this objective?

5. If you were asked to identify people who are classic workaholics (work addicts), what would you look for?

6. A friend says that he is burned out by his job. What questions might you ask this friend to determine whether he is really experiencing job burnout?

7. What should organizations do to reduce employee stress? What is the responsibility of an employee to manage stress effectively? How might fitness programs help employees working in stressful situations?

8. A senior official of a labor union stated, "All stress management does is help people cope with poor management. [Employers] should really be into stress reduction." Discuss the accuracy of this statement.

Case Study 7.1 HOW DID I GET HERE?

Dr. Russell Casey, Clayton State University, and Marc Bacon, Fabgroups Technologies Inc.

Something was not right. John Breckenridge opened his eyes, saw the nurse's face, and closed them once more. Cobwebs slowly cleared from his brain as he woke up from the operation. He felt a hard tube in his nostril, and he tried to lift his hand to pull it out, but it was strapped down to the bed. John tried to speak but could make only a croaking sound. Nurse Thompson spoke soothingly, "Just try to relax, Mr. Breckenridge. You had a heart attack and emergency surgery, but you're going to be OK."

Heart attack? How did I get here? As the anesthesia wore off and the pain set in, John began to recall the events of the past year; and with the memories came another sort of pain—that of remembering a life where success was measured in hours worked and things accomplished, but which of late had not measured up.

John recalled his years in college, where getting good grades had been important, but not so much as his newly developing love for Karen, the girl with auburn hair who got her nursing degree the same year as he graduated with a degree in software engineering. They married the summer after graduation and moved from their sleepy university town in Indiana to Aspen, Colorado. There John got a job with a new software company while Karen worked evenings as a nurse. Although they didn't see much of each other during the week, weekends were a special time, and the surrounding mountains and nature provided a superb quality of life.

Life was good to the Breckenridges. Two years after they were married, Karen gave birth to Josh and two years later to Linda. Karen reduced her nursing to the minimum hours required to maintain her license, and concentrated on rearing the kids. John, on the other hand, was busy providing for the lifestyle they increasingly became used to, which included a house, car, SUV, ski trips, and all of the things a successful engineering career could bring. The company grew in leaps and bounds, and John was one of the main reasons it grew so fast. Work was fun. The company was growing, his responsibilities increased, and he and his team were real buddies. With Karen's help at home, he juggled work, travel, and evening classes that led to a

217

master's degree. The master's degree brought another promotion—this time to vice president of technology at the young (for this company) age of 39.

The promotion had one drawback: It would require working out of the New York office. Karen sadly said goodbye to her friends, convinced the kids that the move would be good to them, and left the ranch house for another one, much more expensive and newer, but smaller and just across the river in New Jersey from the skyscraper where her husband worked. Newark was not much like Aspen, and the kids had a hard time making friends, especially Josh, who was now 16. He grew sullen and withdrawn and began hanging around with a crowd that Karen thought looked very tough. Linda, always the quiet one, stuck mostly to her room.

John's new job brought with it money and recognition, as well as added responsibilities. He now had to not only lead software development but also actively participate in steering the company in the right direction for the future, tailoring its offerings to market trends. Mergers and acquisitions were the big thing in the software business, and John found a special thrill in picking small companies with promising software, buying them out, and adding them to the corporate portfolio. Karen had everything a woman could want and went regularly to a health club. The family lacked for no material need.

At age 41 John felt he had the world by its tail. Sure, he was a bit overweight, but who wouldn't be with the amount of work and entertaining that he did? He drank some, a habit he had developed early in his career. Karen worried about that, but he reassured her by reminding her that he had been really drunk only twice and would never drink and drive. Josh's friends were a worry, but nothing had yet come of it.

Not all was well, however. John had been successful in Colorado because he thought fast on his feet, expressed his opinions, and got people to buy into his decisions. In the New York corporate office things were different. All of the top brass except the president and John had Ivy League, moneyed backgrounds. They spoke of strategy but would take only risks that would further their personal careers. He valued passion, integrity, and action, with little regard for personal advancement. They resented him, rightly surmising that the only reason he had been promoted was because he was more like the president than they were, and he was being groomed as heir apparent.

On November 2, 2004, John Breckenridge's world began to unravel. The company he worked for, the one he had given so much of his life to build, was acquired in a hostile takeover. The president who had been his friend and mentor was let go, and the backstabbing began in earnest. John found himself the odd man out in the office as the others jostled to build status in the new firm. Although his stellar record allowed him to survive the first round of job cuts, that survival only made him more of a pariah to those around him. Going to work was a chore now, and John had no friends like those he had left in Aspen.

Karen was little help. John had spent nearly two decades married more to his job than his wife, and he found she was more of a stranger than a comforter as he struggled in his new role. When he spoke about changing jobs, she blew up. "Why did I have to give up nursing for your career?" she said. "Why do we have to move again, just because you can't get along at work? Can't you see what the move did to our kids?"

Seeing the hurt and anger in Karen's eyes, John stopped sharing and turned to his bottle for comfort. In time that caused even more tension in the home, and it slowed him down at work when he really needed to excel. John would often drink himself into oblivion when on business trips rather than thinking about where his life and career were going. On his last trip he hadn't slept much and had worked far too hard. Midmorning he had been felled by a massive heart attack.

All of this history passed through John Breckenridge's mind as he awoke after the operation. It was time for a change.

Discussion Questions

1. Identify the stressors in John Breckenridge's life. Which ones could he have prevented?

2. What were the results of the stress? Would you consider these to be typical responses to stress situations and lifestyle choices John made, or was John Breckenridge unlucky?

3. Assume you are a career coach retained by John Breckenridge to guide him through his next decisions. How would you recommend that John modify his lifestyle and behavior to reduce stress? Should he change jobs? Do you believe he is capable of reducing his stress alone? If not, where should he seek help?

Case Study 7.2 THE REAL REASONS YOU'RE WORKING SO HARD

BusinessWeek   Do you feel overworked? If so, you are not alone. Surveys estimate that 31 percent of college-educated male workers are regularly logging 50 or more hours a week at work, up from 22 percent in 1980. About 40 percent of American adults get less than seven hours of sleep on weekdays, up from 34 percent in 2001. Almost 60 percent of meals are rushed, and 34 percent of lunches are choked down on the run.

This *BusinessWeek* case study investigates why more Americans are enduring long hours at the workplace. It also looks at ways that companies are trying to reduce unnecessary work hours. Read the full text of this *BusinessWeek* article at www.mhhe.com/mcshane4e and prepare for the discussion questions below.

Discussion Questions

1. What are the main reasons identified in this article as to why Americans are working long hours?

2. Describe ways that companies are trying to reduce these work hours.

Source: M. Mandel, "The Real Reasons You're Working So Hard... and what you can do about it," *Business Week*, 3 October 2005, 60.

Team Exercise 7.3   STAGE FRIGHT!

PURPOSE   This exercise is designed to help you to diagnose a common stressful situation and determine how stress management practices apply to this situation.

BACKGROUND   Stage fright—including the fear of public speaking—is one of the most stressful experiences many people have in everyday life. According to some estimates, nearly three-quarters of us frequently get stage fright, even when speaking or acting in front of a small audience. Stage fright is an excellent topic for this team activity on stress management because the psychological and physiological symptoms of stage fright are really symptoms of stress. In other words, stage fright is the stress experience in a specific context involving a public audience. Based on the personal experiences of team members, your team will be asked to identify the symptoms of stage fright and to determine specific stress management activities that effectively combat stage fright.

INSTRUCTIONS

1. Students are organized into teams of typically four to six students. Ideally each team should have one or more people who acknowledge that they have experienced stage fright.

2. Each team's first task is to identify the symptoms of stage fright. The best way to organize these symptoms is to look at the three categories of stress outcomes described in the textbook: physiological, psychological, and behavioral. The specific stage fright symptoms may be different from the stress outcomes described in the textbook, but the three broad categories are relevant. Teams should be prepared to identify several symptoms and to present one or two specific examples of stage fright symptoms based on personal experiences of team members. (Individual students are not required to describe their experiences to the entire class.)

3. Each team's second task is to identify specific strategies people could or have applied to minimize stage fright. The five categories of stress management presented in the textbook will likely provide a useful template in which to organize the specific stage fright management activities. Each team should document several strategies to minimize stage fright and be able to

present one or two specific examples to illustrate some of these strategies.

4. The class will congregate to hear each team's analysis of symptoms and solutions to stage

fright. This information will then be compared to the stress experience and stress management practices, respectively.

Self-Assessment 7.4

CONNOR–DAVIDSON RESILIENCE SCALE (CD-RISC)

PURPOSE This self-assessment is designed to help you estimate your personal level of resilience.

INSTRUCTIONS See the assessment scale on page 221. Please check the box indicating the extent to which each statement has been true for you *over the past month*. Then use the scoring key in Appendix B of this book to calculate your results. There are no right or wrong answers to these questions. This self-assessment is completed alone so you can use this instrument honestly without concerns of social comparison. However, class discussion will focus on the meaning of resilience and how it relates to workplace stress.

Self-Assessment 7.5

WORK ADDICTION RISK TEST (STUDENT OLC)

This self-assessment is designed to help you identify the extent to which you are a workaholic. This instrument presents several statements and asks you to indicate the extent to which each statement is true of your work habits. You need to be honest with yourself to obtain a reasonable estimate of your level of workaholism.

Self-Assessment 7.6

PERCEIVED STRESS SCALE (STUDENT OLC)

This self-assessment is designed to help you estimate your perceived general level of stress. The items in this scale ask you about your feelings and thoughts during the last month. In each case, please indicate how often you felt or thought a certain way. You need to be honest with yourself to obtain a reasonable estimate of your general level of stress.

Connor-Davidson Resilience Scale (CD-RISC)

To what extent were these statements true about you over the past month?	Not at all true	Rarely true	Sometimes true	Often true	True nearly all of the time
1. I am able to adapt to change.	☐	☐	☐	☐	☐
2. I have close and secure relationships.	☐	☐	☐	☐	☐
3. I take pride in my achievements.	☐	☐	☐	☐	☐
4. I work to attain my goals.	☐	☐	☐	☐	☐
5. I feel in control of my life.	☐	☐	☐	☐	☐
6. I have a strong sense of purpose.	☐	☐	☐	☐	☐
7. I see the humorous side of things.	☐	☐	☐	☐	☐
8. Things happen for a reason.	☐	☐	☐	☐	☐
9. I have to act on a hunch.	☐	☐	☐	☐	☐
10. I can handle unpleasant feelings.	☐	☐	☐	☐	☐
11. Sometimes fate or God can help.	☐	☐	☐	☐	☐
12. I can deal with whatever comes my way.	☐	☐	☐	☐	☐
13. Past success gives me confidence for new challenges.	☐	☐	☐	☐	☐
14. Coping with stress strengthens me.	☐	☐	☐	☐	☐
15. I like challenges.	☐	☐	☐	☐	☐
16. I can make unpopular or difficult decisions.	☐	☐	☐	☐	☐
17. I think of myself as a strong person.	☐	☐	☐	☐	☐
18. When things look hopeless, I don't give up.	☐	☐	☐	☐	☐
19. I give my best effort, no matter what.	☐	☐	☐	☐	☐
20. I can achieve my goals.	☐	☐	☐	☐	☐
21. I am not easily discouraged by failure.	☐	☐	☐	☐	☐
22. I tend to bounce back after a hardship or illness.	☐	☐	☐	☐	☐
23. I know where to turn for help.	☐	☐	☐	☐	☐
24. Under pressure, I focus and think clearly.	☐	☐	☐	☐	☐
25. I prefer to take the lead in problem solving.	☐	☐	☐	☐	☐
	☐	☐	☐	☐	☐

Source: K.M. Connor and J.R.T. Davidson, "Development of a New Resilience Scale: The Connor–Davidson Resilience Scale (CD-RISC)," *Depression and Anxiety* 18, no. 2 (2003), pp. 76–82.

Self-Assessment 7.7

STRESS COPING PREFERENCE SCALE (STUDENT OLC)

This self-assessment is designed to help you identify the type of coping strategy you prefer to use in stressful situations. This scale lists a variety of things you might do when faced with a stressful situation. You are asked how often you tend to react in these ways. You need to be honest with yourself to obtain a reasonable estimate of your preferred coping strategy.

After reading this chapter, if you need additional information, see www.mhhe.com/mcshane4e for more in-depth interactivities that correspond with this material.

Part Three
Team Processes

Chapter 8   Decision Making and Creativity

Chapter 9   Fondations of Team Dynamics

Chapter 10   Developing High-Performance Teams

Chapter 11   Communicating in Teams and Organizations

Chapter 12   Power and Influence in the Workplace

Chapter 13   Conflict and Negotiation in the Workplace

Chapter 14   Leadership in Organizational Settings

What does a swarm of robot bees sound like? Cory Hawthorne tried to figure that out by listening to dozens of sounds and loops. Suddenly the sound effects specialist at Radical Entertainment found the right combination when he mixed his humming through a kazoo with the noise of operating an electric beard trimmer across the surface of his bathtub. The robot bees now had a menacing audio effect in the electronic game that Hawthorne was working on: *The Simpsons: Hit and Run.*

Radical Entertainment founder Ian Wilkinson (third from right) meets with employees every week to reinforce the Vancouver-based games developer's emphasis on creative decision making and employee involvement.

Radical depends on Cory Hawthorne and its other 230 employees to have plenty of such discovery moments to succeed in the competitive video game marketplace. "Hit games are made by people who have the freedom and support to put unconventional ideas in motion," explains Ian Wilkinson, founder and CEO of the Vancouver, Canada, company (now a division of Los Angeles–based Vivendi Universal Games). "So we give our employees the autonomy to drive real change, whatever their role in the company. No other game developer offers this level of creative freedom."

Danielle Michael, Radical's vice president of business development, echoes Wilkinson's view that the best decisions in this fast-paced industry come from employee involvement and autonomy: "People are hugely empowered to be creative, to go beyond the call of duty to come up with great ideas and to actually implement them," says Michael.

To help guide employee decision making, posters hung throughout Radical's headquarters state the company's succinct values, including this one: "Take risks, always learn." Wilkinson takes these values seriously. He lunches with a half dozen employees each week (as shown in this photo—Wilkinson is third from the right), encouraging them to apply the company's values in their everyday decisions.

Creative ideas are also cross-pollinated through Radical's monthly "game fair" day, in which teams show off their products and make presentations to other teams in the organization. "I don't want to be hearing what other companies are doing," Wilkinson advises staff. "I want to do innovative stuff and have some people say we're crazy."[1]

Decision Making and Creativity

After reading this chapter you should be able to

1. Describe the six stages in the rational choice decision process.

2. Explain why people have difficulty identifying problems and opportunities.

3. Explain why people do not follow the rational choice model when evaluating alternative choices.

4. Describe three ways in which emotions influence the selection of alternatives.

5. Outline how intuition operates.

6. Describe four causes of escalation of commitment.

7. Describe four benefits of employee involvement in decision making.

8. Identify four contingencies that affect the optimal level of employee involvement.

9. Outline the four steps in the creative process.

10. Describe the characteristics of employees and the workplace that support creativity.

decision making
A conscious process of making choices among one or more alternatives with the intention of moving toward some desired state of affairs.

Employees at Radical Entertainment are in the creativity business, but every organization depends on creativity to some extent in almost all decisions. **Decision making** is a conscious process of making choices among alternatives with the intention of moving toward some desired state of affairs.[2] This chapter begins by outlining the rational choice paradigm of decision making. Then we examine this perspective more critically by recognizing how people identify problems and opportunities, choose among alternatives, and evaluate the success of their decisions differently from the rational model. Bounded rationality, escalation of commitment, and intuition are three of the more prominent topics in this section. Next we explore the role of employee involvement in decision making, including the benefits of involvement and the factors that determine the optimal level of involvement. The final section of this chapter examines the factors that support creativity in decision making, including characteristics of creative people, work environments that support creativity, and creativity activities.

Learning
Objectives

After reading the next two sections you should be able to

1. **Describe the six stages in the rational choice decision process.**
2. **Explain why people have difficulty identifying problems and opportunities.**

Rational Choice Paradigm of Decision Making

rational choice paradigm
A deeply held view that people should and do make decisions based on pure logic using all necessary information.

How do people make decisions in organizations? For most of written history, philosophers, economists, and scholars in Western societies have stated or assumed that people should—and typically do—make decisions based on pure logic or rationality. This **rational choice paradigm** began 2,500 years ago when Plato and his Greek contemporaries raised logical debate and reasoning to a fine art. A few centuries later Greek and Roman Stoics insisted that one should always "follow where reason leads" rather than fall victim to passion and emotions. About 500 years ago, several European philosophers emphasized that the ability to make logical decisions is one of the most important accomplishments of human beings. By the 1900s, social scientists and mathematicians had developed elegant rational choice models and formulas that are now embedded in operations research and other decision sciences.[3]

Exhibit 8.1 illustrates the rational choice process.[4] The first step is to identify the problem or recognize an opportunity. A problem is a deviation between the current and the desired situation—the gap between "what is" and "what ought to be." This deviation is a symptom of more fundamental root causes that need to be corrected.[5] An opportunity is a deviation between current expectations and a potentially better situation that was not previously expected. In other words, decision makers realize that some decisions may produce results beyond current goals or expectations.

The second step involves deciding how to process the decision.[6] One issue is whether the decision maker has enough information or needs to involve others in the process. Later in this chapter we'll examine whether and how much others should be involved in the decision. Another issue is whether the decision is programmed or nonprogrammed. *Programmed decisions* follow standard operating procedures; they have been resolved in the past, so the optimal solution has already been identified and documented. In contrast, *nonprogrammed decisions* require all steps in the decision model because the problems are new, complex, or ill-defined. The third step is to develop a list of possible solutions. This usually begins by searching for ready-made solutions, such as practices that have worked well on similar problems. If an acceptable solution cannot be found, then decision makers need to design a custom solution or modify an existing one.

Exhibit 8.1
**Rational Choice
Decision-Making
Process**

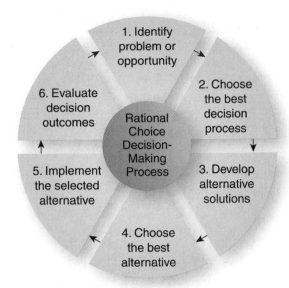

The fourth step is to choose from among the alternatives. The rational choice paradigm assumes that people naturally select the alternative with the highest *subjective expected utility*.[7] Subjective expected utility refers to how much the selected alternative benefits or satisfies the decision maker. Figuring out the alternative with the highest utility (total value or happiness) involves identifying all the outcomes that would occur if the alternative is selected and estimating the amount of satisfaction the person would feel from each of those outcomes. This is incredibly complex, but rational choice assumes that everyone does this calculation without any problem. The fifth step is to implement the selected alternative. This is followed by the sixth step, evaluating whether the gap has narrowed between "what is" and "what ought to be." Ideally this information should come from systematic benchmarks so that relevant feedback is objective and easily observed.

Problems with the Rational Choice Paradigm

The rational choice paradigm seems so logical, yet it is rarely practiced in reality. One reason is that the model assumes people are efficient and logical information-processing machines. But as the next few pages will reveal, people have difficulty recognizing problems; they cannot (or will not) simultaneously process the huge volume of information needed to identify the best solution; and they have difficulty recognizing when their choices have failed. The second reason why the rational model doesn't fit reality is that it focuses on logical thinking and completely ignores the fact that emotions also influence—perhaps even dominate—the decision-making process. As we will discover in this chapter, emotions both support and interfere with our quest to make better decisions.[8] With these points in mind, let's look again at each step of decision making, but with more detail about what really happens.

Identifying Problems and Opportunities

When Albert Einstein was asked how he would save the world in one hour, he replied that the first 55 minutes should be spent defining the problem and the last 5 minutes solving it.[9] Einstein's point was that problem identification is not just the first step in decision making; it is arguably the most important step. But problems and opportunities do not appear on our desks as well-labeled objects. Instead decision makers translate information into evidence that something is wrong or that an opportunity is available.

To some extent this discovery process occurs through conscious evaluation of the facts and persuasive arguments by other people. But what is becoming increasingly apparent is that a fair amount of problem recognition actually occurs during the mostly unconscious processes of perceptual selective attention and attitude formation (described in Chapter 3 and 4, respectively).[10] Specifically we evaluate information as soon as we perceive it by attaching emotional markers (anger, caution, delight,or the like) to that information. These automatic emotional responses, together with logical analysis and the emotions triggered by that analysis, determine whether you perceive something as a problem, as an opportunity, or as irrelevant.

Let's say that a worried-looking colleague tells you that the company's salesperson in Atlanta just quit. Your initial reaction (emotions generated upon hearing the news that the salesperson quit) might be worry and frustration. Meanwhile the rational part of your brain works through this information, recalling that the former salesperson's performance was mediocre and that an excellent salesperson at another company wants to join your firm in that state. What initially felt like a problem was really an opportunity based on your rational analysis of the situation. The initial emotions of worry or frustration might have been wrong in this situation, but sometimes your emotions provide a good indicator of problems or opportunities.

Problems with Problem Identification

The problem identification stage is itself filled with problems. Here are five of the most widely recognized concerns:[11]

1. *Stakeholder framing.*   Employees, clients, and other stakeholders with vested interests try to "frame" the situation by persuading decision makers that the available information points to a problem or an opportunity or has no importance at all. This framing of facts tends to short-circuit the decision maker's full assessment of the situation.

2. *Perceptual defense.*   People sometimes block out bad news as a coping mechanism. Their brains refuse to see information that threatens self-esteem. This phenomenon is not true for everyone. Some people inherently avoid negative information, whereas others are more sensitive to it. Recent studies also report that people are more likely to disregard danger signals when they have limited control over the situation.[12]

3. *Mental models.*   Mental models (cognitive templates of the external world) are essential road maps that provide stability and predictability to guide a person's preferences and behaviors. Unfortunately mental models also produce assumptions and expectations that prevent people from seeing unique problems or opportunities. If an idea doesn't fit the existing mental model of how things should work, then the idea is dismissed as unworkable or undesirable. Connections 8.1 describes how narrow mental models are the source of several famous missed or nearly missed opportunities.

"My team has created a very innovative solution, but we're still looking for a problem to go with it."

Famous Missed Opportunities

Mental models create road maps that guide our decisions. Unfortunately these maps also potentially block our ability to see emerging problems and opportunities. Here are a few famous examples:

- The best television commercial in history (as rated by *Advertising Age*) almost never saw the light of day. The Apple Macintosh "Why 1984 won't be like 1984" clip features a female athlete hurling a sledgehammer at a giant TV screen of an Orwellian Big Brother, liberating thousands of subjugated followers. Apple initially rejected the ad agency's (Chiat-Day) now-memorable phrase in an Apple II newspaper ad, but agreed to use this theme to launch the Macintosh computer during the 1984 Superbowl. The Macintosh team and sales force were ecstatic with rough cuts of the ad, but every outside director on Apple's board despised it. One remarked that it was the worst commercial of all time; another insisted that Apple immediately change its ad agency. Based on the board's reaction, Apple CEO John Sculley asked Chiat-Day to cancel the Superbowl ad space. Fortunately the agency claimed it could sell off only some of the time, so Apple had to show the commercial. The single 60-second ad shown during the Superbowl had such a huge effect that it was featured on evening news programs over the next several days. A month later Apple's board members applauded the Macintosh team for a successful launch and apologized for their misjudgment of the 1984 commercial.
- Graphical user interfaces, mice, windows, pull-down menus, laser printing, distributed computing, and Ethernet technologies weren't invented by Apple, Microsoft, or IBM. These essential elements of contemporary personal computing originated in the 1970s from researchers at Xerox PARC. Unfortunately Xerox executives were so focused on their photocopier business that they didn't bother to patent most of these inventions. Xerox has successfully applied some of its laser technology, but the lost value of Xerox PARC's other computing discoveries is much larger than the entire photocopier industry today.
- Nia Vardalos wrote a comedy screenplay based on incidents involving her Greek Canadian family. Unfortunately none of Hollywood's literary agents were interested. "They all said it's not good; it's not funny," said Vardalos, who honed her writing and acting skills at the Second City comedy group.

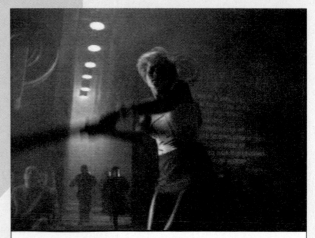

The best television commercial in history—the Apple Macintosh 1984 ad—almost never saw the light of day because it was so different from existing mental models of what a good TV ad should look like.

Undeterred, Vardalos turned the script into a successful one-woman show in Los Angeles. None of Hollywood's talent agents accepted her invitation to see the show, but when actors Rita Wilson and Tom Hanks watched her skits, they immediately supported her in making a movie. Even with Hanks on board, Hollywood studios rejected the script, but HBO agreed to provide a paltry $2.5 million "as a favor" to Hanks. With a budget of only $5 million, *My Big Fat Greek Wedding* became one of the highest-grossing independent films of all time. The screenplay that no one in Hollywood wanted was also nominated for an Oscar.
- When the World Wide Web burst onto the cyberspace scene in the early 1990s, Bill Gates wondered what all the fuss was about. Even as late as 1996, the Microsoft founder lampooned investors for their love-in with companies that made Internet products. However, Gates eventually realized the error in his mental model of computing. Making up for lost time, Microsoft bought Hotmail and other Web-savvy companies and added Internet support to its Windows operating system.

Sources: T. Abate, "Meet Bill Gates, Stand-Up Comic," *San Francisco Examiner*, 13 March 1996, p. D1; O. Port, "Xerox Won't Duplicate Past Errors," *Business Week*, 29 September 1997, p. 98; P. Nason, "A Big Fat Hollywood Success Story," *United Press International*, 12 December 2002; M. McCarthy, "Top 20 in 20 Years: Apple Computer—1984," *Adweek Online*, www.adweek.com/adweek/creative/top20_20years/index.jsp (accessed 16 January 2003); A. Hertzfeld, "1984," www.folklore.org (accessed 31 July 2005); G. James, "The Future That Never Was: Seven Products That Could Have Changed the Industry but Didn't," *Electronic Business* 31 (December 2005), p. 46.

4. *Decisive leadership.*   Studies report that people view leaders as more effective when they are decisive decision makers.[13] Consequently, eager to appear effective, many decision makers zero in on a problem and its solution without sufficiently analyzing the facts.

5. *Solution-focused problems.*   Various studies have found that decision makers often find a solution almost as soon as a problem is identified.[14] Indeed, you will sometimes hear people define problems in terms of their pet solutions, such as "The problem is that we need more control over our suppliers." This solution-focused identification of problems occurs because it provides comforting closure to the otherwise ambiguous and uncertain nature of problems. People with a strong need for cognitive closure (those who feel uncomfortable with ambiguity) are particularly prone to solution-focused problems. Some decision makers take this solution focus a step further by seeing all problems in terms of solutions that have worked well for them in the past, even though they were applied under different circumstances. Again, the familiarity of past solutions makes the current problem less ambiguous or uncertain.

Identifying Problems and Opportunities More Effectively

Recognizing problems and opportunities will always be a challenge, but the process can be improved through awareness of these perceptual and diagnostic limitations. By keeping in mind that mental models restrict a person's perspective of the world, decision makers are more motivated to consider other perspectives of reality. A second method of minimizing perceptual and diagnostic weaknesses is to discuss the situation with colleagues. Decision makers discover blind spots in problem identification by hearing how others perceive certain information and diagnose problems. Opportunities also become apparent when outsiders explore this information from their different mental models. Third, leaders require considerable willpower to resist appearing decisive when a more thoughtful examination of the situation should occur. Finally, successful decision makers experience "divine discontent": They are never satisfied with the status quo, and this aversion to complacency creates a mindset that more actively searches for problems and opportunities.[15]

Learning Objectives

> **After reading the next two sections you should be able to**
>
> 3. **Explain why people do not follow the rational choice model when evaluating alternative choices.**
> 4. **Describe three ways in which emotions influence the selection of alternatives.**
> 5. **Outline how intuition operates.**
> 6. **Describe four causes of escalation of commitment.**

Evaluating and Choosing Alternatives

According to the rational choice paradigm of decision making, people rely on logic to evaluate and choose alternatives. This paradigm assumes that decision makers have well-articulated and agreed-on organizational goals, that they efficiently and simultaneously process facts about all alternatives and the consequences of those alternatives, and that they choose the alternative with the highest payoff.

Nobel Prize–winning organizational scholar Herbert Simon questioned these assumptions half a century ago. He argued that people engage in **bounded rationality**

bounded rationality Processing limited and imperfect information and satisficing rather than maximizing when choosing among alternatives.

Exhibit 8.2   Rational Choice Assumptions versus Organizational Behavior Findings about Choosing Alternatives

Rational Choice Paradigm Assumptions	Observations from Organizational Behavior
Goals are clear, compatible, and agreed upon.	Goals are ambiguous, in conflict, and lack full support.
Decision makers can calculate all alternatives and their outcomes.	Decision makers have limited information processing abilities.
Decision makers evaluate all alternatives simultaneously.	Decision makers evaluate alternatives sequentially.
Decision makers use absolute standards to evaluate alternatives.	Decision makers evaluate alternatives against an implicit favorite.
Decision makers use factual information to choose alternatives.	Decision makers process perceptually distorted information.
Decision makers choose the alternative with the highest payoff.	Decision makers choose the alternative that is good enough (satisficing).

because they process limited and imperfect information and rarely select the best choice.[16] Simon and other OB experts demonstrated that how people evaluate and choose alternatives differs from the rational choice paradigm in several ways, as illustrated in Exhibit 8.2. These differences are so significant that even economists have shifted from rational choice to bounded rationality assumptions in their theories. Let's look at these differences in terms of goals, information processing, and maximization.

Problems with Goals

We need clear goals to choose the best solution. Goals identify "what ought to be" and therefore provide a standard against which each alternative is evaluated. The reality, however, is that organizational goals are often ambiguous or in conflict with each other. One survey found that 25 percent of managers and employees felt decisions are delayed because of difficulty agreeing on what they want the decision to achieve.[17]

Problems with Information Processing

People do not make perfectly rational decisions because they don't process information very well. One problem is that decision makers can't possibly think through all of the alternatives and the outcomes of those alternatives. Consequently, they look at only a few alternatives and only some of the main outcomes of those alternatives.[18] For example, there may be dozens of computer brands to choose from and dozens of features to consider, yet people typically evaluate only a few brands and a few features.

A related problem is that decision makers typically look at alternatives sequentially rather than all at the same time. As a new alternative comes along, it is immediately compared to an **implicit favorite**. An implicit favorite is an alternative that the decision maker prefers and uses as a comparison against which to judge other choices. The implicit favorite is formed early and usually unconsciously in the decision-making process, which means that it is not necessarily the best choice to compare against the others.[19]

Although the implicit favorite comparison process works well some of the time, it more often undermines effective decision making because people unconsciously distort information to favor their implicit favorite over the alternative choices. Specifically, they tend to forget limitations of the implicit favorite and advantages of the alternative. Decision makers also overweight factors where the implicit favorite is better and underweight areas where the alternative is superior.[20] This effect was observed in a study of auditing students who had to decide whether a company described in a case had significant financial problems. Those who decided that the company did have significant problems distorted the available information to make those problems appear worse. Students who felt the financial problems were not significant enough to report in a formal audit minimized any reference to the negative information in their case reports.[21]

Problems with Maximization

Decision makers tend to select the alternative that is acceptable or "good enough" rather than the one with the highest payoff (the highest subjective expected utility). In other words, they engage in **satisficing** rather than maximizing. Satisficing occurs because it isn't possible to identify every alternative, and information about available alternatives is imperfect or ambiguous. Satisficing also occurs because, as mentioned already, decision makers tend to evaluate alternatives sequentially, not all at the same time. They evaluate each alternative against the implicit favorite and eventually select an option that scores above a subjective minimum point considered to be good enough to satisfy their needs or preferences.[22]

Evaluating Opportunities

Opportunities are just as important as problems, but what happens when an opportunity is "discovered" is quite different from the process of problem solving. According to a recent study of decision failures, decision makers do not evaluate several alternatives when they find an opportunity; after all, the opportunity *is* the solution, so why look for others? An opportunity is usually experienced as an exciting and rare revelation, so decision makers tend to have an emotional attachment to the opportunity. Unfortunately this emotional preference motivates decision makers to apply the opportunity and short-circuit any detailed evaluation of it.[23]

Emotions and Making Choices

Herbert Simon and many other experts have presented considerable evidence that people do not evaluate alternatives nearly as well as is assumed by the rational choice paradigm. However, they neglected to mention another glaring weakness with

---

implicit favorite
The decision maker's preferred alternative against which all other choices are judged.

satisficing
Selecting a solution that is satisfactory, or "good enough" rather than optimal or "the best."

rational choice: It completely ignores the effect of emotions in human decision making. Just as both the rational and emotional brain centers alert us to problems, they also influence our choice of alternatives.

Emotions affect the evaluation of alternatives in three ways. First, the emotional marker process described earlier in this chapter as well as in previous chapters (Chapters 3 through 5) determines our preferences for each alternative. Our brain quickly attaches specific emotions to information about each alternative, and our preferred alternative is strongly influenced by those initial emotional markers. Of course, logical analysis also influences which alternative we choose, but it requires strong logical evidence to change our initial preferences (initial emotional markers). But even logical analysis depends on emotions to sway our decision. Specifically, neuroscientific evidence says that information produced from logical analysis is also tagged with emotional markers, which then motivate us to choose or avoid a particular alternative. Ultimately emotions, not rational logic, energize us to make the preferred choice. (People with damaged emotional brain centers have difficulty making choices.)

Second, a considerable body of literature indicates that moods and specific emotions influence the *process* of evaluating alternatives. For instance, we pay more attention to details when in a negative mood, possibly because a negative mood signals that there is something wrong that requires attention. When in a positive mood, on the other hand, we pay less attention to details and rely on a more programmed decision routine. Regarding specific emotions, decision makers rely on stereotypes and other shortcuts to speed up the choice process when they experience anger. Anger also makes them more optimistic about the success of risky alternatives, whereas the emotion of fear tends to make them less optimistic.[24]

The third way that emotions influence the evaluation of alternatives is through a process called "emotions as information." Marketing experts have found that we listen in on our emotions to provide guidance when making choices.[25] Most emotional experiences remain below the radar screen of awareness, but sufficiently intense emotions are picked up consciously and figured into our decision. Suppose that you are in the process of choosing one of several advertising firms to work with your company. You would logically consider several factors, such as previous experience, the agency's resources, and so on. But you would probably also pay attention to your gut feeling about each agency. If you sense positive feelings about a particular advertising firm, those conscious assessments of your emotions tend to get weighted into the decision. Some people pay more attention to these gut feelings, and personality tests such as the Myers-Briggs Type Indicator (see Chapter 2) identify those who listen in on their emotions more than others.[26] But all of us use our emotions as information to some degree. This phenomenon ties directly into our next topic: intuition.

Intuition and Making Choices

Linda, a trainee nurse in the neonatal intensive care unit of a hospital, was responsible for Melissa, a premature baby with no problems other than needing support to grow out of her sensitive condition. One day Melissa was a little sleepier than normal and was a bit lethargic during feeding. A spot on her heel where a blood sample had been taken was bleeding slightly, but that might be due to a sloppy sample prick. Melissa's temperature had also dropped slightly over several checks, but was still within the normal range. None of these conditions would seem unusual to most people, including Linda, the trainee nurse. But when Darlene, an experienced nurse, happened to walk by, she immediately sensed that Melissa "just looked funny," as she put it. After reviewing Melissa's charts and asking Linda a few questions, Darlene rushed to call a physician with the details. The physician immediately prescribed antibiotics to correct what blood tests later confirmed was sepsis.[27]

The gut instinct that helped Darlene save this baby's life is known as **intuition**—the ability to know when a problem or opportunity exists and to select the best course of action without conscious reasoning.[28] Intuition is both an emotional experience and a rapid unconscious analytic process. As was mentioned in the previous section, the gut feelings we experience are emotional signals that have enough intensity to make us consciously aware of them. These signals warn us of impending danger, such as a sick baby, or motivate us to take advantage of an opportunity. Some intuition also directs us to preferred choices relative to other alternatives in that situation.

All gut feelings are emotional signals, but not all emotional signals are intuition. The key distinction is that intuition involves rapidly comparing what we see or otherwise sense with deeply held patterns learned through experience.[29] These templates represent tacit knowledge that has been implicitly acquired over time. When a template fits or doesn't fit the current situation, emotions are produced that motivate us to act. Intuition also relies on mental models—internal representations of the external world that allow us to anticipate future events from current observations. Darlene's years of experience produced mental templates of unhealthy babies that matched what she saw on that fateful day. Studies have also found that chess masters receive emotional signals when they sense an opportunity through quick observation of a chessboard. They can't immediately explain why they see a favorable move on the chessboard; they just sense it.

As mentioned, some emotional signals (gut feelings) are not intuition because they are not based on well-grounded templates or mental models. Instead they occur when we compare the current situation to our templates and mental models of distant circumstances, which may or may not be relevant. Thus whether or not the emotions we experience in a situation represent intuition depends largely on our level of experience in that situation.

So far intuition has been described as an emotional experience (gut feeling) and a process of pattern matching in which we compare the current situation with well-established templates and mental models. Intuition also relies on *action scripts*—preprogrammed routines for responding to pattern matches or mismatches.[30] Action scripts are programmed decision routines; they provide instant road maps to follow without consciously evaluating the alternatives. These action scripts are generic, so we need to consciously adapt them to the specific situation; but they speed up the decision–action process.

Making Choices More Effectively

It is difficult to get around the human limitations of making choices, but a few strategies may help. One important discovery is that decisions tend to have a higher failure rate when leaders are decisive rather than contemplative about the available options. Of course problems also arise when decisions take too long, but research indicates that a lack of logical analysis is a greater concern. By systematically evaluating alternatives, decision makers minimize the implicit favorite and satisficing problems that occur when they rely on general subjective judgments. Intuition still figures into this analysis, but so does careful consideration of relevant information.[31]

Another issue is how to minimize the adverse effects of emotions on the decision process. The first recommendation here is that we need to be constantly aware that decisions are influenced by both rational and emotional processes. With this awareness, some decision makers deliberately revisit important issues so they look at the information in different moods and have allowed their initial emotions to subside.

intuition
The ability to know when a problem or opportunity exists and select the best course of action without conscious reasoning.

scenario planning
A systematic process of thinking about alternative futures, and what the organization should do to anticipate and react to those environments.

Others practice **scenario planning**, in which they anticipate emergencies long before they occur, so that alternative courses of action are evaluated without the pressure and emotions that occur during real emergencies.[32]

Evaluating Decision Outcomes

Contrary to the rational choice paradigm, decision makers aren't completely honest with themselves when evaluating the effectiveness of their decisions. One concern is that after making a choice, decision makers tend to support their choice by forgetting or downplaying the negative features of the selected alternative and emphasizing its positive features. This perceptual distortion, known as **postdecisional justification**, results from the need to maintain our self-esteem.[33] Postdecisional justification gives people an excessively optimistic evaluation of their decisions, but only until they receive clear and undeniable information to the contrary. Unfortunately it also inflates the decision maker's initial evaluation of the decision, so reality often comes as a painful shock when objective feedback is finally received.

postdecisional justification
Justifying choices by unconsciously inflating the quality of the selected option and deflating the quality of the discarded options.

Escalation of Commitment

A second problem when evaluating decision outcomes is **escalation of commitment**—the tendency to repeat an apparently bad decision or allocate more resources to a failing course of action.[34] There are plenty of escalation examples around the world. Tokyo's Metropolitan Transport Bureau promised to build a 20-mile high-speed subway loop under the city in record time and at enormous profit. Instead the multi-

escalation of commitment
The tendency to repeat an apparently bad decision or allocate more resources to a failing course of action.

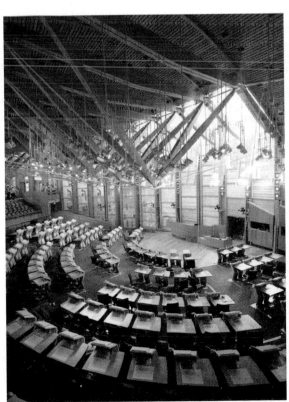

Scottish Parliament Escalates Sky High In 1997 the estimated cost of Scotland's new parliament was £50 million (US $80 million), and it was supposed to be built by 2001. Instead it cost £430 million and was finished three years later than planned. Some writers say that elected officials didn't want to lose face over building contracts they had signed before choosing a different site (Holyrood) and doubling the building size. In spite of warnings from critics, government leaders were also extremely overoptimistic that the many design changes would not escalate costs. The editor of Scottish architecture journal *ARCA* wrote, "The Parliament building will set an all-time world record for waste of money, incompetent management, and covering backsides and political reputations."[35]

billion-dollar project was seriously over budget, more than three years overdue, and won't be profitable until 2040, if ever. Denver's International Airport was supposed to include a state-of-the-art automated baggage handling system. Instead the project was eventually abandoned, causing the airport to open 16 months late and $2 billion over budget. Escalation also occurred years ago when the British government continued funding the Concorde supersonic jet long after its lack of commercial viability was apparent. To this day some fields of science refer to escalation of commitment as the "Concorde fallacy.[36]

Causes of Escalating Commitment

Why are people led deeper and deeper into failing projects? There are several reasons, including self-justification, prospect theory effect, perceptual blinders, and closing costs.

- *Self-justification.* Individuals are motivated to maintain their course of action when they have a high need to justify their decision. This self-justification is particularly evident when decision makers are personally identified with the project and have staked their reputations to some extent on the project's success.[37] The Scottish parliament debacle seems to be partly caused by this factor. Elected officials signed contracts for a smaller building on a different site and were possibly worried that terminating those contracts would symbolize that they had made a mistake.

- *Prospect theory effect.* You would think that people dislike losing $50 just as much as they like receiving $50, but that isn't true for most of us. We actually dislike losing a particular amount more than we like gaining the same amount. We also take fewer risks to receive gains and take more risks to avoid losses. This effect, called **prospect theory**, is a second explanation for escalation of commitment. Stopping a project is a certain loss, which is more painful to most people than the uncertainty of success associated with continuing to fund the project. Given the choice, decision makers choose the less painful option.[38] The prospect theory effect might have been an influence in the escalation of commitment in the Holyrood parliament project. In spite of the numerous setbacks, elected officials in Scotland falsely believed that luck would be on their side in keeping costs low, even after allowing numerous design changes.

- *Perceptual blinders.* Escalation of commitment sometimes occurs because decision makers do not see the problems soon enough. They unconsciously screen out or explain away negative information to protect self-esteem. Serious problems initially look like random errors along the trend line to success. Even when they see that something is wrong, the information is sufficiently ambiguous that it can be misinterpreted or justified.

- *Closing costs.* Even when a project's success is in doubt, decision makers will persist because the costs of ending the project are high or unknown. Terminating a major project may involve large financial penalties, a bad public image, or personal political costs.

These four conditions make escalation of commitment look irrational. Usually it is, but there are exceptions. Recent studies suggest that throwing more money into a failing project is sometimes a logical attempt to further understand an ambiguous situation. This strategy is essentially a variation of testing unknown waters. By adding more resources, the decision maker gains new information about the effectiveness of these funds, which provides more feedback about the project's future success. This strategy is particularly common where the project has high closing costs.[39]

prospect theory
An effect in which losing a particular amount is more disliked than gaining the same amount.

Evaluating Decision Outcomes More Effectively

One of the most effective ways to minimize escalation of commitment and postdecisional justification is to separate decision choosers from decision evaluators. This minimizes the self-justification effect because the person responsible for evaluating the decision is not connected to the original decision. A second strategy is to publicly establish a preset level at which the decision will be abandoned or reevaluated. This is similar to a stop-loss order in the stock market, whereby the stock is sold if it falls below a certain price. The problem with this solution is that conditions are often so complex that it is difficult to identify an appropriate point at which to abandon a project.[40]

A third strategy is to find a source of systematic and clear feedback.[41] For example, elected officials in the Scottish parliament might have avoided some of the cost escalation if they had received less ambiguous and conflicting information about the true costs of the project during the first few years. (In fact, civil servants hid some of these costs from elected officials.) Finally, projects might have less risk of escalation if several people are involved. Co-workers continuously monitor each other and might notice problems sooner than someone working alone on a project. Employee involvement offers these and other benefits to the decision-making process, as we learn next.

Learning Objectives

After reading the next two sections you should be able to

7. **Describe four benefits of employee involvement in decision making.**
8. **Identify four contingencies that affect the optimal level of employee involvement.**
9. **Outline the four steps in the creative process.**
10. **Describe the characteristics of employees and the workplace that support creativity.**

Employee Involvement in Decision Making

Boeing Co. is finding that staying competitive requires the brainwork of every employee, so it is pushing decisions down to the level closest to the activity. At Boeing's subassembly plant in Macon, Georgia, for example, employees identify ways to improve work effectiveness and track their own goals and performance metrics. "We encourage employees to be proactive," says Macon site leader Obie Jones. "When they see a problem or have an idea about process improvements, they take the initiative to start the process improvements, they take the initiative to start the corrective action process or incorporate improvement ideas through the proper channels." Partly due to this high level of employee involvement, *Industry Week* magazine recently named Boeing's Macon facility as one of the 10 best manufacturing plants in the United States.[42]

In this world of rapid change and increasing complexity, leaders rarely have enough information to make the best decisions alone. Whether this information is about reducing costs or improving the customer experience, employee involvement can potentially solve problems or realize opportunities more effectively. **Employee involvement** (also called *participative management*) refers to the degree to which employees influence how their work is organized and carried out.[43] Every organization has some form and various levels of employee involvement. At the lowest level, participation involves asking employees for information. They do not make recommendations and might not even know what the problem is about. At a moderate level of involvement, employees are told about the problem and provide recommendations to the decision maker. At the highest level of involvement, the entire decision-making process is handed over to employees. They identify the problem, choose the best alternative, and implement their choice.

employee involvement
The degree to which employees influence how their work is organized and carried out.

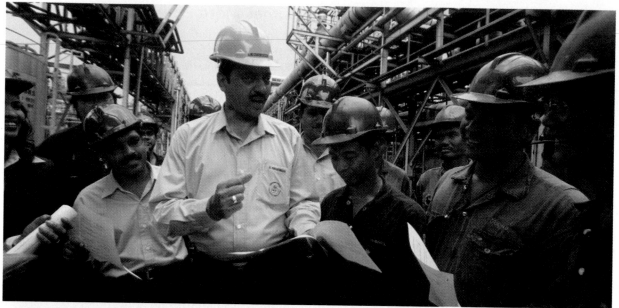

High Involvement Keeps Thai Carbon Black in the Black Thai Carbon Black, which makes the black coloring agent in tires, inks, and many other products, views all of its employees as problem solvers. "The 'can do' attitude of every employee is important," says Subburaman Srinivasan, president of the Thai–Indian joint venture. Each year staff members submit over 600 productivity improvement suggestions, placing their ideas in one of the little red boxes located around the site. Participatory management meetings are held every month, where employees are encouraged to come up with new ideas about ways to improve day-to-day operations. For instance, the company cut its transport costs by more than 10 percent after employees developed a special shipping bag allowing packers to stuff more product into the same volume. Thanks in part to this emphasis on employee involvement, Thai Carbon Black is one of the few companies outside Japan to receive the Deming Prize for total quality management. It has also received the Thailand Quality Class award, *Forbes* magazine's recognition as one of the best managed companies, and Hewitt Associates' ranking as one of the best employers in Asia and Thailand.[44]

Benefits of Employee Involvement

For the past half century organizational behavior scholars have advised that employee involvement potentially improves decision-making quality and commitment.[45] Involved employees can help improve decision quality by recognizing problems more quickly and defining them more accurately. Employees are, in many respects, the sensors of the organization's environment. When the organization's activities misalign with customer expectations, employees are usually the first to know. Employee involvement ensures that everyone in the organization is quickly alerted to these problems.[46]

Employee involvement can also potentially improve the number and quality of solutions generated. In a well-managed meeting, team members create synergy by pooling their knowledge to form new alternatives. In other words, several people working together can potentially generate more and better solutions than the same people working alone. A third benefit is that employee involvement often improves the likelihood of choosing the best alternative. This occurs because the decision is reviewed by people with diverse perspectives and a broader representation of values.[47]

Along with improving decision quality, employee involvement tends to strengthen employee commitment to the decision. Rather than viewing themselves as agents of someone else's decision, staff members feel personally responsible for its success. It also has positive effects on employee motivation, satisfaction, and turnover. A recent study reported that employee involvement also increases skill variety, feelings of autonomy, and task identity, all of which increase job enrichment and potentially employee motivation. Participation is also a critical practice in organizational change because employees are more motivated to implement the decision and less likely to resist changes resulting from the decision. As a respected OB expert concluded, "The new organizational realities are that top-down decision making is not sufficiently responsive to the dynamic organizational environment. Employees must be actively involved in decisions—or completely take over many decisions."[48]

Contingencies of Employee Involvement

If employee involvement is so wonderful, why don't leaders leave all decisions to employees? The answer is that the optimal level of employee involvement depends on the situation. The employee involvement model, shown in Exhibit 8.3, lists four contingencies: decision structure, source of decision knowledge, decision commitment, and risk of conflict in the decision process.

- *Decision structure.* At the beginning of this chapter we learned that some decisions are programmed, whereas others are nonprogrammed. Programmed decisions are less likely to need employee involvement because the solutions are already worked out from past experience. In other words, the benefits of employee involvement increase with the novelty and complexity of the problem or opportunity.

- *Source of decision knowledge.* Subordinates should be involved in some level of decision making when the leader lacks sufficient knowledge and subordinates have additional information to improve decision quality. In many cases employees are closer to customers and production activities, so they often know where the company can save money, improve product or service quality, and realize opportunities. This is particularly true for complex decisions where employees are more likely to possess relevant information.[49]

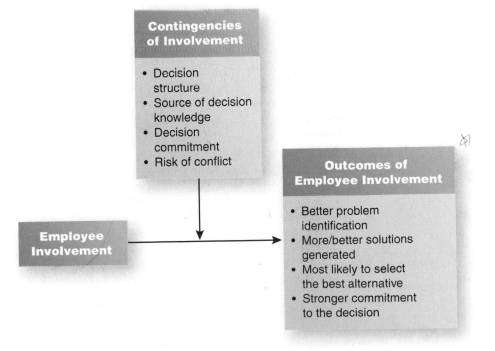

Exhibit 8.3

Model of Employee Involvement in Decision Making

- *Decision commitment.* Participation tends to improve employee commitment to the decision. If employees are unlikely to accept a decision made without their involvement, then some level of participation is usually necessary.

- *Risk of conflict.* Two types of conflict undermine the benefits of employee involvement. First, if employee goals and norms conflict with the organization's goals, then only a low level of employee involvement is advisable. Second, the degree of involvement depends on whether employees will reach agreement on the preferred solution. If conflict is likely, then high involvement (where employees make the decision alone) would be difficult to achieve.

Employee involvement is an important component of the decision-making process. To make the best decisions, we need to involve people who have the most valuable information and who will increase commitment to implement the decision. Another important component of decision making is creativity, which we discuss next.

Creativity

Parcel delivery might seem like a routine business, but that's not how the folks at Yamato Transport Company see it. The Japanese company invented door-to-door next-day parcel delivery in Japan, and its name is now synonymous with the service. Yamato was also the first to offer "cool takkyubin" (delivering chilled or frozen items to any address) and to deliver customers' ski equipment to resorts and homes. To keep better track of shipments, customers receive the mobile telephone numbers of Yamato's delivery personnel, not just distribution centers. One local branch office is testing the use of lockers at train stations around Japan for pickup and delivery locations, notifying customers by e-mail of the delivery times.[50]

creativity
Developing an original product, service, or idea that makes a socially recognized contribution.

Yamato Transport is successful in Japan's fiercely competitive delivery service industry because it relies on creativity for innovative new services. **Creativity** is the development of original ideas that make a socially recognized contribution.[51] Although there are unique conditions for creativity that we discuss over the next few pages, it is really part of the decision-making process described earlier in the chapter. We rely on creativity to find problems, identify alternatives, and implement solutions. Creativity is not something saved for special occasions. It is an integral part of decision making.

The Creative Process Model

One of the earliest and most influential models of creativity is shown in Exhibit 8.4.[52] The first stage is preparation–the person's or group's effort to acquire knowledge and skills regarding the problem or opportunity. Preparation involves developing a clear understanding of what you are trying to achieve through a novel solution, then actively studying information that seems related to the topic.

Exhibit 8.4
The Creative Process Model

Preparation → Incubation → Insight → Verification

The second stage, called incubation, is the stage of reflective thought. We put the problem aside, but our mind is still working on it in the background.[53] The important condition here is to maintain a low-level awareness by frequently revisiting the problem. Incubation does not mean that you forget about the problem or issue. Incubation assists **divergent thinking**—reframing the problem in a unique way and generating different approaches to the issue. This contrasts with convergent thinking—calculating the conventionally accepted "right answer" to a logical problem. Divergent thinking breaks us away from existing mental models so we can apply concepts or processes from completely different areas of life. Consider the following classic example: Years ago the experimental bulbs in Thomas Edison's lab kept falling off their fixtures until a technician wondered whether the threaded caps that screwed down tightly on kerosene bottles would work on lightbulbs. They did, and the design remains to this day.[54]

divergent thinking
Reframing a problem in a unique way and generating different approaches to the issue.

Insight, the third stage of creativity, refers to the experience of suddenly becoming aware of a unique idea.[55] Insight is often visually depicted as a lightbulb, but a better image would be a brief flash of light or perhaps a flickering candle because these bits of inspiration are fleeting and can be quickly lost if not documented. For this reason many creative people keep a journal or notebook nearby at all times, so that they can jot down these ideas before they disappear. Also, these flickering ideas don't keep a particular schedule; they might come to you at any time of day or night. Insights are merely rough ideas. Their usefulness still requires verification through conscious evaluation and experimentation. Thus, although verification is labeled as the final stage of creativity, it is really the beginning of a long process of experimentation and further creativity.

Creative People and Work Environments

Radical Entertainment, which was introduced at the beginning of this chapter, has an impressive list of successful electronic games, including *The Simpsons: Road Rage, Crash Tag Team Racing,* and *The Incredible Hulk.* The company achieves this success by finding creative people and putting them in an environment that encourages creative ideas. In other words, Radical's executives know that creativity is a function of both the person and the situation.

Characteristics of Creative People
Everyone is creative, but some people seem to be more creative than others. Four of the main features of creative people are intelligence, persistence, subject matter knowledge and experience, and inventive thinking style. First, creative people have above-average intelligence to synthesize information, analyze ideas, and apply their ideas.[56] Like the fictional sleuth Sherlock Holmes, creative people recognize the significance of small bits of information and are able to connect them in ways that no one else could imagine. Then they have the capacity to evaluate the potential usefulness of their ideas.

Persistence is the second feature of creative people. The fact is that innovations derive more from trial and error than from intelligence and experience. Persistence drives creative people to continue developing and testing after others have given up. In other words, people who develop more creative products and services are those who develop more ideas that don't work. Thomas Edison emphasized this point in his famous statement that genius is 1 percent inspiration and 99 percent perspiration. Edison and his staff discovered hundreds of ways not to build a lightbulb before they got it right! This persistence is based on a high need for achievement and a moderate or high degree of self-confidence.[57]

Persistence Becomes the Cure for Peptic Ulcers Barry Marshall (left) and Robin Warren (right) faced plenty of doubters when they first proposed that peptic ulcers are caused by specific bacteria. The prevailing belief was that these ulcers are caused by weak stomach linings, gastric acid, and unhealthful diets. Few believed that bacteria could survive, let alone thrive, in the highly acidic stomach environment. Marshall and Warren's initial research supported the bacteria theory, but their paper was rejected because none of the reviewers believed the findings! The paper was eventually published after a British researcher replicated the results in his lab. Bacteria experts soon embraced the theory, but most stomach ulcer experts remained skeptical. To further convince the doubters, Marshall ingested the bacteria into his healthy stomach and developed symptoms within a few days. "It took 10 years and there was a lot of opposition," recalls one expert. "[But Marshall] had this enormous self-belief that what he'd found was right." Marshall and Warren were recently awarded the Nobel Prize in medicine for their discovery. Fittingly, the Nobel committee acknowledged their "tenacity and a prepared mind challenging prevailing dogmas."[58]

A third feature of creative people is that they possess sufficient knowledge and experience in the subject.[59] Creativity experts explain that discovering new ideas requires knowledge of the fundamentals. For example, the 1960s rock group the Beatles produced most of their songs only after they had played together for several years. They developed extensive experience in singing and adapting the music of other people before their creative talents soared.

Although knowledge and experience may be important in one sense, they can also undermine creativity because people develop mental models that lead to "mindless behavior," whereby they stop questioning their assumptions.[60] This explains why some corporate leaders like to hire people from other industries and areas of expertise. For instance, Ballard Power Systems founder Geoffrey Ballard hired a chemist to develop a better battery. When the chemist protested that he didn't know anything about batteries, Ballard replied, "That's fine. I don't want someone who knows batteries. They know what won't work."[61] Ballard explained that he wanted to hire people who would question and investigate what experts stopped questioning.

The fourth characteristic of creative people is that they have an inventive thinking style. Creative types are divergent thinkers and risk takers. They are not bothered by making mistakes or working with ambiguous information. They take a broad view of problems, don't like to abide by rules or status, and are unconcerned about social approval of their actions.[62]

Organizational Conditions Supporting Creativity

Hiring creative people is only part of the creativity equation. Corporate leaders also need to maintain a work environment that supports the creative process for everyone.[63] However, it is overly simplistic to identify one best environment in which creativity flourishes. Instead we need to recognize that it emerges through different combinations of processes, mechanisms, and structures.[64] With this caveat in mind, here are some of the conditions that seem to encourage creative thinking.

One of the most important conditions is that the organization has a learning orientation; that is, leaders recognize that employees make reasonable mistakes as part of the creative process. Motivation from the job itself is another important condition for creativity.[65] Employees tend to be more creative when they believe their work has a substantial impact on the organization and/or society (task significance) and when they have the freedom to pursue novel ideas without bureaucratic delays (autonomy). This emphasis on autonomy is apparent at Radical Entertainment, the Vancouver-based electronic games maker described at the beginning of this chapter. Creativity is about changing things, and change is possible only when employees have the authority to experiment. More generally, jobs encourage creativity when they are challenging and aligned with the employee's competencies.

Along with supporting a learning orientation and intrinsically motivating jobs, companies foster creativity through open communication and sufficient resources. They provide a reasonable level of job security, which explains why creativity suffers during times of downsizing and corporate restructuring.[66] To some degree creativity also improves with support from leaders and co-workers. One recent study reported that effective product champions provide enthusiastic support for new ideas. Other studies suggest that co-worker support can improve creativity in some situations, whereas competition among co-workers improves creativity in other situations.[67] Similarly, it isn't clear how much pressure should be exerted on employees to produce creative ideas. Extreme time pressures are well-known creativity inhibitors, but lack of pressure doesn't seem to produce the highest creativity, either.

Activities That Encourage Creativity

Along with hiring creative people and giving them a supportive work environment, organizations have introduced numerous activities that attempt to crank up the creative potential. One set of activities encourages employees to redefine the problem. This occurs when we revisit old projects that have been set aside. After a few months of neglect, these projects might be seen in new ways.[68] Another strategy involves asking people unfamiliar with the issue (preferably with different expertise) to explore the problem with you. You would state the objectives and give some facts, then let the other person ask questions to further understand the situation. By verbalizing the problem, listening to questions, and hearing what others think, you are more likely to form new perspectives on the issue.[69]

A second set of creativity activities, known as *associative play*, ranges from art classes to impromptu storytelling. Employees at pan-African cellular communications giant Vodacom and South African financial institution ABSA have used Lego blocks to build models that mapped out where they wanted their company to go in the future. These companies also engaged employees in impromptu storytelling, in which participants randomly contributed to the development of characters and storyline. OMD, the British media giant, gets creative juices flowing by sending employees to two-day retreats in the countryside where they play grapefruit croquet, chant like medieval monks, and pretend to be dog collars. "Being creative is a bit like an emotion—we need to be stimulated," explains Harriet Frost, one of OMD's specialists in building creativity. "The same is true for our imagination and its ability to come up with new ideas. You can't just sit in a room and devise hundreds of ideas."[70]

Another associative play activity, called *morphological analysis*, involves listing different dimensions of a system and the elements of each dimension, then looking at each combination. This encourages people to carefully examine combinations that initially seem nonsensical. Tyson Foods, the world's largest poultry producer, applied this activity to identify new ways to serve chicken for lunch. The marketing and research team assigned to this task focused on three categories: occasion, packaging, and taste. Next the team worked through numerous combinations of items in the three categories. This created unusual ideas, such as cheese chicken pasta (taste) in pizza boxes (packaging) for concessions at baseball games (occasion). Later the team looked more closely at the feasibility of these combinations and sent them to customer focus groups for further testing.[71]

A third set of activities that encourages creativity in organizations is known as *cross-pollination*.[72] Cross-pollination occurs when people from different areas of the organization exchange ideas. As described in the opening story to this chapter, Radical Entertainment practices cross-pollination through its monthly "game fair" day, in which teams show off their products and make presentations to other teams in the organization. IDEO, the California-based product design company, has a similar effect by mixing together employees from different past projects so they share new knowledge with each other.

Cross-pollination highlights the fact that creativity rarely occurs alone. Some creative people may be individualistic, but most creative ideas are generated through teams and informal social interaction. This probably explains why Jonathon Ive, the award-winning designer of Apple Computer products, always refers to his team's creativity rather than his own. "The only time you'll hear [Jonathan Ive] use the word 'I' is when he's naming some of the products he helped make famous: iMac, iBook, iPod," says one writer.[73] The next chapter introduces the main concepts in team effectiveness. Then in Chapter 10 we learn about high-performance teams, including ways to improve team decision making and creativity.

Chapter Summary

Decision making is a conscious process of making choices among one or more alternatives with the intention of moving toward some desired state of affairs. The rational choice paradigm of decision making includes identifying problems and opportunities, choosing the best decision style, developing alternative solutions, choosing the best solution, implementing the selected alternative, and evaluating decision outcomes.

Persuasion by stakeholders, perceptual biases, and poor diagnostic skills affect our ability to identify problems and opportunities. We can minimize these challenges by being aware of these human limitations and discussing the situation with colleagues.

Evaluating and choosing alternatives are often challenging because organizational goals are ambiguous or in conflict; human information processing is incomplete and subjective; and people tend to satisfice rather than maximize. Decision makers also short-circuit the evaluation process when faced with an opportunity rather than a problem. Emotions shape our preferences for alternatives and the process we follow to evaluate alternatives. We also listen to our emotions for guidance when making decisions. This latter activity relates to intuition—the ability to know when a problem or opportunity exists and to select the best course of action without conscious reasoning. Intuition is both an emotional experience and a rapid unconscious analytic process that involves both pattern matching and action scripts.

People generally make better choices by systematically evaluating alternatives. Scenario planning can help us make future decisions without the pressure and emotions that occur during real emergencies.

Postdecisional justification and escalation of commitment make it difficult to accurately evaluate decision outcomes. Escalation is mainly caused by self-justification, the prospect theory effect, perceptual blinders, and closing costs. These problems are minimized by separating decision choosers from decision evaluators, establishing a preset level at which the decision is abandoned or reevaluated, relying on more systematic and clear feedback about the project's success, and involving several people in decision making.

Employee involvement (or participation) refers to the degree that employees influence how their work is organized and carried out. The level of participation may range from an employee providing specific information to management without knowing the problem or issue, to complete involvement in all phases of the decision process. Employee involvement may lead to higher decision quality and commitment; but several contingencies need to be considered, including the decision structure, source of decision knowledge, decision commitment, and risk of conflict.

Creativity is the development of original ideas that make a socially recognized contribution. The four creativity stages are preparation, incubation, insight, and verification. Incubation assists divergent thinking, which involves reframing the problem in a unique way and generating different approaches to the issue.

Four of the main features of creative people are intelligence, subject matter knowledge and experience, persistence, and inventive thinking style. Creativity is also strengthened for everyone when the work environment supports a learning orientation, the job has high intrinsic motivation, the organization provides a reasonable level of job security, and project leaders provide appropriate goals, time pressure, and resources. Three types of activities that encourage creativity are redefining the problem, associative play, and cross-pollination.

Key Terms

bounded rationality, p. 230
creativity, p. 240
decision making, p. 226
divergent thinking, p. 241
employee involvement, p. 237

escalation of commitment, p. 235
implicit favorite, p. 232
intuition, p. 234
postdecisional justification, p. 235
prospect theory, p. 236

rational choice paradigm, p. 226
satisficing, p. 232
scenario planning, p. 235

Critical Thinking Questions

1. A management consultant is hired by a manufacturing firm to determine the best site for its next production facility. The consultant has had several meetings with the company's senior executives regarding the factors to consider when making the recommendation. Discuss the decision-making problems that might prevent the consultant from choosing the best site location.

2. You have been asked to personally recommend a new travel agency to handle all airfare, accommodation, and related travel needs for your organization of 500 staff. One of your colleagues, who is responsible for the company's economic planning, suggests that the best travel agent could be selected mathematically by inputting the relevant factors for each agency and the weight (importance) of each factor. What decision-making approach is your colleague recommending? Is this recommendation a good idea in this situation? Why or why not?

3. Intuition is both an emotional experience and an unconscious analytic process. One problem, however, is that not all emotions signaling that there is a problem or opportunity represent intuition. Explain how we would know if our "gut feelings" are intuition or not, and if not intuition, suggest what might be causing them.

4. A developer received financial backing for a new business financial center along a derelict section of the waterfront, a few miles from the current downtown area of a large European city. The idea was to build several high-rise structures, attract large tenants to those sites, and have the city extend transportation systems out to the new center. Over the next decade, the developer believed that others would build in the area, thereby attracting the regional or national offices of many financial institutions. Interest from potential tenants was much lower than initially predicted, and the city did not build transportation systems as quickly as expected. Still the builder proceeded with the original plans. Only after financial support was curtailed did the developer reconsider the project. Using your knowledge of escalation of commitment, discuss three possible reasons why the developer was motivated to continue with the project.

5. Ancient Book Company has a problem with new book projects. Even when others are aware that a book is far behind schedule and may engender little public interest, sponsoring editors are reluctant to terminate contracts with authors whom they have signed. The result is that editors invest more time with these projects than on more fruitful projects.

As a form of escalation of commitment, describe two methods that Ancient Book Company can use to minimize this problem.

6. Employee involvement applies just as well to the classroom as to the office or factory floor. Explain how student involvement in classroom decisions typically made by the instructor alone might improve decision quality. What potential problems may occur in this process?

7. Think of a time when you experienced the creative process. Maybe you woke up with a brilliant (but usually sketchy and incomplete) idea, or you solved a baffling problem while doing something else. Describe this incident to your class and explain how the experience followed the creative process.

8. Two characteristics of creative people are that they have relevant experience and are persistent in their quests. Does this mean that people with the most experience and the highest need for achievement are the most creative? Explain your answer.

Case Study 8.1 EMPLOYEE INVOLVEMENT CASES

Case 1: The Sugar Substitute Research Decision

You are the head of research and development (R&D) for a major beer company. While working on a new beer product, one of the scientists in your unit seems to have tentatively identified a new chemical compound that has few calories but tastes closer to sugar than current sugar substitutes. The company has no foreseeable need for this product, but it could be patented and licensed to manufacturers in the food industry.

The sugar substitute discovery is in its preliminary stages and would require considerable time and resources before it would be commercially viable. This means that it would necessarily take some resources away from other projects in the lab. The sugar substitute project is beyond your technical expertise, but some of the R&D lab researchers are familiar with that field of chemistry. As with most forms of research, it is difficult to determine the amount of research required to further identify and perfect the sugar substitute. You do not know how much demand is expected for this product. Your department has a decision process for funding projects that are behind schedule. However, there are no rules or precedents about funding projects that would be licensed but not used by the organization.

The company's R&D budget is limited, and other scientists in your work group have recently complained that they need more resources and financial support to get their projects completed. Some of these other R&D projects hold promise for future beer sales. You believe that most researchers in the R&D unit are committed to achieving the company's interests.

Case 2: Coast Guard Cutter Decision

You are the captain of a 200-foot Coast Guard cutter, with a crew of 16, including officers. Your mission is general at-sea search and rescue. At 2:00 a.m. this morning, while en route to your home port after a routine 28-day patrol, you received word from the nearest Coast Guard station that a small plane had crashed 60 miles offshore. You obtained all the available information concerning the location of the crash, informed your crew of the mission, and set a new course at maximum speed for the scene to search for survivors and wreckage.

You have now been searching for 20 hours. Your search operation has been increasingly impaired by rough seas, and there is evidence of a severe storm building. The atmospherics associated with the deteriorating weather have made communications with the Coast Guard station impossible. A decision must be made shortly about whether to abandon the search and place your vessel on a course that would ride out the storm (thereby protecting the vessel and your crew, but relegating any possible survivors to almost certain death from exposure) or to continue a potentially futile search and the risks it would entail.

Before losing communications, you received an update weather advisory concerning the severity and duration of the storm. Although your crew members are extremely conscientious about their responsibility, you believe that they would be divided on the decision of leaving or staying.

Discussion Questions (for Both Cases)

1. To what extent should your subordinates be involved in this decision? Select one of the following levels of involvement:

   - *No involvement.* You make the decision alone without any participation from subordinates.
   - *Low involvement.* You ask one or more subordinates for information relating to the problem, but you don't ask for their recommendations and might not mention the problem to them.
   - *Medium involvement.* You describe the problem to one or more subordinates (alone or in a meeting) and ask for any relevant information as well as their recommendations on the issue. However, you make the final decision, which might or might not reflect their advice.

   - *High involvement.* You describe the problem to subordinates. They discuss the matter, identify a solution without your involvement (unless they invite your ideas), and implement that solution. You have agreed to support their decision.

2. What factors led you to choose this level of employee involvement rather than the others?

3. What problems might occur if less or more involvement occurred in this case (where possible)?

Sources: The Sugar Substitute Research Decision is written by Steven L. McShane, ©2002. The Coast Guard cutter case is adapted from V.H. Vroom and A.G. Jago, *The New Leadership: Managing Participation in Organizations* (Englewood Cliffs, NJ: Prentice Hall, 1988), ©1987 V.H. Vroom and A.G. Jago. Used with permission of the authors.

Case Study 8.2 CHAMPIONS OF INNOVATION

 In an era when Six Sigma controls no longer guarantee competitive advantage, when outsourcing to China and India is universal, when creeping commoditization of products, services, and information hammers prices, innovation is the new currency of competition. The most innovative companies rely on champions who are able to bring out more creative thinking in their employees. They know how to select creative types, give them a work environment that supports creativity, and find strategies that boost the creative juices.

This *Business Week* case study describes the practices of five champions of innovation at Google, Old Navy, Procter & Gamble, HP, and Citigroup. The article examines how these champions find creativity in people, work environments, and creativity-enhancing activities. Read the full text of this *Business Week* article at www.mhhe.com/mcshane4e and prepare for the discussion questions below.

Discussion Questions

1. In your opinion, which of these five companies pays the most attention to creativity as a characteristic of individuals?

2. Describe the work environments that these companies create to support creativity and innovation.

3. What special practices are noted in this article that help people to think more creatively?

Source: M. Conlin, "Champions of Innovation", *Business Week*, 19 June 2006, 18.

Class Exercise 8.3 FOR WHAT IT'S WORTH

PURPOSE This exercise is designed to help you understand issues with making perfectly rational decisions.

MATERIALS The instructor will either bring to class or show computer images of three products. Students will need their Social Security numbers (a driver's license or other piece of identity with several numbers can substitute).

INSTRUCTIONS

1. The instructor will show the three products (or images of the products) to the class and describe the features of each product so students are sufficiently informed about their features and functions. The instructor will *not* provide any information about the price paid or market value of these products.

2. Working alone, each student will write at the top of Exhibit 1 the last two digits of his or her identification number. Each student will also write in the left column of Exhibit 1 the name of each product shown by the instructor. Then each student will circle "yes" or "no" in Exhibit 1 for each product, indicating whether he or she

would be willing to pay the dollar equivalent of the two-digit number for each product if seeking to purchase such a product.

3. In the right column of the Exhibit 1 each student (still working alone) will write the maximum dollar value he or she would be willing to pay for each product if seeking to purchase such a product.

4. After completing their calculations alone, students will be organized into four or five groups as specified by the instructor. Group size is unimportant, but the instructor's criterion for organizing teams is important and must be followed. Each team will calculate the average price that students within that group were willing to pay for each product. The team will also calculate the percentage of people within the group who indicated "yes" (willing to purchase at the stated price) for each product.

5. Each team will report its three average maximum willingness-to-pay prices as well as the percentage of students in the team who circled "yes" for each product. The instructor will outline a concept relevant to rational decision making and how that concept relates to this exercise.

Exhibit 1
For What It's Worth Calculation Sheet

Two-Digit Number: _____ _____

Product name (Write in product names below.)	Willing to pay two-digit number price for this product? (Circle your answer.)	Maximum willingness to pay for this product
_____	No Yes	$ _____ : 00
_____	No Yes	$ _____ : 00
_____	No Yes	$ _____ : 00

Source: Based on information in D. Ariely, G. Loewenstein, and D. Prelec, "'Coherent Arbitrariness': Stable Demand Curves without Stable Preferences," *Quarterly Journal of Economics,* February 2003, pp. 73–105.

Team Exercise 8.4 WHERE IN THE WORLD ARE WE?

PURPOSE This exercise is designed to help you understand the potential advantages of involving others in decisions rather than making decisions alone.

MATERIALS Students require an unmarked copy of the map of the United States with grid marks (Exhibit 2). Students are not allowed to look at any other maps or use any other materials. The instructor will provide a list of communities located somewhere on Exhibit 2. The instructor will also provide copies of the answer sheet after students have individually and in teams estimated the locations of communities.

INSTRUCTIONS

1. Write in Exhibit 1 the list of communities identified by your instructor. Then, working alone, estimate the location in Exhibit 2 of these communities, all of which are in the United States. For example, mark a small "1" in Exhibit 2 on the spot where you believe the first community is located. Mark a small "2" where you think the second community is located, and so on. Please be sure to number each location clearly and with numbers small enough to fit within one grid space.

2. The instructor will organize students into roughly equal teams (typically five or six people per team). Working with your team members, reach a consensus on the location of each community listed in Exhibit 1. The instructor might provide teams with a separate copy of the map, or members can identify the team's numbers using a different color pen on the individual maps. The team's decision for each location should occur by consensus, not voting or averaging.

3. The instructor will provide an answer sheet showing the correct locations of the communities. Using this answer sheet, count the minimum number of grid squares between the location you individually marked and the true location of each community. Write the number of grid squares in the third column of Exhibit 1, then add up the total. Next, count the minimum number of grid squares between the location the team marked and the true location of each community. Write the number of grid squares in the fourth column of Exhibit 1, then add up the total.

4. The instructor will ask for information about the totals, and the class will discuss the implications of these results for employee involvement and decision making.

Exhibit 1
List of Selected Communicaties in the United States

Number	Communities	Individual distance in grid units from the true location	Team distance in grid units from the true location
1			
2			
3			
4			
5			
6			
7			
8			
		Total:	Total:

© 2002 Steven L. McShane.

Exhibit 2 Map of the United States

Team Exercise 8.5 WINTER SURVIVAL EXERCISE

PURPOSE This exercise is designed to help you understand the potential advantages of involving others in decisions rather than making decisions alone.

INSTRUCTIONS

1. Read the situation that follows. Then, working alone, rank order the 12 items shown in the accompanying chart according to their importance to your survival. In the "individual ranking" column indicate the most important item with "1" continuing to "12" for the least important. Keep in mind the reasons why each item is or is not important.

2. The instructor will divide the class into small teams (four to six people). Each team will rank order the items in the third column. Team rankings should be based on consensus, not simply averaging the individual rankings.

3. When the teams have completed their rankings, the instructor will provide an expert's ranking, which can be entered in the fourth column.

4. Each student will compute the absolute difference (ignore minus signs) between the individual ranking and the expert's ranking, record this information in column five, and sum the absolute values at the bottom of column five.

5. In column six record the absolute difference between the team's ranking and the expert's ranking, and sum these absolute scores at the bottom. A class discussion will follow regarding the implications of these results for employee involvement and decision making.

SITUATION

You have just crash-landed somewhere in the woods of southern Manitoba or possibly northern Minnesota. It is 11:32 a.m. in mid-January. The small plane in which you were traveling crashed on a small lake. The pilot and copilot were killed. Shortly after the crash, the plane sank completely into the lake with the pilot's

Winter survival tally sheet					
Items	Step 1 Your individual ranking	Step 2 Your team's ranking	Step 3 Survival expert's ranking	Step 4 Difference between steps 1 and 3	Step 5 Difference between steps 2 and 3
Ball of steel wool					
Newspaper					
Compass					
Hand ax					
Cigarette lighter					
45-caliber pistol					
Section air map					
Canvas					
Shirt and pants					
Can of shortening					
Whiskey					
Chocolate bars					
			Total	Your score	Team score

(The lower the score, the better)

Source: Adapted from "Winter Survival" in D. Johnson and F. Johnson, *Joining Together,* 3rd ed. (Englewood Cliffs, NJ: Prentice Hall, 1984).

and copilot's bodies inside. Everyone else on the flight escaped to land dry and without serious injury.

The crash came suddenly before the pilot had time to radio for help or inform anyone of your position. Because your pilot was trying to avoid a storm, you know the plane was considerably off course. The pilot announced shortly before the crash that you were 45 miles northwest of a small town that is the nearest known habitation.

You are in a wilderness area made up of thick woods broken by many lakes and rivers. The snow depth varies from above the ankles in windswept areas to more than knee-deep where it has drifted.

The last weather report indicated that the temperature would reach 5 degrees Fahrenheit in the daytime and minus 15 degrees at night. There are plenty of dead wood scraps and twigs in the area around the lake. You and the other surviving passengers are dressed in winter clothing appropriate for city wear—suits, pantsuits, street shoes, and overcoats. While escaping from the plane, your group salvaged the 12 items listed in the accompanying chart. You may assume that the number of survivors in the group is the same as the number in your class group and that you have agreed to stay together.

Class Exercise 8.6 THE HOPPING ORANGE

PURPOSE This exercise is designed to help you understand the dynamics of creativity and team problem solving.

INSTRUCTIONS
You will be placed in teams of six students. One student serves as the official timer for the team and must have a watch, preferably with a stopwatch timer. The instructor will give each team an orange (or similar object) with a specific task involving use of the orange. The objective is easily understood and nonthreatening and will be described by the instructor at the beginning of the exercise. Each team will have a few opportunities to achieve the objective more efficiently. To maximize the effectiveness of this exercise, no other information is provided here.

Class Exercise 8.7 CREATIVITY BRAINBUSTERS

PURPOSE This exercise is designed to help you understand the dynamics of creativity and team problem solving.

INSTRUCTIONS
This exercise may be completed alone or in teams of three or four people. If teams are formed, students who already know the solutions to one or more of these problems should identify themselves and serve as silent observers. When you have finished (or, more likely, when time is up), the instructor will review the solutions and discuss the implications of this exercise. In particular, be prepared to discuss what you needed to solve these puzzles and what may have prevented you from solving them more quickly (or at all).

1. *Double circle problem.* Draw two circles, one inside the other, with a single line and with neither circle touching the other (as shown here). In other words, you must draw both of these circles without lifting your pen.

2. *Nine dot problem.* Here are nine dots. Without lifting your pen, draw no more than four straight lines that pass through all nine dots.

3. *Nine dot problem revisited.* Referring to the same nine dot exhibit, describe how, without lifting your pen, you could draw a line through all the dots with three or fewer straight lines.

4. *Word search.* In the following line of letters, cross out five letters so that the remaining letters, without altering their sequence, spell a familiar English word.

CFRIVEELATETITEVRSE

5. *Burning ropes.* You have two pieces of rope of unequal lengths and a box of matches. In spite of their different lengths, each piece of rope takes one hour to burn; however, parts of each rope burn at unequal speeds. For example, the first half of one piece might burn in 10 minutes. Use these materials to accurately determine when 45 minutes have elapsed.

Self-Assessment 8.8
MEASURING YOUR CREATIVE PERSONALITY

PURPOSE   This self-assessment is designed to help you measure the extent to which you have a creative personality.

INSTRUCTIONS
Listed on page 254 is an adjective checklist with 30 words that may or may not describe you. Put a mark in the box beside the words that you think accurately describe you. Please *do not* mark the boxes for words that do not describe you. When finished, you can score the test using the scoring key in Appendix B. This exercise is completed alone so you assess yourself without concerns of social comparison. However, class discussion will focus on how this scale might be applied in organizations, as well as the limitations of measuring creativity in work settings.

Self-Assessment 8.9
TESTING YOUR CREATIVE BENCH STRENGTH (STUDENT OLC)

This self-assessment takes the form of a self-scoring quiz. It consists of 12 questions that require divergent thinking to identify the correct answers. For each question, type your answer in the space provided. When finished, look at the correct answer for each question, along with the explanation for that answer.

Source: Adapted from and based on information in H.G. Gough and A.B. Heilbrun Jr., *The Adjective Check List Manual* (Palo Alto, CA: Consulting Psychologists Press, 1965).

Self-Assessment 8.10

DECISION MAKING STYLE INVENTORY (STUDENT OLC)

People have different styles of decision making that are reflected in how they identify problems or opportunities and make choices. This self-assessment estimates your decision-making style through a series of statements describing how individuals go about making important decisions. Please indicate whether you agree or disagree with each statement.

Answer each item as truthfully as possible so that you get an accurate estimate of your decision-making style. This exercise is completed alone so you assess yourself honestly without concerns of social comparison. However, class discussion will focus on the decision-making styles that people prefer in organizational settings.

After reading this chapter, if you need additional information, see **www.mhhe.com/mcshane4e** for more in-depth interactivities that correspond with this material.

A decade ago Paul Tramontano was typical of most Wall Street brokers, single-handedly providing advice to hundreds of clients. Not any more. Today the director of wealth management at Citigroup's Smith Barney heads a 12-person team (called the Topeka Wealth Management Group) that provides expertise in a range of services 24 hours a day. The team includes technical specialists to complement his own focus on financial, estate planning, and advisory business. Tramontano and others at Smith Barney realized that clients needed a wider variety of services than any single person can deliver. "That's why I think the team approach is the model for what this industry will look like," says Tramontano.

Paul Tramontano (second from left) and others in the securities and investment industry are discovering the benefits of teamwork.

Teamwork has become the mantra of success throughout the investment industry. Nearly 40 percent of Smith Barney advisers are now assigned to teams. Merrill Lynch has organized over half of its financial advisers into 3,000 teams. When Mark Mobius, head of the Templeton Emerging Markets Fund, was asked whether individual fund managers are the real "brands" for a mutual fund, Mobius quickly replied, "The funds are actually run by teams of people and do not depend on one person."

Goldman, Sachs & Co. is widely recognized for successfully combining competitive performance with cooperative teamwork. Goldman employees are evaluated annually by their bosses, peers, and subordinates on how well they perform as well as how well they work as team members. Teamwork even extends to leadership roles: Goldman Sachs departments are run by "co-heads"—two people in charge of each unit. "At Goldman's, you have an alpha organization made up of alpha individuals, working together; it's quite something," says Goldman Sachs vice chairwoman Suzanne Nora Johnson.

In spite of the hoopla, getting investment professionals to actually engage in teamwork has not been easy. Robert Fischer, a securities representative with Legg Mason in Richmond, Virginia, has had his share of frustrations, particularly the extra time required to maintain teams as new members are added. "There's a cost to that—the time, the planning element, the learning curve," warns Fischer. Fifth Third Securities also experienced teamwork problems, particularly in encouraging financial experts to share resources. One strategy that particularly helped Fifth Third Securities strengthen team dynamics was to literally move team members into the same room. "It took a lot of work collaborating and colocating these officers into teams," says a senior executive at the Cincinnati-based securities firm.[1]

9

Foundations of Team Dynamics

After reading this chapter you should be able to

1. Define *teams* and distinguish them from informal groups.
2. Discuss the potential benefits of teams in organizations.
3. Outline the model of team effectiveness.
4. Identify six organizational and team environmental elements that influence team effectiveness.
5. Explain how a team's task, size, and composition influence its effectiveness.

6. Summarize the team development process.
7. Discuss how team norms develop and are maintained and how they may be altered.
8. List six factors that influence team cohesiveness.
9. Discuss the limitations of teams.
10. Explain how companies minimize social loafing.

Organizations ultimately consist of individuals, but corporate leaders on Wall Street and throughout the securities industry are discovering that people working alone usually lack sufficient knowledge or capacity to achieve organizational objectives. Instead teams have become a source of competitive advantage. This focus on teamwork extends to most industries. At General Electric's (GE) Aircraft Engines division in Durham, North Carolina, employees are organized into over a dozen 16-member teams who receive feedback and rewards based partially on team performance. Ford Motor Company's legal department was recently identified as one of the best legal departments in the country, partly because almost everything the department does is achieved through project teams. C&S Wholesale Grocers, the second largest grocery wholesaler in the United States, created self-directed work teams throughout its warehouse operation, resulting in significantly higher productivity and lower absenteeism.[2]

This chapter introduces the concept of teams and provides a foundation to understand the complex conditions that make teams more or less effective in organizational settings. We begin by explaining why people join informal groups and why organizations rely on teams. Most of the chapter examines each part of this model, including team and organizational environment, team design, and the team processes of development, norms, roles, and cohesiveness.

Learning Objectives

After reading this section you should be able to

1. **Define** *teams* **and distinguish them from informal groups.**
2. **Discuss the potential benefits of teams in organizations.**

Teams and Groups

teams
Groups of two or more people who interact and influence each other, are mutually accountable for achieving common goals associated with organizational objectives, and perceive themselves as a social entity within an organization.

Teams are groups of two or more people who interact and influence each other, are mutually accountable for achieving common goals associated with organizational objectives, and perceive themselves as a social entity within an organization.[3] All teams exist to fulfill some purpose, such as assembling a product, providing a service, designing a new manufacturing facility, or making an important decision. Team members are held together by their interdependence and need for collaboration to achieve common goals. All teams require some form of communication so members can coordinate and share common objectives. Team members also influence each other, although some members are more influential than others regarding the team's goals and activities.

Exhibit 9.1 briefly describes various types of (usually) formal work teams in organizations. Notice that some teams are permanent, whereas others are temporary. Some are responsible for making products or providing services; others exist to make decisions or share knowledge. Each of these types of teams has been created deliberately to serve an organizational purpose. Some teams, such as skunkworks teams, are not initially sanctioned by management; yet they are called "teams" because members clearly work toward an organization objective.

groups
Two or more people with a unifying relationship.

All teams are **groups** because they consist of people with a unifying relationship. But not all groups are teams; some groups are just people assembled together without any necessary interdependence or organizationally focused objective. Along with formal work teams, organizations consist of *informal groups.* Informal groups are not initiated by the organization and usually do not perform organizational goals (thus they are "informal"). Instead they exist primarily for the

Exhibit 9.1   **Several Types of Formal Teams in Organizations**

Team Type	Description
Departmental teams	Employees have similar or complementary skills located in the same unit of a functional structure; usually minimal task interdependence because each person works with employees in other departments.
Production/service/leadership teams	Typically multiskilled (employees have diverse competencies), team members collectively produce a common product/service or make ongoing decisions; production/service teams typically have an assembly line type of interdependence, whereas leadership teams tend to have tight interactive (reciprocal) interdependence.
Self-directed work teams	Similar to production/service teams except (1) they produce an entire product or subassembly that has low interdependence with other work units, and (2) they have very high autonomy (this type of team has no supervisors and usually controls inputs, flow, and outputs).
Advisory teams	Entities that provide recommendations to decision makers, includes committees, advisory councils, work councils, and review panels; may be temporary, but often permanent, some with frequent rotation of members.
Task force (project) teams	Usually multiskilled, temporary entities whose assignment is to solve a problem, realize an opportunity, or develop a product or service.
Skunkworks	Multiskilled entities that are usually located away from the organization and are relatively free of its hierarchy; these teams are often initiated by an entrepreneurial team leader (*innovation champion*) who borrows people and resources (*bootlegging*) to create a product or develop a service.
Virtual teams	Formal teams whose members operate across space, time, and organizational boundaries and are linked through information technologies to achieve organizational tasks; may be a temporary task force or a permanent service team.
Communities of practice	May be formally designed, but are usually informal groups bound together by shared expertise and passion for a particular activity or interest; often similar to virtual teams in that many rely on information technologies as a main source of interaction, but the purpose is to share information, not make a product or provide a service.

benefit of their members. The groups you meet for lunch and chat with in the hallway are informal groups. In each case you associate with these groups for your own benefit.

Why Rely on Teams?

Goldman Sachs, Fifth Third Securities, C&S Wholesale Grocers, and many other organizations have put a lot of energy into reorganizing their companies around teams. In fact, one major survey of U.S. human resource professionals concluded, "Teams are now an integral part of workplace management." Why all the fuss about teams? The answer to this question has a long history, dating back to research on British coal mining in the 1940s and the Japanese economic miracle of the 1970s.[4] These early studies revealed that *under the right conditions,* teams make better decisions, develop better products and services, and create a more energized workforce compared with employees working alone. "One of the things I think people overlook is the quality of the team," says Rose Marie Bravo, the American executive who engineered the remarkable turnaround of Burberry, the London fashion house. "It isn't one person, and it isn't two people. It is a whole

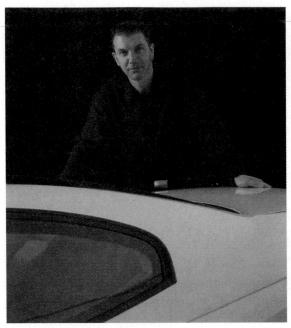

GM Holden's Secret Skunkworks In the late 1990s eight designers at General Motors' small development center in Australia secretly worked on a souped-up coupé, something that was missing from GM's lineup. "It had to stay quiet," recalls Michael Simcoe (shown in this photo), who led the clandestine skunkworks group. "It wasn't an official Holden (GM's Australian company) project, and management hadn't asked us to produce a coupé. It was all after-hours work; people stayed on at the office instead of going straight home at night, and they even came in on weekends to make it happen." The project was so secret that the family room wall at one team member's home was used to complete the first full-size line drawings. When GM Holden executives were notified, they excitedly supported the project, which eventually became the Monaro in Australia and the Pontiac GTO in North America. Members of the skunkworks team are now working with their American colleagues on a new version of the Camaro; Simcoe is now global head of new car design at General Motors' headquarters in Detroit.[5]

group of people—a team that works cohesively toward a goal—that makes something happen or not."[6]

As a form of employee involvement, teams are generally more successful than individuals working alone at identifying problems, developing alternatives, and choosing from those alternatives. For instance, Goldman Sachs teams consist of experts from various disciplines who collectively provide better expertise and service to clients than an individual working alone. Similarly, team members can quickly share information and coordinate tasks, whereas these processes are slower and prone to more errors in traditional departments led by supervisors. Teams typically provide superior customer service because they provide more breadth of knowledge and expertise to customers than individual "stars" can offer.

In many situations people are *potentially* more energized or engaged when working on teams than alone.[7] Employees have a drive to bond and are motivated to fulfill the goals of groups to which they belong. For instance, one study reported that individuals have a stronger sense of belongingness when they work in teams rather than alone. Another consideration is that people potentially have higher motivation in a team environment because they are more accountable to fellow team members, who monitor performance more closely than a traditional supervisor.

Why People Belong to Informal Groups

Employees are not required to join informal groups, yet they exist throughout organizations. One reason is that human beings are social animals. Experts suggest that our drive to bond is a hardwired evolutionary development, which includes the drive to belong to informal groups.[8] This is evidenced by the fact that people invest considerable time and effort in forming and maintaining social relationships without any special circumstances or ulterior motives. A second explanation is provided by social identity theory, which states that individuals define themselves by their group affiliations. Thus we join informal groups—particularly groups viewed favorably by others and that are similar to our existing values—because they shape and reinforce our self-images.[9]

A third reason why people join informal groups is to accomplish tasks that cannot be achieved by individuals working alone. For example, employees will sometimes form a group to oppose organizational changes because the group collectively has more power than individuals complaining alone. A fourth explanation for informal groups is that in stressful situations we are comforted by the mere presence of other people and are therefore motivated to be near them. When in danger, people congregate near each other even though it serves no apparent purpose. Similarly, employees tend to mingle more often when hearing rumors that the company might be sold.[10]

Learning Objectives

After reading the next three sections you should be able to

3. **Outline the model of team effectiveness.**
4. **Identify six organizational and team environmental elements that influence team effectiveness.**
5. **Explain how a team's task, size, and composition influence its effectiveness.**

A Model of Team Effectiveness

You might have noticed that we hedged our glorification of teams by saying that they are "potentially" better than individuals "under the right conditions." The reason for this cautious writing is that many organizations have introduced team structures that later became spectacular failures. Why are some teams effective while others fail? This question has challenged organizational researchers for some time, and as you might expect, numerous models of team effectiveness have been proposed over the years.[11]

team effectiveness
The extent to which a team achieves its objectives, achieves the needs and objectives of its members, and sustains itself over time.

Let's begin by clarifying the meaning of **team effectiveness.** Team effectiveness refers to how a team affects the organization, individual team members, and the team's existence.[12] First, most teams exist to serve some purpose relating to the organization or other system in which the group operates. Some informal groups also have task-oriented (although not organizationally mandated) goals, such as sharing information in an informal community of practice.

Second, team effectiveness relies on the satisfaction and well-being of its members. People join groups to fulfill their personal needs, so effectiveness is partly measured by this need fulfillment. Finally, team effectiveness includes the team's viability—its ability to survive. It must be able to maintain the commitment of its members, particularly during the turbulence of the team's development. Without this commitment, people leave and the team will fall apart. It must also secure sufficient resources and find a benevolent environment in which to operate.

Exhibit 9.2 presents the model of team effectiveness that we will examine closely throughout the rest of this chapter. We begin by looking at elements of the team's and organization's environment that influence team design, processes, and outcomes.

Exhibit 9.2
Model of Team Effectiveness

Organizational and Team Environment

- Reward systems
- Communication systems
- Physical space
- Organizational environment
- Organizational structure
- Organizational leadership

Team Design

- Task characteristics
- Team size
- Team composition

Team Processes

- Task development
- Team norms
- Team roles
- Team cohesiveness

Team Effectiveness

- Achieve organizational goals
- Satisfy member needs
- Maintain team survival

Organizational and Team Environment

The discussion of team effectiveness logically begins with the contextual factors that influence a team's design, processes, and outcomes.[13] Many elements in the organizational and team environment influence team effectiveness. Six of the most important elements are reward systems, communication systems, physical space, organizational environment, organizational structure, and organizational leadership.

- *Reward systems.* Team members tend to work together more effectively when they are at least partly rewarded for team performance.[14] For instance, a large portion of the paycheck earned by Nucor employees is performance pay determined by team results. This doesn't mean that everyone on the team should receive the same amount of pay based on the team's performance. On the contrary, research indicates that employees in the United States and other Western cultures work better on teams when their rewards are based on a combination of individual and team performance.

- *Communication systems.* A poorly designed communication system can starve a team of valuable information and feedback, or it may swamp it with information overload. As we will learn in the next chapter, communication systems are particularly important for geographically dispersed (virtual) teams.

- *Physical space.* The physical layout of an office or manufacturing facility improves team dynamics in at least two ways: (1) It improves communication among team members, and (2) it shapes employee perceptions about being together as a team. Medrad Inc. recently reorganized its production workspace so teams now work in U-shaped "cells" rather than along a straight assembly line. Toyota puts up to 30 people from engineering, design, production, marketing, and other areas in a large room (called an *obeya*) so they have a sense of being a team and can communicate more quickly and effectively. The *obeya* arrangement has cut Toyota's product development time and costs by 25 and 50 percent, respectively. "The reason *obeya* works so well is that it's all about immediate face-to-face human contact," explains the head of Toyota Motor Manufacturing North America."[15]

- *Organizational environment.* Team success depends on the company's external environment. If the organization cannot secure resources, for instance, the team cannot fulfill its performance targets. Similarly, high demand for the team's output creates feelings of success, which motivates team members to stay with the team. A competitive environment can motivate employees to work together more closely.

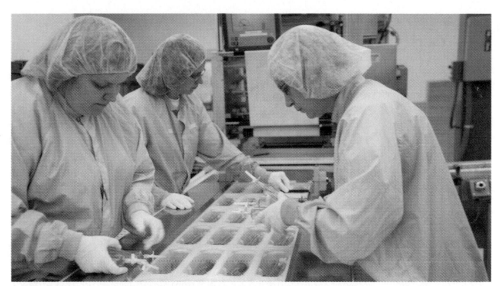

Medrad Sees the U in Team   Medrad Inc. has become a team-based organization, particularly since it adopted the philosophy and practices of lean manufacturing. The Indianola, Pennsylvania, medical device manufacturer relies on cross-functional teams to track down wasted time, space, and distance in the work process. One team also redesigned the production process from a straight-line assembly to clustered structures in which members of each team now work more closely in U-shaped work cells. A successful trial confirmed that the U-shaped cell physical arrangement boosted team performance by improving the ability of team members to observe and assist each other.[16]

- *Organizational structure.* Many teams fail because the organizational structure does not support them. Teams work better when there are few layers of management and teams are given autonomy and responsibility for their work. This structure encourages interaction with team members rather than with supervisors. Teams also flourish when employees are organized around work processes rather than specialized skills. This structure increases interaction among team members.[17]

- *Organizational leadership.* Teams require ongoing support from senior executives to align rewards, organizational structure, communication systems, and other elements of team context. They also require team leaders or facilitators who provide coaching and support. Team leaders are also enablers, meaning that they ensure teams have the authority to solve their own problems and resources to accomplish their tasks.[18] Leaders also maintain a value system that supports team performance more than individual success.

Team Design Features

There are several elements to consider when designing an effective team. Three of the main design elements are task characteristics, team size, and team composition. As we saw in the team effectiveness model (Exhibit 9.2), these design features influence team effectiveness directly as well as indirectly through team processes, described later.

Task Characteristics

What type of work is best handled by teams rather than individuals working alone? OB experts are still figuring out the answer to this question.[19] Some research says that teams are more effective when their tasks are well-structured because the clear structure makes it easier to coordinate work among several people. At the same time, other studies indicate that teams flourish more on complex tasks because the complexity motivates them to work together as a team. The difficulty here is that while task structure and task complexity aren't opposites, it can be difficult to find complex work that is well structured.

Task Interdependence   One task characteristic that is definitely important for teams is **task interdependence**—the extent to which team members must share common inputs to their individual tasks, need to interact in the process of executing their work, or receive outcomes (such as rewards) that are partly determined by the performance of others.[20] The general rule is that the higher the level of task interdependence, the greater the need for teams rather than individuals working alone.

Teams are well suited to highly interdependent tasks because people coordinate better when working together than separately. High task interdependence also tends to increase employee motivation and satisfaction for team members. In other words, high interdependence makes people want to be part of the team, and they feel good about being part of the team. However, this motivation and satisfaction occur only when team members have the same task goals, such as serving the same clients or collectively assembling the same product. In contrast, employees are more likely to experience frustration when each team member is assigned tasks with unique goals (such as serving different clients) but must depend on other team members (high task interdependence) to achieve those unique goals.[21] The bottom line, then, is to assign highly interdependent tasks to teams rather than individuals, but only when those tasks relate to the same goals. If tasks have unique goals, the advantages of teamwork will be less apparent.

Exhibit 9.3 illustrates three levels of task interdependence.[22] Pooled interdependence is the lowest level of interdependence (other than independence), in which

task interdependence
The extent to which team members must share common inputs to their individual tasks, need to interact in the process of executing their work, or receive outcomes (such as rewards) that are partly determined by the performance of others.

Exhibit 9.3
Levels of Task Interdependence

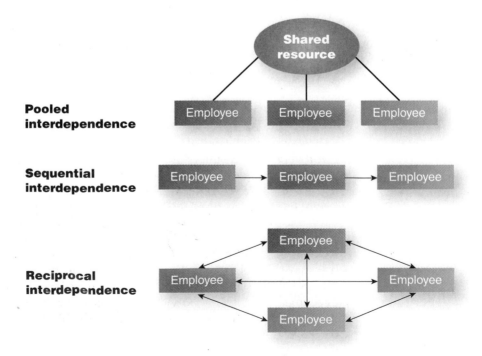

Pooled interdependence

Sequential interdependence

Reciprocal interdependence

individuals operate independently except for reliance on a common resource or authority. Employees share a common payroll, cafeteria, and other organizational resources. In most cases they can work well alone rather than in teams if pooled interdependence is the highest relationship among them.

Sequential interdependence occurs where the output of one person becomes the direct input for another person or unit. This interdependent linkage is found in most assembly lines. Although employees in the production line process usually work alone, they are sufficiently interdependent that Toyota and other companies create teams around these processes. Reciprocal interdependence represents the highest level of interdependence, in which work output is exchanged back and forth among individuals. Employees with reciprocal interdependence should almost always be organized into teams to facilitate coordination in their interwoven relationship.

Team Size

Jim Hassell is a strong believer in teamwork, but the Sun Microsystems executive also recognizes that putting together the best team requires careful consideration of its optimal size. "[A] big challenge in building a team is getting the number of people in the team right. You need to have a balance between having enough people to do all the things that need to be done, while keeping the team small enough so that it is cohesive and can make decisions effectively and speedily."[23]

Team size is an important concern for Jim Hassell and other executives. Some writers claim that team size should be no more than 10 people; but optimal team size really depends on several factors, such as the number of people required to complete the work and the amount of coordination needed to work together. As Hassell described, the general rule is that teams should be large enough to provide the necessary competencies and perspectives to perform the work, yet small enough to maintain efficient coordination and meaningful involvement of each member.[24]

Larger teams are typically less effective because members consume more time and effort coordinating their roles and resolving differences. For instance, some of the continuous improvement process teams at Varian Australia suffered because they had more than a dozen members, making it difficult to reach agreement on ideas. In these larger teams, individuals have less opportunity to participate and consequently are less likely to feel that they are contributing to the team's success. Larger work units tend to break into informal subgroups around common interests and work activities, causing members to form stronger commitments to their subgroups than to the larger team.

Team Composition

When Hewlett-Packard (HP) hires new talent, it doesn't look for just technical skills and knowledge. The high-tech computer manufacturer looks for job applicants who fit into a team environment. "It's important for candidates to prove to us that they can work well with others," explains business development manager Bill Avey. "We're looking for people who value the different perspectives that each individual brings to a team." Avey describes how HP recruiters will ask applicants to recall a time they worked in a group to solve a problem. "Successful candidates tend to show how they got differences out in the open and reached a resolution as a team," says Avey.[25]

Hewlett-Packard has a strong team orientation, so it carefully selects people with the necessary motivation and competencies for teamwork. Royal/Dutch Shell also pays close attention to job applicants who can work effectively in teams. In fact, as Connections 9.1 describes, Shell has developed a unique five-day event, called the Shell Gourami Business Challenge, to help identify university students with both technical and team skills.

Team Diversity Challenges Students in Shell's Gourami Business Challenge

Royal Dutch/Shell (Shell) discovered long ago that a job interview isn't the best way to determine a job applicant's technical skills, nor how well he or she works in a team environment. That's why the global energy company launched the Shell Gourami Business Challenge, a five-day event involving four dozen engineering and business university students. Shell introduced the Gourami Business Challenge a decade ago in Europe and recently in the United States, Asia, and the Middle East.

Students are split into several teams representing different departments, including exploration and production, refining operations, manufacturing, human resources, finance, and sales and marketing. Teams initially develop business plans for their own departments; later they must merge the departmental plans into an organizationwide business strategy. On the final day, the multiteam's strategy is presented to Gourami's board of directors, which consists of senior executives from Shell. Shell leaders emphasize that the Gourami event is not a competition for limited jobs; everyone could be hired if they are qualified.

Throughout the five-day event, Shell assessors evaluate students on how effectively they work in diverse teams, not just on their technical skills. The need for strong social skills is quickly apparent to most participants. Maureen Valencia, a business student from the Philippines who attended the Asian Gourami exercise, admitted feeling some initial tension because the Australians were "more straightforward and tell you right away if you're doing something right or wrong."

Andrew Wang, a Singaporean business student who also attended the Asian Gourami event, says he was easy to get along with—the Filipino participants gave him the nickname *babaero,* which means sweet talker in Tagalog. Yet he admits to a few irritations, including one in which another team member kept interrupting. Eventually, says Wang "my teammate mediated because the atmosphere just got tense."

Team skills were also vital to help students work with people from different specializations. "Coming from a business background, it's most difficult to understand the engineering aspect of the oil industry," admitted Arpan Shah, a University of Texas finance student who attended the Gourami exercise in Rancho Mirage, California. "We have to work together so that both sides understand each other."

Claire Gould, who attended the European session, also noticed the challenges and learning when working with students from other disciplines. "Hard science students can be dismissive of what they see as 'fluffy' disciplines like human resources management and vice versa," admits Gould, a mechanical engineering undergraduate at Imperial College in London. "Dealing with the 'real-life' challenges of Gourami made us all aware of the value of other skills and aptitudes and the need to work as a team."

Sources: P. Wise, "How Shell Finds Student World's Brightest Sparks," *Financial Times* (London), 8 January 2004, p. 12; "Shell Oil Introduces Undergrads to Gourami Business Challenge," University of Texas at Austin news release, 15 August 2005; S. Ganesan, "Reality-Style Recruitment," *Malaysia Star,* 9 October 2005; Z. Nazeer, "You're Hired!" *The New Paper* (Singapore), 31 October 2005; J. Ng, "Shell Uses 'The Apprentice' Contest to Recruit Staff," *Straits Times* (Singapore), 3 October 2005.

Royal Dutch/Shell has found a better way to identify the team skills of prospective job applicants by observing business and engineering students in the Shell Gourami Business Challenge.

What do Royal Dutch/Shell, Hewlett-Packard, and other companies look for in effective team members? First, teams require members who are motivated to remain team members. In particular, they must be motivated to work together rather than alone, abide by the team's rules of conduct, and buy into the team's goals. Employees with a strong collectivist orientation—those who value group goals more than their own personal goals—tend to perform better in work teams.[26] Effective team members also possess valuable skills and knowledge for the team's objectives and can work well with others. Notably, research suggests that high-performing team members have strong social skills and emotional intelligence and generally demonstrate more cooperative behavior toward others.[27]

homogeneous teams
Teams that include members with common technical expertise, demographics (age, sex), ethnicity, experiences, or values.

heterogeneous teams
Teams that include members with diverse personal characteristics and backgrounds.

Team Diversity   Another important dimension of team composition is the diversity of team members.[28] **Homogeneous teams** include members with common technical expertise, demographics (age, sex), ethnicity, experiences, or values, whereas **heterogeneous teams** have members with diverse personal characteristics and backgrounds. Some forms of diversity are apparent on the surface, such as differences in sex and race. *Deep-level diversity,* on the other hand, refers to differences in the personalities, values, attitudes, and other psychological characteristics of team members. *Surface-level diversity* is apparent as soon as the team forms, whereas deep-level diversity emerges over time as team members discover each other's values and beliefs.[29]

Should teams be homogeneous or heterogeneous? Both have advantages and disadvantages, and their relative effectiveness depends on the situation.[30] Heterogeneous teams experience more conflict and take longer to develop. They are susceptible to "faultlines"—hypothetical dividing lines that may split a team into subgroups along gender, ethnic, professional, or other dimensions. Teams with strong faultlines—such as where team members fall into two or more distinct demographic groups—have a higher risk of dysfunctional conflict and other behaviors that undermine team effectiveness. Under these circumstances, leaders need to restructure the work to minimize interaction among these subgroups.[31] In contrast, members of homogeneous teams experience higher satisfaction, less conflict, and better interpersonal relations. Consequently, homogeneous teams tend to be more effective for tasks requiring a high degree of cooperation and coordination, such as emergency response teams.

Although heterogeneous teams have these difficulties, they are generally more effective than homogeneous teams in executive groups and in other situations involving complex problems requiring innovative solutions. One reason is that people from different backgrounds see a problem or opportunity from different perspectives. A second reason is that they usually have a broader knowledge base. For example, Paul Tramontano's team of financial experts at Smith Barney (described in the opening story) is necessarily composed of a diverse group of people who have deep knowledge in several fields, ranging from estate planning to tax planning. Without these heterogeneous characteristics, the team would be much less effective in its assigned task.

A third reason why heterogeneous teams are generally more effective than homogeneous teams is that the diversity provides representation to the team's constituents, such as other departments or clients from similarly diverse backgrounds. When a team represents various professions or departments, those constituents are more likely to accept and support the team's decisions and actions.

After reading this section you should be able to

6. **Summarize the team development process.**
7. **Discuss how team norms develop and are maintained and how they may be altered.**
8. **List six factors that influence team cohesiveness.**

Team Processes

We've looked at two sets of elements in the team effectiveness model so far: (1) organizational and team environment and (2) team design. Over the next few pages we will learn about the third set of team effectiveness elements, collectively known as team processes. These processes—team development, norms, roles, and cohesiveness—are influenced by both team design and organizational and team environment factors.

Team Development

A few years ago the U.S. National Transportation Safety Board (NTSB) studied the circumstances under which airplane cockpit crews were most likely to have accidents and related problems. What they discovered was startling: 73 percent of all incidents took place on the crew's first day, and 44 percent occurred on the crew's very first flight together. This isn't an isolated example. NASA studied fatigue of pilots after returning from multiple-day trips. Fatigued pilots made more errors in the NASA flight simulator, as one would expect. But the NASA researchers didn't expect the discovery that fatigued crews who had previously worked together made fewer errors than did rested crews who had not yet flown together.[32]

The NTSB and NASA studies reveal that team members must resolve several issues and pass through several stages of development before emerging as an effective work unit. They must get to know each other, understand their respective roles, discover appropriate and inappropriate behaviors, and learn how to coordinate their work or social activities. The longer team members work together, the better they develop common mental models, mutual understanding, and effective performance routines to complete their work.

The five-stage model of team development, shown in Exhibit 9.4, provides a general outline of how teams evolve by forming, storming, norming, performing, and eventually adjourning.[33] The model shows teams progressing from one stage to the next in an orderly fashion, but the dashed lines illustrate that they might also fall back to an earlier stage of development as new members join or other conditions disrupt the team's maturity.

1. *Forming*—The first stage of team development is a period of testing and orientation in which members learn about each other and evaluate the benefits and costs of continued membership. People tend to be polite during this stage and will defer to the existing authority of a formal or informal leader who must provide an initial set of rules and structures for interaction. Members try to find out what is expected of them and how they will fit into the team.
2. *Storming*—The storming stage is marked by interpersonal conflict as members become more proactive and compete for various team roles. Coalitions may form to influence the team's goals and means of goal attainment. Members try to establish norms of appropriate behavior and performance standards. This is a

Exhibit 9.4
Stages of Team Development

tenuous stage in the team's development, particularly when the leader is autocratic and lacks the necessary conflict management skills.

3. *Norming*–During the norming stage, the team develops its first real sense of cohesion as roles are established and a consensus forms around group objectives. Members have developed relatively similar mental models, so they have common expectations and assumptions about how the team's goals should be accomplished. They have developed a common team-based mental model that allows them to interact more efficiently so they can move into the next stage, performing.[34]

4. *Performing*–The team becomes more task-oriented in the performing stage. Team members have learned to coordinate and resolve conflicts more efficiently. Further coordination improvements must occasionally be addressed, but the greater emphasis is on task accomplishment. In high-performance teams members are highly cooperative, have a high level of trust in each other, are committed to group objectives, and identify with the team. There is a climate of mutual support in which team members feel comfortable about taking risks, making errors, or asking for help.[35]

5. *Adjourning*–Most work teams and informal groups eventually end. Task forces disband when their projects are completed. Informal work groups may reach this stage when several members leave the organization or are reassigned elsewhere.

Sky-High Team Development Reaching the "performing" stage of team development isn't just a goal for the Blue Angels; it's an absolute necessity to ensure that the U.S. Navy's aerial demonstration team completes its maneuvers with near-perfect timing. Although highly experienced before joining the squad, the pilots put in long hours of practice to reach the pinnacle of team development. The F/A-18A Hornets initially fly with large spaces between them, but the team gradually tightens up the formation over the 10-week training program until the fighter jets are at times only 18 inches apart. Lt. Cdr. John Saccomando, who flies the No. 2 position, explains that the training improves trust and common mental models about each maneuver. "I know exactly what [the lead] jet is going to do, and when," he says. "It takes a while to build that confidence." Team development is also sped up through candid debriefings after every practice. "We close the door, and there's no rank," says Saccomando, who is expected to offer frank feedback to commanding officer and flight leader Cdr. Stephen R. Foley. Foley points out that the safety and success of the Blue Angels depend on how well the team development process works. "The team concept is what makes [everything] here click," Foley emphasizes.[36]

Some teams adjourn as a result of layoffs or plant shutdowns. Whatever the cause of team adjournment, members shift their attention away from task orientation to a socioemotional focus as they realize that their relationship is ending.

The team development model is a useful framework for thinking about how teams develop. Indeed, a recent study suggests that it fits nicely with student recollections of their team development experiences.[37] Still, the model is not a perfect representation of the dynamics of team development. It does not explicitly show that some teams remain in a particular stage longer than others and that team development is a continuous process. As membership changes and new conditions emerge, teams cycle back to earlier stages in the developmental process to regain the equilibrium or balance lost by the changes (as shown by the dashed lines in Exhibit 9.4).

Team Norms

norms
The informal rules and shared expectations that groups establish to regulate the behavior of their members.

Have you ever noticed how employees in one branch office practically run for the exit door the minute the workday ends, whereas their counterparts in another office seem to be competing for who can stay at work the longest? These differences are partly due to **norms**—the informal rules and shared expectations that groups establish to regulate the behavior of their members. Norms apply only to behavior, not to private thoughts or feelings. Moreover, norms exist only for behaviors that are important to the team.[38] Norms guide how team members deal with clients, how they share resources, whether they are willing to work longer hours, and many other behaviors in organizational life. Some norms ensure that employees support organizational goals, whereas other norms might conflict with organizational objectives.

Conformity to Team Norms Everyone has experienced peer pressure at one time or another. Co-workers grimace if we are late for a meeting or make sarcastic comments if we don't have our part of the project completed on time. In more extreme situations, team members may try to enforce norms by temporarily ostracizing deviant co-workers or threatening to terminate their membership. This heavy-handed peer pressure isn't as rare as you might think. One survey revealed that 20 percent of employees have been pressured by their colleagues to slack off at work. Half the time, the peer pressure occurred because colleagues didn't want to look like poor performers against their more productive co-workers.[39]

Norms are also directly reinforced through praise from high-status members, more access to valued resources, or other rewards available to the team. But team members often conform to prevailing norms without direct reinforcement or punishment because they identify with the group and want to align their behavior with the team's expectations. The more tightly the person's social identity is connected to the group, the more the individual is motivated to avoid negative sanctions from that group.[40] This effect is particularly strong in new members because they are uncertain of their status and want to demonstrate their membership in the team.

How Team Norms Develop   Norms develop as soon as teams form because people need to anticipate or predict how others will act. Even subtle events during the team's formation, such as how team members initially greet each other and where they sit in the first meetings, can initiate norms that are later difficult to change. At first most norms are fuzzy, such as "team members should communicate frequently with each other." Over time norms tend to become more specific, such as "check and reply to your e-mail daily."[41]

Norms form as team members discover behaviors that help them function more effectively (such as the need to respond quickly to e-mail). In particular, a critical event in the team's history can trigger formation of a norm or sharpen a previously vague one. As an example, if a co-worker slipped on metal scraps and was seriously injured, team members might develop a strong norm to keep the work area clean. Along with the effect of initial experiences and critical events, a third influence on team norms is the past experiences and values that members bring to the team. If most people who join a new team value work–life balance, then norms are likely to develop that discourage long hours and work overload.[42]

Preventing and Changing Dysfunctional Team Norms   Team norms often become deeply anchored, so the best way to avoid norms that undermine organizational success or employee well-being is to establish desirable norms when teams are first formed. As was just mentioned, norms form from the values that people bring to a team, so one strategy is to select people with appropriate values. If organizational leaders want their teams to have strong safety norms, they should hire people who already value safety.

Another strategy is to clearly state desirable norms as soon as a team is created. For instance, when Four Seasons Hotels & Resorts opens a new hotel, it forms a 35-person task force of respected staff from other Four Seasons hotels to get the new hotel up and running. Their mandate also includes helping to "Four Seasonize" the new staff by watching for behaviors and decisions that are inconsistent with the Four Seasons way of doing things. "The task force helps establish norms [in the new hotel]," explains a Four Seasons manager who has served on these task forces.[43]

Of course most teams are not just starting up, so how can norms change in older teams? One way is for the leader to explicitly discuss the counterproductive norm with team members using persuasive communication tactics. For example, the surgical team of one hospital had developed a norm of arriving late for operations. Patients and other hospital staff often waited 30 minutes or more for the team to arrive. The hospital CEO eventually spoke to the surgical team about their lateness and, through moral suasion, convinced team members to arrive for operating room procedures no more than five minutes late for their appointments.[44]

Team-based reward systems can sometimes weaken counterproductive norms. Unfortunately the pressure to conform to the counterproductive norm is sometimes stronger than the financial incentive. This problem occurred in the classic story of a pajama factory where employees were paid under a piece rate system. Some individuals in the group were able to process up to 100 units per hour and thereby earn more money, but they all chose to abide by the group norm of 50 units per hour. Only after the team was disbanded did the strong performers working alone increase their performance to 100 units per hour.[45]

Finally, a dysfunctional norm may be so deeply ingrained that the best strategy is to disband the group and replace it with people having more favorable norms. Organizational leaders should seize the opportunity to introduce performance-oriented norms when a new team is formed and select members who will bring desirable norms to the group.

Team Roles

role
A set of behaviors that people are expected to perform because they hold certain positions in a team and organization.

Every work team and informal group has various roles necessary to coordinate the team's task and maintain the team's functioning. A **role** is a set of behaviors that people are expected to perform because they hold certain positions in a team and organization.[46] Some roles help a team achieve its goals; other roles maintain relationships so the team survives and team members fulfill their needs. Some team roles are formally assigned to specific people. For example, team leaders are usually expected to initiate discussion, ensure that everyone has an opportunity to present her or his views, and help the team reach agreement on the issues discussed. But team members often take on various roles informally based on their personality, values, and expertise. These role preferences are usually worked out during the storming stage of team development. However, in a dynamic environment, team members often need to assume various roles temporarily as the need arises.[47]

Various team role theories have been proposed over the years, but Meredith Belbin's team role theory is the most popular.[48] The model identifies nine team roles (see Exhibit 9.5) that are related to specific personality characteristics. People have a natural preference for one role or another, although they can adjust to a secondary role. Belbin's model emphasizes that all nine roles must be engaged for optimal team performance. Moreover, certain team roles should dominate over others at various stages of the team's project or activities. For example, shapers and coordinators are key figures when the team is identifying its needs, whereas completers and implementers are most important during the follow-through stage of the team's project.

How accurate is Belbin's team roles model? The evidence is mixed.[49] Research agrees that teams require a balance of roles and that people tend to prefer one type of role. However, Belbin's nine roles typically boil down to six or seven roles in empirical studies. For example, the implementer and completer roles are the same or too similar to distinguish from each other. Scholars have also criticized how Belbin's roles are measured, which creates difficulty in determining the accuracy of the model. Overall, teams do have a variety of roles that must be fulfilled for team effectiveness, but we are still trying to figure out what these roles are and how to measure them.

Team Cohesiveness

team cohesiveness
The degree of attraction people feel toward the team and their motivation to remain members.

Team cohesiveness—the degree of attraction people feel toward the team and their motivation to remain members—is an important factor in a team's success.[50] Employees feel cohesiveness when they believe their team will help them achieve their personal goals, fulfill their need for affiliation or status, or provide social support during times of crisis or trouble. Cohesiveness is an emotional experience, not just

Exhibit 9.5
Belbin's Team Roles

Role Title	Contributions	Allowable Weaknesses
Plant (PL)	Creative, imaginative, unorthodox. Solves difficult problems.	Ignores details. Too preoccupied to communicate effectively.
Resource investigator (RI)	Extrovert, enthusiastic, communicative. Explores opportunities. Develops contacts.	Overoptimistic. Loses interest once initial enthusiasm has passed.
Coordinator (CO)	Mature, confident, a good chairperson. Clarifies goals, promotes decision making, delegates well.	Can be seen as manipulative. Delegates personal work.
Shaper (SH)	Challenging, dynamic, thrives on pressure. Has the drive and courage to overcome obstacles.	Can provoke others. Hurts people's feelings.
Monitor/ evaluator (ME)	Sober, strategic, discerning. Sees all options. Judges accurately.	Lacks drive and ability to inspire others. Overly critical.
Team worker (TW)	Cooperative, mild, perceptive, diplomatic. Listens, builds, averts friction, calms the waters.	Indecisive in crunch situations. Can be easily influenced.
Implementer (IMP)	Disciplined, reliable, conservative, efficient. Turns ideas into practical actions.	Somewhat inflexible. Slow to respond to new possibilities.
Completer/ Finisher (CF)	Painstaking, conscientious, anxious. Searches out errors and omissions. Delivers on time.	Inclined to worry unduly. Reluctant to delegate. Can be a nitpicker.
Specialist (SP)	Single-minded, self-starting, dedicated. Provides knowledge and skills in rare supply.	Contributes on only a narrow front. Dwells on technicalities. Overlooks the "big picture."

Sources: R.M. Belbin, *Team Roles at Work* (Oxford, UK: Butterworth-Heinemann, 1993); www.belbin.com.

a calculation of whether to stay or leave the team. It exists when team members make the team part of their social identity (see Chapter 3). Cohesiveness is the glue or *esprit de corps* that holds the group together and ensures that its members fulfill their obligations.

Influences on Team Cohesiveness   Several factors influence team cohesiveness: member similarity, team size, member interaction, difficult entry, team success, and external competition or challenges. For the most part these factors reflect the individual's social identity with the group and beliefs about how team membership will fulfill personal needs.[51] Several of these factors are related to our earlier discussion about why people join informal groups and how teams develop. Specifically, teams become more cohesive as they reach higher stages of development and are more attractive to potential members.

- *Member similarity.* Earlier in this chapter we learned that highly diverse teams potentially create faultlines that can lead to factious subgroups and higher turnover among team members. Other research has found that people with similar values have a higher attraction to each other. Collectively these findings suggest that homogeneous teams are more cohesive than heterogeneous teams. However, not all forms of diversity reduce cohesion. For example, teams consisting of people from different job groups seem to gel together just as well as teams of people from the same job.[52]

- *Team size.* Smaller teams tend to be more cohesive than larger teams because it is easier for a few people to agree on goals and coordinate work activities. The smallest teams aren't always the most cohesive, however. Small teams are less cohesive when they lack enough members to perform the required tasks. Thus team cohesiveness is potentially greatest when teams are as small as possible, yet large enough to accomplish the required tasks.

- *Member interaction.* Teams tend to be more cohesive when team members interact with each other fairly regularly. This occurs when team members perform highly interdependent tasks and work in the same physical area.

- *Somewhat difficult entry.* Teams tend to be more cohesive when entry to the team is restricted. The more elite the team, the more prestige it confers on its members, and the more they tend to value their membership in the unit. Existing team members are also more willing to welcome and support new members after they have "passed the test," possibly because they have shared the same entry experience. This raises the issue of how difficult the initiation for entry into the team should be. Research suggests that severe initiations can potentially lead to humiliation and psychological distance from the group, even for those who successfully endure the initiation.[53]

- *Team success.* Cohesion is both emotional and instrumental, with the latter referring to the notion that people feel more cohesion to teams that fulfill their needs and goals. Consequently cohesion increases with the team's level of success.[54] Furthermore, individuals are more likely to attach their social identities to successful teams than to those with a string of failures. Team leaders can increase cohesiveness by regularly communicating and celebrating the team's successes. Notice that this can create a positive self-fulfilling prophecy effect. Successful teams are more cohesive, and under certain conditions higher cohesiveness increases a team's success.

- *External competition and challenges.* Team cohesiveness tends to increase when members face external competition or a valued objective that is challenging. This might include a threat from an external competitor or friendly competition from other teams. These conditions tend to increase cohesiveness because employees value the team's ability to overcome the threat or competition if they can't solve the problem individually. They also value their membership as a

A Tight-Knit Lighthouse The staff members at Lighthouse Publishing are a highly cohesive group that successfully keeps its much larger competitors off-guard. "Lighthouse staff members [have] kept us independent in the face of stiff competition and corporate takeovers," says Lynn Hennigar, president of the small publishing company in Bridgewater, Nova Scotia, Canada. Its weekly newspaper, the *Bridgewater Bulletin,* is judged as best in class for Atlantic Canada and one of the top five across Canada. In all, the company received more than two dozen awards over the past year. Lighthouse's mostly female staff often demonstrate their cohesion when faced with new challenges. For instance, the team performed above any reasonable expectations when the press broke down, which threatened to delay getting the paper out on time. On another occasion, when putting together an interactive CD-ROM promoting Nova Scotia tourism, Lighthouse staff displayed skills that Hennigar admits she didn't even know about. "Lighthouse succeeds because of its multitalented, highly dedicated team of employees," says Hennigar. "It's a team that embraces change."[55]

form of social support. We need to be careful about the degree of external threat, however. Evidence suggests that teams seem to be less effective when external threats are severe. Although cohesiveness tends to increase, external threats are stressful and cause teams to make less effective decisions.[56]

Consequences of Team Cohesiveness   Every team must have some minimal level of cohesiveness to maintain its existence. People who belong to high-cohesion teams are motivated to maintain their membership and to help the team perform effectively. Compared to low-cohesion teams, high-cohesion team members spend more time together, share information more frequently, and are more satisfied with each other. They also provide each other with better social support in stressful situations.[57]

Members of high-cohesion teams are generally more sensitive to each other's needs and develop better interpersonal relationships, thereby reducing dysfunctional conflict. When conflict does arise, members tend to resolve these differences swiftly and effectively. With better cooperation and more conformity to norms, high-cohesion teams usually perform better than low-cohesion teams. However, the relationship is a little more complex. Exhibit 9.6 illustrates how the effect of cohesiveness on team performance depends on the extent to which team norms are consistent with organizational goals. Cohesive teams will likely have lower task performance when norms conflict with organizational objectives because cohesiveness motivates employees to perform at a level more consistent with group norms.[58]

Exhibit 9.6
Effect of Team Cohesiveness on Task Performance

	Low ← Team cohesiveness → High	
Team norms support company goals	Moderately high task performance	High task performance
Team norms conflict with company goals	Moderately low task performance	Low task performance

Team cohesiveness

Learning Objectives

After reading this section you should be able to

9. **Discuss the limitations of teams.**
10. **Explain how companies minimize social loafing.**

The Trouble with Teams

As we explained near the beginning of this chapter, organizational leaders are placing a lot more emphasis on teams these days. Although this chapter has outlined the benefits of teams, the reality is that teams sometimes have more costs than benefits.[59] "The now fashionable team in which everybody works with everybody on everything from the beginning rapidly is becoming a disappointment," warned the late management guru Peter Drucker.[60]

For the reasons we outline next, some tasks are performed just as easily and effectively by one person as by a group. As was mentioned earlier, the best tasks for teams are complex (require multiple skill sets), highly interdependent, and have mutual goals. In contrast, tasks should be assigned to individuals when one person has the required skills and ability to perform the work. Similarly, tasks with low interdependence don't usually require a formal team because employees won't benefit from working closely (physically or psychologically) with other people.

Process Losses and Brooks's Law

process losses
Resources (including time and energy) expended toward team development and maintenance rather than the task.

The main problem with teams is that they have additional costs beyond those of individuals working alone. Experts refer to these hidden costs as **process losses**—resources (including time and energy) expended toward team development and maintenance rather than the task.[61] It is much more efficient for an individual to work out an issue alone than to resolve differences of opinion with other people. Teams need to sort out their differences, develop mutual understanding of issues and goals (known as forming a team mental model), and learn to coordinate with each other. The effort to accomplish these team development and maintenance activities is much higher than within one person. Researchers point out that the cost of process losses may be offset by the benefits of teams. Unfortunately few companies conduct a cost–benefit analysis of their team activities.[62]

The process loss problem is particularly apparent when adding new people to the team. The group has to recycle through the team development process to bring everyone up to speed. The software industry even has a name for this. "Brooks's law" (also called the "mythical man-month") says that adding more people to a late software project only makes it later. According to some sources, Apple Computer may have fallen into this trap in the recent development of its professional photography software program, called Aperture. When the project started to fall behind schedule, the manager in charge of the Aperture project increased the size of the team—some sources say it ballooned from 20 to almost 150 engineers and quality assurance staff within a few weeks. Unfortunately adding so many people further bogged down the project. The result? When Aperture was finally released, it was nine months late and considered one of Apple's buggier software offerings.[63]

Along with process loss costs, teams require the right environment to flourish. Many companies forget this point by putting people in teams without changing anything else. As we noted earlier, teams require appropriate rewards, communication systems, team leadership, and other conditions. Without these, the shift to a team structure could be a waste of time. At the same time critics suggest that changing these environmental conditions to improve teamwork could result in higher costs than benefits for the overall organization.[64]

Social Loafing

social loafing
A situation in which people exert less effort (and usually perform at a lower level) when working in groups than when working alone.

Perhaps the best-known limitation of teams is the risk of productivity loss due to **social loafing.** Social loafing occurs when people exert less effort (and usually perform at a lower level) when working in groups than when working alone.[65] A few scholars question whether social loafing is common, but students can certainly report many instances of this problem in their team projects!

Social loafing is most likely to occur in large teams where individual output is difficult to identify. This particularly includes situations in which team members work alone toward a common output pool (that is, they have low task interdependence). Under these conditions, employees aren't as worried that their performance will be noticed. Social loafing is less likely to occur when the task is interesting because individuals have a higher intrinsic motivation to perform their duties. It is less common when the group's objective is important, possibly because individuals experience more pressure from other team members to perform well. Finally, social loafing occurs less frequently among members with a strong collectivist value because they value group membership and believe in working toward group objectives.[66]

How to Minimize Social Loafing   By understanding the causes of social loafing, we can identify ways to minimize this problem. Some of the strategies listed here reduce social loafing by making each member's performance more visible. Others increase each member's motivation to perform his or her tasks within the group:[67]

- *Form smaller teams.* Splitting a team into several smaller groups reduces social loafing because each person's performance becomes more noticeable and important for team performance. A smaller group also potentially increases cohesiveness, so would-be shirkers feel a greater obligation to perform fully for their team.

- *Specialize tasks.* Each person's contribution is easier to see when each team member performs a different work activity. For example, rather than pooling their effort for all incoming customer inquiries, each customer service representative might be assigned a particular type of client.

- *Measure individual performance.* Social loafing is minimized when each member's contribution is measured. Of course, individual performance is difficult to measure in some team activities, such as problem-solving projects in which the team's performance depends on one person discovering the best answer.

- *Increase job enrichment.* Social loafing is minimized when team members are assigned more motivating jobs, such as requiring more skill variety or having direct contact with clients. More generally, social loafing is less common among employees with high job satisfaction.

- *Select motivated employees.* Social loafing can be minimized by carefully selecting job applicants who are motivated by the task and have a collectivist value orientation. Those with a collectivist value are motivated to work harder for the team because they value their membership in the group.

This chapter has laid the foundation for our understanding of team dynamics. To build an effective team requires time, the right combination of team members, and the right environment. We will apply these ingredients of environment and team processes in the next chapter, which looks at high-performance teams, including self-directed teams and virtual teams.

Chapter Summary

Teams are groups of two or more people who interact and influence each other, are mutually accountable for achieving common objectives, and perceive themselves as a social entity within an organization. All teams are groups because they consist of people with a unifying relationship; not all groups are teams because some groups do not have purposive interaction.

Groups can be categorized in terms of their permanence (teams versus informal groups) and formality in the organization. Informal groups exist primarily for the benefit of their members rather than for the organization. Teams have become popular because they tend to make better decisions, support the knowledge management process, and provide superior customer service. In many situations employees are potentially more energized and engaged working in teams rather than alone.

Team effectiveness includes a group's ability to survive, achieve its system-based objectives, and fulfill the needs of its members. The model of team effectiveness considers the team and organizational environment, team design, and team processes. The team or organizational environment influences team effectiveness directly as well as through team design and team processes. Six elements in the organizational and team environment that influence

team effectiveness are reward systems, communication systems, physical space, organizational environment, organizational structure, and organizational leadership.

Three team design elements are task characteristics, team size, and team composition. Teams tend to be more effective when they work on well-structured or complex tasks. The need for teamwork increases with task interdependence. Teams should be large enough to perform the work, yet small enough for efficient coordination and meaningful involvement. Effective teams are composed of people with the competencies and motivation to perform tasks in a team environment. Heterogeneous teams operate best on complex projects and problems requiring innovative solutions.

Teams develop through the stages of forming, storming, norming, performing, and eventually adjourning. Teams develop norms to regulate and guide member behavior. These norms may be influenced by initial experiences, critical events, and the values and experiences that team members bring to the group. Team members also have roles—a set of behaviors they are expected to perform because they hold certain positions in a team and organization.

Cohesiveness is the degree of attraction people feel toward a team and their motivation to remain members.

Cohesiveness increases with member similarity, smaller team size, higher degree of interaction, somewhat difficult entry, team success, and external challenges. Teams need some level of cohesiveness to survive, but highly cohesive units have higher task performance only when their norms do not conflict with organizational objectives.

Teams are not always beneficial or necessary. Moreover, they have hidden costs, known as process losses, and require particular environments to flourish. Teams often fail because they are not set up in supportive environments. Social loafing is another potential problem with teams. This is the tendency for individuals to perform at a lower level when working in groups than when alone. Social loafing can be minimized by making each member's performance more visible and increasing each member's motivation to perform his or her tasks within the group.

Key Terms

groups, p. 258
heterogeneous teams, p. 267
homogeneous teams, p. 267
norms, p. 270

process losses, p. 276
role, p. 272
social loafing, p. 277
task interdependence, p. 264

team cohesiveness, p. 272
team effectiveness, p. 261
teams, p. 258

Critical Thinking Questions

1. Informal groups exist in almost every form of social organization. What types of informal groups exist in your classroom? Why are students motivated to belong to these informal groups?
2. You have been asked to lead a complex software project over the next year that requires the full-time involvement of approximately 100 people with diverse skills and backgrounds. Using your knowledge of team size, how can you develop an effective team under these conditions?
3. You have been put in charge of a cross-functional task force that will develop enhanced Internet banking services for retail customers. The team includes representatives from marketing, information services, customer service, and accounting, all of whom will move to the same location at headquarters for three months. Describe the behaviors you might observe during each stage of the team's development.
4. You have just been transferred from the Kansas office to the Denver office of your company, a national sales organization of electrical products for developers and contractors. In Kansas team members regularly called customers after a sale to ask whether the products arrived on time and whether they were satisfied. But when you moved to the Denver office, no one seemed to make these follow-up calls. A recently hired co-worker explained that other co-workers discouraged her from making those calls. Later another co-worker suggested that your follow-up calls were making everyone else look lazy. Give three possible reasons why the norms in Denver might be different from those in the Kansas office even though the customers, products, sales commissions, and other characteristics of the workplace are almost identical.
5. An employee at a financial services firm recently made the following comment about his team, using a baseball metaphor: "Our team has a great bunch of people. But just like a baseball team, some people need to hit the home run, whereas others have to play catcher. Some need to be coaches and others have to be experts at fixing the equipment every day. The problem with our team is that we don't have people in some of these other jobs. As a result, our team isn't performing as well as it should." What team dynamics topic is this person mainly referring to, and what is he saying about his team in the context of that topic?
6. You have been assigned to a class project with five other students, none of whom you have met before. To what extent would team cohesiveness improve your team's performance on this project? What actions would you recommend to build team cohesiveness among student team members in this situation?
7. The Blue Angels demonstration flight team was described in this chapter as highly cohesive. From the description provided, what factors contribute to this cohesion?
8. The late management guru Peter Drucker said, "The now-fashionable team in which everybody works with everybody on everything from the beginning rapidly is becoming a disappointment." Discuss three problems associated with teams.

Case Study 9.1 TREETOP FOREST PRODUCTS

Treetop Forest Products Ltd. is a sawmill operation in Oregon that is owned by a major forest products company but operates independently of headquarters. It was built 30 years ago and was completely updated with new machinery five years ago. Treetop receives raw logs from the area for cutting and planing into building-grade lumber, mostly 2-by-4 and 2-by-6 pieces of standard lengths. Higher-grade logs leave Treetop's sawmill department in finished form and are sent directly to the packaging department. The remaining 40 percent of sawmill output are cuts from lower-grade logs, requiring further work by the planing department.

Treetop has one general manager, 16 supervisors and support staff, and 180 unionized employees. The unionized employees are paid an hourly rate specified in the collective agreement, whereas management and support staff are paid monthly salaries. The mill is divided into six operating departments: boom, sawmill, planer, packaging, shipping, and maintenance. The sawmill, boom, and packaging departments operate a morning shift starting at 6 a.m. and an afternoon shift starting at 2 p.m. Employees in these departments rotate shifts every two weeks. The planer and shipping departments operate only morning shifts. Maintenance employees work the night shift (starting at 10 p.m.).

Each department, except for packaging, has a supervisor on every work shift. The planer supervisor is responsible for the packaging department on the morning shift, and the sawmill supervisor is responsible for the packaging department on the afternoon shift. However, the packaging operation is housed in a separate building from the other departments, so supervisors seldom visit the packaging department. This is particularly true for the afternoon shift because the sawmill supervisor is farthest from the packaging building.

Packaging Quality

Ninety percent of Treetop's product is sold on the international market through Westboard Co., a large marketing agency. Westboard represents all forest products mills owned by Treetop's parent company as well as several other clients in the region. The market for building-grade lumber is very price competitive because there are numerous mills selling a relatively undifferentiated product. However, some differentiation does occur in product packaging and presentation. Buyers look closely at the packaging when deciding whether to buy from Treetop or another mill.

To encourage its clients to package their products better, Westboard sponsors a monthly package quality award. The marketing agency samples and rates its clients' packages daily, and the sawmill with the highest score at the end of the month is awarded a plaque. Package quality is a combination of how the lumber is piled (such as defects turned in), where the bands and dunnage are placed, how neatly the stencil and seal are applied, the stencil's accuracy, and how neatly and tightly the plastic wrap is attached.

Treetop Forest Products won Westboard's packaging quality award several times over the past five years and received high ratings in the months that it didn't win. However, the mill's ratings have started to decline over the past year or two, and several clients have complained about the appearance of the finished product. A few large customers switched to competitors' lumber, saying that the decision was based on the substandard appearance of Treetop's packaging when it arrived in their lumberyards.

Bottleneck in Packaging

The planing and sawmilling departments have significantly increased productivity over the past couple of years. The sawmill operation recently set a new productivity record for a single day. The planer operation has increased productivity to the point where last year it reduced operations to just one (rather than two) shifts per day. These productivity improvements are due to better operator training, fewer machine breakdowns, and better selection of raw logs. (Sawmill cuts from high-quality logs usually do not require planing work.)

Productivity levels in the boom, shipping, and maintenance departments have remained constant. However, the packaging department has recorded decreasing productivity over the past couple of years, with the result that a large backlog of finished product is typically stockpiled outside the packaging building. The morning shift of the packaging department is unable to keep up with the combined production of the sawmill and planer departments, so the unpackaged output is left for the afternoon shift. Unfortunately the afternoon shift packages even less product than the morning shift, so the backlog continues to build. The backlog adds to Treetop's inventory costs and increases the risk of damaged stock.

Treetop has added Saturday overtime shifts as well as extra hours before and after the regular shifts for the packaging department employees to process this backlog. Last month the packaging department employed 10 percent of the workforce but accounted for 85 percent of the overtime. This is frustrating to Treetop's management because time and motion studies recently confirmed that the packaging department is capable of processing all of the daily sawmill and planer production without overtime. Moreover, with employees earning one and a half or two times their regular pay on overtime, Treetop's cost competitiveness suffers.

Employees and supervisors at Treetop are aware that people in the packaging department tend to extend lunch by 10 minutes and coffee breaks by 5 minutes. They also typically leave work a few minutes before the end of shift. This abuse has worsened recently, particularly on the afternoon shift.

Employees who are temporarily assigned to the packaging department also seem to participate in this time loss pattern after a few days. Although they are punctual and productive in other departments, these temporary employees soon adopt the packaging crew's informal schedule when assigned to that department.

Discussion Questions

1. Based on your knowledge of team dynamics, explain why the packaging department is less productive than other teams at Treetop.

2. How should Treetop change the nonproductive norms that exist in the packaging group?

3. What structural and other changes would you recommend that may improve this situation in the long term?

Source: ©Copyright 1995 Steven L. McShane and David Lebeter. This case is based on actual events, but names and some characteristics have been changed to maintain anonymity.

Case Study 9.2 MOSH PITS OF CREATIVITY

 The Razr, Motorola's highly successful ultralight cell phone, was designed through a process that differed from the electronics company's traditional research and development center. Much of the critical work on the phone was done in an innovation lab where cross-functional teams of engineers, marketers, and others work together in funky open-space offices that foster information sharing. Mattel, Steelcase, Boeing, Wrigley, Procter & Gamble, and many other firms are also turning to cross-functional teams to creatively and efficiently design new products or solve perplexing problems. Some companies have also designed their workplace to improve informal group dynamics that support the creative process.

This *BusinessWeek* case study examines this trend toward collaborative cross-functional teamwork in product development. It describes the characteristics of these "mosh pits," including their separation from the normal corporate bureaucracy and how employees are rotated through these special centers for inspiration. Read the full text of this *BusinessWeek* article at www.mhhe.com/mcshane4e and prepare for the discussion questions below.

Discussion Questions

1. What elements of the team dynamics model are Motorola, Procter & Gamble, and other companies applying to make these product development teams successful?

2. Identify the potential team dynamics challenges these product development teams might face in the situations described in this case study.

3. How are these companies supporting informal groups, and how might these groups aid the creative process?

Source: J. Weber, "'Mosh Pits' of Creativity," *BusinessWeek*, 7 November 2005, 98.

Team Exercise 9.3 TEAM TOWER POWER

PURPOSE This exercise is designed to help you understand team roles, team development, and other issues in the development and maintenance of effective teams.

MATERIALS The instructor will provide enough Lego® pieces or similar materials for each team to complete the assigned task. All teams should have identical (or very similar) amounts and types of pieces. The instructor will need a measuring tape and stopwatch. Students may use writing materials during the design stage (Step 2). The instructor will distribute a Team Objectives Sheet and Tower Specifications Effectiveness Sheet to each team.

INSTRUCTIONS

1. The instructor will divide the class into teams. Depending on class size and space available, teams may have four to seven members, but all should be approximately equal size.

2. Each team is given 20 minutes to design a tower that uses only the materials provided, is freestanding, and provides an optimal return on investment. Team members may wish to draw their tower on paper or a flip chart to assist in the tower's design. Teams are free to practice building their towers during this stage. Preferably teams should be assigned to their own rooms so the designs can be created privately. During this stage each team will complete the Team Objectives Sheet distributed by the instructor. This sheet requires the Tower Specifications Effectiveness Sheet, also distributed by the instructor.

3. Each team will show the instructor that it has completed its Team Objectives Sheet. Then, with all teams in the same room, the instructor will announce the start of the construction phase. The time elapsed for construction will be closely monitored, and the instructor will occasionally call out time elapsed (particularly if there is no clock in the room).

4. Each team will notify the instructor as soon as it has completed its tower. The team will write down the time elapsed that the instructor has determined. It may be asked to help the instructor by counting the number of blocks used and height of the tower. This information is also written on the Team Objectives Sheet. Then the team calculates its profit.

5. After presenting the results, the class will discuss the team dynamics elements that contribute to team effectiveness. Team members will discuss their strategy, division of labor (team roles), expertise within the team, and other elements of team dynamics.

Source: Several published and online sources describe variations of this exercise, but there is no known origin of this activity.

Self-Assessment 9.4

TEAM ROLES PREFERENCES SCALE

PURPOSE This self-assessment is designed to help you identify your preferred roles in meetings and similar team activities.

INSTRUCTIONS Read each of the following statements and circle the response that you believe best reflects your position regarding each statement. Then use the scoring key in Appendix B to calculate your results for each team role. This exercise is completed alone so you can assess yourself honestly without concerns of social comparison. However, class discussion will focus on the roles that people assume in team settings. This scale assesses only a few team roles.

Team Roles Preferences Scale

Circle the number that best reflects your position regarding each of these statements	Does not describe me at all ▼	Does not describe me very well ▼	Describes me somewhat ▼	Describes me well ▼	Describes me very well ▼
1. I usually take responsibility for getting the team to agree on what the meeting should accomplish.	1	2	3	4	(5)
2. I tend to summarize to other team members what the team has accomplished so far.	1	2	3	4	(5)
3. I'm usually the person who helps other team members overcome their disagreements.	1	2	3	(4)	5
4. I try to ensure that everyone gets heard on issues.	1	2	3	(4)	5
5. I'm usually the person who helps the team determine how to organize the discussion.	1	2	3	4	(5)
6. I praise other team members for their ideas more than do others in the meetings.	1	(2)	3	4	5
7. People tend to rely on me to keep track of what has been said in meetings.	1	2	3	(4)	5
8. The team typically counts on me to prevent debates from getting out of hand.	1	2	(3)	4	5
9. I tend to say things that make the group feel optimistic about its accomplishments.	1	(2)	3	4	5
10. Team members usually count on me to give everyone a chance to speak.	1	(2)	3	4	5
11. In most meetings, I am less likely than others to criticize the ideas of teammates.	1	(2)	3	4	5
12. I actively help teammates to resolve their differences in meetings.	1	2	(3)	4	5
13. I actively encourage quiet team members to describe their ideas about each issue.	1	2	3	(4)	5
14. People tend to rely on me to clarify the purpose of the meeting.	1	2	2	4	(5)
15. I like to be the person who takes notes or minutes of the meeting.	1	2	(3)	4	5

Source: ©Copyright 2000 Steven L. McShane.

After reading this chapter, if you need additional information, see **www.mhhe.com/mcshane4e** for more in-depth interactivities that correspond with this material.

PricewaterhouseCoopers LLC (PwC) employs more than 200 training professionals in 70 offices across the United States. These professionals, along with many more consultants and academics who provide employee development services, routinely form virtual teams for new projects. "Virtual teaming is the norm for us," says Peter Nicolas, one of PwC's Learning Solutions manager in Florham Park, New Jersey.

PwC's training group supports these virtual teams by offering a variety of information technologies, including electronic calendars, shared databases, computer-based video meetings, virtual classrooms, and e-mail. But even the techno-savvy professionals in PwC's training group know that technology doesn't quite replace the unique ability of face-to-face interaction to bond people together. "I always try to do the kickoff meeting face-to-face," says Scott Patterson, one of PwC's Learning Solutions managers in Atlanta. "We also try to bring the group back together for major milestones in a project."

Peter Nicolas, a Learning Solutions manager for PricewaterhouseCoopers LLP, prepares for a virtual teaming meeting.

While PwC's learning and education department grapples with virtual teams across the United States, the accounting firm's transaction services group is finding ways to improve virtual teams whose members are scattered around the planet. Every 18 months the group brings together hundreds of employees for a dedicated team-building event. One such gathering was recently held at Disney's EPCOT World Showcase in Orlando. The 850 attendees (300 from outside the United States) were organized into 35 diverse teams and given a packet of background information about a fictitious client that required PwC's help. The teams spent one day visiting EPCOT's various pavilions to gather details before submitting their report on the client's acquisition opportunities as well as cultural issues that needed to be addressed.

PwC executives evaluated the 35 team reports, then invited the top 10 teams to join them for a private breakfast the next morning. After breakfast all PwC attendees watched the captains of the top 10 teams on stage explain their teams' analysis. The PwC executives then selected the top three team leaders, who were further interviewed on stage about the previous day's investigation. After watching a video of the previous day's events at EPCOT, PwC's Global Advisory Leader announced the winning team that had been hired by the fictitious client.

"We were overwhelmed with the results of this program," remarked Barbara Jean Cummins, the PwC manager who coordinated the team-building event with Disney Institute. "I've never seen borders come down so quickly, and everyone was completely engaged in the program."[1]

Developing High-Performance Teams

After reading this chapter you should be able to

1. Identify the characteristics of self-directed work teams (SDWTs).

2. Describe the four conditions in sociotechnical systems theory that support SDWTs.

3. Summarize three challenges to SDWTs.

4. Explain why organizations rely increasingly on virtual teams.

5. Describe the roles of communication systems, task structure, team size, and team composition in virtual team effectiveness.

6. Summarize the three foundations of trust in teams.

7. Identify five constraints on team decision making.

8. Describe five team structures that potentially improve creativity and decision making in team settings.

9. Discuss the potential benefits and limitations of brainstorming.

10. Outline the four types of team building.

PricewaterhouseCoopers is forging new directions in building high-performance virtual teams. This chapter extends our discussion of teams by focusing on high-performance teams, including self-directed work teams, virtual teams, effective decision making in teams, and team-building strategies. The first section introduces the features of self-directed work teams as well as the elements of sociotechnical systems theory, upon which these high-performance teams are based. Next we look at the increasing popularity of virtual teams and summarize current research about how to ensure that these virtual teams are effective. We also look at the important topic of trust in virtual teams and other groups. This chapter then focuses on effective decision making in teams, including challenges and strategies to minimize problems with effective team decision making. The last section of this chapter looks at various team-building strategies.

Learning Objectives

After reading this section you should be able to

1. **Identify the characteristics of self-directed work teams (SDWTs).**
2. **Describe the four conditions in sociotechnical systems theory that support SDWTs.**
3. **Summarize three challenges to SDWTs.**

Self-Directed Work Teams

Whole Foods Market isn't your typical grocery retailer. Yes, the company's products are more organic, but so is its approach to managing the business. Whereas some food chains still make most decisions at the top, Whole Foods hands over day-to-day responsibility to the teams in each store. "Whole Foods Market is organized into self-managing work teams," explains CEO John Mackey. Each store has about eight teams, such as the seafood team, prepared foods team, and cashier/front end team. Each team has authority to make decisions for its own part of the business, and the overall store works around its own profit-and-loss statement. "The [store] team is responsible for managing inventory, labor productivity, gross margins; and its members are responsible for many of the product placement decisions," explains Mackey.[2]

self-directed work teams (SDWTs)
Cross-functional work groups organized around work processes that complete an entire piece of work requiring several interdependent tasks, and that have substantial autonomy over the execution of those tasks.

Whole Foods Market and many other organizations have adopted a form of work structure that relies on **self-directed work teams (SDWTs).** Surveys estimate that approximately three-quarters of medium-sized and large organizations in the United States use SDWT structures for part of their operations.[3] SDWTs vary somewhat from one firm to the next, but they are generally defined by two distinctive features. First, they complete an entire piece of work requiring several interdependent tasks.[4] This high interdependence is important because the work clusters the team members together and minimizes their interdependence with employees outside the team. The result is a closely knit group that depends on each other to accomplish their individual tasks. For example, employees in the prepared foods team at a Whole Foods store would naturally work more closely with each other than with members of other teams.

Second, SDWTs have substantial autonomy over the execution of their tasks. In particular, these teams plan, organize, and control work activities with little or no direct involvement of a higher-status supervisor. They tend to control most work input, flow, and output, such as work directly with suppliers and customers. The team's autonomy extends to responsibility for correcting workflow problems as they occur.

With substantial autonomy and responsibility, SDWTs also receive plenty of team-level feedback and rewards. Whole Foods teams make decisions about incoming resources, including working with local suppliers. They also can rearrange the workplace as well as vote on permanently hiring new recruits.

You may have noticed from this description that members of SDWTs have enriched and enlarged jobs. The team's work includes all the tasks required to make an entire product or provide a service. The team is also mostly responsible for scheduling, coordinating, and planning these tasks.[5] Self-directed work teams were initially designed around production processes. However, they are also found in administrative and service activities (such as at Whole Foods), banking services, city government administration, and customer assistance teams in courier services.[6]

Sociotechnical Systems Theory and SDWTs

sociotechnical systems (STS) theory
A theory stating that effective work sites have joint optimization of their social and technological systems, and that teams should have sufficient autonomy to control key variances in the work process.

How do companies create successful self-directed work teams? To answer this question, we need to look at **sociotechnical systems (STS) theory,** which is the main source of current SDWT practices. STS theory was introduced during the 1940s at Britain's Tavistock Institute, where researchers had been studying the effects of technology on coal mining in the United Kingdom.[7]

The Tavistock researchers observed that the new coal mining technology (called the "long wall" method) led to lower, not higher, job performance. They analyzed the causes of this problem and established the idea that organizations need "joint optimization" between the social and technical systems of the work unit. In other words, they need to introduce technology in a way that creates the best structure for semi-autonomous work teams. Furthermore, the Tavistock group concluded that teams should be sufficiently autonomous so that they can control the main "variances" in the system. This means that the team must control the factors with the greatest impact on quality, quantity, and the cost of the product or service. From this overview of STS, we can identify four main conditions for high-performance SDWTs.[8]

Responsible for an Entire Work Process   STS theory suggests that self-directed teams work best when they are responsible for making an entire product, providing a service, or otherwise completing an entire work process. By making an entire product or service, the team is sufficiently independent that it can make adjustments without interfering, or having interference from, other work units. At the same time the primary work unit ensures that employees perform interdependent subtasks within their team so they have a sense of cohesiveness by working toward a common goal.[9]

Sufficient Autonomy   STS theory says that an SDWT must have sufficient autonomy to manage the work process. The team should be able to organize and coordinate work among its members to respond more quickly and effectively to its environment. This autonomy also motivates team members through feelings of empowerment.

Control Key Variances   STS theory says that high-performance SDWTs have control over "key variances." These variances represent the disturbances or interruptions in the work process that affect the quality or performance of the product or service. For instance, the mixture of ingredients would be a key variance for employees in food processing because the mixture is within the team's control and influences the quality of the final product. In contrast, self-directed teams have fewer advantages when the primary causes of good or poor performance are mainly due to technology, supplies, or other factors beyond the team's control.

joint optimization
A key requirement in sociotechnical systems theory that a balance must be struck between social and technical systems to maximize an operation's effectiveness.

Operate under Joint Optimization   Perhaps the most crucial feature of STS theory is **joint optimization**—the notion that the work process needs to balance the social and technical subsystems.[10] In particular, the technological system should be implemented in a way that encourages or facilitates team dynamics, job enrichment, and meaningful feedback. This idea of joint optimization was quite radical in the 1940s when many thought that technology dictated how employees should be organized. In many cases technology resulted in people working alone with little opportunity to directly coordinate their work or share knowledge and ideas. Sociotechnical systems theory, on the other hand, says that companies can and must introduce technology so that it supports a semi-autonomous, team-based structure.

Applying STS Theory and Self-Directed Work Teams

Numerous studies have found that with a few important caveats to consider, self-directed work teams make a difference. A decade ago Canon Inc. introduced self-directed teams at all 29 of its Japanese plants. The camera and copier company claims that a team of a half-dozen people can now produce as much as 30 people in the old assembly line system. One study found that car dealership service garages that organized employees into self-directed teams were significantly more profitable than service garages where employees worked without a team structure. Another reported that both short- and long-term measures of customer satisfaction increased after street cleaning employees in a German city were organized into SDWTs.[11] DaimlerChrysler improved productivity and quality at its Mexican operations by switching to SDWTs. As Connections 10.1 describes, the Chrysler group is now transforming its American plants to "smart manufacturing" with SDWTs.

STS theory provides some guidance for designing self-directed work teams, but it doesn't provide enough detail regarding the optimal alignment of the social and technical systems. Volvo's Uddevalla manufacturing plant in Sweden is an example.[12] Opened in 1988 as a model of sociotechnical design, the Uddevalla plant replaced the traditional assembly line with fixed workstations at which teams of approximately 20 employees assembled and installed components in an unfinished automobile chassis. The work structure created a strong team orientation, but productivity was among the lowest in the automobile industry. (Producing a car at Uddevalla took 50 hours versus 25 hours at a traditional Volvo plant and 13 hours at a Toyota plant.)

The Uddevalla plant was shut down in 1993 and reopened two years later. The plant still uses highly skilled teams, but they are organized around a more traditional assembly line process (similar to Toyota's production system). Some writers argue that organizational politics and poor market demand closed the Uddevalla experiment prematurely. However, Federal Signal recently had a similar experience in its truck assembly plant in the United States. It seems that both Volvo and Federal Signal failed to identify the best alignment of the social and technical subsystems.

Challenges to Self-Directed Work Teams

Along with determining the best combination of social and technical subsystems, corporate leaders need to recognize and overcome at least three potential barriers to self-directed work teams: cross-cultural issues, management resistance, and employee and labor union resistance.

Cross-Cultural Issues   SDWTs are more difficult to implement in high power distance cultures.[13] Employees in these cultures are more comfortable when supervisors give them directions, whereas low power distance employees value their involvement in decisions. One study reported that SDWTs may be more difficult to introduce in

Chrysler's Lean Self-Directed Work Teams

The "Big Three" automakers—General Motors, Ford, and Chrysler—are under intense pressure to improve productivity and quality. Chrysler CEO Tom La Sorda believes one of the key ingredients to the company's future is "smart manufacturing," which includes introducing lean manufacturing in plants operated by self-directed work teams (SDWTs).

SDWTs were introduced a decade ago at Chrysler's operations in Mexico, where management and employees were determined to make the team-based process successful. The plant in Saltillo, Mexico, for instance, organizes employees into teams of a dozen people responsible for a specific set of integrated tasks, including maintenance, quality control, safety, and productivity in that work area. Team members operate a workstation within their team for a few hours before rotating to another workstation. This mandatory rotation process increases skill flexibility, minimizes repetitive strain, and creates a sense of team ownership over the tasks within their mandate. Saltillo's productivity has increased by almost 30 percent since the team-based structure was introduced.

Now Chrysler is introducing SDWTs in its U.S. plants, including the assembly plants in Toledo, Ohio, and Belvidere, Illinois, where union members voted in favor of more flexible work arrangements. "The people within Belvidere say we should have done this a long time ago," says United Auto Workers union vice president Nate Gooden. "The boredom and everything they have (had) on the job—it's a different culture. You don't have to come to work every day and do the same job over and over again."

To assist the culture change, team leaders completed 40 hours of training to understand their new role as service leaders—serving the teams rather than vice versa. The physical workspace was also rearranged to create a more intimate team environment. Even the lockers were relocated near the teams' work area to maximize efficiency and create a sense of common team space. "Since the plant went to teams, [the assembly area] feels smaller," says Le Etta Bush, a team member at the Belvidere assembly plant.

The transformation to SDWTs has already had a noticeable effect. Scott Dahle, a supervisor on a traditional assembly line, discovered the change when he was asked to cover one day for Margo Barr, a team leader of one of Belvidere's new SDWTs. "The day he filled in for Margo, his pager

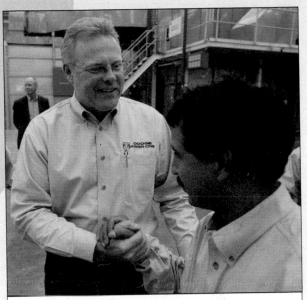

Chrysler CEO Tom La Sorda is pushing the automaker into an era of "smart manufacturing" that relies more on self-directed work teams (SDWTs). This photo shows La Sorda meeting employees at the company's plant in Saltillo, Mexico, which has already introduced SDWTs.

never went off, his phone never rang, and no one called him on his radio. He even checked the batteries to see if they were dead," recalls Belvidere plant manager Kurt Kavajecz. "This traditional first-line supervisor, who is used to putting out fires and reacting to crises, came into the new area and was amazed because the team members and the team leaders were running the area. They were taking care of business."

Sources: M. Connelly, "Chrysler Wants to Put Team Assembly in All Plants," *Automotive News*, 30 May 2005, p. 53; J.B. White, "LaSorda's Chrysler Challenge," *The Wall Street Journal*, 15 August 2005, p. B5; J. Leute, "Union, Management Work in Lockstep at Belvidere, Ill., Plant," *Janesville Gazette* (Illinois), 18 July 2005; J. Smith, "Building Cars, Building Teams," *Plant Engineering*, 1 December 2005; M. Connelly, "Chrysler Boosts Belvidere Flexibility," *Automotive News*, 13 February 2006, p. 44.

Mexico because employees in that country (which has a high power distance culture) expect managers to make decisions affecting their work. However, as Connections 10.1 described, Chrysler was able to introduce these teams at its Mexican operations almost a decade before they were introduced in the United States. One explanation may be that Chrysler's Mexican employees and managers were more motivated to improve productivity due to competitive threats from other low-wage countries. Also, Mexico has relatively high collectivism, so employees may feel more comfortable working in teams compared to their American counterparts. Overall, cultural values might be an impediment to SDWTs, but they are unlikely to completely prevent them in most countries.

Management Resistance

Poet Robert Frost once wrote, "The brain is a wonderful organ; it starts working the moment you get up in the morning and does not stop until you get into the office." Frost's humor highlights the fact that many organizations expect employees to park their brains at the door. Consistent with this view, studies report that supervisors and higher-level managers are often the main source of resistance to the transition to self-directed work teams. Their main worry is losing power when employees gain power through empowered teams. Some are concerned that their jobs will lose value, whereas others believe that they will not have any jobs at all.[14]

Self-directed teams operate best when supervisors shift from "hands-on" controllers to "hands-off" facilitators, but many supervisors have difficulty changing their style. This was one of the biggest stumbling blocks to self directed work teams at a TRW auto parts plant. Many supervisors kept slipping back into their command-and-control supervisory style. As one TRW employee explains, "One of the toughest things for some of them was to shift from being a boss to a coach, moving from saying, 'I know what's good for you' to 'How can I help you?'" Research suggests that supervisors are less likely to resist self-directed work teams when they have personally worked in a high-involvement workplace and receive considerable training in their new facilitation role.[15]

Employee and Labor Union Resistance

Employees sometimes oppose SDWTs because they require new skills or appear to require more work. Many feel uncomfortable as they explore their new roles, and they may be worried that they lack the

Learning to Lead Self-Directed Teams When Standard Motor Products (SMP) introduced self-directed work teams at its Edwardsville, Kansas, plant, supervisors had a tough challenge replacing their command-and-control management style with something closer to a mentor or facilitator. "It wasn't easy for managers who were raised in the top-down authority model," recalls Darrel Ray, the nationally recognized consultant who worked with the auto parts company during the transition. "It is far easier to be a tyrant than it is to be a psychologist or a teacher," explains distribution manager Don Wakefield. Steve Domann was one of the managers who had difficulty adjusting. "I thought about quitting when the changes were announced," says Domann, who now oversees plant work teams as a team developer. "Some of the old management team couldn't conform to the team, but I'm glad I did."[16]

skills to adapt to the new work requirements. For instance, professional surveyors at a Swedish company reported increased stress when their company introduced customer-focused self-directed teams.[17] Chrysler employees in Belvidere, Illinois, initially rejected the switch to self-directed work teams, possibly fearing increased workload due to job rotation and multiskilling requirements under the proposed flexible agreement.

Labor unions supported the early experiments in sociotechnical change in Europe and India, but some unions in other parts of the world have reservations about SDWTs.[18] One concern is that teams improve productivity at the price of higher stress levels among employees, which is sometimes true. Another worry is that SDWTs require more flexibility by reversing work rules and removing job categories that unions have negotiated over the years. Labor union leaders are therefore concerned that regaining these hard-fought union member rights will be a difficult battle.

In spite of these challenges, self-directed work teams offer enormous potential for organizations when they are implemented under the right conditions, as specified by sociotechnical systems theory. Meanwhile information technologies and knowledge work have enabled virtual teams to gain popularity. The next section examines this new breed of team, including strategies to create high-performance virtual teams.

After reading the next two sections you should be able to

4. **Explain why organizations rely increasingly on virtual teams.**
5. **Describe the roles of communication systems, task structure, team size, and team composition in virtual team effectiveness.**
6. **Summarize the three foundations of trust in teams.**

Virtual Teams

virtual teams
Teams whose members operate across space, time and organizational boundaries and who are linked through information technologies to achieve organizational goals.

As was described in the opening vignette to this chapter, PricewaterhouseCoopers relies on plenty of **virtual teams.** Virtual teams are teams whose members operate across space, time, and organizational boundaries and are linked through information technologies to achieve organizational tasks.[19] Virtual teams are similar to face-to-face teams in the sense that they consist of two or more people who interact and influence each other, are mutually accountable for achieving common goals associated with organizational objectives, and perceive themselves as a social entity within an organization. However, virtual teams differ from traditional teams in two ways: (1) they are not usually colocated (they do not work in the same physical area), and (2) due to their lack of colocation, members of virtual teams depend primarily on information technologies rather than face-to-face interaction to communicate and coordinate their work effort.

Virtual teams are one of the most significant developments in organizations over the past decade. One reason for their popularity is that the Internet, intranets, instant messaging, virtual whiteboards, and other products have made it easier to communicate with and coordinate people at a distance.[20] The shift from production-based to knowledge-based work has also made virtual teamwork feasible. Information technologies allow people to exchange knowledge work, such as software code, product development plans, and ideas for strategic decisions. In contrast, relying on virtual teams for production work, in which people develop physical objects, is less feasible.

Information technologies and knowledge-based work make virtual teams possible, but two other factors—globalization and knowledge management—make them increasingly necessary. As Chapter 1 described, companies are opening businesses overseas, forming tight alliances with companies located elsewhere, and serving customers who want global support. These global conditions require a correspondingly global response in the form of virtual teams that coordinate these operations. As one IBM manager stated, "IBM is a global company working in 170 countries in the world. Just that alone would dictate that we do work with people we've never met face-to-face and may never meet."[21]

Along with aiding global coordination, virtual teams support knowledge management by allowing and encouraging employees to share and use knowledge in distributed operations. This is one of the main drivers behind the popularity of virtual teams at PricewaterhouseCoopers. The global operations of PwC's transaction services group connects employees together because they need to share valuable information that resides throughout the organization.

Designing High-Performance Virtual Teams

As with all teams, high-performance virtual teams are influenced by the elements of the team effectiveness model in Chapter 9. Exhibit 10.1 outlines the key design issues for virtual teams that we discuss over the next couple of pages.

Virtual Team Environment   Reward systems, communication systems, organizational environment, organizational structure, and leadership influence the effectiveness of all teams, including virtual teams. Communication systems are particularly important because, unlike conventional teams, virtual teams cannot rely on face-to-face meetings whenever they wish. As we will learn in the next chapter, face-to-face communication transfers the highest volume and complexity of information and offers the timeliest feedback. In contrast, e-mail, telephone, and other information technologies fall far behind in their ability to exchange information. "Having a four- to five-hour discussion is hard to do by phone, especially where you need to read body language," says an executive at accounting giant PricewaterhouseCoopers. Even videoconferencing, which seems similar to face-to-face meetings, actually communicates much less than we realize.[22]

Exhibit 10.1   **Designing High-Performance Virtual Teams**

Team design element	Special virtual team requirements
Team environment	• Virtual teams need several communication channels available to offset lack of face-to-face communication.
Team tasks	• Virtual teams operate better with structured rather than complex and ambiguous tasks.
Team size and composition	• Virtual teams usually require smaller team size than conventional teams. • Virtual team members must have skills in communicating through information technology and be able to process multiple threads of conversation. • Virtual team members are more likely than conventional team members to require cross-cultural awareness and knowledge.
Team processes	• Virtual team development and cohesiveness require some face-to-face interaction, particularly when the team forms.

Invensys Employees Are Virtually There Invensys PLC, the British-based process and control engineering company, relies on information technologies to make the best use of its far-reaching talent, often organizing employees into virtual teams at a moment's notice. "Our development projects operate in a virtual mode and [gather] people from multiple sites based on project needs," explains Joe Ayers, a manager at Invensys's process simulation unit in Lake Forest, California. "It is common for projects to utilize developers from three different time zones in a 'follow the sun' development mode." To assist the virtual teams that routinely develop out of this global business structure, Invensys provides a variety of communication tools, such as desktop sharing tools, voice over IP telephony, instant messaging, and video conferencing.[23]

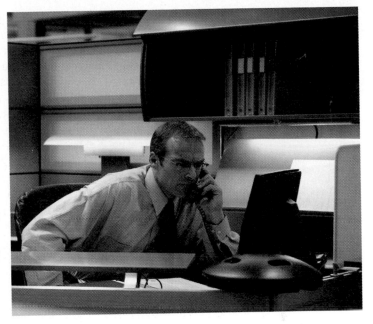

To support high-performance virtual teams, organizations need to provide a variety of communication media so that virtual team members have the freedom to creatively combine these media to match the task demands.[24] For instance, virtual team members might rely on e-mail to coordinate routine tasks but quickly switch to videoconferences and electronic whiteboards when emergencies arise. The lack of face-to-face communication isn't all bad news for virtual teams. Working through e-mail or intranet systems can minimize status differences. Team members whose first language is not English may be overwhelmed into silence in face-to-face meetings but have time to craft persuasive messages in cyberspace.

Virtual Team Tasks Experts suggest that virtual teams operate best with structured tasks requiring only moderate levels of task interdependence.[25] Consider the task structure of client service engineers at BakBone Software. Each day BakBone engineers in San Diego pick up customer support problems passed on from colleagues in Maryland and England. At the end of the workday they pass some of these projects on to BakBone co-workers in Tokyo. The assignments sent on to Tokyo must be stated clearly because overseas co-workers can't ask questions in the middle of San Diego's night.

BakBone's virtual team works well with these structured tasks, whereas the lack of colocation makes it difficult for them to consult and communicate about complex and ambiguous tasks. "You don't have the time for open-ended conversation [in a virtual team]," admits BakBone engineer Roger Rodriguez. "You can't informally brainstorm with someone."[26] Generally, complex and ambiguous tasks should be assigned to colocated teams. Similarly, virtual teams should work on tasks requiring moderate levels of interdependence among team members. High levels of interdependence require more intense communication, so they are better assigned to colocated teams.

Virtual Team Size and Composition   The problems of team size described in the previous chapter are amplified in virtual teams due to the limits of information technologies. In other words, virtual teams need to be smaller than comparable co-located teams to develop as quickly and coordinate as effectively. The team composition issues covered in Chapter 9 also apply to virtual teams, with the added requirement that virtual team members need additional communication skills. They need to be sensitive to emotional reactions to e-mails and listen to more subtle nonverbal signals in teleconferences. "On a call, I use subtle listening," explains Procter & Gamble executive Karim Ladak, whose virtual team members live in six cities around the world. "I listen for a quiver or a pause. And even then I know that I can very quickly miss something."[27]

Virtual teams often span cultures, so team members must also be aware of cross-cultural issues. For example, one study reported that virtual teams of American and Belgian college students were easily confused by differing conventions in the use of commas versus decimal points in numbers (such as $2.953 million versus $2,953 million). They also experienced cultural differences in socializing. The American students were willing to engage in social communication after they completed the assignment, whereas the Belgian students were more interested in developing a relationship with their partners before beginning work on the project.[28]

Team Processes   Team development and cohesiveness are particular concerns for virtual teams because they lack the face-to-face interaction that supports these processes. For example, one recent university study found that face-to-face teams communicate better than virtual teams during the early stages of a project; only after gaining experience did virtual teams share information as openly as face-to face teams. Other studies have reported that employees who work at a distance (such as through telecommuting) from other team members tend to feel less connected with their teams.[29]

Some companies try to ensure that virtual team members have good skills for communicating across distances. Others attempt to create virtual social events. For example, Grant Marshall, Australian country manager for California-based Agilent Technologies, strengthens the bonding process with his virtual team by scheduling a virtual "coffee pot chat" meeting once each month. "All the virtual team [members] call in via a conference line," explains Marshall, whose team members live throughout Asia. "There is no specific preplanned business agenda—the objective is to discuss general activities of what we have been doing." The casual meeting lasts 15 minutes to half an hour and includes such topics as "personal accomplishments, sporting activities, films, holidays, etc.—the type of discussion that you might have around the coffee station."[30]

Another solution, ironically, is to have virtual team members meet face-to-face once in a while. This is what leaders at PricewaterhouseCoopers discovered long ago. As the opening vignette described, PwC virtual teams in the training and development unit meet every few months, whereas global teams in PwC's transaction services group rendezvous every 18 months.

Team Trust

Any relationship—including the relationship among virtual team members—depends on a certain degree of trust between the parties.[31] **Trust** is a psychological state comprising the intention to accept vulnerability based on positive expectations of the intent or behavior of another person. A high level of trust occurs when others affect you in situations where you are at risk, but you believe they will not harm you.

trust
A psychological state comprising the intention to accept vulnerability based on positive expectations of the intent or behavior of another person.

Exhibit 10.2

Three Foundations of Trust in Teams

	Type of trust	Description
High — Identification-based trust		• Based on common mental models and values. • Increases with person's social identity with team.
Potential level of trust — Knowledge-based trust		• Based on predictability and competence. • Fairly robust.
Low — Calculus-based trust		• Based on deterrence. • Fragile and limited potential because dependent on punishment.

Trust has been discussed as both beliefs and conscious feelings about the relationship and other party. In other words, a person both logically evaluates the situation as trustworthy and feels that it is trustworthy.[32] Trust can also be understood in terms of the foundation of that trust. From this perspective, people trust others based on three foundations: calculus, knowledge, and identification (see Exhibit 10.2):

- *Calculus-based trust.* This minimal level of trust refers to an expected consistency of behavior based on deterrence. Each party believes that the other will deliver on its promises because punishments will be administered if they fail.[33] For example, most employees have at least calculus-based trust because co-workers could get fired if they attempt to undermine another employee's work effort.

- *Knowledge-based trust.* Knowledge-based trust is grounded on the other party's predictability. The more we understand others and can predict what they will do in the future, the more we trust them, up to a moderate level. For instance, employees are more willing to trust leaders who "walk the talk" because their actions are aligned with their words. Even if we don't agree with the leaders, this consistency generates some level of trust. Knowledge-based trust also relates to confidence in the other person's ability or competence. People trust others based on their known or perceived expertise, such as when they trust a physician.[34]

- *Identification-based trust.* This third foundation of trust is a mutual understanding and emotional bond between the parties. This identification occurs when one party thinks like, feels like, and responds like the other party. High-performance teams exhibit this level of trust because they share the same values and mental models. Identification-based trust is connected to the concept of social identity; the more you define yourself in terms of membership in the team, the more trust you have in that team.[35]

These three foundations of trust are arranged in a hierarchy. Calculus-based trust offers the lowest potential trust and is easily broken by a violation of expectations. Generally calculus-based trust alone cannot sustain a team's relationship because it relies on deterrence. Relationships don't become strong when based only on the threat of punishment if one party fails to deliver its promises. Knowledge-based trust offers a higher potential level of trust and is more stable because it develops over time. Suppose that another member of your virtual team submitted documentation to you on schedule in the past, but it arrived late this time. Knowledge-based trust might be dented, but not broken, in this incident. Through knowledge-based trust, you "know" that the late delivery is probably an exception because it deviates from the co-worker's past actions.

Identification-based trust is potentially the strongest and most robust of all three. The individual's self-image (social identity) is based partly on membership in the team, and he or she believes the team's values highly overlap; so any transgressions by other team members are quickly forgiven. People are more reluctant to acknowledge a violation of this high-level trust because it strikes at the heart of their self-image.

Individual Differences in Trust

Along with these three foundations of trust, the level of trust depends on a person's general *propensity to trust*.[36] Some people are inherently more willing than others to trust in a given situation. When joining a new work team, you might initially have very high trust in your new teammates, whereas another new team member might only feel a moderate level of trust. This difference is due to each individual's personality, values, and socialization experiences. Our willingness to trust others also varies with the emotions experienced at the moment. In particular, we trust people more when experiencing pleasant emotions than when angry, even if those emotions aren't connected with the other person.

Dynamics of Trust in Teams

A common misconception is that team members build trust from a low level when they first join the team. In truth, people typically join a virtual or conventional team with a moderate or high level—not a low level—of trust in their new co-workers. The main explanation for the initially high trust (called *swift trust*) in organizational settings is that people usually believe their teammates are reasonably competent (knowledge-based trust), and they tend to develop some degree of social identity with the team (identification-based trust). Even when working with strangers, most of us display some level of trust, if only because this supports our self-impression of being a nice person.[37]

However, trust is fragile in new relationships because it is based on assumptions rather than experience. Consequently, recent studies of virtual teams report that trust tends to decrease rather than increase over time. In other words, new team members experience trust violations, which pushes their trust to a lower level. Employees who join the team with identification-based trust tend to drop back to knowledge-based or perhaps calculus-based trust. Declining trust is particularly challenging in virtual teams because research identifies communication among team members as an important condition for sustaining trust. Equally important, employees become less forgiving and less cooperative toward others as their level of trust decreases, which undermines team and organizational effectiveness.[38]

Learning Objectives

After reading the next two sections you should be able to

7. Identify five constraints on team decision making.
8. Describe five team structures that potentially improve creativity and decision making in team settings.
9. Discuss the potential benefits and limitations of brainstorming.
10. Outline the four types of team building.

Team Decision Making

Self-directed work teams, virtual teams, and practically all other groups are involved to some degree in making decisions. Under certain conditions teams are more effective than individuals at identifying problems, choosing alternatives, and evaluating their decisions. To leverage these benefits, however, we first need to understand the constraints on effective team decision making. Then we look at specific team structures that try to overcome these constraints.

Constraints on Team Decision Making

Anyone who has spent enough time in a workplace can list several ways in which teams stumble in decision making. The five most common problems are time constraints, evaluation apprehension, pressure to conform, groupthink, and group polarization.

Time Constraints   There's a saying that "committees keep minutes and waste hours." This reflects the fact that teams take longer than individuals to make decisions.[39] Unlike individuals, teams require extra time to organize, coordinate, and socialize. The larger the group, the more time required to make a decision. Team members need time to learn about each other and build rapport. They need to manage an imperfect communication process so that there is sufficient understanding of each other's ideas. They also need to coordinate roles and rules of order within the decision process.

Another time-related constraint found in most team structures is that only one person can speak at a time.[40] This problem, known as **production blocking,** undermines idea generation in several ways. First, team members need to listen to the conversation to find an opportune time to speak up, and this monitoring makes it difficult for them to concentrate on their own ideas. Second, ideas are fleeting, so the longer they wait to speak up, the more likely these flickering ideas will die out. Third, team members might remember their fleeting thoughts by concentrating on them, but this causes them to pay less attention to the conversation. By ignoring what others are saying, team members miss other potentially good ideas as well as the opportunity to convey their ideas to others in the group.

production blocking
A time constraint in team decision making due to the procedural requirement that only one person may speak at a time.

Evaluation Apprehension   Individuals are reluctant to mention ideas that seem silly because they believe (often correctly) that other team members are silently evaluating them.[41] This **evaluation apprehension** is based on the individual's desire to create a favorable self-presentation and need to protect self-esteem. It is most common in meetings attended by people with different levels of status or expertise, or when members formally evaluate each other's performance throughout the year (as in 360-degree feedback). Creative ideas often sound bizarre or illogical when presented, so evaluation apprehension tends to discourage employees from mentioning them in front of co-workers.

evaluation apprehension
When individuals are reluctant to mention ideas that seem silly because they believe (often correctly) that other team members are silently evaluating them.

Pressure to Conform   Recall from the previous chapter that cohesiveness leads individual members to conform to the team's norms. This control keeps the group organized around common goals, but it may also cause team members to suppress their dissenting opinions, particularly when a strong team norm is related to the issue. When someone does state a point of view that violates the majority opinion, other members might punish the violator or try to persuade him or her that the opinion is incorrect. Conformity can also be subtle. To some extent, we depend on the opinions that others hold to validate our own views. If co-workers don't agree with us, then we begin to question our own opinions even without overt peer pressure.

Groupthink   One team decision-making problem that most people have heard about is **groupthink**—the tendency of highly cohesive groups to value consensus at the price of decision quality.[42] Groupthink goes beyond the problem of conformity by focusing on how decisions go awry when team members try to maintain harmony. This desire for harmony exists as a group norm and is most apparent when team members have a strong social identity with the group. Along with a desire for harmony, groupthink supposedly occurs when the team is isolated from outsiders, the team leader is opinionated (rather than impartial), the team is under stress due to an external threat, the team has experienced recent failures or other decision-making problems, and the team lacks clear guidance from corporate policies or procedures.

Although the word *groupthink* is now part of everyday language, the concept is quickly losing favor among OB experts. The main problem is that groupthink includes the complex cluster of team characteristics. Recent studies have found that some of the groupthink characteristics just mentioned actually improve the team decision-making process in some situations.[43] However, a few elements of this concept do create problems in team decision making, so we need to be aware of them. One of these is team confidence. Studies consistently report that highly confident teams are less attentive in decision making than moderately confident teams. As a consequence, overly confident executive groups make sloppy decisions because they are complacent and have a false sense of invulnerability.[44]

Group Polarization   **Group polarization** refers to the tendency of teams to make more extreme decisions than individuals working alone.[45] Suppose a group of people meets to decide the future of a new product. Individual team members might come to the meeting with various degrees of support or opposition to the product's future. Yet by the end of the meeting, chances are that the team will agree on a more extreme solution than the average person had when the meeting began.

There are three reasons why group polarization occurs (see Exhibit 10.3). First, team members become comfortable with more extreme positions when they realize that co-workers also generally support the same position. Second, persuasive arguments favoring the dominant position convince doubtful members and help form a consensus around the extreme option. Finally, individuals feel less personally responsible for the decision consequences because the decision is made by the team. Social

groupthink
The tendency of highly cohesive groups to value consensus at the price of decision quality.

group polarization
The tendency of teams to make more extreme decisions than individuals working alone.

Exhibit 10.3
The Group Polarization Process

support, persuasion, and shifting responsibility explain why teams make extreme decisions, but they also make *riskier* decisions due to the natural tendency to take higher risks when facing certain losses. This higher risk preference is caused by the prospect theory effect described in Chapter 8—people try to avoid losses because they are more painful than the equivalent gain.[46]

Team Structures to Improve Creativity and Decision Making

The constraints on team decision making are potentially serious, but several solutions also emerge from these bad-news studies. Team members need to be confident in their decision making, but not so confident that they collectively feel invulnerable. This calls for team norms that encourage critical thinking as well as team membership that maintains sufficient diversity. Team leaders and other powerful members can sway the rest of the group, so checks and balances need to be in place to avoid the adverse effects of this power. Another practice is to maintain an optimal team size. The group should be large enough that members possess the collective knowledge to resolve the problem, yet small enough that the team doesn't consume too much time or restrict individual input.

Team structures also help to minimize the problems described over the previous few pages. Five team structures potentially improve creativity and decision making in team settings: constructive conflict, brainstorming, electronic brainstorming, Delphi method, and nominal group technique.

Constructive Conflict

constructive conflict
Occurs when team members debate their different perceptions about an issue in a way that keeps the conflict focused on the task rather than people.

Constructive Conflict Executives at Corning Inc. rely on several strategies to strengthen team decision making and creativity, but one of their favorites is to assign promising ideas to two-person teams, who spend up to four months analyzing the feasibility of their assigned idea. The unique feature about this process is that the team is deliberately designed so that one person is from marketing, while the other has technical expertise. This oil-and-water combination sometimes ruffles feathers, but it seems to generate better team decision making. "We find great constructive conflict this way," says Deborah Mills, who leads Corning's early-stage marketing team.[47]

Constructive conflict refers to conflict in which team members debate their different perceptions about an issue in a way that keeps the conflict focused on the task rather than people. This conflict is called "constructive" because participants pay attention to facts and logic and avoid statements that generate emotional conflict. The main advantage of this debate is that it presents different points of view, which encourages everyone to reexamine their assumptions and logic.

One problem with constructive conflict is that it is difficult to apply; healthy debate can slide into personal attacks. Also, the effect of constructive conflict on team decision making is inconsistent. Some research indicates that debate—even criticism—can be good for team decision making, whereas others say that all forms of conflict can be detrimental to teams. Constructive conflict will be discussed in more detail in Chapter 13, which also identifies specific strategies to minimize the emotional effects of conflict while maintaining a constructive debate.[48]

Brainstorming

brainstorming
A free-wheeling, face-to-face meeting where team members aren't allowed to criticize, but are encouraged to speak freely, generate as many ideas as possible, and build on the ideas of others.

Brainstorming In the 1950s, advertising executive Alex Osborn wanted to find a better way for teams to generate creative ideas.[49] Osborn's solution, called **brainstorming**, requires team members to abide by four rules. Osborn believed that these rules encourage divergent thinking while minimizing evaluation apprehension and other team dynamics problems:

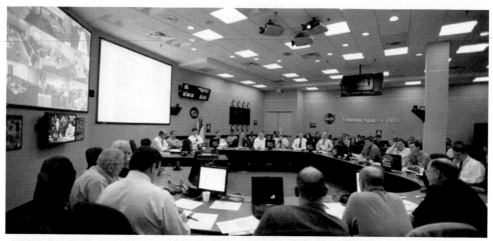

NASA's Constructive Conflict Room   The ill-fated flight of the space shuttle *Columbia* was a wake-up call for how NASA's mission management team makes decisions. The *Columbia* accident investigation team concluded that concerns raised by engineers were either deflected or watered down because the mission management team appeared to be "immersed in a culture of invincibility" and hierarchical authority discouraged constructive debate. If top decision makers had more fully considered the extent of damage during takeoff, they might have been able to save *Columbia's* seven crew members. To foster more open communications and constructive debate, the mission management team's assigned seating rectangular table has been replaced by a C-shaped arrangement where people sit wherever they want (shown in photo). None of the 24 members stands out above the others in the new setup. Around the walls of the room are pearls of wisdom reminding everyone of the pitfalls of team decision making. "People in groups tend to agree on courses of action which, as individuals, they know are stupid," warns one poster.[50]

- *Speak freely.* Brainstorming welcomes wild and wacky ideas because these become the seeds of divergent thinking in the creative process. Crazy suggestions are sometimes crazy only because they break out of the mold set by existing mental models.

- *Don't criticize.* Team members are more likely to contribute wild ideas if no one tries to mock or criticize them. Thus a distinctive rule in brainstorming is that no one is allowed to criticize any ideas that are presented.

- *Provide as many ideas as possible.* Brainstorming is based on the idea that quantity breeds quality. In other words, teams generate better ideas when they generate many ideas. This relates to the belief that divergent thinking occurs after traditional ideas have been exhausted. Therefore the group should think of as many possible solutions as it can and go well beyond the traditional solutions to a problem.

- *Build on the ideas of others.* Team members are encouraged to "piggyback" or "hitchhike"—that is, combine and improve on the ideas already presented. Building on existing ideas encourages the synergy of employee involvement that was mentioned in Chapter 8.

Brainstorming is a well-known team structure for encouraging creative ideas. Yet for several years researchers concluded that this practice is ineffective. Lab studies found that brainstorming groups generate fewer ideas, largely because production blocking and evaluation apprehension still interfere with team dynamics. However, these conclusions contrast with more recent real-world evidence that highly creative firms such as IDEO, the Silicon Valley product design firm, thrive on brainstorming. "Brainstorming is the idea engine of IDEO's culture," says IDEO general manager Tom Kelley. "The more productive the group, the more it brainstorms regularly and effectively."[51]

There are a few explanations why the lab studies differ from real-world evidence.[52] First, the lab studies measured the number of ideas generated, whereas brainstorming seems to provide more creative ideas—which is the main reason why companies use brainstorming. Evaluation apprehension may be a problem for students brainstorming in lab experiments, but it is less of a problem in high-performing teams that trust each other and embrace a learning orientation culture. The lab studies also overlooked the fact that brainstorming participants interact and participate directly, thereby increasing decision acceptance and team cohesiveness.

Brainstorming sessions also provide valuable nonverbal communication that spreads enthusiasm, which in turn provides a more creative climate. Clients are sometimes involved in brainstorming sessions, so these positive emotions may produce higher customer satisfaction than if people are working alone on a product. Overall, although brainstorming might not always be the best team structure, it seems to be more valuable than some of the earlier research studies indicated.

electronic brainstorming
Using special computer software, participants share ideas while minimizing the team dynamics problems inherent in traditional brainstorming sessions.

Electronic Brainstorming   **Electronic brainstorming** tries to minimize many of the problems described above with face-to-face brainstorming by having people generate and share ideas through computers. A facilitator begins the process by posting a question. Participants then enter their answers or ideas on their computer terminal. Soon after, everyone's ideas are posted anonymously and randomly on the computer screens or at the front of the room. Participants eventually vote electronically on the ideas presented. Face to face discussion usually follows the electronic brainstorming process.

Research indicates that electronic brainstorming generates more ideas than traditional brainstorming and more creative ideas than traditionally interacting teams. Participants also tend to be more satisfied, motivated, and confident in the decision-making exercise than in other team structures.[53] One reason for these favorable outcomes is that electronic brainstorming significantly reduces production blocking. Participants are able to document their ideas as soon as they pop into their heads, rather than wait their turn to communicate.[54] The process also supports creative synergy because participants can easily develop new ideas from those generated by other people. Electronic brainstorming also minimizes the problem of evaluation apprehension because ideas are posted anonymously.

Despite these numerous advantages, electronic brainstorming is not widely used by corporate leaders. One possible reason is that it might be too structured and technology-bound for some executives. Furthermore, some decision makers may feel threatened by the honesty of statements generated through this process and by their limited ability to control the discussion. A third explanation is that electronic brainstorming may work best for certain types of decisions, but not for others. For example, electronic brainstorming may be less effective than face-to-face meetings where effective decision making is less important than social bonding and emotional interaction.[55] Overall, electronic brainstorming can significantly improve decision making under the right conditions, but more research is required to identify those conditions.

Delphi method
A structured team decision-making process of systematically pooling the collective knowledge of experts on a particular subject to make decisions, predict the future, or identify opposing views.

Delphi Method   The **Delphi method** was developed by the RAND think tank in the 1950s and has regained attention over the past decade. Delphi systematically pools the collective knowledge of experts on a particular subject to make decisions, predict the future, identify opposing views (called *dissensus*), or identify multiple causes of events.[56] One recent example is a Delphi analysis of the challenges facing agriculture in Finland. Another developed and prioritized a list of indicators that people use to evaluate ecotourism in Taiwan. A third study of 50 experts identified a range of causes of obesity in Australia, then in a second round rank ordered the importance of each cause, along with an explanation of their rankings. The results revealed a dissensus of opinion about why Australians are gaining weight.[57]

There are a few variations, but most Delphi groups have the following features. They do not meet face-to-face; in fact, participants are often located in different parts of the world and may not know each other's identity. As with electronic brainstorming, Delphi participants do not know who "owns" the ideas submitted. Typically Delphi group members submit possible solutions or comments regarding an issue to the central convener, although computer technology is turning this stage into an automatic compilation process. The compiled results are returned to the panel for a second round of comments. This process may be repeated a few more times until consensus or dissensus emerges.

nominal group technique
A structured team decision-making process whereby team members independently write down ideas, describe and clarify them to the group, and then independently rank or vote on them.

Nominal Group Technique   The **nominal group technique** is a variation of traditional brainstorming that tries to combine individual efficiencies with team dynamics.[58] The method is called nominal because participants form a group in name only during two stages of decision making. This process, shown in Exhibit 10.4, first involves the individual, then the group, and finally the individual again. After the problem is described, team members silently and independently write down as many solutions as they can. During the group stage, participants describe their solutions to the other team members, usually in a round-robin format. As with brainstorming, there is no criticism or debate, although members are encouraged to ask for clarification of the ideas presented. In the final stage, participants silently and independently rank order or vote on each proposed solution.

Nominal group technique tends to generate more and better-quality ideas compared with traditionally interacting and possibly brainstorming groups.[59] Due to its high degree of structure, nominal group technique usually maintains a high task orientation and relatively low potential for conflict within the team. However, team cohesiveness is generally lower in nominal decisions because the structure minimizes social interaction. Production blocking and evaluation apprehension still occur to some extent.

Exhibit 10.4   **Nominal Group Technique**

Team Building

HellermanTyton's 60 senior marketing executives recently gathered in what appeared to be the middle of a South American jungle. In reality the executives at the global maker of wire and cable products were participating in a team-building exercise located in a private wildlife reserve in Naples, Florida, complete with giraffes, leopards, chimpanzees, and alligators. "You would never think we were still in Naples, but we were," says Terry Tuttle, HellermannTyton's vice president of marketing. The safari-themed program tested the managers' teamwork, communication, and leadership skills in a realistic setting. One activity even put participants up close with a live Florida alligator. "Although many were skeptical at first, you could see the teams form and build with each exercise," says Tuttle. "By the end, everyone was pumped up. We established camaraderie as a group that is essential to getting business goals accomplished throughout the year."[60]

The executives at HellermannTyton rejuvenated team dynamics more quickly through **team building**—formal activities intended to improve the development and functioning of a work team.[61] Some team-building activities also reshape team norms

team building
Any formal activity intended to improve the development and functioning of a work team.

Volunteering Builds Better Teams When E.ON UK, the United Kingdom's largest integrated energy company, recently formed a social and corporate affairs team, it didn't rely on firewalking, camping in the woods, or the other usual forms of team building. Instead team members spent time creating pathways, tree guards, and fencing in parks operated by the National Trust. "We wanted to give something back to the local community, and as we were a new team we also wanted to bond," says team member Suzanne Doxey. "When we got back to the office we were more relaxed and had better relationships with each other." Community volunteering has become the latest trend in team building. Lockheed Martin employees, including the team shown in this photo helping with the New Orleans clean up following hurricune Katrina, have logged more than 2 million hours over the past three years, volunteering their services for environmental and community improvement projects while improving interpersonal relationships back at work. PricewaterhouseCoopers is another company that sees the dual benefits of volunteering. "It's a great opportunity for people to get to know each other in an environment where they're all doing exactly the same task so there's no hierarchy," says an executive at the global accounting firm. "It really does help people to understand each other and build teams."[62]

and strengthen cohesiveness. Team building is sometimes applied to newly established teams because team members are at the earliest stages of team development. However, it is more common among existing teams, such as at HellermannTyton, where employees need to reestablish camaraderie or where the team has regressed to earlier stages of team development. Team building is therefore most appropriate when the team experiences high membership turnover or members have lost focus on their respective roles and team objectives.

Types of Team Building

There are four main types of team building: goal setting, role definition, interpersonal processes, and problem solving.[63]

- *Goal setting.* Some team-building interventions clarify the team's performance goals, increase the team's motivation to accomplish these goals, and establish a mechanism for systematic feedback on the team's goal performance. This is very similar to individual goal setting described in Chapter 5, except that the goals are applied to teams.

- *Role definition.* Clarifying role definitions is often associated with goal-setting team building. Role definition team building involves clarifying and reconstructing members' perceptions of their roles as well as the role expectations they have of other team members. Various interventions may be applied, ranging from open discussion to structured analysis of the work process. Role definition encompasses the emerging concept of *team mental models.* Recall from Chapter 3 that mental models are internal representations of the external world. Research studies indicate that team processes and performance depend on how well teammates share common mental models about how they should work together.[64] Team-building activities help team members clarify and form a more unified perspective of their team mental models.

- *Interpersonal processes.* This category of team building covers a broad territory. Conflict management fits under this heading, both as a symptom to identify the team's underlying weaknesses and as an ongoing interpersonal process that team members learn to continuously manage constructively. Early team-building interventions relied on direct confrontation sessions to give the sources of conflict an airing. This can work with professional facilitation, but experts warn that open dialogue is not always the most effective way to solve team conflicts.[65] Another interpersonal process is building (or rebuilding) trust among team members. Popular interventions such as wilderness team activities, paintball wars, and obstacle course challenges are typically offered to build trust. "If two colleagues hold the rope for you while you're climbing 10 meters up, that is truly team-building," explains Jan Antwerpes, a partner in a German communications consulting firm.[66]

- *Problem solving.* This type of team building focuses on decision making, including the issues mentioned earlier in this chapter and the decision-making process described in Chapter 8. To improve their problem-solving skills, some teams participate in simulation games that require team decisions in hypothetical situations. PwC's adventure at Disney's EPCOT Center, which was described at the beginning of this chapter, is one such example of team building that improves problem-solving skills among team members.

Is Team Building Effective?

Are team-building interventions effective? Is the money well spent? So far the answer is an equivocal "maybe." Studies suggest that some team-building activities are successful, but just as many fail to build high-performance teams.[67] One problem is that corporate leaders assume team-building activities are general solutions to general team problems. No one bothers to diagnose the team's specific needs (such as problem solving or interpersonal processes) because the team-building intervention is assumed to be a broad-brush solution. A better approach is to begin with a sound diagnosis of the team's health, then select team-building interventions that address weaknesses.[68]

Another problem is that corporate leaders tend to view team building as a one-shot medical inoculation that every team should receive when it is formed. In truth, team building is an ongoing process, not a three-day jump start. Some experts suggest, for example, that wilderness experiences often fail because they rarely include follow-up consultation to ensure that team learning is transferred back to the workplace.[69]

Finally, we must remember that team building occurs on the job, not just on an obstacle course or in a national park. Organizations should encourage team members to reflect on their work experiences and to experiment with just-in-time learning for team development. This dialogue requires open communication, so employees can clarify expectations, coordinate work activities, and build common mental models of working together. The next chapter looks at the dynamics of communicating in teams and organizations.

Chapter Summary

Self-directed work teams (SDWTs) complete an entire piece of work requiring several interdependent tasks and have substantial autonomy over the execution of these tasks. Sociotechnical systems (STS) theory identifies four main conditions for high-performance SDWTs. SDWTs must be responsible for an entire work process have sufficient autonomy, have control over key variances, and operate under joint optimization. STS theory has been widely supported since its origins in the 1950s. However, it is not very helpful at identifying the optimal alignment of the social and technical system. SDWTs also face cross-cultural issues, management resistance, and labor union and employee resistance.

Virtual teams are teams whose members operate across space, time, and organizational boundaries and are linked through information technologies to achieve organizational tasks. Unlike conventional teams, virtual team members are not colocated, so they are more dependent on information technologies rather than face-to-face interaction. Virtual teams are becoming more popular because information technology and knowledge-based work makes it easier to collaborate from a distance. Virtual teams are becoming increasingly necessary because they represent a natural part of the knowledge management process. Moreover, as companies globalize, they must rely more on virtual teams than colocated teams to coordinate operations at distant sites.

Several elements in the team effectiveness model stand out as important issues for virtual teams. High-performance virtual teams require a variety of communication media, and virtual team members need to creatively combine these media to match the task demands. Virtual teams operate better with structured rather than complex and ambiguous tasks. They usually cannot maintain as large a team as is possible in conventional teams. Members of virtual teams require special skills in communication systems and should be aware of cross-cultural issues. Virtual team members should also meet face-to-face, particularly when the team forms, to assist team development and cohesiveness.

Trust is important in team dynamics, particularly in virtual teams. Trust is a psychological state comprising the intention to accept vulnerability based on positive expectations of the intent or behavior of another person. The minimal level of trust is calculus-based trust, which is based on deterrence. Teams cannot survive with this level of trust. Knowledge-based trust is a higher level of trust and is grounded on the other party's predictability. The highest level of trust, called identification-based trust, is based on mutual understanding and emotional bond between the parties. Most employees join a team with a fairly high level of trust, which tends to decline over time.

Team decisions are impeded by time constraints, evaluation apprehension, conformity to peer pressure, groupthink, and group polarization. Production blocking —where only one person typically speaks at a time—is a form of time constraint on teams. Evaluation apprehension occurs when employees believe that others are silently evaluating them, so they avoid stating seemingly silly ideas. Conformity keeps team members aligned with team goals, but it also tends to suppress dissenting opinions. Groupthink is the tendency of highly cohesive groups to value consensus at the price of decision quality. Group polarization refers to the tendency of teams to make more extreme decisions than individuals working alone.

To minimize decision-making problems, teams should be moderately (not highly) confident, ensure that the team leader does not dominate, maintain an optimal team size, and ensure that team norms support critical thinking. Five team structures that potentially improve team decision making are constructive conflict, brainstorming, electronic brainstorming, the Delphi method, and the nominal group technique. Constructive conflict occurs when team members debate their different perceptions about an issue in a way that keeps the conflict focused on the task rather than people. Brainstorming requires team members to speak freely, avoid criticism, provide as many ideas as possible, and build on the ideas of others. Electronic brainstorming uses computer software to share ideas while minimizing team dynamics problems. The Delphi method systematically pools the collective knowledge of experts on a particular subject without face-to-face meetings. In the nominal group technique participants write down ideas alone, describe these ideas in a group, then silently vote on these ideas.

Team building is any formal activity intended to improve the development and functioning of a work team. Four team-building strategies are goal setting, role definition, interpersonal processes, and problem solving. Some team-building events succeed, but companies often fail to consider the contingencies of team building.

Key Terms

brainstorming, p. 299

constructive conflict, p. 299

Delphi method, p. 301

electronic brainstorming, p. 301

evaluation apprehension, p. 297

group polarization, p. 298

groupthink, p. 298

joint optimization, p. 288

nominal group technique, p. 302

production blocking, p. 297

self-directed work teams (SDWTs), p. 286

sociotechnical systems (STS) theory, p. 287

team building, p. 303

trust, p. 294

virtual teams, p. 291

Critical Thinking Questions

1. How do self-directed work teams differ from conventional teams?

2. Advanced Telecom Inc. has successfully introduced self-directed work teams at its operations throughout the United States. The company now wants to introduce SDWTs at its plants in Thailand and Malaysia. What potential cross-cultural challenges might Advanced Telecom experience as it introduces SDWTs in these high power distance countries?

3. A chicken processing company wants to build a processing plant designed around sociotechnical systems principles. In a traditional chicken processing plant, employees work in separate departments—cleaning and cutting, cooking, packaging, and warehousing.

The cooking and packaging processes are controlled by separate workstations in the traditional plant. How would the company change this operation according to sociotechnical systems design?

4. What can organizations do to reduce management resistance to self-directed work teams?

5. Suppose the instructor for this course assigned you to a project team consisting of three other students who are currently taking similar courses in Ireland, India, and Brazil. All students speak English and have similar expertise of the topic. Use your knowledge of virtual teams to discuss the problems that your team might face, compared with a team of local students who can meet face-to-face.

6. What can virtual teams do to sustain trust among team members?

7. Some firms in your region have turned to volunteering as a form of team building, whereby a group of employees spends a day working together on a community project, often outside their expertise. In what ways might volunteering be an effective team-building activity?

8. Bangalore Technologies wants to use brainstorming with its employees and customers to identify new uses for its technology. Advise Bangalore's president about the potential benefits of brainstorming, as well as its potential limitations.

Case Study 10.1 THE SHIPPING INDUSTRY ACCOUNTING TEAM

For the past five years I have been working at McKay, Sanderson, and Smith Associates, a mid-sized accounting firm in Boston that specializes in commercial accounting and audits. My particular specialty is accounting practices for shipping companies, ranging from small fishing fleets to a couple of the big firms with ships along the East Coast.

About 18 months ago McKay, Sanderson, and Smith Associates became part of a large merger involving two other accounting firms. These firms have offices in Miami, Seattle, Baton Rouge, and Los Angeles. Although the other two accounting firms were much larger than McKay, all three firms agreed to avoid centralizing the business around one office in Los Angeles. Instead the new firm—called Goldberg, Choo, and McKay Associates—would rely on teams across the country to "leverage the synergies of our collective knowledge" (an often-cited statement from the managing partner soon after the merger).

The merger affected me a year ago when my boss (a senior partner and vice president of the merger firm) announced that I would be working more closely with three people from the other two firms to become the firm's new shipping industry accounting team. The other team members were Elias in Miami, Susan in Seattle, and Brad in Los Angeles. I had met Elias briefly at a meeting in New York City during the merger but had never met Susan or Brad, although I knew that they were shipping accounting professionals at the other firms.

Initially the shipping team activities involved e-mailing each other about new contracts and prospective clients. Later we were asked to submit joint monthly reports on accounting statements and issues. Normally I submitted my own monthly reports to summarize activities involving my own clients. Coordinating the monthly report with three other people took much more time, particularly because different accounting documentation procedures across the three firms were still being resolved. It took numerous e-mail messages and a few telephone calls to work out a reasonable monthly report style.

During this aggravating process it became apparent—to me at least—that this team business was costing me more time than it was worth. Moreover, Brad in Los Angeles didn't have a clue about how to communicate with the rest of us. He rarely replied to e-mail. Instead he often used the telephone voice mail system, which resulted in lots of telephone tag. Brad arrived at work at 9:30 a.m. in Los Angeles (and was often late), which is early afternoon in Boston. I typically have a flexible work schedule from 7:30 a.m. to 3:30 p.m. so I can chauffeur my kids after school to sports and music lessons. So Brad and I have a window of less than three hours to share information.

The biggest nuisance with the shipping specialist accounting team started two weeks ago when the firm asked the four of us to develop a new strategy for attracting more shipping firm business. This new strategic plan is a messy business. Somehow we have to share our thoughts on various approaches, agree on a new plan, and write a unified submission to the managing partner. Already the project is taking most of my time just writing and responding to e-mail and talking in conference calls (which none of us did much before the team formed).

Susan and Brad have already had two or three misunderstandings via e-mail about their different perspectives on delicate matters in the strategic plan. The worst of these disagreements required a conference call with all of us to resolve. Except for the most basic matters, it seems that we can't understand each other, let alone agree on key issues. I have come to the conclusion that I would never want Brad to work in my Boston office (thank goodness he's on the other side of the country). Although Elias and I seem to agree on most points, the overall team can't form a common vision or strategy. I don't know how Elias, Susan, or Brad feel, but I would be quite happy to work somewhere that did not require any of these long-distance team headaches.

Discussion Questions

1. What type of team was formed here? Was it necessary, in your opinion?

2. Use the team effectiveness model in Chapter 9 and related information in this chapter to identify the strengths and weaknesses of this team's environment, design, and processes.

3. Assuming that these four people must continue to work as a team, recommend ways to improve the team's effectiveness.

Source: Copyright © 2004 Steven L. McShane.

Case Study 10.2 SEAGATE'S MORALE-ATHON

 Team building activities come in many forms and are widely practiced, but few companies go as far as Seagate Technology. Each year, the giant American computer storage hardware manufacturer has been sending hundreds of employees from a dozen countries to a week-long team-building program called Eco-Seagate. CEO Bill Watkins championed the event to break down barriers, boost confidence, and make staffers better team players. "Some of you will learn about teamwork because you have a great team," Watson advises one group of participants. "Some of you will learn because your team is a disaster."

This *BusinessWeek* case study details the team-building events that "tribes" of employees participated in throughout a recent Eco-Seagate program in New Zealand. It describes how employees react to these activities, including the marathon race on the final day. Read the full text of this *BusinessWeek* article at www.mhhe.com/mcshane4e and prepare for the discussion questions below.

Discussion Questions

1. What type(s) of team building would you categorize the Eco-Seagate event? In your opinion, is this type of event effective for teambuilding? Why or why not?

2. What practices in the Eco-Seagate help team members to become more cohesive?

Source: S. Max, "Seagate's Morale-athon," *BusinessWeek,* 3 April 2006, 110

Team Exercise 10.3 EGG DROP EXERCISE

PURPOSE This exercise is designed to help you understand the dynamics of high-performance teams.

MATERIALS The instructor will provide various materials with which to complete this task. The instructor will also distribute a cost sheet to each team and will post the rules for managers and workers. Rule violations will attract penalties that increase the cost of production.

TEAM TASK The team's task is to design and build a protective device that will allow a raw egg (provided by the instructor) to be dropped from a great height without breaking. The team wins if its egg does not break using the lowest-priced device.

INSTRUCTIONS

1. The instructor will divide the class into teams of approximately six people. Team members will divide into groups of "managers" and "workers." The team can have as many people as it thinks is needed for managers and workers as long as all team members are assigned to one of these roles. Please note from the cost sheet that managers and workers represent a cost to your project's budget.

2. Within the time allotted by the instructor, each team's managers will design the device to protect the egg. Workers and managers will purchase supplies from the store, and workers will then build the egg protection device. Team members should read the rules carefully to avoid penalty costs.

Source: This exercise, which is widely available in many forms, does not seem to have any known origin.

Self-Assessment 10.4

THE TEAM PLAYER INVENTORY

Theresa Kline, University of Calgary

PURPOSE This exercise is designed to help you estimate the extent to which you are positively predisposed to working in teams.

INSTRUCTIONS Read each of the following statements and circle the response that you believe best indicates the extent to which you agree or disagree with that statement. Then use the scoring key in Appendix B to calculate your results for each scale. This exercise is completed alone so you can assess yourself honestly without concerns of social comparison. However, class discussion will focus on the characteristics of individuals who are more or less compatible with working in self-directed work teams.

The Team Player Inventory

To what extent do you agree or disagree that	Completely disagree	Disagree somewhat	Neither agree nor disagree	Agree somewhat	Completely agree
1. I enjoy working on team projects.	☒	☐	☐	☐	☐
2. Team project work easily allows others to "pull their weight."	☐	☒	☐	☐	☐
3. Work that is done as a team is better than work done individually.	☒	☐	☐	☐	☐
4. I do my best work alone rather than in a team.	☐	☐	☐	☐	☒
5. Team work is overrated in terms of the actual results produced.	☐	☐	☐	☒	☐
6. Working in a team gets me to think more creatively.	☐	☐	☒	☐	☐
7. Teams are used too often when individual work would be more effective.	☐	☐	☐	☒	☐
8. My own work is enhanced when I am in a team situation.	☐	☒	☐	☐	☐
9. My experiences working in team situations have been primarily negative.	☐	☐	☐	☒	☐
10. More solutions or ideas are generated when working in a team situation than when working alone.	☐	☐	☐	☒	☐

Source: T.J.B. Kline, "The Team Player Inventory: Reliability and Validity of a Measure of Predisposition toward Organizational Team Working Environments," *Journal for Specialists in Group Work* 24 (1999), pp. 102–12.

Self-Assessment 10.5

PROPENSITY TO TRUST SCALE (STUDENT OLC)

Trust is a psychological state comprising the intention to accept vulnerability based on positive expectations of the intent or behavior of another person. Although trust varies from one situation to the next, some people have a higher or lower propensity to trust. In other words, some people are highly trusting of others, even when first meeting them, whereas others have difficulty trusting any-

one, even over a long time. This self-assessment provides an estimate of your propensity to trust. Indicate your preferred response to each statement, being honest with yourself for each item. This self-assessment is completed alone; class discussion will focus on the meaning of propensity to trust, why it varies from one person to the next, and how it affects teamwork.

After reading this chapter, if you need additional information, see www.mhhe.com/mcshane4e for more in-depth interactivities that correspond with this material.

How can corporate leaders conduct a casual conversation with 38,000 staff in dozens of countries? Sun Microsystems president Jonathan Schwartz handles the task through his own Weblog. Blogs (as Weblogs are commonly called) are online journals or diaries. Schwartz writes in his blog each week about a variety of topics, ranging from competition to new technology. Most viewers—up to 20,000 every day—are clients, suppliers, and curious Web surfers, but Schwartz also sees the value of his blogs for Sun's own workforce.

"There are 38,000 people at Sun," Schwartz explains. "I can't have an all-hands meeting. I'd love to put everybody in one room and say, 'Here's the strategy, here are the challenges, here are the obstacles, here's what you need to do to get around them.' I can't do that. But my blog gives me the best proxy for doing exactly that." Schwartz adds that blogging is better than writing memos or newsletters because it gives the information more of a personal touch. "There's an immediacy of interaction you can get with your audience through blogging that's hard to get any other way, except by face-to-face communication."

Sun, IBM, Google, and a few other companies also provide resources for employees to create their own personal blogs. IBM has several outward-facing blogs for customers, but its inward-facing (restricted to IBM employees) BlogCentral hosts more than 3,000 personal blogs created by employees who want to share their thoughts and experiences with co-workers. Google's inward-facing blog has created a gigantic office water cooler effect. "We have seen a lot of different uses of blogs within the firewall," says Jason Goldman, Blogger product manager at Google. "People keeping track of meeting notes, sharing diagnostics information and sharing snippets of code, as well as more personal uses, like letting co-workers know what they're thinking about and what they're up to."

Meanwhile Children's Hospital and Regional Medical Center in Seattle is applying blogs in another way to improve employee communication. Rather than having professionals write employee newsletters or e-zines, the hospital keeps staff up-to-date through volunteer bloggers scattered throughout the organization. Dozens of Children's Hospital staff are authorized to post news and events in their departments to a central blog site that employees visit to learn what's happening. "The distributed authorship of people from different departments means the content is fresher" than the hospital's previous newsletter or e-zine, says Children's Hospital Web services manager Christian Watson.[1]

Sun Microsystems president Jonathan Schwartz says that blogs have a lot to offer as a communication medium in organizations.

Communicating in Teams and Organizations

After reading this chapter you should be able to

1. Explain the importance of communication and diagram the communication process.
2. Describe problems with communicating through electronic mail.
3. Identify two ways in which nonverbal communication differs from verbal communication.
4. Identify two conditions requiring a channel with high media richness.
5. Identify four common communication barriers.
6. Discuss the degree to which men and women communicate differently.
7. Outline the key elements of active listening.
8. Summarize four communication strategies in organizational hierarchies.

communication
The process by which information is transmitted and understood between two or more people.

Information technologies have transformed communication in organizations in recent years, yet we may still be at the beginning of this revolution. Wire cablegrams and telephones introduced a century ago are giving way to e-mail, instant messaging, Weblogs, and podcasting. Each of these inventions creates fascinating changes in how people interact with each other in the workplace. **Communication** refers to the process by which information is transmitted and *understood* between two or more people. We emphasize the word *understood* because transmitting the sender's intended meaning is the essence of good communication.

Sun Microsystems, IBM, Google, and other large organizations require innovative strategies to keep communication pathways open. In fact, a communication audit of several large organizations reported that only 23 percent of employees agree that executives communicate well, and only 15 percent agree that the head office in general communicates effectively.[2] Smaller businesses may have fewer structural bottlenecks, but they too can suffer subtle communication problems.

Effective communication is vital to all organizations because it coordinates employees, fulfills employee needs, supports knowledge management, and improves decision making.[3] First, the ability to exchange information is an essential part of the coordination process, allowing employees to develop common mental models that synchronize their work. Second, communication is the glue that holds people together. It helps people satisfy their drive to bond and, as part of the dynamics of social support, eases work-related stress.

Communication is also a key driver in knowledge management. It brings knowledge into the organization and distributes it to employees who require that information. As such, it minimizes the "silos of knowledge" problem that undermines an organization's potential. Fourth, communication influences the quality of decision making. Individuals rarely have enough information alone to make decisions about the complex matters facing businesses today. Instead problem solvers require information from co-workers, subordinates, and anyone else with relevant knowledge.

This chapter begins by presenting a model of the communication process and discussing several communication barriers. Next, the different types of communication channels, including computer-mediated communication, are described, followed by factors to consider when choosing a communication medium. This chapter then examines cross-cultural and gender differences in communication and outlines strategies to improve interpersonal communication. The latter part of the chapter presents some options for communicating in organizational hierarchies and describes the pervasive organizational grapevine.

Learning
Objectives

After reading this section you should be able to

1. **Explain the importance of communication and diagram the communication process.**
2. **Describe problems with communicating through electronic mail.**
3. **Identify two ways in which nonverbal communication differs from verbal communication.**

A Model of Communication

The communication model presented in Exhibit 11.1 provides a useful "conduit" metaphor for thinking about the communication process.[4] According to this model, communication flows through channels between the sender and receiver. The sender

Exhibit 11.1
The Communication Process Model

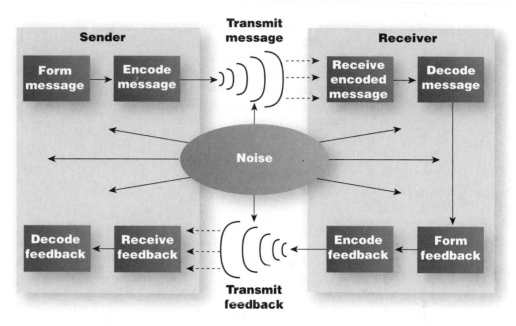

forms a message and encodes it into words, gestures, voice intonations, and other symbols or signs. Next the encoded message is transmitted to the intended receiver through one or more communication channels (media). The receiver senses the incoming message and decodes it into something meaningful. Ideally the decoded meaning is what the sender intended.

In most situations the sender looks for evidence that the other person received and understood the transmitted message. This feedback may be a formal acknowledgment, such as "Yes, I know what you mean," or indirect evidence from the receiver's subsequent actions. Notice that feedback repeats the communication process. Intended feedback is encoded, transmitted, received, and decoded from the receiver to the sender of the original message.

This model recognizes that communication is not a free-flowing conduit. Rather, the transmission of meaning from one person to another is hampered by noise—the psychological, social, and structural barriers that distort and obscure the sender's intended message. If any part of the communication process is distorted or broken, the sender and receiver will not have a common understanding of the message.

Communication Channels

A critical part of the communication model is the channel or medium through which information is transmitted. There are two main types of channels: verbal and nonverbal. Verbal communication includes any oral or written means of transmitting meaning through words. Nonverbal communication, which we discuss later, is any part of communication that does not use words.

Verbal Communication

Different forms of verbal communication should be used in different situations. Face-to-face interaction is usually better than written methods for transmitting emotions and persuading the receiver. This is because nonverbal cues accompany oral communications, such as voice intonation and facial expressions. Furthermore, face-to-face interaction provides the sender with immediate feedback from the receiver and the opportunity to adjust the emotional tone of the message accordingly. Written communication is more appropriate for recording and presenting technical details. This is because ideas are easier to follow when written down than when communicated aurally. Traditionally, written communication has been slow to develop and transmit, but electronic mail, Weblogs, and other computer-mediated communication channels have significantly improved written communication efficiency.

Electronic Communication

Electronic mail (e-mail) is revolutionizing the way we communicate in organizational settings. It has also become the medium of choice in most workplaces because messages are quickly formed, edited, and stored. Information can be appended and transmitted to many people with a simple click of a mouse. E-mail is asynchronous (messages are sent and received at different times), so there is no need to coordinate a communication session. This technology also allows fairly random access to information: You can select any message in any order, skip to different parts of a message, and search for any word in any message on your computer.

E-mail tends to be the preferred medium for coordinating work (such as confirming a co-worker's production schedule) and for sending well-defined information for decision making. It often increases the volume of communication and significantly alters the flow of information within groups and throughout the organization.[5] Specifically, it reduces some face-to-face and telephone communication but increases communication with people further up the hierarchy. Some social and organizational status differences still exist with e-mail, but they are less apparent than in face-to-face communication. E-mail also reduces many selective attention biases because it hides our age, race, weight, and other features that are observable in face-to-face meetings.

flaming
The act of sending an emotionally charged e-mail message to others.

Problems with E-Mail   In spite of the wonders of e-mail, anyone who has used this communication medium knows that it has limitations. One problem is that e-mail is an ineffective medium for communicating emotions. People rely on facial expressions and other nonverbal cues to interpret the emotional meaning of words, and e-mail lacks this parallel communication medium. E-mail aficionados try to clarify the emotional tone of their messages by inserting graphic faces called emoticons or "smileys."[6]

A second problem with e-mail is that it seems to reduce our politeness and respect for others. This is mostly evident through the increased frequency of **flaming**—the act of sending an emotionally charged message to others. There are two explanations for this lack of diplomacy. First, people can quickly write and post e-mail messages before their emotions subside, whereas cooler thoughts might prevail before traditional memos or letters are sent. Second, e-mail is an impersonal medium, allowing employees to write things that they would never say verbally in face-to-face conversation. Fortunately, research has found that politeness and respect increase as team members get to know each other and when companies establish explicit norms and rules of communication.[7]

A third problem is that e-mail is an inefficient medium for communicating in ambiguous, complex, and novel situations. When two people lack mutual mental models, they need to transmit many e-mail messages to share enough information. Two-way face-to-face communication is a much more effective medium under these circumstances, but many employees are reluctant to break out of the e-mail dialogue. Realizing this, executives at St. Joseph's Regional Medical Center in Paterson, New Jersey, banned e-mail for one day in an attempt to "repersonalize the health care business." Similar bans have occurred at Liverpool City Council in the United Kingdom. John Caudwell become so fed up with e-mail that the CEO of British cell phone company

Flaming E-mail   Executives at Admiral Insurance are concerned that the electronic communication medium is making staff at the Welsh company less polite to each other and to customers. "It is much easier to have a row by e-mail than it is face-to-face, and people are often ruder as a result," says Admiral spokesperson Justin Beddows. "Orders can be issued out and people can be quite abrupt because they feel protected by the distance the e-mail provides. But once an abusive e-mail is sent out, there is no getting it back and it can cause a rift that cannot be resolved easily." Along with reminding employees of e-mail's limitations as a communication medium, Admiral executives occasionally try to wean staff from e-mail dependence. "We hold 'no e-mail days' to encourage people to get off their backsides and visit people face-to-face," says Beddows.[8]

Phones 4U banned his 2,500 employees from e-mailing each other at all. Although the ban was short-lived, Caudwell claimed soon after the ban that "the quality and efficiency of communication have increased in one fell swoop."[9]

A fourth difficulty with e-mail is that it contributes to information overload, which we'll discuss in more detail later in this chapter. Many e-mail users are overwhelmed by hundreds of messages each week, many of which are either unnecessary or irrelevant to the receiver. This occurs because e-mail can be easily created and copied to thousands of people through group mailbox systems. E-mail overload may eventually decrease as people become more familiar with it, but this trend may take a while.

Other Computer-Mediated Communication

Intranets, extranets, Blackberry wireless e-mailing, instant messaging, blogging, podcasting, and other forms of computer-mediated communication are fueling the hyperfast world of corporate information sharing. The opening story to this chapter described how blogs enable executives to more personally communicate with employees. Sun Microsystems and a few other firms support employee blogs because they empower staff to share information both internally and externally and let co-workers know more about each other. Blogs also allow firms to archive discussions, something that is less easily done in instant messaging. Podcasting may become another electronic communication medium that gains interest in organizations. Although primarily aimed at the public, podcasts—radiolike programs formatted for digital music players and computer music software—are starting to appear as messages from executives to employees and customers alike.[10]

Instant messaging (IM) is another emerging form of electronic communication that has gained popularity in some organizations. IM is more efficient than e-mail because messages are brief (usually just a sentence or two with acronyms and sound-alike letters for words) and appear on the receiver's screen as soon as they are sent. IM also creates real-time communities of practice as employees form clustered conversations around specific fields of expertise. Another advantage is that employees soon develop the capability of carrying on several IM conversations at the same time. "No matter how good you are on the phone, the best you can do is carry on two conversations at once," says one New York City broker. "With IM, I can have six going at once.... That allows me to get my job done and serve clients better."[11]

Nonverbal Communication

Nonverbal communication includes facial gestures, voice intonation, physical distance, and even silence. This communication channel is necessary where noise or physical distance prevents effective verbal exchanges and the need for immediate feedback precludes written communication. But even in quiet face-to-face meetings, most information is communicated nonverbally. Rather like a parallel conversation, nonverbal cues signal subtle information to both parties, such as reinforcing their interest in the verbal conversation or demonstrating their relative status in the relationship.[12]

Nonverbal communication differs from verbal communication in a couple of ways. First, it is less rule-bound than verbal communication. We receive a lot of formal training in how to understand spoken words but very little in understanding the nonverbal signals that accompany those words. Consequently nonverbal cues are generally more ambiguous and susceptible to misinterpretation. At the same time many facial expressions (such as smiling) are hardwired and universal, thereby providing the only reliable means of communicating across cultures. This point is powerfully illustrated in Connections 11.1. To overcome language and physical noise barriers, the quick-thinking leader of a coalition forces unit during the Iraq war relied on nonverbal communication to communicate its friendly intentions, thereby narrowly avoiding a potentially deadly incident.

The other difference between verbal and nonverbal communication is that the former is typically conscious, whereas most nonverbal communication is automatic and unconscious. We normally plan the words we say or write, but we rarely plan every blink, smile, or other gesture during a conversation. Indeed, as we just mentioned, many of these facial expressions communicate the same meaning across cultures because they are hardwired unconscious or preconscious responses to human emotions.[13] For example, pleasant emotions cause the brain center to widen the mouth, whereas negative emotions produce constricted facial expressions (squinting eyes, pursed lips, and the like).

emotional contagion
The automatic and unconscious tendency to mimic and synchronize one's own nonverbal behaviors with those of other people.

Emotional Contagion   One of the most fascinating effects of emotions on nonverbal communication is the phenomenon called **emotional contagion,** which is the automatic process of "catching" or sharing another person's emotions by mimicking that person's facial expressions and other nonverbal behavior. Consider what happens when you see a co-worker accidentally bang his or her head against a filing cabinet. Chances are that you wince and put your hand on your own head as if you had hit the cabinet. Similarly, while listening to someone describe a positive event, you tend to smile and exhibit other emotional displays of happiness. While some of our nonverbal communication is planned, emotional contagion represents unconscious behavior—we automatically mimic and synchronize our nonverbal behaviors with other people.[14]

Emotional contagion serves three purposes. First, mimicry provides continuous feedback, communicating that we understand and empathize with the sender. To consider the significance of this, imagine employees remaining expressionless after watching a co-worker bang his or her head! The lack of parallel behavior conveys a lack of understanding or caring. Second, mimicking the nonverbal behaviors of other people seems to be a way of receiving emotional meaning from those people. If a

Nonverbal Gestures Help Crowd Control during Iraq War

The southern Iraqi city of Najaf is home to one of Islam's holiest sites, the Ali Mosque. The site is believed to be the final resting place of Ali, son-in-law of the prophet Mohammed. It is also home to Grand Ayatollah Ali Hussein Sistani, one of the most revered Shiites in the Muslim world and a potential supporter of U.S. efforts to introduce a more moderate government in Iraq.

One week before Saddam Hussein's regime was overthrown, Sistani sent word that he wanted to meet with senior officers of the American forces. Fearing assassination, he also asked for soldiers to secure his compound, located along the Golden Road near the mosque. But when 130 soldiers from the 101st Airborne's 2nd Battalion, 327th Infantry, and their gun trucks turned onto the Golden Road to provide security, hundreds of Iraqis in the area started to get angry. Clerics tried to explain to the crowd why the Americans were approaching, but they were drowned out. The crowd assumed the Americans would try to enter and possibly attack the sacred mosque.

The chanting got louder as the quickly growing crowd approached the soldiers. Anticipating a potentially deadly situation, Lieutenant Colonel Christopher Hughes, the battalion's commander, picked up a loudspeaker and called out the unit's nickname: "No Slack Soldiers!" Then he commanded, "All No Slack

Soldiers, take a knee." According to journalists witnessing this incident, every soldier almost immediately knelt down on one knee. Hughes then called out, "All No Slack Soldiers, point your weapons at the ground." Again the soldiers complied.

With the crowd still chanting in anger, Hughes spoke through the loudspeaker a third time: "All No Slack Soldiers, smile," he commanded. "Smile guys, everybody smile." And in this intensely difficult situation, the kneeling troops showed the friendliest smiles they could muster toward the crowd.

Eyewitnesses say that these nonverbal gestures started to work; some people in the crowd smiled back at the Americans and stopped chanting. But insurgents in the crowd (apparently Hussein supporters planted to misinform the crowd) continued to yell. So Hughes spoke one more time: "All vehicles, all No Slack Soldiers, calmly stand up and withdraw from this situation," he said. "We'll go so the people understand we are not trying to hurt him. C'mon, Bravo, back off. Smile and wave and back off." And with that, the soldiers walked backward 100 yards, then turned around and returned to their compound.

Sources: W. Allison, "March to Mosque Provokes Worst Fears," *St. Petersburg Times* (Florida), 4 April 2003, p. 1A; "All Things Considered," National Public Radio (NPR), 4 April 2003; R. Chilcote, "Iraqis Mistakenly Believe Soldiers Have Their Sights on Sacred Landmark," CNN, 4 April 2003.

---

co worker is angry with a client, your tendency to frown and show anger while listening helps you share that emotion more fully. In other words, we receive meaning by expressing the sender's emotions as well as by listening to the sender's words.

The third function of emotional contagion is to fulfill the drive to bond that was described in Chapter 5. Social solidarity is built out of each member's awareness of a collective sentiment. Through nonverbal expressions of emotional contagion, people see others share the same emotions that we feel. This strengthens team cohesiveness by providing evidence of member similarity.[15]

Learning Objectives

After reading the next three sections, you should be able to

4. **Identify two conditions requiring a channel with high media richness.**
5. **Identify four common communication barriers.**
6. **Discuss the degree to which men and women communicate differently.**

Choosing the Best Communication Channels

Employees perform better if they can quickly determine the best communication channels for a situation and are flexible enough to use different methods as the occasion requires. But which communication channels are most appropriate? We partly answered this question in our evaluation of the different communication channels. However, two additional contingencies worth noting are media richness and symbolic meaning.

Media Richness

media richness
The data-carrying capacity of a communication medium, including the volume and variety of information that can be transmitted during a specific time.

A critical factor to consider when selecting a communication channel is **media richness**. Media richness refers to the medium's data-carrying capacity—the volume and variety of information that can be transmitted during a specific time.[16] Exhibit 11.2 illustrates various communication channels arranged in a hierarchy of richness, with face-to-face interaction at the top and lean data-only reports at the bottom.

The media richness hierarchy is determined by three factors. First, rich media allow a person to simultaneously send messages in different ways. For instance, face-to-face communication scores high on media richness because it allows people to transmit their messages both verbally and nonverbally at the same. In contrast, financial reports have low media richness because the message is transmitted only one way (written). Second, rich media allow immediate feedback from receiver to sender, whereas feedback in lean media is delayed or nonexistent. Again this is apparent in face-to-face communication, in which the sender can quickly determine whether the receiver understood the message; in contrast, someone sending a financial report might never find out whether the message was received, let alone understood. Third, rich media allow the sender to customize the message to the receiver. People can

Exhibit 11.2   Media Richness Hierarchy

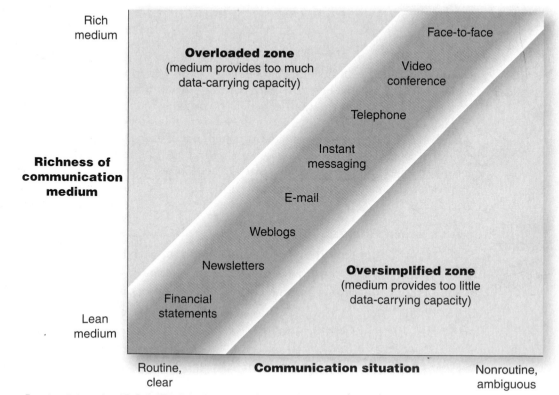

Source: Based on R. Lengel and R. Daft, "The Selection of Communication Media as an Executive Skill," *Academy of Management Executive* 2, no. 3 (August, 1988), p. 226; R.L. Daft and R.H. Lengel, "Information Richness: A New Approach to Managerial Behavior and Organization Design," *Research in Organizational Behavior*, 1984, p. 199.

quickly adjust their face-to-face conversations to suit the situation (such as the receiver's status or interest in the topic), whereas financial reports have low media richness because one size fits all—everyone gets the same information.

Exhibit 11.2 shows that rich media are better than lean media when the communication situation is nonroutine and ambiguous. In nonroutine situations (such as an unexpected and unusual emergency) the sender and receiver have little common experience, so they need to transmit a large volume of information with immediate feedback. Lean media work well in routine situations because the sender and receiver have common expectations through shared mental models. Ambiguous situations also require rich media because the parties must share large amounts of information with immediate feedback to resolve multiple and conflicting interpretations of their observations and experiences.[17]

What happens when we choose the wrong level of media richness for a situation? When the situation is routine or clear, using a rich medium—such as holding a special meeting—would seem like a waste of time. On the other hand, if a unique and ambiguous issue is handled through e-mail or another lean medium, then issues take longer to resolve and misunderstandings are more likely to occur.

Evaluating Media Richness Theory   Research studying traditional channels (face-to-face communication, written memos, and so forth) generally supports the media richness proposition: Rich media are better than lean media when the situation is nonroutine or ambiguous. But the evidence is mixed when emerging information technologies are studied. One reason for this inconsistency is that we need to take into account the communicator's previous experience with e-mail, IM, and other means of communication that do not exist naturally. People who have plenty of experience with a particular communication medium can "push" the amount of media richness normally possible through that information channel. Experienced Blackberry users, for instance, can whip through messages in a flash, whereas new users struggle to type e-mail notes and organize incoming messages. Experience is less relevant with verbal conversation, report writing, and other traditional methods because they are learned early in life and, indeed, may be hardwired in our evolutionary development.[18]

A second factor to consider is the communicator's previous experience with the receiver. The more two or more people share common mental models, the less information exchange is required to communicate new meaning. People who know each other have similar "codebooks," so the sender can communicate with fewer words or other symbols and doesn't need to check as closely that the message has been understood. Without this common codebook, the sender needs to add in more redundancy (such as saying the same thing in two different ways) and requires more efficient feedback to ensure that the receiver understood the message.

Symbolic Meaning of the Medium

"The medium is the message."[19] This famous phrase by communications guru Marshall McLuhan means that the channel of communication has social consequences as much as (or perhaps more than) the content that passes through that medium. McLuhan was referring mainly to the influence of television and other "new media" on society; but this concept applies equally well to how the symbolic meaning of a communication medium influences our interpretation of the message and the relationship between sender and receiver.

The medium-as-message principle was apparent when KPMG gave layoff notices to hundreds of its British employees via e-mail. The public swiftly criticized the consulting firm—not because of the content of the message but because of the medium through which it was transmitted. Ironically KPMG delivered the bad news by e-mail because most employees had specifically asked for this method. Yet even the KPMG executives who sent the layoff notices were hesitant. "I was horrified about telling staff via e-mail as I knew it would make us look callous," admitted one executive.[20] The point here is that we need to be sensitive to the symbolic meaning of the communication medium to ensure that it amplifies rather than misinterprets the meaning found in the message content.

Communication Barriers (Noise)

In spite of the best intentions of sender and receiver to communicate, several barriers inhibit the effective exchange of information. As author George Bernard Shaw wrote, "The greatest problem with communication is the illusion that it has been accomplished." Four pervasive communication barriers (called "noise" earlier in Exhibit 11.1) are perceptions, filtering, language, and information overload. Later we will also investigate cross-cultural and gender communication barriers.

Perceptions

The perceptual process determines what messages we select or screen out, as well as how the selected information is organized and interpreted. This can be a significant source of noise in the communication process if the sender and receiver have different perceptual frames and mental models. For instance, corporate leaders are watched closely by employees, and the most inane words or gestures are interpreted with great meaning even though they often occur without intention.

Filtering

Some messages are filtered or stopped altogether on their way up or down the organizational hierarchy. Filtering may involve deleting or delaying negative information or using less harsh words so that events sound more favorable.[21] Employees and supervisors usually filter communication to create a good impression of themselves to superiors. Filtering is most common where the organization rewards employees who communicate mainly positive information and punishes those who convey bad news. John Stewart admits that reducing filtering isn't easy. "We have been trying hard to get people to be more open," says the chief executive of National Australia Bank. "To do that, you have to make sure your senior people are listening to staff when they bring problems to them, and not killing the messenger.... You have to do it—otherwise people will stop telling you and then nothing gets fixed."[22]

Language Barriers

Language problems can be a huge source of communication noise. Recall from Exhibit 11.1 that the sender encodes the message and the receiver decodes it. To make this process work, both parties need to have the same "codebook"; that is, they need to have a mutual understanding of what the words or other symbols being sent mean. Even when both people speak the same language, they might interpret words and phrases differently. If someone says "Would you like to check the figures again?" he or she may be politely *telling* you to double-check the figures or might be merely *asking* if you want to do this.

This language ambiguity isn't always dysfunctional noise.[23] Corporate leaders sometimes rely on metaphors and other vague language to describe ill-defined or complex ideas. Ambiguity is also used to avoid conveying or creating undesirable emotions. For example, one recent study reported that people rely on more ambiguous language when communicating with people who have different values and beliefs. In these situations ambiguity minimizes the risk of conflict.

Along with ambiguity, people who generally speak the same language might not understand specific jargon within that language. **Jargon** consists of technical language and acronyms as well as recognized words with specialized meaning in specific organizations or social groups. Some jargon can improve communication efficiency when both sender and receiver understand this specialized language. But technical experts (including organizational behavior teachers!) sometimes use jargon without realizing that listeners don't have the codebook to translate those special words. In fact, one recent survey found that people react negatively to unnecessary jargon, which is probably contrary to the sender's intention to look "cool" using the latest buzzwords.[24]

jargon
The technical language and acronyms as well as recognized words with specialized meaning in specific organizations or social groups.

Information Overload

Toni Ballard is busy enough with her music career in Massachusetts, but the continuous flow of 50 to 75 e-mail messages each day also takes a huge chunk of her time. To keep up, she will read through the high-priority items and move them into folders; but others might sit in Ballard's e-mail inbox for several days. "It's nice to be kept informed, but obviously, if you read it all the time, you'd never get anything done," says Ballard. In fact, some people *don't* get much else done beyond processing their e-mail! One estimate is that 22.3 trillion e-mail messages are now transmitted annually, up from just 1.1 trillion in 1998. A major U.S. survey recently revealed that professionals send and receive an average of 19,200 e-mail messages annually and spend an average of two hours per day processing e-mail.[25]

E-mail is only one source of communication. Add in voice mail, cell phone text messages, Web site scanning, PDF file downloads, hard copy documents, and other sources of incoming information, and you have a perfect recipe for **information overload**.[26] Information overload occurs when the volume of information received exceeds a person's capacity to get through it. Employees have a certain *information processing capacity*—the amount of information that they are able to process in a fixed unit of time. At the same time, jobs have a varying *information load*—the amount of information to be processed per unit of time.[27] As Exhibit 11.3 illustrates, information overload occurs whenever a job's information load exceeds an individual's information processing capacity.

information overload
A condition in which the volume of information received exceeds a person's capacity to get through it.

Information overload creates noise in the communication system because information gets overlooked or misinterpreted when people can't process it fast enough. It has also become a common cause of workplace stress. These problems can be minimized by increasing our information processing capacity, reducing the job's information load, or a combination of both. Information processing capacity increases when we learn to read faster, scan through documents more efficiently, and remove distractions that slow information processing speed. Time management also increases information processing capacity. When information overload is temporary, we can increase information processing capacity by working longer hours.

© 2001 Ted Goff

"That's my commendation for deciphering all the sales talk when we needed to upgrade the computer."

Exhibit 11.3
Dynamics of Information Overload

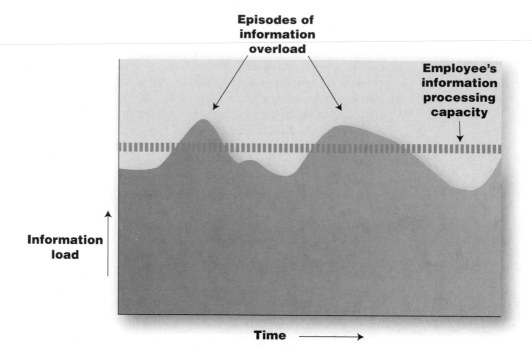

Three strategies help us to reduce information load: buffering, omitting, and summarizing.[28] Consider Microsoft chairman Bill Gates. Gates receives approximately 300 e-mail messages daily from Microsoft addresses that are outside a core group of people; these messages are buffered—routed to an assistant who reads each and sends Gates only the 30 or so messages considered essential. Gates also applies the omitting strategy by using software rules to redirect e-mail messages from distribution lists, nonessential sources, and junk mail (spam). These messages are dumped into preassigned folders to be read later, if ever. Gates likely also relies on the summarizing strategy by reading executive summaries rather than entire reports on some issues.

Perceptions, filtering, language barriers, and information overload are not the only sources of noise in the communication process; but they are probably the most common. Noise also occurs when we communicate across cultures or genders, both of which are discussed next.

Cross-Cultural and Cross-Gender Communication

In a world of increasing globalization and cultural diversity, organizations face new opportunities as well as communication challenges.[29] Language is the most obvious cross-cultural communication challenge. Words are easily misunderstood in verbal communication either because the receiver has a limited vocabulary or because the sender's accent distorts the usual sound of some words. The issue is further complicated in global organizations where employees from non-English countries often rely on English as the common business language. The problem discussed earlier of ambiguous language becomes amplified across cultures. For example, a French executive might call an event a "catastrophe" as a casual exaggeration, whereas someone in Germany usually interprets this word literally as an earth-shaking event.[30]

Mastering the same language improves one dimension of cross-cultural communication, but problems may still occur when interpreting voice intonation. Middle

Easterners tend to speak loudly to show sincerity and interest in the discussion, whereas Japanese people tend to speak softly to communicate politeness or humility. These different cultural norms regarding voice loudness may cause one person to misinterpret the other.

Nonverbal Differences

Nonverbal communication is more important in some cultures than in others. For example, people in Japan interpret more of a message's meaning from nonverbal cues. To avoid offending or embarrassing the receiver (particularly outsiders), Japanese people will often say what the other person wants to hear (called *tatemae*) but send more subtle nonverbal cues indicating the sender's true feelings (called *honne*). A Japanese colleague might politely reject your business proposal by saying "I will think about that" while sending nonverbal signals that he or she is not really interested. "In Japan, they have seven ways to say no; they never want to offend," advises Rick Davidson, global CIO at Manpower, Inc. "Sometimes they nod their head, and you think you have an agreement, but they're just saying, 'I hear you.'"[31]

Many unconscious or involuntary nonverbal cues (such as smiling) have the same meaning around the world, but deliberate gestures often have different interpretations. For example, most of us shake our head from side to side to say "No," but a variation of head shaking means "I understand" to many people in India. Filipinos raise their eyebrows to give an affirmative answer, yet Arabs interpret this expression (along with clicking one's tongue) as a negative response. Most Westerners are taught to maintain eye contact with the speaker to show interest and respect; yet Native Americans, Australian Aborigines, and others learn at an early age to show respect by looking down when an older or more senior person is talking to them.[32]

Even the common handshake communicates different meaning across cultures. Westerners tend to appreciate a firm handshake as a sign of strength and warmth in a friendship or business relationship. In contrast, many Asians and Middle Easterners favor a loose grip and regard a firm clench as aggressive. Germans prefer one good

Thumbs-Up for Cross-Cultural (Mis)communication Patricia Oliveira made several cultural adjustments when she moved from Brazil to Australia. One of the more humorous incidents occurred in the Melbourne office where she works. A co-worker would stick his thumbs up when asked about something, signaling that everything was OK. But the gesture had a totally different meaning to Oliveira and other people from Brazil. "He asked me why I was laughing and I had to explain that in Brazil, that sign means something not very nice," recalls Oliveira. "After that, everyone started doing it to the boss. It was really funny."[33]

handshake stroke, whereas anything less than five or six strokes may symbolize a lack of trust in Spain. If this isn't confusing enough, people from some cultures view any touching in public—including handshakes—as a sign of rudeness.

Silence and Conversational Overlaps Communication includes silence, but its use and meaning varies from one culture to another.[34] A recent study estimated that silence and pauses represented 30 percent of conversation time between Japanese doctors and patients, compared to only 8 percent of the time between American doctors and patients. Why is there more silence in Japanese conversations? In Japan silence symbolizes respect and indicates that the listener is thoughtfully contemplating what has just been said.[35] Empathy is also important in Japan, and this shared understanding is demonstrated without using words. In contrast, most people in the United States and many other cultures view silence as a *lack* of communication and often interpret long breaks as a sign of disagreement.

Conversational overlaps also send different messages in different cultures. Japanese people usually stop talking when they are interrupted, whereas talking over the other person's speech is more common in Brazil and some other countries. The difference in communication behavior is again due to interpretations. Talking while someone is speaking to you is considered quite rude in Japan, whereas Brazilians are more likely to interpret this as a person's interest and involvement in the conversation.

Gender Differences in Communication

A number of popular books about gender differences in communication seem to conclude that men and women are completely different life forms from different planets.[36] In reality men and women have similar communication practices, but there are subtle distinctions that can occasionally lead to misunderstanding and conflict. One distinction is that men are more likely than women to view conversations as negotiations of relative status and power. They assert their power by directly giving advice to others ("You should do the following") and using combative language. There is also evidence that men dominate the talk time in conversations with women, as well as interrupt more, and adjust their speaking style less than women.[37]

Men also engage in more "report talk," in which the primary function of the conversation is impersonal and efficient information exchange. Women also use report talk, particularly when conversing with men; but conversations among women have a higher incidence of relationship building through "rapport talk." This emphasis on rapport rather than report talk is also apparent in studies of how women communicate in e-mail and other forms of online communication. Another gender distinction is that women use indirect requests such as "Have you considered... ?" Similarly, women apologize more often and seek advice from others more quickly than do men. Finally, research fairly consistently indicates that women are more sensitive than men to nonverbal cues in face-to-face meetings.[38]

Both men and women usually understand each other, but these subtle differences are occasional irritants. For instance, female scientists have complained that male scientists use a competitive debating style that makes it difficult for women to participate in meaningful dialogue.[39] Another irritant occurs when women seek empathy but receive male dominance in response. Specifically, women sometimes discuss their personal experiences and problems to develop closeness with the receiver. But when men hear problems, they quickly suggest solutions because this asserts their control over the situation. As well as frustrating a woman's need for common understanding, the advice actually says, "You and I are different; you have the problem and I have the answer." Meanwhile men become frustrated because they can't understand why women don't appreciate their advice.

After reading the next three sections, you should be able to

7. **Outline the key elements of active listening.**
8. **Summarize four communication strategies in organizational hierarchies.**

Improving Interpersonal Communication

Effective interpersonal communication depends on the sender's ability to get the message across and the receiver's performance as an active listener. In this section we outline these two essential features of effective interpersonal communication.

Getting Your Message Across

This chapter began with the statement that effective communication occurs when the other person receives and understands the message. To accomplish this difficult task the sender must learn to empathize with the receiver, repeat the message, choose an appropriate time for the conversation, and be descriptive rather than evaluative:

- *Empathize.* Recall from earlier chapters that empathy is a person's ability to understand and be sensitive to the feelings, thoughts, and situation of others. In conversations this involves putting yourself in the receiver's shoes when encoding the message. For instance, be sensitive to words that may be ambiguous or trigger the wrong emotional response.

- *Repeat the message.* Rephrase the key points a couple of times. The saying "Tell them what you're going to tell them; tell them; then tell them what you've told them" reflects this need for redundancy.

- *Use timing effectively.* Your message competes with other messages and noise, so find a time when the receiver is less likely to be distracted by these other matters.

- *Be descriptive.* Focus on the problem, not the person, if you have negative information to convey. People stop listening when the information attacks their self-esteem. Also, suggest things the listener can do to improve, rather than point to him or her as a problem.

Active Listening

"Nature gave people two ears but only one tongue, which is a gentle hint that they should listen more than they talk." Henry Schacht has followed this sage advice for most of his career. "The experience of doing nothing but being a very good listener for as long as you can stand it is the most important thing to do," advises the former CEO of Lucent Technologies in New Jersey.[40] To follow this advice, we need to recognize that listening is a process of actively sensing the sender's signals, evaluating them accurately, and responding appropriately. These three components of listening—sensing, evaluating, and responding—reflect the listener's side of the communication model described at the beginning of this chapter. Listeners receive the sender's signals, decode them as intended, and provide appropriate and timely feedback to the

Exhibit 11.4

Active Listening Process and Strategies

Sensing
- Postpone evaluation.
- Avoid interruptions.
- Maintain interest.

Active listening

Responding
- Show interest.
- Clarify the message.

Evaluating
- Empathize.
- Organize information.

sender (see Exhibit 11.4). Active listeners constantly cycle through sensing, evaluating, and responding during the conversation and engage in various activities to improve these processes.[41]

Sensing   Sensing is the process of receiving signals from the sender and paying attention to them. These signals include the words spoken, the nature of the sounds (speed of speech, tone of voice, and so on), and nonverbal cues. Active listeners improve sensing by postponing evaluation, avoiding interruptions, and maintaining interest:

- *Postpone evaluation.* Many listeners become victims of first impressions. They quickly form an opinion of the speaker's message and subsequently screen out important information. Active listeners, on the other hand, try to stay as open-minded as possible by delaying evaluation of the message until the speaker has finished.

- *Avoid interruptions.* Interrupting the speaker's conversation has two negative effects on the sensing process. First, it disrupts the speaker's idea, so the listener does not receive the entire message. Second, interruptions tend to second-guess what the speaker is trying to say, which contributes to the problem of evaluating the speaker's ideas too early.

- *Maintain interest.* As with any behavior, active listening requires motivation. Too often we close our minds soon after a conversation begins because the subject is boring. Instead active listeners maintain interest by taking the view—probably an accurate one—that there is always something of value in a conversation; it's just a matter of actively looking for it.

Evaluating   This component of listening includes understanding the message meaning, evaluating the message, and remembering the message. To improve their evaluation of the conversation, active listeners empathize with the speaker and organize information received during the conversation:

- *Empathize.* Active listeners try to understand and be sensitive to the speaker's feelings, thoughts, and situation. Empathy is a critical skill in active listening because the verbal and nonverbal cues from the conversation are accurately interpreted from the other person's point of view.

- *Organize information.* Listeners process information three times faster than the average rate of speech (450 words per minute versus 125 words per minute), so they are easily distracted. Active listeners use this spare time to organize the information into key points. In fact, it's a good idea to imagine that you must summarize what people have said after they are finished speaking.

Responding Responding, the third component of listening, is feedback to the sender, which motivates and directs the speaker's communication. Active listeners do this by showing interest and clarifying the message:

- *Show interest.* Active listeners show interest by maintaining sufficient eye contact and sending back channel signals such as "Oh, really!" and "I see" during appropriate breaks in the conversation.
- *Clarify the message.* Active listeners provide feedback by rephrasing the speaker's ideas at appropriate breaks ("So you're saying that...?"). This further demonstrates interest in the conversation and helps the speaker determine whether you understand the message.

Communicating in Organizational Hierarchies

So far we have focused on "micro-level" issues in the communication process—namely the dynamics of sending and receiving information between two people in various situations. But in this era where knowledge is competitive advantage, corporate leaders also need to maintain an open flow of communication up, down, and across the organization. This section introduces four organizationwide communication strategies: workspace design, e-zines/blogs/wikis, employee surveys, and direct communication with top management.

Workspace Design

The ability and motivation to communicate is to some extent influenced by the physical space in which employees work. The location and design of hallways, offices, cubicles, and communal areas (cafeterias, elevators) all shape whom we speak to as

Pixar Building Animates Communication Communication was a top priority when Pixar Animation Studios designed its new campus in Emeryville, California, a few years ago. The animation company that brought us *The Incredibles, Finding Nemo,* and other blockbuster films created work areas that cluster team members and encourage ongoing informal communication. At the same time the campus is designed so that employees share knowledge through happenstance interactions with people on other teams. Pixar executives call this the "bathroom effect": Team members must leave their isolated pods to fetch their mail, have lunch, or visit the restroom. The building also invites staff to mingle in the central airy atrium. "It promotes that chance encounter," says Pixar creative director John Lasseter. "You run into people constantly. It worked from the minute we arrived. We just blossomed here."[42]

well as the frequency of that communication. Some companies try to encourage communication within the team by organizing employees into clusters. This cluster approach is used at product design firm IDEO. The physical space literally groups employees together so face-to-face communication within the team is easy, whereas interaction with people in other teams is minimized.

Another increasingly popular workspace strategy is to replace traditional offices with open space arrangements in which all employees (including management) work in the same open area. Anecdotal evidence suggests that people do communicate more often with fewer walls between them. However, research also suggests that open office design potentially increases employee stress due to the loss of privacy and personal space. According to an analysis of 13,000 employee surveys in 40 major organizations, the most important function of workspace is to provide a place to concentrate on work without distraction. The second most important function is to support informal communication with co-workers.[43] In other words, workspace needs to balance privacy with opportunities for social interaction.

E-Zines, Blogs, and Wikis

For decades, employees have received official company news through hard copy newsletters and magazines. Many firms still use these communication devices, but most have supplemented or replaced them completely with Web-based information sources. Web-based or PDF-only format newsletters, called *e-zines*, are inexpensive and allow companies to post new information quickly. However, information from e-zines tends to be brief because many employees have difficulty reading long articles on a computer screen.[44]

The opening story to this chapter described how *blogs* are entering the corporate world as another communication vehicle. One recent survey reported that while only 7 percent of CEOs engage in blogging, 59 percent believed that blogs are useful for communicating with employees.[45] Blogs written by senior executives offer direct communication to employees and, if written casually, have a personal touch that makes the information more credible than formal magazines. Executive blogs also allow employees to submit their comments, which isn't possible in e-zines or newsletters. In addition to executive blogs, Matsushita and a few other firms are turning to employee blogs in which people in a work unit post updates about events in their areas.

Wikis (Hawaiian for "fast") are a collaborative variation of blogs in which anyone in a group can write, edit, or remove material from the Web site. Wikipedia, the popular online encyclopedia, is a massive example of a wiki. Wikis are also slowly finding their way into traditional organizations. Employees at Aperture Technologies Inc. in Stamford, Connecticut, use wikis to write documentation, brainstorm ideas, and coordinate marketing projects. "Wikis allow this collaboration much better than anything else, so we get things done faster," says Aperture founder Nicholas Pisarro Jr.[46]

Employee Surveys

Almost all of the "best companies to work for," as well as the majority of large firms throughout the United States and several other countries, conduct employee surveys at least once each year. In fact, leaders in two-thirds of high-performing companies claim that surveying employees is one of their most effective ways to strengthen employee engagement levels. Surveys are useful upward communication devices for a variety of purposes. Tennessee Valley Authority surveys its employees annually using a 60-item "cultural health index" that the energy producer found predicts subsequent

Kowloon Shangri-La's "State of the Hotel" Meetings Communicating with employees can be a challenge when the organization is a large hotel that operates around the clock. But these conditions haven't prevented senior management at Kowloon Shangri-La from holding "state of the hotel" meetings with all 700 staff twice each year. Two sessions are held—one in the morning, the other in the afternoon—so all employees at the Hong Kong hotel can attend without leaving the hotel short-staffed. General manager Mark Heywood conducts no-holds-barred sessions in which employees are updated about the hotel's financial performance, upcoming events, and renovations. "It's a chance to communicate about the good, the bad, and the ugly," says Heywood. "We don't just share good news and positive things." He also outlines his vision for the hotel and reinforces its "one team-one way" culture.[47]

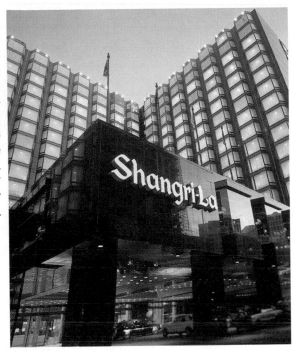

productivity in each work unit. Bell Canada surveys its 60,000 employees each year using 84 questions about several themes, including career mobility, job challenge, information sharing, and trust in the company's leadership. Canada's largest telephone company also has quarterly "pulse surveys" that measure attitudes about specific policies such as early retirement.[18]

Direct Communication with Top Management

"The best fertilizer in any field is that of the farmer's footsteps!" This old Chinese saying means that farms are most successful when the farmers spend time in the fields directly observing the crop's development. In an organizational context this means that to fully understand the issues, senior executives need to get out of the executive suite and meet directly with employees at all levels and on their turf. Nearly 40 years ago people at Hewlett-Packard coined a phrase for this communication strategy: **management by walking around (MBWA)**.[49] Greg Aasen, chief operating officer and cofounder of PMC-Sierra, does his MBWA by running with employees during lunch. "Even the senior guys I've worked with for 10 years, they tell you a lot more running out on the trails than they would in your office. It's less intimidating, I guess," says Aasen.[50]

Along with MBWA, executives are getting more direct communication with employees through "town hall meetings," where large groups of employees hear about a merger or other special news directly from the key decision makers. For example, soon after becoming chief executive of McDonald's in the UK, Peter Beresford instituted a monthly online town hall event where board members answer questions from any McDonald's staff.[51] Some executives also conduct employee roundtable forums to hear opinions from a small representation of staff about various issues. All of these direct communication strategies potentially minimize filtering because executives listen directly to employees. They also help executives acquire a deeper, quicker understanding of internal organizational problems. A third benefit of direct communication is that employees might have more empathy for decisions made further up the corporate hierarchy.

management by walking around (MBWA)

A communication practice in which executives get out of their offices and learn from others in the organization through face-to-face dialogue.

Communicating through the Grapevine

No matter how much corporate leaders try to communicate through e-zines, blogs, wikis, surveys, MBWA, and other means, employees will still rely on the oldest communication channel: the corporate **grapevine**. The grapevine is an unstructured, informal network founded on social relationships rather than organizational charts or job descriptions. What do employees think about the grapevine? Surveys of employees in two U.S. firms—one in Florida, the other in California—provide the answer. Both surveys found that almost all employees use the grapevine, but very few of them prefer this source of information. The California survey also reported that only one-third of employees believe grapevine information is credible. In other words, employees turn to the grapevine when they have few other options.[52]

grapevine
An unstructured, informal network founded on social relationships rather than organizational charts or job descriptions.

Grapevine Characteristics

Research conducted several decades ago reported that the grapevine transmits information very rapidly in all directions throughout the organization. The typical pattern is a cluster chain, whereby a few people actively transmit rumors to many others. The grapevine works through informal social networks, so it is more active where employees have similar backgrounds and can communicate easily. Many rumors seem to have at least a kernel of truth, possibly because they are transmitted through media-rich communication channels (face-to-face) and employees are motivated to communicate effectively. Nevertheless, the grapevine distorts information by deleting fine details and exaggerating key points of the story.[53]

Some of these characteristics might still be true, but other features of the grapevine have changed due to the dramatic effects of information technologies in the workplace. E-mail, instant messages, and even blogs have replaced the traditional water cooler as sources of gossip. Social networks have expanded as employees communicate with each other around the globe, not just around the next cubicle. Public blogs and Web forums have extended gossip to anyone—not just employees connected to social networks.

Grapevine Benefits and Limitations

Should the grapevine be encouraged, tolerated, or quashed? The difficulty in answering this question is that the grapevine has both benefits and limitations.[54] One benefit, as was mentioned earlier, is that employees rely on the grapevine when information is not available through formal channels. It is also the main conduit through which organizational stories and other symbols of the organization's culture are communicated. A third benefit of the grapevine is that this social interaction relieves anxiety. This explains why rumor mills are most active during times of uncertainty.[55] Finally, the grapevine is associated with the drive to bond. Being a recipient of gossip is a sign of inclusion, according to evolutionary psychologists. Trying to quash the grapevine is, in some respects, an attempt to undermine the natural human drive for social interaction.[56]

Although the grapevine offers these benefits, it is not the preferred communication medium. Grapevine information is sometimes so distorted that it escalates rather than reduces employee anxiety. Furthermore, employees develop more negative attitudes toward the organization when management is slower than the grapevine in communicating information. What should corporate leaders do with the grapevine? The best advice seems to be to listen to the grapevine as a signal of employee anxiety, then correct the cause of this anxiety. Some companies also listen to the grapevine and step in to correct blatant errors and fabrications. Most important, corporate leaders need to view the grapevine as a competitor—and eventually win the challenge to inform employees before they receive the news through the grapevine.

Chapter Summary

Communication refers to the process by which information is transmitted and understood between two or more people. Communication supports work coordination, employee well-being, knowledge management, and decision making. The communication process involves forming, encoding, and transmitting the intended message to a receiver, who then decodes the message and provides feedback to the sender. Effective communication occurs when the sender's thoughts are transmitted to and understood by the intended receiver.

Electronic mail (e-mail) is an increasingly popular way to communicate, and it has changed communication patterns in organizational settings. However, e-mail is an ineffective channel for communicating emotions; tends to reduce politeness and respect; is an inefficient medium for communicating in ambiguous, complex, and novel situations; and contributes to information overload. Instant messaging, blogs, and podcasts are also gaining popularity in organizations.

Nonverbal communication includes facial gestures, voice intonation, physical distance, and even silence. Unlike verbal communication, nonverbal communication is less rule-bound and is mostly automatic and unconscious. Emotional contagion refers to the automatic and unconscious tendency to mimic and synchronize our nonverbal behaviors with other people. The most appropriate communication medium depends on its data-carrying capacity (media richness) and its symbolic meaning to the receiver. Nonroutine and ambiguous situations require rich media.

Several barriers create noise in the communication process. People misinterpret messages because of perceptual biases. Some information is filtered out as it gets passed up the hierarchy. Jargon and ambiguous language are barriers when the sender and receiver have different interpretations of the words and symbols used. People also screen out or misinterpret messages due to information overload.

Globalization and workforce diversity have brought new communication challenges. Words are easily misunderstood in verbal communication if the receiver has a limited vocabulary or if the sender's accent distorts the usual sound of some words. Voice intonation, silence, and nonverbal cues have different meanings and importance in other cultures. There are also some communication differences between men and women, such as the tendency for men to exert status and engage in report talk in conversations, whereas women use more rapport talk and are more sensitive than are men to nonverbal cues.

To get a message across, the sender must learn to empathize with the receiver, repeat the message, choose an appropriate time for the conversation, and be descriptive rather than evaluative. Listening includes sensing, evaluating, and responding. Active listeners support these processes by postponing evaluation, avoiding interruptions, maintaining interest, empathizing, organizing information, showing interest, and clarifying the message.

Some companies try to encourage informal communication through workspace design, although open offices run the risk of increasing stress and reducing the ability to concentrate on work. Many larger organizations also rely on e-zines to communicate corporate news. Employee surveys are widely used to measure employee attitudes or involve employees in corporate decisions. Some executives also meet directly with employees, through either management by walking around or other arrangements, to facilitate communication across the organization.

In any organization employees rely on the grapevine, particularly during times of uncertainty. The grapevine is an unstructured, informal network founded on social relationships rather than organizational charts or job descriptions. Although early research identified several unique features of the grapevine, some of these features may be changing as the Internet plays an increasing role in grapevine communication.

Key Terms

communication, p. 314

emotional contagion, p. 318

flaming, p. 316

grapevine, p. 331

information overload, p. 323

jargon, p. 323

management by walking around (MBWA), p. 331

media richness, p. 319

Critical Thinking Questions

1. A company in a country that is just entering the information age intends to introduce electronic mail for office staff at its three buildings located throughout the city. Describe two benefits as well as two potential problems that employees will likely experience with this medium.

2. Corporate and employee blogs might become increasingly popular over the next few years. What

are the advantages and disadvantages of this communication medium?

3. Marshall McLuhan coined the popular phrase "The medium is the message." What does this phrase mean, and why should we be aware of it when communicating in organizations?

4. Why is emotional contagion important in organizations? What effect does the increasing reliance on e-mail have on this phenomenon?

5. Under what conditions, if any, do you think it is appropriate to use e-mail to notify an employee that he or she has been laid off or fired? Why is e-mail usually considered an inappropriate channel to convey such information?

6. Explain why men and women are sometimes frustrated with each other's communication behaviors.

7. In your opinion, has the introduction of e-mail and other information technologies increased or decreased the amount of information flowing through the corporate grapevine? Explain your answer.

8. Wikis are collaborative Web sites where anyone in a group can post, edit, or delete any information. Where might this communication technology be most useful in organizations?

Case Study 11.1 BRIDGING THE TWO WORLDS— THE ORGANIZATIONAL DILEMMA

William Todorovic, Purdue University

I had been hired by Aluminum Elements Corp. (AEC), and it was my first day of work. I was 26 years old, and I was now the manager of AEC's customer service group, which looked after customers, logistics, and some of the raw material purchasing. My superior, George, was the vice president of the company. AEC manufactured most of its products, a majority of which were destined for the construction industry, from aluminum.

As I walked around the shop floor, the employees appeared to be concentrating on their jobs, barely noticing me. Management held daily meetings in which various production issues were discussed. No one from the shop floor was invited to these meetings unless there was a specific problem. Later I also learned that management had separate washrooms and separate lunchrooms, as well as other perks that floor employees did not have. Most of the floor employees felt that management, although polite on the surface, did not really feel they had anything to learn from the floor employees.

John, who worked on the aluminum slitter, a crucial operation required before any other operations could commence, had suffered a number of unpleasant encounters with George. As a result George usually sent written memos to the floor to avoid a direct confrontation with John. Because the directions in the memos were complex, these memos were often more than two pages in length.

One morning as I was walking around, I noticed that John was very upset. Feeling that perhaps there was something I could do, I approached John and asked him if I could help. He indicated that everything was just fine. From the looks of the situation and John's body language, I felt that he was willing to talk, but John knew that this was not the way things were done at AEC. Tony, who worked at the machine next to John's, then cursed and said that the office guys cared only about schedules, not about the people down on the floor. I just looked at him, and then said that I began working here only last week, and I thought that I could address some of their issues. Tony gave me a strange look, shook his head, and went back to his machine. I could hear him still swearing as I left. Later I realized that most of the office staff were also offended by Tony's language.

On the way back to my office Lesley, a recently hired engineer from Russia, approached me and pointed out that the employees were not accustomed to managers talking to them. Managers only issued orders and made demands. As we discussed the different perceptions between office and floor staff, we were interrupted by a loud lunch bell, which startled me. I was happy to join Lesley for lunch, but she asked me why I was not eating in the office lunchroom. I replied that if I was going to understand how AEC worked, I had to get to know all the people better. In addition, I realized that this was not how

334

things were done, and I wondered about the nature of this apparent division between the managers and the floor workers. In the lunchroom the other workers were amazed to see me there, commenting that I was just new and had not learned the ropes yet.

After lunch, when I asked George, my supervisor, about his recent confrontation with John, George was surprised that John got upset, and exclaimed, "I just wanted John to know that he did a great job, and as a result, we will be able to ship on time one large order to the West Coast. In fact, I thought I was complimenting him."

Earlier, Lesley had indicated that certain behavior was expected from managers and therefore from me. I reasoned that I do not think that this behavior works, and besides it is not what I believe or how I care to behave. For the next couple of months I simply walked around the floor and took every opportunity to talk to the shop floor employees. Often when the employees related specific information about their workplaces, I felt that it went over my head. Frequently I had to write down the information and revisit it later. I made a point of listening to them, identifying where they were coming from, and trying to understand them. I needed to keep my mind open to new ideas. Because the shop employees expected me to make requests and demands, I made a point of not doing any of that. Soon enough the employees became friendly and started to accept me as one of their own, or at least as a different type of management person.

During my third month of work the employees showed me how to improve the scheduling of jobs, especially those on the aluminum slitter. In fact, the greatest contribution was made by John, who demonstrated better ways to combine the most common slitting sizes and reduce waste by retaining some of the "common-sized" material for new orders. Seeing the opportunity, I programmed a spreadsheet to calculate and track inventory. This, in addition to better planning and forecasting, allowed us to reduce our new order turnarounds from four to five weeks to one or two days.

By the time I was employed for four months, I realized that members from other departments came to me and asked me to relay messages to the shop employees. When I asked why they were delegating this task to me, they stated that I spoke the same language as the shop employees. Increasingly I became the messenger for the office-to-floor shop communication.

One morning George called me into his office and complimented me on the levels of customer service and the improvements that had been achieved. As we talked, I mentioned that we could not have done it without John's help. "He really knows his stuff, and he is good," I said. I suggested that we consider him for some type of promotion. Also, I hoped that this would be a positive gesture that would improve the communication between the office and shop floor.

George turned and pulled a flyer out of his desk: "Here is a management skills seminar. Do you think we should send John to it?"

"That is a great idea," I exclaimed. "Perhaps it would be good if he were to receive the news from you directly, George." George agreed, and after discussing some other issues, we parted company.

That afternoon John came into my office, upset and ready to quit. "After all my effort and work, you guys are sending me for training seminars. So am I not good enough for you?"

Discussion Questions

1. What barriers to effective communication existed in Aluminum Elements Corp? How did the author deal with these? What would you do differently?

2. Identify and discuss why John was upset at the end of the case. What should the writer do at this time?

Case Study 11.2 INTO THE WILD BLOG YONDER

Defense contractors and aerospace companies aren't known for their openness, but Boeing Co. is embracing a level of transparency that would be unthinkable a few years ago. In some divisions of the Chicago-based company, executives are bearing their

335

personal thoughts through internal Web logs (blogs) and sharing their public opinions through external blogs. James F. Albaugh, the chief executive of Boeing Integrated Defense Systems, uses an internal blog to get conversations going and allow employees to raise issues anonymously. Randy Baseler, vice president for marketing at Boeing Commercial Airplanes, got rapped when he started a Web log that wasn't personal enough, but has since "found his voice."

This *BusinessWeek* case study case study details the experiences of blogging at Boeing, including its potential benefits and problems. Read the full text of this *BusinessWeek* article at www.mhhe.com/mcshane4e and prepare for the discussion questions below.

Discussion Questions

1. Describe the main advantages that Boeing executives say that blogging offer the organization and its employees.

2. Some blogs work and some don't. Based on the information in this article, as well as your own opinions, what are the characteristics of successful blogs?

Source: S. Holmes, "Into the Wild Blog Yonder," *BusinessWeek*, 22 May 2006, 84.

Team Exercise 11.3 ANALYZING THE BLOGOSPHERE

PURPOSE This exercise is designed to help you understand the dynamics of corporate blogs as a way to communicate around organizations.

INSTRUCTIONS This activity is usually conducted between classes as a homework assignment. The instructor will divide the class into teams (although this exercise can also be conducted by individuals). Each team will identify a corporate blog (written by a company or government executive and aimed at customers, employees, or the wider community).

The team will analyze content in the selected blog and answer the following questions for class (preferably with brief samples where applicable):

1. Who is the main intended audience of the selected blog?

2. To what extent do you think this blog attracts the interest of its intended audience? Please explain.

3. What are the main topics in recent postings about this organization? Are they mostly good or bad news? Why do you think this has occurred?

Team Exercise 11.4 ACTIVE LISTENING EXERCISE

Mary Gander, Winona State University

PURPOSE This exercise is designed to help you understand the dynamics of active listening in conversations and to develop active listening skills.

INSTRUCTIONS For each of the four vignettes presented here, student teams (or students working individually) will compose three statements that demonstrate active listening. Specifically, one statement will indicate that you show empathy for the

situation; the second will ask for clarification and detail in a nonjudgmental way; and the third statement will provide nonevaluative feedback to the speaker. Here are details about each of these three types of responses:

Showing empathy: acknowledge feelings. Sometimes it sounds like a speaker wants you to agree with him or her, but in reality the speaker mainly wants you to understand how he or she feels. "Acknowledging feelings" involves taking in the speaker's statements while looking at the "whole message" including body language, tone of voice, and level of arousal, and trying to determine what emotion the speaker is conveying. Then you let the speaker know that you realize what he or she is feeling by acknowledging it in a sentence.

Asking for clarification and detail while withholding your judgment and own opinions. This conveys that you are trying to understand and not just trying to push your opinions onto the speaker. To formulate a relevant question in asking for more clarification, you will have to listen carefully to what the speaker says. Frame your question as someone trying to understand in more detail; often asking for a specific example is useful. This also helps the speaker evaluate his or her own opinions and perspective.

Providing nonevaluative feedback: feeding back the message you heard. This will allow the speaker to determine if he or she conveyed the message to you and will help prevent troublesome miscommunication. It will also help the speaker become more aware of how he or she is coming across to another person (self-evaluation). Just think about what the speaker is conveying; paraphrase it in your own words, and say it back to the speaker (without judging the correctness or merit of what was said), asking him or her if that is what was meant.

After teams (or individual students) have prepared the three statements for each vignette, the instructor will ask them to present their statements and explain how these statements satisfy the active listening criteria.

VIGNETTE #1 A colleague stops by your desk and says, "I am tired of the lack of leadership around here. The boss is so wishy-washy, he can't get tough with some of the slackers around here. They just keep milking the company, living off the rest of us. Why doesn't management do something about these guys? And *you* are always so supportive of the boss; he's not as good as you make him out to be."

Develop three statements that respond to the speaker in this vignette by (a) showing empathy, (b)

seeking clarification, and (c) providing nonevaluative feedback.

VIGNETTE #2 Your co-worker stops by your cubicle; her voice and body language show stress, frustration, and even some fear. You know she has been working hard and has a strong need to get her work done on time and done well. You are trying to concentrate on some work and have had a number of interruptions already. She abruptly interrupts you and says, "This project is turning out to be a mess. Why can't the other three people on my team quit fighting with each other?"

Develop three statements that respond to the speaker in this vignette by (a) showing empathy, (b) seeking clarification, and (c) providing nonevaluative feedback.

VIGNETTE #3 One of your subordinates is working on an important project. He is an engineer who has good technical skills and knowledge and was selected for the project team because of that. He stops by your office and appears to be quite agitated: His voice is loud and strained, and his face has a look of bewilderment. He says, "I'm supposed to be working with four other people from four other departments on this new project, but they never listen to my ideas and seem to hardly know I'm at the meeting!"

Develop three statements that respond to the speaker in this vignette by (a) showing empathy, (b) seeking clarification, and (c) providing nonevaluative feedback.

VIGNETTE #4 Your subordinate comes into your office in a state of agitation, asking if she can talk to you. She is polite and sits down. She seems calm and does not have an angry look on her face. However, she says, "It seems like you consistently make up lousy schedules; you are unfair and unrealistic in the kinds of assignments you give certain people, me included. Everyone else is so intimidated they don't complain, but I think you need to know that this isn't right and it's got to change."

Develop three statements that respond to the speaker in this vignette by (a) showing empathy, (b) seeking clarification, and (c) providing nonevaluative feedback.

Team Exercise 11.5 CROSS-CULTURAL COMMUNICATION GAME

PURPOSE This exercise is designed to develop and test your knowledge of cross-cultural differences in communication and etiquette.

MATERIALS The instructor will provide one set of question-and-answer cards to each pair of teams.

INSTRUCTIONS

1. The class is divided into an even number of teams. Ideally each team would have three students. (Two- or four-student teams are possible if matched with an equal-sized team.) Each team is then paired with another team, and the paired teams (teams "A" and "B") are assigned a private space away from other matched teams.

2. The instructor will hand each pair of teams a stack of cards with the multiple-choice questions face down. These cards have questions and answers about cross-cultural differences in communication and etiquette. No books or other aids are allowed.

3. The exercise begins with a member of team A picking up one card from the top of the pile and posing the question on that card to members of team B. The information given to team B includes the question and all alternatives listed on the card. Team B has 30 seconds to give an answer after the question and alternatives have been read. Team B earns one point if the correct answer is given. If team B's answer is incorrect, however, team A earns that point. Correct answers to each question are indicated on the card and, of course, should not be revealed until the question is correctly answered or time is up. Whether or not team B answers correctly, it picks up the next card on the pile and asks its question to members of team A. In other words, cards are read alternately to each team. This procedure is repeated until all of the cards have been read or time has elapsed. The team receiving the most points wins.

Important note: The textbook provides little information pertaining to the questions in this exercise. Rather, you must rely on past learning, logic, and luck to win.

Source: ©2001 Steven L. McShane.

Self-Assessment 11.6

ACTIVE LISTENING SKILLS INVENTORY

PURPOSE This self-assessment is designed to help you estimate your strengths and weaknesses in various dimensions of active listening.

INSTRUCTIONS Think back to face-to-face conversations you have had with a co-worker or client in the office, hallway, factory floor, or other setting. Indicate the extent to which each item in the accompanying chart describes your behavior during those conversations. Answer each item as truthfully as possible to get an accurate estimate of where your active listening skills need improvement. Then use the scoring key in Appendix B to calculate your results for each scale. This exercise is completed alone so you can assess yourself honestly without concerns of social comparison. However, class discussion will focus on the important elements of active listening.

Active Listening Skills Inventory

Check the response to the right that best indicates the extent to which each statement describes you when listening to others.	Not at all	A little	Some-what	Very much
1. I keep an open mind about the speaker's point of view until he or she has finished talking.	☐	☐	☒	☐
2. While listening, I mentally sort out the speaker's ideas in a way that makes sense to me.	☐	☐	☐	☒
3. I stop the speaker and give my opinion when I disagree with something he or she has said.	☐	☐	☒	☐
4. People can often tell when I'm not concentrating on what they are saying.	☒	☐	☐	☐
5. I don't evaluate what a person is saying until he or she has finished talking.	☒	☐	☐	☐
6. When someone takes a long time to present a simple idea, I let my mind wander to other things.	☐	☒	☐	☐
7. I jump into conversations to present my views rather than wait and risk forgetting what I wanted to say.	☐	☒	☐	☐
8. I nod my head and make other gestures to show I'm interested in the conversation.	☐	☐	☐	☒
9. I can usually keep focused on what people are saying to me even when they don't sound interesting.	☐	☒	☐	☐
10. Rather than organizing the speaker's ideas, I usually expect the person to summarize them for me.	☐	☒	☐	☐
11. I always say things like "I see" or "uh-huh" so people know that I'm really listening to them.	☐	☐	☐	☒
12. While listening, I concentrate on what is being said and regularly organize the information.	☐	☐	☒	☐
13. While a speaker is talking, I quickly determine whether I like or dislike his or her ideas.	☐	☐	☒	☐
14. I pay close attention to what people are saying even when they are explaining something I already know.	☐	☒	☐	☐
15. I don't give my opinion until I'm sure the other person has finished talking.	☐	☒	☐	☐

Source: ©Copyright 2000 Steven L. McShane.

After reading this chapter, if you need additional information, see **www.mhhe.com/mcshane4e** for more in-depth interactivities that correspond with this material.

For three long days junior trader Dennis Gentilin received the cold shoulder from his boss, Luke Duffy. Duffy, who ran National Australia Bank's (NAB) foreign currency options desk in Melbourne, had discovered that Gentilin complained to Duffy's boss, Gary Dillon, that Duffy was altering transaction records to "smooth" his group's profits. Smoothing (which includes carrying forward trading losses) was apparently common at one time, but traders had recently been warned to stop the practice.

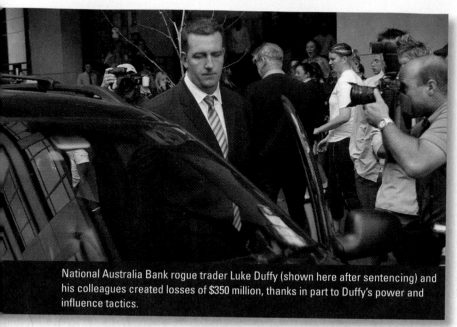

National Australia Bank rogue trader Luke Duffy (shown here after sentencing) and his colleagues created losses of $350 million, thanks in part to Duffy's power and influence tactics.

On the fourth day, Duffy called Gentilin into a private meeting and, according to Gentilin, launched into a tirade: "I felt like … killing someone the other day," Duffy said pointedly to Gentilin. "If you want to stay in the team, I demand loyalty and don't want you going to Dillon about what's happening in the team."

Duffy was apparently accustomed to getting his way. Gentilin explained that Duffy, Dillon, and a few other senior traders were "untouchables" who were given free rein at NAB due to their expertise. "They just created this power base where they were laws unto themselves," claims Gentilin.

Anyone who interfered with Duffy's plans was apparently mocked into submission. For example, Duffy taunted a co-worker in London who he thought was too skeptical and conservative. Duffy called him "the London stench boy" because he "was always making a stink about things whether they were going on, both good and bad, and you could smell the stink coming from London," Duffy admitted in court.

Soon after his private meeting with Duffy, Gentilin was transferred to NAB's London office, still working in the foreign exchange group. Duffy's unit in Melbourne continued to fudge the numbers so upper management wouldn't notice any problems with the trading results. But when the group bet the wrong way against a rising Australian dollar, the cover-ups escalated, including creation of fictitious trades to offset the losses. The idea was that they could recover the losses and receive their cherished bonuses by year-end.

Fatefully, Gentilin got wind from London of these subsequent trading problems, so he asked Vanessa McCallum, a junior NAB trader in Melbourne, to have other people look into Duffy's transactions. McCallum later acknowledged that she was terrified about asking for the audit. "My greatest fear was, if nothing is wrong I'm going to have to leave the desk because you had to be loyal to Luke [Duffy]," explained McCallum, who no longer works at the bank.

What senior NAB executives discovered shook the Australian bank to its core. Duffy and other senior traders had become a rogue team that amassed $350 million in losses in one year. Their unrestrained power and influence kept everyone (except Gentilin and McCallum) in line, resulting in countless transaction record irregularities and over 800 breaches of the bank's trading limits. Duffy and a few other traders were jailed for securities violations. Several executives, including both NAB's chief executive and chairman, lost their jobs.[1]

Power and Influence in the Workplace

LEARNING OBJECTIVES

After reading this chapter you should be able to

1. Define the meaning of *power* and *counterpower*.
2. Describe the five bases of power in organizations.
3. Explain how information relates to power in organizations.
4. Discuss the four contingencies of power.
5. Summarize the eight types of influence tactics.
6. Discuss three contingencies to consider when deciding which influence tactic to use.
7. Distinguish influence from organizational politics.
8. Describe the organizational conditions and personal characteristics that support organizational politics.
9. Identify ways to minimize organizational politics.

The National Australia Bank saga illustrates how power and influence can have profound consequences for employee behavior and the organization's success. Although this story has an unhappy ending, power and influence can equally influence ethical conduct and improve corporate performance. The reality is that no one escapes from organizational power and influence. They exist in every business and, according to some writers, in every decision and action.

This chapter unfolds as follows: First we define *power* and present a basic model depicting the dynamics of power in organizational settings. The chapter then discusses the five bases of power, as well as information as a power base. Next we look at the contingencies that amplify or weaken the potential of those sources of power. The latter part of this chapter examines the various types of influence in organizational settings as well as the contingencies of effective influence strategies. The final section of this chapter looks at situations in which influence becomes organizational politics, as well as ways of minimizing dysfunctional politics.

Learning Objectives

After reading the next three sections you should be able to

1. **Define the meaning of *power* and *counterpower*.**
2. **Describe the five bases of power in organizations.**
3. **Explain how information relates to power in organizations.**
4. **Discuss the four contingencies of power.**

The Meaning of Power

power
The capacity of a person, team, or organization to influence others.

Power is the capacity of a person, team, or organization to influence others.[2] Power is not the act of changing others' attitudes or behavior; it is only the potential to do so. People frequently have power they do not use; they might not even know they have power.

The most basic prerequisite of power is that one person or group believes it is dependent on another person or group for something of value.[3] This relationship is shown in Exhibit 12.1, where Person A has power over Person B by controlling something that Person B needs to achieve his or her goals. You might have power over others by controlling a desired job assignment, useful information, important resources, or even the privilege of being associated with you! In the opening story Luke Duffy wielded power because he controlled the job security and workplace resources of the NAB foreign exchange staff. To make matters more complex, power is ultimately a perception, so people might gain power simply by convincing others that they have something of value. Thus power exists when others believe that you control resources they want.[4]

Exhibit 12.1
Dependence in the Power Relationship

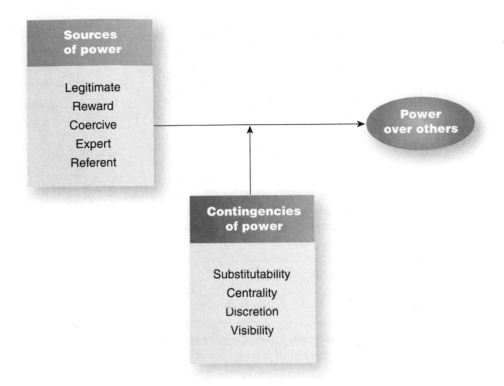

Exhibit 12.2
A Model of Power within Organizations

Sources of power

Legitimate
Reward
Coercive
Expert
Referent

Power over others

Contingencies of power

Substitutability
Centrality
Discretion
Visibility

counterpower
The capacity to a person, team, or organization to keep a more powerful person or group in the exchange relationship

Although power requires dependence, it is really more accurate to say that the parties are interdependent. One party may be more dependent than the other, but the relationship exists only when each party has something of value to the other. Exhibit 12.1 shows a dashed line to illustrate the weaker party's (Person B's) power over the dominant participant (Person A). This **counterpower**, as it is known, is strong enough to maintain Person A's participation in the exchange relationship. For example, executives have power over subordinates by controlling their job security and promotional opportunities. At the same time, employees have counterpower by controlling their ability to work productively and thereby creating a positive impression of the supervisor to his or her boss. Counterpower usually motivates executives to apply their power judiciously so that the relationship is not broken.

A Model of Power in Organizations

Power involves more than just dependence. As we see in Exhibit 12.2, the model of power includes both power sources and contingencies. It indicates that power is derived from five sources: legitimate, reward, coercive, expert, and referent. The model also shows that these sources yield power only under certain conditions. The four contingencies of power include the employee's or department's substitutability, centrality, discretion, and visibility. Finally, as we will discuss later, the type of power applied affects the type of influence the power holder has over the other person or work unit.

Sources of Power in Organizations

More than 40 years ago social scientists John French and Bertrand Raven listed five sources of power within organizations: legitimate, reward, coercive, expert, and referent. Many researchers have studied these five power bases and searched for others.

For the most part, French and Raven's list remains intact.[5] The first three power bases are derived from the power holder's position; that is, the person receives these power bases because of the specific authority or roles he or she is assigned in the organization. The latter two sources of power originate from the power holder's own characteristics. In other words, people bring these power bases to the organization.

Legitimate Power

Legitimate power is the capacity to influence others through formal authority. This perceived right partly comes from formal job descriptions as well as informal rules of conduct. Executives have considerable legitimate power, but all employees also have this power based on company rules and government laws.[6] For example, an organization might give employees the right to request customer files if this information is required for their job.

Legitimate power depends on more than job descriptions. It also depends on mutual agreement from those expected to abide by this authority. Your boss's power to make you work overtime partly depends on your agreement to this power. Stories and movies about mutinies, such as *The Caine Mutiny* and *Crimson Tide*, illustrate this point; mutinies occur when bosses step too far outside the range of authority that employees deem acceptable. More frequently, employees question their bosses' right to make them stay late or perform unsafe tasks and other activities. Thus, legitimate power is a person's authority to make discretionary decisions as long as followers accept this discretion.[7]

People in high power distance cultures (that is, those who accept an unequal distribution of power) are more likely to comply with legitimate power than are people in low power distance cultures. Legitimate power is also stronger in some organizations than in others. A 3M scientist might continue to work on a project after being told by

Legitimate Power Meets a Mutiny *Crimson Tide* is a riveting novel and film about the limits of legitimate power. When radical Russian nationalists threaten World War III, the nuclear submarine *USS Alabama* is sent to prepare for retaliation with its own nuclear arsenal. The signal to launch does come in, but the message is incomplete before the submarine goes into silent mode. Alabama's commander, Captain Frank Ramsey (Gene Hackman, right in photo), is ready to have his crew push the button, whereas Lieutenant Commander Ron Hunter (Denzel Washington, left in photo), opposes this decision. What ensues is a mutiny that divides the loyalties of the *Alabama's* crew. The story illustrates how Captain Ramsey's decision and its consequences tested the limits of his legitimate power over his crew.

superiors to stop working on it because the 3M culture supports an entrepreneurial spirit, which includes ignoring your boss's authority from time to time. More generally, employees are becoming less tolerant of legitimate power. They increasingly expect to be involved in decisions rather than being told what to do.[8] Thus the command style of leadership that often guided employee behavior in the past must be replaced by other forms, particularly expert and referent power, which are described below.

Reward Power

Reward power is derived from a person's ability to control the allocation of rewards valued by others and to remove negative sanctions (negative reinforcement). Managers have formal authority that gives them power over the distribution of organizational rewards such as pay, promotions, time off, vacation schedules, and work assignments. Employees also have reward power over their bosses through the use of 360-degree feedback systems. Employee feedback affects supervisors' promotions and other rewards, so they tend to behave differently toward employees after 360-degree feedback is introduced.

Coercive Power

Coercive power is the ability to apply punishment. In the opening story to this chapter, Luke Duffy demonstrated his coercive power by reprimanding and threatening employees into submission. Employees also have coercive power, ranging from sarcasm to ostracism, to ensure that co-workers conform to team norms. Many firms also rely on the coercive power of team members to control co-worker behavior.

For instance, when asked how AirAsia maintained attendance and productivity when the Kuala Lumpur–based discount airline removed the time clocks, chief executive Tony Fernandes replied, "Simple. Peer pressure sees to that. The fellow employees, who are putting their shoulders to the wheel, will see to that." General Electric's Aircraft Engines division also relies on co-workers to guide employee behavior. "There is no better pressure than peer pressure," says GE's team plant manager in Durham, North Carolina.[9]

Expert Power

Legitimate, reward, and coercive power mainly originate from the individual's position in the organization. In contrast, expert power originates from within each person. It is an individual's or work unit's capacity to influence others by possessing knowledge or skills that they value. Luke Duffy and other "untouchables" mentioned in the opening story had expert power over more senior executives at National Australia Bank, apparently to the point that they performed much of their work with minimal checks and balances. Employees are also gaining expert power as our society moves from an industrial to a knowledge-based economy.[10] The reason is that employee knowledge becomes the means of production and is ultimately outside the control of those who own the company. And without this control over production, owners are more dependent on employees to achieve their corporate objectives.

Referent Power

referent power
The capacity to influence others based on the identification and respect they have for the power holder.

People have **referent power** when others identify with them, like them, or otherwise respect them. Like expert power, referent power comes from within a person. It is largely a function of the person's interpersonal skills and usually develops slowly. Referent power is usually associated with charismatic leadership. *Charisma* is often defined as a form of interpersonal attraction whereby followers develop respect for and trust in the charismatic individual.[11]

Information and Power

Information is power.[12] This phrase, which is increasingly relevant in a knowledge-based economy, exists in two forms. First, people gain information power when they control the flow of information to others. These information gatekeepers can alter perceptions of the situation and restrict information as a resource that others need to accomplish their work. For example, supervisors tend to have more information power in a centralized hierarchy where information flows through them to employees. But when information systems (such as intranets and corporate blogs) bypass supervisors, their information power declines.[13]

Second, information power is higher for those who seem to be able to cope with organizational uncertainties. Organizations value the ability to cope with environmental uncertainties because it allows them to more easily secure resources, introduce more efficient work processes, and estimate demand for their outputs. In other words, coping increases the organization's adaptability to its environment. Individuals and work units gain power by offering one or more of the following ways to cope with uncertainty, with the first being the most powerful:[14]

- *Prevention.* The most effective strategy is to prevent environmental changes from occurring. For example, financial experts acquire power by preventing the organization from experiencing a cash shortage or defaulting on loans.

- *Forecasting.* The next best strategy is to predict environmental changes or variations. In this respect, marketing specialists gain power by predicting changes in consumer preferences.

- *Absorption.* People and work units also gain power by absorbing or neutralizing the impact of environmental shifts as they occur. An example is the ability of maintenance crews to come to the rescue when machines break down and the production process stops.

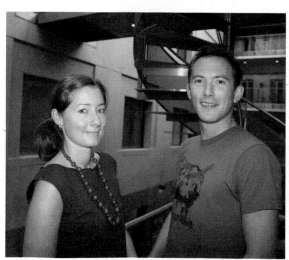

Trend Spotters Have Information Power People who can forecast the future are worth their weight in gold. The reason is this: Information about the future helps companies cope with environmental uncertainties. Corporate leaders can ramp up production to cash in on growing demand and can take corrective action to minimize damage from falling demand. "It's good to have advance-warning radar about what's happening among consumers," says London-based trend spotter Zoe Lazarus. Lazarus and Richard Welch in New York (both shown here) jointly lead a trend analysis unit for Lowe Worldwide, one of several ad agencies that have recently introduced trend analysis teams that peer into the future. Along with scanning offbeat magazines *(Sleazenation, Relax)*, Lazarus and Welch anticipate social changes by listening to more than 500 bartenders, photographers, disc jockeys, architects, journalists, designers, and other "influencers" in 52 cities across several countries. "[We're] looking for leading-edge trends that will eventually filter into the mainstream in one to two years' time, changing patterns in leisure behavior, holiday destinations, music choices, as well as fashion trends," Lazarus explains.[15]

Contingencies of Power

Let's say that you have expert power by virtue of your ability to forecast and possibly even prevent dramatic changes in the organization's environment. Does this expertise mean that you are influential? Not necessarily. As we saw earlier in Exhibit 12.2, power bases generate power only under certain conditions. The four conditions—called the *contingencies of power*—include substitutability, centrality, discretion, and visibility.[16] These are not sources of power; rather, they determine the extent to which people can leverage their power bases. You may have lots of expert power, but you won't be able to influence others with this power base if the contingency factors are not in place.

Substitutability

substitutability
The extent to which people dependent on a resource have alternatives.

Substitutability refers to the availability of alternatives. Power is strongest when someone has a monopoly over a valued resource. Conversely, power decreases as the number of alternative sources of the critical resource increases. If only you have expertise across the organization on an important issue, you would be more powerful than if several people in your company possessed this valued knowledge. Substitutability refers not only to other sources that offer the resource, but also to substitutions for the resource itself. For instance, labor unions are weakened when companies introduce technologies that replace the need for their union members. At one time a strike by telephone employees would have shut down operations, but computerized systems and other technological innovations now ensure that telephone operations continue during labor strikes and reduce the need for telephone operators during normal operations. Technology is a substitute for employees and consequently reduces union power.

How do people and work units increase their power through nonsubstitutability? There are several ways, although not all of them are ethical. We describe some of them here for your information—not necessarily for you to practice:

- *Controlling tasks.* Governments pass laws that give certain professions an exclusive right to perform particular tasks. As an example, most countries require publicly traded corporations to have their financial statements audited by a specific accounting group (certified public accountants, chartered accountants, or the like). The simmering conflict between medical doctors and nurse practitioners in some countries is also based on the exclusive rights of doctors to perform specific medical procedures that nurse practitioners want within their mandate.

- *Controlling knowledge.* Professions control access to the knowledge of their work domain, such as through restricted enrollment in educational programs. Knowledge is also restricted on the job. Several years ago maintenance workers in a French tobacco processing plant had become very powerful because they controlled the knowledge required to repair the tobacco machines.[17] The maintenance manuals had mysteriously disappeared, and the machines had been redesigned enough that only the maintenance staff knew how to fix them if they broke down (which they often did). Knowing the power of nonsubstitutability, maintenance staff carefully avoided documenting the repair procedures and didn't talk to production employees about their trade knowledge.

- *Controlling labor.* Aside from their knowledge resource, people gain power by controlling the availability of their labor. Labor unions attempt to organize as many people as possible within a particular trade or industry so that employers have no other source of labor supply. Unions have an easier time increasing wages when their members produce almost all of a particular product or service in the industry. The union's power during a strike is significantly weakened when the employer can continue production through outside contractors or other nonunion facilities.

- *Differentiation.* Differentiation occurs when an individual or work unit claims to have a unique resource—such as raw materials or knowledge—that others would want. By definition, the uniqueness of this resource means no one else has it. The tactic here isn't so much the nonsubstitutability of the resource, but making others believe that the resource is unique. Some people claim that consultants use this tactic. They take skills and knowledge that many consulting firms can provide and wrap them into a package (with the latest buzzwords, of course) so that it looks like a service that no one else can offer.

Centrality

centrality
The degree and nature of interdependence between the power holder and others.

Centrality refers to the degree and nature of interdependence between the power holder and others.[18] Think about your own centrality for a moment: If you decided not to show up for work or school tomorrow, how many people would be affected, and how much time would pass before they were affected? If you have high centrality, most people in the organization would be adversely affected by your absence, and they would be affected quickly. This centrality was apparent when, as Connections 12.1 describes, New York City transit workers staged an illegal walkout. Within hours, commuters and businesses were affected. When it ended three days later, the strike had cost the city and its businesses more than $1 billion. Notice, however, that the power of centrality in the New York transit strike was partly offset by its substitutability—dedicated and sometimes ingenious New York commuters and business leaders found ways during the strike to reduce their dependence on the transit system.

Discretion

The freedom to exercise judgment—to make decisions without referring to a specific rule or receiving permission from someone else—is another important contingency of power in organizations. Consider the plight of first-line supervisors. It may seem that they have legitimate and reward power over employees, but this power is often curtailed by specific rules. This lack of discretion makes supervisors largely powerless even though they may have access to some of the power bases described earlier in this chapter. "Middle managers are very much 'piggy-in-the-middle,'" complains a middle manager at Britain's National Health System. "They have little power, only what senior managers are allowed to give them."[19]

Visibility

Several years ago as a junior copywriter at advertising agency Chiat/Day, Mimi Cook submitted an idea for a potential client to her boss, who then presented it to co-founder Jay Chiat. Chiat was thrilled with the concept, but Cook's boss "never mentioned the idea came from me," recalls Cook. Cook confronted her boss, who claimed the oversight was unintentional. But when a similar incident occurred a few months later, Cook left the agency for another firm.[20]

Mimi Cook, who has since progressed to associate creative director at another ad agency, knows that power does not flow to unknown people in the organization. Those who control valued resources or knowledge will yield power only when others are aware of these power bases—in other words, when it is visible. One way to increase visibility is to take people-oriented jobs and work on projects that require

New York Transit Strike Reveals Its Centrality, But Also Its Substitutability

New York City's 7 million commuters were recently on the receiving end of centrality of power when transit workers illegally walked off the job for three days (legislation bans transit strikes in New York). The strike's effect on commuters and businesses was immediate and widespread, amplified by the fact that the strike occurred during peak Christmas shopping and while the weather was cold and blustery. Roads were clogged just hours after the strike began, even though cars with fewer than four passengers were denied entry to the city center. Downtown department stores were noticeably quieter in spite of one-day sales to counter the strike's effect. Some businesses estimated that half of their employees did not arrive to work or were very late. Some public schools started two hours later than usual. New York's mayor estimated the three-day stoppage cost the city and its businesses more than $1 billion.

"[The Metropolitan Transit Authority] told us we got no power, but we got power," said striking transit worker Fausto Fienco. "We got the power to stop the city." The strike ended after three days because courts imposed heavy fines on the transit union and promised jail terms for its leaders.

Although some newspaper headlines claimed the strike "paralyzed" New York City, it did not cause mass chaos, largely because the union's centrality was offset by substitutability as determined commuters found alternative ways to get to work. New Jersey residents took the less well-known PATH transit system into New York City, tripling the usual number of riders on the first day. Some Wall Street securities firms arranged special busing for their staff. Television stations booked hotel rooms nearby so key staff could avoid the need for any commuting. Telecommuting at American Express and other firms shot up for the strike's three days.

For many others, the only alternative to an expensive taxi ride was to walk dozens of city blocks or bicycle even farther. "I live in Brooklyn and I walked all the way here," says Giovanni Magana, a security guard at Macy's downtown store. "It took me about three hours, and I'll have to walk back home tonight."

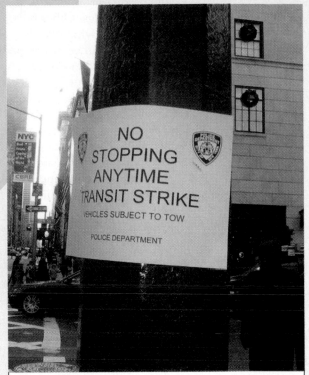

Seven million New York City commuters felt the effects of the transit union's centrality when its members walked off the job just before Christmas.

Sources: "N.Y. Transit Strike Sends TV, Film Biz Scrambling," *Reuters News,* 20 December 2005, J. Frankston, "PATH Ridership Spikes during Strike, Authority Chairman Pushes for New Service," *Associated Press,* 24 December 2005; S. D. Harrington and B. Ivry, "For Commuters, a Day to Adapt," *The Record* (Bergen, New Jersey), 21 December 2005, p. A01; S. McCarthy, "Transit Strike Cripples New York," *Globe & Mail* (Toronto), 21 December 2005, p. A17; R. Richmond, "During Strike, Some New Yorkers Go to Work Virtually," *Dow Jones Newswires,* 21 December 2005.

frequent interaction with senior executives. "You can take visibility in steps," advises an executive at a U.S. pharmaceutical firm. "You can start by making yourself visible in a small group, such as a staff meeting. Then when you're comfortable with that, seek out larger arenas."[21]

Employees also gain visibility by being, quite literally, visible. Some people strategically move into offices or cubicles where co-workers pass most often (such as closest to the elevator or office lunchroom). People often use public symbols as subtle (and not-so-subtle) cues to make their power sources known to others. Many professionals display their educational diplomas and awards on office walls to

349

remind visitors of their expertise. Medical professionals wear white coats with a stethoscope around their necks to symbolize their legitimate and expert power in hospital settings. Other people play the game of "face time"—spending more time at work and showing that they are working productively. One engineer working on a color laser printer project made a habit of going to the office once each week at 2 a.m. after her boss once saw her working at that hour. "[A]fter the reaction I got from my manager I decided it was important to do that early morning work in the office," explains the engineer. "It is better to be seen here if you are going to work in the middle of the night."[22]

mentoring
The process of learning the ropes of organizational life from a senior person within the company.

Another way to increase visibility is through **mentoring**—the process of learning the ropes of organizational life from a senior person within the company. Mentors give protégés more visible and meaningful work opportunities and open doors for them to meet more senior people in the organization. Mentors also teach these newcomers influence tactics supported by the organization's senior decision makers.[23]

Networking and Power

networking
Cultivating social relationships with others to accomplish one's goals.

"It's not what you know, but whom you know that counts!" This often-heard statement reflects the reality that employees get ahead not just by developing their competencies, but by **networking**—cultivating social relationships with others to accomplish one's goals. Networking increases a person's power in three ways. First, networks represent a critical component of *social capital*—the knowledge and other resources available to people or social units (teams, organizations) due to a durable network that connects them to others. Networks consist of people who trust each other, which increases the flow of knowledge among those within the network. The more you network, the more likely you will receive valuable information that increases your expert power in the organization.[24]

Second, people tend to identify more with partners within their own networks, which increases referent power among people within each network. This network-based referent power may lead to more favorable decisions by others in the network. Finally, effective networkers are better known by others in the organization, so their talents are more readily recognized. This power increases when networkers place themselves in strategic positions in the network, thereby gaining centrality.[25] For example, these people might be regarded as the main person who distributes information in the network or who keeps the network connected through informal gatherings.

Networking is a natural part of the informal organization, yet it can create a formidable barrier to those who are not actively connected to it.[26] Women are often excluded from powerful networks because they do not participate in golf games and other male-dominated social events. That's what Deloitte and Touche executives discovered when they investigated why so many junior female employees left the accounting and consulting firm before reaching partnership level. Deloitte and Touche now relies on mentoring, formal women's network groups, and measurement of career progress to ensure that female staff members have the same career development opportunities as their male colleagues.[27]

Learning Objectives

After reading the next section you should be able to

5. **Summarize the eight types of influence tactics.**
6. **Discuss three contingencies to consider when deciding which influence tactic to use.**

Influencing Others

Up to this point we have focused on the sources and contingencies of power. But power is only the capacity to influence others. It represents the potential to change someone's attitudes and behavior. Influence, on the other hand, refers to any behavior that attempts to alter someone's attitudes or behavior.[28] Influence is power in motion. It applies one or more power bases to get people to alter their beliefs, feelings, and activities. Consequently our focus in the remainder of this chapter is on how people use power to influence others.

Influence tactics are woven throughout the social fabric of all organizations. This is because influence is an essential process through which people coordinate their effort and act in concert to achieve organizational objectives. Indeed, influence is central to the definition of leadership. Influence operates down, across, and up the corporate hierarchy. Executives ensure that subordinates complete required tasks. Employees influence co-workers to help them with their job assignments. Subordinates engage in upward influence tactics so corporate leaders make decisions compatible with subordinates' needs and expectations.

Types of Influence Tactics

Organizational behavior researchers have devoted considerable attention to the various types of influence tactics found in organizational settings. A groundbreaking study over 25 years ago identified several influence strategies, but recent evidence suggests that some of them overlap.[29] The original list also seems to have a Western bias that ignores influence tactics used in Asian and other cultures.[30] With these caveats in mind, we will focus on the following influence tactics identified in the current literature (see Exhibit 12.3): silent authority, assertiveness, information control, coalition formation, upward appeal, ingratiation and impression management, persuasion, and exchange. The first five are known as *hard influence tactics* because they force behavior change through position power (legitimate, reward, and coercion).

Exhibit 12.3

Types of Influence Tactics in Organizations

Influence Tactic	Description
Silent authority	Influencing behavior through legitimate power without explicitly referring to that power base.
Assertiveness	Actively applying legitimate and coercive power by applying pressure or threats.
Information control	Explicitly manipulating someone else's access to information for the purpose of changing their attitudes and/or behavior.
Coalition formation	Forming a group that attempts to influence others by pooling the resources and power of its members.
Upward appeal	Gaining support from one or more people with higher authority or expertise.
Ingratiation/impression management	Attempting to increase liking by, or perceived similarity to, some targeted person.
Persuasion	Using logical arguments, factual evidence, and emotional appeals to convince people of the value of a request.
Exchange	Promising benefits or resources in exchange for the target person's compliance.

The latter three—ingratiation and impression management, persuasion, and exchange—are called *soft tactics* because they rely more on personal sources of power (referent, expert) and appeal to the target person's attitudes and needs.

Silent Authority

The silent application of authority occurs when someone complies with a request because of the requester's legitimate power as well as the target person's role expectations. We often refer to this condition as *deference to authority*.[31] This deference occurs when you comply with your boss's request to complete a particular task. If the task is within your job scope and your boss has the right to make this request, then this influence strategy operates without negotiation, threats, persuasion, or other tactics.

Silent authority is often overlooked as an influence strategy in the United States, but it is the most common form of influence in high power distance cultures. Employees comply with supervisor requests without question because they respect the supervisor's higher authority in the organization. Silent authority also occurs when leaders influence subordinates through role modeling. One study reported that Japanese managers typically influence subordinates by engaging in the behaviors that they want employees to mimic.[32]

Assertiveness

In contrast to silent authority, assertiveness might be called *vocal authority* because it involves actively applying legitimate and coercive power to influence others. Assertiveness includes persistently reminding a target of his or her obligations, frequently checking the target's work, confronting the target, and using threats of sanctions to force compliance. Assertiveness typically applies or threatens to apply punishment if the target does not comply. Explicit or implicit threats range from job loss to losing face by letting down the team. Extreme forms of assertiveness include blackmailing colleagues, such as by threatening to reveal the other person's previously unknown failures unless he or she complies with your request. Associates claim that Luke Duffy influenced his staff at National Australia Bank largely through assertiveness, including threatening to fire them if they didn't keep quiet and follow his wishes.

Information Control

Luke Duffy also used information control as an influence tactic. Specifically, the rogue National Australia Bank trader hid hundreds of illegal transactions from his boss and other executives to avoid their involvement in the unit's trading problems. Information control involves explicitly manipulating others' access to information for the purpose of changing their attitudes or behavior. With limited access to potentially valuable information, others are at a disadvantage. Although the NAB incident is more extreme than most, hiding information isn't unusual in organizations. Almost half of the employees in one major survey believe people keep their colleagues in the dark about work issues if it helps their own cause. Employees also influence executive decisions by screening out (filtering) information flowing up the hierarchy. Indeed, one recent study found that CEOs also influence their board of directors by selectively feeding information to board members.[33]

Coalition Formation

coalition
An informal group that attempts to influence people outside the group by pooling the resources and power of its members.

When people lack sufficient power alone to influence others in the organization, they might form a **coalition** of people who support the proposed change. A coalition is influential in three ways.[34] First, it pools the power and resources of many people, so the coalition potentially has more influence than any number of people operating alone. Second, the coalition's mere existence can be a source of power by symbolizing the legitimacy of the issue. In other words, a coalition creates a sense that the issue deserves attention because it has broad support. Third, coalitions tap into the power of the social identity process introduced in Chapter 3. A coalition is essentially an informal group that advocates a new set of norms and behaviors. If the coalition has a broad-based membership (that is, if its members come from various parts of the organization), then other employees are more likely to identify with that group and consequently accept the ideas the coalition is proposing.

Upward Appeal   Have you ever had a disagreement with a colleague in which one of you eventually says, "I'm sure the boss (or teacher) will agree with me on this. Let's find out!" This tactic—called **upward appeal**—is a form of coalition in which at least one member is someone with higher authority or expertise. Upward appeal ranges from a formal alliance to the perception of informal support from someone with higher authority or expertise. Upward appeal also includes relying on the authority of the firm as an entity without approaching anyone further up the hierarchy. For instance, one study reported that Japanese managers influence employees by reminding them of their obligation to support the organization's objectives.[35] By reminding the target that your request is consistent with the organization's overarching goals, you are implying support from senior executives without formally involving anyone with higher authority in the situation.

Ingratiation and Impression Management   Silent authority, assertiveness, information control, coalitions, and upward appeals are forceful ways to influence other people. At the opposite extreme is a "soft" influence tactic called **ingratiation**, which includes any attempt to increase liking by, or perceived similarity to, some targeted person.[36] Flattering your boss in front of others, helping co-workers with their work, exhibiting similar attitudes (such as agreeing with your boss's proposal to change company policies), and seeking the other person's counsel (perhaps asking for his or her "expert" advice) are all examples of ingratiation. Collectively, ingratiation behaviors are better than most other forms of influence at predicting career success (performance appraisal feedback, salaries, and promotions).[37]

Ingratiation is potentially influential because it increases the perceived similarity of the source of ingratiation to the target person, which causes the target person to form more favorable opinions of the ingratiator. However, people who are obvious in their ingratiation risk losing any influence because their behaviors are considered insincere and self-serving. The derogatory terms "apple polishing" and "brown-nosing" are applied to those who ingratiate to excess or in ways that suggest selfish motives for the ingratiation. Sure enough, research indicates that people who engage in high levels of ingratiation are less (not more) influential and are less likely to get promoted.[38]

Ingratiation is part of a larger influence tactic known as **impression management**, which is the practice of actively shaping our public images.[39] These public images might be crafted as being important, vulnerable, threatening, or pleasant. For the most part employees routinely engage in pleasant impression management behaviors to satisfy the basic norms of social behavior, such as the way they dress and how they behave toward colleagues and customers. Impression management is a common strategy for people trying to get ahead in the workplace. For instance, almost all job applicants in a recent study relied on one or more types of impression management.

As with ingratiation, employees who use too much impression management tend to be less influential because their behaviors are viewed as insincere.[40] However, until they are caught, some people have successfully gained influence by exaggerating their credentials. Somewhere between 25 and 50 percent of application forms and résumés contain false information. Although most of these inaccuracies are minor, there are also many high-profile misrepresentations.[41] For example, a former CEO of Radio

---

upward appeal
A type of coalition in which one or more members have higher authority or expertise.

ingratiation
Any attempt to increase liking by, or perceived similarity to, the targeted person.

impression management
The practice of actively shaping one's public image.

Shack, an executive at NASA, a football coach at the University of Notre Dame, and a mayor of Rancho Mirage, California, embellished their educational credentials. Lucent Technologies discovered that a former executive had lied about having a PhD from Stanford University and hid his criminal past involving forgery and embezzlement. Ironically the executive was Lucent's director of recruiting!

One of the most elaborate misrepresentations occurred a few years ago when a Singaporean entrepreneur sent out news releases claiming to be a renowned artificial intelligence researcher, the author of several books, and the recipient of numerous awards from MIT and Stanford University (one of the awards was illustrated on his Web site). These falsehoods were so convincing that the entrepreneur almost received a real award, the "Internet Visionary of the Year" at the Internet World Asia Industry Awards.

persuasion
Using logical arguments, facts, and emotional appeals to encourage people to accept a request or message.

Persuasion   Along with ingratiation, **persuasion** is one of the most effective influence strategies for career success. The ability to present facts, logical arguments, and emotional appeals to change another person's attitudes and behavior is not just an acceptable way to influence others; in many societies it is a noble art and a quality of effective leaders. The literature about influence strategies has typically described persuasion as the use of reason through factual evidence and logical arguments. However, recent studies have begun to adopt a "dual process" perspective in which persuasion is influenced by both the individual's emotional reaction and rational interpretation of incoming information.[42] Thus persuasion is an attempt to convince people by using emotional appeals as well as factual evidence and logical arguments.

The effectiveness of persuasion as an influence tactic depends on characteristics of the persuader, message content, communication medium, and the audience being persuaded.[43] What makes one person more persuasive than another? One factor is the person's perceived expertise. Persuasion attempts are more successful when listeners believe the speaker is knowledgeable about the topic. People are also more persuasive when they demonstrate credibility, such as when the persuader does not seem to profit from the persuasion attempt and states a few points against the position.[44]

Steve Jobs's Persuasiveness Creates a Reality Distortion Field
Wearing his trademark black turtleneck and faded blue jeans, Apple Computer cofounder and CEO Steve Jobs is famous for stirring up crowds with evangelical fervor as he draws them into his "reality distortion field." A reality distortion field occurs when people are caught in Steve Jobs's visionary headlights. Apple Computer manager Bud Tribble borrowed the phrase from the TV series *Star Trek* to describe Jobs's overwhelming persuasiveness. "In his presence, reality is malleable," Tribble explained to newly hired Andy Hertzfeld in 1981. " He [Steve Jobs] can convince anyone of practically anything. It wears off when he's not around, but it makes it hard to have realistic schedules." As one journalist wrote, "Drift too close to Jobs in the grip of one of his manias and you can get sucked in, like a wayward asteroid straying into Jupiter's gravitational zone."[45]

Message content is more important than the messenger when the issue is important to the audience. Persuasive message content acknowledges several points of view so the audience does not feel cornered by the speaker. The message should also be limited to a few strong arguments, which are repeated a few times, but not too frequently. The message content should use emotional appeals (such as graphically showing the unfortunate consequences of a bad decision), but only in combination with logical arguments so the audience doesn't feel manipulated. Also, emotional appeals should always be accompanied with specific recommendations to overcome the threat. Finally, message content is more persuasive when the audience is warned about opposing arguments. This **inoculation effect** causes listeners to generate counterarguments to the anticipated persuasion attempts, which makes opponents' subsequent persuasion attempts less effective.[46]

inoculation effect
A persuasive communication strategy of warning listeners that others will try to influence them in the future and that they should be wary of the opponent's arguments.

Two other considerations when persuading people are the medium of communication and characteristics of the audience. Generally, persuasion works best in face-to-face conversations and through other media-rich communication channels. The personal nature of face-to-face communication increases the persuader's credibility, and the richness of this channel provides faster feedback about whether the influence strategy is working. With respect to audience characteristics, it is more difficult to persuade people who have high self-esteem and intelligence, as well as those whose targeted attitudes are strongly connected to their self-identities.[47]

Exchange Exchange activities involve the promise of benefits or resources in exchange for a target person's compliance with your request. This tactic also includes reminding the target of past benefits or favors with the expectation that the target will now make up for that debt. The norm of reciprocity is a central and explicit theme in exchange strategies. According to the *norm of reciprocity*, individuals are expected to help those who have helped them.[48] Negotiation, which we discuss more fully in Chapter 13, is also an integral part of exchange influence activities. For instance, you might negotiate with your boss for a day off in return for working a less desirable shift at a future date. Networking is another form of exchange as an influence strategy. Active networkers build up "exchange credits" by helping colleagues in the short term for reciprocal benefits in the long term.

Networking as an influence strategy is a deeply ingrained practice in several cultures. The Chinese term *guanxi* refers to special relationships and active interpersonal connectedness. It is based on traditional Confucian values of helping others without expecting future repayment. However, some writers suggest that the original interpretation and practice of guanxi has shifted to include implicit long-term reciprocity, which can slip into cronyism. As a result, some Asian governments are discouraging guanxi-based decisions, preferring more arms-length transactions in business and government decisions.[49] *Blat* is a Russian word that also refers to special relationships or connections. Unlike guanxi, however, blat was originally associated with survival during times of scarcity and continues to have a connotation of self-interest and possible illegality.[50]

Consequences and Contingencies of Influence Tactics

Now that the main influence strategies have been described, you are probably wondering which ones are best. The best way to answer this question is to identify the three ways in which people react when others try to influence them: resistance, compliance, or commitment.[51] *Resistance* occurs when people or work units oppose the behavior desired by the influencer and consequently refuse, argue, or delay engaging in the behavior. *Compliance* occurs when people are motivated to implement the influencer's request at a minimal level of effort and for purely instrumental reasons. Without external

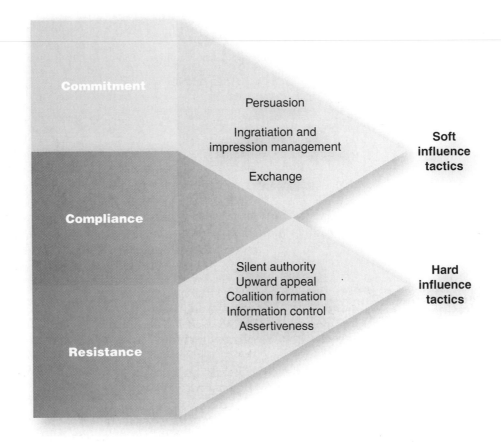

Exhibit 12.4
Consequences of Hard and Soft Influence Tactics

Commitment

Compliance

Resistance

Persuasion

Ingratiation and impression management

Exchange

Soft influence tactics

Silent authority
Upward appeal
Coalition formation
Information control
Assertiveness

Hard influence tactics

sources to prompt the desired behavior, it would not occur. *Commitment* is the strongest form of influence, whereby people identify with the influencer's request and are highly motivated to implement it even when extrinsic sources of motivation are no longer present.

Research has found that people generally react more favorably to "soft" tactics such as friendly persuasion and subtle ingratiation than to "hard" tactics such as upward appeal and assertiveness (see Exhibit 12.4). Soft tactics rely on personal power bases (expert and referent power), which tend to build commitment to the influencer's request. For example, co-workers tend to "buy in" to your ideas when you apply moderate levels of ingratiation and impression management tactics or use persuasion based on expertise. In contrast, hard influence tactics rely on position power (legitimate, reward, and coercion), so they tend to produce compliance or, worse, resistance. Hard tactics also tend to undermine trust, which can hurt future relationships. For example, the potential influence of coalitions is sometimes limited when the group's forcefulness is threatening to those being influenced.[52]

Upward, Downward, or Lateral Influence   Aside from the general preference for soft rather than hard tactics, the most appropriate influence strategy depends on a few contingencies. One consideration is whether the person being influenced is higher, lower, or at the same level in the organization. Employees have some legitimate power over their boss, but they may face adverse career consequences by being too assertive with this power. Similarly, it may be more acceptable for supervisors to control information access than for employees to control what information they distribute to co-workers and people at higher levels in the organization.

The Influencer's Power Base   A second contingency is the influencer's power base. Those with expertise tend to be more successful using persuasion, whereas those with a strong legitimate power base are usually more successful applying silent authority.[53]

Personal and Cultural Values   Studies indicate that personal values guide our preference for some influence methods more than others.[54] The general trend in the United States and elsewhere is toward softer influence tactics because younger employees tend to have more egalitarian values compared with those near retirement. As such, silent authority and assertiveness are tolerated less than a few decades ago. Acceptance of influence tactics also varies across cultures. Research indicates that American managers and subordinates alike often rely on ingratiation because it minimizes conflict and supports a trusting relationship. In contrast, managers in Hong Kong and other high power distance cultures rely less on ingratiation, possibly because this tactic disrupts the more distant roles that managers and employees expect in these cultures. Instead, as we noted earlier, influence through exchange tends to be more common and accepted in Asian cultures because of the importance of interpersonal relationships (guanxi).

Gender Differences in Influence Tactics

Men and women seem to differ in their use of influence tactics. Some writers say that men are more likely than women to rely on direct impression management tactics. Specifically, men tend to advertise their achievements and take personal credit for successes of others reporting to them, whereas women are more reluctant to force the spotlight on themselves, preferring instead to share the credit with others. At the same time, women are more likely to apologize—personally take blame—even for problems not caused by them. Men are more likely to assign blame and less likely to assume it.[55]

Some research also suggests that women generally have difficulty exerting some forms of influence in organizations, and this has limited their promotional opportunities. In particular, women are viewed as less (not more) influential when they try to directly influence others by exerting their authority or expertise. In job interviews, for example, direct and assertive female job applicants were less likely to be hired than were male applicants using the same influence tactics. Similarly, women who directly disagreed in conversations were less influential than women who agreed with the speaker.[56] These findings suggest that women may face problems applying "hard" influence tactics such as assertiveness. Instead, until stereotypes change, women need to rely on softer and more indirect influence strategies, such as ingratiation.

Learning Objectives

After reading this section you should be able to

7. **Distinguish influence from organizational politics.**
8. **Describe the organizational conditions and personal characteristics that support organizational politics.**
9. **Identify ways to minimize organizational politics.**

Influence Tactics and Organizational Politics

You might have noticed that organizational politics has not been mentioned yet, even though some of the practices or examples described over the past few pages are usually considered political tactics. This phrase was carefully avoided because, for the most part, "organizational politics" is in the eye of the beholder. I might perceive your attempt to influence our boss as normal behavior, whereas someone else might perceive your tactic as brazen organizational politics. This is why experts mainly discuss influence tactics as behaviors and organizational politics as perceptions. The influence tactics described earlier are behaviors that might be considered organizational politics, or they might be considered normal behavior. It all depends on the observer's perception of the situation.[57] Of course, some tactics are so blatantly selfish that almost everyone views them as political. However, many incidents of using influence are viewed from different perspectives; some think the employee is helping the company whereas others think the employee is helping himself or herself. For these reasons organizational politics should be considered a perception.

When are influence tactics perceived as **organizational politics**? Increasingly OB researchers say that influence tactics are organizational politics when they seem to benefit the perpetrators at the expense of others and usually the entire organization or work unit. Organizational politics has a number of negative effects. Those who believe their organization is steeped in organizational politics have lower job satisfaction, organizational commitment, and organizational citizenship, as well as high levels of work-related stress. Employees affected by organizational politics also engage in more "neglect" behaviors, such as reducing work effort, paying less attention to quality, and increasing absenteeism and lateness.[58]

Some incidents involving organizational politics have devastating effects on the organization. The opening story to this chapter is one such example. Luke Duffy's political acts of hiding transactions and threatening or criticizing those who attempted to report the wrongdoing ultimately resulted in huge losses for the bank. Connections 12.2 describes an even more extreme example, whereby WorldCom executives used their assertiveness, information control, and other influence practices to protect their financial interests. Ultimately these actions led to the largest accounting fraud and bankruptcy in American history.

organizational politics
Behaviors that others perceive as self-serving tactics for personal gain at the expense of other people and possibly the organization.

Conditions Supporting Organizational Politics

Organizational politics flourishes under the right conditions.[59] One of those conditions is scarce resources. When budgets are slashed, people rely on political tactics to safeguard their resources and maintain the status quo. Office politics also flourishes when resource allocation decisions are ambiguous, complex, or lack formal rules. This occurs because decision makers are given more discretion over resource allocation, so potential recipients of those resources use political tactics to influence the factors that should be considered in the decision. Organizational change encourages political behaviors for this reason. Change creates uncertainty and ambiguity as the company moves from an old set of rules and practices to a new set. During these times, employees apply political strategies to protect their valued resources, positions, and self-images.[60]

Organizational politics also becomes commonplace when it is tolerated and transparently supported by the organization.[61] Companies sometimes promote people who are the best politicians, not necessarily the best talent to run the company. If left unchecked, organizational politics can paralyze an organization as people focus more on protecting themselves than fulfilling their roles. Political activity becomes self-reinforcing unless the conditions supporting political behavior are altered.

Personal Characteristics   Several personal characteristics affect a person's motivation to engage in organizational politics.[62] Some people have a strong need for personal as opposed to socialized power. They seek power for its own sake and use political tactics to acquire more power. People with an internal locus of control are more likely than those with an external locus of control to engage in political behaviors.

Politics at WorldCom Leads to Record-Breaking Accounting Fraud

Bernie Ebbers built WorldCom, Inc. (since acquired by Verizon Communications, Inc.), into one of the world's largest telecommunications firms. Yet he and chief financial officer (CFO) Scott Sullivan have become better known for creating a massive corporate accounting fraud that led to the largest bankruptcy in U.S. history. Two investigative reports and subsequent court cases concluded that WorldCom executives were responsible for billions in fraudulent or unsupported accounting entries. How did this mammoth accounting scandal occur without anyone raising the alarm? Evidence suggests that Ebbers and Sullivan held considerable power and influence that prevented accounting staff from complaining, or even knowing, about the fraud.

Ebbers's inner circle held tight control over the flow of all financial information. The geographically dispersed accounting groups were discouraged from sharing information. Ebbers's group also restricted distribution of company-level financial reports and prevented sensitive reports from being prepared at all. Accountants didn't even have access to the computer files where some of the largest fraudulent entries were made. As a result, employees had to rely on Ebbers's executive team to justify the accounting entries that were requested.

Another reason why employees complied with questionable accounting practices was that CFO Scott Sullivan wielded immense personal power. He was considered a "whiz kid" with impeccable integrity who had won the prestigious "CFO Excellence Award." Thus when Sullivan's office asked staff to make questionable entries, some accountants assumed Sullivan had found an innovative—and legal—accounting loophole. If Sullivan's expert power didn't work, other executives took a more coercive approach. Employees cited incidents where they were publicly berated for questioning headquarters' decisions and intimidated if they asked for more information. When one employee at a branch refused to alter an accounting entry, WorldCom's controller threatened to fly in from WorldCom's Mississippi headquarters to make the change himself. The employee changed the entry.

Ebbers wielded similar influence over WorldCom's board of directors. Sources indicate that his personal charisma and intolerance of dissension produced a passive board that rubber-stamped most of his recommendations. As one report concluded, "The Board of Directors appears to have embraced suggestions by Mr. Ebbers without question or dissent, even under circumstances where its members now readily acknowledge they had significant misgivings regarding his recommended course of action."

Sources: United States Bankruptcy Court, Southern District of New York. In Re: WorldCom, Inc., et al., Debtors. Chapter 11 Case No. 02-15533 (AJG) Jointly Administered Second Interim Report of Dick Thornburgh, Bankruptcy Court Examiner, June 9, 2003; Report of Investigation by the Special Investigative Committee of the Board of Directors of WorldCom, Inc. Dennis R. Beresford, Nicholas Deb. Katzenbach, C.B. Rogers, Jr., Counsel, Wilmer, Cutler & Pickering, Accounting Advisors, PricewaterhouseCoopers LLP, March 31, 2003. Also see T. Catan et al., "Before the Fall," *Financial Times* (London), 19 December 2002, p. 17; J. O'Donnell and A. Backover, "Ebbers's High-Risk Act Came Crashing Down on Him," *USA Today,* 12 December 2002, p. B1; C. Stern, "Ebbers Dominated Board, Report Says," *Washington Post,* 5 November 2002, p. E1; D.S. Hilzenrath, "How a Distinguished Roster of Board Members Failed to Detect Company's Problems," *Washington Post,* 16 June 2003, p. E1; S. Pulliam and A. Latour, "Lost Connection," *The Wall Street Journal,* 12 January 2005, p. A1; S. Rosenbush, "Five Lessons of the WorldCom Debacle," *Business Week Online,* 16 March 2005.

Former WorldCom CEO Bernard Ebbers (left), chief financial officer Scott Sullivan (right), and other executives perpetrated one of the largest cases of accounting fraud in history by using influence tactics for personal gain.

This does not mean that internals are naturally political; rather, they are more likely to use influence tactics when political conditions are present because, unlike externals, they feel very much in charge of their own destiny.

Some individuals have strong **Machiavellian values**. Machiavellianism is named after Niccolò Machiavelli, the 16th-century Italian philosopher who wrote *The Prince*, a famous treatise about political behavior. People with high Machiavellian values are comfortable with getting more than they deserve, and they believe that deceit is a natural and acceptable way to achieve this goal. They seldom trust co-workers and tend to use cruder influence tactics, such as bypassing their bosses or being assertive, to get their own way.[63] The opening vignette to this chapter suggests that National Australia Bank's rogue trader displayed Machiavellian characteristics, including rough assertiveness and controlling information.

Machiavellian values
The belief that deceit is a natural and acceptable way to influence others.

Minimizing Organizational Politics and its Consequences   The conditions that fuel organizational politics also give us some clues about how to control dysfunctional political activities.[64] One strategy to keep organizational politics in check is to introduce clear rules and regulations to specify the use of scarce resources. Corporate leaders also need to actively support the all-channels communication structure described earlier in this chapter so that political employees do not misuse power through information control. As mentioned, organizational politics can become a problem during times of organizational change. Effective organizational change practices—particularly education and involvement—can minimize uncertainty and consequently politics during the change process.

Organizational politics is either supported or punished, depending on team norms and the organization's culture. Thus leaders need to actively manage group norms to curtail self-serving influence activities. They also need to support organizational values that oppose political tactics, such as altruism and customer focus. One of the most important strategies is for leaders to become role models of organizational citizenship rather than symbols of successful organizational politicians.

Along with minimizing organizational politics, companies can limit the adverse effects of political perceptions by giving employees more control over their work and keeping them informed about organizational events. Research has found that employees who know what is going on in the organization and who are involved in organizational decisions are less likely to experience stress, job dissatisfaction, and absenteeism as a result of organizational politics.

Chapter Summary

Power is the capacity to influence others. It exists when one party perceives that he or she is dependent on another for something of value. However, the dependent person must also have counterpower—some power over the dominant party—to maintain the relationship.

There are five power bases. Legitimate power is the capacity to influence others through formal authority, but only to the extent employees agree to this authority. Reward power is derived from the ability to control the allocation of rewards valued by others and to remove negative sanctions. Coercive power is the ability to apply punishment. Expert power is the capacity to influence

others by possessing knowledge or skills that they value. People have referent power when others identify with them, like them, or otherwise respect them.

Information plays an important role in organizational power. Employees gain power by controlling the flow of information that others need and by being able to cope with uncertainties related to important organizational goals.

Four contingencies determine whether these power bases translate into real power. Individuals and work units are more powerful when they are nonsubstitutable—that is, there is a lack of alternatives. Employees, work units, and organizations reduce substitutability by controlling tasks, knowledge, and labor and by differentiating themselves from competitors. A second contingency is centrality. People have more power when they have high centrality: They affect many people quickly by their actions. Discretion, the third contingency of power, refers to the freedom to exercise judgment. Power increases when people are free to use it. The fourth contingency, visibility, refers to the idea that power increases to the extent that a person's or work unit's competencies are known to others.

Networking involves cultivating social relationships with others to accomplish one's goals. This activity increases an individual's expert and referent power as well as visibility and possibly centrality. However, networking can limit opportunities for people outside the network, as many women in senior management positions have discovered.

Influence refers to any behavior that attempts to alter someone's attitudes or behavior. The most widely studied influence tactics are silent authority, assertiveness, information control, coalition formation, upward appeal, ingratiation and impression management, persuasion, and exchange. "Soft" influence tactics such as friendly persuasion and subtle ingratiation are more acceptable than "hard" tactics such as upward appeal and assertiveness. However, the most appropriate influence tactic also depends on the influencer's power base; whether the person being influenced is higher, lower, or at the same level in the organization; and personal and cultural values regarding influence behavior.

Organizational politics refers to influence tactics that others perceive to be self-serving behaviors at the expense of others and sometimes contrary to the interests of the entire organization or work unit. Organizational politics is more prevalent when scarce resources are allocated using complex and ambiguous decisions and when the organization tolerates or rewards political behavior. Individuals with a high need for personal power, an internal locus of control, and strong Machiavellian values have a higher propensity to use political tactics.

Organizational politics can be minimized by providing clear rules for resource allocation, establishing a free flow of information, using education and involvement during organizational change, supporting team norms and a corporate culture that discourage dysfunctional politics, and having leaders who model organizational citizenship rather than political savvy.

Key Terms

centrality, p. 348

coalition, p. 352

counterpower, p. 343

impression management, p. 353

ingratiation, p. 353

inoculation effect, p. 355

legitimate power, p. 344

Machiavellian values, p. 360

mentoring, p. 350

networking, p. 350

organizational politics, p. 358

persuasion, p. 354

power, p. 342

referent power, p. 345

substitutability, p. 347

upward appeal, p. 353

Critical Thinking Questions

1. What role does counterpower play in the power relationship? Give an example of your own encounter with counterpower at school or work.

2. Several years ago the major league baseball players' association went on strike in September, just before the World Series started. The players' contract expired at the beginning of the season (May), but they held off the strike until September when they would lose only one-sixth of their salaries. In contrast, a September strike would hurt the owners financially because they earn a larger portion of their revenue during the playoffs. As one player explained, "If we strike next spring, there's nothing stopping [the club owners] from letting us go until next June or July because they don't have that much at stake." Use your knowledge of the sources and contingencies of power to explain why the baseball players' association had more power in negotiations by walking out in September rather than in March.

3. You have just been hired as a brand manager of toothpaste for a large consumer products company. Your job mainly involves encouraging the advertising and production groups to promote and manufacture your product more effectively. These departments aren't under your direct authority, although company procedures indicate that they must complete certain tasks requested by brand managers. Describe the sources of power you can use to ensure that the advertising and production departments will help you make and sell toothpaste more effectively.

4. How does networking increase a person's power? What networking strategies could you initiate now to potentially enhance your future career success?

5. Discuss how the eight influence tactics described in this chapter are used by students to influence their university teachers. Which influence tactic is applied most often? Which is applied least often, in your opinion? To what extent is each influence tactic considered legitimate behavior or organizational politics?

6. How do cultural differences affect the following influence factors: (a) silent authority and (b) upward appeal?

7. A few years ago the CEO of Apple Computer invited Steve Jobs (who was not associated with the company at the time) to serve as a special adviser and raise morale among Apple employees and customers. While doing this, Jobs spent more time advising the CEO on how to cut costs, redraw the organization chart, and hire new people. Before long, most of the top people at Apple were Jobs's colleagues, who began to systematically evaluate and weed out teams of Apple employees. While publicly supporting Apple's CEO, Jobs privately criticized him and, in a show of nonconfidence, sold 1.5 million shares of Apple stock he had received. This action caught the attention of Apple's board of directors, who soon after decided to replace the CEO with Steve Jobs. The CEO claimed Jobs was a conniving backstabber who used political tactics to get his way. Others suggest that Apple would be out of business today if he hadn't taken over the company. In your opinion, were Steve Jobs's actions examples of organizational politics? Justify your answer.

8. This book frequently emphasizes that successful companies engage in knowledge management. How do political tactics interfere with knowledge management objectives?

Case Study 12.1 RHONDA CLARK: TAKING CHARGE AT THE SMITH FOUNDATION

Joseph C. Santora, Essex County College and TST, Inc.

Dr. Rhonda Clark was ecstatic as she hung up the telephone. Bennett Mitchell, chairperson of KLS Executive Search firm, had just informed her that she landed the coveted position of chief executive officer (CEO) at the Smith Foundation, a nonprofit organization whose mission was to fund public awareness campaigns and research programs about eye care. Clark knew that she had just pulled off a major coup. Her appointment to this new, challenging position would indeed be *the* high point in a long, arduous climb to the executive suite. As an organizational outsider—one with no work experience within the hiring organization—she assumed that her appointment as CEO signaled a strong desire by the board to shake up the organizational status quo. However, she heard from a reliable inside source that the same board that hired her and charged her with the responsibility of transforming the foundation was extremely fragmented. The often rambunctious board had forced the last five CEOs to resign after short tenures. Clark's feeling of exhilaration was rapidly being replaced by cautious optimism. As a new CEO, she pondered the rather thorny question of how she could take charge of the board of directors to ensure the mission of the organization would be accomplished.

Background

Charlie Smith, an industrialist and philanthropist, had founded the Smith Foundation 40 years ago with a multimillion-dollar endowment. Despite this generous financial start-up capital and additional income derived from several financial investments and major corporate donations, in recent years the foundation's endowment has been slowly dwindling as a result of significant funding awards to academics, community organizations, and smaller, less well-funded foundations. Board members had held some preliminary discussions about developing new innovative strategies to strengthen the balance sheet of the organization. Currently the foundation was operating on an annual budget of slightly less than $1,500,000 (USD).

In the last five years some foundation board members had begun to abandon many of their fiduciary responsibilities. Over the past few months several board meetings had been canceled because the meetings lacked a quorum. In general, this 13-member board seemed to drift aimlessly in one direction or another. The board had been operating at only 70 percent capacity for the past two years with nine active board members—five men and four women.

Challenges

Dr. Rhonda Clark believed she was the one who could lead the Smith Foundation. She had great academic credentials and management experience that would help her tackle her new position as the foundation head. In the last 30 years the 54-year-old Clark, who held a PhD in political science and policy analysis from a major U.S. West Coast university, had gained an enviable amount of managerial experience in the nonprofit and public sectors. Past professional experiences included a graduate school professorship, as well as being a director of research for a major statewide political office holder, the director of planning in a large metropolitan hospital, and the director of programs at a small foundation.

Immediately upon taking office, Clark was astounded to learn that a small but active and influential faction on the board had withdrawn its initial verbal promise to assist her in working closely with the corporate community. Essentially, she was informed that she was solely responsible for all external corporate relations. Clark thought to herself, "I wonder if they hired me because they thought they would get a 'do-nothing' female leader. These folks want me to either sink or swim on my own. Perhaps they set me up for failure by giving me a one-year appointment." She lamented, "I won't let this happen. I really need to learn about the key decision makers and stakeholders on the board and in the larger community, and fast."

At the last board meeting Clark detailed the major elements of her latest proposal. Yet several board members seemed totally unfazed by it. Soon she began to encounter stiff resistance from some male board members. Jim Jackson, in particular, told Clark, "We are disappointed that you failed to win a city contract to conduct a feasibility study to determine if we can erect a facility in another section of town. We're not certain if you have the right stuff to run this foundation, and we certainly won't help you to gain financial support for the foundation by using our personal, corporate, or political contacts."

Jackson thought to himself, "We've removed CEOs before; we can remove Clark, too."

After hearing Jackson's comments, Clark decided to take another tack. She began to focus on making external and internal inroads that she believed could result in some modest gains for the foundation. For example, she identified and developed a close relationship with a few well-connected city agency executives, persuaded some supporters to nominate her for membership on two influential boards, and forged a relationship with two key foundation decision makers and political power brokers. She reconfigured the internal structure of the foundation to increase maximum productivity from the staff, and she tightened budgetary controls by changing some fiscal policies and procedures.

Clark also sought the support of Susan Frost, a board member who likely had been instrumental in Clark's appointment as CEO. Clark said to herself, "If I can develop a strong symbiotic relationship with some female board members, like Sue, to support my plan, then maybe I get some traction." To do this Clark held a number of late evening meetings with Sue and another female board member. They indicated their willingness to help her, but only if she would consider implementing a few of their ideas for the foundation as well as recommending their close friend for a current staff vacancy. Clark knew they were trying to exercise their political influence; yet she believed that everyone could benefit from this *quid quo pro* relationship. She said to herself, "I guess it's a matter of you scratch my back, and I scratch yours." She eagerly agreed to move their agenda along. In a matter of a few weeks, as promised, they began working on a couple of relatively sympathetic board members. One day Clark got a terse but crucial telephone call from Sue. "Several of us support you. Proceed!"

Once she heard this, Clark began to move at lightning speed. She formed a 15-member coalition of community, educational, and quasi-governmental agencies that would apply for a collaborative federal grant to create a public awareness campaign for children's eye health. Through the dissemination of various media, coalition members would help to inform the community about various eye diseases that afflict young children. Shortly afterward Clark received notification from a federal agency that this multi-agency project would be awarded a million-dollar grant. Clark would serve as the administrative and fiscal agent of the grant, and as a result, she would be able to earmark a considerable amount of the administrative oversight dollars for the foundation's budget. For her efforts in coordinating this project, Clark received high marks from coalition and community members alike.

Yet despite this important initial accomplishment, Clark had the unpleasant task of notifying the full board that due to some unforeseen problems and their lack of support on certain key initiatives, the foundation would still experience a financial deficit. She heard several rumors that her next employment contract would not be renewed by the executive committee of the board. At this point she thought about directly confronting the obstructionists on the board by telling them that they were unreasonable and in fact that they were why the foundation had not recovered during the past year … but she hesitated: She had signed on to do a job, and she was unsure if this was the wisest action to take at this time.

Despite this latest conflict between herself and certain board members, she paused to reflect on what she believed to have been a tumultuous year as CEO.

Discussion Questions

1. Does Clark have any sources of power and any contingencies of power? If so, list and discuss them.

2. To what degree were Clark's methods of influencing board members the most effective possible under the circumstances presented in the case?

3. Do you think her methods of getting things done at the foundation were ethical? Why or why not?

Note: The names and some managerial actions in this case have been altered to preserve the integrity and anonymity of the organization. This case is intended to be used as a basis for class discussion rather than to illustrate either effective or ineffective handling of a management situation.

©Joseph C. Santora. *Source:* Joseph C. Santora, Essex County College and TST, Inc.

Case Study 12.2 SHAKING UP OXFORD

John Hood may be soft-spoken, but the New Zealand-born vice chancellor of Oxford University shows flashes of the steely determination that first convinced Oxford's search committee to hire him to give the place a top-to-bottom management overhaul. Hood's decisive actions have created few friends among the scholars, but he claims he is merely working in the university community's best interests. "I am here as the servant of the scholars," says Hood. "One has no power or authority in this job."

This *BusinessWeek* case study describes the changes that John Hood is making at Oxford and how academics at the British university are responding to those changes. The article looks at Hood's influence strategies, the methods used by Oxford's professors to resist those changes, and some of the politics of change that has occurred. Read the full text of this *BusinessWeek* article at www.mhhe.com/mcshane4e and prepare for the discussion questions below.

Discussion Questions

1. John Hood claims that he has no power or authority in his job. Is he correct? What other sources of power work for and against him during this change process?

2. What influence tactics has Hood used that are most apparent in this case study?

3. What influence tactics have professors and other stakeholders used to resist Hood's changes? Would you call any of these influence tactics "organizational politics"?

Source: S. Reed, "Shaking Up Oxford," *BusinessWeek*, 5 December 2005, 48.

Team Exercise 12.3 BUDGET DELIBERATIONS

Sharon Card

PURPOSE This exercise is designed to help you understand some of the power dynamics and influence tactics that occur across hierarchical levels in organizations.

MATERIALS This activity works best where one small room leads to a larger room, which leads to a larger area.

INSTRUCTIONS These exercise instructions are based on a class size of about 30 students. The instructor may adjust the size of the first two groups slightly for larger classes. The instructor will organize students as follows: A few (three or four) students are assigned the position of executives. They are preferably located in a secluded office or corner of a large classroom. Another six to eight students are assigned positions as middle managers. These people will ideally be located in an adjoining room or space, allowing privacy for the executives. The remaining students represent the nonmanagement employees in the organization. They are located in an open area outside the executive and management rooms.

RULES Members of the executive group are free to enter the space of either the middle management or nonmanagement groups and to communicate whatever they wish, whenever they wish. Members of the middle management group may enter the space of the nonmanagement group whenever they wish, but must request permission to enter the executive group's space. The executive group can refuse the middle management group's request. Members of the nonmanagement group are not allowed to disturb the top group in any way unless specifically invited by members of the executive group. The nonmanagement group does have the right to request permission to communicate with the middle management group. The middle management group can refuse the lower group's request.

TASK Your organization is in the process of preparing a budget. The challenge is to balance needs with financial resources. Of course the needs are greater than the resources. The instructor will distribute a budget sheet showing a list of budget requests and their costs. Each group has control over a portion of the budget and must decide how to spend the money over which they have control. Nonmanagement staff members have discretion over a relatively small portion, and the executive group has discretion over the greatest portion. The exercise is finished when the organization has negotiated a satisfactory budget, or when the instructor calls time out. The class will then debrief with the following questions and others the instructor might ask.

Discussion Questions

1. What can you learn from this exercise about power in organizational hierarchies?
2. How is this exercise similar to relations in real organizations?
3. How did students in each group feel about the amount of power they held?
4. How did they exercise their power in relations with the other groups?

Self-Assessment 12.4

UPWARD INFLUENCE SCALE

PURPOSE This exercise is designed to help you understand several ways of influencing people up the organizational hierarchy as well as estimate your preferred upward influence tactics.

INSTRUCTIONS Read each of the following statements and circle the response that you believe best indicates how often you engaged in that behavior over the past six months. Then use the scoring key in Appendix B to calculate your results. This exercise is completed alone so you can assess yourself honestly without concerns of social comparison. However, class discussion will focus on the types of influence in organizations and the conditions under which particular influence tactics are most and least appropriate.

Upward Influence Scale

How often in the past six months have you engaged in these behaviors?	Never ▼	Seldom ▼	Occasionally ▼	Frequently ▼	Amost always ▼
1. I obtain the support of my co-workers in persuading my manager to act on my request.	1	2	3	4	5
2. I offer an exchange in which I will do something that my manager wants if he or she will do what I want.	1	2	3	4	5
3. I act very humble and polite while making my request.	1	2	3	4	5
4. I appeal to higher management to put pressure on my manager.	1	2	3	4	5
5. I remind my manager of how I have helped him or her in the past and imply that now I expect compliance with my request.	1	2	3	4	5
6. I go out of my way to make my manager feel good about me before asking him or her to do what I want.	1	2	3	4	5
7. I use logical arguments to convince my manager.	1	2	3	4	5
8. I have a face-to-face confrontation with my manager in which I forcefully state what I want.	1	2	3	4	5
9. I act in a friendly manner toward my manager before making my request.	1	2	3	4	5
10. I present facts, figures, and other information to my manager in support of my position.	1	2	3	4	5
11. I obtain the support and cooperation of my subordinates to back up my request.	1	2	3	4	5
12. I obtain the informal support of higher management to back me.	1	2	3	4	5
13. I offer to make a personal sacrifice such as giving up my free time if my manager will do what I want.	1	2	3	4	5
14. I very carefully explain to my manager the reasons for my request.	1	2	3	4	5
15. I verbally express my anger to my manager in order to get what I want.	1	2	3	4	5
16. I use a forceful manner; I try such things as demands, the setting of deadlines, and the expression of strong emotion.	1	2	3	4	5
17. I rely on the chain of command—on people higher up in the organization who have power over my supervisor.	1	2	3	4	5
18. I mobilize other people in the organization to help me in influencing my supervisor.	1	2	3	4	5

Source: C. Schriesheim and T. Hinkin, "Influence Tactics Used by Subordinates: A Theoretical and Empirical Analysis and Refinement of the Kipnis, Schmidt, and Wilkinson Subscales," *Journal of Applied Psychology* 75 (1990), pp. 246–57.

Self-Assessment 12.5

GUANXI ORIENTATION SCALE (STUDENT OLC)

Guanxi, which is translated as interpersonal connections, is an important element of doing business in China and some other Asian countries with strong Confucian cultural values. Guanxi is based on traditional Confucian values of helping others without expecting future repayment. This instrument estimates your guanxi orientation—that is, the extent to which you accept and apply guanxi values. This self-assessment is completed alone so you can rate yourself honestly without concerns of social comparison. However, class discussion will focus on the meaning of guanxi and its relevance for organizational power and influence.

Self-Assessment 12.6

MACHIAVELLIANISM SCALE (STUDENT OLC)

Machiavellianism is named after Niccolò Machiavelli, the 16th-century Italian philosopher who wrote *The Prince,* a famous treatise about political behavior. Out of Machiavelli's work emerged this instrument that estimates the degree to which you have a Machiavellian personality. Indicate the extent to which you agree or disagree that each statement in this instrument describes you. Complete each item honestly to get the best estimate of your level of Machiavellianism.

Self-Assessment 12.7

PERCEPTIONS OF POLITICS SCALE (POPS) (STUDENT OLC)

Organizations have been called "political arenas"—environments where political tactics are common because decisions are ambiguous and resources are scarce. This instrument estimates the degree to which you believe the school where you attend classes has a politicized culture. This scale consists of several statements that might or might not describe the school where you are attending classes. These statements refer to the administration of the school, not the classroom. Please indicate the extent to which you agree or disagree with each statement.

After reading this chapter, if you need additional information, see www.mhhe.com/mcshane4e for more in-depth interactivities that correspond with this material.

By any measure, Microsoft Corp. is a monolithic money machine. Its $12 billion annual earnings exceed those of Cisco, Dell, Google, and Apple combined. And although most of these profits come from its computer operating system (Windows) and software (Office), Microsoft is reaching into new markets, such as Xbox for games and MSN for online portals.

Yet various sources conclude that Microsoft is riddled with dysfunctional conflict that could soon hamper its ability to remain competitive. One source of strife is between employees and management. "We have over 61,000 employees, only 8,000 of whom are developers," quips a computer science graduate who recently joined Microsoft. "Doesn't sound right, does it? Not to me anyway." Jeff B. Erwin, who left the company after five years, agrees. "Microsoft has some of the smartest people in the world, but they [managers] are just crushing them."

Various sources conclude that Microsoft is riddled with dysfunctional conflict that could soon hamper its ability to remain competitive.

The rift between management and employees may widen under a new reward system that pays management substantial bonuses while most staff continue to receive market rates. Even within project teams, a bell-curved performance system pits one employee against another. If the entire team performs well to get the product completed, the reward system still forces some team members into the low performance category. "It creates competition in the ranks, when people really want community," says a former Microsoft vice president.

But conflict between management and employees and within groups is subtle compared to the almost vicious infighting across product groups. The squabbling is amplified by top management's strategy of "integrated innovation"; in other words, the groups are expected to work more closely together than ever before. "Pretty much across the board people are saying that Microsoft is dysfunctional," concludes one industry analyst. "They are not cooperating across business groups."

For example, MSN delayed releasing search software to compete against Google Desktop because the Windows group, which has a similar search tool for its long-delayed Vista operating system, objected. The two groups negotiated for more than a month to reach a compromise. The MSN group also fought against the Office people over MSN's desire to connect their online calendar with the calendar in Office. The Office group balked because "then MSN could cannibalize Office," says an employee who recently left Microsoft. "Windows and Office would never let MSN have more budget or more control."[1]

Conflict and Negotiation in the Workplace

After reading this chapter you should be able to

1. Outline the conflict process.
2. Distinguish constructive from socioemotional conflict.
3. Discuss the advantages and disadvantages of conflict in organizations.
4. Identify six sources of organizational conflict.
5. Outline the five interpersonal styles of conflict management.
6. Summarize six structural approaches to managing conflict.
7. Outline four situational influences on negotiations.
8. Describe four behaviors that are characteristic of effective negotiators.
9. Compare and contrast the three types of third-party dispute resolution.

Most organizations experience some backbiting and infighting among employees and across business groups, but Microsoft's current situation illustrates the importance of understanding the causes and consequences of conflict before it becomes a dysfunctional disease that seeps into a company's cultural mindset. This chapter investigates the dynamics of conflict in organizational settings, beginning with a description of the conflict process. Next, this chapter discusses the consequences and sources of conflict in organizational settings. Five conflict management styles are then described, followed by a discussion of the structural approaches to conflict management. The last two sections of this chapter introduce two procedures for resolving conflict: negotiation and third-party resolution.

Learning Objectives

After reading this section you should be able to

1. **Outline the conflict process.**
2. **Distinguish constructive from socioemotional conflict.**
3. **Discuss the advantages and disadvantages of conflict in organizations.**

The Conflict Process

conflict
The process in which one party perceives that its interests are being opposed or negatively affected by another party.

Conflict is a process in which one party perceives that its interests are being opposed or negatively affected by another party.[2] Conflict was reported between Microsoft's MSN and Office groups, for example, because they viewed the other division's product development activities as a threat to their own interests. Similarly, frontline technical employees experience conflict with management's heavy-handed control systems that seem to further delay product development.

When describing an incident involving conflict, we are usually referring to the observable part of conflict—the angry words, shouting matches, and actions that symbolize opposition. But this manifest conflict is only a small part of the conflict process. As Exhibit 13.1 illustrates, the conflict process begins with the sources of conflict.[3] Incompatible goals, different values, and other conditions lead one or both parties to perceive that conflict exists. We will look closely at these sources of conflict later in this chapter because understanding and changing them is the key to effective conflict management.

Exhibit 13.1
The Conflict Process

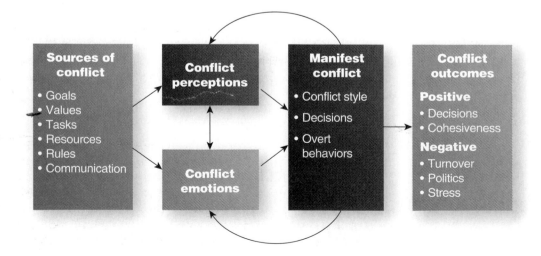

Conflict Perceptions and Emotions

At some point the sources of conflict lead one or both parties to perceive that conflict exists. They become aware that one party's statements and actions are incompatible with their own goals. These perceptions usually interact with emotions experienced about the conflict. Infighting at Microsoft is likely stoked with emotions, such as the anger employees experience when they work late completing monthly performance reports for management rather than spending more time meeting customers. "Instead of promoting the product to customers, I'd get stuck in the office until midnight preparing slides for my monthly product review," complains a frustrated Windows XP marketing employee.[4]

Manifest Conflict

Conflict perceptions and emotions usually manifest themselves in the decisions and overt behaviors of one party toward the other. These conflict episodes may range from subtle nonverbal behaviors to warlike aggression. Particularly when people experience high levels of conflict emotions, they have difficulty finding words and expressions that communicate effectively without further irritating the relationship.[5] Conflict is also manifested by the style each side uses to resolve the conflict. Some people tend to avoid the conflict, whereas others try to defeat those with opposing views. Conflict management styles will be described later in this chapter. At this point you should know that these styles influence the other party's perceptions and actions regarding the conflict, which then either defuse or further escalate the conflict.

Conflict Escalation Cycle   The conflict process in Exhibit 13.1 shows arrows looping back from manifest conflict to conflict perceptions and emotions. These loops represent the fact that the conflict process is really a series of episodes that potentially link in an escalation cycle or spiral.[6] It doesn't take much to start this conflict cycle— just an inappropriate comment, a misunderstanding, or action that lacks diplomacy. These behaviors communicate to the other party in a way that creates a perception of conflict. If the first party did not intend to demonstrate conflict, the second party's response may create that perception.

If the conflict remains focused on perceptions, both parties can often resolve the conflict through logical analysis. However, the communication process has enough ambiguity that a wrong look or word may trigger strong emotions and set the stage for further conflict escalation. These distorted beliefs and emotions reduce each side's motivation to communicate, making it more difficult for them to discover common ground and ultimately resolve the conflict. The parties then rely more on stereotypes and emotions to reinforce their perceptions of the other party. Some structural conditions increase the likelihood of conflict escalation. Employees who are more confrontational and less diplomatic also tend to escalate conflict.[7]

Conflict Outcomes

Recent events at Microsoft illustrate some of the dysfunctional consequences of conflict: delayed product releases because one group obstructs another group's product launch; restricted flow of information across divisions; lower morale and higher turnover of key employees. Employees are often distracted from their work by internal feuds and, in some cases, engage in dysfunctional behaviors such as withholding valuable knowledge and other resources. Ongoing conflict also increases stress and turnover while reducing organizational commitment and job satisfaction. At the

Constructive Confrontation Inside Intel Former Goldman Sachs president John Thornton has had his share of executive debates, but even he was surprised after joining the board of Intel Corp. regarding the "constructive confrontation" that permeates the chipmaker's culture. "It can be kind of shocking at first," says Thornton. "You realize quickly that [Intel managers] practice a form of honesty that borders on brutality." Intel cofounder and former chairman Andy Grove nurtured constructive confrontation many years ago when he noticed that meetings generate better ideas when staff actively debate rather than politely defer to ideas that others put forward. But Grove emphasizes that this conflict is constructive only under specific circumstances. "Constructive confrontation does not mean being loud, unpleasant, or rude, and it is not designed to affix blame," warns Grove. "The essence of it is to attack a problem by speaking up in a businesslike way." Intel also holds confrontation training seminars to help staff become more comfortable with the brutal honesty in its meetings.[8]

intergroup level, conflict with people outside the team may cause the team to become more insular—increasing their cohesiveness while distancing themselves from outsiders who are critical of the team's past decisions.[9]

Given these problems, it's not surprising that people normally associate **conflict management** with reducing or removing conflict. However, conflict management refers to interventions that alter the level and form of conflict in ways that maximize its benefits and minimize its dysfunctional consequences. This sometimes means increasing the level of **constructive conflict** (also known as *task-related conflict*).[10] Recall from Chapter 10 that constructive conflict occurs when team members debate their different perceptions about an issue in a way that keeps the conflict focused on the task rather than people. This form of conflict tests the logic of arguments and encourages participants to reexamine their basic assumptions about the problem and its possible solution.

To some extent Microsoft encourages constructive conflict. For instance, Microsoft employees can openly complain on their employee blogs, whereas Google has a reputation for firing employees who dissent in public. When Ray Ozzie, a renowned programmer who developed Lotus Notes and more recently Groove Networks, recently joined Microsoft's executive team, one of his first observations was Microsoft executives engaged in "vigorous disagreement" over business models. Microsoft has a history of encouraging this constructive conflict because senior management believes debate generates better decisions and ultimately better strategies and products.

The challenge is to engage in constructive conflict without having it escalate into **socioemotional conflict** (also known as *relationship conflict*). When socioemotional conflict dominates, differences are viewed as personal attacks rather than attempts to resolve an issue. The parties become defensive and competitive toward each other, which motivates them to reduce communication and information sharing.

Minimizing Socioemotional Conflict

The solution here seems obvious: Encourage constructive conflict for better decision making and minimize socioemotional conflict to avoid dysfunctional emotions and behaviors. This sounds good in theory, but recent evidence suggests that separating these two types of conflict isn't easy. Most of us experience some degree of socioemotional conflict during or after any constructive debate.[11] In other words, it is difficult to suppress defensive emotions when trying

---

conflict management
Interventions that alter the level and form of conflict in ways that maximize its benefits and minimize its dysfunctional consequences.

constructive conflict
Occurs when team members debate their different perceptions about an in issue in a way that keeps the conflict focused on the task rather than people.

socioemotional conflict
A negative outcome that occurs when differences are viewed as personal attacks rather than attempts to resolve an issue.

to resolve conflicts calmly and rationally. Fortunately conflict management experts have identified three strategies that might reduce the level of socioemotional conflict during constructive conflict episodes.[12]

- *Emotional intelligence.* Socioemotional conflict is less likely to occur, or is less likely to escalate, when team members have high levels of emotional intelligence. Emotionally intelligent employees are better able to regulate their emotions during debate, which reduces the risk of escalating perceptions of interpersonal hostility. People with high emotional intelligence are also more likely to view a co-worker's emotional reaction as valuable information about that person's needs and expectations, rather than as a personal attack.

- *Cohesive team.* Socioemotional conflict is suppressed when the conflict occurs within a highly cohesive team. The longer people work together, get to know each other, and develop mutual trust, the more latitude they give to each other to show emotions without being personally offended. Strong cohesion also allows each person to know about and anticipate the behaviors and emotions of teammates. Another benefit is that cohesion produces a stronger social identity with the group, so team members are motivated to avoid escalating socioemotional conflict during otherwise emotionally turbulent discussions.

- *Supportive team norms.* Various team norms can hold socioemotional conflict at bay during constructive debate. When team norms encourage openness, for instance, team members learn to appreciate honest dialogue without personally reacting to any emotional display during the disagreements. Other norms might discourage team members from displaying negative emotions toward co-workers. Team norms also encourage tactics that defuse socioemotional conflict when it first appears. For instance, research has found that teams with low socioemotional conflict use humor to maintain positive group emotions, which offsets negative feelings team members might develop toward some co-workers during debate.

Learning Objectives

After reading the next three sections you should be able to

4. **Identify six sources of organizational conflict.**
5. **Outline the five interpersonal styles of conflict management.**
6. **Summarize six structural approaches to managing conflict.**

Sources of Conflict in Organizations

Manifest conflict is really the tip of the proverbial iceberg. What we really need to understand are the sources of this conflict, which lie under the surface. The six main conditions that cause conflict in organizational settings are shown in Exhibit 13.2.

Incompatible Goals

A common source of conflict is goal incompatibility.[13] Goal incompatibility occurs when personal or work goals seem to interfere with another person's or department's goals. This source of conflict is apparent in the opening story. Managers in each Microsoft division are rewarded for the success of their products, so conflict results when other divisions threaten that success with similar products. Incompatible goals also explain conflict between employees and management. Microsoft managers are

Exhibit 13.2
**Sources of Conflict
in Organizations**

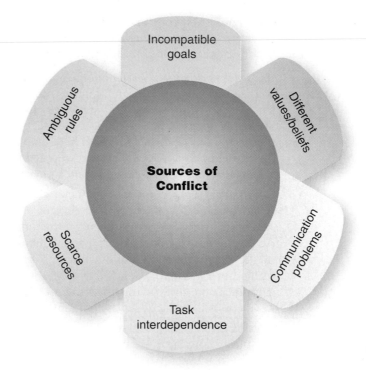

cutting costs and pushing for more accountability through performance management reports, yet employees believe these activities interfere with their own goals of developing or selling products and of taking home better paychecks.

Differentiation

Not long ago a British automotive company proposed a friendly buyout of an Italian firm. Executives at both companies were excited about the opportunities for sharing distribution channels and manufacturing technologies. But the grand vision of a merged company turned to a nightmare as executives began meeting over the details. Their backgrounds and experiences were so different that they were endlessly confused and constantly apologizing to the other side for oversights and misunderstandings. At one meeting—the last as it turned out—the president of the Italian firm stood up and, smiling sadly, said, "I believe we all know what is the problem here … it seems your forward is our reverse; your down, our up; your right, our wrong. Let us finish now, before war is declared."[14]

These automobile executives discovered that conflict is often caused by different values and beliefs due to unique backgrounds, experiences, or training. Mergers often produce conflict because they bring together people with divergent corporate cultures. Employees fight over the "right way" to do things because of their unique experiences in the separate companies. The British and Italian automobile executives probably also experienced conflict due to different national cultures. Cultural diversity makes it difficult to understand or accept the beliefs and values that other people hold toward organizational decisions and events.

Along with conflict generated from cultural diversity, many companies are experiencing a rising incidence of cross-generational conflict.[15] Younger and older employees have different needs, different expectations, and somewhat different values, which sometimes produce conflicting preferences and actions. Generational gaps have always existed, but this source of conflict is more common today because employees across age groups work together more than ever before. Virtual teams represent a third area where conflict is amplified due to differentiation. Recent investigations indicate that virtual teams have a high incidence of conflict because, in addition to increased cultural diversity, they have more difficulty than face-to-face (colocated) teams in establishing common mental models, norms, and temporal rhythms.[16]

Task Interdependence

Conflict tends to increase with the level of task interdependence. Task interdependence exists when team members must share common inputs to their individual tasks, need to interact in the process of executing their work, or receive outcomes (such as rewards) that are partly determined by the performance of others. The higher the level of task interdependence, the greater the risk of conflict because there is a greater chance that each side will disrupt or interfere with the other side's goals.[17]

Other than complete independence, employees tend to have the lowest risk of conflict when working with others in a pooled interdependence relationship. Pooled interdependence occurs where individuals operate independently except for reliance on a common resource or authority (see Chapter 9). The potential for conflict is higher in sequential interdependence work relationships, such as an assembly line. The highest risk of conflict tends to occur in reciprocal interdependence situations. With reciprocal interdependence, employees are highly dependent on each other and consequently have a higher probability of interfering with each other's work and personal goals. This increased interdependence partly accounts for the escalating conflict at Microsoft. As top management expects divisions to work more closely together, they have moved from pooled to sequential and reciprocal interdependence, thereby increasing perceptions of interference from each other's goals.

Scarce Resources

Resource scarcity generates conflict because each person or unit that requires the same resource necessarily undermines others who also need that resource to fulfill their goals. Consider the feud among employees and divisional managers at Microsoft, described in the opening vignette to this chapter. Although the Redmond, Washington–based software company may dominate several markets, its staff members still fight over limited resources, including budgets, personnel, and customers. Some of this conflict escalated when Microsoft introduced cost-cutting measures within the past few years when its growth and profitability flattened out.

Ambiguous Rules

Ambiguous rules—or the complete lack of rules—breed conflict. This occurs because uncertainty increases the risk that one party intends to interfere with the other party's goals. Ambiguity also encourages political tactics, and in some cases employees enter a free-for-all battle to win decisions in their favor. This explains why conflict is more common during mergers and acquisitions. Employees from both companies have conflicting practices and values, and few rules have developed to minimize the maneuvering for power and resources.[18] When clear rules exist, on the other hand, employees know what to expect from each other and have agreed to abide by those rules. Connections 13.1 illustrates how ambiguity bred conflict at Arthur Andersen. The now defunct accounting and consulting firm lacked clear guidelines to determine

Ambiguous Fee Structure Creates Fractious Divisions at Arthur Andersen

To outsiders, Arthur Andersen's "One Firm" policy was solid. The Chicago-based accounting firm provided the same quality of work anywhere in the world by the same type of people trained the same way. But when Barbara Toffler joined Andersen as an ethics consultant in 1996, she discovered plenty of infighting. Arthur Andersen is now gone because of accounting fraud at its client Enron; but internal conflict may have contributed to the accounting firm's demise as well.

Much of the dysfunctional conflict was caused by Arthur Andersen's ambiguous fee structure, which generously rewarded one engagement partner (the person in charge of the overall project) at the expense of other partners who provided services to the client. To maximize fees, executives fought over who should be the project's engagement partner and played games that would minimize the fees going to other groups. "While I was at Arthur Andersen, the fight for fees defined my existence," recalls Toffler.

In one incident a partner demanded that he should be the engagement partner because he had made the initial connection with a client, even though the project relied mainly on expertise from Barbara Toffler's ethical practices group. The two argued all the way to the airport and in several subsequent "violent" phone arguments. In another client proposal Toffler flew to Japan, only to spend two days of her time there negotiating through a translator with Andersen's Japanese engagement partner over how to split fees.

In a third incident several Arthur Andersen partners met with a potential client, supposedly to discuss their services. Instead the partners openly criticized each other during the pitch so the client would spend more money on their particular specialization. A couple of partners also extended the length of their presentations so other partners would have less time to convince the client of their particular value in the project. "Eventually I learned to screw someone else before they screwed me," says Toffler. "The struggle to win fees for your office and your group—and not someone else's—came to define the firm."

Source: Adapted from B.L. Toffler, *Final Accounting: Ambition, Greed, and the Fall of Arthur Andersen* (New York: Broadway Books, 2003).

Although Arthur Andersen employees put up a united front during the firm's dying days (as this photo shows), its ambiguous fee structure generated internal conflict that undermined the accounting firm's performance.

who would be the engagement partner (the person who gets financial credit for solic-iting a customer), so partners and associates battled and postured over who would get this coveted position.

Communication Problems

Conflict often occurs due to the lack of opportunity, ability, or motivation to communicate effectively. Let's look at each of these causes. First, when two parties lack the opportunity to communicate, they tend to use stereotypes to explain past behaviors and anticipate future actions. Unfortunately stereotypes are sufficiently subjective that emotions can negatively distort the meaning of an opponent's actions, thereby escalating perceptions of conflict. Furthermore, without direct interaction the two sides have less psychological empathy for each other. Second, some people lack the necessary skills to communicate in a diplomatic, nonconfrontational manner. When one party communicates its disagreement in an arrogant way, opponents are more likely to heighten their perception of the conflict. Arrogant behavior also sends a message that one side intends to be competitive rather than cooperative. This may lead the other party to reciprocate with a similar conflict management style.[19] Consequently, as we explained earlier, ineffective communication often escalates the conflict cycle.

Ineffective communication can also lead to a third problem: less motivation to communicate in the future. Socioemotional conflict is uncomfortable, so people avoid interacting with others in a conflicting relationship. Unfortunately less communication can further escalate conflict because there is less opportunity to empathize with the opponent's situation, and opponents are more likely to rely on distorted stereotypes of the other party. In fact, conflict tends to further distort these stereotypes through the process of social identity (see Chapter 3). We begin to see competitors less favorably so that our self-image remains strong during these uncertain times.[20]

The lack of motivation to communicate also explains (along with different values and beliefs, described earlier) why conflict is more common in cross-cultural relationships. People tend to feel uncomfortable or awkward interacting with co workers from different cultures, so they are less motivated to engage in dialogue with them. With limited communication, people rely more on stereotypes to fill in missing information. They also tend to misunderstand each other's verbal and nonverbal signals, further escalating the conflict.[21]

Interpersonal Conflict Management Styles

win–win orientation
The belief that conflicting parties will find a mutually beneficial solution to their disagreement.

The six structural conditions just described set the stage for conflict. The conflict process identified in Exhibit 13.1 illustrates that these sources of conflict lead to perceptions and emotions. Some people enter a conflict with a **win–win orientation**. This is the perception that the parties will find a mutually beneficial solution to their disagreement. They believe that the resources at stake are expandable rather than fixed if the parties work together to find a creative solution. Other people enter a conflict with a **win–lose orientation**. They adopt the belief that the parties are drawing from a fixed pie, so the more one party receives, the less the other party will receive.

win–lose orientation
The belief that conflicting parties are drawing from a fixed pie, so the more one party receives, the less the other party will receive.

Conflict tends to escalate when the parties develop a win–lose orientation because they rely on power and politics to gain advantage. A win–lose orientation may occasionally be appropriate when the conflict really is over a fixed resource, but few organizational conflicts are due to perfectly opposing interests with fixed resources. Some degree of win–win orientation is usually advantageous—that is, believing that each side's goals are not perfectly opposing. One possibility is that each party needs different parts of the resource. Another possibility is that various parts of the shared resource have different levels of value to each side.

Consider the example of a supplier and customer resolving a disagreement over the price of a product. Initially this seems like a clear win–lose situation—the supplier wants to receive more money for the product, whereas the customer wants to pay less money for it. Yet further discussion may reveal that the customer would be willing to pay more if the product could be provided earlier than originally arranged. The vendor may actually value that earlier delivery because it saves inventory costs. By looking at the bigger picture, both parties can often discover common ground.[22]

Adopting a win–win or win–lose orientation influences our conflict management style—that is, how we act toward the other person. The five conflict resolution styles described next can be placed in a two-dimensional grid reflecting the person's degree of concern for his or her own interests and concern for the other party's interests (see Exhibit 13.3). Problem solving is the only style that represents a purely win–win orientation. The other four styles represent variations of the win–lose approach.

- *Problem solving.* Problem solving tries to find a mutually beneficial solution for both parties. Information sharing is an important feature of this style because parties collaborate to identify common ground and potential solutions that satisfy all of them.

Exhibit 13.3
Interpersonal Conflict Management Styles

Source: C.K.W. de Dreu, A. Evers, B. Beersma, E.S. Kluwer, and A. Nauta, "A Theory-Based Measure of Conflict Management Strategies in the Workplace," *Journal of Organizational Behavior* 22 (2001), pp. 645–68. For earlier variations of this model, see T.L. Ruble and K. Thomas, "Support for a Two-Dimensional Model of Conflict Behavior," *Organizational Behavior and Human Performance* 16 (1976), p. 145.

NHLPA Shifts from Forcing to Problem Solving Bob Goodenow (left in photo) was called the Darth Vader of hockey. As the National Hockey League Players' Association (NHLPA) boss, his forcing style catapulted NHL player salaries from an average of $210,000 in the early 1990s to $1.3 million today. But while Goodenow's uncompromising approach rewarded players handsomely, critics say it also helped sink the public's image of NHL players, priced professional hockey out of smaller markets, and contributed to the cancellation of an entire season due to the recent player's strike. Goodenow stepped down when players agreed to the NHL owners' request to cap team salaries. Taking his place is Ted Saskin (right in photo), whose diplomatic problem-solving conflict resolution style couldn't be more different from Goodenow's. "We've got to be able to work more cooperatively (with the NHL) in the future," Saskin announced on the day he took over. NHL board of governors chairman Harley Hotchkiss thinks Saskin's approach to resolving differences is good for the sport's future. "I will say nothing bad about Bob Goodenow," insists Hotchkiss. "I just think that in any business you need a spirit of cooperation to move forward, and I think Ted Saskin will handle that well."[23]

- *Avoiding.* Avoiding tries to smooth over or avoid conflict situations altogether. It represents a low concern for both self and the other party; in other words, avoiders try to suppress thinking about the conflict. For example, some employees will rearrange their work area or tasks to minimize interaction with certain co-workers.[24]

- *Forcing.* Forcing tries to win the conflict at the other's expense. This style, which has the strongest win–lose orientation, relies on some of the "hard" influence tactics described in Chapter 12, particularly assertiveness, to get your own way.

- *Yielding.* Yielding involves giving in completely to the other side's wishes, or at least cooperating with little or no attention to your own interests. This style involves making unilateral concessions and unconditional promises, as well as offering help with no expectation of reciprocal help.

- *Compromising.* Compromising involves looking for a position in which your losses are offset by equally valued gains. It involves matching the other party's concessions, making conditional promises or threats, and actively searching for a middle ground between the interests of the two parties.[25]

Choosing the Best Conflict Management Style

Most of us have a preferred conflict management style, but the best style varies with the situation.[26] The problem-solving style is the preferred approach to resolving conflict in many situations because it is the only one that actively tries to optimize the value for both parties. However, this style works well only when the parties do not have perfectly opposing interests and when they have enough trust and openness to share information.

You might think that avoiding is an ineffective conflict management strategy, but it is actually the best approach where conflict has become socioemotional or where negotiating has a higher cost than the benefits of conflict resolution.[27] At the same time, conflict avoidance should not be a long-term solution where the conflict persists because it increases the other party's frustration. The forcing style of conflict resolution is usually inappropriate because organizational relationships rarely involve complete opposition. However, forcing may be necessary when you know you are correct and the dispute requires a quick solution. For example, a forcing style may be necessary when the other party engages in unethical conduct because any degree of unethical behavior is unacceptable. The forcing style may also be necessary where the other party would take advantage of more cooperative strategies.

The yielding style may be appropriate when the other party has substantially more power or the issue is not as important to you as to the other party. On the other hand, yielding behaviors may give the other side unrealistically high expectations, thereby motivating them to seek more from you in the future. In the long run, yielding may produce more conflict rather than resolve it. The compromising style may be best when there is little hope for mutual gain through problem solving, both parties have equal power, and both are under time pressure to settle their differences. However, compromise is rarely a final solution and may cause the parties to overlook options for mutual gain.

Cultural and Gender Differences in Conflict Management Styles

Cultural differences are more than just a source of conflict. Cultural background also affects the preferred conflict management style.[28] Some research suggests that people from collectivist cultures—where group goals are valued more than individual goals—are motivated to maintain harmonious relations and consequently are more likely than those from low collectivism cultures to manage disagreements through avoidance or problem solving. However, this view may be somewhat simplistic because people in some collectivist cultures are also more likely to publicly shame those whose actions conflict with expectations.[29]

Some writers suggest that men and women also tend to rely on different conflict management styles.[30] Generally speaking, women pay more attention than do men to the relationship between the parties. Consequently they tend to adopt a problem-solving style in business settings and are more willing to compromise to protect the relationship. Men tend to be more competitive and take a short-term orientation to the relationship. Of course we must be cautious about these observations because gender has a weak influence on conflict management style.

Structural Approaches to Conflict Management

Conflict management styles refer to how we approach the other party in a conflict situation. But conflict management also involves altering the underlying structural causes of potential conflict. The main structural approaches are identified in Exhibit 13.4. Although this section discusses ways to reduce conflict, we should keep in mind that conflict management sometimes calls for increasing conflict. This occurs mainly by reversing the strategies described over the next few pages.[31]

Emphasizing Superordinate Goals

A decade ago salespeople at Microchip Technology acted more like opponents than colleagues. As clients moved business to Asia, the U.S. and Asian sales reps would often compete for the same business, sometimes even undercutting each other's proposals. To minimize the dysfunctional conflict, the Mountain View, California, company made an unprecedented decision: It completely replaced sales commissions with stocks and bonuses based on the company's overall performance. Today sales staff are much more cooperative through mutual regard for the bigger picture—Microchip's long-term success.[32]

Exhibit 13.4
Structural Approaches to Conflict Management

Emphasize superordinate goals

Reduce differentiation

Clarify rules and procedures

Minimizing Dysfunctional Conflict

Improve communication /understanding

Increase resources

Reduce task interdependence

superordinate goals
Common objectives held by conflicting parties that are more important than their conflicting departmental or individual goals.

Microchip's executives minimized conflict among sales staff by getting them to focus on the company's superordinate goals rather than their conflicting subordinate goals. **Superordinate goals** are common objectives held by conflicting parties that are more important than the departmental or individual goals on which the conflict is based. By increasing commitment to corporatewide goals, employees place less emphasis on and therefore feel less conflict with co-workers over competing individual or departmental-level goals. They also potentially reduce the problem of differentiation by establishing a common frame of reference. For example, one study revealed that marketing managers in Hong Kong, China, Japan, and the United States were more likely to develop a collaborative conflict management style when executives aligned departmental goals with corporate objectives.[33]

Reducing Differentiation

Another way to minimize dysfunctional conflict is to reduce the differences that produce the conflict in the first place. The more employees think they have common backgrounds or experiences with co-workers, the more motivated they are to coordinate their activities and resolve conflict through constructive discussion with those co-workers.[34] One way to increase this commonality is by creating common experiences. The Manila Diamond Hotel in the Philippines accomplishes this by rotating staff across different departments. Hibernia Management and Development Company, which operates a large oil platform off the coast of Newfoundland, Canada, removed the "destructive differences" between hourly and salaried personnel by putting employees on salary rather than hourly wages. Multinational peacekeeping forces reduce differentiation among troops from the representative nations by providing opportunities for them to socialize and engage in common activities, including eating together.[35]

Toyota Drums Out Differences Employees at Toyota Motor Sales U.S.A. are drumming their way to a common bond and cooperation. Over the past three years, more than 3,000 Toyota employees have visited the automaker's training center (University of Toyota) in Torrance, California, to participate in drum circles. Typically in groups of 15 to 50 from one department, employees begin banging on one of the 150 percussion instruments available in the drum room. Few have played a percussion instrument before, so the first attempt rarely is worth recording. "At first it sounds pretty terrible, with everyone competing to be the loudest," admits Ron Johnson, Toyota's resident drum guru and a training center manager in Torrance. But most groups soon find a common beat without any guidance or conductor. Johnson recalls his first drum circle experience: "I'll never forget the spirit that came alive inside me. In a matter of moments, perfect strangers came together in synchronistic rhythm to share a common vision." By the end of the hourlong event most groups have formed a special bond that apparently increases their cooperation and sense of unity when they return to their jobs.[36]

Improving Communication and Understanding

A third way to resolve dysfunctional conflict is to give the conflicting parties more opportunities to communicate and understand each other. This recommendation relates back to the contact hypothesis described in Chapter 3. Specifically, the more meaningful interaction we have with someone, the less we rely on stereotypes to understand that person.[37] This positive effect is more pronounced when people work closely and frequently together on a shared goal in a meaningful task where they need to rely on each other (that is, cooperate rather than compete with each other). Another important ingredient is that the parties have equal status in that context.

There are two important caveats regarding the communication–understanding strategy. First, this strategy should be applied only *after* differentiation between the two sides has been reduced. If perceived differentiation remains high, attempts to manage conflict through dialogue might have the opposite effect because defense mechanisms are more likely to kick into action. These self-preservation forces increase stereotyping and tend to distort incoming sensory information. In other words, when forced to interact with people who we believe are quite different and in conflict with us, we tend to select information that reinforces that view.[38] Thus communication and understanding interventions are effective only when differentiation is sufficiently low.

Second, resolving differences through direct communication with the opposing party is a distinctly Western strategy that is not as comfortably applied in most parts of Asia and in other collectivist cultures.[39] As noted earlier, people in high collectivism cultures prefer an avoidance conflict management style because it is the most consistent with harmony and saving face. Direct communication is a high-risk strategy because it easily threatens the need to save face and maintain harmony.

Talking Circles   Where avoidance is ineffective in the long run, some collectivist groups engage in structured forms of dialogue that enable communication with less risk of upsetting harmony. One such practice in Native American culture is the talking circle.[40] A talking circle is an ancient group process used to educate, make decisions, and repair group harmony due to conflict. Participants sit in a circle and often begin with song, prayer, shaking hands with the next person, or some other communal activity. Then they share their experiences, information, and stories relating to the issue.

A talking stick or other natural object (such as a rock or feather) is held by the person speaking, which minimizes interruptions and dysfunctional verbal reactions by others. Talking circles are not aimed at solving problems through negotiated discussion. In fact, talking circle norms usually discourage participants from responding to someone else's statements. Rather, the emphasis is on healing relationships and restoring harmony, typically through the circle's communal experience and improved understanding of each person's views. Talking circles are still rare in business organizations, but they have been applied in meetings between aboriginal people and government representatives in several countries.

Reducing Task Interdependence

Conflict increases with the level of interdependence, so minimizing dysfunctional conflict might involve reducing the level of interdependence between the parties. If cost-effective, this might occur by dividing the shared resource so that each party has exclusive use of part of it. Sequentially or reciprocally interdependent jobs might be combined to form a pooled interdependence. For example, rather than having one employee serve customers and another operate the cash register, each employee could handle both customer activities alone. Buffers also help to reduce task interdependence between people. Buffers include resources, such as adding more inventory between people who perform sequential tasks.

Organizations also use human buffers—people who serve as intermediaries between interdependent people or work units who do not get along through direct interaction. For instance, one business school dean worked effectively with corporate leaders but held little affection for faculty. To minimize potential conflict, the dean hired a faculty-friendly associate dean to fulfill the internal leadership role. The associate dean became an intermediary who minimized the amount of time during which the dean and faculty needed to directly interact with each other.

Increasing Resources

An obvious way to reduce conflict due to resource scarcity is to increase the amount of resources available. Corporate decision makers might quickly dismiss this solution because of the costs involved. However, they need to carefully compare these costs with the costs of dysfunctional conflict arising out of resource scarcity.

Clarifying Rules and Procedures

Conflicts that arise from ambiguous rules can be minimized by establishing rules and procedures. Armstrong World Industries Inc. applied this strategy when consultants and information systems employees clashed while working together on development of a client–server network. Information systems employees at the flooring and building materials company thought they should be in charge, whereas consultants believed they had the senior role. Also, the consultants wanted to work long hours and take Friday off to fly home, whereas Armstrong employees wanted to work regular hours. The company reduced these conflicts by having both parties agree on specific responsibilities and roles. The agreement also assigned two senior executives at the companies to establish rules if future disagreements arose.[41]

Rules establish changes to the terms of interdependence, such as an employee's hours of work or a supplier's fulfillment of an order. In most cases the parties affected by these rules are involved in the process of deciding these terms of interdependence. By redefining the terms of interdependence, the strategy of clarifying rules is part of the larger process of negotiation.

Learning Objectives

After reading the next two sections you should be able to

7. **Outline four situational influences on negotiations.**
8. **Describe four behaviors that are characteristic of effective negotiators.**
9. **Compare and contrast the three types of third-party dispute resolution.**

Resolving Conflict through Negotiation

Think back through yesterday's events. Maybe you had to work out an agreement with other students about what tasks to complete for a team project. Chances are that you shared transportation with someone, so you had to clarify the timing of the ride. Then perhaps there was the question of who made dinner. Each of these daily events created potential conflict, and they were resolved through negotiation. **Negotiation** occurs whenever two or more conflicting parties attempt to resolve their divergent goals by redefining the terms of their interdependence. In other words, people negotiate when they think that discussion can produce a more satisfactory arrangement (at least for them) in their exchange of goods or services.

negotiation
Two or more conflicting parties attempt to resolve their divergent goals by redefining the terms of their interdependence.

As you can see, negotiation is not an obscure practice reserved for labor and management bosses when hammering out a collective agreement. Everyone negotiates daily. Most of the time you don't even realize that you are in negotiations. Negotiation is particularly evident in the workplace because employees work interdependently with each other. They negotiate with their supervisors over next month's work assignments, with customers over the sale and delivery schedules of their product, and with co-workers over when to have lunch. And yes, they occasionally negotiate with each other in labor disputes and workplace agreements.

Some writers suggest that negotiations are more successful when the parties adopt a problem-solving style, whereas others caution that this conflict management style is sometimes costly.[42] We know that any win–lose style (forcing, yielding, or the like) is unlikely to produce the optimal solution because the parties have not shared information necessary to discover a mutually satisfactory solution. On the other hand, we must be careful about adopting an open problem-solving style until mutual trust has been established.

Exhibit 13.5   **Bargaining Zone Model of Negotiations**

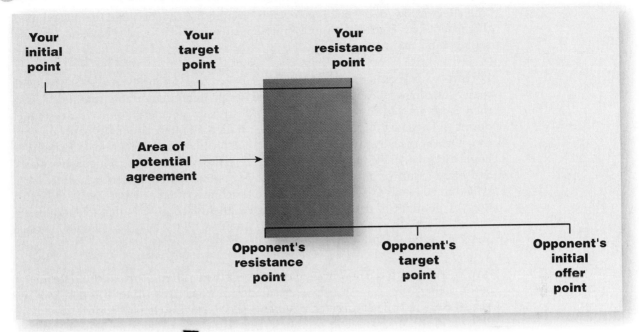

The concern with the problem-solving style is that information is power, so information sharing gives the other party more power to leverage a better deal if the opportunity occurs. Skilled negotiators often adopt a cautious problem-solving style at the outset by sharing information slowly and determining whether the other side will reciprocate. In this respect they try to establish trust with the other party.[13] They switch to one of the win–lose styles only when it becomes apparent that a win–win solution is not possible or the other party is unwilling to share information with a cooperative orientation.

Bargaining Zone Model of Negotiations

The negotiation process moves each party along a continuum with an area of potential overlap called the *bargaining zone*.[44] Exhibit 13.5 displays one possible bargaining zone situation. This linear diagram illustrates a purely win–lose situation—one side's gain will be the other's loss. However, the bargaining zone model can also be applied to situations in which both sides potentially gain from the negotiations. As this model illustrates, the parties typically establish three main negotiating points. The *initial offer point* is the team's opening offer to the other party. This may be its best expectation or a pie-in-the-sky starting point. The *target point* is the team's realistic goal or expectation for a final agreement. The *resistance point* is the point beyond which the team will make no further concessions.

The parties begin negotiations by describing their initial offer points for each item on the agenda. In most cases the participants know that this is only a starting point that will change as both sides offer concessions. In win–lose situations neither the target nor the resistance point is revealed to the other party. However, people try to discover the other side's resistance point because this knowledge helps them determine how much they can gain without breaking off negotiations. When the parties have a win–win orientation, on the other hand, the objective is to find a creative solution that keeps everyone close to their initial offer points. They hope to find an arrangement by which each side loses relatively little value on some issues and gains significantly more on other issues.

Situational Influences on Negotiations

The effectiveness of negotiating depends on both the situation and the behaviors of the negotiators. Four of the most important situational factors are location, physical setting, time, and audience.

Location

It is easier to negotiate on your own turf because you are familiar with the negotiating environment and are able to maintain comfortable routines.[45] Also, there is no need to cope with travel-related stress or depend on others for resources during the negotiation. Of course you can't walk out of negotiations as easily on your own turf, but this is usually a minor issue. Considering these strategic benefits of home turf, many negotiators agree to neutral territory. Telephones, videoconferences, and other forms of information technology potentially avoid territorial issues, but skilled negotiators usually prefer the media richness of face-to-face meetings. Frank Lowy, cofounder of retail property giant Westfield Group, says that telephones are "too cold" for negotiating. "From a voice I don't get all the cues I need. I go by touch and feel, and I need to see the other person."[46]

Physical Setting

The physical distance between the parties and the formality of the setting can influence their orientation toward each other and the disputed issues. So can the seating arrangements. People who sit face-to-face are more likely to develop a win–lose orientation toward the conflict situation. In contrast, some negotiation groups deliberately intersperse participants around the table to convey a win–win orientation. Others arrange the seating so that both parties face a white board, reflecting the notion that both parties face the same problem or issue.

Time Passage and Deadlines

The more time people invest in negotiations, the stronger their commitment becomes to reaching an agreement. This increases the motivation to resolve the conflict, but it also fuels the escalation of commitment problems described in Chapter 8. For example, the more time put into negotiations, the stronger the tendency to make unwarranted concessions so that the negotiations do not fail.

Time deadlines may be useful to the extent that they motivate the parties to complete negotiations. However, time pressures are usually a liability in negotiations.[47] One problem is that time pressure inhibits a problem-solving conflict management style because the parties have less time to exchange information or present flexible offers. Negotiators under time pressure also process information less effectively, so they have less creative ability to discover a win–win solution to the conflict. There is also anecdotal evidence that negotiators make excessive concessions and soften their demands more rapidly as a deadline approaches.

Audience Characteristics

Most negotiators have audiences—anyone with a vested interest in the negotiation outcomes, such as executives, other team members, or the general public. Negotiators tend to act differently when their audience observes the negotiation or has detailed information about the process, compared to situations in which the audience sees only the end results.[48] When the audience has direct surveillance over the proceedings, negotiators tend to be more competitive, less willing to make concessions, and more likely to engage in political tactics against the other party. This "hard-line" behavior shows the audience that the negotiator is working for their interests. With their audience watching, negotiators also have more interest in saving face.

Negotiator Behaviors

Negotiator behaviors play an important role in resolving conflict. Four of the most important behaviors are setting goals, gathering information, communicating effectively, and making concessions.

- *Preparation and goal setting.* Research consistently reports that people have more favorable negotiation results when they prepare for the negotiation and set goals.[49] In particular, negotiators should carefully think through their initial offer, target, and resistance points. They need to consider alternative strategies in case the negotiation fails. Negotiators also need to check their underlying assumptions, as well as goals and values. Equally important is the need to research what the other party wants from the negotiation. "You have to be prepared every which way about the people, the subject, and your fallback position," advises former Bombardier CEO Tellier. "Before walking into the room for the actual negotiation, I ask my colleagues to throw some curve balls at me," he says.[50]

- *Gathering information.* "Seek to understand before you seek to be understood." This popular philosophy from management guru Stephen Covey applies to effective negotiations. It means that we should spend more time listening closely to the other party and asking for details.[51] One way to improve the information-gathering process is to have a team of people participate in negotiations. Asian companies tend to have large negotiation teams for this purpose.[52] With more information about the opponent's interests and needs, negotiators are better able to discover low-cost concessions or proposals that will satisfy the other side.

- *Communicating effectively.* Effective negotiators communicate in a way that maintains effective relationships between the parties. Specifically, they minimize socioemotional conflict by focusing on issues rather than people. Effective negotiators also avoid irritating statements such as "I think you'll agree that this is a generous offer." Third, effective negotiators are masters of persuasion. They structure the content of their message so it is accepted by others, not merely understood.[53]

- *Making concessions.* Concessions are important because they (1) enable the parties to move toward the area of potential agreement, (2) symbolize each party's motivation to bargain in good faith, and (3) tell the other party the relative importance of the negotiating items.[54] How many concessions should you make? This varies with the other party's expectations and the level of trust between you. For instance, many Chinese negotiators are wary of people who change their position during the early stages of negotiations. Similarly, some writers warn that Russian negotiators tend to view concessions as a sign of weakness, rather than a sign of trust.[55] Generally the best strategy is to be moderately tough and give just enough concessions to communicate sincerity and motivation to resolve the conflict.[56] Being too tough can undermine relations between the parties; giving too many concessions implies weakness and encourages the other party to use power and resistance.

Third-Party Conflict Resolution

third-party conflict resolution
Any attempt by a relatively neutral person to help the parties resolve their differences.

Most of this chapter has focused on people directly involved in a conflict, yet many disputes in organizational settings are resolved with the assistance of a third party. **Third-party conflict resolution** is any attempt by a relatively neutral person to help the parties resolve their differences. There are generally three types of third-party dispute resolution activities: arbitration, inquisition, and mediation. These activities can be classified by their level of control over the process and control over the decision (see Exhibit 13.6).[57]

Exhibit 13.6
Types of Third-Party Intervention

Level of process control — High / Low

Mediation — Inquisition — Arbitration

Level of decision control — Low / High

- *Arbitration.* Arbitrators have high control over the final decision but low control over the process. Executives engage in this strategy by following previously agreed rules of due process, listening to arguments from the disputing employees, and making a binding decision. Arbitration is applied as the final stage of grievances by unionized employees, but it is also becoming more common in nonunion conflicts.

- *Inquisition.* Inquisitors control all discussion about the conflict. Like arbitrators, they have high decision control because they choose the form of conflict resolution. However, they also have high process control because they choose which information to examine and how to examine it, and they generally decide how the conflict resolution process will be handled.

- *Mediation.* Mediators have high control over the intervention process. In fact, their main purpose is to manage the process and context of interaction between the disputing parties. However, the parties make the final decision about how to resolve their differences. Thus mediators have little or no control over the conflict resolution decision.

Choosing the Best Third-Party Intervention Strategy

Team leaders, executives, and co-workers regularly intervene in disputes between employees and departments. Sometimes they adopt a mediator role; other times they serve as arbitrators. However, research suggests that people in positions of authority (like managers) usually adopt an inquisitional approach whereby they dominate the intervention process as well as making a binding decision.[58] Managers like the inquisition approach because it is consistent with the decision-oriented nature of managerial jobs, gives them control over the conflict process and outcome, and tends to resolve disputes efficiently.

However, the inquisitional approach to third-party conflict resolution is usually the least effective in organizational settings.[59] One problem is that leaders who take an inquisitional role tend to collect limited information about the problem using this approach, so their imposed decision may produce an ineffective solution to the conflict. Also, employees often view inquisitional procedures and outcomes as unfair because they have little control over this approach.

Which third-party intervention is most appropriate in organizations? The answer partly depends on the situation, such as the type of dispute, the relationship between the manager and employees, and cultural values such as power distance.[60] But generally speaking, for everyday disputes between two employees, the mediation approach is usually best because this gives employees more responsibility for resolving their own disputes. The third-party representative merely establishes an appropriate context for conflict resolution. Although not as efficient as other strategies, mediation potentially offers the highest level of employee satisfaction with the conflict process and outcomes.[61] When employees cannot resolve their differences, arbitration seems to work best because the predetermined rules of evidence and other processes create a higher sense of procedural fairness. Moreover, arbitration is preferred where the organization's goals should take priority over individual goals.

Alternative Dispute Resolution   After a two-year educational leave, Michael Kenney returned to Eastman Kodak Co. as a contractor, not the permanent position he previously held. A year later Kodak announced that Kenney's digitizing technician

U.S. Air Force Staff Resolve Workplace Battles through ADR Rather than battle each other in court or external arbitration, the U.S. Air Force and its civilian staff have resolved most workplace conflicts quickly and with improved mutual understanding through alternative dispute resolution (ADR). "The parties, in essence, maintain control over the [ADR] process and its outcome," explains Air Mobility Command civilian programs branch chief Diana Hendrix. Some Air Force bases retain a mediator to identify issues and explore options with the parties without imposing a solution. Other bases use peer review panels consisting of four to six union and nonunion employees who examine facts, listen to the parties, and make a final binding decision. The U.S. Air Force's goal is to use ADR for at least half of its employee disputes. ADR currently processes most disputes in less than one month. But even with these formal third-party systems in place, Diana Hendrix explains that supervisors are the first line of defense in resolving workplace conflict. "Ultimately, it's about Air Force employees and supervisors resolving conflicts in an efficient and effective manner so they can continue performing the Air Force mission of supporting and defending the United States of America," she says.[62]

position would disappear and that he would soon be jobless. Kenney didn't think losing his permanent position status was fair, so he took his dispute to Kodak's Resolution Support Services program. The program gives trained employees and managers the right to hear both sides of the conflict and, if appropriate, overturn management's decision. A trained adjudicator listened to Kenney's side of the story and then, with Kenney excused, listened to the supervisor and other witnesses. The adjudicator decided that Kenney should have a permanent position because Kodak applied its educational leave policy inconsistently.[63]

Eastman Kodak has joined a long list of firms that have taken third-party resolution one step further through an **alternative dispute resolution** (**ADR**) process. ADR combines third-party dispute resolution in an orderly sequence. ADR typically begins with a meeting between the employee and employer to clarify and negotiate their differences. If this fails, a mediator is brought in to help the parties reach a mutually agreeable solution. If mediation fails, the parties submit their case to an arbitrator whose decision may be either binding or voluntarily accepted by the employer. Although most ADR systems rely on professional arbitrators, some firms, such as Eastman Kodak and some U.S. Air Force bases, prefer peer arbitrations, which include a panel of co-workers and managers who are not involved in the dispute.[64] Overall, ADR helps the parties solve their own problems and tends to be more conciliatory than courtroom battles.

Whether resolving conflict through third-party dispute resolution or direct negotiation, we need to recognize that many solutions come from the sources of conflict that were identified earlier in this chapter. This may seem obvious; but in the heat of conflict, people often focus on each other rather than the underlying causes. Recognizing these conflict sources is the role of effective leadership, which is discussed in the next chapter.

alternative dispute resolution (ADR)
A third-party dispute resolution process that includes mediation, typically followed by arbitration.

Chapter Summary

Conflict is the process in which one party perceives that its interests are being opposed or negatively affected by another party. The conflict process begins with the sources of conflict. These sources lead one or both sides to perceive a conflict and to experience conflict emotions. This, in turn, produces manifest conflict, such as behaviors toward the other side. The conflict process often escalates through a series of episodes.

Conflict management maximizes the benefits and minimizes the dysfunctional consequences of conflict. Constructive conflict, a possible benefit of conflict, occurs when team members debate their different perceptions about an issue in a way that keeps the conflict focused on the task rather than people. Socioemotional conflict, a negative outcome, occurs when differences are viewed as personal attacks rather than attempts to resolve an issue. Socioemotional conflict tends to emerge in most constructive conflict episodes, but it is less likely to dominate when the parties are emotionally intelligent, have a cohesive team, and have supportive team norms. The main problems with conflict are that it may lead to job stress, dissatisfaction, and turnover.

Conflict tends to increase when people have incompatible goals, differentiation (different values and beliefs), interdependent tasks, scarce resources, ambiguous rules, and problems communicating with each other. Conflict is more common in a multicultural workforce because of greater differentiation and communication problems among employees.

People with a win–win orientation believe the parties will find a mutually beneficial solution to their disagreement. Those with a win–lose orientation adopt the belief that the parties are drawing from a fixed pie. The latter tends to escalate conflict. Among the five interpersonal conflict management styles, only problem solving represents a purely win–win orientation. The four other styles—avoiding, forcing, yielding, and compromising—adopt some variation of a win–lose orientation. Women and people with high collectivism tend to use a problem-solving or avoidance style more than men and people with high individualism.

Structural approaches to conflict management include emphasizing superordinate goals, reducing differentiation, improving communication and understanding, reducing task interdependence, increasing resources, and clarifying rules and procedures. These elements can also be altered to stimulate conflict.

Negotiation occurs whenever two or more conflicting parties attempt to resolve their divergent goals by redefining the terms of their interdependence. Negotiations are influenced by several situational factors, including location, physical setting, time passage and deadlines, and audience. Important negotiator behaviors include preparation and goal setting, gathering information, communicating effectively, and making concessions.

Third-party conflict resolution is any attempt by a relatively neutral person to help the parties resolve their differences. The three main forms of third-party dispute resolution are mediation, arbitration, and inquisition. Managers tend to use an inquisition approach, although mediation and arbitration are more appropriate, depending on the situation. Alternative dispute resolution applies mediation but may also involve negotiation and eventually arbitration.

Key Terms

alternative dispute resolution (ADR), p. 390

conflict, p. 370

conflict management, p. 372

constructive conflict, p. 372

negotiation, p. 384

socioemotional conflict, p. 372

superordinate goals, p. 381

third-party conflict resolution, p. 387

win–lose orientation, p. 377

win–win orientation, p. 377

Critical Thinking Questions

1. Distinguish constructive conflict from socioemotional conflict and explain how to apply the former without having the latter become a problem.

2. The chief executive officer of Creative Toys Inc. has read about cooperation in Japanese companies and vows to bring this same philosophy to the company. The goal is to avoid all conflict so that employees will work cooperatively and be happier at Creative Toys. Discuss the merits and limitations of the CEO's policy.

3. Conflict among managers emerged soon after a French company acquired a Swedish firm. The Swedes perceived the French management as hierarchical and arrogant, whereas the French thought the Swedes were naive, cautious, and lacking in achievement orientation. Describe ways to reduce dysfunctional conflict in this situation.

4. This chapter describes three levels of task interdependence that exist in interpersonal and intergroup relationships. Identify examples of these three levels in your work or school activities. How do these three levels affect potential conflict for you?

5. Jane has just been appointed as purchasing manager of Tacoma Technologies Corp. The previous purchasing manager, who recently retired, was known for his "winner-take-all" approach to suppliers. He continually fought for more discounts and was skeptical about any special deals that suppliers would propose.

A few suppliers refused to do business with Tacoma Technologies, but senior management was confident that the former purchasing manager's approach minimized the company's costs. Jane wants to try a more collaborative approach to working with suppliers. Will her approach work? How should she adopt a more collaborative approach in future negotiations with suppliers?

6. You are a special assistant to the commander-in-chief of a peacekeeping mission to a war-torn part of the world. The unit consists of a few thousand peacekeeping troops from the United States, France, India, and four other countries. The troops will work together for approximately one year. What strategies would you recommend to improve mutual understanding and minimize conflict among these troops?

7. Suppose you head one of five divisions in a multinational organization and are about to begin this year's budget deliberations at headquarters. What are the characteristics of your audience in these negotiations, and what effect might they have on your negotiation behavior?

8. Managers tend to use an inquisitional approach to resolving disputes between employees and departments. Describe the inquisitional approach and discuss its appropriateness in organizational settings.

Case Study 13.1 CONFLICT IN CLOSE QUARTERS

A team of psychologists at Moscow's Institute for Biomedical Problems (IBMP) wanted to learn more about the dynamics of long-term isolation in space. This knowledge would be applied to the International Space Station, a joint project of several countries that would send people into space for more than six months. It would eventually include a trip to Mars taking up to three years.

IBMP set up a replica of the *Mir* space station in Moscow. They then arranged for three international researchers from Japan, Canada, and Austria to spend 110 days isolated in a chamber the size of a train car. This chamber joined a smaller chamber where four Russian cosmonauts had already completed half of their 240 days of isolation. This was the first time an international crew was involved in the studies. None of the participants spoke English as their first language, yet they communicated throughout their stay in English at varying levels of proficiency.

Judith Lapierre, a French–Canadian, was the only female in the experiment. Along with obtaining a PhD in public health and social medicine, Lapierre had studied space sociology at the International Space University in France and conducted isolation research in the Antarctic. This was her fourth trip to Russia, where she had learned the language. The mission was supposed to have a second female participant from the Japanese space program, but she was not selected by IBMP.

The Japanese and Austrian participants viewed the participation of a woman as a favorable factor, says Lapierre. For example, to make the surroundings more comfortable, they rearranged the furniture, hung posters on the wall, and put a tablecloth on the kitchen table. "We adapted our environment, whereas the Russians just viewed it as something to be endured," she explains. "We decorated for Christmas because I'm the kind of person who likes to host people."

New Year's Eve Turmoil

Ironically, it was at one of those social events, the New Year's Eve party, that events took a turn for the worse. After drinking vodka (allowed by the Russian space agency), two of the Russian cosmonauts got into a fistfight that left blood splattered on the chamber walls. At one point a colleague hid the knives in the station's kitchen because of fears that the two

Russians were about to stab each other. The two cosmonauts, who generally did not get along, had to be restrained by other men. Soon after that brawl, the Russian commander grabbed Lapierre, dragged her out of view of the television monitoring cameras, and kissed her aggressively—twice. Lapierre fought him off, but the message didn't register. He tried to kiss her again the next morning.

The next day the international crew complained to IBMP about the behavior of the Russian cosmonauts. The Russian institute apparently took no action against any of the aggressors. Instead the institute's psychologists replied that the incidents were part of the experiment. They wanted crew members to solve their personal problems with mature discussion without asking for outside help. "You have to understand that *Mir* is an autonomous object, far away from anything," Vadim Gushin, the IBMP psychologist in charge of project, explained after the experiment had ended in March. "If the crew can't solve problems among themselves, they can't work together."

Following IBMP's response, the international crew wrote a scathing letter to the Russian institute and the space agencies involved in the experiment. "We had never expected such events to take place in a highly controlled scientific experiment where individuals go through a multistep selection process," they wrote. "If we had known … we would not have joined it as subjects." The letter also complained about IBMP's response to their concerns.

Informed about the New Year's Eve incident, the Japanese space program convened an emergency meeting on January 2 to address the incidents. Soon after the Japanese team member quit, apparently shocked by IBMP's inaction. He was replaced with a Russian researcher on the international team. Ten days after the fight—a little over a month after the international team began the mission—the doors between the Russian and international crews' chambers were barred at the request of the international research team. Lapierre later emphasized that this action was taken because of concerns about violence, not the incident involving her.

A Stolen Kiss or Sexual Harassment

By the end of the experiment in March, news of the fistfight between the cosmonauts and the commander's

392

attempts to kiss Lapierre had reached the public. Russian scientists attempted to play down the kissing incident by saying that it was one fleeting kiss, a clash of cultures, and a female participant who was too emotional.

"In the West, some kinds of kissing are regarded as sexual harassment. In our culture it's nothing," said Russian scientist Vadim Gushin in one interview. In another interview he explained, "The problem of sexual harassment is given a lot of attention in North America but less in Europe. In Russia it is even less of an issue, not because we are more or less moral than the rest of the world; we just have different priorities."

Judith Lapierre says the kissing incident was tolerable compared to this reaction from the Russian scientists who conducted the experiment. "They don't get it at all," she complains. "They don't think anything is wrong. I'm more frustrated than ever. The worst thing is that they don't realize it was wrong."

Norbert Kraft, the Austrian scientist on the international team, also disagreed with the Russian interpretation of events. "They're trying to protect themselves," he says. "They're trying to put the fault on others. But this is not a cultural issue. If a woman doesn't want to be kissed, it is not acceptable."

Discussion Questions

1. Identify the different conflict episodes that exist in this case. Who was in conflict with whom?

2. What are the sources of conflict for these conflict incidents?

3. What conflict management style(s) did Lapierre, the international team, and Gushin use to resolve these conflicts? What style(s) would have worked best in these situations?

4. What conflict management interventions were applied here? Did they work? What alternative strategies would work best in this situation and in the future?

The facts of this case were pieced together by Steven L. McShane from the following sources: G. Sinclair Jr., "If You Scream in Space, Does Anyone Hear?" *Winnipeg Free Press*, 5 May 2000, p. A4; S. Martin, "Reining in the Space Cowboys," *Globe & Mail*, 19 April 2000, p. R1; M. Gray, "A Space Dream Sours," *Maclean's*, 17 April 2000, p. 26; E. Niiler, "In Search of the Perfect Astronaut," *Boston Globe*, 4 April 2000, p. E4; J. Tracy, "110-Day Isolation Ends in Sullen … Isolation," *Moscow Times*, 30 March 2000, p. 1; M. Warren, "A Mir Kiss?" *Daily Telegraph* (London), 30 March 2000, p. 22; G. York, "Canadian's Harassment Complaint Scorned," *Globe & Mail*, 25 March 2000, p. A2; S. Nolen, "Lust in Space," *Globe & Mail*, 24 March 2000, p. A3.

Case Study 13.2 THE HOUSE OF PRITZKER

BusinessWeek Just four years after the death of patriarch Jay Pritzker, one of America's wealthiest families is being torn apart by sibling rivalry and resentment. At the heart of the dispute is a rift over control of the family businesses and fortune, which include Hyatt Hotels, thousands of apartment units, industrial conglomerate Marmon Group, and stakes in Reliant Pharmaceuticals and First Health Group. Tom, the eldest son, was groomed to lead the family business and had demonstrated the ability to invest and negotiate. But even Tom could not prevent the escalating disputes among other Pritzker family members.

This *BusinessWeek* case study examines the feud in one of America's wealthiest families. It describes the tensions that have built up in recent years, and identifies the solutions that Jay Pritzker and his son, Tom, have tried to use to diffuse the conflict. Read through this *BusinessWeek* article at www.mhhe.com/mcshane4e and prepare for the discussion questions below.

Discussion Questions

1. Identify the sources of conflict that explain current relations in the Pritzker family.

2. What did Tom do to try to minimize the conflict among family members? Did any of it work? Why or why not?

3. What other organizational behavior concepts seem to be relevant to this story about rivalries in the Pritzker family and its businesses?

Source: J. Weber, "The House of Pritzker," *BusinessWeek*, 17 March 2003, 58.

Class Exercise 13.3 THE CONTINGENCIES OF CONFLICT HANDLING

Gerard A. Callanan and David F. Perri, West Chester University of Pennsylvania

PURPOSE This exercise is designed to help you understand the contingencies of applying conflict handling styles in organizational settings.

INSTRUCTIONS

1. Participants will read each of the five scenarios presented here and select the most appropriate response from among the five alternatives. Each scenario has a situationally correct response.

2. *(Optional)* The instructor may ask each student to complete the Dutch Test for conflict handling self-assessment in this chapter (Self-Assessment 13.5) or a similar instrument. This instrument will provide an estimate of your preferred conflict handling style.

3. As a class, participants will give their feedback on the responses to each of the scenarios, with the instructor guiding discussion on the contextual factors embodied in each scenario. For each scenario the class should identify the response selected by the majority. In addition, participants will discuss how they decided on the choices they made and the contextual factors they took into account in making their selections.

4. Students will compare their responses to the five scenarios with their results from the conflict handling self-assessment. Discussion will focus on the extent to which each person's preferred conflict handling style influenced his or her choices in this activity, as well as the implications of this style preference for managing conflict in organizations.

SCENARIO #1

SETTING You are a manager of a division in the accounting department of a large eastern U.S. bank. Nine exempt-level analysts and six nonexempt clerical staff report to you. Recently one of your analysts, Jane Wilson, has sought the bank's approval for tuition reimbursement for the cost of an evening MBA program specializing in organizational behavior. The bank normally encourages employees to seek advanced degrees on a part-time basis. Indeed, through your encouragement, nearly all members of your staff are pursuing additional schoolwork. You consult the bank's policy manual and discover that two approvals are necessary for reimbursement—yours and that of the manager of training and development, Kathy Gordon. Further, the manual states that approval for reimbursement will be granted only if the coursework is "reasonably job related." Based on your review of the matter, you decide to approve Jane's request for reimbursement. However, Kathy Gordon rejects it outright by claiming that coursework in organizational behavior is not related to an accounting analyst position. She states that the bank will reimburse the analyst only for a degree in either accounting or finance. In your opinion, however, the interpersonal skills and insights to be gained from a degree in organizational behavior are job related and can also benefit the employee in future assignments. The analyst job requires interaction with a variety of individuals at different levels in the organization, and it is important that interpersonal and communication skills be strong.

After further discussion it becomes clear that you and Kathy Gordon have opposite views of the matter. Because both of you are at the same organizational level and have equal status, it appears that you are at an impasse. Although the goal of reimbursement is important, you are faced with other pressing demands on your time. In addition, the conflict has diverted the attention of your work group away from its primary responsibilities. Because the school term is about to begin, it is essential that you and Kathy Gordon reach a timely agreement to enable Jane to pursue her coursework.

ACTION ALTERNATIVES FOR SCENARIO #1
Please indicate your first (1) and second (2) choices from among the following alternatives by writing the appropriate numbers in the space provided.

Action Alternative	Ranking (1st and 2nd)
1. You go along with Kathy Gordon's view and advise Jane Wilson to select either accounting or finance as a major for her MBA.	_____
2. You decide to withdraw from the situation completely and tell Jane to work it out with Kathy Gordon on her own.	_____
3. You decide to take the matter to those in higher management levels and argue forcefully for your point of view. You do everything in your power to ensure that a decision will be made in your favor.	_____
4. You decide to meet Kathy Gordon halfway to reach an agreement. You advise Jane to pursue her MBA in accounting or finance, but also recommend that she minor in organizational behavior by taking electives in that field.	_____
5. You decide to work more closely with Kathy Gordon by attempting to get a clear as well as flexible policy written that reflects both of your views. Of course this will require a significant amount of your time.	_____

SCENARIO #2

SETTING You are the vice president of a relatively large division (300 employees) in a medium-sized consumer products company. Due to the recent turnover of minority staff, your division has fallen behind in meeting the company's goal for Equal Employment Opportunity (EEO) hiring. Because of a scarcity of qualified minority candidates, it appears that you may fall further behind in achieving the stated EEO goals.

Although you are aware of the problem, you believe that the low level of minority hiring is due to increased attrition in minority staff as well as the lack of viable replacement candidates. However, the EEO officer believes that your hiring criteria are too stringent, resulting in the rejection of minority candidates with the basic qualifications to do the job. You support the goals and principles of EEO; however, you are concerned that hiring less qualified candidates will weaken the performance of your division. The EEO officer believes that your failure to hire minority employees is damaging to the company in the short term because corporate goals will not be met, and in the long term because it will restrict the pool of minority candidates available for upward mobility. Both of you regard your concerns as important. Further, you recognize that both of you have the company's best interests in mind and that you have a mutual interest in resolving the conflict.

ACTION ALTERNATIVES FOR SCENARIO #2
Please indicate your first (1) and second (2) choices from among the following alternatives by writing the appropriate numbers in the space provided.

Action Alternative	Ranking (1st and 2nd)
1. You conclude that the whole problem is too complex an issue for you to handle right now. You put it on the "back burner" and decide to reconsider the problem at a later date.	_____
2. You believe that your view outweighs the perspective of the EEO officer. You decide to argue your position more vigorously and hope that your stance will sway the EEO officer to agree with your view.	_____
3. You decide to accept the EEO officer's view. You agree to use less stringent selection criteria and thereby hire more minority employees.	_____
4. You give in to the EEO officer somewhat by agreeing to relax your standards a little bit. This would allow slightly more minority hiring (but not enough to satisfy the EEO goal) and could cause a small reduction in the overall performance of your division.	_____
5. You try to reach a consensus that addresses each of your concerns. You agree to work harder at hiring more minority applicants and request that the EEO officer agree to help find the most qualified minority candidates available.	_____

SCENARIO #3

SETTING   You are the manager in charge of the financial reporting section of a large insurance company. It is the responsibility of your group to make periodic written and oral reports to senior management regarding the company's financial performance. The company's senior management has come to rely on your quick and accurate dissemination of financial data as a way to make vital, timely decisions. This has given you a relatively high degree of organizational influence. You rely on various operating departments to supply financial information according to a pre-established reporting schedule.

In two days you must make your quarterly presentation to the company's board of directors. However, the claims department has failed to supply several key pieces of information that are critical to your presentation. You check the reporting schedule and realize that you should have had the information two days ago. When you call Bill Jones, the claims department manager, he informs you that he cannot possibly get you the data within the next two days. He states that other pressing work has a higher priority. Although you explain the critical need for this data, he is unwilling to change his position. You believe that your presentation is vital to the company's welfare and explain this to Bill Jones. Although Bill has less status than you, he has been known to take advantage of individuals who are unwilling or unable to push their point of view. With your presentation less than two days away, it is critical that you receive information from the claims department within the next 24 hours.

ACTION ALTERNATIVES FOR SCENARIO #3
Please indicate your first (1) and second (2) choices from among the following alternatives by writing the appropriate numbers in the space provided.

Action Alternative	Ranking (1st and 2nd)
1. Accept the explanation from Bill Jones and try to get by without the figures by using your best judgment as to what they would be.	_____
2. Tell Bill Jones that unless you have the data from his department on your desk by tomorrow morning, you will be forced to go over his head to compel him to give you the numbers.	_____
3. Meet Bill Jones halfway by agreeing to receive part of the needed figures and using your own judgment on the others.	_____
4. Try to get your presentation postponed until a later date, if possible.	_____
5. Forget about the short-term need for information and try to achieve a longer-term solution, such as adjusting the reporting schedule to better accommodate your mutual needs.	_____

SCENARIO #4

SETTING   You are the production manager of a medium-sized building products company. You control a production line that runs on a three-shift basis. Recently Ted Smith, the materials handling manager, asked you to accept a different packaging of the raw materials for the production process than what has been customary. He states that new machinery he has installed makes it much easier to provide the material in 100-pound sacks instead of the 50-pound bags that you currently receive. Ted further explains that providing the material in the 50-pound bags would put an immense strain on his operation, and he therefore has a critical need for you to accept the change. You know that accepting materials in the new packaging will cause some minor disruption in your production process but should not cause long-term problems for any of the three shifts. However, you are a little annoyed by the proposed change because Ted did not consult with you before he installed the new equipment. In the past you and he have been open in your communication. You do not think that this failure to consult you represents a change in your relationship.

Because you work closely with Ted, it is essential that you maintain the harmonious and stable working relationship that you have built over the past few years. In addition, you may need some help from him in the future: You already know that your operation will have special material requirements in about two months. You also know that Ted has influence at higher levels of the organization.

ACTION ALTERNATIVES FOR SCENARIO #4
Please indicate your first (1) and second (2) choices from among the following alternatives by writing the appropriate numbers in the space provided.

Action Alternative	Ranking (1st and 2nd)
1. Agree to accept the raw material in the different format.	_____
2. Refuse to accept the material in the new format because it would disrupt your operation.	_____
3. Propose a solution in which you accept material in the new format during the first shift but not during the second and third.	_____
4. Tell Ted Smith that you do not wish to deal with the issue at this time, but that you will consider his request and get back to him at a later date.	_____
5. Tell Ted Smith about your concern regarding his failure to consult with you before installing new equipment. You inform him that you wish to find longer-term solutions to the conflict between you.	_____

SCENARIO #5

SETTING You supervise the compensation and benefits section in the human resources department of a medium-sized pharmaceutical company. Your staff of three clerks is responsible for maintaining contacts with the various benefits providers and answering related questions from the company's employees. Your section shares secretarial, word processing, and copier resources with the training and development section of the department. Recently a disagreement has arisen between you and Beth Hanson, the training and development supervisor, over when the secretarial staff should take their lunch breaks. Beth would like the secretarial staff to take their breaks an hour later to coincide with the time most of her people go to lunch. You know that the secretaries do not want to change their lunchtimes. Further, the current time is more convenient for your staff.

At this time you are hard-pressed to deal with the situation. You have an important meeting with the provider of dental insurance in two days. It is critical that you are well prepared for this meeting, and these other tasks are a distraction.

ACTION ALTERNATIVES FOR SCENARIO #5 Please indicate your first (1) and second (2) choices from among the following alternatives by writing the appropriate numbers in the space provided.

Action Alternative	Ranking (1st and 2nd)
1. Take some time over the next day and propose a solution in which three days a week the secretaries take their lunch at the earlier time and two days at the later.	_____
2. Tell Beth Hanson you will deal with the matter in a few days after you have addressed the more pressing issues.	_____
3. Let Beth Hanson have her way by agreeing to a later lunch hour for the secretarial staff.	_____
4. Tell Beth Hanson that you will not agree to a change in the secretaries' lunchtime.	_____
5. Devote more time to the issue. Attempt to achieve a broad-based consensus with Beth Hanson that meets her needs as well as yours and those of the secretaries.	_____

Source: G.A. Callanan and D.F. Perri, "Teaching Conflict Management Using a Scenario-Based Approach," *Journal of Education for Business* 81 (January/February 2006), pp. 131–39.

Team Exercise 13.4 UGLI ORANGE ROLE-PLAY

PURPOSE This exercise is designed to help you understand the dynamics of interpersonal and intergroup conflict as well as the effectiveness of negotiation strategies under specific conditions.

MATERIALS The instructor will distribute roles for Dr. Roland, Dr. Jones, and a few observers. Ideally each negotiation should occur in a private area away from other negotiations.

INSTRUCTIONS

1. The instructor will divide the class into an even number of teams of three people each, with one participant left over for each team formed (for example, there will be six observers if there are six teams). Half of the teams will take the role of Dr. Roland and the other half will be Dr. Jones. The instructor will distribute roles after these teams have been formed.

2. Members within each team are given 10 minutes (or another time limit stated by the instructor) to learn their roles and choose a negotiating strategy.

3. After reading their roles and discussing strategy, each Dr. Jones team is matched with a Dr. Roland team to conduct negotiations. Observers will receive observation forms from the instructor, and two observers will be assigned to watch the paired teams during prenegotiations and subsequent negotiations.

4. As soon as Roland and Jones reach agreement or at the end of the time allotted for the negotiation (whichever comes first), the Roland and Jones teams report to the instructor for further instruction.

5. At the end of the exercise the class will congregate to discuss the negotiations. Observers, negotiators, and the instructor will then discuss their observations and experiences and the implications for conflict management and negotiation.

Source: This exercise was developed by Robert J. House, Wharton Business School, University of Pennsylvania. A similar activity is also attributed to earlier writing by R.R. Blake and J.S. Mouton.

Self-Assessment 13.5

THE DUTCH TEST FOR CONFLICT HANDLING

PURPOSE This self-assessment is designed to help you identify your preferred conflict management style.

INSTRUCTIONS Read each of the following statements and circle the response that you believe best reflects your position regarding each statement.

Then use the scoring key in Appendix B to calculate your results for each conflict management style. This exercise is completed alone so you can assess yourself honestly without concerns of social comparison. However, class discussion will focus on the different conflict management styles and the situations in which each is most appropriate.

Dutch Test for Conflict Handling

When I have a conflict at work, I do the following:	Not at all ▼				Very much ▼
1. I give in to the wishes of the other party.	1	2	3	4	5
2. I try to reach a middle-of-the-road solution.	1	2	3	4	5
3. I push my own point of view.	1	2	3	4	5
4. I examine issues until I find a solution that really satisfies me and the other party.	1	2	3	4	5
5. I avoid confrontation about our differences.	1	2	3	4	5
6. I concur with the other party.	1	2	3	4	5
7. I emphasize that we have to find a compromise solution.	1	2	3	4	5
8. I search for gains.	1	2	3	4	5
9. I stand for my own and the other's goals and interests.	1	2	3	4	5
10. I avoid differences of opinion as much as possible.	1	2	3	4	5
11. I try to accommodate the other party.	1	2	3	4	5
12. I insist that we both give in a little.	1	2	3	4	5
13. I fight for a good outcome for myself.	1	2	3	4	5
14. I examine ideas from both sides to find a mutually optimal solution.	1	2	3	4	5
15. I try to make differences loom less severe.	1	2	3	4	5
16. I adapt to the parties' goals and interests.	1	2	3	4	5
17. I strive whenever possible toward a 50–50 compromise.	1	2	3	4	5
18. I do everything to win.	1	2	3	4	5
19. I work out a solution that serves my own and the other's interests as well as possible.	1	2	3	4	5
20. I try to avoid a confrontation with the other.	1	2	3	4	5

Source: C.K.W. de Dreu, A. Evers, B. Beersma, E.S. Kluwer, and A. Nauta, "A Theory-Based Measure of Conflict Management Strategies in the Workplace," *Journal of Organizational Behavior* 22 (2001), pp. 645–68.

After reading this chapter, if you need additional information, see **www.mhhe.com/mcshane4e** for more in-depth interactivities that correspond with this material.

Infosys has grown into one of India's largest and most successful information technology companies, and chief executive Nandan Nilekani wants to maintain that momentum by focusing his attention on leadership development. "Given our pace of growth, transferring the values and beliefs, the DNA of the organization, to the next generations of leaders is one of my most important functions," says Nilekani, who is actively involved in the company's leadership development workshops and mentoring activities.

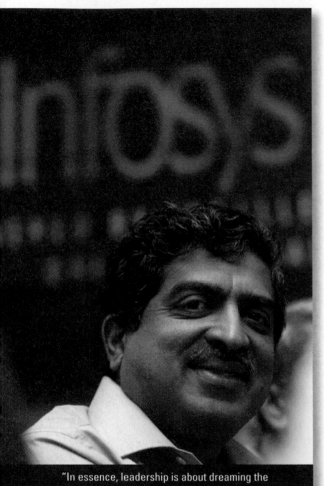

"In essence, leadership is about dreaming the impossible and helping followers achieve the same," says Nandan Nilekani, chief executive of Infosys, one of India's largest and most successful information technology companies.

Building a strong cadre of leaders required Nilekani and his executive team to carefully think about the meaning of effective leadership. "We believe our future leaders need to learn how to set direction, to create a shared vision, encourage execution excellence, embrace inclusive meritocracy," he says. Nilekani particularly emphasizes the importance of values and vision. "In essence, leadership is about dreaming the impossible and helping followers achieve the same. Moreover, the dream has to be built on sound and context-invariant values to sustain the enthusiasm and energy of people over a long time."

Nilekani's definition of leadership bears an uncanny resemblance to the one formed by Pacific Gas & Electric Company (PG&E) CEO Peter Darbee. "A leader needs to first be able to dream great dreams, and establish a vision," he says. Furthermore, great leaders translate that broad vision into more precise objectives, goals, and metrics, all of which are guided by strategy and supported by the organization's culture. Darbee also advises that "the glue that holds this all together is your values. You have to lead from your values."

Richard Brajer, CEO of Lioposcience Inc., adds another view of leadership. He suggests that leadership isn't about being front-and-center, but nurturing an environment where everyone can achieve their potential. "I think the power and role of a leader are to release the potential of an organization," he says. "This means not to take my brain and replicate it in the brains of the people around me, but to release their potential to work toward an agreed-upon direction." Microsoft Australia chief executive Steve Vamos makes a similar observation. "It's not about having all the answers. The role of the leader is to create environments where others can do great work—and then to get out of the way."[1]

Leadership in Organizational Settings

LEARNING OBJECTIVES

After reading this chapter you should be able to

1. Define *leadership* and *shared leadership*.
2. List seven competencies of effective leaders.
3. Describe the people-oriented and task-oriented leadership styles.
4. Outline the path–goal theory of leadership.
5. Summarize leadership substitutes theory.
6. Distinguish transformational leadership from transactional and charismatic leadership.
7. Describe the four elements of transformational leadership.
8. Describe the implicit leadership perspective.
9. Discuss the influence of culture on perceptions of effective leaders.
10. Discuss similarities and differences in the leadership styles of women and men.

After reading the next three sections you should be able to

1.   Define *leadership* and *shared leadership*.
2.   List seven competencies of effective leaders.

What Is Leadership?

The world is changing, and so is our concept of leadership. Gone is yesteryear's image of the command-and-control boss. Also gone is the more recent view that leaders are front-and-center charismatic heroes. Instead, as Nandan Nilekani, Peter Darbee, Richard Brajer, and Steve Vamos stated in the opening vignette, leadership is about values, vision, enabling, and coaching. A few years ago 54 leadership experts from 38 countries reached a consensus that **leadership** is about influencing, motivating, and enabling others to contribute toward the effectiveness and success of the organizations of which they are members.[2] Leaders apply various forms of influence—from subtle persuasion to direct application of power—to ensure that followers have the motivation and role clarity to achieve specified goals. Leaders also arrange the work environment—such as allocating resources and altering communication patterns—so employees can achieve corporate objectives more easily.

Shared Leadership

Leadership isn't restricted to the executive suite. Anyone in the organization may be a leader in various ways and at various times.[3] This view is variously known as **shared leadership** or the leaderful organization. Effective self-directed work teams, for example, consist of members who share leadership responsibilities or otherwise allocate this role to a responsible coordinator. W.L. Gore & Associates is a case in point. The

leadership
Influencing, motivating, and enabling others to contribute toward the effectiveness and success of the organizations of which they are members.

shared leadership
The view that leadership is broadly distributed rather than assigned to one person, such that people within the team and organization lead each other.

Shared Leadership at Semco If anyone can say they lead a company of leaders, it would be Ricardo Semler, CEO of Semco Corporation, SA. Headquartered in Sao Paulo, Brazil, the manufacturing and services conglomerate delegates almost total responsibility to its 3,000 employees. Organized into small groups of 6 to 10 people, Semco employees choose their objectives every six months, hire their co-workers, work out their budgets, set their own salaries, decide when to come to work, and even elect their own bosses. This may seem radical, but Semler says that the company is "only 50 or 60 percent where we'd like to be." Semler (shown here with head office staff) believes that replacing the head office with several satellite offices around Sao Paulo would give employees even more opportunity to lead themselves.[4]

company's 6,500 employees are organized around self-directed work teams and consequently have few formal leaders. Yet the company has no shortage of leaders. When asked in the company's annual survey "Are you a leader?" more than 50 percent of Gore employees answered "Yes."[5]

Shared leadership also extends to organizational clients, as was dramatically illustrated in the recent revival of St. Magloire. The small village in Quebec, Canada, near the Maine border, had suffered population decline as children grew up and moved to larger population centers. When the Quebec government threatened to close the only school, Julie Bercier and a handful of other citizens rallied to attract new residents. At first people were skeptical, suggesting that Bercier and her friends were dreaming to think that anyone could reverse the rural exodus. But persistence paid off as people eventually got involved in marketing and developing St. Magloire as a better lifestyle for city folks. Newspaper campaigns, a new resident welcoming program, and government support attracted 54 people within a year. The school remained open as enough children enrolled the following year. Although the village mayor and school leaders played important roles, Bercier and others became leaders by providing the passion and vision of what the small community could become with enough ingenuity and effort.[6]

Perspectives of Leadership

Leadership has been contemplated since the days of Greek philosophers, and it is one of the most popular research topics among organizational behavior scholars. This has resulted in an enormous volume of leadership literature, most of which can be organized into the five perspectives shown in Exhibit 14.1.[7] Although some of these perspectives are currently more popular than others, each helps us to more fully understand this complex issue.

Exhibit 14.1
Perspectives of Leadership

Some researchers examine leadership competencies, whereas others look at leadership behaviors. More recent studies have looked at leadership from a contingency approach by considering the appropriate leader behaviors in different settings. Currently the most popular perspective is that leaders transform organizations through their vision, communication, and ability to build commitment. Finally, an emerging perspective suggests that leadership is mainly a perceptual bias. We distort reality and attribute events to leaders because we feel more comfortable believing that a competent individual is at the organization's helm. This chapter explores each of these five perspectives of leadership. In the final section we also consider cross-cultural and gender issues in organizational leadership.

Competency Perspective of Leadership

When Helene Gayle was recently appointed president of CARE, the Atlanta-based global aid agency, numerous colleagues and observers were quick to point out several attributes that make her an excellent leader. She has a deep knowledge of global health issues, has drive and determination to bring about meaningful change, is highly trusted, and demonstrates a high level of emotional intelligence. These characteristics of Helene Gayle reflect the notion that people require specific competencies to fulfill leadership roles.

Since the beginning of recorded civilization, people have been interested in the personal characteristics that distinguish great leaders from the rest of us. A major review in the late 1940s concluded that no consistent list of traits could be distilled from the hundreds of studies conducted up to that time. A subsequent review suggested that a few traits are consistently associated with effective leaders, but most are unrelated to effective leadership.[8] These conclusions caused many scholars to give up their search for personal characteristics that distinguish effective leaders.

Over the past decade leadership researchers and consultants have returned to the notion that leadership requires specific personal characteristics. One recent study established that inherited personality characteristics significantly influence *leadership*

CAREing Leadership Competencies By all accounts Helene Gayle has the competencies of an effective leader. Recently appointed as president of CARE, the Atlanta-based global aid agency, Gayle brings a wealth of experience from her previous executive positions with the Bill & Melinda Gates Foundation and the Centers for Disease Control (CDC). "Her leadership, commitment, and talents are well demonstrated," says CARE board chairman Lincoln Chen. William Foege, who worked with Gayle when he was head of the CDC, also points to her incredible drive and motivation. "Helene has the capacity to go full-tilt day after day and week after week," he notes. "It's almost as if she doesn't know what fatigue is like." Others have commented on her high degree of integrity. "Helene Gayle may be the most trusted public health leader in the world," says David Satcher, who has served as CDC director and U.S. surgeon-general. Still others describe Gayle's high level of emotional intelligence. "Helene has a tremendous natural empathy," says Ashok Alexander, director of the Gates' Foundation AIDS program in India.[9]

Exhibit 14.2

**Seven Competencies
of Effective Leaders**

Leadership trait	Description
Emotional intelligence	The leader's ability to monitor his or her own and others' emotions, discriminate among them, and use the information to guide his or her thoughts and actions.
Integrity	The leader's truthfulness and tendency to translate words into deeds.
Drive	The leader's inner motivation to pursue goals.
Leadership motivation	The leader's need for socialized power to accomplish team or organizational goals.
Self-confidence	The leader's belief in his or her own leadership skills and ability to achieve objectives.
Intelligence	The leader's above-average cognitive ability to process enormous amounts of information.
Knowledge of the business	The leader's tacit and explicit knowledge about the company's environment, enabling him or her to make more intuitive decisions.

emergence—the perception that someone is a leader in a leaderless situation.[10] More striking, however, is the resurgence in interest in discovering leadership *competencies* that enable companies to select and develop future leaders.[11] Competencies encompass a broad range of personal characteristics, including knowledge, skills, abilities, and values. The recent leadership literature identifies several leadership competencies, most of which can be grouped into the seven categories listed in Exhibit 14.2 and described next.[12]

- *Emotional intelligence.* Research points to emotional intelligence as an important attribute of effective leaders.[13] They have the ability to perceive and express emotion, assimilate emotion in thought, understand and reason with emotion, and regulate emotion in themselves and others (see Chapter 4). Helene Gayle and other leaders can empathize, build rapport, and network with others. The contingency leadership perspective described later in this chapter assumes that effective leaders have sufficient emotional intelligence to know when to adjust their behavior so it matches the situation.

- *Integrity.* Integrity refers to the leader's truthfulness and tendency to translate words into deeds. This characteristic is sometimes called *authentic leadership* because the individual acts with sincerity. He or she has a high moral capacity to judge dilemmas based on sound values and to act accordingly. Several large-scale studies have reported that integrity or honesty is the most important characteristic of effective leaders. Employees and other stakeholders want honest leaders whom they can trust.[14] Helene Gayle is known as a highly trustworthy leader because she engages in honest dialogue, demonstrates knowledge of the subject matter, and shows sincere interest in the needs of others. "I have been impressed with her ability—not just in Africa and Asia, but everywhere—to work with people from different cultures and to gain their trust. She has a way of relating to others," says former surgeon-general David Satcher. Unfortunately Gayle is in the minority regarding authentic leadership. Two recent surveys reported that only about a third of American employees believe top managers display integrity and morality. Another recent survey reported that fewer than a third of the 115,000 Asian workers polled are satisfied with their level of trust in management.[15]

- *Drive.* Helene Gayle and other successful leaders have a high need for achievement (see Chapter 5). This drive represents the inner motivation that leaders possess to pursue their goals and encourage others to move forward with theirs. Drive inspires inquisitiveness, an action orientation, and boldness to take the company into uncharted waters. A recent survey of 3,600 bosses identified a "drive for results" as one of the five most important competencies of effective middle managers. This evidence is backed up by Larry Bossidy's experience leading thousands of managers. "When assessing candidates, the first thing I looked for was energy and enthusiasm for execution," says the former CEO of Honeywell and Allied Signal. Bossidy says that this bias for action is so important that "if you have to choose between someone with a staggering IQ...and someone with a lower IQ who is absolutely determined to succeed, you'll always do better with the second person."[16]

- *Leadership motivation.* Leaders have a strong need for power because they want to influence others (see Chapter 5). However, they tend to have a need for "socialized power" because their motivation is constrained by a strong sense of altruism and social responsibility. In other words, effective leaders try to gain power so they can influence others to accomplish goals that benefit the team or organization.[17]

- *Self-confidence.* Leaders demonstrate confidence in their leadership skills and ability to achieve objectives. Effective leaders are typically extroverted—outgoing, sociable, talkative, and assertive—but they also remain humble.

- *Intelligence.* Leaders have above-average cognitive ability to process enormous amounts of information. Leaders aren't necessarily geniuses; rather, they have superior ability to analyze a variety of complex alternatives and opportunities.

- *Knowledge of the business.* Effective leaders possess tacit and explicit knowledge of the business environment in which they operate. Consider once again the characteristics of CARE president Helene Gayle. With a quarter century of experience at the Centers for Disease Control and the Bill & Melinda Gates Foundation, Gayle has gained tremendous knowledge and experience working with health foundations and political leaders around the world, particularly in the fight against AIDS. This knowledge and experience support Gayle's intuition to recognize opportunities and understand the organization's capacity to capture those opportunities.

Competency (Trait) Perspective Limitations and Practical Implications

Although the competency perspective is gaining popularity (again), it assumes that all leaders have the same personal characteristics and that all of these qualities are equally important in all situations. This is probably a false assumption; leadership is far too complex to have a universal list of traits that apply to every condition. Some competencies might not be important all the time. Another limitation is that alternative combinations of competencies may be equally successful. In other words, people with two different sets of competencies might be equally good leaders.[18]

As we discuss later in this chapter, several leadership researchers have also warned that some personal characteristics might only influence our perception that someone is a leader—not determine whether the individual really makes a difference to the organization's success. People who exhibit self-confidence, extroversion, and other traits are called leaders because they fit our stereotype of an effective leader. Or we might see a successful person, call that person a leader, and then attribute unobservable traits that we consider essential for great leaders.

Aside from these limitations, the competency perspective recognizes that some people possess personal characteristics that offer them a higher potential to be great leaders. The most obvious implication of this is that organizations are turning to competency-based methods to hire people with strong leadership potential. The competency perspective of leadership does not necessarily imply that leadership is something you are either born with or must live without. On the contrary, competencies indicate only leadership potential, not leadership performance. People with these characteristics become effective leaders only after they have developed and mastered the necessary leadership behaviors. People with somewhat lower leadership competencies may become effective leaders because they have leveraged their potential more fully.

Learning Objectives

After reading the next three sections you should be able to

3.   **Describe the people-oriented and task-oriented leadership styles.**
4.   **Outline the path–goal theory of leadership.**

Behavioral Perspective of Leadership

In the 1940s and 1950s leadership experts at several universities launched an intensive research investigation to answer the question "What behaviors make leaders effective?" Questionnaires were administered to subordinates, asking them to rate their supervisors on a large number of behaviors. These studies distilled two clusters of leadership behaviors from literally thousands of leadership behavior items.[19]

One cluster represented people-oriented behaviors. This included showing mutual trust and respect for subordinates, demonstrating a genuine concern for their needs, and having a desire to look out for their welfare. Leaders with a strong people-oriented style listen to employee suggestions, do personal favors for employees, support their interests when required, and treat employees as equals. The other cluster represented a task-oriented leadership style and included behaviors that define and structure work roles. Task-oriented leaders assign employees to specific tasks, clarify their work duties and procedures, ensure that they follow company rules, and push them to reach their performance capacity. They establish stretch goals and challenge employees to push beyond those high standards.

Choosing Task-Oriented versus People-Oriented Leadership

Should leaders be task-oriented or people-oriented? This is a difficult question to answer because each style has advantages and disadvantages. Recent evidence suggests that both styles are positively associated with leader effectiveness, but differences are often apparent only in very high or very low levels of each style. Absenteeism, grievances, turnover, and job dissatisfaction are higher among employees who work for supervisors with very low levels of people-oriented leadership. Job performance is lower among employees who work for supervisors with low levels of task-oriented leadership.[20] Research also suggests that university students value task-oriented instructors because they want clear objectives and well-prepared lectures that abide by the unit's objectives.[21]

One problem with the behavioral leadership perspective is that the two categories are broad generalizations that mask specific behaviors within each category. For instance, task-oriented leadership includes planning work activities, clarifying roles, and monitoring operations and performance. These clusters of activities are fairly distinct and likely have different effects on employee well-being and performance. A second concern is that the behavioral approach assumes that high levels of both styles are best in all situations. In reality the best leadership style depends on the situation.[22] On a positive note, the behavioral perspective lays the foundation for two of the main leadership styles—people-oriented and task-oriented—found in many contemporary leadership theories. These contemporary theories, which adopt a contingency perspective, are described next.

Contingency Perspective of Leadership

The contingency perspective of leadership is based on the idea that the most appropriate leadership style depends on the situation. Most (although not all) contingency leadership theories assume that effective leaders must be both insightful and flexible.[23] They must be able to adapt their behaviors and styles to the immediate situation. This isn't easy to do, however. Leaders typically have a preferred style. It takes considerable effort for leaders to learn when and how to alter their styles to match the situation. As we noted earlier, leaders must have high emotional intelligence so they can diagnose the circumstances and match their behaviors accordingly.

Path–Goal Theory of Leadership

path–goal leadership theory
A contingency theory of leadership based on expectancy theory of motivation that relates several leadership styles to specific employee and situational contingencies.

Several contingency theories have been proposed over the years, but **path–goal leadership theory** has withstood scientific critique better than most others. The theory has roots in the expectancy theory of motivation (see Chapter 5).[24] Early research incorporated expectancy theory into the study of how leader behaviors influence employee perceptions of expectancies (paths) between employee effort and performance (goals). Out of this early work was born path–goal theory as a contingency leadership model.

Using the language of expectancy theory, path–goal theory states that effective leaders strengthen the performance-to-outcome expectancy and valences of those outcomes, thereby ensuring that employees who perform their jobs well have a higher degree of need fulfillment than employees who perform poorly. Effective leaders also strengthen the effort-to-performance expectancy by providing the information, support, and other resources necessary to help employees complete their tasks.[25]

servant leadership
The belief that leaders serve followers by understanding their needs and facilitating their work performance.

In other words, path–goal theory advocates **servant leadership**.[26] Servant leaders do not view leadership as a position of power; rather they are coaches, stewards, and facilitators. Leadership is an obligation to understand employee needs and to facilitate their work performance. Servant leaders ask, "How can I help you?" rather than expecting employees to serve them. As Microsoft Australia chief executive Steve Vamos stated at the beginning of this chapter, "The role of the leader is to create environments where others can do great work—and then to get out of the way." Similarly, when Financial Planning Association president Jim Barnash was recently asked about his leadership style, he replied, "I try to live a servant leader's life, which means being more interested in your needs than my needs."[27]

Path–Goal Leadership Styles

Exhibit 14.3 presents the path–goal theory of leadership. This model specifically highlights four leadership styles and several contingency factors leading to three indicators of leader effectiveness. The four leadership styles are[28]

Exhibit 14.3
Path–Goal
Leadership Theory

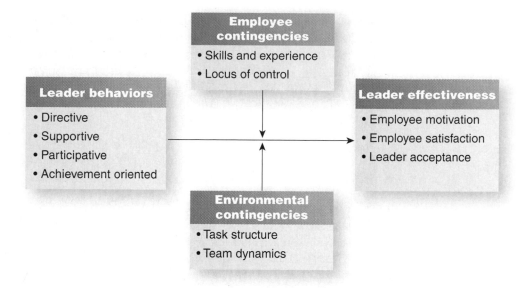

The following are the four leader behaviors described in the text below the figure:

*   *Directive.* These are clarifying behaviors that provide a psychological structure for subordinates. The leader clarifies performance goals, the means to reach those goals, and the standards against which performance will be judged. This style also includes judicious use of rewards and disciplinary actions. Directive leadership is the same as task-oriented leadership (described earlier) and echoes our discussion in Chapter 2 about the importance of clear role perceptions in employee performance.

*   *Supportive.* These behaviors provide psychological support for subordinates. The leader is friendly and approachable; makes the work more pleasant; treats employees with equal respect; and shows concern for the status, needs, and well-being of employees. Supportive leadership is the same as people-oriented leadership (described earlier) and reflects the benefits of social support to help employees cope with stressful situations.

*   *Participative.* These behaviors encourage and facilitate subordinate involvement in decisions beyond their normal work activities. The leader consults with employees, asks for their suggestions, and takes these ideas into serious consideration before making a decision. Participative leadership relates to involving employees in decisions (see Chapter 8).

*   *Achievement-oriented.* These behaviors encourage employees to reach their peak performance. The leader sets challenging goals, expects employees to perform at their highest levels, continuously seeks improvement in employee performance, and shows a high degree of confidence that employees will assume responsibility and accomplish challenging goals. Achievement-oriented leadership applies goal-setting theory (Chapter 5) as well as positive expectations in self-fulfilling prophecy (Chapter 3).

The path–goal model contends that effective leaders are capable of selecting the most appropriate behavioral style (or styles) for a situation. Leaders might simultaneously use two or more styles. For example, they might be both supportive and participative in a specific situation.

Supportive Leader Takes Britain's Top Spot   What does it take to be voted the best boss in Great Britain? You will likely find the answer by watching Bruce Draper at work. The managing director of Geotechnical Instruments was recently named Britain's best boss. According to personal assistant Hannah Delany, Draper provides plenty of supportive leadership to the company's 85 staff members. "Bruce cares about his staff and never takes them for granted," she says. "He appears friendly, approachable, and kind and makes sure everyone is content in their job." Fiona Cannon, head of equality and diversity at Lloyds TSB, the financial institution that cosponsored the award, says that supportive leadership is vital in organizations today. "Having a good boss can make a huge difference, not only to the success of a business but also to the happiness and well-being of those who work for them." She adds, "Bruce Draper particularly stood out from the crowd."[29]

Contingencies of Path–Goal Theory

As a contingency theory, path–goal theory states that each of these four leadership styles will be effective in some situations but not in others. The path–goal leadership model specifies two sets of situational variables that moderate the relationship between a leader's style and effectiveness: (1) employee characteristics and (2) characteristics of the employee's work environment. Several contingencies have already been studied within the path–goal framework, and the model is open for more variables in the future.[30] However, only four contingencies are reviewed here (see Exhibit 14.4).

Skill and Experience   A combination of directive and supportive leadership is best for employees who are (or perceive themselves to be) inexperienced and unskilled.[31] Directive leadership gives subordinates information about how to accomplish the task, whereas supportive leadership helps them cope with the uncertainties of unfamiliar work situations. Directive leadership is detrimental when employees are skilled and experienced because it introduces too much supervisory control.

Locus of Control   Recall from Chapter 2 that people with an internal locus of control believe that they have control over their work environment. Consequently these employees prefer participative and achievement-oriented leadership styles and may become frustrated with a directive style. In contrast, people with an external locus of control believe that their performance is due more to luck and fate, so they tend to be more satisfied with directive and supportive leadership.

Exhibit 14.4 Selected Contingencies of Path–Goal Theory

	Directive	Supportive	Participative	Achievement-oriented
Employee contingencies				
Skill, experience	Low	Low	High	High
Locus of control	External	External	Internal	Internal
Environmental contingencies				
Task structure	Nonroutine	Routine	Nonroutine	???
Team dynamics	Negative norms	Low cohesion	Positive norms	???

Task Structure Leaders should adopt the directive style when a task is nonroutine because this style minimizes the role ambiguity that tends to occur in these complex work situations (particularly for inexperienced employees).[32] The directive style is ineffective when employees have routine and simple tasks because the manager's guidance serves no purpose and may be viewed as unnecessarily close control. Employees in highly routine and simple jobs may require supportive leadership to help them cope with the tedious nature of the work and lack of control over the pace of work. Participative leadership is preferred for employees performing nonroutine tasks because the lack of rules and procedures gives them more discretion to achieve challenging goals. The participative style is ineffective for employees in routine tasks because they lack discretion over their work.

Team Dynamics Cohesive teams with performance-oriented norms act as a substitute for most leader interventions. High team cohesiveness substitutes for supportive leadership, whereas performance-oriented team norms substitute for directive and possibly achievement-oriented leadership. Thus when team cohesiveness is low, leaders should use the supportive style. Leaders should apply a directive style to counteract team norms that oppose the team's formal objectives. For example, the team leader may need to use legitimate power if team members have developed a norm to "take it easy" rather than get a project completed on time.

Practical Implications and Limitations of Path–Goal Theory

Path–goal theory has received more research support than other contingency leadership models, but the evidence is far from complete. A few contingencies (such as task structure) do not have a clear-cut association with any leadership style. Other contingencies and leadership styles in the path–goal leadership model haven't received research investigation at all, as indicated by the question marks in Exhibit 4.4.[33] The path–goal model was expanded a few years ago to include more leadership styles and contingencies, but these additions have received limited investigation.

Another concern is that as path–goal theory expands, the model may become too complex for practical use. Although the expanded model provides a closer representation of the complexity of leadership, it may become too cumbersome for training people in leadership styles. Few people would be able to remember all the contingencies and appropriate leadership styles for those contingencies. In spite of these limitations, path–goal theory remains a relatively robust contingency leadership theory.

After reading the next two sections you should be able to

5. **Summarize leadership substitutes theory.**
6. **Distinguish transformational leadership from transactional and charismatic leadership.**
7. **Describe the four elements of transformational leadership.**

Other Contingency Theories

At the beginning of this chapter we noted that numerous leadership theories have developed over the years. Most of them are found in the contingency perspective of leadership. Some overlap with the path–goal model in terms of leadership styles, but most use simpler and more abstract contingencies. We will briefly mention just two here because of their popularity and historical significance to the field.

Situational Leadership Theory

situational leadership theory (SLT)
Development by Hersey and Blanchard, this model suggests that effective leaders vary their styles with the "readiness" of followers.

One of the most popular contingency theories among practitioners is the **situational leadership theory (SLT)**, also called the life cycle theory of leadership, developed by Paul Hersey and Ken Blanchard.[34] SLT suggests that effective leaders vary their style with the "readiness" of followers. (An earlier version of the model called this "maturity.") Readiness refers to the employee's or work team's ability and willingness to accomplish a specific task. *Ability* refers to the extent to which the follower has the skills and knowledge to perform the task without the leader's guidance. *Willingness* refers to the follower's self-motivation and commitment to performing the assigned task. The model compresses these distinct concepts into a single situational condition.

The situational leadership model also identifies four leadership styles–telling, selling, participating, and delegating–that Hersey and Blanchard distinguish in terms of the amount of directive and supportive behavior provided. For example, "telling" has high task behavior and low supportive behavior. The situational leadership model has four quadrants, with each quadrant showing the leadership style that is most appropriate under different circumstances.

In spite of its popularity, several studies and at least three reviews have concluded that the situational leadership model lacks empirical support.[35] Only one part of the model apparently works–namely that leaders should use "telling" (that is, directive style) when employees lack motivation and ability. (Recall that this is also documented in path–goal theory.) The model's elegant simplicity is attractive and entertaining, but most parts don't represent reality well.

Fiedler's Contingency Model

Fiedler's contingency model
Development by Fred Fiedler, a model that suggests that leader effectiveness depends on whether the person's natural leadership style is appropriately matched to the situation.

Fiedler's contingency model, developed by Fred Fiedler and his associates, is the earliest contingency theory of leadership.[36] According to this model, leader effectiveness depends on whether the person's natural leadership style is appropriately matched to the situation. The theory examines two leadership styles that essentially correspond to the previously described people-oriented and task-oriented styles. Unfortunately Fiedler's model relies on a questionnaire that does not measure either leadership style well.

Fiedler's model suggests that the best leadership style depends on the level of *situational control*–that is, on the degree of power and influence the leader possesses in a particular situation. Situational control is affected by three factors in the following order of importance: leader–member relations, task structure, and position power.[37] *Leader–member relations* refers to how much employees trust and respect the leader and are willing to follow his or her guidance. *Task structure* refers to the clarity or ambiguity of operating procedures. *Position power* is the extent to which the leader possesses legitimate, reward, and coercive power over subordinates. These three contingencies form the eight possible combinations of *situation favorableness* from the leader's viewpoint. Good leader–member relations, high task structure, and strong position power create the most favorable situation for the leader because he or she has the most power and influence under these conditions.

Fiedler has gained considerable respect for pioneering the first contingency theory of leadership. However, his theory has fared less well. As mentioned, the leadership style scale used by Fiedler has been widely criticized. There is also no scientific justification for placing the three situational control factors in a hierarchy. Moreover, it seems that leader–member relations are actually an indicator of leader effectiveness (as in path–goal theory) rather than a situational factor. Finally, the theory considers only two leadership styles, whereas other models present a more complex and realistic array of behavior options. These concerns explain why the theory has limited empirical support.[38]

Changing the Situation to Match the Leader's Natural Style   Fiedler's contingency model may have become a historical footnote, but it does make an important and lasting contribution by suggesting that leadership style is related to the individual's personality and consequently is relatively stable over time. Leaders might be able to alter their style temporarily, but they tend to use a preferred style in the long term. More recent scholars have also proposed that leadership styles are "hard-wired" more than most contingency leadership theories assume.[39]

If leadership style is influenced by personality, then organizations should engineer situations to fit the leader's dominant style, rather than expect leaders to change their style with situations. A directive leader might be assigned inexperienced employees who need direction rather than seasoned people who work less effectively under a directive style. Alternatively, companies might transfer supervisors to workplaces where their dominant styles fit best. For instance, directive leaders might be parachuted into work teams with counterproductive norms, whereas leaders who prefer a supportive style should be sent to departments in which employees face work pressures and other stressors.

Leadership Substitutes

leadership substitutes
A theory that identifies conditions that either limit a leader's ability to influence subordinates or make that particular leadership style unnecessary.

So far we have looked at theories that recommend using different leadership styles in various situations. But one theory, called **leadership substitutes**, identifies conditions that either limit a leader's ability to influence subordinates or make that particular leadership style unnecessary. The literature identifies several conditions that possibly substitute for task-oriented or people-oriented leadership. For example, performance-based reward systems keep employees directed toward organizational goals, so they might replace or reduce the need for task-oriented leadership. Task-oriented leadership is also less important when employees are skilled and experienced. Notice how these propositions are similar to path–goal leadership theory: Directive leadership is unnecessary—and may be detrimental—when employees are skilled or experienced.[40]

Some research suggests that effective leaders help team members learn to lead themselves through leadership substitutes; in other words, co-workers substitute for leadership in high involvement team structures.[41] Co-workers instruct new employees, thereby providing directive leadership. They also provide social support, which reduces stress among fellow employees. Teams with norms that support organizational goals may substitute for achievement-oriented leadership, because employees encourage (or pressure) co-workers to stretch their performance levels.[42]

Self-leadership—the process of influencing oneself to establish the self-direction and self-motivation needed to perform a task (see Chapter 6)—is another possible leadership substitute.[43] Employees with high self-leadership set their own goals, reinforce their own behavior, maintain positive thought processes, and monitor their own performance, thereby managing both personal motivation and abilities. As employees become more proficient in self-leadership, they presumably require less supervision to keep them energized and focused toward organizational objectives.

The leadership substitutes model has intuitive appeal, but the evidence so far is mixed. Some studies show that a few substitutes do replace the need for task- or people-oriented leadership, but others do not. The difficulties of statistically testing for leadership substitutes may account for some problems; however, a few writers contend that the limited support is evidence that leadership plays a critical role regardless of the situation.[44] At this point we can conclude that a few conditions such as self-directed work teams, self-leadership, and reward systems might reduce the importance of task- or people-oriented leadership, but they probably won't completely replace leaders in these roles.

Transformational Perspective of Leadership

transformational leadership

A leadership perspective that explains how leaders change teams or organizations by creating, communicating, and modeling a vision for the organization or work unit and inspiring employees to strive for that vision.

In the opening vignette to this chapter, Infosys chief executive Nandan Nilekani stated that effective leaders create a shared vision and encourage excellent execution toward that vision. Leadership, he explains, is essentially "about dreaming the impossible and helping followers achieve the same." Nandan Nilekani is referring to **transformational leadership**. Transformational leaders are agents of change. They create, communicate, and model a shared vision for the team or organization, inspiring followers to strive for that vision.[45]

Transformational versus Transactional Leadership

transactional leadership

Leadership that helps organizations achieve their current objectives more efficiently, such as linking job performances to valued rewards and ensuring that employees have the resources needed to get the job done.

Transformational leadership differs from **transactional leadership**.[46] Transactional leadership is "managing"—helping organizations achieve their current objectives more efficiently, such as by linking job performance to valued rewards and ensuring that employees have the resources needed to get the job done. The contingency and behavioral theories described earlier adopt the transactional perspective because they focus on leader behaviors that improve employee performance and satisfaction. In contrast, transformational leadership is about "leading"—changing the organization's strategies and culture so they fit better with the surrounding environment.[47] Transformational leaders are change agents who energize and direct employees to a new set of corporate values and behaviors.

Organizations require both transactional and transformational leadership.[48] Transactional leadership improves organizational efficiency, whereas transformational leadership steers companies into a better course of action. Transformational leadership is particularly important in organizations that require significant alignment with the external environment. Unfortunately too many leaders get trapped in the daily managerial activities that represent transactional leadership.[49] They lose touch with the transformational aspect of effective leadership. Without transformational leaders, organizations stagnate and eventually become seriously misaligned with their environments.

Transformational versus Charismatic Leadership

One topic that has generated some confusion and controversy is the distinction between transformational and charismatic leadership.[50] Many researchers either use the words interchangeably, as if they have the same meaning, or view charismatic leadership as an essential ingredient of transformational leadership. Others take this view further by suggesting that charismatic leadership is the highest degree of transformational leadership.

However, the emerging view, which this book adopts, comes from a third group of experts who contend that charisma is distinct from transformational leadership. These academics point out that charisma is a personal trait that provides referent power over followers, whereas transformational leadership is a set of behaviors that people use to lead the change process.[51] Charismatic leaders might be transformational leaders; indeed, their personal power through charisma is a tool to change the behavior of followers. However, some research points out that charismatic or "heroic" leaders easily build allegiance in followers, but they do not necessarily change the organization. Other research suggests that charismatic leaders produce dependent followers, whereas transformational leaders have the opposite effect—they support follower empowerment, which tends to reduce dependence on the leader.[52]

The distinction between charismatic and transformational leadership is illustrated in recent leadership dynamics at Procter & Gamble. The American household goods company lost market share and innovativeness under the previous charismatic leader. Yet as Connections 14.1 describes, it has experienced a dramatic turnaround under Alan G. Lafley, who is not known for being charismatic. Instead Lafley applies the classic elements of transformational leadership, which we describe next.

Elements of Transformational Leadership

There are several descriptions of transformational leadership, but most include the four elements illustrated in Exhibit 14.5. These elements include creating a strategic vision, communicating the vision, modeling the vision, and building commitment to the vision.

Creating a Strategic Vision   Transformational leaders shape a strategic vision of a realistic and attractive future that bonds employees together and focuses their energy toward a superordinate organizational goal. A shared strategic vision represents the substance of transformational leadership. It reflects a future for the company or work unit that is ultimately accepted and valued by organizational members. Strategic vision creates a "higher purpose" or superordinate goal that energizes and unifies employees.[53] A strategic vision might originate with the leader, but it is just as likely to emerge from employees, clients, suppliers, or other constituents. A shared strategic vision plays an important role in organizational effectiveness.[54] Visions offer the motivational benefits of goal setting, but they are compelling future states that bond employees and motivate them to strive for those objectives. Visions are typically described in a way that distinguishes them from the current situation, yet makes the goal both appealing and achievable.

Communicating the Vision   If vision is the substance of transformational leadership, then communicating that vision is the process. Transformational leaders communicate meaning and elevate the importance of the visionary goal to employees. They frame messages around a grand purpose with emotional appeal that captivates employees and other corporate stakeholders. Framing helps transformational leaders establish a common mental model so that the group or organization will act collectively toward the desirable goal.[55]

Procter & Gamble Trades Charisma for Transformational Substance

A few days after becoming CEO of Procter & Gamble (P&G), Alan George Lafley made an impression by walking unannounced into a dinner party of executives who had left P&G for other companies. This act was highly symbolic because the household goods giant famously promoted from within and treated anyone who left the company before retirement as outcasts. P&G was in trouble: It lacked new products, and its existing offerings were under siege from competitors. So Lafley's visit to P&G alumni (the first such visit by a P&G CEO) quickly signaled that the company would embrace ideas and people from outside the organization.

In addition to greeting former employees, Lafley incessantly communicates the mantra that "the consumer is boss" and that the company's future depends on creativity. Far from the heroic, charismatic style of P&G's previous CEO, who failed to turn the company around and was ousted in just 18 months, Lafley is distinctly "unassuming" with "a humble demeanor that belies his status." One industry observer is more blunt: "If there were 15 people sitting around the conference table, it wouldn't be obvious that he was the CEO."

Yet Lafley has transformed P&G where others could not. His calm self-assurance, consistent vision, and symbolic and strategic actions toward a more customer-friendly and innovative organization have provided the direction and clarity that the company lacked. Lafley also walks the talk—his behavior is closely aligned with the message that he conveys. He restructured the company, pruned costs, made significant acquisitions (Gillette and Clairol), and rekindled a spirit of innovation through special creativity teams. Lafley is also out in the field 10 to 15 days each year, meeting with customers and closely observing what they like and don't like about the company's and competitor's products.

To instill the creative spirit at the top, Lafley took P&G's entire 40-person leadership council to a one-day innovation workshop in San Francisco led by design firm IDEO. IDEO also built an innovation center (called "the Gym") where P&G staff

A.G. Lafley has turned around beleaguered Procter & Gamble through transformational leadership behaviors without being charismatic or heroic.

learn brainstorming, prototyping, observation, and other ways to become more innovative. Lafley revamped the executive offices into an open-space plan that improves information sharing. He has also hired an army of creative types from other organizations and paired them with long-service P&G staff. The result: P&G has become the industry's hot spot for innovation, its market share and profitability have experienced sustained growth, and its stock price has soared.

Sources: K. Brooker and J. Schlosser, "The Un-CEO," *Fortune*, 16 September 2002, pp. 88–93; B. Nussbaum, "The Power of Design," *BusinessWeek*, 17 May 2004, p. 86; N. Buckley, "The Calm Reinventor," *Financial Times* (London), 29 January 2005, p. 11; S. Ellison, "Women's Touch Guides P&G Chief's Firm Hand in Company Turnaround," *The Wall Street Journal Europe*, 1 June 2005, p. A1; S. Hill Jr., "P&G's Turnaround Proves Listening to Customer Pays," *Manufacturing Business Technology*, July 2005, p. 64; J. Tylee, "Procter's Creative Gamble," *Campaign*, 18 March 2005, pp. 24–26.

Transformational leaders bring their visions to life through symbols, metaphors, stories, and other vehicles that transcend plain language. Metaphors borrow images of other experiences, thereby creating richer meaning of the vision that has not yet been experienced. As an example, McDonald's executive George Cohen was handed the difficult task of opening the fast-food company's first restaurants in Russia during the 1980s, when the Soviet Union had limited infrastructure and poor quality standards. To communicate a higher purpose of this challenging initiative, Cohen reminded staff that they were establishing "hamburger diplomacy."[56]

Modeling the Vision   Transformational leaders not only talk about a vision; they enact it. They "walk the talk" by stepping outside the executive suite and doing things that symbolize the vision.[57] They are also reliable and persistent in their actions, thereby legitimizing the vision and providing further evidence that they can be trusted. For example, when Chick-fil-A opens a new store, many customers camp out the day before opening, hoping to be among the first 100 adults to receive a year's worth of free Chick-fil-A combo meal coupons. CEO Dan Cathy participates in the grand opening by bringing his own tent, mingling with the crowd throughout the night, and, when the store opens, putting on his customer service hat to greet customers entering the store. "I'll camp out this year about 40 times," says Cathy. "I like to model the practice I stand for."[58]

Leaders walk the talk through significant events such as camping out with customers, moving their offices closer to employees or customers, and holding ceremonies to destroy outdated policy manuals. However, they also alter mundane activities—meeting agendas, office locations, executive schedules—so they are more consistent with the vision and its underlying values. Modeling the vision is important because employees and other stakeholders are executive watchers who look for behaviors that symbolize values and expectations. The greater the consistency between the leader's words and actions, the more employees will believe and follow the leader. Walking the talk also builds employee trust because it is partly determined by the consistency of the person's actions.

"As an executive, you're always being watched by employees, and everything you say gets magnified—so you teach a lot by how you conduct yourself," advises Carl Bass, CEO of California software company Autodesk. Peter Farrell, founder and chief executive of San Diego–based ResMed, agrees. "There are lots of people who talk a good story, but very few deliver one," he warns. "You've got to mean what you say, say what you mean, and be consistent." Surveys suggest that some employees don't see this consistency in their leaders. In one global poll, only 48 percent of employees in Germany and the United Kingdom believed management decisions are consistent

Exhibit 14.5

**Elements of
Transformational
Leadership**

with the company's core values. This figure was higher in the United States (64 percent) and Canada (76 percent). Another recent survey estimated that only 28 percent of Taiwanese employees believe senior management behaves in accordance with the company's core values.[59]

Building Commitment to the Vision   Transforming a vision into reality requires employee commitment. Transformational leaders build this commitment in several ways. Their words, symbols, and stories build a contagious enthusiasm that energizes people to adopt the vision as their own. Leaders demonstrate a "can do" attitude by enacting their vision and staying on course. Their persistence and consistency reflect an image of honesty, trust, and integrity. Finally, leaders build commitment by involving employees in the process of shaping the organization's vision.

Evaluating the Transformational Leadership Perspective

Transformational leaders do make a difference. Subordinates are more satisfied and have higher affective organizational commitment under transformational leaders. They also perform their jobs better, engage in more organizational citizenship behaviors, and make better or more creative decisions. One study of bank branches also reported that organizational commitment and financial performance seem to increase where the branch manager completed a transformational leadership training program.[60]

Transformational leadership is currently the most popular leadership perspective, but it faces a number of challenges. One problem is that some writers engage in circular logic by defining transformational leadership in terms of the leader's success.[61] They suggest that leaders are transformational when they successfully bring about change, rather than whether they engage in certain behaviors we call transformational. Another concern is that the transformational leadership model seems to be universal rather than contingency-oriented. Only very recently have writers begun to explore the idea that transformational leadership is more appropriate in some situations than others.[62] For instance, transformational leadership is probably more appropriate when organizations need to adapt than when environmental conditions are stable. Preliminary evidence suggests that the transformational leadership perspective is relevant across cultures. However, specific elements of transformational leadership, such as the way visions are formed and communicated, may be more appropriate in North America than in other cultures.

Learning
Objectives

After reading the next two sections you should be able to

8. **Describe the implicit leadership perspective.**
9. **Discuss the influence of culture on perceptions of effective leaders.**
10. **Discuss similarities and differences in the leadership styles of women and men.**

Implicit Leadership Perspective

The competency, behavior, contingency, and transformational leadership perspectives make the basic assumption that leaders make a difference. Certainly there is evidence that senior executives influence organizational performance. However, leaders might have less influence than most of us would like to believe. Some

implicit leadership theory

A theory hypothesizing that perceptual processes cause people to inflate the importance of leadership as the cause of organizational events.

leadership experts suggest that people inflate the importance of leadership in explaining organizational events. These processes, including stereotyping, attribution errors, and the need for situational control, are collectively called **implicit leadership theory**.[63]

Stereotyping Leadership

Implicit leadership theory states that everyone has preconceived notions about the features and behaviors of an effective leader. These perceptions are stereotypes or prototypes of idealized leadership that develop through socialization within the family and society.[64] Mental images of an ideal leader shape our expectations and acceptance of people as leaders, which in turn affect their ability to influence us as followers. We rely on leadership stereotypes partly because a leader's success might not be apparent for months or possibly years. Consequently employees depend on immediate information to decide whether a leader is effective. If the leader fits the mold, then employees are more confident that the leader is effective.[65]

Attributing Leadership

Implicit leadership is also influenced by attribution errors. Research has found that (at least in Western cultures) people tend to attribute organizational events to the leader, even when those events are largely caused by factors beyond the leader's control. This attribution is partly caused by fundamental attribution error (see Chapter 3) in which leaders are given credit or blame for the company's success or failure because employees do not readily see the external forces that also influence these events. Leaders reinforce this belief by taking credit for organizational successes.[66]

Need for Situational Control

A third perceptual distortion of leadership suggests that people want to believe leaders make a difference. There are two basic reasons for this belief.[67] First, leadership is a useful way for us to simplify life events. It is easier to explain organizational successes and failures in terms of the leader's ability than by analyzing a complex array of other forces. For example, there are usually many reasons why a company fails to change quickly enough in the marketplace, yet we tend to simplify this explanation down to the notion that the company president or some other corporate leader was ineffective.

Second, there is a strong tendency in the United States and other Western cultures to believe that life events are generated more from people than from uncontrollable natural forces.[68] This illusion of control is satisfied by believing that events result from the rational actions of leaders. In short, employees feel better believing that leaders make a difference, so they actively look for evidence that this is so.

The implicit leadership perspective questions the importance of leadership, but it also provides valuable advice to improve leadership acceptance. This approach highlights the fact that leadership is a perception of followers as much as the actual behaviors and characteristics of people calling themselves leaders. Potential leaders must be sensitive to this fact, understand what followers expect, and act accordingly. Individuals who do not make an effort to fit leadership prototypes will have more difficulty bringing about necessary organizational change.

Leading with *Ubuntu* Values in Africa Woven into the fabric of African society is the concept of *ubuntu,* a collection of values representing harmony, compassion, respect, human dignity, and collective unity. It is "that profound African sense that each of us is human through the humanity of other human beings," explains former South African president Nelson Mandela. *Ubuntu* is about connectedness, so leaders must be comfortable with the highly participative process of making decisions through consensus. It requires leaders to coach, facilitate, and possibly mediate as the group moves toward mutual agreement. *Ubuntu* also values a collective respect for everyone in the system, so leaders must view their role as someone who supports followers, not the other way around. The heroic leader who steps in front—and typically looks down from a higher plateau—is not consistent with *ubuntu.*[69]

Cross-Cultural and Gender Issues in Leadership

Along with the five perspectives of leadership presented throughout this chapter, we need to keep in mind that societal cultural values and practices affect what leaders do. Culture shapes the leader's values and norms, which influence his or her decisions and actions. These cultural values also shape the expectations that followers have of their leaders. This is apparent in Africa, where *ubuntu* values shape the preferred leadership behaviors and style. *Ubuntu* stands for harmony and connectedness, which is incompatible with the heroic leadership styles that are still common in some Western cultures.

An executive who acts inconsistently with cultural expectations is more likely to be perceived as an ineffective leader. Furthermore, leaders who deviate from those values may experience various forms of influence to get them to conform to the leadership norms and expectations of that society. In other words, implicit leadership theory (described in the previous section of this chapter) explains differences in leadership practices across cultures.

Over the past few years 150 researchers from dozens of countries have worked together on Project GLOBE (Global Leadership and Organizational Behavior Effectiveness) to identify the effects of cultural values on leadership.[70] The project organized countries into 10 regional clusters, of which the United States, Great Britain, and similar countries are grouped into the "Anglo" cluster. The results of this massive investigation are just beginning to appear, but preliminary work suggests that some features of leadership are universal and some differ across cultures.

Specifically the GLOBE project reports that "charismatic visionary" is a universally recognized concept, and that middle managers around the world believe that it is characteristic of effective leaders. Charismatic visionary represents a cluster of concepts including visionary, inspirational, performance orientation, integrity, and decisiveness.[71] In contrast, participative leadership is perceived as characteristic of effective leadership in low power distance cultures but less so in high power distance cultures. For instance, one study reported that Mexican employees expect managers to make decisions affecting their work. Mexico is a high power distance culture, so followers expect leaders to apply their authority rather than delegate their power most of the time.[72] In summary, there are similarities and differences in the concepts and preferred practices of leadership across cultures.

Gender Differences in Leadership

Do women lead differently than men? Several writers think so. They suggest that women have an interactive style that includes more people-oriented and participative leadership.[73] They also believe that women are more relationship-oriented, cooperative, nurturing, and emotional in their leadership roles. They further assert that these qualities make women particularly well suited to leadership roles when companies are adopting a stronger emphasis on teams and employee involvement. These arguments are consistent with sex role stereotypes—namely that men tend to be more task-oriented whereas women are more people-oriented.

Are these stereotypes true? Do women adopt more people-oriented and participative leadership styles? The answer is no and yes, respectively. Leadership studies outside university labs (that is, in real work settings) have generally found that male and female leaders do not differ in their levels of task-oriented or people-oriented leadership. The main explanation is that real-world jobs require similar behavior from male and female job incumbents.[74]

However, women do adopt a participative leadership style more readily than their male counterparts. One possible reason is that compared to boys, girls are often raised to be more egalitarian and less status-oriented, which is consistent with being participative. There is also some evidence that women have somewhat better interpersonal skills than men, and this translates into their relatively greater use of the participative leadership style. A third explanation is that subordinates expect female leaders to be more participative, based on their own sex stereotypes, so female leaders comply with follower expectations to some extent.

Several recent surveys report that women are rated higher than men on the emerging leadership qualities of coaching, teamwork, and empowering employees.[75] Yet research also suggests that women are evaluated negatively when they try to apply the full range of leadership styles, particularly more directive and autocratic approaches. Thus, ironically, women may be well suited to contemporary leadership roles, yet they often continue to face limitations of leadership through the gender stereotypes and prototypes of leaders held by followers.[76] Overall both male and female leaders must be sensitive to the fact that followers have expectations about how leaders should act, and negative evaluations may go to leaders who deviate from those expectations.

Chapter Summary

Leadership is a complex concept that is defined as the ability to influence, motivate, and enable others to contribute toward the effectiveness and success of the organizations of which they are members. Leaders use influence to motivate followers and arrange the work environment so that they can do the job more effectively. Leaders exist throughout the organization, not just in the executive suite.

The competency perspective tries to identify the characteristics of effective leaders. Recent writing suggests that leaders have emotional intelligence, integrity, drive, leadership motivation, self-confidence, above-average intelligence, and knowledge of the business. The behavioral perspective of leadership has identified two clusters of leader behavior—people-oriented and task-oriented. People-oriented behaviors include showing mutual trust and respect for subordinates, demonstrating a genuine concern for their needs, and having a desire to look out for their welfare. Task-oriented behaviors include assigning employees to specific tasks, clarifying their work duties and procedures, ensuring that they follow company rules, and pushing them to reach their performance capacity.

The contingency perspective of leadership takes the view that effective leaders diagnose the situation and adapt their style to fit that situation. The path–goal model is the prominent contingency theory that identifies four leadership styles–directive, supportive, participative, and achievement-oriented–and several contingencies relating to the characteristics of the employee and of the situation.

Two other contingency leadership theories include the situational leadership theory and Fiedler's contingency theory. Research support is quite weak for both theories. However, a lasting element of Fiedler's theory is the idea that leaders have natural styles and that companies consequently need to change leaders' environments to suit their style. Leadership substitutes theory identifies contingencies that either limit the leader's ability to influence subordinates or make a particular leadership style unnecessary.

Transformational leaders create a strategic vision, communicate that vision through framing and use of metaphors, model the vision by "walking the talk" and acting consistently, and build commitment to the vision. This contrasts with transactional leadership, which involves linking job performance to valued rewards and ensuring that employees have the resources needed to do their jobs. The contingency and behavioral perspectives adopt the transactional view of leadership.

According to the implicit leadership perspective, people inflate the importance of leadership through attribution, stereotyping, and fundamental needs for human control. Implicit leadership theory is evident across cultures because cultural values shape the behaviors that followers expect of their leaders.

Cultural values also influence the leader's personal values, which in turn influence his or her leadership practices. The GLOBE project data reveal that there are similarities and differences in the concepts and preferred practices of leadership across cultures. Women generally do not differ from men in the degree of people-oriented or task-oriented leadership. However, female leaders more often adopt a participative style. Research also suggests that people evaluate female leaders based on gender stereotypes, which may result in higher or lower ratings.

Key Terms

Fiedler's contingency model, p. 412

implicit leadership theory, p. 419

leadership, p. 402

leadership substitutes, p. 413

path–goal leadership theory, p. 408

servant leadership, p. 408

shared leadership, p. 402

situational leadership theory (SLT), p. 412

transactional leadership, p. 414

transformational leadership, p. 414

Critical Thinking Questions

1. Why is it important for top executives to value and support leadership demonstrated at all levels of the organization?

2. Find two newspaper ads for management or executive positions. What leadership competencies are mentioned in these ads? If you were on the selection panel, what methods would you use to identify these competencies in job applicants?

3. Consider your favorite teacher. What people-oriented and task-oriented leadership behaviors did he or she use effectively? In general, do you think students prefer an instructor who is more people-oriented or task-oriented? Explain your preference.

4. Your employees are skilled and experienced customer service representatives who perform nonroutine tasks, such as solving unique customer problems or special needs with the company's equipment. Use path–goal theory to identify the most appropriate leadership style(s) you should use in this situation. Be sure to fully explain your answer and discuss why other styles are inappropriate.

5. Transformational leadership is currently the most popular perspective of leadership. However, it is far from perfect. Discuss the limitations of transformational leadership.

6. This chapter emphasized that charismatic leadership is not the same as transformational leadership. Still, charisma is often mentioned in discussions of leadership. In your opinion, how does charisma relate to leadership?

7. Identify a current political leader (president, governor, mayor) and his or her recent accomplishments. Now, using the implicit leadership perspective, think of ways that these accomplishments of the leader may be overstated. In other words, explain why they may be due to factors other than the leader.

8. You hear two people debating the merits of women as leaders. One person claims that women make better leaders than do men because women are more sensitive to their employees' needs and involve them in organizational decisions. The other person counters that although these leadership styles may be increasingly important, most women have trouble gaining acceptance as leaders when they face tough situations in which a more autocratic style is required. Discuss the accuracy of the comments made in this discussion.

Case Study 14.1 A WINDOW ON LIFE

For Gilbert LaCrosse, there is nothing quite as beautiful as a handcrafted wood-framed window. LaCrosse's passion for windows goes back to his youth in Eau Claire, Wisconsin, where he learned from an elderly carpenter how to make residential windows. He learned about the characteristics of good wood, the best tools to use, and how to choose the best glass from local suppliers. LaCrosse apprenticed with the carpenter in his small workshop, and when the carpenter retired, he was given the opportunity to operate the business himself.

LaCrosse hired his own apprentice as he built up business in the local area. His small operation soon expanded as the quality of windows built by LaCrosse Industries Inc. became better known. Within eight years the company employed nearly 25 people, and the business had moved to larger facilities to accommodate the increased demand from Wisconsin. In these early years LaCrosse spent most of his time in the production shop, teaching new apprentices the unique skills that he had mastered and applauding the workers for their accomplishments. He would constantly repeat the point that LaCrosse products had to be of the highest quality because they gave families a "window on life."

After 15 years LaCrosse Industries employed over 200 people. A profit-sharing program was introduced to give employees a financial reward for their contribution to the organization's success. Due to the company's expansion, headquarters had to be moved to another area of the city; but the founder never lost touch with the workforce. Although new apprentices were now taught entirely by the master carpenters and other craftspeople, LaCrosse would still chat with plant and office employees several times each week.

When a second work shift was added, LaCrosse would show up during the evening break with coffee and boxes of doughnuts and discuss how the business was doing and how it became so successful through quality work. Production employees enjoyed the times when he would gather them together to announce new contracts with developers from Chicago and New York. After each announcement LaCrosse would thank everyone for making the business a success. They knew that LaCrosse quality had become a standard of excellence in window manufacturing across the eastern part of the country.

It seemed that almost every time he visited, LaCrosse would repeat the now well-known phrase that LaCrosse products had to be of the highest quality because they provided a window on life to so many families. Employees never grew tired of hearing this from the company founder. However, it gained extra meaning when LaCrosse began posting photos of families looking through LaCrosse windows. At first LaCrosse would personally visit developers and homeowners with a camera in hand. Later, as the "window on life" photos became known by developers and customers, people would send in photos of their own families looking through elegant front windows made by LaCrosse Industries. The company's marketing staff began using this idea, as well as LaCrosse's famous phrase, in their advertising. After one such marketing campaign, hundreds of photos were sent in by satisfied customers. Production and office employees took time after work to write personal letters of thanks to those who had submitted photos.

As the company's age reached the quarter-century mark, LaCrosse, now in his mid-fifties, realized that the organization's success and survival depended on expansion to other parts of the United States. After consulting with employees, LaCrosse made the difficult decision to sell a majority share to Build-All Products Inc., a conglomerate with international marketing expertise in building products. As part of the agreement, Build-All brought in a vice president to oversee production operations while LaCrosse spent more time meeting with developers. LaCrosse would return to the plant and office at every opportunity, but often this would be only once a month.

Rather than visiting the production plant, Jan Vlodoski, the new production vice president, would rarely leave his office in the company's downtown headquarters. Instead production orders were sent to supervisors by memorandum. Although product quality had been a priority throughout the company's history, less attention had been paid to inventory controls. Vlodoski introduced strict inventory guidelines and outlined procedures on using supplies for each shift. Goals were established for supervisors to meet specific inventory targets. Whereas employees previously could have tossed out several pieces of warped wood, they would now have to justify this action, usually in writing.

Vlodoski also announced new procedures for purchasing production supplies. LaCrosse Industries had highly trained purchasing staff who worked closely with senior craftspeople when selecting suppliers, but Vlodoski wanted to bring in Build-All's procedures. The new purchasing methods removed production leaders from the decision process and, in some cases, resulted in trade-offs that LaCrosse's employees would not have made earlier. A few employees quit during this time, saying that they did not feel comfortable about producing a window that would not stand the test of time. However, there were few jobs for carpenters, so most staff members remained with the company.

After one year inventory expenses decreased by approximately 10 percent, but the number of defective windows returned by developers and wholesalers had increased markedly. Plant employees knew that the number of defective windows would increase as they used somewhat lower-quality materials to reduce inventory costs. However, they heard almost no news about the seriousness of the problem until Vlodoski sent a memo to all production staff saying that quality must be maintained. During the latter part of the first year under Vlodoski, a few employees had the opportunity to personally ask LaCrosse about the changes and express their concerns. LaCrosse apologized, saying due to his travels to new regions, he had not heard about the problems, and he would look into the matter.

Exactly 18 months after Build-All had become majority shareholder of LaCrosse Industries, LaCrosse called together five of the original staff in the plant. The company founder looked pale and shaken as he said that Build-All's actions were inconsistent with his vision of the company, and for the first time in his career, he did not know what to do. Build-All was not pleased with the arrangement either. Although LaCrosse windows still enjoyed a healthy market share and were competitive for the value, the company did not quite provide the minimum 18 percent return on equity that the conglomerate expected. LaCrosse asked his long-time companions for advice.

Discussion Questions

1. Identify the symptoms indicating that problems exist at LaCrosse Industries Inc.

2. Use one or more leadership theories to analyze the underlying causes of the current problems at LaCrosse Industries. What other organizational behavior theories might also help to explain some of the problems?

3. What should Gilbert LaCrosse do in this situation?

© Copyright 2000 Steven L. McShane.

Case Study 14.2 MACK ATTACK

 John J. Mack, who had left Morgan Stanley four years earlier, was back as CEO, replacing Philip J. Purcell, who had resigned weeks earlier after mounting criticism that he was mismanaging the once-mighty investment bank. Whereas Purcell was a top-down strategist and tended to hole up in his office, Mack is drawing on his skills as a salesman and operator to make Morgan Stanley as nimble and dynamic as possible. He also hired key people to help him put the new culture in place.

This *BusinessWeek* case study examines the leadership of Morgan Stanley CEO John J. Mack. It describes his actions to change the investment bank's culture and to redirect decision making so it is more aggressive rather than timid. Read through this *BusinessWeek* article at www.mhhe.com/mcshane4e and prepare for the discussion questions below.

Discussion Questions

1. Based on the information in this case study, describe the competencies that seem strongest in John Mack.

2. To what extent has John Mack exhibited transformational leadership behaviors to shift Morgan Stanley's culture and decision making?

Source: E. Thornton, Mack Attack, *BusinessWeek*, 3 July 2006, 88.

Team Exercise 14.3 LEADERSHIP DIAGNOSTIC ANALYSIS

PURPOSE To help students learn about the different path–goal leadership styles and when to apply each style.

INSTRUCTIONS

1. Students should individually write down two incidents in which someone was an effective manager or leader over them. The leader and situation might be from work, a sports team, a student work group, or any other setting where leadership might emerge. For example, students might describe how their supervisor in a summer job pushed them to reach higher performance goals than they would have done otherwise. Each incident should state the actual behaviors that the leader used, not just general statements (for example, "My boss sat down with me and we agreed on specific targets and deadlines, then he said several times over the next few weeks that I was capable of reaching those goals"). Each incident only requires two or three sentences.

2. After everyone has written their incidents, the instructor will form small groups (typically four to five students). Each team will answer the following questions for each incident presented in that team:

   a. Which path–goal theory leadership style(s)—directive, supportive, participative, or achievement-oriented—did the leader apply in this incident?

   b. Ask the person who wrote the incident about the conditions that made this leadership style (or these styles, if more than one was used) appropriate in this situation. The team should list these contingency factors clearly and, where possible, connect them to the contingencies described in path–goal theory. (*Note:* The team might identify path–goal leadership contingencies that are not described in the book. These too should be noted and discussed.)

3. After the teams have diagnosed the incidents, each team will describe to the entire class the most interesting incidents as well as the team's diagnosis of that incident. Other teams will critique the diagnosis. Any leadership contingencies not mentioned in the textbook should also be presented and discussed.

Self-Assessment 14.4 LEADERSHIP DIMENSIONS INSTRUMENT

PURPOSE This assessment is designed to help you understand two important dimensions of leadership and identify which of these dimensions is more prominent in your supervisor, team leader, coach, or other person to whom you are accountable.

INSTRUCTIONS Read each of the following statements and circle the response that you believe best describes your supervisor. You may substitute for "supervisor" anyone else to whom you are accountable, such as a team leader, CEO, course instructor, or sports coach. Then use the scoring key in Appendix B to calculate the results for each leadership dimensions. After completing this assessment, be prepared to discuss in class the distinctions between these leadership dimensions.

Leadership Dimensions Instrument

My Supervisor	Strongly agree ▼	Agree ▼	Neutral ▼	Disagree ▼	Strongly disagree ▼
1. Focuses attention on irregularities, mistakes, exceptions, and deviations from what is expected of me.	5	4	3	2	1
2. Engages in words and deeds that enhance his or her image of competence.	5	4	3	2	1
3. Monitors performance for errors needing correction.	5	4	3	2	1
4. Serves as a role model for me.	5	4	3	2	1
5. Points out what I will receive if I do what is required.	5	4	3	2	1
6. Instills pride in being associated with him or her.	5	4	3	2	1
7. Keeps careful track of mistakes.	5	4	3	2	1
8. Can be trusted to help me overcome any obstacle.	5	4	3	2	1
9. Tells me what to do to be rewarded for my efforts.	5	4	3	2	1
10. Makes me aware of strongly held values, ideals, and aspirations that are shared in common.	5	4	3	2	1
11. Is alert for failure to meet standards.	5	4	3	2	1
12. Mobilizes a collective sense of mission.	5	4	3	2	1
13. Works out agreements with me on what I will receive if I do what needs to be done.	5	4	3	2	1
14. Articulates a vision of future opportunities.	5	4	3	2	1
15. Talks about special rewards for good work.	5	4	3	2	1
16. Talks optimistically about the future.	5	4	3	2	1

Source: Items and dimensions are adapted from D.N. Den Hartog, J.J. Van Muijen, and P.L. Koopman, "Transactional versus Transformational Leadership: An Analysis of the MLQ," *Journal of Occupational & Organizational Psychology* 70 (March 1997), pp. 19–34. Den Hartog et al. label transactional leadership as "rational–objective leadership" and label transformational leadership as "inspirational leadership." Many of their items may have originated from B.M. Bass and B.J. Avolio, *Manual for the Multifactor Leadership Questionnaire* (Palo Alto, CA: Consulting Psychologists Press, 1989).

After reading this chapter, if you need additional information, see **www.mhhe.com/mcshane4e** for more in-depth interactivities that correspond with this material.

Part four
Organizational Processes

Chapter 15   Organizational Structure

Chapter 16   Organizational Culture

Chapter 17   Organizational Change

Globalization is playing havoc with the organizational structures of advertising agencies. Some multinational firms, such as Samsung, have centralized marketing decisions, requiring ad firms to also concentrate their expertise globally. Other companies, such as Coca-Cola and Procter & Gamble, have positioned their advertising decisions at the regional level, so agencies serving these clients need to offer both regional and global expertise. Meanwhile, believing that global advertising firms are too bureaucratic, several client companies are turning to boutique agencies for local expertise.

Boutique advertising firm Nitro relies on an organizational structure that keeps it nimble and responsive to customer needs.

Nitro may have found an organizational structure that satisfies this mishmash of client needs. Each local Nitro office has account service staff, but a global creative team is parachuted in as required. This micro-network structure began in Shanghai, China, and within three years had expanded to New York, London, Taipei, Hong Kong, Sydney, and Melbourne. Its global billings have already reached US $300 million, catapulting it to the 66th spot in the global ranking of ad agencies.

Nitro's balance of regional decentralization and global centralization gives clients direct access to the agency's top creatives, who move from one office to the next, solving client issues and contributing their specialized knowledge as needed. Founder Chris Clarke also intends to keep Nitro boutique-size by limiting the number of clients. "We want to remain small, as a certain size gives us the ability to be fast and nimble," he says. Wei Wei Chen, Nitro's head of operations for Greater China, says that the company's unique structure minimizes the bureaucracy of most global agencies. "The speed at which we can move gives us a competitive edge. We believe in erasing the lines between departments and between us and the client."

Nitro isn't alone in designing an organizational structure aligned with the need for global and regional balance. Lowe Worldwide recently introduced a "lighthouse structure" that reorganized its offices in 91 countries around a dozen "lighthouses" or centers of creativity in key markets. "The Lighthouse structure eliminates the bureaucratic system of regional management and pools resources, talent, and processes," explains one executive at the ad agency, which operates out of London and New York. Another adds, "[The Lighthouse structure] means access to top-flight talent around the world—talent that has access to local markets and the creativity and flexibility to execute."[1]

Organizational Structure

After reading this chapter you should be able to

1. Describe three types of coordination in organizational structures.
2. Justify the optimal span of control in a given situation.
3. Discuss the advantages and disadvantages of centralization and formalization.
4. Distinguish organic from mechanistic organizational structures.
5. Identify and evaluate five pure types of departmentalization.
6. Describe three variations of divisionalized structure and explain which one should be adopted in a particular situation.
7. Diagram the matrix structure for a project-based organization and a large global business.
8. Describe the features of team-based organizational structures.
9. Identify four characteristics of external environments and discuss the preferred organizational structure for each environment.
10. Summarize the influences of organizational size, technology, and strategy on organizational structure.

organizational structure
The division of labor
and the patterns of
coordination,
communication, work
flow, and formal power
that direct organizational
activities.

There is something of a revolution occurring in how organizations are structured. Nitro, Lowe Worldwide, and other companies are rethinking their organizational charts and trying out new designs that they hope will achieve organizational objectives more effectively. **Organizational structure** refers to the division of labor as well as the patterns of coordination, communication, workflow, and formal power that direct organizational activities. An organizational structure reflects the organization's culture and power relationships.[2]

Organizational structures are frequently used as tools for change because they establish new communication patterns and align employee behavior with the corporate vision.[3] For example, to steer Charles Schwab Co. out of its financial trouble, founder Charles Schwab held a two-day marathon session in which the company's top executives were asked to redraw the organization chart in a way that would make the company simpler, more decentralized, and refocused on the customer. Every executive in the room, including those whose jobs would be erased from the new structure, was asked for her or his input.[4]

We begin this chapter by considering the two fundamental processes in organizational structure: division of labor and coordination. This is followed by a detailed investigation of the four main elements of organizational structure: span of control, centralization, formalization, and departmentalization. The latter part of this chapter examines the contingencies of organizational design, including organizational size, technology, external environment, and strategy.

Learning Objectives

After reading the next two sections you should be able to

1. **Describe three types of coordination in organizational structures.**
2. **Justify the optimal span of control in a given situation.**
3. **Discuss the advantages and disadvantages of centralization and formalization.**
4. **Distinguish organic from mechanistic organizational structures.**

Division of Labor and Coordination

All organizational structures include two fundamental requirements: the division of labor into distinct tasks and the coordination of that labor so that employees can accomplish common goals.[5] Organizations are groups of people who work interdependently toward some purpose. To efficiently accomplish their goals, these groups typically divide the work into manageable chunks, particularly when there are many different tasks to perform. They also introduce various coordinating mechanisms to ensure that everyone is working effectively toward the same objectives.

Division of Labor

Division of labor refers to the subdivision of work into separate jobs assigned to different people. Subdivided work leads to job specialization because each job now includes a narrow subset of the tasks necessary to complete the product or service. Launching a space shuttle at NASA, for example, involves tens of thousands of specific tasks that are divided among thousands of people. Tasks are also divided vertically, such as having supervisors coordinate work while employees perform the work.

Work is divided into specialized jobs because this potentially increases work efficiency.[6] Job incumbents can master their tasks quickly because work cycles are very short. Less time is wasted changing from one task to another. Training costs are

Exhibit 15.1 Coordinating Mechanisms in Organizations

Form of coordination	Description	Subtypes
Informal communication	Sharing information about mutual tasks; forming common mental models to synchronize work activities.	• Direct communication. • Liaison roles. • Integrator roles.
Formal hierarchy	Assigning legitimate power to individuals, who then use this power to direct work processes and allocate resources.	• Direct supervision. • Corporate structure.
Standardization	Creating routine patterns of behavior or output.	• Standardized skills. • Standardized processes. • Standardized output.

Source: Based on information in J. Galbraith, *Designing Complex Organizations* (Reading, MA: Addison-Wesley, 1973), pp. 8–19; H. Mintzberg, *The Structuring of Organizations* (Englewood Cliffs, NJ: Prentice Hall, 1979), Chapter 1; D.A. Nadler and M.L. Tushman, *Competing by Design: The Power of Organizational Architecture* (New York: Oxford University Press, 1997), Chapter 6.

reduced because employees require fewer physical and mental skills to accomplish the assigned work. Finally, job specialization makes it easier to match people with specific aptitudes or skills to the jobs for which they are best suited.

Coordinating Work Activities

As soon as people divide work among themselves, coordinating mechanisms are needed to ensure that everyone works in concert. Every organization—from the two-person corner convenience store to the largest corporate entity—uses one or more of the following coordinating mechanisms:[7] informal communication, formal hierarchy, and standardization (see Exhibit 15.1).

Coordination through Informal Communication Informal communication is a coordinating mechanism in all organizations. This includes sharing information about mutual tasks as well as forming common mental models so that employees synchronize work activities using the same mental road map.[8] Informal communication is vital in nonroutine and ambiguous situations because employees can exchange a large volume of information through face-to-face communication and other media-rich channels.

Coordination through informal communication is easiest in small firms such as Nitro, although information technologies have further leveraged this coordinating mechanism in large organizations. Companies employing thousands of people, such as auto parts manufacturer Magna International, also support informal communication by keeping each production site small (usually fewer than 200 employees). Toyota and other automakers further support this coordinating mechanism by occasionally moving dozens of employees responsible for developing a new product into one large room.[9]

Larger organizations also encourage coordination through informal communication by creating *integrator roles.* These people are responsible for coordinating a work process by encouraging employees in each work unit to share information and informally coordinate work activities. Integrators do not have authority over the people involved in that process, so they must rely on persuasion and commitment. Brand managers at Procter & Gamble coordinate work among marketing, production, and design groups.[10]

Coordination through Formal Hierarchy

Informal communication is the most flexible form of coordination, but it can be time-consuming. Consequently, as organizations grow, they develop a second coordinating mechanism: formal hierarchy. Hierarchy assigns legitimate power to individuals, who then use this power to direct work processes and allocate resources. In other words, work is coordinated through direct supervision. Any organization with a formal structure coordinates work to some extent through formal hierarchy. For instance, team leaders at computer chip maker Intel are responsible for ensuring that employees on their team remain on schedule and that their respective tasks are compatible with tasks completed by other team members.

Formal hierarchy also coordinates work among executives through the division of organizational activities. If the organization is divided into geographic areas, this structure gives regional group leaders legitimate power over executives responsible for production, customer service, and other activities in those areas. If the organization is divided into product groups, the heads of those groups have the right to coordinate work across regions.

Formal hierarchy has traditionally been applauded as the optimal coordinating mechanism for large organizations. A century ago administrative scholars argued that organizations are most effective where managers exercise their authority and employees receive orders from only one supervisor. Coordination should occur through the chain of command—that is, up the hierarchy and across to the other work units.[11]

Coordination through formal hierarchy may have been popular with classic organizational theorists, but it can be an inefficient coordinating mechanism. Without relying on other coordinating mechanisms, managers can supervise only a limited number of employees. As the business grows, the number of supervisors and layers of management must also increase, resulting in a costly bureaucracy. Also, communicating through the chain of command is rarely as fast or accurate as direct communication between employees. A third concern is that today's workforce is less tolerant of rigid structures. For instance, Wegmans Food Market is one of the best places to work partly because the Rochester, New York–based grocery chain minimizes formal hierarchy as a coordinating mechanism.

Coordination through Standardization

Standardization, the third means of coordination, involves creating routine patterns of behavior or output. This coordinating mechanism takes three distinct forms:

"Shipwrecked or not, Bradley, we must maintain the chain of command."

- *Standardized processes.* Quality and consistency of a product or service can often be improved by standardizing work activities through job descriptions and procedures.[12] This coordinating mechanism is feasible when the work is routine (such as mass production) or simple (such as making pizzas) but is less effective in nonroutine and complex work such as product design.

- *Standardized outputs.* This form of standardization involves ensuring that individuals and work units have clearly defined goals and output measures (such as customer satisfaction and production efficiency). For instance, to coordinate the work of salespeople, companies assign sales targets rather than specific behaviors.

- *Standardized skills.* When work activities are too complex to standardize through processes or goals, companies often coordinate work efforts by extensively training employees or hiring people who have learned precise role behaviors from educational programs. This form of coordination is used in hospital operating rooms. Surgeons, nurses, and other operating room professionals coordinate their work more through training than through goals or company rules.

Division of labor and coordination of work represent the two fundamental ingredients of all organizations. How work is divided, who makes decisions, which coordinating mechanisms are emphasized, and other issues are related to the four elements of organizational structure.

Elements of Organizational Structure

Every company is configured in terms of four basic elements of organizational structure. This section introduces three of them: span of control, centralization, and formalization. The fourth element—departmentalization—is presented in the next section.

Span of Control

span of control
The number of people directly reporting to the next level in the organizational hierarchy.

Span of control refers to the number of people directly reporting to the next level in the hierarchy. Almost 100 years ago French engineer and administrative theorist Henri Fayol strongly recommended formal hierarchy as the primary coordinating mechanism. Consequently he prescribed a relatively narrow span of control: typically no more than 20 employees per supervisor and 6 supervisors per manager. These prescriptions were based on the assumption that managers simply cannot monitor and control any more subordinates closely enough. Today we know better. The best-performing manufacturing plants currently have an average of 38 production employees per supervisor.[13]

What's the secret here? Did Fayol and others miscalculate the optimal span of control? The answer is that Fayol and many other scholars sympathetic to hierarchical control believed that employees should do the work, whereas supervisors and other management personnel should monitor employee behavior and make most of the decisions. In contrast, the best-performing manufacturing operations today rely on self-directed work teams, so direct supervision (formal hierarchy) is just a backup coordinating mechanism. The underlying principle is that the optimal span of control depends on the presence of other coordinating mechanisms. Self-directed work teams supplement direct supervision with informal communication and specialized knowledge.[14]

Along with the presence of other coordinating mechanisms, the best span of control depends on the nature of the task. A wider span of control is possible when employees perform routine tasks, whereas a narrower span of control is required when employees perform novel or complex tasks. Routine tasks have few exceptions, so there is less need for direction or advice from supervisors; in contrast, novel or complex tasks tend to require more supervisory decisions or coaching. This principle is illustrated in a survey of American property and casualty insurers. The average span of control in commercial policy processing departments is around 15 employees per supervisor, whereas the span of control is 6.1 in claims service and 5.5 in commercial underwriting. Staff members in the latter two departments perform more technical work, so they have more novel and complex tasks. Commercial policy processing, on the other hand, is production-like work where tasks are routine and have few exceptions.[15]

A third influence on span of control is the degree of interdependence among employees within the department or team. One recent study of airline flight departure crews reported that supervisors responsible for highly interdependent teams need to provide more feedback and coaching than where employees are less interdependent. When tasks are highly linked, employees lack unique performance indicators for their own work, so supervisory feedback must be introduced. This increased coaching and feedback means that supervisors need a narrower span of control when managing highly interdependent teams.[16]

Tall and Flat Structures   A few years ago BASF's European Seal Sands plant organized employees into self-directed work teams and dramatically restructured the work process. These actions did much more than increase efficiency and lower costs at the bulk chemical plant. They also chopped out several layers of hierarchy. "Seven levels of management have been cut basically to two," says a BASF executive.[17]

BASF's European Seal Sands plant joins a long list of companies that are moving toward flatter organizational structures. This trend toward delaying—moving from a tall to flat structure—is partly in response to the recommendations of management gurus. Twenty years ago, for example, management guru Tom Peters challenged corporate leaders to cut the number of layers to three within a facility and to five within the entire organization.[18] The main reasons why BASF and other companies are moving toward flatter organizational structures is that it potentially cuts overhead costs and puts decision makers closer to front-line staff and information about customer needs. With fewer managers, employees might also experience more empowerment due to greater autonomy over their work roles.

However, some organizational experts warn that corporate leaders may be cutting out too much hierarchy. They argue that the much-maligned "middle managers" serve a valuable function by controlling work activities and managing corporate growth. Furthermore, companies will always need hierarchy because someone has to make quick decisions and represent a source of appeal over conflicts.[19] The conclusion here is that there is an optimal level of delayering in most organizations. Flatter structures offer several benefits, but cutting out too much management can offset these benefits.

One last point before leaving this topic: The size of an organization's hierarchy depends on both the average span of control and the number of people employed by the organization. Exhibit 15.2 illustrates this principle. A tall structure has many hierarchical levels, each with a relatively narrow span of control, whereas a flat structure has few levels, each with a wide span of control. Larger organizations that depend on hierarchy for coordination necessarily develop taller structures. For instance, HP is considered a high-involvement organization, yet it has 8 levels of corporate hierarchy (recently reduced from 11 levels) to coordinate its tens of thousands of employees.[20]

Centralization and Decentralization

centralization
The degree to which formal decision authority is held by a small group of people, typically those at the top of the organizational hierachy.

Centralization and decentralization represent a second element of organizational design. **Centralization** means that formal decision-making authority is held by a small group of people, typically those at the top of the organizational hierarchy. Most organizations begin with centralized structures because the founder makes most decisions and tries to direct the business toward his or her vision. But as organizations grow, they diversify and their environments become more complex. Senior executives aren't able to process all the decisions that significantly influence the business.

Consequently, larger organizations tend to *decentralize*; that is, they disperse decision authority and power throughout the organization. Barrick Gold Corp., the world's largest gold producer, is a case in point. "Barrick had always been run on this command-

Exhibit 15.2   **Span of Control and Tall/Flat Structures**

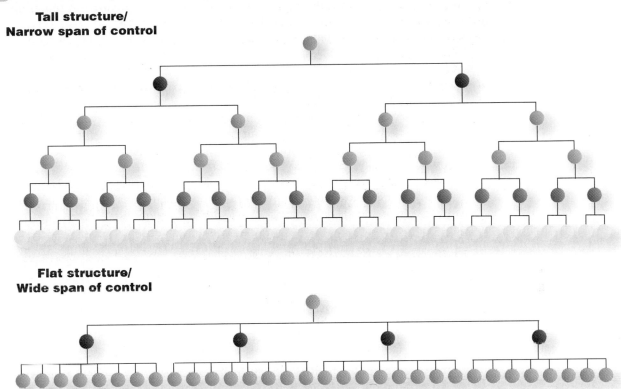

**Tall structure/
Narrow span of control**

**Flat structure/
Wide span of control**

and-control model, a centrist approach that saw all the decision making made in Toronto," says CEO Greg Wilkins. "That worked while the company was small and operating only in North America. But all of a sudden we are in four continents and seven countries, and it becomes pretty clear that you just can't do it any more." The company has since decentralized its operations around three regions of the world.[21]

The optimal level of centralization or decentralization depends on several contingencies that we will examine later in this chapter. However, we also need to keep in mind that different degrees of decentralization can occur simultaneously in different parts of the organization. Nestlé has decentralized marketing decisions to remain responsive to local markets. At the same time the Swiss-based food company has centralized production, logistics, and supply chain management activities to improve cost efficiencies and avoid having too much complexity across the organization. "If you are too decentralized, you can become too complicated—you get too much complexity in your production system," explains Nestlé CEO Peter Brabeck.[22] Firms also tend to rapidly centralize during times of turbulence and organizational crisis. When the problems are over, the company should decentralize decisions again, although this reversal tends to occur slowly because leaders are reluctant to give up decision-making power.

Formalization

Have you ever wondered why McDonald's hamburgers in Seattle look and taste the same as the McDonald's hamburgers in Singapore? The reason is that the fast-food company has engineered out all variation through formalization. **Formalization** is

formalization
The degree to which organizations standardize behavior through rules, procedures, formal training, and related mechanisms.

the degree to which organizations standardize behavior through rules, procedures, formal training, and related mechanisms.[23] In other words, formalization represents the establishment of standardization as a coordinating mechanism.

McDonald's restaurants have a formalized structure because they rely heavily on standardization of work processes as a coordinating mechanism. Employees have precisely defined roles, right down to how much mustard should be dispensed, how many pickles should be applied, and how long each hamburger should be cooked. In contrast, Nitro, described in the opening story to this chapter, has relatively little formalization because job descriptions and output expectations are broadly defined to accommodate varying tasks and responsibilities.

Older companies tend to become more formalized because work activities become routinized, making them easier to document into standardized practices. Larger companies formalize as a coordinating mechanism because direct supervision and informal communication among employees do not operate as easily. External influences, such as government safety legislation and strict accounting rules, also encourage formalization.

Problems with Formalization   Formalization may increase efficiency and compliance, but it can also create problems. Rules and procedures reduce organizational flexibility, so employees follow prescribed behaviors even when the situation clearly calls for a customized response. Thus, high levels of formalization undermine a learning orientation required for knowledge management and creativity. Some work rules become so convoluted that organizational efficiency would decline if they were actually followed as prescribed. Labor unions sometimes invoke work-to-rule strikes in which their members closely follow the formalized rules and procedures established by an organization. This tactic is effective if the company's productivity falls when employees follow the rules that are supposed to guide their behavior.

Formalized structures are fine for employees who value a stable workplace, but many employees today feel disempowered—they lack feelings of self-determination, meaning, competence, and impact of their organizational role—when working in highly formalized organizations. Finally, rules and procedures have been known to take on a life of their own in some organizations. They become the focus of attention rather than the organization's ultimate objectives of producing a product or service and serving the dominant stakeholders.

Mechanistic versus Organic Structures

We have discussed span of control, centralization, and formalization together because they usually cluster into two forms: mechanistic and organic structures.[24] A **mechanistic structure** is characterized by a narrow span of control and high degree of formalization and centralization. Mechanistic structures have many rules and procedures, limited decision making at lower levels, tall hierarchies of people in specialized roles, and vertical rather than horizontal communication flows. Tasks, which are rigidly defined, are altered only when this is sanctioned by higher authorities.

Companies with an **organic structure** have the opposite characteristics. Nitro, the boutique advertising firm described at the beginning of this chapter, is a clear example of an organic structure because it has a wide span of control, decentralized decision making, and little formalization. Tasks are fluid, adjusting to new situations and organizational needs. The organic structure supports knowledge management practices, particularly the view that information may be located anywhere in the organization rather than among senior executives. Thus, communication flows in all directions with little concern for formal hierarchy.

mechanistic structure
An organizational structure with a narrow span of control and high degrees of formalization and centralization.

organic structure
An organizational structure with a wide span of control, with little formalization, and decentralized decision making.

Harbinger Partners is a "manager-free zone." That's because the business intelligence and creative services company has no bosses. All 20 employees (actually they're partners) own a piece of the company and are involved in making company decisions. Harbinger doesn't even have a formal headquarters—just a post office box number in St. Paul, Minnesota. The company's partners work either from their homes or in clients' offices. This arrangement might give some executives sleepless nights, but not Scott Grausnick (center), who founded Harbinger in 1999. Instead he deliberately created this highly organic structure so staff could cater more effectively to customer needs while satisfying their entrepreneurial spirit. The structure seems to work: Harbinger Partners weathered the downturn that affected other firms and receives very high satisfaction ratings from customers and staff alike.[25]

As a general rule, mechanistic structures operate better in stable environments because they rely on efficiency and routine behaviors, whereas organic structures work better in rapidly changing (dynamic) environments because they are more flexible and responsive to these changes. Organic structures are also more compatible with knowledge and quality management because they emphasize information sharing rather than hierarchy and status.[26] However, the benefits of organic structures in dynamic environments occur only when employees have developed well-established roles and expertise.[27] In other words, effective organic companies rely on employee expertise and team development. Without these conditions, employees are unable to coordinate effectively with each other, resulting in errors and gross inefficiencies.

Start-up companies, particularly those in new industries, often face this problem, known as the "liability of newness." Newness makes start-up firms more organic, but their employees often lack industry experience and their teams have not developed sufficiently for peak performance. As a result, the organic structures of new companies cannot compensate for the poorer coordination and significantly lower efficiencies caused by this lack of structure from past experience and team mental models. Nitro is an excellent counterexample because, although a new firm, the ad agency relies on a team of highly experienced industry creatives who swoop into a local office to assist the new operations with specific accounts. Thus, Nitro enjoys an organic structure yet has the foundations of well-established roles and expertise to deliver service.

After reading this section you should be able to

5. Identify and evaluate five pure types of departmentalization.
6. Describe three variations of divisionalized structure and explain which one should be adopted in a particular situation.
7. Diagram the matrix structure for a project-based organization and a large global business.
8. Describe the features of team-based organizational structures.

Forms of Departmentalization

Span of control, centralization, and formalization are important elements of organizational structure, but most people think about organizational charts when the discussion of organizational structure arises. The organizational chart represents the fourth element in the structuring of organizations, called *departmentalization*. Departmentalization specifies how employees and their activities are grouped together. It is a fundamental strategy for coordinating organizational activities because it influences organizational behavior in the following ways:[28]

- Departmentalization establishes the chain of command—the system of common supervision among positions and units within the organization. It frames the membership of formal work teams and typically determines which positions and units must share resources. Thus, departmentalization establishes interdependencies among employees and subunits.

- Departmentalization focuses people around common mental models or ways of thinking, such as serving clients, developing products, or supporting a particular skill set. This focus is typically anchored around the common budgets and measures of performance assigned to employees within each departmental unit.

- Departmentalization encourages coordination through informal communication among people and subunits. With common supervision and resources, members within each configuration typically work near each other, so they can use frequent and informal interaction to get the work done.

There are almost as many organizational charts as there are businesses, but we can identify five pure types of departmentalization: simple, functional, divisional, matrix, and team-based. In addition, this section describes the network structure, which extends beyond internal departments.

Simple Structure

Most companies begin with a *simple structure*.[29] They employ only a few people and typically offer only one distinct product or service. There is minimal hierarchy—usually just employees reporting to the owners. Employees are grouped into broadly defined roles because there are insufficient economies of scale to assign them to specialized roles. The simple structure is highly flexible and minimizes the walls that form between employees in other structures. However, the simple structure usually depends on the owner's direct supervision to coordinate work activities, so it is difficult to operate as the company grows and becomes more complex.

Functional Structure

Organizations that grow large enough use functional structures at some level of the hierarchy or at some time in their history. A **functional structure** organizes employees around specific knowledge or other resources. Employees with marketing expertise are grouped into a marketing unit; those with production skills are located in manufacturing; engineers are found in product development; and so on. Organizations with functional structures are typically centralized to coordinate their activities effectively. Standardization of work processes is the most common form of coordination used in a functional structure.

Evaluating the Functional Structure   The functional structure encourages specialization and increases employees' identification with their profession. It permits greater specialization so that the organization has expertise in each area. Direct supervision is easier because managers have backgrounds in that functional area, and employees approach them with common problems and issues. Finally, the functional structure creates common pools of talent that typically serve everyone in the organization. This provides more economies of scale than if functional specialists are spread over different parts of the organization.[30]

The functional structure also has limitations.[31] Grouping employees around their skills tends to focus attention on those skills and related professional needs rather than on the company's product, service, and client needs. Unless people are transferred from one function to the next, they might not develop a broader understanding of the business. Compared with other structures, the functional structure usually produces higher dysfunctional conflict and poorer coordination in serving clients or developing products. These problems occur because employees need to work with co-workers in other departments to complete organizational tasks, yet they have different subgoals and mental models of ideal work. Together these problems require substantial formal controls and coordination when people are organized around functions.

Divisional Structure

The **divisional structure** groups employees around geographic areas, outputs (products and services), or clients. This type of structure creates minibusinesses that may operate as subsidiaries rather than departments (sometimes called *strategic business units*); they are far more autonomous than functional departments. Exhibit 15.3 illustrates the three variations of divisional structure. The *geographic structure* organizes employees around distinct regions of the country or globe. Exhibit 15.3(a) illustrates a geographic divisionalized structure recently adopted by Barrick Gold Corp. The *product/service structure* organizes work around distinct outputs. Exhibit 15.3(b) illustrates this type of structure at Philips. The Dutch electronics company divides its workforce mainly into five product divisions, ranging from consumer electronics to semiconductors. The *client structure* represents the third form of divisional structure, in which employees are organized around specific customer groups. Exhibit 15.3(c) illustrates the customer-focused structure similar to one adopted by the U.S. Internal Revenue Service.[32]

Which form of divisionalization should large organizations adopt? The answer depends mainly on the primary source of environmental diversity or uncertainty.[33] Suppose an organization sells one type of product to people across the country. If customer needs vary across regions, or if state governments impose different regulations on the product, then a geographic structure would be best to be more vigilant of

Exhibit 15.3   Three Types of Divisional Structure

(a) Geographic structure

Chief executive officer

- North American operations
- South American operations
- Australian/ African operations

(b) Product structure

Chief executive officer

- Consumer electronics
- Domestic appliances
- Lighting products
- Medical systems
- Semiconductors

(c) Client structure

Commissioner (chief executive)

- Wages and investments (individual taxpayers)
- Small business and self-employed
- Large and medium-sized business
- Tax-exempt and government entities

this diversity. On the other hand, if the company sells several types of products across the country and customer preferences and government regulations are similar everywhere, then a product structure would likely work best.

Coca-Cola, Nestlé, and many other food and beverage companies are organized mainly around geographic regions because consumer tastes and preferred marketing strategies vary considerably around the world. Even though McDonald's makes the same Big Mac around the planet, it has more fish products in Hong Kong and more vegetarian products in India in line with traditional diets in those countries. Philips, on the other hand, is organized around products because consumer preferences are similar within each group. Hospitals from Geneva, Switzerland, to Santiago, Chile, purchase similar medical equipment from Philips, whereas manufacturing and sales of these products are quite different from Philips' semiconductor business.

Many divisionalized companies are moving away from geographical structures.[34] One reason is that clients can purchase online and communicate with businesses from almost anywhere in the world, so local representation is less critical. Reduced geographic variation is another reason for the shift away from geographical structures; freer trade has reduced government intervention for many products, and consumer preferences for many products and services are becoming more similar (converging) around the world. The third reason is that large companies increasingly have global business customers who demand one global point of purchase, not one in every country or region.

Evaluating the Divisionalized Structure   The divisional form is a building block structure in that it accommodates growth relatively easily. Related products or clients can be added to existing divisions with little need for additional learning. Different products, services, or clients can be accommodated by sprouting a new division. Organizations typically reorganize around divisional structures as they expand into distinct products, services, and domains of operation because coordinating functional units becomes too unwieldy with increasing diversity.[35]

These advantages are offset by a number of limitations. First, the divisionalized structure tends to duplicate resources, such as production equipment and engineering or information technology expertise. Also, unless the division is quite large, resources are not used as efficiently as in functional structures where resources are pooled across the entire organization. The divisionalized structure also creates silos of knowledge. Expertise is spread throughout the various business units, which reduces the ability and perhaps motivation of these people to share their knowledge with counterparts in other divisions. In contrast, a functional structure groups experts together, which supports knowledge sharing.

Finally, as was already explained, the preferred divisionalized structure depends on the company's primary source of environmental diversity or uncertainty. This principle seems to be applied easily enough at Coca-Cola, McDonald's, and Philips. But the decision of whether to choose a geographic, product, or client structure is really quite difficult because global organizations experience diversity and uncertainties in many ways. The decision also affects political dynamics in the organization. If corporate leaders switch from a geographic to product structure, people who led the geographical fiefdoms suddenly get demoted under the product chiefs. Consequently, global organizations revise their structures back and forth, with each transition usually resulting in one or more executives leaving the company.

Matrix Structure

Electronic games developer BioWare launched its business with a simple or team structure in which everyone worked together to create BioWare's first game, *Shattered Steel.* But when the company launched a second project, *Baldur's Gate,* founders Ray Muzyka and Greg Zeschuk had to decide on a new structure. One option would be to simply have two teams working independently; but this multiteam structure would duplicate resources, possibly undermine information sharing among people with the same expertise across teams, and weaken employee loyalty to the overall company.

Alternatively, the game developer could create departments around the various specializations, including art, programming, audio, quality assurance, and design. This would allow employees with similar technical expertise to share information and create new ideas within their specialization. However, employees would not have the same level of teamwork or commitment to the final product as they would in a team-based project structure.

matrix structure
A type of departmentalization that overlays two organizational forms in order to leverage the benefits of both.

To gain the benefits of both alternatives, BioWare adopted a **matrix structure** in which employees belonged to departments but were assigned to specific teams based on needs. A matrix structure overlays two organizational forms to leverage the benefits that each has to offer. BioWare's matrix structure, which is similar to the diagram

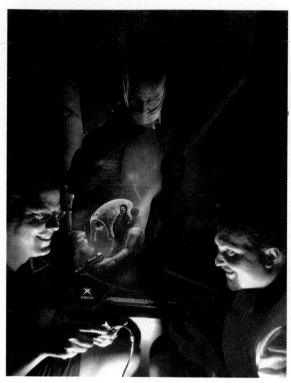

BioWare Enters the Matrix Executives at electronic games developer BioWare adopted a matrix organizational structure to gain the benefits of both a functional structure and a team or project-based structure. BioWare employees belong to departments but are assigned to specific projects for several months or longer. A matrix structure can be challenging, so BioWare holds "synchronization meetings" where functional and project leaders resolve conflicts. They also carefully select applicants who can work with the ambiguity of a matrix structure. The result is a company that has a much higher success rate than most companies in the competitive electronic games business. "They've been amazingly successful," the editor of one electronic games magazine recently applauded. "Anything that comes out of [BioWare] is on everyone's radar."[36]

in Exhibit 15.4, is organized around both functions (art, audio, programming, and so on) and products (games). Employees are assigned to a cross-functional team responsible for a specific game project, yet they also belong to a permanent functional unit from which they are redistributed when their work is completed on a particular project.[37] Muzyka and Zeschuk say the matrix structure encourages employees to think in terms of the final product, yet keeps them organized around their expertise to encourage knowledge sharing. "The matrix structure also supports our overall company culture where BioWare is the team, and everyone is always willing to help each other whether they are on the same project or not," explain Muzyka and Zeschuk.

BioWare's structure, in which project teams overlap with functional departments, is just one form of matrix structure. Another variation, which is common in large firms with global business, is to have geography on one dimension and products/services or client groups on the other. General Motors applies this global matrix structure in its information technology group.[38] One dimension consists of GM's five regional operations (North America, Europe, Asia, and so forth) led by chief information officers (CIOs) who provide IT support in their appointed regions. The other dimension consists of five business processes (services), including production, customer experience, supply chain, product development, and business services. Each process is led by a "process information officer" who is responsible for global IT support in that particular business activity. Thus, a manager who oversees supply chain information systems in Brazil would report to both the CIO for Latin America and the process information officer who heads the supply chain group.

Evaluating the Matrix Structure   The matrix structure usually optimizes the use of resources and expertise, making it ideal for project-based organizations with fluctuating workloads. When properly managed, it improves communication efficiency, project flexibility, and innovation compared to purely functional or divisional designs.

Exhibit 15.4   **Project-Based Matrix Structure (Similar to BioWare's Structure)**

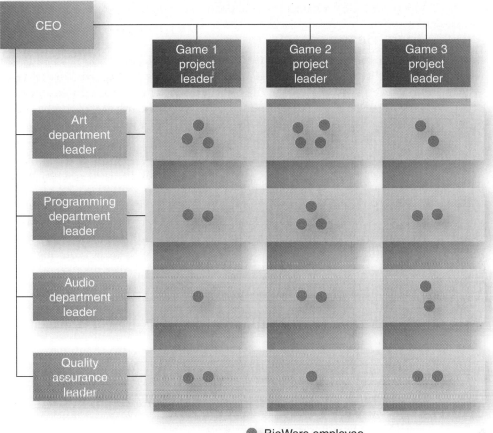

● BioWare employee

It focuses employees on serving clients or creating products, yet keeps expertise organized around their specialization so knowledge sharing improves and resources are used more efficiently. The matrix structure is also a logical choice when, as in the case of GM's IT group, two different dimensions (regions and processes) are equally important. Structures determine executive power and what is important; the matrix structure works when two different dimensions deserve equal attention.

In spite of these advantages, the matrix structure has several well-known problems.[39] One concern is that it increases goal conflict and ambiguity. Employees working at the matrix level have two bosses and, consequently, two sets of priorities that aren't always aligned with each other. Project leaders might squabble over specific employees who are assigned to other projects. They may also disagree with employee decisions, but the employee's functional leader has more say than the project leader about the individual's technical competence. Aware of these concerns, BioWare holds several "synchronization meetings" each year involving all department directors (art, design, audio, and so on), producers (game project leaders), and the human resources manager. These meetings sort out differences and ensure that staff members are properly assigned to each game project.

Another challenge is that the existence of two bosses can dilute accountability. In a functional or divisionalized structure, one manager is responsible for everything, even the most unexpected issues. But in a matrix structure the unusual problems don't get resolved because neither manager takes ownership for them.[40] The result of conflict and ambiguity in matrix structures is that some employees experience more stress, and some managers are less satisfied with their work arrangements.

Team-Based Structure

Medrad Inc. threw out the traditional assembly line when it recently consolidated some of its manufacturing operations into a new facility. For several years the Indianola, Pennsylvania, maker of medical devices has nurtured a team culture, and the new site provided an opportunity to add more structure to this emphasis on teamwork. Rather than a supervised long-line assembly, the new facility relies on clusters of work cells in which self-directed work teams manage the process with minimal involvement from management. Within two years of the changeover, productivity at Medrad's new facility increased by 30 percent compared to the previous plants, while employee satisfaction shot up due to higher autonomy and opportunities for cross-training.[41]

Medrad Inc. has adopted a **team-based structure** in its production operations. The team-based structure has a few distinguishing features from other organizational forms. First, it is built around self-directed work teams (SDWTs) rather than traditional teams or departments. SDWTs complete an entire piece of work requiring several interdependent tasks, and they have substantial autonomy over the execution of their tasks. The teams operating at Medrad plan, organize, and control their own work activities without traditional supervision. Second, these teams are typically organized around work processes, such as making a specific product or serving a specific client group.

A third distinguishing feature of the team-based organizational structure is that it has a very flat hierarchy, usually with no more than two or three management levels. This flatter structure is possible because self-directed teams do not rely on direct supervision to coordinate their work. Finally, the team-based structure has very little formalization. Almost all day-to-day decisions are made by team members rather than someone further up the organizational hierarchy. Teams are given relatively few rules about how to organize their work. Instead the executive team typically assigns output goals to the team, such as the volume and quality of product or service, or productivity improvement targets for the work process. Teams are then encouraged to use available resources and their own initiative to achieve those objectives.

Team-based structures are usually found within the manufacturing operations of larger divisionalized structures. For example, automobile parts giant TRW Automotive has a team-based structure in many of its 200 plants, but these plants are linked together within the company's divisionalized structure. However, a few firms apply the team-based structure from top to bottom. Perhaps the most famous example of this is W. L. Gore & Associates, whose extreme team-based structure is described in Connections 15.1.

Evaluating the Team-Based Structure   The team-based organization represents an increasingly popular structure because it is usually more responsive and flexible than traditional functional or divisionalized structures.[42] It tends to reduce costs because teams have less reliance on formal hierarchy (direct supervision). A cross-functional team structure improves communication and cooperation across traditional boundaries. With greater autonomy, this structure also allows quicker and more informed decision making.[43] For this reason, some hospitals have shifted from functional departments to cross-functional teams. Teams composed of nurses, radiologists, anesthesiologists, a pharmacology representative, and possibly social workers, a rehabilitation therapist, and other specialists communicate and coordinate more efficiently, therefore reducing delays and errors.[44]

The Extreme Team Structure of W. L. Gore & Associates Inc.

Diane Davidson admits that her first few months at W. L. Gore & Associates Inc. were a bit frustrating. "When I arrived at Gore, I didn't know who did what," recalls the apparel industry sales executive hired to market Gore-Tex fabrics to brand name designers. "I wondered how anything got done here. It was driving me crazy." Davidson kept asking her "starting sponsor" who her boss was, but the sponsor firmly replied, "Stop using the B-word." Gore must have managers, she thought, but they probably downplay their status. But there really aren't any bosses, not in the traditional sense. "Your team is your boss because you don't want to let them down," Davidson eventually learned. "Everyone's your boss, and no one's your boss."

From its beginnings in 1958, the Newark, Delaware-based manufacturer of fabrics (Gore-Tex), electronics, and industrial and medical products has adopted an organizational structure in which most employees (or "associates" as they are known) are organized around self-directed teams. The company has an incredibly flat hierarchy with a high degree of decentralized authority. Associates make day-to-day decisions within their expertise without approval from anyone higher up. Bigger issues, such as hiring and compensating staff, are decided by teams. "We make our own decisions and everything is discussed as well," explains Phyllis Tait, a medical business support leader at Gore's U.K. business unit.

The company has a divisional structure, organized around products and clients, such as fabrics, medical, electronics, and industrial. But most of Gore's 7,000 associates work at 45 self-sufficient manufacturing and sales offices around the world. Each facility is deliberately limited to about 200 people so they can coordinate more effectively through informal communication. Within those units, new projects are started through individual initiative and support from others. "There is no positional power," explains a Gore team leader. "You are a leader only if teams decide to respect and follow you."

As Diane Davidson discovered, Gore operates without job titles, job descriptions, or a formal chain of command. This ambiguous structure was established so associates can be creative and responsive by coordinating directly with people in other areas of the organization. "You go to whomever you need to get things done," says Gore sales veteran Tom Erickson (left in photo with colleague John Cusick). "If I want to talk to a

W. L. Gore & Associates Inc. has an extreme team-based organizational structure that eliminates traditional hierarchy. "There's no fear of any person going over another's head," says Gore sales veteran Tom Erickson, shown here (left) with co-worker John Cusick in Gore's testing room.

person on the manufacturing line about a particular job, I just go out and talk to him. That's one thing that sets us apart. There's no fear of any person going over another's head."

Sources: "The Firm That Lets Staff Breathe," Sunday Times (London), 24 March 2002; A. Brown, "Satisfaction All in a Day's Work for Top 3," Evening News (Edinburgh, Scotland), 23 March 2002, p. 13; M. Weinreb, "Power to the People," Sales & Marketing Management, April 2003, pp. 30–35; L.D. Maloney, "Smiles in the Workplace," Test & Measurement World, March 2004, p. 5; A. Deutschman, "The Fabric of Creativity," Fast Company, December 2004, pp. 54–59; M.L. Diamond, "Change in Management for Medical Device Company," Asbury Park Press (New Jersey), 6 February 2006; P.J. Kiger, "Power of the Individual," Workforce Management, 27 February 2006, pp. 1–7.

Against these benefits, the team-based structure can be costly to maintain due to the need for ongoing interpersonal skills training. Teamwork potentially takes more time to coordinate than formal hierarchy during the early stages of team development. Employees may experience more stress due to increased ambiguity in their roles. Team leaders also experience more stress due to increased conflict, loss of functional power, and unclear career progression ladders.[45]

Network Structure

network structure
An alliance of several organizations for the purpose of creating a product or serving a client.

BMW isn't eager to let you know this, but some of its vehicles designed and constructed with Germanic precision are neither designed nor constructed by BMW or in Germany. The BMW X3, for example, was not only assembled by auto parts giant Magna International in Austria, but much of the vehicle's engineering was designed by Magna specialists. BMW is the hub organization that owns and markets the BMW brand, whereas Magna and other supplier firms are spokes around the hub that provide production, engineering, and other services that get BMW products to customers.[46]

BMW is moving toward a **network structure** as it creates an alliance of several organizations for the purpose of creating a product or serving a client.[47] Exhibit 15.5 illustrates how this collaborative structure typically consists of several satellite organizations beehived around a hub or core firm. The core firm orchestrates the network process and provides one or two other core competencies, such as marketing or product development. In our example, BMW is the hub that provides marketing and distribution, whereas other firms perform most other functions. The core firm might be the main contact with customers, but most of the product or service delivery and support activities are farmed out to satellite organizations located anywhere in the world. Extranets (Web-based networks with partners) and other technologies ensure that information flows easily and openly between the core firm and its array of satellites.[48]

One of the main forces pushing toward a network structure is the recognition that an organization has only a few *core competencies*. A core competency is a knowledge base that resides throughout the organization and provides a strategic advantage. As companies discover their core competency, they "unbundle" noncritical tasks to other organizations that have a core competency in performing those tasks.

Companies are also more likely to form network structures when technology is changing quickly and production processes are complex or varied.[49] Many firms cannot keep up with the hyperfast changes in information technology, so they have

Exhibit 15.5
A Network Structure

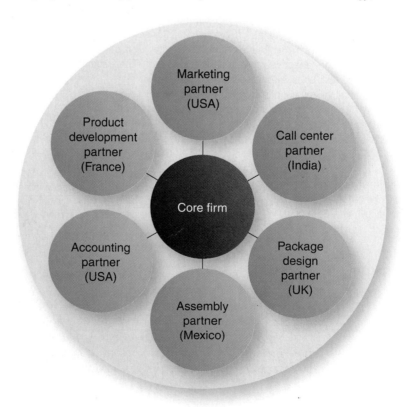

outsourced their entire information systems departments to IBM, EDS, and other firms that specialize in information systems services. Similarly, many high-technology firms form networks with Solectron, Celestica, and other electronics equipment manufacturers because they have expertise in diverse production processes.

Virtual Corporations   The network structure generally performs a patterned set of tasks for all clients. In contrast, some network structures—known as **virtual corporations**—represent several independent companies that form unique partnership teams to provide customized products or services, usually to specific clients, for a limited time.[50] A good example of this is host universal. The British advertising firm (which spells its name all lowercase) has no employees or clients. Instead it serves a specific project by forming a unique team of partners, who then disband when the project is finished. "At host we have no clients or employees, which enables us to pull the most effective teams together from our network without foisting redundant skills, fees, and hierarchy onto clients," explains one of host's founding partners.[51]

Virtual corporations exist temporarily and reshape themselves quickly to fit immediate needs. When an opportunity emerges, a unique combination of partners in the alliance forms a virtual corporation that works on the assignment until it is completed. Virtual corporations are self-organizing, meaning that they rearrange their own communication patterns and roles to fit the situation. The relationship among the partners is mutually determined rather than imposed by a core firm.

Evaluating the Network Structure   For several years organizational behavior theorists have argued that organizational leaders must develop a metaphor of organizations as plasma-like organisms rather than rigid machines.[52] Network structures come close to the organism metaphor because they offer the flexibility to realign their structures with changing environmental requirements. If customers demand a new product or service, the core firm forms new alliances with other firms offering the appropriate resources. For example, by working with Magna International, BMW was probably able to develop and launch the X3 vehicle much sooner than if it had performed these tasks on its own. When BMW needs a different type of manufacturing, it isn't saddled with nonessential facilities and resources. Network structures also offer efficiencies because the core firm becomes globally competitive as it shops worldwide for subcontractors with the best people and the best technology at the best price. Indeed, the pressures of global competition have made network structures more vital, and computer-based information technology has made them possible.[53]

A potential disadvantage of network structures is that they expose the core firm to market forces. Other companies may bid up the price for subcontractors, whereas the short-term cost would be lower if the company hired its own employees to provide this function. Another problem is that although information technology makes worldwide communication much easier, it will never replace the degree of control organizations have when manufacturing, marketing, and other functions are in-house. The core firm can use arm's-length incentives and contract provisions to maintain the subcontractor's quality, but these actions are relatively crude compared to those used to maintain performance of in-house employees.

virtual corporations
Network structures representing several independent companies that form unique partnership teams to provide customized products or services, usually to specific clients, for a limited time.

Learning
Objectives

After reading the next section you should be able to

9. **Identify four characteristics of external environments and discuss the preferred organizational structure for each environment.**

10. **Summarize the influences of organizational size, technology, and strategy on organizational structure.**

Contingencies of Organizational Design

Most organizational behavior theories and concepts have contingencies: Ideas that work well in one situation might not work as well in another situation. This contingency approach is certainly relevant when firms choose the most appropriate organizational structure.[54] In this section we introduce four contingencies of organizational design: external environment, size, technology, and strategy.

External Environment

The best structure for an organization depends on its external environment. The external environment includes anything outside the organization, including most stakeholders (clients, suppliers, government), resources (raw materials, human resources, information, finances), and competitors. Four characteristics of external environments influence the type of organizational structure best suited to a particular situation: dynamism, complexity, diversity, and hostility:[55]

- *Dynamic versus stable environments.* Dynamic environments have a high rate of change, leading to novel situations and a lack of identifiable patterns. Organic structures, including the team-based structure at Nitro, are better suited to this type of environment so that the organization can adapt more quickly to changes, but only if employees are experienced and coordinate well in teamwork.[56] In contrast, stable environments are characterized by regular cycles of activity and steady changes in supply and demand for inputs and outputs. Events are more predictable, enabling the firm to apply rules and procedures. Mechanistic structures are more efficient when the environment is predictable, so they tend to work better than organic structures under these conditions.

- *Complex versus simple environments.* Complex environments have many elements, whereas simple environments have few things to monitor. As an example, a major university library operates in a more complex environment than a small town public library. The university library's clients require several types of services—book borrowing, online full-text databases, research centers, course reserve collections, and so on. A small town public library experiences fewer of these demands. The more complex the environment, the more decentralized the organization should become. Decentralization is a logical response to complexity because decisions are pushed down to people and subunits with the necessary information to make informed choices.

- *Diverse versus integrated environments.* Organizations located in diverse environments have a greater variety of products or services, clients, and regions. In contrast, an integrated environment has only one client, product, and geographic area. The more diversified the environment, the more a firm needs to use a divisionalized form aligned with that diversity. If it sells a single product around the world, a geographic divisionalized structure would align best with the firm's geographic diversity, for example.

- *Hostile versus munificent environments.* Firms located in a hostile environment face resource scarcity and more competition in the marketplace. Hostile environments are typically dynamic ones because they reduce the predictability of access to resources and demand for outputs. Organic structures tend to be best in hostile environments. However, when the environment is extremely hostile—such as a severe shortage of supplies or lower market share—organizations tend to temporarily centralize so that decisions can be made more

7-Eleven's Centralized–Decentralized Structure 7-Eleven tries to leverage the buying power and efficiencies of its 25,000 stores in 19 countries by centralizing decisions about information technology and supplier purchasing. At the same time, the convenience store chain's customers have diverse preferences from Australia to Japan to North America. This diversity exists even within countries. For example, weather and special events can be dramatically different from one city to the next, which means that product demand will also vary. To thrive in this diverse and complex environment, 7-Eleven's business in the United States has what it calls a "centrally decentralized" structure in which store managers make local inventory decisions using a centralized inventory management system. Along with ongoing product training and guidance from regional consultants, store managers have the best information about their customers and can respond quickly to local market needs. "We could never predict a busload of football players on a Friday night, but the store manager can," explains 7-Eleven president and CEO Jim Keyes, shown in this photo with a 7-Eleven employee.[57]

quickly and executives feel more comfortable being in control.[58] Ironically, centralization may result in lower-quality decisions during organizational crises because top management has less information, particularly when the environment is complex.

Organization Size

Larger organizations should have different structures from smaller organizations.[59] As the number of employees increases, job specialization increases due to a greater division of labor. This greater division of labor requires more elaborate coordinating mechanisms. Thus larger firms make greater use of standardization (particularly work processes and outcomes) to coordinate work activities. These coordinating mechanisms create an administrative hierarchy and greater formalization. Historically, larger organizations have made less use of informal communication as a coordinating mechanism. However, emerging information technologies and increased emphasis on empowerment have caused informal communication to regain its importance in large firms.[60]

Larger organizations also tend to be more decentralized. Executives have neither sufficient time nor expertise to process all the decisions that significantly influence the business as it grows. Therefore, decision-making authority is pushed down to lower levels, where incumbents can cope with the narrower range of issues under their control.

Technology

Technology is another factor to consider when designing the best organizational structure for the situation.[61] *Technology* refers to the mechanisms or processes by which an organization turns out its products or services. One technological contingency is its *variability*—the number of exceptions to standard procedure that tend to occur. In work processes with low variability, jobs are routine and follow standard operating procedures. Another contingency is *analyzability*—the predictability or difficulty of the required work. The less analyzable the work, the more it requires experts with sufficient discretion to address the work challenges.

Assembly line technology has low variability and high analyzability; the jobs are routine and highly predictable. This type of technology works best with a structure consisting of high formalization and centralization. When employees perform tasks with high variety and low analyzability, they apply their skills to unique situations with little opportunity for repetition. Research project teams operate under these conditions. These situations call for an organic structure with low formalization, highly decentralized decision-making authority, and coordination mainly through informal communication among team members.

High-variety and high-analyzability tasks have many exceptions to routines, but these exceptions can usually be resolved through standard procedures. Maintenance groups and engineering design teams experience these conditions. Work units that fall into this category should use an organic structure, but it is possible to have somewhat greater formalization and centralization due to the analyzability of problems. Skilled trades people tend to work in situations with low variety and low analyzability. Their tasks involve few exceptions, but the problems that arise are difficult to resolve. This situation allows more centralization and formalization than in a purely organic structure, but coordination must include informal communication among the skilled employees so that unique problems can be resolved.

Organizational Strategy

organizational strategy
The way an organization positions itself in its setting in relation to its stakeholders, given the organization's resources, capabilities, and mission.

Organizational strategy refers to the way an organization positions itself in its setting in relation to its stakeholders, given the organization's resources, capabilities, and mission.[62] In other words, strategy represents the decisions and actions applied to achieve the organization's goals. Although size, technology, and environment influence the optimal organizational structure, these contingencies do not necessarily determine structure. Instead corporate leaders formulate and implement strategies that shape both the characteristics of these contingencies as well as the organization's resulting structure.

This concept is summed up with the simple phrase "Structure follows strategy."[63] Organizational leaders decide how large to grow and which technologies to use. They take steps to define and manipulate their environments rather than letting the organization's fate be entirely determined by external influences. Furthermore, organizational structures don't evolve as a natural response to these contingencies. Instead they result from organizational decisions. Thus organizational strategy influences both the contingencies of structure and the structure itself.

The structure follows strategy thesis that has become the dominant perspective of business policy and strategic management. An important aspect of this view is that organizations can choose the environments in which they want to operate. Some businesses adopt a *differentiation strategy* by bringing unique products to the market or attracting clients who want customized goods and services. They try to distinguish their outputs from those provided by other firms through marketing, providing special services, and innovation. Others adopt a *cost leadership strategy* in which they maximize productivity and are thereby able to offer popular products or services at a competitive price.[64]

The type of organizational strategy selected leads to the best organizational structure to adopt.[65] Organizations with a cost leadership strategy should adopt a mechanistic, functional structure with high levels of job specialization and standardized work processes. This is similar to the routine technology category described earlier because this approach maximizes production and service efficiency. A differentiation strategy, on the other hand, requires more customized relations with clients. A matrix or team-based structure with less centralization and formalization is most appropriate here so that technical specialists can coordinate their work activities more closely with clients' needs. Overall, it is now apparent that organizational structure is influenced by size, technology, and environment, but the organization's strategy may reshape these elements and loosen their connection to organizational structure.

Chapter Summary

Organizational structure refers to the division of labor as well as the patterns of coordination, communication, workflow, and formal power that direct organizational activities. All organizational structures divide labor into distinct tasks and coordinate that labor to accomplish common goals. The primary means of coordination are informal communication, formal hierarchy, and standardization.

The four basic elements of organizational structure include span of control, centralization, formalization, and departmentalization. At one time scholars suggested that firms should have a tall hierarchy with a narrow span of control. However, span of control can be much wider when other coordinating mechanisms are present. Span of control should be narrower when employees perform novel or complex tasks and where their work is highly interdependent with co-workers.

Centralization occurs when formal decision authority is held by a small group of people, typically senior executives. Many companies decentralize as they become larger and more complex because senior executives lack the necessary time and expertise to process all the decisions that significantly influence the business. Formalization is the degree to which organizations standardize behavior through rules, procedures, formal training, and related mechanisms. Companies become more formalized as they grow older and larger.

Span of control, centralization, and formalization cluster into mechanistic and organic structures. Mechanistic structures are characterized by a narrow span of control and high degree of formalization and centralization. Companies with an organic structure have the opposite characteristics.

Departmentalization specifies how employees and their activities are grouped together. It establishes the chain of command, focuses people around common mental models, and encourages coordination through informal communication among people and subunits. A functional structure organizes employees around specific knowledge or other resources. This fosters greater specialization, improves direct supervision, but increases conflict in serving clients or developing products. It also focuses employee attention on functional skills rather than on the company's product/service or client needs.

A divisional structure groups employees around geographic areas, clients, or outputs. This structure accommodates growth and focuses employee attention on products or customers rather than on tasks. However, this structure creates silos of knowledge and duplication of resources.

The matrix structure combines two structures to leverage the benefits of both types of structure. However, this approach requires more coordination than functional or pure divisional structures, may dilute accountability, and increases conflict.

Team-based structures are very flat with low formalization and organize self-directed teams around work processes rather than functional specialties. A network structure is an alliance of several organizations for the purpose of creating a product or serving a client. Virtual corporations are network structures that can quickly reorganize themselves to suit the client's requirements.

The best organizational structure depends on the firm's external environment, size, technology, and strategy. The optimal structure depends on whether the environment is dynamic or stable, complex or simple, diverse or integrated, and hostile or munificent. As organizations increase in size, they become more decentralized and more formalized, with greater job specialization and more elaborate coordinating mechanisms. The work unit's technology—including variety of work and analyzability of problems—influences whether to adopt an organic or mechanistic structure. These contingencies influence but do not necessarily determine structure. Instead corporate leaders formulate and implement strategies that shape both the characteristics of these contingencies as well as the organization's resulting structure.

Key Terms

centralization, p. 434

divisional structure, p. 439

formalization, p. 435

functional structure, p. 439

matrix structure, p. 441

mechanistic structure, p. 436

network structure, p. 446

organic structure, p. 436

organizational strategy, p. 450

organizational structure, p. 450

span of control, p. 433

team-based structure, p. 444

virtual corporations, p. 447

Critical Thinking Questions

1. Boutique advertising agency Nitro has an organic, team-based structure. What coordinating mechanism dominates in this type of organizational structure? Describe the extent and form in which the other two forms of coordination might be apparent at Nitro.

2. Think about the business school or other organizational unit whose classes you are currently attending. What is the dominant coordinating mechanism used to guide or control the instructor? Why is this coordinating mechanism used the most here?

3. Administrative theorists concluded many decades ago that the most effective organizations have a narrow span of control. Yet today's top-performing manufacturing firms have a wide span of control. Why is this possible? Under what circumstances, if any, should manufacturing firms have a narrow span of control?

4. If we could identify trends in organizational structure, one of them would be decentralization. Why is decentralization becoming more common in contemporary organizations? What should companies consider when determining their degree of decentralization?

5. Diversified Technologies LLC (DTL) makes four types of products, each type to be sold to different types of clients. For example, one product is sold exclusively to automobile repair shops, whereas another is used mainly in hospitals. Customer expectations and needs are surprisingly similar throughout the world. However, the company has separate marketing, product design, and manufacturing facilities in Asia, North America, Europe, and South America because, until recently, each jurisdiction had unique regulations governing the production and sales of these products. Now several governments have begun the process of deregulating the products that DTL designs and manufactures, and trade agreements have opened several markets to foreign-made products. Which form of departmentalization might be best for DTL if deregulation and trade agreements occur?

6. Why are many organizations moving away from geographic divisional structures?

7. From an employee perspective, what are the advantages and disadvantages of working in a matrix structure?

8. Suppose that you have been hired as a consultant to diagnose the environmental characteristics of your college or university. How would you describe the school's external environment? Is the school's existing structure appropriate for this environment?

Case Study 15.1 FTCA—REGIONAL AND HEADQUARTERS RELATIONS

Swee C. Goh, University of Ottawa

The FTCA is a government agency that provides services to the public but also serves an enforcement role. It employs over 20,000 people who are located at headquarters and in many regional offices across the country. Most staff members are involved with direct counter-type services for both individuals and businesses. These services include collections, inquiries, payments, and audits. The agency also has large centers in various parts of the country to process forms and payments submitted by individuals and businesses.

FTCA is a typical federal government agency; many employees are unionized and have experienced numerous changes over the years. Because of the increasing complexity of regulations and the need to be more cost-effective in service delivery, FTCA has evolved into an organization that uses technology to a great extent. The agency's leaders increasingly emphasize the need for easier and faster service and turnaround in dealing with clients. They also expect staff to depend more on electronic means of communication for interaction with the public.

As the population has grown over the years, the regional offices of this government organization have expanded. Each regional office is headed by an assistant director (AD) who has a budget and an increasing number of staff for the various functional activities related to the region, such as a manager for information systems. Every region also has offices located in the major cities. The managers of these city center offices report directly to the regional AD. The regional ADs report to the director who is the overall head of the agency.

FTCA has a strong emphasis on centralized control, particularly in the functional units. This emphasis occurs because of legal requirements as well as the fact that the agency has extensive direct interaction with the public. For example, one functional unit at headquarters (HQ) is responsible for collections and enforcement. If a regional manager has the same functional activity, FTCA executives believe that person should be accountable to the HQ functional AD. However, as mentioned earlier, the regional manager also reports directly to the regional AD; and the budget for the agency comes from the regional budget allocations, not from the HQ functional group.

This arrangement produces a dual reporting relationship for regional functional managers. Regional managers complain that this situation is awkward. Who is the real boss under the circumstances: the regional AD or the functional HQ AD for these managers? Also, who should be responsible for evaluating the work performance of these dual-reporting regional managers? And if a regional manager makes a serious error, which of the two supervisors of that manager is ultimately accountable?

The potential for confusion about responsibility and accountability has made the roles and reporting relationships of the senior managers vague. This has also increased conflict between regional managers and HQ managers.

To address this growing problem, a consultant was brought in to do an independent evaluation of the current organization structure of FTCA. The consultant asked for an organization chart of FTCA, which is shown here. The consultant became aware of the concerns just described by conducting interviews with various staff members throughout the agency. Other information such as budgets and financial allocations, some earlier organizational studies, the mandate of the agency, and the like were also provided to the consultant.

The discussions with staff members were interesting. Some viewed this issue as a people problem and not a structural one. That is, if regional and HQ managers learned how to cooperate and work with each other, this would not be an issue at all: They should take a shared responsibility approach and try to work together. But the view of the HQ functional groups was quite different. They argued that FTCA is a functional organization, so these functional unit leaders should have authority and power over regional managers performing the same function. In effect, these regional managers should report to the functional unit ADs or at least be accountable to HQ policies and objectives.

To compound the problem, the regional managers saw this problem completely differently. They argued that the functional HQ managers should have a policy development function. On an annual basis they should develop broad objectives and targets in consultation with regional managers. Once these were approved, it should be the responsibility of the regional managers to carry them out in light of the environment and constraints they face. The functional unit ADs opposed the regional managers' position, pointing out that if the regional managers did not achieve their objectives, the functional ADs would suffer the consequences.

After hearing these views, the consultant formed the opinion that this was an intractable and complex problem that could be related to both people and structure. The consultant also noted that the regional budgets were huge, sometimes larger than the budgets for functional groups at HQ. Regional ADs also met infrequently—only once a month—with the director and functional ADs at HQ. Most of the time the regions seemed to operate fairly autonomously, whereas the director seemed to have ongoing involvement with the functional ADs.

An HQ staff member observed that over time the regional offices seemed to be getting bigger and had become fairly autonomous with functional staff mirroring the staff functions at HQ. The implication was that the regional staff would soon view the functional units at headquarters as a distant group that only set policy for the regions to interpret or ignore as they pleased.

A functional AD with several years of seniority at FTCA warned that the functional units must have some control audit and other functional activities in the region. The AD explained that without clear roles, reporting relationships, and accountabilities between the regions and HQ, FTCA could not provide citizens with transparent and fair treatment in the services under its mandate.

The regional ADs, however, saw their responsibilities as facilitating horizontal coordination within the regions to ensure that actions and decisions were consistent and reflected the legislative responsibility of the agency.

After a month of study and discussions with FTCA staff, the consultant realized that this was not going to be an easy problem to resolve. There were also rumblings as the project progressed that some regional ADs did not like the idea of restructuring FTCA to deal with these issues. They seemed to have considerable clout and power in the organization as a group and would resist any change to the status quo.

As the consultant sat down to write the report, a number of critical questions became apparent: Was FTCA a purely functional organization? Could the accountability issues be resolved through an acceptable organizational process and people training without the need for restructuring? What about power, politics, and conflict in this situation? Finally, would resistance to change become a problem as well?

Discussion Questions

1. Describe the current organization structure of FTCA. What is it? What are the strengths and weaknesses of such a structure?

2. Can FTCA operate effectively as a purely functional structure?

3. What roles do power and politics play in the current situation?

4. What kind of conflict is FTCA experiencing between HQ and regional managers?

5. Suggest a practical, workable solution to the problem at FTCA. If restructuring is part of your solution, describe what the structure would look like and justify from your knowledge of organization theory and design why it would work—that is, how it would improve the working relationship between headquarters and regional staff.

Materials in this case are based on factual and nonfactual information about a government agency. This case is written for classroom discussion and not to demonstrate effective or ineffective management of an organization.©2005 Swee C. Goh.

Case Study 15.2 BALLMER'S MICROSOFT

BusinessWeek It didn't take long after Bill Gates handed over Microsoft's top job to his buddy Steve Ballmer that Ballmer realized things had to change. In particular, Microsoft had become a very large organization that was not moving as quickly as it should in the marketplace. To make Microsoft more responsive, Ballmer restructured the organization and introduced practices to ensure those structural changes worked well.

This *BusinessWeek* case study looks at the changes that Steve Ballmer is making at Microsoft. It describes specific adjustments to the company's organizational structure, as well as coordination mechanisms to support that structure. Read through this *BusinessWeek* article at www.mhhe.com/mcshane4e and prepare for the discussion questions below.

Discussion Questions

1. What symptoms or conditions suggested that Microsoft's current organizational structure wasn't sufficiently effective?

2. What changes did Steve Ballmer ultimately make to Microsoft's departmentalization? What problems occurred with the initial changes in departmentalization?

3. Along with changing the organizational chart, what other organizational structure changes did Steve Ballmer make at Microsoft? Do these changes seem reasonable under the circumstances?

Source: J. Greene, S. Hamm, and J. Kerstetter, "Ballmer's Microsoft," *BusinessWeek,* 17 June 2002, 66–72.

Team Exercise 15.3 THE CLUB ED EXERCISE

Cheryl Harvey and Kim Morouney, Wilfred Laurier University

PURPOSE This exercise is designed to help you understand the issues to consider when designing organizations at various stages of growth.

MATERIALS Each student team should have enough overhead transparencies or flip chart sheets to display several organizational charts.

INSTRUCTIONS Each team discusses the scenario presented. The first scenario is presented next. The instructor will facilitate discussion and notify teams when to begin the next step. The exercise and debriefing require approximately 90 minutes, although fewer scenarios can reduce the time somewhat.

1. Students are placed in teams (typically four or five people).

2. After reading Scenario #1 presented here, each team will design an organizational chart (departmentalization) that is most appropriate for this situation. Students should be able to describe the type of structure drawn and explain why it is appropriate. The structure should be drawn on an overhead transparency or flip chart for others to see during later class discussion. The instructor will set a fixed time (perhaps 15 minutes) to complete this task.

Scenario #1 Determined never to shovel snow again, you are establishing a new resort business on a small Caribbean island. The resort is under construction and is scheduled to open one year from now. You decide it is time to draw up an organizational chart for this new venture, called Club Ed.

3. At the end of the time allowed, the instructor will present Scenario #2 and each team will be asked to draw another organizational chart to suit that situation. Again, students should be able to describe the type of structure drawn and explain why it is appropriate.

4. At the end of the time allowed, the instructor will present Scenario #3 and each team will be asked to draw another organizational chart to suit that situation.

5. Depending on the time available, the instructor might present a fourth scenario. The class will gather to present their designs for each scenario.

During each presentation, teams should describe the type of structure drawn and explain why it is appropriate.

Source: Adapted from C. Harvey and K. Morouney, *Journal of Management Education* 22 (June 1998), pp. 425–29. Used with permission of the authors.

Self-Assessment 15.4

IDENTIFYING YOUR PREFERRED ORGANIZATIONAL STRUCTURE

PURPOSE This exercise is designed to help you understand how an organization's structure influences the personal needs and values of people working in that structure.

INSTRUCTIONS Personal values influence how comfortable you are working in different organizational structures. You might prefer an organization with clearly defined rules or no rules at all. You might prefer a firm where almost any employee can make important decisions, or where

important decisions are screened by senior executives. Read the following statements and indicate the extent to which you would like to work in an organization with that characteristic. When finished, use the scoring key in Appendix B to calculate your results. This self-assessment is completed alone so you can complete it honestly without concerns of social comparison. However, class discussion will focus on the elements of organizational design and their relationship to personal needs and values.

Organizational Structure Preference Scale

I would like to work in an organization where…	Not at all	A little	Some-what	Very much	Score
1. A person's career ladder has several steps toward higher status and responsibility.	☐	☐	☐	☐	___
2. Employees perform their work with few rules to limit their discretion.	☐	☐	☐	☐	___
3. Responsibility is pushed down to employees who perform the work.	☐	☐	☐	☐	___
4. Supervisors have few employees, so they work closely with each person.	☐	☐	☐	☐	___
5. Senior executives make most decisions to ensure that the company is consistent in its actions.	☐	☐	☐	☐	___
6. Jobs are clearly defined so there is no confusion over who is responsible for various tasks.	☐	☐	☐	☐	___
7. Employees have their say on issues, but senior executives make most of the decisions.	☐	☐	☐	☐	___
8. Job descriptions are broadly stated or nonexistent.	☐	☐	☐	☐	___
9. Everyone's work is tightly synchronized around top management operating plans.	☐	☐	☐	☐	___
10. Most work is performed in teams without close supervision.	☐	☐	☐	☐	___
11. Work gets done through informal discussion with co-workers rather than through formal rules.	☐	☐	☐	☐	___
12. Supervisors have so many employees that they can't watch anyone very closely.	☐	☐	☐	☐	___
13. Everyone has clearly understood goals, expectations, and job duties.	☐	☐	☐	☐	___
14. Senior executives assign overall goals but leave daily decisions to frontline teams.	☐	☐	☐	☐	___
15. Even in a large company, the CEO is only three or four levels above the lowest position.	☐	☐	☐	☐	___

After reading this chapter, if you need additional information, see **www.mhhe.com/mcshane4e** for more in-depth interactivities that correspond with this material.

During the peak of the dot-com boom, Charles Schwab & Co. then-CEO David Pottruck was convinced that as investors grew wealthier they would migrate from the San Francisco—based discount broker to full-service firms that offered more personalized service. So Schwab paid top dollar to acquire U.S. Trust, a high-brow New York–based private bank that served only clients with at least $10 million to invest. Schwab customers who became wealthy would be shunted over to U.S. Trust for more personalized service.

The strategy backfired—partly because Schwab's customers still wanted cheap trades as they grew wealthier, and partly because Schwab ignored the acquisition's cultural dynamics. Schwab's employees valued rapid change, cost-cutting frugality, process efficiency, and egalitarianism. In contrast, U.S. Trust was an exclusive club that was slow to adopt technology and preferred to admit new clients through referrals from existing clients. Clients were pampered by "wealth advisers" who earned huge bonuses and worked in an environment that reeked of luxury.

While negotiating the takeover, U.S. Trust executives expressed concern about these cultural differences, so Schwab agreed to leave the firm as a separate entity. This separation strategy didn't last long. Schwab cut U.S. Trust employees' lucrative bonuses and tied their annual rewards to Schwab's financial performance. U.S. Trust executives were pushed to cut costs and set more aggressive goals. Schwab even tried to acculturate several hundred U.S. Trust employees with a board game that used a giant mat showing hills, streams, and a mountain with founder Charles Schwab's face carved into the side. U.S. Trust staff complained that the game was demeaning, particularly wearing smocks as they played the role of investors.

Executives at Charles Schwab & Co. underestimated the influence of organizational culture on behavior when they acquired U.S. Trust.

In meetings immediately following the acquisition, U.S. Trust executives winced when Schwab frequently used the term *customers*. They reminded Schwab's staff that U.S. Trust has *clients*, which implies much more of a long-term relationship. U.S. Trust advisers also resisted Schwab's referrals of newly minted millionaires in blue jeans. "We were flabbergasted," said one Schwab board member of the cultural clash. "Some of the U.S. Trust officers simply refused to accept our referrals."

When the depth of cultural intransigence became apparent, Pottruck replaced U.S. Trust's CEO with Schwab executive Alan Weber. Weber later insisted that "there is no culture clash" because Schwab "never tried to change the nature of the organization." Meanwhile, sources say that more than 300 U.S. Trust wealth advisers have defected to competitors since the acquisition, taking many valued clients with them. Pottruck lost his job as Schwab CEO, in part because the U.S. Trust acquisition stumbled. The acquisition is now worth less than half of its purchase price.

"Here are two first-class companies, but structural and cultural problems keep the combination from the kind of success they expected," explains a financial adviser in Florida.[1]

Organizational Culture

After reading this chapter you should be able to

1. Describe the elements of organizational culture.

2. Discuss the importance of organizational subcultures.

3. List four categories of artifacts through which corporate culture is deciphered.

4. Identify three functions of organizational culture.

5. Discuss the conditions under which cultural strength improves corporate performance.

6. Compare and contrast four strategies for merging organizational cultures.

7. Identify four strategies to strengthen an organization's culture.

8. Describe the stages of organizational socialization.

9. Explain how realistic job previews assist the socialization process.

organizational culture
The basic pattern of shared values and assumptions governing the way employees within an organization think about and act on problems and opportunities.

Schwab's acquisition of U.S. Trust is a classic tale of the perils of ignoring organizational culture. **Organizational culture** consists of the values and assumptions shared within an organization.[2] It defines what is important and unimportant in the company and consequently directs everyone in the organization toward the "right way" of doing things. You might think of it as the organization's DNA—invisible to the naked eye, yet a powerful template that shapes what happens in the workplace.[3]

This chapter begins by examining the elements of organizational culture and how culture is deciphered through artifacts. This is followed by a discussion of the relationship between organizational culture and corporate performance, including the effects of cultural strength, fit, and adaptability. Then we turn to the issue of mergers and corporate culture, followed by specific strategies for maintaining a strong organizational culture. The last section of this chapter zooms in on employee socialization, which is identified as one of the more important ways to strengthen organizational culture.

Learning Objectives

After reading the next two sections you should be able to

1. **Describe the elements of organizational culture.**
2. **Discuss the importance of organizational subcultures.**
3. **List four categories of artifacts through which corporate culture is deciphered.**

Elements of Organizational Culture

Exhibit 16.1 illustrates how the shared values and assumptions of an organization's culture relate to each other and are associated with artifacts, which are discussed later in this chapter. *Values*, which we introduced in Chapter 1, are stable, evaluative beliefs that guide our preferences for outcomes or courses of action in a variety of situations.[4] They are conscious perceptions about what is good or bad, right or wrong. Values exist as a component of organizational culture in the form of *shared values*. Shared values are values that people within the organization or work unit have in common and place near the top of their hierarchy of values.[5] At Charles Schwab & Co., employees place a high priority on rapid change, cost-cutting frugality, process efficiency, and egalitarianism.

It has become trendy for leaders to determine and publicly announce their company's shared values. Yahoo, the online portal company, is no exception. Its Web site proudly says that six values represent "what makes it tick": excellence, innovation, customer fixation, teamwork, community, and fun. Do these values really represent the content of Yahoo's culture? Maybe, but what companies say they value—their *espoused values*—isn't necessarily what they actually value (called *enacted values*). Values are socially desirable, so people create a positive public image by claiming to believe in values that others expect them to embrace (see Chapter 2).

For instance, one large international corporation hung signs around its headquarters proclaiming that its culture embraced "trust"; yet the same company required all employees to be searched whenever they entered or exited the building. Even if an organization's dozen or so top executives embrace the stated values, they are not necessarily the values held by most people throughout the organization. *Enacted values*, on the other hand, represent the values that people actually rely on to guide their decisions and actions. These values-in-use are apparent by watching people in action. An organization's culture consists of these enacted values, not espoused values.[6]

Exhibit 16.1
Organizational Culture Assumptions, Values, and Artifacts

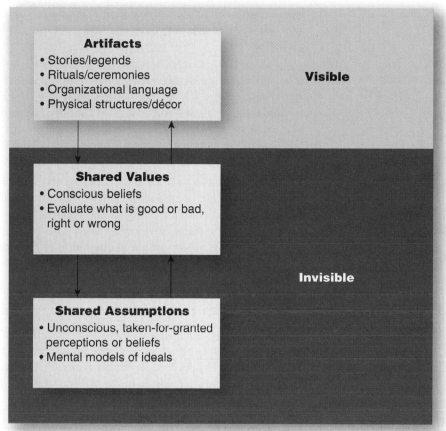

Source: Based on information in E.H. Schein, *Organizational Culture and Leadership: A Dynamic View* (San Francisco: Jossey-Bass, 1985).

Along with shared values, corporate culture consists of a deeper element—some experts believe it is really the essence of culture—called *shared assumptions.* These are unconscious taken-for-granted perceptions or beliefs that have worked so well in the past that they are considered the correct way to think and act toward problems and opportunities. Shared assumptions are so deeply ingrained that you probably wouldn't discover them by surveying employees. Only by observing employees, analyzing their decisions, and debriefing them about their actions would these assumptions rise to the surface.

Content of Organizational Culture

Organizations differ in their cultural content—that is, the relative ordering of values and assumptions. The culture of Charles Schwab & Co. values rapid change, cost-cutting frugality, process efficiency, and egalitarianism. At U.S. Trust employees embrace stability, dedicated service, and reputation. Here are a few more companies and their apparent dominant cultures:

- *SAS Institute.* Spend some time at SAS Institute and you will soon discover that the world's largest privately held software company has one of the most employee-friendly cultures on the planet. Located on a 200-acre campus in Cary, North Carolina, SAS supports employee well-being with free on-site medical care, unlimited sick days, heavily subsidized day care, ski trips, personal trainers, inexpensive gourmet cafeterias, and tai chi classes. Unlike other software companies, SAS encourages its employees to stick to a 35-hour workweek.[7]

- *ICICI Bank.* India's second largest bank exudes a performance-oriented culture. Its organizational practices place a premium on training, career development, goal setting, and pay for performance, all with the intent of maximizing employee performance and customer service. "We believe in defining clear performance for employees and empowering them to achieve their goals," says ICICI Bank executive director Kalpana Morparia. "This has helped to create a culture of high performance across the organization."[8]

- *JetBlue.* JetBlue has soared higher and faster than other new airlines because its culture "humanizes" air travel by providing comfort and service at low prices. As JetBlue quickly expands operations, Founder and CEO David Neeleman wants to ensure that the New York–based airline maintains this culture, so all new staff members receive a deep education in JetBlue's shared values. "The cultural aspects of our training programs are at least as important as the technical aspects," says Mike Barger, vice president of JetBlue University. "The People Department will find the right people, and we will inculcate the culture into them and nurture that culture until we release them out into the operation."[9]

Employee-friendly. Performance-oriented. Customer-focused. How many corporate cultural values are there? Some writers and consultants have attempted to classify organizational cultures into several categories. One of these models claims that there are seven corporate cultures in the world: attention to detail, outcome orientation, people orientation, team orientation, aggressiveness, stability, and innovation and risk taking. Another organizational culture model identifies eight cultures organized around a circle, indicating that some cultures are opposite to each other. A rules-oriented culture is opposite to an innovation culture; an internally focused culture is opposed to an externally focused culture; a controlling culture is opposite to a flexible culture; and a goal-oriented culture is opposite to a supportive culture.[10]

These organizational culture models may help to sort out organizational values to some extent, but unfortunately they also oversimplify the diversity of cultural values in organizations. The fact is, there are dozens of individual values, so there are likely

Cirque du Soleil's High-Wire Risk Culture Cirque du Soleil, the entertainment company that combines circus with theater, thrives on a culture of risk and creativity. This culture is apparent in the size and grandeur of its performances. Its most recent production, Ka, is a $150 million extravaganza representing the largest entertainment gamble ever made in Las Vegas. Cirque du Soleil also has a permanent show at Disney World in Florida and five traveling events around the world. Cirque du Soleil also took risks when it opened its first Las Vegas show, Mystère, which was dark and moody—a sharp contrast to the upbeat style of Las Vegas entertainment. Mystère had sellout crowds soon after its opening night. "(We stop growing) if we start being afraid of taking risks and if we start diminishing our creative pertinence," says Guy Laliberté, who founded Cirque du Soleil in 1984.[11]

as many organizational values. Thus we need to be wary of models that reduce the variety of organizational cultures into a few simple categories with catchy labels. They would certainly reflect the values of many organizations, but they may also distort rather than clarify our attempts to diagnose corporate culture.

Organizational Subcultures

When discussing organizational culture, we are actually referring to the *dominant culture*—that is, the themes shared most widely by the organization's members. However, organizations are also comprised of *subcultures* located throughout their various divisions, geographic regions, and occupational groups.[12] Some subcultures enhance the dominant culture by espousing parallel assumptions, values, and beliefs; others are called *countercultures* because they directly oppose the organization's core values.

Subcultures, particularly countercultures, potentially create conflict and dissension among employees, but they also serve two important functions.[13] First, they maintain the organization's standards of performance and ethical behavior. Employees who hold countercultural values are an important source of surveillance and critique over the dominant order. They encourage constructive conflict and more creative thinking about how the organization should interact with its environment. Subcultures prevent employees from blindly following one set of values and thereby help the organization to abide by society's ethical values.

The second function of subcultures is that they are the spawning grounds for emerging values that keep the firm aligned with the needs of customers, suppliers, society, and other stakeholders. Companies eventually need to replace their dominant values with ones that are more appropriate for the changing environment. If subcultures are suppressed, the organization may take longer to discover and adopt values aligned with the emerging environment.

Deciphering Organizational Culture through Artifacts

We can't directly see an organization's cultural assumptions and values. Instead, as Exhibit 16.1 illustrated earlier, we decipher organizational culture indirectly through **artifacts**. Artifacts are the observable symbols and signs of an organization's culture, such as the way visitors are greeted, the organization's physical layout, and how employees are rewarded.[14] Some experts suggest that these artifacts are the essence of organizational culture, whereas others view artifacts as symbols or indicators of culture. Either way, artifacts are important because, as we will learn later, they reinforce and potentially support changes to an organization's culture.

artifacts
The observable symbols and signs of an organization's culture.

Artifacts are also important because they offer the best evidence about a company's culture. Discovering an organization's culture isn't accomplished just by surveying its executives or employees. Instead, to accurately understand the company's dominant values and assumptions, we need to observe workplace behavior, listen to everyday conversations among staff and with customers, study written documents and e-mails, and interview staff about corporate stories. In other words, we need to conduct an anthropological investigation of the company. [15]

The Mayo Clinic recently took this approach to learning about its corporate culture. The Rochester, Minnesota, clinic brought in an anthropologist, who interviewed managers, shadowed employees on duty, joined physicians on patient visits, and posed as a patient to observe what happens in waiting rooms. So, understanding a company's culture involves sampling information from the broad range of organizational artifacts. In this section, we review the four broad categories of artifacts: organizational stories and legends, rituals and ceremonies, language, and physical structures and symbols.

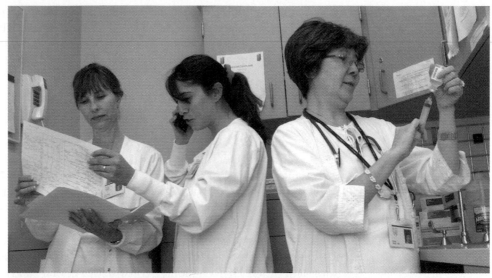

Mayo Clinic's Cultural Expedition The Mayo Clinic has a well-established culture at its original clinic in Rochester, Minnesota; but maintaining that culture in its expanding operations in Florida and Arizona has been challenging. "We were struggling with growing pains; we didn't want to lose the culture, and we were looking at how to keep the heritage alive," explains Matt McElrath, Mayo Clinic human resources director in Arizona. The Mayo Clinic retained anthropologist Linda Catlin to decipher Mayo's culture and identify ways to reinforce it at the two newer sites. Catlin shadowed employees and posed as a patient to observe what happens in waiting rooms. "She did countless interviews, joined physicians on patient visits, and even spent time in the operating room," says McElrath. At the end of her six-week cultural expedition, Catlin submitted a report outlining Mayo's culture and how its satellite operations varied from that culture. The Mayo Clinic adopted all of Catlin's 11 recommendations, such as requiring all new physicians at the three sites to attend an orientation in Rochester where they learn about Mayo's history and values.[16]

Organizational Stories and Legends

Stories permeate strong organizational cultures. Some tales recount heroic deeds by employees; others ridicule past events that deviated from the firm's core values. These stories and legends serve as powerful social prescriptions of the way things should (or should not) be done. They provide human realism to corporate expectations, individual performance standards, and the criteria for getting fired. These stories also create emotions in listeners, which tends to improve their memory of the lessons within the stories. Stories have the greatest effect at communicating corporate culture when they describe real people, are assumed to be true, and are known by employees throughout the organization.[17]

Rituals and Ceremonies

rituals
The programmed routines of daily organizational life that dramatize the organization's culture.

Rituals are the programmed routines of daily organizational life that dramatize an organization's culture. They include how visitors are greeted, how often senior executives visit subordinates, how people communicate with each other, how much time employees take for lunch, and so on. For instance, BMW's fast-paced culture is quite literally apparent in the way employees walk around the German carmaker's offices. "When you move through the corridors and hallways of other companies' buildings, people kind of crawl; they walk slowly," says BMW board of management chairman Helmut Panke. "But BMW people tend to move faster."[18] **Ceremonies** are more formal artifacts than rituals. Ceremonies are planned activities conducted specifically for the benefit of an audience. This would include publicly rewarding (or punishing) employees or celebrating the launch of a new product or newly won contract.

ceremonies
Planned and usually dramatic displays of organizational culture, conducted specifically for the benefit of an audience.

Organizational Language

The language of the workplace speaks volumes about the company's culture. How employees address co-workers, describe customers, express anger, and greet stakeholders are all verbal symbols of cultural values. Employees at The Container Store compliment each other about "being Gumby," meaning that they are being as flexible as the once-popular green toy—going outside their regular jobs to help a customer or another employee. (A human-sized Gumby is displayed at the retailer's headquarters.)[19] Language as a cultural artifact is also apparent in the opening story to this chapter. U.S. Trust executives insisted on using the term *clients* rather than *customers*, the term Schwab executives used freely. This language reflects the long–term, deep relationships that U.S. Trust staff members have with their clients, compared with the more impersonal connections between Schwab's staff members and their customers.

Language also highlights values held by organizational subcultures. For instance, consultants working at Whirlpool kept hearing employees talk about the appliance company's "PowerPoint culture." This phrase, which names Microsoft's presentation software, is a critique of Whirlpool's hierarchical culture in which communication is one-way (from executives to employees.).[20]

Physical Structures and Symbols

Winston Churchill once said, "We shape our buildings; thereafter, they shape us."[21] The former British prime minister was reminding us that buildings both reflect and influence an organization's culture. The size, shape, location, and age of buildings might suggest a company's emphasis on teamwork, environmental friendliness, flexibility, or any other set of values. An extreme example is the "interplanetary headquarters" of Oakley, Inc. The ultrahip eyewear and clothing company built a vaultlike structure in Foothills Ranch, California, complete with towering metallic walls studded with oversize bolts, to represent its secretive and protective culture. "We've always had a fortress mentality," says an Oakley executive. "What we make is gold, and people will do anything to get it, so we protect it."[22]

Even if the building doesn't make much of a statement, there is a treasure trove of physical artifacts inside. Desks, chairs, office space, and wall hangings (or lack of them) are just a few of the items that might convey cultural meaning. Stroll through Wal-Mart's headquarters in Bentonville, Arkansas, and you will find a workplace that almost screams frugality and efficiency. The world's largest retailer has a spartan waiting room for suppliers, rather like government office waiting areas. Visitors pay for their own soft drinks and coffee. In each of the building's inexpensive cubicles, employees sit at inexpensive desks finding ways to squeeze more efficiencies and lower costs out of suppliers as well as their own work processes.[23] Each of these artifacts alone might not say much, but put enough of them together and the company's cultural values become easier to decipher.

After reading the next two sections you should be able to

4. **Identify three functions of organizational culture.**
5. **Discuss the conditions under which cultural strength improves corporate performance.**
6. **Compare and contrast four strategies for merging organizational cultures.**

Is Organizational Culture Important?

Why do executives at the Mayo Clinic, the Container Store, Oakley, BMW, and other companies pay so much attention to organizational culture? The answer is that they believe a strong culture is a competitive advantage. "Culture is one of the most precious things a company has, so you must work harder on it than anything else," says Herb Kelleher, founder of Southwest Airlines. Does corporate culture really make a difference? The answer is yes … potentially. Various studies indicate that companies with strong cultures are more likely to be successful, but only under a particular set of conditions.[24] The explanation of how organizational culture influences corporate prosperity and employee well-being has a few twists and turns, which we walk through in this section.

To begin, the effect of organizational culture depends partly on its strength. Corporate culture *strength* refers to how widely and deeply employees hold the company's dominant values and assumptions. In a strong organizational culture, most employees across all subunits hold the dominant values. These values are also institutionalized through well-established artifacts, thereby making it difficult for those values to change. Furthermore, strong cultures tend to be long-lasting; some can be traced back to the company founder's values and assumptions. In contrast, companies have weak cultures when the dominant values are short-lived and held mainly by a few people at the top of the organization. A strong corporate culture potentially increases a company's success by serving three important functions:

1. *Control system.* Organizational culture is a deeply embedded form of social control that influences employee decisions and behavior.[25] Culture is pervasive and operates unconsciously. You might think of it as an automatic pilot, directing employees in ways that are consistent with organizational expectations.
2. *Social glue.* Organizational culture is the "social glue" that bonds people together and makes them feel part of the organizational experience.[26] Employees are motivated to internalize the organization's dominant culture because this helps fulfill their need for social identity. This social glue is increasingly important as a way to attract new staff and retain top performers.
3. *Sense-making.* Organizational culture assists the sense-making process.[27] It helps employees understand what goes on and why things happen in the company. Corporate culture also makes it easier for them to understand what is expected of them and to interact with other employees who know the culture and believe in it.

Contingencies of Organizational Culture and Performance

Strong cultures are *potentially* good for business, as we just explained, but studies have found only a modestly positive relationship between culture strength and success.[28] Why the weak relationship? One reason is that a strong culture increases organizational performance only when the cultural content is appropriate for the organization's environment (see Exhibit 16.2). Recall from a few pages back that culture *content*

Exhibit 16.2
**Organizational
Culture and
Performance**

refers to the relative ordering of values and assumptions. Trouble occurs when the relative ordering of cultural values is misaligned with its environment. This lack of fit causes employees to make decisions and engage in behaviors that are inconsistent with the company's best interests. Strong cultures create a greater risk than weak cultures when values are misaligned because culture strength indicates that a greater number of employees will be guided by those values and assumptions.

Consider the problems described at the beginning of this chapter regarding Charles Schwab & Co.'s acquisition of U.S. Trust. Schwab's frugal and egalitarian culture helped it to succeed as a discount broker. But when this culture was imposed on U.S. Trust, top-performing brokers defected with their clients. U.S. Trust's existing culture was not perfectly adapted to the times (it lagged competitors with new financial products and was fined for poor record keeping), but Schwab's culture would have been an even worse fit for U.S. Trust's competitive space.

A second reason why companies with strong cultures aren't necessarily more effective is that strong cultures lock decision makers into mental models that blind them to new opportunities and unique problems. Thus strong cultures might cause decision makers to overlook or incorrectly define subtle misalignments between the organization's activities and the changing environment. Several bankrupt steel manufacturers apparently suffered from this problem. "It was 100 years of integrated culture," recalls Mittal Steel vice president John Mang III, who worked at one of the now-bankrupt firms for three decades. "People in the organization are inbreds, including myself. You grew up in the culture; you didn't see anything else. You didn't typically see people even at very high levels in the steel organization coming in from the outside—even financial, executive, or management. It is a culture from within, so you have these rose-colored glasses that everything's fine."[29]

A third consideration is that very strong cultures tend to suppress dissenting subcultural values. As we noted earlier, subcultures encourage constructive conflict, which improves creative thinking and offers some level of ethical vigilance over the dominant culture. In the long run the subculture's nascent values could become important dominant values as the environment changes. Strong cultures suppress subcultures, thereby undermining these benefits.

Adaptive Cultures

adaptive culture
An organizational culture in which employees focus on the changing needs of customers and other stakeholders, and support initiatives to keep pace with those changes.

So far we have learned that strong cultures are more effective when the cultural values are aligned with the organization's environment. Also, no corporate culture should be so strong that it blinds employees to alternative viewpoints or completely suppresses dissenting subcultures. One last point to add to this discussion is that organizations are more likely to succeed when they have an adaptive culture.[30] An **adaptive culture** exists when employees focus on the changing needs of customers and other stakeholders, supporting initiatives to keep pace with these changes. Adaptive cultures have an external focus, and employees assume responsibility for the organization's performance. As a result, they are proactive and quick. Employees seek opportunities rather than waiting for them to arrive. They act quickly to learn through discovery rather than engaging in "paralysis by analysis."

Organizational culture experts are starting to piece together the elements of adaptive cultures.[31] First and foremost, adaptive cultures have an external focus. Employees hold a common mental model that the organization's success depends on continuous change to support stakeholders. Nortel Networks has shifted from telephones to Internet gear. Nokia has moved from toilet paper and rubber boots to cellular telephones. Both of these firms have maintained an adaptive culture because employees believe that change is both necessary and inevitable to keep pace with a changing external environment.

Second, employees in adaptive cultures pay as much attention to organizational processes as they do to organizational goals. They engage in continuous improvement of internal processes (production, customer service, and the like) to serve external stakeholders. Third, employees in adaptive cultures have a strong sense of ownership. They assume responsibility for the organization's performance. In other words, they believe "it's our job" rather than "it's not my job."

Organizational Culture and Business Ethics

Along with other forms of performance, an organization's culture can potentially influence ethical conduct. In fact, in one recent survey executives identified organizational culture as one of the three main influences on ethical conduct at work. (The other two were executive leadership and personal commitment to ethical principles.)[32] This makes sense because, as we learned in Chapter 2, good behavior is driven by ethical values. An organization can guide the conduct of its employees by embedding ethical values in its dominant culture.

Citibank's Culture Pushes Ethical Boundaries Citibank Japan director Koichiro Kitade thrived in Citigroup's intensely bottom-line corporate culture. Each year his group handily exceeded the ever-increasing targets set by Citigroup's top executives in New York. Over six years Citibank Japan increased its clientele tenfold and delivered profits that outscored all other private banks in the company's huge network. Unfortunately the Japanese government's financial watchdog recently concluded that Citibank's culture also encouraged Kitade to push aside ethical and financial compliance rules. Japan's regulator accused Citibank of constructing "a law-evading sales system," citing infractions ranging from grossly overcharging clients to helping them to falsify profit and manipulate stock. With 83 infractions, Citigroup was told to close some of its Japanese operations. "It's our fault, because all we talk about is delivering the numbers. We've done this forever," admits Citigroup chief executive Charles Prince. This photo shows Prince (right) with a colleague bowing at a Tokyo news conference in apology for the violations. Prince fired several top executives in Tokyo and New York and is now on a mission to change Citibank's culture. He has a major challenge ahead of him. Dow Jones news service reports that Citigroup has an "established reputation for pushing the limits of acceptable banking behavior."[34]

Organizational culture is also potentially a source of ethical problems when it applies excessive control over employees. All organizations require some values congruence. As explained in Chapter 2, this congruence ensures that employees make decisions that are compatible with organizational objectives. Congruence also improves employee satisfaction, loyalty, and longevity (that is, it helps create low turnover). But a few organizations imprint their cultural values so strongly on employees that they risk becoming corporate cults. They take over employees' lives and rob people's individualism.

This cultlike phenomenon was apparently one of the factors that led to the downfall of Arthur Andersen. The accounting firm's uniting principle, called "One Firm," emphasized consistent service throughout the world by developing Andersen employees the same way. Andersen carefully selected university graduates with compatible values, then subjected these "green beans" to a powerful indoctrination process to further imprint Andersen's culture. This production of Andersen think-alikes, called "Androids," improved service consistency, but it also undermined the ethics of individualism.[33] Thus an organization's culture should be consistent with society's ethical values, and the culture should not be so strong that it undermines individual freedom.

Merging Organizational Cultures

4C Corporate Culture Clash and Chemistry is a company with an unusual name and mandate. The Dutch consulting firm helps clients determine whether their culture is aligned ("chemistry") or incompatible with ("clash") a potential acquisition or merger partner. The firm also analyzes the company's culture with its strategy. There should be plenty of demand for 4C's expertise. According to various studies, the majority of corporate mergers and acquisitions fail, mostly because corporate leaders are so focused on the financial or marketing logistics of a merger that they fail to conduct due diligence audits on their respective corporate cultures.[35]

Schwab's acquisition of U.S. Trust, described at the beginning of this chapter, is one example. The marriage of AOL Time Warner is another. AOL's culture valued youthful, high-flying, quick deal making, whereas Time Warner had a buttoned-down, hierarchical, and systematic culture.[36] For both Schwab and AOL, the culture clash undermined job performance, increased dysfunctional conflict, and resulted in lost talent.

IBM's acquisition of PricewaterhouseCooper's (PwC) consulting business has recently turned into yet another well-publicized culture clash. IBM employees tend to be cost conscious and flexible, whereas PwC staff are accustomed to flying business class and having large personal offices (IBM workers tend to share office space, called "hot desking"). PwC staff are also much more conservative than their IBM counterparts. At one event in Australia, a senior IBM executive was dressed as American tennis star Andre Agassi. "The IBMers went mad that time—nuts, standing and cheering. They loved it," recalls one onlooker. "The PwC folk were stunned. Silent." Less than two years after IBM had acquired PwC's consulting business, up to a quarter of PwC's partners had apparently quit.[37]

Bicultural Audit

bicultural audit
A diagnosis of cultural relations between companies prior to a merger and a determination of the extent to which cultural clashes are likely to occur.

Organizational leaders can minimize these cultural collisions and fulfill their duty of due diligence by conducting a bicultural audit. A **bicultural audit** diagnoses cultural relations between companies and determines the extent to which cultural clashes will likely occur.[38] The bicultural audit process begins by identifying cultural differences between the merging companies. Next the bicultural audit data are analyzed to determine which differences between the two firms will result in conflict and which cultural values provide common ground on which to build a cultural foundation in the merged organization. The final stage involves identifying strategies and preparing action plans to bridge the two organizations' cultures.

A few years ago pulp and paper conglomerate Abitibi-Price applied a bicultural audit before it agreed to merge with rival Stone Consolidated. Specifically, Abitibi developed the Merging Cultures Evaluation Index (MCEI), an evaluation system that helped Abitibi executives compare its culture with other companies in the industry. The MCEI analyzed several dimensions of corporate culture, such as concentration of power versus diffusion of power, innovation versus tradition, wide versus narrow flow of information, and consensus versus authoritative decision making. Abitibi and Stone executives completed the questionnaire to assess their own culture, then compared the results. The MCEI results, along with financial and infrastructural information, served as the basis for Abitibi-Price to merge with Stone Consolidated to become Abitibi-Consolidated, the world's largest pulp and paper firm.[39]

Strategies to Merge Different Organizational Cultures

In some cases a bicultural audit results in a decision to end merger talks because the two cultures are too different to merge effectively. However, even with substantially different cultures, two companies may form a workable union if they apply the appropriate merger strategy. The four main strategies for merging different corporate cultures are assimilation, deculturation, integration, and separation (see Exhibit 16.3).[40]

Assimilation   Assimilation occurs when employees at the acquired company willingly embrace the cultural values of the acquiring organization. Typically this strategy works best when the acquired company has a weak, dysfunctional culture, whereas the acquiring company's culture is strong and aligned with the external environment. Cultural clashes are less common with assimilation because the acquired firm's culture is weak and employees are looking for better cultural alternatives. Research in Motion (RIM), the Canadian company that makes Blackberry wireless devices, applies the assimilation strategy by

Exhibit 16.3   **Strategies for Merging Different Organizational Cultures**

Merger strategy	Description	Works best when:
Assimilation	Acquired company embraces acquiring firm's culture.	Acquired firm has a weak culture.
Deculturation	Acquiring firm imposes its culture on unwilling acquired firm.	Rarely works—may be necessary only when acquired firm's culture doesn't work but employees don't realize it.
Integration	Combining the two or more cultures into a new composite culture.	Existing cultures can be improved.
Separation	Merging companies remain distinct entities with minimal exchange of culture or organizational practices.	Firms operate successfully in different businesses, requiring different cultures.

Source: Based on ideas in A.R. Malekazedeh and A. Nahavandi, "Making Mergers Work by Managing Cultures," *Journal of Business Strategy,* May/June 1990, pp. 55–57; K.W. Smith, "A Brand-New Culture for the Merged Firm," *Mergers and Acquisitions* 35 (June 2000), pp. 45–50.

deliberately acquiring only small start-up firms. "Small companies...don't have cultural issues," says RIM co-CEO Jim Balsillie, adding that they are typically absorbed into RIM's culture with little fuss or attention.[41]

Deculturation
Assimilation is rare. Employees usually resist organizational change, particularly when they are asked to throw away personal and cultural values. Under these conditions some acquiring companies apply a *deculturation* strategy by imposing their culture and business practices on the acquired organization. The acquiring firm strips away artifacts and reward systems that support the old culture. People who cannot adopt the acquiring company's culture are often terminated.

Deculturation may be necessary when the acquired firm's culture doesn't work but employees aren't convinced of this. However, this strategy is difficult to apply effectively because the acquired firm's employees resist the cultural intrusions from the buying firm, thereby delaying or undermining the merger process. These problems were apparent at U.S. Trust after it was acquired by Charles Schwab & Co.

Integration
A third strategy is to combine the cultures into a new composite culture that preserves the best features of the previous ones. Integration is slow and potentially risky because many forces preserve the existing cultures. Still, this strategy should be considered when the companies have relatively weak cultures or when their cultures include several overlapping values. Integration also works best when people realize that their existing cultures are ineffective and are therefore motivated to adopt a new set of dominant values.

Separation
A separation strategy occurs if the merging companies agree to remain distinct entities with minimal exchange of culture or organizational practices. This strategy is most appropriate when the two merging companies are in unrelated industries or operate in different countries: The most appropriate cultural values tend to differ by industry and national culture. Charles Schwab & Co. tried to apply a separation strategy with U.S. Trust. However, in many companies that attempt this approach, executives in the acquiring firm have difficulty keeping their hands off the acquired firm. It's not surprising, therefore, that only 15 percent of acquisitions leave the purchased organization as a stand-alone unit.[42]

A Marriage of Cultural Separation Cisco Systems, the California-based Internet equipment maker, has acquired approximately 90 companies over the past two decades, most of them small, privately held start-up firms with technical expertise in high-growth niches compatible with Cisco's own products. Cisco typically assimilates the smaller firm into its own culture. Linksys, the home wireless network company was an exception. Linksys employs 400 people and was just a few years younger than Cisco. Furthermore, unlike Cisco, Linksys had developed a low-cost business with mass-market retail channels. To avoid disrupting its success, Cisco made sure that Linksys kept its own culture. Cisco executives were so concerned about this that a "filtering team" was formed to prevent Cisco's culture or its leaders from taking over the smaller enterprise. So far the strategy has worked. Linksys continues to thrive in a competitive low-cost market even though it is wholly owned by Cisco, which focuses on high-end networks.[43]

After reading the next two sections you should be able to

7.   **Identify four strategies to strengthen an organization's culture.**

8.   **Describe the stages of organizational socialization.**

9.   **Explain how realistic job previews assist the socialization process.**

Changing and Strengthening Organizational Culture

Is it possible to change an organization's culture? Yes, but it isn't easy, it rarely occurs quickly, and often the culture ends up changing (or replacing) corporate leaders. Consider the plight of Hewlett-Packard. As Connections 16.1 describes, board members hired outsider Carly Fiorina with specific instructions to change the high-technology firm's famous "HP way" culture. The strategy backfired according to several observers. Why? Because corporate culture is deeply embedded in the collective mindset. Employees don't even question why they believe certain values are appropriate and corresponding behaviors are the right thing to do. Indeed, when outsiders critique those culturally congruent decisions and actions, employees often respond with disbelief that anyone would doubt such logical courses of action. Artifacts further reinforce this cultural mindset.

The lesson here is that changing an organization's culture can be a leader's greatest challenge. At the same time, as we noted earlier, organizational culture can be a powerful influence on a company's success. So how do some people successfully change and strengthen organizational culture? Over the next few pages we highlight four strategies that have had some success. This list, outlined in Exhibit 16.4, is not exhaustive; but each activity seems to work well under the right circumstances.

Exhibit 16.4   **Strategies to Change and Strengthen Organizational Culture**

Actions of founders and leaders

- Symbolize the new culture (or need for one) through memorable events.
- Model the new culture through subtle decisions and actions.

Culturally consistent rewards

- Reward employees for culturally consistent behaviors.
- Reward managers who help employees understand the culture.

Changing and Strengthening Organizational Culture

Selecting and socializing employees

- Hire people whose values are consistent with the culture.
- Inform and indoctrinate new staff about what the culture means.

Aligning artifacts

- Share stories supporting the culture.
- Celebrate goals/milestones to support the culture.
- Inhabit buildings that reflect the culture.

Defeated by the HP Way

Many executives have been driven out of organizations because they tried to change the organization's culture. Carly Fiorina, the former CEO of Hewlett-Packard (HP), was one such casualty. The California-based technology company's legendary culture, known as the "HP Way," revered innovation, employee well-being, and collegial teamwork. It was a role model for cultures in other Silicon Valley companies. But Hewlett-Packard started to lose ground to Dell, Compaq, and other competitors who were responding with more agility and efficiency to customer demands. Furthermore, an internal assessment revealed that Hewlett-Packard's culture had shifted. "The HP Way has been misinterpreted and twisted as a gentle bureaucracy of entitlement instead of a performance-based meritocracy," said Fiorina soon after becoming Hewlett-Packard's CEO.

As Hewlett-Packard's first CEO hired from outside the company, Fiorina's task was to alter the HP Way so the company would become more competitive. She launched "The Rules of the Garage," a set of cultural values with symbolic reference to the Palo Alto garage where founders William Hewlett and David Packard started the company in 1939. Fiorina reinforced these performance-focused values with a customer-driven bonus system and organizational structure. Her biggest initiative was acquiring Compaq, a fast-paced and aggressive competitor from Texas. The merger was intended to inject "a little of Compaq's DNA into the HP Way, especially speed and agility," said a Compaq executive who later took an executive position at Hewlett-Packard.

Hewlett-Packard's acquisition of Compaq seems to have had some effect on Hewlett-Packard's culture—but at a cost. Both board members from the founding families (Hewlett and Packard) quit over the changed culture; Hewlett-Packard lost its status as one of the top 10 best places to work in America (it isn't even on the top 100 today); and Fiorina was ousted as CEO. On the surface, Hewlett-Packard's board lost confidence in Fiorina because she failed to raise the company's profitability and achieve related targets. But sources say that Fiorina also tried to change more of the HP Way than was necessary, which battered employee loyalty, productivity, and ultimately profitability. "A little of the HP Way would probably work pretty well right now," says Quantum CEO and former Hewlett-Packard executive Richard E. Belluzzo soon after Fiorina was fired. "The strength of HP has always been its culture and its people."

Sources: B. Pimentel, "Losing Their Way?" *San Francisco Chronicle*, 6 September 2001; P. Burrows, *Backfire: Carly Fiorina's High-Stakes Battle for the Soul of Hewlett-Packard* (New York: John Wiley & Sons, 2003); C. Swett, "HP Seems to Have Digested Compaq," *Sacramento Bee* (California), 13 May 2003, p. D1; P. Burrows, "The HP Way out of a Morass," *BusinessWeek Online*, 14 February 2005; D. Gillmor, "Getting Back the HP Way," *Computerworld*, 7 March 2005, pp. 24–25.

Actions of Founders and Leaders

An organization's culture begins with its founders and leaders.[44] You can see this at Charles Schwab & Co., where founder Charles Schwab has established a culture that is frugal, egalitarian, and fast-paced. Founders set the tone and develop compatible systems and structures, emphasizing what is most important and what should receive a lower priority. They are often visionaries who provide a powerful role model for others to follow. Experts suggest that a company's culture sometimes reflects the founder's personality, and that this cultural imprint often remains with the organization for decades.

Founders establish an organization's culture, but they and subsequent CEOs can sometimes reshape that culture if they apply the transformational leadership concepts that were described in Chapter 14 and organizational change practices described in Chapter 17. Transformational leaders alter and strengthen organizational culture by communicating and enacting their vision of the future.[45]

Introducing Culturally Consistent Rewards

Reward systems strengthen corporate culture when they are consistent with cultural values. If Carly Fiorina had any success at infusing a performance-oriented culture at Hewlett-Packard, it was in large part because she introduced reward systems that reinforced employee performance. John Deere took a similar approach. When the farm implement manufacturer was reorganized into a team-based structure a few years ago, it replaced its individual-oriented incentive plan with a team-based continuous improvement plan. The team bonus helped to shift John Deere's cultural values so that employees now think in terms of team dynamics and work flow efficiencies.[46]

Aligning Artifacts

Artifacts represent more than just the visible indicators of a company's culture. They are also mechanisms that keep the culture in place. Thus by altering artifacts—or creating new ones—leaders can potentially adjust organizational culture. Consider how Louis Gerstner began the long journey of transforming IBM's culture in the 1990s. Gerstner showed up on the first day wearing a blue shirt. What's so symbolic about the incoming CEO wearing a blue shirt? Quite a lot at IBM, where every male employee wore a neatly starched white shirt. (Several decades earlier, IBM founder Thomas Watson had disapproved of anyone wearing shirts that weren't white.) Gerstner's blue shirt attire wasn't accidental. It was a deliberate signal that he intended to break the technology firm's culture of following mindless rules. He also made the point to everyone that IBM employees are not evaluated by the color of their shirts. Instead they should wear attire appropriate for the occasion, and they are rewarded for their performance.[47]

Buildings and décor are artifacts of an organization's culture, but some leaders are moving into offices that reflect what they want the company's culture to become. National Australia Bank's (NAB) National@Docklands, a low-rise campuslike building in Melbourne's docklands area, is a case in point. The building's open design and colorful décor symbolize a more open, egalitarian, and creative culture, compared to the closed hierarchical culture that NAB executives are trying to shed. The docklands building project was initiated when executives realized that MLC, a financial services firm that NAB had acquired a few years earlier, was able to change its culture after moving into its funky headquarters in Sydney. "There's no doubt that MLC has moved its culture over the last few years to a more open and transparent style which is a good example for the rest of the group to follow," admits a NAB executive.[48]

Corporate cultures are also altered and strengthened through the artifacts of stories and behaviors. According to Max De Pree, former CEO of furniture manufacturer Herman Miller Inc., every organization needs "tribal storytellers" to keep the organization's history and culture alive.[49] Leaders play a role by creating memorable events that symbolize the cultural values they want to develop or maintain. At Wall Street investment firm Goldman Sachs, this leadership function is so important that such people are called "culture carriers." Goldman's senior executives live and breathe the company's culture so much that they can effectively transmit and reinforce that culture.[50] Companies also strengthen culture in new operations by transferring current employees who abide by the culture.

Selecting and Socializing Employees

People at Bristol-Myers noticed that executives hired from the outside weren't as successful as those promoted from within. Within a year, many quit or were fired. When managers looked closely at the problem, they arrived at the following conclusion: "What came through was, those who left were uncomfortable in our culture or violated some core area of our value system," says a Bristol-Myers executive. From this discovery, Bristol-Myers assessed its culture—it's team-oriented, consistent with the firm's research and development roots. Now applicants are carefully screened to ensure that they have compatible values.[51]

Bristol-Myers and a flock of other organizations strengthen and sometimes re-shape their corporate cultures by hiring people with beliefs, values, and assumptions similar to those cultures. They realize that a good fit of personal and organizational values makes it easier for employees to adopt the corporate culture. A good person–organization fit also improves job satisfaction and organizational loyalty because new hires with values compatible to the corporate culture adjust more quickly to the organization.[52]

Job applicants also pay attention to corporate culture during the hiring process. They realize that as employees, they must feel comfortable with the company's values, not just the job duties and hours of work. Thus job applicants tend to look at corporate culture artifacts when deciding whether to join a particular organization. By diagnosing the company's dominant culture, they are more likely to determine whether its values are compatible to their own.

Along with selecting people with compatible values, companies maintain strong cultures through the process of organizational socialization. **Organizational socialization** refers to the process by which individuals learn the values, expected behaviors, and social knowledge necessary to assume their roles in the organization.[53] If a company's dominant values are clearly communicated, job candidates and new hires are more likely to internalize these values quickly and deeply. Socialization is an important process for absorbing corporate culture as well as helping newcomers to adjust to co-workers, work procedures, and other corporate realities. Thus the final section of this chapter looks more closely at the organizational socialization process.

organizational socialization
The process by which individuals learn the values, expected behaviors, and social knowledge necessary to assume their roles in the organization.

Whole Foods Spreads Its Culture like Yogurt How do companies maintain their corporate culture when expanding operations? At Whole Foods Market the solution is yogurt. "One of our secrets is what I refer to as our 'yogurt culture,'" explains Whole Foods cofounder John McKey. This strategy involves transferring employees who carry Whole Foods' unique culture to new stores so recently hired employees learn and embrace that cultural milieu quickly. "For example, in our Columbus Circle store in New York, about 25 percent of the team members transferred from existing stores," McKey recalls. "They were the starting culture for the fermentation that turned Columbus Circle into a true Whole Foods store." Some employees even took lesser titles just to help Columbus Circle adopt Whole Foods' cultural values. For example, the store's two associate store team leaders previously operated their own stores in Georgetown, Maryland, and Albuquerque, New Mexico, before coming to New York.[54]

Organizational Socialization

Nadia Ramos had plenty of job opportunities after she graduated from business school, but Bank of Nova Scotia won the contest hands down. Ramos was impressed by the panel interview with senior commercial banking managers and by the many opportunities to work overseas. But it was the little things that really won Ramos over to the Canadian financial institution. Rather than seeing only the company boardroom and company recruiters, Ramos toured the offices where she would actually work and met with fellow international banking associates, who immediately welcomed her to the team and offered advice for apartment hunting in Toronto. ScotiaBank also assigned a buddy to help Ramos adjust to the workplace over the first two years. "We have to make sure, once they are in the door, that they start having a great experience as an employee—and that we haven't overpromised," says Sylvia Chrominska, ScotiaBank's executive vice president of human resources.[55]

ScotiaBank successfully brings employees into the organization by going beyond selecting applicants with the right competencies. It relies on several organizational socialization practices to help newcomers learn about and adjust to the company's culture, physical layout, procedures, and so on. Research indicates that when employees are effectively socialized into an organization, they tend to perform better and have higher job satisfaction.[56]

Organizational socialization is a process of both learning and adjustment. It is a learning process because newcomers try to make sense of the company's physical workplace, social dynamics, and strategic and cultural environment. They learn about the organization's performance expectations, power dynamics, corporate culture, company history, and jargon. Organizational socialization is also a process of adjustment because individuals need to adapt to their new work environment. They develop new work roles that reconfigure their social identity, adopt new team norms, and practice new behaviors. Research reports that the adjustment process is fairly rapid for many people—usually within a few months. However, newcomers with diverse work experience seem to adjust better than those with limited previous experience, possibly because diverse work experience provides a larger toolkit of knowledge and skills to make the adjustment easier.[57]

Newcomers absorb the organization's dominant culture to varying degrees. Some people deeply internalize the company's culture; a few others rebel against these attempts to change their mental models and values. Ideally newcomers adopt a level of "creative individualism" in which they accept the essential elements of the organization's culture and team norms, yet maintain a healthy individualism that challenges the allegedly dysfunctional elements of organizational life.

Stages of Socialization

Socialization is a continuous process, beginning long before the first day of employment and continuing throughout a person's career within the company. However, it is most intense when people move across organizational boundaries, such as when they first join a company or get transferred to an international assignment. Each of these transitions is a process that can be divided into three stages. Our focus here is on the socialization of new employees, so the three stages are called preemployment socialization, encounter, and role management (see Exhibit 16.5). These stages parallel the individual's transition from outsider to newcomer and then to insider.[58]

Exhibit 16.5 **Stages of Organizational Socialization**

Preemployment socialization (outsider)	**Encounter (newcomer)**	**Role management (insider)**	**Socialization outcomes**
• Learn about the organization and job. • Form employment relationship expectations.	• Test expectations against perceived realities.	• Strengthen work relationships. • Practice new role behaviors. • Resolve work–nonwork conflicts.	• Higher motivation. • Higher loyalty. • Higher satisfaction. • Lower stress. • Lower turnover.

Stage 1: Preemployment Socialization Think back to the months and weeks before you began working in a new job (or attending a new school). You actively searched for information about the company, formed expectations about working there, and felt some anticipation about fitting into that environment. The preemployment socialization stage encompasses all of the learning and adjustment that occurs prior to the first day of work in a new position. In fact, a large part of the socialization adjustment process occurs before the first day of work.[59]

The main problem with preemployment socialization is that individuals are outsiders, so they must rely on friends, employment interviews, recruiting literature, and other indirect information to form expectations about what it is like to work in the organization. Furthermore, the information exchange between applicants and employers is usually less than perfectly honest.[60] Job applicants might distort their résumés, whereas employers hide their blemishes by presenting overly positive images of organizational life. Job applicants avoid asking sensitive questions—such as pay increases and faster promotions—to maintain a good image to recruiters.

To make matters worse, job applicants tend to engage in postdecisional justification during preemployment socialization. Before the first day of work they tend to increase the importance of favorable elements of the job and justify or completely forget about some negative elements. At the same time they reduce the perceived quality of job offers that they turned down. Employers often distort their expectations of new hires in the same way. The result is that both parties develop higher expectations of each other than they will actually experience during the encounter stage.

Stage 2: Encounter The first day on the job typically marks the beginning of the encounter stage of organizational socialization. This is the stage in which newcomers test their prior expectations with the perceived realities. Many companies fail the test because newcomers often believe that their employers are not delivering the promised employment experience. To varying degrees these people have experienced **reality shock**—the stress that results when employees perceive discrepancies between their preemployment expectations and on-the-job reality.[61] The larger the gap, the stronger the reality shock. Reality shock doesn't necessarily occur on the first day; it might develop over several weeks or even months as newcomers form a better understanding of their new work environment. Along with experiencing unmet expectations,

reality shock
Perceived discrepancies between preemployment expectations and on-the-job reality.

reality shock occurs when newcomers are overwhelmed by the experience of sudden entry into a new work environment. In other words, reality shock also includes the stress of information overload and the challenges of adjusting quickly to new roles.

Stage 3: Role Management   During the role management stage in the socialization process, employees settle in as they make the transition from newcomers to insiders. They strengthen relationships with co-workers and supervisors, practice new role behaviors, and adopt attitudes and values consistent with their new positions and organizations. Role management also involves resolving the conflicts between work and nonwork activities. In particular, employees must redistribute their time and energy between work and family, reschedule recreational activities, and deal with changing perceptions and values in the context of other life roles. They must address any discrepancies between their existing values and those emphasized by the organizational culture. New self-identities are formed that are more compatible with the work environment.

Improving the Socialization Process

Before hiring people for its new computer assembly plant in Winston-Salem, North Carolina, Dell Inc. invites applicants to understand the company and the jobs better. "We will discuss the soul of Dell, give them a realistic job preview, and give them the opportunity to complete a job application," explains Ann Artzer, Dell's human resource manager for the plant. "It will be a chance to determine the mutual interest between the candidates and Dell."[62]

realistic job preview (RJP)

The process of giving job applicants a balance of positive and negative information about the job and work context.

Dell improves the socialization process by providing a **realistic job preview (RJP)**—a balance of positive and negative information about the job and work context.[63] As described at the beginning of this section on organizational socialization, the ScotiaBank human resource executive also tries to make sure that the financial institution hasn't overpromised to job applicants. Unfortunately many companies do overpromise. They often exaggerate positive features of a job and neglect to mention undesirable elements, hoping that the best applicants will get "stuck" on the organization. In contrast, an RJP helps job applicants decide for themselves whether their skills, needs, and values are compatible with a job and organization.

Although RJPs scare away some applicants, they tend to reduce turnover and increase job performance.[64] This occurs because RJPs help applicants develop more accurate preemployment expectations, which in turn minimize reality shock. RJPs represent a type of vaccination by preparing employees for the more challenging and troublesome aspects of work life. There is also some evidence that RJPs increase organizational loyalty. A possible explanation for this is that companies providing candid information are easier to trust. They also show respect for the psychological contract and concern for employee welfare.[65]

Socialization Agents   Nadia Ramos received plenty of support to help her adjust to a career at ScotiaBank. As was mentioned at the beginning of this section, Ramos's future co-workers welcomed her to the team and offered advice on finding an apartment. ScotiaBank also assigned an experienced employee (a buddy) to offer Ramos special assistance and guidance. ScotiaBank leaders seem to be aware that a lot of organizational socialization occurs informally through socialization agents, including co-workers, bosses, and friends who work for the company.

Supervisors tend to provide technical information, performance feedback, and information about job duties. They also improve the socialization process by giving newcomers reasonably challenging first assignments, buffering them from excessive demands, and helping them to form social ties with co-workers.[66] Co-workers are particularly important socialization agents because they are easily accessible, can answer questions when problems arise, and serve as role models for appropriate behavior. New employees tend to receive this information and support when co-workers integrate them into the work team. Co-workers also aid the socialization process by being flexible and tolerant in their interactions with these new hires. Newcomers who quickly form social relations with co-workers tend to have a less traumatic socialization experience and are less likely to quit their jobs within the first year of employment.[67] However, co-workers sometimes engage in hazing—the practice of fooling or intimidating newcomers as a practical joke or initiation ritual.

The challenge is for organizations to ensure that co-workers offer the necessary support. ScotiaBank and many other organizations rely on a "buddy system" whereby newcomers are assigned to co-workers as sources of information and social support. Progressive Inc., the Mayfield, Ohio–based insurance firm, relies on current employees to recruit and socialize job applicants. "I think candidates can trust and respect people who already work here," says Jennifer Cohen, Progressive's national employment director. "They get a lot of honest information about the company." ExtendMedia also has a formal buddy system, but equally valuable is the box of doughnuts put on every newcomer's desk on the first day of work. "The [doughnuts] are there to break the ice so that other people come and talk to them. We are introducing people through their stomachs," explains an executive at the interactive media company.[68]

Chapter Summary

Organizational culture is the basic pattern of shared assumptions and values that governs behavior within a particular organization. Assumptions are the shared mental models or theories-in-use on which people rely to guide their perceptions and behaviors. Values are more stable, long-lasting beliefs about what is important. They help us define what is right or wrong, or good or bad, in the world. Culture content refers to the relative ordering of shared values and assumptions.

Organizations have subcultures as well as dominant cultures. Subcultures maintain the organization's standards of performance and ethical behavior. They are also the source of emerging values that replace aging core values.

Artifacts are the observable symbols and signs of an organization's culture. Four broad categories of artifacts include organizational stories and legends, rituals and ceremonies, language, and physical structures and symbols. Understanding an organization's culture requires assessment of many artifacts because they are subtle and often ambiguous.

Organizational culture has three main functions. It is a deeply embedded form of social control. It is also the "social glue" that bonds people together and makes them feel part of the organizational experience. Third, corporate culture helps employees make sense of the workplace.

Companies with strong cultures generally perform better than those with weak cultures, but only when the cultural content is appropriate for the organization's environment. Also, the culture should not be so strong that it drives out dissenting values, which may form emerging values for the future. Organizations should have adaptive cultures so that employees focus on the need for change and support initiatives and leadership that keep pace with these changes.

Mergers should include a bicultural audit to diagnose the compatibility of the organizational cultures. The four main strategies for merging different corporate cultures are integration, deculturation, assimilation, and separation.

Organizational culture may be altered and strengthened through the actions of founders and leaders, the introduction of culturally-consistent rewards, the alignment of artifacts, and the selection and socialization of employees.

Organizational socialization is the process by which individuals learn the values, expected behaviors, and social knowledge necessary to assume their roles in the organization. It is a process of both learning about the work context and adjusting to new work roles, team norms, and behaviors. Employees typically pass through three socialization stages: preemployment, encounter, and role management. To improve the socialization process, organizations should introduce realistic job previews (RJPs) and recognize the value of socialization agents in the process.

Key Terms

adaptive culture, p. 467

artifacts, p. 463

bicultural audit, p. 469

ceremonies, p. 465

organizational culture, p. 460

organizational socialization, p. 475

realistic job preview (RJP), p. 478

reality shock, p. 477

rituals, p. 464

Critical Thinking Questions

1. The Superb Consultants company has submitted a proposal to analyze the cultural values of your organization. The proposal states that Superb has developed a revolutionary new survey to tap a company's true culture. The survey takes just 10 minutes to complete, and the consultants say results can be based on a small sample of employees. Discuss the merits and limitations of this proposal.

2. Some people suggest that the most effective organizations have the strongest cultures. What do we mean by the "strength" of organizational culture, and what possible problems are there with a strong organizational culture?

3. The CEO of a manufacturing firm wants everyone to support the organization's dominant culture of lean efficiency and hard work. The CEO has introduced a new reward system to reinforce this culture and personally interviews all professional and managerial applicants to ensure that they bring similar values to the organization. Some employees who criticized these values had their careers sidelined until they left. Two midlevel managers were fired for supporting contrary values, such as work–life balance. Based on your knowledge of organizational subcultures, what potential problems is the CEO creating?

4. Identify at least two artifacts you have observed in your department or school from each of the four broad categories: (a) organizational stories and legends; (b) rituals and ceremonies; (c) language; and (d) physical structures and symbols.

5. "Organizations are more likely to succeed when they have an adaptive culture." What can an organization do to foster an adaptive culture?

6. Acme Corp. is planning to acquire Beta Corp., which operates in a different industry. Acme's culture is entrepreneurial and fast-paced, whereas Beta employees value slow, deliberate decision making by consensus. Which merger strategy would you recommend to minimize culture shock when Acme acquires Beta? Explain your answer.

7. Suppose you are asked by senior officers of a city government to identify ways to reinforce a new culture of teamwork and collaboration. The senior executive group clearly supports these values, but it wants everyone in the organization to embrace them. Identify four types of activities that would strengthen these cultural values.

8. Progressive, Inc., ExtendMedia, and other organizations rely on current employees to socialize new recruits. What are the advantages of relying on this type of socialization agent? What problems can you foresee (or you have personally experienced) with co-worker socialization practices?

Case Study 16.1 HILLTON'S TRANSFORMATION

Twenty years ago Hillton was a small city (about 70,000 residents) that served as an outer suburb to a large Midwest metropolitan area. The city treated employees like family and gave them a great deal of autonomy in their work. Everyone in the organization (including the two labor unions representing employees) implicitly agreed that the leaders and supervisors of the organization should rise through the ranks based on their experience. Few people were ever hired from the outside into middle or senior positions. The rule of employment at Hillton was to learn the job skills, maintain a reasonably good work record, and wait your turn for promotion.

Hillton has grown rapidly since the mid-1970s. As the population grew, so did the municipality's workforce to keep pace with the increasing demand for municipal services. This meant that employees were promoted fairly quickly and were almost guaranteed employment. In fact, until recently Hillton had never laid off any employee. The organization's culture could be described as one of entitlement and comfort. Neither the elected city council members nor the city manager bothered the department managers about their work. There were few cost controls because rapid growth forced emphasis on keeping up with the population expansion. The public became somewhat more critical of the city's poor service, including road construction at inconvenient times and the apparent lack of respect some employees showed toward taxpayers.

During these expansion years Hillton put most of its money into "outside" (also called "hard") municipal services such as road building, utility construction and maintenance, fire and police protection, recreational facilities, and land use control. This emphasis occurred because an expanding population demanded more of these services, and most of Hillton's senior people came from the outside services group. For example, Hillton's city manager for many years was a road development engineer. The "inside" workers (taxation, community services, and the like) tended to have less seniority, and their departments were given less priority.

As commuter and road systems developed, Hillton attracted more upwardly mobile professionals to the community. Some infrastructure demands continued, but now these suburban dwellers wanted more "soft" services, such as libraries, social activities, and community services. They also began complaining about how the municipality was being run. The population had more than doubled between the 1970s and 1990s, and it was increasingly apparent that the city organization needed more corporate planning, information systems, organization development, and cost control systems. Residents voiced their concerns in various ways that the municipality was not providing the quality of management that they would expect from a city of its size.

In 1996 a new mayor and council replaced most of the previous incumbents, mainly on the platform of improving the municipality's management structure. The new council gave the city manager, along with two other senior managers, an early retirement buyout package. Rather than promoting from the lower ranks, council decided to fill all three positions with qualified candidates from large municipal corporations in the region. The following year several long-term managers left Hillton, and at least half of those positions were filled by people from outside the organization.

In less than two years Hillton had eight senior or departmental managers hired from other municipalities who played a key role in changing the organization's value system. These eight managers became known (often with negative connotations) as the "professionals." They worked closely with each other to change the way middle and lower-level managers had operated for many years. They brought in a new computer system and emphasized cost controls where managers previously had complete autonomy. Promotions were increasingly based more on merit than seniority.

These managers frequently announced in meetings and newsletters that municipal employees must provide superlative customer service, and that Hillton would become one of the most customer-friendly places for citizens and those doing business with the municipality. To this end these managers were quick to support the public's increasing demand for more soft services, including expanded library services and recreational activities. And when population growth flattened for a few years, the city manager and the other professionals gained council support to lay off a few outside workers due to lack of demand for hard services.

One of the most significant changes was that the outside departments no longer held dominant positions in city management. Most of the professional managers had worked exclusively in administrative and related inside jobs. Two had Master of Business Administration degrees. This led to some tension between the professional managers and the older outside managers.

Even before the layoffs, managers of outside departments resisted the changes more than others. These managers complained that their employees with the highest seniority were turned down for promotions. They argued for more budget and warned that infrastructure problems would cause liability problems. Informally these outside managers were supported by the labor union representing outside workers. The union leaders tried to bargain for more job guarantees, whereas the union representing inside workers focused more on improving wages and benefits. Leaders of the outside union made several statements in the local media that the city had "lost its heart" and that the public would suffer from the actions of the new professionals.

DISCUSSION QUESTIONS

1. Contrast Hillton's earlier corporate culture with the emerging set of cultural values.

2. Considering the difficulty in changing organizational culture, why did Hillton's management seem to be successful at this transformation?

3. Identify two other strategies that the city might consider to reinforce the new set of corporate values.

Case Study 16.2 IKEA: SWEDISH FOR CORPORATE CULTURE

BusinessWeek Ikea is the quintessential global cult brand. The furniture retailer has more than 200 stores in several countries, but is just beginning to grow in the United States (where it had only one store in 2000, 25 stores by 2005, and an expected 50 stores by 2010). But Ikea is also a role model of how to nurture an effective corporate culture. Its chief cheerleader is founder Ingvar Kamprad. Although officially retired, Kamprad remains a vital link to the company's culture. For instance, Ikea is still run by managers who were trained and groomed by Kamprad himself.

This *BusinessWeek* case study describes the success of Ikea and provides some insight into its organizational culture. Read through this *BusinessWeek* article at www.mhhe.com/mcshane4e and prepare for the discussion questions below.

Discussion Questions

1. What are the values that dominate Ikea's culture?

2. How does Ikea seem to maintain a strong organizational culture?

3. Ikea is accelerating store rollouts around the world. In this context, how can Ikea maintain its cultural values and ensure that they are embedded in the newly opened stores?

Source: K. Capell, "Ikea: How the Swedish Retailer became a Global Cult Brand," *BusinessWeek,* 14 November 2005, 96

Web Exercise 16.3 DIAGNOSING CORPORATE CULTURE PROCLAMATIONS

PURPOSE To understand the importance and context in which corporate culture is identified and discussed in organizations.

INSTRUCTIONS This exercise is a take-home activity, although it can be completed in classes with computers and Internet connections. The instructor will divide the class into small teams (typically four to five people per team). Each team is assigned a specific industry such as energy, biotechnology, or computer hardware.

The team's task is to search Web sites of several companies in the selected industry for company statements about corporate culture. Use company

Web site search engines (if they exist) to find documents with key phrases such as "corporate culture" or "company values."

DISCUSSION QUESTIONS

1. What values seem to dominate the corporate cultures of the companies you searched? Are these values similar or diverse across companies in the industry?

2. What was the broader content of the Web pages where these companies described or mentioned their corporate cultures?

3. Do companies in this industry refer to their corporate cultures on their Web sites more or less than companies in other industries searched by teams in this class?

Team Exercise 16.4 TRUTH IN ADVERTISING

PURPOSE This team activity is designed to help you diagnose the degree to which recruitment advertisements and brochures provide realistic previews of jobs and organizations.

MATERIALS The instructor will bring to class either recruiting brochures or newspaper advertisements.

INSTRUCTIONS The instructor will place students into teams and give them copies of recruiting brochures and/or advertisements. The instructor might assign one lengthy brochure; alternatively several newspaper advertisements may be assigned. All teams should receive the same materials so that everyone is familiar with the items and results can be compared.

Teams will evaluate the recruiting material(s) and answer the following questions for each item.

DISCUSSION QUESTIONS

1. What information in the text of this brochure or advertisement identifies conditions or activities in this organization or job that some applicants may not like?

2. If there are photographs or images of people at work, do they show only positive conditions, or do any show conditions or events that some applicants may not like?

3. After reading this item, would you say that it provides a realistic preview of the job and/or organization?

Self-Assessment 16.5

CORPORATE CULTURE PREFERENCE SCALE

PURPOSE This self-assessment is designed to help you identify a corporate culture that fits most closely with your personal values and assumptions.

INSTRUCTIONS Read each pair of the statements in the Corporate Culture Preference Scale and circle the statement that describes the organization you would prefer to work in. Then use the scoring key in Appendix B to calculate your results for each subscale. The

scale does not attempt to measure your preference for every corporate culture—just a few of the more common varieties. Also keep in mind that none of these corporate cultures is inherently good or bad. The focus here is on how well you fit within each of them. This exercise is completed alone so you can assess yourself honestly without concerns of social comparison. However, class discussion will focus on the importance of matching job applicants to the organization's dominant values.

Corporate Culture Preference Scale

I would prefer to work in an organization:

1a.	Where employees work well together in teams.	*or* 1b.	That produces highly respected products or services.
2a.	Where top management maintains a sense of order in the workplace.	*or* 2b.	Where the organization listens to customers and responds quickly to their needs.
3a.	Where employees are treated fairly.	*or* 3b.	Where employees continuously search for ways to work more efficiently.
4a.	Where employees adapt quickly to new work requirements.	*or* 4b.	Where corporate leaders work hard to keep employees happy.
5a.	Where senior executives receive special benefits not available to other employees.	*or* 5b.	Where employees are proud when the organization achieves its performance goals.
6a.	Where employees who perform the best get paid the most.	*or* 6b.	Where senior executives are respected.
7a.	Where everyone gets their jobs done like clockwork.	*or* 7b.	That is on top of innovations in the industry.
8a.	Where employees receive assistance to overcome any personal problems.	*or* 8b.	Where employees abide by company rules.
9a.	That is always experimenting with new ideas in the marketplace.	*or* 9b.	That expects everyone to put in 110 percent for peak performance.
10a.	That quickly benefits from market opportunities.	*or* 10b.	Where employees are always kept informed about what's happening in the organization.
11a.	That can quickly respond to competitive threats.	*or* 11b.	Where most decisions are made by the top executives.
12a.	Where management keeps everything under control.	*or* 12b.	Where employees care for each other.

©Copyright 2000 Steven L. McShane.

After reading this chapter, if you need additional information, see www.mhhe.com/mcshane4e for more in-depth interactivities that correspond with this material.

A half-dozen years ago, district and store managers at Home Depot made their own decisions, routinely ignored directives from the head office, and opposed anything that looked like bureaucracy or hierarchy. "Whether it was an aisle, department, or store, you were truly in charge of it," recalls a former store operations manager. This decentralized, freewheeling culture likely fueled Home Depot's phenomenal growth, but it turned into a liability when Lowe's and Wal-Mart brought more intense competition to the marketplace. Home Depot needed more structure and efficiency, so the board of directors plucked Robert Nardelli from General Electric (GE) to become the new CEO and chief architect for change. His objective, not surprisingly, was to "GE-ize" Home Depot, turning it into a much more regimented, centralized, and measurement-focused organization.

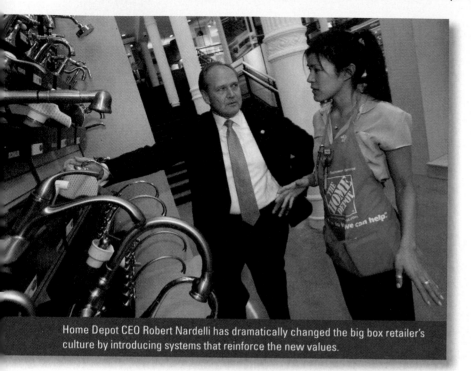

Home Depot CEO Robert Nardelli has dramatically changed the big box retailer's culture by introducing systems that reinforce the new values.

Nardelli took a structural approach to change by introducing precise measures of corporate performance and drilling managers with weekly performance objectives around those metrics. The previous hodge-podge of subjective performance reviews was replaced with one centralized fact-based system to evaluate store managers and weed out poor performers. Nardelli instituted quarterly business review meetings in which objective measures of revenue, margins, inventory turns, cash flow, and other key indicators were analyzed across stores and regions. A two-hour weekly conference call became a ritual in which Home Depot's top executives were held accountable for the previous week's goals.

These changes occurred with lightning speed. "The rate of change internally has to be greater than the rate of change externally or else you're pedaling backward," advises Nardelli. For example, Dennis Donovan, one of several GE alumni Nardelli hired into key management posts, was given 90 days to develop a centralized purchasing system that would leverage more buying power than the existing decentralized process. "In the game of change, velocity is your friend," says Donovan, adding that Nardelli works by a stopwatch, not a time clock.

These rapid structural change interventions have helped Home Depot increase operating efficiency and double sales and profits over Nardelli's first five years. Employee engagement scores initially suffered, but they have now risen above the industry average. However, critics point out that these changes resulted in the departure of almost all of Home Depot's top management as well as ongoing turnover rates well above those at Lowe's. "[Nardelli's] lost so much good talent out of that place," observes one former executive. "The guys I still talk to there say they're waiting for the next shoe to drop."

Equally troubling is that Home Depot's customer service levels have sunk to new lows (one survey ranks Home Depot dead last among major U.S. retailers). "[Nardelli's] made Home Depot much more profitable and more streamlined, but messed up everything that has to do with serving the customer," complains one retail consultant. Wall Street isn't impressed, either; Home Depot's share price hasn't budged since Nardelli arrived.[1]

Organizational Change

After reading this chapter you should be able to

1. Describe the elements of Lewin's force field analysis model.

2. Outline six reasons why people resist organizational change.

3. Discuss six strategies to minimize resistance to change.

4. Outline the conditions for effectively diffusing change from a pilot project.

5. Describe the action research approach to organizational change.

6. Outline the "Four-D" model of appreciative inquiry and explain how this approach differs from action research.

7. Explain how parallel learning structures assist the change process.

8. Discuss four ethical issues in organizational change.

Robert Nardelli's extraordinary effort to transform Home Depot into a more performance-oriented and fact-based organization illustrates several practices, as well as the risks and complexities, of managing organizational change. Nardelli's relative success is due in part to his clear vision and careful realignment of information and reward systems to match the desired future state. At the same time, the change process was punctuated with various forms of resistance—only some of which Nardelli's parachuted team of former GE executives was able to offset.

This chapter investigates the dynamics of change and how to actively manage the change process in organizational settings. It begins by introducing Lewin's model of change and its component parts, including sources of resistance to change, ways to minimize this resistance, and ways to stabilize desired behaviors. Next, this chapter examines three approaches to organizational change: action research, appreciative inquiry, and parallel learning structures. The last section of this chapter considers both cross-cultural and ethical issues in organizational change.

Learning Objectives

After reading this section you should be able to

1. **Describe the elements of Lewin's force field analysis model.**
2. **Outline six reasons why people resist organizational change.**

Lewin's Force Field Analysis Model

Social psychologist Kurt Lewin developed the force field analysis model to help us understand how the change process works (see Exhibit 17.1).[2] Although developed more than 50 years ago, Lewin's **force field analysis** model remains the preeminent way of viewing this process.

One side of the force field model represents the *driving forces* that push organizations toward a new state of affairs. Chapter 1 described some of the driving forces in the external environment, including globalization, virtual work, and a changing workforce. Along with these external forces, corporate leaders create driving forces within the organization so the organization anticipates the external forces. These

force field analysis
Lewin's model of system-wide change that helps change agents diagnose the forces that drive and restrain proposed organizational change.

Exhibit 17.1
Lewin's Force Field Analysis Model

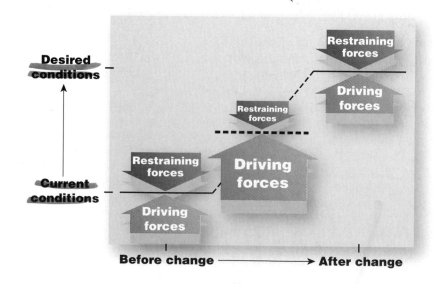

internally originated forces are difficult to apply because they lack external justifications, so effective transformational leadership as well as structural change mechanisms are necessary to legitimate and support internal driving forces.

The other side of Lewin's model represents the *restraining forces* that maintain the status quo. These restraining forces are commonly called "resistance to change" because they appear as employee behaviors that block the change process. Stability occurs when the driving and restraining forces are roughly in equilibrium—that is, when they are of approximately equal strength in opposite directions.

Lewin's force field model emphasizes that effective change occurs by **unfreezing** the current situation, moving to a desired condition, and then **refreezing** the system so that it remains in this desired state. Unfreezing involves producing disequilibrium between the driving and restraining forces. As we describe later, this may occur by increasing the driving forces, reducing the restraining forces, or having a combination of both. Refreezing occurs when the organization's systems and structures are aligned with the desired behaviors. They must support and reinforce the new role patterns and prevent the organization from slipping back into the old ways of doing things. Over the next few pages we use Lewin's model to understand why change is blocked and how the process can evolve more smoothly.

unfreezing
The first part of the change process whereby the change agent produces disequilibrium between the driving and restraining forces.

refreezing
The latter part of the change process in which systems and conditions are introduced that reinforce and maintain the desired behaviors.

Restraining Forces

Economist John Kenneth Galbraith once quipped that when faced with the prospect of changing or proving why change isn't needed, most people get busy on the proof! Jacques Nasser, the former CEO of Ford Motor Company, would likely attest to the

FBI Meets Its Own Resistance In 1993, following the first terrorist attacks on the World Trade Center, the U.S. Federal Bureau of Investigation (FBI) promised to refocus itself from a reactive law enforcement agency (solving crimes) to a proactive domestic intelligence agency (preventing terrorism). Yet two government reports recently concluded that resistance from FBI staff has hampered this change process. One report even stated that the FBI (as well as CIA) "seem to be working harder and harder just to maintain a status quo that is increasingly irrelevant to the new challenges." The reports claim that FBI employees and managers are unable or unwilling to change because solving crimes (rather than intelligence gathering) is burned into their mindset, routines, career paths, and decentralized structure. Most FBI field managers were trained in law enforcement, so they continue to give preferential treatment and resources to enforcement rather than to terrorist prevention initiatives. An information access barrier called "the wall" further isolates FBI intelligence officers from the mainstream criminal investigation staff. Historical turf wars with the CIA have also undermined FBI respect for the bureau's intelligence-gathering initiative. "One of the most difficult things one has to do is to bring an entity through the development of a change of business practices," FBI director Robert Mueller recently admitted.[3]

accuracy of that statement. Over two tumultuous years Nasser tried to shift the auto-maker from engineering prowess to "cyber-savviness," from quality to efficiency, and from an old boys' club to a performance-focused competitor. In one year he rammed through a performance review system that took General Electric nearly a decade to implement. The changes were too much for many Ford employees. Some engineers grumbled that quality had declined; employees stung by the performance system launched age discrimination lawsuits. "When you induce change, you get a reaction," explained a senior Ford executive. "I have letters from employees congratulating us. I have letters from employees doing the opposite." In the latter group was the Ford family, who eventually replaced Nasser with William Clay Ford as CEO.[4]

Of course Ford Motor Company employees aren't the only ones to engage in resistance to change. According to various surveys, more than 40 percent of executives identify employee resistance as the most important barrier to corporate restructuring or improved performance. This is consistent with a recent survey in which most employees admitted they don't follow through with organizational changes because they "like to keep things the way they are" or the changes seem to be too complicated or time-wasting.[5] Robert Nardelli experienced this and other forms of resistance when changing Home Depot's culture and practices. Disenchanted staff began calling the company "Home Despot" because the changes took away their autonomy. Others named it "Home GEpot," a cutting reference to the many former GE executives Nardelli hired into top positions.

Employee resistance takes many forms, including passive noncompliance, complaints, absenteeism, turnover, and collective action (such as strikes and walkouts). In extreme cases of resistance, the chief change agent eventually leaves or is pushed out. This resistance is a symptom of deeper problems in the change process; so rather than directly correcting incidents of passive noncompliance, change agents need to understand why employees are not changing their behavior in the desired ways.[6] In some situations employees may be worried about the *consequences* of change, such as how the new conditions will take away their power and status. In other situations employees show resistance because of concerns about the *process* of change itself, such as the effort required to break old habits and learn new skills. The main reasons why people resist change are shown in Exhibit 17.2 and described on the next page.[7]

Exhibit 17.2
Forces Resisting Organizational Change

- *Direct costs.* People tend to block actions that result in higher direct costs or lower benefits than the existing situation. Many Home Depot employees resisted the change that CEO Robert Nardelli was pushing through because it threatened their autonomy, job security, and career opportunities.

- *Saving face.* Some people resist change as a political strategy to "prove" that the decision is wrong or that the person encouraging change is incompetent. This occurred when senior executives in a manufacturing firm bought a computer other than the system recommended by the information systems department. Soon after the system was in place, several information systems employees let minor implementation problems escalate to demonstrate that senior management had made a poor decision.

- *Fear of the unknown.* People resist change out of worry that they cannot adjust to the new work requirements. This fear of the unknown increases the risk of personal loss. For example, one company owner wanted sales staff to telephone rather than personally visit prospective customers. With no experience in telephone sales, they complained about the changes. Some even avoided the training program that taught them how to make telephone sales.[8]

- *Breaking routines.* Chapter 1 described how organizations need to unlearn, not just learn. This means employees need to abandon behavioral routines that are no longer appropriate. Unfortunately people are creatures of habit. They like to stay within comfort zones by continuing routine role patterns that make life predictable. Consequently many people resist organizational changes that force them out of their comfort zones and require investing time and energy learning new role patterns.

- *Incongruent organizational systems.* Rewards, selection, training, and other control systems ensure that employees maintain desired role patterns. Yet the organizational systems that maintain stability also discourage employees from adopting new ways. The implication, of course, is to do what Nardelli did at Home Depot—alter organizational systems to fit the desired future state. Unfortunately control systems can be difficult to change, particularly when they have supported role patterns that worked well in the past.[9]

- *Incongruent team dynamics.* Teams develop and enforce conformity to a set of norms that guide behavior. However, conformity to existing team norms may discourage employees from accepting organizational change. Team norms that conflict with the desired changes need to be altered.

Learning Objectives

After reading the next two sections you should be able to

3. **Discuss six strategies to minimize resistance to change.**
4. **Outline the conditions for effectively diffusing change from a pilot project.**

Unfreezing, Changing, and Refreezing

According to Lewin's force field analysis model, effective change occurs by unfreezing the current situation, moving to a desired condition, and then refreezing the system so it remains in this desired state. Unfreezing occurs when the driving forces are stronger than the restraining forces. This happens by making the driving forces stronger, weakening or removing the restraining forces, or a combination of both.

With respect to the first option, driving forces must increase enough to motivate change. Change rarely occurs by increasing driving forces alone, however, because the restraining forces often adjust to counterbalance the driving forces. This is rather like the coils of a spring. The harder corporate leaders push for change, the more strongly the restraining forces push back. This antagonism threatens the change effort by producing tension and conflict within the organization. The change effort at Home Depot was likely hampered to some extent by Nardelli's strategy of forcefully pushing the change through without sufficiently addressing the sources of resistance to that change. Only a year or two later, when resistance was still apparent, did Home Depot's executive team address some of the sources of resistance, as will be described later. The preferred option is to both increase the driving forces and reduce or remove the restraining forces. Increasing the driving forces creates an urgency for change, whereas reducing the restraining forces minimizes resistance to change.

Creating an Urgency for Change

It is by now cliché to say that organizations today operate in more dynamic, fast-paced environments than they did a few decades ago. These environmental pressures represent the driving forces that push employees out of their comfort zones. They energize people to face the risks that change creates. In many organizations, however, corporate leaders buffer employees from the external environment to such an extent that these driving forces are hardly felt by anyone below the top executive level. The result is that employees don't understand why they need to change, and leaders are surprised when their change initiatives do not have much effect. Thus the change process must begin by ensuring that employees feel an urgency to change; this typically occurs by informing them about competitors, changing consumer trends, impending government regulations, and other driving forces.[10]

DaimlerChrysler took this approach after its initial attempt to create a team-based organizational structure met with resistance at its Belvidere, Illinois, assembly plant. "There is a need to change," says Belvidere plant manager Kurt Kavajecz. The problem, he explains, is that employees didn't see the need for change. They knew that "we build cars pretty well...So why do we have to change?" To develop a stronger urgency to change, Kavajecz told employees about the challenges the company faced. "If you show them what's going on in the industry, if you give them the information, the data on why we are changing, at the end of the presentation, they get it. They see that plants are closing and jobs are going away. We talk very openly about those things, and they understand why we're changing." The Belvidere plant eventually introduced team-based work.[11]

Customer-Driven Change   Another way to fuel the urgency to change is by putting employees in direct contact with customers. Dissatisfied customers represent a compelling driving force for change because of the adverse consequences for the organization's survival and success. Customers also provide a human element that further energizes employees to change current behavior patterns.[12]

Executives at Shell Europe applied customer-driven change when they discovered that middle managers seemed blissfully unaware that Shell was neither achieving its financial goals nor satisfying customer needs. So to create an urgency for change, the European managers were loaded onto buses and taken out to talk with customers and employees who worked with customers every day. "We called these 'bus rides.' The idea was to encourage people to think back from the customer's perspective rather than from the head office," explains Shell Europe's vice president of retailing. "The

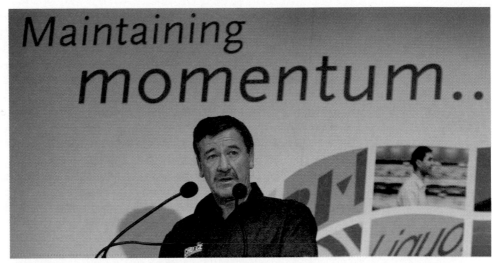

Coles Myer Chief Maintains the Momentum for Change Coles Myer chief executive John Fletcher has led the challenging task of transforming Australia's second largest retailer into a more nimble and customer-focused organization. The change process is starting to show positive results, including a more engaged workforce and better customer service. But Fletcher points out that as the company becomes more successful, his role as a change agent becomes even more difficult. "The thing now is to maintain momentum; it's critical in change programs when things start to look good," Fletcher advises. "Change programs are easier when things are bad. When things improve, people relax and think, we're there."[13]

bus rides were difficult for a lot of people who, in their work history, had hardly ever had to talk to a customer and find out what was good and not so good about Shell from the customer's standpoint."[14]

Urging Change without External Forces   Exposing employees to external forces can strengthen the urgency for change, but leaders often need to begin the change process before problems come knocking at the company's door. "You want to create a burning platform for change even when there isn't a need for one," says Steve Bennett, CEO of financial software company Intuit.[15] Creating an urgency for change when the organization is riding high requires a lot of persuasive influence that helps employees visualize future competitive threats and environmental shifts.

For instance, Apple Computer's iPod dominates the digital music market, but Steve Jobs wants the company to be its own toughest competitor. Just when sales of the iPod Mini were soaring, Jobs challenged a gathering of 100 top executives and engineers to develop a better product to replace it. "Playing it safe is the most dangerous thing we can do," Jobs warned. Nine months later, the company launched the iPod Nano, which replaced the still-popular iPod Mini before competitors could offer a better alternative.[16]

Reducing the Restraining Forces

Effective change requires more than making employees aware of the driving forces. It also involves reducing or removing the restraining forces. Exhibit 17.3 summarizes six ways to overcome employee resistance. Communication, learning, employee

Exhibit 17.3   Strategies to Minimize Resistance to Change

Strategy	Example	When Used	Problem
Communication	Customer complaint letters are shown to employees.	When employees don't feel an urgency for change, or don't know how the change will affect them.	Time-consuming and potentially costly.
Learning	Employees learn how to work in teams as company adopts a team-based structure.	When employees need to break old routines and adopt new role patterns.	Time-consuming and potentially costly.
Employee involvement	Company forms a task force to recommend new customer service practices.	When the change effort needs more employee commitment, some employees need to save face, or employee ideas would improve decisions about the change strategy.	Very time-consuming. Might also lead to conflict and poor decisions if employees' interests are incompatible with organizational needs.
Stress management	Employees attend sessions to discuss their worries about the change.	When communication, training, and involvement do not sufficiently ease employee worries.	Time-consuming and potentially expensive. Some methods may not reduce stress for all employees.
Negotiation	Employees agree to replace strict job categories with multiskilling in return for increased job security.	When employees will clearly lose something of value from the change and would not otherwise support the new conditions. Also necessary when the company must change quickly.	May be expensive, particularly if other employees want to negotiate their support. Also tends to produce compliance but not commitment to the change.
Coercion	Company president tells managers to "get on board" the change or leave.	When other strategies are ineffective and the company needs to change quickly.	Can lead to more subtle forms of resistance, as well as long-term antagonism with the change agent.

Sources: Adapted from J.P. Kotter and L.A. Schlesinger, "Choosing Strategies for Change," *Harvard Business Review* 57 (1979), pp. 106–14; P.R. Lawrence, "How to Deal With Resistance to Change," *Harvard Business Review,* May–June 1954, pp. 49–57.

involvement, and stress management try to reduce the restraining forces and, if feasible, should be attempted first.[17] However, negotiation and coercion are necessary for people who will clearly lose something from the change and when the speed of change is critical.

Communication   Honest and frequent communication is the highest priority and first strategy required for any organizational change.[18] Communication improves the change process in at least two ways. First, as was mentioned earlier, leaders develop an urgency to change by candidly telling employees about the driving forces for change. Whether through town hall meetings with senior management or by directly meeting with disgruntled customers, employees become energized to change. Second, communication can potentially reduce fear of the unknown. The more corporate leaders communicate their images of the future, the more easily employees can visualize their own role in that future. This effort may also begin the process of adjusting team norms to be more consistent with the new reality.

Learning

Learning is an important process in most change initiatives because employees need new knowledge and skills to fit the organization's evolving requirements. When a company introduces a new sales database, for instance, representatives must learn how to adapt their previous behavior patterns to benefit from the new system. Action learning, which was described in Chapter 3, is another potentially powerful learning process for organizational change because it develops management skills while discovering ways to improve the organization.[19] Coaching is yet another form of learning that provides more personalized feedback and direction during the learning process. Coaching and other forms of learning are time-consuming, but they help employees break routines by learning new role patterns.

Employee Involvement

Except in times of extreme urgency or where employee interests are highly incompatible with the organization's needs, employee involvement is almost an essential part of the change process. Rather than viewing themselves as agents of someone else's decision, employees prefer to feel personally responsible for the success of the change effort.[20] Involvement also minimizes problems of saving face and fear of the unknown. Furthermore, the complexity of today's work environment demands that more people provide ideas regarding the best direction of the change effort.

Employee involvement was not part of Robert Nardelli's game plan for change when he first arrived at Home Depot (see the opening vignette to this chapter). But after 18 months of resistance from store and district managers, Home Depot's senior management team held several five-day "learning forums" that tried to make these managers feel more involved in the change process. In particular, the sessions challenged staff members to think through how they would change the home improvement retailer. "Large-scale organizational change is not a spectator sport, and it's easy to be a cynic when you're in the stands," says Dennis Donovan, the Home Depot executive who led the learning forums.

The problem with Home Depot's "learning forum" strategy is that the sessions began long after Nardelli had launched many of the changes, thereby making it difficult for managers to feel that they were part of the change initiative. In contrast, Carlos Ghosn relied on employee involvement from the outset of an important change process at Nissan Motor Company. As Connections 17.1 describes, Ghosn formed a dozen cross-functional management teams and gave them three months to identify ways to save the company from possible bankruptcy.

Minimizing resistance to change through employee involvement is also possible in large organizations through **future search** events. Future search conferences "put the entire system in the room," meaning that they try to involve as many employees and other stakeholders as possible associated with the organizational system. These multiday events ask participants to identify trends or issues and establish strategic solutions for those conditions.[21]

In the corporate world, Microsoft, the U.S. Forest Service, and Peco Energy have used future search conferences to assist the change process. Every five years Whole Foods Market gathers together several hundred employees, shoppers, and shareholders for a future search meeting to help identify new directions for the food retailer. Search conferences have been more widely used as a form of community involvement. The State of Washington Department of Corrections recently held a future search event in which a representative 75 employees and managers reached a consensus about the department's future direction. Specific executives in the department were then assigned specific recommendations to ensure that the conference results were put into place.[22]

future search
Systemwide group sessions, usually lasting a few days, in which participants identify trends and identify ways to adapt to those changes.

Carlos Ghosn Relies on High Involvement to Transform Nissan

Nissan Motor Company was on the brink of bankruptcy when French automaker Renault purchased a controlling interest and installed Carlos Ghosn as the effective head of the Japanese automaker. Along with Nissan's known problems of high debt and plummeting market share, Ghosn (pronounced "gone") saw that Nissan managers had no apparent sense of urgency for change. "Even though the evidence is against them, they sit down and they watch the problem a little bit longer," says Ghosn.

Ghosn's challenge was to act quickly, yet minimize the inevitable resistance that arises when an outsider tries to change traditional Japanese business practices. "I was non-Nissan, non-Japanese," he says. "I knew that if I tried to dictate changes from above, the effort would backfire, undermining morale and productivity. But if I was too passive, the company would simply continue its downward spiral."

To resolve this dilemma, Ghosn formed nine cross-functional teams of 10 middle managers each, giving them the mandate to identify innovative proposals for a specific area (marketing, manufacturing, and so on) within three months. Each team could form subteams with additional people to analyze issues in more detail. In all, over 500 middle managers and other employees were involved in the so-called "Nissan Revival Plan."

After a slow start—Nissan managers weren't accustomed to such authority or working with colleagues across functions or cultures—ideas began to flow as Ghosn stuck to his deadline, reminded team members of the automaker's desperate situation, and encouraged teams to break traditions. Three months later the nine teams submitted a bold plan to close three assembly plants, eliminate thousands of jobs, cut the number of suppliers by half, reduce purchasing costs by 20 percent, return to profitability, cut the company's debt by half, and introduce 22 new models within the next two years.

Although risky, Ghosn accepted all of the proposals. Moreover, when revealing the plan publicly on the eve of the annual Tokyo Motor Show, Ghosn added his own commitment to the plan: "If you ask people to go through a difficult period of time, they have to trust that you're sharing it with them," Ghosn explains. "So I said that if we did not fulfill our commitments, I would resign."

Ghosn's strategy for organizational change and the Nissan Revival Plan worked. Within 12 months the automaker had increased sales and market share and posted its first profit in seven years. The company has introduced innovative models and expanded operations. Ghosn has received high praise throughout Japan and abroad and has since become head of Renault.

Sources: C. Lebner, "Nissan Motor Co.," *Fast Company,* July 2002, p. 80; C. Dawson, "On Your Marks," *Business Week,* 17 March 2003, p. 52; D. Magee, *Turn Around: How Carlos Ghosn Rescued Nissan* (New York: HarperCollins, 2003); C. Ghosn and P. Riès, *Shift: Inside Nissan's Historic Revival* (New York: Currency Doubleday, 2005).

Carlos Ghosn launched a turnaround at Nissan Motor Company that saved the Japanese automaker and relied on change management practices rarely seen in Japan.

Future search meetings potentially minimize resistance to change and assist the quality of the change process, but they also have limitations.[23] One problem is that involving so many people invariably limits the opportunity to contribute and increases the risk that a few people will dominate the process. Another concern is that these events generate high expectations about an ideal future state that is difficult to satisfy in practice. Furthermore, some executives forget that future search conferences and other forms of employee involvement require follow-up action. If employees do not see meaningful decisions and actions resulting from these meetings, they begin to question the credibility of the process and are more cynical of similar subsequent change management activities.[24]

Stress Management   Organizational change is a stressful experience for many people because it threatens self-esteem and creates uncertainty about the future. Communication, learning, and employee involvement can reduce some of these stressors. However, research indicates that companies also need to introduce stress management practices to help employees cope with the changes.[25] In particular, stress management minimizes resistance by removing some of the direct costs and fear of the unknown of the change process. Stress also saps energy, so minimizing stress potentially increases employee motivation to support the change process.

Wachovia Corp. was aware of the need for stress management when it merged with First Union Corp. The Charlotte, North Carolina–based financial institution set up a toll-free telephone number that employees and other stakeholders could call for updates on the merger process. It also dispatched 400 middle and upper-level managers called "ambassadors" to keep everyone informed. Wachovia offered special sessions to help employees cope with change and stress. Shortly after the merger was announced, the company sent out a memo reminding people about the company's employee assistance counseling service.[26]

Negotiation   As long as people resist change, organizational change strategies will require some influence tactics. Negotiation is a form of influence that involves the promise of benefits or resources in exchange for the target person's compliance with the influencer's request. This strategy potentially activates those who would otherwise lose out from the change. However, it tends to merely gain compliance rather than commitment to the change effort, so it might not be effective in the long term.

Coercion   If all else fails, leaders can use coercion to change organizations. Coercion can include persistently reminding people of their obligations, frequently monitoring behavior to ensure compliance, confronting people who do not change, and using threats of sanctions to force compliance. Replacing people who will not support the change is an extreme step, but this is fairly common in senior management ranks. The opening story to this chapter described how almost all of Home Depot's top management team departed within one year after Robert Nardelli arrived. Many of these people did not leave voluntarily.

Replacing staff is a radical form of organizational "unlearning" (see Chapter 1) because replacing executives removes knowledge of the organization's past routines. This potentially opens up opportunities for new practices to take hold.[27] At the same time, coercion is a risky strategy because survivors (employees who are not fired) may have less trust in corporate leaders and engage in more political tactics to protect their own job security. Forcing people to leave isn't always necessary, even during times of radical change. One of the notable features of the turnaround at Nissan Motor Company, described earlier in Connections 17.1, was that few executives were replaced. More generally, various forms of coercion may change behavior through compliance, but they won't develop commitment to the change effort (see Chapter 12).

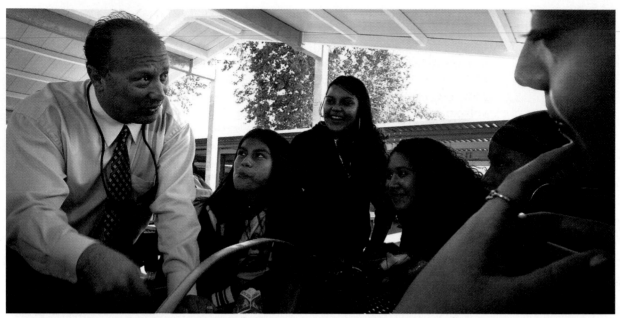

Change the School by Changing the Principal A few years ago, test results at Sun Valley Middle School were so low that the San Fernando Valley, California, school was put on a U S. federal government watch list for closer scrutiny. The Los Angeles unified school district tried to help the principal and staff to improve, but to no avail. When a state audit reported that the school suffered from poor management, unsanitary conditions, and uneven classroom instruction, the school district applied a more radical change strategy: It replaced Sun Valley's principal and four assistant principals with new leaders. Sun Valley's new principal, Jeff Davis (shown with students in this photo), introduced extra English language instruction, reorganized class locations, and launched team teaching to foster a more collegial atmosphere among staff. Sun Valley still has a long way to go, but student test scores in math and English have tripled over the past three years. "That school is absolutely headed in the right direction," says Sue Shannon, superintendent of schools in the eastern San Fernando Valley.[28]

Refreezing the Desired Conditions

Unfreezing and changing behavior patterns won't result in lasting change. People are creatures of habit, so they easily slip back into past patterns. Therefore leaders need to refreeze the new behaviors by realigning organizational systems and team dynamics with the desired changes.[29] This is the main change strategy that helped Robert Nardelli transform Home Depot. The former GE executive introduced new information systems and realigned the reward system to support the desired future state. Feedback, organizational structures, and physical layout of buildings are among the other tools used to refreeze desired behaviors.

Strategic Visions, Change Agents, and Diffusing Change

Kurt Lewin's force field analysis model is a useful template to explain the dynamics of organizational change. But it overlooks three other ingredients in effective change processes: strategic visions, change agents, and diffusing change. Every successful change requires a well-articulated and appealing vision of the desired future state.[30] We can see this critical element in the opening vignette. Robert Nardelli had a clear vision of what he wanted Home Depot to become. Similarly, A.G. Lafley was able to revive Procter & Gamble's flagging sales by describing and finding ways to support a much more creative and customer-focused culture. Generally the leader's vision provides a sense of direction and establishes the critical success factors against which the real changes are evaluated. It also minimizes employee fear of the unknown and provides a better understanding of what behaviors employees must learn for the future state.

Change Agents

Every organizational change, whether large or small, requires one or more change agents. A **change agent** is anyone who possesses enough knowledge and power to guide and facilitate the change effort. Change agents come in different forms, and more than one person is often required to serve in these different roles. Transformational leaders such as Robert Nardelli and A.G. Lafley are the primary agents of change because they form a vision of the desired future state, communicate that vision in ways that are meaningful to others, behave in ways that are consistent with the vision, and build commitment to the vision.[31] Transformational leaders are the architects who shape the overall direction for the change effort and motivate employees to achieve that objective.

Organizational change also requires transactional leaders who implement the change by aligning the daily behavior of individual employees with the organization's new goals.[32] If a company wants to provide better customer service, then supervisors and other transactional leaders need to arrange rewards, resources, feedback, and other conditions that support better customer service behaviors in employees. Consultants from either inside or outside the organization represent a third change agent role. Consultants typically bring unique expertise to the change process through a toolkit of change processes, some of which we introduce later in this chapter. Finally, just as employees are encouraged to become leaders anytime and anywhere, they also can assist the change process as role models for others to follow.

Diffusion of Change

Change agents often test the transformation process with a pilot project, and then diffuse what has been learned from this experience to other parts of the organization. Unlike centralized, systemwide changes, pilot projects are more flexible and less risky.[33] The pilot project approach also makes it easier to select organizational groups that are most ready for change, which increases the pilot project's success.

But how do we ensure that the change process started in the pilot project is adopted by other segments of the organization? The MARS model introduced in Chapter 2 offers a useful template to organize the answer to this question. First, employees are more likely to adopt the practices of a pilot project when they are motivated to do so.[34] This occurs when they see that the pilot project is successful and people in the pilot project receive recognition and rewards for changing their previous work practices. Diffusion also requires supervisor support and reinforcement of the desired behaviors. More generally, change agents need to minimize the sources of resistance to change that we discussed earlier in this chapter.

Second, employees must have the ability—the required skills and knowledge—to adopt the practices introduced in the pilot project. According to innovation diffusion studies, people adopt ideas more readily when they have an opportunity to interact and learn from others who have already applied the new practices.[35] Thus pilot projects get diffused when employees in the original pilot are dispersed to other work units as role models and knowledge sources.

Third, pilot projects get diffused when employees have clear role perceptions; that is, they understand how the practices in a pilot project apply to them even though the change is applied in a completely different functional area. For instance, accounting department employees won't easily recognize how they can adopt quality improvement practices developed by employees in the production department. The challenge here is for change agents to provide guidance that is neither too specific (because it might not seem relevant to other areas of the organization) nor too abstract (because this makes the instructions too vague). Finally, employees require supportive situational factors, including the resources and time necessary to adopt the practices demonstrated in the pilot project.

Learning Objectives

After reading the next two sections you should be able to

5. **Describe the action research approach to organizational change.**

6. **Outline the "Four-D" model of appreciative inquiry and explain how this approach differs from action research.**

7. **Explain how parallel learning structures assist the change process.**

8. **Discuss four ethical issues in organizational change.**

Three Approaches to Organizational Change

So far this chapter has examined the dynamics of change that occur every day in organizations. However, organizational change agents and consultants also apply various approaches to organizational change. This section introduces three of the leading approaches to organizational change: action research, appreciative inquiry, and parallel learning structures.

Action Research Approach

action research

A data-based, problem-oriented process that diagnoses the need for change, introduces the intervention, and then evaluates and stabilizes the desired changes.

Along with introducing the force field model, Kurt Lewin recommended an **action research** approach to the change process. Action research takes the view that meaningful change is a combination of action orientation (changing attitudes and behavior) and research orientation (testing theory).[36] On one hand, the change process needs to be action-oriented because the ultimate goal is to bring about change. An action orientation involves diagnosing current problems and applying interventions that resolve those problems. On the other hand, the change process is a research study because change agents apply a conceptual framework (such as team dynamics or organizational culture) to a real situation. As with any good research, the change process involves collecting data to diagnose problems more effectively and to systematically evaluate how well the theory works in practice. In other words, action research embraces the notion of organizational learning and knowledge management (see Chapter 1).[37]

Within this dual framework of action and research, the action research approach adopts an open systems view. It recognizes that organizations have many interdependent parts, so change agents need to anticipate both the intended and unintended consequences of their interventions. Action research is also a highly participative process because open systems change requires both the knowledge and commitment of members within that system. Indeed, employees are essentially co-researchers as well as participants in the intervention. Overall, action research is a data-based, problem-oriented process that diagnoses the need for change, introduces the intervention, and then evaluates and stabilizes the desired changes (see Exhibit 17.4).[38]

Exhibit 17.4   **The Action Research Process**

| Form client–consultant relationship. | **Diagnose need for change**
• Gather data.
• Analyze data.
• Decide objectives. | **Introduce intervention**
• Implement the desired incremental or quantum change. | **Evaluate and stabilize change**
• Determine the change effectiveness.
• Refreeze new conditions. | Disengage consultant's services. |

1. *Form client–consultant relationship*–Action research usually assumes that the change agent originates outside the system (as does a consultant), so the process begins by forming the client–consultant relationship. Consultants need to determine the client's readiness for change, including whether people are motivated to participate in the process, are open to meaningful change, and possess the abilities to complete the process.

2. *Diagnose the need for change*–Action research is a problem-oriented activity that carefully diagnoses the problem through systematic analysis of the situation. Organizational diagnosis identifies the appropriate direction for the change effort by gathering and analyzing data about an ongoing system, such as through interviews and surveys of employees and other stakeholders. Organizational diagnosis also includes employee involvement in agreeing on the appropriate change method, the schedule for these actions, and the expected standards of successful change.

3. *Introduce intervention*–This stage in the action research model applies one or more actions to correct the problem. It may include any of the prescriptions mentioned in this textbook, such as building more effective teams, managing conflict, building a better organizational structure, or changing the corporate culture. An important issue is how quickly the changes should occur.[39] Some experts recommend *incremental change* in which the organization fine-tunes the system and takes small steps toward a desired state. Others claim that *quantum change* is often required, in which the system is overhauled decisively and quickly. Quantum change is usually traumatic to employees and offers little opportunity for correction. But incremental change is also risky when the organization is seriously misaligned with its environment, thereby threatening its survival.

4. *Evaluate and stabilize change*–Action research recommends evaluating the effectiveness of the intervention against the standards established in the diagnostic stage. Unfortunately, even when these standards are clearly stated, the effectiveness of an intervention might not be apparent for several years or might be difficult to separate from other factors. If the activity has the desired effect, the change agent and participants need to stabilize the new conditions. This refers to the refreezing process that was described earlier. Rewards, information systems, team norms, and other conditions are redesigned to support the new values and behaviors.

The action research approach has dominated organizational change thinking since it was introduced in the 1940s. However, some experts complain that the problem-oriented nature of action research–in which something is wrong that must be fixed–focuses on the negative dynamics of a group or system rather than its positive opportunities and potential. This concern with action research has led to the development of a more positive approach to organizational change called *appreciative inquiry*.[40]

Appreciative Inquiry Approach

appreciative inquiry
An organizational change process that directs attention away from the group's own problems and focuses participant's on the group's potential and positive elements.

Appreciative inquiry tries to break out of the problem-solving mentality of traditional change management practices by reframing relationships around the positive and the possible. It searches for organizational (or team) strengths and capabilities, then adapts or applies that knowledge for further success and well-being. Appreciative inquiry is therefore deeply grounded in the emerging philosophy of *positive organizational behavior* (a variation of *positive psychology*), which focuses on building positive qualities and traits within individuals or institutions as opposed to focusing just on trying to fix what might be wrong with them. In other words, this approach emphasizes building on strengths rather than trying to correct weaknesses.[41]

Appreciative inquiry typically directs its inquiry toward successful events and successful organizations or work units. This external focus becomes a form of behavioral modeling, but it also increases open dialogue by redirecting the group's attention away from its own problems. Appreciative inquiry is especially useful when participants are aware of their "problems" or already suffer from negativity in their relationships. The positive orientation of appreciative inquiry enables groups to overcome these negative tensions and build a more hopeful perspective of their future by focusing on what is possible. [42]

The "Four-D" model of appreciative inquiry (named after its four stages) shown in Exhibit 17.5 begins with *discovery*—identifying the positive elements of the observed events or organization.[43] This might involve documenting positive customer experiences elsewhere in the organization. Or it might include interviewing members of another organization to discover its fundamental strengths. As participants discuss their findings, they shift into the *dreaming* stage by envisioning what might be possible in an ideal organization. By directing their attention to a theoretically ideal

Canadian Tire's Appreciative Journey After effectively battling the American juggernauts Wal-Mart and Home Depot over the past decade, Canadian Tire's executive team wanted to hear from employees and store owners about what made the Canadian hardware and auto parts retailer so successful, then rebuild its core values around those positive experiences. Appreciative inquiry played an important role in this re-envisioning process. Internal consultants conducted detailed interviews with 377 staff members across the organization, asking each to describe occasions where they felt Canadian Tire was working at its best and what they valued most about the company. Some people described the excitement of holiday season where products were flying out the door. Others recalled the teamwork of employees volunteering to work late to clean up a store after a major delivery. These appreciative incidents were organized around six team values (owners, driven, accountable, and so on), which the executive team discussed and affirmed. Canadian Tire then held a one-day conference in which middle and senior managers developed a common understanding of these values. Next, store managers discussed the six team values with their staff members and participated in an appreciative exercise in which employees visualized a good news story about Canadian Tire's success.[44]

Exhibit 17.5   The "Four-D" Model of Appreciative Inquiry

Source: Based on F.J. Barrett and D.L. Cooperrider, "Generative Metaphor Intervention: A New Approach for Working with Systems Divided by Conflict and Caught in Defensive Perception," *Journal of Applied Behavioral Science* 26 (1990), p. 229; D. Whitney and C. Schau, "Appreciative Inquiry: An Innovative Process for Organization Change," *Employment Relations Today* 25 (Spring 1998), pp.11–21; J. M. Watkins and B.J. Mohr, *Appreciative Inquiry: Change at the Speed of Imagination* (San Francisco: Jossey-Bass, 2001), pp. 25, 42–45.

organization or situation, participants feel safer revealing their hopes and aspirations than if they were discussing their own organization or predicament.

As participants make their private thoughts public to the group, the process shifts into the third stage, called *designing*. Designing involves dialogue in which participants listen with selfless receptivity to each other's models and assumptions and eventually form a collective model for thinking within the team. In effect, they create a common image of what should be. As this model takes shape, group members shift the focus back to their own situation. In the final stage of appreciative inquiry, called *delivering*, participants establish specific objectives and direction for their own organization based on their model of what will be.

Appreciative inquiry was developed 20 years ago, but it really gained popularity only within the past few years, partly due to success stories at the U.S. Environmental Protection Agency, AVON Mexico, American Express, Green Mountain Coffee Roasters, and Hunter Douglas, among others.[45] At AVON Mexico, for example, a team of employees and consultants interviewed people for their stories illustrating best practices in gender equality. These stories were presented at two day sessions, and participants built on these best practices to discover how AVON could extend these experiences. Over the next few years the company won the Catalyst award for gender equality; its profits increased dramatically (attributed partly to the appreciative inquiry process); and women found their way into more senior positions at AVON Mexico.

Although appreciative inquiry shows promise as an approach to organizational change, experts warn that it requires a particular mindset among participants in which they are willing to let go of the problem-oriented approach and in which leaders are willing to accept appreciative inquiry's less structured process.[46] Another concern is that research has not yet examined the contingencies of this approach.[47] Specifically, we don't yet know under what conditions appreciative inquiry is the best approach to organizational change or under what conditions it is less effective. Overall, appreciative inquiry has much to offer the organizational change process, but we are just beginning to understand its potential and limitations.

Parallel Learning Structure Approach

parallel learning structures
Highly participative groups constructed alongside (i.e., parallel to) the formal organization with the purpose of increasing the organization's learning and producing meaningful organizational change.

Parallel learning structures are highly participative arrangements composed of people from most levels of the organization who follow the action research model to produce meaningful organizational change. They are social structures developed alongside the formal hierarchy with the purpose of increasing the organization's learning.[48] Ideally participants in parallel learning structures are sufficiently free from the constraints of the larger organization so they can effectively solve organizational issues.

Royal Dutch/Shell relied on a parallel learning structure to introduce a more customer-focused organization.[49] Rather than try to change the entire organization at once, executives held weeklong "retail boot camps" with six country teams of frontline people (such as gas station managers, truck drivers, and marketing professionals). Participants learned about competitive trends in their regions and were taught powerful marketing tools to identify new opportunities. The teams then returned home to study their markets and develop proposals for improvement.

Four months later, boot camp teams returned for a second workshop in which each proposal was critiqued by Royal/Dutch Shell executives. Each team had 60 days to put its ideas into action, then return for a third workshop to analyze what worked and what didn't. This parallel learning process did much more than introduce new marketing ideas. It created enthusiasm in participants that spread contagiously to their co-workers, including managers above them, when they returned to their home countries.

Cross-Cultural and Ethical Issues in Organizational Change

One significant concern with some organizational change interventions is that they originate in the United States and other Western countries and may conflict with cultural values in some other countries.[50] A few experts point out that this Western perspective of change is linear, as is Lewin's force field model shown earlier. It also assumes that the change process is punctuated by tension and overt conflict. Indeed, some organizational change practices encourage open display of conflict.

But change as a linear and conflict-ridden process is incompatible with cultures that view change as a natural cyclical process with harmony and equilibrium as the objectives.[51] For instance, people in many Asian countries try to minimize conflict in order to respect others and save face.[52] These concerns do not mean that Western-style change interventions are necessarily ineffective elsewhere. Rather, it suggests that we need to develop a more contingency-oriented perspective with respect to the cultural values of participants.

Ethical Issues with Organizational Change   Some organizational change practices also face ethical issues.[53] One ethical concern is threats to the privacy rights of individuals. The action research model is built on the idea of collecting information from organizational members, yet this requires employees to provide personal information and emotions that they may not want to divulge.[54] A second ethical concern is that some change activities potentially increase management's power by inducing compliance and conformity in organizational members. This power shift occurs because change creates uncertainty and may reestablish management's position in directing the organization. For instance, action research is a systemwide activity that requires employee participation rather than allowing individuals to get involved voluntarily.

A third concern is that some organizational change interventions undermine the individual's self-esteem. The unfreezing process requires participants to disconfirm their existing beliefs, sometimes including their own competence at certain tasks or interpersonal relations. Some specific change practices involve direct exposure to personal critique by co-workers as well as public disclosure of one's personal limitations and faults. A fourth ethical concern is the change management consultant's role in the change process. Ideally consultants should occupy "marginal" positions with the clients they are serving. This means that they must be sufficiently detached from the organization to maintain objectivity and avoid having the client become too dependent on them. However, some consultants tend to increase, rather than decrease, clients' dependence for financial gain. Others have difficulty maintaining neutrality because they often come to the situation with their own biases and agendas.

Organizational change is a complex process with a variety of approaches and issues. Many corporate leaders have promised more change than they were able to deliver because they underestimated the time and challenges involved with this process. Yet the dilemma is that most organizations operate in hyperfast environments that demand continuous and rapid adaptation. As Home Depot CEO Robert Nardelli stated in the opening story to this chapter, "The rate of change internally has to be greater than the rate of change externally or else you're pedaling backward." Organizations survive and gain competitive advantage by mastering the complex dynamics of moving people through the continuous process of change faster than the external environment is changing.

Personal Change for the Road Ahead

In this last section of this textbook we thought it would be a good idea to shift attention from organizational change to a few practical ideas about personal change and development in organizations. Whether you are just starting your career or are already well along the trail, the following principles should help you improve both your prospects and your long-term career satisfaction. These points do not cover everything you need to remember about developing your career. Instead they highlight some key strategies that will help you along the road ahead.

Understand Your Needs and Values

The first piece of advice regarding personal growth and development is to understand your needs and values. How do you know what path is most fulfilling for you? This involves doing self-assessments of your vocational interests and recounting experiences you have enjoyed. Holland's occupational choice model presented in Chapter 2 helps to align your personality and interests with the work environment. It may also be useful to get feedback from others regarding activities that they notice you like or dislike, or that they see you excelling at. This applies the Johari Window model described in Chapter 3, whereby you learn more about yourself through information presented by close associates.

Understand Your Competencies

Knowing yourself also involves knowing what you are capable of doing.[55] Although you might visualize your future as an Albert Einstein, the head of a *Fortune* 500 company, or the political leader of your country, you need to take your potential abilities into account. The more closely the work you perform is aligned with your personal competencies, the more you will develop feelings of satisfaction and empowerment. Self-assessments, performance results, and constructive feedback from friends can help identify your capabilities. Also keep in mind that competencies extend beyond technical skills: Employers also look for generic competencies, such as communication, problem solving, and emotional intelligence.

Set Career Goals

Goal setting is a powerful way to motivate and achieve results, and this applies as much to careers as to any other activity. Career goals are benchmarks against which we evaluate our progress and identify strategies to develop our competencies. Career consultant Barbara Moses emphasizes that career goal setting is a fundamental element in becoming a "career activist." It involves writing your own script rather than waiting for someone to write it for you, being vigilant by identifying and preparing for opportunities, and becoming an independent agent by separating your self-identity from your job title, your organization, or what other people think you should be.[56]

Maintain Networks

Networking makes a difference in personal career growth. This observation is supported by several research studies and from evidence in executive placement firms. One large placement firm reported that 64 percent of the 7,435 clients in its executive career transition program found new employment through networking. As one successful job hunter advises, "Be prepared, know your story, and network, network, network."[57] Some networks are more effective than others, however. Specifically, job seekers tend to be more successful with large nonredundant networks. Networks that extend beyond your current sphere of work are also critical. Careers change much more today than in the past, so you need to establish connections to other fields where you may someday find yourself.[58]

Get a Mentor

Thus far our discussion has emphasized self-leadership in personal development. We need to set our own goals, motivate ourselves for career advancement, and visualize where we want to go. But personal development in organizational settings also benefits from the help of others. Mentoring is the process of learning the ropes of organizational life from a senior person within the company. Mentors give protégés more visible and meaningful work opportunities, and they also provide ongoing career guidance. You might think of them as career coaches because they provide ongoing advice and feedback.[59]

Organizational Behavior: The Journey Continues

Nearly 100 years ago American industrialist Andrew Carnegie said, "Take away my people, but leave my factories, and soon grass will grow on the factory floors. Take away my factories, but leave my people, and soon we will have a new and better factory." Carnegie's statement reflects the message woven throughout this textbook that organizations are not buildings, machinery, or financial assets. Rather they are the people in them. Organizations are human entities—full of life, sometimes fragile, always exciting.

Chapter Summary

Lewin's force field analysis model states that all systems have driving and restraining forces. Change occurs through the process of unfreezing, changing, and refreezing. Unfreezing produces disequilibrium between the driving and restraining forces. Refreezing realigns the organization's systems and structures with the desired behaviors.

Restraining forces are manifested as employee resistance to change. The main reasons why people resist change are direct costs, saving face, fear of the unknown, breaking routines, incongruent organizational systems, and incongruent team dynamics. Resistance to change may be minimized by keeping employees informed about what to expect from the change effort (communicating); teaching employees valuable skills for the desired future (learning); involving them in the change process; helping employees cope with the stress of change; negotiating trade-offs with those who will clearly lose from the change effort; and using coercion (sparingly and as a last resort).

Organizational change also requires driving forces. This means employees need to feel an urgency for change by becoming aware of the environmental conditions that demand change in the organization. The change process also requires refreezing the new behaviors by realigning organizational systems and team dynamics with the desired changes.

Every successful change requires a clear, well-articulated vision of the desired future state. Change agents rely on transformational leadership to develop a vision, communicate that vision, and build commitment to the vision of a desirable future state. The change process also often applies a diffusion process in which change begins as a pilot project and eventually spreads to other areas of the organization.

Action research is a highly participative, open-systems approach to change management that combines action orientation (changing attitudes and behavior) with research orientation (testing theory). It is a data-based, problem-oriented process that diagnoses the need for change, introduces the intervention, and then evaluates and stabilizes the desired changes.

Appreciative inquiry embraces the positive organizational behavior philosophy by focusing participants on the positive and possible. It tries to break out of the problem-solving mentality that dominates organizational change through the action research model. The four stages of appreciative inquiry include discovery, dreaming, designing, and delivering. A third approach, parallel learning structures, relies on social structures developed alongside the formal hierarchy with the purpose of increasing the organization's learning. These are highly participative arrangements, composed of people from most levels of the organization who follow the action research model to produce meaningful organizational change.

One significant concern is that organizational change theories developed with a Western cultural orientation potentially conflict with cultural values in some other countries. Also, organizational change practices can raise ethical concerns, including increasing management's power over employees, threatening individual privacy rights, undermining individual self-esteem, and making clients dependent on the change consultant.

Five strategies that assist personal development in organizational settings are understanding your needs and values, understanding your competencies, setting career goals, maintaining networks, and getting a mentor.

Key Terms

action research, p. 500

appreciative inquiry, p. 502

change agent, p. 499

force field analysis, p. 488

future search, p. 495

parallel learning structure, p. 503

refreezing, p. 489

unfreezing, p. 489

Critical Thinking Questions

1. Chances are that the school you attend is currently undergoing some sort of change to adapt more closely with its environment. Discuss the external forces that are driving these changes. What internal drivers for change also exist?

2. Use Lewin's force field analysis to describe the dynamics of organizational change at Nissan Motor Company (Connections 17.1).

3. Employee resistance is a *symptom*, not a *problem*, in the change process. What are some of the real problems that may underlie employee resistance?

4. Senior managers of a large multinational corporation are planning to restructure the organization. Currently the organization is decentralized around geographical areas so that the executive responsible for each area has considerable autonomy over manufacturing and

sales. The new structure will transfer power to the executives responsible for different product groups; the executives responsible for each geographic area will no longer be responsible for manufacturing in their areas but will retain control over sales activities. Describe two types of resistance senior managers might encounter from this organizational change.

5. Web Circuits is a Malaysia-based custom manufacturer for high-technology companies. Senior managers want to introduce lean management practices to reduce production costs and remain competitive. A consultant has recommended that the company start with a pilot project in one department and, when successful, diffuse these practices to other areas of the organization. Discuss the advantages of this recommendation and identify three ways (other than the pilot project's success) to make diffusion of the change effort more successful.

6. Suppose you are vice president of branch services at the Bank of East Lansing. You notice that several branches have consistently low customer service ratings even though there are no apparent differences in resources or staff characteristics. Describe an appreciative inquiry process in one of these branches that might help to overcome these problems.

7. This chapter suggests that some organizational change activities create ethical concerns. Yet several consultants actively use these processes because they believe they benefit the organization and do less damage to employees than it seems on the surface. For example, some activities try to open up the employees' hidden areas (see the discussion of the Johari Window in Chapter 3) so there is better mutual understanding with co-workers. Discuss this argument and identify where you think organizational change interventions should limit this process.

8. Career activism is a concept that is gaining interest because it emphasizes managing your own development in organizations. What concepts introduced throughout this book are compatible with the career activist concept? In what ways might a person be a career activist?

Case Study 17.1 THE EXCELLENT EMPLOYEE

Mary Gander, Winona State University

Emily, who had the reputation of being an excellent worker, was a machine operator in a furniture manufacturing plant that had been growing at a rate of between 15 percent and 20 percent each year for the past decade. New additions were built onto the plant, new plants opened in the region, workers hired, new product lines developed—lots of expansion—but with no significant change in overall approaches to operations, plant layout, ways of managing workers, or design processes. Plant operations as well as organizational culture were rooted in traditional Western management practices and logic, based largely on the notion of mass production and economies of scale. Over the past four years the company had grown in number and variety of products and in market penetration; however, profitability was flattening and showing signs of decline. As a result, managers were beginning to focus on production operations (internal focus) rather than mainly focusing on new market strategies, new products, and new market segments (external focus) in developing their strategic plans. They hoped to reduce

manufacturing costs, improving consistency of quality and ability to meet delivery times better while decreasing inventory and increasing flexibility.

One of several new programs initiated by managers in this effort to improve flexibility and lower costs was to get workers cross-trained. However, when a representative from Human Resources explained this program to Emily's supervisor, Jim, he reluctantly agreed to cross-train most of his workers, but *not* Emily.

Jim explained to the Human Resources person that Emily worked on a machine that was very complex and not easy to effectively operate. She had to "babysit" it much of the time. He had tried to train many workers on it, but Emily was the only person who could consistently get products through the machine that were within specifications and still meet production schedules. When anyone else tried to operate the machine, which performed a key function in the manufacturing process, it ended up either being a big bottleneck or producing excessive waste, which created a lot of trouble for Jim.

Jim went on to explain that Emily knew this sophisticated and complicated machine inside and out; she had been running it for five years. She liked the challenge, and she said it made the day go by faster, too. She was meticulous in her work—a skilled employee who really cared about the quality of her work. Jim told the HR person that he wished all of his workers were like Emily. In spite of the difficulty of running this machine, Emily could run it so well that product piled up at the next workstation in the production process, which couldn't keep up with her!

Jim was adamant about keeping Emily on this machine and not cross-training her. The HR person was frustrated. He could see Jim's point, but he had to follow executive orders: "Get these people cross-trained."

Around the same time a university student was doing a field study in the section of the plant where Emily worked, and Emily was one of the workers he interviewed. Emily told the student that in spite of the fact that the plant had some problems with employee morale and excessive employee turnover, she really liked working there. She liked the piece-rate pay system and hoped she did not have to participate in the recent "program of the month," which was having operators learn each other's jobs. She told the student that it would just create more waste if they tried to have other employees run her machine. She told him that other employees had tried to learn how to operate her machine but couldn't do it as well as she could.

Emily seemed to like the student and began to open up to him. She told him that her machine really didn't need to be so difficult and touchy to operate: With a couple of minor design changes in the machine and better maintenance, virtually anyone could run it. She had tried to explain this to her supervisor a couple of years ago, but he just told her to "do her work and leave operations to the manufacturing engineers." She also said that if workers upstream in the process would spend a little more time and care to keep the raw material in slightly tighter specifications, it would go through her machine much more easily; but they were too focused on speed and making more piece-rate pay. She expressed a lack of respect for the managers who couldn't see this and even joked about how "managers didn't know anything."

Discussion Questions

1. Identify the sources of resistance to change in this case.

2. Discuss whether this resistance is justified or could be overcome.

3. Recommend ways to minimize resistance to change in this incident or in future incidents.

Source: Copyright 2001 Mary J. Gander. This case is based on actual events, but names have been changed to maintain anonymity.

Case Study 17.2 INSIDE INTEL

BusinessWeek For years, Intel thrived on a business model that co-founder Andy Grove perfected and reinforced under his leadership and the leadership of his successor, Craig Barrett. But Intel's latest CEO, Paul Otellini has different plans. Rather than continuing to build faster chips just for PC computers, Otellini sees bigger opportunities in new "platforms." Otellini also wants to raise the profile of marketing, rather than let engineers determine what products

are developed. Even the famous Intel logo (with a lowered "e") is being ditched for a more contemporary design.

This *BusinessWeek* case study reviews the changes that Paul Otellini is introducing at Intel and explains how he is building momentum toward these changes. The article also describes how employees are responding to these changes. Read through this *BusinessWeek* article at www.mhhe.com/mcshane4e and prepare for the discussion questions below.

1. What change management strategies has Paul Otellini used to help introduce the various changes at Intel?

2. Discuss evidence that some employees are resisting these changes? What, if anything, can Otellini do to minimize this resistance?

Source: C. Edwards, "Inside Intel," *BusinessWeek*, 9 January 2006, 46.

Team Exercise 17.3 STRATEGIC CHANGE INCIDENTS

PURPOSE This exercise is designed to help you identify strategies to facilitate organizational change in various situations.

INSTRUCTIONS

1. The instructor will place students into teams, and each team will be assigned one of the scenarios presented here.

2. Each team will diagnose its assigned scenario to determine the most appropriate set of change management practices. Where appropriate, these practices should (a) create an urgency to change, (b) minimize resistance to change, and (c) refreeze the situation to support the change initiative. Each of these scenarios is based on real events.

3. Each team will present and defend its change management strategy. Class discussion of the appropriateness and feasibility of each strategy will occur after all teams assigned the same scenario have presented their recommendations. The instructor will then describe what the organizations actually did in these situations.

SCENARIO 1: GREENER TELCO

The board of directors at a large telephone company wants its executives to make the organization more environmentally friendly by encouraging employees to reduce waste in the workplace. There are also expectations by government and other stakeholders for the company to take this action and be publicly successful. Consequently, the managing director wants to significantly reduce the use of paper, as well as refuse and other waste throughout the company's many widespread offices. Unfortunately, a survey indicates that employees do not value environmental objectives and do not know how to "reduce, reuse, recycle." As the executive responsible for this change, you have been asked to develop a strategy that might bring about meaningful behavioral change toward these environmental goals. What would you do?

SCENARIO 2: GO FORWARD AIRLINE

A major airline has experienced a decade of rough turbulence, including two bouts of bankruptcy protection, 10 chief executives, and morale so low that employees have ripped company logos off their uniforms out of embarrassment. Service is terrible, and the airplanes rarely arrive or leave the terminal on time. This is costing the airline significant amounts of money in passenger layovers. Managers are paralyzed by anxiety, and many have been with the firm so long that they don't know how to set strategic goals that work. One-fifth of all flights lose money, and the company overall is near financial collapse (just three months to defaulting on payroll obligations). The newly hired CEO and you must get employees to quickly improve operational efficiency and customer service. What actions would you take to bring about these changes in time?

Self-Assessment 17.4

TOLERANCE OF CHANGE SCALE

PURPOSE This exercise is designed to help you understand how people differ in their tolerance for change.

INSTRUCTIONS Read each of the following statements and circle the response that best fits your personal beliefs. Then use the scoring key in Appendix B of this book to calculate your results. This self-assessment is completed alone so you can rate yourself honestly without concerns of social comparison. Class discussion will focus on the meaning of the concept measured by this scale and its implications for managing change in organizational settings.

After reading this chapter, if you feel that you need additional information, see www.mhhe.com/ mcshane4e for more in-depth interactivities that correspond to this material.

Tolerance of Change

To what extent does each statement describe you? indicate your level of agreement by marking the appropriate response on the right	Strongly agree	Moderately agree	Slightly agree	Neutral	Slightly disagree	Moderately disagree	Strongly disagree
1. An expert who doesn't come up with a definite answer probably doesn't know too much.	☐	☐	☐	☐	☐	☐	☐
2. I would like to live in a foreign country for a while.	☐	☐	☐	☐	☐	☐	☐
3. There is really no such thing as a problem that can't be solved.	☐	☐	☐	☐	☐	☐	☐
4. People who fit their lives into a schedule probably miss most of the joy of living.	☐	☐	☐	☐	☐	☐	☐
5. A good job is one where it is always clear what is to be done and how it is to be done.	☐	☐	☐	☐	☐	☐	☐
6. It is more fun to tackle a complicated problem than to solve a simple one.	☐	☐	☐	☐	☐	☐	☐
7. In the long run, it is possible to get more done by tackling small, simple problems rather than large, complicated ones.	☐	☐	☐	☐	☐	☐	☐
8. Often the most interesting and stimulating people are those who don't mind being different and original.	☐	☐	☐	☐	☐	☐	☐
9. What we are used to is always preferable to what is unfamiliar.	☐	☐	☐	☐	☐	☐	☐
10. People who insist on a yes or no answer just don't know how complicated things really are.	☐	☐	☐	☐	☐	☐	☐
11. A person who leads an even, regular life in which few surprises or unexpected happenings arise really has a lot to be grateful for.	☐	☐	☐	☐	☐	☐	☐
12. Many of our most important decisions are based on insufficient information.	☐	☐	☐	☐	☐	☐	☐
13. I like parties where I know most of the people more than ones where all or most of the people are complete strangers.	☐	☐	☐	☐	☐	☐	☐
14. Teachers or supervisors who hand out vague assignments give people a chance to show initiative and originality.	☐	☐	☐	☐	☐	☐	☐
15. The sooner everyone acquires similar values and ideals, the better.	☐	☐	☐	☐	☐	☐	☐
16. A good teacher is one who makes you wonder about your way of looking at things.	☐	☐	☐	☐	☐	☐	☐

Source: Adapted from S. Budner, "Intolerance of Ambiguity as a Personality Variable," *Journal of Personality* 30 (1962), pp. 29–50.

additional cases

Case 1   Arctic Mining Consultants

Case 2   Big Screen's Big Failure

Case 3   High Noon at Alpha Mills

Case 4   Keeping Suzanne Chalmers

Case 5   Magic Cable

Case 6   MexFabrics

Case 7   Nirvana Art Gallery

Case 8   Woodland Community Center Corporation

                Video Cases

Case1: ARCTIC MINING CONSULTANTS

Tom Parker enjoyed working outdoors. At various times in the past he had worked as a ranch hand, high steel rigger, headstone installer, prospector, and geological field technician. Now 43, Parker was a geological field technician and field coordinator with Arctic Mining Consultants. He had specialized knowledge and experience in all nontechnical aspects of mineral exploration, including claim staking, line cutting and grid installation, soil sampling, prospecting, and trenching. He was responsible for hiring, training, and supervising field assistants for all of Arctic Mining Consultants' programs. Field assistants were paid a fairly low daily wage (no matter how long they worked, which might be up to 12 hours or more) and were provided meals and accommodation. Many of the programs were operated by a project manager who reported to Parker.

Parker sometimes acted as a project manager, as he did on a job that involved staking 15 claims near Eagle Lake, Alaska. He selected John Talbot, Greg Boyce, and Brian Millar, all of whom had previously worked with Parker, as the field assistants. To stake a claim, the project team marked a line with flagging tape and blazes along the perimeter of the claim, cutting a claim post every 500 yards (called a "length"). The 15 claims would require almost 60 miles of line in total. Parker had budgeted seven days (plus mobilization and demobilization) to complete the job. This meant that each of the four stakers

(Parker, Talbot, Boyce, and Millar) would have to complete a little over seven "lengths" each day. The following is a chronology of the project.

Day 1

The Arctic Mining Consultants crew assembled in the morning and drove to Eagle Lake, from where they were flown by helicopter to the claim site. On arrival they set up tents at the edge of the area to be staked and agreed on a schedule for cooking duties. After supper they pulled out the maps and discussed the job—how long it would take, the order in which the areas were to be staked, possible helicopter landing spots, and areas that might be more difficult to stake.

Parker pointed out that with only a week to complete the job, everyone would have to average seven and a half lengths per day. "I know that is a lot," he said, "but you've all staked claims before, and I'm confident that each of you is capable of it. And it's only for a week. If we get the job done in time, there's a $300 bonus for each man." Two hours later Parker and his crew members had developed what seemed to be a workable plan.

Day 2

Millar completed six lengths, Boyce six lengths, Talbot eight, and Parker eight. Parker was not

513

pleased with Millar's or Boyce's production. However, he didn't make an issue of it, thinking they would develop their rhythm quickly.

Day 3

Millar completed five and a half lengths, Boyce four, and Talbot seven. Parker, who was nearly twice as old as the other three, completed eight lengths. He also had enough time remaining to walk over and check the quality of stakes that Millar and Boyce had completed, then walk back to his own area for helicopter pickup back to the tent site.

That night Parker exploded with anger. "I thought I told you that I wanted seven and a half lengths a day!" he shouted at Boyce and Millar. Boyce said that he was slowed down by unusually thick underbrush in his assigned area. Millar said that he had done his best and would try to pick up the pace. Parker did not mention that he had inspected their work. He explained that as far as he was concerned, the field assistants were supposed to finish their assigned area for the day, no matter what.

Talbot, who was sharing a tent with Parker, talked to him later. "I think that you're being a bit hard on them, you know. I know that it has been more by luck than anything else that I've been able to do my quota. Yesterday I had only five lengths done after the first seven hours and there was only an hour before I was supposed to be picked up. Then I hit a patch of really open bush and was able to do three lengths in 70 minutes. Why don't I take Millar's area tomorrow and he can have mine? Maybe that will help."

"Conditions are the same in all of the areas," replied Parker, rejecting Talbot's suggestion. "Millar just has to try harder."

Day 4

Millar did seven lengths and Boyce completed six and a half. When they reported their production that evening, Parker grunted uncommunicatively. Parker and Talbot did eight lengths each.

Day 5

Millar completed six lengths, Boyce six, Talbot seven and a half, and Parker eight. Once again Parker blew up, but he concentrated his diatribe on Millar. "Why don't you do what you say you are going to do? You

know that you have to do seven and a half lengths a day. We went over that when we first got here, so why don't you do it? If you aren't willing to do the job, you never should have taken it in the first place!"

Millar replied by saying that he was doing his best, that he hadn't even stopped for lunch, and that he didn't know how he could possibly do any better. Parker launched into him again: "You have got to work harder! If you put enough effort into it, you will get the area done!"

Later Millar commented to Boyce, "I hate getting dumped on all the time! I'd quit if it didn't mean that I'd have to walk 50 miles to the highway. And besides, I need the bonus money. Why doesn't he pick on you? You don't get any more done than me; in fact, you usually get less. Maybe if you did a bit more he wouldn't be so bothered about me."

"I work only as hard as I have to," Boyce replied.

Day 6

Millar raced through breakfast, was the first one to be dropped off by the helicopter, and arranged to be the last one picked up. That evening the production figures were Millar eight and a quarter lengths, Boyce seven, and Talbot and Parker eight each. Parker remained silent when the field assistants reported their performance for the day.

Day 7

Millar was again the first out and last in. That night he collapsed in an exhausted heap at the table, too tired to eat. After a few moments he announced in an abject tone, "Six lengths. I worked like a dog all day and I got only a lousy six lengths!" Boyce completed five lengths, Talbot seven, and Parker seven and a quarter.

Parker was furious. "That means we have to do a total of 34 lengths tomorrow if we are to finish this job on time!" With his eyes directed at Millar, he added, "Why is it that you never finish the job? Don't you realize that you are part of a team, and that you are letting the rest of the team down? I've been checking your lines and you're doing too much blazing and wasting too much time making picture-perfect claim posts! If you worked smarter, you'd get a lot more done!"

Day 8

Parker cooked breakfast in the dark. The helicopter dropoffs began as soon as morning light appeared on the horizon. Parker instructed each assistant to complete eight lengths and, if they finished early, to help the others. Parker said that he would finish the other ten lengths. Helicopter pickups were arranged for one hour before dark.

By noon, after working as hard as he could, Millar had completed only three lengths. "Why bother," he thought to himself, "I'll never be able to do another five lengths before the helicopter comes, and I'll catch the same amount of abuse from Parker for doing six lengths as for seven and a half." So he sat down and had lunch and a rest. "Boyce won't finish his eight lengths either, so even if I did finish mine, I still wouldn't get the bonus. At least I'll get one more day's pay this way."

That night Parker was livid when Millar reported that he had completed five and a half lengths. Parker had done ten and a quarter lengths, and Talbot had completed eight. Boyce proudly announced that he finished seven and a half lengths, but he sheepishly added that Talbot had helped him with some of it. All that remained were the two and a half lengths that Millar had not completed.

The job was finished the next morning, and the crew demobilized. Millar has never worked for Arctic Mining Consultants again, despite being offered work several times by Parker. Boyce sometimes does staking for Arctic, and Talbot works full-time with the company.

Source: © Copyright Steven L. McShane and Tim Neale. This case is based on actual events, but names and some characteristics have been changed to maintain anonymity.

Case 2: BIG SCREEN'S BIG FAILURE

Fiona McQuarrie, University College of the Fraser Valley

Bill Brosnan stared at the financial statements in front of him and shook his head. The losses from *Conquistadors,* the movie that was supposed to establish Big Screen Studios as a major Hollywood power, were worse than anyone had predicted. In fact, the losses were so huge that Brosnan's predecessor, Buck Knox, had been fired as a result of this colossal failure. Brosnan had wanted to be the head of a big movie production company for as long as he could remember, and he was thrilled to have been chosen by the board of directors to be the new president. But he had never expected that the first task in his dream job would be to deal with the fallout from one of the most unsuccessful movies ever.

The driving force behind *Conquistadors* was its director, Mark Frazier. Frazier had made several profitable movies for other studios and had a reputation as being a maverick with a "vision." He was a director with clearly formulated ideas of what his movies should look like, and he also had no hesitation about being forceful with producers, studios, actors, and technical staff to ensure that his ideas came to life as he envisioned them. For several years, while Frazier had been busy on other projects, he had also been working on a script about two Spanish aristocrats in the 16th century who set out for America to find riches and gold, encountering many amazing adventures on their travels. Frazier was something of an amateur historian, which led to his interest in the real-life stories of the Spanish conquistadors and bringing those stories to life for a 21st-century audience. But he also felt that creating an epic tale like this would establish him as a serious writer and filmmaker in the eyes of Hollywood, some of whose major powers had dismissed his past work as unimaginative or hackneyed.

When Big Screen Studios approached Frazier to see if he would be interested in working for them, the company was going through something of a rough spot. Through several years of hard work and mostly successful productions, Buck Knox, the president of Big Screen, had established Big Screen as a studio that produced cost-efficient and profitable films. The studio also had a good reputation for supporting the creative side of filmmaking; actors, writers, directors, and producers generally felt that Big Screen trusted them enough to give them autonomy in making decisions appropriate for their

515

productions. (Other studios had reputations for keeping an overly tight rein on production budgets and for dictating choices based on cost rather than artistic considerations.) However, in the last two years Big Screen had invested in several major productions–a musical, a horror film, and the sequel to a wildly successful film adaptation of a comic book–that for various reasons had all performed well below expectations. Knox had also heard through the grapevine that several of the studio's board members were prepared to join together to force him out of the presidency if Big Screen did not come up with a hit soon.

Knox knew that Frazier was being wooed by several other studios for his next project, and he decided to contact Frazier to see if he was interested in directing any of the productions Big Screen was considering in the next year or so. After hearing Knox's descriptions of the upcoming productions, Frazier said, "What I'd really be interested in doing is directing this script I've been writing." He described the plot of *Conquistadors* to Knox, and Knox was enchanted by the possibilities–two strong male lead characters, a beautiful woman the men encountered in South America whose affections they fought over, battles, sea journeys, and challenging journeys over mountains and through jungles. However, Knox could also see that this movie might be extremely expensive to produce. He expressed this concern to Frazier, and Frazier replied, "Yes, but it will be an investment that will pay off. I know this movie will work. And I've mentioned it to two other studios and they are interested in it. I would prefer to make it with Big Screen, but if I have to, I will go somewhere else to get it made. That is how strongly I believe in it. However, any studio I work with has to trust me. I won't make the film without adequate financial commitment from the studio, I want final approval over casting, and I won't make the film if I don't get final cut." ("Final cut" means the director, not the studio, edits the version of the movie that is released to theaters, and the studio cannot release a version of the movie that the director does not approve.)

Knox told Frazier that he would get back to him later that week, and he asked Frazier not to commit to any other project until then. He spent several days mulling over the possibilities. Like Frazier, he believed that *Conquistadors* could be a huge success. It certainly sounded like it had more potential than anything else Big Screen had in development. How-

ever, Knox was still concerned about the potential cost and the amount of control over the project that Frazier was demanding. Frazier's reputation as a maverick meant that he likely would not compromise on his demands. Knox was also concerned about his own vulnerability if the movie failed. But on the other hand, Big Screen needed a big hit soon. Big Screen would look bad if it turned down *Conquistadors* and the movie became a gigantic hit for some other studio. Frazier had a respectable track record of producing moneymakers, so even if he might be difficult to work with, the end product usually was successful. At the end of the week Knox phoned Frazier and told him that Big Screen was willing to produce *Conquistadors*. Frazier thanked Knox, adding, "This film is going to redeem me, and it's going to redeem Big Screen as well."

Preproduction on the film started almost immediately after Frazier and the studio negotiated a budget of $50 million. This was slightly higher than Knox had anticipated, but he believed this was not an excessive amount to permit Frazier to realize the grand vision he had described. Knox further reassured himself by assigning John Connor, one of his trusted vice presidents, to act as the studio's liaison with Frazier and to be executive producer on the film. Connor was a veteran of many years in the movie production industry and was experienced in working with directors and budgets. Knox trusted Connor to make Frazier contain the costs of the production within the agreed limits.

The first major problem the film encountered involved casting. The studio gave Frazier final approval over casting as he had requested. Frazier's first signing was Cole Rogan, a famous action star, to be one of the male leads. The studio did not object to this choice; in fact, Knox and Connor felt that Rogan was an asset because he had a reputation as a star that could "open" a film (in other words, audiences would come to a movie just because he was in it). However, Frazier then decided to cast Frank Monaco as the other male lead. Monaco had made only a few films to date, and those were fluffy romantic comedies. Frazier said that Monaco would bring important qualities of vulnerability and innocence to the role, which would be a strong contrast to Rogan's rugged machismo. However, Connor told Knox that he saw two major problems with Monaco's casting: Monaco had never proven himself in an epic adventure role, and he was an accomplished enough actor that he would make the rather wooden Rogan look bad. Knox told Connor to suggest to Frazier that Rogan's role be recast. Unfortunately Frazier had signed Rogan to a "pay or play" deal, meaning that if the studio released Rogan from the project, the studio would have to pay him a considerable sum of money. Knox was somewhat bothered that Frazier had made this deal with Rogan without consulting either him or Connor. But he told Connor to instruct Frazier to release Rogan and recast the role, and the studio would just accept the payment to Rogan as part of the production costs. Although Frazier complained, he did as the studio asked and chose as a replacement Marty Jones, who had had some success in films but mostly in supporting roles. However, Jones was thrilled to be cast in a major role, and Connor felt that he would be capable of convincingly playing the part.

A few weeks after casting was completed, Connor called Knox and asked to see him immediately. "Buck," he told him once he arrived at Knox's office, "we have a really big problem." Connor said Frazier was insisting that the majority of the production be filmed in the jungles of South America, where most of the action took place, rather than on a studio soundstage or in a more accessible location that resembled the South American locale. Not only that, but Frazier was also insisting that he needed to bring along most of the crew that had worked on his previous films, rather than staffing the production locally. "Why does he want that? That's going to cost a hell of a lot," Knox said. "I know," Connor said, "but he says it's the only way the film is going to work. He says it just won't be the same if the actors are in a studio or in some swamp in the southern United States. According to him, the actors and the crew need to be in the real location to truly understand what the conquistadors went through, and audiences won't believe it's a real South American jungle if the film isn't made in one."

Knox told Connor that Frazier had to provide an amended budget to reflect the increased costs before he would approve the location filming. Connor took the request to Frazier, who complained that the studio was weakening its promise to support the film adequately, and added that he might be tempted to take the film to another studio if he was not allowed to film on location in South America. After a few weeks he produced an amended budget of $75 million. Knox was horrified that the budget for *Conquistadors* had grown by half in a few weeks.

He told Connor that he would accept the amended budget only under two conditions: First, Connor would go on the location shoot to ensure that costs stayed within the amended budget, and second, if the costs exceeded Frazier's estimates, he would have to pay any excess himself. Frazier again complained that the studio was attempting to compromise his vision, but he grudgingly accepted the modified terms.

Frazier, Connor, and the cast and crew then headed off to the South American jungles for a scheduled two-month shoot. Immediately it became apparent that there was more trouble. Connor, who reported daily to Knox, told him after two weeks that Frazier was shooting scenes several times over—not because the actors or the crew were making mistakes or because there was something wrong with the scene, but because the output just didn't meet his artistic standards. This attention to detail meant that the filming schedule was nearly a week behind after only the first week's work. Also, because the filming locations were so remote, the cast and crew were spending nearly four hours of a scheduled seven-hour workday traveling to and from location, leaving only three hours in which they could work at regular pay rates. Work beyond those hours meant they had to be paid overtime; and because Frazier's demanding vision required shooting 10 or 12 hours each day, the production was incurring huge overtime costs. As if that wasn't bad enough, the "rushes" (the finished film produced each day) showed that Monaco and Jones didn't have any chemistry as a pair; and Gia Norman, the European actress Frazier had cast as the love interest, had such a heavy accent that most of her lines couldn't be understood.

Knox told Connor that he was coming to the location right away to meet with Frazier. After several days of arduous travel, Knox, Connor, and Frazier met in the canvas tent that served as the director's office in the middle of the jungle. Knox didn't waste any time with pleasantries. "Mark," he told Frazier, "there is no way you can bring this film in for the budget you have promised or within the deadline you agreed to. John has told me how this production is being managed, and it's just not acceptable. I've done some calculations, and at the rate you are going, this picture is going to cost $85 million and have a running time of four and a half hours. Big Screen is not prepared to support that. We need a film that's a commercially viable length, and we need it at a reasonable cost."

"It needs to be as long as it is," replied Frazier, "because the story has to be told. And if it has to cost this much, it has to cost this much. Otherwise it will look like crap and no one will buy a ticket to see it."

"Mark," replied Knox, "we are prepared to put $5 million more into this picture, and that is it. You have the choice of proceeding under those terms and keeping John fully aware of the costs so he can help you stay within the budget. If you don't agree to that, you can leave the production, and we will hire another director and sue you for breach of contract."

Frazier looked as though he was ready to walk into the jungle and head back to California that very minute, but the thought of losing his dream project was too much for him. He muttered, "OK, I'll finish it."

Knox returned to California, nursing several nasty mosquito bites, and Connor stayed in the jungle and reported to him regularly. Unfortunately it didn't seem like Frazier was paying much attention to the studio's demands. Connor estimated that the shoot would run three months rather than two, and that the total cost of the shoot would be $70 million. This left only $10 million of the budget for postproduction, distribution, and marketing, which was almost nothing for an epic adventure. To add to Knox's problems, he got a phone call from Richard Garrison, the chairman of Big Screen's board of directors. Garrison had heard gossip about what was going on with *Conquistadors* in the jungles of South America, and he wanted to know what Knox was going to do to curb Frazier's excesses. Knox told Garrison that Frazier was operating under clearly understood requirements, and that Connor was on the set to monitor the costs. Unfortunately, Knox thought, Connor was doing a good job of reporting, but he didn't seem to be doing much to correct the problems he was observing.

Frazier eventually came back to California after three and a half months of shooting, and he started editing the several hundred hours of film he had produced. Knox requested that Frazier permit Connor or himself to participate in the editing, but Frazier retorted that permitting that would infringe on his right to "final cut"; he refused to allow anyone associated with the studio to be in the editing room. Knox scheduled a release date for the film in six months' time and asked the studio's publicity department to start working on an ad campaign for the film; but not much could be done on either of these tasks without at least a rough cut of the finished product.

Three weeks into the editing, Connor called Knox. "I heard from Mark today," he said. "He wants to do some reshoots." "Is that a problem?" Knox asked. "No," said Connor, "most of it is interior stuff that we can do here. But he wants to add a prologue. He says that the story doesn't make sense without more development of how the two lead characters sailed from Spain to South America. He wants to hire a ship."

"He wants to WHAT?" exclaimed Knox.

"He wants to hire a sailing ship, like the conquistadors traveled on. There's a couple of tall ships that would do, but the one he wants is in drydock in Mexico and would cost at least a million to make seaworthy and sail up to Southern California. And that's on top of the cost of bringing the actors and crew back for a minimum of a week. I suggested to him that we try some special effects or a computerized animation for the scenes of the ship on the ocean, and shoot the shipboard scenes in the studio, but he says that won't be the same and it needs to be authentic."

At this point Knox was ready to drive over to the editing studios and take care of Frazier himself. Instead he called Garrison and explained the situation. "I won't commit any more money to this without the board's approval. But we've already invested $80 million into this already, so is a few more million that much of a deal if it gets the damn thing finished and gets Frazier out of our hair? If we tell him no, we'll have to basically start all over again, or just dump the whole thing and kiss $80 million goodbye." At the other end of the line, Garrison sighed, and said, "Do whatever you have to do to get it done."

Knox told Connor to authorize the reshoots, with a schedule of two months and the expectation that Frazier would have a rough cut of the film ready for the studio executives to view in three months. However, because of the time Frazier had already spent in editing, Knox had to change the release date, which meant changing the publicity campaign as well—and releasing the film at the same time that one of Big Screen's major competitors was releasing another epic adventure that was considered a surefire hit. However, Knox felt he had no choice. If he didn't enforce some deadline, Frazier might sit in the editing room and tinker with his dream forever.

Connor supervised the reshoots and reported that they went as well as could be expected. The major problem was that Gia Norman had had plastic surgery on her nose after the first shoot was completed, and she looked considerably different than she had in the jungles of South America. However, creative lighting, makeup, and costuming managed to minimize the change in her appearance. By all accounts the (very expensive) sailing ship looked spectacular in the rushes, and Frazier was satisfied that his vision had been sufficiently dramatized.

Amazingly, Frazier delivered the rough cut of the film at the agreed time. Knox, Connor, Garrison, and the rest of the studio's executives crowded into the screening room to view the realization of Frazier's dream. Five and a half hours later, they were in shock. No one could deny that the movie looked fantastic and that it was an epic on a grand scale. But there was no way the studio could commercially release a film that was over five hours long—plus Frazier had agreed to produce a movie that was at most two and a half hours long. Knox was at his wits' end. He cornered Garrison in the hallway outside the screening room. "Will you talk to Mark? He won't listen to me, he won't listen to John. But we can't release this. It won't work." Garrison agreed, contacting Frazier the next day. He reported back to Knox that Frazier, amazingly, had agreed to cut the film to two hours and fifteen minutes. Knox, heartened by this news, proceeded with the previously set release date, which by now was a month away, and got the publicity campaign going.

Two days before the scheduled release date, Frazier provided an advance copy of his shortened version of *Conquistadors* for a studio screening. Knox had asked him to provide a copy sooner, but Frazier said he could not produce anything that quickly. As a consequence, the version of the film that the studio executives were seeing for the first time was the version that already had thousands of copies duplicated for distribution to movie theaters all across North America. In fact, those copies were on their way by courier to the theaters as the screening started.

At the end of the screening, the studio executives were stunned. The movie was shorter, but now it made no sense. Characters appeared and disappeared randomly, the plot was impossible to follow, and the dialogue did not make sense at several key points in the small parts of plot that were discernible. The film was a disaster. Several of the executives present voiced the suspicion that Frazier had deliberately edited the movie this way to get revenge on the studio for not respecting his vision and forcing him to reduce the film's length. Others suggested that Frazier was simply a lunatic who never should have been given so much autonomy in the first place.

Knox, Garrison, and Connor held a hastily called meeting the next morning. What could the studio do? Recall the film and force Frazier to produce a more coherent shorter version? Recall the film and release the five-and-a-half-hour version? Or let the shorter version be released as scheduled and hope that it wouldn't be too badly received? Knox argued that the film should be recalled and Frazier should be forced to produce the product he agreed to produce. Connor said that he thought Frazier had been doing his best to do what the studio wanted, based on what Connor saw on the set, and that making Frazier cut the movie so short compromised the vision that Frazier wanted to achieve. He said the studio should release the long version and present it as a "special cinematic event." Garrison, as chairman of the board, listened to both sides, and after figuring out the costs of recalling and/or reediting the film—not to mention the less tangible costs of further worsening the film's reputation—said, "Gentlemen, we really don't have any choice. *Conquistadors* will be released tomorrow."

Knox immediately canceled the critics' screenings of *Conquistadors* scheduled for that afternoon so that bad reviews would not appear on the day of the film's release. Despite that preemptive step and an extensive advertising campaign, *Conquistadors* was a complete and utter flop. On a total outlay of $90 million, the studio recouped less than $9 million. The reviews of the film were terrible, and audiences just didn't arrive. The only place *Conquistadors* was even close to successful was in some parts of Europe, where film critics called the edited version an example of American studios' crass obsession with making money by compromising the work of a genius. The studio attempted to capitalize on this note of hope by releasing the five-and-a-half-hour version of *Conquistadors* for screening at some overseas film festivals and cinema appreciation societies; but the revenues from these screenings were so small that they made no difference to the overall financial results.

Three months after *Conquistadors* was released, Garrison called Knox in and told him he was fired. Garrison told Knox the board appreciated what a difficult production *Conquistadors* had been to manage, but that the costs of the production had been unchecked to a degree that the board no longer had confidence in Knox's ability to operate Big Screen Studios efficiently. Connor was offered a generous early retirement package, and he accepted it. The board then hired Bill Brosnan, a vice president at another studio, as Knox's replacement.

After reviewing *Conquistadors'* financial records and the notes that Knox had kept throughout the production, Brosnan was determined that a disaster like this would not undermine his career as it had Knox's. But what could he do to ensure this would not happen?

Case 3: HIGH NOON AT ALPHA MILLS

Arif Hassan and Thivagar Velayutham, International Islamic University Malaysia

Alpha Plantations was an oil palm plantation located in Malaysia. It consisted of an oil palm estate and one palm oil mill. It was a wholly owned subsidiary of a British multinational company and was founded with the purpose of supplying crude palm oil for its parent company's detergent manufacturing business. Since its formation, most of the managers had been recruited from the United Kingdom, with many British ex-soldiers and police officers joining up. Ang Siow Lee first joined Alpha Mill in 1965 at the age of 15 as a laborer, rising through the ranks to become the most senior nonmanagerial staff member in Alpha. Ang was now the senior production supervisor in Alpha's palm oil mill. His immediate superior was the mill manager, and he had two junior supervisors to assist him. The mill operated on a three-shift cycle of 25 operators each, and each supervisor (including Ang) was in charge of one shift.

Ang was responsible for the smooth daily palm oil processing operations. He coordinated the activities of all three shifts with the two supervisors, prepared the daily production reports, addressed short-term human resource planning issues and minor discipline issues, and set and evaluated short-term performance targets for the three shifts. In addition, he acted as the "gatekeeper": Any mill workers who wished to see the mill manager had to first see Ang, who tried to solve the problem, which could be anything from house repairs to a request for an advance on wages. Only in rare cases when Ang could not resolve the issue was the matter brought up to the mill manager. Ang ran a tight ship, and he never let anyone forget it. His superb technical competency helped him keep the mill in top shape. He was accustomed to receiving the highest appraisal ratings from the mill manager, who appreciated his firm, methodical, and almost militarily efficient way of running the mill.

The palm oil industry in Malaysia faced many challenges in 1999. World oil prices plunged due to oversupply; palm oil prices hit a 15-year low. This cut the profit margins of all palm oil producers and caused Alpha Mill to post losses regularly.

Captain Chubb, the 54-year-old ex–Royal Engineer and mill manager, had no idea how to improve performance. "We are doing nothing wrong, and have met all our efficiency targets. It's this market that is killing us!" he exasperatedly explained during the annual year-end visit of the directors from London. Soon Captain Chubb was given his marching orders. In early 2000 a new mill manager was appointed who was different from his predecessors. Ian Davison, a 32-year-old from Edinburgh, Scotland, was not a career plantation engineer and had never managed an agricultural product processing mill before. He was actually an electronics engineer with an Ivy League MBA on the fast track to a top management position. His previous appointment was as factory manager of a detergent factory in Egypt, where he managed to streamline and modernize operations and increase financial performance drastically. Headquarters in London hoped he would be able to do the same with Alpha Mill and return it to profitability. His first action was to analyze operations at Alpha Mill and look for ways to reduce production costs and increase profits. He arrived at the following conclusions:

- Current performance standards allowed too much machine breakdown and changeover time. Better standards were achievable with the latest technology.
- Waste could be reduced and yield improved drastically by installing machinery based on new technology.
- Personnel numbers were too high–they could be reduced with technology and multitasking and unleashing the full potential of workers.

- Personnel were just "cruising along"; they were not fully committed to achieving better performance.

- Hygiene needs were not being met.

- The old colonial, hierarchical company culture was not conducive to performance improvement.

- Information was not shared across the mill. Operators knew about only their own little areas in the mill and almost nothing about the company as a whole.

Davison proposed to remedy the situation with the following initiatives:

- Empower operators by reorganizing the shifts into self-directed production teams where the supervisors would now play the role of "facilitators," thereby gaining commitment.

- Install new technology and automation.

- Adopt more stringent performance measures.

Davison implemented and executed these initiatives by first organizing an excursion to a local picnic spot for the entire factory. After the icebreakers, games, and lunch, he held a briefing session on the beach, where he explained the situation Alpha Mill was in and the need to make changes. He then unveiled his plan. The response was enthusiastic, although some operators privately confessed to not understanding some of the terminology Davison used. At the end of the excursion, when there was some time allocated for feedback, Ang expressed his full support for Davison's plan. "We in Alpha Mill have full confidence in you, our new leader, and we assure you of our 110 percent support to make your plan a success!" he said at the end of his speech.

When the new machinery had been installed and each shift had been reorganized into self-directed work teams, the plan was put into motion. Whenever the team faced a problem during processing and tried to find a solution using the techniques that had been taught, Ang would step in after some time, issue instructions, and take over the process. "This is a simple problem, no need to waste time over it. Just do it . . ." His instructions were always followed, and the immediate problem was always solved. However, the production team reverted to the old ways of working, and none of the expected benefits of teaming were realized. Given the new tighter performance standards and reduced staffing levels, the teams consistently underperformed. Team meetings were one-way affairs where Ang would tell everyone else what had gone wrong.

Ang's response was to push himself harder. He was always the first to arrive and the last to leave. He would spend a lot of time troubleshooting process problems. He pushed his operators even harder, but he felt that he had less control over his operators now that they had direct access to the mill manager and most of their minor needs were taken care of by him. Sometimes he became annoyed at his operators' mistakes and would resort to shouting and cursing, which had the immediate effect of moving people in the direction he wanted. This was in contrast to the mere glare that would have sufficed previously.

The continued poor performance of Alpha Mill affected Ang's midyear appraisal rating, which fell from excellent to merely adequate. During the appraisal interview, an annoyed Davison bluntly told Ang that he needed to understand clearly what the initiatives were all about, and that he had to let the team take some responsibility, make mistakes, and learn from them. "With your knowledge of this mill, you should be able to provide them with all the technical input they need," he said. Davison also added, "It might help if you treated our people with a little more respect. We aren't living in the 1940s anymore, you know." Ang was thunderstruck by the appraisal but did not raise any objections on the spot. He silently deferred to Davison's judgment and promised to do better. He also reiterated his utmost support for Davison and his plan.

After the midyear appraisal there was a noticeable change in Ang's demeanor. He became very quiet and began to take a less active role in the daily running of the mill. He was superficially polite to the operators and answered most requests for help with "Get the team together and discuss it among yourselves. Show the boss that you can solve it for yourselves." At first the teams were at a loss and mill performance suffered badly, but within two weeks the teams had found their feet and performance began to improve. One of Ang's junior supervisors, Mr. Raman, was able to coordinate between production teams to ensure that the performance gains were maintained. The effect on Ang was devastating. He became withdrawn and began to drink more than usual. His presence at team meetings became a mere formality and he contributed next to nothing, taking a back seat to other team members. He spoke little to mill personnel and became a mere shadow of his former self.

Davison was aware of the changes taking place on the mill floor. He decided that it was time to remove Ang from his position. He began to plan for a reshuffling of Alpha Mill's organization chart where Ang would be promoted to the new position of mill executive, a staff position with a small pay raise. His responsibility would be to advise the mill manager on technical, quality, and efficiency problems faced by the mill. He would be assigned to carry out minor improvement projects and performance audits from time to time. Raman would be promoted to supervisor and would report directly to the mill manager. Ang would no longer have any line authority over the production team. This reorganization was quickly approved by the head office, and Davison proceeded to lay the groundwork for the announcements and the necessary paperwork. Little did he foresee what was to follow.

Ang was in the head office one morning when the personnel executive's clerk congratulated him on his imminent promotion. A surprised Ang inquired further and learned of the plans that Davison had in store for him. It was the final straw. He rushed back to Alpha Mill just as Davison was about to conduct his noon mill inspection. The confrontation was loud, acrimonious, and public. It ended with Ang being terminated for insubordination and gross misconduct.

After Ang had left, Davison felt that the obstacle to better commitment and morale was gone and that performance would improve greatly. He was wrong. Team performance began to deteriorate, and no amount of pep talks could improve it. He began to wonder what had gone wrong.

Case 4: KEEPING SUZANNE CHALMERS

Thomas Chan hung up the telephone and sighed. The vice president of software engineering at Advanced Photonics Inc. (API) had just spoken to Suzanne Chalmers, who had called to arrange a meeting with Chan later that day. She didn't say what the meeting was about, but Chan almost instinctively knew that Suzanne was going to quit after working at API for the past four years. Chalmers was a software engineer in Internet Protocol (IP), the software that directed fiber optic light through API's routers. It was very specialized work, and Suzanne was one of API's top talents in that area.

Thomas Chan had been through this before. A valued employee would arrange a private meeting. The meeting would begin with a few pleasantries; then the employee would announce that he or she wanted to quit. Some employees said they were leaving because of the long hours and stressful deadlines. They said they needed to decompress, get to know the kids again, or whatever. But that was not usually the real reason. Almost every organization in this industry was scrambling to keep up with technological advances and the competition. They would just leave one stressful job for another one.

Also, many of the people who left API joined a start-up company a few months later. These start-up firms could be pressure cookers where everyone worked 16 hours each day and had to perform a variety of tasks. For example, engineers in these small firms might have to meet customers or work on venture capital proposals rather than focus on specialized tasks related to their knowledge. API had over 1,000 employees, so it was easier to assign people to work matching their technical competencies.

No, the problem wasn't the stress or long hours, Chan thought. The problem was money—too much money. Most of the people who left were millionaires. Suzanne Chalmers was one of them. Thanks to generous stock options that had skyrocketed on the NASDAQ stock market, many employees at API had more money than they could use. Most were under 40 years old, so they were too young to retire. But their financial independence gave them less reason to remain with API.

The Meeting

The meeting with Suzanne Chalmers took place a few hours after the telephone call. It began like the others, with the initial pleasantries and brief discussion about progress on the latest fiber optic router project. Then Suzanne made her well-rehearsed statement: "Thomas, I've really enjoyed working here, but I'm going to leave Advanced Photonics." Suzanne took a breath, then looked at Chan. When he didn't reply after a few seconds, she continued, "I need to take time off. You know, get away to recharge my batteries. The project's nearly done and the team can complete it without me. Well, anyway, I'm thinking of leaving."

Chan spoke in a calm voice. He suggested that Suzanne take an unpaid leave for two or maybe three months, complete with paid benefits, then return refreshed. Suzanne politely rejected that offer, saying that she needed to get away from work for a while. Thomas then asked Suzanne whether she was unhappy with her work environment—whether she was getting the latest computer technology to do her work and whether there were problems with co-workers. The workplace was fine, Susanne replied. The job was getting a bit routine at times, but she had a comfortable workplace with excellent co-workers.

Chan then apologized for the cramped work space, due mainly to the rapid increase in the number of people hired over the past year. He suggested that if Suzanne took a couple of months off, API would have a larger work space with a better view of the park behind the campuslike building when she returned. She politely thanked Chan for that offer, but it wasn't what she needed. Besides, it wouldn't be fair to have a large work space when other team members worked in smaller quarters.

Chan was running out of tactics, so he tried his last hope: money. He asked whether Suzanne had higher offers. Suzanne replied that she regularly received calls from other companies, and some of them offered more money. Most were start-up firms that offered a lower salary but higher potential gains in stock options. Chan knew from market surveys that Suzanne was already paid well in the industry. He also knew that API couldn't compete on stock option potential. Employees working in start-up firms sometimes saw their shares increase by 5 or 10 times their initial value, whereas shares at API and other large firms increased more slowly. However, Chan promised Suzanne that he would recommend that she receive a significant raise—maybe 25 percent—and more stock options. Chan added that Chalmers was one of API's most valuable employees and that the company would suffer if she left the firm.

The meeting ended with Chalmers promising to consider Chan's offer of higher pay and stock options. Two days later Chan received her resignation in writing. Five months later Chan learned that after a few months of travel with her husband, Chalmers joined a start-up software firm in the area.

Case 5: MAGIC CABLE

Joseph Kavanaugh, Henry S. Maddux III, and Harry Gene Redden,
Sam Houston State University

"I think I've found what I'm looking for," Gary Roberts said.

"Oh yeah, what is that?" Jim Handley asked, as he handed Roberts a pair of vise-grip pliers.

"I'm thinking I might have found a way out of this dump. No more tile dust, no more 40-mile-an-hour winds blowing through the plant, and no more Al Wright for me," Roberts replied.

Wright, the plant manager, and Roberts, maintenance mechanic for Tile-Elite, had been at odds for years. Roberts had been hired during a manufacturing plant expansion at Tile-Elite, and Wright had promised Roberts a production supervisor's job upon its completion. However, when the expansion was completed and the last production line was ready, Wright told Roberts to forget the supervisor's job because he was more valuable to the company as a maintenance mechanic.

"I know what I said, Gary, but I think you're going to be a mechanic here even if you stay 20 years," Wright had stated at the time.

After that encounter almost five years ago, Wright and Roberts had mixed like oil and water. Roberts had to admit that he was probably more valuable to the company as a maintenance mechanic in the short run, but he had been looking at the long run. He wanted to be more involved in the production process. He had just turned 40, was recently divorced, and had been involved in maintenance of some type since his military service in Vietnam 20 years earlier. While working full-time at his previous job, Roberts had completed his bachelor's degree in business. His major had been management, and it had taken him six long years to graduate. He had then wanted a position where he could use his management education. The company for which he was working while going to school had promised him a supervisor's position when he graduated, but that promise had evaporated when the company went bankrupt during the oil recession of the 1980s.

During his years with Tile-Elite Roberts had searched for another company that would give him a chance as a supervisor, but it seemed no one wanted a man his age with minimal management experience. The oil recession had left the employment market flooded with unemployed managers with significant supervisory experience. Consequently Roberts decided he would stick with what he knew best, maintenance, because jobs were more plentiful and the pay was reasonably good.

"Magic Cable in Fresno is looking for a maintenance mechanic. I've got an interview tomorrow morning," Roberts said to Handley.

"I've seen their plant over on Cook Street, behind the county barn, but I've never been in it. What do they build there?" Handley asked.

"Shoot, I don't know and I don't really care. All machines are alike. Just some are bigger than other ones, so my job will be basically the same. What I want is better working conditions and a chance for advancement. I'd even take a slight cut in pay to get out of here," Roberts answered.

"I understand where you're coming from, but don't tell Magic Cable that! Well, good luck tomorrow, Gair. I hope you get that job," Handley said as he closed his toolbox and started moving toward the time clock.

Roberts hated it when Handley called him "Gair". It sounded so trite. The only reason he hadn't said something was because Jim was such a good friend and he had taught him a lot.

Magic Cable was just two miles farther from Roberts's home than Tile-Elite. The facility was considerably smaller, but the grounds were kept neatly trimmed, and Roberts considered that a good sign. The parking was also directly in front of the plant, which would be good during bad weather.

"I've got a good feeling about this place," Roberts muttered to himself as he drove through the gate.

After parking in a vacant visitor parking space, Roberts gathered his resume and the completed employment application, took a couple of deep breaths, and headed toward the door labeled "Personnel." Once inside, all he saw was a doorbell mounted on a wall, a door with a peephole and mail slot, and a poster that displayed a picture of the building and a narrative describing the company's history. The poster was on the outside wall opposite the bell. Above the doorbell was a small sign: "Ring for Personnel." There was also a sign below the button that read, "We are NOT accepting applications." The word "not" was hanging loosely so it could be removed if needed. "Lucky I've got an appointment," Roberts thought.

After pushing the button produced no sound, Roberts said out loud to himself, "Just my luck. The stupid thing is broken and no one even knows I'm here."

Almost immediately the door opened partially and a neatly dressed young woman stuck her head out and asked, "Gary Roberts?" Roberts nodded his head in reply. "Bill Lindsey, the manufacturing engineer, will be right with you," she added before shutting the door again.

"Great, more waiting," Roberts thought. After looking around the sparsely furnished lobby for a minute, Roberts occupied himself by reading the narrative written on the poster. It said Magic Cable had been started in a small warehouse in Oakland in 1977 by a group of friends with a good idea. They started manufacturing throttle and drive cables for outdoor equipment. The business grew very fast, and in 1979 the plant was moved to Fresno. Now they were producing push–pull cables for cars and aircraft with a workforce consisting of about 300 employees.

Just as Roberts finished reading the poster, the inside door swung open a second time and a tall gray-haired man in an open-collared shirt emerged.

"Hi, I'm Bill Lindsey, the manufacturing engineer. You must be Gary Roberts. Come in here." As Roberts edged through the door, Lindsey added, "We need to go up and meet Bob Walters. He's our manufacturing manager. We'll both be interviewing you." And with that Lindsey turned to go up the set of stairs to his right. "Have you ever met Bob Walters?"

Roberts remembered seeing Bob Walters's name on the list of people who started Magic Cable. "No, sir, I haven't," he answered.

"He's kind of rough around the edges, so don't let him run you off," Lindsey said with a wry smile. Roberts smiled back and said that he wouldn't.

Lindsey and Roberts went up one flight of stairs and proceeded down the hall. One wall of the corridor was glass, and Roberts could see the entire production floor. The floor was organized into small production cells. Each group of operators in a work cell was busy at their machines doing their individual tasks. He noticed that many of the workers were female and of various minorities.

"They really look overworked, don't they?" Lindsey asked while showing a slight sarcastic smile. Roberts noticed that Lindsey walked with a slight limp. He had to make a conscious effort to walk slowly and not pass him. "He must be disabled somehow," Roberts thought to himself. Magic Cable appeared to be a lot different than the ceramic tile plant with all of its dust, heat, noisy conveyors, and frantic production pace. Gary Roberts had his second good feeling about Magic Cable.

As the pair approached the third office, Gary noticed the expression on Bill Lindsey's face change. It became somber, almost showing agony. Lindsey turned and knocked on the door facing the hall. Roberts maintained his position behind Lindsey while they both stood quietly and waited to be acknowledged.

"Bill, ya'll come on in," the man inside the office said. As Lindsey and Roberts entered the office, Bob Walters rose so he could shake Roberts's hand. "This is Gary Roberts, Bob. He's here to interview for the mechanic position."

"Great, have a seat, Gary," said Walters, gesturing to an empty office chair across from his desk. He was a good bit taller than Roberts and appeared to be in his middle fifties. He was dressed in Western style and had an air of arrogance in his manner and speech, which gave Gary an uneasy feeling.

"First, Gary, tell me why you want to leave Tile-Elite," Walters said. In reply Roberts described the working conditions at Tile-Elite, explaining that there was no overtime and little chance for advancement. He purposely omitted his feeling about Al Wright, the plant manager. Walters sat almost motionless and listened.

"What about the people you work for?" Walters asked, expecting Roberts to add to his explanation. So Roberts related that he and management had had some differences, but said that he preferred not to expound upon them. Walters seemed satisfied with that explanation. He knew Gary's present boss personally and understood the problems. He also knew that if Gary had said there were no problems, he would have been lying, and there was no room at Magic Cable for a liar.

Walters began to explain what Magic Cable had to offer a plant employee. He compared Magic Cable to the tile plant. Magic Cable's working conditions were fairly pleasant. He described how the building was air-conditioned, clean, and reasonably quiet. Maintenance staff members always got overtime because they were required to work six shifts of 10 hours each per week, with no exceptions. If the production floor was not working, maintenance people could always find something to do. The hourly pay was not quite up to Tile-Elite's level, but Walters explained that Roberts could expect to catch up in salary after a 90-day probationary period. Magic Cable paid an incentive bonus every three months, and the maintenance department was included in that program.

"I've got one final question," Walters added. "How do you feel working with women? We have around 150 women on first shift and about 100 on second shift, so if there's going to be a problem in that area, I need to know it now."

"It's not a problem for me. I don't believe in dating anyone where I work," Roberts replied.

"Great, as far as I'm concerned you've got the job if you want it. What do you think, Bill?" Walters said, after turning to face Lindsey.

"Sounds great to me. Gary, you ready for work?" Lindsey asked.

"Let me give Tile-Elite a week's notice and I'll be here with bells on," Roberts answered, smiling broadly.

Roberts loved his new job. When people asked him what he did at Magic Cable, he would reply that he was semiretired. The work was easy, the machines were simple, and the 60 hours a week did wonders for his bank account. On the sixth day, Saturday, most of his time was spent in the machine shop teaching himself to run the machines. He had some small conflicts with the way things were run, but nothing serious. The most significant problem was that he wanted to be given formal training relating to the new electronics being integrated into production processes. However, Magic Cable had shown no interest in providing that training. Roberts hoped that attitude would change. He knew he had to have patience.

As the months passed, the machine repair procedures became routine. As a result the days became boring, and the sixth 10-hour shift of every week felt more like 20 hours. Roberts suggested to his maintenance supervisor that the mechanics could take turns being off on Saturday. That would give everyone some recreational time and save Magic Cable some money.

When the supervisor voiced the proposal to Walters, he went ballistic. He did not bother relaying his reply through the supervisor; he came to the floor himself to find Roberts. As the manager quickly strode through the maintenance shop gate with the supervisor right behind him, Roberts thought to himself, "Uh-oh!"

Walters stopped in front of the workbench where Roberts was putting seals in a gearbox. He pointed his finger at the mechanic and said tensely, "When you came to work here you agreed to work six 10-hour shifts a week, and that is what you are going to work. The choice is not yours. If you do not want to live up to your agreement, you need to load up your toolbox and move on."

Roberts had no reply other than a rather weak "Yes, sir." With that response, Walters turned and left the maintenance shop without speaking another word.

For the next two years Roberts and the other members of the maintenance department worked within the work schedule guidelines set by Walters. Although some weekends off would have been nice, the steady overtime pay enabled them to have a higher standard of living. One mechanic purchased a newer, larger home, and Roberts purchased the new sports car he had been wishing for.

Then one Monday morning a new production supervisor, Dale Wood, met Roberts at the time clock just inside the plant door. He appeared to be a different type of person than Walters. Wood handed Roberts a white sheet of paper folded in half so that the print was covered. As he did this, he said, "This memo outlines the new policy covering the work schedule of the maintenance department and machine shop. Rick Tanal is over the maintenance department and the machine shop from now on. He broke the news to me this morning and told me to pass it on to you and the other guys."

Tanal was the plant manager. He was a retired major from the military and had a terrible attitude toward the guys, but he was sweet as sugar to the girls. One indicator of his personality was that he would shoot armadillos and rabbits while hunting on the company deer lease with his .458 magnum rifle (elephant gun) and then brag to everyone about how many pieces they were blown into. Roberts disliked him immensely and did not try to hide it.

His "big me, little you" attitude had caused more than a few problems and clashes with male employees. His favorite reply, when asked about something the company had promised but had not delivered, was "You got that in writing?" The hourly personnel had not signed a contract, so their answer was always no. His typical comment was that if the promise was not in writing it was not binding.

Roberts opened the folded sheet and read the memo. It stated that as of the previous Friday evening the maintenance department and the machine shop were not part of engineering anymore; they were now a part of the production department. The memo also stated that the personnel in those two departments would be limited to 40 hours of work per week for an indefinite period. As he read the memo, Roberts's temperature skyrocketed. He yelled, almost screamed, several vulgar words and made derogatory statements concerning Tanal and his parentage as he headed for the production office.

When Roberts got to Tanal's office he did not even knock on the door. He rushed in through the doorway, causing the plant manager to abruptly stop a telephone conversation in midsentence.

Holding the memo up in Tanal's face, he asked, "What the hell is this crap?"

"New orders from the front office," Tanal replied, smiling slightly. Tanal told the party on the other end of the phone line goodbye and hung up the phone.

"This is not what I agreed on when I went to work here. Bob Walters said that overtime was a requirement of the job. When I tried to get him to cut the hours back, he threatened to fire me," Roberts almost yelled.

"That is in the past and has nothing to do with what is required at this time," Tanal answered. "You and the rest of the department need to learn how to live on 40 hours a week," he continued. "If you had been doing that all along, you would not be hurt by the cutback in working hours."

"I don't know who the hell you think you are, but don't tell me how to live. I spend as I see fit, whether I make my money here. . . or somewhere else." Roberts paused, and then added, "I'll tell you what, I'll give you a week, unless you don't want it, then I'm out of here."

"Are you saying that you quit?" Tanal asked.

"That's what I'm saying. I don't want to work for a thief, and I consider you a thief," Gary stated.

"A thief. How do you get that?" Tanal asked.

"Whenever you take something away you promised without discussing it, you're stealing—and that's what you did. As far as I'm concerned, you stole my overtime hours from me, which amounts to about half of my check, " Roberts returned.

Tanal did not have a chance to reply to this conjecture because Roberts turned abruptly and exited the office.

Roberts worked his last week grudgingly. He did not want to stay at Magic Cable, but he said he would, so he did. By the end of the week he had secured a job as a line mechanic for a local bottling plant, loaded his toolboxes in his truck, and moved on.

Case 6: MEXFABRICS

Martha Burkle, Monterrey Institute of Technology*

Juan Diego Martinez watched the sunset over the city of Guadalajara. It was not only the heat that made the human resources manager at MexFabrics sweat during the day. Production orders from head quarters in Mexico City were far more a problem for him. After the Easter holidays another seven workers had quit work without a particular reason. High turnover of MexFabrics' production employees, most of whom were women, had been a constant problem since Martinez started his job two years ago. Now the problem had turned into a serious matter threatening the company's reputation. How could he finish orders on time and also maintain high standards of quality without the experienced people he needed? The work was highly dependent on handwork because automation was almost nonexistent in most of the small manufacturing plants in Mexico; and MexFabrics' most important competitive advantage was the high quality of its products.

People at the head office in Mexico City expected excellent results this year, and Martinez knew that this could not be achieved until he solved the problem of the high staff turnover. He thought that this was especially difficult looking at the personal situations of many of his female workers and the specific context in Mexico. A strategy had to be developed whereby the situation was radically improved and a stable, well-trained, experienced workforce established.

MexFabrics: The Company

The company had started its operation in 1938 by importing fine Italian, French, and Spanish ties under the names of several recognized brands. Years after that the MexFabrics group decided to manufacture high-quality ties in Mexico. By the 1970s the company's production became an addition to the already large clothes manufacturing industry in Mexico, which had begun in 1966 with the purpose of promoting foreign investment and technology transfer in the country. Manufacturing industries in Mexico had enjoyed a large growth spurt during the 1990s, supported by the implementation of NAFTA, foreign investment from other countries (particularly the United States, Canada, and Japan), and cheap hand labor. Currently there were over 4,500 garment manufacturing plants employing over 2 million people in Mexico. So MexFabrics had entered an already large industry sector. Over the years compatible products were added to the line of ties: fine shirts, trousers, cuff links, belts, and scarves.

Now MexFabrics was one of the largest and best-known manufacturers of fine clothes in Mexico. The company manufactured and marketed 30 different high-quality products for men. In total, the company employed 1,000 people in Mexico, of which almost 400 manufactured 80 percent of the products in Guadalajara. The operations were divided between formal and casual wear, which were then further divided into several subgroups. In both fields shirts and ties were among the most important products. Last year MexFabrics had sold around a million articles with a sales volume of more than 300 million Mexican pesos (30 million US dollars). Shirts represented 35 percent of sales, followed by ties with 30 percent and trousers with 15 percent. MexFabrics was the number one supplier to the two largest mall chains in Mexico in relation to sales and prestige.

The work performed at MexFabrics could appear easy and repetitive; employees simply received raw materials, and after sewing and cutting, a final piece of work was produced. But nothing was further from the truth. In fact, being an employee at MexFabrics was a challenging task. The manufacture of quality clothing demands high levels of employee skills and special abilities supported by regular training to be able to produce a high-quality piece quickly.

Operations and Human Resources Challenges for Group MexFabrics

In 1991 the first shirt factory of the group was built in Guadalajara in response to the company's need to offer better service to the group and to improve quality control standards. In 1994 the leather and ties factory was transferred from Mexico City to Guadalajara, and in 1997 the plant for casual shirts and trousers began operations. Daily production in these plants consisted of approximately 1,300 shirts, 1,200 ties, 300 trousers, and 950 leather products such as belts and wallets.

The production process started with the production order, which documented the specifications and quantities, and the receipt of the raw material, which was imported from Italy, France, or Spain and received at the general warehouse in Mexico City. After the first quality inspection, the raw materials were sent to production, where the forms were designed and the product fabricated. Product quality was maintained by frequently inspecting random samples throughout the production process.

After packing, products were sent to the distribution center in Guadalajara and then shipped to the different outlets around Mexico.

MexFabrics had recently experienced a number of challenges and opportunities regarding employees. The high turnover among personnel (up to 20 percent per month by the end of 2004) threatened product quality as inexperienced employees filled jobs vacated by expert staff. The problem of fulfilling the planned production output, together with the time required for recruiting new personnel, was also putting a great deal of pressure on plant managers and on the human resources manager.

MexFabrics received many job applicants, but selecting the appropriate personnel for the demanding production process was a difficult task. Out of every 100 applications, the human resources department in Guadalajara selected about 50 for individual interviews and chose about 10 people for employment in the plants. There they received specific training in manufacturing MexFabrics' different products, from shirts to trousers. After about two weeks of this training, the new recruits began working in assigned production jobs, receiving advice and instruction for several more weeks. It took about six months for a typical worker to be fully trained.

All workers received salary increases based on the number of weeks they had worked for the company. These increases were proportional to the country's general inflation rate. To give an example, during the first semester last year, inflation had been 0.8 percent. So after 8 weeks the salary increased 0.5 percent, and this increase reached 1 percent after 48 weeks. After that the salary increase policy was replaced by a bonus policy that encouraged employees' loyalty to the company over a period of 18 months. Employees also received bonuses for punctuality and attendance. Moreover, there was an incentive for the different operation units, trousers or belts for example, in which workers earned more money by improving productivity (total pieces produced per person-hour). However, employees seldom received these productivity bonuses because high turnover kept productivity too low.

MexFabrics' Organizational Culture

Buses operated on specific routes every morning to facilitate workers' transportation to the plant. For those who lived far from the bus routes, a certain amount of money was designated to pay for public transportation. Because women represented a large percentage of the workforce, MexFabrics had a child care center, which was offered to workers who had been employed for at least five years in the company and had a good work record. This strategy created satisfaction among the women who could enjoy the benefit but was not well seen by those who were still new to the company. Moreover, to reduce the turnover of workers during the first weeks while they were still in training, MexFabrics paid a special bonus for those who learned their jobs quickly.

An internal magazine promoted MexFabrics' organizational culture. Boards across the plant also stated the company's values and mission: to be a flexible, dynamic, and efficient company that responded to market needs. Distributed information also promoted employee loyalty to the company.

However, promoting loyalty was a difficult task for the HR department. Low literacy skills and lack of responsibility seemed to be a constant characteristic among many manufacturing employees in developing countries. Coming from poor families, many employees just wanted to survive day-to-day and had no vision of the possibilities that working in the sector could give them, such as skills development and economic stability.

Personal problems among the workers or social problems within their households were seen as the main reasons for the high turnover, resulting in a shortage of experienced personnel. Many employees lacked the necessary education to perform the work, whereas others lacked commitment to the company. Often without any reason people would fail to show up for work for a day or would suddenly quit. There was an urgent need to analyze and overcome these problems.

Martinez, MexFabrics' human resources manager, was not too keen to go to bed that night; he knew the problem of chronic employee turnover would not let him sleep well. At a meeting scheduled on Monday morning, MexFabrics' directors expected Martinez to outline a decisive strategy to significantly reduce turnover. He would certainly present some things that he thought were crucial. But within the context of the firm, the economic and social climate of Mexican industry, and the day-to-day personal and social challenges experienced by the mainly female workers, things were not always so easy to realize.

*Jaschar Saedi of the Otto Beisheim Graduate School of Management, Germany, assisted in developing this case study.

Case 7: NIRVANA ART GALLERY

Christine Ho, University of Adelaide

It was an irony not lost on many of the employees of Nirvana Art Gallery. This gallery was far from being a place of harmony and joy. In fact, some of the employees preferred to refer to management using the acronym "NAG" in a derogatory manner.

Nirvana was regarded as one of the leading art museums in Australia. The collection of Australian art was one of the oldest and best known in the country. This museum also housed an enviable aboriginal collection and an international collection of considerable breadth and depth.

Rod was the assistant curator for the curatorial unit. Despite his job title, his time was divided between the curatorial and research units because there was not enough work in the former to keep him occupied from week to week. It was agreed between the managers of the two units that he work Mondays through Wednesdays at curatorial and then the remaining days at research. Although Rod would have preferred to work solely for curatorial because that was where his interests lay, he was in no position to argue with either manager. He hoped that when he finished his PhD in art history he would be employed full-time in curatorial, where he could fully use his specialized knowledge and meet his aspiration to be a curator.

Rod did not particularly enjoy coming to work on Thursdays. The research he was asked to do was okay. It was not that stimulating, but he convinced himself that it was useful to understand the functions of the different units in the gallery and not restrict himself to purely curatorial issues. The research unit was quite small, and the staff were very serious. Because they were located within close proximity to each other, he tried initially to be friendly to them while they worked.

When he kept getting frowns and annoyed looks from his colleagues, it became obvious that they did not like being interrupted. Further, they assumed he did not have enough work to do, so they kept giving him more tasks. Rod found himself falling behind and having to ask for permission to stay late to finish his work. Because the gallery housed expensive art works, security was tight. All staff members were expected to leave by 5 p.m. and not return until the following morning after 8 a.m. Managers were strict about granting this special permission because security had to be notified so that alarm systems could be adjusted and monitored accordingly. Because the research manager, Nelly, often stayed late she did not mind granting Rod permission as well.

On Friday morning Rod met with Nelly to give her the report he had written about business plans.

529

"Thanks Rod, it looks good," said Nelly, as she flipped through the document. "You're still working on that draft document on the current spending and budget allocation for this year, aren't you? Andrew can help you with this."

Rod hesitated. "Oh, I think I have all the necessary information, and I'm sure Andrew is busy anyway. If I stay late tonight, I might be able to give it to you before I leave work."

"What's wrong?" asked Nelly.

"It's nothing. I just always get the impression that I'm disturbing everyone in research. They seem really busy all the time and don't seem to have time for anything else. I'm more of a sociable and friendly person, and I like to talk with others while I work."

Nelly gave him a look that Rod did not know how to decipher. I hope she does not think I am complaining about my job or my colleagues, Rod thought to himself as he walked out of her office. He liked the fact that no one was breathing down his neck all the time. And the last thing he needed was to create animosity between himself and the rest of research. It was bad enough that they always went out for lunch together and never invited him. But at least they could say hello whenever he was there.

The following Thursday, when Nelly came into the research area to talk to one of the researchers, she came by his desk to say that she had read both his reports that he finished last week, thanked him for his hard work, and asked how his work was going. He appreciated the attention. Over the following weeks when he was in research, she would come by and talk to him. This sometimes included complimenting him on his appearance. How his shirt color emphasized his eyes, or his new stylish haircut made him look more handsome. At least someone was talking to me, thought Rod. He did not think her comments were appropriate, but he accepted them graciously with a smile, making sure he kept his comments professional. He also tried to minimize how often he had to stay late at work so as not to give the wrong impression. But usually that was not possible given his workload.

It was not long before the other researchers noticed the attention she gave him. He started noticing the surreptitious looks and frowns he received whenever she spoke to him. Rod thought he was being paranoid. A couple of times when he had walked into the research area, some of the researchers were talking in low voices, but they would stop when they noticed him.

Rod wondered what was going on. It was not like he was not pulling his own weight around here. He got the projects done on time even though he worked only two days each week in research, and Nelly had told him numerous times that he was doing a good job. Rod put his thoughts aside and focused on his day's tasks. He went home that weekend pleased for once that he did not have to work late.

He arrived at work on Monday in good spirits. He had studied all weekend and nearly completed his final draft of his PhD thesis. He always enjoyed working in the curatorial unit. He found his work preparing upcoming exhibitions interesting. Further, he liked the curatorial team. His manager, Sarah, was approachable; and despite his being the most junior team member, his colleagues regularly asked for his input during the weekly Monday meetings. The team was friendly, and he found he had a lot in common with many of them. Sometimes he would be invited to lunch when he was there on one of his curatorial days. Working in curatorial also meant that he was not in research. He would not have to put up with Nelly's comments, which were beginning to really make him feel uncomfortable, and he did not have to put up with the whispers or silent stares he got from his research colleagues. Rod was looking forward to working on a catalog for an aboriginal exhibition the gallery was to host next month when Nelly walked in.

"Rod, you're looking sexy today. Andrew is away sick. Can you come and work in research today?" she asked.

"Um, I can't, Nelly. I'm supposed to work in curatorial today, and it's really busy at the moment. We've got this exhibition coming up and we're behind. Claire is on maternity leave, and two others in curatorial are sick as well with that flu that's going around at the moment. Sorry, but I can't."

Nelly frowned and left without a backward glance. I'll be at research soon enough on Thursday anyway, thought Rod.

Later that day Rod received an e-mail message from Nelly:

Rod,

There has been a change in your work arrangement to start this week. The assistant director and I have decided that instead of working in curatorial three days and research two days, you will now work in curatorial only two days, and then on Wednesday switch over to research for the rest of the week.

Nelly.

Rod began to feel panicky. The whole point of this job was to gain curatorial experience, which was why he had changed his PhD status to part-time. He went to see Sarah to see if she could get his work days changed back. Unfortunately Sarah just confirmed the arrangement.

"There's nothing I can do about this, Rod. I wish I could, but Nelly helped me get this job. You're a valuable member of curatorial, and we both know everyone on the team is flat out with the others away sick or on leave. Nelly has more authority than me and is good friends with the assistant director."

When Rod arrived in research on Wednesday, Nelly told him that the desk arrangements were to be changed around. His desk was now visible from her office at all times. Other things began to change in research as well. Nelly rarely spoke to him except to pass on job assignments. And because he was there an extra day each week, he was able to complete his tasks without having to stay after hours. Rod was pleased about that. However, as the weeks passed, there were not enough tasks to keep him occupied, and he was told to find something to do.

He felt as if he was wasting his time, especially because curatorial continued to be short-staffed and research was now brimming with staff and limited work. Rod hated that sometimes he had to pretend to be busy.

To make matters worse, when he would arrive at work Nelly had started to remark, "So *now* you've decided to turn up to work" or "Getting your beauty sleep, were we?" His fellow researchers began to chime in with similar snide remarks, like "While you've been having your coffee, we've been at work since 8 a.m."

It was getting unbearable in research for Rod. Even though his colleagues were talking to him now, he much preferred it when they were not.

Rod was unhappy. He was at lunch with some of the curatorial staff and told them about the e-mail message.

"You'll just have to do the time with research and hope that you get back on the good side of Nelly. She may eventually change things back so that you can work more in curatorial. She's a NAG who likes to use her power over others. It's happened before."

Case 8: WOODLAND COMMUNITY CENTER CORPORATION

Joseph C. Santora, Essex County College & TST, Inc.

Fred Chambers, the recently appointed executive director of the Woodland Community Center Corporation (WCCC), leaned back in his overstuffed executive chair and contemplated his new job. At 60 years old, he felt young and fit. His career as a nonprofit executive director had spanned more than 25 years at five diverse nonprofit organizations. Once he believed his job was done at an organization, he moved on to accept the challenges of a new executive position. Most of all, Chambers resisted complacency, and he wanted to avoid getting stale in the saddle.

After retiring about four years ago, Chambers heard the trumpet's call to lead once again, so he sought short-term or interim leadership positions in nonprofit organizations. He enjoyed the challenges of the unique organizational niche he had carved out for himself. His last three interim executive director appointments had lasted six months, two years, and one year respectively and served both him and the

hiring boards of directors well. By hiring Chambers on an interim basis, boards of directors, many of whom lacked the foresight to prepare an executive succession plan, could conduct a more thorough executive search for a permanent replacement rather than hastily appointing someone who did not fit the organization.

Once appointed, Chambers was given carte blanche by the boards to make the necessary internal organizational changes; and despite some initial rocky starts, things had worked out well for both him and the nonprofits he led. Chambers got an opportunity to travel to different locations throughout the country, met some interesting people, received a lucrative compensation package, and enjoyed a fixed-term contract agreement; on the other hand, the boards got the opportunity to hire an outsider—someone with diversified senior administrative experiences—to develop and implement a strategy for organizational change. The overall assessment of

Chambers as a "gun for hire" by his various board employers was quite respectable.

But unlike past situations, Chambers felt uneasy about this new executive appointment. This time, against his wife's advice, he had taken a full-time permanent executive director position as a replacement for Alain Yates, the articulate, charismatic, long-term executive director at the WCCC. From time to time, the community center board had heard some internal rumblings about the organizational culture at the agency, but it failed to act because Yates held considerable power over the board as a result of his longevity in office and the constant turnover of board members. Chambers's appointment as executive director signaled the community center board's earnest desire to change the organizational culture at the agency. As Chambers conducted his fact-finding mission, he uncovered what the board in general seemed to know about the organizational culture: Yates had encouraged policies of "double standards" that demotivated some long-term and industrious agency employees. Perhaps Chambers should have heeded his wife's warning about taking a full-time position. After assessing his situation, he now thought, "Be careful what you wish for—you just might get it."

Gail Katz, a social worker, had founded the Woodland Community Center Corporation (WCCC) in 1926 to deliver a variety of social and human services to the indigent population of Woodland, an East Coast seaport city. Over time the organization had a series of executive directors. Alain Yates had been the longest-reigning executive director and had led the WCCC for the past 25 years. Yates assumed the leadership of the agency after a tumultuous internal struggle almost caused the agency to cease operations. He gained support for the position from several powerful administrative and staff members in the agency. This internal groundswell forced the board of directors to appoint Yates as the executive director of the agency. Once the board approved his three-year contract as executive director, Yates immediately began repaying the political debts he owed these in-group members for their support. He simultaneously initiated a number of bold steps to clean up the agency, and through his adroitness the local media turned Yates into a savior figure; yet some agency employees began to say quietly that Yates was just an ordinary leader who now began to display a new attitude toward employees. One employee who was especially critical of Yates's leadership stated, "Yates *believes* his own newspaper clippings."

Alain Yates, more so than any previous WCCC executive director, had shaped the organizational culture of the agency. For him seniority was sacrosanct, and neither creativity nor hard work replaced it. Many employees enjoyed a secure work environment, and few employees were fired for a poor work ethic. The key to employee survival and its attendant rewards was loyalty, not competency. Furthermore, loyalty was the sole way to advance in the agency or to receive a pay increase for the agency's over 100 employees. However, not all employees felt comfortable with Yates's leadership style. For example, some employees were upset with Yates's decision to give certain employees reserved parking spaces while they had to walk a considerable distance to the agency—a policy that irked them particularly during inclement weather. In addition, other employees became vexed after Yates denied their requests to attend a local off-site management seminar; he often quipped, "We really don't have enough money in the budget" or "Do you really need to attend this seminar? Nothing in management has changed that much." One employee was so outraged when she discovered that Yates had on the same day approved a request for an in-group employee to attend a high-priced, out-of-state conference that she announced to some colleagues, "I'll do my job, but nothing more as long as Yates is here."

This two-tiered structure created a further wedge between the agency's so-called "haves and have nots." Yates's actions resulted in a small but noticeable agency fissure that led to a growing rift between employees who sought to excel and those who just got by on their loyalty. One long-time employee opined, "I simply do not believe in just getting by, but . . ."

Despite this, many employees decided not to leave the agency because, as a result of Yates's external political contacts and connections with philanthropic funding agencies, employee salaries were superior to those in similar organizations. Moreover, members of the out-group—employees not part of the agency in-group elite whom Yates constantly rewarded—decided to remain at the agency because as one employee succinctly put it, "We are committed to working for the betterment of the agency and its clients, and we will stay despite *his* preferential treatment of 'pet' employees." But over time, as employees retired or slowly trickled out of the agency because they could no longer tolerate what one employee called "employment injustices," they were replaced by new employees who were connected to agency in-group members or financial contributors to the agency. Both, regardless of how they arrived at the agency, had one characteristic in common: They swore undying loyalty to Yates. The agency was becoming more incestuous and a breeding ground for a groupthink mentality. At this month's staff meeting Yates had informed staff about some serious agency problems. However, no one dared mention that these problems and their negative organizational impact were a result of several major strategic leadership blunders Yates had made. One astute observer sitting in the last row of the cavernous room where staff meetings were held whispered in a muffled voice, "I guess I am the only one who noticed that the emperor has no clothes."

Yates also informed managers and staff that he was retiring as the executive director of the agency. But prior to announcing his retirement plans after his 25th year in office, Yates had recommended to the board of directors a successor from among his most trusted managers to continue his legacy. Agency managers and employees prepared several lavish retirement celebrations for Yates—they held a formal retirement dinner, hosted several large parties, and even etched Yates's name in gold leaf on the glass entrance doors to the agency.

Despite all the hoopla and festive mood, the board of directors dealt Yates a major blow when it announced that Fred Chambers would succeed him. Board members had been quietly working behind the scenes, waiting for the right opportunity to create an environment for changing the organizational culture. Board members believed that their change to Chambers would do this. They had already exerted strong pressure on him to reduce costs, to begin downsizing the nonessential politically connected staff, and to restore a new sense of professionalism to the agency. Chambers knew that he was a good leader, knew he had the confidence of the board, and most important, knew he had to change the organizational culture that had existed in the organization for last quarter of a century. He thought to himself, "My legacy won't be etched on any glass doors." But first he had to begin the process of changing the organizational culture that was so deeply embedded in the WCCC.

Note: The names and some managerial actions in this case have been altered to preserve the integrity and anonymity of the organization. This case is intended to be used as a basis for class discussion rather than to illustrate either effective or ineffective handling of a management situation.

Source: ©Joseph C. Santora.

VIDEO CASES FOR PART ONE

TROUBLES AT GENERAL MOTORS

General Motors Corporation isn't bankrupt, but the once-great automaker is on the rocks, laying off employees and recently losing $4 billion. Its market share, which was almost 50 percent a few decades ago, has dropped to 25 percent. While part of this problem may be due to poor strategy, a major burden is GM's legacy costs. The company spends $5.2 billion annually on health care for its 145,000 workers and more than 1 million retirees. That equates to a cost disadvantage of $1,500 for every car that GM makes. This video program describes GM's current woes and how it got there.

Discussion Questions

1. Describe General Motors' current problems in terms of the demands from its various stakeholders.

2. Rather than laying off redundant workers, GM has a jobs bank in which employees can transfer to other jobs or remain fully paid while serving the community until a job becomes available. Discuss this practice in terms of corporate social responsibility.

NEW BELGIUM BREWERY

This video program outlines the various ways in which New Belgium Brewery in Fort Collins, Colorado, tries to operate an environmentally sustainable business. The company accomplishes impressive environmental standards through new technology, alternative forms of energy, and waste minimization. The program reveals these environmentally sustainable strategies and describes how employees buy into this model of doing business.

Discussion Questions

1. Describe the various ways that New Belgium Brewery supports environmental sustainability.

2. How did New Belgium Brewery's founders gain employee support for environmental sustainability?

VIDEO CASES FOR PART TWO

GOOD BUSINESS DEEDS

You might not expect to see British American Tobacco, McDonald's, and Microsoft at a meeting on corporate social responsibility, but in their own way these firms are taking steps to become better employers and citizens in the community. This video program describes how these and other firms are embracing values and corporate social responsibility. It particularly highlights a few firms that serve as role models in this regard. One of these is Greyston Bakery, a multimillion dollar gourmet operation that takes people who need help and turns them into contributing members of the organization and society. Another is Eileen Fisher Company, which promotes good labor practices both at home and overseas, and helps customers meet their needs. In each case, the company's values are aligned more closely with employee values than at your typical organization.

Discussion Questions

1. Employees at Greyston Bakery, Eileen Fisher Company, Feed the Children, Green@Work, and other organizations described in this video program seem to have a strong congruence of their personal values with the organization's values. What are the apparent benefits of this values congruence?

2. Discuss the implications of corporate social responsibility in terms of employer branding. What companies come to mind whose employer brand is "doing good" for the community?

WORKPLACE BIAS

Wal-Mart is known for its low prices, but many former and current female employees claim the company also has discriminatory low pay and promotional opportunities for women. This video program presents the views of several women who have joined in one of the largest class action sex discrimination lawsuits in history. They claim that qualified women at Wal-Mart receive fewer promotions than their male counterparts. Others say they were fired for launching a sexual harassment complaint. The program describes statistics showing that male district managers earn significantly more than their female counterparts.

Discussion Questions

1. Use your knowledge of social identity theory, stereotyping, and prejudice to explain how sex discrimination might exist at Wal-Mart and in other large retail organizations. Be sure to note any evidence described in this program to support your explanation.

2. If you were a senior manager at Wal-Mart and believed that some of these complaints are due to stereotyping and other biases among middle managers, what interventions would you recommend to correct these biases?

MONEY & ETHICS

Is business ethics an oxymoron? Although stock manipulation and other forms of business fraud have occurred for hundreds of years, Barbara Toffler, an ethics professor and former ethics consultant at Arthur Andersen, believes that business can be more ethical. Still, she acknowledges that being ethical isn't easy. Most executives know right from wrong, yet they make unethical decisions when the financial rewards and pressure to perform are high enough. This video case study documents Toffler's experience at Arthur Andersen, where greed overwhelmed ethical values. It also tells the story of grocer Stew Leonard, Sr., who was jailed for tax fraud just two years after being featured in an ethics video.

Discussion Questions

1. Identify the various strategies described in this video program to encourage ethical conduct and discourage or punish wrongdoing. Explain why each of these practices is, or is not, effective.

2. Use the expectancy theory of motivation, discussed in Chapter 5, to explain why people engage in unethical behavior even though they know it is wrong.

NOW WHO'S BOSS?

Jonathan Tisch, CEO of Loews Hotels, had plenty of opportunity to empathize with staff when he spent five days performing a variety of frontline jobs. Although Tisch began his career working on the front desk, times have changed. Tisch discovered the complexities of computer technology as well as the challenges of greeting irritable guests, making beds, and working in sweaty polyester outfits. In this video program Tisch recalls his five-day experience.

Discussion Questions

1. Relate the frontline experience that Tisch went through to the Johari Window model.

2. Is working on the frontlines an effective way for executives to understand the business? Why or why not?

PIKE PLACE FISH MARKET

Fifteen years ago, Pike Place Fish Market in Seattle had unhappy employees and was in financial trouble. Rather than close shop, owner John Yokoyama sought help from consultant Jim Bergquist to improve his leadership and energize the workforce. Rather than rule as a tyrant, Yokoyama learned how to actively involve employees in the business. Soon,

staff felt more empowered and gained more enjoyment from their work. They also began to actively have fun at work, including setting goals as a game, throwing fish to each other as sport, and pretending they are "world famous". Today, thanks to these and other strategies described in this video case, Pike Place is world famous. The little shop has become a tourist attraction and customers from California to New York call in orders.

Discussion Questions

1. Based on the model of emotions and attitudes in Chapter 4, explain how the changes at Pike Place Fish Market improved job satisfaction and reduced turnover. How did these attitude changes affect customer satisfaction?

2. Goal setting is discussed as an important activity at Pike Place. Evaluate the effectiveness of this goal setting process in the context of the characteristics of effective goals described in Chapter 5 of this textbook.

3. How is coaching applied at Pike Place, and how does this coaching influence employee performance?

STRESS IN JAPAN

Stress from overwork has become an epidemic in Japan. This video program consists of two segments that illustrate the degree to which some Japanese employees are overworked, as well as the consequences of their overwork. The first segment follows a typical day of a Japanese manager, from his two-hour morning commute to his late night working hours. The program also shows how he is under constant pressure to improve efficiency, and experiences a heavy burden and responsibility to do better. The second segment describes how karoshi–death from overwork–took the life of 23-year-old Yoshika. It reconstructs Yoshiko's work life as a graphic artist up to the time when she died suddenly on the job due to a brain hemorrhage.

Discussion Questions

1. Identify the various sources of stress (i.e. stressors) that the Japanese manager in the first segment likely experiences each day. Does he do anything to try to manage his stress?

2. What conditions led up to the karoshi death of Yoshika? Are these conditions commonly found in the country where you live?

AMERICA: AN OVERWORKED NATION (WORKING SMART)

Americans are working more hours, even when not at the office (thanks to technology). E-mails alone consume up to one full day each week. In this video program, you'll hear from people on the street about their long work days. The program cites surveys on how many hours people work, how much of their vacation they use, and what are the consequences of overwork. The program closes by recommending several steps to reduce work overload.

Discussion Questions

1. What seems to be the main causes of work overload? Which jobs would likely have these conditions more than others?

2. This program identifies several strategies to minimize work overload. Organize these recommendations into the various stress management categories described in Chapter 7. Does this program overlook any of the stress management categories in its recommendations? If so, what recommendations can you generate from those overlooked categories regarding overwork?

VIDEO CASES FOR PART THREE

BULLY BROADS

Women executives in Silicon Valley who seem to be over-aggressive are sent to (or voluntarily join) a reform program called the Bully Broads Program. The program provides executive coaching as well as group activities to curb the impulse to influence others through too much assertiveness. But while the program tries to change women, its founder and participants also believe there is a double standard; aggressive male executives aren't sent to similar programs, whereas women are expected to act more genteel.

Discussion Questions

1. Use your knowledge of leadership theories to explain why aggressive women are told to be less aggressive whereas this behavior is acceptable in men.

2. Are there situations where employees are more likely to accept aggressive female leaders?

CELEBRITY CEO CHARISMA

Does the cult of CEO charisma really make a difference to company profits? This NBC program takes a brief look at chief executives who acted like superheroes but failed to deliver, as well as a few low-key executives who really made a difference. The program hears from Harvard business school professor Rakesh Khurana, author of "Searching for a Corporate Savior", a book warning that charismatic leaders are not necessarily effective leaders.

Discussion Questions

1. Why do company boards tend to hire charismatic CEOs?

2. What can corporate boards do to minimize the charisma effect when filling chief executive officer and other senior executive positions?

SOUTHWEST CEO: GET TO KNOW GARY KELLY

Southwest Airlines remains one of the most successful airlines in the United States. Its secret to success? Treat customers as kings and queens, and treat employees even better. This video program shows how Southwest Airlines CEO Gary Kelly keeps in touch with day-to-day activities at the airline. It also describes some of the challenges that Kelly and his executive team have ahead of them.

Discussion Questions

1. Discuss the transactional and transformational leadership of Gary Kelly.

2. How does Gary Kelly's leadership reinforce Southwest Airlines' organizational culture?

VIDEO CASE FOR PART FOUR

JETBLUE AIRWAYS

JetBlue Airways is one of America's great aviation success stories. In just a few short years after its startup, the New York-based discount airline has become both profitable and highly popular among customers. Founder David Neeleman claims that the notion of a "JetBlue experience" emerged from customer feedback about their travels on JetBlue. This unique experience is based on the company's customer-focused culture and the many decisions focused on giving customers the best possible encounters.

Discussion Questions

1. Identify the activities or conditions that have developed and maintained JetBlue's customer service culture.

2. How has JetBlue's culture and explicit values influenced its decision making?

appendix A

Theory Building and Systematic Research Methods

People need to make sense of their world, so they form theories about how the world operates. A **theory** is a general set of propositions that describes interrelationships among several concepts. We form theories for the purpose of predicting and explaining the world around us.[1] What does a good theory look like? First, it should be stated as clearly and simply as possible so that the concepts can be measured and there is no ambiguity regarding the theory's propositions. Second, the elements of the theory must be logically consistent with each other because we cannot test anything that doesn't make sense. Finally, a good theory provides value to society; it helps people understand their world better than without the theory.[2]

Theory building is a continuous process that typically includes the inductive and deductive stages shown in Exhibit A.1.[3] The inductive stage draws on personal experience to form a preliminary theory, whereas the deductive stage uses the scientific method to test the theory.

The inductive stage of theory building involves observing the world around us, identifying a pattern of relationships, and then forming a theory from these personal observations. For example, you might casually notice that new employees want their supervisor to give direction, whereas this leadership style irritates long-service employees. From these observations you form a theory about the effectiveness of directive leadership. (See Chapter 14 for a discussion of this leadership style.)

Positivism versus Interpretivism

Research requires an interpretation of reality, and researchers tend to perceive reality in one of two ways. A common view, called **positivism**, is that reality exists independent of people. It is "out there" to be discovered and tested. Positivism is the foundation for most quantitative research (statistical analysis). It assumes that we can measure variables and that those variables have fixed relationships with other variables. For example, the positivist perspective says that we could study whether a supportive style of leadership reduces stress. If we find evidence of this, then someone else studying leadership and stress would "discover" the same relationship.

Interpretivism takes a different view of reality. It suggests that reality comes from shared meaning among people in that environment. For example, supportive leadership is a personal interpretation of

Exhibit A.1   **Theory Building and Theory Testing**

reality, not something that can be measured across time and people. Interpretivists rely mainly on qualitative data, such as observation and nondirective interviews. They particularly listen to the language people use to understand the common meaning that people have toward various events or phenomena. For example, they might argue that you need to experience and observe supportive leadership to effectively study it. Moreover, you can't really predict relationships because the specific situation shapes reality.[4]

Most OB scholars identify themselves somewhere between the extreme views of positivism and interpretivism. Many believe that inductive research should begin with an interpretivist angle. We should enter a new topic with an open mind and search for the shared meaning of people in that situation. In other words, researchers should let the participants define reality rather than let the researcher's preconceived notions shape that reality. This process involves gathering qualitative information and letting this information shape the theory.[5] After the theory emerges, researchers shift to the positivist perspective by quantitatively testing relationships in that theory.

Theory Testing: The Deductive Process

Once a theory has been formed, we shift into the deductive stage of theory building. This process includes forming hypotheses, defining and measuring constructs, and testing hypotheses (see Exhibit A.1). **Hypotheses** make empirically testable declarations that certain variables and their corresponding measures are related in a specific way proposed by the theory. For instance, to find support for the directive leadership theory described earlier, we need to form and then test a specific hypothesis from that theory. One such hypothesis might be this: "New employees are more satisfied with supervisors who exhibit a directive rather than a nondirective leadership style." Hypotheses are indispensable tools of scientific research because they provide the vital link between theory and empirical verification.

Defining and Measuring Constructs   Hypotheses are testable only if we can define and then form measurable indicators of the concepts stated in those hypotheses. Consider the hypothesis in the previous paragraph about new employees and directive leadership. To test this hypothesis, we first need to define the concepts, such as *new employees, directive leadership,* and *supervisor.* These are known as **constructs** because they are abstract ideas constructed by the

researcher that can be linked to observable information. Organizational behavior researchers developed the construct called *directive leadership* to help them understand the different effects that leaders have over followers. We can't directly see, taste, or smell directive leadership; instead we rely on indirect indicators that it exists, such as observing someone giving directions, maintaining clear performance standards, and ensuring that procedures and practices are followed.

As you can see, defining constructs well is important: These definitions become the foundation for finding or developing acceptable measures of those constructs. We can't measure directive leadership if we have only a vague idea about what this concept means. The better a construct is defined, the better our chances of finding or developing a good measure of that construct. However, even with a good definition, constructs can be difficult to measure because the empirical representation must capture several elements in the definition. A measure of directive leadership must be able to identify not only people who give directions, but also those who maintain performance standards and ensure that procedures are followed.

Testing Hypotheses   The third step in the deductive process is to collect data for the empirical measures of the variables. Following our directive leadership example, we might conduct a formal survey in which new employees indicate the behavior of their supervisors and their attitudes toward their supervisors. Alternatively, we might design an experiment in which people work with someone who applies either a directive or nondirective leadership style. When the data have been collected, we can use various procedures to statistically test our hypotheses.

A major concern in theory building is that some researchers might inadvertently find support for their theory simply because they use the same information used to form the theory during the inductive stage. Consequently, the deductive stage must collect new data that are completely independent of the data used during the inductive stage. For instance, you might decide to test your theory of directive leadership by studying employees in another organization. Moreover, the inductive process may have relied mainly on personal observation, whereas the deductive process might use survey questionnaires. By studying different samples and using different measurement tools, we minimize the risk of conducting circular research.

Using the Scientific Method

Earlier we said that the deductive stage of theory building follows the scientific method. The **scientific method** is systematic, controlled, empirical, and critical investigation of hypothetical propositions about the presumed relationships among natural phenomena.[6] There are several elements to this definition, so let's look at each one. First, scientific research is *systematic* and *controlled* because researchers want to rule out all but one explanation for a set of interrelated events. To rule out alternative explanations, we need to control them in some way, such as by keeping them constant or removing them entirely from the environment.

Second, we say that scientific research is *empirical* because researchers need to use objective reality—or as close as we can get to it—to test theory. They measure observable elements of the environment, such as what a person says or does, rather than relying on their own subjective opinions to draw conclusions. Moreover, scientific research analyzes these data using accepted principles of mathematics and logic.

Finally, scientific research involves *critical investigation*. This means that the study's hypotheses, data, methods, and results are openly described so that other experts in the field can properly evaluate the research. It also means that scholars are encouraged to critique and build on previous research. Eventually the scientific method encourages the refinement and eventually the replacement of a particular theory with one that better suits our understanding of the world.

Grounded Theory: An Alternative Approach

The scientific method dominates the quantitative approach to systematic research; but another approach, called **grounded theory**, dominates research using qualitative methods.[7] Grounded theory is a process of developing knowledge through the constant interplay of data collection, analysis, and theory development. It relies mainly on qualitative methods to form categories and variables, analyze relationships among these concepts, and form a model based on the observations and analysis. Grounded theory combines the inductive stages of theory development by cycling back and forth between data collection and analysis to converge on a robust explanatory model. This ongoing reciprocal process results in theory that is grounded in the data (thus the name *grounded theory*).

Like the scientific method, grounded theory is a systematic and rigorous process of data collection and analysis. It requires specific steps and documentation and adopts a positivist view by assuming that the results are generalizable to other settings. However, grounded theory also takes an interpretivist view by building categories and variables from the perceived realities of the subjects rather than from an assumed universal truth.[8] It also recognizes that personal biases are not easily removed from the research process.

Selected Issues in Organizational Behavior Research

There are many issues to consider in theory building, particularly when we use the deductive process to test hypotheses. Some of the more important issues are sampling, causation, and ethical practices in organizational research.

Sampling in Organizational Research   When finding out why things happen in organizations, we typically gather information from a few sources and then draw conclusions about the larger population. If we survey several employees and determine that older employees are more loyal to their company, then we would like to generalize this statement to all older employees in our population, not just those whom we surveyed. Scientific inquiry generally requires researchers to engage in **representative sampling**—that is, sampling a population in such a way that we can extrapolate the results of that sample to the larger population.

One factor that influences representativeness is whether the sample is selected in an unbiased way from the larger population. Let's suppose you want to study organizational commitment among employees in your organization. A casual procedure might result in sampling too few employees from the head office and too many located elsewhere in the country. If head office employees actually have higher loyalty than employees located elsewhere, then the biased sampling would cause the results to underestimate the true level of loyalty among employees in the company. If you repeat the process again next year but somehow overweight employees from the head office, the results might wrongly suggest that employees have increased their organizational commitment over the past year. In reality, the only change may be the direction of sampling bias.

How do we minimize sampling bias? The answer is to randomly select the sample. A randomly drawn sample gives each member of the population an equal probability of being chosen, so there is less likelihood that a subgroup within that population dominates the study's results.

The same principle applies to random assignment of subjects to groups in experimental designs. If we want to test the effects of a team development training program, we need to randomly place some employees in the training group and randomly place others in a group that does not receive training. Without this random selection, each group might have different types of employees, so we wouldn't know whether the training explained the differences between the two groups. Moreover, if employees were to respond differently to the training program, we couldn't be sure that the training program results were representative of the larger population. Of course random sampling does not necessarily produce a perfectly representative sample; but we do know that this is the best approach to ensure unbiased selection.

The other factor that influences representativeness is sample size. Whenever we select a portion of the population, there will be some error in our estimate of the population values. The larger the sample, the less error will occur in our estimate. Let's suppose you want to find out how employees in a 500-person firm feel about smoking in the workplace. If you asked 400 of those employees, the information would provide a very good estimate of how the entire workforce in that organization feels. If you survey only 100 employees, the estimate might deviate more from the true population. If you ask only 10 people, the estimate could be quite different from what all 500 employees feel.

Notice that sample size goes hand-in-hand with random selection. You must have a sufficiently large sample size for the principle of randomization to work effectively. In our example of attitudes toward smoking, we would do a poor job of random selection if our sample consisted of only 10 employees from the 500-person organization. The reason is that these 10 people probably wouldn't capture the diversity of employees throughout the organization. In fact, the more diverse the population, the larger the sample size should be to provide adequate representation through random selection.

Causation in Organizational Research Theories present notions about relationships among constructs. Often these propositions suggest a causal relationship—

namely, that one variable has an effect on another variable. When discussing causation, we refer to variables as being independent or dependent. *Independent* variables are the presumed causes of *dependent* variables, which are the presumed effects. In our earlier example of directive leadership, the main independent variable (there might be others) would be the supervisor's directive or nondirective leadership style because we presume that it causes the dependent variable (satisfaction with supervision).

In laboratory experiments (described later), the independent variable is always manipulated by the experimenter. In our research on directive leadership, we might have subjects (new employees) work with supervisors who exhibit directive or nondirective leadership behaviors. If subjects are more satisfied under the directive leaders, then we would be able to infer an association between the independent and dependent variables.

Researchers must satisfy three conditions to provide sufficient evidence of causality between two variables.[9] The first condition of causality is that the variables are empirically associated with each other. An association exists whenever one measure of a variable changes systematically with a measure of another variable. This condition of causality is the easiest to satisfy because there are several well-known statistical measures of association. A research study might find, for instance, that heterogeneous groups (in which members come from diverse backgrounds) produce more creative solutions to problems. This might be apparent because the measure of creativity (such as number of creative solutions produced within a fixed time) is higher for teams that have a high score on the measure of group heterogeneity. They are statistically associated or correlated with each other.

The second condition of causality is that the independent variable precedes the dependent variable in time. Sometimes this condition is satisfied through simple logic. In our group heterogeneity example, it doesn't make sense to say that the number of creative solutions caused the group's heterogeneity because the group's heterogeneity existed before it produced the creative solutions. In other situations, however, the temporal relationship among variables is less clear. One example is the ongoing debate about job satisfaction and organizational commitment. Do companies develop more loyal employees by increasing their job satisfaction, or do changes in organizational loyalty cause changes in job satisfaction?

Simple logic does not answer these questions; instead researchers must use sophisticated longitudinal studies to build up evidence of a temporal relationship between these two variables.

The third requirement for evidence of a causal relationship is that the statistical association between two variables cannot be explained by a third variable. There are many associations that we quickly dismiss as being causally related. For example, perhaps there is a statistical association between the number of storks in an area and the birthrate in that area. We know that storks don't bring babies, so something else must cause the association between these two variables. The real explanation is that both storks and births have a higher incidence in rural areas.

In other studies, the third variable effect is less apparent. Many years ago, before polio vaccines were available, a study in the United States reported a surprisingly strong association between consumption of a certain soft drink and the incidence of polio. Was polio caused by drinking this pop, or did people with polio have an unusual craving for this beverage? Neither. Both polio and consumption of the soft drink were caused by a third variable: climate. There was a higher incidence of polio in the summer months and in warmer climates, and people drink more liquids in these climates.[10] As you can see from this example, researchers have a difficult time supporting causal inferences because third variable effects are sometimes difficult to detect.

Ethics in Organizational Research   Organizational behavior researchers need to abide by the ethical standards of the society in which the research is conducted. One of the most important ethical considerations is the individual subjects' freedom to participate in the study. For example, it is inappropriate to force employees to fill out a questionnaire or attend an experimental intervention for research purposes only. Moreover, researchers have an obligation to tell potential subjects about any potential risks inherent in the study so that participants can make an informed choice about whether to be involved.

Finally, researchers must be careful to protect the privacy of those who participate in the study. This usually includes letting people know when they are being studied as well as guaranteeing that their individual information will remain confidential (unless publication of identities is otherwise granted). Researchers maintain anonymity through careful security of data. The research results usually aggregate data in numbers large enough that they do not reveal the opinions or characteristics of any specific individual. For example, we would report the average absenteeism of employees in a department rather than state the absence rates of each person. When sharing data with other researchers, it is usually necessary to specially code each case so that individual identities are not known.

Research Design Strategies

So far we have described how to build a theory, including the specific elements of empirically testing that theory within the standards of scientific inquiry. But what are the different ways to design a research study so that we get the data necessary to achieve our research objectives? There are many strategies, but they mainly fall under three headings: laboratory experiments, field surveys, and observational research.

Laboratory Experiments   A **laboratory experiment** is any research study in which independent variables and variables outside the researcher's main focus of inquiry can be controlled to some extent. Laboratory experiments are usually located outside the everyday work environment, such as in a classroom, simulation lab, or any other artificial setting in which the researcher can manipulate the environment. Organizational behavior researchers sometimes conduct experiments in the workplace (called *field experiments*) in which the independent variable is manipulated. However, the researcher has less control over the effects of extraneous factors in field experiments than in laboratory situations.

Advantages of Laboratory Experiments   Laboratory experiments have many advantages. By definition this research method offers a high degree of control over extraneous variables that would otherwise confound the relationships being studied. Suppose we wanted to test the effects of directive leadership on the satisfaction of new employees. One concern might be that employees are influenced by how much leadership is provided, not just the type of leadership style. An experimental design would allow us to control how often the supervisor exhibited this style so that this extraneous variable does not confound the results.

A second advantage of lab studies is that the independent and dependent variables can be developed more precisely than in a field setting. For example, the researcher can ensure that supervisors in a lab study apply specific directive or nondirective behaviors, whereas real-life supervisors would use a more complex mixture of leadership behaviors. By using more precise measures, we can be more certain that we are measuring the intended construct. Thus if new employees are more satisfied with supervisors in the directive leadership condition, we are more confident that the independent variable was directive leadership rather than some other leadership style.

A third benefit of laboratory experiments is that the independent variable can be distributed more evenly among participants. In our directive leadership study, we can ensure that approximately half of the subjects have a directive supervisor, whereas the other half have a nondirective supervisor. In natural settings we might have trouble finding people who have worked with a nondirective leader, and consequently we couldn't determine the effects of this condition.

Disadvantages of Laboratory Experiments

With these powerful advantages, you might wonder why laboratory experiments are the least appreciated form of organizational behavior research.[11] One obvious limitation of this research method is that it lacks realism, so the results might differ in the real world. Another argument is that laboratory experiment subjects are less involved than their counterparts in an actual work situation. This is sometimes true, although many lab studies have highly motivated participants. An additional criticism is that the extraneous variables controlled in the lab setting might produce a different effect of the independent variable on the dependent variables. This might also be true, but remember that the experimental design controls variables in accordance with the theory and its hypotheses. Consequently this concern is really a critique of the theory, not the lab study.

Finally, there is the well-known problem that participants are aware they are being studied, and this causes them to act differently than they normally would. Some participants try to figure out how the researcher wants them to behave and then deliberately try to act that way. Other participants try to upset the experiment by doing just the opposite of what they believe the researcher expects. Still others might act unnaturally simply because they know they are being observed. Fortunately experimenters are well aware of these potential problems and are usually (although not always) successful at disguising the study's true intent.

Field Surveys

Field surveys collect and analyze information in a natural environment—an office, factory, or other existing location. The researcher takes a snapshot of reality and tries to determine whether elements of that situation (including the attitudes and behaviors of people in that situation) are associated with each other as hypothesized. Everyone does some sort of field research. You might think that people from some states are better drivers than others, so you "test" your theory by looking at how people with out-of-state license plates drive. Although your methods of data collection might not satisfy scientific standards, this is a form of field research because it takes information from a naturally occurring situation.

Advantages and Disadvantages of Field Surveys

One advantage of field surveys is that the variables often have a more powerful effect than they would in a laboratory experiment. Consider the effect of peer pressure on the behavior of members within the team. In a natural environment, team members would form strong cohesive bonds over time, whereas a researcher would have difficulty replicating this level of cohesiveness and corresponding peer pressure in a lab setting.

Another advantage of field surveys is that the researcher can study many variables simultaneously, thereby permitting a fuller test of more complex theories. Ironically this is also a disadvantage of field surveys; it is difficult for the researcher to contain his or her scientific inquiry. There is a tendency to shift from deductive hypothesis testing to more inductive exploratory browsing through the data. If these two activities become mixed together, the researcher can lose sight of the strict covenants of scientific inquiry.

The main weakness with field surveys is that it is difficult to satisfy the conditions for causal conclusions. One reason is that the data are usually collected at one point in time, so the researcher must rely on logic to decide whether the independent variable really preceded the dependent variable. Contrast this with the lab study, in which the researcher can usually be confident that the independent variable was applied before the dependent variable occurred. Increasingly organizational behavior studies use longitudinal research to provide a better indicator of temporal relations among variables; but this is still not as precise as the lab setting. Another reason why causal analysis is difficult in field surveys is that extraneous variables are not controlled as they are in lab studies. Without this control, there is a higher chance that a third variable might explain the relationship between the hypothesized independent and dependent variables.

Observational Research

In their study of brainstorming and creativity, Robert Sutton and Andrew Hargadon observed 24 brainstorming sessions at IDEO, a product design firm in Palo Alto, California. They also attended a dozen "Monday morning meetings," conducted 60 semistructured interviews with IDEO executives and designers, held hundreds of informal discussions with these people, and read through several dozen magazine articles about the company.[12]

Sutton and Hargadon's use of observational research and other qualitative methods was quite appropriate for their research objectives, which were to reexamine the effectiveness of brainstorming beyond the number of ideas generated. Observational research generates a wealth of descriptive accounts about the drama of human existence in organizations. It is a useful vehicle for learning about the complex dynamics of people and their activities, such as brainstorming. (The results of Sutton and Hargadon's study are discussed in Chapter 10.)

Participant observation takes the observation method one step further by having the observer take part in the organization's activities. This experience gives the researcher a fuller understanding of the activities compared to just watching others participate in those activities.

Disadvantages of Observational Research   In spite of its intuitive appeal, observational research has a number of weaknesses. The main problem is that the observer is subject to the perceptual screening and organizing biases that we discuss in Chapter 3 of this textbook. There is a tendency to overlook the routine aspects of organizational life, even though they may prove to be the most important data for research purposes. Instead observers tend to focus on unusual information, such as activities that deviate from what the observer expects. Because observational research usually records only what the observer notices, valuable information is often lost.

Another concern with the observation method is that the researcher's presence and involvement may influence the people whom he or she is studying.

This can be a problem in short-term observations, but in the long term people tend to return to their usual behavior patterns. With ongoing observations, such as Sutton and Hargadon's study of brainstorming sessions at IDEO, employees eventually forget that they are being studied.

Finally, observation is usually a qualitative process, so it is more difficult to empirically test hypotheses with the data. Instead observational research provides rich information for the inductive stages of theory building. It helps us form ideas about how things work in organizations. We begin to see relationships that lay the foundation for new perspectives and theory. We must not confuse this inductive process of theory building with the deductive process of theory testing.

Notes

[1]F.N. Kerlinger, *Foundations of Behavioral Research* (New York: Holt, Rinehart, & Winston, 1964), p. 11.

[2]J.B. Miner, *Theories of Organizational Behavior* (Hinsdale, IL: Dryden, 1980), pp. 7–9.

[3]Miner, *Theories of Organizational Behavior,* pp. 6–7.

[4]J. Mason, *Qualitative Researching* (London: Sage, 1996).

[5]A. Strauss and J. Corbin (eds.), *Grounded Theory in Practice* (London: Sage, 1997); B.G. Glaser and A. Strauss, *The Discovery of Grounded Theory: Strategies for Qualitative Research* (Chicago: Aldine, 1967).

[6]Kerlinger, *Foundations of Behavioral Research*, p. 13.

[7]Strauss and Corbin (eds.), *Grounded Theory in Practice;* Glaser and Strauss, *The Discovery of Grounded Theory.*

[8]W.A. Hall and P. Callery, "Enhancing the Rigor of Grounded Theory: Incorporating Reflexivity and Relationality," *Qualitative Health Research* 11 (March 2001), pp. 257–72.

[9]P. Lazarsfeld, *Survey Design and Analysis* (New York: The Free Press, 1955).

[10]This example is cited in D.W. Organ and T.S. Bateman, *Organizational Behavior*, 4th ed. (Homewood, IL: Irwin, 1991), p. 42.

[11]Organ and Bateman, *Organizational Behavior*, p. 45

[12]R.I. Sutton and A. Hargadon, "Brainstorming Groups in Context: Effectiveness in a Product Design Firm," *Administrative Science Quarterly* 41 (1996), pp. 685–718.

appendix B

Scoring Keys for Self-Assessment Activities

The following pages provide scoring keys for self-assessments that are presented in this textbook. Most (although not all) of these self-assessments, as well as the self-assessments that are summarized in this book, are scored on the student Online Learning Center.

Chapter 2

Scoring Key for Self-Monitoring Scale

Scoring Instructions: Use the following table to assign numbers to each box you checked. Insert the number for each statement on the appropriate line after the table. For example, if you checked "somewhat false" for statement #1 ("In social situations, I have the ability..."), you would write a "2" on the line with "(1)" underneath it. After assigning numbers for all 13 statements, add up your scores to estimate your self-monitoring personality.

For statement items 1, 2, 3, 4, 5, 6, 7, 8, 10, 11, 13	For statement items 9, 12
Very true = 6	Very true = 1
Somewhat true = 5	Somewhat true = 2
Slightly more true than false = 4	Slightly more true than false = 3
Slightly more false than true = 3	Slightly more false than true = 4
Somewhat false = 2	Somewhat false = 5
Very false = 1	Very false = 6

Sensitive to expressive behavior of others

$$\frac{5}{(2)} + \frac{6}{(4)} + \frac{5}{(5)} + \frac{5}{(6)} + \frac{5}{(8)} + \frac{5}{(11)} = \frac{31}{(A)}$$

Ability to modify self-presentation

$$\frac{5}{(1)} + \frac{4}{(3)} + \frac{5}{(7)} + \frac{6}{(9)} + \frac{6}{(10)} + \frac{5}{(12)} +$$

$$\frac{0}{(13)} = \frac{}{(B)} \; 39$$

Self-monitoring total score

$$\frac{}{(A)} + \frac{}{(B)} = \frac{}{Total}$$

Interpreting Your Score: Self-monitoring consists of two dimensions: (a) sensitivity to expressive behavior of others and (b) ability to modify self-presentation. These two dimensions as well as the total score are defined in the following table, along with the range of scores for high, medium, and low levels of each scale:

Self-monitoring dimension and definition	Score interpretation
Sensitive to expressive behavior of others: This scale indicates the extent to which you are aware of the feelings and perceptions of others, as expressed by their facial expressions, subtle statements, and other behaviors.	High: 25 to 36 Medium: 18 to 24 Low: Below 18
Ability to modify self-presentation: This scale indicates the extent to which you are adept at modifying your behavior in a way that is most appropriate for a situation or social relationship.	High: 30 to 42 Medium: 21 to 29 Low: Below 21
Self-monitoring total: Self-monitoring refers to an individual's level of sensitivity to the expressive behavior of others and ability to adapt appropriately to these situational cues.	High: 55 to 78 Medium: 39 to 54 Low: Below 39

Chapter 3

Scoring Key for Assessing Your Personal Need for Structure

Scoring Instructions: Use the following table to assign numbers to each box you checked. For example, if you checked "moderately disagree" for statement #3 ("I enjoy being spontaneous."), you would assign a "5" to that statement. After assigning numbers for all 12 statements, add up your scores to estimate your personal need for structure.

For statement items 1, 5, 6, 7, 8, 9, 10, 12	For statement items 2, 3, 4, 11
Strongly agree = 6	Strongly agree = 1
Moderately agree = 5	Moderately agree = 2
Slightly agree = 4	Slightly agree = 3
Slightly disagree = 3	Slightly disagree = 4
Moderately disagree = 2	Moderately disagree = 5
Strongly disagree = 1	Strongly disagree = 6

Interpreting Your Score: Some people need to "make sense" of things around them more quickly or completely than do other people. This personal need for perceptual structure relates to selective attention as well as perceptual organization and interpretation. For instance, people with a strong personal need for closure might form first impressions, fill in missing pieces, and rely on stereotyping more quickly than people who don't mind incomplete perceptual situations.

This scale, called the personal need for structure (PNS) scale, assesses the degree to which people are motivated to structure their world in a simple and unambiguous way. Scores range from 12 to 72, with higher scores indicating a high personal need for structure. PNS norms vary from one group to the next. For instance, a study of Finnish nurses reported a mean PNS score of 34, whereas a study of 236 male and 303 female undergraduate psychology students in the United States had a mean score of 42. The norms in the following table are based on scores from these undergraduate students:

Personal need for structure score	Interpretation
58 to 72	High need for personal structure.
47 to 57	Above-average need for personal structure.
38 to 46	Average need for personal structure.
27 to 37	Below- average need for personal structure.
12 to 26	Low need for personal structure.

Chapter 4

Scoring Key for School Commitment Scale

Scoring Instructions: Use the following table to assign numbers to each box you checked. Insert the number for each statement on the appropriate line after the table. For example, if you checked "moderately disagree" for statement #1 ("I would be very happy..."), you would write a "2" on the line with "(1)" underneath it. After assigning numbers for all 12 statements, add up your scores to estimate your affective and continuance school commitment.

For statement items 1, 2, 3, 4, 6, 8, 10, 11, 12	For statement items 5, 7, 9
Strongly agree = 7	Strongly agree = 1
Moderately agree = 6	Moderately agree = 2
Slightly agree = 5	Slightly agree = 3
Neutral = 4	Neutral = 4
Slightly disagree = 3	Slightly disagree = 5
Moderately disagree = 2	Moderately disagree = 6
Strongly disagree = 1	Strongly disagree = 7

Affective commitment

$$\underline{\quad} + \underline{\quad} + \underline{\quad} + \underline{\quad} + \underline{\quad} + \underline{\quad} = \underline{\quad}$$
$$(1) \quad (3) \quad (5) \quad (7) \quad (9) \quad (11)$$

Continuance commitment

$$\underline{\quad} + \underline{\quad} + \underline{\quad} + \underline{\quad} + \underline{\quad} + \underline{\quad} = \underline{\quad}$$
$$(2) \quad (4) \quad (6) \quad (8) \quad (10) \quad (12)$$

Interpreting Your Affective Commitment Score: This scale measures both affective commitment and continuance commitment. *Affective commitment* refers to a person's emotional attachment to, identification with, and involvement in a particular organization. In this scale, the organization is the school you are attending. How high or low is your affective commitment? The ideal would be to compare your score with the collective results of other students in your class. You can also compare your score with the following results, which are based on a sample of employees:

Affective commitment score	Interpretation
Above 36	High level of affective commitment.
32 to 36	Above-average level of affective commitment.
28 to 31	Average level of affective commitment.
20 to 27	Below-average level of affective commitment.
Below 20	Low level of affective commitment.

Interpreting Your Continuance Commitment Score: *Continuance commitment* occurs when people believe it is in their own personal interest to remain with an organization. People with a high continuance commitment have a strong calculative bond with the organization. In this scale, the organization is the school you are attending. How high or low is your continuance commitment? The ideal would be to compare your score with the collective results of other students in your class. You can also compare your score with the following results, which are based on a sample of employees:

Continuance commitment score	Interpretation
Above 31	High level of continuance commitment.
26 to 31	Above-average level of continuance commitment.
21 to 25	Average level of continuance commitment.
13 to 20	Below-average level of continuance commitment.
Below 13	Low level of continuance commitment.

Chapter 5

Scoring Key for Equity Sensitivity

Scoring Instructions: To score this scale, called the equity preference questionnaire (EPQ), complete these three steps:

1. Write your circled numbers for the following items and add them up:

$$\frac{}{(1)} + \frac{}{(2)} + \frac{}{(3)} + \frac{}{(4)} + \frac{}{(5)} + \frac{}{(6)} + \frac{}{(7)} + \frac{}{(10)} = \frac{}{\text{Subtotal A}}$$

2. The remaining items in the equity preference questionnaire need to be reverse-scored. To calculate a reverse score, subtract the direct score from 6. For example, if you circled 4 in one of these items, the reverse score would be 2 (i.e., $6 - 4 = 2$). If you circled 1, the reverse score

would be 5 (i.e., $6 - 1 = 5$). Calculate the reverse score for each of the following items and write them in the spaces provided. Then calculate Subtotal B by adding up these reverse scores:

$$\frac{}{(8)} + \frac{}{(9)} + \frac{}{(11)} + \frac{}{(12)} + \frac{}{(13)} + \frac{}{(14)} + \frac{}{(15)} + \frac{}{(16)} = \frac{}{\text{Subtotal B}}$$

3. Calculate the total score by summing Subtotal A and Subtotal B:

$$\frac{}{\text{(Subtotal A)}} + \frac{}{\text{(Subtotal B)}} = \frac{}{\text{TOTAL}}$$

Interpreting Your Score: The equity preference questionnaire measures the extent to which you are a "benevolent," "equity sensitive," or "entitled." Generally, people who score as follows fall into one of these categories:

EPQ score	Equity preference category
59 to 80	Benevolents—are tolerant of situations where they are underrewarded.
38 to 58	Equity sensitives—want an outcome-input ratio equal to the ratio of the comparison other.
16 to 37	Entitleds—want to receive proportionally more than others (like to be overrewarded).

Chapter 6

Scoring Key for the Money Attitude Scale

Scoring Instructions: This instrument presents three dimensions with a smaller set of items than the original money attitude scale. To calculate your score on each dimension, write the number you circled in the scale above the corresponding item number in the scoring key at the top of the next page. For example, write the number you circled for the scale's first statement ("I sometimes purchase things…") on the line above "Item 1." Then add up the numbers for that dimension. The money attitude total score is calculated by adding up all scores and all dimensions.

Money attitude dimension	Calculation	Your score
Money as power/prestige	Item 1 + Item 4 + Item 7 + Item 10 =	
Retention time	Item 2 + Item 5 + Item 8 + Item 11 =	
Money anxiety	Item 3 + Item 6 + Item 9 + Item 12 =	
Money attitude total	Add up all dimension scores =	

(handwritten above items: 5 4 5 1 = 15 (9); 2 2 2 3 = 9; 4 4 3 3 = 14; total 38)

Interpreting Your Score: The three money attitude scale dimensions measured here, as well as the total score, are defined as follows:

Money as power/prestige: People with higher scores on this dimension tend to use money to influence and impress others.

Retention time: People with higher scores on this dimension tend to be careful financial planners.

Money anxiety: People with higher scores on this dimension tend to view money as a source of anxiety.

Money attitude total: This is a general estimate of how much respect and attention you give to money.

The following table shows how a sample of MBA students scored on the money attitude scale. The table shows percentiles, that is, the percentage of people with the same or lower scores. For example, the table indicates that a score of 12 on the retention scale is quite low because only 20 percent of students would have scored at this level or lower (80 percent scored higher). However, a score of 12 on the prestige scale is quite high because 80 percent of students scored at or below this number (only 20 percent scored higher).

Chapter 7

Scoring Key for the Connor–Davidson Resilience Scale

Scoring Instructions: Use the following values to assign numbers to each box you checked in the Connor–Davidson resilience scale; then add up the scores for all 25 items:
0 = Not at all true
1 = Rarely true
2 = Sometimes true
3 = Often true
4 = True nearly all of the time

Interpreting Your Score: Resilience is the capability of individuals to cope successfully in the face of significant change, adversity, or risk. Everyone has some resilience; it occurs every time we pull through

Percentile (% with scores at or below this number)	Prestige score	Retention score	Anxiety score	Total money score
Average score	9.89	14.98	12.78	37.64
Highest score	17	20	18	53
90	13	18	16	44
80	12	17	15	42
70	11	17	14	40
60	10	16	14	39
50	10	15	13	38
40	9	14	12	36
30	8	14	11	34
20	7	12	10	32
10	7	11	8	29
Lowest score	4	8	6	23

stressful experiences. Although everyone needs to recuperate to some extent following a stressful experience, people with high resilience are better able to maintain equilibrium and, consequently, have lost little ground in the first place. The Connor–Davidson resilience scale was recently developed to estimate levels of resilience. Scores range from 0 to 100. Preliminary studies indicate that people with post-traumatic stress disorder score much lower (average score of 48) than primary health care outpatients (average score of 72), who score lower than the general population (average score of 80). The following table allows you to compare your score against the results of 577 people in the general U.S. population:

Resilience score	Interpretation
92 to 100	Top 20th percentile (very high resilience).
86 to 91	21st—40th percentile.
77 to 85	41st—60th percentile (middle of the pack).
65 to 76	61st—80th percentile.
0 to 64	81st—100th percentile (low resilience in general population).

Chapter 8

Scoring Key for Assessing Your Creative Personality

Scoring Instructions: Assign one positive (+1) point to the following words if you put a check mark beside them: *capable, clever, confident, egotistical, humorous, individualistic, informal, insightful, intelligent, inventive, original, reflective, resourceful, self-confident, sexy, snobbish, unconventional, wide interests.*

Assign one negative (–1) point to the following words if you put a check mark beside them: *affected, cautious, commonplace, conservative, conventional, dissatisfied, honest, mannerly, narrow interests, sincere, submissive, suspicious.* Words without check marks receive zero points. Add up the total score, which will range from –12 to +18.

Interpreting Your Score: This instrument estimates your creative potential as a personal characteristic. The scale recognizes that creative people are intelligent, persistent, and possess an inventive thinking

style. Creative personality varies somewhat from one occupational group to the next. The following table provides norms based on undergraduate and graduate university students:

Creative disposition score	Interpretation
Above +9	You have a high creative personality.
+1 to +9	You have an average creative personality.
Below +1	You have a low creative personality.

Chapter 9

Scoring Key for the Team Roles Preferences Scale

Scoring Instructions: Write the scores circled for each item on the appropriate lines here (statement numbers are in parentheses); then add up each scale.

Encourager $\underset{(6)}{2} + \underset{(9)}{2} + \underset{(11)}{2} = 6$

Gatekeeper $\underset{(4)}{4} + \underset{(10)}{2} + \underset{(13)}{4} = 10$

Harmonizer $\underset{(3)}{4} + \underset{(8)}{3} + \underset{(12)}{2} = 10$

Initiator $\underset{(1)}{5} + \underset{(5)}{5} + \underset{(14)}{5} = 15$

Summarizer $\underset{(2)}{5} + \underset{(7)}{4} + \underset{(15)}{3} = 12$

Interpreting Your Score: The five team roles measured here are different from Belbin's roles described in the textbook. However, these roles are also based on academic writing. These five roles are defined as follows, along with the range of scores for high, medium, and low levels of each role. These norms are based on results from a sample of MBA students:

Team role and definition	Interpretation
Encourager: People who score high on this dimension have a strong tendency to praise and support the ideas of other team members, thereby showing warmth and solidarity to the group.	High: 12 and above Medium: 9 to 11 Low: 8 and below

Team role and definition	Interpretation
Gatekeeper: People who score high on this dimension have a strong tendency to encourage all team members to participate in a discussion.	High: 12 and above Medium: 9 to 11 Low: 8 and below
Harmonizer: People who score high on this dimension have a strong tendency to mediate intragroup conflicts and reduce tension.	High: 11 and above Medium: 9 to 10 Low: 8 and below
Initiator: People who score high on this dimension have a strong tendency to identify goals for a meeting, including ways to work on those goals.	High: 12 and above Medium: 9 to 11 Low: 8 and below
Summarizer: People who score high on this dimension have a strong tendency to keep track of what was said in a meeting (that is, act as the team's memory).	High: 10 and above Medium: 8 to 9 Low: 7 and below

Chapter 10

Scoring Key for the Team Player Inventory

Scoring Instructions: To calculate your score on the team player inventory, use the following table to assign numbers to each box that you checked. Then add up the numbers to determine your total score.

For statement items 1, 3, 6, 8, 10	For statement items 2, 4, 5, 7, 9
Completely agree = 5	Completely agree = 1
Agree somewhat = 4	Agree somewhat = 2
Neither agree nor disagree = 3	Neither agree nor disagree =3
Disagree somewhat = 2	Disagree somewhat = 4
Completely disagree = 1	Completely disagree = 5

Interpreting Your Score: The team player inventory estimates the extent to which you are positively predisposed to working on teams. The higher your score, the more you enjoy working in teams and believe that teamwork is beneficial. The following table allows you to compare your team player inventory score against the norms for this scale. These norms are derived from undergraduate psychology students:

Team player inventory score	Interpretation
40 to 50	You have a strong predisposition or preference for working in teams.
21 to 39	You are generally ambivalent about working in teams.
10 to 20	You have a low predisposition or preference for working in teams.

Chapter 11

Scoring Key for the Active Listening Skills Inventory

Scoring Instructions: Use the following table to score the response you checked for each statement. Write the score for each item on the appropriate line below the table (statement numbers are in parentheses), and add up each subscale. For example, if you checked "A little" for statement #1 ("I keep an open mind…"), you would write a "1" on the line with "(1)" underneath it. Then calculate the overall active listening inventory score by summing all subscales.

For statement items 3, 4, 6, 7, 10, 13	For statement items 1, 2, 5, 8, 9, 11, 12, 14, 15
Not at all = 3	Not at all = 0
A little = 2	A little = 1
Somewhat = 1	Somewhat = 2
Very much = 0	Very much = 3

Avoiding interruption(AI) $\underline{1}_{(3)} + \underline{2}_{(7)} + \underline{1}_{(15)} = \underline{4}$

Maintaining interest(MI) $\underline{2}_{(6)} + \underline{1}_{(9)} + \underline{1}_{(14)} = \underline{4}$

Postponing evaluation(PE) $\underline{2}_{(1)} + \underline{0}_{(5)} + \underline{1}_{(13)} = \underline{3}$

Organizing information(OI) $\underline{2}_{(2)} + \underline{3}_{(10)} + \underline{2}_{(12)} = \underline{7}$

Showing interest(SI) $\underline{2}_{(4)} + \underline{3}_{(8)} + \underline{5}_{(11)} = \underline{9}$

Active listening (total score): $\underline{27}$

Interpreting Your Score: The five active listening dimensions and the overall active listening scale measured here are defined in the following table, along with the range of scores for high, medium, and low levels of each dimension based on a sample of MBA students:

Active listening dimension and definition	Score interpretation
Avoiding interruption: People with high scores on this dimension have a strong tendency to let a speaker finish his or her statements before responding.	High: 8 to 9 Medium: 5 to 7 Low: Below 5
Maintaining interest: People with high scores on this dimension have a strong tendency to remain focused and concentrate on what a speaker is saying even when the conversation is boring or the information is well known.	High: 6 to 9 Medium: 3 to 5 Low: Below 3
Postponing evaluation: People with high scores on this dimension have a strong tendency to keep an open mind and avoid evaluating what a speaker is saying until the speaker has finished.	High: 7 to 9 Medium: 4 to 6 Low: Below 4
Organizing information: People with high scores on this dimension have a strong tendency to actively organize a speaker's ideas into meaningful categories.	High: 8 to 9 Medium: 5 to 7 Low: Below 5
Showing interest: People with high scores on this dimension have a strong tendency to use nonverbal gestures or brief verbal acknowledgments to demonstrate that they are paying attention to the speaker.	High: 7 to 9 Medium: 5 to 6 Low: Below 5
Active listening (total): People with high scores on this total active listening scale have a strong tendency to actively sense a sender's signals, evaluate them accurately, and respond appropriately.	High: Above 31 Medium: 26 to 31 Low: Below 26

Note: The active listening inventory does not explicitly measure two other dimensions of active listening, namely, empathizing and providing feedback. Empathizing is difficult to measure with behaviors; providing feedback involves similar behaviors as showing interest.

Chapter 12

Scoring Key for the Upward Influence Scale

Scoring Instructions: To calculate your scores on the upward influence scale, write the number circled for each statement on the appropriate line here (statement numbers are in parentheses), and add up each scale.

Assertiveness $\frac{\quad}{(8)} + \frac{\quad}{(15)} + \frac{\quad}{(16)} = \frac{\quad}{}$

Exchange $\frac{\quad}{(2)} + \frac{\quad}{(5)} + \frac{\quad}{(13)} = \frac{\quad}{}$

Coalition formation $\frac{\quad}{(1)} + \frac{\quad}{(11)} + \frac{\quad}{(18)} = \frac{\quad}{}$

Upward appeal $\frac{\quad}{(4)} + \frac{\quad}{(12)} + \frac{\quad}{(17)} = \frac{\quad}{}$

Ingratiation $\frac{\quad}{(3)} + \frac{\quad}{(6)} + \frac{\quad}{(9)} = \frac{\quad}{}$

Persuasion $\frac{\quad}{(7)} + \frac{\quad}{(10)} + \frac{\quad}{(14)} = \frac{\quad}{}$

Interpreting Your Score: *Influence* refers to any behavior that attempts to alter someone else's attitudes or behavior. There are several types of influence, including the following six measured by this instrument: assertiveness, exchange, coalition formation, upward appeal, ingratiation, and persuasion. This instrument assesses your preference for using each type of influence on your boss or other people at higher levels in the organization. Each scale has a potential score ranging from 3 to 15 points. Higher scores indicate that a person has a greater preference for that particular tactic. The six upward influence dimensions measured are defined here, along with the range of scores for high, medium, and low levels of each tactic:

Influence tactic and definition	Score interpretation
Assertiveness: Assertiveness involves actively applying legitimate and coercive power to influence others. This tactic includes persistently reminding others of their obligations, frequently checking their work, confronting them, and using threats of sanctions to force compliance.	High: 8 to 15 Medium: 5 to 7 Low: 3 to 4
Exchange: Exchange involves the promise of benefits or resources in exchange for the target person's compliance with your request. This tactic also includes reminding the target of past benefits or favors with the expectation that the target will now make up for that debt. Negotiation is also part of the exchange strategy.	High: 10 to 15 Medium: 6 to 9 Low: 3 to 5

Influence tactic and definition	Score interpretation
Coalition formation: Coalition formation occurs when a group of people with common interests band together to influence others. This tactic pools the power and resources of many people, so the coalition potentially has more influence than if each person operated alone.	High: 11 to 15 Medium: 7 to 10 Low: 3 to 6
Upward appeal: Upward appeal occurs when you rely on support from a higher-level person to influence others. In effect, this is a form of coalition in which one or more members are people with higher authority or expertise.	High: 9 to 15 Medium: 6 to 8 Low: 3 to 5
Ingratiation: Flattering your boss in front of others, helping your boss with his or her work, agreeing with your boss's ideas, and asking for your boss's advice are all examples of ingratiation. This tactic increases the perceived similarity of the source of ingratiation to the target person.	High: 13 to 15 Medium: 9 to 12 Low: 3 to 8
Persuasion: Persuasion refers to using logical and emotional appeals to change others' attitudes. According to several studies, it is also the most common upward influence strategy.	High: 13 to 15 Medium: 9 to 12 Low: 3 to 8

Chapter 13

Scoring Key for the Dutch Test for Conflict Handling

Scoring Instructions: Write the number circled for each item on the appropriate line here (the statement number is under the line), and add up each subscale:

Interpreting Your Score: The five conflict handling dimensions are defined here, along with the range of scores for high, medium, and low levels of each dimension:

Conflict handling dimension and definition	Score interpretation
Yielding: Yielding involves giving in completely to the other side's wishes, or at least cooperating with little or no attention to your own interests. This style involves making unilateral concessions, and unconditional promises, as well as offering help with no expectation of reciprocal help.	High: 14 to 20 Medium: 9 to 13 Low: 4 to 8
Compromising: Compromising involves looking for a position in which your losses are offset by equally valued gains. It involves matching the other party's concessions, making conditional promises or threats, and actively searching for a middle ground between the interests of the two parties.	High: 17 to 20 Medium: 11 to 16 Low: 4 to 10
Forcing: Forcing involves trying to win the conflict at the other's expense. It includes "hard" influence tactics, particularly assertiveness, to get your own way.	High: 15 to 20 Medium: 9 to 14 Low: 4 to 8
Problem solving: Problem solving tries to find a mutually beneficial solution for all parties. Information sharing is an important feature of this style because the parties need to identify common ground and potential solutions that satisfy all of them.	High: 17 to 20 Medium: 11 to 16 Low: 4 to 10
Avoiding: Avoiding tries to smooth over or avoid conflict situations altogether. It represents a low concern for both self and the other party. In other words, avoiders try to suppress thinking about the conflict.	High: 13 to 20 Medium: 8 to 12 Low: 4 to 7

Conflict handling dimension	Calculation	Your score
Yielding	____ + ____ + ____ + ____ = Item 1 + Item 6 + Item 11 + Item 16	_____
Compromising	____ + ____ + ____ + ____ = Item 2 + Item 7 + Item 12 + Item 17	_____
Forcing	____ + ____ + ____ + ____ = Item 3 + Item 8 + Item 13 + Item 18	_____
Problem solving	____ + ____ + ____ + ____ = Item 4 + Item 9 + Item 14 + Item 19	_____
Avoiding	____ + ____ + ____ + ____ = Item 5 + Item 10 + Item 15 + Item 20	_____

Chapter 14

Scoring Key for Leadership Dimensions Instrument: Transactional Leadership

Scoring Instructions: Add up the scores for the odd-numbered items. The maximum score here is 40.

Interpreting Your Score: Transactional leadership is "managing"—helping organizations to achieve their current objectives more efficiently, such as by linking job performance to valued rewards and ensuring that employees have the resources needed to do their jobs. The following table shows the range of scores for high, medium, and low levels of transactional leadership:

Transactional leadership score	Interpretation
32 to 40	The person you evaluated seems to be a highly transactional leader.
25 to 31	The person you evaluated seems to be a moderately transactional leader.
Below 25	The person you evaluated seems to display few characteristics of a transactional leader.

Scoring Key for Leadership Dimensions Instrument: Transformational Leadership

Scoring Instructions: Add up the scores for the even numbered items. The maximum score here is 40. Higher scores indicate that your supervisor has a strong inclination toward transformational leadership.

Interpreting Your Score: Transformational leadership involves changing teams or organizations by creating, communicating, and modelling a vision for the organization or work unit, and inspiring employees to strive for that vision. The following table shows the range of scores for high, medium, and low levels of transformational leadership:

Transformational leadership score	Interpretation
32 to 40	The person you evaluated seems to be a highly transformational leader.
25 to 31	The person you evaluated seems to be a moderately transformational leader.
Below 25	The person you evaluated seems to display few characteristics of a transformational leader.

Chapter 15

Scoring Key for the Organizational Structure Preference Scale

Scoring Instructions: Use the following table to assign numbers to each response you checked. Insert the number for each statement on the appropriate line after the table. For example, if you checked "Not at all" for item #1 ("A person's career ladder..."), you would write a "0" on the line with "(1)" underneath it. After assigning numbers for all 15 statements, add up the scores to estimate your degree of preference for a tall hierarchy, formalization, and centralization. Then calculate your overall score by summing all scales.

For statement items 2, 3, 8, 10, 11, 12, 14, 15	For statement Items 1, 4, 5, 6, 7, 9, 13
Not at all = 3	Not at all = 0
A little = 2	A little = 1
Somewhat = 1	Somewhat = 2
Very much = 0	Very much = 3

Tall hierarchy (H) $\underline{\quad} + \underline{\quad} + \underline{\quad} = \underline{\quad} + \underline{\quad} = \underline{\quad}$
(1) (4) (10) (12) (15) (H)

Formalization (F) $\underline{\quad} + \underline{\quad} + \underline{\quad} = \underline{\quad} + \underline{\quad} = \underline{\quad}$
(2) (6) (8) (11) (13) (F)

Centralization (C) $\underline{\quad} + \underline{\quad} + \underline{\quad} = \underline{\quad} + \underline{\quad} = \underline{\quad}$
(3) (5) (7) (9) (14) (C)

Total score (mechanistic) $\underline{\quad} + \underline{\quad} + \underline{\quad} = \underline{\quad}$
(H) (F) (C) Total

Interpreting Your Score: The three organizational structure dimensions and the overall score are defined here, along with the range of scores for high, medium, and low levels of each dimension based on a sample of MBA students:

Organizational structure dimension and definition	Interpretation
Tall hierarchy: People with high scores on this dimension prefer to work in organizations with several levels of hierarchy and a narrow span of control (few employees per supervisor).	High: 11 to 15 Medium: 6 to 10 Low: Below 6
Formalization: People with high scores on this dimension prefer to work in organizations where jobs are clearly defined with limited discretion.	High: 12 to 15 Medium: 9 to 11 Low: Below 9
Centralization: People with high scores on this dimension prefer to work in organizations where decision making occurs mainly among top management rather than being spread out to lower-level staff.	High: 10 to 15 Medium: 7 to 9 Low: Below 7
Total score (mechanistic): People with high scores on this dimension prefer to work in mechanistic organizations, whereas those with low scores prefer to work in organic organizational structures. Mechanistic structures are characterized by a narrow span of control and a high degree of formalization and centralization. Organic structures have a wide span of control, little formalization, and decentralized decision making.	High: 30 to 45 Medium: 22 to 29 Low: Below 22

cultures. Also, keep in mind that none of these subscales is inherently good or bad. Each is effective in different situations. The four corporate cultures are defined here, along with the range of scores for high, medium, and low levels of each dimension based on a sample of MBA students:

Corporate culture dimension and definition	Score interpretation
Control culture: This culture values the role of senior executives to lead the organization. The goal is to keep everyone aligned and under control.	High: 3 to 6 Medium: 1 to 2 Low: 0
Performance culture: This culture values individual and organizational performance and strives for effectiveness and efficiency.	High: 5 to 6 Medium: 3 to 4 Low: 0 to 2
Relationship culture: This culture values nurturing and well-being. It considers open communication, fairness, teamwork, and sharing a vital part of organizational life.	High: 6 Medium: 4 to 5 Low: 0 to 3
Responsive culture: This culture values its ability to keep in tune with the external environment, including being competitive and realizing new opportunities.	High: 6 Medium: 4 to 5 Low: 0 to 3

Chapter 16

Scoring Key for the Corporate Culture Preference Scale

Scoring Instructions: In each space here, write in a "1" if you circled the statement and a "0" if you did not. Then add up your scores for each subscale.

Interpreting Your Score: These corporate cultures may be found in many organizations, but they represent only four of many possible organizational

Chapter 17

Scoring Key for the Tolerance of Change Scale

Scoring Instructions: Use the following table to assign numbers to each box you checked. For example, if you checked "Moderately disagree" for statement #1 ("An expert who doesn't come up …"), you would write a "2" beside that statement. After assigning numbers for all 16 statements, add up your scores to estimate your tolerance for change.

Control culture   ___ + ___ + ___ = ___ + ___ + ___ = ___
                   (2a)   (5a)   (6b)   (8b)   (11b)   (12a)

Performance culture   ___ + ___ + ___ = ___ + ___ + ___ = ___
                   (1b)   (3b)   (5b)   (6a)   (7a)   (9b)

Relationship culture   ___ + ___ + ___ = ___ + ___ + ___ = ___
                   (1a)   (3a)   (4b)   (8a)   (10b)   (12b)

Responsive culture   ___ + ___ + ___ + ___ + ___ + ___ = ___
                   (2b)   (4a)   (7b)   (9a)   (10a)   (11a)

For statement items 2, 4, 6, 8, 10, 12, 14, 16	For statement items 1, 3, 5, 7, 9, 11, 13, 15
Strongly agree = 7	Strongly agree = 1
Moderately agree = 6	Moderately agree = 2
Slightly agree = 5	Slightly agree = 3
Neutral = 4	Neutral = 4
Slightly disagree = 3	Slightly disagree = 5
Moderately disagree = 2	Moderately disagree = 6
Strongly disagree = 1	Strongly disagree = 7

Interpreting Your Score: This measurement instrument is formally known as the "tolerance of ambiguity" scale. Although it was developed over 40 years ago, the instrument is still used today in research. People with a high tolerance for ambiguity are comfortable with uncertainty, sudden change, and new situations. These are characteristics of the hyperfast changes occurring in many organizations today. The following table indicates the range of scores for high, medium, and low tolerance for change. These norms are based on results for MBA students:

Tolerance for change score	Interpretation
81 to 112	You seem to have a high tolerance for change.
63 to 80	You seem to have a moderate level of tolerance for change.
Below 63	You seem to have a low degree of tolerance for change. Instead, you prefer stable work environments.

glossary

The number(s) in parentheses indicates the chapter(s) where the term is formally defined. See the subject index for other places in the textbook where the term is discussed.

A

ability   Both the natural aptitudes and learned capabilities required to successfully complete a task. (2)

absorptive capacity   The ability to recognize the value of new information, assimilate it, and apply it to commercial ends. (1)

achievement–nurturing orientation   A competitive versus cooperative view of relations with other people. (2)

action learning   A variety of experiential learning activities in which employees are involved in a "real, complex, and stressful problem," usually in teams, with immediate relevance to the company. (3)

action research   A data-based, problem-oriented process that diagnoses the need for change, introduces the intervention, and then evaluates and stabilizes the desired changes. (17)

adaptive culture   An organizational culture in which employees focus on the changing needs of customers and other stakeholders, and support initiatives to keep pace with those changes. (16)

alternative dispute resolution (ADR)   A third-party dispute resolution process that includes mediation, typically followed by arbitration. (13)

appreciative inquiry   An organizational change process that directs attention away from the group's own problems and focuses participant's on the group's potential and positive elements. (17)

artifacts   The observable symbols and signs of an organization's culture. (16)

attitudes   The cluster of beliefs, assessed feelings, and behavioral intentions toward an object. (4)

attribution process   The perceptual process of deciding whether an observed behavior or event is caused largely by internal or by external factors. (3)

autonomy   The degree to which a job gives employees the freedom, independence, and discretion to schedule their work and determine the procedures used in completing it. (6)

B

balanced scorecard (BSC)   A reward system that pays bonuses for improved results on a composite of financial, customer, internal process, and employee factors. (6)

behavior modification   A theory that explains learning in terms of the antecedents and consequences of behavior. (3)

bicultural audit   A diagnosis of cultural relations between companies prior to a merger and a determination of the extent to which cultural clashes are likely to occur. (16)

"Big Five" personality dimensions   The five abstract dimensions representing most personality traits: conscientiousness, agreeableness, neuroticism, openness to experience, and extroversion (CANOE). (2)

bounded rationality   Processing limited and imperfect information and satisficing rather than maximizing when choosing among alternatives. (8)

brainstorming   A free-wheeling, face-to-face meeting where team members aren't allowed to criticize, but are encouraged to speak freely, generate as many ideas as possible, and build on the ideas of others. (10)

C

categorical thinking   The mostly unconscious process of organizing people and objects into preconceived categories that are stored in our long-term memory. (3)

centrality   The degree and nature of interdependence between the power holder and others. (12)

centralization   The degree to which formal decision authority is held by a small group of people, typically those at the top of the organizational hierarchy. (15)

ceremonies   Planned and usually dramatic displays of organizational culture, conducted specifically for the benefit of an audience. (16)

change agent   Anyone who possesses enough knowledge and power to guide and facilitate the organizational change effort. (17)

coalition   An informal group that attempts to influence people outside the group by pooling the resources and power of its members. (12)

cognitive dissonance   A psychological tension that occurs when people perceive an inconsistency between their beliefs, feelings, and behavior. (4)

collectivism   The extent to which people value duty to groups to which they belong, and to group harmony. (2)

communication   The process by which information is transmitted and understood between two or more people. (11)

communities of practice   Informal groups bound together by shared expertise and passion for a particular activity or intrest. (1)

competencies   Skills, knowledge, aptitudes, and other characteristics of people that lead to superior performance. (2)

conflict   The process in which one party perceives that its interests are being opposed or negatively affected by another party. (13)

conflict management   Interventions that alter the level and form of conflict in ways that maximize its benefits and minimize its dysfunctional consequences. (13)

constructive conflict   Occurs when team members debate their different perceptions about an issue in a way that keeps the conflict focused on the task rather than people. (10) (13)

contact hypothesis   A theory stating that the more we interact with someone, the less we rely on stereotypes to understand that person. (3)

contingency approach   The idea that a particular action may have different consequences in different situations. (1)

contingent work   Any job in which the individual does not have an explicit or implicit contract for long-term employment, or one in which the minimum hours of work can vary in a nonsystematic way. (1)

continuance commitment   A calculative decision to remain with an organization because quitting would be costly. (4)

corporate social responsibility (CSR)   An organization's moral obligation towards its stakeholders. (1)

counterpower   The capacity to a person, team, or organization to keep a more powerful person or group in the exchange relationship. (12)

counterproductive work behaviors (CWBs)   Voluntary behaviors that are potentially harmful to the organization's effectiveness. (2)

creativity   Developing an original product, service, or idea that makes a socially recognized contribution. (8)

D

decision making A conscious process of making choices among one or more alternatives with the intention of moving toward some desired state of affairs. (8)

deep-level diversity The differences in the psychological characteristics of employees, including personalities, beliefs, values, and attitudes. (1)

Delphi method A structured team decision-making process of systematically pooling the collective knowledge of experts on a particular subject to make decisions, predict the future, or identify opposing views. (10)

distributive justice The perceived fairness in outcomes we receive relative to our contributions and the outcomes and contributions of others. (5)

divergent thinking Reframing a problem in a unique way and generating different approaches to the issue. (8)

divisional structure An organizational structure that groups employees around geographic areas, clients, or outputs. (15)

drives Instinctive or innate tendencies to seek certain goals or maintain internal stability. (5)

E

electronic brainstorming Using special computer software, participants share ideas while minimizing the team dynamics problems inherent in traditional brainstorming sessions. (10)

emotional contagion The automatic and unconscious tendency to mimic and synchronize one's own nonverbal behaviors with those of other people. (11)

emotional dissonance A conflict between a person's required and true emotions. (4)

emotional intelligence (EI) The ability to perceive and express emotion, assimilate emotion in thought, understand and reason with emotion, and regulate emotion in oneself and others. (4)

emotional labor The effort, planning, and control needed to express organizationally desired emotions during interpersonal transactions. (4)

emotions Psychological, behavioral, and physiological episodes experienced toward an object, person, or event that create a state of readiness. (4)

empathy A person's understanding and sensitivity to the feelings, thoughts, and situation of others. (3)

employability An employment relationship in which people perform a variety of work activities rather than hold specific jobs, and are expected to continuously learn skills that will keep them employed. (1)

employee assistance programs (EAPs) Counseling services that help employees overcome personal or organizational stressors and adopt more effective coping mechanisms. (7)

employee engagement Employees' emotional and cognitive (rational) motivation, their ability to perform their jobs, their possessing a clear understanding of the organization's vision and their specific roles in that vision, and a belief that they have been given the resources to get their jobs done. (2)

employee involvement The degree to which employees influence how their work is organized and carried out. (8)

employee stock ownership plans (ESOPs) A reward system that encourages employees to buy stock in the company. (6)

empowerment A psychological concept in which people experience more self-determination, meaning, competence, and impact regarding their role in the organization. (6)

equity sensitivity A person's outcome/input preferences and reaction to various outcome/input ratios. (5)

equity theory A theory that explains how people develop perceptions of fairness in the distribution and exchange of resources. (5)

ERG theory A needs hierarchy theory consisting of three instinctive needs—existence, relatedness, and growth. (5)

escalation of commitment The tendency to repeat an apparently bad decision or allocate more resources to a failing course of action. (8)

ethical sensitivity A personal characteristic that enables people to recognize the presence and determine the relative importance of an ethical issue. (2)

ethics The study of moral principles or values that determine whether actions are right or wrong and outcomes are good or bad. (1) (2)

evaluation apprehension When individuals are reluctant to mention ideas that seem silly because they believe (often correctly) that other team members are silently evaluating them. (10)

executive coaching A helping relationship using behavioral methods to assist clients in identifying and achieving goals for their professional performance and personal satisfaction. (5)

exit-voice-loyalty-neglect (EVLN) model The four ways, as indicated in the name, employees respond to job dissatisfaction. (4)

expectancy theory The motivation theory based on the idea that work effort is directed toward behaviors that people believe will lead to desired outcomes. (5)

extinction Occurs when the target behavior decreases because no consequence follows it. (3)

extroversion A "Big Five" personality dimension that characterizes people who are outgoing, talkative, sociable, and assertive. (2)

F

feedback Any information that people receive about the consequences of their behavior. (5)

Fiedler's contingency model Development by Fred Fiedler, a model that suggests that leader effectiveness depends on whether the person's natural leadership style is appropriately matched to the situation. (14)

flaming The act of sending an emotionally charged e-mail message to others. (11)

force field analysis Lewin's model of systemwide change that helps change agents diagnose the forces that drive and restrain proposed organizational change. (17)

formalization The degree to which organizations standardize behavior through rules, procedures, formal training, and related mechanisms. (15)

four-drive theory A motivation theory based on the innate drives to acquire, bond, learn, and defend that incorporates both emotions and rationality. (5)

functional structure An organizational structure that organizes employees around specific knowledge or other resources. (15)

fundamental attribution error The tendency to attribute the behavior of other people more to internal than to external factors. (3)

future search Systemwide group sessions, usually lasting a few days, in which participants identify trends and identify ways to adapt to those changes. (17)

G

gainsharing plan A reward system in which team members earn bonuses for reducing costs and increasing labor efficiency in their work process. (6)

general adaptation syndrome A model of the stress experience, consisting of three stages: alarm, resistance, and exhaustion. (7)

globalization Economic, social, and cultural connectivity (and interdependence) with people in other parts of the world. (1)

goal setting The process of motivating employees and clarifying their role perceptions by establishing performance objectives. (5)

grapevine An unstructured, informal network founded on social relationships rather than organizational charts or job descriptions. (11)

grounded theory A process of developing theory through the constant interplay between data gathering and the development of theoretical concepts. (1)

group polarization The tendency of teams to make more extreme decisions than individuals working alone. (10)

groups Two or more people with a unifying relationship. (9)

groupthink The tendency of highly cohesive groups to value consensus at the price of decision quality. (10)

H

halo effect A perceptual error whereby our general impression of a person, usually based on one prominent characteristic, colors the perception of other characteristics of that person. (3)

heterogeneous teams Teams that include members with diverse personal characteristics and backgrounds. (9)

homogeneous teams Teams that include members with common technical expertise, demographics (age, sex), ethnicity, experiences, or values. (9)

I

implicit favorite The decision maker's preferred alternative against which all other choices are judged. (8)

implicit leadership theory A theory hypothesizing that perceptual processes cause people to inflate the importance of leadership as the cause of organizational events. (14)

impression management The practice of actively shaping one's public image. (12)

individualism The extent to which a person values independence and personal uniqueness. (2)

information overload A condition in which the volume of information received exceeds a person's capacity to get through it. (11)

ingratiation Any attempt to increase liking by, or perceived similarity to, the targeted person. (12)

inoculation effect A persuasive communication strategy of warning listeners that others will try to influence them in the future and that they should be wary of the opponent's arguments. (12)

intellectual capital The sum of an organization's human capital, structural capital, and relationship capital. (1)

introversion A "Big Five" personality dimension that characterizes people who are quiet, shy, and cautious. (2)

intuition The ability to know when a problem or opportunity exists and select the best course of action without conscious reasoning. (8)

J

jargon The technical language and acronyms as well as recognized words with specialized meaning in specific organizations or social groups. (11)

job burnout The process of emotional exhaustion, cynicism, and reduced efficacy (lower feelings of personal accomplishment) resulting from prolonged exposure to stress. (7)

job characteristics model A job design model that relates the motivational properties of jobs to specific personal and organizational consequences of those properties. (6)

job design The process of assigning tasks to a job, including the interdependency of those tasks with other jobs. (6)

job enlargement Increasing the number of tasks employees perform within their job. (6)

job enrichment Giving employees more responsibility for scheduling, coordinating, and planning their own work. (6)

job evaluation Systematically evaluating the worth of jobs within an organization by measuring their required skill, effort, responsibility, and working conditions. (6)

job rotation The practice of moving employees from one job to another. (6)

job satisfaction A person's evaluation of his or her job and work context. (2) (4)

job specialization The result of division of labor in which each job includes a subset of the tasks required to complete the product or service. (6)

Johari Window The model of personal and interpersonal understanding that encourages disclosure and feedback to increase the open area and reduce the blind, hidden, and unknown areas of oneself. (3)

joint optimization A key requirement in sociotechnical systems theory that a balance must be struck between social and technical systems to maximize an operation's effectiveness. (10)

K

knowledge management Any structured activity that improves an organization's capacity to acquire, share, and use knowledge in ways that improve its survival and success. (1)

L

leadership Influencing, motivating, and enabling others to contribute toward the effectiveness and success of the organizations of which they are members. (14)

leadership substitutes A theory that identifies conditions that either limit a leader's ability to influence subordinates or make that particular leadership style unnecessary. (14)

learning A relatively permanent change in behavior (or behavior tendency) that occurs as a result of a person's interaction with the environment. (3)

learning orientation The extent that an organization or individual supports knowledge management, particularly opportunities to acquire knowledge through experience and experimentation. (3)

legitimate power The capacity to influence others through formal authority. (12)

locus of control A personality trait referring to the extent to which people believe events are within their control. (2)

M

Machiavellian values The belief that deceit is a natural and acceptable way to influence others. (12)

management by walking around (MBWA) A communication practice in which executives get out of their offices and learn from others in the organization through face-to-face dialogue. (11)

Maslow's needs hierarchy theory Maslow's motivation theory of five instinctive needs arranged in a hierarchy, whereby people are motivated to fulfill a higher need as a lower one becomes gratified. (5)

matrix structure A type of departmentalization that overlays two organizational forms in order to leverage the benefits of both. (15)

mechanistic structure A organizational structure with a narrow span of control and high degrees of formalization and centralization. (15)

media richness The data-carrying capacity of a communication medium, including the volume and variety of information that can be transmitted during a specific time. (11)

mental imagery Mentally practicing a task and visualizing its successful completion. (6)

mental models The broad worldviews or "theories in-use" that people rely on to guide their perceptions and behaviors. (3)

mentoring The process of learning the ropes of organizational life from a senior person within the company. (12)

moral intensity The degree to which an issue demands the application of ethical principles. (2)

motivation The forces within a person that affect his or her direction, intensity, and persistence of voluntary behavior. (2) (5)

motivator–hygiene theory Herzberg's theory stating that employees are primarily motivated by growth and esteem needs, not by lower-level needs. (6)

multisource (360-degree) feedback Performance feedback received from a full circle of people around an employee. (5)

Myers-Briggs Type Indicator (MBTI) A personality inventory designed to identify individuals' basic preferences for perceiving and processing information. (2)

N

need for achievement (nAch) A learned need in which people want to accomplish reasonably challenging goals, and desire unambiguous feedback and recognition for their success. (5)

need for affiliation (nAff) A learned need in which people seek approval from others, conform to their wishes and expectations, and avoid conflict and confrontation. (5)

need for power (nPow) A learned need in which people want to control their environment, including people and material resources, to benefit either themselves (personalized power) or others (socialized power). (5)

needs Deficiencies that energize or trigger behaviors to satisfy those needs. (5)

negative reinforcement Occurs when the removal or avoidance of a consequence increases or maintains the frequency or future probability of a behavior. (3)

negotiation Two or more conflicting parties attempt to resolve their divergent goals by redefining the terms of their interdependence. (13)

networking Cultivating social relationships with others to accomplish one's goals. (12)

network structure An alliance of several organizations for the purpose of creating a product or serving a client. (15)

nominal group technique A structured team decision-making process whereby team members independently write down ideas, describe and clarify them to the group, and then independently rank or vote on them. (10)

norms The informal rules and shared expectations that groups establish to regulate the behavior of their members. (9)

O

open systems Organizations that take their sustenance from the environment and, in turn, affect that environment through their output. (1)

organic structure An organizational structure with a wide span of control, with little formalization and decentralized decision making. (15)

organizational behavior (OB) The study of what people think, feel, and do in and around organizations. (1)

organizational citizenship Behaviors that extend beyond the employee's normal job duties. (2)

organizational commitment The employee's emotional attachment to, identification with, and involvement in a particular organization. (4)

organizational culture The basic pattern of shared assumptions, values, and beliefs governing the way employees within an organization think about and act on problems and opportunities. (16)

organizational politics Behaviors that others perceive as self-serving tactics for personal gain at the expense of other people and possibly the organization. (12)

organizational socialization The process by which individuals learn the values, expected behaviors, and social knowledge necessary to assume their roles in the organization. (16)

organizational strategy The way an organization positions itself in its setting in relation to its stakeholders, given the organization's resources, capabilities, and mission. (15)

organizational structure The division of labor and the patterns of coordinations, communications, work flow, and formal power that direct organizational activities. (15)

organizations Groups of people who work interdependently toward some purpose. (1)

P

parallel learning structures Highly participative groups constructed alongside (i.e., parallel to) the formal organization with the purpose of increasing the organization's learning and producing meaningful organizational change. (17)

path–goal leadership theory A contingency theory of leadership based on expectancy theory of motivation that relates several leadership styles to specific employee and situational contingencies. (14)

perception The process of receiving information about and making sense of the world around us. (3)

personality The relatively stable pattern of behaviors and consistent internal states that explain a person's behavioral tendencies. (2)

persuasion Using logical arguments, facts, and emotional appeals to encourage people to accept a request or message. (12)

positive organizational behavior An emerging philosophy that focuses on building positive qualities and traits within individuals or institutions as opposed to focusing on just trying to fix what might be wrong with them. (3) (5)

positive reinforcement Occurs when the introduction of a consequence increases or maintains the frequency or future probability of a behavior. (3)

postdecisional justification Justifying choices by unconsciously inflating the quality of the selected option and deflating the quality of the discarded options. (8)

power The capacity of a person, team, or organization to influence others. (12)

power distance The extent to which people accept unequal distribution of power in a society. (2)

prejudice The unfounded negative emotions and attitudes toward people belonging to a particular stereotyped group. (3)

primacy effect A perceptual error in which we quickly form an opinion of people based on the first information we receive about them. (3)

procedural justice The fairness of the procedures used to decide the distribution of resources. (5)

process losses Resources (including time and energy) expended toward team development and maintenance rather than the task. (9)

production blocking A time constraint in team decision making due to the procedural requirement that only one person may speak at a time. (10)

profit sharing plans A reward system that pays bonuses to employees based on the previous year's level of corporate profits. (6)

projection bias A perceptual error in which we believe that other people have the same beliefs and behaviors that we do. (3)

prospect theory An effect in which losing a particular amount is more disliked than gaining the same amount. (8)

psychological contract The individual's beliefs about the terms and conditions of a reciprocal exchange agreement between that person and another party. (4)

psychological harassment Repeated and hostile or unwanted conduct, verbal comments, actions, or gestures that affect an employee's dignity or psychological or physical integrity and that result in a harmful work environment for the employee. (7)

punishment Occurs when a consequence decreases the frequency or future probability of a behavior. (3)

R

rational choice paradigm A deeply held view that people should and do make decisions based on pure logic using all necessary information. (8)

realistic job preview (RJP) The process of giving job applicants a balance of positive and negative information about the job and work context. (16)

reality shock Perceived discrepancies between preemployment expectations and on the job reality. (16)

recency effect A perceptual error in which the most recent information dominates one's perception of others. (3)

referent power The capacity to influence others based on the identification and respect they have for the power holder. (12)

refreezing The latter part of the change to the process in which systems and conditions are introduced that reinforce and maintain the desired behaviors. (17)

resilience The capability of individuals to cope successfully in the face of significant change, adversity, or risk. (7)

rituals The programmed routines of daily organizational life that dramatize the organization's culture. (16)

role A set of behaviors that people are expected to perform because they hold certain positions in a team and organization. (9)

role ambiguity A lack of clarity and predictability of the outcomes of a person's behavior. (7)

role conflict Incongruity or incompatibility of expectations associated with a person's role. (7)

S

satisficing Selecting a solution that is satisfactory, or "good enough" rather than optimal or "the best." (8)

scenario planning A systematic process of thinking about alternative futures, and what the organization should do to anticipate and react to those environments. (8)

scientific management Involves systematically partitioning work into its smallest elements and standardizing tasks to achieve maximum efficiency. (6)

scientific method A set principles and procedures that help researchers to systematically understand previously unexplained events and conditions. (1)

selective attention The process of filtering information received by our senses. (3)

self-actualization The need for self-fulfillment—a sense that a person's potential has been realized. (5)

self-directed work teams (SDWTs) Cross-functional work groups organized around work processes that complete an entire piece of work requiring several interdependent tasks, and that have substantial autonomy over the execution of those tasks. (10)

self-fulfilling prophecy Occurs when our expectations about another person cause that person to act in a way that is consistent with those expectations. (3)

self-leadership The process of influencing oneself to establish the self-direction and self-motivation needed to perform a task. (6)

self-monitoring A personality trait referring to an individual's level of sensitivity behavior of others and the ability to adapt appropriately to these situational cues. (2)

self-reinforcement Occurs whenever someone has control over a reinforcer but delays it until a self-set goal has been completed. (3)

self-serving bias A perceptual error whereby people tend to attribute their favorable outcomes to internal factors and their failures to external factors. (3)

self-talk Talking to ourselves about our own thoughts or actions for the purpose of increasing our self-confidence and navigating through decisions in a future event. (6)

servant leadership The belief that leaders serve followers by understanding their needs and facilitating their work performance. (14)

sexual harassment Unwelcome conduct of a sexual nature that detrimentally affects the work environment or leads to adverse job-related consequences for its victims. (7)

shared leadership The view that leadership is broadly distributed rather than assigned to one person, such that people within the team and organization lead each other. (14)

situational leadership theory (SLT) Development by Hersey and Blanchard, this model suggests that effective leaders vary their styles with the "readiness" of followers. (14)

skill variety The extent to which employees must use different skills and talents to perform tasks within their job. (6)

social identity theory A conceptual framework based on the idea that how we perceive the world depends on how we define ourselves in terms of our membership in various social groups. (3)

social learning theory A theory stating that much learning occurs by observing others and then modeling the behaviors that lead to favorable outcomes and avoiding the behaviors that lead to punishing consequences. (3)

social loafing A situation in which people exert less effort (and usually perform at a lower level) when working in groups than when working alone. (9)

socioemotional conflict A negative outcome that occurs when differences are viewed as personal attacks rather than attempts to resolve an issue. (13)

sociotechnical systems (STS) theory A theory stating that effective work sites have joint optimization of their social and technological systems, and that teams should have sufficient autonomy to control key variances in the work process. (10)

span of control The number of people directly reporting to the next level in the organizational hierarchy. (15)

stakeholders Shareholders, customers, suppliers, governments, and any other groups with a vested interest in the organization. (1)

stereotyping The process of assigning traits to people based on their membership in a social category. (3)

stock options A reward system that gives employees the right to purchase company stock at a future date at a predetermined price. (6)

stress An individual's adaptive response to a situation that is perceived as challenging or threatening to the person's well-being. (7)

stressors The causes of stress, including any environmental conditions that place a physical or emotional demand on the person. (7)

substitutability The extent to which people dependent on a resource have alternatives. (12)

superordinate goals Common objectives held by conflicting parties that are more important than their conflicting departmental or individual goals. (13)

surface-level diversity Observable demographic or physiological differences in people, such as their race, ethnicity, gender, age, and physical disabilities. (1)

T

tacit knowledge Knowledge embedded in our actions and ways of thinking, and transmitted only through observation and experience. (3)

task identity The degree to which a job requires completion of a whole or an identifiable piece of work. (6)

task interdependence The extent to which team members must share common inputs to their individual tasks, need to interact in the process of executing their work, or receive outcomes (such as rewards) that are partly determined by the performance of others. (9)

task significance The degree to which the job has a substantial impact on the organization and/or larger society. (6)

team-based structure A type of departmentalization with a flat hierarchy and relatively little formalization, consisting of self-directed work teams responsible for various work processes. (15)

team building Any formal activity intended to improve the development and functioning of a work team. (10)

team cohesiveness The degree of attraction people feel toward the team and their motivation to remain members. (9)

team effectiveness The extent to which a team achieves its objectives, achieves the needs and objectives of its members, and sustains itself over time. (9)

teams Groups of two or more people who interact and influence each other, are mutually accountable for achieving common goals associated with organizational objectives, and perceive themselves as a social entity within an organization. (9)

third-party conflict resolution Any attempt by a relatively neutral person to help the parties resolve their differences. (13)

transactional leadership Leadership that helps organizations achieve their current objectives more efficiently, such as linking job performances to valued rewards and ensuring that employees have the resources needed to get the job done. (14)

transformational leadership A leadership perspective that explains how leaders change teams or organizations by creating, communicating, and modeling a vision for the organization or work unit and inspiring employees to strive for that vision. (14)

trust A person's positive expectations toward another person in situations involving risk. (4) (10)

Type A behavior pattern A behavior pattern associated with people having premature coronary heart disease; Type As tend to be impatient, lose their temper, talk rapidly, and interrupt others. (7)

U

uncertainty avoidance The degree to which people tolerate ambiguity or feel threatened by ambiguity and uncertainty. (2)

unfreezing The first part of the change process whereby the change agent produces disequilibrium between the driving and restraining forces. (17)

upward appeal A type of coalition in which one or more members have higher authority or expertise. (12)

V

valence The anticipated satisfaction or dissatisfaction that an individual feels toward an outcome. (5)

values Stable, long-lasting beliefs about what is important in a variety of situations, that guide our decisions and actions. (1) (2)

values congruence A situation wherein two or more entities have similar value systems. (2)

virtual corporations Network structures representing several independent companies that form unique partnership teams to provide customized products or services, usually to specific clients, for a limited time. (15)

virtual teams Teams whose members operate across space, time, and organizational boundaries and who are linked through information technologies to achieve organizational goals. (10)

virtual work Work practices whereby employees use information technology to perform their jobs away from the traditional physical workplace. (1)

W

win–lose orientation The belief that conflicting parties are drawing from a fixed pie, so the more one party receives, the less the other party will receive. (13)

win–win orientation The belief that conflicting parties will find a mutually beneficial solution to their disagreement. (13)

work–life balance Minimizing conflict between work and nonwork demands. (1)

workaholic A person who is highly involved in work, feels compelled to work, and has a low enjoyment of work. (7)

references

CHAPTER 1

1. J. McHugh, "Google vs. Evil," *Wired,* January 2003; A. Hermida, "Google Looks to See Off Rivals," *BBC News Online,* 30 March 2004; M. Liedtke, "Google vs. Yahoo: Heavyweights Attack from Different Angles," *Associated Press Newswires,* 18 December 2004; F. Vogelstein, "Google @ $165," *Fortune,* 13 December 2004, pp. 98–104; R. Basch, "Doing Well by Doing Good," *Searcher Magazine,* January 2005, pp. 18–28; K. Coughlin, "Goooood Move," *Star-Ledger (Newark, NJ),* 5 June 2005, p. 1; A. Ignatius and L.A. Locke, "In Search of the Real Google," *Time,* 20 February 2006, p. 36.

2. M. Warner, "Organizational Behavior Revisited," *Human Relations* 47 (October 1994), pp. 1151–66; R. Westwood and S. Clegg, "The Discourse of Organization Studies: Dissensus, Politics, and Peradigms," in *Debating Organization: Point–Counterpoint in Organization Studies,* ed. R. Westwood and S. Clegg (Malden, MA: Blackwood, 2003), pp. 1–42. Some of the historical bases of OB mentioned in this paragraph are described in J.A. Conger, "Max Weber's Conceptualization of Charismatic Authority: Its Influence on Organizational Research," *The Leadership Quarterly* 4, no. 3–4 (1993), pp. 277–88; R. Kanigel, *The One Best Way: Frederick Winslow Taylor and the Enigma of Efficiency* (New York: Viking, 1997); J.H. Smith, "The Enduring Legacy of Elton Mayo," *Human Relations* 51, no. 3 (1998), pp. 221–49; T. Takala, "Plato on Leadership," *Journal of Business Ethics* 17 (May 1998), 785–98; and J.A. Fernandez, "The Gentleman's Code of Confucius: Leadership by Values," *Organizational Dynamics* 33, no. 1 (February 2004), pp. 21–31.

3. J. Micklethwait and A. Wooldridge, *The Company: A Short History of a Revolutionary Idea* (New York: Random House, 2003).

4. B. Schlender, "The Three Faces of Steve," *Fortune,* 9 November 1998, pp. 96–101.

5. D.K. Katz, R.L., *The Social Psychology of Organizations* (New York: Wiley, 1966), Chapter 2; R.N. Stern and S.R. Barley, "Organizations as Social Systems: Organization Theory's Neglected Mandate," *Administrative Science Quarterly* 41 (1996), pp. 146–62.

6. N. Hooper, "Call Me Irresistible," *Australian Financial Review,* 5 December 2003, p. 38.

7. J. Pfeffer, *New Directions for Organization Theory* (New York: Oxford University Press, 1997), pp. 7–9.

8. P.R. Lawrence and N. Nohria, *Driven: How Human Nature Shapes Our Choices* (San Francisco: Jossey-Bass, 2002), Chapter 6.

9. P.R. Lawrence "Historical Development of Organizational Behavior," in *Handbook of Organizational Behavior,* ed. L.W. Lorsch (Englewood Cliffs, NJ: Prentice Hall, 1987), pp. 1–9; S.A. Mohrman, C.B. Gibson, and A.M. Mohrman Jr., "Doing Research That Is Useful to Practice: A Model and Empirical Exploration," *Academy of Management Journal* 44 (April 2001), pp. 357–75. For a contrary view, see A.P. Brief and J.M. Dukerich, "Theory in Organizational Behavior: Can It Be Useful?" *Research in Organizational Behavior* 13 (1991), pp. 327–52.

10. M.S. Myers, *Every Employee a Manager* (New York: McGraw-Hill, 1970).

11. D. Yankelovich, "Got to Give to Get," *Mother Jones* 22 (July 1997), pp. 60–63; D. MacDonald, "Good Managers Key to Buffett's Acquisitions," *Montreal Gazette,* 16 November 2001. The two studies on OB and financial performance are B.N. Pfau and I.T. Kay, *The Human Capital Edge* (New York: McGraw-Hill, 2002); and I.S. Fulmer, B. Gerhart, and K.S. Scott, "Are the 100 Best Better? An Empirical Investigation of the Relationship between Being a 'Great Place to Work' and Firm Performance," *Personnel Psychology* 56, no. 4 (Winter 2003), pp. 965–93.

12. V. Kopytoff, "Google Making Its Mark Worldwide," *San Francisco Chronicle,* 20 September 2004, p. H1.

13. J. Guyon, "David Whitwam (CEOs on Managing Globally)," *Fortune,* 26 July 2004, p. 174; P. Loewe and J. Rufat-Latre, "The Changing Face of Global Business," *Optimize* (June 2004), pp. 32–37; L. Uchitelle, "Globalization: It's Not Just Wages," *New York Times,* 17 June 2005, pp. C1, C4.

14. S. Fischer, "Globalization and Its Challenges," *American Economic Review* (May 2003), pp. 1–29. For discussion of the diverse meanings of *globalization,* see M.F. Guillén, "Is Globalization Civilizing, Destructive or Feeble? A Critique of Five Key Debates in the Social Science Literature," *Annual Review of Sociology* 27 (2001), pp. 235–60.

15. The ongoing debate regarding the advantages and disadvantages of globalization is discussed in Guillén, "Is Globalization Civilizing, Destructive or Feeble?"; D. Doane, "Can Globalization Be Fixed?" *Business Strategy Review* 13, no. 2 (2002), pp. 51–58; J. Bhagwati, *In Defense of Globalization* (New York: Oxford University Press, 2004); and M. Wolf, *Why Globalization Works* (New Haven, CT: Yale University Press, 2004).

16. C.L. Cooper and R. J. Burke, *The New World of Work: Challenges and Opportunities* (Oxford: Blackwell, 2002); C. Higgins and L. Duxbury, *The 2001 National Work–Life Conflict Study: Report One, Final Report* (Ottawa: Health Canada, March 2002).

17. K. Ohmae, *The Next Global Stage* (Philadelphia: Wharton School Publishing, 2005).

18. R. House, M. Javidan, and P. Dorfman, "Project Globe: An Introduction," *Applied Psychology: An International Journal* 50 (2001), pp. 489–505; M.A. Von Glinow, E.A. Drost, and M.B. Teagarden, "Converging on IHRM Best Practices: Lessons Learned from a Globally Distributed Consortium on Theory and Practice," *Human Resource Management* 41, no. 1 (April 2002), pp. 123–40; M.M. Javidan et al., "In the Eye of the Beholder: Cross-Cultural Lessons in Leadership from Project Globe," *Academy of Management Perspectives* 20, no. 1 (February 2006), pp. 67–90.

19. Verizon, *Making Connections: Verizon Corporate Responsibility Report 2004* (New York: Verizon, December 2004); J. Carlton, "Dig In: At Google, a Global Workforce Translates into a Global Cafeteria Menu," *The Wall Street Journal,* 14 November 2005, p. R9; P. Goffney, "Champions of Diversity: The Path to Corporate Enlightenment," *Essence,* May 2005, pp. 149–57.

20. M.F. Riche, "America's Diversity and Growth: Signposts for the 21st Century," *Population Bulletin* (June 2000), pp. 3–43; U.S. Census Bureau, *Statistical Abstract of the United States: 2004–2005* (Washington: U.S. Census Bureau, May 2005).

21. Association of American Medical Colleges, "Table 1: Women Applicants, Enrollees–Selected Years 1949–1950 through 2002–2003" (14 July 2003), http://www.aamc.org/members/wim/statistics/stats03/start.htm (accessed 20 June 2005); U.S. Census Bureau, *Statistical Abstract of the United States: 2004–2005,* (Table no. 570, p. 371).

22. D.A. Harrison et al., "Time, Teams, and Task Performance: Changing Effects of Surface- and Deep-Level Diversity on Group Functioning," *Academy of Management Journal* 45, no. 5 (2002), pp. 1029–46.

23. R. Zemke, C. Raines, and B. Filipczak, *Generations at Work: Managing the Clash of Veterans, Boomers, Xers, and Nexters in Your Workplace* (New York: Amacom, 2000); M.R. Muetzel, *They're Not Aloof, Just Generation X* (Shreveport, LA: Steel Bay, 2003); S.H. Applebaum, M. Serena, and B.T. Shapiro, "Generation X and the Boomers: Organizational Myths and Literary Realities," *Management Research News* 27, no. 11/12 (2004), pp. 1–28.

24. O.C. Richard, "Racial Diversity, Business Strategy, and Firm Performance: A Resource-Based View," *Academy of Management Journal* 43 (2000), pp. 164–77; D.D. Frink et al., "Gender Demography and Organization Performance: A Two Study Investigation with Convergence," *Group & Organization Management* 28 (March 2003), pp. 127–47; T. Kochan et al., "The Effects of Diversity on Business Performance: Report of the Diversity Research Network," *Human Resource Management* 42 (2003), pp. 3–21.

25. C. Hymowitz, "The New Diversity," *The Wall Street Journal,* 14 November 2005, p. R1; Sempra Energy, "Case History: Putting Diversity to Work," (San Diego, CA: Sempra Energy, 2005), www.sempra.com/diversity.htm (accessed 21 June 2005).

26. R.J. Ely and D.A. Thomas, "Cultural Diversity at Work: The Effects of Diversity Perspectives on Work Group Processes and Outcomes," *Administrative Science Quarterly* 46 (June 2001), pp. 229–73; T. Kochan et al., "The Effects of Diversity on Business Performance: Report of the Diversity Research Network," *Human Resource Management* 42, no. 1 (2003), pp. 3–21; D. van Knippenberg and S.A. Haslam, "Realizing the Diversity Dividend: Exploring the Subtle Interplay between Identity, Ideology and Reality," in *Social Identity at Work: Developing Theory for Organizational Practice,* ed. S.A. Haslam et al.

(New York: Taylor and Francis, 2003), pp. 61–80; D. van Knippenberg, C.K. W. De Dreu, and A.C. Homan, "Work Group Diversity and Group Performance: An Integrative Model and Research Agenda," *Journal of Applied Psychology* 89, no. 6 (2004), pp. 1008–22; E. Molleman, "Diversity in Demographic Characteristics, Abilities, and Personality Traits: Do Faultlines Affect Team Functioning?" *Group Decision and Negotiation* 14, no. 3 (2005), pp. 173–93.

27. A. Birritteri, "Workplace Diversity: Realizing the Benefits of an All-Inclusive Employee Base," *New Jersey Business,* November 2005, p. 36.

28. S.-A. Chia and E. Toh, "Give Employees a Break," *Straits Times (Singapore),* 23 July 2005.

29. W.G. Bennis and R.J. Thomas, *Geeks and Geezers* (Boston: Harvard Business School Press, 2002), pp. 74–79; E.D.Y. Greenblatt, "Work–Life Balance: Wisdom or Whining," *Organizational Dynamics* 31, no. 2 (2002), pp. 177–93.

30. Basch, "Doing Well by Doing Good"; Coughlin, "Goooood Move."

31. M.V. Roehling et al., "The Nature of the New Employment Relationship(s): A Content Analysis of the Practitioner and Academic Literatures," *Human Resource Management* 39 (2000), pp. 305–20; W.R. Boswell et al., "Responsibilities in the 'New Employment Relationship': An Empirical Test of an Assumed Phenomenon," *Journal of Managerial Issues* 13 (Fall 2001), 307–27; M. Fugate, A.J. Kinicki, and B.E. Ashforth, "Employability: A Psycho-Social Construct, Its Dimensions, and Applications," *Journal of Vocational Behavior* 65, no. 1 (2004), pp. 14–38.

32. M. Jenkins, "Yours for the Taking," *Boeing Frontiers,* June 2004, http://www.boeing.com/news/frontiers/index.html.

33. A.E. Polivka, "Contingent and Alternative Work Arrangements, Defined," *Monthly Labor Review* 119 (October 1996), pp. 3–10; D.H. Pink, *Free Agent Nation* (New York: Time Warner, 2002); C.E. Connelly and D.G. Gallagher, "Emerging Trends in Contingent Work Research," *Journal of Management* 30, no. 6 (2004), pp. 959–83.

34. B.A. Lautsch, "Uncovering and Explaining Variance in the Features and Outcomes of Contingent Work," *Industrial & Labor Relations Review* 56 (October 2002), pp. 23–43; S. Ang, L. Van Dyne, and T.M. Begley, "The Employment Relationships of

Foreign Workers versus Local Employees: A Field Study of Organizational Justice, Job Satisfaction, Performance, and OCB," *Journal of Organizational Behavior* 24 (2003), pp. 561–83; A.L. Kalleberg, "Flexible Firms and Labor Market Segmentation," *Work and Occupations* 30, no. 2 (May 2003), pp. 154–75; B.A. Lautsch, "The Influence of Regular Work Systems on Compensation for Contingent Workers," *Industrial Relations* 42, no. 4 (October 2003), pp. 565–88; Connelly and Gallagher, "Emerging Trends in Contingent Work Research"; B. Pocock, J. Buchanan, and I. Campbell, "Meeting the Challenge of Casual Work in Australia: Evidence, Past Treatment and Future Policy," *Australian Bulletin of Labour* 30, no. 1 (March 2004), pp. 16–32.

35. S. de Castro and Y.-C. Tham, "Home Work," *Digital Life,* 8 February 2005.

36. Australian Telework Advisory Committee (ATAC), *Telework—International Developments (Paper III)* (Canberra: Commonwealth of Australia, March 2005); M. Conlin, "The Easiest Commute of All," *Business Week,* 12 December 2005, p. 78.

37. "AT&T Telecommute Survey Indicates Productivity Is Up," AT&T News release, (New York: 6 August 2002); L. Duxbury and C. Higgins, "Telecommute: A Primer for the Millennium Introduction," in *The New World of Work: Challenges and Opportunities,* ed. C.L. Cooper and R.J. Burke (Oxford: Blackwell, 2002), pp. 157–99; V. Illegems and A. Verbeke, "Telework: What Does It Mean for Management?" *Long Range Planning* 37 (2004), pp. 319–34; S. Raghuram and B. Wiesenfeld, "Work–Nonwork Conflict and Job Stress among Virtual Workers," *Human Resource Management* 43, no. 2/3 (Summer/Fall 2004), pp. 259–77.

38. D.E. Bailey and N.B. Kurland, "A Review of Telework Research: Findings, New Directions, and Lessons for the Study of Modern Work," *Journal of Organizational Behavior* 23 (2002), pp. 383–400; D.W. McCloskey and M. Igbaria, "Does 'Out of Sight' Mean 'Out of Mind'? An Empirical Investigation of the Career Advancement Prospects of Telecommuters," *Information Resources Management Journal* 16 (April–June 2003), pp. 19–34; Sensis, *Sensis® Insights Report: Teleworking,* (Melbourne: Sensis, June 2005).

39. J. Lipnack and J. Stamps, *Virtual Teams: People Working across Boundaries with Technology* (New York: John Wiley & Sons, 2001); L.L. Martins, L.L. Gilson, and

M.T. Maynard, "Virtual Teams: What Do We Know and Where Do We Go from Here?" *Journal of Management* 30, no. 6 (2004), pp. 805–35; G. Hertel, S. Geister, and U. Konradt, "Managing Virtual Teams: A Review of Current Empirical Research," *Human Resource Management Review* 15, no. 1 (2005), pp. 69–95.

40. C. Kelly et al., *Deriving Value from Corporate Values* (The Aspen Institute and Booz Allen Hamilton Inc., February 2005).

41. B.M. Meglino and E.C. Ravlin, "Individual Values in Organizations: Concepts, Controversies, and Research," *Journal of Management* 24, no. 3 (1998), pp. 351–89; B.R. Agle and C.B. Caldwell, "Understanding Research on Values in Business," *Business and Society* 38, no. 3 (September 1999), pp. 326–87; S. Hitlin and J.A. Pilavin, "Values: Reviving a Dormant Concept," *Annual Review of Sociology* 30 (2004), pp. 359–93.

42. Some of the popular books that emphasize the importance of values include J.C. Collins and J.I. Porras, *Built to Last: Successful Habits of Visionary Companies* (London: Century, 1995); C.A. O'Reilly III and J.Pfeffer, *Hidden Value* (Cambridge, MA: Harvard Business School Press, 2000); J.M. Kouzes and B.Z. Posner, *The Leadership Challenge*, 3rd ed. (San Francisco: Jossey-Bass, 2002).

43. The role of values as a control system is discussed in T.M. Begley and D.P. Boyd, "Articulating Corporate Values through Human Resource Policies," *Business Horizons* 43, no. 4 (July 2000), pp. 8–12; and M.G. Murphy and K.M. Davey, "Ambiguity, Ambivalence and Indifference in Organizational Values," *Human Resource Management Journal* 12 (2002), pp. 17–32.

44. Middle East Company News, "Accountability, Teamwork, and Continuous Improvement Define Core Operating Values at DED," Middle East Company News News release (Dubai: 4 January 2005).

45. "Believe It," *BC Business,* July 2004, p. 130; "Multi-Year Study Finds 21% Increase in Americans Who Say Corporate Support of Social Issues Is Important in Building Trust," *Business Wire,* 9 December 2004; J. Milne, "Do the Right Thing," *MIS UK,* 1 December 2005, p. 20.

46. M. van Marrewijk, "Concepts and Definitions of CSR and Corporate Sustainability: Between Agency and Commu-

nion," *Journal of Business Ethics* 44 (May 2003), pp. 95–105.

47. S. Zadek, *The Civil Corporation: The New Economy of Corporate Citizenship* (London: Earthscan, 2001), Chapter 9; The Warehouse, *This Way Forward: Society and Environment Report* 2005 (2005); S. Zambon and A. Del Bello, "Toward a Stakeholder Responsible Approach: The Constructive Role of Reporting," *Corporate Governance* 5, no. 2 (2005), pp. 130–42.

48. "Wal-Mart to Cut Ties with Bangladesh Factories Using Child Labour," *CBC News (Toronto),* 30 November 2005; P. Foster, "Heaven Can Wait," *National Post,* 2 July 2005, p. FP17.

49. A. Brown, "Trust Makes the Difference," *Evolution–The Business and Technology Magazine from SKF,* 25 May 2004; J. Reingold, "Walking the Talk," *Fast Company,* November 2005, pp. 80–85.

50. M.N. Zald, "More Fragmentation? Unfinished Business in Linking the Social Sciences and the Humanities," *Administrative Science Quarterly* 41 (1996), pp. 251–61. Concerns about the "trade deficit" in OB are raised in C. Heath and S.B. Sitkin, "Big-B versus Big-O: What Is Organizational about Organizational Behavior?" *Journal of Organizational Behavior* 22 (2001), pp. 43–58.

51. N. Nicholson, "Evolutionary Psychology: Toward a New View of Human Nature and Organizational Society," *Human Relations* 50 (September 1997), pp. 1053–78; B.D. Pierce and R. White, "The Evolution of Social Structure: Why Biology Matters," *Academy of Management Review* 24 (October 1999), pp. 843–53; Lawrence and Nohria, *Driven: How Human Nature Shapes Our Choices.*

52. A.C. Strauss, J., *Grounded Theory in Practice* (London: Sage Publications, 1997). For an overview of the importance of qualitative methods in organizational behavior, see R.P. Gephart Jr., "Qualitative Research and the *Academy of Management Journal,*" *Academy of Management Journal* 47 (2004), pp. 454–62.

53. C.M. Christensen and M.E. Raynor, "Why Hard-Nosed Executives Should Care about Management Theory," *Harvard Business Review* (September 2003), pp. 66–74. For an excellent critique of the "one best way" approach in early management scholarship, see P.F. Drucker, "Management's New Paradigms," *Forbes* (5 October 1998), pp. 152–77.

54. H.L. Tosi and J.W. Slocum Jr., "Contingency Theory: Some Suggested Directions," *Journal of Management* 10 (1984), pp. 9–26.

55. D.M.H. Rousseau, "Meso Organizational Behavior: Avoiding Three Fundamental Biases," in *Trends in Organizational Behavior,* ed. C.L. Cooper and D.M. Rousseau (Chichester, UK: John Wiley & Sons, 1994), pp. 13–30.

56. E. Zore, "When We Grow Together, We Grow Stronger," *Executive Speeches,* October 2005, p. 20.

57. F.E. Kast and J.E. Rosenweig, "General Systems Theory: Applications for Organization and Management," *Academy of Management Journal* (1972), pp. 447–65; P.M. Senge, *The Fifth Discipline: The Art and Practice of the Learning Organization* (New York: Doubleday Currency, 1990); A. De Geus, *The Living Company* (Boston: Harvard Business School Press, 1997); R.T. Pascale, M. Millemann, and L. Gioja, *Surfing on the Edge of Chaos* (London: Texere, 2000).

58. V.P. Rindova and S. Kotha, "Continuous 'Morphing': Competing through Dynamic Capabilities, Form, and Function," *Academy of Management Journal* 44 (2001), pp. 1263–80; J. McCann, "Organizational Effectiveness: Changing Concepts for Changing Environments," *Human Resource Planning* 27, no. 1 (2004), pp. 42–50.

59. R. Martin, "The Virtue Matrix: Calculating the Return on Corporate Responsibility," *Harvard Business Review* 80 (March 2002), pp. 68–85.

60. M.L. Tushman, M.B. Nadler, and D.A. Nadler, *Competing by Design: The Power of Organizational Architecture* (New York: Oxford University Press, 1997).

61. G. Huber, "Organizational Learning: The Contributing Processes and Literature," *Organizational Science* 2 (1991), pp. 88–115; E.C. Nevis, A.J. DiBella, and J.M. Gould, "Understanding Organizations as Learning Systems," *Sloan Management Review* 36 (1995), pp. 73–85; G. Miles et al., "Some Conceptual and Research Barriers to the Utilization of Knowledge," *California Management Review* 40 (Spring 1998), pp. 281–88; D.A. Garvin, *Learning in Action: A Guide to Putting the Learning Organization to Work* (Boston: Harvard Business School Press, 2000).

62. T.A. Stewart, *Intellectual Capital: The New Wealth of Organizations* (New York:

Currency/Doubleday, 1997); H. Saint-Onge and D. Wallace, *Leveraging Communities of Practice for Strategic Advantage* (Boston: Butterworth-Heinemann, 2003), pp. 9–10; J.-A. Johannessen, B. Olsen, and J. Olaisen, "Intellectual Capital as a Holistic Management Philosophy: A Theoretical Perspective," *International Journal of Information Management* 25, no. 2 (2005), pp. 151–71.

63. There is no complete agreement on the meaning of *organizational learning* (or *learning organization*), and the relationship between organizational learning and knowledge management is still somewhat ambiguous. For example, see S.C. Goh, "The Learning Organization: An Empirical Test of a Normative Perspective," *International Journal of Organization Theory & Behavior* 4, no. 3/4 (August 2001), pp. 329–55; and B.R. McElyea, "Knowledge Management, Intellectual Capital, and Learning Organizations: A Triad of Future Management Integration," *Futurics* 26 (2002), pp. 59–65.

64. C.W. Wick and L.S. Leon, "From Ideas to Actions: Creating a Learning Organization," *Human Resource Management* 34 (Summer 1995), pp. 299–311; L. Falkenberg et al., "Knowledge Acquisition Processes for Technology Decisions," in *Proceedings of the Academy of Management 2002 Annual Conference* (2002), pp. J1–J6; S. Lloyd, "Smarter Spending Habits," *Business Review Weekly*, 10 November 2005, p. 130.

65. W. Cohen and D. Levinthal, "Absorptive Capacity: A New Perspective on Learning and Innovation," *Administrative Science Quarterly* 35 (1990), pp. 128–52; J.L. Johnson, R.S. Sohi, and R. Grewal, "The Role of Relational Knowledge Stores in Interfirm Partnering," *Journal of Marketing* 68 (July 2004), pp. 21–36; M. Rogers, "Absorptive Capacity and Economic Growth: How Do Countries Catch Up?" *Cambridge Journal of Economics* 28, no. 4 (July 2004), pp. 577–96.

66. G.S. Richards and S.C. Goh, "Implementing Organizational Learning: Toward a Systematic Approach," *The Journal of Public Sector Management* (Autumn 1995), pp. 25–31; C. O'Dell and C.J. Grayson, "If Only We Knew What We Know: Identification and Transfer of Internal Best Practices," *California Management Review* 40 (Spring 1998), pp. 154–74; R. Ruggles, "The State of the Notion: Knowledge Management in Practice," *California Management Review* 40 (Spring 1998), pp. 80–89.

67. R. Garud and A. Kumaraswamy, "Vicious and Virtuous Circles in the Management of Knowledge: The Case of Infosys Technologies," *MIS Quarterly* 29, no. 1 (March 2005), pp. 9–33.

68. E.C. Wenger and W.M. Snyder, "Communities of Practice: The Organizational Frontier," *Harvard Business Review* 78 (January–February 2002), pp. 139–45; Saint-Onge and Wallace, *Leveraging Communities of Practice for Strategic Advantage;* M. Thompson, "Structural and Epistemic Parameters in Communities of Practice," *Organization Science* 16, no. 2 (March–April 2005), pp. 151–64.

69. Saint-Onge and Wallace, *Leveraging Communities of Practice for Strategic Advantage,* Chapter 5.

70. B.P. Sunoo, "The Sydney Challenge," *Workforce,* September 2000, pp. 70–73; N. Bita and J. Lehmann, "Five-Ring Circuit for Olympic Organisers," *The Australian,* 12 September 2005, p. 27; E. Scmertzaki, "A Brief but Intense Job," *Information Outlook,* May 2005, pp. 29–35.

71. H. Beazley, J. Boenisch, and D. Harden, "Knowledge Continuity: The New Management Function," *Journal of Organizational Excellence* 22 (2003), pp. 65–81.

72. D. Cline, "On a Roll," *Augusta Chronicle,* 2 February 2003, p. D1.

73. M.E. McGill and J.W. Slocum Jr., "Unlearn the Organization," *Organizational Dynamics* 22, no. 2 (1993), pp. 67–79; D. Lei, J.W. Slocum, and R.A. Pitts, "Designing Organizations for Competitive Advantage: The Power of Unlearning and Learning," *Organizational Dynamics* 27 (Winter 1999), pp. 24–38.

CHAPTER 2

1. "Owens Corning Makes Smart Investments in Employee Training," *The Resource (Newsletter of Jackson State's Division of Economic and Community Development),* Fall 2004, p. 1; M. Millar, "Getting the Measure of Its People," *Personnel Today,* 14 December 2004, p. 6; J. Robison, "ASB Bank: Good Isn't Good Enough," *Gallup Management Journal,* 12 August 2004; V. Ratanjee, "Wake-up Call for Thailand, Inc.," *Gallup Management Journal,* 12 May 2005; T.J. Tschida, "Creating an Employee-Centric Call Center," *Gallup Management Journal,* 13 October 2005; "Employee Engagement Levels Are Focus of Global Towers Perrin Study," *Towers Perrin Monitor (Online),* January 2006, www.towersperrin.com; "Gallup Study: Feeling Good Matters in the Workplace," *Gallup Management Journal,* 12 January 2006.

2. Thanks to senior officers in the Singapore Armed Forces for discovering the handy "MARS" acronym. Thanks also to Chris Perryer at the University of Western Australia for pointing out that the full model should be called the "MARS BAR" because the outcomes are "behavior and results"! The MARS model is a variation of earlier models and writing by several sources, including E.E. Lawler III and L.W. Porter, "Antecedent Attitudes of Effective Managerial Performance," *Organizational Behavior and Human Performance* 2, no. 2 (1967), pp. 122–42; and K.F. Kane, "Special Issue: Situational Constraints and Work Performance," *Human Resource Management Review* 3 (Summer 1993), pp. 83–175.

3. T.A. Judge and R. Illies, "Relationship of Personality to Performance Motivation: A Meta-Analytic Review," *Journal of Applied Psychology* 87, no. 4 (2002), pp. 797–807; S. Roccas et al., "The Big Five Personality Factors and Personal Values," *Personality and Social Psychology* 28 (June 2002), pp. 789–801.

4. C.C. Pinder, *Work Motivation in Organizational Behavior* (Upper Saddle River, NJ: Prentice-Hall, 1998); G.P. Latham and C.C. Pinder, "Work Motivation Theory and Research at the Dawn of the Twenty-First Century," *Annual Review of Psychology* 56 (2005), pp. 485–516.

5. K. Brown, "Putting Leadership Rubber to the Manager Road," *Human Resources Magazine (Australia),* 15 June 2005.

6. R. Jacobs, "Using Human Resource Functions to Enhance Emotional Intelligence," in *The Emotionally Intelligent Workplace,* ed. C. Cherniss and D. Goleman (San Francisco: Jossey-Bass, 2001), pp. 159–81.

7. "New Euro 16m Centre to Train 1,000 Toyota Staff a Year," *Just-Auto,* 24 March 2006; Y. Kageyama, "Toyota Workers Learn Knack of Auto Production in New Global Push," *Associated Press Newswires,* 17 April 2006.

8. S. Brady, "Deep in the Heart of AT&T Dallas," *Cable World,* 7 October 2002, p. 37.

9. J. Waresh, "750 Workers Log 16-Hour Days to Restore Power," *Palm Beach Post (Florida),* 9 November 2005, p. 1.

10. Kane, "Special Issue: Situational Constraints and Work Performance"; S.B. Bacharach and P. Bamberger, "Beyond Situational Constraints: Job Resources

Inadequacy and Individual Performance at Work," *Human Resource Management Review* 5, no. 2 (1995), pp. 79–102; G. Johns, "Commentary: In Praise of Context," *Journal of Organizational Behavior* 22 (2001), pp. 31–42.

11. J.P. Campbell, "The Definition and Measurement of Performance in the New Age," in *The Changing Nature of Performance: Implications for Staffing, Motivation, and Development,* ed. D.R. Ilgen and E.D. Pulakos (San Francisco: Jossey-Bass, 1999), pp. 399–429; R.D. Hackett, "Understanding and Predicting Work Performance in the Canadian Military," *Canadian Journal of Behavioural Science* 34, no. 2 (2002), pp. 131–40.

12. D.W. Organ, "Organizational Citizenship Behavior: It's Construct Clean-up Time," *Human Performance* 10 (1997), pp. 85–97; J.A. LePine, A. Erez, and D.E. Johnson, "The Nature and Dimensionality of Organizational Citizenship Behavior: A Critical Review and Meta-Analysis," *Journal of Applied Psychology* 87 (February 2002), pp. 52–65; B. Erickson, "Nature Times Nurture: How Organizations Can Optimize Their People's Contributions," *Journal of Organizational Excellence* 24, no. 1 (Winter 2004), pp. 21–30; M.A. Vey and J.P. Campbell, "In-Role or Extra-Role Organizational Citizenship Behavior: Which Are We Measuring?" *Human Performance* 17, no. 1 (2004), pp. 119–35.

13. M. Rotundo and P. Sackett, "The Relative Importance of Task, Citizenship, and Counterproductive Performance to Global Ratings of Job Performance: A Policy-Capturing Approach," *Journal of Applied Psychology* 87 (February 2002), pp. 66–80; P. D. Dunlop and K. Lee, "Workplace Deviance, Organizational Citizenship Behaviour, and Business Unit Performance: The Bad Apples Do Spoil the Whole Barrel," *Journal of Organizational Behavior* 25 (2004), pp. 67–80.

14. B. Carey, "Truckload's New Recruiting Routes," *Traffic World,* 22 August 2005; D. Simanoff, "Hotels Plagued by Staff Vacancies," *Tampa Tribune,* 30 January 2006, p. 1.

15. Watson Wyatt, "U.S. Workers City Hypocrisy and Favoritism–Rather Than Financial Misdeeds–as Biggest Ethical Lapses at Work," Watson Wyatt News release (Washington, DC: 12 January 2005); Watson Wyatt, *WorkCanada 2004/2005– Pursuing Productive Engagement* (Toronto: Watson Wyatt, January 2005).

16. T.R. Mitchell, B.C. Holtom, and T.W. Lee, "How to Keep Your Best Employees: Developing an Effective Retention Policy," *Academy of Management Executive* 15 (November 2001), pp. 96–108.

17. D.A. Harrison and J.J. Martocchio, "Time for Absenteeism: A 20-Year Review of Origins, Offshoots, and Outcomes," *Journal of Management* 24 (Spring 1998), pp. 305–50; C.M. Mason and M.A. Griffin, "Group Absenteeism and Positive Affective Tone: A Longitudinal Study," *Journal of Organizational Behavior* 24, no. 6 (2003), pp. 667–87; A. Vaananen et al., "Job Characteristics, Physical and Psychological Symptoms, and Social Support as Antecedents of Sickness Absence among Men and Women in the Private Industrial Sector," *Social Science & Medicine* 57, no. 5 (2003), pp. 807–24.

18. J. Miller, "Tom's of Maine Co-Founder, in Portsmouth, Relates His Philosophy," *Union-Leader (Manchester, NH),* 22 May 2003, p. D8.

19. Some of the more popular books that encourage executives to develop values statements include J.C. Collins and J.I. Porras, *Built to Last: Successful Habits of Visionary Companies* (London: Century, 1995); C. A. O'Reilly III and J. Pfeffer, *Hidden Value* (Cambridge, MA: Harvard Business School Press, 2000); and J.M. Kouzes and B.Z. Posner, *The Leadership Challenge,* 3rd ed. (San Francisco: Jossey-Bass, 2002).

20. B.M. Meglino and E.C. Ravlin, "Individual Values in Organizations: Concepts, Controversies, and Research," *Journal of Management* 24, no. 3 (1998), pp. 351–89; B.R. Agle and C.B. Caldwell, "Understanding Research on Values in Business," *Business and Society* 38, no. 3 (September 1999), pp. 326–87; S. Hitlin and J.A. Pilavin, "Values: Reviving a Dormant Concept," *Annual Review of Sociology* 30 (2004), pp. 359–93.

21. D. Lubinski, D.B. Schmidt, and C.P. Benbow, "A 20-Year Stability Analysis of the Study of Values for Intellectually Gifted Individuals from Adolescence to Adulthood," *Journal of Applied Psychology* 81 (1996), pp. 443–51.

22. B. Kabanoff and J. Daly, "Espoused Values in Organizations," *Australian Journal of Management* 27, Special issue (2002), pp. 89–104.

23. S.H. Schwartz, "Universals in the Content and Structure of Values: Theoretical Advances and Empirical Tests in 20 Countries," *Advances in Experimental Social Psychology* 25 (1992), pp. 1–65; S.H. Schwartz, "Are There Universal Aspects in the Structure and Contents of Human Values?" *Journal of Social Issues* 50 (1994), pp. 19–45; M. Schwartz, "The Nature of the Relationship between Corporate Codes of Ethics and Behavior," *Journal of Business Ethics* 32, no. 3 (2001), p. 247; D. Spini, "Measurement Equivalence of 10 Value Types from the Schwartz Value Survey across 21 Countries," *Journal of Cross-Cultural Psychology* 34, no. 1 (January 2003), pp. 3–23; S.H. Schwartz and K. Boehnke, "Evaluating the Structure of Human Values with Confirmatory Factor Analysis," *Journal of Research in Personality* 38, no. 3 (2004), pp. 230–55.

24. "Building a Solid Foundation on Value-Driven Principles," *Business Leader* 14 (June 2003), p. 6.

25. G.R. Maio and J.M. Olson, "Values as Truisms: Evidence and Implications," *Journal of Personality and Social Psychology* 74, no. 2 (1998), pp. 294–311; G.R. Maio et al., "Addressing Discrepancies between Values and Behavior: The Motivating Effect of Reasons," *Journal of Experimental Social Psychology* 37, no. 2 (2001), pp. 104–17; B. Verplanken and R.W. Holland, "Motivated Decision Making: Effects of Activation and Self-Centrality of Values on Choices and Behavior," *Journal of Personality and Social Psychology* 82, no. 3 (2002), pp. 434–47; A. Bardi and S.H. Schwartz, "Values and Behavior: Strength and Structure of Relations," *Personality and Social Psychology Bulletin* 29, no. 10 (October 2003), pp. 1207–20; M.M. Bernard and G.R. Maio, "Effects of Introspection about Reasons for Values: Extending Research on Values-as-Truisms," *Social Cognition* 21, no. 1 (2003), pp. 1–25.

26. M.L.A. Hayward, V.P. Rindova, and T.G. Pollock, "Believing One's Own Press: The Causes and Consequences of CEO Celebrity," *Strategic Management Journal* 25, no. 7 (July 2004), pp. 637–53.

27. K.F. Alam, "Business Ethics in New Zealand Organizations: Views from the Middle and Lower Level Managers," *Journal of Business Ethics* 22 (November 1999), pp. 145–53; S.R. Chatterjee and C.A.L. Pearson, "Indian Managers in Transition: Orientations, Work Goals, Values and Ethics," *Management International Review* (January 2000), pp. 81–95.

28. A.L. Kristof, "Person–Organization Fit: An Integrative Review of Its Conceptualizations, Measurement, and Implications," *Personnel Psychology* 49, no. 1 (Spring 1996), pp. 1–49; M.L. Verquer, T.A. Beehr, and

S.H. Wagner, "A Meta-Analysis of Relations between Person–Organization Fit and Work Attitudes," *Journal of Vocational Behavior* 63 (2003), pp. 473–89; J.W. Westerman and L.A. Cyr, "An Integrative Analysis of Person–Organization Fit Theories," *International Journal of Selection and Assessment* 12, no. 3 (September 2004), pp. 252–61; D. Bouckenooghe et al., "The Prediction of Stress by Values and Value Conflict," *Journal of Psychology* 139, no. 4 (2005), pp. 369–82.

29. K.M. Eisenhardt, J.L. Kahwajy, and L.J. Bourgeois III, "Conflict and Strategic Choice: How Top Management Teams Disagree," *California Management Review* 39 (Winter 1997), pp. 42–62; D. Arnott, *Corporate Cults* (New York: AMACOM, 1999).

30. Coles Myer Ltd., *Corporate Social Responsibility Report 2005* (Tooronga, Victoria: Coles Myer, July 2005); F. Smith et al., "25 True Leaders," *Australian Financial Review,* 12 August 2005, p. 62.

31. T. Simons, "Behavioral Integrity: The Perceived Alignment between Managers' Words and Deeds as a Research Focus," *Organization Science* 13, no. 1 (January–February 2002), pp. 18–35. Values at Meyners & Co. are described in K.A. McDonald, "Meyners Does a Reality Check," *Journal of Accountancy* 201, no. 2 (2006), p. 51.

32. T.A. Joiner, "The Influence of National Culture and Organizational Culture Alignment on Job Stress and Performance: Evidence from Greece," *Journal of Managerial Psychology* 16 (2001), pp. 229–42; Z. Aycan, R.N. Kanungo, and J.B.P. Sinha, "Organizational Culture and Human Resource Management Practices: The Model of Culture Fit," *Journal of Cross-Cultural Psychology* 30 (July 1999), pp. 501–26.

33. W. Sekiguchi, "Managing Means People, Visions," *Nikkei Weekly (Japan),* 12 December 2005.

34. D. Oyserman, H.M. Coon, and M. Kemmelmeier, "Rethinking Individualism and Collectivism: Evaluation of Theoretical Assumptions and Meta-Analyses," *Psychological Bulletin* 128 (2002), pp. 3–72; C.P. Earley and C.B. Gibson, "Taking Stock in Our Progress on Individualism–Collectivism: 100 Years of Solidarity and Community," *Journal of Management* 24 (May 1998), pp. 265–304; F.S. Niles, "Individualism–Collectivism Revisited," *Cross-Cultural Research* 32 (November 1998), pp. 315–41.

35. Oyserman, Coon, and Kemmelmeier, "Rethinking Individualism and Collectivism: Evaluation of Theoretical Assumptions and Meta-Analyses." The relationship between individualism and collectivism is still being debated. Some researchers suggest that there are different types of individualism and collectivism, and some of these types may be opposites. Others say the lack of association is due to the way we measure these concepts. See E.G.T. Green, J.-C. Deschamps, and D. Paez, "Variation of Individualism and Collectivism within and between 20 Countries," *Journal of Cross-Cultural Psychology* 36, no. 3 (May 2005), pp. 321–39; S. Oishi et al., "The Measurement of Values across Cultures: A Pairwise Comparison Approach," *Journal of Research in Personality* 39, no. 2 (2005), pp. 299–305.

36. M.H. Bond, "Reclaiming the Individual from Hofstede's Ecological Analysis—A 20-Year Odyssey," *Psychological Bulletin* 128 (2002), pp. 73–77; M. Voronov and J.A. Singer, "The Myth of Individualism–Collectivism: A Critical Review," *Journal of Social Psychology* 142 (August 2002), pp. 461–80.

37. J. Chao, "Culture Clash Looms as Lenovo Gobbles IBM Unit," *Palm Beach Post,* 19 December 2004, p. 3F; D. Roberts and L. Lee, "East Meets West, Big Time," *BusinessWeek,* 9 May 2005, p. 74.

38. H. Trinca, "It's about Soul, but Don't Get Too Soft," *Australian Financial Review,* 12 August 2005, p. 56.

39. G. Hofstede, *Culture's Consequences: Comparing Values, Behaviors, Institutions, and Organizations across Nations,* 2nd ed. (Thousand Oaks, CA: Sage, 2001).

40. G. Hofstede, *Cultures and Organizations: Software of the Mind* (New York: McGraw-Hill, 1991). Hofstede used the terms *masculinity* and *femininity* for achievement and nurturing orientation, respectively. We have adopted the latter terms to minimize the sexist perspective of these concepts.

41. J.S. Osland et al., "Beyond Sophisticated Stereotyping: Cultural Sensemaking in Context," *Academy of Management Executive* 14 (February 2000), pp. 65–79; S.S. Sarwono and R.W. Armstrong, "Microcultural Differences and Perceived Ethical Problems: An International Business Perspective," *Journal of Business Ethics* 30 (March 2001), pp. 41–56; Voronov and Singer, "The Myth of Individualism–Collectivism: A Critical Review";

N. Jacob, "Cross-Cultural Investigations: Emerging Concepts," *Journal of Organizational Change Management* 18, no. 5 (2005), pp. 514–28.

42. C. Savoye, "Workers Say Honesty Is Best Company Policy," *Christian Science Monitor,* 15 June 2000; Kouzes and Posner, *The Leadership Challenge;* J. Schettler, "Leadership in Corporate America," *Training & Development,* September 2002, pp. 66–73.

43. J. Moir, "Dishing the Dirt on China's Corporate Criminals," *South China Morning Post (Hong Kong),* 20 August 2005, p. 1; M. Wilkinson and D. Snow, "Going against the Grain," *Sydney Morning Herald,* 5 November 2005, p. 28; J. Spencer and K. Scannell, "Gemstar Ex-CEO Is Ordered to Pay $22.3 Million," *The Wall Street Journal,* 9 May 2006, p. A3.

44. P.L. Schumann, "A Moral Principles Framework for Human Resource Management Ethics," *Human Resource Management Review* 11 (Spring–Summer 2001), pp. 93–111; J. Boss, *Analyzing Moral Issues,* 3rd ed. (New York: McGraw-Hill, 2005), Chapter 1; M.G. Velasquez, *Business Ethics: Concepts and Cases,* 6th ed. (Upper Saddle River, NJ: Prentice-Hall, 2006), Chapter 2.

45. T.J. Jones, "Ethical Decision Making by Individuals in Organizations: An Issue Contingent Model," *Academy of Management Review* 16 (1991), pp. 366–95; B.H. Frey, "The Impact of Moral Intensity on Decision Making in a Business Context," *Journal of Business Ethics* 26 (August 2000), pp. 181–95; D.R. May and K.P. Pauli, "The Role of Moral Intensity in Ethical Decision Making," *Business and Society* 41 (March 2002), pp. 84–117.

46. J.R. Sparks and S.D. Hunt, "Marketing Researcher Ethical Sensitivity: Conceptualization, Measurement, and Exploratory Investigation," *Journal of Marketing* 62 (April 1998), pp. 92–109.

47. Alam, "Business Ethics in New Zealand Organizations: Views from the Middle and Lower Level Managers"; K. Blotnicky, "Is Business in Moral Decay?," *Chronicle-Herald (Halifax),* 11 June 2000; B. Stoneman and K.K. Holliday, "Pressure Cooker," *Banking Strategies,* January–February 2001, p. 13.

48. S. Greengard, "Golden Values," *Workforce Management,* March 2005, pp. 52–53.

49. B. Farrell, D.M. Cobbin, and H.M. Farrell, "Codes of Ethics: Their Evolution, Development and Other Controversies," *Journal of Management Development* 21,

no. 2 (2002), pp. 152–63; G. Wood and M. Rimmer, "Codes of Ethics: What Are They Really and What Should They Be?" *International Journal of Value-Based Management* 16, no. 2 (2003), p. 181.

50. P. J. Gnazzo and G.R. Wratney, "Are You Serious about Ethics?" *Across the Board* 40 (July/August 2003), p. 46ff; T.F. Lindeman, "A Matter of Choice," *Pittsburgh Post-Gazette,* 30 March 2004; B. Schultz, "Ethics under Investigation," *Network World,* 26 April 2004; K. Tyler, "Do the Right Thing," *HRMagazine* 50, no. 2 (February 2005), pp. 99–103.

51. E. Aronson, "Integrating Leadership Styles and Ethical Perspectives," *Canadian Journal of Administrative Sciences* 18 (December 2001), pp. 266–76; D.R. May et al., "Developing the Moral Component of Authentic Leadership," *Organizational Dynamics* 32 (2003), pp. 247–60. The Vodafone director quotation is from R. Van Lee, L. Fabish, and N. McGaw, "The Value of Corporate Values," *Strategy+Business* (Summer 2005), pp. 1–13.

52. Roccas et al., "The Big Five Personality Factors and Personal Values,"

53. H.C. Triandis and E.M. Suh, "Cultural Influences on Personality," *Annual Review of Psychology* 53 (2002), pp. 133–60.

54. B. Reynolds and K. Karraker, "A Big Five Model of Disposition and Situation Interaction: Why a 'Helpful' Person May Not Always Behave Helpfully," *New Ideas in Psychology* 21 (April 2003), pp. 1–13; W. Mischel, "Toward an Integrative Science of the Person," *Annual Review of Psychology* 55 (2004), pp. 1–22.

55. W. Immen, "Prospective Hires Put to the Test," *Globe & Mail,* 26 January 2005, p. C1.

56. R.M. Guion and R.F. Gottier, "Validity of Personnel Measures in Personnel Selection," *Personnel Psychology* 18 (1965), pp. 135–64; N. Schmitt et al., "Meta-Analyses of Validity Studies Published between 1964 and 1982 and the Investigation of Study Characteristics," *Personnel Psychology* 37 (1984), pp. 407–22.

57. P.G. Irving, "On the Use of Personality Measures in Personnel Selection," *Canadian Psychology* 34 (April 1993), pp. 208–14.

58. K.M. DeNeve and H. Cooper, "The Happy Personality: A Meta-Analysis of 137 Personality Traits and Subjective Well-Being," *Psychological Bulletin* 124 (September 1998), pp. 197–229; T.A. Judge et al., "Personality and Leadership: A Qualitative and Quantitative Review," *Journal of Applied*

Psychology 87, no. 4 (2002), pp. 765–80; R. Ilies, M.W. Gerhardt, and H. Le, "Individual Differences in Leadership Emergence: Integrating Meta-Analytic Findings and Behavioral Genetics Estimates," *International Journal of Selection and Assessment* 12, no. 3 (September 2004), pp. 207–19.

59. This historical review, and the trait descriptions in this section, are discussed in J.M. Digman, "Personality Structure: Emergence of the Five-Factor Model," *Annual Review of Psychology* 41 (1990), pp. 417–40; M.K. Mount and M.R. Barrick, "The Big Five Personality Dimensions: Implications for Research and Practice in Human Resources Management," *Research in Personnel and Human Resources Management* 13 (1995), pp. 153–200; R.J. Schneider and L.M. Hough, "Personality and Industrial/Organizational Psychology," *International Review of Industrial and Organizational Psychology* 10 (1995), pp. 75–129.

60. T.A. Judge and R. Ilies, "Relationship of Personality to Performance Motivation: A Meta-Analytic Review," *Journal of Applied Psychology* 87, no. 4 (2002), pp. 797–807; A. Witt, L.A. Burke, and M.R. Barrick, "The Interactive Effects of Conscientiousness and Agreeableness on Job Performance," *Journal of Applied Psychology* 87 (February 2002), pp. 164–69.

61. C.G. Jung, *Psychological Types,* trans. H.G. Baynes (Princeton, NJ: Princeton University Press, 1971); I.B. Myers, *The Myers-Briggs Type Indicator* (Palo Alto, CA: Consulting Psychologists Press, 1987).

62. M. Gladwell, "Personality Plus," *New Yorker,* 20 September 2004, pp. 42–48; R.B. Kennedy and D.A. Kennedy, "Using the Myers-Briggs Type Indicator in Career Counseling," *Journal of Employment Counseling* 41, no. 1 (March 2004), pp. 38–44. The Portsmouth City and Dell Computer examples are found in E. Ross, "Enough Chiefs," *BRW,* 6 October 2005, p. 66; M. Hoyer, "The Quiet Man of Portsmouth: City Manager James Oliver," *Public Management,* April 2006, p. 28.

63. W.L. Johnson et al., "A Higher-Order Analysis of the Factor Structure of the Myers-Briggs Type Indicator," *Measurement and Evaluation in Counseling and Development* 34 (July 2001), pp. 96–108; R.M. Capraro and M.M. Capraro, "Myers-Briggs Type Indicator Score Reliability across Studies: A Meta-Analytic Reliability Generalization Study," *Educational and Psychological Measurement* 62 (August 2002), pp. 590–602;

J. Michael, "Using the Myers-Briggs Type Indicator as a Tool for Leadership Development? Apply with Caution," *Journal of Leadership & Organizational Studies* 10 (Summer 2003), pp. 68–81.

64. P.E. Spector, "Behavior in Organizations as a Function of Employees' Locus of Control," *Psychological Bulletin* 91 (1982), pp. 482–97; J.M. Howell and B.J. Avolio, "Transformational Leadership, Transactional Leadership, Locus of Control, and Support for Innovation: Key Predictors of Consolidated-Business-Unit Performance," *Journal of Applied Psychology* 78 (1993), pp. 891–902; P.E. Spector et al., "Do National Levels of Individualism and Internal Locus of Control Relate to Well-Being: An Ecological Level International Study," *Journal of Organizational Behavior* 22 (2001), pp. 815–32.

65. M. Snyder, *Public Appearances/Private Realities: The Psychology of Self-Monitoring* (New York: W. H. Freeman, 1987).

66. R.J. Ellis and S.E. Cronshaw, "Self-Monitoring and Leader Emergence: A Test of Moderator Effects," *Small Group Research* 23 (1992), pp. 113–29; M. Kilduff and D.V. Day, "Do Chameleons Get Ahead? The Effects of Self-Monitoring on Managerial Careers," *Academy of Management Journal* 37 (1994), pp. 1047–60; M.A. Warech et al., "Self-Monitoring and 360-Degree Ratings," *Leadership Quarterly* 9 (Winter 1998), pp. 449–73; A. Mehra, M. Kilduff, and D.J. Brass, "The Social Networks of High and Low Self-Monitors: Implications for Workplace Performance," *Administrative Science Quarterly* 46 (March 2001), pp. 121–46.

67. J.L. Holland, *Making Vocational Choices: A Theory of Careers* (Englewood Cliffs, NJ: Prentice Hall, 1973).

68. G.D. Gottfredson and J.L. Holland, "A Longitudinal Test of the Influence of Congruence: Job Satisfaction, Competency Utilization, and Counterproductive Behavior," *Journal of Counseling Psychology* 37 (1990), pp. 389–98; A. Furnham, "Vocational Preference and P-O Fit: Reflections on Holland's Theory of Vocational Choice," *Applied Psychology: An International Review* 50 (2001), pp. 5–29.

69. J. Tupponce, "Listening to Those Inner Voices," *Richmond Times-Dispatch,* 11 May 2003, p. S3.

70. Furnham, "Vocational Preference and P-O Fit: Reflections on Holland's Theory of Vocational Choice"; R.P. Tett and D.D. Burnett, "A Personality Trait-Based Interactionist Model of Job Performance," *Journal of Applied Psychology* 88, no. 3 (2003),

pp. 500–517; W. Yang, G.S. Stokes, and C.H. Hui, "Cross-Cultural Validation of Holland's Interest Structure in Chinese Population," *Journal of Vocational Behavior* (2005), In Press.

71. G.D. Gottfredson, "John L. Holland's Contributions to Vocational Psychology: A Review and Evaluation," *Journal of Vocational Behavior* 55, no. 1 (1999), pp. 15–40.

CHAPTER 3

1. J. Lynch and M. Dagostino, "Man in Motion," *People Magazine,* 26 August 2002, p. 89; N. Hooper, "Call Me Irresistible," *Australian Financial Review,* 5 December 2003, p. 38; D. Knight, "Hands-on CEO Gets IPL Back on Track," *Indianapolis Star,* 21 November 2004; K. Capell, "Ikea; How the Swedish Retailer Became a Global Cult Brand," *BusinessWeek,* 14 November 2005, p. 96; W. Frey, "Rubbish Boy Doing Well as Junk Man," *Metro-Vancouver,* 25 April 2005, p. 11; L. Morrell, "Taking the Floor," *Retail Week,* 18 November 2005.

2. Plato, *The Republic,* trans. D. Lee (Harmondsworth, England: Penguin, 1955).

3. R.H. Fazio, D.R. Roskos-Ewoldsen, and M.C. Powell, "Attitudes, Perception, and Attention," in *The Heart's Eye: Emotional Influences in Perception and Attention,* ed. P.M. Niedenthal and S. Kitayama (San Diego, CA: Academic Press, 1994), pp. 197–216.

4. The effect of the target in selective attention is known as "bottom-up selection"; the effect of the perceiver's psychodynamics on this process is known as "top down selection." C.E. Connor, H.E. Egeth, and S. Yantis, "Visual Attention: Bottom-Up Versus Top-Down," *Current Biology* 14, no. 19 (2004), pp. R850–R852.

5. A. Mack et al., "Perceptual Organization and Attention," *Cognitive Psychology* 24, no. 4 (1992), pp. 475–501; A.R. Damasio, *Descartes' Error: Emotion, Reason, and the Human Brain* (New York: Putnam Sons, 1994).

6. R. Henry, "Police Departments Scale Back 'Always Armed' Policies," *Associated Press,* 26 November 2005.

7. C.N. Macrae et al., "Tales of the Unexpected: Executive Function and Person Perception," *Journal of Personality and Social Psychology* 76 (1999), pp. 200–13; C. Frith, "A Framework for Studying the Neural Basis of Attention," *Neuropsychologia* 39, no. 12 (2001), pp. 1367–71;

N. Lavie, "Distracted and Confused? Selective Attention under Load," *Trends in Cognitive Sciences* 9, no. 2 (2005), pp. 75–82.

8. E. Byron, "To Master the Art of Solving Crimes, Cops Study Vermeer," *The Wall Street Journal,* 27 July 2005, p. A1; D.J. Hall, "The Justice System Isn't Always Just," *Capital Times & Wisconsin State Journal,* 27 November 2005, p. D1.

9. C.N. Macrae and G.V. Bodenhausen, "Social Cognition: Thinking Categorically about Others," *Annual Review of Psychology* 51 (2000), pp. 93–120. For literature on the automaticity of the perceptual organization and interpretation process, see J.A. Bargh, "The Cognitive Monster: The Case against the Controllability of Automatic Stereotype Effects," in *Dual Process Theories in Social Psychology,* ed. S. Chaiken and Y. Trope (New York: Guilford, 1999), pp. 361–82; J.A. Bargh and M.J. Ferguson, "Beyond Behaviorism: On the Automaticity of Higher Mental Processes," *Psychological Bulletin* 126, no. 6 (2000), pp. 925–45; and M. Gladwell, *Blink: The Power of Thinking without Thinking* (New York: Little, Brown, 2005).

10. E.M. Altmann and B.D. Burns, "Streak Biases in Decision Making: Data and a Memory Model," *Cognitive Systems Research* 6, no. 1 (2005), pp. 5–16. For discussion of cognitive closure and perception, see A.W. Kruglanski and D.M. Webster, "Motivated Closing of the Mind: 'Seizing' and 'Freezing,'" *Psychological Review* 103, no. 2 (1996), pp. 263–83.

11. N. Ambady and R. Rosenthal, "Half a Minute: Predicting Teacher Evaluations from Thin Slices of Nonverbal Behavior and Physical Attractiveness," *Journal of Personality and Social Psychology* 64, no. 3 (March 1993), pp. 431–41. For other research on thin slices, see N. Ambady and R. Rosenthal, "Thin Slices of Expressive Behavior as Predictors of Interpersonal Consequences: A Meta-Analysis," *Psychological Bulletin* 111, no. 2 (1992), pp. 256–74; and N. Ambady et al., "Surgeons' Tone of Voice: A Clue to Malpractice History," *Surgery* 132, no. 1 (July 2002), pp. 5–9.

12. P.M. Senge, *The Fifth Discipline: The Art and Practice of the Learning Organization* (New York: Doubleday Currency, 1990), Chapter 10; P.N. Johnson-Laird, "Mental Models and Deduction," *Trends in Cognitive Sciences* 5, no. 10 (2001), pp. 434–42; A.B. Markman and D. Gentner, "Thinking," *Annual Review of Psychology* 52 (2001), pp. 223–47; T.J. Chermack, "Mental

Models in Decision Making and Implications for Human Resource Development," *Advances in Developing Human Resources* 5, no. 4 (2003), pp. 408–22.

13. H. Tajfel, *Social Identity and Intergroup Relations* (Cambridge: Cambridge University Press, 1982); B.E. Ashforth and F. Mael, "Social Identity Theory and the Organization," *Academy of Management Review* 14 (1989), pp. 20–39; M.A. Hogg and D.J. Terry, "Social Identity and Self-Categorization Processes in Organizational Contexts," *Academy of Management Review* 25 (January 2000), pp. 121–40; S.A. Haslam, R.A. Eggins, and K.J. Reynolds, "The Aspire Model: Actualizing Social and Personal Identity Resources to Enhance Organizational Outcomes," *Journal of Occupational and Organizational Psychology* 76 (2003), pp. 83–113. Although this topic is labeled *social identity theory,* it also incorporates an extension of social identity theory, called *self-categorization theory.*

14. J.E. Dutton, J.M. Dukerich, and C.V. Harquail, "Organizational Images and Member Identification," *Administrative Science Quarterly* 39 (June 1994), pp. 239–63; B. Simon and C. Hastedt, "Self-Aspects as Social Categories: The Role of Personal Importance and Valence," *European Journal of Social Psychology* 29 (1999), pp. 479–87.

15. M.A. Hogg et al., "The Social Identity Perspective: Intergroup Relations, Self-Conception, and Small Groups," *Small Group Research* 35, no. 3 (June 2004), pp. 246–76; J. Jetten, R. Spears, and T. Postmes, "Intergroup Distinctiveness and Differentiation: A Meta-Analytic Integration," *Journal of Personality and Social Psychology* 86, no. 6 (2004), pp. 862–79.

16. J.W. Jackson and E.R. Smith, "Conceptualizing Social Identity: A New Framework and Evidence for the Impact of Different Dimensions," *Personality & Social Psychology Bulletin* 25 (January 1999), pp. 120–35.

17. L. Falkenberg, "Improving the Accuracy of Stereotypes within the Workplace," *Journal of Management* 16 (1990), pp. 107–18; S.T. Fiske, "Stereotyping, Prejudice, and Discrimination," in *Handbook of Social Psychology,* ed. D.T. Gilbert, S.T. Fiske, and G. Lindzey, 4th ed. (New York: McGraw-Hill, 1998), pp. 357–411; Macrae and Bodenhausen, "Social Cognition: Thinking Categorically about Others."

18. C.N. Macrae, A.B. Milne, and G.V. Bodenhausen, "Stereotypes as Energy-

Saving Devices: A Peek inside the Cognitive Toolbox," *Journal of Personality and Social Psychology* 66 (1994), pp. 37–47; J.W. Sherman et al., "Stereotype Efficiency Reconsidered: Encoding Flexibility under Cognitive Load," *Journal of Personality and Social Psychology* 75 (1998), pp. 589–606; Macrae and Bodenhausen, "Social Cognition: Thinking Categorically about Others."

19. L. Sinclair and Z. Kunda, "Motivated Stereotyping of Women: She's Fine If She Praised Me but Incompetent If She Criticized Me," *Personality and Social Psychology Bulletin* 26 (November 2000), pp. 1329–42; J.C. Turner and S.A. Haslam, "Social Identity, Organizations, and Leadership," in *Groups at Work: Theory and Research,* ed. M.E. Turner (Mahwah, NJ: Lawrence Erlbaum Associates, 2001), pp. 25–65.

20. Y. Lee, L.J. Jussim, and C.R. McCauley, *Stereotype Accuracy: Toward Appreciating Group Differences* (Washington, DC: American Psychological Association, 1996); S. Madon et al., "The Accuracy and Power of Sex, Social Class, and Ethnic Stereotypes: A Naturalistic Study in Person Perception," *Personality & Social Psychology Bulletin* 24 (December 1998), pp. 1304–18; F.T. McAndrew, "A Multicultural Study of Stereotyping in English-Speaking Countries," *Journal of Social Psychology* (August 2000), pp. 487–502.

21. A.L. Friedman and S.R. Lyne, "The Beancounter Stereotype: Towards a General Model of Stereotype Generation," *Critical Perspectives on Accounting* 12, no. 4 (2001): 423–451

22. "Employers Face New Danger: Accidental Age Bias," *Omaha World-Herald,* 10 October 2005, p. D1; "Tiptoeing through the Employment Minefield of Race, Sex, and Religion? Here's Another One," *North West Business Insider (Manchester, UK),* February 2006.

23. S.O. Gaines and E.S. Reed, "Prejudice: From Allport to Dubois," *American Psychologist* 50 (February 1995), pp. 96–103; Fiske, "Stereotyping, Prejudice, and Discrimination"; M. Billig, "Henri Tajfel's 'Cognitive Aspects of Prejudice' and the Psychology of Bigotry," *British Journal of Social Psychology* 41 (2002), pp. 171–88; M Hewstone, M. Rubin, and H. Willis, "Intergroup Bias," *Annual Review of Psychology* 53 (2002), pp. 575–604.

24. J. Sinclair, "Breaking Down the Barriers," *The Age (Melbourne),* 30 January 2002, p. 14; L. Giovanelli, "Gender Divide," *Winston-Salem Journal,* 3 July

2005, p. 1; V. Reitman, "Caltech to Harvard: Redo the Math," *Los Angeles Times,* 20 June 2005.

25. "Army Chief's Warning KKK Photo May Lead to Officers' Dismissals," *Townsville Bulletin,* 25 June 2005, p. 7; M. Patriquin, "Quebec Farm Segregated Black Workers," *Globe & Mail,* 30 April 2005, p. A1; C. Spivak and D. Bice, "Looks Like Some to Face Bias Up North," *Milwaukee Journal Sentinel,* 16 October 2005, p. A2; J.W. Anderson, "French Firm Tests Colorblind Hiring," *Washington Post,* 29 January 2006, p. A20.

26. J.A. Bargh and T.L. Chartrand, "The Unbearable Automaticity of Being," *American Psychologist* 54, no. 7 (July 1999), pp. 462–79; S.T. Fiske, "What We Know Now About Bias and Intergroup Conflict, the Problem of the Century," *Current Directions in Psychological Science* 11, no. 4 (August 2002), pp. 123–28. For recent evidence that shows that intensive training can minimize stereotype activation, see K. Kawakami et al., "Just Say No (to Stereotyping): Effects of Training in the Negation of Stereotypic Associations on Stereotype Activation," *Journal of Personality and Social Psychology* 78, no. 5 (2000), pp. 871–88; and E.A. Plant, B.M. Peruche, and D.A. Butz, "Eliminating Automatic Racial Bias: Making Race Non-Diagnostic for Responses to Criminal Suspects," *Journal of Experimental Social Psychology* 41, no. 2 (2005), pp. 141–56.

27. M. Bendick, M.L. Egan, and S.M. Lofhjelm, "Workforce Diversity Training: From Anti-Discrimination Compliance to Organizational Development HR," *Human Resource Planning* 24 (2001), pp. 10–25; L. Roberson, C.T. Kulik, and M.B. Pepper, "Using Needs Assessment to Resolve Controversies in Diversity Training Design," *Group & Organization Management* 28, no. 1 (March 2003), pp. 148–74; D.E. Hogan and M. Mallott, "Changing Racial Prejudice through Diversity Education," *Journal of College Student Development* 46, no. 2 (March/April 2005), pp. 115–25.

28. P. Babcock, "Detecting Hidden Bias," *HRMagazine,* February 2006, p. 50.

29. T.F. Pettigrew, "Intergroup Contact Theory," *Annual Review of Psychology* 49 (1998), pp. 65–85; S. Brickson, "The Impact of Identity Orientation on Individual and Organizational Outcomes in Demographically Diverse Settings," *Academy of Management Review* 25 (January 2000), pp. 82–101; J. Dixon and K. Durrheim, "Contact and the Ecology

of Racial Division: Some Varieties of Informal Segregation," *British Journal of Social Psychology* 42 (March 2003), pp. 1–23.

30. B.F. Reskin, "The Proximate Causes of Employment Discrimination," *Contemporary Sociology* 29 (March 2000), pp. 319–28.

31. T. Phillips, "UPS Sends Executives on Diversity Sabbaticals," *Indianapolis Business Journal,* November 2004, p. 10; S. Teicher, "Corner-Office Volunteers," *Christian Science Monitor,* 19 July 2004, pp. 14–15; "Walking in Their Shoes," *Training,* June 2005, p. 19; C. Darden, "Pursuing Excellence–Constructive Dissatisfaction," *Executive Speeches,* February 2005, p. 1.

32. H.H. Kelley, *Attribution in Social Interaction* (Morristown, NJ: General Learning Press, 1971).

33. J.M. Feldman, "Beyond Attribution Theory: Cognitive Processes in Performance Appraisal," *Journal of Applied Psychology* 66 (1981), pp. 127–48.

34. J.M. Crant and T.S. Bateman, "Assignment of Credit and Blame for Performance Outcomes," *Academy of Management Journal* 36 (1993), pp. 7–27; B. Weiner, "Intrapersonal and Interpersonal Theories of Motivation from an Attributional Perspective," *Educational Psychology Review* 12 (2000), pp. 1–14; N. Bacon and P. Blyton, "Worker Responses to Teamworking: Exploring Employee Attributions of Managerial Motives," *International Journal of Human Resource Management* 16, no. 2 (February 2005), pp. 238–55.

35. Fundamental attribution error is part of a larger phenomenon known as correspondence bias. See D.T. Gilbert and P.S. Malone, "The Correspondence Bias," *Psychological Bulletin* 117, no. 1 (1995), pp. 21–38.

36. I. Choi, R.E. Nisbett, and A. Norenzayan, "Causal Attribution across Cultures: Variation and Universality," *Psychological Bulletin* 125, no. 1 (1999), pp. 47–63; D.S. Krull et al., "The Fundamental Attribution Error: Correspondence Bias in Individualist and Collectivist Cultures," *Personality and Social Psychology Bulletin* 25, no. 10 (October 1999), pp. 1208–19; R.E. Nisbett, *The Geography of Thought: How Asians and Westerners Think Differently–and Why* (New York: Free Press, 2003), Chapter 5.

37. F. Lee and L.Z. Tiedens, "Who's Being Served? 'Self-Serving' Attributions in Social Hierarchies," *Organizational Behavior and Human Decision Processes* 84, no. 2 (2001), pp. 254–87; E.W.K. Tsang, "Self-

Serving Attributions in Corporate Annual Reports: A Replicated Study," *Journal of Management Studies* 39, no. 1 (January 2002), pp. 51–65.

38. Similar models are presented in D. Eden, "Self-Fulfilling Prophecy as a Management Tool: Harnessing Pygmalion," *Academy of Management Review* 9 (1984), pp. 64–73; R.H.G. Field and D.A. Van Seters, "Management by Expectations (MBE): The Power of Positive Prophecy," *Journal of General Management* 14 (Winter 1988), pp. 19–33; D.O. Trouilloud et al., "The Influence of Teacher Expectations on Student Achievement in Physical Education Classes: Pygmalion Revisited," *European Journal of Social Psychology* 32 (2002), pp. 591–607.

39. D. Eden, "Interpersonal Expectations in Organizations," in *Interpersonal Expectations: Theory, Research, and Applications* (Cambridge, UK: Cambridge University Press, 1993), pp. 154–78.

40. D. Eden, "Pygmalion Goes to Boot Camp: Expectancy, Leadership, and Trainee Performance," *Journal of Applied Psychology* 67 (1982), pp. 194–99; R.P. Brown and E.C. Pinel, "Stigma on My Mind: Individual Differences in the Experience of Stereotype Threat," *Journal of Experimental Social Psychology* 39, no. 6 (2003), pp. 626–33.

41. S. Madon et al., "Self-Fulfilling Prophecies: The Synergistic Accumulative Effect of Parents' Beliefs on Children's Drinking Behavior," *Psychological Science* 15, no. 12 (2005), pp. 837–45 A.E. Smith, L. Jussim, and J. Eccles, "Do Self-Fulfilling Prophecies Accumulate, Dissipate, or Remain Stable over Time?" *Journal of Personality and Social Psychology* 77, no. 3 (1999), pp. 548–65.

42. S. Madon, L. Jussim, and J. Eccles, "In Search of the Powerful Self-Fulfilling Prophecy," *Journal of Personality and Social Psychology* 72, no. 4 (April 1997), pp. 791–809.

43. A.R. Remo, "Nurture the Good to Create an Asset," *Philippine Daily Inquirer*, 6 December 2004.

44. D. Eden et al., "Implanting Pygmalion Leadership Style through Workshop Training: Seven Field Experiments," *Leadership Quarterly* 11 (2000), pp. 171–210; S.S. White and E.A. Locke, "Problems with the Pygmalion Effect and Some Proposed Solutions," *Leadership Quarterly* 11 (Autumn 2000), pp. 389–415; H.A. Wilkinson, "Hope, False Hope, and Self-Fulfilling Prophecy," *Surgical Neurology* 63,

no. 1 (2005), pp. 84–86. For literature on positive organizational behavior, see K. Cameron, J.E. Dutton, and R.E. Quinn, *Positive Organizational Scholarship: Foundations of a New Discipline* (San Francisco: Berrett Koehler, 2003).

45. C.L. Kleinke, *First Impressions: The Psychology of Encountering Others* (Englewood Cliffs, NJ: Prentice Hall, 1975); E.A. Lind, L. Kray, and L. Thompson, "Primacy Effects in Justice Judgments: Testing Predictions from Fairness Heuristic Theory," *Organizational Behavior and Human Decision Processes* 85 (July 2001), pp. 189–210; O. Ybarra, "When First Impressions Don't Last: The Role of Isolation and Adaptation Processes in the Revision of Evaluative Impressions," *Social Cognition* 19 (October 2001), pp. 491–520.

46. D.D. Steiner and J.S. Rain, "Immediate and Delayed Primacy and Recency Effects in Performance Evaluation," *Journal of Applied Psychology* 74 (1989), pp. 136–42; K.T. Trotman, "Order Effects and Recency: Where Do We Go from Here?" *Accounting & Finance* 40 (2000), pp. 169–82; W. Green, "Impact of the Timing of an Inherited Explanation on Auditors' Analytical Procedures Judgments," *Accounting and Finance* 44 (2004), pp. 369–92.

47. W.H. Cooper, "Ubiquitous Halo," *Psychological Bulletin* 90 (1981), pp. 218–44; K.R. Murphy, R.A. Jako, and R.L. Anhalt, "Nature and Consequences of Halo Error: A Critical Analysis," *Journal of Applied Psychology* 78 (1993), pp. 218–25; T.H. Feeley, "Comment on Halo Effects in Rating and Evaluation Research," *Human Communication Research* 28, no. 4 (October 2002), pp. 578–86.

48. G.G. Sherwood, "Self-Serving Biases in Person Perception: A Re-Examination of Projection as a Mechanism of Defense," *Psychological Bulletin* 90 (1981), pp. 445–59; R.L. Gross and S.E. Brodt, "How Assumptions of Consensus Undermine Decision Making," *Sloan Management Review* (January 2001), pp. 86–94.

49. C. Duan and C.E. Hill, "The Current State of Empathy Research," *Journal of Counseling Psychology* 43 (1996), pp. 261–74; W.G. Stephen and K.A. Finlay, "The Role of Empathy in Improving Intergroup Relations," *Journal of Social Issues* 55 (Winter 1999), pp. 729–43; S.K. Parker and C.M. Axtell, "Seeing Another Viewpoint: Antecedents and Outcomes of Employee Perspective Taking," *Academy of Management Journal* 44 (December 2001),

pp. 1085–1100; G.J. Vreeke and I.L. van der Mark, "Empathy, an Integrative Model," *New Ideas in Psychology* 21, no. 3 (2003), pp. 177–207.

50. D. Goleman, R. Boyatzis, and A. McKee, *The New Leaders* (London: Little, Brown, 2002).

51. T.W. Costello and S.S. Zalkind, *Psychology in Administration: A Research Orientation* (Englewood Cliffs, NJ: Prentice Hall, 1963), pp. 45–46; J.M. Kouzes and B.Z. Posner, *The Leadership Challenge,* 3rd ed. (San Francisco: Jossey-Bass, 2002), Chapter 3.

52. J. Luft, *Group Processes* (Palo Alto, CA: Mayfield Publishing, 1984). For a variation of this model, see J. Hall, "Communication Revisited," *California Management Review* 15 (Spring 1973), pp. 56–67.

53. L.C. Miller and D.A. Kenny, "Reciprocity of Self-Disclosure at the Individual and Dyadic Levels: A Social Relations Analysis," *Journal of Personality and Social Psychology* 50 (1986), pp. 713–19.

54. "Wipro: Leadership in the Midst of Rapid Growth," *Knowledge@Wharton,* February 2005.

55. I. Nonaka and H. Takeuchi, *The Knowledge-Creating Company* (New York: Oxford University Press, 1995); E.N. Brockmann and W.P. Anthony, "Tacit Knowledge and Strategic Decision Making," *Group & Organization Management* 27 (December 2002), pp. 436–55; P. Duguid, "'The Art of Knowing': Social and Tacit Dimensions of Knowledge and the Limits of the Community of Practice," *The Information Society* 21 (2005), pp. 109–18.

56. B.F. Skinner, *About Behaviorism* (New York: Alfred A. Knopf, 1974); J. Komaki, T. Coombs, and S. Schepman, "Motivational Implications of Reinforcement Theory," in *Motivation and Leadership at Work,* ed. R.M. Steers, L.W. Porter, and G.A. Bigley (New York: McGraw-Hill, 1996), pp. 34–52; R.G. Miltenberger, *Behavior Modification: Principles and Procedures* (Pacific Grove, CA: Brooks/Cole, 1997).

57. T.K. Connellan, *How to Improve Human Performance* (New York: Harper & Row, 1978), pp. 48–57; F. Luthans and R. Kreitner, *Organizational Behavior Modification and Beyond* (Glenview, Ill.: Scott, Foresman, 1985), pp. 85–88

58. Miltenberger, *Behavior Modification: Principles and Procedures,* Chapters 4–6.

59. Punishment can also include removing a pleasant consequence, such as when

employees must switch from business to economy class flying when their sales fall below the threshold for top-tier sales "stars."

60. T.R. Hinkin and C.A. Schriesheim, "'If You Don't Hear from Me You Know You Are Doing Fine,'" *Cornell Hotel & Restaurant Administration Quarterly* 45, no. 4 (November 2004), pp. 362–72.

61. L.K. Trevino, "The Social Effects of Punishment in Organizations: A Justice Perspective," *Academy of Management Review* 17 (1992), pp. 647–76; L.E. Atwater et al., "Recipient and Observer Reactions to Discipline: Are Managers Experiencing Wishful Thinking?" *Journal of Organizational Behavior* 22, no. 3 (May 2001), pp. 249–70.

62. G.P. Latham and V.L. Huber, "Schedules of Reinforcement: Lessons from the Past and Issues for the Future," *Journal of Organizational Behavior Management* 13 (1992), pp. 125–49; B.A. Williams, "Challenges to Timing-Based Theories of Operant Behavior," *Behavioural Processes* 62 (April 2003), pp. 115–23.

63. S. Overman, "Many Offer Basic Wellness Initiatives, Few Track Results," *Employee Benefit News*, 15 April 2006; H. Wecsler, "Sick Day Incentive Plan Favored by NLR Board," *Arkansas Democrat Gazette,* 17 February 2006, p. 14.

64. T.C. Mawhinney, "Philosophical and Ethical Aspects of Organizational Behavior Management: Some Evaluative Feedback," *Journal of Organizational Behavior Management* 6 (Spring 1984), pp. 5–13; G.A. Merwin, J.A. Thomason, and E.E. Sandford, "A Methodological and Content Review of Organizational Behavior Management in the Private Sector: 1978–1986," *Journal of Organizational Behavior Management* 10 (1989), pp. 39–57; "New Warnings on the Fine Points of Safety Incentives," *Pay for Performance Report,* September 2002.

65. Bargh and Ferguson, "Beyond Behaviorism: On the Automaticity of Higher Mental Processes." Some writers argue that behaviorists long ago accepted the relevance of cognitive processes in behavior modification. See I. Kirsch et al., "The Role of Cognition in Classical and Operant Conditioning," *Journal of Clinical Psychology* 60, no. 4 (April 2004), pp. 369–92.

66. ExxonMobil, *UK and Ireland Corporate Citizenship* (ExxonMobil, August 2004); "ExxonMobil Recognizes Employees, Contractors for Outstanding," *Bernama Daily Malaysian News,* 27 June 2005.

67. A. Bandura, *Social Foundations of Thought and Action: A Social Cognitive Theory* (Englewood Cliffs, NJ: Prentice Hall, 1986).

68. A. Pescuric and W.C. Byham, "The New Look of Behavior Modeling," *Training & Development* 50 (July 1996), pp. 24–30.

69. M.E. Schnake, "Vicarious Punishment in a Work Setting," *Journal of Applied Psychology* 71 (1986), pp. 343–45; Trevino, "The Social Effects of Punishment in Organizations: A Justice Perspective"; J.B. DeConinck, "The Effect of Punishment on Sales Managers' Outcome Expectancies and Responses to Unethical Sales Force Behavior," *American Business Review* 21, no. 2 (June 2003), pp. 135–40.

70. A. Bandura, "Self-Reinforcement: Theoretical and Methodological Considerations," *Behaviorism* 4 (1976), pp. 135–55; C.A. Frayne and J.M. Geringer, "Self-Management Training for Improving Job Performance: A Field Experiment Involving Salespeople," *Journal of Applied Psychology* 85, no. 3 (June 2000), pp. 361–72; J.B. Vancouver and D.V. Day, "Industrial and Organisation Research on Self-Regulation: From Constructs to Applications," *Applied Psychology* 54, no. 2 (April 2005), pp. 155–85.

71. D. Woodruff, "Putting Talent to the Test," *The Wall Street Journal Europe,* November 14 2000, p. 25. The simulation events described here were experienced by the author of this article, but we reasonably assume that Mandy Chooi, who also completed the simulation, experienced similar scenarios.

72. D.A. Kolb, *Experiential Learning* (Englewood Cliffs, NJ: Prentice-Hall, 1984); S. Gherardi, D. Nicolini, and F. Odella, "Toward a Social Understanding of How People Learn in Organizations," *Management Learning* 29 (September 1998), pp. 273–97; D.A. Kolb, R.E. Boyatzis, and C. Mainemelis, "Experiential Learning Theory: Previous Research and New Directions," in *Perspectives on Thinking, Learning, and Cognitive Styles*, ed. R.J. Sternberg and L.F. Zhang (Mahwah, NJ: Lawrence Erlbaum, 2001), pp. 227–48.

73. J. Jusko, "Always Lessons to Learn," *Industry Week* (15 February 1999), p. 23; R. Farson and R. Keyes, "The Failure-Tolerant Leader," *Harvard Business Review* 80 (August 2002), pp. 64–71.

74. I. Teotonio, "Rescuers Pull 'Victims' from Rubble," *Toronto Star,* 8 April 2005, pp. B01, B03.

75. R.W. Revans, *The Origin and Growth of Action Learning* (London: Chartwell Bratt, 1982), pp. 626–27; M.J. Marquardt, *Optimizing the Power of Action Learning: Solving Problems and Building Leaders in Real Time* (Palo Alto, CA: Davies-Black, 2004).

76. J.A. Conger and K. Xin, "Executive Education in the 21st Century," *Journal of Management Education* (February 2000), pp. 73–101; R.M. Fulmer, P. Gibbs, and M. Goldsmith, "Developing Leaders: How Winning Companies Keep on Winning," *Sloan Management Review* (October 2000), pp. 49–59; "Strategies Needed to Nurture Top Talent," *South China Morning Post (Hong Kong),* 7 August 2004, p. 4; M.J. Marquardt, "Harnessing the Power of Action Learning," *T+D,* June 2004, pp. 26–32.

CHAPTER 4

1. F. Bilovsky, "Wegmans Is Named America's No. 1 Employer," *Democrat & Chronicle* (Rochester,New York), 11 January 2005; M. Boyle, "The Wegmans Way," *Fortune,* 24 January 2005, 62; B. Niedt, "Wegmans Reaches No. 1 on List of Workplaces," *Post Standard* (Syracuse), 11 January 2005, p. A1; M. Sommer and J.F. Bonfatti, "Wegmans Employees Feel Challenged, Valued," *Buffalo News,* 16 January 2005, p. B7.

2. The centrality of emotions in marketing, economics, and sociology is discussed in G. Loewenstein, "Emotions in Economic Theory and Economic Behavior," *American Economic Review* 90, no. 2 (May 2000), pp. 426–32; D.S. Massey, "A Brief History of Human Society: The Origin and Role of Emotion in Social Life," *American Sociological Review* 67 (February 2002), pp. 1–29; and J. O'Shaughnessy and N.J. OShaughnessy, *The Marketing Power of Emotion* (New York: Oxford University Press, 2003).

3. The definition presented here is constructed from information in the following sources: N.M. Ashkanasy, W.J. Zerbe, and C.E.J. Hartel, "Introduction: Managing Emotions in a Changing Workplace," in *Managing Emotions in the Workplace*, ed. N.M. Ashkanasy, W.J. Zerbe, and C.E.J. Hartel (Armonk, NY: M.E. Sharpe, 2002), pp. 3–18; H.M. Weiss, "Conceptual and Empirical Foundations for the Study of Affect at Work," in *Emotions in the Workplace*, ed. R.G. Lord, R.J. Klimoski, and R. Kanfer (San Francisco: Jossey-Bass, 2002), pp. 20–63. However, the

meaning of emotions is still being debated. See, for example, M. Cabanac, "What Is Emotion?" *Behavioural Processes* 60 (2002), pp. 69–83.

4. R. Kanfer and R.J. Klimoski, "Affect and Work: Looking Back to the Future," in *Emotions in the Workplace*, ed. R.G. Lord, R.J. Klimoski, and R. Kanfer (San Francisco: Jossey-Bass, 2002), pp. 473–90; J.A. Russell, "Core Affect and the Psychological Construction of Emotion," *Psychological Review* 110, no. 1 (2003), pp. 145–72.

5. R.B. Zajonc, "Emotions," in *Handbook of Social Psychology*, ed. D.T. Gilbert, S.T. Fiske, and L. Gardner (New York: Oxford University press, 1998), pp. 591–634.

6. N.A. Remington, L.R. Fabrigar, and P.S. Visser, "Reexamining the Circumplex Model of Affect," *Journal of Personality and Social Psychology* 79, no. 2 (2000), pp. 286–300; R.J. Larson, E. Diener, and R.E. Lucas, "Emotion: Models, Measures, and Differences," in *Emotions in the Workplace*, ed. R.G. Lord, R.J. Klimoski, and R. Kanfer (San Francisco: Jossey- Bass, 2002), pp. 64–113.

7. A.H. Eagly and S. Chaiken, *The Psychology of Attitudes* (Orlando, FL: Harcourt Brace Jovanovich, 1993); A.P. Brief, *Attitudes in and around Organizations* (Thousand Oaks, CA: Sage, 1998) There is ongoing debate about whether attitudes represent only feelings or all three components described here. However, those who adopt the single-factor perspective still refer to beliefs as the cognitive *component* of attitudes. For example, see I. Ajzen, "Nature and Operation of Attitudes," *Annual Review of Psychology* 52 (2001), pp. 27–58.

8. S.D. Farley and M.F. Stasson, "Relative Influences of Affect and Cognition on Behavior: Are Feelings or Beliefs More Related to Blood Donation Intentions?" *Experimental Psychology* 50, no. 1 (2003), pp. 55–62.

9. C.D. Fisher, "Mood and Emotions While Working: Missing Pieces of Job Satisfaction?" *Journal of Organizational Behavior* 21 (2000), pp. 185–202; M. Pergini and R.P. Bagozzi, "The Role of Desires and Anticipated Emotions in Goal-Directed Behaviors: Broadening and Deepening the Theory of Planned Behavior," *British Journal of Social Psychology* 40 (March 2001), pp. 79–; J.D. Morris et al., "The Power of Affect: Predicting Intention," *Journal of Advertising Research* 42 (May-June 2002), pp. 7–17. For a review

of the predictability of the traditional attitude model, see C.J. Armitage and M. Conner, "Efficacy of the Theory of Planned Behavior: A Meta-Analytic Review," *British Journal of Social Psychology* 40 (2001), pp. 471–99.

10. This explanation refers to a singular "cognitive (logical reasoning) center" and "emotional center." Although many scholars refer to a single location for most emotional transactions, an emerging view is that both the emotional and rational "centers" are distributed throughout the brain. J. Schulkin, B.L. Thompson, and J. B. Rosen, "Demythologizing the Emotions: Adaptation, Cognition, and Visceral Representations of Emotion in the Nervous System," *Brain and Cognition (Affective Neuroscience)* 52 (June 2003), pp. 15–23.

11. J.A. Bargh and M.J. Ferguson, "Beyond Behaviorism: On the Automaticity of Higher Mental Processes," *Psychological Bulletin* 126, no. 6 (2000), pp. 925–45; R. H. Fazio, "On the Automatic Activation of Associated Evaluations: An Overview," *Cognition and Emotion* 15, no. 2 (2001), pp. 115–41; M. Gladwell, *Blink: The Power of Thinking without Thinking* (New York: Little, Brown, 2005).

12. A.R. Damasio, *Descartes' Error: Emotion, Reason, and the Human Brain* (New York: Putnam Sons, 1994); A. Damasio, *The Feeling of What Happens* (New York: Harcourt Brace and Co., 1999); P. Ekman, "Basic Emotions," in *Handbook of Cognition and Emotion*, ed. T. Dalgleish and M. Power (San Francisco: Jossey-Bass, 1999), pp. 45–60; J.E. LeDoux, "Emotion Circuits in the Brain," *Annual Review of Neuroscience* 23 (2000), pp. 155–84; R.J. Dolan, "Emotion, Cognition, and Behavior," *Science* 298, no. 5596 (8 November 2002), pp. 1191–94.

13. H.M. Weiss and R. Cropanzano, "Affective Events Theory: A Theoretical Discussion of the Structure, Causes, and Consequences of Affective Experiences at Work," *Research in Organizational Behavior* 18 (1996), pp. 1–74.

14. N. Schwarz, "Emotion, Cognition, and Decision Making," *Cognition and Emotion* 14, no. 4 (2000), pp. 433–40; M.T. Pham, "The Logic of Feeling," *Journal of Consumer Psychology* 14, no. 4 (2004), pp. 360–69.

15. G.R. Maio, V.M. Esses, and D.W. Bell, "Examining Conflict between Components of Attitudes: Ambivalence and Inconsistency Are Distinct Constructs," *Canadian Journal of Behavioural Science* 32, no. 2 (2000), pp. 71–83.

16. P.C. Nutt, *Why Decisions Fail* (San Francisco: Berrett-Koehler, 2002); S. Finkelstein, *Why Smart Executives Fail* (New York: Viking, 2003); P.C. Nutt, "Search during Decision Making," *European Journal of Operational Research* 160 (2005), pp. 851–76.

17. Weiss and Cropanzano, "Affective Events Theory."

18. L. Festinger, *A Theory of Cognitive Dissonance* (Evanston, IL: Row, Peterson, 1957); G.R. Salancik, "Commitment and the Control of Organizational Behavior and Belief," in *New Directions in Organizational Behavior*, ed. B.M. Staw and G.R. Salancik (Chicago: St. Clair, 1977), pp. 1–54; A.D. Galinsky, J. Stone, and J. Cooper, "The Reinstatement of Dissonance and Psychological Discomfort Following Failed Affirmation," *European Journal of Social Psychology* 30, no. 1 (2000), pp. 123–47.

19. T.A. Judge, E.A. Locke, and C.C. Durham, "The Dispositional Causes of Job Satisfaction: A Core Evaluations Approach," *Research in Organizational Behavior* 19 (1997), pp. 151–88; A.P. Brief and H.M. Weiss, "Organizational Behavior: Affect in the Workplace," *Annual Review of Psychology* 53 (2002), pp. 279–307.

20. C.M. Brotheridge and A.A. Grandey, "Emotional Labor and Burnout: Comparing Two Perspectives of 'People Work,'" *Journal of Vocational Behavior* 60 (2002), pp. 17–39; P.G. Irving, D.F. Coleman, and D.R. Bobocel, "The Moderating Effect of Negative Affectivity in the Procedural Justice-Job Satisfaction Relation," *Canadian Journal of Behavioural Science* 37, no. 1 (January 2005), pp. 20–32.

21. J. Schaubroeck, D.C. Ganster, and B. Kemmerer, "Does Trait Affect Promote Job Attitude Stability?" *Journal of Organizational Behavior* 17 (1996), pp. 191–96; C. Dormann and D. Zapf, "Job Satisfaction: A Meta-Analysis of Stabilities," *Journal of Organizational Behavior* 22 (2001), pp. 483–504.

22. R. Corelli, "Dishing Out Rudeness," *Maclean's*, 11 January 1999, pp. 44–47; D. Matheson, "A Vancouver Cafe Where Rudeness Is Welcomed," *Canada AM, CTV Television* (11 January 2000).

23. B.E. Ashforth and R.H. Humphrey, "Emotional Labor in Service Roles: The Influence of Identity," *Academy of Management Review* 18 (1993), pp. 88–115. For a recent review of the emotional labor concept, see T.M. Glomb and M.J. Tews,

"Emotional Labor: A Conceptualization and Scale Development," *Journal of Vocational Behavior* 64, no. 1 (2004), pp. 1–23.

24. R. Strauss, "Seminar on Smiling Brightens the Shore," *The New York Times*, 28 August 2005, p. 8.

25. J.A. Morris and D.C. Feldman, "The Dimensions, Antecedents, and Consequences of Emotional Labor," *Academy of Management Review* 21 (1996), pp. 986–1010; D. Zapf, "Emotion Work and Psychological Well-Being: A Review of the Literature and Some Conceptual Considerations," *Human Resource Management Review* 12 (2002), pp. 237–68.

26. E. Forman, "'Diversity Concerns Grow as Companies Head Overseas,' Consultant Says," *Sun-Sentinel (Fort Lauderdale, Florida)*, 26 June 1995. Cultural differences in emotional expression are discussed in F. Trompenaars, "Resolving International Conflict: Culture and Business Strategy," *Business Strategy Review* 7, no. 3 (Autumn 1996), pp. 51–68; F. Trompenaars and C. Hampden-Turner, *Riding the Waves of Culture*, 2nd ed. (New York: McGraw-Hill, 1998), Chapter 6.

27. R. Hallowell, D. Bowen, and C. I. Knoop, "Four Seasons Goes to Paris," *Academy of Management Executive* 16, no. 4 (November 2002), pp. 7–24.

28. This relates to the automaticity of emotion, which is summarized in P. Winkielman and K.C. Berridge, "Unconscious Emotion," *Current Directions in Psychological Science* 13, no. 3 (2004), pp. 120–23; K.N. Ochsner and J.J. Gross, "The Cognitive Control of Emotions," *TRENDS in Cognitive Sciences* 9, no. 5 (May 2005), pp. 242–49.

29. W.J. Zerbe, "Emotional Dissonance and Employee Well-Being," in *Managing Emotions in the Workplace*, ed. N.M. Ashkanasy, W.J. Zerbe, and C.E.J. Hartel (Armonk, NY: M.E. Sharpe, 2002), pp. 189–214; R. Cropanzano, H.M. Weiss, and S.M. Elias, "The Impact of Display Rules and Emotional Labor on Psychological Well-Being at Work," *Research in Occupational Stress and Well Being* 3 (2003), pp. 45–89.

30. A. Schwitzerlette, "Cici's Pizza Coming to Beckley," *Register-Herald* (Beckley, West Virginia), 24 August 2003.

31. Brotheridge and Grandey, "Emotional Labor and Burnout: Comparing Two Perspectives of 'People Work'"; Zapf, "Emotion Work and Psychological

Well-Being"; J.M. Diefendorff, M.H. Croyle, and R.H. Gosserand, "The Dimensionality and Antecedents of Emotional Labor Strategies," *Journal of Vocational Behavior* 66, no. 2 (2005), pp. 339–57.

32. C. Fox, "Shifting Gears," *Australian Financial Review*, 13 August 2004, p. 28; J. Thomson, "True Team Spirit," *Business Review Weekly*, 18 March 2004, p. 92.

33. J.D. Mayer, P. Salovey, and D.R. Caruso, "Models of Emotional Intelligence," in *Handbook of Human Intelligence*, ed. R.J. Sternberg, 2nd ed. (New York: Cambridge University Press, 2000), pp. 396–420. This definition is also recognized in C. Cherniss, "Emotional Intelligence and Organizational Effectiveness," in *The Emotionally Intelligent Workplace*, ed. C. Cherniss and D. Goleman (San Francisco: Jossey-Bass, 2001), pp. 3–12; and M. Zeidner, G. Matthews, and R.D. Roberts, "Emotional Intelligence in the Workplace: A Critical Review," *Applied Psychology: An International Review* 53, no. 3 (2004), pp. 371–99.

34. These four dimensions of emotional intelligence are discussed in detail in D. Goleman, R. Boyatzis, and A. McKee, *Primal Leadership* (Boston: Harvard Business School Press, 2002), Chapter 3. Slight variations of this model are presented in R. Boyatzis, D. Goleman, and K.S. Rhee, "Clustering Competence in Emotional Intelligence," in *The Handbook of Emotional Intelligence*, ed. R. Bar-On and J.D.A. Parker (San Francisco: Jossey-Bass, 2000), pp. 343–62; and D. Goleman, "An EI-Based Theory of Performance," in *The Emotionally Intelligent Workplace*, ed. C. Cherniss and D. Goleman (San Francisco: Jossey-Bass, 2001), pp. 27–44.

35. H.A. Elfenbein and N. Ambady, "Predicting Workplace Outcomes from the Ability to Eavesdrop on Feelings," *Journal of Applied Psychology* 87, no. 5 (2002), pp. 963–71.

36. The hierarchical nature of the four EI dimensions is discussed by Goleman but is more explicit in the Salovey and Mayer model. See D.R. Caruso and P. Salovey, *The Emotionally Intelligent Manager* (San Francisco: Jossey-Bass, 2004).

37. P.J. Jordan et al., "Workgroup Emotional Intelligence: Scale Development and Relationship to Team Process Effectiveness and Goal Focus," *Human Resource Management Review* 12 (2002), pp. 195–214; H. Nel, W.S. De Villiers, and A.S. Engelbrecht, "The Influence of Emotional Intelligence on Performance in a Call

Centre Environment," in *First International Conference on Contemporary Management*, ed. A. Travaglione et al. (Adelaide, Australia, 1–2 September 2003), pp. 81–90; P.N. Lopes et al., "Emotional Intelligence and Social Interaction," *Personality and Social Psychology Bulletin* 30, no. 8 (August 2004), pp. 1018–34; C.S. Daus and N.M. Ashkanasy, "The Case for the Ability-Based Model of Emotional Intelligence in Organizational Behavior," *Journal of Organizational Behavior* 26 (2005), pp. 453–66. Not all studies have found that EI predicts job performance. See S. Newsome, A.L. Day, and V.M. Catano, "Assessing the Predictive Validity of Emotional Intelligence," *Personality and Individual Differences*, no. 29 (December 2000), pp. 1005–16; A.L. Day and S.A. Carroll, "Using an Ability-Based Measure of Emotional Intelligence to Predict Individual Performance, Group Performance, and Group Citizenship Behaviours," *Personality and Individual Differences* 36 (2004), pp. 1443–58.

38. S.C. Clark, R. Callister, and R. Wallace, "Undergraduate Management Skills Courses and Students' Emotional Intelligence," *Journal of Management Education* 27, no. 1 (February 2003), pp. 3–23; B. Carey, "Measuring Emotions," *Journal Gazette* (Fort Wayne, Indiana), 20 April 2004, p. 8B.

39. E.A. Locke, "The Nature and Causes of Job Satisfaction," in *Handbook of Industrial and Organizational Psychology*, ed. M. Dunnette (Chicago: Rand McNally, 1976), pp. 1297–1350; H.M. Weiss, "Deconstructing Job Satisfaction: Separating Evaluations, Beliefs, and Affective Experiences," *Human Resource Management Review* no. 12 (2002), pp. 173–94. Some definitions still include emotion as an element of job satisfaction, whereas the definition presented in this book views emotion as a cause of job satisfaction. Also, this definition views job satisfaction as a "collection of attitudes," not several "facets" of job satisfaction.

40. Ipsos-Reid, "Ipsos-Reid Global Poll Finds Major Differences in Employee Satisfaction around the World," news release (Toronto: 8 January 2001); International Survey Research, *Employee Satisfaction in the World's 10 Largest Economies: Globalization or Diversity?* (Chicago: International Survey Research, 2002); Watson Wyatt Worldwide, "Asia-Pacific Workers Satisfied with Jobs Despite Some Misgivings with Management and Pay," Watson Wyatt news release (Singapore: 16 November

2004); "Most U.S. Workers Satisfied with Their Jobs: Study," *Reuters News*, 31 August 2005.

41. "Hudson Employment Index Data Suggest Suggests U.S. Workers Will Jump Ship," *PR Newswire* (New York), 7 January 2004; Watson Wyatt Worldwide, "Malaysian Workers More Satisfied with Their Jobs Than Their Companies' Leadership and Supervision Practices," Watson Wyatt Worldwide news release, (Kuala Lumpur), 30 November 2004; K. Keis, "HR Needs Happy Staff to Show Its Success," *Canadian HR Reporter*, 14 February 2005, p. 14.

42. The problems with measuring attitudes and values across cultures are discussed in G. Law, "If You're Happy & You Know It, Tick the Box," *Management-Auckland* 45 (March 1998), pp. 34–37; P.E. Spector et al., "Do National Levels of Individualism and Internal Locus of Control Relate to Well-Being? An Ecological Level International Study," *Journal of Organizational Behavior* 22 (2001), pp. 815–32; L. Saari and T.A. Judge, "Employee Attitudes and Job Satisfaction," *Human Resource Management* 43, no. 4 (Winter 2004), pp. 395–407.

43. M.J. Withey and W.H. Cooper, "Predicting Exit, Voice, Loyalty, and Neglect," *Administrative Science Quarterly* 34 (1989), pp. 521–39, W.H. Turnley and D.C. Feldman, "The Impact of Psychological Contract Violations on Exit, Voice, Loyalty, and Neglect," *Human Relations* 52 (July 1999), pp. 895–922.

44. T.R. Mitchell, B.C. Holtom, and T.W. Lee, "How to Keep Your Best Employees: Developing an Effective Retention Policy," *Academy of Management Executive* 15 (November 2001), pp. 96–108; C.P. Maertz and M.A. Campion, "Profiles of Quitting: Integrating Process and Content Turnover Theory," *Academy of Management Journal* 47, no. 4 (2004), pp. 566–82.

45. A.A. Luchak, "What Kind of Voice Do Loyal Employees Use?" *British Journal of Industrial Relations* 41 (March 2003), pp. 115–34.

46. J.D. Hibbard, N. Kumar, and L.W. Stern, "Examining the Impact of Destructive Acts in Marketing Channel Relationships," *Journal of Marketing Research* 38 (February 2001), pp. 45–61; J. Zhou and J.M. George, "When Job Dissatisfaction Leads to Creativity: Encouraging the Expression of Voice," *Academy of Management Journal* 44 (August 2001), pp. 682–96.

47. M.J. Withey and I.R. Gellatly, "Situational and Dispositional Determinants of Exit, Voice, Loyalty, and Neglect," *Proceedings of the Administrative Sciences Association of Canada, Organizational Behaviour Division* (June 1998); M.J. Withey and I.R. Gellatly, "Exit, Voice, Loyalty and Neglect: Assessing the Influence of Prior Effectiveness and Personality," *Proceedings of the Administrative Sciences Association of Canada, Organizational Behaviour Division* 20 (1999), pp. 110–19.

48. D.P. Schwab and L.L. Cummings, "Theories of Performance and Satisfaction: A Review," *Industrial Relations* 9 (1970), pp. 408–30; M.T. Iaffaldano and P.M. Muchinsky, "Job Satisfaction and Job Performance: A Meta-Analysis," *Psychological Bulletin* 97 (1985), pp. 251–73.

49. T.A. Judge et al., "The Job Satisfaction-Job Performance Relationship: A Qualitative and Quantitative Review," *Psychological Bulletin* 127 (2001), pp. 376–407; Saari and Judge, "Employee Attitudes and Job Satisfaction."

50. Judge et al., "The Job Satisfaction–Job Performance Relationship: A Qualitative and Quantitative Review."

51. "The Greatest Briton in Management and Leadership," *Personnel Today* (18 February 2003), p. 20. The Wegmans motto is mentioned in R. Levering and M. Moskowitz, "The Best 100 Companies to Work For," *Fortune*, 24 January 2005, pp. 90–96.

52. J.I. Heskett, W.E. Sasser, and L.A. Schlesinger, *The Service Profit Chain* (New York: Free Press, 1997); D.J. Koys, "The Effects of Employee Satisfaction, Organizational Citizenship Behavior, and Turnover on Organizational Effectiveness: A Unit-Level, Longitudinal Study," *Personnel Psychology* 54 (April 2001), pp. 101–14; W.-C. Tsai and Y.-M. Huang, "Mechanisms Linking Employee Affective Delivery and Customer Behavioral Intentions," *Journal of Applied Psychology* 87, no. 5 (2002), pp. 1001–8; T. DeCotiis et al., "How Outback Steakhouse Created a Great Place to Work, Have Fun, and Make Money," *Journal of Organizational Excellence* 23, no. 4 (Autumn 2004), pp. 23–33; G.A. Gelade and S. Young, "Test of a Service Profit Chain Model in the Retail Banking Sector," *Journal of Occupational & Organizational Psychology* 78 (2005), pp. 1–22. However, some studies have found only a weak relationship between employee attitudes and sales outcomes.

53. P. Guenzi and O. Pelloni, "The Impact of Interpersonal Relationships on Customer Satisfaction and Loyalty to the Service Provider," *International Journal of Service Industry Management* 15, no. 3–4 (2004), pp. 365–84; S.J. Bell, S. Auh, and K. Smalley, "Customer Relationship Dynamics: Service Quality and Customer Loyalty in the Context of Varying Levels of Customer Expertise and Switching Costs," *Journal of the Academy of Marketing Science* 33, no. 2 (Spring 2005), pp. 169–83.

54. DeCotiis et al., "How Outback Steakhouse Created a Great Place to Work, Have Fun, and Make Money."

55. R.T. Mowday, L.W. Porter, and R.M. Steers, *Employee Organization Linkages: The Psychology of Commitment, Absenteeism, and Turnover* (New York: Academic Press, 1982).

56. J.P. Meyer, "Organizational Commitment," *International Review of Industrial and Organizational Psychology* 12 (1997), pp. 175–228. Along with affective and continuance commitment, Meyer identifies *normative commitment*, which refers to employee feelings of obligation to remain with the organization. This commitment has been excluded here so that students focus on the two most common perspectives of commitment.

57. R.D. Hackett, P. Bycio, and P.A. Hausdorf, "Further Assessments of Meyer and Allen's (1991) Three-Component Model of Organizational Commitment," *Journal of Applied Psychology* 79 (1994), pp. 15–23.

58. F.F. Reichheld, *The Loyalty Effect* (Boston: Harvard Business School Press, 1996), Chapter 4; J.P. Meyer et al., "Affective, Continuance, and Normative Commitment to the Organization: A Meta-Analysis of Antecedents, Correlates, and Consequences," *Journal of Vocational Behavior* 61 (2002), pp. 20–52; M. Riketta, "Attitudinal Organizational Commitment and Job Performance: A Meta-Analysis," *Journal of Organizational Behavior* 23 (2002), pp. 257–66.

59. B.L. Toffler, *Final Accounting: Ambition, Greed, and the Fall of Arthur Andersen* (New York: Broadway Books, 2003).

60. J. Churchill, "To the Bitter End," *Registered Rep*, March 2006, p. 59.

61. J.P. Meyer et al., "Organizational Commitment and Job Performance: It's the Nature of the Commitment That Counts," *Journal of Applied Psychology* 74 (1989), pp. 152–56; A.A. Luchak and I.R. Gellatly, "What Kind of Commitment Does a Final-Earnings Pension Plan Elicit?" *Relations Industrielles* 56 (Spring 2001), pp. 394–417; Z.X. Chen and A.M.

Francesco, "The Relationship between the Three Components of Commitment and Employee Performance in China," *Journal of Vocational Behavior* 62, no. 3 (2003), pp. 490–510; D.M. Powell and J.P. Meyer, "Side-Bet Theory and the Three-Component Model of Organizational Commitment," *Journal of Vocational Behavior* 65, no. 1 (2004), pp. 157–77.

62. E.W. Morrison and S.L. Robinson, "When Employees Feel Betrayed: A Model of How Psychological Contract Violation Develops," *Academy of Management Review* 22 (1997), pp. 226–56; J.E. Finegan, "The Impact of Person and Organizational Values on Organizational Commitment," *Journal of Occupational and Organizational Psychology* 73 (June 2000), pp. 149–69.

63. D.M. Cable and T.A. Judge, "Person-Organization Fit, Job Choice Decisions, and Organizational Entry," *Organizational Behavior and Human Decision Processes* 67, no. 3 (1996), pp. 294–311; T.J. Kalliath, A.C. Bluedorn, and M.J. Strube, "A Test of Value Congruence Effects," *Journal of Organizational Behavior* 20, no. 7 (1999), pp. 1175–98; J.W. Westerman and L.A. Cyr, "An Integrative Analysis of Person-Organization Fit Theories," *International Journal of Selection and Assessment* 12, no. 3 (September 2004), pp. 252–61.

64. D.M. Rousseau et al., "Not So Different after All: A Cross-Discipline View of Trust," *Academy of Management Review* 23 (1998), pp. 393–404.

65. S. Ashford, C. Lee, and P. Bobko, "Content, Causes, and Consequences of Job Insecurity: A Theory-Based Measure and Substantive Test," *Academy of Management Journal* 32 (1989), pp. 803–29; C. Hendry, Chris, and R. Jenkins, "Psychological Contracts and New Deals," *Human Resource Management Journal* 7 (1997), pp. 38–44.

66. T.S. Heffner and J.R. Rentsch, "Organizational Commitment and Social Interaction: A Multiple Constituencies Approach," *Journal of Vocational Behavior* 59 (2001), pp. 471–90.

67. E. White, "Know Your Duties, the Firm to Reduce New-Job Surprises," *The Wall Street Journal*, 27 December 2005, p. A16.

68. P. Kruger, "Betrayed by Work," *Fast Company*, November 1999, p. 182.

69. S.L. Robinson, M.S. Kraatz, and D.M. Rousseau, "Changing Obligations and the Psychological Contract: A Longitudinal Study," *Academy of Management Journal* 37 (1994), pp. 137–52; Morrison and Robinson, "When Employees Feel Betrayed: A Model of How Psychological Contract Violation Develops."

70. D.M. Rousseau, *Psychological Contracts in Organizations* (Thousand Oaks, CA: Sage, 1995); M. Janssens, L. Sels, and I. Van den Brande, "Multiple Types of Psychological Contracts: A Six-Cluster Solution," *Human Relations* 56, no. 11 (2003), pp. 1349–78.

71. "Officials Worry as Younger Japanese Embrace 'Freeting,'" *Taipei Times* (Korea), 4 June 2003, p. 12; "Ministry Scheme Lets You Test-Drive a Job," *Yomiuri Shimbun* (Tokyo), 22 April 2005; C. Fujioka, "Idle Young Adults Threaten Japan's Workforce," *Reuters News*, 28 February 2005; "40% of Students Accept Becoming 'Freeters' to Realize Dreams: Survey," *Kyodo News* (Tokyo), 2 May 2006.

72. P.R. Sparrow, "Reappraising Psychological Contracting: Lessons for the Field of Human Resource Development from Cross-Cultural and Occupational Psychology Research," *International Studies of Management & Organization* 28 (March 1998), pp. 30–63; D.C. Thomas, K. Au, and E.C. Ravlin, "Cultural Variation and the Psychological Contract," *Journal of Organizational Behavior* 24 (2003), pp. 451–71.

73. W.H. Whyte, *Organization Man* (New York: Simon & Schuster, 1956), p. 129; C. Hendry and R. Jenkins, "Psychological Contracts and New Deals," *Human Resource Management Journal* 7 (1997), pp. 38–44.

74. R.J. Burke, "Organizational Transitions," in *The New World of Work: Challenges and Opportunities,* ed. C.L. Cooper and R.J. Burke (Oxford: Blackwell, 2002), pp. 3–28; F. Patterson, "Developments in Work Psychology: Emerging Issues and Future Trends," *Journal of Occupational and Organizational Psychology* 74 (November 2001), pp. 381–90.

75. L. Uchitelle, "As Job Cuts Spread, Tears Replace Anger," *The New York Times*, 5 August 2001. Psychological contract expectations of young employees are discussed in P. Herriot and C. Pemberton, "Facilitating New Deals," *Human Resource Management Journal* 7 (1997), pp. 45–56; and P.R. Sparrow, "Transitions in the Psychological Contract: Some Evidence from the Banking Sector," *Human Resource Management Journal* 6 (1996), pp. 75–92.

CHAPTER 5

1. D. Creelman, "Interview: Bob Catell & Kenny Moore," *HR.com*, February 2005; W.L. Lee, "Net Value: That Loving Feeling," *The Edge Financial Daily* (Malaysia), 25 April 2005; N. Mwaura, "Honour Staff for Good Work," *Daily Nation* (Nairobi, Kenya), 27 September 2005; E. White, "Praise from Peers Goes a Long Way," *The Wall Street Journal*, 19 December 2005, p. B3.

2. C.C. Pinder, *Work Motivation in Organizational Behavior* (Upper Saddle River, NJ: Prentice-Hall, 1998); R.M. Steers, R.T. Mowday, and D.L. Shapiro, "The Future of Work Motivation Theory," *Academy of Management Review* 29 (2004), pp. 379–87.

3. "Towers Perrin Study Finds, Despite Layoffs and Slow Economy, a New, More Complex Power Game Is Emerging between Employers and Employees," *Business Wire* news release, (New York: 30 August 2001); K.V. Rondeau and T.H. Wagar, "Downsizing and Organizational Restructuring: What Is the Impact on Hospital Performance?" International Journal of Public Administration 26 (2003), pp. 1647–68.

4. C. Lachnit, "The Young and the Dispirited," *Workforce* 81 (August 2002), p. 18; S.H. Applebaum, M. Serena, and B.T. Shapiro, "Generation X and the Boomers: Organizational Myths and Literary Realities," *Management Research News* 27, no. 11/12 (2004), pp. 1–28. Motivation and needs across generations are also discussed in R. Zemke and B. Filipczak, *Generations at Work: Managing the Clash of Veterans, Boomers, Xers, and Nexters in Your Workplace* (New York: AMACOM, 2000).

5. T.V. Sewards and M.A. Sewards, "Fear and Power-Dominance Drive Motivation: Neural Representations and Pathways Mediating Sensory and Mnemonic Inputs, and Outputs to Premotor Structures," *Neuroscience and Biobehavioral Reviews* 26 (2002), pp. 553–79; K.C. Berridge, "Motivation Concepts in Behavioral Neuroscience," *Physiology & Behavior* 81, no. 2 (2004), pp. 179-209.

6. A.H. Maslow, "A Theory of Human Motivation," *Psychological Review* 50 (1943), pp. 370–96; A.H. Maslow, *Motivation and Personality* (New York: Harper & Row, 1954).

7. D.T. Hall and K.E. Nougaim, "An Examination of Maslow's Need Hierarchy in an Organizational Setting," *Organizational Behavior and Human Performance* 3, no. 1

(1968), p. 12; M.A. Wahba and L.G. Bridwell, "Maslow Reconsidered: A Review of Research on the Need Hierarchy Theory," *Organizational Behavior and Human Performance* 15 (1976), pp. 212–40; E. L. Betz, "Two Tests of Maslow's Theory of Need Fulfillment," *Journal of Vocational Behavior* 24, no. 2 (1984), pp. 204–20; P.A. Corning, "Biological Adaptation in Human Societies: A 'Basic Needs' Approach," *Journal of Bioeconomics* 2, no. 1 (2000), pp. 41–86.

8. A.H. Maslow, "A Preface to Motivation Theory," Psychsomatic Medicine 5 (1943), pp. 85-92.

9. K. Dye, A.J. Mills, and T.G. Weatherbee, "Maslow: Man Interrupted–Reading Management Theory in Context," February 2005, Wolfville, Nova Scotia. As Maslow acknowledged, self-actualization was introduced with a broader meaning by fellow psychologist Kurt Goldstein.

10. A.H. Maslow, *Maslow on Management* (New York: John Wiley & Sons, 1998).

11. F.F. Luthans, "Positive Organizational Behavior: Developing and Managing Psychological Strengths," *The Academy of Management* Executive 16, no. 1 (2002), pp. 57–72; S.L. Gable and J. Haidt, "What (and Why) Is Positive Psychology?" *Review of General Psychology* 9, no. 2 (2005), pp. 103–10; M.E.P. Seligman et al., "Positive Psychology Progress: Empirical Validation of Interventions," *American Psychologist* 60, no. 5 (2005), pp. 410–21.

12. C.P. Alderfer, *Existence, Relatedness, and Growth* (New York: Free Press, 1972).

13. J. Rauschenberger, N. Schmitt, and J.E. Hunter, "A Test of the Need Hierarchy Concept by a Markov Model of Change in Need Strength," *Administrative Science Quarterly* 25, no. 4 (December 1980), pp. 654–70; J.P. Wanous and A.A. Zwany, "A Cross-Sectional Test of Need Hierarchy Theory," *Organizational Behavior and Human Performance* 18 (1977), pp. 78–97.

14. B.A. Agle and C.B. Caldwell, "Understanding Research on Values in Business," *Business and Society* 38 (September 1999), pp. 326–87; B. Verplanken and R.W. Holland, "Motivated Decision Making: Effects of Activation and Self-Centrality of Values on Choices and Behavior," *Journal of Personality and Social Psychology* 82, no. 3 (2002), pp. 434–47; S. Hitlin and J.A. Pilavin, "Values: Reviving a Dormant Concept," *Annual Review of Sociology* 30 (2004), pp. 359–93.

15. P.R. Lawrence and N. Nohria, Driven: *How Human Nature Shapes Our Choices* (San Francisco: Jossey-Bass, 2002).

16. R.E. Baumeister and M.R. Leary, "The Need to Belong: Desire for Interpersonal Attachments as a Fundamental Human Motivation," *Psychological Bulletin* 117 (1995), pp. 497–529; S. Kirkey, "Being Shy, Unsociable Is Bad for Your Health, Study Finds," *Ottawa Citizen*, 21 November 2005, p. A1.

17. W.H. Bexton, W. Heron, and T.H. Scott, "Effects of Decreased Variation in the Sensory Environment," *Canadian Journal of Psychology* 8 (1954), pp. 70–76; G. Loewenstein, "The Psychology of Curiosity: A Review and Reinterpretation," *Psychological Bulletin* 116, no. 1 (1994), pp. 75–98.

18. A.R. Damasio, *Descartes' Error: Emotion, Reason, and the Human Brain* (New York: Putnam Sons, 1994); J.E. LeDoux, "Emotion Circuits in the Brain," *Annual Review of Neuroscience* 23 (2000), pp. 155–84; P. Winkielman and K.C. Berridge, "Unconscious Emotion," *Current Directions in Psychological Science* 13, no. 3 (2004), pp. 120–23.

19. Lawrence and Nohria, *Driven: How Human Nature Shapes Our Choices*, pp. 145–47.

20. D.C. McClelland, *The Achieving Society* (New York: Van Nostrand Reinhold, 1961).

21. S. Shane, E.A. Locke, and C.J. Collins, "Entrepreneurial Motivation," *Human Resource Management Review* 13, no. 2 (2003), pp. 257–79.

22. D.C. McClelland and D.H. Burnham, "Power Is the Great Motivator," *Harvard Business Review* 73 (January–February 1995), pp. 126–39; J.L. Thomas, M.W. Dickson, and P.D. Bliese, "Values Predicting Leader Performance in the U.S. Army Reserve Officer Training Corps Assessment Center: Evidence for a Personality-Mediated Model," *The Leadership Quarterly* 12, no. 2 (2001), pp. 181–96.

23. D. Vredenburgh and Y. Brender, "The Hierarchical Abuse of Power in Work Organizations," *Journal of Business Ethics* 17 (September 1998), pp. 1337–47.

24. D. Miron and D.C. McClelland, "The Impact of Achievement Motivation Training on Small Business," *California Management Review* 21 (1979), pp. 13–28.

25. Lawrence and Nohria, *Driven: How Human Nature Shapes Our Choices*, Chapter 11.

26. P. Dvorak, "Out of Tune," *The Wall Street Journal*, 29 June 2005, p. A1.

27. R. Turcsik, "The Prince of Tidewater," *Progressive Grocer*, 15 April 2003.

28. Expectancy theory of motivation in work settings originated in V.H. Vroom, *Work and Motivation* (New York: Wiley, 1964). The version of expectancy theory presented here was developed by Edward Lawler. Lawler's model provides a clearer presentation of the model's three components. P-to-O expectancy is similar to "instrumentality" in Vroom's original expectancy theory model. The difference is that instrumentality is a correlation, whereas P-to-O expectancy is a probability. See J.P. Campbell et al., *Managerial Behavior, Performance, and Effectiveness* (New York: McGraw-Hill, 1970); E.E. Lawler III, *Motivation in Work Organizations* (Monterey, CA: Brooks-Cole, 1973); and D.A. Nadler and E.E. Lawler, "Motivation: A Diagnostic Approach," in *Perspectives on Behavior in Organizations*, 2nd edition, ed. J.R. Hackman, E.E. Lawler III, and L.W. Porter (New York: McGraw-Hill, 1983), pp. 67–78.

29. M. Zeelenberg et al., "Emotional Reactions to the Outcomes of Decisions: The Role of Counterfactual Thought in the Experience of Regret and Disappointment," *Organizational Behavior and Human Decision Processes* 75, no. 2 (1998), pp. 117–41; B.A. Mellers, "Choice and the Relative *Pleasure of Consequences*," Psychological Bulletin 126, no. 6 (November 2000), pp. 910–24; R.P. Bagozzi, U.M. Dholakia, and S. Basuroy, "How Effortful Decisions Get Enacted: The Motivating Role of Decision Processes, Desires, and Anticipated Emotions," *Journal of Behavioral Decision Making* 16, no. 4 (October 2003), pp. 273–95.

30. Nadler and Lawler, "Motivation: A Diagnostic Approach."

31. T. Janz, "Manipulating Subjective Expectancy through Feedback: A Laboratory Study of the Expectancy-Performance Relationship," *Journal of Applied Psychology* 67 (1982), p. 480–85; K.A. Karl, A.M. O' Leary-Kelly, and J.J. Martoccio, "The Impact of Feedback and Self-Efficacy on Performance in Training," *Journal of Organizational Behavior* 14 (1993), pp. 379–94; R.G. Lord, P.J. Hanges, and E.G. Godfrey, "Integrating Neural Networks into Decision-Making and Motivational Theory: Rethinking Vie Theory," *Canadian Psychology* 44, no. 1 (2003), pp. 21–38.

32. P.W. Mulvey et al., *The Knowledge of Pay Study: E-Mails from the Frontline* (Scottsdale, Arizona: WorldatWork, 2002).

33. M.L. Ambrose and C.T. Kulik, "Old Friends, New Faces: Motivation Research in the 1990s," *Journal of Management* 25 (May 1999), pp. 231–92; C.L. Haworth and P.E. Levy, "The Importance of Instrumentality Beliefs in the Prediction of Organizational Citizenship Behaviors," *Journal of Vocational Behavior* 59 (August 2001), pp. 64–75; Y. Chen, A. Gupta, and L. Hoshower, "Marketing Students' Perceptions of Teaching Evaluations: An Application of Expectancy Theory," *Marketing Education Review* 14, no. 2 (Summer 2004), pp. 23–36.

34. T. Matsui and I. Terai, "A Cross-Cultural Study of the Validity of the Expectancy Theory of Motivation," *Journal of Applied Psychology* 60 (1979), pp. 263–65; D.H.B. Welsh, F. Luthans, and S.M. Sommer, "Managing Russian Factory Workers: The Impact of U.S.-Based Behavioral and Participative Techniques," *Academy of Management Journal* 36 (1993), pp. 58–79.

35. L. Hollman, "Seeing the Writing on the Wall," *Call Center* (August 2002), p. 37; S. Zeller, "Good Calls," *Government Executive*, 15 May 2005.

36. K.H. Doerr and T.R. Mitchell, "Impact of Material Flow Policies and Goals on Job Outcomes," *Journal of Applied Psychology* 81 (1996), pp. 142–52; L.A. Wilk and W.K. Redmon, "The Effects of Feedback and Goal Setting on the Productivity and Satisfaction of University Admissions Staff," *Journal of Organizational Behavior Management* 18 (1998), pp. 45–68.

37. A. Prayag, "All Work...and More Play," *Business Line (The Hindu)*, 13 June 2005, p. 4; S. Rajagopalan, "Bangalore to Hawaii, an All-Paid Holiday," *Hindustan Times*, 7 May 2005; J.A. Singh, "Hola for Success!" *Business Standard* (India), 4 June 2005.

38. G.P. Latham, "Goal Setting: A Five-Step Approach to Behavior Change," *Organizational Dynamics* 32, no. 3 (2003), pp. 309–18; E.A. Locke and G.P. Latham, *A Theory of Goal Setting and Task Performance* (Englewood Cliffs, NJ: Prentice Hall, 1990). Some practitioners rely on the acronym "SMART" goals, referring to goals that are specific, measurable, acceptable, relevant, and timely. However, this list overlaps key elements (for example, specific goals are measurable *and* timely) and overlooks the key elements of being challenging and feedback-related.

39. K. Tasa, T. Brown, and G.H. Seijts, "The Effects of Proximal, Outcome, and Learning Goals on Information Seeking and Complex Task Performance," *Proceedings of the Annual Conference of the Administrative Sciences Association of Canada, Organizational Behavior Division* 23, no. 5 (2002), pp. 11–20.

40. K.R. Thompson, W.A. Hochwarter, and N.J. Mathys, "Stretch Targets: What Makes Them Effective?" *Academy of Management Executive* 11 (August 1997), pp. 48–60; S. Kerr and S. Landauer, "Using Stretch Goals to Promote Organizational Effectiveness and Personal Growth: General Electric and Goldman Sachs," *Academy of Management Executive* 18, no. 4 (2004), pp. 134–38.

41. A. Li and A.B. Butler, "The Effects of Participation in Goal Setting and Goal Rationales on Goal Commitment: An Exploration of Justice Mediators," Journal of Business and Psychology 19, no. 1 (Fall 2004), pp. 37-51.

42. Locke and Latham, *A Theory of Goal Setting and Task Performance*, Chapters 6 and 7; J. Wegge, "Participation in Group Goal Setting: Some Novel Findings and a Comprehensive Model as a New Ending to an Old Story," *Applied Psychology: An International Review* 49 (2000), pp. 498–516.

43. M. London, E.M. Mone, and J.C. Scott, "Performance Management and Assessment: Methods for Improved Rater Accuracy and Employee Goal Setting," *Human Resource Management* 43, no. 4 (Winter 2004), pp. 319–36; G.P. Latham and C.C. Pinder, "Work Motivation Theory and Research at the Dawn of the Twenty-First Century," *Annual Review of Psychology* 56 (2005), pp. 485–516.

44. S.P. Brown, S. Ganesan, and G. Challagalla, "Self-Efficacy as a Moderator of Information-Seeking Effectiveness," *Journal of Applied Psychology* 86, no. 5 (2001), pp. 1043–51; P.A. Heslin and G.P. Latham, "The Effect of Upward Feedback on Managerial Behaviour," *Applied Psychology: An International Review* 53, no. 1 (2004), pp. 23–37; D. Van-Dijk and A.N. Kluger, "Feedback Sign Effect on Motivation: Is It Moderated by Regulatory Focus?" Applied Psychology: *An International Review* 53, no. 1 (2004), pp. 113–35; J.E. Bono and A.E. Colbert, "Understanding Responses to Multi-Source Feedback: The Role of Core Self-Evaluations," *Personnel Psychology* 58, no. 1 (Spring 2005), pp. 171–203.

45. Hollman, "Seeing the Writing on the Wall."

46. C. Mabey, "Closing the Circle: Participant Views of a 360-Degree Feedback Programme," *Human Resource Management Journal* 11 (2001), pp. 41–53. However, one recent study reported that fewer than half of the 55 human resource executives surveyed (most from *Fortune* 500 companies) use 360-degree feedback. See E.E. Lawler III and M. McDermott, "Current Performance Management Practices," *WorldatWork Journal* 12 (Second Quarter 2003), pp. 49–60.

47. W.W. Tornow and M. London, *Maximizing the Value of 360-Degree Feedback: A Process for Successful Individual and Organizational Development* (San Francisco: Jossey-Bass, 1998); L.E. Atwater, D.A. Waldman, and J.F. Brett, "Understanding and Optimizing Multisource Feedback," *Human Resource Management Journal* 41 (Summer 2002), pp. 193–208; J.W. Smither, M. London, and R.R. Reilly, "Does Performance Improve Following Multisource Feedback? A Theoretical Model, Meta-Analysis, and Review of Empirical Findings," *Personnel Psychology* 58, no. 1 (2005), pp. 33–66.

48. A.S. DeNisi and A.N. Kluger, "Feedback Effectiveness: Can 360-Degree Appraisals Be Improved?" *Academy of Management Executive* 14 (February 2000), pp. 129–39; M.A. Peiperl, "Getting 360-Degree Feedback Right," *Harvard Business Review* 79 (January 2001), pp. 142–47; "Perils & Payoffs of Multi-Rater Feedback Programs," *Pay for Performance Report* (May 2003), p. 1; M.-G. Seo, L.F. Barrett, and J.M. Bartunek, "The Role of Affective Experience in Work Motivation," *Academy of Management Review* 29 (2004), pp. 423–49.

49. E. Ross, "Know Yourself," *Business Review Weekly*, 17 March 2005, p. 86.

50. J.W. Smither et al., "Can Working with an Executive Coach Improve Multisource Feedback Ratings over Time? A Quasi-Experimental Field Study," *Personnel Psychology* 56 (Spring 2003), pp. 23–44; C. Udy, "Coaching a Winner," *Bay of Pleny Times* (New Zealand), 23 November 2005, p. P01.

51. S.J. Ashford and G.B. Northcraft, "Conveying More (or Less) Than We Realize: The Role of Impression Management in Feedback Seeking," *Organizational Behavior and Human Decision Processes* 53 (1992), pp. 310–34; M. London, "Giving Feedback: Source-Centered Antecedents

and Consequences of Constructive and Destructive Feedback," *Human Resource Management Review* 5 (1995), pp. 159–88; J.R. Williams et al., "Increasing Feedback Seeking in Public Contexts: It Takes Two (or More) to Tango," *Journal of Applied Psychology* 84 (December 1999), pp. 969–76.

52. A. Dragoon, "Sleepless in Manhattan," CIO, April 2005, p. 1; S.E. Ante, "Giving the Boss the Big Picture," *Business Week*, 13 February 2006, p. 48.

53. J.B. Miner, "The Rated Importance, Scientific Validity, and Practical Usefulness of Organizational Behavior Theories: A Quantitative Review," *Academy of Management Learning and Education* 2, no. 3 (2003), pp. 250–68. Also see C.C. Pinder, *Work Motivation in Organizational Behavior* (Upper Saddle River, NJ: Prentice-Hall, 1997), p. 384.

54. P.M. Wright, "Goal Setting and Monetary Incentives: Motivational Tools That Can Work Too Well," *Compensation and Benefits Review* 26 (May–June 1994), pp. 41–49; E.A. Locke and G.P. Latham, "Building a Practically Useful Theory of Goal Setting and Task Motivation: A 35-Year Odyssey," *American Psychologist* 57, no. 9 (2002), pp. 705–17.

55. "Boeing Settles Sex Discrimination Suit for up to $73m," *Puget Sound Business Journal*, 16 July 2004; S. Holmes, "A New Black Eye for Boeing?" *BusinessWeek*, 26 April 2004, p. 90; S. Holt, "Boeing Gender-Bias Lawsuit Brings Women's Buried Stories to Surface," *Knight Ridder/Tribune Business News*, 6 July 2004; S. Holt and D. Bowermaster, "Rare Trial Nears: 28,000 Women Accuse Boeing of Gender Bias," *The Seattle Times*, 14 May 2004, p. A1.

56. J. Greenberg and E.A. Lind, "The Pursuit of Organizational Justice: From Conceptualization to Implication to Application," in *Industrial and Organizational Psychology: Linking Theory with Practice*, ed. C.L. Cooper and E.A. Locke (London: Blackwell, 2000), pp. 72–108; R. Cropanzano and M. Schminke, "Using Social Justice to Build Effective Work Groups," in *Groups at Work: Theory and Research*, ed. M.E. Turner (Mahwah, NJ: Lawrence Erlbaum Associates, 2001), pp. 143–71; D.T. Miller, "Disrespect and the Experience of Injustice," *Annual Review of Psychology* 52 (2001), pp. 527–53.

57. Adams, "Toward an Understanding of Inequity"; Mowday, "Equity Theory Predictions of Behavior in Organizations"; Cropanzano, "Progress in Organizational Justice: Tunneling through the Maze";

Powell, "Justice Judgments as Complex Psychocultural Constructions: An Equity-Based Heuristic for Mapping Two- and Three-Dimensional Fairness Representations in Perceptual Space."

58. C.T. Kulik and M.L. Ambrose, "Personal and Situational Determinants of Referent Choice," *Academy of Management Review* 17 (1992), pp. 212–37; G. Blau, "Testing the Effect of Level and Importance of Pay Referents on Pay Level Satisfaction," *Human Relations* 47 (1994), pp. 1251–68.

59. T.P. Summers and A.S. DeNisi, "In Search of Adams' Other: Reexamination of Referents Used in the Evaluation of Pay," *Human Relations* 43 (1990), pp. 497–511.

60. Y. Cohen-Charash and P.E. Spector, "The Role of Justice in Organizations: A Meta-Analysis," *Organizational Behavior and Human Decision Processes* 86 (November 2001), pp. 278–321.

61. Canadian Press, "Pierre Berton, Canadian Cultural Icon, Enjoyed Long and Colourful Career," *Times Colonist* (Victoria, B.C.), 30 November 2004.

62. K.S. Sauleya and A.G. Bedeian, "Equity Sensitivity: Construction of a Measure and Examination of Its Psychometric Properties," *Journal of Management* 26 (September 2000), pp. 885–910.

63. B. Murphy, "Rising Fortunes," *Milwaukee Journal Sentinel*, 10 October 2004, p. 1; S. Greenhouse, "How Costco Became the Anti-Wal-Mart," *The New York Times*, 17 July 2005, p. BU1.

64. The meaning of these three groups has evolved over the years. These definitions are based on W.C. King Jr. and E.W. Miles, "The Measurement of Equity Sensitivity," *Journal of Occupational and Organizational Psychology* 67 (1994), pp. 133–42.

65. M. Ezzamel and R. Watson, "Pay Comparability across and within UK Boards: An Empirical Analysis of the Cash Pay Awards to CEOs and Other Board Members," *Journal of Management Studies* 39, no. 2 (March 2002), pp. 207–32; J. Fizel, A.C. Krautman, and L. Hadley, "Equity and Arbitration in Major League Baseball," *Managerial and Decision Economics* 23, no. 7 (October–November 2002), pp. 427–35.

66. Miner, "The Rated Importance, Scientific Validity, and Practical Usefulness of Organizational Behavior Theories: A Quantitative Review."

67. Cohen-Charash and Spector, "The

Role of Justice in Organizations: A Meta-Analysis"; J.A. Colquitt et al., "Justice at the Millennium: A Meta-Analytic Review of 25 Years of Organizational Justice Research," *Journal of Applied Psychology* 86 (2001), pp. 425–45.

68. Several types of justice have been identified, and there is some debate over whether they represent forms of procedural justice or are distinct from procedural and distributive justice. The discussion here adopts the former view, which seems to dominate the literature. See C. Viswesvaran and D.S. Ones, "Examining the Construct of Organizational Justice: A Meta-Analytic Evaluation of Relations with Work Attitudes and Behaviors," *Journal of Business Ethics* 38 (July 2002), 193.

69. Greenberg and Lind, "The Pursuit of Organizational Justice: From Conceptualization to Implication to Application." For a recent study of voice and injustice, see J.B. Olson-Buchanan and W.R. Boswell, "The Role of Employee Loyalty and Formality in Voicing Discontent," *Journal of Applied Psychology* 87, no. 6 (2002), pp. 1167–74.

70. R. Folger and J. Greenberg, "Procedural Justice: An Interpretive Analysis of Personnel Systems," *Research in Personnel and Human Resources Management* 3 (1985), pp. 141–83; L.B. Bingham, "Mediating Employment Disputes: Perceptions of Redress at the United States Postal Service," *Review of Public Personnel Administration* 17 (Spring 1997), pp. 20–30.

71. R. Hagey et al., "Immigrant Nurses' Experience of Racism," *Journal of Nursing Scholarship* 33 (Fourth Quarter 2001), pp. 389–95; K. Roberts and K.S. Markel, "Claiming in the Name of Fairness: Organizational Justice and the Decision to File for Workplace Injury Compensation," *Journal of Occupational Health Psychology* 6 (October 2001), pp. 332–47; D.A. Jones and D.P. Skarlicki, "The Effects of Overhearing Peers Discuss an Authority's Fairness Reputation on Reactions to Subsequent Treatment," *Journal of Applied Psychology* 90, no. 2 (2005), pp. 363–72.

72. Miller, "Disrespect and the Experience of Injustice."

73. S. Fox, P.E. Spector, and E.W. Miles, "Counterproductive Work Behavior (CWB) in Response to Job Stressors and Organizational Justice: Some Mediator and Moderator Tests for Autonomy and Emotions," *Journal of Vocational Behavior* 59 (2001), pp. 291–309; I.M. Jawahar, "A Model of Organizational Justice and

Workplace Aggression," *Journal of Management* 28, no. 6 (2002), pp. 811–34; M.M. LeBlanc and J. Barling, "Workplace Aggression," *Current Directions in Psychological Science* 13, no. 1 (2004), pp. 9–12.

74. M.L. Ambrose, M.A. Seabright, and M. Schminke, "Sabotage in the Workplace: The Role of Organizational Injustice," *Organizational Behavior and Human Decision Processes* 89, no. 1 (2002), pp. 947–65.

75. N.D. Cole and G.P. Latham, "Effects of Training in Procedural Justice on Perceptions of Disciplinary Fairness by Unionized Employees and Disciplinary Subject Matter Experts," *Journal of Applied Psychology* 82 (1997), pp. 699–705 D.P. Skarlicki and G.P. Latham, "Increasing Citizenship Behavior within a Labor Union: A Test of Organizational Justice Theory," *Journal of Applied Psychology* 81 (1996), pp. 161–69.

CHAPTER 6

1. V.L. Parker, "Org Charts Turn around with Teams," *News & Observer* (Raleigh, North Carolina), 21 July 2005, p. D1; N. Byrnes and M. Arndt, "The Art of Motivation," *BusinessWeek*, 1 May 2006, p. 56.

2. H. Das, "The Four Faces of Pay: An Investigation into How Canadian Managers View Pay," *International Journal of Commerce & Management* 12 (2002), pp. 18–40. For recent ratings of the importance of pay and benefits, see P. Babcock, "Find What Workers Want," *HRMagazine*, April 2005, pp. 50–56.

3. R. Lynn, *The Secret of the Miracle Economy* (London: SAE, 1991), cited in A. Furnham and R. Okamura, "Your Money or Your Life: Behavioral and Emotional Predictors of Money Pathology," *Human Relations* 52 (September 1999), pp. 1157–77. The opinion polls are summarized in J. O'Rourke, "Show Boys the Money and Tell Girls You Care," *Sun-Herald* (Sydney, Australia), 10 December 2000, p. 43; M. Steen, "Study Looks at What Good Employees Want from a Company," *San Jose Mercury*, 19 December 2000.

4. A. Furnham, B.D. Kirkcaldy, and R. Lynn, "National Attitudes to Competitiveness, Money, and Work among Young People: First, Second, and Third World Differences," *Human Relations* 47 (January 1994), pp. 119–32; V.K.G. Lim, "Money Matters: An Empirical Investigation of Money, Face, and the Confucian Work Ethic," *Personality and Individual Differences* 35 (2003), pp. 953–70; T.L.-P. Tang, A. Furnham, and G.M.-T. Davis, "A Cross-Cultural Comparison of the Money Ethic, the Protestant Work Ethic, and Job Satisfaction: Taiwan, the USA, and the UK," *International Journal of Organization Theory and Behavior* 6, no. 2 (Summer 2003), pp. 175–94.

5. J.L. Sanchez Jr., "City OKs Police Pay Hikes," *Press Democrat* (Santa Rosa, California), 18 October 2005, p. B1; J. Castellucci, "Longevity Bonus Now a Bone of Contention," *Providence Journal*, 31 January 2006, p. C01.

6. "Seniority Pay System Seeing Revival," *Kyodo News* (Tokyo), 29 March 2004; "More Firms Offering Childbirth Allowances," *Daily Yomiuri* (Tokyo), 29 September 2005, p. 4.

7. D.M. Figart, "Equal Pay for Equal Work: The Role of Job Evaluation in an Evolving Social Norm," *Journal of Economic Issues* 34 (March 2000), pp. 1–19; G.T. Milkovich, J.M. Newman, and C. Milkovich, *Compensation* (Burr Ridge, IL: McGraw-Hill/Irwin, 2002).

8. E.E. Lawler III, *Rewarding Excellence: Pay Strategies for the New Economy* (San Francisco: Jossey-Bass, 2000), pp. 30–35, 109–19; R. McNabb and K. Whitfield, "Job Evaluation and High Performance Work Practices: Compatible or Conflictual?" *Journal of Management Studies* 38 (March 2001), pp. 293–312.

9. "Syracuse's Restructured Flexible Pay Plan Makes Managing Employees Easier," *HR On Campus*, 5 December 2002. For discussion of why companies are shifting to competency-based pay, see R.L. Heneman, G.E. Ledford Jr., and M.T. Gresham, "The Changing Nature of Work and Its Effects on Compensation Design and Delivery," in *Compensation in Organizations: Current Research and Practice*, ed. S. Rynes and B. Gerhart (San Francisco: Jossey-Bass, 2000), pp. 195–240.

10. E.E. Lawler III, "From Job-Based to Competency-Based Organizations," *Journal of Organizational Behavior* 15 (1994), pp. 3–15; B. Murray and B. Gerhart, "Skill-Based Pay and Skill Seeking," *Human Resource Management Review* 10 (August 2000), pp. 271–87; J.D. Shaw et al., "Success and Survival of Skill-Based Pay Plans," *Journal of Management* 31, no. 1 (February 2005), pp. 28–49.

11. E.B. Peach and D.A. Wren, "Pay for Performance from Antiquity to the 1950s," *Journal of Organizational Behavior Management* (1992), pp. 5–26.

12. L. Spiers, "Piece by Piecemeal," *Lawn & Landscape Magazine*, 5 August 2003; H.-H. Pai, "'Our Eyes Have Been Opened to the Abuse,'" *The Guardian* (London), 29 April 2006, p. 2.

13. C. Petrie, "PCCW Puts the Focus on Rewarding Staff," *South China Morning Post* (Hong Kong), 17 July 2004, p. 4.

14. H. Stock Jr. "At National City, Reps Are Judged on a Whole Lot More Than Their Production," *Bank Investment Consultant*, 1 December 2004, p. 26; K. Whitehouse, "More Employers Link Pay to Performance," *Dow Jones Commodities Service*, 7 December 2005.

15. J.M. Welch, "Gainsharing Returns: Hospitals and Physicians Join to Reduce Costs," *Journals of Health Care Compliance* 7, no. 3 (May/June 2005), pp. 39–42; D. Jacobson, "Best-Kept Secrets of the World's Best Companies: Gainsharing," *Business 2.0*, April 2006, p. 82. For evaluations of gainsharing programs, see L.R. Gomez-Mejia, T.M. Welbourne, and R.M. Wiseman, "The Role of Risk Sharing and Risk Taking under Gainsharing," *Academy of Management Review* 25 (July 2000), pp. 492–507; and K.M. Bartol and A. Srivastava, "Encouraging Knowledge Sharing: The Role of Organizational Reward System," *Journal of Leadership & Organizational Studies* 9 (Summer 2002), pp. 64–76.

16. C. Rukuni, "Employee Share Schemes Change Workers' Fortunes," *LiquidAfrica*, 9 October 2004.

17. "Nucor Pays $200m in Bonuses to Employees," *Steel Business Briefing*, 16 December 2005.

18. "KT Seeks New Growth Engines," *Korea Herald*, 2 March 2004.

19. J. Chelius and R.S. Smith, "Profit Sharing and Employment Stability," *Industrial and Labor Relations Review* 43 (1990), pp. 256s–273s; S.H. Wagner, C.P. Parkers, and N.D. Christiansen, "Employees That Think and Act Like Owners: Effects of Ownership Beliefs and Behaviors on Organizational Effectiveness," *Personnel Psychology* 56, no. 4 (Winter 2003), pp. 847–71; G. Ledford, M. Lucy, and P. Leblanc, "The Effects of Stock Ownership on Employee Attitudes and Behavior: Evidence from the Rewards at Work Studies," *Perspectives (Sibson)*, January 2004; P. Andon, J. Baxter, and H. Mahama, "The Balanced Scorecard: Slogans, Seduction, and State of Play,"

Australian Accounting Review 15, no. 1 (March 2005), pp. 29–38.

20. T. Lester, "Performance at Hugo Boss," *Executive Briefing (Economist Intelligence Unit)*, 4 May 2006, 1

21. A.J. Maggs, "Enron, ESOPs, and Fiduciary Duty," *Benefits Law Journal* 16, no. 3 (Autumn 2003), pp. 42–52; C. Brodzinski, "ESOP's Fables Can Make Coverage Risky," *National Underwriter P & C*, 13 June 2005, pp. 16–17.

22. J. Pfeffer, *The Human Equation* (Boston: Harvard Business School Press, 1998); B.N. Pfau and I.T. Kay, *The Human Capital Edge* (New York: McGraw-Hill, 2002). The problems with performance-based pay are discussed in W.C. Hammer, "How to Ruin Motivation with Pay," *Compensation Review* 7, no. 3 (1975), pp. 17–27; A. Kohn, Punished by *Rewards* (Boston: Houghton Mifflin, 1993); M. O'Donnell and J. O' Brian, "Performance-Based Pay in the Australian Public Service," *Review of Public Personnel Administration* 20 (Spring 2000), pp. 20–34; and M. Beer and M.D. Cannon, "Promise and Peril of Implementing Pay-for-Performance," *Human Resource Management* 43, no. 1 (Spring 2004), pp. 3–48.

23. M. Buckingham and D.O. Clifton, *Now, Discover Your Strengths* (New York: Free Press, 2001); Watson Wyatt, *WorkMalaysia* (Kuala Lumpur: Watson Wyatt, 2004), http://www.watsonwyatt.com/asia-pacific/research/workasia/workmy_key-findings.asp (accessed 2 December 2005).

24. S. Kerr, "Organization Rewards: Practical, Cost-Neutral Alternatives That You May Know, but Don't Practice," *Organizational Dynamics* 28 (Summer 1999), pp. 61–70.

25. J.S. DeMatteo, L.T. Eby, and E. Sundstrom, "Team-Based Rewards: Current Empirical Evidence and Directions for Future Research," *Research in Organizational Behavior* 20 (1998), pp. 141–83; S. Rynes, B. Gerhart, and L. Parks, "Personnel Psychology: Performance Evaluation and Pay for Performance," *Annual Review of Psychology* 56 (2005), pp. 571–600.

26. "Dream Teams," *Human Resources Professional*, November 1994, pp. 17–19.

27. D.R. Spitzer, "Power Rewards: Rewards That Really Motivate," *Management Review* May 1996, pp. 45–50. For a classic discussion of the unintended consequences of pay, see S. Kerr, "On the Folly of Rewarding A, While Hoping for

B," *Academy of Management Journal* 18 (1975), pp. 769–83.

28. "Strong Leaders Make Great Workplaces," *CityBusiness*, 28 August 2000; P.M. Perry, "Holding Your Top Talent," *Research Technology Management* 44 (May 2001), pp. 26–30.

29. J.R. Edwards, J.A. Scully, and M.D. Brtek, "The Nature and Outcomes of Work: A Replication and Extension of Interdisciplinary Work-Design Research," *Journal of Applied Psychology* 85, no. 6 (2000), pp. 860–68; F.P. Morgeson and M.A. Campion, "Minimizing Trade-offs When Redesigning Work: Evidence from a Longitudinal Quasi-Experiment," *Personnel Psychology* 55, no. 3 (Autumn 2002), pp. 589–612.

30. P. Siekman, "This Is Not a BMW Plant," *Fortune*, 18 April 2005, p. 208.

31. Accel-Team, "Scientific Management: Lessons from Ancient History through the Industrial Revolution," www.accel-team.com; A. Smith, *The Wealth of Nations* (London: Dent, 1910).

32. H. Fayol, *General and Industrial Management*, trans. C. Storrs (London: Pitman, 1949); E.E. Lawler III, *Motivation in Work Organizations* (Monterey, CA: Brooks/Cole, 1973), Chapter 7; M.A. Campion, "Ability Requirement Implications of Job Design: An Interdisciplinary Perspective," *Personnel Psychology* 42 (1989), pp. 1–24.

33. F.W. Taylor, *The Principles of Scientific Management* (New York: Harper & Row, 1911); R. Kanigel, *The One Best Way: Frederick Winslow Taylor and the Enigma of Efficiency* (New York: Viking, 1997).

34. C.R. Walker and R.H. Guest, *The Man on the Assembly Line* (Cambridge, MA: Harvard University Press, 1952); W.F. Dowling, "Job Redesign on the Assembly Line: Farewell to Blue-Collar Blues?" *Organizational Dynamics* (Autumn 1973), pp. 51–67; E.E. Lawler III, *High-Involvement Management* (San Francisco: Jossey-Bass, 1986).

35. M. Keller, *Rude Awakening* (New York: Harper Perennial, 1989), p. 128.

36. F. Herzberg, B. Mausner, and B.B. Snyderman, *The Motivation to Work* (New York: Wiley, 1959).

37. S.K. Parker, T.D. Wall, and J.L. Cordery, "Future Work Design Research and Practice: Toward an Elaborated Model of Work Design," *Journal of Occupational and Organizational Psychology* 74 (November 2001), pp. 413–40. For a

decisive critique of motivator–hygiene theory, see N. King, "Clarification and Evaluation of the Two Factor Theory of Job Satisfaction," *Psychological Bulletin* 74 (1970), pp. 18–31.

38. J.R. Hackman and G. Oldham, *Work Redesign* (Reading, MA: Addison-Wesley, 1980).

39. D. Whitford, "A Human Place to Work," *Fortune*, 8 January 2001, pp. 108–19.

40. J.E. Champoux, "A Multivariate Test of the Job Characteristics Theory of Work Motivation," *Journal of Organizational Behavior* 12, no. 5 (September 1991), pp. 431–46; R.B. Tiegs, L.E. Tetrick, and Y. Fried, "Growth Need Strength and Context Satisfactions as Moderators of the Relations of the Job Characteristics Model," *Journal of Management* 18, no. 3 (September 1992), pp. 575–93.

41. "Region Positioned among DCX Leaders in Advanced Manufacturing," *Toledo Business Journal*, August 2004, p. 1; M. Connelly, "Chrysler Wants to Put Team Assembly in All Plants," *Automotive News*, 20 May 2005, p. 53.

42. M.A. Campion and C.L. McClelland, "Follow-up and Extension of the Interdisciplinary Costs and Benefits of Enlarged Jobs," *Journal of Applied Psychology* 78 (1993), pp. 339–51; N.G. Dodd and D.C. Ganster, "The Interactive Effects of Variety, Autonomy, and Feedback on Attitudes and Performance," *Journal of Organizational Behavior* 17 (1996), pp. 329–47.

43. J.R. Hackman et al., "A New Strategy for Job Enrichment," *California Management Review* 17, no. 4 (1975), pp. 57–71; R.W. Griffin, *Task Design: An Integrative Approach* (Glenview, IL: Scott Foresman, 1982).

44. P.E. Spector and S.M. Jex, "Relations of Job Characteristics from Multiple Data Sources with Employee Affect, Absence, Turnover Intentions, and Health," *Journal of Applied Psychology* 76 (1991), pp. 46–53; P. Osterman, "How Common Is Workplace Transformation and Who Adopts It?" *Industrial and Labor Relations Review* 47 (1994). pp. 173–88; R. Saavedra and S.K. Kwun, "Affective States in Job Characteristics Theory," *Journal of Organizational Behavior* 21 (2000), pp. 131–46.

45. Hackman and Oldham, *Work Redesign*, pp. 137–38.

46. A. Hertting et al., "Personnel Reductions and Structural Changes in Health Care: Work–Life Experiences of Medical Secretaries," *Journal of Psychosomatic Research* 54 (February 2003), pp. 161–70.

47. Business Wire, "WKRN-TV and KRON-TV to Become First U.S. Broadcast Stations to Utilize Video Journalism Model to Maximize News Gathering Capabilities and Branding," *Business Wire* news release (San Francisco: 29 June 2005); DV Dojo, "Michael Rosenblum" (2005), http://www.dvdojo.com/who.php (accessed 27 July 2005).

48. K. Tyler, "The Boss Makes the Weather," *HRMagazine*, May 2004, pp. 93–96.

49. This definition is based mostly on G.M. Spreitzer and R.E. Quinn, *"A Company of Leaders: Five Disciplines for Unleashing the Power in Your Workforce "* (2001). However, most elements of this definition appear in other discussions of empowerment. See, for example, R. Forrester, "Empowerment: Rejuvenating a Potent Idea," *Academy of Management Executive* 14 (August 2000), pp. 67–80; W.A. Randolph, "Re-Thinking Empowerment: Why Is It So Hard to Achieve?" *Organizational Dynamics* 29 (November 2000), pp. 94–107; and S.T. Menon, "Employee Empowerment: An Integrative Psychological Approach," *Applied Psychology: An International Review* 50 (2001), pp. 153–80.

50. The positive relationship between these structural empowerment conditions and psychological empowerment is reported in H.K.S. Laschinger et al., "A Longitudinal Analysis of the Impact of Workplace Empowerment on Work Satisfaction," *Journal of Organizational Behavior* 25, no. 4 (June 2004), pp. 527–45.

51. C. S. Koberg et al., "Antecedents and Outcomes of Empowerment," *Group and Organization Management* 24 (1999), pp. 71–91; Y. Melhem, "The Antecedents of Customer-Contact Employees' Empowerment," *Employee Relations* 26, no. 1/2 (2004), pp. 72–93.

52. B.J. Niehoff et al., "The Influence of Empowerment and Job Enrichment on Employee Loyalty in a Downsizing Environment," *Group and Organization Management* 26 (March 2001), pp. 93–113; J. Yoon, "The Role of Structure and Motivation for Workplace Empowerment: The Case of Korean Employees," Social *Psychology Quarterly* 64 (June 2001), pp. 195–206; T.D. Wall, J.L. Cordery, and C.W. Clegg, "Empowerment, Performance, and Operational Uncertainty: A Theoretical Integration," *Applied Psychology: An International Review* 51 (2002), pp. 146–69.

53. R. Semler, *The Seven-Day Weekend* (London: Century, 2003), p. 61. The organizational factors affecting empowerment are discussed in G.M. Spreitzer, "Social Structural Characteristics of Psychological Empowerment," *Academy of Management Journal* 39 (April 1996), pp. 483–504; J. Godard, "High Performance and the Transformation of Work? The Implications of Alternative Work Practices for the Experience and Outcomes of Work," *Industrial & Labor Relations Review* 54 (July 2001), pp. 776–805; and P.A. Miller, P. Goddard, and H.K. Spence Laschinger, "Evaluating Physical Therapists' Perception of Empowerment Using Kanter's Theory of Structural Power in Organizations," *Physical Therapy* 81 (December 2001), pp. 1880–88.

54. D. Furlonger, "Best Company to Work For," *Financial Mail* (South Africa), 30 September 2005, p. 20; A. Hogg, "John Gomersall: CEO, PPC" (South Africa, 26 October 2005), http://www.money-web.co.za/specials/corp_gov/509689.htm (accessed 4 January 2006); Pretoria Portland Cement, "PPC Wins Best Company to Work for 2005," *Meropa Communications* news release (Sandton, South Africa: 29 September 2005). Information was also collected from the 2003, 2004, and 2005 annual reports of Pretoria Portland Cement.

55. J.-C. Chebat and P. Kollias, "The Impact of Empowerment on Customer Contact Employees' Role in Service Organizations," *Journal of Service Research* 3 (August 2000), pp. 66–81; H.K.S. Laschinger, J. Finegan, and J. Shamian, "The Impact of Workplace Empowerment, Organizational Trust on Staff Nurses' Work Satisfaction and Organizational Commitment," *Health Care Management Review* 26 (Summer 2001), pp. 7–23.

56. D. Czurak, "Cool Places to Work... Universal Insurance: Where You Rate Yourself," *Grand Rapids Business Journal*, 29 August 2005, p. E8; "Bosses Love Team Workers," *Lancashire Evening Post* (U.K.), 25 May 2006.

57. C.P. Neck and C.C. Manz, "Thought Self-Leadership: The Impact of Mental Strategies Training on Employee Cognition, Behavior, and Affect," *Journal of Organizational Behavior* 17 (1996), pp. 445–67.

58. C.C. Manz, "Self-Leadership: Toward an Expanded Theory of Self-Influence Processes in Organizations," *Academy of Management Review* 11 (1986), pp. 585–600; C.C. Manz and C. Neck, *Mastering Self-Leadership*, 3rd ed. (Upper Saddle River, NJ: Prentice Hall, 2004).

59. O.J. Strickland and M. Galimba, "Managing Time: The Effects of Personal Goal Setting on Resource Allocation Strategy and Task Performance," *Journal of Psychology* 135 (July 2001), pp. 357–67.

60. R.M. Duncan and J.A. Cheyne, "Incidence and Functions of Self-Reported Private Speech in Young Adults: A Self-Verbalization Questionnaire," *Canadian Journal of Behavioral Science* 31 (April 1999), pp. 133–36.

61. J.E. Driscoll, C. Copper, and A. Moran, "Does Mental Practice Enhance Performance?" *Journal of Applied Psychology* 79 (1994), pp. 481–92; C.P. Neck, G.L. Stewart, and C.C. Manz, "Thought Self-Leadership as a Framework for Enhancing the Performance of Performance Appraisers," *Journal of Applied Behavioral Science* 31 (September 1995), pp. 278–302. Some research separates mental imagery from mental practice, whereas most studies combine both into one concept.

62. A. Joyce, "Office Parks: Re-Energize to Get through the Blahs," *Washington Post*, 28 August 2005, p. F05.

63. A. Wrzesniewski and J.E. Dutton, "Crafting a Job: Revisioning Employees as Active Crafters of Their Work," *Academy of Management Review* 26 (April 2001). pp. 179–201.

64. M.I. Bopp, S.J. Glynn, and R.A. Henning, *Self-Management of Performance Feedback during Computer-Based Work by Individuals and Two-Person Work Teams.* Paper presented at the APA-NIOSH conference (March 1999).

65. A.W. Logue, *Self-Control: Waiting until Tomorrow for What You Want Today* (Englewood Cliffs, NJ: Prentice-Hall, 1995).

66. P. Mannion, "Never Lose Focus," *Electronic Engineering Times*, 30 May 2005, p. 1.

67. Neck and Manz, "Thought Self-Leadership: The Impact of Mental Strategies Training on Employee Cognition, Behavior, and Affect"; A.M. Saks and B.E. Ashforth, "Proactive Socialization and Behavioral Self-Management," *Journal of Vocational Behavior* 48 (1996), pp. 301–23; L. Morin and G. Latham, "The Effect of Mental Practice and Goal Setting as a Transfer of Training Intervention on Supervisors' Self-Efficacy and Communication Skills: An Exploratory Study," *Applied Psychology: An International Review* 49 (July 2000), pp. 566–78; J.S. Hickman and E.S. Geller, "A Safety Self-Management Intervention

for Mining Operations," *Journal of Safety Research* 34 (2003), pp. 299–308.

68. S. Ming and G.L. Martin, "Single-Subject Evaluation of a Self-Talk Package for Improving Figure Skating Performance," *Sport Psychologist* 10 (1996), pp. 227–38; D. Landin and E.P. Hebert, "The Influence of Self-Talk on the Performance of Skilled Female Tennis Players," *Journal of Applied Sport Psychology* 11 (September 1999), pp. 263–82; K.E. Thiese and S. Huddleston, "The Use of Psychological Skills by Female Collegiate Swimmers," *Journal of Sport Behavior* (December 1999), pp. 602–10; J. Bauman, "The Gold Medal Mind," *Psychology Today* 33 (May 2000), pp. 62–69; A. Papaioannou et al., "Combined Effect of Goal Setting and Self-Talk in Performance of a Soccer-Shooting Task," *Perceptual and Motor Skills* 98, no. 1 (February 2004), pp. 89–99.

69. J. Houghton, D. et al., "The Relationship between Self Leadership and Personality: A Comparison of Hierarchical Factor Structures," *Journal of Managerial Psychology* 19, no. 4 (2004), pp. 427–41. For discussion of constructive thought patterns in the context of organizations, see J. Godwin, C.P. Neck, and J. Houghton, "The Impact of Thought Self-Leadership on Individual Goal Performance: A Cognitive Perspective," *Journal of Management Development* 18 (1999), pp. 153–69.

CHAPTER 7

1. E. Frauenheim, "For Developers, It's Not All Fun and Games," *CNET News.com*, 18 November 2004; A. Pham, "Video Game Programmers Get Little Time to Play," *Houston Chronicle*, 21 November 2004, p. 6; N. Davidson, "Vancouver Developer Looks to Make Video Games without Burning Out Staff," *Canadian Press*, 21 February 2006; N. Wong, "Exclusive: Nicole Wong Reveals Identity of EA Spouse," *Mercury News* (San Jose), 25 April 2006.

2. T. Haratani, "Job Stress Trends in Japan," in *Job Stress Trends in East Asia (Proceedings of the First East Asia Job Stress Meeting)*, ed. A. Tsutsumi (Tokyo: Waseda University, 8 January 2000), pp. 4–10; "New Survey: Americans Stressed More Than Ever," *PR Newswire*, 26 June 2003; "Hong Kong People Still Most Stressed in Asia–Survey," *Reuters News*, 2 November 2004; E. Galinsky et al., *Overwork in America: When the Way We Work Becomes Too Much* (New York: Families and Work Institute, March 2005);

M. Mandel, "The Real Reasons You're Working So Hard . . . And What You Can Do about It," *BusinessWeek*, 3 October 2005, p. 60; Mind, *Stress and Mental Health in the Workplace* (London: Mind, May 2005); D. Passmore, "We're All Sick of Work," *Sunday Mail* (Brisbane), 27 November 2005, p. 45.

3. J.C. Quick et al., *Preventive Stress Management in Organizations* (Washington, DC: American Psychological Association, 1997), pp. 3–4; R.S. DeFrank and J.M. Ivancevich, "Stress on the Job: An Executive Update," *Academy of Management Executive* 12 (August 1998), pp. 55–66.

4. Quick et al., *Preventive Stress Management in Organizations*, pp. 5–6; B.L. Simmons and D.L. Nelson, "Eustress at Work: The Relationship between Hope and Health in Hospital Nurses," *Health Care Management Review* 26, no. 4 (October 2001), p. 7ff.

5. H. Selye, *Stress without Distress* (Philadelphia: J.B. Lippincott, 1974).

6. S.E. Taylor, R.L. Repetti, and T. Seeman, "Health Psychology: What Is an Unhealthy Environment and How Does It Get under the Skin?" *Annual Review of Psychology* 48 (1997), pp. 411–47.

7. K. Danna and R.W. Griffin, "Health and Well-Being in the Workplace: A Review and Synthesis of the Literature," *Journal of Management* (Spring 1999), pp. 357–84.

8. N. Wager, G. Fieldman, and T. Hussey, "The Effect on Ambulatory Blood Pressure of Working under Favourably and Unfavourably Perceived Supervisors," *Occupational and Environmental Medicine* 60, no. 7 (1 July 2003), pp. 468–74. For further details on the stressful effects of bad bosses, see E.K. Kelloway et al., "Poor Leadership," in *Handbook of Workplace Stress*, ed. J. Barling, E.K. Kelloway, and M. Frone (Thousand Oaks, CA: Sage, 2005), pp. 89–112.

9. Bureau of Labor Statistics, "National Census of Fatal Occupational Injuries in 2004," U.S. Department of Labor news release (Washington, DC: 25 August 2005); N. Paton, "Nurses on the Verge of Breakdown," *Occupational Health*, April 2006, p. 4.

10. This is a slight variation of the definition in the Quebec antiharassment legislation. See www.cnt.gouv.qc.ca. For related definitions and discussion of workplace incivility, see H. Cowiea et al., "Measuring Workplace Bullying," *Aggression and Violent Behavior* 7 (2002), pp. 33–51;

C.M. Pearson and C.L. Porath, "On the Nature, Consequences, and Remedies of Workplace Incivility: No Time for 'Nice'? Think Again," *Academy of Management Executive* 19, no. 1 (February 2005), pp. 7–18.

11. Pearson and Porath, "On the Nature, Consequences, and Remedies of Workplace Incivility"; J. Przybys, "How Rude!" *Las Vegas Review-Journal*, 25 April 2006, p. 1E.

12. "HR Bullied Just as Much as Anyone Else," *Personnel Today*, November 2005, p. 3; T. Goldenberg, "Thousands of Workers Intimidated on Job: Study," *Montreal Gazette*, 11 June 2005, p. A9; S. Toomey, "Bullying Alive and Kicking," *The Australian*, 16 July 2005, p. 9; V. Raman, "One Worker in Three Has Experienced Bullying," *National Business Review* (New Zealand), 10 March 2006.

13. H.-H. Pai, "'Our Eyes Have Been Opened by the Abuse'" *The Guardian* (London), 29 April 2006, p. 2.

14. V. Schultz, "Reconceptualizing Sexual Harassment," *Yale Law Journal* 107 (April 1998), pp. 1683–1805; M. Rotundo, D.-H. Nguyen, and P.R. Sackett, "A Meta-Analytic Review of Gender Differences in Perceptions of Sexual Harassment," *Journal of Applied Psychology* 86 (October 2001), pp. 914–922.

15. E.K. Kelloway and J. Barling, "Job Characteristics, Role Stress, and Mental Health," *Journal of Occupational Psychology* 64 (1991), pp. 291–304; M. Siegall and L.L. Cummings, "Stress and Organizational Role Conflict," *Genetic, Social, and General Psychology Monographs* 12 (1995), pp. 65–95; J. Lait and J.E. Wallace, "Stress at Work: A Study of Organizational-Professional Conflict and Unmet Expectations," *Relations Industrielles* 57, no. 3 (Summer 2002), pp. 463–87; E. Grunfeld et al., "Job Stress and Job Satisfaction of Cancer Care Workers," *Psycho-Oncology* 14, no. 1 (May 2005), pp. 61–69.

16. A.M. Saks and B.E. Ashforth, "Proactive Socialization and Behavioral Self-Management," *Journal of Vocational Behavior* 48 (1996), pp. 301–23; A. Nygaard and R. Dahlstrom, "Role Stress and Effectiveness in Horizontal Alliances," *Journal of Marketing* 66 (April 2002), pp. 61–82.

17. Past predictions of future work hours are described in B.K. Hunnicutt, *Kellogg's Six-Hour Day* (Philadelphia: Temple University Press, 1996).

18. C.B. Meek, "The Dark Side of Japanese Management in the 1990s: Karoshi

and Ijime in the Japanese Workplace," *Journal of Managerial Psychology* 19, no. 3 (2004), pp. 312–31; J. Shi, "Beijing's High Flyers Dying to Get Ahead," *South China Morning Post* (Hong Kong), 8 October 2005, p. 8; N. You, "Mantra: Work for Life, Rather Than Live to Work," *China Daily*, 26 March 2005.

19. R. Drago, D. Black, and M. Wooden, *The Persistence of Long Work Hours*, Melbourne Institute Working Paper Series (Melbourne: Melbourne Institute of Applied Economic and Social Research, University of Melbourne, August 2005).

20. L. Wahyudi S., "'Traffic Congestion Makes Me Crazy," *Jakarta Post*, 18 March 2003. Traffic congestion is linked to stress in G.W. Evans, R.E. Wener, and D. Phillips, "The Morning Rush Hour: Predictability and Commuter Stress," *Environment and Behavior* 34 (July 2002), pp. 521–30.

21. F. Kittell et al., "Job Conditions and Fibrinogen in 14,226 Belgian Workers: The Belstress Study," *European Heart Journal* 23 (2002), pp. 1841–48; S.K. Parker, "Longitudinal Effects of Lean Production on Employee Outcomes and the Mediating Role of Work Characteristics," *Journal of Applied Psychology* 88, no. 4 (2003), pp. 620–34.

22. R.J. Burke and C.L. Cooper, *The Organization in Crisis: Downsizing, Restructuring, and Privatization* (Oxford, UK: Blackwell, 2000); M. Kivimaki et al., "Factors Underlying the Effect of Organizational Downsizing on Health of Employees: Longitudinal Cohort Study," *British Medical Journal* 320 (8 April 2000), pp. 971–75; M. Sverke, J. Hellgren, and K. N"swall, "No Security: A Meta-Analysis and Review of Job Insecurity and Its Consequences," *Journal of Occupational Health Psychology* 7 (July 2002), pp. 242–64; R.J. Burke, "Correlates of Nursing Staff Survivor Responses to Hospital Restructuring and Downsizing," *Health Care Manager* 24, no. 2 (2005), pp. 141–49.

23. L.T. Eby et al., "Work and Family Research in IO/OB: Content Analysis and Review of the Literature (1980–2002)," *Journal of Vocational Behavior* 66, no. 1 (2005), pp. 124–97.

24. N. Chesley, "Blurring Boundaries? Linking Technology Use, Spillover, Individual Distress, and Family Satisfaction," *Journal of Marriage and Family* 67, no. 5 (2005), pp. 1237–48; T. Taylor, "Hard-Working Canadians Find It Tough to Disconnect," *Calgary Herald*, 18 May 2005,

p. A10; R. Parloff, "Secrets of Greatness-How I Work: Amy W. Schulman," *Fortune*, 20 March 2006, p. 66.

25. C. Higgins and L. Duxbury, *The 2001 National Work-Life Conflict Study: Report One, Final Report* (Ottawa: Health Canada, March 2002); M. Shields, "Shift Work and Health," *Health Reports (Statistics Canada)* 13 (Spring 2002), pp. 11–34.

26. E.K. Kelloway, B.H. Gottlieb, and L. Barham, "The Source, Nature, and Direction of Work and Family Conflict: A Longitudinal Investigation," *Journal of Occupational Health Psychology* 4 (October 1999), pp. 337–46; C.M. Brotheridge and R.T. Lee, "Impact of Work-Family Interference on General Well-Being: A Replication and Extension," *International Journal of Stress Management* 12, no. 3 (2005), pp. 203-21.

27. A.S. Wharton and R.J. Erickson, "Managing Emotions on the Job and at Home: Understanding the Consequences of Multiple Emotional Roles," *Academy of Management Review* (1993), pp. 457–86.

28. B. Keil, "The 10 Most Stressful Jobs in NYC," *New York Post*, 6 April 1999, p. 50; A. Smith et al., *The Scale of Occupational Stress: A Further Analysis of the Impact of Demographic Factors and Type of Job* (Sudbury, Suffolk: United Kingdom, Health & Safety Executive, 2000).

29. J.L. Hernandez, "What's the Buzz in Schuyler? Just Ask Beekeeper Finster," *Observer-Dispatch* (Utica, New York), 23 June 2003.

30. S.J. Havlovic and J.P. Keenen, "Coping with Work Stress: The Influence of Individual Differences; Handbook on Job Stress [Special Issue]," *Journal of Social Behavior and Personality* 6 (1991), pp. 199–212.

31. S.C. Segerstrom et al., "Optimism Is Associated with Mood, Coping, and Immune Change in Response to Stress," *Journal of Personality & Social Psychology* 74 (June 1998), pp. 1646–55; S.M. Jex et al., "The Impact of Self-Efficacy on Stressor-Strain Relations: Coping Style as an Explanatory Mechanism," *Journal of Applied Psychology* 86 (2001), pp. 401–9.

32. S.S. Luthar, D. Cicchetti, and B. Becker, "The Construct of Resilience: A Critical Evaluation and Guidelines for Future Work," *Child Development* 71, no. 3 (May–June 2000), pp. 543–62; F. Luthans, "The Need for and Meaning of Positive Organizational Behavior," *Journal of Organizational Behavior* 23 (2002), pp. 695–706; G.A. Bonanno, "Loss, Trauma, and Human

Resilience: Have We Underestimated the Human Capacity to Thrive after Extremely Aversive Events?" *American Psychologist* 59, no. 1 (2004), pp. 20–28.

33. K.M. Connor and J.R.T. Davidson, "Development of a New Resilience Scale: The Connor–Davidson Resilience Scale (CD-RISC)," *Depression and Anxiety* 18, no. 2 (2003), pp. 76–82; M.M. Tugade, B.L. Fredrickson, and L. Feldman Barrett, "Psychological Resilience and Positive Emotional Granularity: Examining the Benefits of Positive Emotions on Coping and Health," *Journal of Personality* 72, no. 6 (2004), pp. 1161-90; L. Campbell-Sills, S.L. Cohan, and M.B. Stein, "Relationship of Resilience to Personality, Coping, and Psychiatric Symptoms in Young Adults," *Behaviour Research and Therapy*, in press (2006).

34. M. Beasley, T. Thompson, and J. Davidson, "Resilience in Response to Life Stress: The Effects of Coping Style and Cognitive Hardiness," *Personality and Individual Differences* 34, no. 1 (2003), pp. 77–95; I. Tsaousis and I. Nikolaou, "Exploring the Relationship of Emotional Intelligence with Physical and Psychological Health Functioning," *Stress and Health* 21, no. 2 (2005), pp. 77–86.

35. Y. Kim and L. Seidlitz, "Spirituality Moderates the Effect of Stress on Emotional and Physical Adjustment," *Personality and Individual Differences* 32, no. 8 (June 2002), pp. 1377–90; G.E. Richardson, "The Metatheory of Resilience and Resiliency," *Journal of Clinical Psychology* 58, no. 3 (2002), pp. 307–21.

36. J.T. Spence, and A.S. Robbins, "Workaholism: Definition, Measurement, and Preliminary Results," *Journal of Personality Assessment* 58 (1992), pp. 160–78; R.J. Burke, "Workaholism in Organizations: Psychological and Physical Well-Being Consequences," *Stress Medicine* 16, no. 1 (2000), pp. 11–16; I. Harpaz and R. Snir, "Workaholism: Its Definition and Nature," *Human Relations* 56 (2003), pp. 291–319; R.J. Burke, A.M. Richardson, and M. Martinussen, "Workaholism among Norwegian Senior Managers: New Research Directions," *International Journal of Management* 21, no. 4 (December 2004), pp. 415–26.

37. R.J. Burke and G. MacDermid, "Are Workaholics Job Satisfied and Successful in Their Careers?" *Career Development International* 4 (1999), pp. 277–82; R.J. Burke and S. Matthiesen, "Short Communication: Workaholism among Norwegian

Journalists: Antecedents and Consequences," *Stress and Health* 20, no. 5 (2004), pp. 301–8.

38. D. Ganster, M. Fox, and D. Dwyer, "Explaining Employees' Health Care Costs: A Prospective Examination of Stressful Job Demands, Personal Control, and Physiological Reactivity," *Journal of Applied Psychology* 86 (May 2001), pp. 954–64.

39. M. Kivimaki et al., "Work Stress and Risk of Cardiovascular Mortality: Prospective Cohort Study of Industrial Employees," *British Medical Journal* 325 (19 October 2002), pp. 857–60; "Banishing the Blues Could Cut the Chances of Cancer," *The Scotsman* (23 June 2003); I. Hajjar and T.A. Kotchen, "Trends in Prevalence, Awareness, Treatment, and Control of Hypertension in the United States, 1988–2000," *JAMA: Journal of the American Medical Association* 290 (9 July 2003), pp. 199–206; A. Rosengren et al., "Association of Psychosocial Risk Factors with Risk of Acute Myocardial Infarction in 11,119 Cases and 13,648 Controls from 52 Countries (the Interheart Study): Case–Control Study," *The Lancet* 364, no. 9438 (11 September 2004), pp. 953–62; S. Yusuf et al., "Effect of Potentially Modifiable Risk Factors Associated with Myocardial Infarction in 52 Countries (the Interheart Study): Case–Control Study," *The Lancet* 364, no. 9438 (11 September 2004), pp. 937–52.

40. R.C. Kessler, "The Effects of Stressful Life Events on Depression," *Annual Review of Psychology* 48 (1997), pp. 191–214; M. Jamal and V.V. Baba, "Job Stress and Burnout among Canadian Managers and Nurses: An Empirical Examination," *Canadian Journal of Public Health* 91, no. 6 (November-December 2000). pp. 454–58.

41. C. Maslach, W.B. Schaufeli, and M.P. Leiter, "Job Burnout," *Annual Review of Psychology* 52 (2001), pp. 397–422; J.R.B. Halbesleben and M.R. Buckley, "Burnout in Organizational Life," *Journal of Management* 30, no. 6 (2004), pp. 859–79.

42. M. Jamal, "Job Stress and Job Performance Controversy: An Empirical Assessment," *Organizational Behavior and Human Performance* 33 (1984), pp. 1–21; G. Keinan, "Decision Making under Stress: Scanning of Alternatives under Controllable and Uncontrollable Threats," *Journal of Personality and Social Psychology* 52 (1987), pp. 638–44. The positive effects of moderate stress are reported in L. Van Dyne, K.A. Jehn, and A. Cummings, "Differential Effects of Strain on Two

Forms of Work Performance: Individual Employee Sales and Creativity," *Journal of Organizational Behavior* 23, no. 1 (2002), pp. 57–74; E. Chajut and D. Algom, "Selective Attention Improves under Stress: Implications for Theories of Social Cognition," *Journal of Personality and Social Psychology* 85, no. 2 (2003), pp. 231–48.

43. R.D. Hackett and P. Bycio, "An Evaluation of Employee Absenteeism as a Coping Mechanism among Hospital Nurses," *Journal of Occupational & Organizational Psychology* 69 (December 1996), pp. 327–38; A. Vaananen et al., "Job Characteristics, Physical and Psychological Symptoms, and Social Support as Antecedents of Sickness Absence among Men and Women in the Private Industrial Sector," *Social Science & Medicine* 57, no. 5 (September 2003), pp. 807–24; L. Tourigny, V.V. Baba, and T.R. Lituchy, "Job Burnout among Airline Employees in Japan: A Study of the Buffering Effects of Absence and Supervisory Support," *International Journal of Cross Cultural Management* 5, no. 1 (April 2005), pp. 67–85.

44. L. Greenburg and J. Barling, "Predicting Employee Aggression against Coworkers, Subordinates, and Supervisors: The Roles of Person Behaviors and Perceived Workplace Factors," *Journal of Organizational Behavior* 20 (1999), pp. 897–913; H. Steensma, "Violence in the Workplace: The Explanatory Strength of Social (In)Justice Theories," in *The Justice Motive in Everyday Life*, ed. M. Ross and D.T. Miller (New York: Cambridge University Press, 2002), pp. 149–67; J.D. Leck, "Violence in the Canadian Workplace," *Journal of the American Academy of Business* 7, no. 2 (September 2005), pp. 308–15.

45. Siegall and Cummings, "Stress and Organizational Role Conflict."

46. "Employee Wellness," *Canadian HR Reporter*, 23 February 2004, pp. 9–12.

47. J.L. Howard, "Workplace Violence in Organizations: An Exploratory Study of Organizational Prevention Techniques," *Employee Responsibilities and Rights Journal* 13 (June 2001), pp. 57–75.

48. C.R. Cunningham and S.S. Murray, "Two Executives, One Career," *Harvard Business Review* 83, no. 2 (February 2005), pp. 125–31.

49. C. Reister, "Schedule Flexing," *Grand Rapids Press* (Michigan), 11 September 2005, p. H1; K. Rives, "Deloitte Offers up to 5 Years Away," *News & Observer*

(Raleigh, North Carolina), 10 July 2005, p. E1.

50. S.R. Madsen, "The Effects of Home-Based Teleworking on Work-Family Conflict," *Human Resource Development Quarterly* 14, no. 1 (2003), pp. 35–58.

51. B. Pettit and J. Hook, "The Structure of Women's Employment in Comparative Perspective," *Social Forces* 84, no. 2 (December 2005), pp. 779–801.

52. M. Secret, "Parenting in the Workplace: Child Care Options for Consideration," *The Journal of Applied Behavioral Science* 41, no. 3 (September 2005), pp. 326–47.

53. M. Blair-Loy and A.S. Wharton, "Employees' Use of Work-Family Policies and the Workplace Social Context," *Social Forces* 80 (March 2002), pp. 813–45; M. Jackson, "Managers Measured by Charges' Work-Life Accountability Programs Let Firms Calculate Progress," *Boston Globe*, 2 February 2003, p. G1.

54. "Office Stress? Just Sleep on It," *Western Mail* (Cardiff, Wales), 2 November 2004, p. 12; K. Redford, "Is It Time to Get Bossy?" *Employee Benefits* (U.K.), 7 December 2005, p. S25; J. Saranow, "Anybody Want to Take a Nap?" *The Wall Street Journal*, 24 January 2005, p. R5.

55. S. Overman, "Sabbaticals Benefit Companies as Well as Employees," *Employee Benefit News*, 15 April 2006.

56. M. Waung, "The Effects of Self-Regulatory Coping Orientation on Newcomer Adjustment and Job Survival," *Personnel Psychology* 48 (1995), pp. 633–50; Saks and Ashforth, "Proactive Socialization and Behavioral Self-Management."

57. S. Moreland, "Strike Up Creativity," *Crain's Cleveland Business*, 14 April 2003. p. 3.

58. W.M. Ensel and N. Lin, "Physical Fitness and the Stress Process," *Journal of Community Psychology* 32, no. 1 (January 2004), pp. 81–101.

59. S. Armour, "Rising Job Stress Could Affect Bottom Line," *USA Today*, 29 July 2003; V.A. Barnes, F.A. Treiber, and M.H. Johnson, "Impact of Transcendental Meditation on Ambulatory Blood Pressure in African-American Adolescents," *American Journal of Hypertension* 17, no. 4 (2004), pp. 366–69; M.S. Lee et al., "Effects of Qi-Training on Anxiety and Plasma Concentrations of Cortisol, Acth, and Aldosterone: A Randomized Placebo-Controlled Pilot Study," *Stress and Health* 20, no. 5 (2004), pp. 243–48; P. Manikonda

et al., "Influence of Non-Pharmacological Treatment (Contemplative Meditation and Breathing Technique) on Stress Induced Hypertension—A Randomized Controlled Study," *American Journal of Hypertension* 18, no. 5, Supplement 1 (2005), pp. A89–A90.

60. L. Chordes, "Here's to Your Health," *Best's Review*, April 2006, pp. 52–55; D. Gill, "Get Healthy . . . Or Else," *Inc.*, April 2006, pp. 35–38; J. Wojcik, "Pitney Bowes Tool Encourages Workers to Live Healthier," *Business Insurance*, 3 April 2006, p. 4.

61. T. Rotarius, A. Liberman, and J.S. Liberman, "Employee Assistance Programs: A Prevention and Treatment Prescription for Problems in Health Care Organizations," *Health Care Manager* 19 (September 2000), pp. 24–31; J.J.L. van der Klink et al., "The Benefits of Interventions for Work-Related Stress," *American Journal of Public Health* 91 (February 2001), pp. 270–76.

62. S.E. Taylor et al., "Biobehavioral Responses to Stress in Females: Tend-and-Befriend, Not Fight-or-Flight," *Psychological Review* 107, no. 3 (July 2000), pp. 411–29; R. Eisler and D.S. Levine, "Nurture, Nature, and Caring: We Are Not Prisoners of Our Genes," *Brain and Mind* 3 (2002), pp. 9–52; J.T. Deelstra et al., "Receiving Instrumental Support at Work: When Help Is Not Welcome," *Journal of Applied Psychology* 88, no. 2 (2003), pp. 324–31.

63. J.S. House, *Work Stress and Social Support* (Reading, MA: Addison-Wesley, 1981).

64. S. Schachter, *The Psychology of Affiliation* (Stanford, CA: Stanford University Press, 1959).

CHAPTER 8

1. P. Withers, "Few Rules Rule," *B.C. Business,* January 2002, p. 24; G. Huston, I. Wilkinson, and D. Kellogg, "Dare to Be Great," *B.C. Business*, May 2004, pp. 28–29; P. Withers and L. Kloet, "The Best Companies to Work for in B.C.," *B C. Business*, December 2004, pp. 37–53; M. Andrews, "How to Make Robot Bees, and Other Sound Secrets," *National Post*, 5 March 2005, p. TO32; P. Wilson, "Radical Entertainment to Hire Staff, Expand Studio," *Vancouver Sun*, 6 May 2005, p. C3.

2. F.A. Shull Jr., A.L. Delbecq, and L.L. Cummings, *Organizational Decision Making* (New York: McGraw-Hill, 1970), p. 31.

3. R.E. Nisbett, *The Geography of Thought: How Asians and Westerners Think Differently—and Why* (New York: Free Press, 2003); D. Baltzly, "Stoicism" (Stanford Encyclopedia of Philosophy, 2004), http://plato.stanford.edu/entries/stoicism/ (accessed 8 March 2005); R. Hanna, "Kant's Theory of Judgment" (Stanford Encyclopedia of Philosophy, 2004), http://plato.stanford.edu/entries/kant-judgment/ (accessed 12 March 2005).

4. This model is adapted from several sources, including H.A. Simon, *The New Science of Management Decision* (New York: Harper & Row, 1960); H. Mintzberg, D. Raisinghani, and A. Théorét, "The Structure of 'Unstructured' Decision Processes," *Administrative Science Quarterly* 21 (1976), pp. 246–75; W.C. Wedley and R. H.G. Field, "A Predecision Support System," *Academy of Management Review* 9 (1984), pp. 696–703.

5. P.F. Drucker, *The Practice of Management* (New York: Harper & Brothers, 1954), pp. 353–57; B.M. Bass, *Organizational Decision Making* (Homewood, IL: Irwin, 1983), Chapter 3.

6. L.R. Beach and T.R. Mitchell, "A Contingency Model for the Selection of Decision Strategies," *Academy of Management Review* 3 (1978), pp. 439–49; I.L. Janis, *Crucial Decisions* (New York: The Free Press, 1989), pp. 35–37; W. Zhongtuo, "Meta-Decision Making: Concepts and Paradigm," *Systematic Practice and Action Research* 13, no. 1 (February 2000), pp. 111–15.

7. J.G. March and H.A. Simon, *Organizations* (New York: John Wiley & Sons, 1958).

8. N. Schwarz, "Social Judgment and Attitudes: Warmer, More Social, and Less Conscious," *European Journal of Social Psychology* 30 (2000), pp. 149–76; N.M. Ashkanasy and C.E.J. Hartel, "Managing Emotions in Decision Making," in *Managing Emotions in the Workplace*, ed. N.M. Ashkanasy, W.J. Zerbe, and C.E.J. Hartel (Armonk, NY: M.E. Sharpe, 2002); S. Maitlis and H. Ozcelik, "Toxic Decision Processes: A Study of Emotion and Organizational Decision Making," *Organization Science* 15, no. 4 (July–August 2004), pp. 375–93.

9. A. Howard, "Opinion," *Computing* (8 July 1999), p. 18.

10. A.R. Damasio, *Descartes' Error: Emotion, Reason, and the Human Brain* (New York: Putnam Sons, 1994); P. Winkielman and K.C. Berridge, "Unconscious Emotion," *Current Directions in Psychological Science* 13, no. 3 (2004), pp. 120–23; A. Bechara and A.R. Damasio, "The Somatic Marker Hypothesis: A Neural Theory of Economic Decision," *Games and Economic Behavior* 52, no. 2 (2005), pp. 336–72.

11. T.K. Das and B.S. Teng, "Cognitive Biases and Strategic Decision Processes: An Integrative Perspective," *Journal of Management Studies* 36, no. 6 (November 1999), pp. 757–78; P. Bijttebier, H. Vertommen, and G.V. Steene, "Assessment of Cognitive Coping Styles: A Closer Look at Situation-Response Inventories," *Clinical Psychology Review* 21, no. 1 (2001), pp. 85–104; P.C. Nutt, "Expanding the Search for Alternatives during Strategic Decision Making," *Academy of Management Executive* 18, no. 4 (November 2004), pp. 13–28.

12. J. Brandtstadter, A. Voss, and K. Rothermund, "Perception of Danger Signals: The Role of Control," *Experimental Psychology* 51, no. 1 (2004), pp. 24–32; M. Hock and H.W. Krohne, "Coping with Threat and Memory for Ambiguous Information: Testing the Repressive Discontinuity Hypothesis," *Emotion* 4, no. 1 (2004), pp. 65–86.

13. P.C. Nutt, *Why Decisions Fail* (San Francisco: Berrett-Koehler, 2002); S. Finkelstein, *Why Smart Executives Fail* (New York: Viking, 2003).

14. E. Witte, "Field Research on Complex Decision-Making Processes—the Phase Theorum," *International Studies of Management and Organization* (1972), pp. 156–82; J.A. Bargh and T.L. Chartrand, "The Unbearable Automaticity of Being," *American Psychologist* 54, no. 7 (July 1999), pp. 462–79.

15. R. Rothenberg, "Ram Charan: The Thought Leader Interview," *strategy + business* (Fall 2004).

16. H.A. Simon, *Administrative Behavior*, 2nd ed. (New York: The Free Press, 1957); H.A. Simon, "Rational Decision Making in Business Organizations," *American Economic Review* 69, no. 4 (September 1979), pp. 493–513.

17. D. Sandahl and C. Hewes, "Decision Making at Digital Speed," *Pharmaceutical Executive* 21 (August 2001), p. 62.

18. Simon, Administrative *Behavior*, pp. xxv, 80–84.

19. P.O. Soelberg, "Unprogrammed Decision Making," *Industrial Management Review* 8 (1967), pp. 19–29; J.E. Russo, V.H. Medvec, and M.G. Meloy, "The Distortion of Information during Decisions," *Organizational Behavior & Human Decision Processes* 66 (1996), pp. 102–10.

20. A.L. Brownstein, "Biased Predecision Processing," *Psychological Bulletin 129, no.* 4 (2003), pp. 545–68.

21. F. Phillips, "The Distortion of Criteria after Decision Making," *Organizational Behavior and Human Decision Processes* 88 (2002), pp. 769–84.

22. H.A. Simon, "Rational Choice and the Structure of Environments," *Psychological Review* 63 (1956), pp. 129–38; H. Schwartz, "Herbert Simon and Behavioral Economics," *Journal of Socio-Economics* 31 (2002), pp. 181–89.

23. P.C. Nutt, "Search during Decision Making," *European Journal of Operational Research* 160 (2005), pp. 851–76.

24. J.P. Forgas, "Affective Intelligence: Toward Understanding the Role of Affect in Social Thinking and Behavior," in *Emotional Intelligence in Everyday Life*, ed. J.V. Ciarrochi, J.P. Forgas, and J.D. Mayer (New York: Psychology Press, 2001), pp. 46–65; J.P. Forgas and J.M. George, "Affective Influences on Judgments and Behavior in Organizations: An Information Processing Perspective," *Organizational Behavior and Human Decision Processes* 86 (September 2001), pp. 3–34; G. Loewenstein and J.S. Lerner, "The Role of Affect in Decision Making," in *Handbook of Affective Sciences*, ed. R.J. Davidson, K.R. Scherer, and H.H. Goldsmith (New York: Oxford University Press, 2003), pp. 619–42; J.S. Lerner, D.A. Small, and G. Loewenstein, "Heart Strings and Purse Strings: Carryover Effects of Emotions on Economic Decisions," *Psychological Science* 15, no. 5 (2004), pp. 337–41.

25. M.T. Pham, "The Logic of Feeling," *Journal of Consumer Psychology* 14 (September 2004), pp. 360–69; N. Schwarz, "Metacognitive Experiences in Consumer Judgment and Decision Making," *Journal of Consumer Psychology* 14 (September 2004), pp. 332–49.

26. L. Sjöberg, "Intuitive vs. Analytical Decision Making: Which Is Preferred?" *Scandinavian Journal of Management* 19 (2003), pp. 17–29.

27. G. Klein, *Intuition at Work* (New York: Currency/Doubleday, 2003), pp. 3–7.

28. W.H. Agor, "The Logic of Intuition," *Organizational Dynamics* (Winter 1986), pp. 5–18; H.A. Simon, "Making Management Decisions: The Role of Intuition and Emotion," *Academy of Management Executive* (February 1987), pp. 57–64; O. Behling and N.L. Eckel, "Making Sense out of Intuition," *Academy of Management Executive* 5 (February 1991), pp. 46–54.

29. M.D. Lieberman, "Intuition: A Social Cognitive Neuroscience Approach," *Psychological Bulletin* 126 (2000), pp. 109–37; Klein, *Intuition at Work*; E. Dane and M.G. Pratt, "Intuition: Its Boundaries and Role in Organizational Decision Making," in *Academy of Management Best Papers Proceedings* (New Orleans, 2004), pp. A1–A6.

30. Klein, *Intuition at Work*, pp. 12–13, 16–17.

31. Y. Ganzach, A.H. Kluger, and N. Klayman, "Making Decisions from an Interview: Expert Measurement and Mechanical Combination," *Personnel Psychology* 53 (Spring 2000), pp. 1–20; A.M. Hayashi, "When to Trust Your Gut," *Harvard Business Review* 79 (February 2001), pp. 59–65. Evidence of high failure rates from quick decisions is reported in Nutt, *Why Decisions Fail*; and Nutt, "Search during Decision Making."

32. P. Goodwin and G. Wright, "Enhancing Strategy Evaluation in Scenario Planning: A Role for Decision Analysis," *Journal of Management Studies* 38 (January 2001), pp. 1–16; R. Bradfield et al., "The Origins and Evolution of Scenario Techniques in Long-Range Business Planning," *Futures* 37, no. 8 (2005), pp. 795–812.

33. R.N. Taylor, *Behavioral Decision Making* (Glenview, IL: Scott, Foresman, 1984), pp. 163–66.

34. G. Whyte, "Escalating Commitment to a Course of Action: A Reinterpretation," *Academy of Management Review* 11 (1986), pp. 311–21; J. Brockner, "The Escalation of Commitment to a Failing Course of Action: Toward Theoretical Progress," *Academy of Management Review* 17, no. 1 (January 1992), pp. 39–61.

35. I. Macwhirter, "Let's Build a Parliament," *The Scotsman* (17 July 1997), p. 19; "Macdome," *Mail on Sunday* (16 December 2001); P. Gallagher, "New Bid to Rein in Rising Costs of Scots Parliament," *Aberdeen Press and Journal* (Scotland), 11 June 2003, p. 1; I. Swanson, "Holyrood Firms Face Grilling over Costs," *Evening News* (Edinburgh), 6 June 2003, p. 2.

36. P. Ayton and H. Arkes, "Call It Quits," *New Scientist* (20 June 1998); M. Fackler, "Tokyo's Newest Subway Line a Saga of Hubris, Humiliation," *Associated Press Newswires* (20 July 1999).

37. F.D. Schoorman and P.J. Holahan, "Psychological Antecedents of Escalation Behavior: Effects of Choice, Responsibility, and Decision Consequences," *Journal of Applied Psychology* 81 (1996), pp. 786–93.

38. G. Whyte, "Escalating Commitment in Individual and Group Decision Making: A Prospect Theory Approach," *Organizational Behavior and Human Decision Processes* 54 (1993), pp. 430–55; D.J. Sharp and S.B. Salter, "Project Escalation and Sunk Costs: A Test of the International Generalizability of Agency and Prospect Theories," *Journal of International Business Studies* 28, no. 1 (1997), pp. 101–21.

39. J.D. Bragger et al., "When Success Breeds Failure: History, Hysteresis, and Delayed Exit Decisions," *Journal of Applied Psychology* 88, no. 1 (2003), pp. 6–14. A second logical reason for escalation, called the martingale strategy, is described in J.A. Aloysius, "Rational Escalation of Costs by Playing a Sequence of Unfavorable Gambles: The Martingale," *Journal of Economic Behavior & Organization* 51 (2003), pp. 111–29.

40. I. Simonson and B.M. Staw, "Deescalation Strategies: A Comparison of Techniques for Reducing Commitment to Losing Courses of Action," *Journal of Applied Psychology* 77 (1992), pp. 419–26; W. Boulding, R. Morgan, and R. Staelin, "Pulling the Plug to Stop the New Product Drain," *Journal of Marketing Research* 34 (1997), pp. 164–76; B.M. Staw, K.W. Koput, and S.G. Barsade, "Escalation at the Credit Window: A Longitudinal Study of Bank Executives' Recognition and Write-Off of Problem Loans," *Journal of Applied Psychology* 82 (1997), pp. 130–42; M. Keil and D. Robey, "Turning around Troubled Software Projects: An Exploratory Study of the Deescalation of Commitment to Failing Courses of Action," *Journal of Management Information Systems* 15 (Spring 1999), pp. 63–87.

41. D. Ghosh, "Deescalation Strategies: Some Experimental Evidence," *Behavioral Research in Accounting* 9 (1997), pp. 88–112.

42. M. Bruno, "Macon: Big Acclaim for a Small Facility," *Boeing Frontiers Online*, June 2005.

43. M. Fenton-O'Creevy, "Employee Involvement and the Middle Manager: Saboteur or Scapegoat?" *Human Resource Management Journal* 11 (2001), pp. 24–40. Also see V.H. Vroom and A.G. Jago, *The New Leadership: Managing Participation in Organizations* (Englewood Cliffs, NJ: Prentice Hill, 1988).

44. S.W. Crispin, "Workers' Paradise," *Far Eastern Economic Review*, 17 April 2003, pp. 40–41; "Thai Carbon Black: Worker-Driven Focus Key to Firm's Success," *The Nation* (Thailand), 3 June 2004.

45. Some of the early OB writing on employee involvement includes C. Argyris, *Personality and Organization* (New York: Harper & Row, 1957); D. McGregor, *The Human Side of Enterprise* (New York: McGraw-Hill, 1960); and R. Likert, *New Patterns of Management* (New York: McGraw-Hill, 1961).

46. A.G. Robinson and D.M. Schroeder, *Ideas Are Free* (San Francisco: Berrett-Koehler, 2004).

47. A. Kleingeld, H. Van Tuijl, and J.A. Algera, "Participation in the Design of Performance Management Systems: A Quasi-Experimental Field Study," *Journal of Organizational Behavior* 25, no. 7 (2004), pp. 831–51.

48. K.T. Dirks, L.L. Cummings, and J.L. Pierce, "Psychological Ownership in Organizations: Conditions under Which Individuals Promote and Resist Change," *Research in Organizational Change and Development* 9 (1996), pp. 1–23; J.P. Walsh and S.-F. Tseng, "The Effects of Job Characteristics on Active Effort at Work," *Work & Occupations* 25 (February 1998), pp. 74–96; B. Scott-Ladd and V. Marshall, "Participation in Decision Making: A Matter of Context?" *Leadership & Organization Development Journal* 25, no. 8 (2004), pp. 646–62. The quotation is from E.E. Lawler III, *Rewarding Excellence: Pay Strategies for the New Economy* (San Francisco: Jossey-Bass, 2000), pp. 23–24.

49. G.P. Latham, D.C. Winters, and E.A. Locke, "Cognitive and Motivational Effects of Participation: A Mediator Study," *Journal of Organizational Behavior* 15 (1994), pp. 49–63; J.A. Wagner III et al., "Cognitive and Motivational Frameworks in U.S. Research on Participation: A Meta-Analysis of Primary Effects," *Journal of Organizational Behavior* 18 (1997), pp. 49–65.

50. Y. Utsunomiya, "Yamato Continues to Deliver New Ideas," *Japan Times*, 8 July 2003; "Yamato Transport Co., Ltd.–

SWOT Analysis," *Datamonitor Company Profiles*, 7 July 2004.

51. J. Zhou and C.E. Shalley, "Research on Employee Creativity: A Critical Review and Directions for Future Research," *Research in Personnel and Human Resources Management* 22 (2003), pp. 165–217; M.A. Runco, "Creativity," *Annual Review of Psychology* 55 (2004), pp. 657–87.

52. B. Kabanoff and J.R. Rossiter, "Recent Developments in Applied Creativity," *International Review of Industrial and Organizational Psychology* 9 (1994), pp. 283–24.

53. R.S. Nickerson, "Enhancing Creativity," in *Handbook of Creativity*, ed. R.J. Sternberg (New York: Cambridge University Press, 1999), pp. 392–430.

54. R.I. Sutton, *Weird Ideas That Work* (New York: Free Press, 2002), p. 26.

55. For a thorough discussion of insight, see R.J. Sternberg and J.E. Davidson, *The Nature of Insight* (Cambridge, MA: MIT Press, 1995).

56. R.J. Sternberg and L.A. O'Hara, "Creativity and Intelligence," in *Handbook of Creativity*, ed. R.J. Sternberg (New York: Cambridge University Press, 1999), pp. 251–72; S. Taggar, "Individual Creativity and Group Ability to Utilize Individual Creative Resources: A Multilevel Model," *Academy of Management Journal* 45 (April 2002), pp. 315–30.

57. G.J. Feist, "The Influence of Personality on Artistic and Scientific Creativity," in *Handbook of Creativity*, ed. R.J. Sternberg (New York: Cambridge University Press, 1999), pp. 273–96; Sutton, *Weird Ideas That Work*, pp. 8–9, Chapter 10.

58. V. Laurie, "Gut Instinct," *The Australian Magazine*, 10 December 2005, p. 1; J. Robotham, "Of Guts and Glory," *Sydney Morning Herald*, 5 October 2005, p. 16; M. Irving, "Nobel Deeds, Words of Praise," *West Australian* (Perth), 14 January 2006, p. 4. Some facts are also found in Robin Warren's 2005 Nobel lecture. See J. Robin Warren, "Nobel Lecture: The Ease and Difficulty of a New Discovery," RealVideo presentation at http://nobelprize.org/medicine/laureates/2005/warren-lecture.html.

59. R.W. Weisberg, "Creativity and Knowledge: A Challenge to Theories," in *Handbook of Creativity*, ed. R.J. Sternberg (New York: Cambridge University Press, 1999), pp. 226–50.

60. Sutton, *Weird Ideas That Work*, pp. 121, 153–54; C. Andriopoulos, "Six Paradoxes in Managing Creativity: An Embracing

Act," *Long Range Planning* 36 (2003), pp. 375–88.

61. T. Koppell, *Powering the Future* (New York: Wiley, 1999), p. 15.

62. D.K. Simonton, "Creativity: Cognitive, Personal, Developmental, and Social Aspects," *American Psychologist* 55 (January 2000), pp. 151–58.

63. M.D. Mumford, "Managing Creative People: Strategies and Tactics for Innovation," *Human Resource Management Review* 10 (Autumn 2000), pp. 313–51; T.M. Amabile et al., "Leader Behaviors and the Work Environment for Creativity: Perceived Leader Support," *The Leadership Quarterly* 15, no. 1 (2004), pp. 5–32; C.E. Shalley, J. Zhou, and G.R. Oldham, "The Effects of Personal and Contextual Characteristics on Creativity: Where Should We Go from Here?" *Journal of Management* 30, no. 6 (2004), pp. 933–58.

64. R. Westwood and D.R. Low, "The Multicultural Muse: Culture, Creativity and Innovation," *International Journal of Cross Cultural Management* 3, no. 2 (2003), pp. 235–59.

65. T.M. Amabile, "Motivating Creativity in Organizations: On Doing What You Love and Loving What You Do," *California Management Review* 40 (Fall 1997), pp. 39–58; A. Cummings and G.R. Oldham, "Enhancing Creativity: Managing Work Contexts for the High-Potential Employee," *California Management Review* 40 (Fall 1997), pp. 22–38.

66. T.M. Amabile, "Changes in the Work Environment for Creativity during Downsizing," *Academy of Management Journal* 42 (December 1999), pp. 630–40.

67. J.M. Howell and K. Boies, "Champions of Technological Innovation: The Influence of Contextual Knowledge, Role Orientation, Idea Generation, and Idea Promotion on Champion Emergence," *The Leadership Quarterly* 15, no. 1 (2004), pp. 123–43; Shalley, Zhou, and Oldham, "The Effects of Personal and Contextual Characteristics on Creativity."

68. A. Hiam, "Obstacles to Creativity– and How You Can Remove Them," *Futurist* 32 (October 1998), pp. 30–34.

69. M.A. West, *Developing Creativity in Organizations* (Leicester, UK: BPS Books, 1997), pp. 33–35.

70. S. Hemsley, "Seeking the Source of Innovation," *Media Week*, 16 August 2005, p. 22; S. Planting, "When You Need to Get Serious, Get Playful," *Financial Mail* (South Africa), 4 February 2005, p. 14.

71. J. Neff, "At Eureka Ranch, Execs Doff Wing Tips, Fire up Ideas," *Advertising Age,* 9 March 1998, pp. 28–29.

72. A. Hargadon and R.I. Sutton, "Building an Innovation Factory," *Harvard Business Review* 78 (May–June 2000), pp. 157–66; T. Kelley, *The Art of Innovation* (New York: Currency Doubleday, 2001), pp. 158–62.

73. K.S. Brown, "The Apple of Jonathan Ive's Eye," *Investor's Business Daily,* 19 September 2003.

CHAPTER 9

1. S. Konig, "The Challenge of Teams," *On Wall Street,* August 2003; D. Jamieson, "8 Most Common Myths about Teams," *On Wall Street,* May 2005; H.J. Stock, "A 'Cheat Sheet' to Cross Sell," *Bank Investment Consultant,* April 2005, p. 28; L. Wei, "Brokers Increasingly Use Teamwork," *The Wall Street Journal,* 23 February 2005; V. Knight, "Wealth Managers Sell Their Clients Safety, Security," *The Wall Street Journal,* 3 May 2006, p. B3E; M. Santoli, "The Goldman Sachs Way: Minting Money," *Barron's,* 10 April 2006, p. 22; R. Wachman, "Wall Street's Alpha Female Wants to Smash Glass Ceilings," *The Observer* (London), 15 January 2006, p. 7.

2. V.L. Parker, "Org Charts Turn Around with Teams," *News & Observer* (Raleigh, North Carolina), 21 July 2005, p. D1; J. Springer, "Eyes on the Prize," *Supermarket News,* 1 August 2005, p. 12; D. Hechler, "Teamwork Is Job One at Ford," *Fulton County Daily Report* (Atlanta), 16 May 2006, p. 16.

3. This definition and very similar variations are found in M.E. Shaw, *Group Dynamics,* 3rd ed. (New York: McGraw-Hill, 1981), p. 8; S.A. Mohrman, S.G. Cohen, and A.M. Mohrman Jr., *Designing Team-Based Organizations: New Forms for Knowledge Work* (San Francisco: Jossey-Bass, 1995), pp. 39–40; M.A. West, "Preface: Introducing Work Group Psychology," in *Handbook of Work Group Psychology,* ed. M.A. West (Chichester, UK: Wiley, 1996), p. xxvi; S.G. Cohen and D.E. Bailey, "What Makes Teams Work: Group Effectiveness Research from the Shop Floor to the Executive Suite," *Journal of Management* 23 (May 1997), pp. 239–90; and E. Sundstrom, "The Challenges of Supporting Work Team Effectiveness," in *Supporting Work Team Effectiveness,* ed. E. Sundstrom and Associates (San Francisco: Jossey-Bass, 1999), pp. 6–9.

4. M. Moldaschl and W. Weber, "The 'Three Waves' of Industrial Group Work: Historical Reflections on Current Research on Group Work," *Human Relations* 51 (March 1998), pp. 347–88. The survey quotation is found in J.N. Choi, "External Activities and Team Effectiveness: Review and Theoretical Development," *Small Group Research* 33 (April 2002), pp. 181–208. Several popular books in the 1980s encouraged teamwork, based on the Japanese economic miracle. These books included W. Ouchi, *Theory Z: How American Management Can Meet the Japanese Challenge* (Reading, MA: Addison-Wesley, 1981); and R.T. Pascale and A.G. Athos, *Art of Japanese Management* (New York: Simon and Schuster, 1982).

5. A. Doak, "New-Age Style, Old-Fashioned Grunt, but How Will It Look with Fluffy Dice?" *The Age* (Melbourne), 16 October 1998, p. 4; W. Webster, "How a Star Was Born," *Daily Telegraph* (Sydney), 17 October 1998, p. 11; R. Edgar, "Designers Front up to World Stage," *The Age* (Melbourne), 11 February 2004, p. 6; P. Gover, "The Camaro Commandos," *Herald-Sun* (Melbourne), 7 April 2006, p. G07.

6. S. Beatty, "Bass Talk: Plotting Plaid's Future," *The Wall Street Journal,* 9 September 2004, p. B1

7. J. Godard, "High Performance and the Transformation of Work? The Implications of Alternative Work Practices for the Experience and Outcomes of Work" *Industrial & Labor Relations Review* 54 (July 2001), pp. 776–805; J. Pfeffer, "Putting People First," *Stanford Social Innovation Review* 3, no. 1 (Spring 2005), pp. 26–33.

8. B.D. Pierce and R. White, "The Evolution of Social Structure: Why Biology Matters," *Academy of Management Review* 24 (October 1999), pp. 843–53; P.R. Lawrence and N. Nohria, *Driven: How Human Nature Shapes Our Choices* (San Francisco: Jossey-Bass, 2002); J.R. Spoor and J.R. Kelly, "The Evolutionary Significance of Affect in Groups: Communication and Group Bonding," *Group Processes & Intergroup Relations* 7, no. 4 (2004), pp. 398–412.

9. M.A. Hogg et al., "The Social Identity Perspective: Intergroup Relations, Self-Conception, and Small Groups," *Small Group Research* 35, no. 3 (June 2004), pp. 246–76; N. Michinov, E. Michinov, and M.-C. Toczek-Capelle, "Social Identity, Group Processes, and Performance in Synchronous Computer-Mediated Communication," *Group Dynamics: Theory, Research, and Practice* 8, no. 1 (2004), pp. 27–39; M. Van Vugt and C.M. Hart, "Social Identity as Social Glue: The Origins of Group Loyalty," *Journal of Personality and Social Psychology* 86, no. 4 (2004), pp. 585–98.

10. S. Schacter, *The Psychology of Affiliation* (Stanford, CA: Stanford University Press, 1959), pp. 12–19; R. Eisler and D.S. Levine, "Nurture, Nature, and Caring: We Are Not Prisoners of Our Genes," *Brain and Mind* 3 (2002), pp. 9–52; A.C. DeVries, E.R. Glasper, and C.E. Detillion, "Social Modulation of Stress Responses," *Physiology & Behavior* 79, no. 3 (August 2003), pp. 399–407.

11. M.A. West, C.S. Borrill, and K.L. Unsworth, "Team Effectiveness in Organizations," *International Review of Industrial and Organizational Psychology* 13 (1998), pp. 1–48; R. Forrester and A.B. Drexler, "A Model for Team-Based Organization Performance," *Academy of Management Executive* 13 (August 1999), pp. 36–49; J.E. McGrath, H. Arrow, and J.L. Berdahl, "The Study of Groups: Past, Present, and Future," *Personality & Social Psychology Review* 4, no. 1 (2000), pp. 95–105; M.A. Marks, J.E. Mathieu, and S.J. Zaccaro, "A Temporally Based Framework and Taxonomy of Team Processes," *Academy of Management Review* 26, no. 3 (July 2001), pp. 356–76.

12. G.P. Shea and R.A. Guzzo, "Group Effectiveness: What Really Matters?" *Sloan Management Review* 27 (1987), pp. 33–46; J.R. Hackman et al., "Team Effectiveness in Theory and in Practice," in *Industrial and Organizational Psychology: Linking Theory with Practice,* ed. C.L. Cooper and E.A. Locke (Oxford, UK: Blackwell, 2000), pp. 109–29.

13. Choi, "External Activities and Team Effectiveness: Review and Theoretical Development"; T.L. Doolen, M.E. Hacker, and E.M. Van Aken, "The Impact of Organizational Context on Work Team Effectiveness: A Study of Production Teams," *IEEE Transactions on Engineering Management* 50, no. 3 (August 2003), pp. 285–96.

14. J.S. DeMatteo, L.T. Eby, and E. Sundstrom, "Team-Based Rewards: Current Empirical Evidence and Directions for Future Research," *Research in Organizational Behavior* 20 (1998), pp. 141–83; E.E. Lawler III, *Rewarding Excellence: Pay Strategies for the New Economy* (San Francisco: Jossey-Bass, 2000), pp. 207–14; G. Hertel, S. Geister, and U. Konradt, "Managing Virtual Teams: A Review of Current Em-

pirical Research," *Human Resource Management Review* 15 (2005), pp. 69–95.

15. A. Niimi, "The Slow and Steady Climb toward True North," Toyota Motor Manufacturing North America news release, 7 August 2003; B. Andrews, "Room with Many Views," *Business Review Weekly*, 15 January 2004, p. 68; L. Chappell, "Toyota Trims Development Time," *Automotive News*, 4 August 2005, p. 14.

16. L. Adams, "Medrad Works and Wins as a Team," *Quality Magazine*, October 2004, p. 42; "Lean Manufacturing Increases Productivity, Decreases Cycle Time," *Industrial Equipment News*, October 2005.

17. R. Wageman, "Case Study: Critical Success Factors for Creating Superb Self-Managing Teams at Xerox," *Compensation and Benefits Review* 29 (September–October 1997), pp. 31–41; G. Gard, K. Lindström, and M. Dallner, "Toward a Learning Organization: The Introduction of a Client-Centered Team-Based Organization in Administrative Surveying Work," *Applied Ergonomics* 34 (2003), pp. 97–105.

18. S.D. Dionne et al., "Transformational Leadership and Team Performance," *Journal of Organizational Change Management* 17, no. 2 (2004), pp. 177–93.

19. M.A. Campion, E.M. Papper, and G.J. Medsker, "Relations between Work Team Characteristics and Effectiveness: A Replication and Extension," *Personnel Psychology* 49 (1996), pp. 429–52; D.C. Man and S.S.K. Lam, "The Effects of Job Complexity and Autonomy on Cohesiveness in Collectivistic and Individualistic Work Groups: A Cross-Cultural Analysis," *Journal of Organizational Behavior* 24 (2003), pp. 979–1001.

20. R. Wageman, "The Meaning of Interdependence," in *Groups at Work: Theory and Research*, ed. M.E. Turner (Mahwah, NJ: Lawrence Erlbaum Associates, 2001), pp. 197–217.

21. R. Wageman, "Interdependence and Group Effectiveness," *Administrative Science Quarterly* 40 (1995), pp. 145–80; G.S. Van der Vegt, J.M. Emans, and E. Van de Vliert, "Patterns of Interdependence in Work Teams: A Two-Level Investigation of the Relations with Job and Team Satisfaction," *Personnel Psychology* 54 (Spring 2001), pp. 51–69; S.M. Gully et al., "A Meta-Analysis of Team-Efficacy, Potency, and Performance: Interdependence and Level of Analysis as Moderators of Observed Relationships," *Journal Of Applied Psychology* 87, no. 5 (October 2002), pp. 819–32.

22. J.D. Thompson, *Organizations in Action* (New York: McGraw-Hill, 1967), pp. 54–56. One concern with Thompson's typology is that it isn't clear how much more interdependence is created by each of these three forms. See G. Van der Vegt and E. Van de Vliert, "Intragroup Interdependence and Effectiveness: Review and Proposed Directions for Theory and Practice," *Journal of Managerial Psychology* 17, no. 1/2 (2002), pp. 50–67.

23. J. O'Toole and D. Tessmann-Keys, "The Power of Many: Building a High-Performance Management Team," *ceoforum.com.au*, March 2003.

24. G. Stasser, "Pooling of Unshared Information during Group Discussion," in *Group Process and Productivity*, ed. S. Worchel, W. Wood, and J.A. Simpson (Newbury Park, CA: Sage, 1992); J.R. Katzenbach and D.K. Smith, *The Wisdom of Teams: Creating the High-Performance Organization* (Boston: Harvard University Press, 1993), pp. 45–47.

25. S.E. Nedleman, "Recruiters Reveal Their Top Interview Questions," *Financial News Online*, 16 February 2005.

26. P.C. Earley, "East Meets West Meets Mideast: Further Explorations of Collectivistic and Individualistic Work Groups," *Academy of Management Journal* 36 (1993), pp. 319–48; L.T. Eby and G.H. Dobbins, "Collectivist Orientation in Teams: An Individual and Group-Level Analysis," *Journal of Organizational Behavior* 18 (1997), pp. 275–95; S.B. Alavi and J. McCormick, "Theoretical and Measurement Issues for Studies of Collective Orientation in Team Contexts," *Small Group Research* 35, no. 2 (April 2004), pp. 111–27.

27. M.R. Barrick et al., "Relating Member Ability and Personality to Work-Team Processes and Team Effectiveness," *Journal of Applied Psychology* 83 (1998), pp. 377–91; S. Sonnentag, "Excellent Performance: The Role of Communication and Cooperation Processes," *Applied Psychology: An International Review* 49 (2000), pp. 483–97; F.P. Morgenson, M.H. Reider, and M.A. Campion, "Selecting Individuals in Team Settings: The Importance of Social Skills, Personality Characteristics, and Teamwork Knowledge," *Personnel Psychology* 58, no. 3 (2005), pp. 583–611.

28. S.E. Jackson and A. Joshi, "Diversity in Social Context: A Multi-Attribute, Multilevel Analysis of Team Diversity and Sales Performance," *Journal of Organizational Behavior* 25 (2004), pp. 675–702; D. van Knippenberg, C.K. W. De Dreu,

and A.C. Homan, "Work Group Diversity and Group Performance: An Integrative Model and Research Agenda," *Journal of Applied Psychology* 89, no. 6 (2004), pp. 1008–22.

29. D.A. Harrison et al., "Time, Teams, and Task Performance: Changing Effects of Surface- and Deep-Level Diversity on Group Functioning," *Academy of Management Journal* 45 (October 2002), pp. 1029–45.

30. K.Y.O.R. Williams, C.A., "Demography and Diversity in Organizations: A Review of 40 Years of Research," in *Research in Organizational Behavior*, ed. B.M. Staw and L.L. Cummings (Greenwich, CT: JAI, 1998), pp. 77–140; C.M. Riodan, "Relational Demography within Groups: Past Developments, Contradictions, and New Directions," in *Research in Personnel and Human Resources Management*, ed. G.R. Ferris (Greenwich, CT: JAI, 2000), pp. 131–73.

31. D.C. Lau and J.K. Murnighan, "Interactions within Groups and Subgroups: The Effects of Demographic Faultlines," *Academy of Management Journal* 48, no. 4 (August 2005), pp. 645–59.

32. The NTSB and NASA studies are summarized in J.R. Hackman, "New Rules for Team Building," *Optimize*, July 2002, pp. 50–62.

33. B.W. Tuckman and M.A.C. Jensen, "Stages of Small-Group Development Revisited," *Group and Organization Studies* 2 (1977), pp. 419–42.

34. J.E. Mathieu and G.F. Goodwin, "The Influence of Shared Mental Models on Team Process and Performance," *Journal of Applied Psychology* 85 (April 2000), pp. 273–84.

35. A. Edmondson, "Psychological Safety and Learning Behavior in Work Teams," *Administrative Science Quarterly* 44 (1999), pp. 350–83.

36. W.B. Scott, "Blue Angels," *Aviation Week & Space Technology*, 21 March 2005, pp. 50–57.

37. D.L. Miller, "The Stages of Group Development: A Retrospective Study of Dynamic Team Processes," *Canadian Journal of Administrative Sciences* 20, no. 2 (2003), pp. 121–34. For other models of team development, see J.G. Gersick, "Time and Transition in Work Teams: Toward a New Model of Group Development," *Academy of Management Journal* 31 (March 1988), pp. 9–41; J.E. Jones and W.L. Bearley, "Facilitating Team Development: A View

from the Field," *Group Facilitation* 3 (Spring 2001), pp. 56–65; and H. Arrow et al., "Time, Change, and Development: The Temporal Perspective on Groups," *Small Group Research* 35, no. 1 (February 2004), pp. 73–105.

38. D.C. Feldman, "The Development and Enforcement of Group Norms," *Academy of Management Review* 9 (1984), pp. 47-53; E. Fehr and U. Fischbacher, "Social Norms and Human Cooperation," *Trends in Cognitive Sciences* 8, no. 4 (2004), pp. 185-90.

39. "Employees Terrorized by Peer Pressure in the Workplace," Morgan & Banks news release, September 2000. For further discussion of sanctions applied to people who outperform others in the group, see J.J. Exline and M. Lobel, "The Perils of Outperformance: Sensitivity about Being the Target of a Threatening Upward Comparison," *Psychological Bulletin* 125, no. 3 (1999), pp. 307–37.

40. N. Ellemers and F. Rink, "Identity in Work Groups: The Beneficial and Detrimental Consequences of Multiple Identities and Group Norms for Collaboration and Group Performance," *Advances in Group Processes* 22 (2005), pp. 1–41.

41. C.R. Graham, "A Model of Norm Development for Computer-Mediated Teamwork," *Small Group Research* 34, no. 3 (June 2003), pp. 322–52.

42. J.J. Dose and R.J. Klimoski, "The Diversity of Diversity: Work Values Effects on Formative Team Processes," *Human Resource Management Review* 9, no. 1 (Spring 1999), pp. 83–108.

43. R. Hallowell, D. Bowen, and C.-I. Knoop, "Four Seasons Goes to Paris," *Academy of Management Executive* 16, no. 4 (November 2002), pp. 7–24.

44. L.Y. Chan and B.E. Lynn, "Operating in Turbulent Times: How Ontario's Hospitals Are Meeting the Current Funding Crisis," *Health Care Management Review* 23, no. 3 (1998), pp. 7–18.

45. L. Coch and J. French Jr., "Overcoming Resistance to Change," *Human Relations* 1 (1948), pp. 512–32.

46. A.P. Hare, "Types of Roles in Small Groups: A Bit of History and a Current Perspective," *Small Group Research* 25 (1994), pp. 443–48.

47. S.H.N. Leung, J.W.K. Chan, and W.B. Lee, "The Dynamic Team Role Behavior: The Approaches of Investigation," *Team Performance Management* 9 (2003), pp. 84–90.

48. R.M. Belbin, *Team Roles at Work* (Oxford, UK: Butterworth-Heinemann, 1993).

49. W.G. Broucek and G. Randell, "An Assessment of the Construct Validity of the Belbin Self-Perception Inventory and Observer's Assessment from the Perspective of the Five-Factor Model," *Journal of Occupational and Organizational Psychology* 69 (December 1996), pp. 389–40; S.G. Fisher, T.A. Hunter, and W.D.K. Macrosson, "The Structure of Belbin's Team Roles," *Journal of Occupational and Organizational Psychology* 71 (September 1998), pp. 283–88; J.S. Prichard and N.A. Stanton, "Testing Belbin's Team Role Theory of Effective Groups," *Journal of Management Development* 18 (1999), pp. 652–65; G. Fisher, T.A. Hunter, and W.D.K. Macrosson, "Belbin's Team Role Theory: For Non-Managers Also?" *Journal of Managerial Psychology* 17 (2002), pp. 14–20.

50. C.R. Evans and K.L. Dion, "Group Cohesion and Performance: A Meta Analysis," *Small Group Research* 22 (1991), pp. 175–86; B. Mullen and C. Copper, "The Relation between Group Cohesiveness and Performance: An Integration," *Psychological Bulletin* 115 (1994), pp. 210–27; A.V. Carron et al., "Cohesion and Performance in Sport: A Meta-Analysis," *Journal of Sport and Exercise Psychology* 24 (2002), pp. 168–88; D.J. Beal et al., "Cohesion and Performance in Groups: A Meta-Analytic Clarification of Construct Relations," *Journal of Applied Psychology* 88, no. 6 (2003), pp. 989–1004.

51. N. Ellemers, R. Spears, and B. Doosie, "Self and Social Identity," *Annual Review of Psychology* 53 (2002), pp. 161–86; K.M. Sheldon and B.A. Bettencourt, "Psychological Need Satisfaction and Subjective Well-Being within Social Groups," *British Journal of Social Psychology* 41 (2002), pp. 25-38.

52. K.A. Jehn, G.B. Northcraft, and M.A. Neale, "Why Differences Make a Difference: A Field Study of Diversity, Conflict, and Performance in Workgroups," *Administrative Science Quarterly* 44, no. 4 (1999), pp. 741–63; van Knippenberg, De Dreu, and Homan, "Work Group Diversity and Group Performance: An Integrative Model and Research Agenda." For evidence that diversity/similarity does not always influence cohesion, see S.S. Webber and L.M. Donahue, "Impact of Highly and Less Job-Related Diversity on Work Group Cohesion and Performance: A Meta-Analysis," *Journal of Management* 27, no. 2 (2001), pp. 141–62.

53. E. Aronson and J. Mills, "The Effects of Severity of Initiation on Liking for a Group," *Journal of Abnormal and Social Psychology* 59 (1959), pp. 177–81; J.E. Hautaluoma and R.S. Enge, "Early Socialization into a Work Group: Severity of Initiations Revisited," *Journal of Social Behavior & Personality* 6 (1991), pp. 725–48.

54. Mullen and Copper, "The Relation between Group Cohesiveness and Performance: An Integration."

55. F. Piccolo, "Brownie Points," *Atlantic Business*, October/November 2004, p. 22.

56. M. Rempel and R.J. Fisher, "Perceived Threat, Cohesion, and Group Problem Solving in Intergroup Conflict," *International Journal of Conflict Management* 8 (1997), pp. 216-34; M.E. Turner and T. Horvitz, "The Dilemma of Threat: Group Effectiveness and Ineffectiveness under Adversity," in *Groups at Work: Theory and Research*, ed. M.E. Turner (Mahwah, NJ: Lawrence Erlbaum Associates, 2001), pp. 445–70.

57. W. Piper et al., "Cohesion as a Basic Bond in Groups," *Human Relations* 36 (1983), pp. 93-108; C.A. O'Reilly, D.E. Caldwell, and W.P. Barnett, "Work Group Demography, Social Integration, and Turnover," *Administrative Science Quarterly* 34 (1989), pp. 21–37.

58. C. Langfred, "Is Group Cohesiveness a Double-Edged Sword? An Investigation of the Effects of Cohesiveness on Performance," *Small Group Research* 29 (1998), pp. 124-43; K.L. Gammage, A.V. Carron, and P.A. Estabrooks, "Team Cohesion and Individual Productivity: The Influence of the Norm for Productivity and the Identifiability of Individual Effort," *Small Group Research* 32 (February 2001), pp. 3–18.

59. "The Trouble with Teams," *Economist*, 14 January 1995, p. 6; H. Robbins and M. Finley, *Why Teams Don't Work* (Princeton, NJ: Peterson's/Pacesetters, 1995), Chapter 20; E.A. Locke et al., "The Importance of the Individual in an Age of Groupism," in *Groups at Work: Theory and Research*, ed. M.E. Turner (Mahwah, NJ: Lawrence Erbaum Associates, 2001), pp. 501–28; N.J. Allen and T.D. Hecht, "The 'Romance of Teams': Toward an Understanding of Its Psychological Underpinnings and Implications," *Journal of Occupational and Organizational Psychology* 77 (2004), pp. 439–61.

60. P. Panchak, "The Future Manufacturing," *Industry Week* 247 (September 21 1998), pp. 96–105.

61. I.D. Steiner, *Group Process and Productivity* (New York: Academic Press, 1972); N.L. Kerr and S.R. Tindale, "Group Performance and Decision Making," *Annual Review of Psychology* 55 (2004), pp. 623–55.

62. D. Dunphy and B. Bryant, "Teams: Panaceas or Prescriptions for Improved Performance?" *Human Relations* 49 (1996), pp. 677–99. For discussion of Brooks's Law, see F.P. Brooks, ed., *The Mythical Man-Month: Essays on Software Engineering*, 2nd ed. (Reading, MA: Addison-Wesley, 1995).

63. J. Gruber, "More Aperture Dirt" (Daring Fireball, 4 May 2006), http://daringfireball.net/2006/05/more_aperture_dirt (accessed 7 June 2006); J. Gruber, "Aperture Dirt" (Daring Fireball, 28 April 2006), http://daringfireball.net/2006/04/aperture_dirt (accessed 30 April 2006).

64. R. Cross, "Looking before You Leap: Assessing the Jump to Teams in Knowledge-Based Work," *Business Horizons* (September 2000); Q.R. Skrabec Jr., "The Myth of Teams," *Industrial Management* (September–October 2002), pp. 25-27.

65. S.J. Karau and K.D. Williams, "Social Loafing: A Meta-Analytic Review and Theoretical Integration," *Journal of Personality and Social Psychology* 65 (1993), pp. 681–706; R.C. Liden et al., "Social Loafing: A Field Investigation," *Journal of Management* 30 (2004), pp. 285–304.

66. M. Erez and A. Somech, "Is Group Productivity Loss the Rule or the Exception? Effects of Culture and Group-Based Motivation," *Academy of Management Journal* 39 (1996), pp. 1513–37; Kerr and Tindale, "Group Performance and Decision Making."

67. E. Kidwell and N. Bennett, "Employee Propensity to Withhold Effort: A Conceptual Model to Intersect Three Avenues of Research," *Academy of Management Review* 19 (1993), pp. 429–56; J.M. George, "Asymmetrical Effects of Rewards and Punishments: The Case of Social Loafing," *Journal of Occupational and Organizational Psychology* 68 (1995), pp. 327–38; T.A. Judge and T.D. Chandler, "Individual-Level Determinants of Employee Shirking," *Relations Industrielles* 51 (1996), pp. 468–86.

CHAPTER 10

1. J. Gordon, "Do Your Virtual Teams Deliver Only Virtual Performance?" *Training*, June 2005, pp. 20–24; A. Graham, "Team-building Reveals Its Serious Side," *Corporate Meetings & Incentives*, May 2005, pp. S6–S11.

2. C. Fishman, "The Anarchist's Cookbook," *Fast Company*, July 2004, p. 70; J. Mackey, "Open Book Company," *Newsweek*, 28 November 2005, p. 42.

3. S.G. Cohen, J. Ledford, G.E., and G.M. Spreitzer, "A Predictive Model of Self-Managing Work Team Effectiveness," *Human Relations* 49 (1996), pp. 643–76; E.E. Lawler, *Organizing for High Performance* (San Francisco: Jossey-Bass, 2001); V.U. Druskat and J.V. Wheeler, "How to Lead a Self-Managing Team," *MIT Sloan Management Review* 45, no. 4 (Summer 2004), pp. 65–71.

4. S.A. Mohrman, S.G. Cohen, and J. Mohrman, A.M., *Designing Team-Based Organizations: New Forms for Knowledge Work* (San Francisco: Jossey-Bass, 1995); B.L. Kirkman and D.L. Shapiro, "The Impact of Cultural Values on Employee Resistance to Teams: Toward a Model of Globalized Self-Managing Work Team Effectiveness," *Academy of Management Review* 22 (July 1997), pp. 730–57; D.E. Yeatts and C. Hyten, *High-Performing Self-Managed Work Teams: A Comparison of Theory and Practice* (Thousand Oaks, CA: Sage, 1998).

5. P.S. Goodman, R. Devadas, and T.L.G. Hughson, "Groups and Productivity: Analyzing the Effectiveness of Self-Managing Teams," in *Productivity in Organizations*, ed. J.P. Campbell, R.J. Campbell, and associates (San Francisco: Jossey-Bass, 1988), pp. 295–327.

6. D. Tjosvold, *Teamwork for Customers* (San Francisco: Jossey-Bass, 1993); J. Childs, "Five Years and Counting: The Path to Self-Directed Work Teams," *Hospital Materiel Management Quarterly* 18 (May 1997), pp. 34–43; A. de Jong and K. de Ruyter, "Adaptive versus Proactive Behavior in Service Recovery: The Role of Self-Managing Teams," *Decision Sciences* 35, no. 3 (2004), pp. 457–91.

7. E.L. Trist et al., *Organizational Choice* (London: Tavistock, 1963); N. Adler and P. Docherty, "Bringing Business into Sociotechnical Theory and Practice," *Human Relations* 51, no. 3 (1998), pp. 319–45; R.J. Torraco, "Work Design Theory: A Review and Critique with Implications for Human Resource Development," *Human Resource Development Quarterly* 16, no. 1 (Spring 2005), pp. 85–109.

8. The main components of sociotechnical systems are discussed in M. Moldaschl and W.G. Weber, "The 'Three Waves' of Industrial Group Work: Historical Reflections on Current Research on Group Work," *Human Relations* 51 (March 1998), pp. 259–87; and W. Niepce and E. Molleman, "Work Design Issues in Lean Production from Sociotechnical System Perspective: Neo-Taylorism or the Next Step in Sociotechnical Design?" *Human Relations* 51, no. 3 (March 1998), pp. 259–87.

9. E. Ulich and W.G. Weber, "Dimensions, Criteria, and Evaluation of Work Group Autonomy," in *Handbook of Work Group Psychology*, ed. M.A. West (Chichester, UK: John Wiley and Sons, 1996), pp. 247–82.

10. K.P. Carson and G.L. Stewart, "Job Analysis and the Sociotechnical Approach to Quality: A Critical Examination," *Journal of Quality Management* 1 (1996), pp. 49–65; C.C. Manz and G.L. Stewart, "Attaining Flexible Stability by Integrating Total Quality Management and Socio-Technical Systems Theory," *Organization Science* 8 (1997), pp. 59–70.

11. C.R. Emery and L.D. Fredendall, "The Effect of Teams on Firm Profitability and Customer Satisfaction," *Journal of Service Research* 4 (February 2002), pp. 217–29; I.M. Kunii, "He Put the Flash Back in Canon," *Business Week* (16 September 2002), p. 40; A. Krause and H. Dunckel, "Work Design and Customer Satisfaction: Effects of the Implementation of Semi-Autonomous Group Work on Customer Satisfaction Considering Employee Satisfaction and Group Performance (Translated Abstract)," *Zeitschrift fur Arbeits-und Organisationspsychologie* 47, no. 4 (2003), pp. 182–93.

12. J.P. Womack, D.T. Jones, and D. Roos, *The Machine That Changed the World* (New York: MacMIllan, 1990); P.S. Adler and R.E. Cole, "Designed for Learning: A Tale of Two Auto Plants," *Sloan Management Review* 34 (Spring 1993), pp. 85–94; C. Berggren, "Volvo Uddevalla: A Dead Horse or a Car Dealer's Dream?" in *Actes du GERPISA* (May 1993), pp. 129–43; J.Å. Granath, "Torslanda to Uddevalla Via Kalmar: A Journey in Production Practice in Volvo," Paper presented at Seminário Internacional Reestruturação Produtiva, Flexibilidade do Trabalho e Novas Competências Profissionais COPPE/UFRJ, Rio de Janeiro, Brasil, 24–25 August 1998; Emery and Fredendall, "The Effect of Teams on Firm Profitability and Customer Satisfaction"; J. Boudreau et al., "On the Interface between Operations and Human Resources Management," *Manufacturing & Service Operations Management* 5, no. 3 (Summer 2003), pp. 179–202.

13. C.E. Nicholls, H.W. Lane, and M.B. Brechu, "Taking Self-Managed Teams to Mexico," *Academy of Management Executive* 13 (August 1999), pp. 15–25; B.L. Kirkman and D.L. Shapiro, "The Impact of Cultural Values on Job Satisfaction and Organizational Commitment in Self-Managing Work Teams: The Mediating Role of Employee Resistance," *Academy of Management Journal* 44 (June 2001), pp. 557–69.

14. C.C. Manz, D.E. Keating, and A. Donnellon, "Preparing for an Organizational Change to Employee Self-Management: The Managerial Transition," *Organizational Dynamics* 19 (Autumn 1990), pp. 15–26; J.D. Orsburn and L. Moran, *The New Self-Directed Work Teams: Mastering the Challenge* (New York: McGraw-Hill, 2000), Chapter 11. The Robert Frost quotation is found at www.quoteland.com.

15. M. Fenton-O'Creevy, "Employee Involvement and the Middle Manager: Saboteur or Scapegoat?" *Human Resource Management Journal* 11 (2001), pp.24–40; R. Wageman, "How Leaders Foster Self-Managing Team Effectiveness," *Organization Science* 12, no. 5 (September–October 2001), pp. 559–77; C. Douglas and W. L. Gardner, "Transition to Self-Directed Work Teams: Implications of Transition Time and Self-Monitoring for Managers' Use of Influence Tactics," *Journal of Organizational Behavior* 25 (2004), pp. 47–65. The TRW quotation is found in J. Jusko, "Always Lessons to Learn," Industry Week (15February 1999), pp. 23–30.

16. D. Stafford, "Sharing the Driver's Seat," *Kansas City Star*, 11 June 2002, p. D1.

17. G. Garda, K. Lindstrom, and M. Dallnera, "Toward a Learning Organization: The Introduction of a Client-Centered Team-Based Organization in Administrative Surveying Work," *Applied Ergonomics* 34 (2003), pp. 97–105.

18. R. Hodson, "Dignity in the Workplace under Participative Management: Alienation and Freedom Revisited," *American Sociological Review* 61 (1996), pp. 719–38; R. Yonatan and H. Lam, "Union Responses to Quality Improvement Initiatives: Factors Shaping Support and Resistance," *Journal of Labor Research* 20 (Winter 1999), pp. 111–31.

19. J. Lipnack and J. Stamps, *Virtual Teams: People Working across Boundaries with Technology* (New York: John Wiley and Sons, 2001); B.S. Bell and W.J. Kozlowski, "A Typology of Virtual Teams: Implications for Effective Leadership," *Group & Organization Management* 27 (March 2002), pp. 14–49; G. Hertel, S. Geister, and U. Konradt, "Managing Virtual Teams: A Review of Current Empirical Research," *Human Resource Management Review* 15 (2005), pp. 69–95.

20. G. Gilder, *Telecosm: How Infinite Bandwidth Will Revolutionize Our World* (New York: Free Press, 2001); L.L. Martins, L.L. Gilson, and M.T. Maynard, "Virtual Teams: What Do We Know and Where Do We Go Form Here?" *Journal of Management* 30, no. 6 (2004), pp. 805–35. The Novartis quotation is from S. Murray, "Pros and Cons of Technology: The Corporate Agenda: Managing Virtual Teams," *Financial Times (London)*, 27 May 2002, p. 6.

21. J.S. Lureya and M.S. Raisinghani, "An Empirical Study of Best Practices in Virtual Teams," *Information & Management* 38 (2001), pp. 523–44; Y.L. Doz, J.F.P. Santos, and P.J. Williamson, "The Metanational Advantage," *Optimize* (May 2002), p. 45ff; K. Marron, "Close Encounters of the Faceless Kind," *Globe & Mail*, 9 February 2005, p. C1.

22. Martins, Gilson, and Maynard, "Virtual Teams." The quotation is found in S. Gasper, "Virtual Teams, Real Benefits," *Network World*, 24 September 2001, p. 45.

23. D. Robb, "Global Workgroups," *Computerworld*, 15 August 2005, pp. 37–38.

24. D. Robey, H.M. Khoo, and C. Powers, "Situated Learning in Cross-Functional Virtual Teams," *Technical Communication* (February 2000), pp. 51–66.

25. Lureya and Raisinghani, "An Empirical Study of Best Practices in Virtual Teams."

26. S. Alexander, "Virtual Teams Going Global," *InfoWorld* (13 November 2000), pp. 55–56.

27. S. Prashad, "Building Trust Tricky for 'Virtual' Teams," *Toronto Star*, 23 October 2003, p. K06.

28. S. Van Ryssen and S.H. Godar, "Going International without Going International: Multinational Virtual Teams," *Journal of International Management* 6 (2000), pp. 49–60.

29. B.J. Alge, C. Wiethoff, and H.J. Klein, "When Does the Medium Matter? Knowledge-Building Experiences and Opportunities in Decision-Making Teams," *Organizational Behavior and Human Decision Processes* 91, no. 1 (2003), pp. 26–37; D. Robey, K.S. Schwaig, and L. Jin, "Intertwining Material and Virtual Work," *Information & Organization* 13 (2003), pp. 111–29; U. Bernard, R. Gfrörer, and B. Staffelbach, "Der Einfluss Von Telearbeit Auf Das Team: Empirisch Analysiert Am Beispiel Eines Versicherungsunternehmens (translated abstract)," *Zeitschrift für Personalforschung* 19, no. 2 (2005), pp. 120–38.

30. "Leading a Virtual Team: Agilent's Grant Marshall," ceoforum.com.au, March 2005; "Supporting Australian Innovation," *Electronics News*, 11 January 2005; M. Conlin, "The Easiest Commute of All," *Business Week*, 12 December 2005, p. 78.

31. S.L. Robinson, "Trust and Breach of the Psychological Contract," Administrative Science Quarterly 41 (1996), pp. 574–99; D.M. Rousseau et al., "Not So Different After All: A Cross-Discipline View of Trust," *Academy of Management Review* 23 (1998), pp. 393–404; D.L. Duarte and N. T. Snyder, *Mastering Virtual Teams: Strategies, Tools, and Techniques That Succeed*, 2nd ed. (San Francisco, CA: Jossey-Bass, 2000), pp. 139–55; A.C. Costa, "Work Team Trust and Effectiveness," *Personnel Review* 32, no. 5 (2003), pp. 605–24; S. Kiffin-Petersen, "Trust: A Neglected Variable in Team Effectiveness Research," *Journal of the Australian and New Zealand Academy of Management* 10, no. 1 (2004), pp. 38–53.

32. D.J. McAllister, "Affect- and Cognition-Based Trust as Foundations for Interpersonal Cooperation in Organizations," *Academy of Management Journal* 38, no. 1 (February 1995), pp. 24–59; M. Williams, "In Whom We Trust: Group Membership as an Affective Context for Trust Development," *Academy of Management Review* 26, no. 3 (July 2001), pp. 377–96.

33. O.E. Williamson, "Calculativeness, Trust, and Economic Organization," *Journal of Law and Economics* 36, no. 1 (1993), pp. 453–86.

34. E.M. Whitener et al., "Managers as Initiators of Trust: An Exchange Relationship Framework for Understanding Managerial Trustworthy Behavior," *Academy of Management Review* 23 (July 1998), pp. 513–30; J.M. Kouzes and B.Z. Posner, *The Leadership Challenge*, 3rd ed. (San Francisco: Jossey-Bass, 2002), Chapter 2; T. Simons, "Behavioral Integrity: The Perceived Alignment between Managers' Words and Deeds as a Research Focus," *Organization Science* 13, no. 1 (January–February 2002), pp. 18–35.

35. M.A. Hogg et al., "The Social Identity Perspective: Intergroup Relations, Self-Conception, and Small Groups," *Small Group Research* 35, no. 3 (June 2004), pp. 246–76.

36. J.R. Dunn and M.E. Schweitzer, "Feeling and Believing: The Influence of Emotion on Trust," *Journal of Personality and Social Psychology* 88, no. 5 (May 2005), pp. 736–48;

H. Gill et al., "Antecedents of Trust: Establishing a Boundary Condition for the Relation between Propensity to Trust and Intention to Trust," *Journal of Business and Psychology* 19, no. 3 (Spring 2005), pp. 287–302.

37. T.K. Das and B. Teng, "Between Trust and Control: Developing Confidence in Partner Cooperation in Alliances," *Academy of Management Review* 23 (1998), pp. 491–512; S.L. Jarvenpaa and D.E. Leidner, "Communication and Trust in Global Virtual Teams," *Organization Science* 10 (1999), pp. 791–815; J.K. Murnighan, J.M. Oesch, and M. Pillutla, "Player Types and Self-Impression Management in Dictatorship Games: Two Experiments," *Games and Economic Behavior* 37, no. 2 (2001), pp. 388–414; M.M. Pillutla, D. Malhotra, and J. Keith Murnighan, "Attributions of Trust and the Calculus of Reciprocity," *Journal of Experimental Social Psychology* 39, no. 5 (2003), pp. 448–55.

38. K.T. Dirks and D.L. Ferrin, "The Role of Trust in Organizations," *Organization Science* 12, no. 4 (July-August 2004), pp. 450–67.

39. V.H. Vroom and A.G. Jago, *The New Leadership* (Englewood Cliffs, NJ: Prentice-Hall, 1988), pp. 28–29.

40. M. Diehl and W. Stroebe, "Productivity Loss in Idea-Generating Groups: Tracking Down the Blocking Effects," *Journal of Personality and Social Psychology* 61 (1991), pp. 392–403; R.B. Gallupe et al., "Blocking Electronic Brainstorms," *Journal of Applied Psychology* 79 (1994), pp. 77–86; B.A. Nijstad, W. Stroebe, and H.F.M. Lodewijkx, "Production Blocking and Idea Generation: Does Blocking Interfere with Cognitive Processes?" *Journal of Experimental Social Psychology* 39, no. 6 (November 2003), pp. 531–48.

41. B.E. Irmer, P. Bordia, and D. Abusah, "Evaluation Apprehension and Perceived Benefits in Interpersonal and Database Knowledge Sharing," *Academy of Management Proceedings* (2002), pp. B1–B6.

42. I.L. Janis, *Groupthink: Psychological Studies of Policy Decisions and Fiascoes*, 2nd ed. (Boston: Houghton Mifflin, 1982); J.K. Esser, "Alive and Well after 25 Years: A Review of Groupthink Research," *Organizational Behavior and Human Decision Processes* 73, no. 2–3 (1998), pp. 116–41.

43. J.N. Choi and M.U. Kim, "The Organizational Application of Groupthink and Its Limitations in Organizations," *Journal of Applied Psychology* 84, no. 2 (April 1999), pp. 297–306; N.L. Kerr and S.R. Tindale,

"Group Performance and Decision Making," *Annual Review of Psychology* 55 (2004), pp. 623–55.

44. D. Miller, *The Icarus Paradox: How Exceptional Companies Bring About Their Own Downfall* (New York: HarperBusiness, 1990); S. Finkelstein, *Why Smart Executives Fail* (New York: Viking, 2003); K. Tasa and G. Whyte, "Collective Efficacy and Vigilant Problem Solving in Group Decision Making: A Non-Linear Model," *Organizational Behavior and Human Decision Processes* 96, no. 2 (March 2005), pp. 119–29.

45. D. Isenberg, "Group Polarization: A Critical Review and Meta-Analysis," *Journal of Personality and Social Psychology* 50 (1986), pp. 1141–51; C. McGarty et al., "Group Polarization as Conformity to the Prototypical Group Member," *British Journal of Social Psychology* 31 (1992), pp. 1–20; C.R. Sunstein, "Deliberative Trouble? Why Groups Go to Extremes," *Yale Law Journal* 110, no. 1 (October 2000), pp. 71–119.

46. D. Friedman, "Monty Hall's Three Doors: Construction and Deconstruction of a Choice Anomaly," *American Economic Review* 88 (September 1998), pp. 933–46; D. Kahneman, "Maps of Bounded Rationality: Psychology for Behavioral Economics," *American Economic Review* 93, no. 5 (December 2003), pp. 1449–75.

47. H. Collingwood, "Best-Kept Secrets of the World's Best Companies: Outside-in R&D," *Business* 2.0, April 2006, p. 82.

48. K.M. Eisenhardt, J.L. Kahwajy, and L. J. Bourgeois III, "Conflict and Strategic Choice: How Top Management Teams Disagree," *California Management Review* 39 (1997), pp. 42–62; R. Sutton, *Weird Ideas That Work* (New York: Free Press, 2002); C.J. Nemeth et al., "The Liberating Role of Conflict in Group Creativity: A Study in Two Countries," *European Journal of Social Psychology* 34, no. 4 (2004), pp. 365–74. For discussion on how all conflict is potentially detrimental to teams, see C.K.W. De Dreu and L.R. Weingart, "Task Versus Relationship Conflict, Team Performance, and Team Member Satisfaction: A Meta-Analysis," *Journal of Applied Psychology* 88 (August 2003), pp. 587–604; P. Hinds and D.E. Bailey, "Out of Sight, Out of Sync: Understanding Conflict in Distributed Teams," *Organization Science* 14, no. 6 (2003), pp. 615–32.

49. A.F. Osborn, *Applied Imagination* (New York: Scribner, 1957).

50. K. Darce, "Ground Control: NASA Attempts a Cultural Shift," *The Seattle*

Times, 24 April 2005, p. A3; R. Shelton, "NASA Attempts to Change Mindset in Wake of Columbia Tragedy," *Macon Telegraph* (Macon, GA), 7 July 2005.

51. C. Stewart, "Six Degrees of Innovation," *Orange County Register* (California), 22 March 2006. The problems with brainstorming are described in B. Mullen, C. Johnson, and E. Salas, "Productivity Loss in Brainstorming Groups: A Meta-Analytic Integration," *Basic and Applied Psychology* 12 (1991), pp. 2–23. For recent evidence that group brainstorming is beneficial, see V.R. Brown and P.B. Paulus, "Making Group Brainstorming More Effective: Recommendations from an Associative Memory Perspective," *Current Directions in Psychological Science* 11, no. 6 (2002), pp. 208–12; K. Leggett Dugosh and P.B. Paulus, "Cognitive and Social Comparison Processes in Brainstorming," *Journal of Experimental Social Psychology* 41, no. 3 (2005), pp. 313–20.

52. R.I. Sutton and A. Hargadon, "Brainstorming Groups in Context: Effectiveness in a Product Design Firm," *Administrative Science Quarterly* 41 (1996), pp. 685–718; T. Kelley, *The Art of Innovation* (New York: Currency Doubleday, 2001), Chapter 4.

53. R.B. Gallupe, L.M. Bastianutti, and W.H. Cooper, "Unblocking Brainstorms," *Journal of Applied Psychology* 76 (1991), pp. 137–42; W.H. Cooper et al., "Some Liberating Effects of Anonymous Electronic Brainstorming," *Small Group Research* 29, no. 2 (April 1998), pp. 147–78; A.R. Dennis, B.H. Wixom, and R.J. Vandenberg, "Understanding Fit and Appropriation Effects in Group Support Systems via Meta-Analysis," *MIS Quarterly* 25, no. 2 (June 2001), pp. 167–93; D.S. Kerr and U.S. Murthy, "Divergent and Convergent Idea Generation in Teams: A Comparison of Computer-Mediated and Face-to-Face Communication," *Group Decision and Negotiation* 13, no. 4 (July 2004), pp. 381–99.

54. P. Bordia, "Face-to-Face versus Computer-Mediated Communication: A Synthesis of the Experimental Literature," *Journal of Business Communication* 34 (1997), pp. 99–120; P.B. Paulus and H.-C. Yang, "Idea Generation in Groups: A Basis for Creativity in Organizations," *Organizational Behavior and Human Decision Processes* 82, no. 1 (2000), pp. 76–87; R.R.E. Potter, "The Role of Individual Memory and Attention Processes during Electronic Brainstorming," *MIS Quarterly* 28, no. 4 (December 2004), pp. 621–43.

55. B. Kabanoff and J.R. Rossiter, "Recent Developments in Applied Creativity," *International Review of Industrial and Organizational Psychology* 9 (1994), pp. 283–324; A. Pinsoneault et al., "Electronic Brainstorming: The Illusion of Productivity," *Information Systems Research* 10 (1999), pp. 110–33.

56. H.A. Linstone and M. Turoff, *The Delphi Method: Techniques and Applications* (Reading, MA: Addison-Wesley, 1975); P. M. Mullen, "Delphi: Myths and Reality," *Journal of Health Organization and Management* 17, no. 1 (2003), pp. 37–51; J. Landeta, "Current Validity of the Delphi Method in Social Sciences," *Technological Forecasting and Social Change* 73, no. 5 (June 2006), pp. 467–82.

57. C. Banwell et al., "Reflections on Expert Consensus: A Case Study of the Social Trends Contributing to Obesity," *The European Journal of Public Health* 15, no. 6 (December 2005), pp. 564–68; P. Rikkonen, J. Aakkula, and J. Kaivo oja, "How Can Future Long-Term Changes in Finnish Agriculture and Agricultural Policy Be Faced? Defining Strategic Agendas on the Basis of a Delphi Study," *European Planning Studies* 14, no. 2 (February 2006), pp. 147–68; S.-H. Tsaur, Y.-C. Lin, and J.-H. Lin, "Evaluating Ecotourism Sustainability from the Integrated Perspective of Resource, Community and Tourism," *Tourism Management* 27, no. 4 (2006), pp. 640–53.

58. A.L. Delbecq, A.H. Van de Ven, and D.H. Gustafson, *Group Techniques for Program Planning: A Guide to Nominal Group and Delphi Processes* (Middleton, WI: Green Briar Press, 1986).

59. S. Frankel, "NGT + MDS: An Adaptation of the Nominal Group Technique for Ill-Structured Problems," *Journal of Applied Behavioral Science* 23 (1987), pp. 543–51; H. Barki and A. Pinsonneault, "Small Group Brainstorming and Idea Quality: Is Electronic Brainstorming the Most Effective Approach?" *Small Group Research* 32, no. 2 (April 2001), pp. 158–205.

60. Graham, "Teambuilding Reveals Its Serious Side."

61. W.G. Dyer, *Team Building: Current Issues and New Alternatives*, 3rd ed. (Reading, MA: Addison-Wesley, 1995); C.A. Beatty and B.A. Barker, *Building Smart Teams: Roadmap to High Performance* (Thousand Oaks, CA: Sage Publications, 2004).

62. J. Murray, "Office Hours," *The Guardian* (London), 5 September 2005, p. 4; S. Williams, "Thanks, but No Thanks,"

Australian Financial Review, 20 August 2005, p. 32; "Lockheed Volunteers Get Bush Nod," *Los Angeles Daily News*, 9 May 2006, p. AV2.

63. M. Beer, *Organizational Change and Development: A Systems View* (Santa Monica, CA: Goodyear, 1980), pp. 143–46; E. Sundstrom, K.P. De Meuse, and D. Futrell, "Work Teams: Applications and Effectiveness," *American Psychologist* 45 (1990), pp. 120–33.

64. J. Langan-Fox and J. Anglim, "Mental Models, Team Mental Models, and Performance: Process, Development, and Future Directions," *Human Factors and Ergonomics in Manufacturing* 14, no. 4 (2004), pp. 331–52; J.E. Mathieu et al., "Scaling the Quality of Teammates' Mental Models: Equifinality and Normative Comparisons," *Journal of Organizational Behavior* 26 (2005), pp. 37–56.

65. R. Beckhard, "The Confrontation Meeting," *Harvard Business Review* 45, no. 4 (1967), pp. 159–65; H.D. Glover, "Organizational Change and Development: The Consequences of Misuse," *Leadership & Organization Development Journal* 13, no. 1 (1992), pp. 9–16. For recent discussion about problems with confrontation in teams, see M.A. Von Glinow, D.L. Shapiro, and J.M. Brett, "Can We *Talk*, and Should We? Managing Emotional Conflict in Multinational Teams," *Academy of Management Review* 29, no. 4 (2004), pp. 578–92.

66. "German Businesswoman Demands End to Fun at Work," *Reuters* (9 July 2003).

67. R.W. Woodman and J.J. Sherwood, "The Role of Team Development in Organizational Effectiveness: A Critical Review," *Psychological Bulletin* 88 (1980), pp. 166–86.

68. L. Mealiea and R. Baltazar, "A Strategic Guide for Building Effective Teams," *Personnel Management* 34, no. 2 (Summer 2005), pp. 141–60.

69. G.E. Huszczo, "Training for Team Building," *Training and Development Journal* 44 (February 1990), pp. 37–43; P. McGraw, "Back from the Mountain: Outdoor Management Development Programs and How to Ensure the Transfer of Skills to the Workplace," *Asia Pacific Journal of Human Resources* 31 (Spring 1993), pp. 52–61.

CHAPTER 11

1. J.C. Perez, "Google Sees Benefits in Corporate Blogging," *Network World*, 29 November 2004, p. 28; E. Cone, "Rise of

the Blog," *CIO Insight*, April 2005, p. 54; M. Delio, "The Enterprise Blogosphere," *InfoWorld*, 28 March 2005, pp. 42–47; S. Stern, "Word on the Blog Says Sun King Rules," *Daily Telegraph* (London), 5 January 2006, p. 3.

2. R. Gray, "Finding the Right Direction," *Communication World*, November–December 2004, pp. 26-32.

3. I. Nonaka and H. Takeuchi, *The Knowledge–Creating Company* (New York: Oxford University Press, 1995); R.T. Barker and M.R. Camarata, "The Role of Communication in Creating and Maintaining a Learning Organization: Preconditions, Indicators, and Disciplines," *Journal of Business Communication* 35 (October 1998), pp. 443-67; D. Te'eni, "A Cognitive–Affective Model of Organizational Communication for Designing It," *MIS Quarterly* 25 (June 2001), pp. 251–312.

4. C.E. Shannon and W. Weaver, *The Mathematical Theory of Communication* (Urbana, IL: University of Illinois Press, 1949); K.J. Krone, F.M. Jablin, and L.L. Putnam, "Communication Theory and Organizational Communication: Multiple Perspectives," in *Handbook of Organizational Communication: An Interdisciplinary Perspective*, ed. F.M. Jablin et al. (Newbury Park, CA: Sage, 1987), pp. 18–40.

5. W. Lucas, "Effects of E-Mail on the Organization," *European Management Journal* 16, no. 1 (February 1998), pp. 18–30; D. A. Owens, M.A. Neale, and R.I. Sutton, "Technologies of Status Management Status Dynamics in E Mail Communications," *Research on Managing Groups and Teams* 3 (2000), pp. 205–30; N. Ducheneaut and L.A. Watts, "In Search of Coherence: A Review of E-Mail Research," *Human–Computer Interaction* 20, no. 1–2 (2005), pp. 11–48.

6. J.B. Walther, "Language and Communication Technology: Introduction to the Special Issue," *Journal of Language and Social Psychology* 23, no. 4 (December 2004), pp. 384–96; J.B. Walther, T. Loh, and L. Granka, "Let Me Count the Ways: The Interchange of Verbal and Nonverbal Cues in Computer–Mediated and Face-to-Face Affinity," *Journal of Language and Social Psychology* 24, no. 1 (March 2005), pp. 36–65.

7. G. Hertel, S. Geister, and U. Konradt, "Managing Virtual Teams: A Review of Current Empirical Research," *Human Resource Management Review* 15 (2005), pp. 69–95; H. Lee, "Behavioral Strategies

for Dealing with Flaming in an Online Forum," *The Sociological Quarterly* 46, no. 2 (2005), pp. 385–403.

8. S. Williams, "Apologies and Rows by E-mail Are a New Sin for Hi-Tech Cowards," *Western Mail* (Cardiff, Wales), 1 April 2006, p. 11.

9. "A Day without E-Mail?" *Modern Healthcare*, 30 June 2003, p. 36; M. Greenwood, "I Have Banned E-mails: They Are a Cancer of Modern Business," *The Mirror* (London), 19 September 2003, p. 11.

10. K. Restivo, "Coming to an iPod near You," *National Post*, 16 July 2005, p. FP4.

11. D. Robb, "Ready or Not…Instant Messaging Has Arrived as a Financial Planning Tool," *Journal of Financial Planning* (July 2001), pp. 12–14; J. Black, "Why Offices Are Now Open Secrets," *Business Week*, 17 September 2003; A.F. Cameron and J. Webster, "Unintended Consequences of Emerging Communication Technologies: Instant Messaging in the Workplace," *Computers in Human Behavior* 21, no. 1 (2005), pp. 85–103.

12. L.Z. Tiedens and A.R. Fragale, "Power Moves: Complementarity in Dominant and Submissive Nonverbal Behavior," *Journal of Personality and Social Psychology* 84, no. 3 (2003), pp. 558–68.

13. P. Ekman and E. Rosenberg, *What the Face Reveals: Basic and Applied Studies of Spontaneous Expression Using the Facial Action Coding System* (Oxford, England: Oxford University Press, 1997); P. Winkielman and K.C. Berridge, "Unconscious Emotion," *Current Directions in Psychological Science* 13, no. 3 (2004), pp. 120–23.

14. E. Hatfield, J.T. Cacioppo, and R.L. Rapson, *Emotional Contagion* (Cambridge, England: Cambridge University Press, 1993); S.G. Barsade, "The Ripple Effect: Emotional Contagion and Its Influence on Group Behavior," *Administrative Science Quarterly* 47 (December 2002), pp. 644–75; M. Sonnby-Borgstrom, P. Jonsson, and O. Svensson, "Emotional Empathy as Related to Mimicry Reactions at Different Levels of Information Processing," *Journal of Nonverbal Behavior* 27 (Spring 2003), pp. 3–23.

15. J.R. Kelly and S.G. Barsade, "Mood and Emotions in Small Groups and Work Teams," *Organizational Behavior and Human Decision Processes* 86 (September 2001), pp. 99–130.

16. R.L. Daft and R.H. Lengel, "Information Richness: A New Approach to Managerial Behavior and Organization Design," *Research in Organizational Behavior* 6 (1984), pp. 191–233; R.H. Lengel and R.L. Daft, "The Selection of Communication Media as an Executive Skill," *Academy of Management Executive* 2 (1988), pp. 225–32.

17. R.E. Rice, "Task Analyzability, Use of New Media, and Effectiveness: A Multi-Site Exploration of Media Richness," *Organization Science* 3 (1992), pp. 475–500.

18. J.R. Carlson and R.W. Zmud, "Channel Expansion Theory and the Experiential Nature of Media Richness Perceptions," *Academy of Management Journal* 42 (April 1999), pp. 153–170; N. Kock, "Media Richness or Media Naturalness? The Evolution of Our Biological Communication Apparatus and Its Influence on Our Behavior toward E-Communication Tools," *IEEE Transactions on Professional Communication* 48, no. 2 (June 2005), pp. 117–30.

19. M. McLuhan, *Understanding Media: The Extensions of Man* (New York: McGraw-Hill, 1964).

20. K. Griffiths, "KPMG Sacks 670 Employees by E-Mail," *The Independent* (London), 5 November 2002, p. 19; P. Nelson, "Work Practices," *Personnel Today*, 12 November 2002, p. 2.

21. D. Goleman, R. Boyatzis, and A. McKee, *Primal Leaders* (Boston: Harvard Business School Press, 2002), pp. 92–95.

22. J. Kavanaugh, "National Emergency," *Business Review Weekly*, 3 November 2005, p. 32.

23. L.L. Putnam, N. Phillips, and P. Chapman, "Metaphors of Communication and Organization," in *Handbook of Organization Studies*, ed. S.R. Clegg, C. Hardy, and W.R. Nord (London: Sage, 1996), pp. 373–408; G. Morgan, *Images of Organization*, 2nd ed. (Thousand Oaks, CA: Sage, 1997); M. Rubini and H. Sigall, "Taking the Edge Off of Disagreement: Linguistic Abstractness and Self-Presentation to a Heterogeneous Audience," *European Journal of Social Psychology* 32 (2002), pp. 343–51.

24. K.M. Jackson, "Buzzword Backlash Looks to Purge Jibba-Jabba from Corporate-Speak," *Boston Globe*, 17 April 2005, p. G1.

25. L. Eckelbecker, "Click Tricks: Taming the E-mail Monster," *Worcester Telegram & Gazette*, 3 March 2006, p. A1; K. Hilpern, "Office Hours: Cc Me in on That," *The Guardian* (London), 9 January 2006, p. 3; "New Survey Reveals: Enterprises and Employees Continue to Struggle with Growing E-mail Overload Burden," *PR Newswire* (Richmond, Virginia), 7 December.

26. T. Koski, "Reflections on Information Glut and Other Issues in Knowledge Productivity," *Futures* 33 (August 2001), pp. 483–95; D.D. Dawley and W.P. Anthony, "User Perceptions of E-Mail at Work," *Journal of Business and Technical Communication* 17, no. 2 (April 2003), pp. 170–200; "E-mail Brings Costs and Fatigue," *Western News* (University of Western Ontario, London, Ontario), 9 July 2004.

27. A.G. Schick, L.A. Gordon, and S. Haka, "Information Overload: A Temporal Approach," *Accounting, Organizations & Society* 15 (1990), pp. 199–220; A. Edmunds and A. Morris, "The Problem of Information Overload in Business Organizations: A Review of the Literature," *International Journal of Information Management* 20 (2000), pp. 17–28.

28. D. Kirkpatrick, "Gates and Ozzie: How to Escape E-Mail Hell," *Fortune*, 27 June 2005, pp. 169–71.

29. D.C. Thomas and K. Inkson, *Cultural Intelligence: People Skills for Global Business* (San Francisco: Berrett-Koehler, 2004), Chapter 6; D. Welch, L. Welch, and R. Piekkari, "Speaking in Tongues," *International Studies of Management & Organization* 35, no. 1 (Spring 2005), pp. 10–27.

30. D. Woodruff, "Crossing Culture Divide Early Clears Merger Paths," *The Asian Wall Street Journal*, 28 May 2001, p. 9.

31. M. Brandel, "Global CIO," *Computerworld*, 21 November 2005, pp. 39–41. *Tatamae* and *hone* are discussed in H. Yamada, *American and Japanese Business Discourse: A Comparison of Interaction Styles* (Norwood, NJ: Ablex, 1992), p. 34; and R.M. March, *Reading the Japanese Mind* (Tokyo: Kodansha International, 1996), Chapter 1.

32. P. Harris and R. Moran, *Managing Cultural Differences* (Houston: Gulf, 1987); H. Blagg, "A Just Measure of Shame?" *British Journal of Criminology* 37 (Autumn 1997), pp. 481–501; R.E. Axtell, *Gestures: The Do's and Taboos of Body Language around the World*, revised ed. (New York: Wiley, 1998).

33. M. Griffin, "The Office, Australian Style," *Sunday Age*, 22 June 2003, p. 6.

34. S. Ohtaki, T. Ohtaki, and M.D. Fetters, "Doctor–Patient Communication:

A Comparison of the USA and Japan," *Family Practice* 20 (June 2003), pp. 276–82; M. Fujio, "Silence during Intercultural Communication: A Case Study," *Corporate Communications* 9, no. 4 (2004), pp. 331–39.

35. D.C. Barnlund, *Communication Styles of Japanese and Americans: Images and Realities* (Belmont,CA: Wadsworth, 1988); Yamada, *American and Japanese Business Discourse: A Comparison of Interaction Styles*, Chapter 2; H. Yamada, *Different Games, Different Rules* (New York: Oxford University Press, 1997), pp. 76–79.

36. This stereotypical notion is prevalent throughout J. Gray, *Men Are from Mars, Women Are from Venus* (New York: Harper Collins, 1992). For a critique of this view see J.T. Wood, "A Critical Response to John Gray's Mars and Venus Portrayals of Men and Women," *Southern Communication Journal* 67 (Winter 2002), pp. 201–10.

37. D. Tannen, *You Just Don't Understand: Men and Women in Conversation* (New York: Ballentine Books, 1990); D. Tannen, *Talking from 9 to 5* (New York: Avon, 1994); M. Crawford, *Talking Difference: On Gender and Language* (Thousand Oaks, CA: Sage, 1995), pp. 41–44; L.L. Namy, L.C. Nygaard, and D. Sauerteig, "Gender Differences in Vocal Accommodation: The Role of Perception," *Journal of Language and Social Psychology* 21, no. 4 (December 2002), pp. 422–32.

38. A. Mulac et al., "'Uh-Huh. What's That All About?' Differing Interpretations of Conversational Backchannels and Questions as Sources of Miscommunication across Gender Boundaries," *Communication Research* 25 (December 1998), pp. 641–68; N.M. Sussman and D.H. Tyson, "Sex and Power: Gender Differences in Computer-Mediated Interactions," *Computers in Human Behavior* 16 (2000), pp. 381–94; D.R. Caruso and P. Salovey, *The Emotionally Intelligent Manager* (San Francisco: Jossey-Bass, 2004), p. 23; D. Fallows, *How Women and Men Use the Internet* (Washington, DC: Pew Internet and American Life Project, 28 December 2005).

39. P. Tripp-Knowles, "A Review of the Literature on Barriers Encountered by Women in Science Academia," *Resources for Feminist Research* 24 (Spring/Summer 1995), pp. 28–34.

40. The opening quotation is cited in K. Davis and J.W. Newstrom, *Human Behavior at Work: Organizational Behavior*, 7th ed.

(New York: McGraw-Hill, 1985), p. 438. Henry Schacht's quotation is found in T. Neff and J. Citrin, "You're in Charge. Now What?" *Fortune*, 24 January 2005, pp. 109–15.

41. The three components of listening discussed here are based on several recent studies in the field of marketing, including S.B. Castleberry, C.D. Shepherd, and R. Ridnour, "Effective Interpersonal Listening in the Personal Selling Environment: Conceptualization, Measurement, and Nomological Validity," *Journal of Marketing Theory and Practice* 7 (Winter 1999), pp. 30–38; L.B. Comer and T. Drollinger, "Active Empathetic Listening and Selling Success: A Conceptual Framework," *Journal of Personal Selling & Sales Management* 19 (Winter 1999), pp. 15–29; and K. de Ruyter and M.G.M. Wetzels, "The Impact of Perceived Listening Behavior in Voice-to-Voice Service Encounters," *Journal of Service Research* 2 (February 2000), pp. 276–84.

42. S.P. Means, "Playing at Pixar," *Salt Lake Tribune* (Utah), 30 May 2003, p. D1; G. Whipp, "Swimming against the Tide," *Daily News of Los Angeles*, 30 May 2003, p. U6.

43. G. Evans and D. Johnson, "Stress and Open-Office Noise," *Journal of Applied Psychology* 85 (2000), pp. 779–83; F. Russo, "My Kingdom for a Door," *Time Magazine*, 23 October 2000, p. B1.

44. B. Sosnin, "Digital Newsletters 'E-Volutionize' Employee Communications," *HRMagazine*, May 2001, pp. 99–107.

45. E. Booker, "Rethinking the Blogosphere," *B to B*, 14 November 2005, p. 10.

46. R.D. Hof, "Something Wiki Comes This Way," *BusinessWeek*, 7 June 2004, p. 128; K. Swisher, "Boomtown: 'Wiki' May Alter How Employees Work Together," *The Wall Street Journal*, 29 July 2004, p. B1; Delio, "The Enterprise Blogosphere."

47. S. Greengard, "Employee Surveys: Ask the Right Questions, Probe the Answers for Insight," *Workforce Management*, December 2004, p. 76; A. Kover, "And the Survey Says…" *Industry Week*, September 2005, pp. 49–52.

48. R. Rodwell, "Regular Staff Meetings Help Build Morale," *South China Morning Post* (Hong Kong), 27 August 2005, p. 4.

49. The original term is "management by *wandering* around," but this has been replaced with "walking" over the years. See W. Ouchi, *Theory Z* (New York: Avon

Books, 1981), pp. 176–77; T. Peters and R. Waterman, *In Search of Excellence* (New York: Harper and Row, 1982), p. 122.

50. D. Penner, "Putting the Boss Out Front," *Vancouver Sun*, 7 June 2002.

51. D. Thomas, "HR Challenges…I'm Lovin' It," *Personnel Today*, 6 September 2005, p. 11.

52. R. Rousos, "Trust in Leaders Lacking at Utility," *The Ledger* (Lakeland, Florida), 29 July 2003, p. B1; B. Whitworth and B. Riccomini, "Management Communication: Unlocking Higher Employee Performance," *Communication World*, March–April 2005, pp. 18–21.

53. K. Davis, "Management Communication and the Grapevine," *Harvard Business Review* 31 (September-October 1953), pp. 43–49; W.L. Davis and J.R. O'Connor, "Serial Transmission of Information: A Study of the Grapevine," *Journal of Applied Communication Research* 5 (1977), pp. 61 72.

54. H. Mintzberg, *The Structuring of Organizations* (Englewood Cliffs, NJ: Prentice Hall, 1979), pp. 46–53; D. Krackhardt and J.R. Hanson, "Informal Networks: The Company Behind the Chart," *Harvard Business Review* 71 (July-August 1993), pp. 104–11.

55. C.J. Walker and C.A. Beckerle, "The Effect of State Anxiety on Rumor Transmission," *Journal of Social Behaviour & Personality* 2 (August 1987), pp. 353–60; R.L. Rosnow, "Inside Rumor: A Personal Journey," *American Psychologist* 46 (May 1991), pp. 484–96; M. Noon and R. Delbridge, "News from Behind My Hand: Gossip in Organizations," *Organization Studies* 14 (1993), pp. 23–36.

56. N. Nicholson, "Evolutionary Psychology: Toward a New View of Human Nature and Organizational Society," *Human Relations* 50 (September 1997), pp. 1053–78.

CHAPTER 12

1. R. Gluyas, "Fear and Loathing in NAB's Forex Fiasco," *The Australian*, 6 August 2005, p. 35; E. Johnston, "'Anything Goes,' Ex-Trader Says," *Australian Financial Review*, 2 August 2005, p. 3; E. Johnston, "Expletives and Stench in Hothouse of NAB Dealers," *Australian Financial Review*, 6 August 2005, p. 3.

2. For a discussion of the definition of power, see H. Mintzberg, *Power in and around Organizations* (Englewood Cliffs,

NJ: Prentice Hall, 1983), Chapter 1; J. Pfeffer, *Managing with Power* (Boston: Harvard Business University Press, 1992), pp. 17, 30; J. Pfeffer, *New Directions in Organizational Theory* (New York: Oxford University Press, 1997), Chapter 6; J.M. Whitmeyer, "Power through Appointment," *Social Science Research* 29 (2000), pp. 535–55.

3. R.A. Dahl, "The Concept of Power," *Behavioral Science* 2 (1957), pp. 201–18; R.M. Emerson, "Power-Dependence Relations," *American Sociological Review* 27 (1962), pp. 31-41; A.M. Pettigrew, *The Politics of Organizational Decision-Making* (London: Tavistock, 1973).

4. K.M. Bartol and D.C. Martin, "When Politics Pays: Factors Influencing Managerial Compensation Decisions," *Personnel Psychology* 43 (1990), pp. 599–614; D.J. Brass and M.E. Burkhardt, "Potential Power and Power Use: An Investigation of Structure and Behavior," *Academy of Management Journal* 36 (1993), pp. 441–70.

5. J.R.P. French and B. Raven, "The Bases of Social Power," in *Studies in Social Power*, ed. D. Cartwright (Ann Arbor, MI: University of Michigan Press, 1959), pp. 150-67; P. Podsakoff and C. Schreisheim, "Field Studies of French and Raven's Bases of Power: Critique, Analysis, and Suggestions for Future Research," *Psychological Bulletin* 97 (1985), pp. 387–411; S. Finkelstein, "Power in Top Management Teams: Dimensions, Measurement, and Validation," *Academy of Management Journal* 35 (1992), pp. 505–38; P.P. Carson and K.D. Carson, "Social Power Bases: A Meta-Analytic Examination of Interrelationships and Outcomes," *Journal of Applied Social Psychology* 23 (1993), pp. 1150–69.

6. B.H. Raven, "The Bases of Power: Origins and Recent Developments," *Journal of Social Issues* 49 (1993), pp. 227–51; G.A. Yukl, *Leadership in Organizations*, 3rd ed. (Englewood Cliffs, NJ: Prentice Hall, 1994), p. 13.

7. C. Barnard, *The Function of the Executive* (Cambridge, MA: Harvard University Press, 1938); C. Hardy and S.R. Clegg, "Some Dare Call It Power," in *Handbook of Organization Studies*, ed. S.R. Clegg, C. Hardy, and W.R. Nord (London: Sage, 1996), pp. 622–41.

8. L.A. Conger, *Winning 'Em Over: A New Model for Managing in the Age of Persuasion* (New York: Simon & Schuster, 1998), Appendix A.

9. V.L. Parker, "Org Charts Turn Around with Teams," *News & Observer* (Raleigh, North Carolina), 21 July 2005, p. D1; L.S. Sya, "Flying to Greater Heights," *New Sunday Times* (Kuala Lumpur), 31 July 2005, p. 14.

10. P.F. Drucker, "The New Workforce," *The Economist*, 3 November 2001, pp. 8–12.

11. J.D. Kudisch and M.L. Poteet, "Expert Power, Referent Power, and Charisma: Toward the Resolution of a Theoretical Debate," *Journal of Business & Psychology* 10 (Winter 1995), pp. 177–95; H.L. Tosi et al., "CEO Charisma, Compensation, and Firm Performance," *Leadership Quarterly* 15, no. 3 (2004), pp. 405–20.

12. G. Yukl and C.M. Falbe, "Importance of Different Power Sources in Downward and Lateral Relations," *Journal of Applied Psychology* 76 (1991), pp. 416-23; B.H. Raven, "Kurt Lewin Address: Influence, Power, Religion, and the Mechanisms of Social Control," *Journal of Social Issues* 55 (Spring 1999), pp. 161–86.

13. P.L. Dawes, D.Y. Lee, and G.R. Dowling, "Information Control and Influence in Emergent Buying Centers," *Journal of Marketing* 62, no. 3 (July 1998), pp. 55-68; D.J. Brass et al., "Taking Stock of Networks and Organizations: A Multilevel Perspective," *Academy of Management Journal* 47, no. 6 (December 2004), pp. 795–817.

14. C.R. Hinings et al., "Structural Conditions of Intraorganizational Power," *Administrative Science Quarterly* 19 (1974), pp. 22–44. Also see C.S. Saunders, "The Strategic Contingency Theory of Power: Multiple Perspectives," *The Journal of Management Studies* 27 (1990), pp. 1–21.

15. S. Elliott, "Hunting for the Next Cool in Advertising," *The New York Times*, 1 December 2003, p. C19; S. Delaney, "Predicting the Birth of the Cool," *The Independent* (London), 5 September 2005, p. 15; A. McMains, "Trend-Spotting Division Adds to Lowe's Evolution," *Adweek*, 11 April 2005, p. 11.

16. D.J. Hickson et al., "A Strategic Contingencies' Theory of Intraorganizational Power," *Administrative Science Quarterly* 16 (1971), pp. 216-27; Hinings et al., "Structural Conditions of Intraorganizational Power"; R.M. Kanter, "Power Failure in Management Circuits," *Harvard Business Review* (July-August 1979), pp. 65–75.

17. M. Crozier, *The Bureaucratic Phenomenon* (London: Tavistock, 1964).

18. Hickson et al., "A Strategic Contingencies' Theory of Intraorganizational Power"; J.D. Hackman, "Power and Centrality in the Allocation of Resources in Colleges and Universities," *Administrative Science Quarterly* 30 (1985), pp. 61–77; Brass and Burkhardt, "Potential Power and Power Use: An Investigation of Structure and Behavior."

19. Kanter, "Power Failure in Management Circuits"; B.E. Ashforth, "The Experience of Powerlessness in Organizations," *Organizational Behavior and Human Decision Processes* 43 (1989), pp. 207–42; L. Holden, "European Managers: HRM and an Evolving Role," *European Business Review* 12 (2000).

20. J. Voight, "When Credit Is Not Due," *Adweek*, 1 March 2004, p. 24.

21. R. Madell, "Ground Floor," *Pharmaceutical Executive (Women in Pharma Supplement)*, June 2000, pp. 24–31.

22. L.A. Perlow, "The Time Famine: Toward a Sociology of Work Time," *Administrative Science Quarterly* 44 (March 1999), pp. 5–31.

23. B.R. Ragins, "Diversified Mentoring Relationships in Organizations: A Power Perspective," *Academy of Management Review* 22 (1997), pp. 482–521; M.C. Higgins and K.E. Kram, "Reconceptualizing Mentoring at Work: A Developmental Network Perspective," *Academy of Management Review* 26 (April 2001), pp. 264–88.

24. D. Krackhardt and J.R. Hanson, "Informal Networks: The Company behind the Chart," *Harvard Business Review* 71 (July-August 1993), pp. 104–11; P.S. Adler and S.-W. Kwon, "Social Capital: Prospects for a New Concept," *Academy of Management Review* 27, no. 1 (2002), pp. 17–40.

25. A. Mehra, M. Kilduff, and D.J. Brass, "The Social Networks of High and Low Self-Monitors: Implications for Workplace Performance," *Administrative Science Quarterly* 46 (March 2001), pp. 121–46.

26. B.R. Ragins and E. Sundstrom, "Gender and Power in Organizations: A Longitudinal Perspective," *Psychological Bulletin* 105 (1989), pp. 51–88; M. Linehan, "Barriers to Women's Participation in International Management," *European Business Review* 13 (2001).

27. D.M. McCracken, "Winning the Talent War for Women: Sometimes It Takes a Revolution," *Harvard Business Review* (November–December 2000), pp. 159–67; D.L. Nelson and R.J. Burke, "Women

Executives: Health, Stress, and Success," *Academy of Management Executive* 14 (May 2000), pp. 107–21.

28. K. Atuahene-Gima and H. Li, "Marketing's Influence Tactics in New Product Development: A Study of High Technology Firms in China," *Journal of Product Innovation Management* 17 (2000), pp. 451–70; A. Somech and A. Drach-Zahavy, "Relative Power and Influence Strategy: The Effects of Agent/Target Organizational Power on Superiors' Choices of Influence Strategies," *Journal of Organizational Behavior* 23 (2002), pp. 167–79.

29. D. Kipnis, S.M. Schmidt, and I. Wilkinson, "Intraorganizational Influence Tactics: Explorations in Getting One's Way," *Journal of Applied Psychology* 65 (1980), pp. 440–52. Also see C. Schriesheim and T. Hinkin, "Influence Tactics Used by Subordinates: A Theoretical and Empirical Analysis and Refinement of the Kipnis, Schmidt, and Wilkinson Subscales," *Journal of Applied Psychology* 75 (1990), pp. 246–57; W.A. Hochwarter et al., "A Reexamination of Schriesheim and Hinkin's (1990) Measure of Upward Influence," *Educational and Psychological Measurement* 60 (October 2000), pp. 755–71.

30. Some of the more thorough lists of influence tactics are presented in A. Rao and K. Hashimoto, "Universal and Culturally Specific Aspects of Managerial Influence: A Study of Japanese Managers," *Leadership Quarterly* 8 (1997), pp. 295–312; L.A. McFarland, A.M. Ryan, and S.D. Kriska, "Field Study Investigation of Applicant Use of Influence Tactics in a Selection Interview," *Journal of Psychology* 136 (July 2002), pp. 383–98.

31. R.B. Cialdini and N.J. Goldstein, "Social Influence: Compliance and Conformity," *Annual Review of Psychology* 55 (2004), pp. 591–621.

32. Rao and Hashimoto, "Universal and Culturally Specific Aspects of Managerial Influence." Silent authority as an influence tactic in non-Western cultures is also discussed in S.F. Pasa, "Leadership Influence in a High Power Distance and Collectivist Culture," *Leadership & Organization Development Journal* 21 (2000), pp. 414–26.

33. "Be Part of the Team If You Want to Catch the Eye," *Birmingham Post* (U.K.), 31 August 2000, p. 14; S. Maitlis, "Taking It from the Top: How CEOs Influence

(and Fail to Influence) Their Boards," *Organization Studies* 25, no. 8 (2004), pp. 1275–1311.

34. A.T. Cobb, "Toward the Study of Organizational Coalitions: Participant Concerns and Activities in a Simulated Organizational Setting," *Human Relations* 44 (1991), pp. 1057–79; E.A. Mannix, "Organizations as Resource Dilemmas: The Effects of Power Balance on Coalition Formation in Small Groups," *Organizational Behavior and Human Decision Processes* 55 (1993), pp. 1–22; D.J. Terry, M.A. Hogg, and K.M. White, "The Theory of Planned Behavior: Self-Identity, Social Identity, and Group Norms," *British Journal of Social Psychology* 38 (September 1999), pp. 225–44.

35. Rao and Hashimoto, "Universal and Culturally Specific Aspects of Managerial Influence."

36. D. Strutton and L.E. Pelton, "Effects of Ingratiation on Lateral Relationship Quality within Sales Team Settings," *Journal of Business Research* 43 (1998), pp. 1–12; R. Vonk, "Self-Serving Interpretations of Flattery: Why Ingratiation Works," *Journal of Personality and Social Psychology* 82 (2002), pp. 515–26.

37. C.A. Higgins, T.A. Judge, and G.R. Ferris, "Influence Tactics and Work Outcomes: A Meta-Analysis," *Journal of Organizational Behavior* 24 (2003), pp. 90–106.

38. D. Strutton, L.E. Pelton, and J. Tanner Jr., "Shall We Gather in the Garden? The Effect of Ingratiatory Behaviors on Buyer Trust in Salespeople," *Industrial Marketing Management* 25 (1996), pp. 151–62; J. O'Neil, "An Investigation of the Sources of Influence of Corporate Public Relations Practitioners," *Public Relations Review* 29 (June 2003), pp. 159–69.

39. A. Rao and S.M. Schmidt, "Upward Impression Management: Goals, Influence Strategies, and Consequences," *Human Relations* 48 (1995), pp. 147–67.

40. A.P.J. Ellis et al., "The Use of Impression Management Tactics in Structured Interviews: A Function of Question Type?" *Journal of Applied Psychology* 87 (December 2002), pp. 1200–8; M.C. Bolino and W.H. Tunley, "More Than One Way to Make an Impression: Exploring Profiles of Impression Management," *Journal of Management* 29 (2003), pp. 141–60.

41. S.L. McShane, "Applicant Misrepresentations in Résumés and Interviews in Canada," *Labor Law Journal*, January

1994, pp. 15–24; J. Jaucius, "Internet Guru's Credentials a True Work of Fiction," *Ottawa Citizen*, 12 June 2001; S. Romero and M. Richtel, "Second Chance," *The New York Times*, 5 March 2001, p. C1; "Up to 40 Percent of U.S. Workers Pad Their Résumés," *Agence France Presse* (Washington, D.C.), 22 February 2006; P. Sabatini, "Fibs on Résumés Commonplace," *Pittsburgh Post-Gazette*, 24 February 2006.

42. J. Dillard and E. Peck, "Persuasion and the Structure of Affect: Dual Systems and Discrete Emotions as Complementary Models," *Human Communication Research* 27 (2000), pp. 38–68; S. Fox and Y. Amichai-Hamburger, "The Power of Emotional Appeals in Promoting Organizational Change Programs," *Academy of Management Executive* 15 (November 2001), pp. 84–94; E.H.H.J. Das, J.B.F. de Wit, and W. Stroebe, "Fear Appeals Motivate Acceptance of Action Recommendations: Evidence for a Positive Bias in the Processing of Persuasive Messages," *Personality and Social Psychology Bulletin* 29 (May 2003), pp. 650–64; R. Buck et al., "Emotion and Reason in Persuasion: Applying the ARI Model and the CASC Scale," *Journal of Business Research* 57, no. 6 (2004), pp. 647–56.

43. A.P. Brief, *Attitudes in and Around Organizations* (Thousand Oaks, CA: Sage, 1998), pp. 69–84; D.J. O'Keefe, *Persuasion: Theory and Research* (Thousand Oaks, CA: Sage Publications, 2002).

44. Conger, *Winning 'Em Over: A New Model for Managing in the Age of Persuasion*; J.J. Jiang, G. Klein, and R.G. Vedder, "Persuasive Expert Systems: The Influence of Confidence and Discrepancy," *Computers in Human Behavior* 16 (March 2000), pp. 99–109.

45. S. Gilmor, "Ahead of the Curve," *Infoworld*, 13 January 2003, p. 58; M. Hiltzik, "Apple CEO's Visions Don't Guarantee Sustained Gains," *Los Angeles Times*, 14 April 2003, p. C1. The origin of the term *reality distortion field* is described at www.folklore.org.

46. These and other features of message content in persuasion are detailed in R. Petty and J. Cacioppo, *Attitudes and Persuasion: Classic and Contemporary Approaches* (Dubuque, IA: W.C. Brown, 1981); D.G. Linz and S. Penrod, "Increasing Attorney Persuasiveness in the Courtroom," *Law and Psychology Review* 8 (1984), pp. 1–47; M. Pfau, E.A. Szabo, and J. Anderson, "The Role and Impact

of Affect in the Process of Resistance to Persuasion," *Human Communication Research* 27 (April 2001), pp. 216–52; O'Keefe, *Persuasion: Theory and Research*, Chapter 9.

47. N. Rhodes and W. Wood, "Self-Esteem and Intelligence Affect Influenceability: The Mediating Role of Message Reception," *Psychological Bulletin* 111, no. 1 (1992), pp. 156–71.

48. A.W. Gouldner, "The Norm of Reciprocity: A Preliminary Statement," *American Sociological Review* 25 (1960), pp. 161–78.

49. Y. Fan, "Questioning Guanxi: Definition, Classification, and Implications," *International Business Review* 11 (2002), pp. 543–61; D. Tan and R.S. Snell, "The Third Eye: Exploring Guanxi and Relational Morality in the Workplace," *Journal of Business Ethics* 41 (December 2002), pp. 361–84; W.R. Vanhonacker, "When Good Guanxi Turns Bad," *Harvard Business Review* 82, no. 4 (April 2004), pp. 18–19.

50. A. Ledeneva, *Russia's Economy of Favors: Blat, Networking and Informal Exchange* (New York: Cambridge University Press, 1998); S. Michailova and V. Worm, "Personal Networking in Russia and China: Blat and Guanxi," *European Management Journal* 21 (2003), pp. 509–19.

51. C.M. Falbe and G. Yukl, "Consequences for Managers of Using Single Influence Tactics and Combinations of Tactics," *Academy of Management Journal* 35 (1992), pp. 638–52.

52. Falbe and Yukl, "Consequences for Managers of Using Single Influence Tactics and Combinations of Tactics"; Atuahene-Gima and Li, "Marketing's Influence Tactics in New Product Development."

53. R.C. Ringer and R.W. Boss, "Hospital Professionals' Use of Upward Influence Tactics," *Journal of Managerial Issues* 12 (2000), pp. 92–108.

54. G. Blickle, "Do Work Values Predict the Use of Intraorganizational Influence Strategies?" *Journal of Applied Social Psychology* 30, no. 1 (January 2000), pp. 196–205; P.P. Fu et al., "The Impact of Societal Cultural Values and Individual Social Beliefs on the Perceived Effectiveness of Managerial Influence Strategies: A Meso Approach," *Journal of International Business Studies* 35, no. 4 (July 2004), pp. 284–305.

55. D. Tannen, *Talking from 9 to 5* (New York: Avon, 1994), Chapter 2; M. Crawford, *Talking Difference: On Gender and Language* (Thousand Oaks, CA: Sage, 1995), pp. 41–44.

56. S. Mann, "Politics and Power in Organizations: Why Women Lose Out," *Leadership & Organization Development Journal* 16 (1995), pp. 9–15; E.H. Buttner and M. McEnally, "The Interactive Effect of Influence Tactic, Applicant Gender, and Type of Job on Hiring Recommendations," *Sex Roles* 34 (1996), pp. 581–91; L.L. Carli, "Gender, Interpersonal Power, and Social Influence," *Journal of Social Issues* 55 (Spring 1999), pp. 81–99.

57. This definition of organizational politics has become the dominant perspective over the past 15 years. See G.R. Ferris and K.M. Kacmar, "Perceptions of Organizational Politics," *Journal of Management* 18 (1992), pp. 93–116; R. Cropanzano et al., "The Relationship of Organizational Politics and Support to Work Behaviors, Attitudes, and Stress," *Journal of Organizational Behavior* 18 (1997), pp. 159–80; E. Vigoda and A. Cohen, "Influence Tactics and Perceptions of Organizational Politics: A Longitudinal Study," *Journal of Business Research* 55 (2002), pp. 311–24. However, organizational politics was previously viewed as influence tactics outside the formal role that could be either selfish or altruistic. This older definition is less common today, possibly because it is incongruent with popular views of politics and because it overlaps too much with the concept of influence. For the older perspective of organizational politics, see J. Pfeffer, *Power in Organizations* (Boston: Pitman, 1981); Mintzberg, *Power in and around Organizations*.

58. K.M. Kacmar and R.A. Baron, "Organizational Politics: The State of the Field, Links to Related Processes, and an Agenda for Future Research," in *Research in Personnel and Human Resources Management*, ed. G.R. Ferris (Greenwich, CT: JAI Press, 1999), pp. 1–39; L.A. Witt, T.F. Hilton, and W.A. Hochwarter, "Addressing Politics in Matrix Teams," *Group & Organization Management* 26 (June 2001), pp. 230–47; E. Vigoda, "Stress-Related Aftermaths to Workplace Politics: The Relationships among Politics, Job Distress, and Aggressive Behavior in Organizations," *Journal of Organizational Behavior* 23 (2002), pp. 571–91.

59. C. Hardy, *Strategies for Retrenchment and Turnaround: The Politics of Survival* (Berlin: Walter de Gruyter, 1990), Chapter 14; M.C. Andrews and K.M. Kacmar, "Discriminating among Organizational Politics, Justice, and Support," *Journal of Organizational Behavior* 22 (2001), pp. 347–66.

60. S. Blazejewski and W. Dorow, "Managing Organizational Politics for Radical Change: The Case of Beiersdorf–Lechia S.A., Poznan," *Journal of World Business* 38 (August 2003), pp. 204–23.

61. H. Mitzberg, "The Organization as Political Arena," *Journal of Management Studies* 22 (1985), pp. 133–54; G.R. Ferris, G.S. Russ, and P.M. Fandt, "Politics in Organizations," in *Impression Management in the Organization*, ed. R.A. Giacalone and P. Rosenfeld (Hillsdale, NJ: Erlbaum, 1989), pp. 143–70.

62. L.W. Porter, R.W. Allen, and H.L. Angle, "The Politics of Upward Influence in Organizations," *Research in Organizational Behavior* 3 (1981), pp. 120–22; R.J. House, "Power and Personality in Complex Organizations," *Research in Organizational Behavior* 10 (1988), pp. 305–57.

63. R. Christie and F. Geis, *Studies in Machiavellianism* (New York: Academic Press, 1970); S.M. Farmer et al., "Putting Upward Influence Strategies in Context," *Journal of Organizational Behavior* 18 (1997), pp. 17–42; K.S. Sauleya and A.G. Bedeian, "Equity Sensitivity: Construction of a Measure and Examination of Its Psychometric Properties," *Journal of Management* 26 (September 2000), pp. 885–910.

64. G.R. Ferris et al., "Perceptions of Organizational Politics: Prediction, Stress-Related Implications, and Outcomes," *Human Relations* 49 (1996), pp. 233–63.

CHAPTER 13

1. B. Dudley, "Bring Back the Dazzle," *The Seattle Times*, 23 September 2005; J. Greene, "Troubling Exits at Microsoft," *Business-Week*, 26 September 2005, p. 98; A. Linn, "Microsoft Reorganizes to Compete Better with Google, Yahoo," *Associated Press Newswires*, 21 September 2005; V. Murphy, "Microsoft's Midlife Crisis," *Forbes*, 3 October 2005, p. 88; L. Vaas, "Microsoft Expands Bureaucracy, Crowns MSN King," *eWeek*, 20 September 2005; J.L. Yang, "Microsoft's New Brain," *Fortune*, 1 May 2006, p. 56.

2. J.A. Wall and R.R. Callister, "Conflict and Its Management," *Journal of Management*, 21 (1995), pp. 515–58; M.A. Rahim, "Toward a Theory of Managing Organizational Conflict," *International Journal of Conflict Management* 13, no. 3 (2002), pp. 206–35.

3. L. Pondy, "Organizational Conflict: Concepts and Models," *Administrative Science Quarterly* 2 (1967), pp. 296–320; K.W. Thomas, "Conflict and Negotiation Processes in Organizations," in *Handbook of Industrial and Organizational Psychology*, ed. M.D. Dunnette and L.M. Hough, 2nd ed. (Palo Alto, CA: Consulting Psychologists Press, 1992), pp. 651–718.

4. Murphy, "Microsoft's Midlife Crisis."

5. M.A. Von Glinow, D.L. Shapiro, and J.M. Brett, "Can We Talk, and Should We? Managing Emotional Conflict in Multicultural Teams," *Academy of Management Review* 29, no. 4 (2004), pp. 578–92.

6. G.E. Martin and T.J. Bergman, "The Dynamics of Behavioral Response to Conflict in the Workplace," *Journal of Occupational & Organizational Psychology* 69 (December 1996), pp. 377–87; J.M. Brett, D.L. Shapiro, and A.L. Lytle, "Breaking the Bonds of Reciprocity in Negotiations," *Academy of Management Journal* 41 (August 1998), pp. 410–24.

7. H. Witteman, "Analyzing Interpersonal Conflict: Nature of Awareness, Type of Initiating Event, Situational Perceptions, and Management Styles," *Western Journal of Communications* 56 (1992), pp. 248–80; Wall and Callister, "Conflict and Its Management."

8. A. Grove, "How to Make Confrontation Work for You," in *The Book of Management Wisdom*, ed. P. Krass (New York: John Wiley & Sons, 2000), pp. 83–89; B. Schlender, "Inside Andy Grove's Latest Crusade," *Fortune*, 23 August 2004, p. 68.

9. M. Rempel and R.J. Fisher, "Perceived Threat, Cohesion, and Group Problem Solving in Intergroup Conflict," *International Journal of Conflict Management* 8 (1997), pp. 216–34.

10. D. Tjosvold, *The Conflict-Positive Organization* (Reading, MA: Addison-Wesley, 1991); K.M. Eisenhardt, J.L. Kahwajy, and L.J. Bourgeois III, "Conflict and Strategic Choice: How Top Management Teams Disagree," *California Management Review* 39 (Winter 1997), pp. 42–62; L.H. Pelled, K.M. Eisenhardt, and K.R. Xin, "Exploring the Black Box: An Analysis of Work Group Diversity, Conflict, and Performance," *Administrative Science Quarterly* 44 (March 1999), pp. 1–28; S. Schulz-Hardt, M. Jochims, and D. Frey, "Productive Conflict in Group Decision Making: Genuine and Contrived Dissent as Strategies to Counteract Biased Information Seeking," *Organizational Behavior and Human Decision Processes* 88 (2002), pp. 563–86.

11. C.K.W. De Dreu and L.R. Weingart, "Task versus Relationship Conflict, Team Performance, and Team Member Satisfaction: A Meta-Analysis," *Journal of Applied Psychology* 88 (August 2003), pp. 587–604.

12. J. Yang and K.W. Mossholder, "Decoupling Task and Relationship Conflict: The Role of Intergroup Emotional Processing," *Journal of Organizational Behavior* 25 (2004), pp. 589–605.

13. R.E. Walton and J.M. Dutton, "The Management of Conflict: A Model and Review," *Administrative Science Quarterly* 14 (1969), pp. 73–84.

14. D.M. Brock, D. Barry, and D.C. Thomas, "'Your Forward Is Our Reverse, Your Right, Our Wrong': Rethinking Multinational Planning Processes in Light of National Culture," *International Business Review* 9 (2000), pp. 687–701.

15. R. Zemke and B. Filipczak, *Generations at Work: Managing the Clash of Veterans, Boomers, Xers, and Nexters in Your Workplace* (New York: Amacom, 1999); P. Harris, "Boomers vs. Echo Boomer: The Work War," *T+D*, May 2005, pp. 44–49.

16. P. Hinds and D.E. Bailey, "Out of Sight, Out of Sync: Understanding Conflict in Distributed Teams," *Organization Science* 14, no. 6 (2003), pp. 615–32; P. Hinds and M. Mortensen, "Understanding Conflict in Geographically Distributed Teams: The Moderating Effects of Shared Identity, Shared Context, and Spontaneous Communication," *Organization Science* 16, no. 3 (May–June 2005), pp. 290–307.

17. P.C. Earley and G.B. Northcraft, "Goal Setting, Resource Interdependence, and Conflict Management," in *Managing Conflict: An Interdisciplinary Approach*, ed. M.A. Rahim (New York: Praeger, 1989), pp. 161–70; K. Jelin, "A Multimethod Examination of the Benefits and Detriments of Intragroup Conflict," *Administrative Science Quarterly* 40 (1995), pp. 245–82.

18. A. Risberg, "Employee Experiences of Acquisition Processes," *Journal of World Business* 36 (March 2001), pp. 58–84.

19. K.A. Jehn and C. Bendersky, "Intragroup Conflict in Organizations: A Contingency Perspective on the Conflict–Outcome Relationship," *Research in Organizational Behavior* 25 (2003), pp. 187–242.

20. J. Jetten, R. Spears, and T. Postmes, "Intergroup Distinctiveness and Differentiation: A Meta-Analytic Integration," *Journal of Personality and Social Psychology* 86, no. 6 (2004), pp. 862–79.

21. Von Glinow, Shapiro, and Brett, "Can We Talk, and Should We?"

22. J.M. Brett, *Negotiating Globally: How to Negotiate Deals, Resolve Disputes, and Make Decisions across Cultural Boundaries* (San Francisco: Jossey-Bass, 2001); R.J. Lewicki et al., *Negotiation*, 4th ed. (Burr Ridge, IL: McGraw-Hill/Irwin, 2003), Chapter 4.

23. D. Cox, "Goodenow's Downfall," *Toronto Star*, 29 July 2005, p. A1; A. Maki, "NHLPA's New Leader Is a Peacemaker, Not Warrior," *Globe & Mail*, 29 July 2005, p. S1; M. Spector, "Players: He Is Your Father," *National Post*, 29 July 2005, p. B8.

24. Jelin, "A Multimethod Examination of the Benefits and Detriments of Intragroup Conflict."

25. C.K.W. De Dreu et al., "A Theory-Based Measure of Conflict Management Strategies in the Workplace," *Journal of Organizational Behavior* 22 (2001), pp. 645–68.

26. D.W. Johnson et al., "Effects of Cooperative, Competitive, and Individualistic Goal Structures on Achievement: A Meta-Analysis," *Psychological Bulletin* 89 (1981), pp. 47–62; D. Tjosvold, *Working Together to Get Things Done* (Lexington, MA: Lexington, 1986); C.K.W. De Dreu, E. Giebels, and E. Van de Vliert, "Social Motives and Trust in Integrative Negotiation: The Disruptive Effects of Punitive Capability," *Journal of Applied Psychology* 83, no. 3 (June 1998), pp. 408–22; G.A. Callanan and D.F. Perri, "Teaching Conflict Management Using a Scenario-Based Approach," *Journal of Education for Business* 81, no. 3 (2006), pp. 131–39.

27. C.K.W. De Dreu and A.E.M. Van Vianen, "Managing Relationship Conflict and the Effectiveness of Organizational Teams," *Journal of Organizational Behavior* 22 (2001), pp. 309–28; Lewicki et al., *Negotiation*, pp. 35–36.

28. M.W. Morris and H.-Y. Fu, "How Does Culture Influence Conflict Resolution? Dynamic Constructivist Analysis," *Social Cognition* 19 (June 2001), pp. 324–49; S. Ting Toomey, J.G. Oetzel, and K. Yee-Jung, "Self-Construal Types and Conflict Management Styles," *Communication Reports* 14 (Summer 2001), pp. 87–104; C.H. Tinsley, "How Negotiators Get to Yes: Predicting the Constellation of Strategies Used across Cultures to Negotiate Conflict," *Journal of Applied Psychology* 86, no. 4 (2001), pp. 583–93.

29. C.H. Tinsley and E. Weldon, "Responses to a Normative Conflict among American and Chinese Managers,"

International Journal of Conflict Management 3, no. 2 (2003), pp. 183–94. Also see D.A. Cai and E.L. Fink, "Conflict Style Differences between Individualists and Collectivists," *Communication Monographs* 69 (March 2002), pp. 67–87.

30. N. Brewer, P. Mitchell, and N. Weber, "Gender Role, Organizational Status, and Conflict Management Styles," *International Journal of Conflict Management* 13 (2002), pp. 78–95; N.B. Florea et al., "Negotiating from Mars to Venus: Gender in Simulated International Negotiations," *Simulation & Gaming* 34 (June 2003), pp. 226–48.

31. E. Van de Vliert, "Escalative Intervention in Small Group Conflicts," *Journal of Applied Behavioral Science* 21 (Winter 1985), pp. 19–36.

32. M. Alva, "Teamwork Means Getting All Hands Ready for a Touchdown," *Investor's Business Daily*, 12 June 2006, p. A07.

33. M. Sherif, "Superordinate Goals in the Reduction of Intergroup Conflict," *American Journal of Sociology* 68 (1958), pp. 349–58; K.M. Eisenhardt, J.L. Kahwajy, and L.J. Bourgeois III, "How Management Teams Can Have a Good Fight," *Harvard Business Review*, July–August 1997, pp. 77–85; X.M. Song, J. Xile, and B. Dyer, "Antecedents and Consequences of Marketing Managers' Conflict-Handling Behaviors," *Journal of Marketing* 64 (January 2000), pp. 50–66.

34. H.C. Triandis, "The Future of Workforce Diversity in International Organizations: A Commentary," *Applied Psychology: An International Journal* 52, no. 3 (2003), pp. 486–95.

35. E. Elron, B. Shamir, and E. Bem-Ari, "Why Don't They Fight Each Other? Cultural Diversity and Operational Unity in Multinational Forces," *Armed Forces & Society* 26 (October 1999), pp. 73–97; "How Hibernia Helped Its Hourly Employees Make a Leap to PFP," *Pay for Performance Report*, January 2000, p. 2; "Teamwork Polishes This Diamond," *Philippine Daily Inquirer*, 4 October 2000, p. 10.

36. K.R. Lewis, "(Drum) Beatings Build Corporate Spirit," *Star Tribune* (Minneapolis), 3 June 2003, p. 3E; "Oh What a Feeling!" *Music Trades*, May 2004, pp. 94–95; D. Cole, "Joining the Tom-Tom Club," *U.S. News & World Report*, 22 March 2004, p. D12.

37. T.F. Pettigrew, "Intergroup Contact Theory," *Annual Review of Psychology* 49 (1998), pp. 65–85; S. Brickson, "The Impact of Identity Orientation on Individual and Organizational Outcomes in Demographically Diverse Settings," *Academy of Management Review* 25 (January 2000), pp. 82–101; J. Dixon and K. Durrheim, "Contact and the Ecology of Racial Division: Some Varieties of Informal Segregation," *British Journal of Social Psychology* 42 (March 2003), pp. 1–23.

38. Triandis, "The Future of Workforce Diversity in International Organizations."

39. Von Glinow, Shapiro, and Brett, "Can We Talk, and Should We?"

40. P.O. Walker, "Decolonizing Conflict Resolution: Addressing the Ontological Violence of Westernization," *American Indian Quarterly* 28, no. 3/4 (July 2004), pp. 527–49; Native Dispute Resolution Network, "Glossary of Terms" (Tucson, Arizona, 2005), http://nativenetwork.ecr.gov (accessed 15 September 2005).

41. E. Horwitt, "Knowledge, Knowledge, Who's Got the Knowledge," *Computerworld*, 8 April 1996, pp. 80, 81, 84.

42. For a critical view of the problem-solving style in negotiation, see J.M. Brett, "Managing Organizational Conflict," *Professional Psychology: Research and Practice* 15 (1984), pp. 664–78.

43. R.E. Fells, "Developing Trust in Negotiation," *Employee Relations* 15 (1993), pp. 33–45; R.E. Fells, "Overcoming the Dilemmas in Walton and McKersie's Mixed Bargaining Strategy," *Industrial Relations* (Laval) 53 (March 1998), pp. 300–25.

44. R. Stagner and H. Rosen, *Psychology of Union–Management Relations* (Belmont, CA: Wadsworth, 1965), pp. 95–96, 108–10; R.E. Walton and R.B. McKersie, *A Behavioral Theory of Labor Negotiations: An Analysis of a Social Interaction System* (New York: McGraw-Hill, 1965), pp. 41–46; L. Thompson, *The Mind and Heart of the Negotiator* (Upper Saddle River, NJ: Prentice-Hall, 1998), Chapter 2.

45. J.W. Salacuse and J.Z. Rubin, "Your Place or Mine? Site Location and Negotiation," *Negotiation Journal* 6 (January 1990), pp. 5–10; J. Mayfield et al., "How Location Impacts International Business Negotiations," *Review of Business* 19 (December 1998), pp. 21–24.

46. J. Margo, "The Persuaders," *Boss Magazine*, 29 December 2000, p. 38. For a full discussion of the advantages and disadvantages of face-to-face and alternative negotiations situations, see M.H. Bazerman et al., "Negotiation," *Annual Review of Psychology* 51 (2000), pp. 279–314.

47. A.F. Stuhlmacher, T.L. Gillespie, and M.V. Champagne, "The Impact of Time Pressure in Negotiation: A Meta-Analysis," *International Journal of Conflict Management* 9, no. 2 (April 1998), pp. 97–116; C.K.W. De Dreu, "Time Pressure and Closing of the Mind in Negotiation," *Organizational Behavior and Human Decision Processes* 91 (July 2003), pp. 280–95. However, one recent study reported that speeding up these concessions leads to better negotiated outcomes. See D.A. Moore, "Myopic Prediction, Self-Destructive Secrecy, and the Unexpected Benefits of Revealing Final Deadlines in Negotiation," *Organizational Behavior and Human Decision Processes* 94, no. 2 (2004), pp. 125–39.

48. Lewicki et al., *Negotiation*, pp. 298–322.

49. S. Doctoroff, "Reengineering Negotiations," *Sloan Management Review* 39 (March 1998), pp. 63–71; D.C. Zetik and A.F. Stuhlmacher, "Goal Setting and Negotiation Performance: A Meta-Analysis," *Group Processes & Intergroup Relations* 5 (January 2002), pp. 35–52.

50. B. McRae, *The Seven Strategies of Master Negotiators* (Toronto: McGraw-Hill Ryerson, 2002), pp. 7–11.

51. L.L. Thompson, "Information Exchange in Negotiation," *Journal of Experimental Social Psychology* 27 (1991), pp. 161–79.

52. L. Thompson, E. Peterson, and S.E. Brodt, "Team Negotiation: An Examination of Integrative and Distributive Bargaining," *Journal of Personality and Social Psychology* 70 (1996), pp. 66–78; Y. Paik and R.L. Tung, "Negotiating with East Asians: How to Attain "Win–Win" Outcomes," *Management International Review* 39 (1999), pp. 103–22.

53. D.J. O'Keefe, *Persuasion: Theory and Research* (Thousand Oaks, CA: Sage Publications, 2002).

54. Lewicki et al., *Negotiation*, pp. 90–96; S. Kwon and L.R. Weingart, "Unilateral Concessions from the Other Party: Concession Behavior, Attributions, and Negotiation Judgments," *Journal of Applied Psychology* 89, no. 2 (2004), pp. 263–78.

55. J.J. Zhao, "The Chinese Approach to International Business Negotiation," *Journal of Business Communication*, July 2000, pp. 209–37; N. Crundwell, "U.S.–Russian Negotiating Strategies," *BISNIS Bulletin*, October 2003, pp. 5–6.

56. J.Z. Rubin and B.R. Brown, *The Social Psychology of Bargaining and Negotiation* (New York: Academic Press, 1976), Chapter 9.

57. L.L. Putnam, "Beyond Third Party Role: Disputes and Managerial

Intervention," *Employee Responsibilities and Rights Journal* 7 (1994), pp. 23–36; A.R. Elangovan, "The Manager as the Third Party: Deciding How to Intervene in Employee Disputes," in *Negotiation: Readings, Exercises, and Cases*, ed. R.J. Lewicki, J.A. Litterer, and D. Saunders, 3rd ed. (New York: McGraw-Hill, 1999), pp. 458–69. For a somewhat different taxonomy of managerial conflict intervention, see P.G. Irving and J.P. Meyer, "A Multidimensional Scaling Analysis of Managerial Third-Party Conflict Intervention Strategies," *Canadian Journal of Behavioural Science* 29, no. 1 (January 1997), pp. 7–18.

58. B.H. Sheppard, "Managers as Inquisitors: Lessons from the Law," in *Bargaining inside Organizations*, ed. M.H. Bazerman and R.J. Lewicki (Beverly Hills, CA: Sage, 1983); N.H. Kim, D.W. Sohn, and J.A. Wall, "Korean Leaders' (and Subordinates') Conflict Management," *International Journal of Conflict Management* 10, no. 2 (April 1999), pp. 130–53.

59. R. Karambayya and J.M. Brett, "Managers Handling Disputes: Third Party Roles and Perceptions of Fairness," *Academy of Management Journal* 32 (1989), pp. 687–704; R. Cropanzano et al., "Disputant Reactions to Managerial Conflict Resolution Tactics," *Group & Organization Management* 24 (June 1999), pp. 124–53.

60. A.R. Elangovan, "Managerial Intervention in Organizational Disputes: Testing a Prescriptive Model of Strategy Selection," *International Journal of Conflict Management* 4 (1998), pp. 301–35; P.S. Nugent, "Managing Conflict: Third-Party Interventions for Managers," *Academy of Management Executive* 16, no. 1 (February 2002), pp. 139–54.

61. J.P. Meyer, J.M. Gemmell, and P.G. Irving, "Evaluating the Management of Interpersonal Conflict in Organizations: A Factor-Analytic Study of Outcome Criteria," *Canadian Journal of Administrative Sciences* 14 (1997), pp. 1–13.

62. "AMC Uses Alternative Dispute Resolution to Solve Workplace Conflicts," Department of Defense, U.S. Air Force news release (Scott Air Force Base, IL), 13 July 2005.

63. K. Downey, "With Its Dispute Resolution Process, Kodak Joins a Trend," *Washington Post*, 21 September 2003, p. F1.

64. C. Hirschman, "Order in the Hearing," *HRMagazine* 46 (July 2001), p. 58; D. Hechler, "No Longer a Novelty: ADR Winning Corporate Acceptance," *Fulton County Daily Report*, 29 June 2001; S.L.

Hayford, "Alternative Dispute Resolution," *Business Horizons* 43 (January–February 2000), pp. 2–4.

CHAPTER 14

1. "Building a Solid Foundation on Value-Driven Principles," *Business Leader*, June 2003, p. 6; N. Nilekani, "How Do I Develop Next Generation Leaders?" *Economic Times* (India), 25 November 2005; D. Tarrant, "The Leading Edge," *The Bulletin*, 15 November 2005; R. Stavros, "The Ultimate CEOs," *Public Utilities Fortnightly*, 1 June 2006, p. 40.

2. R. House, M. Javidan, and P. Dorfman, "Project Globe: An Introduction," *Applied Psychology: An International Review* 50 (2001), pp. 489–505; R. House et al., "Understanding Cultures and Implicit Leadership Theories across the Globe: An Introduction to Project Globe," *Journal of World Business* 37 (2002), pp. 3–10.

3. R.G. Issac, W.J. Zerbe, and D.C. Pitt, "Leadership and Motivation: The Effective Application of Expectancy Theory," *Journal of Managerial Issues* 13 (Summer 2001), pp. 212–26; C.L. Pearce and J.A. Conger, eds., *Shared Leadership: Reframing the Hows and Whys of Leadership* (Thousand Oaks, CA: Sage, 2003); J.S. Nielson, *The Myth of Leadership* (Palo Alto, CA: Davies-Black, 2004)

4. S. Caulkin, "Who's in Charge Here?" *The Observer* (London), 27 April 2003, p. 9; D. Gardner, "A Boss Who's Crazy about His Workers," *Sunday Herald* (Glasgow, Scotland), 13 April 2003, p. 6; S. Moss, "Portrait: 'Idleness Is Good,'" *The Guardian* (London), 17 April 2003, p. 8; R. Semler, *The Seven-Day Weekend* (London: Century, 2003); "Ricardo Semler Set Them Free," *CIO Insight*, April 2004, p. 30.

5. J. Raelin, "Preparing for Leaderful Practice," *T&D*, March 2004, p. 64.

6. L. Gyulai, "It Takes Children to Raise a Village," *Montreal Gazette*, 30 July 2005, p. A14.

7. Many of these perspectives are summarized in R.N. Kanungo, "Leadership in Organizations: Looking Ahead to the 21st Century," *Canadian Psychology* 39 (Spring 1998), pp. 71–82; G.A. Yukl, *Leadership in Organizations*, 6th ed. (Upper Saddle River, NJ: Pearson Education, 2006).

8. R.M. Stogdill, *Handbook of Leadership* (New York: The Free Press, 1974), Chapter 5.

9. "Care Board Names Dr. Helene Gayle as New President/CEO," CARE news release, (Atlanta), 2 December 2005; M. Bixler, "Chief's Global View to Influence Goals," *Atlanta Journal-Constitution*, 12 April 2006, p. F1; P. Bock, "In Every Way, Helene Gayle Cares in All Capital Letters," *Washington Post*, 1 January 2006, p. D01.

10. R. Ilies, M.W. Gerhardt, and H. Le, "Individual Differences in Leadership Emergence: Integrating Meta-Analytic Findings and Behavioral Genetics Estimates," *International Journal of Selection and Assessment* 12, no. 3 (September 2004), pp. 207–19.

11. J. Intagliata, D. Ulrich, and N. Smallwood, "Leveraging Leadership Competencies to Produce Leadership Brand: Creating Distinctiveness by Focusing on Strategy and Results," *Human Resources Planning* 23, no. 4 (2000), pp. 12–23; J.A. Conger and D.A. Ready, "Rethinking Leadership Competencies," *Leader to Leader*, Spring 2004, pp. 41–47; S.J. Zaccaro, C. Kemp, and P. Bader, "Leader Traits and Attributes," in *The Nature of Leadership*, ed. J. Antonakis, A.T. Cianciolo, and R.J. Sternberg (Thousand Oaks, CA: Sage, 2004), pp. 101–24.

12. This list is based on S.A. Kirkpatrick and E.A. Locke, "Leadership: Do Traits Matter?" *Academy of Management Executive* 5 (May 1991), pp. 48–60; R.M. Aditya, R.J. House, and S. Kerr, "Theory and Practice of Leadership: Into the New Millennium," in *Industrial and Organizational Psychology: Linking Theory with Practice*, ed. C.L. Cooper and E.A. Locke (Oxford, UK: Blackwell, 2000), pp. 130–65; D. Goleman, R. Boyatzis, and A. McKee, *Primal Leaders* (Boston: Harvard Business School Press, 2002); T.A. Judge et al., "Personality and Leadership: A Qualitative and Quantitative Review," *Journal of Applied Psychology* 87, no. 4 (August 2002), pp. 765–80; T.A. Judge, A.E. Colbert, and R. Ilies, "Intelligence and Leadership: A Quantitative Review and Test of Theoretical Propositions," *Journal of Applied Psychology* 89, no. 3 (June 2004), pp. 542–52; Zaccaro, Kemp, and Bader, "Leader Traits and Attributes."

13. J. George, "Emotions and Leadership: The Role of Emotional Intelligence," *Human Relations* 53 (August 2000), pp. 1027–55; Goleman, Boyatzis, and McKee, *Primal Leaders*; R.G. Lord and R.J. Hall, "Identity, Deep Structure, and the Development of Leadership Skill,"

Leadership Quarterly 16, no. 4 (August 2005), pp. 591–615; C. Skinner and P. Spurgeon, "Valuing Empathy and Emotional Intelligence in Health Leadership: A Study of Empathy, Leadership Behavior, and Outcome Effectiveness," *Health Services Management Research* 18, no. 1 (February 2005), pp. 1–12.

14. D.R. May et al., "The Moral Component of Authentic Leadership," *Organizational Dynamics* 32 (August 2003), pp. 247–60. The large-scale studies are reported in C. Savoye, "Workers Say Honesty Is Best Company Policy," *Christian Science Monitor*, 15 June 2000; J.M. Kouzes and B.Z. Posner, *The Leadership Challenge*, 3rd ed. (San Francisco: Jossey-Bass, 2002), Chapter 2; J. Schettler, "Leadership in Corporate America," *Training & Development*, September 2002, pp. 66–73.

15. Watson Wyatt Worldwide, "Asia-Pacific Workers Satisfied with Jobs Despite Some Misgivings with Management and Pay," Watson Wyatt Worldwide news release, (Singapore), 16 November 2004; J. Cremer, "Asian Workers Give Low Marks to Leaders," *South China Morning Post* (Hong Kong), 30 July 2005, p. 8; D. Jones, "Optimism Puts Rose-Colored Tint in Glasses of Top Execs," *USA Today*, 16 December 2005, p. B1; E. Pondel, "Friends & Bosses?" *Seattle Post-Intelligencer*, 10 April 2006, p. C1.

16. R. Charan, C. Burke, and L. Bossidy, *Execution: The Discipline of Getting Things Done* (New York: Crown Business, 2002). The survey of managerial competencies is reported in D. Nilsen, B. Kowske, and A. Kshanika, "Managing Globally," *HRMagazine*, August 2005, pp. 111–15.

17. R.J. House and R.N. Aditya, "The Social Scientific Study of Leadership: Quo Vadis?" *Journal of Management* 23 (1997), pp. 409–73.

18 R. Jacobs, "Using Human Resource Functions to Enhance Emotional Intelligence," in *The Emotionally Intelligent Workplace*, ed. C. Cherniss and D. Goleman (San Francisco: Jossey-Bass, 2001), pp. 161–63; Conger and Ready, "Rethinking Leadership Competencies."

19. P.G. Northouse, *Leadership: Theory and Practice*, 3rd ed. (Thousand Oaks, CA: Sage, 2004), Chapter 4; Yukl, *Leadership in Organizations*, Chapter 3.

20. A.K. Korman, "Consideration, Initiating Structure, and Organizational Criteria-A Review," *Personnel Psychology* 19 (1966), pp. 349–62; E.A. Fleishman,

"Twenty Years of Consideration and Structure," in *Current Developments in the Study of Leadership*, ed. E.A. Fleishman and J.C. Hunt (Carbondale, IL: Southern Illinois University Press, 1973), pp. 1–40; T.A. Judge, R.F. Piccolo, and R. Ilies, "The Forgotten Ones? The Validity of Consideration and Initiating Structure in Leadership Research," *Journal of Applied Psychology* 89, no. 1 (2004), pp. 36–51; Yukl, *Leadership in Organizations*, pp. 62–75.

21. V.V. Baba, "Serendipity in Leadership: Initiating Structure and Consideration in the Classroom," *Human Relations* 42 (1989), pp. 509–25.

22. S. Kerr et al., "Toward a Contingency Theory of Leadership Based upon the Consideration and Initiating Structure Literature," *Organizational Behavior and Human Performance* 12 (1974), pp. 62–82; L.L. Larson, J.G. Hunt, and R.N. Osbom, "The Great Hi-Hi Leader Behavior Myth: A Lesson from Occam's Razor," *Academy of Management Journal* 19 (1976), pp. 628–41.

23. R. Tannenbaum and W.H. Schmidt, "How to Choose a Leadership Pattern," *Harvard Business Review*, May-June 1973, pp. 162–80.

24. For a thorough study of how expectancy theory of motivation relates to leadership, see R.G. Isaac, W.J. Zerbe, and D.C. Pitt, "Leadership and Motivation: The Effective Application of Expectancy Theory," *Journal of Managerial Issues* 13 (Summer 2001), pp. 212–26.

25. R.J. House, "A Path-Goal Theory of Leader Effectiveness," *Administrative Science Quarterly* 16 (1971), pp. 321–38; M.G. Evans, "Extensions of a Path-Goal Theory of Motivation," *Journal of Applied Psychology* 59 (1974), pp. 172–78; R.J. House and T.R. Mitchell, "Path-Goal Theory of Leadership," *Journal of Contemporary Business*, Autumn 1974, pp. 81–97; M.G. Evans, "Path-Goal Theory of Leadership," in *Leadership*, ed. L.L. Neider and C.A. Schriesheim (Greenwich, CT: Information Age Publishing, 2002), pp. 115–38.

26. Various thoughts about servant leadership are presented in L.C. Spears and M. Lawrence, eds., *Focus on Leadership: Servant Leadership* (New York: John Wiley & Sons, 2002).

27. "2006 Movers & Shakers," *Financial Planning*, January 2006, p. 1.

28. R.J. House, "Path-Goal Theory of Leadership: Lessons, Legacy, and a

Reformulated Theory," *Leadership Quarterly* 7 (1996), pp. 323–52.

29. "Why Geotechnical Instruments Boss Draper Is One in a Million," *Birmingham Post* (United Kingdom), 2 June 2006, p. 26; N. Whitten, "Best Boss Sets Examples to Staff," *Evening Chronicle* (Newcastle, U.K.), 15 June 2006, p. 24.

30. J. Indvik, "Path-Goal Theory of Leadership: A Meta-Analysis," *Academy of Management Proceedings*, 1986, pp. 189–92; J.C. Wofford and L.Z. Liska, "Path-Goal Theories of Leadership: A Meta-Analysis," *Journal of Management* 19 (1993), pp. 857–76.

31. J.D. Houghton and S.K. Yoho, "Toward a Contingency Model of Leadership and Psychological Empowerment: When Should Self-Leadership Be Encouraged?" *Journal of Leadership & Organizational Studies* 11, no. 4 (2005), pp. 65–83.

32. R.T. Keller, "A Test of the Path-Goal Theory of Leadership with Need for Clarity as a Moderator in Research and Development Organizations," *Journal of Applied Psychology* 74 (1989), pp. 208–12.

33. C.A. Schriesheim and L.L. Neider, "Path-Goal Leadership Theory: The Long and Winding Road," *Leadership Quarterly* 7 (1996), pp. 317–21.

34. P. Hersey and K.H. Blanchard, *Management of Organizational Behavior: Utilizing Human Resources*, 5th ed. (Englewood Cliffs, NJ: Prentice Hall, 1988).

35. R.P. Vecchio, "Situational Leadership Theory: An Examination of a Prescriptive Theory," *Journal of Applied Psychology* 72 (1987), pp. 444–51; W. Blank, J.R. Weitzel, and S.G. Green, "A Test of the Situational Leadership Theory," *Personnel Psychology* 43 (1990), pp. 579–97; C.L. Graeff, "Evolution of Situational Leadership Theory: A Critical Review," *Leadership Quarterly* 8 (1997), pp. 153–70.

36. F.E. Fiedler, *A Theory of Leadership Effectiveness* (New York: McGraw-Hill, 1967); F.E. Fiedler and M.M. Chemers, *Leadership and Effective Management* (Glenview, IL: Scott, Foresman, 1974).

37. F.E. Fiedler, "Engineer the Job to Fit the Manager," *Harvard Business Review* 43, no. 5 (1965), pp. 115–22.

38. For a summary of criticisms, see Yukl, *Leadership in Organizations*, pp. 217–18.

39. N. Nicholson, *Executive Instinct* (New York: Crown, 2000).

40. This observation has also been made by C.A. Schriesheim, "Substitutes-for-

Leadership Theory: Development and Basic Concepts," *Leadership Quarterly* 8 (1997), pp. 103–8.

41. D.F. Elloy and A. Randolph, "The Effect of Superleader Behavior on Autonomous Work Groups in a Government Operated Railway Service," *Public Personnel Management* 26 (Summer 1997), pp. 257–72; C.C. Manz and H. Sims Jr., *The New SuperLeadership: Leading Others to Lead Themselves* (San Francisco: Berrett-Koehler, 2001).

42. M.L. Loughry, "Co-workers Are Watching: Performance Implications of Peer Monitoring," *Academy of Management Proceedings* (2002), pp. O1–O6.

43. C.C. Manz and C. Neck, *Mastering Self-Leadership*, 3rd ed. (Upper Saddle River, NJ: Prentice Hall, 2004).

44. P.M. Podsakoff and S.B. MacKenzie, "Kerr and Jermier's Substitutes for Leadership Model: Background, Empirical Assessment, and Suggestions for Future Research," *Leadership Quarterly* 8 (1997), pp. 117–32; S.D. Dionne et al., "Neutralizing Substitutes for Leadership Theory: Leadership Effects and Common-Source Bias," *Journal of Applied Psychology* 87, no. 3 (June 2002), pp. 454–64; J.R. Villa et al., "Problems with Detecting Moderators in Leadership Research Using Moderated Multiple Regression," *Leadership Quarterly* 14, no. 1 (February 2003), pp. 3–23; S.D. Dionne et al., "Substitutes for Leadership, or Not," *The Leadership Quarterly* 16, no. 1 (2005), pp. 169–93.

45. J.M. Burns, *Leadership* (New York: Harper & Row, 1978); B.M. Bass, *Transformational Leadership: Industrial, Military, and Educational Impact* (Hillsdale, NJ: Erlbaum, 1998); S.B. Proctor-Thomson and K.W. Parry, "What the Best Leaders Look Like," in *Leadership in the Antipodes: Findings, Implications, and a Leader Profile*, ed. K.W. Parry (Wellington, N.Z.: Institute of Policy Studies and Centre for the Study of Leadership, 2001), pp. 166–91; B.J. Avolio and F.J. Yammarino, eds., *Transformational and Charismatic Leadership: The Road Ahead* (Greenwich, CT: JAI Press, 2002).

46. V.L. Goodwin, J.C. Wofford, and J.L. Whittington, "A Theoretical and Empirical Extension to the Transformational Leadership Construct," *Journal of Organizational Behavior* 22 (November 2001), pp. 759–74.

47. A. Zaleznik, "Managers and Leaders: Are They Different?" *Harvard Business Review* 55, no. 5 (1977), pp. 67–78; W.

Bennis and B. Nanus, *Leaders: The Strategies for Taking Charge* (New York: Harper & Row, 1985). For a recent discussion regarding managing versus leading, see G. Yukl and R. Lepsinger, "Why Integrating the Leading and Managing Roles Is Essential for Organizational Effectiveness," *Organizational Dynamics* 34, no. 4 (2005), pp. 361–75.

48. Both transformational and transactional leadership improve work unit performance. See B.M. Bass et al., "Predicting Unit Performance by Assessing Transformational and Transactional Leadership," *Journal of Applied Psychology* 88 (April 2003), pp. 207–18. This point is also argued in Yukl and Lepsinger, "Why Integrating the Leading and Managing Roles Is Essential for Organizational Effectiveness."

49. For discussion of the tendency to slide from transformational to transactional leadership, see W. Bennis, *An Invented Life: Reflections on Leadership and Change* (Reading, MA: Addison-Wesley, 1993).

50. R.J. House, "A 1976 Theory of Charismatic Leadership," in *Leadership: The Cutting Edge*, ed. J.G. Hunt and L.L. Larson (Carbondale, IL.: Southern Illinois University Press, 1977), pp. 189–207; J.A. Conger, "Charismatic and Transformational Leadership in Organizations: An Insider's Perspective on These Developing Streams of Research," *Leadership Quarterly* 10 (Summer 1999), pp. 145–79.

51. J. Barbuto, J.E., "Taking the Charisma out of Transformational Leadership," *Journal of Social Behavior & Personality* 12 (September 1997), p. 689–97; Y.A. Nur, "Charisma and Managerial Leadership: The Gift That Never Was," *Business Horizons* 41 (July 1998), pp. 19–26; M.D. Mumford and J.R. Van Doorn, "The Leadership of Pragmatism-Reconsidering Franklin in the Age of Charisma," *Leadership Quarterly* 12, no. 3 (Fall 2001), pp. 279–309.

52. R.E. De Vries, R.A. Roe, and T.C.B. Taillieu, "On Charisma and Need for Leadership," *European Journal of Work and Organizational Psychology* 8 (1999), pp. 109–33; R. Khurana, *Searching for a Corporate Savior: The Irrational Quest for Charismatic CEOs* (Princeton, NJ: Princeton University Press, 2002).

53. Bennis and Nanus, *Leaders*, pp. 27–33, 89; I.M. Levin, "Vision Revisited," *Journal of Applied Behavioral Science* 36 (March 2000), pp. 91–107; J.R. Sparks and J.A.

Schenk, "Explaining the Effects of Transformational Leadership: An Investigation of the Effects of Higher-Order Motives in Multilevel Marketing Organizations," *Journal of Organizational Behavior* 22 (2001), pp. 849–69; D. Christenson and D.H.T. Walker, "Understanding the Role of 'Vision' in Project Success," *Project Management Journal* 35, no. 3 (September 2004), pp. 39–52; R.E. Quinn, *Building the Bridge as You Walk on It: A Guide for Leading Change* (San Francisco: Jossey-Bass, 2004), Chapter 11.

54. J.R. Baum, E.A. Locke, and S.A. Kirkpatrick, "A Longitudinal Study of the Relation of Vision and Vision Communication to Venture Growth in Entrepreneurial Firms," *Journal of Applied Psychology* 83 (1998), pp. 43–54; S.L. Hoe and S.L. McShane, "Leadership Antecedents of Informal Knowledge Acquisition and Dissemination," *International Journal of Organisational Behaviour* 5 (2002), pp. 282–91.

55. J.A. Conger, "Inspiring Others: The Language of Leadership," *Academy of Management Executive* 5 (February 1991), pp. 31–45; G.T. Fairhurst and R.A. Sarr, *The Art of Framing: Managing the Language of Leadership* (San Francisco: Jossey-Bass, 1996); A.E. Rafferty and M.A. Griffin, "Dimensions of Transformational Leadership: Conceptual and Empirical Extensions," *Leadership Quarterly* 15, no. 3 (2004), pp. 329–54.

56. L. Black, "Hamburger Diplomacy," *Report on Business Magazine*, August 1988, pp. 30–36.

57. D.E. Berlew, "Leadership and Organizational Excitement," *California Management Review* 17, no. 2 (Winter 1974), pp. 21–30; Bennis and Nanus, *Leaders*, pp. 43–55; T. Simons, "Behavioral Integrity: The Perceived Alignment between Managers' Words and Deeds as a Research Focus," *Organization Science* 13, no. 1 (January-February 2002), pp. 18–35.

58. C. Salter, "Customer-Centered Leader Chick-fil-A," *Fast Company*, October 2004, pp. 83–84; L. Cannon, "2005 Golden Chain: Dan T. Cathy," *Nation's Restaurant News*, 19 September 2005; H. Jett, "Businesses Use Grand Openings to Attract Audience, Establish Roots," *Free Lance-Star* (Fredericksburg, Virginia), 24 March 2005.

59. M. Webb, "Executive Profile: Peter C. Farrell," *San Diego Business Journal*, 24 March 2003, p. 32; P. Benesh, "He Likes Them Breathing Easy," *Investor's Business*

Daily, 13 September 2005, p. A04; C. Hymowitz, "Today's Bosses Find Mentoring Isn't Worth the Time and Risks," *The Wall Street Journal*, 13 March 2006, p. B1. The two surveys are reported in ISR, "Driving an Innovative Culture: Insights from Global Research and Implications for Businesses in Hong Kong" (ISR, 2004), www.isrsurveys.com.au/pdf/insight/IHRM%20Show-18Nov04.pdf (accessed 22 December 2005); Watson Wyatt Worldwide, "Worktaiwan: Key Findings" (Singapore: Watson Wyatt Worldwide, 2004), www.watsonwyatt.com/asia-pacific/research/workasia/worktw_keyfindings.asp (accessed 2 December 2005).

60. J. Barling, T. Weber, and E.K. Kelloway, "Effects of Transformational Leadership Training on Attitudinal and Financial Outcomes: A Field Experiment," *Journal of Applied Psychology* 81 (1996), pp. 827–32.

61. A. Bryman, "Leadership in Organizations," in *Handbook of Organization Studies*, ed. S.R. Clegg, C. Hardy, and W.R. Nord (Thousand Oaks, CA: Sage, 1996), pp. 276–92.

62. B.S. Pawar and K.K. Eastman, "The Nature and Implications of Contextual Influences on Transformational Leadership: A Conceptual Examination," *Academy of Management Review* 22 (1997), pp. 80–109; C.P. Egri and S. Herman, "Leadership in the North American Environmental Sector: Values, Leadership Styles, and Contexts of Environmental Leaders and Their Organizations," *Academy of Management Journal* 43, no. 4 (2000), pp. 571–604.

63. J.R. Meindl, "On Leadership: An Alternative to the Conventional Wisdom," *Research in Organizational Behavior* 12 (1990), pp. 159–203; L.R. Offermann, J.K. Kennedy, and P.W. Wirtz, "Implicit Leadership Theories: Content, Structure, and Generalizability," *Leadership Quarterly* 5, no. 1 (1994), pp. 43–58; R.J. Hall and R.G. Lord, "Multi-Level Information Processing Explanations of Followers' Leadership Perceptions," *Leadership Quarterly* 6 (1995), pp. 265–87; O. Epitropaki and R. Martin, "Implicit Leadership Theories in Applied Settings: Factor Structure, Generalizability, and Stability over Time," *Journal of Applied Psychology* 89, no. 2 (2004), pp. 293–310.

64. L.M.A. Chong and D.C. Thomas, "Leadership Perceptions in Cross-Cultural Context: Pakeha and Pacific Islanders in New Zealand," *Leadership Quarterly* 8 (1997), pp. 275–93; R.G. Lord et al., "Contextual Constraints on Prototype Generation and Their Multilevel Consequences for Leadership Perceptions," *The Leadership Quarterly* 12, no. 3 (2001), p. 311–38; T. Keller, "Parental Images as a Guide to Leadership Sensemaking: An Attachment Perspective on Implicit Leadership Theories," *Leadership Quarterly* 14 (2003), pp. 141–60.

65. S.F. Cronshaw and R.G. Lord, "Effects of Categorization, Attribution, and Encoding Processes on Leadership Perceptions," *Journal of Applied Psychology* 72 (1987), pp. 97–106; J.L. Nye and D.R. Forsyth, "The Effects of Prototype-Based Biases on Leadership Appraisals: A Test of Leadership Categorization Theory," *Small Group Research* 22 (1991), pp. 360–79.

66. R. Weber et al., "The Illusion of Leadership: Misattribution of Cause in Coordination Games," *Organization Science* 12, no. 5 (2001), pp. 582–98; N. Ensari and S.E. Murphy, "Cross-Cultural Variations in Leadership Perceptions and Attribution of Charisma to the Leader," *Organizational Behavior and Human Decision Processes* 92 (2003), pp. 52–66; M.L.A. Hayward, V.P. Rindova, and T.G. Pollock, "Believing One's Own Press: The Causes and Consequences of CEO Celebrity," *Strategic Management Journal* 25, no. 7 (July 2004), pp. 637–53.

67. Meindl, "On Leadership: An Alternative to the Conventional Wisdom," p. 163.

68. J. Pfeffer, "The Ambiguity of Leadership," *Academy of Management Review* 2 (1977), pp. 102–12.

69. M.P. Mangaliso, "Building Competitive Advantage from *Ubuntu*: Management Lessons from South Africa," *Academy of Management Executive* 15 (August 2001), pp. 23–43; L. van der Colff, "Leadership Lessons from the African Tree," *Management Decision* 41 (2003), pp. 257–61; L.L. Karsten and H. Illa, "*Ubuntu* as a Key African Management Concept: Contextual Background and Practical Insights for Knowledge Application," *Journal of Managerial Psychology* 20, no. 7 (July 2005), pp. 607–20. Speech by President Nelson Mandela at his 80th birthday party, Kruger National Park, 16 July 1998.

70. Six of the Project GLOBE clusters are described in a special issue of the *Journal of World Business* 37 (2000). For an overview of Project GLOBE, see House, Javidan, and Dorfman, "Project Globe: An Introduction"; House et al., "Understanding Cultures and Implicit Leadership Theories across the Globe: An Introduction to Project Globe."

71. J.C. Jesiuno, "Latin Europe Cluster: From South to North," *Journal of World Business* 37 (2002), p. 88. Another GLOBE study of Iranian managers also reported that charismatic visionary stands out as a primary leadership dimension. See A. Dastmalchian, M. Javidan, and K. Alam, "Effective Leadership and Culture in Iran: An Empirical Study," *Applied Psychology: An International Review* 50 (2001), pp. 532–58.

72. D.N. Den Hartog et al., "Culture Specific and Cross-Cultural Generalizable Implicit Leadership Theories: Are Attributes of Charismatic/Transformational Leadership Universally Endorsed?" *Leadership Quarterly* 10 (1999), pp. 219–56; F.C. Brodbeck et al., "Cultural Variation of Leadership Prototypes across 22 European Countries," *Journal of Occupational and Organizational Psychology* 73 (2000), pp. 1–29; E. Szabo et al., "The Europe Cluster: Where Employees Have a Voice," *Journal of World Business* 37 (2002), pp. 55–68. The Mexican study is reported in C.E. Nicholls, H.W. Lane, and M.B. Brechu, "Taking Self-Managed Teams to Mexico," *Academy of Management Executive* 13 (August 1999), pp. 15–25.

73. J.B. Rosener, "Ways Women Lead," *Harvard Business Review* 68 (November-December 1990), pp. 119–25; S.H. Appelbaum and B.T. Shaprio, "Why Can't Men Lead Like Women?" *Leadership and Organization Development Journal* 14 (1993), pp. 28–34; N. Wood, "Venus Rules," *Incentive* 172 (February 1998), pp. 22–27.

74. G.N. Powell, "One More Time: Do Female and Male Managers Differ?" *Academy of Management Executive* 4 (1990), pp. 68–75; M.L. van Engen and T.M. Willemsen, "Sex and Leadership Styles: A Meta-Analysis of Research Published in the 1990s," *Psychological Reports* 94, no. 1 (February 2004), pp. 3–18.

75. R. Sharpe, "As Leaders, Women Rule," *BusinessWeek*, 20 November 2000, p. 74; M. Sappenfield, "Women, It Seems, Are Better Bosses," *Christian Science Monitor*, 16 January 2001; A.H. Eagly and L.L. Carli, "The Female Leadership Advantage: An Evaluation of the Evidence," *The Leadership Quarterly* 14, no. 6 (December 2003), pp. 807–34; A.H. Eagly, M.C. Johannesen-Schmidt, and M.L. van Engen, "Transformational, Transactional,

and Laissez-Faire Leadership Styles: A Meta-Analysis Comparing Women and Men," *Psychological Bulletin* 129 (July 2003), pp. 569–91.

76. A.H. Eagly, S.J. Karau, and M.G. Makhijani, "Gender and the Effectiveness of Leaders: A Meta-Analysis," *Psychological Bulletin* 117 (1995), pp. 125–45; J.G. Oakley, "Gender-Based Barriers to Senior Management Positions: Understanding the Scarcity of Female CEOs," *Journal of Business Ethics* 27 (2000), pp. 821–34; N.Z. Stelter, "Gender Differences in Leadership: Current Social Issues and Future Organizational Implications," *Journal of Leadership Studies* 8 (2002), pp. 88–99; M. E. Heilman et al., "Penalties for Success: Reactions to Women Who Succeed at Male Gender-Typed Tasks," *Journal of Applied Psychology* 89, no. 3 (2004), pp. 416–27; A.H. Eagly, "Achieving Relational Authenticity in Leadership: Does Gender Matter?" *The Leadership Quarterly* 16, no. 3 (June 2005), pp. 459–74.

CHAPTER 15

1. L. Sinclair, "Morris Vows to Aid and Abet Nitro," *The Australian*, 30 September 2004, p. 21; "Nimble Nitro Steals a March on the Big Networks," *Marketing Week*, 9 June 2005, p. 13; P. Chatterjee, "'India Vital Part of Our Jigsaw,'" *Business Line* (The Hindu, India), 17 November 2005, p. 1; S. Elliott, "Watch Out, Giant Agencies. Boutique Shops Like Nitro Are Winning Some Big Clients," *The New York Times*, 4 April 2005, p. 6; F. Hall, "Nitro Takes 'Substantial' Chunk of UK's Soul," *Advertising Age*, 18 April 2005, p. 22; A. Hargrave-Silk, "Chen Named Chairman for Nitro Greater China," *Media*, 6 May 2005; N. Shatrujeet, "The Light at Lowe," *Economic Times* (India), 29 June 2005. Also see www.nitro-group.com.

2. S. Ranson, R. Hinings, and R. Greenwood, "The Structuring of Organizational Structure," *Administrative Science Quarterly* 25 (1980), pp. 1–14.

3. J.-E. Johanson, "Intraorganizational Influence," *Management Communication Quarterly* 13 (February 2000), pp. 393–435.

4. B. Morris, "Charles Schwab's Big Challenge," *Fortune*, 30 May 2005, p. 88.

5. H. Mintzberg, *The Structuring of Organizations* (Englewood Cliffs, NJ: Prentice Hall, 1979), pp. 2–3.

6. E.E. Lawler III, *Motivation in Work Organizations* (Monterey, CA: Brooks/ Cole, 1973); M.A. Campion, "Ability Requirement Implications of Job Design: An Interdisciplinary Perspective," *Personnel Psychology* 42 (1989), pp. 1–24.

7. Mintzberg, *The Structuring of Organizations*, pp. 2–8; D.A. Nadler and M.L. Tushman, *Competing by Design: The Power of Organizational Architecture* (New York: Oxford University Press, 1997), Chapter 6.

8. C. Downs, P. Clampitt, and A.L. Pfeiffer, "Communication and Organizational Outcomes," in *Handbook of Organizational Communication*, ed. G. Goldhaber and G. Barnett (Norwood, NJ: Ablex, 1988), pp. 171–211; I. Nonaka and H. Takeuchi, *The Knowledge-Creating Company* (New York: Oxford University Press, 1995).

9. A.L. Patti, J.P. Gilbert, and S. Hartman, "Physical Co-Location and the Success of New Product Development Projects," *Engineering Management Journal* 9 (September 1997), pp. 31–37; M. Hoque, M. Akter, and Y. Monden, "Concurrent Engineering: A Compromise Approach to Develop a Feasible and Customer-Pleasing Product," *International Journal of Production Research* 43, no. 8 (15 April 2005), pp. 1607–24.

10. For a discussion of the role of brand manager at Procter & Gamble, see C. Peale, "Branded for Success," *Cincinnati Enquirer* (20 May 2001), p. A1. Details about how to design integrator roles in organizational structures are presented in J.R. Galbraith, *Designing Organizations* (San Francisco: Jossey-Bass, 2002), pp. 66–72.

11. Fayol's work is summarized in J.B. Miner, *Theories of Organizational Structure and Process* (Chicago: Dryden, 1982), pp. 358–66.

12. Y.-M. Hsieh and A. Tien-Hsieh, "Enhancement of Service Quality with Job Standardisation," *Service Industries Journal* 21 (July 2001), pp. 147–66.

13. D. Drickhamer, "Lessons from the Leading Edge," *Industry Week*, 21 February 2000, pp. 23–26.

14. D.D. Van Fleet and B.A.G., "A History of the Span of Management," *Academy of Management Review* 2 (1977), pp. 356–72; Mintzberg, *The Structuring of Organizations*, Chapter 8.

15. J. Greenwald, "Ward Compares the Best with the Rest," *Business Insurance*, 26 August 2002, p. 16.

16. J.H. Gittell, "Supervisory Span, Relational Coordination, and Flight Departure Performance: A Reassessment of Postbureaucracy Theory," *Organization Science* 12, no. 4 (July–August 2001), pp. 468–83.

17. "BASF Culling Saves (GBP) 4M," *Personnel Today* (19 February 2002), p. 3.

18. T. Peters, *Thriving on Chaos* (New York: Knopf, 1987), p. 359.

19. Q.N. Huy, "In Praise of Middle Managers," *Harvard Business Review* 79 (September 2001), pp. 72–79; H.J. Leavitt, *Top Down: Why Hierarchies Are Here to Stay and How to Manage Them More Effectively* (Cambridge: Harvard Business School Press, 2005).

20. A. Lashinsky, "The Hurd Way," *Fortune*, 17 April 2006, p. 92.

21. W. Stueck, "Revamped Barrick Keeps Eyes on the Hunt for the Golden Prize," *Globe & Mail*, 17 September 2005, p. B4.

22. P. Brabeck, "The Business Case against Revolution: An Interview with Nestle's Peter Brabeck," *Harvard Business Review* 79 (February 2001), p. 112; H.A. Richardson et al., "Does Decentralization Make a Difference for the Organization? An Examination of the Boundary Conditions Circumscribing Decentralized Decision Making and Organizational Financial Performance," *Journal of Management* 28, no. 2 (2002), pp. 217–44; C. Masado, "To Centralize or Decentralize?" *Optimize*, May 2005, p. 58.

23. Mintzberg, *The Structuring of Organizations*, Chapter 5.

24. T. Burns and G. Stalker, *The Management of Innovation* (London: Tavistock, 1961).

25. D. Youngblood, "Computer Consultants Win Business with Creative Strategies," *Star Tribune* (Minneapolis, MN), 15 July 2001; S. Brouillard, "Right at Home," *Minneapolis-St. Paul Business Journal*, 23 August 2002; J. Fure, "Staying Connected," *Minneapolis-St. Paul Business Journal*, 20 August 2004.

26. J. Tata, S. Prasad, and R. Thom, "The Influence of Organizational Structure on the Effectiveness of TQM Programs," *Journal of Managerial Issues* 11, no. 4 (Winter 1999), pp. 440–53; A. Lam, "Tacit Knowledge, Organizational Learning and Societal Institutions: An Integrated Framework," *Organization Studies* 21 (May 2000), pp. 487–513.

27. W.D. Sine, H. Mitsuhashi, and D.A. Kirsch, "2006," *Academy of Management Journal* 49, no. 1, pp. 121–32.

28. Mintzberg, *The Structuring of Organizations*, p. 106.

29. Mintzberg, *The Structuring of Organizations*, Chapter 17.

30. Galbraith, *Designing Organizations*, pp. 23–25.

31. E.E. Lawler III, *Rewarding Excellence: Pay Strategies for the New Economy* (San Francisco: Jossey-Bass, 2000), pp. 31–34.

32. These structures were identified from corporate Web sites and annual reports. These companies include a mixture of other structures, so the charts shown are adapted for learning purposes.

33. M. Goold and A. Campbell, "Do You Have a Well-Designed Organization?" *Harvard Business Review* 80 (March 2002), pp. 117–24.

34. J.R. Galbraith, "Structuring Global Organizations," in *Tomorrow's Organization*, ed. S.A. Mohrman et al. (San Francisco: Jossey-Bass, 1998), pp. 103–29; C. Homburg, J.P. Workman Jr., and O. Jensen, "Fundamental Changes in Marketing Organization: The Movement toward a Customer-focused Organizational Structure," *Academy of Marketing Science. Journal* 28 (Fall 2000), pp. 459–78; T. H. Davenport, J.G. Harris, and A.K. Kohli, "How Do They Know Their Customers So Well?" *Sloan Management Review* 42 (Winter 2001), pp. 63–73; J.R. Galbraith, "Organizing to Deliver Solutions," *Organizational Dynamics* 31 (2002), pp. 194–207.

35. D. Robey, *Designing Organizations*, 3rd ed. (Homewood, IL: Irwin, 1991), pp. 191–97.

36. R. Muzyka and G. Zeschuk, "Managing Multiple Projects," *Game Developer*, March 2003, pp. 34–42; M. Saltzman, "The Ex-Doctors Are In," *National Post*, 24 March 2004, p. AL4; R. McConnell, "For Edmonton's Bioware, Today's the Big Day," *Edmonton Journal*, 14 April 2005, p. C1.

37. R.C. Ford and W.A. Randolph, "Cross-Functional Structures: A Review and Integration of Matrix Organization and Project Management," *Journal of Management* 18 (1992), pp. 267–94.

38. J. Teresko, "Transforming GM," *Industry Week*, December/January 2002, pp. 34–38; E. Prewitt, "GM's Matrix Reloads," *CIO Magazine*, 1 September 2003.

39. G. Calabrese, "Communication and Cooperation in Product Development: A Case Study of a European Car Producer,"

R & D Management 27 (July 1997), pp. 239–52; T. Sy and L.S. D'Annunzio, "Challenges and Strategies of Matrix Organizations: Top-Level and Mid-Level Managers' Perspectives," *Human Resource Planning* 28, no. 1 (2005), pp. 39–48.

40. Nadler and Tushman, *Competing by Design*, Chapter 6; M. Goold and A. Campbell, "Structured Networks: Toward the Well-Designed Matrix," *Long Range Planning* 36, no. 5 (October 2003), pp. 427–39.

41. "Lean Manufacturing Increases Productivity, Decreases Cycle Time," *Industrial Equipment News*, October 2005.

42. J.R. Galbraith, E.E. Lawler III, and Associates, *Organizing for the Future: The New Logic for Managing Complex Organizations* (San Francisco, CA: Jossey-Bass, 1993); R. Bettis and M. Hitt, "The New Competitive Landscape," *Strategic Management Journal* 16 (1995), pp. 7–19.

43. P.C. Ensign, "Interdependence, Coordination, and Structure in Complex Organizations: Implications for Organization Design," *Mid-Atlantic Journal of Business* 34 (March 1998), pp. 5–22.

44. M.M. Fanning, "A Circular Organization Chart Promotes a Hospital-Wide Focus on Teams," *Hospital & Health Services Administration* 42 (June 1997), pp. 243–54; L.Y. Chan and B.E. Lynn, "Operating in Turbulent Times: How Ontario's Hospitals Are Meeting the Current Funding Crisis," *Health Care Management Review* 23 (June 1998), pp. 7–18.

45. R. Cross, "Looking before You Leap: Assessing the Jump to Teams in Knowledge-Based Work," *Business Horizons* (September 2000); M. Fenton-O'Creevy, "Employee Involvement and the Middle Manager: Saboteur or Scapegoat?" *Human Resource Management Journal* 11 (2001), pp. 24–40; G. Garda, K. Lindstrom, and M. Dallnera, "Toward a Learning Organization: The Introduction of a Client-Centered Team-Based Organization in Administrative Surveying Work," *Applied Ergonomics* 34 (2003), pp. 97–105; C. Douglas and W.L. Gardner, "Transition to Self-Directed Work Teams: Implications of Transition Time and Self-Monitoring for Managers' Use of Influence Tactics," *Journal of Organizational Behavior* 25 (2004), pp. 47–65.

46. P. Siekman, "This Is Not a BMW Plant," *Fortune*, 18 April 2005, p. 208.

47. R.F. Miles and C.C. Snow, "The New

Network Firm: A Spherical Structure Built on a Human Investment Philosophy," *Organizational Dynamics* 23, no. 4 (1995), pp. 5–18; C. Baldwin and K. Clark, "Managing in an Age of Modularity," *Harvard Business Review* 75 (September–October 1997), pp. 84–93.

48. J. Hagel III and M. Singer, "Unbundling the Corporation," *Harvard Business Review* 77 (March–April 1999), pp. 133–41; R. Hacki and J. Lighton, "The Future of the Networked Company," *McKinsey Quarterly* 3 (2001), pp. 26–39.

49. M.A. Schilling and H.K. Steensma, "The Use of Modular Organizational Forms: An Industry-Level Analysis," *Academy of Management Journal* 44 (December 2001), pp. 1149–68.

50. W.H. Davidow and T.W. Malone, *The Virtual Corporation* (New York: Harper Business, 1992); L. Fried, *Managing Information Technology in Turbulent Times* (New York: John Wiley and Sons, 1995).

51. C. Taylor, "Agency Teams Balancing in an Ever-Changing Media World," *Media Week* (1 June 2001), p. 20.

52. G. Morgan, *Images of Organization*, 2nd ed. (Newbury Park, CA: Sage, 1996); G. Morgan, *Imagin-I-Zation: New Mindsets for Seeing, Organizing, and Managing* (Thousand Oaks, CA: Sage, 1997).

53. H. Chesbrough and D.J. Teece, "When Is Virtual Virtuous? Organizing for Innovation," *Harvard Business Review* (January–February 1996), pp. 65–73; P.M.J. Christie and R. Levary, "Virtual Corporations: Recipe for Success," *Industrial Management* 40 (July 1998), pp. 7–11.

54. L. Donaldson, *The Contingency Theory of Organizations* (Thousand Oaks, CA: Sage, 2001); J. Birkenshaw, R. Nobel, and J. Ridderstråle, "Knowledge as a Contingency Variable: Do the Characteristics of Knowledge Predict Organizational Structure?" *Organization Science* 13, no. 3 (May–June 2002), pp. 274–89.

55. P.R. Lawrence and J.W. Lorsch, *Organization and Environment* (Homewood, IL: Irwin, 1967); Mintzberg, *The Structuring of Organizations*, Chapter 15.

56. Burns and Stalker, *The Management of Innovation*; Lawrence and Lorsch, Organization and Environment.

57. J.G. Kelley, "Slurpees and Sausages: 7-Eleven Holds School," *Richmond (Virginia) Times-Dispatch*, 12 March 2004, p. C1; S. Marling, "The 24-Hour Supply Chain," *InformationWeek*, 26 January 2004, p. 43.

58. Mintzberg, *The Structuring of Organizations*, p. 282.

59. D.S. Pugh and C.R. Hinings, *Organizational Structure: Extensions and Replications* (Farnborough, England: Lexington Books, 1976); Mintzberg, *The Structuring of Organizations*, Chapter 13.

60. G. Hertel, S. Geister, and U. Konradt, "Managing Virtual Teams: A Review of Current Empirical Research," *Human Resource Management Review* 15 (2005), pp. 69–95.

61. C. Perrow, "A Framework for the Comparative Analysis of Organizations," *American Sociological Review* 32 (1967), pp. 194–208; D. Gerwin, "The Comparative Analysis of Structure and Technology: A Critical Appraisal," *Academy of Management Review* 4, no. 1 (1979), pp. 41–51; C.C. Miller et al., "Understanding Technology–Structure Relationships: Theory Development and Meta-Analytic Theory Testing," *Academy of Management Journal* 34, no. 2 (1991), pp. 370–99.

62. R.H. Kilmann, *Beyond the Quick Fix* (San Francisco: Jossey-Bass, 1984), p. 38.

63. A.D. Chandler, *Strategy and Structure* (Cambridge, MA: MIT Press, 1962).

64. A.M. Porter, *Competitive Strategy* (New York: The Free Press, 1980).

65. D. Miller, "Configurations of Strategy and Structure," *Strategic Management Journal* 7 (1986), pp. 233–49.

CHAPTER 16

1. F. Vogelstein and E. Florian, "Can Schwab Get Its Mojo Back?" *Fortune*, 17 September 2001, p. 93; B. Morris, "When Bad Things Happen to Good Companies," *Fortune*, 8 December 2003, p. 78; S. Craig and K. Brown, "Schwab Ousts Pottruck as CEO," *The Wall Street Journal*, 21 July 2004, p. A1; R. Frank, "U.S. Trust Feels Effects of Switch," *The Wall Street Journal*, 21 July 2004, p. A8; R. Frank and S. Craig, "White-Shoe Shuffle," *The Wall Street Journal*, 15 September 2004, p. A1; C. Harrington, "Made in Heaven? Watching the Watchovia–Tanager Union," *Accounting Today*, 20 December 2004, p. 18; J. Kador, "Cultures in Conflict," *Registered Rep.*, October 2004, p. 43.

2. A. Williams, P. Dobson, and M. Walters, *Changing Culture: New Organizational Approaches* (London: Institute of Personnel Management, 1989); E.H. Schein, "What Is Culture?" in *Reframing Organizational Culture*, ed. P.J. Frost et al. (Beverly Hills, CA: Sage, 1991), pp. 243–53.

3. Williams, Dobson, and Walters, *Changing Culture: New Organizational Approaches*; Schein, "What Is Culture?"

4. B.M. Meglino and E.C. Ravlin, "Individual Values in Organizations: Concepts, Controversies, and Research," *Journal of Management* 24, no. 3 (1998), pp. 351–89; B.R. Agle and C.B. Caldwell, "Understanding Research on Values in Business," *Business and Society* 38, no. 3 (September 1999), pp. 326–87; S. Hitlin and J.A. Pilavin, "Values: Reviving a Dormant Concept," *Annual Review of Sociology* 30 (2004), pp. 359–93.

5. N.M. Ashkanasy, "The Case for Culture," in *Debating Organization*, ed. R. Westwood and S. Clegg (Malden, MA: Blackwell, 2003), pp. 300–10.

6. Edgar Schein's original model suggested that organizational culture consists of espoused values; but others have subsequently pointed out that enacted values are a more logical part of culture because enacted values are consistent with other elements of the model, namely shared assumptions on one side and artifacts on the other. See D. Denison, "Organizational Culture: Can It Be a Key Lever for Driving Organizational Change?" in *International Handbook of Culture and Climate*, ed. C. Cooper, S. Cartwright, and P.C. Earley (New York: John Wiley & Sons, 2000).

7. M. Fan, "Cary, N.C., Software Firm Posts Steady Growth without IPO," *San Jose Mercury News*, 29 July 2001; B. Darrow, "James Goodnight, Founder and CEO, SAS Institute," *Computer Reseller News*, 12 December 2005, p. 23.

8. "New Age Banks Bet on Variable Pay Plan," *Business Line* (India), 22 September 2003; "Golden Handshake, the ICICI Bank Way," *Financial Express* (India), 6 July 2003.

9. S. Huettel, "Soaring Ahead," *St. Petersburg Times* (Florida), 24 October 2005, p. 1D; E.P. Lima, "Winning Cultures," *Air Transport World*, 1 February 2006, p. 54.

10. J.J. van Muijen, "Organizational Culture," in *A Handbook of Work and Organizational Psychology: Organizational Psychology*, ed. P.J.D. Drenth, H. Thierry, and C.J. de Wolff, 2nd ed. (East Sussex, UK: Psychology Press, 1998), pp. 113–32.

11. M. Miller, "The Acrobat," *Forbes*, 15 March 2004, pp. 100n3; R. Ouzounian, "Cirque's Dream Factory," *Toronto Star*, 1 August 2004; "Cirque Du Soleil's Creator Goes from a Busker to a Billionaire," *Knight Ridder Tribune Business News*, 9 January 2005, p. 1; P. Donnelly, "Grandiose at the Grand," *The Gazette* (Montreal), 29 January 2005, p. D1; L. Tischler, "Join the Circus," *Fast Company*, July 2005, pp. 52–58.

12. J.S. Ott, *The Organizational Culture Perspective* (Pacific Grove, CA: Brooks/ Cole, 1989), pp. 45–47; S. Sackmann, "Culture and Subcultures: An Analysis of Organizational Knowledge," *Administrative Science Quarterly* 37 (1992), pp. 140–61.

13. A. Sinclair, "Approaches to Organizational Culture and Ethics," *Journal of Business Ethics* 12 (1993); A. Boisnier and J. Chatman, "The Role of Subcultures in Agile Organizations," in *Leading and Managing People in Dynamic Organizations*, ed. R. Petersen and E. Mannix (Mahwah, NJ: Lawrence Erlbaum Associates, 2003), pp. 87–112.

14. Ott, *The Organizational Culture Perspective*, Chapter 2; J.S. Pederson and J.S. Sorensen, *Organizational Cultures in Theory and Practice* (Aldershot, England: Gower, 1989), pp. 27–29; M.O. Jones, *Studying Organizational Symbolism: What, How, Why?* (Thousand Oaks, CA: Sage, 1996).

15. E.H. Schein, "Organizational Culture," *American Psychologist*, February 1990, pp. 109–19; A. Furnham and B. Gunter, "Corporate Culture: Definition, Diagnosis, and Change," *International Review of Industrial and Organizational Psychology* 8 (1993), pp. 233–61; E.H. Schein, *The Corporate Culture Survival Guide* (San Francisco: Jossey-Bass, 1999), Chapter 4.

16. M. Doehrman, "Anthropologists—Deep in the Corporate Bush," *Daily Record* (Kansas City, MO), 19 July 2005, p. 1.

17. A.L. Wilkins, "Organizational Stories as Symbols Which Control the Organization," in *Organizational Symbolism*, ed. L.R. Pondy et al. (Greenwich, CT: JAI Press, 1984), pp. 81–92; R. Zemke, "Storytelling: Back to a Basic," *Training* 27 (March 1990), pp. 44–50; J.C. Meyer, "Tell Me a Story: Eliciting Organizational Values from Narratives," *Communication Quarterly* 43 (1995), pp. 210–24; W. Swap et al., "Using Mentoring and Storytelling to Transfer Knowledge in the Workplace," *Journal of Management Information Systems* 18 (Summer 2001), pp. 95–114.

18. "The Ultimate Chairman," *Business Times Singapore*, 3 September 2005.

19. D. Roth, "My Job at the Container Store," *Fortune*, 10 January 2000, pp. 74–78.

20. R.E. Quinn and N.T. Snyder, "Advance Change Theory: Culture Change at Whirlpool Corporation," in *The Leader's Change Handbook*, ed. J.A. Conger, G.M. Spreitzer, and E.E. Lawler III (San Francisco: Jossey-Bass, 1999), pp. 162–93.

21. Churchill apparently made this statement on October 28, 1943, in the British House of Commons, when London, damaged by bombings in World War II, was about to be rebuilt.

22. P. Roberts, "The Empire Strikes Back," *Fast Company* 22 (February–March 1999), pp. 122-31. Some details are also found at www.oakley.com and americahurrah.com/Oakley/Entry.htm.

23. A. D'Innocenzio, "Wal-Mart's Town Becomes New Address for Corporate America," *Associated Press*, 19 September 2003; J. Useem, "One Nation under Wal-Mart," *Fortune*, 3 March 2003, pp. 65–78.

24. T.E. Deal and A.A. Kennedy, *Corporate Cultures* (Reading, MA: Addison-Wesley, 1982); J.B. Barney, "Organizational Culture: Can It Be a Source of Sustained Competitive Advantage?" *Academy of Management Review* 11 (1986), pp. 656–65; C. Siehl and J. Martin, "Organizational Culture: A Key to Financial Performance?" in *Organizational Climate and Culture*, ed. B. Schneider (San Francisco: Jossey-Bass, 1990), pp. 241–81; C.P.M. Wilderom, U. Glunk, and R. Maslowski, "Organizational Culture as a Predictor of Organizational Performance," in *Handbook of Organizational Culture and Climate*, ed. N.M. Ashkanasy, C.P.M. Wilderom, and M.F. Peterson (Thousand Oaks, CA: Sage, 2000), pp. 193–210; C.F. Fey and D.R. Denison, "Organizational Culture and Effectiveness: Can American Theory Be Applied to Russia?" *Organization Science* 14, no. 6 (2003), pp. 686–706; A. Carmeli and A. Tishler, "The Relationships between Intangible Organizational Elements and Organizational Performance," *Strategic Management Journal* 25 (2004), pp. 1257–78.

25. C.A. O'Reilly and J.A. Chatman, "Culture as Social Control: Corporations, Cults, and Commitment," *Research in Organizational Behavior* 18 (1996), pp. 157–200; J.C. Helms Mills and A.J. Mills, "Rules, Sensemaking, Formative Contexts, and Discourse in the Gendering of Organizational Culture," in *International Handbook of Organizational Climate and Culture*, ed. N. Ashkanasy, C. Wilderom, and M. Peterson (Thousand Oaks, CA: Sage, 2000), pp. 55–70; J.A. Chatman and S.E. Cha, "Leading by Leveraging Culture," *California Management Review* 45 (Summer 2003), pp. 20–34.

26. B. Ashforth and F. Mael, "Social Identity Theory and the Organization," *Academy of Management Review* 14 (1989), pp. 20–39.

27. M.R. Louis, "Surprise and Sensemaking: What Newcomers Experience in Entering Unfamiliar Organizational Settings," *Administrative Science Quarterly* 25 (1980), pp. 226–51; S.G. Harris, "Organizational Culture and Individual Sensemaking: A Schema-Based Perspective," *Organization Science* 5 (1994), pp. 309–21.

28. D.R. Denison, *Corporate Culture and Organizational Effectiveness* (New York: Wiley, 1990); G.G. Gordon and N. DiTomasco, "Predicting Corporate Performance from Organizational Culture," *Journal of Management Studies* 29 (1992), pp. 783–98; J.P. Kotter and J.L. Heskett, *Corporate Culture and Performance* (New York: Free Press, 1992).

29. A. Holeck, "Griffith, Ind., Native Takes over as Steel Plant Manager," *The Times* (Munster, Ind.), 24 May 2003.

30. Kotter and Heskett, *Corporate Culture and Performance*; J.P. Kotter, "Cultures and Coalitions," *Executive Excellence* 15 (March 1998), pp. 14–15.

31. The features of adaptive cultures are described in W.F. Joyce, *MegaChange: How Today's Leading Companies Have Transformed Their Workforces* (New York: Free Press, 1999), pp. 44–47.

32. M. Acharya, "A Matter of Business Ethics," *Kitchener-Waterloo Record*, 23 March 1999, p. C2.

33. D. Griesing, "'Boot Camp' Failed to Teach All They Could Be," *Chicago Tribune*, 21 April 2002, p. C1; B.L. Toffler, *Final Accounting: Ambition, Greed, and the Fall of Arthur Andersen* (New York: Broadway Books, 2003).

34. "Japanese Officials Order Citibank to Halt Some Operations," *Dow Jones Business News*, 17 September 2004; "Citigroup CEO Prince Holds Press Conference in Japan," *Business Wire* (Tokyo), 25 October 2004; A. Morse, "Citigroup Extends Apology to Japan," *The Wall Street Journal*, 26 October 2004, p. A3; M. Pacelle, M. Fackler, and A. Morse, "Mission Control," *The Wall Street Journal*, 22 December 2004, p. A1.

35. M.L. Marks, "Adding Cultural Fit to Your Diligence Checklist," *Mergers &* *Acquisitions* 34, no. 3 (November–December 1999), pp. 14–20; Schein, *The Corporate Culture Survival Guide*, Chapter 8; M.L. Marks, "Mixed Signals," *Across the Board*, May 2000, pp. 21–26; J.P. Daly, R.W. Pouder, and B. Kabanoff, "The Effects of Initial Differences in Firms' Espoused Values on Their Postmerger Performance," *Journal of Applied Behavioral Science* 40, no. 3 (September 2004), pp. 323–43.

36. A. Klein, "A Merger Taken AO-Ill," *Washington Post*, 21 October 2002, p. E1; A. Klein, *Stealing Time: Steve Case, Jerry Levin, and the Collapse of AOL Time Warner* (New York: Simon & Shuster, 2003).

37. E. Connors, "Not Drowning, Dancing," *Australian Financial Review*, 12 November 2004, p. 22.

38. S. Greengard, "Due Diligence: The Devil in the Details," *Workforce*, October 1999, p. 68; Marks, "Adding Cultural Fit to Your Diligence Checklist."

39. Greengard, "Due Diligence: The Devil in the Details"; Marks, "Adding Cultural Fit to Your Diligence Checklist."

40. A.R. Malekazedeh and A. Nahavandi, "Making Mergers Work by Managing Cultures," *Journal of Business Strategy*, May–June 1990, pp. 55–57; K.W. Smith, "A Brand-New Culture for the Merged Firm," *Mergers and Acquisitions* 35 (June 2000), pp. 45–50.

41. T. Hamilton, "RIM on a Roll," *Toronto Star*, 22 February 2004, p. C01.

42. Hewitt Associates, "Mergers and Acquisitions May Be Driven by Business Strategy–But Often Stumble over People and Culture Issues," *PR Newswire news release*, (Lincolnshire, Illinois), 3 August 1998.

43. I. Mount, "Be Fast Be Frugal Be Right," *Inc* 26, no. 1 (January 2004), pp. 64–70; S. Anthony and C. Christensen, "Mind over Merger," *Optimize*, February 2005, pp. 22–27.

44. E.H. Schein, "The Role of the Founder in Creating Organizational Culture," *Organizational Dynamics* 12, no. 1 (Summer 1983), pp. 13–28; R. House, M. Javidan, and P. Dorfman, "Project Globe: An Introduction," *Applied Psychology: An International Review* 50 (2001), pp. 489–505; R. House et al., "Understanding Cultures and Implicit Leadership Theories across the Globe: An Introduction to Project Globe," *Journal of World Business* 37 (2002), pp. 3–10.

45. T.J. Peters, "Symbols, Patterns, and Settings: An Optimistic Case for Getting

Things Done," *Organizational Dynamics* 7, no. 2 (Autumn 1978), pp. 2–23; E.H. Schein, *Organizational Culture and Leadership* (San Francisco: Jossey-Bass, 1985), Chapter 10.

46. J. Kerr and J. W. Slocum Jr., "Managing Corporate Culture through Reward Systems," *Academy of Management Executive* 1 (May 1987), pp. 99–107; K.R. Thompson and F. Luthans, "Organizational Culture: A Behavioral Perspective," in *Organizational Climate and Culture*, ed. B. Schneider (San Francisco: Jossey-Bass, 1990), pp. 319–44. John Deere's reward system is described in G.B. Sprinkle and M.G. Williamson, "The Evolution from Taylorism to Employee Gainsharing: A Case Study Examining John Deere's Continuous Improvement Pay Plan," *Issues in Accounting Education* 19, no. 4 (November 2004), pp. 487–503.

47. "Big Blue Is Finally Living up to Its Name," *Charleston Daily Mail*, 9 February 1995, p. 5H.

48. J. Hewett, "Office Politics," *Australian Financial Review*, 27 September 2003, p. 29.

49. M. De Pree, *Leadership Is an Art* (East Lansing, MI: Michigan State University Press, 1987).

50. B. McLean, "Inside the Money Machine," *Fortune*, 6 September 2004, p. 84.

51. C. Daniels, "Does This Man Need a Shrink?" *Fortune*, 5 February 2001, pp. 205–8.

52. Chatman and Cha, "Leading by Leveraging Culture"; A.E.M. Van Vianen, "Person–Organization Fit: The Match between Newcomers' and Recruiters' Preferences for Organizational Cultures," *Personnel Psychology* 53 (Spring 2000), pp. 113–49; C.A. O'Reilly III, J. Chatman, and D.F. Caldwell, "People and Organizational Culture: A Profile Comparison Approach to Assessing Person–Organization Fit," *Academy of Management Journal* 34 (1991), pp. 487–516.

53. J. Van Maanen, "Breaking In: Socialization to Work," in *Handbook of Work, Organization, and Society*, ed. R. Dubin (Chicago: Rand McNally, 1976).

54. C. Fishman, "The Anarchist's Cookbook," *Fast Company*, July 2004, p. 70; "World's Finest Food Retailers: Whole Foods, Not Holy Food," *The Grocer*, 12 November 2005, p. 32.

55. V. Galt, "Kid-Glove Approach Woos New Grads," *Globe & Mail*, 9 March 2005, p. C1.

56. C.L. Adkins, "Previous Work Experience and Organizational Socialization: A Longitudinal Examination," *Academy of Management Journal* 38 (1995), pp. 839–62; J.D. Kammeyer-Mueller and C.R. Wanberg, "Unwrapping the Organizational Entry Process: Disentangling Multiple Antecedents and Their Pathways to Adjustment," *Journal of Applied Psychology* 88, no. 5 (2003), pp. 779–94.

57. J.M. Beyer and D.R. Hannah, "Building on the Past: Enacting Established Personal Identities in a New Work Setting," *Organization Science* 13 (November/December 2002), pp. 636–52; H.D.C. Thomas and N. Anderson, "Newcomer Adjustment: The Relationship between Organizational Socialization Tactics, Information Acquisition and Attitudes," *Journal of Occupational and Organizational Psychology* 75 (December 2002), pp. 423–37.

58. L.W. Porter, E.E. Lawler III, and J R Hackman, *Behavior in Organizations* (New York: McGraw-Hill, 1975), pp. 163–67; Van Maanen, "Breaking In: Socialization to Work"; D.C. Feldman, "The Multiple Socialization of Organization Members," *Academy of Management Review* 6 (1981), pp. 309–18.

59. B.E. Ashforth and A.M. Saks, "Socialization Tactics: Longitudinal Effects on Newcomer Adjustment," *Academy of Management Journal* 39 (1996), pp. 149–78; Kammeyer-Mueller and Wanberg, "Unwrapping the Organizational Entry Process."

60. Porter, Lawler, and Hackman, *Behavior in Organizations*, Chapter 5.

61. Louis, "Surprise and Sensemaking: What Newcomers Experience in Entering Unfamiliar Organizational Settings."

62. R. Craver, "Dell Thinning out List of Job Candidates," *Winston-Salem Journal*, 23 April 2005.

63. J.A. Breaugh, *Recruitment: Science and Practice* (Boston: PWS-Kent, 1992); J.P. Wanous, *Organizational Entry* (Reading, MA: Addison-Wesley, 1992).

64. J.M. Phillips, "Effects of Realistic Job Previews on Multiple Organizational Outcomes: A Meta-Analysis," *Academy of Management Journal* 41 (December 1998), pp. 673–90.

65. Y. Ganzach et al., "Social Exchange and Organizational Commitment: Decision-Making Training for Job Choice as an Alternative to the Realistic Job Preview," *Personnel Psychology* 55 (Autumn 2002), pp. 613–37.

66. C. Ostroff and S.W.J. Koslowski, "Organizational Socialization as a Learning Process: The Role of Information Acquisition," *Personnel Psychology* 45 (1992), pp. 849–74; E.W. Morrison, "Newcomer Information Seeking: Exploring Types, Modes, Sources, and Outcomes," *Academy of Management Journal* 36 (1993). pp. 557–89; U. Anakwe and J.H. Greenhaus, "Effective Socialization of Employees: Socialization Content Perspective," *Journal of Managerial Issues* 11, no. 3 (Fall 1999), pp. 315–29.

67. S.L. McShane, *Effect of Socialization Agents on the Organizational Adjustment of New Employees* (Big Sky, MT: Annual Conference of the Western Academy of Management, March 1988).

68. D. Francis, "Work Is a Warm Puppy," *National Post*, 27 May 2000, p. W20; C. Goforth, "Still Recruiting Staff," *Akron Beacon Journal*, 15 July 2001.

CHAPTER 17

1. D. Howell, "Nardelli Nears Five-Year Mark with Riveting Record," *DSN Retailing Today*, 9 May 2005, pp. 1, 38; R. Charan, "Home Depot's Blueprint for Culture Change," *Harvard Business Review*, April 2006, pp. 61–70; R. DeGross, "Five Years of Change: Home Depot's Results Mixed under Nardelli," *Atlanta Journal-Constitution*, 1 January 2006, p. F1; B. Grow, D. Brady, and M. Arndt, "Renovating Home Depot," *BusinessWeek*, 6 March 2006, pp. 50–57.

2. K. Lewin, *Field Theory in Social Science* (New York: Harper & Row, 1951).

3. "The Wrong People Doing the Right Job: Reforming the FBI," *The Economist*, 17 April 2004, p. 371; National Commission on Terrorist Attacks upon the United States, *The 9/11 Commission Report* (Washington, DC: U.S. Government Printing Office, July 2004); D. Eggen, "FBI Fails to Transform Itself, Panel Says," *Washington Post*, 7 June 2005, p. A04; C. Ragavan and C.S. Hook, "Fixing the FBI," *U.S. News & World Report*, 28 March 2005, pp. 18–24, 26, 29–30; The Commission on the Intelligence Capabilities of the United States Regarding Weapons of Mass Destruction, *Report to the President of the United States* (Washington, DC: 31 March 2005).

4. M. Riley, "High-Revving Nasser Undone by a Blind Spot," *Sydney Morning Herald*, 3 November 2001; J. McCracken, "Nasser Out; Ford In," *Detroit Free Press*, 30 October 2001; M. Truby, "Can Ford Chief

Ride Out Storm?" *Detroit News*, 24 June 2001; M. Truby, "Ford Revolution Spawns Turmoil," *Detroit News*, 29 April 2001.

5. C.O. Longenecker, D.J. Dwyer, and T.C. Stansfield, "Barriers and Gateways to Workforce Productivity," *Industrial Management*, March-April 1998, pp. 21–28; J. Seifman, "Middle Managers-the Meat in the Corporate Sandwich," *China Staff*, June 2002, p. 7; *Bosses Want Change but Workers Want More of the Same!* (Sydney: Talent2, 29 June 2005).

6. E.B. Dent and S.G. Goldberg, "Challenging 'Resistance to Change,'" *Journal of Applied Behavioral Science* 35 (March 1999), pp. 25–41; D.B. Fedor, S. Caldwell, and D.M. Herold, "The Effects of Organizational Changes on Employee Commitment: A Multilevel Investigation," *Personnel Psychology* 59, no. 1 (2006), pp. 1–29.

7. D.A. Nadler, "The Effective Management of Organizational Change," in *Handbook of Organizational Behavior*, ed. J.W. Lorsch (Englewood Cliffs, NJ: Prentice Hall, 1987), pp. 358–69; R. Maurer, *Beyond the Wall of Resistance: Unconventional Strategies to Build Support for Change* (Austin, TX: Bard Books, 1996); P. Strebel, "Why Do Employees Resist Change?" *Harvard Business Review*, May-June 1996, pp. 86–92; D.A. Nadler, *Champions of Change* (San Francisco: Jossey-Bass, 1998).

8. "Making Change Work for You-Not against You," *Agency Sales Magazine* 28 (June 1998), pp. 24–27.

9. D. Miller, "What Happens after Success: The Perils of Excellence," *Journal of Management Studies* 31 (1994), pp. 325–58.

10. T.G. Cummings, "The Role and Limits of Change Leadership," in *The Leader's Change Handbook*, ed. J.A. Conger, G.M. Spreitzer, and E.E. Lawler III (San Francisco: Jossey-Bass, 1999), pp. 301–20; J.P. Kotter and D.S. Cohen, *The Heart of Change* (Boston: Harvard Business School Press, 2002), pp. 15–36.

11. J. Smith, "Building Cars, Building Teams," *Plant Engineering*, December 2005, pp. 41–50.

12. L.D. Goodstein and H.R. Butz, "Customer Value: The Linchpin of Organizational Change," *Organizational Dynamics* 27 (June 1998), pp. 21–35.

13. F. Smith et al., "25 True Leaders," *Australian Financial Review*, 12 August 2005, p. 62.

14. I.J. Bozon and P.N. Child, "Refining Shell's Position in Europe," *McKinsey Quarterly*, no. 2 (2003), pp. 42–51.

15. D. Darlin, "Growing Tomorrow," *Business 2.0*, May 2005, p. 126.

16. L. Grossman and S. Song, "Stevie's Little Wonder," *Time*, 19 September 2005, p. 63; S. Levy, "Honey, I Shrunk the iPod. A Lot," *Newsweek*, 19 September 2005, p. 58.

17. J.P. Kotter and L.A. Schlesinger, "Choosing Strategies for Change," *Harvard Business Review*, March-April 1979, pp. 106–14.

18. B. Nanus and S.M. Dobbs, *Leaders Who Make a Difference* (San Francisco: Jossey-Bass, 1999); Kotter and Cohen, *The Heart of Change*, pp. 83–98.

19. M.J. Marquardt, *Optimizing the Power of Action Learning: Solving Problems and Building Leaders in Real Time* (Palo Alto, CA: Davies-Black, 2004).

20. K.T. Dirks, L.L. Cummings, and J.L. Pierce, "Psychological Ownership in Organizations: Conditions under Which Individuals Promote and Resist Change," *Research in Organizational Change and Development* 9 (1996), pp. 1–23.

21. B.B. Bunker and B.T. Alban, *Large Group Interventions: Engaging the Whole System for Rapid Change* (San Francisco: Jossey-Bass, 1996); M. Weisbord and S. Janoff, *Future Search: An Action Guide to Finding Common Ground in Organizations and Communities* (San Francisco: Berrett-Koehler, 2000). For a description of the first future search conference, see M.R. Weisbord, "Inventing the Search Conference: Bristol Siddeley Aircraft Engines, 1960," in *Discovering Common Ground*, ed. M.R. Weisbord (San Francisco: Berret-Koehler, 1992), pp. 19–33.

22. W. Kaschub, "Peco Energy Redesigns HR," *HR Focus* 74 (March 1997), p. 3; R. Larson, "Forester Defends 'Feel-Good' Meeting," *Washington Times*, 28 November 1997, p. A9; R.E. Purser and S. Cabana, *The Self-Managing Organization* (New York: Free Press, 1998); T. Shapley, "Trying to Fix What Everyone Else Has Broken," *Seattle Post-Intelligencer*, 16 November 2005, p. B8.

23. For criticism of a recent search conference for lacking innovative or realistic ideas, see A. Oels, "Investigating the Emotional Roller-Coaster Ride: A Case Study-Based Assessment of the Future Search Conference Design," *Systems Research and Behavioral Science* 19 (July-August 2002), pp. 347–55; M.F.D. Polanyi, "Communicative Action in Practice: Future Search and the Pursuit of an Open, Critical and Non-Coercive Large-Group Process," *Systems Research*

and Behavioral Science 19 (July 2002), pp. 357–66.

24. S.M. Weber, "the Dangers of Success: Diffusion and Transition of Large Group Interventions in German-Speaking Countries," *Journal of Applied Behavioral Science*, 41 (March 2005), 111–121.

25. M. McHugh, "The Stress Factor: Another Item for the Change Management Agenda?" *Journal of Organizational Change Management* 10 (1997), pp. 345–62; D. Buchanan, T. Claydon, and M. Doyle, "Organisation Development and Change: The Legacy of the Nineties," *Human Resource Management Journal* 9 (1999), pp. 20–37.

26. T. Joyner, "Merger Toil Replaced Fun in Sun," *Atlanta Journal and Constitution*, 5 August 2001, p. A1.

27. D. Nicolini and M.B. Meznar, "The Social Construction of Organizational Learning: Conceptual and Practical Issues in the Field," *Human Relations* 48 (1995), pp. 727–46.

28. D. Helfand, "School Is Down but Looking Up," *Los Angeles Times*, 14 October 2004, p. B1; "Mrs. Bush Remarks on Helping America's Youth in Sun Valley, California," The White House news release (Sun Valley, CA: 27 April 2005), http://www.whitehouse.gov/news/releases/2005/04/20050427-5.html.

29. R.H. Miles, "Leading Corporate Transformation: Are You up to the Task?" in *The Leader's Change Handbook*, ed. J.A. Conger, G.M. Spreitzer, and E.E. Lawler III (San Francisco: Jossey-Bass, 1999), pp. 221–67; E.E. Lawler III, "Pay Can Be a Change Agent," *Compensation & Benefits Management* 16 (Summer 2000), pp. 23–26; Kotter and Cohen, *The Heart of Change*, pp. 161–77.

30. R.E. Quinn, *Building the Bridge as You Walk on It: A Guide for Leading Change* (San Francisco: Jossey-Bass, 2004), Chapter 11.

31. J.P. Kotter, "Leading Change: Why Transformation Efforts Fail," *Harvard Business Review*, March-April 1995, pp. 59–67; J.P. Kotter, "Leading Change: The Eight Steps to Transformation," in *The Leader's Change Handbook*, ed. J.A. Conger, G.M. Spreitzer, and E.E. Lawler III (San Francisco: Jossey-Bass, 1999), pp.221–67.

32. R. Caldwell, "Models of Change Agency: A Fourfold Classification," *British Journal of Management* 14 (June 2003), pp. 131–42.

33. M. Beer, R.A. Eisenstat, and B. Spector, *The Critical Path to Corporate Renewal* (Boston, MA: Harvard Business School Press, 1990).

34. R.E. Walton, "Successful Strategies for Diffusing Work Innovations," *Journal of Contemporary Business*, Spring 1977, pp. 1–22; R.E. Walton, *Innovating to Compete: Lessons for Diffusing and Managing Change in the Workplace* (San Francisco: Jossey-Bass, 1987); Beer, Eisenstat, and Spector, *The Critical Path to Corporate Renewal*, Chapter 5.

35. E.M. Rogers, *Diffusion of Innovations*, 4th ed. (New York: Free Pree, 1995).

36. P. Reason and H. Bradbury, *Handbook of Action Research* (London: Sage, 2001); D. Coghlan and T. Brannick, "Kurt Lewin: The 'Practical Theorist' for the 21st Century," *Irish Journal of Management* 24, no. 2 (2003), pp. 31-37; C. Huxham and S. Vangen, "Researching Organizational Practice through Action Research: Case Studies and Design Choices," *Organizational Research Methods* 6 (July 2003), pp. 383-403.

37. V.J. Marsick and M.A. Gephart, "Action Research: Building the Capacity for Learning and Change," *Human Resource Planning* 26 (2003), pp. 14–18.

38. L. Dickens and K. Watkins, "Action Research: Rethinking Lewin," *Management Learning* 30 (June 1999), pp. 127–40; J. Heron and P. Reason, "The Practice of Cooperative Inquiry: Research 'with' Rather Than 'on' People," in *Handbook of Action Research*, ed. P. Reason and H. Bradbury (Thousand Oaks, CA: Sage, 2001), pp. 179–88.

39. D.A. Nadler, "Organizational Frame Bending: Types of Change in the Complex Organization," in *Corporate Transformation: Revitalizing Organizations for a Competitive World*, ed. R.H. Kilmann, T.J. Covin, and Associates (San Francisco: Jossey-Bass, 1988), pp. 66–83; K.E. Weick and R.E. Quinn, "Organizational Change and Development," *Annual Review of Psychology*, 1999, pp. 361–86.

40. T.M. Egan and C.M. Lancaster, "Comparing Appreciative Inquiry to Action Research: OD Practitioner Perspectives," *Organization Development Journal* 23, no. 2 (Summer 2005), pp. 29–49.

41. F.F. Luthans, "Positive Organizational Behavior: Developing and Managing Psychological Strengths," *The Academy of Management Executive* 16, no. 1 (2002), pp. 57–72; N. Turner, J. Barling, and A. Zacharatos, "Positive Psychology at Work," in *Handbook of Positive Psychology*, ed. C.R. Snyder and S. Lopez (Oxford, UK: Oxford University Press, 2002), pp. 715–30; K. Cameron, J.E. Dutton, and R.E. Quinn, eds., *Positive Organizational Scholarship: Foundation of a New Discipline* (San Francisco: Berrett Koehler Publishers, 2003); J.I. Krueger and D.C. Funder, "Toward a Balanced Social Psychology: Causes, Consequences, and Cures for the Problem-Seeking Approach to Social Behavior and Cognition," *Behavioral and Brain Sciences* 27, no. 3 (June 2004), pp. 313–27; S.L. Gable and J. Haidt, "What (and Why) Is Positive Psychology?" *Review of General Psychology* 9, no. 2 (2005), pp. 103–10; M.E.P. Seligman et al., "Positive Psychology Progress: Empirical Validation of Interventions," *American Psychologist* 60, no. 5 (2005), pp. 410–21.

42. D. Whitney and D.L. Cooperrider, "The Appreciative Inquiry Summit: Overview and Applications," *Employment Relations Today* 25 (Summer 1998), pp. 17–28; J.M. Watkins and B.J. Mohr, *Appreciative Inquiry: Change at the Speed of Imagination* (San Francisco: Jossey-Bass, 2001).

43. F.J. Barrett and D.L. Cooperrider, "Generative Metaphor Intervention: A New Approach for Working with Systems Divided by Conflict and Caught in Defensive Perception," *Journal of Applied Behavioral Science* 26 (1990), pp. 219–39; Whitney and Cooperrider, "The Appreciative Inquiry Summit: Overview and Applications", Watkins and Mohr, *Appreciative Inquiry: Change at the Speed of Imagination*, pp. 15–21.

44. Canadian Tire, *Team Values Development Process*, Powerpoint File (Toronto: Canadian Tire, 24 September 2001); Canadian Tire, *Leadership Guide* (Toronto: Canadian Tire, 2002).

45. M. Schiller, "Case Study: Avon Mexico," in *Appreciative Inquiry: Change at the Speed of Imagination*, ed. J.M. Watkins and B.J. Mohr (San Francisco: Jossey-Bass, 2001), pp. 123–26; D. Whitney and A. Trosten-Bloom, *The Power of Appreciative Inquiry: A Practical Guide to Positive Change* (San Francisco: Berrett-Koehler Publishers, 2003); P. Babcock, "Seeing a Brighter Future," *HRMagazine* 50, no. 9 (September 2005), p. 48; D.S. Bright, D.L. Cooperrider, and W.B. Galloway, "Appreciative Inquiry in the Office of Research and Development: Improving the Collaborative Capacity of Organization," *Public Performance & Management Review* 29, no. 3 (2006), p. 285.

46. T.F. Yaeger, P.F. Sorensen, and U. Bengtsson, "Assessment of the State of Appreciative Inquiry: Past, Present, and Future," *Research in Organizational Change and Development* 15 (2004), pp. 297–319; G.R. Bushe and A.F. Kassam, "When Is Appreciative Inquiry Transformational? A Meta-Case Analysis," *Journal of Applied Behavioral Science* 41, no. 2 (June 2005), pp. 161–81.

47. G.R. Bushe, "Five Theories of Change Embedded in Appreciative Inquiry," in *18th Annual World Congress of Organization Development* (Dublin, Ireland: July 14–18, 1998).

48. G.R. Bushe and A.B. Shani, *Parallel Learning Structures* (Reading, MA: Addison-Wesley, 1991); E.M. Van Aken, D.J. Monetta, and S.D. Sink. "Affinity Groups: The Missing Link in Employee Involvement," *Organization Dynamics* 22 (Spring 1994), pp. 38–54.

49. D.J. Knight, "Strategy in Practice: Making It Happen," *Strategy & Leadership* 26 (July-August 1998), pp. 29–33; R.T. Pascale, "Grassroots Leadership-Royal Dutch/Shell," *Fast Company* 14 (April-May 1998), pp. 110–20; R.T. Pascale, "Leading from a Different Place," in *The Leader's Change Handbook*, ed. J.A. Conger, G.M. Spreitzer, and E.E. Lawler III (San Francisco: Jossey-Bass, 1999), pp. 301–20; R. Pascale, M. Millemann, and L. Gioja, *Surfing on the Edge of Chaos* (London: Texere, 2000).

50. C.M. Lau, "A Culture-Based Perspective of Organization Development Implementation," *Research in Organizational Change and Development* 9 (1996), pp. 49–79.

51. T.C. Head and P.F. Sorensen, "Cultural Values and Organizational Development: A Seven-Country Study," *Leadership and Organization Development Journal* 14 (1993), pp. 3–7; R.J. Marshak, "Lewin Meets Confucius: A Review of the OD Model of Change," *Journal of Applied Behavioral Science* 29 (1993), pp. 395–415; C.M. Lau and H.Y. Ngo, "Organization Development and Firm Performance: A Comparison of Multinational and Local Firms," *Journal of International Business Studies* 32, no. 1 (2001), pp. 95–114.

52. For an excellent discussion of conflict management and Asia values, see several articles in K. Leung and D. Tjosvold, eds., *Conflict Management in the Asian Pacific: Assumptions and Approaches in Diverse Cultures* (Singapore: John Wiley & Sons, 1998).

53. M. McKendall, "The Tyranny of Change: Organizational Development Revisited," *Journal of Business Ethics* 12 (February 1993), pp. 93–104; C.M.D. Deaner, "A Model of Organization Development Ethics," *Public Administration Quarterly* 17 (1994), pp. 435–46.

54. G.A. Walter, "Organization Development and Individual Rights," *Journal*

of Applied Behavioral Science 20 (1984),
pp. 423–39.

55. B. Moses, "Give People Belief in the
Future," *Workforce,* June 2000, pp. 134–41.

56. B. Moses, "Career Activists Take
Command," *Globe & Mail,* 20 March
2000, p. B6.

57. Drake Beam Morin, *1999 DBM
Career Transition Study* (Drake Beam
Morin, November 2000); F.T. McCarthy,
"Career Evolution," *The Economist,* 29
January 2000.

58. B. Moses, *The Good News about Careers:
How You'll Be Working in the Next Decade*
(San Francisco: Jossey-Bass, 1999); S.E.
Sullivan, "The Changing Nature of Ca-
reers: A Review and Research Agenda,"
Journal of Management 25 (May 1999),
pp. 457–84.

59. S.C. Van Collie, "Moving up through
Mentoring," *Workforce,* March 1998,
pp. 36–40; N. Beech and A. Brockbank,
"Power/Knowledge and Psychosocial
Dynamics in Mentoring," *Management
Learning* 30 (March 1999), pp. 7–24.

photo credits

CHAPTER 1

page 2:   AP/Wide World Photos

page 7:   © Hans Rudolf Oeser/The New York Times

page 14:   Department of Economic Development, Government of Dubai

page 16:   © John Gillooly, Professional Event Images, Inc.

page 23:   © The Augusta Chronicle

CHAPTER 2

page 32:   Reprinted with permission of Owens Corning. All Rights Reserved.

page 36:   AP/Wide World Photos

page 40:   © Norbert von der Groeben/ The Image Works

page 44:   © PARRAMATTA/Newspix

page 47:   © Cancan Chu/Getty Images

page 50:   Courtesy of Molson Coors

page 55:   © C. Blanchard, Richmond Times-Dispatch

CHAPTER 3

page 66:   © Bob Finlayson/Newspix

page 70:   AP/Wide World Photos

page 74:   © Mel Melcon, 2005, Los AngelesTimes; Reprinted with permission.

page 77:   © Melanie Stetson Freeman/ The Christian Science Monitor/Getty Images

page 81:   Courtesy of Cocoplans

page 88:   Courtesy of Exxon Mobil

page 91:   © Michael Stuparyk, Toronto Star

CHAPTER 4

page 102:   Courtesy of Wegmans

page 104:   Copyright © Ted Goff, 2001 www.tedgoff.com. Used with permission.

page 109:   Courtesy of CXtec

page 112:   Courtesy of Four Seasons Hotels and Resorts

page 117:   Photo Courtesy of Outback Steakhouse

page 122:   © Yuriko Nakao/Reuters/ Landov

CHAPTER 5

page 132:   Courtesy of Sarova Panafric Hotel

page 137:   © Ed Wheeler Photography, Inc.

page 142:   AP/Wide World Photos

page 147:   Photo courtesy of Akamai

page 151:   Courtesy of Verizon

page 154:   © The New Yorker Collection 2001 Barbara Smaller from cartoonbank. com. All rights reserved.

page 155:   © Peter Yates/The New York Times

CHAPTER 6

page 166:   © Will Crockett, Shoot Smarter

page 170:   © Jason Dewey/Getty Images

page 173:   Wolfgang von Brauchitsch/ Bloomberg News/Landov

page 182:   Photo by Kevin Adler, Kron 4

page 184:   Courtesy of Pretoria Portland Cement Company

page 187:   Courtesy of eSilicon Corporation

CHAPTER 7

page 196 (top):   Courtesy of Buena Vista Games

page 196 (bottom):   Munshi Ahmed/Bloomberg News/Landov

page 202:   © Wolfgang Schmidt/Peter Arnold, Inc.

page 203:   © Larry Dale Gordon/Getty Images

page 205:   Photo by Mikael Kjellstrom/ Calgary Herald, May 18, 2005

page 207:   © Observer Dispatch

page 212:   Image courtesy of Deloitte

page 214:   Photo courtesy of Liggett Stashower

CHAPTER 8

page 224:   Ron Sangha Photography

page 228:   Copyright © Randy Glasbergen. Reprinted with special permission from www.glasbergen.com.

page 229:   © Apple Computer, Inc. Use with permission. All rights reserved. Apple® and the Apple logo are registered trademarks of Apple Computer, Inc.

page 235:   © Scottish Parliamentary Corporate Body – 2006

page 238:   © Yvan Cohen/OnAsia Images Pte. Ltd.

page 242:   AP/Wide World Photos

CHAPTER 9

page 256:   Courtesy of Paul Tramontano, Smith Barney

page 260:   Car Design News Ltd.

page 263:   MEDRAD INC.

page 266:   Photo courtesy of Shell International Ltd.

page 270:   U.S. Navy photo by Photographer's Mate 1st Class Casey Akins

page 275:   Courtesy of Lighthouse Publishing Limited, Robert Hirtle, photographer

CHAPTER 10

page 284:   Photo Courtesy of PricewaterhouseCoopers LLP. Visit us on the Web at www.pwc.com/us.

page 289:   AP/Wide World Photos

page 290:   Photo Courtesy of Standard Motor Company

page 293:   © Royalty Free/Corbis

page 300:   Johnson Space Center/ NASA

page 303:   Courtesy of Lockheed Martin Corporation

CHAPTER 11

page 312:   Photo Courtesy of Sun Microsystems, Inc.

page 317:   Photo courtesy of Admiral Insurance

page 323:   © Ted Goff

page 325:   © Mark M. Lawrence/ Corbis

page 329:   Photo courtesy of www.aintitcool.com

page 331:   Courtesy of Shangri-La Hotels & Resorts

CHAPTER 12

page 340: Craig Abraham/Fairfax Photos

page 344: ©Topham/The Image Works

page 346: Photo courtesy of Lowe Worldwide

page 349: © Scott Sendrow, Bridge and Tunnel Club

page 354: AP/Wide World Photos

page 359: © Martin H. Simon/Corbis

CHAPTER 13

page 368: © Reuters/Corbis

page 372: © Reza Estakhrian/Getty Images

page 376: AP/Wide World Photos

page 379: AP/Wide World Photos

page 382: Edward Carreon/Newhouse News Service

page 389: U.S. Air Force photo by Tech. Sgt. Bob Oldham

CHAPTER 14

page 400: AP/Wide World Photos

page 402: Photo courtesy of Semco

page 404: AP/Wide World Photos

page 410: © Empics

page 415: AP/Wide World Photos

page 420: © ADREES LATIF/Reuters/Corbis

CHAPTER 15

page 428: Photo courtesy of Nitro Group

page 432: Edward Smith/Artizans.com. Reprinted with permission.

page 437: The Minnesota Business Journal/Used with permission by Harbinger Partners Inc.

page 442: © The Edmonton Journal

page 445: © Bill Cramer

page 449: Photo courtesy of 7-Eleven, Inc.

CHAPTER 16

page 458: AP/Wide World Photos

page 462: © Munson, John/Star Ledger/Corbis

page 464: Courtesy of Mayo Clinic

page 469: Yuriko Nakao/Reuters

page 471: Noah Berger/Bloomberg News/Landov

page 475: AP/Wide World Photos

CHAPTER 17

page 486: © Najlah Feanny/Corbis

page 489: AP/Wide World Photos

page 493: William West/AFP/Getty Images

page 496: © Eriko Sugita/Reuters/Corbis

page 498: © Brian Vander Brug, 2004, Los Angeles Times. Reprinted with permission.

page 502: Norm Betts/Bloomberg News/Landov

organization index

A

Abitibi-Consolidated, 470
Abitibi-Price, 470
ABSA, 243
Admiral Insurance, 213, 317
Adolph Coors Co., 50
Agilent Technologies, 13, 294
Airbus, 45
Akamai, 147
Allied Signal, 406
Amcor, 21–22
American Express, 36, 349, 503
AOL, 469
AOL Time Warner, 469
Aperture Technologies Inc., 330
Apple Computer, 5, 142, 229, 244, 277, 354, 368, 493
Armstrong World Industries Inc., 384
Arthur Andersen, 119, 375, 376, 468, 534–535
ASB Bank, 32–33, 37
Association of Technology Staffing Companies, 74
Astral Media Inc., 51–52
AstraZeneca, 215
AT&T, 13,36
Australian Olympic Committee, 22
Australian Wheat Board (AWB), 48
Autodesk, 417
AVON Mexico, 503
AWB (Australian Wheat Board), 48
AXA, 75

B

BakBone Software, 293
Ballard Power Systems, 242
Bank of America New Jersey, 10
Bank of Nova Scotia (ScotiaBank), 476, 478, 479
Barrick Gold Corp., 434–435, 439
BASF, 434
BBC (British Broadcasting Company), 182
BB&T Corp., 114
Bell Canada, 330
Bell Labs, 2
Best Buy, 172
Best Practices Project, 8
Bethlehem Steel, 166
Bill & Melinda Gates Foundation, 404, 406
BioWare, 441, 442
Blue Angels, 270
BMW, 446, 447, 464, 465, 466
Boeing Co., 12, 92, 152, 153, 237
Bombardier, 387
Bristol-Myers, 474–475
British American Tobacco, 534
British Broadcasting Company (BBC), 182

Buena Vista Games, 196
Burberry, 259

C

CalTech, 74
Campbell Soup Company, 175
Canadian Tire, 502
Canon Inc., 288
CARE, 404, 406
Casino Reinvestment Development Authority (CRDA), 111
CDC (Centers for Disease Control), 404, 406
Celestica, 447
Centers for Disease Control (CDC), 404, 406
Central Intelligence Agency (CIA), 489
Charles Schwab & Co., 430, 458, 460, 461, 465, 467, 469, 471, 473
Chiat/Day, 229, 348
Chick-fil-A, 417
Chrysler Corporation, 176, 177, 180, 289, 291
CIA (Central Intelligence Agency), 489
CiCi's Pizza, 112
Cirque du Soleil, 462
Cisco Systems, 368, 471
Citibank, 469
Citigroup, 256, 469
Citigroup Australia/New Zealand, 47
Clairol, 415
Clarica Life Insurance Company, 22
Coca-Cola, 428, 440, 441
Cocoplans, 81
Coles Myer, 44, 493
Compaq Computer, 473
The Container Store, 465, 466
Contract Freighters, 39
Corning Inc., 299
Costco Wholesale, 155
CRDA (Casino Reinvestment Development Authority), 111
Crown Castle, 172
C&S Wholesale Grocers, 258, 259
Culinary Institute of America, 102
CXtec, 109

D

DaimlerChrysler, 288, 492
Dairibord Zimbabwe, 172
Daiwa House Industry Co., 170
Dallas Area Rapid Transit (DART), 88
DART (Dallas Area Rapid Transit), 88
Debenhams, 66
DED (Department of Economic Development; Dubai), 14
Dell Computer, Inc., 14, 54, 368, 473, 478

Deloitte & Touche, 212, 350
Denver International Airport, 236
Department of Corrections, State of Washington, 495
Department of Economic Development (DED; Dubai), 14
DLA Piper Rudnick Gray Cary, 205
Donnelly Mirrors, 175
Dow Jones, 469

E

EA (Electronic Arts), 196, 198, 203
Eastman Kodak Co., 389–390
EDS, 447
EEOC (Equal Employment Opportunity Commission), 202
Eileen Fisher Company, 534
Elbow Room Café, 110
Electronic Arts (EA), 196, 198, 203
Enron Corporation, 48, 50, 376
Environmental Protection Agency, U.S. (EPA), 503
E.ON UK, 303
EPA (Environmental Protection Agency, U.S.), 503
Equal Employment Opportunity Commission (EEOC), 202
Ericsson, 211
eSilicon Corp., 187
Evercare, 23
ExtendMedia, 479
ExxonMobil, 88

F

Fabgroups Technologies Inc., 217
Families and Work Institute, 198
Farm Fresh Supermarkets, 142–143
Fawley Refinery (ExxonMobil UK), 88
FBI (Federal Bureau of Investigation), 489
FDA (Food and Drug Administration), 58–60
Federal Bureau of Investigation (FBI), 489
Federal Signal, 288
Feed the Children, 534
Fifth Third Securities, 256, 259
Financial Planning Association, 408
Finster Honey Farms, 207
First Union Corp., 497
Florida Power & Light (FPL), 37
Food and Drug Administration (FDA), 58–60
Ford Motor Company, 258, 289, 489–490
Forest Service, U.S.,495
4C Corporate Culture Clash and Chemistry, 468
Four Seasons Hotels & Resorts, 112, 271
FPL (Florida Power & Light), 37
Fuji Xerox, 11

G

Gallup Organization, 174
GE Aircraft Engines, 258
GE (General Electric), 92, 147, 258, 486,
    488, 490, 498
Gemstar-TV Guide International Inc., 48
General Electric (GE), 92, 147, 258, 486,
    488, 490, 498
General Motors (GM), 113, 260, 289,
    442, 443, 533
General Union (Gr. Britain), 202
Geotechnical Instruments, 410
Gillette, 415
GM (General Motors), 113, 260, 289,
    442, 443, 533
GM Holden, 113, 114, 260
Golden Inn, 111
Goldman, Sachs & Co., 147, 256, 259,
    260, 372, 474
Golwing Lafleur Henderson, 205
Google, 2, 4, 5, 7, 8, 12, 14, 21, 39, 40,
    314, 368, 372
Gore, W. L. & Associates, 444, 445
Gray Plant Mooty, 11
Green Mountain Coffee Roasters, 503
Green@Work, 534
Greyston Bakery, 534

H

H. J. Heinz Co., 50–51
Harbinger Partners, 437
HBI (Hugo Boss Industries), 173
HBO, 229
Heavy Urban Search and Rescue
    (HUSAR), 91
Heineken, 92
Hellerman Tyton, 303, 304
Helmac, 23
Herman Miller Inc., 474
Hewitt Associates, 239
Hewlett-Packard (HP), 13, 265, 331, 434,
    472, 473
Hibernia Management and Development
    Company, 381
Home Depot, 171, 486, 488, 490, 491,
    492, 495, 497, 498–499, 502, 505
Honeywell, 406
host universal, 447
Hotmail, 229
HP (Hewlett-Packard), 13, 265, 331, 434,
    472, 473
Hugo Boss Industries (HBI), 173
Hunter Douglas, 503
HUSAR (Heavy Urban Search and
    Rescue), 91

I

IBM, 47, 48, 229, 292, 314, 447, 469, 474
IBMP (Institute for Biomedical
    Problems), 392

ICICI Bank, 462
IDEO, 244, 301, 329, 415, 540
Ikea, 66
Imation Corp., 176
Indianapolis Power & Light (IPL), 66
Infosys, 400, 414
Ingersoll-Rand, 172
Institute for Biomedical Problems
    (IBMP), 392
Intel Corporation, 372, 432
Interface, 15
Internal Revenue Service, U.S., 439
International Labor Organization, 201
Invensys PLC, 293
IPL (Indianapolis Power & Light), 66
Ipsos-Reid, 11, 116
Israeli Defense Force, 80

J

JetBlue, 66, 462, 537
John Deere, 473–474
J.P. Morgan Chase, 155

K

Kenexa, 38
Keyspan Corporation, 132, 134
KFC, 132
Korea Telecom (KT), 172–173
Kowloon Shangri-La hotel, 331
KPMG, 321
KRON-TV, 182
KT (Korea Telecom), 172–173

L

The Lawn Mowgul, 171
Legg Mason, 256
Lenovo Group, 47
Liggett-Stashower Inc., 214
Lighthouse Publishing, 275
Linksys, 471
LipoScience Inc., 43, 400
Liverpool City Council (U.K.), 316
Lloyds TSB, 410
Lockheed Martin, 91, 303
Loew's Hotels, 535
Lowe's, 486
Lowe Worldwide, 346, 428, 430
Lucent Technologies, 327, 354

M

McDonald's Corp., 110, 112, 214, 331,
    417, 435, 436, 440, 441, 534
Macquarie Bank, 210
Macy's, 349
Maersk Line, 150
Magna International, 175, 431, 446, 447
Magna Steyr, 176
Manila Diamond Hotel, 381
Manpower Inc., 325
Marks & Spencer, 32
Marriott International, 66

Mayo Clinic, 463, 464, 466
Medrad Inc., 262, 263, 444
Medtronic, 179
Merck, 58–60
Mercury Interactive, 203
Merrill Lynch, 256
Metropolitan Transit Authority (NYC), 349
Metropolitan Transport Bureau (Tokyo),
    235
Meyners & Co., 45
Microchip Technology, 380–381
Microsoft Australia, 400, 408
Microsoft Corporation, 161, 229, 323–324,
    368, 370, 371, 372, 373–374, 375, 495,
    534
Microsoft's MSN Group, 368, 370
Microsoft's Office Group, 370
Minitab Inc., 215
Mittal Steel, 467
MLC, 474
Motorola, 90, 123
MSN Group (Microsoft), 368, 370
MTR Corporation, 92

N

NAB (National Australia Bank), 322, 340,
    342, 345, 352, 360, 474
NASA (National Aeronautics & Space
    Administration), 268, 300, 354, 430
National Aeronautics & Space
    Administration (NASA), 268, 300,
    354, 430
National Australia Bank (NAB), 322, 340,
    342, 345, 352, 360, 474
National Broadcasting Company
    (NBC), 536
National City Bank, 171
National Health System (UK), 348
National Hockey League (NHL), 379
National Hockey League Players
    Association (NHLPA), 379
National Steel, 166
National Transportation Safety Board,
    U.S. (NTSB), 268
National Trust (U.K.), 303
NBC (National Broadcasting Company),
    536
Nestlé, 435, 440
New Belgium Brewery, 533–534
New York Police Department, 70
New Zealand Institute of Chartered
    Accountants, 11
NHL (National Hockey League), 379
NHLPA (National Hockey League
    Players Association), 379
Nissan Motor Company, 495, 496, 497
Nitro, 428, 430, 431, 436, 437, 448
Nokia, 468
Nortel Networks, 13, 468
North Little Rock School Board, 88
Northwestern Mutual, 19

NTSB (National Transportation Safety
  Board, U.S.), 268
Nucor, 166, 168, 171, 172, 174, 262
Nuvation, 109
NYT-TV, 182

O

Oakley, Inc., 465, 466
Office Group (Microsoft), 370
OMD, 243
1-800-GOT-JUNK?, 66
Oracle Corporation, 71, 72
Outback Steakhouse, Inc., 117
Owens Corning, 32
Oxygen Business Solutions, 214
Oxygen network, 182

P

Pacific Gas & Electric (PG&E), 400
Panafric Hotel, 132, 134
Pawtucket, R.I., City of, 169
PCCW, 171
Peco Energy, 495
PepsiCo, 10
Pfizer, 58–60
PG&E (Pacific Gas & Electric), 400
P&G (Procter & Gamble), 294, 415, 416,
  428, 431, 499
Philips Electronics, 439, 440, 441
Phones4U, 317
Pike Place Fish Market, 108, 535
Pitney Bowes, 215
Pixar Animation Studios, 5, 329
Pizza Hut, 132
PMC-Sierra, 331
P&O Nedlloyd, 150
PPC (Pretoria Portland Cement),
  171, 184
Pretoria Portland Cement (PPC), 171, 184
PricewaterhouseCoopers (PwC), 213, 284,
  286, 291, 292, 294, 303, 304, 469
Procter & Gamble (P&G), 294, 415, 416,
  428, 431, 499
Progressive Inc., 479
Project GLOBE, 8
Propaganda Games, 196
PwC. *See* PricewaterhouseCoopers

Q

Quebecor, 109

R

Radical Entertainment, 224, 226, 241,
  243, 244
Radio Shack, 353–354
RAND (think tank), 301
Renault, 496

Research in Motion (RIM), 470–471
ResMed, 417
RIM (Research in Motion), 470–471
Ritz-Carlton Hotels, 111, 132, 134
Royal Bank of Scotland, 32
Royal Dutch/Shell, 265, 266, 504
RSM McGladrey, Inc., 213
Ryanair, 75

S

St. Joseph's Regional Medical Center, 316
The Saltwater Institute, 41
Samsung, 428
SAS Institute, 213, 461–462
Scope International, 109
ScotiaBank (Bank of Nova Scotia), 476,
  478, 479
Scottish Parliament, 235
Sears Roebuck & Co., 172
Segal Co., 213
Semco Corporation, SA, 183, 402
7-Eleven, 449
Shell Europe, 492–493
Smith Barney, 256, 267
SMP (Standard Motor Products), 290
SOCOG (Sydney Organizing Committee
  for the Olympic Games), 22–23
Solectron, 447
Sony, 142
Southern California Gas Co., 10
Southwest Airlines, 466, 536
Speedera Network, 147
Standard Chartered Bank, 109
Standard Motor Products (SMP), 290
Standard & Poor's, 166
Stone Consolidated, 470
Sun Microsystems, 13, 50, 265, 314, 317
Sun Valley Middle School, 498
Sydney Organizing Committee for the
  Olympic Games (SOCOG), 22–23
Syracuse University, 171

T

Taco Bell, 132
Tavistock Institute, 287
Templeton Emerging Markets Fund, 256
Tennessee Valley Authority, 330
Thai Carbon Black, 238
3M, 344–345
Tickles Child Care Center, 150
Timberland Co., 15, 16
Time Warner, 469
Tokai Rubber Industries Ltd., 170
Tom's of Maine, 41, 44
Topeka Wealth Management Group, 256
Toyota Motor Company, 36, 175, 262,
  265, 288

Toyota Motor Manufacturing North
  America, 262
Toyota Motor Sales U.S.A., 382
TRW Automotive, 290, 444
TST, Inc., 362, 364
Tyco, 48, 50
Tyson Foods, 243–244

U

UBS Warburg, 137
United Auto Workers, 289
United Parcel Service (UPS), 77, 172
Universal Insurance Services, Inc., 184
Universum Communications, 11
UPS (United Parcel Service), 77, 172
U.S. Air Force, 389, 390
U.S. Navy, 270
U.S. Trust, 458, 460, 461, 465, 467,
  469, 471

V

Varian Australia, 265
Verizon Communications, 8, 161
Vielife, 213
Virgin Group, 118
Vivendi Universal Games, 224
Vodacom, 243
Vodafone, 5, 14, 51, 66
Volvo, 288

W

W. L. Gore & Associates, 402–403, 444,
  445
Wachovia Corp., 497
Wal-Mart, 5, 15, 174, 465, 486, 502, 534
Walt Disney Company, 196, 284, 304
The Warehouse, 15
Wegmans Food Market, 102, 104, 108,
  110, 118, 432
Westfield Group, 386
Whirlpool, 7, 465
Whole Foods Market, 171–172, 286, 287,
  475, 495
Wipro Technologies, 85
Wisconsin Innocence Project, 70
WorldCom, Inc., 48, 50, 358, 359

X

Xerox, 14, 176, 229

Y

Yahoo!, 460
Yamato Transport Company, 240
Yum Brands Inc., 132, 134

Z

Zebra Technologies, 109

name index

A

Aakkula, J., 595
Aasen, Greg, 331
Abate, T., 229
Abusah, D., 594
Acharya, M., 610
Adams, L., 590
Aditya, R. N., 603, 604
Adkins, C. L., 611
Adler, N., 592
Adler, P. S., 592, 598
Agassi, Andre, 469
Agle, B. R., 564, 566, 577, 609
Agor, W. H., 587
Agovino, T., 60
Ajzen, I., 573
Akter, M., 607
Alam, K., 606
Alam, K. F., 566, 567
Alavi, S. B., 590
Alban, B. T., 612
Alderfer, C. P., 577
Alexander, Ashok, 404
Alexander, S., 593
Alge, B. J., 593
Algera, J. A., 588
Algom, D., 585
Ali (son-in-law of Mohammed), 319
Allen, N. J., 129, 591
Allen, R. W., 600
Allison, W., 319
Aloysius, J. A., 587
Altmann, E. M., 569
Alva, M., 602
Amabile, T. M., 588
Ambady, N., 569, 574
Ambrose, M. L., 578, 579, 580
Amichai-Hamburger, Y., 599
Anakwe, U., 611
Anderson, J., 599–600
Anderson, J. W., 570
Anderson, N., 611
Anderson, Patti, 152, 153
Andon, P., 581
Andrews, B., 590
Andrews, M., 586
Andrews, M. C., 600
Andriopoulos, C., 588
Ang, S., 563
Angle, H. L., 600
Anglim, J., 595
Anhalt, R. L., 571
Ante, S. E., 578
Anthony, S., 610
Anthony, W. P., 571, 596
Antonitis, Mark, 182
Appelbaum, S. H., 563, 576, 606

Argyris, C., 588
Ariely, D., 248
Arkes, H., 587
Armitage, C. J., 573
Armour, S., 585
Armstrong, R. W., 567
Arndt, M., 580, 611
Arnott, D., 567
Aronson, E., 568, 591
Arrow, H., 589, 591
Artzer, Ann, 478
Ashford, S. J., 576, 578–579
Ashforth, B. E., 563, 569, 573, 582, 583, 585, 598, 610, 611
Ashkanasy, N. M., 572, 574, 586, 609
Ashworth, C. L., 578
Athos, A. G., 589
Atuahene-Gima, K., 599, 600
Atwater, L. E., 572, 578
Au, K., 576
Auh, S., 575
Avolio, B. J., 426, 568, 605
Axtell, C. M., 571
Axtell, R. E., 596
Aycan, Z., 567
Ayers, Charlie, 8
Ayers, Joe, 293
Ayton, P., 587

B

Baba, V. V., 585, 604
Babcock, P., 570, 580, 613
Bacharach, S. B., 565–566
Backover, A., 359
Bacon, Marc, 217
Bacon, N., 570
Bader, P., 603
Bael, F., 610
Bagozzi, R. P., 573, 577
Bagshaw, Wesley, 91
Bailey, D. E., 563, 589, 594, 601
Baldwin, C., 608
Ballard, Geoffrey, 242
Ballard, Toni, 323
Ballmer, Steve, 151
Balsillie, Jim, 471
Baltazar, R., 595
Baltzly, D., 586
Bamberger, P., 565–566
Bandura, A., 572
Banwell, C., 595
Barbuto, J., E., Jr., 605
Bardi, A., 566
Barger, Mike, 462
Bargh, J. A., 569, 570, 572, 573, 586
Barham, L., 584
Barker, B. A., 595
Barker, R. T., 595

Barki, H., 595
Barley, S. R., 562
Barling, J., 580, 583, 585, 606, 613
Barnard, C., 598
Barnash, Jim, 408
Barnes, V. A., 585
Barnett, W. P., 591
Barney, J. B., 610
Barnlund, D. C., 597
Baron, R. A., 600
Baroni, Mark, 32
Barr, Margo, 289
Barrett, F. J., 503, 613
Barrett, L. Feldman, 578, 584
Barrick, M. R., 568, 590
Barry, D., 601
Barsade, S. G., 587, 596
Bartol, K. M., 580, 598
Bartunek, J. M., 578
Basch, R., 562, 563
Bass, B. M., 426, 586, 605
Bass, Carl, 417
Bastianutti, L. M., 594
Basuroy, S., 577
Bateman, T. S., 544, 574
Bates, Tony, 210–211
Baum, J. R., 605
Bauman, J., 583
Baumeister, R. E., 577
Baxter, J., 581
Bazerman, M. H., 602
Beach, L. R., 586
Beal, D. J., 591
Bearley, W. L., 590–591
Beasley, M., 584
Beatty, C. A., 595
Beatty, S., 589
Beazley, H., 565
Bebear, Claude, 75
Bechara, A., 586
Becker, B., 584
Beckerle, C. A., 597
Beckhard, R., 595
Beddows, Justin, 317
Bedeian, A. G., 164, 579, 600, 607
Beech, N., 614
Beehr, T. A., 567
Beer, M., 581, 595, 613
Beersma, B., 378, 399
Begley, T. M., 563, 564
Behling, O., 587
Belbin, R. Meredith, 272, 273, 591
Bell, B. S., 593
Bell, D. W., 573
Bell, S. J., 575
Belluzzo, Richard E., 473
Ben-Ari, E., 602
Benbow, C. P., 566

Bendersky, C., 601
Bendick, M., 570
Benesh, P., 605–606
Bengtsson, U., 613
Bennett, N., 592
Bennett, Steve, 493
Bennis, W. G., 563, 605
Bercier, Julie, 403
Berdahl, J. L., 589
Beresford, Dennis R., 359
Beresford, Peter, 331
Berggren, C., 592
Bergman, T. J., 601
Bergquist, Jim, 535
Berlew, D. E., 605
Bernard, M. M., 566
Bernard, U., 593
Berridge, K. C., 574, 576, 577, 586, 596
Bettencourt, B. A., 591
Bettis, R., 608
Betz, E. L., 577
Bexton, W. H., 577
Beyer, J. M., 611
Bhagwati, J., 562
Bice, D., 570
Bijttebier, P., 586
Billig, M., 570
Bilovsky, F., 572
Bingham, L. B., 579
Birkenshaw, J., 608
Birritteri, A., 563
Bita, N., 565
Bixler, M., 603
Black, D., 583–584
Black, J., 596
Black, L., 605
Blagg, H., 596
Blair Loy, M., 585
Blake, R. R., 398
Blanchard, Ken II., 412, 604
Blank, W., 604
Blau, G., 579
Blazejewski, S., 600
Blickle, G., 600
Bliese, P. D., 577
Blotnicky, K., 567
Bluedorn, A. C., 576
Blyton, P., 570
Bobko, P., 576
Bobocel, D. R., 573
Bock, P., 603
Bodenhausen, G. V., 569–570
Boehnke, K., 566
Boenisch, J., 565
Boies, K., 588
Boisnier, Alicia, 94, 609
Bolino, M. C., 599
Bonanno, G. A., 584
Bond, M. H., 567
Bonfatti, J. F., 572
Bono, J. E., 578

Booker, E., 597
Bopp, M. I., 582
Bordia, P., 594
Borrill, C. S., 589
Boss, J., 567
Boss, R. W., 600
Bossidy, Lawrence A., 406, 604
Boswell, W. R., 563, 579
Botsman, P., 612
Bouckenooghe, D., 567
Boudreau, J., 592
Boulding, W., 587
Bourgeois, L. J., III, 567, 594, 601, 602
Bowen, D., 574, 591
Bowermaster, D., 579
Boyatzis, R. E., 113, 571, 572, 574, 596, 603
Boyd, D. P., 564
Boyle, M., 572
Bozon, I. J., 612
Brabeck, Peter, 435, 607
Bradbury, H., 613
Bradfield, R., 587
Bradford, S., 9
Brady, D., 611
Brady, S., 565
Bragger, J. D., 587
Brajer, Richard, 43, 400, 402
Brandel, M., 596
Brandtstadter, J., 586
Brannick, T., 613
Branson, Richard, 118
Brass, D. J., 568, 598
Bravo, Rose Marie, 259
Breaugh, J. A., 611
Brechu, M. B., 593, 606
Brender, Y., 577
Brett, J. F., 578
Brett, J. M., 595, 601, 602, 603
Brewer, N., 602
Brickson, S., 570, 602
Bridwell, L. G., 577
Brief, A. P., 562, 573, 599
Briggs, Katherine, 54
Briggs-Myers, Isabel, 54
Bright, D. S., 613
Brin, Sergey, 49
Brock, D. M., 601
Brockbank, A., 614
Brockmann, E. N., 571
Brockner, J., 587
Brodbeck, F. C., 606
Brodt, S. E., 571, 602
Brodzinski, C., 581
Bromley, Dave, 37
Brooker, K., 415
Brooks, F. P., 592
Brotheridge, C. M., 573, 574, 584
Broucek, W. G., 591
Brougham, Devin, 51
Brouillard, S., 607

Brown, A., 445, 564
Brown, B. R., 602
Brown, K., 565, 609
Brown, K. S., 589
Brown, R. P., 571
Brown, S. P., 578
Brown, T., 578
Brown, V. R., 594
Brownstein, A. L., 587
Brtek, M. D., 581
Bruno, M., 587
Bryant, B., 592
Bryman, A., 606
Buchanan, D., 612
Buchanan, J., 563
Buck, R., 599
Buckingham, M., 581
Buckley, M. R., 585
Buckley, N., 415
Budner, S., 512
Buffett, Warren, 6
Bunker, B. B., 612
Burke, C., 604
Burke, L. A., 568
Burke, R. J., 562, 576, 584–585, 598–599
Burkhardt, M. E., 598
Burkle, Martha, 527
Burnett, D. D., 568–569
Burnham, D. H., 577
Burns, B. D., 569
Burns, J. M., 605
Burns, T., 607, 608
Burrows, P., 473
Burton, Pierre, 154
Bush, Le Etta, 289
Bushe, G. R., 613
Butler, A. B., 578
Buttner, E. H., 600
Butz, D. A., 570
Butz, H. R., 612
Bycio, P., 575, 585
Byham, W. C., 572
Byrne, J. A., 175
Byrnes, N., 580
Byron, E., 569

C

Cabana, S., 612
Cabanac, M., 573
Cable, D. M., 576
Cacioppo, J. T., 596, 599
Cai, D. A., 602
Calabrese, G., 608
Caldwell, C. B., 564, 566, 577, 609
Caldwell, D. E., 591
Caldwell, D. F., 611
Caldwell, R., 612–613
Caldwell, S., 612
Callanan, Gerard A., 394, 397, 601
Callery, P., 544

Callister, R. R., 574, 600, 601
Camarata, M. R., 595
Cameron, A. F., 596
Cameron, K., 571, 613
Campbell, A., 608
Campbell, I., 563
Campbell, J. P., 566, 577
Campbell-Sills, L., 584
Campion, M. A., 575, 581, 590, 607
Cannon, Fiona, 410
Cannon, L., 605
Cannon, M. D., 581
Capell, K., 569
Capraro, M. M., 568
Capraro, R. M., 568
Card, Sharon, 364
Carey, B., 566, 574
Carli, L. L., 600, 606
Carlson, J. R., 596
Carlton, J., 562
Carmeli, A., 610
Carnegie, Andrew, 506
Carroll, S. A., 574
Carron, A. V., 591
Carson, K. D., 598
Carson, K. P., 592
Carson, P. P., 598
Caruso, D. R., 574, 597
Casey, Russell, 160, 217
Castellucci, J., 580
Castleberry, S. B., 597
Catan, T., 359
Catano, V. M., 574
Catell, Bob, 132
Catellier, Brigitte, 51–52
Cathy, Dan, 417
Catlin, Linda, 464
Caudwell, John, 316–317
Caulkin, S., 603
Certain, Katherine, 121
Cha, S. E., 610, 611
Chaiken, S., 573
Chajut, E., 585
Challagalla, G., 578
Champagne, M. V., 602
Champoux, J. E., 581
Chan, J. W. K., 591
Chan, L. Y., 591, 608
Chandler, A. D., 609
Chandler, T. D., 592
Chao, J., 567
Chapman, P., 596
Chappell, Kate, 41
Chappell, L., 590
Chappell, Tom, 41
Charan, R., 604, 611
Chartrand, T. L., 570, 586
Chatman, J. A., 609, 610, 611
Chatterjee, P., 607
Chatterjee, S. R., 566
Chebat, J.-C., 582

Chelius, J., 580
Chemers, M. M., 604
Chen, Lincoln, 404
Chen, Wei Wei, 428
Chen, Y., 578
Chen, Z. X., 575–576
Chermack, T. J., 569
Cherniss, C., 574
Chesbrough, H., 608
Chesley, N., 584
Cheyne, J. A., 582
Chia, S.-A., 11, 563
Chiat, Jay, 348
Chilcote, R., 319
Child, P. N., 612
Childs, J., 592
Cho, Jeewon, 94
Choi, I., 570
Choi, J. N., 589, 594
Chong, Ivy, 91
Chong, L. M. A., 606
Chooi, Mandy, 90, 572
Chordes, L., 586
Christensen, C., 610
Christensen, C. M., 564
Christenson, D., 605
Christie, P. M. J., 608
Christie, R., 600
Chrominska, Sylvia, 476
Churchill, J., 575
Churchill, Winston, 465, 610
Cialdini, R. B., 599
Cicchetti, D., 584
Citrin, J., 597
Clampitt, P., 607
Clark, Alison, 150
Clark, K., 608
Clark, S. C., 574
Clarke, Chris, 428
Claydon, T., 612
Clegg, C. W., 582
Clegg, S. R., 562, 598
Clifton, D. C., 581
Cline, D., 565
Cobb, A. T., 599
Cobbin, D. M., 567
Coblin, Jim, 166
Coch, L., 591
Cochran, Karin, 212
Coghlan, D., 613
Cohan, S. L., 584
Cohen, A., 600
Cohen, D. S., 612
Cohen, George, 417
Cohen, Jennifer, 479
Cohen, Jo-Ann, 74
Cohen, S. G., 589, 592
Cohen, W., 565
Cohen-Charash, Y., 579
Colbert, A. E., 578, 603
Cole, D., 602

Cole, N. D., 580
Cole, R. E., 592
Coleman, D. F., 573
Collingwood, H., 594
Collins, C. J., 577
Collins, J. C., 564, 566
Colquitt, J. A., 579
Comer, L. B., 597
Cone, E., 595
Confucius, 4
Conger, J. A., 562, 572, 598, 599,
    603, 604, 605
Conlin, M., 563, 593
Connellan, T. K., 86, 571
Connelly, C. E., 563
Connelly, M., 289, 581
Conner, M., 573
Connon, H., 175
Connor, C. E., 569
Connor, K. M., 221, 584
Connors, E., 610
Cook, Mimi, 348
Coombs, T., 571
Coon, H. M., 46, 567
Cooper, C. L., 562, 579, 584, 603
Cooper, H., 568
Cooper, J., 573
Cooper, W. H., 571, 575, 594
Cooperrider, D. L., 503, 613
Copper, C., 582, 591
Corbin, J., 544
Cordery, J. L., 581, 582
Corelli, R., 573
Corinthios, Antoine, 112
Corning, P. A., 577
Costa, A. C., 593
Costello, T. W., 571
Coughlin, K., 562, 563
Covey, Stephen, 387
Cowiea, H., 583
Cox, D., 601
Craig, S., 609
Cramer, K. L., 98
Crant, J. M., 570
Craver, R., 611
Crawford, M., 597, 600
Creelman, D., 576
Cremer, J., 604
Crispin, S. W., 588
Cronshaw, S. E., 568
Cronshaw, S. F., 606
Cropanzano, R., 573, 574, 579, 600, 603
Cross, R., 592, 608
Crowl, David, 112
Croyle, M. H., 574
Crozier, M., 598
Crundwell, N., 602
Cummings, A., 585, 588
Cummings, L. L., 575, 583, 585,
    586, 588, 612
Cummings, T. G., 612

Cummins, Barbara Jean, 284
Cunningham, C. R., 585
Cusick, John, 445
Cyr, L. A., 567, 576
Czurak, D., 582

D

Daft, R. L., 320, 596
Dagostino, M., 569
Dahl, R. A., 598
Dahle, Scott, 289
Dahlstrom, R., 583
Dallnera, M., 590, 593, 608
Daly, J., 566
Daly, J. P., 610
Damasio, A. R., 569, 573, 577, 586
Dane, E., 587
Daniels, C., 611
Danna, K., 583
D'Annunzio, L. S., 608
Darbee, Peter, 400, 402
Darce, K., 594
Darden, C., 570
Darlin, D., 612
Darrow, B., 609
Das, E. H. H. J., 599
Das, H., 580
Das, T. K., 586, 594
Dastmalchian, A., 606
Daus, C. S., 574
Davenport, T. H., 608
Davey, K. M., 564
Davidow, W. H., 608
Davidson, Diane, 445
Davidson, J., 584
Davidson, J. E., 588
Davidson, J. R. T., 221, 584
Davidson, N., 583
Davidson, Rick, 325
Davis, G. M.-T., 580
Davis, Jeff, 498
Davis, K., 597
Davis, W. L., 597
Dawes, P. L., 598
Dawley, D. D., 596
Dawson, C., 496
Day, A. L., 574
Day, D. V., 568, 572
Deal, T. E., 610
Deaner, C. M. D., 614
Debecq, A. L., 586
de Castro, S., 563
DeConinck, J. B., 572
DeCotiis, T., 575
De Dreu, C. K. W., 378, 399, 563,
    590, 591, 594, 601, 602
Deelstra, J. T., 586
De Frank, R. S., 583
De Geus, A., 564
DeGross, R., 611
de Jong, A., 592

Delaney, K. J., 49
Delaney, S., 598
Delany, Hannah, 410
Delbecq, A. L., 595
Del Bello, A., 564
Delbridge, R., 597
Delio, M., 595, 597
Dell, Michael, 54
DeMatteo, J. S., 581, 589
De Meuse, K. P., 595
DeNeve, K. M., 568
Den Hartog, D. N., 426, 606
DeNisi, A. S., 578, 579
Denison, D., 609
Denison, D. R., 610
Dennis, A. R., 594
Dennis, Ron, 142–143
Dent, E. B., 612
DePeters, Jack, 102
De Pree, Max, 474, 611
de Ruyter, K., 592, 597
Deruyter, R., 109
Deschamps, J.-C., 567
Detillion, C. E., 589
Deutschman, A., 445
Devadas, R., 592
De Villiers, W. S., 574
DeVries, A. C., 589
De Vries, R. E., 605
de Wit, J. B. F., 599
Dholakia, U. M., 577
Diamond, M. L., 445
DiBella, A. J., 564
Dickens, L., 613
Dickson, M. W., 577
Diefendorff, J. M., 574
Diehl, M., 594
Diener, E., 105, 573
Digh, P., 62
Digman, J. M., 568
Dillard, J., 599
D'Innocenzio, A., 610
Dion, K. L., 591
Dionne, S. D., 590, 605
Dirks, K. T., 588, 594, 612
DiTomasco, N., 610
Dixon, J., 570, 602
Doak, A., 589
Doane, D., 562
Dobbins, G. H., 590
Dobbs, S. M., 612
Dobson, P., 609
Docherty, P., 592
Doctoroff, S., 602
Dodd, N. G., 581
Doehrman, M., 609
Doerr, K. H., 578
Dojo, D. V., 582
Dokey, Suzanne, 303
Dolan, R. J., 573
Domann, Steve, 290

Donahue, L. M., 591
Donaldson, L., 608
Donnellon, A., 593
Donnelly, P., 609
Donovan, Dennis, 486, 495
Doolen, T. L., 589
Doosie, B., 591
Dorfman, P., 562, 603, 606, 610
Dormann, C., 573
Dorow, W., 600
Dose, J. J., 591
Douglas, C., 593, 608
Dowling, G. R., 598
Dowling, W. F., 581
Downey, K., 603
Downs, C., 607
Doyle, M., 612
Doz, Y. L., 593
Drach-Zahavy, A., 599
Drago, R., 583–584
Dragoon, A., 578
Draper, Bruce, 410
Drexler, A. B., 589
Drickhamer, D., 607
Driscoll, J. E., 582
Drollinger, T., 597
Drost, E. A., 562
Drucker, Peter F., 276, 564, 586, 598
Druskat, V. U., 592
Duan, C., 571
Duarte, D. L., 593
Ducheneaut, N., 595
Dudley, B., 600
Duffy, Luke, 340, 342, 345, 352, 358
Dugosh, K. Leggett, 594
Duguid, P., 571
Dukerich, J. M., 562, 569
Duncan, R. M., 582
Dunckel, H., 592
Dunlop, P. D., 566
Dunn, J. R., 593
Dunphy, D., 592
Durham, C. C., 573
Durrheim, K., 570, 602
Dutton, J. E., 569, 571, 582, 613
Dutton, J. M., 601
Duxbury, L., 562, 563, 584
Dvorak, P., 577
Dwyer, D., 585
Dwyer, D. J., 612
Dye, K., 577
Dyer, B., 602
Dyer, W. G., 595

E

Eagly, A. H., 573, 606–607
Earley, C. P., 567
Earley, P. C., 590, 601
Eastman, K. K., 606
Ebbers, Bernie, 359
Eby, L. T., 581, 584, 589, 590

Eccles, J., 571
Eckel, N. L., 587
Eckelbecker, L., 596
Eden, D., 571
Edgar, R., 589
Edison, Thomas, 241
Edmondson, A., 590
Edmunds, A., 596
Edwards, J. R., 581
Egan, M. L., 570
Egan, T. M., 613
Egeth, H. E., 569
Eggen, D., 612
Eggins, R. A., 569
Egri, C. P., 606
Einstein, Albert, 227, 505
Eisenhardt, K. M., 567, 594, 601, 602
Eisenstat, R. A., 613
Eisler, R., 586, 589
Ekman, P., 573, 596
Elangovan, A. R., 603
Elfenbein, H. A., 574
Elias, S. M., 574
Ellemers, N., 591
Elliott, J., 109
Elliott, S., 598, 607
Ellis, A. P. J., 599
Ellis, R. J., 568
Ellison, John, 111
Ellison, S., 415
Elloy, D. F., 605
Elron, E., 602
Ely, R. J., 563
Emans, J. M., 590
Emerson, R. M., 598
Emery, C. R., 592
Enge, R. S., 591
Engelbrecht, A. S., 574
Ensari, N., 606
Ensel, W. M., 585
Ensign, P. C., 608
Epitropaki, O., 606
Erez, A., 566
Erez, M., 592
Erickson, B., 566
Erickson, R. J., 584
Erickson, Tom, 445
Erikson, Bill, 38
Erwin, Jeff B., 368
Esser, J. K., 594
Esses, V. M., 573
Estabrooks, P. A., 591
Evans, C. R., 591
Evans, G., 597
Evans, G. W., 584
Evans, M. G., 604
Evers, A., 378, 399
Ewasyshyn, Frank, 180
Exline, J. J., 591
Ezzamel, M., 579

F

Fabish, L., 568
Fabrigar, L. R., 573
Fackler, M., 587, 610
Fairhurst, G. T., 605
Falbe, C. M., 598, 600
Falkenberg, L., 565, 569
Fallows, D., 597
Fan, M., 609
Fan, Y., 600
Fandt, P. M., 600
Fanning, M. M., 608
Farley, S. D., 573
Farmer, S. M., 600
Farrell, B., 567
Farrell, H. M., 567
Farrell, Peter, 417
Farson, R., 572
Fayol, Henri, 433, 607
Fazio, R. H., 569, 573
Feder, B. J., 60
Fedor, D. B., 612
Feeley, T. H., 571
Fehr, E., 591
Feist, G. J., 588
Feldman, D. C., 574, 575, 591
Feldman, J. M., 570
Fells, R. E., 602
Fenton-O'Creevy, M., 588, 593, 608
Ferguson, M. J., 569, 572, 573
Fernandes, Tony, 345
Fernandez, J. A., 562
Ferrin, D. L., 594
Ferris, G. R., 599, 600
Festinger, L., 573
Fetters, M. D., 596–597
Fey, C. F., 610
Fiedler, F. E., 412–413, 604
Field, R. H. G., 571, 586
Fieldman, G., 583
Fienco, Fausto, 349
Figart, D. M., 580
Filipczak, B., 563, 576, 601
Findley, Keith, 70
Finegan, J. E., 576, 582
Fink, E. L., 602
Finkelstein, S., 594, 598
Finlay, K. A., 571
Finley, M., 591
Fiorina, Carly, 472, 473
Fischbacher, U., 591
Fischer, Robert, 256
Fischer, S., 562
Fisher, C. D., 573
Fisher, G., 591
Fisher, R. J., 591, 601
Fisher, S. G., 591
Fishman, C., 592, 611
Fiske, S. T., 569, 570
Fizel, J., 579

Fleishman, E. A., 604
Fletcher, John, 44, 493
Florea, N. B., 602
Florian, E., 609
Flynn, Kristen, 214
Foege, William, 404
Foley, Stephen R., 270
Folger, R., 579
Ford, R. C., 608
Ford, William Clay, 490
Forgas, J. P., 587
Forman, E., 574
Forrester, R., 582, 589
Forsyth, D. R., 606
Foster, P., 564
Fox, C., 574
Fox, M., 585
Fox, S., 579, 599
Fragale, A. R., 596
Francesco, A. M., 575–576
Francis, D., 611
Frank, R., 609
Frankel, S., 595
Frankston, J., 349
Frauenheim, E., 583
Frayne, C. A., 572
Fredendall, L. D., 592
Fredrickson, B. L., 584
French, J., Jr., 591
French, John R. P., 343–344, 598
Frey, B. H., 567
Frey, D., 601
Frey, W., 569
Fricke, Dirk, 77
Fried, L., 608
Fried, Y., 581
Friedman, A. L., 570
Friedman, D., 594
Friedman, Milton, 15
Frink, D. D., 563
Frith, C., 569
Frost, Harriet, 243
Frost, Robert, 290
Fu, H.-Y., 601
Fu, P. P., 600
Fugate, M., 563
Fujii, Akira, 170
Fujio, M., 597
Fujioka, C., 576
Fulmer, L. S., 562
Fulmer, R. M., 572
Funder, D. C., 613
Fure, J., 607
Furlonger, D., 582
Furnham, A., 568, 580, 609
Fursman, Mark, 102
Futrell, D., 595

G

Gable, S. L., 577, 613
Gachuru, David, 132

Gaines, S. O., 570
Galbraith, J. R., 431, 607, 608
Galbraith, John Kenneth, 489
Galimba, M., 582
Galinsky, A. D., 573
Galinsky, E., 583
Gallagher, D. G., 563
Gallagher, P., 587
Galloway, W. B., 613
Gallupe, R. B., 594
Galt, V., 611
Gamer, Bill, 102
Gammage, K. L., 591
Gander, Mary J., 336, 508, 509
Ganesan, S., 266, 578
Ganster, D. C., 573, 581, 585
Ganzach, Y., 587, 611
Garda, G., 590, 593, 608
Gardner, D., 603
Gardner, W. L., 593, 608
Garlick, Rick, 182–183
Garud, R., 565
Garvin, D. A., 564
Gates, Bill, 229, 323–324
Gayle, Helene, 404, 405, 406
Geis, F., 600
Geister, S., 564, 589–590, 593, 595, 609
Gellatly, I. R., 575
Geller, E. S., 582–583
Gemmell, J. M., 603
Gentilin, Dennis, 340
Gentner, D., 569
George, J., 603
George, J. M., 575, 587, 592
Gephart, M. A., 613
Gephart, R. P., Jr., 564
Gerhardt, M. W., 568, 603
Gerhart, B., 562, 580, 581
Geringer, J. M., 572
Gersick, J. G., 590
Gerstner, Louis, 474
Gerwin, D., 609
Gfrörer, R., 593
Gherardi, S., 572
Ghosh, D., 587
Ghosn, Carlos, 495, 496
Gibbs, P., 572
Gibson, C. B., 562, 567
Giebels, E., 601
Gilbert, D. T., 570
Gilbert, J. P., 607
Gilbert, Judy, 49
Gilder, G., 593
Gill, D., 586
Gill, H., 594
Gillespie, T. L., 602
Gillmor, D., 473
Gilmor, S., 599
Gilson, L. L., 563–564, 593
Gioja, L., 564, 613
Giovanelli, L., 74, 570

Giron, Michelle, 74
Gittell, J. H., 607
Glade, G. A., 575
Gladwell, M., 568, 569, 573
Glasper, E. R., 589
Glomb, T. M., 573–574
Glover, H. D., 595
Glunk, U., 610
Gluyas, R., 597
Glynn, S. J., 582
Gnazzo, P. J., 568
Godar, S. H., 593
Godard, J., 582, 589
Goddard, P., 582
Godfrey, E. G., 577
Godwin, J., 583
Goffney, P., 562
Goforth, C., 611
Goh, Swee C., 452, 454, 565
Goldberg, S. G., 612
Goldenberg, T., 583
Goldman, Jason, 312
Goldsmith, M., 572
Goldstein, Kurt, 577
Goldstein, N. J., 599
Goleman, D., 113, 571, 574, 596, 603
Gomersall, John, 184
Gomez-Mejia, L. R., 580
Gooden, Nate, 289
Goodenow, Bob, 379
Goodman, P. S., 592
Goodnough, A., 60
Goodstein, L. D., 612
Goodwin, G. F., 590
Goodwin, P., 587
Goodwin, V. L., 605
Goold, M., 608
Gordon, G. G., 610
Gordon, J., 592
Gordon, L. A., 596
Gosserand, R. H., 574
Gottfredson, G. D., 568, 569
Gottier, R. F., 568
Gottlieb, B. H., 584
Gough, H. G., 253
Gould, Claire, 266
Gould, J. M., 564
Gouldner, A. W., 600
Gover, P., 589
Grace, S. L., 98
Graeff, C. L., 604
Graham, A., 592, 595
Graham, C. R., 591
Granath, J. Å., 592
Grandey, A. A., 573, 574
Granka, L., 595
Grausnick, Scott, 437
Gray, J., 597
Gray, M., 393
Gray, R., 595
Grayson, C. J., 565

Green, E. G. T., 567
Green, S. G., 604
Green, W., 571
Greenberg, J., 579
Greenblatt, E. D. Y., 563
Greenburg, L., 585
Greene, J., 600
Greengard, S., 568, 597, 610
Greenhaus, J. H., 56, 611
Greenhouse, S., 579
Greenwald, J., 607
Greenwood, M., 596
Greenwood, R., 607
Gresham, M. T., 580
Grewal, R., 565
Griesing, D., 610
Griffin, M., 596
Griffin, M. A., 566, 605
Griffin, R. W., 581, 583
Griffiths, K., 596
Gross, J. J., 574
Gross, R. L., 571
Grossi, David, 70
Grossman, L., 612
Grove, Andrew, 372, 601
Grow, B., 611
Gruber, J., 592
Grunfeld, E., 583
Guenzi, P., 575
Guest, R. H., 581
Guillén, M. F., 562
Guion, R. M., 568
Gully, S. M., 590
Gunter, B., 609
Gunterman, Haluna, 74
Gupta, Ajit, 147, 578
Gushin, Vadim, 392–393
Gustafson, D. H., 595
Guyon, J., 562
Guzzo, R. A., 589
Gyulai, L., 603

H

Hackett, R. D., 566, 575, 585
Hacki, R., 608
Hackman, Gene, 344
Hackman, J. R., 178, 192, 581, 582,
    589, 590, 598, 611
Hadley, L., 579
Hagel, J., III, 608
Hagey, R., 579
Haidt, J., 577, 613
Hajjar, I., 585
Haka, S., 596
Halbesleben, J. R. B., 585
Hall, D. J., 569
Hall, D. T., 576–577
Hall, E., 607
Hall, J., 571
Hall, R. J., 603–604, 606
Hall, W. A., 544

Hallowell, R., 574, 591
Hamilton, T., 610
Hammer, W. C., 581
Hampden-Turner, C., 574
Hanges, P. J., 577
Hanks, Tom, 229
Hanna, R., 586
Hannah, D. R., 611
Hanson, J. R., 597, 598
Haratani, T., 583
Harden, D., 565
Harding, Jack, 187
Hardy, C., 598, 600
Hare, A. P., 591
Hargadon, Andrew, 544, 593, 598
Hargrave-Silk, A., 607
Harpaz, I., 584
Harquail, C. V., 569
Harrington, C., 609
Harrington, S. D., 349
Harris, J. G., 608
Harris, P., 596, 601
Harris, S. G., 610
Harrison, D. A., 563, 566, 590
Harrison, William B., Jr., 155
Hart, C. M., 589
Hartel, C. E. J., 572, 586
Hartman, S., 607
Hartnett, Rich, 12
Harvey, Cheryl, 455
Hashimoto, K., 599
Haslam, S. A., 563, 569, 570
Hassan, Arif, 520
Hastedt, C., 569
Hasty, Leander, 196
Hatfield, E., 596
Hausdorf, P. A., 575
Hautaluoma, J. E., 591
Havlovic, S. J., 584
Hawthorne, Cory, 224
Hayashi, A. M., 587
Hayford, S. L., 603
Hayward, M. L. A., 566, 606
Head, T. C., 613
Healey, D., 11
Heath, C., 564
Hebert, E. P., 583
Hechler, D., 589, 603
Hecht, T. D., 591
Heffner, T. S., 576
Heilbrun, A. B., Jr., 253
Helfand, D., 612
Hellgren, J., 584
Helms-Mills, J. C., 610
Hemsley, S., 588
Hendrix, Diana, 389
Hendry, C., 576
Heneman, R. L., 580
Hennigar, Lynn, 275
Henning, R. A., 582
Henry, R., 569

Herman, S., 606
Hermida, A., 562
Hernandez, J. L., 584
Herold, D. M., 612
Heron, J., 613
Heron, W., 577
Hersey, Paul, 412, 604
Hertel, G., 564, 589–590, 593, 595, 609
Hertting, A., 582
Hertzfeld, Andy, 229, 354
Herzberg, Frederick, 178, 581
Heskett, J. L., 575, 610
Heslin, P. A., 578
Hetzel, Bill, 44
Hewes, C., 586
Hewett, J., 611
Hewlett, William, 473
Hewstone, M., 570
Heywood, Mark, 331
Hiam, A., 588
Hibbard, J. D., 575
Hickman, J. S., 582–583
Hickson, D. J., 598
Hidalgo, Brenda, 102
Hielman, M. E., 607
Higgins, C., 562, 563, 584
Higgins, C. A., 599
Higgins, M. C., 598
Hill, C. E., 571
Hill, S., Jr., 415
Hilpern, K., 596
Hilton, T. F., 600
Hiltzik, M., 599
Hilzenrath, D. S., 359
Hinds, P., 594, 601
Hinings, C. R., 598, 607, 609
Hinkin, T. R., 572, 599
Hinklin, T., 366
Hirschman, C., 603
Hitlin, S., 564, 566, 577, 609
Hitt, M., 608
Ho, Christine, 529
Ho, Lisa, 189
Hochwarter, W. A., 578, 599, 600
Hock, M., 586
Hodson, R., 593
Hoe, S. L., 605
Hof, R. D., 597
Hoffman, Erin, 196
Hofstede, G., 567
Hogan, D. E., 570
Hogg, M. A., 569, 589, 593, 599
Holahan, P. J., 587
Holden, L., 598
Holeck, A., 175, 610
Holland, John L., 55, 56, 505, 568
Holland, R. W., 566, 577
Holliday, K. K., 567
Hollman, L., 578
Holmes, Josh, 196
Holmes, S., 579

Holt, S., 579
Holtom, B. C., 566, 575
Homan, A. C., 563, 590, 591
Homburg, C., 608
Hook, C. S., 612
Hook, J., 585
Hooper, N., 562, 569
Hoque, M., 607
Horvitz, T., 591
Horwitt, E., 602
Hoshower, L., 578
Hotchkiss, Harley, 379
Hough, L. M., 568
Houghton, J., 583
Houghton, J. D., 604
House, J. S., 586
House, Robert J., 398, 562, 600, 603, 604, 605, 606, 610
Howard, A., 586
Howard, Gary L., 123
Howard, J. L., 585
Howell, D., 611
Howell, J. M., 568, 588
Howley, Ray, 36
Hoyer, M., 568
Hsieh, S., 11
Hsieh, Y.-M., 607
Huang, Y.-M., 575
Huber, G., 564
Huber, V. L., 572
Huddleston, S., 583
Huettel, S., 609
Hughes, Christopher, 319
Hughson, T. L. G., 592
Hui, C. H., 569
Humbert, Gustav, 45
Humphrey, R. H., 573
Hung, J. G., 604
Hunnicutt, B. K., 583
Hunt, S. D., 567
Hunter, J. E., 577
Hunter, T. A., 591
Hussein, Saddam, 48, 319
Hussey, T., 583
Huston, G., 586
Huszczo, G. E., 595
Huxham, C., 613
Huy, Q. N., 607
Hymowitz, C., 49, 563, 606
Hyodo, Kazuo, 36
Hyten, C., 592

I

Iaffaldano, M. T., 575
Igbaria, M., 563
Ignatius, A., 562
Ilies, R., 565, 568, 603, 604
Illa, H., 606
Illegems, V., 563
Indvik, J., 604
Ingram, Harry, 83

Inkson, K., 596
Intagliata, J., 603
Irmer, B. E., 594
Irving, M., 588
Irving, P. G., 568, 573, 603
Isenberg, D., 594
Issac, R. G., 603, 604
Ivancevich, J. M., 583
Ive, Jonathan, 255
Ivry, B., 349

J

Jablin, F. M., 595
Jackson, J. W., 569
Jackson, K. M., 596
Jackson, M., 585
Jackson, S. E., 590
Jacob, N., 567
Jacobs, R., 565, 604
Jacobson, D., 580
Jago, A. G., 247, 588, 594
Jako, R. A., 571
Jamal, M., 585
James, G., 229
Jamieson, D., 589
Janis, I. L., 586, 594
Janoff, S., 612
Janssens, M., 576
Janz, T., 577
Jarvenpaa, S. L., 594
Jaucius, J., 599
Javidan, M., 562, 603, 606, 610
Jawahar, I. M., 579–580
Jehn, K. A., 585, 591, 601
Jelin, K., 601
Jenkins, M., 563
Jenkins, R., 576
Jensen, M. A. C., 590
Jensen, O., 608
Jesuino, J. C., 606
Jett, H., 605
Jetten, J., 569, 601
Jex, S. M., 581, 584
Jiang, J. J., 599
Jin, L., 593
Jobs, Steven, 5, 354, 493
Jochims, M., 601
Johannesen-Schmidt, M. C., 606–607
Johannessen, J.-A., 565
Johanson, J.-E., 607
Johns, G., 566
Johnson, C., 594
Johnson, D., 251, 597
Johnson, D. E., 566
Johnson, D. W., 601
Johnson, F., 251
Johnson, J. L., 565
Johnson, M. J., 585
Johnson, Ron, 382
Johnson, Suzanne Nora, 256
Johnson, W. L., 568

Johnson-Laird, P. N., 569
Johnston, E., 597
Joiner, T. A., 567
Jones, D., 604
Jones, D. A., 579
Jones, D. T., 592
Jones, J. E., 590–591
Jones, M. O., 609
Jones, Obie, 237
Jones, T. J., 567
Jonsson, P., 596
Jordan, P. J., 574
Joshi, A., 590
Joyce, A., 582
Joyce, W. F., 610
Joyner, T., 612
Judge, T. A., 565, 568, 573, 575, 576, 592, 599, 603, 604
Jung, Carl G., 53–54, 568
Jusko, J., 572, 593
Jussim, L. J., 570, 571

K

Kabanoff, B., 566, 588, 595, 610
Kacmar, K. M., 600
Kador, J., 609
Kageyama, Y., 565
Kahn, R. L., 562
Kahneman, D., 594
Kahwajy, J. L., 567, 594, 601, 602
Kaivo-oja, J., 595
Kalleberg, A. L., 563
Kalliath, T. J., 576
Kammeyer-Mueller, J. D., 611
Kane, K. F., 565
Kanfer, R., 573
Kanigel, R., 562, 581
Kanter, R. M., 598
Kanungo, R. N., 567, 603
Karambayya, R., 603
Karau, S. J., 592, 607
Karl, K. A., 577
Karraker, K., 568
Karsten, L. L., 606
Kaschub, W., 612
Kassam, A. F., 613
Kast, F. E., 564
Katz, D. K., 562
Katzenbach, J. R., 590
Katzenbach, Nicholas D., 359
Kavajecz, Kurt, 289, 492
Kavanaugh, J., 596
Kavanaugh, Joseph, 523
Kawakami, K., 570
Kay, I. T., 562, 581
Keating, D. E., 593
Keenen, J. P., 584
Keil, B., 584
Keil, M., 587
Keinan, G., 585
Keis, K., 575

Kelleher, Herb, 466
Keller, M., 581
Keller, R. T., 604
Keller, T., 606
Kelley, H. H., 570
Kelley, J. G., 608
Kelley, T., 589, 594
Kelley, Tom, 301
Kellogg, D., 586
Kelloway, E. K., 583, 584, 606
Kelly, C., 564
Kelly, Gary, 536
Kelly, J. R., 589
Kemmelmeier, M., 46, 567
Kemmerer, B., 573
Kemp, Bob, 150
Kemp, C., 603
Kennedy, A. A., 610
Kennedy, D. A., 568
Kennedy, J. K., 606
Kennedy, R. B., 568
Kenney, Michael, 389–390
Kenny, D. A., 571
Kerlinger, F. N., 544
Kerr, D. S., 594
Kerr, J., 611
Kerr, N. L., 592, 594
Kerr, S., 578, 581, 603, 604
Kessler, R. C., 585
Keyes, Jim, 449
Keycs, R., 572
Kheradpir, Shaygan, 151
Khoo, H. M., 593
Khurana, R., 605
Khurana, Rakesh, 536
Kidwell, E., 592
Kiffin-Petersen, S., 593
Kiger, P. J., 445
Kilduff, M., 568, 598
Kilmann, R. H., 609
Kim, M. U., 594
Kim, N. H., 603
Kim, Y., 584
King, N., 581
King, W. C., Jr., 579
Kinicki, A. J., 563
Kipnis, D., 599
Kirkcaldy, B. D., 580
Kirkey, S., 577
Kirkman, B. L., 592, 593
Kirkpatrick, D., 596
Kirkpatrick, S. A., 603, 605
Kirsch, D. A., 607
Kirsch, I., 572
Kitade, Koichiro, 469
Kittel, F., 584
Kivimaki, M., 584, 585
Klayman, N., 587
Klein, A., 610
Klein, G., 587, 599
Klein, H. J., 593

Kleingeld, A., 588
Kleinke, C. L., 571
Klimoski, R. J., 573, 591
Kline, Theresa J. B., 309, 310
Kloet, L., 586
Kluger, A. H., 587
Kluger, A. N., 578
Kluwer, E. S., 378, 399
Knauss, T., 109
Knight, D., 569
Knight, D. J., 613
Knight, V., 589
Knoop, C. I., 574, 591
Koberg, C. S., 582
Kochan, T., 563
Kock, N., 596
Kohli, A. K., 608
Kohn, A., 581
Kolb, D. A., 90, 92, 93, 572
Kollias, P., 582
Komaki, J., 571
Konig, S., 589
Konradt, U., 564, 589–590, 593,
    595, 609
Koopman, P. L., 426
Koppel, T., 588
Koput, K. W., 587
Kopytoff, V., 49, 562
Korman, A. K., 604
Koski, T., 596
Koslowski, S. W. J., 611
Kotchen, T. A., 585
Kotha, S., 564
Kotter, J. P., 494, 610, 612
Kouzes, J. M., 564, 566, 567,
    571, 593, 604
Kover, A., 597
Kowske, B., 604
Kozlowski, W. J., 593
Kraatz, M. S., 576
Krackhardt, D., 597, 598
Kraft, Norbert, 393
Kram, K. E., 598
Krause, A., 592
Krautman, A. C., 579
Kray, L., 571
Kreitner, R., 86, 571
Kriska, S. D., 599
Kristof, A. L., 567
Krohne, H. W., 586
Krone, K. J., 595
Krueger, J. I., 613
Kruger, P., 576
Kruglanski, A. W., 569
Krull, D. S., 570
Kshanika, A., 604
Kudisch, J. D., 598
Kuhn, M. H., 98
Kulik, C. T., 570, 578, 579
Kumar, N., 575
Kumaraswamy, A., 565

Kunda, Z., 570
Kunii, I. M., 592
Kurland, N. B., 563
Kwon, S., 602
Kwon, S.-W., 598
Kwun, S. K., 581

L

Lachnit, C., 576
Lackas, Werner, 173
Ladak, Karim, 294
Lafley, Alan George, 415, 416, 499
Lait, J., 583
Lalibert, Guy, 462
Lam, A., 607
Lam, H., 593
Lam, S. S. K., 590
Lancaster, C. M., 613
Landauer, S., 578
Landeta, J., 595
Landin, D., 583
Lane, H. W., 593, 606
Langan-Fox, J., 595
Langfred, C., 591
Lapierre, Judith, 392–393
Larson, J., 105
Larson, J. R., Jr., 61
Larson, L. L., 604
Larson, R., 612
Larson, R. J., 573
Laschinger, H. K. S., 582
Lashinsky, A., 607
La Sorda, Tom, 289
Lasseter, John, 329
Last, Kirsty, 74
Latham, G. P., 565, 572, 578,
    579, 580, 582, 588
Latour, A., 359
Lau, C. M., 613
Lau, D. C., 590
Laurie, V., 588
Lautsch, B. A., 563
Lavie, N., 569
Law, G., 575
Lawler, Edward E., III, 565, 577,
    578, 580, 581, 588, 589, 592, 607,
    608, 611, 612
Lawrence, M., 604
Lawrence, Paul R., 138, 140, 142,
    494, 562, 564, 577, 589, 608
Lay, C., 98
Lazarsfeld, P., 544
Lazarus, Zoe, 346
Le, H., 568, 603
Leary, M. R., 577
Leavitt, H. J., 607
Lebeter, David, 281
LeBlanc, M. M., 580
Leblanc, P., 580–581
Lebner, C., 496
Leck, J. D., 585

Ledeneva, A., 600
Ledford, G., 580–581
Ledford, G. E., Jr., 580, 592
LeDoux, J. E., 573, 577
Lee, C., 576
Lee, D. Y., 598
Lee, Edna, 74
Lee, F., 570
Lee, H., 595–596
Lee, K., 566
Lee, L., 567
Lee, M. S., 585
Lee, R. T., 584
Lee, T. W., 566, 575
Lee, W. B., 591
Lee, W. L., 576
Lee, Y., 570
Lehmann, J., 565
Lei, D., 565
Leibowitz, Z. B., 56
Leidner, D. E., 594
Leiter, M. P., 585
Lengel, R. H., 320, 596
Lennox, R. D., 64
Leon, L. S., 565
LePine, J. A., 566
Lepsinger, R., 605
Lerner, J. S., 587
Lester, T., 580
Leung, K., 613
Leung, S. H. N., 591
Leute, J., 289
Levary, R., 608
Levering, R., 575
Levin, I. M., 605
Levine, D. S., 586, 589
Levinthal, D., 565
Levy, P. E., 578
Levy, S., 612
Lewicki, R. J., 601, 602
Lewin, Kurt, 488, 489, 491, 498,
    500, 504, 507, 611
Lewis, K. R., 602
Lewis, Shannon, 74
Li, A., 578
Li, H., 599, 600
Liberman, A., 586
Liberman, J. S., 586
Liden, R. C., 592
Lieberman, M. D., 587
Liedke, M., 562
Lighton, J., 608
Likert, R., 588
Lim, V. K. G., 580
Lima, E. P., 609
Limberg, Ann M., 10
Lin, J.-H., 595
Lin, N., 585
Lin, Y.-C., 595
Lind, E. A., 571, 579
Lindeman, T. F., 568

Lindstrom, K., 590, 593, 608
Linehan, M., 598
Linn, A., 600
Linstone, H. A., 595
Linz, D. G., 599
Lipnack, J., 563, 593
Liska, L. Z., 604
Lituchy, T. R., 585
Lloyd, S., 565
Lobel, M., 591
Lochhead, Christopher, 203
Locke, E. A., 562, 571, 573, 574, 577,
    578, 579, 588, 591, 603, 605
Loden, M., 9
Lodewijkx, H. F. M., 594
Loewe, P., 562
Loewenstein, G., 248, 572, 577, 587
Lofhjelm, S. M., 570
Logue, A. W., 582
Loh, T., 595
London, M., 578, 579
Longenecker, C. O., 611
Lopes, P. N., 574
Lord, R. G., 577, 603–604, 606
Lorsch, J. W., 562, 608, 612
Loughry, M. L., 605
Louis, M. R., 610, 611
Loutfy, Rafik O., 176
Low, D. R., 588
Lowy, Frank, 386
Lubinski, D., 566
Lucas, R. E., 105, 573
Lucas, W., 595
Luchak, A. A., 575
Lucy, M., 580–581
Luft, Joseph, 83, 84, 571
Lureya, J. S., 593
Luthans, F. F., 86, 571, 577, 578,
    584, 611, 613
Luthar, S. S., 584
Lynch, J., 569
Lyne, S. R., 570
Lynn, B. E., 591, 608
Lynn, R., 580
Lytle, A. L., 601

M

Mabey, C., 578
McAllister, D. J., 593
McAndrew, F. T., 570
McCallum, Vanessa, 340
McCann, J., 564
McCarthy, F. T., 614
McCarthy, M., 229
McCarthy, S., 349
McCauley, C. R., 570
McClelland, C. L., 581
McClelland, David C., 134, 140,
    141, 158, 577
McCloskey, D. W., 563
McConnell, R., 608

McCormick, J., 590
McCracken, D. M., 598
McCracken, J., 611
MacDermid, G., 584
McDermott, M., 578
MacDonald, D., 562
McDonald, K. A., 567
McElrath, Matt, 464
McElyea, B. R., 565
McEnally, M., 600
McFarland, L. A., 599
McGargy, C., 594
McGaw, N., 568
McGill, M. E., 565
McGrath, J. E., 589
McGraw, P., 595
McGregor, D., 588
Machiavelli, Niccolò, 360, 367
McHugh, J., 562
McHugh, M., 612
Mack, A., 569
McKee, A., 113, 571, 574, 596, 603
McKendall, M., 613–614
MacKenzie, S. B., 605
McKersie, R. B., 602
Mackey, J., 592
Mackey, John, 286, 475
McLatchey, Craig, 22
McLean, B., 611
McLuhan, Marshall, 321, 596
McMains, A., 598
McMichen, Caroline, 50
McNabb, R., 580
McPartland, T. S., 98
McQuarrie, Fiona, 25, 515
McRae, B., 602
Macrae, C. N., 569–570
Macrosson, W. D. K., 591
McShane, Steven L., 189, 247, 249, 281,
    283, 308, 337, 338, 393, 424, 456,
    482, 484, 515, 599, 605, 611
Macwhirter, I., 587
Maddux, Henry S., III, 523
Madell, R., 598
Madon, S., 571
Madonet, S., 570
Madsen, S. R., 585
Mael, F., 569
Maellaro, Rosemary, 125
Maertz, C. P., 575
Magana, Giovanni, 349
Magee, D., 496
Maggs, A. J., 581
Mahama, H., 581
Maher, Grahame, 5, 66, 68
Mainemelis, C., 572
Maio, G. R., 566, 573
Maitlis, S., 586, 599
Makhijani, M. G., 607
Maki, A., 601
Malekazedeh, A. R., 470, 610

Malhotra, D., 594
Mallott, M., 570
Malmquist, Warren, 50
Malone, P. S., 570
Malone, T. W., 608
Maloney, L. D., 445
Man, D. C., 590
Mandel, M., 583
Mandela, Nelson, 420, 606
Mang, John, III, 467
Mangaliso, M. P., 606
Manikonda, P., 585–586
Mann, S., 600
Mannion, P., 582
Mannix, E. A., 599
Manz, C. C., 582, 592, 593, 605
March, J. G., 586
March, R. M., 596
Margo, J., 602
Markel, K. S., 579
Markman, A. B., 569
Marks, M. A., 589
Marks, M. L., 610
Marling, S., 608
Marquardt, M. J., 572, 612
Marron, K., 593
Marshak, R. J., 613
Marshall, Barry, 242
Marshall, Grant, 294
Marshall, V., 588
Marsick, V. J., 613
Martin, D. C., 598
Martin, G. E., 601
Martin, G. L., 583
Martin, J., 610
Martin, R., 564, 606
Martin, S., 393
Martins, L. L., 563–564, 593
Martinussen, M., 584
Martocchio, J. J., 566, 577
Masado, G., 607
Maslach, C., 585
Maslow, Abraham H., 134, 135, 136–137,
    138, 158, 208, 576, 577
Maslowski, R., 610
Mason, C. M., 566
Mason, J., 544
Massey, D. S., 572
Matheson, D., 573
Mathieu, J. E., 589, 590, 595
Mathys, N. J., 578
Matsui, T., 578
Matthews, G., 574
Matthiack, Ed, 77
Matthiesen, S., 584–585
Maurer, R., 612
Mausner, B., 581
Mawhinney, T. C., 572
Maxon, Tom, 180
May, D. R., 567, 568, 604
Mayer, J. D., 574

Mayfield, J., 602
Maynard, M. T., 563–564, 593
Mayo, Elton, 4
Mealiea, L., 595
Means, S. P., 597
Medsker, G. J., 590
Medvec, V. H., 587
Meek, C. B., 584
Meglino, B. M., 564, 566, 609
Mehra, A., 568, 598
Meindl, J. R., 606
Melhem, Y., 582
Mellers, B. A., 577
Meloy, M. G., 587
Mencius, 177
Menon, S. T., 582
Merwin, G. A., 572
Meyer, J. C., 609
Meyer, J. P., 129, 575, 576, 603
Meznar, M. B., 612
Michael, Danielle, 224
Michael, J., 568
Michailova, S., 600
Michalak, Michael, 77
Michelena, Caesar T., 81
Michinov, E., 589
Michinov, N., 589
Micklethwait, J., 562
Miles, E. W., 579
Miles, G., 564
Miles, R. F., 608
Miles, R. H., 612
Milkovich, C., 580
Milkovich, G. T., 580
Millar, M., 565
Millemann, M., 564, 613
Miller, C. C., 609
Miller, D., 594, 609, 612
Miller, D. L., 590
Miller, D. T., 579
Miller, J., 566
Miller, L. C., 571
Miller, M., 609
Miller, P. A., 582
Miller, Paula, 109
Mills, A. J., 577, 610
Mills, Deborah, 299
Mills, J., 591
Milne, A. B., 569–570
Milne, J., 564
Miltenberger, R. G., 571
Miner, J. B., 544, 583, 611
Ming, S., 583
Mintzberg, H., 431, 586, 597–598,
    600, 607, 608, 609
Miron, D., 577
Mischel, W., 568
Mitchell, P., 602
Mitchell, T. R., 61, 566, 575, 578, 586, 604
Mitsuhashi, H., 607
Mobius, Mark, 256

Mohammed, 319
Mohr, B. J., 503, 613
Mohrman, A. M., Jr., 562, 589, 592
Mohrman, S. A., 562, 589, 592
Moir, J., 567
Moldaschl, M., 589, 592
Molleman, E., 563, 592
Monahan, William, 176
Monden, Y., 607
Mone, E. M., 578
Monetta, D. J., 613
Montross, D. H., 56
Moore, Alf, 113
Moore, D. A., 602
Moore, John, 23
Moran, A., 582
Moran, L., 593
Moran, R., 596
Moreland, S., 585
Morgan, G., 596, 608
Morgan, John Pierpont, 155
Morgan, R., 587
Morgenson, F. P., 581, 590
Morin, L., 582
Morouney, Kim, 455
Morparia, Kalpana, 462
Morrell, L., 569
Morris, A., 596
Morris, B., 607, 609
Morris, J. A., 574
Morris, J. D., 573
Morris, M. W., 601
Morrison, E. W., 576, 611
Morse, A., 610
Mortensen, M., 601
Moses, Barbara, 506, 614
Moskowitz, M., 575
Moss, S., 603
Mossholder, K. W., 601
Mount, I., 610
Mount, M. K., 568
Mouton, J. S., 398
Mowday, R. T., 575, 576, 579
Moyale, Matayo, 132
Muchinsky, P. M., 575
Mueller, Robert, 489
Muetzel, M. R., 563
Mulac, A., 597
Mulcahy, Anne, 14
Mullen, B., 591, 594
Mullen, P. M., 595
Mulvey, P. W., 578
Mumford, M. D., 588, 605
Murnighan, J. Keith, 590, 594
Murphy, B., 579
Murphy, K. R., 571
Murphy, M. G., 564
Murphy, S. E., 606
Murphy, V., 600, 601
Murray, B., 580
Murray, J., 595

Murray, S., 593
Murray, S. S., 585
Murthy, U. S., 594
Murtlow, Ann, 66, 68
Muzycka, Ray, 441, 442, 608
Mwaura, N., 576
Myers, I. B., 568
Myers, M. S., 562

N

Naccarato, M. E., 99
Nadler, D. A., 431, 564, 577, 607,
    608, 612, 613
Nadler, M. B., 564
Nahavandi, A., 470, 610
Namy, L. L., 597
Nanus, B., 605, 612
Nardelli, Robert, 486, 488, 490,
    491, 492, 495, 497, 498–499, 505
Nason, P., 229
Nasser, Jacques, 489–490
Nauta, A., 378, 399
Nazeer, Z., 266
Neale, M. A., 591, 595
Neale, Tim, 515
Neck, C. P., 582, 583, 605
Nedleman, S. E., 590
Neeleman, David, 66, 68, 462, 536
Neff, J., 589
Neff, T., 597
Neider, L. L., 604
Nel, H., 574
Nelson, D. L., 583, 598–599
Nelson, P., 596
Nemeth, C. J., 594
Nevis, E. C., 564
Newman, J. M., 580
Newsome, S., 574
Newstrom, J. W., 597
Ng, J., 266
Ngo, H. Y., 613
Nguyen, D.-H., 583
Nicholls, C. E., 593, 606
Nicholson, N., 564, 597, 604
Nickerson, R. S., 588
Nicolas, Peter, 284
Nicolini, D., 572, 612
Niehoff, B. J., 582
Nielson, J. S., 603
Niepce, W., 592
Niiler, E., 393
Niimi, A., 590
Nijstad, B. A., 594
Nikolaou, I., 584
Nilekani, Nandan, 400, 402, 414, 603
Niles, F. S., 567
Nilsen, D., 604
Nisbett, R. E., 570, 586
Nobel, R., 608
Nohria, Nitin, 138, 140, 142, 562,
    564, 577, 589

Nolen, S., 393
Nonaka, I., 571, 595, 607
Noon, M., 597
Norenzayan, A., 570
Northcraft, G. B., 578–579, 591, 601
Northouse, P. G., 604
Nougaim, K. E., 576–577
Nugent, P. S., 603
Nur, Y. A., 605
Nussbaum, B., 415
Nutt, P. C., 573, 586, 587
Nye, J. L., 606
Nygaard, A., 583
Nygaard, L. C., 597

O

Oakley, J. G., 607
O'Brian, J., 581
Ochsner, K. N., 574
O'Connor, J. R., 597
O'Dell, C., 565
Odella, F., 572
O'Donnell, J., 359
O'Donnell, M., 581
Oels, A., 612
Oesch, J. M., 594
Oetzel, J. G., 601
Offerman, L. R., Jr., 606
O'Hara, L. A., 588
Ohmae, K., 562
Ohtaki, S., 596–597
Ohtaki, T., 596–597
Oishi, S., 567
O'Keefe, D. J., 599, 600, 602
Olaisen, J., 565
Oldham, G. R., 178, 192, 581, 582, 588
O'Leary-Kelly, A. M., 577
Oliveira, Patricia, 325
Olsen, B., 565
Olsen, S., 49
Olson, J. M., 566
Olson-Buchanan, J. B., 579
O'Malley, Steve, 102
O'Neil, J., 599
Ones, D. S., 579
Onodera, Mika, 122
O'Reilly, C. A., III, 564, 566, 590, 591, 610, 611
Organ, D. W., 544, 570
O'Rourke, J., 580
Orsburn, J. D., 593
Osborn, Alex F., 299, 594
Osborn, R. N., 604
O'Shaughnessy, J., 572
O'Shaughnessy, N. J., 572
Osland, J. S., 567
Osterman, P., 581
Ostroff, C., 611
O'Toole, J., 590
Ott, J. S., 609
Ouchi, W., 589, 597

Ouzounian, R., 609
Overman, S., 572, 585
Owens, D. A., 595
Oyserman, D., 46, 567
Ozcelik, H., 586
Ozzie, Ray, 372

P

Pacelle, M., 610
Packard, David, 473
Paez, D., 567
Pai, H.-H., 580, 583
Paik, Y., 602
Panchak, P., 591
Panke, Helmut, 465
Papaioannou, A., 583
Papper, E. M., 590
Parker, K. E., 99
Parker, S. K., 571, 581, 584
Parker, V. L., 580, 589, 598
Parkers, C. P., 580
Parks, J. M., 121
Parks, L., 581
Parloff, R., 584
Parry, K. W., 605
Pasa, S. F., 599
Pascale, R. T., 564, 589, 613
Passmore, D., 583
Paton, N., 583
Patriquin, M., 570
Patterson, F., 576
Patterson, Scott, 284
Patti, A. L., 607
Paul, Vivek, 85
Pauli, K. P., 567
Paulus, P. B., 594
Pawar, B. S., 606
Peach, E. B., 580
Peale, C., 607
Pearce, C. L., 603
Pearson, C. A. L., 566
Pearson, C. M., 583
Peck, E., 599
Pederson, J. S., 609
Pehlic, Hakija, 207
Peiperl, M. A., 578
Pelled, L. H., 601
Pelloni, O., 575
Pelton, L. E., 599
Penner, D., 597
Penrod, S., 599
Pepper, M. B., 570
Perez, J. C., 595
Pergini, M., 573
Perlow, L. A., 598
Perri, D. F., 601
Perri, David F., 394, 397
Perrow, C., 609
Perry, M., 11
Perry, P. M., 581
Perryer, Chris, 565

Peruche, B. M., 570
Pescuric, A., 572
Peters, T. J., 610–611
Peters, Tom, 434, 597, 607
Peterson, E., 602
Petrie, C., 580
Pettigrew, A. M., 598
Pettigrew, T. F., 570, 602
Pettit, B., 585
Petty, R., 599
Pfau, B. N., 562, 581
Pfau, M., 599–600
Pfeffer, J., 562, 564, 566, 581, 589, 598, 600, 606
Pfeiffer, A. L., 607
Pham, A., 583
Pham, M. T., 573, 587
Phillips, C., 62
Phillips, D., 584
Phillips, F., 587
Phillips, J. M., 611
Phillips, N., 596
Phillips, T., 570
Piccolo, F., 591
Piccolo, R. F., 604
Piekkari, R., 596
Pierce, B. D., 564, 589
Pierce, J. L., 588, 612
Pike, Rob, 2, 21
Pilavin, J. A., 564, 566, 577, 609
Pillutla, M., 594
Pimentel, B., 473
Pinder, C. C., 565, 576, 578, 579
Pinel, E. C., 571
Pink, D. H., 563
Pinsonneault, A., 595
Piper, W., 591
Pisarro, Nicholas, Jr., 330
Pitt, D. C., 603, 604
Pitts, R. A., 565
Plant, E. A., 570
Planting, S., 588
Plato, 4, 52, 68, 177, 226, 569
Podsakoff, P. M., 598, 605
Polanyi, M. F. D., 612
Polivka, A. E., 563
Pollock, T. G., 566, 606
Pondel, E., 604
Pondy, L., 601
Porath, C. L., 583
Porras, J. I., 564, 566
Port, O., 229
Porter, A. M., 609
Porter, L. W., 565, 575, 600, 611
Porzio, Dan, 55
Posner, B. Z., 564, 566, 567, 571, 593
Postmes, T., 569, 601
Poteet, M. L., 598
Potter, R. R. E., 594
Pottruck, David, 458
Pouder, R. W., 610

Powell, D. M., 576
Powell, G. N., 606
Powell, M. C., 569
Powers, C., 593
Prasad, S., 607
Prashad, S., 593
Pratt, M. G., 587
Prayag, A., 578
Prelec, D., 248
Prewitt, E., 608
Prichard, J. S., 591
Prince, Charles, 469
Proctor-Thomson, S. B., 605
Przybys, J., 583
Pugh, D. S., 609
Puliyenthuruthel, J., 49
Pulliam, S., 359
Purser, R. E., 612
Putnam, L. L., 595, 596, 602–603

Q

Quick, J. C., 583
Quinn, R. E., 571, 582, 605, 610,
    612, 613

R

Radke, Jack W., 51
Raelin, J., 603
Rafferty, A. E., 605
Ragavan, C., 612
Raghuram, S., 563
Ragins, B. R., 598
Rahim, M. A., 600
Raikes, Jeff, 151
Rain, J. S., 571
Raines, C., 563
Raisinghani, D., 586
Raisinghani, M. S., 593
Rajagopalan, S., 578
Raman, V., 583
Ramos, Nadia, 476, 478
Rance, C., 612
Randell, G., 591
Randolph, A., 605
Randolph, W. A., 582, 608
Ranson, S., 607
Rao, A., 599
Rapson, R. L., 596
Ratanjee, V., 565
Rauschenberger, J., 577
Raven, Bertrand H., 343–344, 598
Ravlin, E. C., 564, 566, 576, 609
Ray, Darrel, 290
Raynor, M. E., 564
Ready, D. A., 603, 604
Reason, P., 613
Redden, Harry Gene, 523
Redford, K., 585
Redmon, W. K., 578
Reed, E. S., 570
Reichheld, F. F., 175, 575

Reider, M. H., 590
Reilly, R. R., 578
Reingold, J., 564
Reister, C., 585
Reitman, V., 74, 570
Remington, N. A., 573
Remo, A. R., 571
Rempel, M., 591, 601
Rentsch, J. R., 576
Repetti, R. L., 583
Reskin, B. F., 570
Restivo, K., 596
Revans, R. W., 572
Reyes, George, 2, 21
Reynolds, B., 568
Reynolds, K. J., 569
Rhee, K. S., 574
Rhodes, N., 600
Riccomini, B., 597
Rice, R. E., 596
Richard, O. C., 563
Richards, G. S., 565
Richardson, A. M., 584
Richardson, G. E., 584
Richardson, H. A., 607
Riche, M. F., 562
Richmond, R., 349
Richtel, M., 599
Ridderstråle, J., 608
Ridnour, R., 597
Riès, P., 496
Riketta, M., 575
Rikkonen, P., 595
Riley, M., 611
Rimmer, M., 567–568
Rindova, V. P., 564, 566, 606
Ringer, R. C., 600
Rink, F., 591
Riordan, C. M., 590
Risberg, A., 601
Rives, K., 585
Robb, D., 593, 596
Robbins, A. S., 584
Robbins, H., 591
Roberson, L., 570
Roberts, D., 567
Roberts, J. A., 194
Roberts, K., 579
Roberts, P., 610
Roberts, R. D., 574
Roberts, Stephen, 46–47
Robey, D., 587, 593, 608
Robinson, A. G., 588
Robinson, S. L., 576, 593
Robison, J., 565
Robotham, J., 588
Roccas, S., 565, 568
Rodriguez, Roger, 293
Rodwell, R., 597
Roe, R. A., 605
Roehling, M. V., 563

Rogers, C. B., Jr., 359
Rogers, E. M., 613
Rogers, M., 565
Rollins, Kevin, 54
Romero, S., 599
Rondeau, K. V., 576
Roos, D., 592
Rosen, H., 602
Rosen, J. B., 573
Rosen, R., 62
Rosenberg, E., 596
Rosenblum, Michael, 182
Rosenbush, S., 359
Rosener, J. B., 606
Rosengren, A., 585
Rosenthal, R., 569
Rosenweig, J. E., 564
Roskos-Ewoldsen, D. R., 569
Rosnow, R. L., 597
Ross, E., 568, 578
Rossiter, J. R., 588, 595
Rotarius, T., 586
Roth, D., 609
Rothenberg, R., 586
Rothermund, K., 586
Rotundo, M., 566, 583
Rousos, R., 597
Rousseau, D. M. H., 121, 564, 576, 593
Rubin, J. Z., 602
Rubin, M., 570
Rubini, M., 596
Ruble, T. L., 378
Rufat-Latre, J., 562
Ruggles, R., 565
Rukuni, C., 580
Runco, M. A., 588
Russ, G. S., 600
Russell, J. A., 105, 573
Russo, F., 597
Russo, J. E., 587
Ryan, A. M., 599
Rynes, S., 581

S

Saari, L., 575
Saavedra, R., 581
Sabatini, P., 599
Saccomando, John, 270
Sackett, P. R., 566, 583
Sackmann, S., 609
Saedi, Jaschar, 529
Sagie, G., 42
Saint-Onge, H., 565
Saks, A. M., 582, 583, 585, 611
Salacuse, J. W., 602
Salancik, G. R., 573
Salas, E., 594
Salaysay, Nick, 205
Salovey, P., 574, 597
Salter, C., 605
Salter, S. B., 587

Saltzman, M., 608
Sanchez, J. L., Jr., 580
Sandahl, D., 586
Sandford, E. E., 572
Santoli, E. M., 589
Santora, Joseph C., 362, 364, 531, 533
Santos, J. F. P., 593
Sappenfield, M., 606
Saranow, J., 585
Sarr, R. A., 605
Sarwono, S. S., 567
Saskin, Ted, 379
Sasser, W. E., 575
Satcher, David, 404, 405
Sauerteig, D., 597
Sauleya, K. S., 164, 579, 600
Saunders, C. S., 598
Savoie, Patrick, 110
Savoye, C., 567, 604
Scannell, K., 567
Schacht, Henry, 327, 597
Schachter, S., 586, 589
Schau, C., 503
Schaubroeck, J., 573
Schaufeli, W. B., 585
Schein, Edgar H., 461, 609, 610, 611
Schenk, J. A., 605
Schepman, S., 571
Schettler, J., 567
Schetz, Tricia, 212
Schick, A. G., 596
Schiller, M., 613
Schilling, M. A., 608
Schlender, B., 562, 601
Schlesinger, L. A., 494, 575, 612
Schletter, J., 604
Schlosser, J., 415
Schmidt, D. B., 566
Schmidt, Eric, 2
Schmidt, Herb, 39
Schmidt, S. M., 599
Schmidt, W. H., 604
Schminke, M., 579, 580
Schmitt, N., 568, 577
Schnake, M. E., 572
Schneider, R. J., 568
Schoorman, F. D., 587
Schriesheim, C. A., 366, 572, 598, 599, 604–605
Schroeder, D. M., 588
Schulkin, J. Conner, M., 573
Schulman, Amy, 205
Schultz, B., 568
Schultz, V., 583
Schulz-Hardt, S., 601
Schumann, P. L., 567
Schwab, Charles, 430, 473
Schwab, D. P., 575
Schwaig, K. S., 593
Schwartz, H., 587
Schwartz, Jonathan, 312

Schwartz, M., 566
Schwartz, Shalom H., 34, 42–43, 57, 566
Schwarz, N., 573, 586, 587
Schweitzer, M. E., 593
Schwitzerlette, A., 574
Scott, J. C., 578
Scott, K. S., 562
Scott, T. H., 577
Scott, W. B., 591
Scott-Ladd, B., 588
Scudamore, Brian, 66
Sculley, John, 229
Scully, J. A., 581
Seabright, M. A., 580
Secret, M., 585
Seeman, T., 583
Seidlitz, L., 584
Seifman, J., 611
Seijts, G. H., 578
Sekiguchi, W., 567
Seligman, M. E. P., 577, 613
Sels, L., 576
Selye, Hans, 199, 583
Semertzaki, E., 565
Semler, Ricardo, 183, 402, 582, 603
Senge, P. M., 564, 569
Seo, M.-G., 578
Sepulveda, C. J., 194
Serena, M., 563, 576
Sergerstrom, S. C., 584
Sewards, M. A., 570
Sewards, T. V., 576
Shah, Arpan, 266
Shalley, C. E., 588
Shamian, J., 582
Shamir, B., 602
Shane, S., 577
Shani, A. B., 613
Shannon, C. E., 595
Shannon, Sue, 498
Shapiro, B. T., 563, 576, 606
Shapiro, D. L., 576, 592, 593, 595, 601, 602
Shapley, T., 612
Sharp, D. J., 587
Sharpe, R., 606
Shatrujeet, N., 607
Shaw, George Bernard, 322
Shaw, J. D., 580
Shaw, M. E., 589
Shea, G. P., 589
Sheldon, K. M., 591
Shellenbarger, S., 11
Shelton, R., 594
Shepherd, C. D., 597
Sheppard, B. H., 603
Sherbino, Jonathan, 91
Sherif, M., 602
Sherman, J. W., 570
Sherwood, G. G., 571

Sherwood, J. J., 595
Shi, J., 584
Shields, M., 584
Shih, P., 74
Shinkman, C. J., 56
Shull, F. A., Jr., 586
Siegall, M., 583, 585
Siehl, C., 610
Siekman, P., 581, 608
Sigall, H., 596
Simanoff, D., 566
Simcoe, Michael, 260
Simmons, B. L., 583
Simon, B., 569
Simon, Herbert A., 230–231, 232, 586, 587
Simons, T., 567, 593, 605
Simonson, I., 587
Simonton, D. K., 588
Sims, H., Jr., 605
Sinclair, A., 609
Sinclair, G., Jr., 393
Sinclair, J., 570
Sinclair, L., 570, 607
Sine, W. D., 607
Sinegal, Jim, 155
Singer, J. A., 567
Singer, M., 62, 608
Singh, J. A., 578
Sinha, J. B. P., 567
Sistani, Ali Hussein, 319
Sitkin, S. B., 564
Sjöberg, L., 587
Skarlicki, D. P., 579, 580
Skinner, B. F., 571
Skinner, C., 604
Skrabec, Q. R., Jr., 592
Slocum, J. W., Jr., 564, 565, 611
Small, D. A., 587
Smalley, K., 575
Smallwood, N., 603
Smith, A., 581, 584
Smith, A. E., 571
Smith, Adam, 4, 177
Smith, C. A., 129
Smith, D. K., 590
Smith, E. R., 569
Smith, F., 566, 612
Smith, J., 289, 612
Smith, J. H., 562
Smith, K. W., 470, 610
Smith, Mike, 214
Smith, R. S., 580
Smither, J. W., 578
Smith-Holladay, Jennifer, 76
Snell, R. S., 600
Snir, R., 584
Snow, C. C., 608
Snow, D., 567
Snyder, M., 568
Snyder, N. T., 593, 610

Snyder, W. M., 565
Snyderman, B. B., 581
Soelberg, P. O., 587
Sohi, R. S., 565
Sohn, D. W., 603
Somech, A., 592, 599
Sommer, M., 572
Sommer, S. M., 578
Song, S., 612
Song, X. M., 602
Song Young-han, 173
Sonnby-Borgstrom, M., 596
Sorensen, J. S., 609
Sorensen, P. F., 613
Sosnin, B., 597
Sotello, Dan, 77
Southard, Katie, 102
Sparks, J. R., 567, 605
Sparrow, P. R., 576
Spears, L. C., 604
Spears, R., 569, 591, 601
Spector, B., 613
Spector, M., 601
Spector, P. E., 568, 575, 579, 581
Spence, J. T., 584
Spencer, J., 567
Spiers, L., 580
Spini, D., 566
Spitzer, D. R., 175, 581
Spivak, C., 570
Spoor, J. R., 589
Spreitzer, G. M., 582, 592
Springer, J., 589
Sprinkle, G. B., 611
Spurgeon, P., 604
Srinivasan, Subburaman, 238
Srivastava, A., 580
Staelin, R., 587
Staffelbach, B., 593
Stafford, D., 593
Stagner, R., 602
Stalker, G., 607, 608
Stamper, Christine, 58
Stamps, J., 563, 593
Stansfield, T. C., 611
Stanton, N. A., 591
Stasser, G., 590
Stasson, M. F., 573
Stavros, R., 603
Staw, B. M., 587
Steen, M., 580
Steene, G. V., 586
Steensma, H. K., 585, 608
Steers, R. M., 575, 576
Stein, M. B., 584
Steiner, D. D., 571
Steiner, I. D., 592
Stelter, N. Z., 607
Stephen, W. G., 571
Stern, C., 359
Stern, L. W., 575

Stern, R. N., 562
Stern, S., 595
Sternberg, R. J., 588
Stewart, C., 594
Stewart, G. L., 582, 592
Stewart, John, 322
Stewart, T. A., 564–565
Stock, H. J., 580, 589
Stogdill, R. M., 603
Stokes, G. S., 569
Stone, J., 573
Stoneman, B., 567
Straitiff, Joe, 196
Strauss, A., 544
Strauss, A. C., Jr., 564
Strauss, R., 574
Strebel, P., 612
Strickland, O. J., 582
Stroebe, W., 594, 599
Strube, M. J., 576
Strutton, D., 599
Stueck, W., 607
Stuhlmacher, A. F., 602
Suh, E. M., 568
Sullivan, Chris, 117
Sullivan, S. E., 614
Sullivan, Scott, 359
Summers, T. P., 579
Sundstrom, E., 581, 589, 595, 598
Sunoo, B. P., 565
Sunstein, C. R., 594
Sussman, N. M., 597
Sutton, Robert I., 544, 592,
    593, 598, 599
Svensson, O., 596
Sverke, M., 584
Swain, Ann, 74
Swanson, I., 587
Swap, W., 609
Swartz, Jeffrey, 16
Swett, C., 473
Swisher, K., 597
Sy, T., 608
Sya, L. S., 598
Szabo, E. A., 599–600, 606

T

Taggar, S., 588
Taillieu, T. C. B., 605
Tait, Phyllis, 445
Tajfel, H., 569
Takala, T., 562
Takeuchi, H., 571, 595, 607
Tam, P.-W., 49
Tan, D., 600
Tan, M. A., 109
Tang, T. L.-P., 580
Tannen, D., 597
Tannen, F., 600
Tannenbaum, R., 604
Tanner, J., Jr., 599

Tan Swee Hoong, 13
Tarrant, D., 603
Tasa, K., 578, 594
Tata, J., 607
Taylor, C., 608
Taylor, Frederick Winslow, 4, 177, 581
Taylor, R. N., 587
Taylor, S. E., 583, 586
Taylor, T., 584
Teagarden, M. B., 562
Teece, D. J., 608
Te'eni, D., 595
Teicher, S., 570
Tellier, Paul, 387
Templer, D., 194
Teng, B., 586, 594
Teoh, Nancy, 132
Teotonio, I., 572
Terai, I., 578
Teresko, J., 608
Terry, D. J., 569, 599
Tessmann-Keys, D., 590
Tetrick, L. E., 581
Tett, R. P., 568–569
Tews, M. J., 573–574
Tham, Y.-C., 563
Théorét, A., 586
Thiese, K. E., 583
Thom, R., 607
Thomas, D., 597
Thomas, D. A., 563
Thomas, D. C., 576, 596, 601, 606
Thomas, H. D. C., 611
Thomas, J. L., 577
Thomas, K., 378
Thomas, K. W., 601
Thomas, R. J., 563
Thomason, J. A., 572
Thompson, B. L., 573
Thompson, Gloria, 160
Thompson, J. D., 590
Thompson, K. R., 578, 611
Thompson, L., 571, 602
Thompson, L. L., 602
Thompson, M. M., 99, 565
Thompson, T., 584
Thomson, J., 574
Thornburgh, Dick, 359
Thornton, John, 372
Tiedens, L. Z., 570, 596
Tiegs, R. B., 581
Tien-Hsieh, A., 607
Tindale, S. R., 592, 594
Ting-Toomey, S., 601
Tinsley, C. H., 601–602
Tisch, Jonathan, 535
Tischler, L., 609
Tishler, A., 610
Tjosvold, D., 592, 601, 613
Toczek-Capelle, M.-C., 589
Todorovic, William, 334

Toffler, Barbara L., 376, 534–535, 575, 610
Toh, E., 11, 563
Tomaszewski, Barbara, 23
Toomey, S., 583
Tornow, W. W., 578
Torraco, R. J., 592
Tosi, H. L., 564, 598
Tourigny, L., 585
Tracy, J., 393
Tramontano, Paul, 256, 267
Treiber, F. A., 585
Trenwith, C., 74
Trevino, L. K., 572
Triandis, H. C., 568, 602
Tribble, Bud, 354
Trinca, H., 567
Tripp-Knowles, P., 597
Trist, E. L., 592
Trompejnaars, F., 574
Trosten-Bloom, A., 613
Trotman, K. T., 571
Trouilloud, D. O., 571
Truby, M., 611
Tsai, W.-C., 575
Tsang, E. W. K., 570–571
Tsao, Janie, 471
Tsao, Victor, 471
Tsaousis, I., 584
Tsaur, S.-H., 595
Tschida, T. J., 565
Tseng, S.-F., 588
Tsutumi, A., 583
Tuckman, B. W., 590
Tugade, M. M., 584
Tung, R. L., 602
Tunley, W. H., 599
Tupponce, J., 568
Turcsik, R., 577
Turner, J. C., 570
Turner, M. E., 579, 591
Turner, N., 613
Turnley, W. H., 575
Turns, T., 607
Turoff, M., 595
Tushman, M. L., 431, 564, 607, 608
Tuttle, Terry, 303
Tylee, J., 415
Tyler, K., 568, 582
Tyson, D. H., 597

U

Uchitelle, L., 562, 576
Udy, C., 578
Ulich, E., 592
Ulrich, D., 603
Unsworth, K. L., 589
Useem, J., 610
Utsunomiya, Y., 588

V

Vaananen, A., 566, 585
Vaas, L., 600
Valencia, Maureen, 266
Vamos, Steve, 400, 402, 408
Van Aken, E. M., 613
Van Collie, S. C., 614
Vancouver, J. B., 572
Vandenberg, R. J., 594
Van den Brande, I., 576
van der Colff, L., 606
van der Klink, J. J. L., 586
van der Mark, I. L., 571
Van der Vegt, G. S., 590
Van de Ven, A. H., 595
Van de Vliert, E., 590, 601, 602
Van Dijk, D., 578
Van Doorn, J. R., 605
Van Dyne, L., 563, 585
van Engen, M. L., 606–607
Van Fleet, D. D., 607
Vangen, S., 613
Vanhonacker, W. R., 600
van Knippenberg, D., 563, 590, 591
Van Lee, R., 568
Van Maanen, J., 611
van Marrewijk, M., 564
Van Muijen, J. J., 426
van Muijen, J. J., 609
Van Ryssen, S., 593
Van Seters, D. A., 571
Van Tuijl, H., 588
Van Vianen, A. E. M., 601, 611
Van Vugt, M., 589
Vardalos, Nia, 229
Vassileva, Vesselka, 113
Vecchio, R. P., 604
Vedder, R. G., 599
Velasquez, M. G., 567
Velayutham, Thivagar, 520
Verbeke, A., 563
Verkuyten, M., 98
Verplanken, B., 566, 577
Verquer, M. L., 567
Vertommen, H., 586
Vey, M. A., 566
Vigoda, E., 600
Villa, J. R., 605
Visser, P. S., 573
Viswesvaran, C., 579
Vogelstein, F., 562, 609
Voight, J., 598
Von Glinow, M. A., 562, 595, 601, 602
Vonk, R., 599
Voronov, M., 567
Voss, A., 586
Vredenburgh, D., 577
Vreeke, G. J., 571
Vroom, V. H., 247, 577, 588, 594

W

Wachman, R., 589
Wagar, T. H., 576
Wageman, R., 590, 593
Wager, N., 583
Wagner, J. A., III, 588
Wagner, S. H., 567, 580
Wahba, M. A., 577
Wahyudi, L., 584
Wakefield, Don, 290
Waldman, D. A., 578
Walker, C. J., 597
Walker, C. R., 581
Walker, D. H. T., 605
Walker, P. O., 602
Wall, J. A., 600, 601, 603
Wall, T. D., 581, 582
Wallace, D., 565
Wallace, J. E., 583
Wallace, R., 574
Walsh, J. P., 588
Walter, G. A., 614
Walters, M., 609
Walther, J. B., 595
Walton, R. E., 601, 602, 613
Wanberg, C. R., 611
Wang, Tony, 186
Wanous, J. P., 577, 611
Want, Andrew, 266
Warech, M. A., 568
Waresh, J., 565
Warner, M., 562
Warren, J. Robin, 242, 588
Warren, M., 393
Washington, Denzel, 344
Waterman, R., 597
Watkins, J. M., 503, 613
Watkins, K., 613
Watson, Christine, 312
Watson, R., 579
Watson, Thomas, 474
Watts, L. A., 595
Waung, M., 585
Weatherbee, T. G., 577
Weaver, W., 595
Webb, M., 605
Webber, S. S., 591
Weber, Max, 4
Weber, N., 602
Weber, R., 606
Weber, T., 606
Weber, W., 589
Weber, W. G., 592
Webster, D. M., 569
Webster, J., 596
Webster, W., 589
Wecsler, H., 572
Wedley, W. C., 586
Wegge, J., 578

Wei, L., 589
Weick, K. E., 613
Weingart, L. R., 594, 601, 602
Weinreb, M., 445
Weisberg, R. W., 588
Weisbord, M. R., 612
Weiss, H. M., 572, 573, 574
Weitzel, J. R., 604
Welbourne, T. M., 580
Welch, D., 596
Welch, J. M., 580
Welch, L., 596
Welch, Richard, 346
Weldon, E., 601–602
Welsh, D. H. B., 578
Wener, R. E., 584
Wenger, E. C., 565
West, M. A., 588, 589
Westerman, J. W., 567, 576
Westwood, R., 562, 588
Wetzels, M. G. M., 597
Wex, P., 612
Wharton, A. S., 584, 585
Wheeler, J. V., 592
Whipp, G., 597
White, E., 576
White, Geoff, 109
White, J. B., 289
White, K. M., 599
White, R., 564, 589
White, S. S., 571
Whitehouse, K., 580
Whitener, E. M., 593
Whitfield, K., 580
Whitford, D., 581
Whitmeyer, J. M., 598
Whitney, D., 503, 613
Whitten, N., 604
Whittington, J. L., 605
Whitwam, David, 7
Whitworth, B., 597
Whyte, G., 587, 594
Whyte, W. H., 576
Wick, C. W., 565
Wiesenfeld, B., 563
Wiethoff, C., 593
Wilderom, C. P. M., 610
Wilk, L. A., 578
Wilkins, A. L., 609
Wilkins, Greg, 435
Wilkinson, H. A., 571
Wilkinson, I., 586, 599
Wilkinson, Ian, 224
Wilkinson, M., 567

Willemsen, T. M., 606
Williams, A., 609
Williams, B. A., 572
Williams, J. R., 579
Williams, K. D., 592
Williams, K. Y., 590
Williams, Lisa V., 94
Williams, M., 593
Williams, S., 595, 596
Williamson, M. G., 611
Williamson, O. E., 593
Williamson, P. J., 593
Willis, H., 570
Wilson, P., 586
Wilson, Rita, 229
Winkielman, P., 574, 577, 586, 596
Winters, D. C., 588
Wirtz, P. W., 606
Wise, P., 266
Wiseman, R. M., 580
Withers, P., 586
Withey, M. J., 575
Witt, A., 568
Witt, L. A., 600
Witte, E., 586
Witteman, H., 601
Wixom, B. H., 594
Wofford, J. C., 604, 605
Wojcik, J., 586
Wolf, M., 562
Wolfe, R. N., 64
Womack, J. P., 592
Wong, N., 583
Wong, S. K., 109
Wood, G., 567–568
Wood, J. T., 597
Wood, N., 606
Wood, W., 600
Wooden, M., 583–584
Woodman, R. W., 595
Woodruff, D., 572, 596
Wooldridge, A., 562
Workman, J. P., Jr., 608
Worm, V., 600
Wratney, G. R., 568
Wren, D. A., 580
Wright, G., 587
Wright, P. M., 579
Wrzesniewski, A., 582

X

Xile, J., 602
Xin, K., 572
Xin, K. R., 601

Y

Yaeger, T. F., 613
Yamada, H., 596, 597
Yamauchi, K., 194
Yammarino, F. J., 605
Yang, H.-C., 594
Yang, J., 601
Yang, J. L., 600
Yang, W., 569
Yang Yuanqing, 47
Yankelovich, D., 562
Yantis, S., 569
Ybarra, O., 571
Yeatts, D. E., 592
Yee-Jung, K., 601
Yoho, S. K., 604
Yokoyama, John, 535
Yonatan, R., 593
Yoon, J., 582
York, G., 393
You, N., 584
Young, S., 575
Youngblood, D., 607
Yukl, G. A., 598, 600, 603, 604, 605
Yusuf, S., 585

Z

Zaccaro, S. J., 589, 603
Zacharatos, A., 613
Zadek, S., 564
Zajonc, R. B., 573
Zald, M. N., 564
Zaleznik, A., 605
Zalkind, S. S., 571
Zambon, S., 564
Zapf, D., 573, 574
Zeelenberg, M., 577
Zeidner, M., 574
Zemke, R., 563, 576, 601, 609
Zerbe, W. J., 572, 574, 603, 604
Zeschuk, Greg, 441, 442, 608
Zetik, D. C., 602
Zhao, J. J., 602
Zhongtuo, W., 586
Zhou, J., 575, 588
Zmud, R. W., 596
Zodarecky, Terri, 102
Zore, Ed, 19, 564
Zwany, A. A., 577

subject index

A

A-B-Cs of behavior modification, 86
Ability, 34, 36–37, 413
Absenteeism, 88, 177, 210, 490
Absorption of changes, 346
Absorptive capacity, 22
Abstract conceptualization, 90
Abuse of others, 39
Abuse of power, 340, 358, 359, 360
Accountability, 76, 157, 443–444
Achievement, 80
Achievement motivation program, 141
Achievement-nurturing orientation, 47–48
Achievement-oriented leadership style, 409, 411
Acquisition drive, 138, 139
Action learning, 91–92, 495
Action research, 500–502, 504, 507
Action scripts, 234
Active experimentation, 90
Active listening, 327–329
    evaluating, 328
    responding, 329
    sensing, 327–328
Adaptive cultures, 467–468
Adjourning stage, 269
ADR (alternative dispute resolution), 389–390
Advisory teams, 259
Affective commitment, 119, 124
African Americans, 8, 9
Age, stress and, 206
Age discrimination, 75
Aggressive responses, 157, 210
Agreeableness, 52, 53
Alarm reaction, 199
All-channels communication structure, 360
Alternative dispute resolution (ADR), 389–390
Alternatives
    choosing from, 227, 244
    evaluating, 230–235, 244
    implementation of, 227
Ambiguity
    in language, 322
    matrix structure and, 443
    rich media and, 321
    role ambiguity, 202–203
    stress and, 445
    tolerance for, 47, 230
Ambiguous goals, 231
Ambiguous rules, 375–377
Ambiguous structures, 445
Analyzability of technology, 450
Anger in workplace, 121, 233
Antecedents of behavior, 86
Anthropology, relevance to OB, 17
Anticipation, 69

Applied performance practices, 166, 167–188
    empowerment practices, 168, 182–184
    financial reward practices, 168–176, 188
    job design. See Job design
    self-leadership. See Self-leadership
Appreciative inquiry, 502–503, 507
Aptitudes, 36
Arbitration, 387, 388, 389
Arbitrators, 390
Artifacts, 460, 461, 463–465, 479, 609
    aligning, 472, 474
    organizational language, 465
    rituals and ceremonies, 464–465
    stories and legends, 464, 474
    structures and symbols, 465
Artistic personality, 56
Asian Americans, 9
Assembly line technology, 450
Assertiveness, 351, 352
Assimilation, 470–471
Association, causation and, 541
Associative play, 243
Attendance, maintaining, 40–41
Attitude object, 106
Attitudes, 34–35, 106–110, 123, 573
    cognitive dissonance and, 109–110
    cognitive model of, 106–107
    conflict of cognitions and emotions, 107, 108–109, 140
    difficulty of teaching, 112
    formation of, 227
    influence of emotions on, 107–108
Attribution errors, 79, 419, 570
Attribution process, 77, 92
Attribution theory, 77–79
Audience characteristics, 386
Authentic leadership, 405
Autonomy, 179, 187
    creativity and, 224, 243
    of SDWTs, 286–287
    in STS theory, 287
    of team-based structure, 444
Avoiding style, 379

B

Baby boomers, 10
Bad bosses, stress and, 200–201
Balanced scorecard (BSC) strategy, 172–173
Bargaining zone model of negotiation, 385
Barriers to communication, 315, 322–324, 333
    filtering, 322
    information access barriers, 489

information overload, 323–324
    language barriers, 322–323
    perceptions, 322
Behavior, 33–57, 86, 123
    arrogance, conflict and, 377
    cognitive dissonance and, 109–110
    counterproductive work behaviors, 39
    cross-cultural values, 45–48
    ethical values. See Ethics
    hiring and retention, 39–40
    inconsistent with beliefs, 109–110
    influence of emotions on, 107–108, 109
    maintaining attendance, 40–41
    modification of. See Behavior modification
    needs hierarchy models and, 138
    organizational. See Organizational behavior
    organizational citizenship, 38–39
    personality. See Personality
    supporting empowerment, 183–184
    task performance, 38
    types of, in organizations, 38–41, 57
    values, 41–45
    See also MARS model of individual behavior
Behavioral effects of distress, 200, 210, 216
Behavioral intentions, 106–107
Behavioral modeling, 89
    appreciative inquiry, 502
    increasing E-to-P expectancies, 144–145
    social learning theory and, 89, 144–145
    in transformational leadership, 417–418
    See also MARS model of individual behavior
Behavioral perspective of leadership, 403, 404, 407–408
Behavioral routines, 490, 491
Behavior modification, 86–88, 93
    A-B-Cs of, 86
    contingencies of reinforcement, 86–87
    practical aspects of, 88
    reinforcement schedules, 87–88
Beliefs, 106, 109–110, 207
Belongingness, 135, 136, 137
"Benevolents," 155
Biased sampling, 540–541
Bicultural audit, 469–470
Big Five dimensions of personality, 52–53, 57
Blackmail, 352
Blat, 355

Blind area, in Johari Window, 84
Blogs (weblogs), 312, 317, 330
Bonding
emotional contagion and, 319
in identification-based trust, 295, 296
in virtual teams, 294
Bonding drive, 138, 139, 260–261
Bonuses, 166, 169, 170, 172
"Bottom-up selection," 569
Bounded rationality, 230–231
Boutique agencies, 428
Brainstorming, 299–301
"Brooks's law," 277
BSC (balanced scorecard) strategy, 172–173
"Buddy system," 479
Buffering, 323–324, 383
Buildings, 465, 474
Bullying, 201, 202
Business ethics. See Ethics
Business knowledge, 405, 406
Buzzwords, 323

C

Calculus-based trust, 295
Call centers, 146, 149
Cardiovascular disease, stress and, 209
"Career activism," 506
Career goals, 506
Categorical thinking, 69–70, 73, 75
Categorization, 72
Causation
in field surveys, 543–544
research design and, 541–542
Cause–effect relationships, 78
CD-RISC (Connor-Davidson Resilience Scale), 221
Centrality, power and, 348, 349
Centralization
global, 428
munificent environments and, 448–449
of organizational structure, 434–435, 451
Centralized cultures, 486
"Centrally decentralized" structure, 449
Ceremonies, as artifacts, 465
Chain of command, 438
Challenging goals, 147
Change agents, 493, 507
in organizational change, 499
Changing organizational culture, 472–475
actions of founders and leaders, 472, 473
aligning artifacts, 472, 474
culturally consistent rewards, 472, 473–474
role of employees, 472, 474–475
Charisma, 345, 415–416
Charismatic leadership, 415–416
Charismatic visionaries, 420

Childbirth bonuses, 170
Child care support, 213
Child labor, 15
CIP (Community Internship Program), 77
Circumplex model of emotions, 105–106, 123
Clarifying message, 329
Client relationships, 181, 182, 501
Client structure, 439, 440
Closed systems, 19
"Closing costs," 236
Coaching, 115, 150, 495
Coalition formation, 351, 352–353
Coercion, 494, 497
Coercive power, 343, 345, 369
Cognitions, 104, 140
"Cognitive center," 573
Cognitive dissonance, 109–110, 123
Cognitive intelligence (IQ), 114
Cognitive model of attitudes, 106–107
Collaborative conflict management style, 381
Collectivism
comfort with teamwork and, 290
individualism compared, 42, 45–46
social loafing and, 277
talking circles, 383
Command-and-control supervision, 290
Commissions, 171
Commitment, influence and, 356
Communication, 313–333
all-channels structure, 360
conflict management and, 382–383
creativity and, 243
cross-cultural. See Cross-cultural communication
cross-gender, 326–327
effective, by negotiator, 387
electronic, 316–318, 330
improving, 327–329
informal, 431, 438
media richness and, 319–321, 431
model of, 314–315
noise and. See Barriers to communication
nonverbal. See Nonverbal communication
in organic structure, 436
in organizational hierarchies, 329–331
patterns of, structure and, 430
in person. See Face-to-face communication
problems with, conflict and, 377, 390
in reducing restraining forces, 493–494
relevance to OB, 17, 18
through "grapevine," 331–332
written, 315–316
Communication channels, 315–319
choosing, 319–322

electronic, 316–318
nonverbal, 315, 318–319
verbal, 315–316
Communication process, 262, 293–294, 305
Communication systems, 292
Communicator, experience of, 321
Communities of practice, 22, 259
Community Internship Program (CIP), 77
Community volunteering, 303
Comparison other, 153, 154
Compassion fatigue, 209
Competencies, 36
core competencies, 446
emotional intelligence and, 113
empowerment and, 183
individual, 505–506
measuring, 171
resilience and, 208
Competency-based financial rewards, 169, 171, 188
Competency-based hiring, 407
Competency perspective of leadership, 403, 404–407, 421
limitations and practical implications, 406–407
personality characteristics, 404–406
Complex environments, decentralization and, 448
Compliance, 355–356, 490, 497
Compromising style, 379, 380
Concessions, by negotiator, 387
"Concorde fallacy," 236
Concrete experience, 90
"Conduit" model of communication, 314–315
Confidence, in decision making, 298
Conflict, 369–391
conflict process, 370–373
constructive conflict, 299, 372, 390
dysfunctional, 368, 371–373, 375–377, 439
management of. See Conflict management
mergers and acquisitions, 374, 375
risk of, 240, 375, 383
socioemotional, 372–373, 390
sources of. See Sources of conflict
as stressor, 202–205
in team development, 268, 269
Conflict escalation cycle, 370, 371
Conflict management, 372, 390
interpersonal styles, 370, 377–380
structural approaches to, 380–384, 390–391
team building and, 304
third-party resolution, 387–391
through negotiation. See Negotiation
Conflict process, 370–373
manifest conflict, 371
outcomes, 371–373

perceptions and emotions, 370, 371
Conformity, pressure for, 297
Congruence, 55
Connectedness, 420
Connor-Davidson Resilience Scale
    (CD-RISC), 221
Conscientiousness, 52, 53, 187
Conscious drives, 139–140
Consensus, 77–78, 302
Consequences
    of behavior, 86, 89
    of change, fear of, 490
    of organizational commitment,
        119–120
    of organizational politics, 359, 360
    of procedural justice, 157
    of reward systems, 175–176
    of team cohesiveness, 275
    of workforce diversity, 10
Consequential principles, 49
Conservation, 42, 43
Consistency, 77, 78
Constructive conflict, 299, 372, 390
"Constructive confrontation," 372
Constructive thought patterns, 185–186
Constructs, defining, 539
Consultants, 121
Contact hypothesis, 76, 382
Context, 69, 79
Contingencies of influence tactics, 355–357
Contingencies of organizational culture,
    435, 466–467
Contingencies of organizational structure,
    435, 448–451
    external environment, 448–449
    organizational strategy, 450–451
    organization size, 449
    technology, 449–450
Contingencies of power, 347–350,
    360–361
    centrality, 348, 349
    discretion, 348
    networking and, 350
    substitutability, 347–348, 349
    visibility, 348–350
Contingencies of reinforcement, 86–87
Contingencies of self-fulfilling prophecy,
    80–81
Contingency approach to OB, 18–19
Contingency theories of leadership, 403,
    404, 408, 421–422
    Fiedler's model, 412–413
    leadership substitutes, 413–414
    situational leadership theory, 412
Contingent work, 12–13
Continuance commitment, 119–120
Continuous reinforcement, 87
Controlled research, 540
Control system, corporate culture as, 466
Conventional personality, 56
Conversational overlaps, 326

Coordinating mechanisms, 449
Coping strategies, 206–207, 228, 346
Core competencies, in network structure,
    446
Core job characteristics, 179
"Corporate cults," 44, 468
Corporate culture. See Organizational
    culture
Corporate restructuring, employment
    relationship and, 134
Corporate social responsibility (CSR),
    15–16, 24
Corporate vision. See Strategic vision
Corrective feedback, 148
Correspondence bias, 570
Cost leadership strategy, 450–451
Countercultures, 463
Counterpower, 343
Counterproductive work behaviors
    (CWBs), 39, 157
Creative process model, 240–241
Creativity, 240–244, 245
    activities that encourage, 243–244
    autonomy and, 224, 243
    brainstorming and, 301
    creative process model, 240–241
    work environments and, 241–243
Credible feedback, 148
Critical feedback, 150
Critical investigation, 540
Critical psychological states, 179
Criticism, lack of, in brainstorming, 300
Cross-cultural communication,
    324–326, 333
    conflict and, 377
    nonverbal differences, 318, 319,
        325–326
    silence and conversational overlaps,
        326
Cross-cultural issues
    in leadership, 420, 422
    in organizational change, 504, 507
    with SDWTs, 288–290
Cross-cultural values
    achievement-nurturing orientation,
        47–48
    individual behavior and, 45–48
    individualism v. collectivism, 42,
        45–46
    power distance, 46–47
    uncertainty avoidance, 47
Cross-functional teams, 444, 496
Cross-gender communication,
    326–327, 333
Cross-generational conflict, 374–375
Cross-pollination, creativity and, 244
CSR (corporate social responsibility),
    15–16, 24
Cultural content, 461–463
Cultural differences, 294, 325–326,
    374, 380

Culturally consistent rewards, 472,
    473–474
Cultural values, 41
    comparison of job satisfaction and, 115,
        116
    influence tactics and, 357
    meaning and value of money, 168
    ubuntu values, 420
Culture
    conflict management styles and, 380
    cultural norms, 111, 112, 324–325
    emotional display norms and, 111, 112
    expectancy theory and, 146
    multiculturalism, 48
    of organizations. See Organizational
        culture
    psychological contracts and, 122–123
    See also Collectivism; Cross-cultural
        values; Cultural values; Power
        distance
"Culture carriers," 474
Culture clash, 458, 469
Curiosity, 139
Customer-driven change, 492–493
Customer-focused organizational culture,
    462, 473
Customer satisfaction, 118, 175
Customer service, 10, 486
CWBs (counterproductive work
    behaviors), 39, 157
Cycle time, 148, 176
Cynicism, 210

D

Deadlines, in negotiation, 386
Death from overwork, 203, 204
Decentralization
    "centrally decentralized" structure, 449
    complex environments and, 448
    of organizational culture, 486
    of organizational structure, 434–435
    regional, 428
Decentralized cultures, 486
Decision commitment, 240
Decision control, 388
Decision making, 225–245
    accountability for, 76
    alternatives in, 230–235
    brainstorming, 299–301
    clear goals in, 231
    constraints on, 297–299
    constructive conflict and, 299
    creativity and. See Creativity
    delphi method, 301–302
    effective choices, 234–235
    emotions and, 232–233
    employee involvement in, 237–240,
        244–245, 409
    escalation of commitment, 235–236
    evaluating opportunities, 232
    evaluating outcomes, 235–237

Decision making—*Cont.*
  evaluation apprehension and, 297
  group polarization and, 298–299
  groupthink and, 298
  by high-performance teams, 286,
    297–302, 306
  identifying problems and opportunities,
    227–230
  information processing and, 231–232
  intuition and, 233–234
  maximization and, 232
  nominal group technique, 302
  postdecisional justification, 235,
    244, 477
  pressure to conform in, 297
  rational choice paradigm, 226–227,
    230, 231
  team building and, 304
  time constraints on, 297
Decision structure, employee
    involvement and, 239
Decisive leadership, problem
    identification and, 230
Deculturation, as merger strategy, 470,
    471
Deductive process, 538, 539–540
  constructs, 539
  testing hypotheses, 539–540
Deductive stage of theory building, 538
Deep acting, 112
Deep-level diversity, 9–10, 267
Defending drive, 138, 139
Deference to authority, 351, 352
Deferred compensation, 119–120
Deficiency needs, 136
Degree of differentiation, 56
Delivering stage, in "Four-D" model, 503
Delphi method, 301–302
Deming Prize, 238
Demographics, social identity and, 72
Departmentalization, 438–447, 451
  divisional structure, 439–441, 445
  functional structure, 439
  matrix structure, 441–444
  network structure, 446–447
  simple structure, 438
  team-based structure, 444–445
Departmental teams, 259
Dependence, in power relationship,
    342, 343
Dependent variables, 541–542
Depersonalization, 210
Descriptive language, 327
Designing stage, in "Four-D" model, 503
Deterrence, 295
Differentiation
  cultural differences, 294, 325–326, 374,
    380
  degree of, 56
  reducing, 381
  in social perception, 72–73

as source of conflict, 374–375,
    382, 389
  substitutability and, 348
  See also Individual differences
Differentiation strategy, 450, 451
Diffusion of organizational change,
    499–500
Direct communication, 331
Direct costs, 490, 491
Direction of effort, 35
Direction of influence, 356
Directive leadership style, 409, 411, 413
Disclosure, perceptions and, 84
Discovery stage, in "Four-D" model, 502
Discretion, power and, 348
Disparate impact, 75
Display rules, for emotion, 110–111
Dissensus, 302
Distinctiveness, 77, 78
Distress, 198, 199, 208–210, 216
  behavioral effects of, 200, 210
  physiological effects, 199–201, 209
  psychological effects, 196, 200,
    209–210
Distributive justice (equity theory), 48, 49,
    152–156
  correcting inequity feelings, 153–154
  elements of, 152–153
  equity evaluation, 153
  equity sensitivity and, 154–155
  evaluating, 155–156
Divergent thinking, 241
Diverse environments, 448
Diversity. *See* Workforce diversity
Diversity awareness training, 75–76
"Divine discontent," 230
Divisional structure, 439–441, 445, 451
Division of labor, 430–431
Dominant culture, 463
Downward influence, 356
Dreaming stage, in "Four-D" model,
    502–503
Drive(s), 135
  four-drive theory. *See* Four-drive
    theory
  leadership and, 404, 405–406
  practical implications of, 142–143
Drive deprivation, 137
Driving forces, 488–489, 492, 507
Drum circles, 382
Dynamic environments, 448
Dysfunctional conflict, 368
  ambiguous rules and, 375–377
  functional structure and, 439
  outcomes, 371–373
Dysfunctional norms, 271–272

E

EAPs (employee assistance programs),
    215
Economics, relevance to OB, 17

Economy, job satisfaction and, 115–116
Education, influence of, 9–10
Effort-to-performance (E-to-P)
    expectancies, 147
  increasing, 144–145
  model of, 143–144
  path-goal leadership theory and, 408
EI. *See* Emotional intelligence
Electronic brainstorming, 301
Electronic communication (e-mail),
    316–318, 333
  computer-mediated communication,
    317–318
  problems with e-mail, 316–317
Embezzlement, 48
Emoticons ("smileys"), 316
Emotion(s), 34–35, 103–124
  attitudes and. *See* Attitudes
  behavior and, 107–108, 109
  circumplex model of, 105–106, 123
  cognitions and, 107, 108–109, 140
  in conflict process, 370, 371
  effects of, 232–235
  e-mail and, 316
  emotional dissonance, 111–112
  emotional labor, 111
  fun and, 109
  influence on attitudes, 107–108
  as information, 233
  job satisfaction and, 115–118, 574
  managing, 110–112
  organizational commitment and,
    119–120
  personality and, 110
  psychological contracts, 121–123
  rational choice paradigm and, 227
  role in employee behavior, 146
  types of emotions, 105–106
  in workplace, 104–110
  See also Emotional intelligence
Emotional appeals, 355
"Emotional center," 573
Emotional contagion, 318–319
Emotional dissonance, 111–112
Emotional exhaustion, 209
Emotional intelligence (EI), 112, 113–115,
    123–124
  dimensions of, 113–114
  four-drive theory and, 140
  improving, 114–115
  leadership and, 404, 405, 408
  socioemotional conflict and, 373
Emotional labor, 110–112, 123
Emotional markers, 130
  in evaluating information, 227
  in making choices, 233
  in selective attention, 69, 70
"Emotions as information," 233
Empathy, 83, 114, 326–328
Empirical research, 540
Employability, 12

Employee(s)
    adaptive cultures and, 468
    choice of rewards for, 142–143
    control over stressors, 212
    corporate vision and, 418, 430
    with countercultural values, 463
    expertise of, 437, 441
    generation-X/-Y, 10, 11–12, 123,
        134, 170
    high-expectancy, 80
    need for communication, 314
    organizational commitment of, 120
    organizational socialization, 475,
        476–479
    perceptions of disempowerment, 436
    pilot projects and, 499–500
    psychological characteristics of, 9
    replacing staff, 497, 498
    resistance to change, 78, 489–491, 507
    resistance to SDWTs, 290–291
    response to leadership styles, 407
    role in culture change, 172, 174–175
    rotating across departments, 381
    self-fulfilling prophecy, 80
    self-leadership, 402
    surveys of, 32–33, 330
    temporary, 121
    tolerance of legitimate power, 345
    See also Hiring and retention
Employee anxiety, 332
Employee assistance programs (EAPs), 215
Employee behavior, 134, 430
Employee complaints, 490
Employee contingencies, 410, 411
Employee empowerment, 166, 182–184,
    188
Employee engagement, 34, 37, 38, 57, 166
Employee-friendly culture, 461–462
Employee interdependence, 293–294,
    433–434
Employee involvement
    in decision making, 237–240,
        244–245, 409
    organizational commitment and, 120
    in reducing restraining forces, 494,
        495–497
Employee motivation
    in MARS model, 34, 35, 134, 173
    P-to-O expectancy and, 173
    stock options and, 172, 173–174
Employee satisfaction, 117–118, 389
Employee stock ownership plans
    (ESOPs), 172, 173–174
Employee turnover, 177, 486, 490
Employment relationships, 11–13
    contingent work, 12–13
    organizational commitment and, 120
    workforce flexibility, 12, 171
    work–life balance, 11–12
Empowerment, 155, 182–184, 188
Enacted values, 42, 44–45, 460, 609

Encounter, 476, 477–478
"Enlightened management," 137
Enterprising personality, 56
Enthusiastic workaholics, 208
"Entitleds," 155
Environmental changes, 346
Environmental contingencies, 410, 411
Environmental values, 44
Episodes, 104
Equality principle, 152, 157
Equity principle, 152, 157
Equity sensitivity, 154–155
Equity theory, 48, 49, 152–156, 158
    correcting inequity feelings, 153–154
    elements of, 152–153
    equity evaluation, 153
    equity sensitivity and, 154–155
    evaluating, 155–156
ERG theory, 138, 158
Escalation of commitment, 235–236, 244
ESOPs (employee stock ownership
    plans), 172, 173–174
Espoused-enacted values congruence,
    44–45
Espoused values, 42, 45, 460, 609
Esteem, 135, 136
Ethical sensitivity, 50
Ethics, 15, 24, 34, 48–51
    ethical sensitivity, 50
    job satisfaction and, 118
    moral intensity, 49–50
    of organizational change,
        504–505, 507
    organizational culture and, 2, 51, 468,
        469
    in organizational research, 542
    situational factors, 50
    support for ethical behavior, 50–51
    three principles of, 48–49
    values and, 14–16
Ethics codes, 50
E-to-P (effort-to-performance)
    expectancies, 143–145, 147
Eustress, 198–199
Evaluation, in active listening, 328
Evaluation apprehension, 297, 300, 301
Evaluation of alternatives, 230–235, 244
    clear goals in, 231
    effective choices, 234–235
    emotions and, 232–233
    evaluating opportunities, 232
    information processing and, 231–232
    intuition and, 233–234
    maximization and, 232
EVLN (exit-voice-loyalty-neglect) model,
    116–117, 118
Exchange, as influence tactic, 351, 355
Exchange relationship, 343
"Executive dashboards," 149, 151
Exhaustion, 199–200
Exit, job satisfaction and, 116, 117

Exit-voice-loyalty-neglect (EVLN) model,
    116–117, 118
Expectancy theory, 134, 143–146, 158
    model of, 143–144
    path-goal leadership theory and, 408
    in practice, 144–146
    reality and, 146
Expectations
    of generation-X/-Y employees, 170
    positive, power of, 81
    in self-fulfilling prophecy, 80
    social fulfillment, 12
    work–life balance, 11–12
Experienced meaningfulness, 179
Experienced responsibility, 179
Experiences, emotions as, 104–105, 106
Experiential learning, 85, 90–92, 93
    action learning, 91–92
    in practice, 90–92
    steps in, 90
Experimentation, 22
Expert power, 343, 345
Explicit knowledge, 85
External attributions, 77, 78
External competition, 274
External environments
    driving forces for change, 492–493
    environmental diversity, 439–440
    learning from, 21–22
    in open systems, 19, 20
    organizational design and,
        448–449, 451
    organizational strategy and, 450–451
    as situational factor, 37
    stakeholders and, 20
Extinction, 87
Extranets, 446
Extreme decisions, 298–299
Extroversion, 53, 54, 110, 187, 406
E-zines, 330

F

"Face time," 350
Face-to-face communication, 312, 315
    in brainstorming, 301
    coordinating work activities, 431
    in grapevine, 332
    persuasion and, 355
    in virtual teams, 292, 294
Face-to-face (colocated) teams, 375
Fear of unknown, 490, 491
Feedback, 134, 158
    characteristics of, 148
    in communication, 315, 320
    empathy and, 83
    evaluating, 151
    in evaluating outcomes, 237
    executive coaching, 150
    in improving emotional intelligence, 115
    job feedback, 179
    learning and, 85

Feedback—*Cont.*
  media richness and, 320
  multisource (360°), 149–150, 174, 297,
      345, 578
  naturally occurring, 186
  in open systems, 19, 20
  perceptions and, 84
  for personal change, 505
  refreezing and, 498
  reward systems and, 345
  sources of, 149–151, 174
  supportive, 144–145
  team-level, in SDWTs, 287
Feelings, attitudes and, 106
Fiedler's contingency model of
      leadership, 412–413
Field experiments, 542
Field surveys, 543–544
"Fight-or-flight" response, 139, 198, 210
Filtering, 322
Financial health of organizations, 6, 24
Financial reward practices, 168–176, 188
  competency-based, 169, 171, 188
  improving effectiveness, 174–176
  job status-based, 169, 170, 188
  membership- or seniority-based,
      168–170
  monetary incentives, 151
  performance-based, 171–174
Fish! principles, 108
Five-factor model of personality, 34
Five-stage model of team development,
      268–270
Fixed interval schedule, 87
Fixed ratio schedule, 87
Flaming, 316, 317
Flat structures, 434, 435, 444
Flattery, 353
Flexibility. *See* Workforce flexibility
Flexible work time, 212–213
"Follow the sun" development, 293
Force field analysis model, 488–491,
      498, 504, 507
  driving forces, 488–489
  restraining forces, 489–491
Forcing style, 379–380
Forecasting, 346
Formal feedback, 149
Formal hierarchy, 431, 432
Formalization
  of organizational structure,
      435–436, 451
  team-based structure and, 444
Forming stage, 268, 269
Founders, organizational culture and,
      472, 473
"Four-D" model of appreciative inquiry,
      502–503
Four-drive balance, 142–143
Four-drive theory, 134, 138–140, 158
  evaluation of, 140

four-drive balance, 142–143
  fundamental drives, 138–139
  influence on motivation, 139–140
Framing, 228, 417
Fraud, stock options and, 175
Free agency, 12–13
Freedom to speak, in brainstorming, 300
Freelance contractors, 12–13
"Freeters," 122
Friendships, stress relief and, 216
Frontline jobs, 66, 76
Functional structure
  in departmentalization, 439
  matrix structure and, 442, 443
Fundamental attribution error, 79, 570
Fun in workplace, 109
Future search events, 495, 497

G

Gainsharing plans, 171–172
Gender differences
  conflict management styles and, 380
  cross-gender communication,
      326–327
  in influence tactics, 357
  in leadership, 421, 422
  stereotyping and, 74, 75, 80
  workforce diversity and, 9
Gender equality, 503
General adaptation syndrome, 216
  alarm reaction, 199
  exhaustion, 199–200
  resistance, 199
Generation cohorts, 10, 123
Generation-X/-Y employees, 10, 11–12
  employee motivation and, 134
  psychological contracts and, 123
  workplace expectations, 170
Geographic location, values and, 9
Geographic structure, 439–441
Global issues
  centralization, 428
  change management, 496
  individualism v. collectivism, 42,
      45–46
  membership- and seniority-based
      rewards, 169, 170
  nonverbal communication, 325–326
  psychological contracts, 122
  psychological harassment, 201, 202
  telecommuting, 13
  values-based leadership, 14
  work–life balance, 11
Globalization
  competencies and, 36
  employment relationship and, 134
  global point of purchase, 440–441
  importance of values, 14–15
  organizational behavior and, 7–8, 24
  virtual teams and, 292
  work overload and, 203–204

Goal(s)
  ambiguous, 231
  effective, 147–148
  individual, 185, 215506
  relevance of, 5
  shared goals, 156
  "SMART" goals, 578
  superordinate goals, 380–381, 416
  task-oriented, 261, 264
  See also Goal setting
Goal commitment, 147
Goal feedback, 148
Goal incompatiblity
  matrix structure and, 443
  as source of conflict, 373–374, 390
Goal participation, 147–148
Goal quality, 148
Goal setting, 4, 135, 146–151, 158
  characteristics of effective goals,
      147–148
  evaluating, 151
  feedback in, 148, 149–151
  by negotiator, 387
  personal, 185, 215, 506
  role perceptions in, 146
  self-leadership and, 184, 185
  in team building, 304
"Golden handcuffs," 119
"Good guy–bad guy" contrast, 72–73
Gourami Business Challenge, 265–267
Grapevine, 331–332, 333
Grounded theory, 18, 540
Group dynamics, 4
Grouping principles, 70
Group polarization, 298–299
Groups, 258–259, 278
  formal. *See* Team(s)
  informal. *See* Informal groups
  nominal group technique, 302
Group status, in social identity, 72, 271
Groupthink, 298
Growth needs, 136
Guanxi, 355
Guerrilla recruiting, 40
Guilds, 4–5
Guolaosi, 203, 204

H

Halo effect, 81, 82
Handshakes, 325–326
Hard influence tactics, 351, 356, 357, 361
"Hard-line" negotiation, 386
Hazing, 479
Healthy lifestyle, 206, 215
Heterogeneous teams, 267
Hidden area, in Johari Window, 84
High-expectancy employees, 80
High-performance teams, 285–306
  building, 303–305
  decision making by, 286, 297–302, 306
  self-directed. *See* Self-directed work teams

team trust, 294–296, 305–306
virtual teams, 284, 286, 291–294
High power distance cultures
  influence in, 352, 357
  leadership in, 420
  legitimate power and, 344–345
  SDWTs and, 288–290
Hiring and retention
  applicant screening, 202, 474
  competency-based hiring, 407
  of creative people, 242–243
  emotional labor and, 112
  employee turnover, 177, 486, 490
  guerrilla recruiting, 40
  individual behavior and, 39–40
  knowledge acquisition and, 21
  membership- and seniority-based
    rewards, 169, 170
  organizational memory and, 23
  person–job matching and, 36
  psychological tests in, 52
  strengthening corporate culture,
    474–475
Hispanics, 8–9
"Hitchhiking," in brainstorming, 300
Holistic perspective of motivation,
  136–137, 138
Holland's six types of personalities, 56
Homogeneous teams, 267
Homogenization, in social perception, 72
Honne, 325
Hostile environments, 448–449
Hostile work environment, 201
"Hot desking," 469
Human capital, 21
Humanistic perspective of motivation,
  138, 139–140
"Human relations" school of thought, 4
Human rights, 49
Humor, in stress management, 215
Hygienes, 178
Hypercompetitive corporate culture, 142
Hypotheses, testing, 539–540

I

IAT (Implicit Association Test), 76
Idea generation, in brainstorming, 300, 301
"Ideal worker norm," 204
Identification-based trust, 295, 296
Illegal acts
  embezzlement, 48
  fraud, 175
  kickbacks, 48
  sexual harassment, 201–202
  theft, 39
  theft or sabotage, 153, 155
IM (instant messaging), 317–318
Immune system, stress and, 209
Impact, empowerment and, 183
Implementation of alternatives, 227
Implicit Association Test (IAT), 76

Implicit favorites, 232
Implicit leadership theory, 403, 418–419,
  422
Impression management, 351, 353–354
Inclusive meritocracy, 10
Incongruent organizational systems, 490,
  491
Incongruent team dynamics, 490, 491
Incremental change, 501
Incubation, in creative process, 240, 241
Independent variables, 541–542
Individual activity, in nominal groups,
  392
Individual analysis, 19
Individual behavior. See Behavior
Individual differences
  differences in trust and, 296
  equity sensitivity, 154–155
  job design and, 180
  in stress, 206–208
  in value and meaning of money, 168
Individualism, collectivism and, 42,
  45–46
Individual performance measurement,
  278
Individual rewards, 171
Individual rights, 48, 49
Inductive stage of theory building, 538
Industrial engineering, 17
Inequalities, acceptability of, 49
Inequity feelings, 153–154
Influence tactics, 351–357, 361, 600
  assertiveness, 352
  coalition formation, 352–353
  contingencies of, 355–357
  creating urgency for change, 493
  direction of influence, 356
  exchange, 351, 355
  gender differences in, 357
  hard tactics, 351, 356, 357, 361
  impression management, 353–354
  influencer's power base, 357
  information control, 351, 352, 359
  ingratiation, 353
  of leaders, 402
  organizational politics, 200, 342,
    357–360, 361, 600
  personal and cultural values, 357
  persuasion, 354–355
  silent authority, 352
  soft tactics, 351, 352, 356, 361
  types of, 351–355
  upward appeal, 353
Influencing, 5–6
Informal communication, 431, 438
Informal groups
  drive to bond and, 260–261
  nature of, 258–259
  task-oriented goals of, 261
Information
  distorted, 232, 332

emotions as, 233
evaluating, emotional markers in, 227
false, on resumes, 353–354
gained from escalation of commitment,
  236
power and, 346, 360, 385
source of decision knowledge, 239
Information access barriers, 489
Information control, 351, 352, 359
Information flow, in network structure,
  446
Information gathering, 387
Information load, 323
Information overload, 316, 323–324
Information processing, 231–232, 328
Information processing capacity, 323
Information screening, 352
Information systems, 17, 18
Information technologies
  employment relationship and, 134
  grapevine and, 332
  media richness and, 321
  network structure and, 446
  for virtual teams, 284, 291, 292
Ingratiation, 351, 353, 357
Initial offer point, 385, 387
Innate drives, 140
Innovation culture, 462
Inoculation effect, 355
Inputs, 19, 20, 154
Inquisition, 387, 388
Insight, in creativity, 240, 241
Instant messaging (IM), 317–318
Instrumentality, 577
Integrated environments, 448
Integration, as merger strategy, 470, 471
Integrator roles, 431
Integrity, leadership and, 404, 405
Intellectual capital, 21, 22, 23
Intelligence
  cognitive (IQ) or social, 114
  creativity and, 241
  emotional. See Emotional intelligence
  leadership and, 405, 406
Intensity of effort, 35, 146
Interdependence among employees
  span of control and, 433–434
  virtual team members, 293–294
  See also Task interdependence
Interdependence of open systems, 20
Interest, in active listening, 329
Internal attributions, 77–78
Internships, 40
Interpersonal processes, 304
Interpersonal relationships, 275
Interpersonal stressors, 200–202
Interpersonal styles of conflict
  management, 370, 377–380, 390
Interpretivism, 538–539, 540
Interruptions, avoiding, 328
Intervention, in action research, 501

Introversion, 53, 54
Intuition, making choices and, 233–234
Inventive thinking style, 242
Investigative personality, 56

J

Jargon, 323
Job burnout, 196
   stress and, 209–210
   workaholism and, 208
Job characteristics model, 178–179,
      183, 188
Job design, 168, 176–182, 188
   core job characteristics, 179
   critical psychological states, 179
   individual differences, 180
   job enlargement, 180–181, 287
   job enrichment, 181–182, 278, 287
   job rotation, 180
   scientific management, 177–178
   strategies in, 180–182
   work efficiency and, 176–178
   work motivation and, 178–180
Job enlargement, 180–181, 287
Job enrichment, 181–182, 278, 287
Job evaluation, 170
Job feedback, 179
Job redesign, 36–37
Job rotation, 180
Job satisfaction, 39–40, 115–118, 123
   customer satisfaction and, 118
   emotion and, 115–118, 574
   performance and, 117–118
   work behavior and, 116–117
Job sharing, 213
Job specialization, 188
   scientific management and, 177–178
   work efficiency and, 176–177
Job status-based rewards, 169, 170, 188
Johari Window, 83–84, 93, 505
Joint optimization, 287, 288
Judging/perceiving, 54
Judgments, attitudes as, 106
Justice, 579
   equity theory. *See* Distributive justice
   organizational. *See* Organizational
      justice
   organizational commitment and, 120
   procedural, 152, 156–157, 159
   social rules of, 157
   structural rules of, 156–157
"Just-in-time" personal development, 150

K

Karoshi, 203, 204
Key variances, 287
Kickbacks, 48
Knowledge acquisition, 21–22
Knowledge-based trust, 295–296
Knowledge-based work, 291
Knowledge control, 347

Knowledge/experience
   business knowledge, 405, 406
   creativity and, 242
   decision knowledge, 239
   expert power and, 345
   explicit knowledge, 85
   persuasion and, 354
   "silos of knowledge" problem, 314, 441
   tacit knowledge, 85, 89, 234
Knowledge management, 21–23, 24
   communication in, 314
   organizational memory and, 22–23
   processes, 21–22
   virtual teams and, 292
Knowledge of skills, 179
Knowledge sharing, 22
Knowledge use, 22

L

Laboratory experiments
   advantages of, 542–543
   disadvantages of, 543
   variables in, 541
Labor control, substitutability and,
      347–348
Labor unions
   formalized structure and, 436
   power of, 347–348, 349
   resistance to SDWTs, 290–291
"Lagging indicators," 88
Language barriers, 322–323
Lateral influence, 356
Layoffs, employee loyalty and, 120
Leader(s)
   changing organizational culture and,
      472, 473
   influence tactics of, 402
   transformational, 499
   work environments arranged by, 402
Leaderful organization, 402–403
Leader–member relations, 413
Leadership, 401–422
   behavioral perspective of, 403, 404,
      407–408
   competency perspective of, 403,
      404–407, 421
   contingency theories of, 403, 404, 408,
      412–414, 421–422
   cross-cultural issues in, 420
   decisive, 230
   developing through action
      learning, 92
   ethics and, 51
   Fiedler's leadership model, 412–413
   gender differences in, 421, 422
   implicit leadership perspective, 403,
      418–419
   leadership substitutes, 413–414
   nature of, 402–403
   organizational behavior and, 4

path-goal theory of, 408–411, 413,
      421–422
   perspectives of, 403–404
   shared, 402–403
   situational leadership theory, 412
   team effectiveness and, 263
   of teams, 271, 272
   transformational. *See* Transformational
      leadership
   values and, 14, 43
   See also Self-leadership; *specific leadership
      styles*
Leadership development, 400
Leadership emergence, 404–405
Leadership motivation, 404, 405, 406
Leadership substitutes, 413–414
Leadership teams, 259
"Leading indicators," 88
Lean manufacturing, 263, 289
Lean media, 321
Learned capabilities, 36
Learned needs theory, 134, 140–141, 158
Learning, 85, 93
   action learning, 91–92, 495
   behavior modification and, 86–88
   experiential learning, 85, 90–92, 93
   from external environments, 21–22
   of organizational socialization, 476
   parallel learning structures, 503–504
   in reducing restraining forces,
      493–494, 495
   social learning theory. *See* Social
      learning theory
   vicarious learning, 89–90
Learning drive, 138, 139
Learning organizations, 21
Learning orientation, 90
   creativity and, 243
   empowerment and, 183
   formalized structure and, 436
"Leaving the field," 154
Legends, 464
Legitimate power, 343, 344–345
Lewin's force field analysis model,
      488–491, 498, 504, 507
   driving forces, 488–489, 492
   restraining forces, 489–491
"Liability of newness," 437
Life cycle theory of leadership, 412
"Lighthouse structure," 428
Location, negotiations and, 386
Locus of control, 54, 55, 183
   leadership style and, 411
   organizational politics and, 358, 360
Logical reasoning, 108, 234–235
Logical reasons for values, 43
Loyalty, job satisfaction and, 117

M

Machiavellianism, 39
Machiavellian values, 360, 361

Maintaining interest, 328
Management by walking around
    (MBWA), 331
Management resistance to SDWTs, 290
Manifest conflict, 370, 371
Marketing, relevance to OB, 17, 18
MARS model of individual behavior,
    34–37, 57, 106, 499
    ability, 36–37
    employee motivation, 34, 35,
        134, 173
    learning and, 85
    role perceptions, 37
    situational factors, 37
Maslow's needs hierarchy theory,
    135–138
    hierarchy of needs, 135–136
    motivation theories and, 136–138
Matrix structure, 441–444, 451
Maximization, 232
MBWA (management by walking
    around), 331
MCEI (Merging Cultures Evaluation
    Index), 470
Meaning, empowerment and, 183
Meaningful interaction, 76
Mechanistic structures, 436–437, 448, 451
Media-rich channels, 431
Media richness theory
    in communication, 319–321
    evaluating, 321
    persuasion and, 355
Mediation, 387, 388, 389
Mediators, 390
Medium, meaning of, 321–322
Medium-as-message principle, 321
Member interaction/similarity,
    in teams, 274
Membership based financial rewards,
    168–170, 188
Mental imagery, 185–186, 187, 582
Mental models
    corporate culture and, 467
    departmentalization and, 438
    in perceptual organization, 70–71, 92
    in problem identification, 228, 229, 230
Mentoring, 89, 212, 350, 506
Mergers and acquisitions, 460, 468–471,
    479
    bicultural audit, 469–470
    conflict due to ambiguous rules, 375
    conflict due to differentiation, 374
    cultural dynamics and, 458
    strategies for, 470–471
Merger strategies
    assimilation, 470–471
    deculturation, 470, 471
    integration, 470, 471
    separation, 470, 471
Merging Cultures Evaluation Index
    (MCEI), 470

Message
    clarifying, 329
    communicating effectively, 327, 333
    content of, 355
    media richness and, 320
Metaphors, 417
Micro-network structure, 428
Middle managers, 434
Mimicry, 318–319
Mindfulness of values, 43
Mistakes, learning and, 91
Modeling. See Behavioral modeling
Models. See specific models
Monitoring of employee behavior, 134
Moods, 104
Moral intensity, 49–50
Morphological analysis, 243–244
Motivation, 133–159
    challenges in, 134–135
    creativity and, 243
    expectancy theory of, 134, 143–146,
        158, 408
    feedback and. See Feedback
    goal setting. See Goal setting
    leadership motivation, 404, 405, 406
    needs and drives, 135–143
    organizational justice and, 152–158
    praise and recognition, 132
    social loafing and, 278
    in team environment, 260
    in work attendance, 40–41
    See also Employee motivation; Work
        motivation
Motivational potential of jobs, 177–178,
    179
Motivator(s), 178
Motivator-hygiene theory, 178
Multiculturalism, 48
Multidisciplinary anchor of OB, 17–18
Multiple levels of analysis, in OB, 19
Multiskilling, 180
Multisource (360°) feedback, 149–150,
    174, 297, 345, 578
Munificent environments, 448–449
Mutinies, 344
Myers-Briggs Type Indicator (MBTI), 34,
    53–54, 57, 233
"Mythical man-month," 277

N

nAch (need for achievement), 141
nAff (need for affiliation), 141
Natural grouping approach to job
    enrichment, 181, 182
Natural rewards, 186
Need for achievement (nAch), 141
Need for affiliation (nAff), 141
Need for communication, 314
Need for power (nPow), 141
Need for understanding, 73
Need principle, 152, 157

Needs and drives, 135–143
    four-drive theory. See Four-drive theory
Maslow's theory, 135–138
    practical implications of theories,
        142–143
    problems with needs hierarchies, 138
    theory of learned needs, 134, 140–141,
        158
Needs and values, 505
Needs hierarchy theories, 134, 158
    learning needs, 141
    Maslow's theory, 135–138
    practical implications of, 142–143
    problems with, 138
    theory of learned needs, 134, 140–141
Negative emotional traits, 110
Negative impressions, 82
Negative mood, 233
Negative reinforcement, 87
Negative self-talk, 185
Negative valence, 144
Neglect, job satisfaction and, 117
"Neglect" behaviors, 358
Negotiation
    bargaining zone model, 385
    in conflict management, 384–387, 391
    in exchange, 355
    negotiator behaviors, 387
    in reducing restraining forces, 494, 497
    situational influences, 386
Networking, 350, 361, 506
Network structure, 446–447
Neuroscience, 18
Neuroticism, 52, 53
Noise. See Barriers to communication
Nominal group technique, 302
Nonprogrammed decisions, 226, 239
Nonroutine situations, 320–321
Nonsocial sources of feedback, 149, 150
Nonverbal communication, 315, 318–319,
    333
    in brainstorming, 301
    cultural differences in, 325–326
    gender and, 326
Normative commitment, 575
Norming stage, 268, 269
Norms
    cultural, 111, 112, 324–325
    dysfunctional, 271–272
    emotional display norms, 111, 112
    enforcing, 270–271
    "ideal worker norm," 204
    reciprocity, 355
    regarding voice loudness, 324–325
    team norms. See Team norms
nPow (need for power), 141

O

OB. See Organizational behavior
Obeya, 262
Object, in selective attention, 69

Observation, learning by, 89–90
Observational research, 544
"Offshoring," 8
Omitting strategy, 323–324
Open area, in Johari Window, 84
Openness to change, 42, 43
Openness to experience, 53
Open systems, 19–20, 24, 500
Operant conditioning, 86
Opportunities
    evaluating, 232
    identifying, 227–230
Organic structures, 436–437, 448, 451
Organizational behavior (OB), 3–24
    anchors of, 16–20, 24
    choosing alternatives and, 231
    contingency anchor, 18–19
    employment relationships, 11–13
    as field of study, 4–6
    globalization and, 7–8
    knowledge management and, 21–23, 24
    multidisciplinary anchor, 17–18
    multiple levels of analysis, 19
    open systems, 19–20
    personality and, 51–52
    positive, 81, 137–138, 502
    systematic research, 18
    trends in, 7–16, 24
    values and ethics, 14–16
    virtual work, 13–14
    workforce diversity, 8–10
Organizational change, 487–507
    action research approach, 500–502
    appreciative inquiry approach,
        502–503
    change agents, 414, 499
    creating urgency for, 492–493
    cross-cultural issues in, 504
    diffusion of, 499–500
    ethical issues in, 504–505, 507
    force field analysis model, 488–491,
        489, 504, 507
    parallel learning structure approach,
        503–504
    personal change and, 505–506
    reducing restraining forces on, 493–497
    resistance to. See Resistance to change
    strategic vision and, 498–499
    structural approach to, 486
    unfreezing, changing, and refreezing,
        489, 491–498
Organizational citizenship, 38–39
    psychological contracts and, 122
    transformational leadership and, 418
Organizational commitment, 119–120
Organizational comprehension, 120
Organizational crisis, 435
Organizational culture, 459–479, 609
    adaptive, 467–468
    artifacts of. See Artifacts
    bicultural audit, 469–470

BSC strategy and, 173
    campus model, 2
    centralized/decentralized, 486
    changing. See Changing organizational
        culture
    contingencies, 435, 466–467
    as control system, 466
    countercultures, 463
    cultural dynamics and, 458
    elements of, 460–463
    ethics and, 2, 51, 468, 469
    experiential learning in, 22
    hypercompetitive, 142
    importance of, 466–468
    merging cultures, 468–471
    organizational socialization, 475,
        476–479
    positive expectations and, 81
    shared assumptions of, 461, 609
    strong/weak, 466, 479
    subcultures, 463, 467, 479
    See also Culture
Organizational diagnosis, 501
Organizational environment
    creativity and, 242–243
    mechanistic v. organic structure, 437
    stressors in, 204
    team effectiveness and, 262, 277
    for virtual teams, 293–294
Organizational hierarchies
    communication in, 329–331, 333
    formal, 431, 432
    in larger organizations, 449
    size of, factors in, 434, 435
Organizational justice, 39, 135, 152–158
    distributive justice (equity theory),
        152–156
    in practice, 157–158
    procedural justice, 156–157
Organizational language, 465
Organizational learning, 21
Organizational memory, 22–23
Organizational politics, 342, 357–360,
        361, 600
    consequences of, 359, 360
    interpersonal stress and, 200
    minimizing, 360
    supporting conditions, 358, 360
Organizational rewards, 172–174
Organizational socialization, 475, 476–479
    improving process of, 478–479
    stages of, 476–478
Organizational strategy
    balanced scorecard strategy, 172–173
    cost leadership strategy, 450–451
    differentiation strategy, 450, 451
    for mergers, 470–471
    strategies in job design, 180–182
    structure and, 450–451

Organizational structure, 429–451
    centralization/decentralization in,
        434–435
    contingencies of, 435, 448–451
    coordinating work activities in,
        431–433
    departmentalization. See
        Departmentalization
    division of labor in, 430–431
    elements of, 433–437
    external environment and, 448–449
    formal hierarchy, 431, 432
    formalization, 435–436, 444
    informal communication, 431
    mechanistic v. organic structures,
        436–437
    organizational strategy and, 450–451
    organization size and, 449
    refreezing and, 498
    span of control in, 433–434
    standardization, 431, 432–433
    team effectiveness and, 263
    technology and, 449–450
Organizational values, 41
Organization analysis, 19
Organizations, 24
    financial health of, 6
    nature of, 4–5
Organization size, structure and, 449, 451
Outcome/input ratio
    equity sensitivity and, 154–155
    in equity theory, 152–153
Outcomes
    of conflict process, 371–373
    escalation of commitment, 235–236
    evaluating, 235–237
    increasing, 154
Outcome valences (V)
    increasing, 145–146
    model of, 143, 144
Outputs, 19, 20
Overreward inequity, 153
Overt acts, 39, 48
Overtime, 203–204
Overwork, 196, 198

P

Parallel learning structures, 503–504
"Paralysis by analysis," 468
Parental status, influence of, 10
Participant observation, 544
Participative leadership style, 409, 411, 421
Participative management. See Employee
    involvement
Passive noncompliance, 490
Path-goal leadership theory, 408–411,
        421–422
    contingencies of, 410–411
    implications and limitations, 410, 411
    leadership styles, 408–409
    leadership substitutes, 413

"Pay for pulse," 168–170
Peer pressure, 270–271, 345
Peers
  co-workers as socialization agents, 479
  feedback from, 150
  instruction from co-workers, 413–414
Peer-to-peer recognition, 132, 148
People-oriented leadership style,
    407–408, 409
Perceiver, 69
Perception(s), 67–93
  attribution theory, 77–79
  as barrier to communication, 322
  of differentiation, conflict and, 370, 371,
    382
  of disempowerment, 436
  distortion, 235
  errors, 81–82
  improving, 83–84
  learning and. See Learning
  organization and interpretation,
    69–71
  perceived inequities, 153–154
  perceptual process, 68–71
  P-to-O expectancies, 143, 144, 145, 173
  role perceptions, 34, 37, 85, 146
  selective attention, 69
  self-fulfilling prophecy, 79–81
  social identity theory, 71–73
  stereotyping. See Stereotyping
Perceptual blinders, 236
Perceptual defense, 228
Perceptual errors, 81–82, 93
Perceptual interpretation, 107
Perceptual organization, 69–71, 92
Perceptual process, 68–71
  organization and interpretation, 69–71
  selective attention, 69
  stress perceptions, 215
Performance
  E-to-P expectancies, 143–145, 147
  job satisfaction and, 117–118
  P-to-O expectancies, 143, 144, 145, 173
  rewards linked to, 174
  task performance, 38, 261, 275, 276
  See also Applied performance
    practices; High-performance teams
Performance-based reward systems, 145,
    166, 188
  financial rewards, 169, 171–174
  individual rewards, 171
  as leadership substitute, 413
  organizational rewards, 172–174
  team rewards, 171–172
Performance measurement, 171, 174, 278
Performance-oriented organizational
    culture, 462, 473
Performance-to-outcome (P-to-O)
    expectancy
  increasing, 145
  low, employee motivation and, 173

model of, 143, 144
  path-goal leadership theory and, 408
Performing stage, 269, 270
Permanent work teams, 257, 258
Persistence, creativity and, 241, 242
Persistence of effort, 35, 146
Personal accomplishment, 210
Personal change, 507
  competencies, 505–506
  mentoring, 506
  needs and values, 505
  networking, 506
Personal characteristics
  leadership and, 404
  organizational politics and, 358, 360
Personal goal setting, 185, 215, 506
Personal identity, 72
Personality, 34, 51–57
  Big Five dimensions of, 52–53
  competency perspective and,
    404–406
  emotions and, 110
  five-factor model of, 34
  Holland's six types, 56
  leadership emergence and, 404–405
  leadership style and, 413
  locus of control, 54, 55
  Myers-Briggs Type Indicator, 53–54
  organizational behavior and, 51–52
  resilience and, 208
  self-monitoring, 54, 55
  team roles and, 272, 273
  vocational choice and, 55–57
Personalized power, 141, 359
Personal leave, 213
"Personal Pursuits" initiative, 212
Personal values, 14, 41, 43, 357
Personal wealth, influence of, 10
Person–job matching, 36–37
Person–organization values
    congruence, 44
Perspective(s)
  developing multiple perspectives, 70
  holistic, 136–137, 138
  humanistic, 138, 139–140
  of leadership. See Leadership
  single-factor perspective, 573
Perspective taking, 83
Persuasion, 351, 354–355
Physical environment stressors, 204
Physical space
  communication and, 329–330
  influence on negotiations, 386
  refreezing and, 329–330
  team effectiveness and, 262, 263
  team environment and, 289
Physiological effects of distress, 209, 216
  bad bosses and, 200–201
  general adaptation syndrome, 199–200
Physiological needs, 135, 136
"Piggybacking," 300

Pilot projects, 499–500, 507
Podcasting, 317
Political science, OB and, 17
Pooled interdependence, 264–265,
    375, 383
Position power, 413
Positive emotions, 102
Positive expectations, 81
Positive organizational behavior, 81,
    137–138, 502
Positive psychology, 81, 137, 502
Positive reinforcement, 87
Positive self-talk, 185
Positive valence, 144
Positivism, 538
Postdecisional justification, 235, 244, 477
Power, 341–361
  abuse of, 340, 358, 359, 360
  contingencies of. See Contingencies of
    power
  dependence and, 342, 343
  influence and. See Influence tactics
  of labor unions, 347–348, 349
  meaning of power, 342–343
  model of power, 343
  need for power (nPow), 141
  shifting, change and, 504
  socialized power, 141, 406
  sources of. See Sources of power
  symbols as power cues, 349–350
Power base, 357
Power distance, 46–47
  legitimate power and, 344–345
  meaning and value of money and, 168
  See also High power distance cultures
Practice, 115
Praise, 132
Predictability, 295–296
Predicting, 5–6
Preemployment socialization, 176, 177
Prejudice, 75
Preparation, 240, 387
Pressure to conform, 297
Prevention of environmental changes, 346
Primacy effect, 81, 82
Privacy concerns, in research, 504
Proactive drives, 138, 139
Problem identification, 226, 227–230, 244
  difficulties with, 228–230
  effective, 230
  missed opportunities, 229
Problem orientation, of research, 501–502
Problem redefinition, 243
Problem solving, 304
Problem-solving style
  negotiation, 384–385
  win–win orientation, 378, 379
Procedural justice, 152, 158
  consequences of, 157
  social rules of, 157
  structural rules of, 156–157

Process losses, 276–277
Production blocking, 297, 300
Production teams, 259
Productivity, applying STS theory and, 288
Product/service structure, 439, 440
Profit-sharing plans, 172, 173–174
Programmed decisions, 226, 239
Project GLOBE (Global Leadership and Organizational Behavior Effectiveness), 420, 606
Projection bias, 81, 82
Propensity to trust, 296
Prospect theory effect, 236
Psychological characteristics, 9
Psychological contracts, 121–123, 124
    cultural and generational factors, 122–123
    organizational commitment and, 120
    organizational socialization and, 478
    types of, 121–122
Psychological effects of distress, 196, 200, 209–210, 216
Psychological harassment, 201–202
Psychological tests
    CD-RISC, 221
    in hiring and retention, 52
    Implicit Association Test (IAT), 76
    Myers-Briggs Type Indicator (MBTI), 34, 53–54, 57, 233
Psychology
    critical psychological states, 179
    positive psychology, 81, 137, 502
    relevance to OB, 17, 18
P-to-O (performance-to-outcome) expectancies, 143, 144, 145, 173
"Pulse surveys," 330
Punishments, 87, 571–572

Q

Qi Gong, 215
Quantum change, 501
Quid pro quo sexual harassment, 201

R

Radical "behaviorist" philosophy, 88
Random sampling, 541
"Rapport talk," 326
Rational choice paradigm, 226–227, 230, 231
Realistic job preview (RJP), 478, 479
Realistic personality, 56
Reality, perceptual process and, 68–69
Recency effect, 81, 82
Reciprocal interdependence, 264, 265, 375, 383
Reduced personal accomplishment, 210
Reduced professional efficacy, 210
Referent power, 343, 345
Reflective observation, 90
Refreezing, 489, 498

Reinforcement, 85
    contingencies of, 86–87
    feedback as, 148
    schedules of, 87–88
    self-reinforcement, 89–90, 186, 215
Reinforcement theory, 86
Relational contracts, 121, 122
Relationship capital, 21
Relationship conflict, 372–373
Relationship management, 114
Relaxation/meditation, 215
Relevant goals, 147
Relevant rewards, 174
Religion, influence of, 9
Repetition, 327
Repetitive work, 180
"Report talk," 326
Representative sampling, 540–541
Research
    action research, 500–502, 504, 507
    leadership as topic of, 403
    in organizational culture, 463, 464
    privacy concerns in, 504
    problem orientation of, 501–502
    systematic, 18, 540
Research design, 540–544
    causation in, 541–542
    ethics in, 542
    field surveys, 543–544
    laboratory experiments, 542–543
    observational research, 544
    sampling in, 540–541
    strategies for, 542–544
    theory building and. See Theory building
Resilience
    social support and, 216
    stress and, 207–208
Resistance
    in bargaining zone model, 385, 387
    in general adaptation syndrome, 199
    to influence tactics, 355
    to SDWTs, 290–291
Resistance to change, 78, 489–491, 507
    future search meetings and, 497
    kinds of, 489–490
    reasons for, 490, 491
    sources of, 492
Resources
    allocation of, 358
    control of, 342
    creativity and, 243
    increasing, 383
    optimal use of, 442
    scarce, conflict and, 375
Respect, 157
Responding, 329
Responsibility, in STS theory, 287
Restraining forces, 489–491, 507
    coercion, 494, 497
    communication and, 493–494

    employee involvement, 494, 495–497
    learning, 493–494, 495
    negotiation, 494, 497
    reducing, 493–497
    stress management, 494, 497
Restricted entry, 274
Revenue growth, diversity and, 10
Reward(s), 4
    culturally consistent, 472, 473–474
    directive leadership style, 409
    employee choice of, 142–143
    monetary. See Financial reward practices
    natural, 186
    over- or underreward inequity, 153
    self-leadership and, 186, 187
    team-level, 171–172, 287
    See also Performance-based reward systems
Reward effectiveness, 174–176, 188
    linking to performance, 174
    relevance of reward, 174
    team rewards, 174–175, 287
    unintended consequences, 175–176
    value of reward, 175
"Reward inflation," 88
Reward power, 343, 345
Reward systems
    in change initiatives, 498
    team effectiveness and, 262, 272
    See also Performance-based reward systems
Risk of conflict, 240
Risky decisions, 299
Rituals, 464–465
RJP (realistic job preview), 478, 479
Role ambiguity, 202–203
Role behavior conflict, 205
Role conflict, 202–203
Role definition, 304
Role management, 476, 478
Role perceptions
    in goal setting, 146
    learning and, 85
    in MARS model, 34, 37
Role-related stressors, 202–204
    role ambiguity, 202–203
    role behavior conflict, 205
    role conflict, 202
    work overload, 203–204
Roles
    integrator roles, 431
    team roles, 272, 273
    team role theory, 272, 273
Rules and procedures
    ambiguous rules, 375–377
    clarification of, 384
    in mechanistic structure, 436
    rules of justice, 156–157
    rules-oriented cultures, 462
    work-to-rule strikes, 436

S

Sabbaticals, paid, 214
Safety needs, 135, 136
Sample size, 541
Sampling, 540–541
Sampling bias, 540–541
Sarbanes-Oxley Act of 2002, 48
Satisficing, 232
Saving face, 490, 491, 504
Scenario planning, 235
Scientific management, 177–178
Scientific method, 18, 540
SDWTs. *See* Self-directed work teams
Selective attention, 69, 70, 92, 228
Self-actualization, 135–136
Self-awareness, 114
Self-categorization theory, 569
Self-confidence, 405, 406
Self-determination, empowerment and, 183
Self-directed work teams (SDWTs), 259, 286–291, 305
    challenges to, 288–291
    in lean manufacturing, 289
    optimal span of control and, 433
    shared leadership, 402–403
    sociotechnical systems theory and, 287–288
    team-based structure and, 444, 445
Self-enhancement, 42, 43
Self-fulfilling prophecy, 79–81, 92–93
    contingencies of, 80–81
    steps in, 80
Self-interest, equity theory and, 156
Self-justification, 236
Self-leadership, 168, 184–187, 188, 402
    constructive thought patterns, 185–186
    as leadership substitute, 414
    natural rewards, 186
    personal goal setting, 185
    in practice, 186–187
    self-monitoring, 186
    self-reinforcement, 186
    stress perceptions and, 215
Self-management, 114, 184
Self-monitoring, 54, 55, 186
Self-perception, 73–74
Self-reinforcement, 89–90, 186, 215
Self-serving bias, 79
Self-talk, 185
Self-transcendence, 42, 43
Seniority-based financial rewards, 168–170, 188
Sense making, 466
Sensing, in active listening, 327–328
Sensing/intuition, 54
Separation, as merger strategy, 470, 471
Sequential interdependence, 264, 265, 375, 383

Servant leadership, 408
Service industries, contingent work in, 12–13
Service teams, 259
Sexual harassment, 201–202
Shared assumptions, 461, 609
Shared leadership, 402–403
Shared values, 14, 41
    organizational commitment and, 120
    organizational culture and, 460, 461, 462
"Shock events," 40, 116
Sick leave, 41
Silence, 326
Silent authority, 351, 352
"Silos of knowledge" problem, 314, 441
Simple environments, 448
Simple structure, 438
Simulations, in learning, 91
Single-factor perspective, 573
Situational control, 412–413, 419
Situational factors
    in conflict management, 379–380
    in employee involvement, 239–240
    in ethical behavior, 50
    leadership style and, 408
    in MARS model, 34, 37
    in negotiation, 386
    in relevance of rewards, 174
    in third-party conflict resolution, 389
    in values, 44
Situational leadership theory (SLT), 412, 422
Situation favorableness, 413
Skill-based pay, 171
Skill variety, 179
Skunkworks teams, 257, 258, 259
SLT (situational leadership theory), 412, 422
"SMART" goals, 578
Smoothing, 340
Social awareness, 114
Social capital, 350
Social change, anticipating, 346
Social desirability of values, 42
Social fulfillment, 12
"Social glue," 466, 479
Social identity(ies), 71
    drive to bond and, 139
    group status and, 72, 271
    stereotyping and, 73–74
    team cohesiveness and, 272, 273
Social identity theory, 71–73, 261
Social intelligence, 114
Social isolation, virtual work and, 13
Socialization, conflict reduction and, 381
Socialization agents, 478–479
Socialized power, 141, 406
Social learning, 85
Social learning theory, 93
    behavior modeling, 89, 144–145

learning behavior consequences, 89
    self-leadership and, 184
    self-reinforcement, 89–90
Social loafing, 277–278, 279
Social perception, 72–73
Social personality, 56
Social prescriptions, 464, 474
Social rules of justice, 157
Social sources of feedback, 149, 150–151
Social support, 215–216, 274, 414
Social welfare, 303
Socioemotional conflict, 372–373, 390
Sociology, OB and, 17–18
Sociotechnical systems (STS) theory, 286, 287–288, 305
    applications of, 288, 289
    autonomy, 287
    control over key variances, 287
    joint optimization, 288
    responsibility, 287
Soft influence tactics, 351, 352, 356, 361
Solution-focused problems, 230
Solutions, developing, 226
Sources of conflict, 373–377
    ambiguous rules, 375–377
    communication problems, 377
    differentiation, 374–375
    incompatible goals, 373–374
    resource scarcity, 375
    task interdependence, 375
Sources of power, 343–346, 360
    coercive power, 345, 349
    expert power, 345
    information as, 346, 360, 385
    legitimate power, 344–345
    referent power, 345
    reward power, 343, 345
Span of control, 433–434, 451
Specific feedback, 148
Specific goals, 147
Stabilization of change, 501
Stable environments, 448
Stakeholder framing, 228
Stakeholders, 15, 20
Standardization, 431, 432–433, 439
Standardized outputs, 432
Standardized processes, 432
Standardized skills, 432–433
Statistical association between variables, 542
Status
    electronic communication and, 316
    group status, 72, 271
    influence of parental status, 10
    job status-based rewards, 169, 170, 188
    within teams, 271
Stereotyping, 73–76, 92
    conflict and, 377, 382
    female leadership styles, 421
    gender and, 74, 75, 80

Stereotyping—*Cont.*
in implicit leadership theory, 419
minimizing bias from, 75–76
perceptions of leadership and, 406
problems with, 74–75
reasons for, 73–74
Stock options, 172, 173–174, 175
"Stop-loss order," 237
Stories, 417
role of, 464, 474
Storming stage, 268, 269
Strain-based conflict, 205
Strategic business units, 439, 440
Strategic vision, 418, 430
in change management, 498–499
communicating, 417
organizational change and, 498–499
transformational leadership and,
416–418
Strategy. *See* Organizational strategy
Stress, 34–35, 197–216
caused by information overload, 323
coping strategies, 206–207, 213–214,
228, 346
CWBs and, 39
effects of distress. *See* Distress
eustress, 198–199
general adaptation syndrome, 199–200
handling. *See* Stress management
individual differences in, 206–208
informal groups and, 261
managing. *See* Stress management
nature of, 198–200
occupation and, 206
overwork, 196, 198
physiological effects of, 199–201, 209
psychological effects of, 196, 200,
209–210
reasons for, 206–207
resilience and, 207–208
SDWTs and, 291
stressors. *See* Stressors
women's responses to, 215–216
workaholism and, 208
work–life balance and, 212
Stress index, 211
Stress management, 210–216
changing stress perceptions, 215
controlling effects of stress, 215
reducing restraining forces and, 494,
497
removing stressor, 211–213
social support and, 215–216
withdrawal from stressor, 213–214
Stressors, 200–205, 216
ambiguity as, 445
employee control over, 212
interpersonal, 200–202
job burnout, 209–210
occupations and, 204–205
organizational and physical

environment, 204
psychological and sexual harassment,
201–202
role-related, 202–204, 205
strain-based conflict, 205
task control, 204
time-based conflict, 204–205
work–nonwork, 204–205
workplace violence, 201
Stretch goals, 147
Strikes, 348, 349, 436, 490
Strong organizational culture, 466, 479
Structural approaches to conflict
management, 380–384, 390–391
clarifying rules and procedures, 384
communication and understanding,
382–383
increasing resources, 383
reducing differentiation, 381
reducing task interdependence, 383
superordinate goals, 380–381
Structural approach to change, 486
Structural approach to organizational
change, 486
Structural capital, 21, 23
Structural rules of justice, 156–157
Structures (buildings), 465
STS theory. *See* Sociotechnical systems
theory
Subcultures, 463, 467, 479
Subjective expected utility, 227
Substitutability, 347–348, 349
Sufficiently frequent feedback, 148
Summarizing strategy, 323–324
Superordinate goals, 380–381, 416
Supportive leadership style, 409, 410,
411, 413
Support of employees, 120
Surface acting, 112
Surface-level diversity, 8–9, 10, 267
Surveys
employee surveys, 32–33, 330
of job satisfaction, 115–116
Swift trust, 296
Symbolic meaning, 321–322
Symbols, 349–350, 465
Systematic research, 18, 540
Systemic discrimination, 75

T

Tacit knowledge, 85, 89, 234
Talking circles, 383
Tall structures, 434, 435
Target point, 385, 387
Task(s)
ideal for teams, 276
nature of, span of control and, 433
virtual team tasks, 293–294
Task characteristics, 263, 264–265
Task control, 347
Task control stressors, 204

Task force teams, 259, 271
Task identity, 179
Task interdependence
in self-directed work teams, 286
as source of conflict, 375, 383
team design and, 264–265
Task-oriented goals, 261, 264
Task-oriented leadership style, 407–408
Task performance, 38, 261, 275, 276
Task-related conflict, 372
Task significance, 179
Task specialization, 278
Task structure, 411, 413
Tatemae, 325
Team(s), 256, 257–279
"Brooks's law," 277
cross-functional, 444, 496
departmental teams, 259
design of. *See* Team design
diversity in, 265–267, 274
environment, 262–263
groups and, 258–261
heterogeneous/homogeneous, 267
high-performance. *See* High-
performance teams
in matrix structure, 442, 443
membership in, 260–261
problems with, 276–278, 279
processes. *See* Team processes
process losses, 276–277
reliance on, 259–260
skunkworks, 257, 258, 259
social loafing, 277–278
team effectiveness model, 261, 262
Team activity, 392
Team analysis, 19
Team-based bonus systems, 166
Team-based structure, 444–445, 451
Team building, 286, 303–305, 306
effectiveness of, 305
training programs, 284
types of, 304
volunteering and, 303
Team-building exercises, 303
Team cohesiveness, 272–275, 278–279
consequences of, 275
influences on, 273–274
socioemotional conflict and, 373
task performance and, 275, 276
Team composition, 263, 265–267
Team design, 263–267, 278
diversity in, 266, 267, 274
task characteristics, 264–265
team composition, 265–267
team size, 265
Team development, 278
five-stage model of, 268–270
organic structure and, 437
Team dynamics
incongruent, 490, 491
leadership style and, 411

Team effectiveness, 278
　　leadership and, 263
　　model of, 261, 262
　　norms and, 271
　　organizational environment and, 262, 277
　　organizational structure and, 263
　　physical space and, 262, 263
　　reward systems and, 262, 272
　　team size and, 265
Team mental models, 304
Team norms, 270–272
　　conformity to, 270–271, 275, 276
　　decision making and, 299
　　developing, 271
　　dysfunctional, changing, 271–272
　　as leadership substitute, 414
　　organizational politics and, 360
　　supportive, 373
　　work attendance and, 41
Team processes, 268–275
　　cohesiveness, 272–275
　　development, 268–270
　　norms. See Team norms
　　roles, 272, 273
Team rewards, 174–175, 287
Team size
　　decision making and, 277
　　social loafing and, 277
　　team cohesiveness and, 274
　　team design and, 263, 265
　　virtual teams, 294
Team success, 274
Team trust
　　dynamics of, 296
　　foundations of, 295
　　in high-performance teams, 294–296, 305–306
　　individual differences in, 296
　　team building, 304
　　See also Trust
Teamwork, 200
Technology, 19
　　organizational structure and, 449–450, 451
　　strain-based conflict and, 205
　　work overload and, 203–204
Telecommuting (teleworking), 13, 213
Temporary employees, 121
Temporary staffing agencies, 12
Temporary work teams, 257, 258
"Tend and befriend" response, 215–216
Theft, 39
Theory(ies), 538
Theory building, 538–540
　　grounded theory, 540
　　positivism v. interpretivism, 538–539
　　research design and. See Research design
　　using scientific method, 540

Theory testing, 538, 539–540
　　defining and measuring constructs, 539
　　testing hypotheses, 539–540
Thinking/feeling, 54
"Thin-slice" studies, 70
Third-party conflict resolution, 391
　　alternative dispute resolution, 389–390
　　choosing best strategy, 388–390
　　kinds of, 387–388
"13th month" bonus, 169
Threats, 39, 352
360° annual reviews, 213
360° (multisource) feedback, 149–150, 174, 297, 345, 578
Time-based conflict, 204–205
Time constraints, 297
Time passage, 386
Timing, in communication, 327
Tolerance for ambiguity, 47, 230
"Top-down selection," 569
"Town hall meetings," 331
Training
　　in diversity awareness, 75–76
　　drum circles, 382
　　on emotion, 113
　　on emotional intelligence, 114–115
　　ethics programs, 50–51
　　in person–job matching, 36
　　quality management training, 32
　　in standardized skills, 432–433
Training programs
　　achievement motivation program, 141
　　power of positive expectations, 81
　　in procedural justice, 158
　　team-building events, 284
Transactional contracts, 121
Transactional leadership, 414, 499
Transformational leadership, 403, 404, 414–418, 422
　　building commitment, 418
　　change agents, 499
　　charismatic leadership compared, 415–416
　　communicating vision, 417
　　corporate culture and, 473
　　creating strategic vision, 416–418
　　example of, 415
　　modeling vision, 417–418
　　transactional leadership compared, 414
Trend spotters, 346
"Triggers," emotions as, 105
Triple bottom line, 15
Trust
　　building, in transformational leadership, 417–418
　　in conflict resolution, 384
　　organizational commitment and, 120
　　See also Team trust
Type A behavior pattern, 208

U
Ubuntu values, 420
Uncertainties, coping with, 346
Uncertainty avoidance, 47
Underreward inequity, 153
Understanding, 5–6
　　in communication, 314
　　conflict management and, 382–383
Unfreezing, changing, and refreezing, 489, 491–498, 504–505, 507
　　creating urgency, 492–493
　　reducing restraining forces, 493–497
　　refreezing, 498
Unintentional discrimination, 75
Universal theories, 18
Unknown area, in Johari Window, 84
Upward appeal, 351, 353
Upward influence, 356
Urgency for change, creating, 492–493
U.S. Family and Medical Leave Act, 213
Utilitarianism, 48, 49

V
V (outcome valences), 143, 145–146
Valence, 144
Value-expressive functions, 156–157
Value of rewards, 175
Values, 14–16, 24, 41–45, 57
　　corporate social responsibility, 15–16, 24
　　cross-cultural values, 42, 45–48
　　cultural. See Cultural values
　　enacted values, 42, 44–45, 460, 609
　　espoused values, 42, 45, 460, 609
　　ethical values. See Ethics
　　importance in workplace, 14–15
　　individual behavior and, 43–44
　　influences on, 9
　　influence tactics and, 357
　　leading from, 14, 43, 400
　　Machiavellian values, 360, 361
　　misaligned with environment, 466–467
　　needs and, 505
　　organizational culture and, 460
　　personal values, 14, 41, 43, 357
　　shared. See Shared values
　　types of, 42–43
　　ubuntu values, 420
　　values congruence, 44–45
Values circumplex, 42–43
Values congruence, 34, 57
Value system, 41
Variability of technology, 449–450
Variable interval schedule, 87
Variable ratio schedule, 88
Verbal communication, 315–316
Verification, 240, 241
Vicarious learning, 89–90
Videoconferencing, 292
Virtual corporations, 447

Virtual social events, 294
Virtual teams, 14, 259, 284, 305
    conflict due to differentiation, 375
    designing, 292–294
    environment, 292–293
    high-performance, 284, 286, 291–294
    information technologies for, 284, 291,
        292
    processes, 294
    size and composition, 294
    tasks, 293–294
Virtual work, 13–14, 24
Visibility, power and, 348–350
Visions, in transformational leadership, 417
Visualization (mental imagery), 185–186,
    187
VJ model of job enrichment, 182
Vocal authority, 352
Vocational choice, 55–57
Voice
    job satisfaction and, 116–117
    in procedural justice, 156–157
Voice intonation, 324–325
Volunteering, 303

W

Wage gap, 155
"Walking the talk," 416, 417
Walkouts, 490
Weak organizational culture, 466, 479
Web-based sources of communication,
    330
Weblogs (blogs), 312, 317, 330
"Wellness" days, 214
Wellness programs, 215, 216

Wikis, 330
Willingness, 413
Win–lose orientation, 377–379, 384, 390
Win–win orientation, 377–378, 385, 390
Withdrawal behaviors, 157
Withdrawal strategies, 213–214
Women
    networking and, 350
    responses to stress, 215–216
    stereotyping of, 74, 75, 80
    time-based conflict and, 205
    See also Gender differences
Women's studies, 17, 18
Work activities, 431–433
    through formal hierarchy, 432
    through informal communication, 431
    through standardization, 431, 432–433
Work addicts, 208
Workaholics, 208, 216
Work avoidance, 39
Work behavior, 116–117
Work efficiency
    cost of production and, 175
    job design and, 176–178
    job enlargement and, 180–181
    job specialization and, 177
    network structure and, 447
    scientific management and, 177–178
    specialized jobs and, 430–431
Work enthusiasts, 208
Work environments, 241–243, 402
Work experience, influence of, 9–10
Workforce diversity, 8–10, 24
    consequences of, 10
    deep-level diversity, 9–10

    diverse teams, 265–267, 274
    globalization and, 7
    surface-level diversity, 8–9, 10, 267
Workforce flexibility, 12
    competency-based rewards and, 171
    job enlargement and, 180–181
    in work arrangements, 289
Work–life balance, 11–12, 13, 212
Work–life balance initiatives, 212–213
Work motivation, job design and, 178–180
    core job characteristics, 179
    critical psychological states, 179
    individual differences, 180
Work–nonwork stressors
    role behavior conflict, 205
    strain-based conflict, 205
    time-based conflict, 204–205
Work overload, 203–204
Workplace, 14–15, 109
Workplace aggression, 210
Workplace expectations. *See* Expectations
Workplace spirituality, 208
Workplace violence, 201
Work-related stress. *See* Stress; Stressors
Work sabotage, 39
Workspace design, 329–330
Work-to-rule strikes, 436
World Wide Web, 229
Written communication, 315–316

Y

Yielding style, 379, 380

url index

A

aamc.org/members/wim/statistics/
stats03/start.htm, 563
adweek.com/adweek/creative/top20_
20years/index.isp, 229
americahurrah.com/Oakley/Entry.htm, 610

B

boeing.com/news/frontiers/index.
html, 563

C

ceoforum.com, 593

D

daringfireball.net/2006/04/aperture_
dirt, 592
daringfireball.net/2006/05/more_
aperture_dirt, 592

F

folklore.org, 229, 599

G

google.com/codejam/, 40

I

isrsurveys.com.au/pdf/insight/
IHRM%20Show-18Nov04.pdf, 606

M

mmhe.com/mcshane4e, 30, 130, 165, 195,
222, 283, 367, 426, 456, 484
moneyweb.co.za/specials/corp_
gov/509689.htm, 582
MSNBC.com, 60

N

nativenetwork.ecr.gov, 602
nitro-group.com, 607
nobelprize.org/medicine/laureates/2005/
warren lecture.html, 588

O

oakley.com, 610

P

plato.stanford.edu/entries/kant-
judgment/, 586
plato.stanford.edu/entries/stoicism, 586

Q

quoteland.com, 593

S

Scoop.co.nz, 11
sempra.com/diversity.htm, 563

T

towersperrin.com, 565

W

watsonwyatt.com/asia-pacific/research/
workasia/worktw_keyfindings.asp,
606
whitehouse.gov/news/releases/
2005/04/20050427.5.html, 612